Best Jobs for the 21st Century

Second Edition

J. Michael Farr and LaVerne L. Ludden, Ed.D.

With database work by Laurence Shatkin, Ph.D.

jist
Works

Best Jobs for the 21st Century, *Second Edition*

© 2001 by JIST Publishing, Inc.

Published by JIST Works, an imprint of JIST Publishing, Inc.
8902 Otis Avenue
Indianapolis, IN 46216-1033

Phone: 1-800-648-JIST   **Fax: 1-800-JIST-FAX**   **E-Mail: editorial@jist.com**

Visit our Web site at www.jist.com for information on JIST, free job search information and book chapters, and ordering information on our many products.

Some Other Books by the Authors

J. Michael Farr and LaVerne L. Ludden

Best Jobs for the 21st Century for
College Graduates

Enhanced Occupational Outlook Handbook

Guide for Occupational Exploration

J. Michael Farr

The Quick Resume & Cover Letter Book

Getting the Job You Really Want

The Very Quick Job Search

LaVerne L. Ludden

Job Savvy

Supervisor Savvy

Franchise Opportunities Handbook

Quantity discounts are available for JIST books. Please call our sales department at 1-800-648-5478 for a free catalog and more information.

Editors: Susan Pines, Veda Dickerson
Cover and Interior Designer: Aleata Howard
Interior Layout: Carolyn J. Newland
Proofreader: Linda Quigley

Printed in the United States of America
05 04 03 02 01   9 8 7 6 5 4 3 2 1

Library of Congress Cataloging-in-Publication Data
Farr, J. Michael.
    Best jobs for the 21st century / J. Michael Farr and LaVerne L. Ludden ; with database work by Laurence Shatkin.—2nd ed.
        p. cm.
    ISBN 1-56370-735-7
        1. Vocational guidance. 2. Occupations—Forecasting. I. Title: Best jobs for the twenty-first century. II. Ludden, LaVerne,
    1949-   III. Title.
HF5381.15 .F37 2001
331.7'02—dc21

                    2001033167

ISBN 1-56370-735-7

This Is a Big Book, But It Is Very Easy to Use

This book is designed to help you explore career options in a variety of interesting ways. The nice thing about it is that you don't have to read it all. Instead, we designed it to allow you to browse and find information that most interests you.

The table of contents will give you a good idea of what's inside and how to use the book, so we suggest you start there. The first part is made up of interesting lists that help you to explore jobs based on pay, interests, education level, personality type, and many other criteria. The second part provides descriptions for the jobs in the lists. Simple.

How We Selected the Best Jobs

Deciding on the "best" job is a choice that only you can make. But objective criteria can help you identify jobs that are, for example, better paying than other jobs with similar duties. We have sorted through the data for *all* major jobs and selected only those jobs that meet one of the following measures:

▲ Average annual earnings of $40,000 or more

▲ The number of people employed in the occupation is expected to increase by 10 percent or more by 2008

▲ Large enough to create 100,000 or more openings each year

About 500 jobs met our criteria. We are not suggesting that all of them are good ones for you to consider–they are not. But we present such a wide range of jobs that you are likely to find one or more that will stand out, and these are the jobs to consider most in your career planning.

Some Things You Can Do with This Book

▲ Identify more interesting or better-paying jobs that don't require additional training or education.

▲ Develop long-term career plans that may require additional training, education, or experience.

▲ Explore and select a college major or a training program that relates to a career objective.

▲ Find reliable earnings information to negotiate pay.

▲ Prepare for interviews.

These are a few of the many ways you can use this book. We hope you find it as interesting to browse as we did to put together. We have tried to make it easy to use and as interesting as occupational information can be.

When you are done with this book, pass it along or tell someone else about it. We wish you well in your career and in your life.

About This Revision

The first edition of this book was very well received, and we set out to make this new edition even better. As you might expect, we updated all the earnings and other data with the most reliable, current government sources. Using the latest release of the Occupational Information Network (O*NET) database (version 3) from the U.S. Department of Labor gives this book many major changes in job titles and results in all-new job descriptions. In addition, all the best jobs lists are based on new data. We also added new lists, including job lists for all 50 states and the 30 largest metropolitan areas, and best jobs based on personality types. Finally, all text was updated, making it even more interesting. These detailed changes make this book a major new edition.

Credits and Acknowledgments: While the authors created this book, it is based on the work of many others. The occupational information is based on data obtained from the U.S. Department of Labor and the U.S. Census Bureau. These sources provide the most authoritative occupational information available. The job titles and their related descriptions are from the O*NET database, which was developed by researchers and developers under the direction of the U.S. Department of Labor. They, in turn, were assisted by thousands of employers who provided details on the nature of work in the many thousands of job samplings used in the database's development.

The O*NET database is based on the substantial work done on an earlier occupational database, also developed by the U.S. Department of Labor, that was used in the *Dictionary of Occupational Titles* and other information sources. The *Dictionary of Occupational Titles* was first published in 1939, and its underlying database of occupational information has been continuously updated since. All of this work, over many years, forms the basis for much of the occupational information used by employers, job seekers, career counselors, education and training institutions, researchers, policy makers, and others.

Table of Contents

Part I: Lists of the Best Jobs for the 21st Century 9

Following are the titles of all lists in this book. On the pages noted below, browse the lists to find jobs that interest you. Then look up job descriptions in Part II.

Section A: Best Jobs Lists Overall, for Different Groups of People, and by Various Criteria 11

Section B: Best Jobs Lists for All States, Plus the 30 Largest Metropolitan Areas 107

Provides two lists for each geographic area—one
with the 25 jobs employing the most people and a
second with the 25 highest-paying jobs.

Job Lists by State 109

Job Lists for the 30 Largest Metropolitan Areas 160

Part II: The Best Jobs Directory—Descriptions of the 500 Best Jobs for the 21st Century..... 191

⊞ Table of Contents

⊞ Table of Contents

Introduction

The first years of a new millennium seem like a good time to think about the future, and we hope this book will help you do so. This book's first edition was very well received, and we think this second edition is even better. We've updated it using all-new data on employment projections through 2008. We emphasize jobs with the best possibilities for high pay, fast growth, and the most openings. We hope that you find our approach interesting and that the book encourages you to uncover possibilities you may not have considered. We also hope it helps motivate you to take the next step in planning your career, training, or education.

We wrote this introduction to help you better understand and use the rest of the book. We've kept it short (well, relatively short) and nontechnical in hopes that you will read it.

How the Best Jobs in This Book Were Selected

The statement on page iii gives some information on how we selected the occupations included in this book. Here are a few more details:

▲ We started with the jobs included in the new O*NET (for Occupational Information Network) database, which consists of occupational information maintained by the U.S. Department of Labor. The O*NET offers details on about 1,000 occupations and is now the primary source of specific facts on occupations, replacing the earlier *Dictionary of Occupational Titles* database. We used the O*NET as a basis for this book because it provides the most reliable, up-to-date occupational information available from any source.

▲ Because we wanted to include pay data and that is not part of the O*NET, we cross-referenced information on earnings developed by the Bureau of Labor Statistics (BLS) and the U.S. Census Bureau. This source offers the most reliable information we could obtain, but the census uses a different system of job titles than the O*NET. We were able to link the two systems and tie census earnings information to O*NET job titles.

In some cases, this process resulted in our using more general BLS job titles (that had earnings data available) and tying them to several more specific O*NET job titles (where earnings data was not available). An example is the BLS job title "accountants and auditors" that has two separate O*NET job titles of "accountants" and "auditors."

▲ We went through the resulting list of occupations and included those that met one or more of the following criteria:

- ▲ Have earnings of $40,000 or more a year (the average earnings for all workers in 2000 was about $29,000 a year)

- ▲ Are expected to increase employment by 10 percent or more by 2008

- ▲ Are large enough to create 100,000 or more job openings each year

Approximately 500 O*NET occupations met the criteria, and their descriptions appear in Part II. These almost 500 O*NET jobs are arranged under the more general BLS job titles—272 of these met our criteria for this book. The 272 job titles are also the ones used in the lists in Part I.

Part I: Lists of the Best Jobs for the 21st Century

We created lists we think are most likely to interest you. One list, for example, presents the jobs with the highest pay. Another shows jobs with the most openings. All the lists are easy to understand. Simply find the lists that interest you and browse them. We added notes to each list as needed to help you understand how we developed them or to provide tips on using them.

The lists are arranged into groupings within two main sections. For example, one group supplies a list of the best jobs at different levels of education and training—information that many will find useful.

In reviewing the lists, keep in mind that the primary measure for selection as a "best" job is a combination of high pay, high growth, and high number of openings. For example, the best occupations for college graduates have the highest total score for pay, growth, and openings.

The list titles are provided in the table of contents and are summarized here, along with a few additional comments.

Section A: Best Jobs Lists Overall, for Different Groups of People, and by Various Criteria

Section A organizes jobs in many useful ways. We hope these lists get you thinking about your career and education options.

Best of the Best—Jobs with Highest Pay, Fastest Growth, and Largest Number of Openings

These lists use criteria most people consider important in selecting a "best" job—high pay, high growth, and many openings. Of all jobs that met our criteria for inclusion in this book, the jobs on these lists had the highest overall ratings.

▲ 50 Best Jobs for the 21st Century: Occupations with the highest combination scores for pay, growth, and number of openings.

▲ Best-Paying Jobs for the 21st Century: The jobs with the highest average earnings per year.

▲ Fastest Growing Jobs for the 21st Century: The jobs with the highest percentage growth rates projected through 2008.

▲ Jobs with the Most Annual Openings for the 21st Century

Best Jobs Lists for Different Types of Workers

We did some special analysis to create these lists. We began by sorting our lists of jobs with high percentages of people who were older, younger, working part-time, and so on. We then did another sort to identify jobs, within each group, with the highest combination of pay, growth, and number of openings. We provide more details on the criteria used for creating these lists in Part I. The lists include

▲ Best Jobs for Workers 16–24

▲ Best Jobs for Workers 55 and Over

▲ Best Jobs for Part-Time Workers

▲ Best Jobs for Self-Employed Workers

▲ Best Jobs Employing 70 Percent or More Women

▲ Best Jobs Employing 70 Percent or More Men

Best Jobs Lists Based on Levels of Education, Training, and Experience

We used the same categories for training and education that the U.S. Department of Labor assigns to each occupation. These lists will help you identify jobs that pay more or that are more interesting to you at your current level of education. These lists also can help you identify occupations at the education level you are willing to pursue:

▲ Best Jobs Requiring a Graduate or Professional Degree

▲ Best Jobs Requiring a Bachelor's Degree, Plus Experience

▲ Best Jobs Requiring a Bachelor's Degree

▲ Best Jobs Requiring an Associate Degree

- ▲ Best Jobs Requiring Postsecondary Vocational Training
- ▲ Best Jobs Requiring Work Experience in a Related Job
- ▲ Best Jobs Requiring Long-Term, On-the-Job Training
- ▲ Best Jobs Requiring Moderate-Term, On-the-Job Training
- ▲ Best Jobs Requiring Short-Term, On-the-Job Training

Best Jobs Lists Based on Personality Types

John Holland developed one of the most popular career theories. It uses six personality types and relates them to career clusters. We cross-referenced each job in this book to one of the six personality types. The occupations within each type are then rated based on a combined score for pay, growth, and annual openings. We include these lists:

- ▲ Best Jobs for Artistic Personality Types
- ▲ Best Jobs for Conventional Personality Types
- ▲ Best Jobs for Enterprising Personality Types
- ▲ Best Jobs for Investigative Personality Types
- ▲ Best Jobs for Realistic Personality Types
- ▲ Best Jobs for Social Personality Types

Best Jobs Lists Based on Interests

We provide an interesting series of lists that organizes all the jobs in this book into group-ings based on interests. These groupings use a system called the *Guide for Occupational Exploration*, or *GOE*, developed by the U.S. Department of Labor. Exploring career options based on interests has been found to be a very effective way to explore career options, and the *GOE* was developed to provide a useful way to do so. We use the new *GOE* structure from the *Guide for Occupational Exploration*, Third Edition, published by JIST Works. The lists include

- ▲ Best Jobs for People Interested in Arts, Entertainment, and Media
- ▲ Best Jobs for People Interested in Science, Math, and Engineering
- ▲ Best Jobs for People Interested in Plants and Animals
- ▲ Best Jobs for People Interested in Law, Law Enforcement, and Public Safety
- ▲ Best Jobs for People Interested in Mechanics, Installers, and Repairers
- ▲ Best Jobs for People Interested in Construction, Mining, and Drilling
- ▲ Best Jobs for People Interested in Transportation
- ▲ Best Jobs for People Interested in Industrial Production
- ▲ Best Jobs for People Interested in Business Detail

- ▲ Best Jobs for People Interested in Sales and Marketing
- ▲ Best Jobs for People Interested in Recreation, Travel, and Other Personal Services
- ▲ Best Jobs for People Interested in Education and Social Service
- ▲ Best Jobs for People Interested in General Management and Support
- ▲ Best Jobs for People Interested in Medical and Health Services

Section B: Best Jobs Lists for All States, Plus the 30 Largest Metropolitan Areas

The earnings and other data in this book are based on national information. But earnings and the number of people employed in a specific job can vary considerably in different areas of the country. For that reason, we include new lists that provide information for each state, plus the 30 largest metropolitan areas in the United States. There are two lists for each state and each area. One list shows the 25 occupations employing the most people. Another list displays the 25 occupations paying the highest average annual wage. We hope you find these lists helpful.

Some job titles in Section B may vary slightly from those used in Part II's descriptions because states control their own data collection. You should, however, be able to find a similar job described in Part II.

Part II: The Best Jobs Directory— Descriptions of the 500 Best Jobs for the 21st Century

The second major section gives job descriptions for the almost 500 occupations selected for this book. As a reminder, the occupations described were selected because they met one or more of the following criteria:

- ▲ The average annual earnings for the job are equal to or greater than $40,000.
- ▲ The number of job openings for the occupation is expected to increase by 10 percent or more by 2008. This is an indicator of jobs offering high potential for entry and advancement.
- ▲ The occupation has 100,000 or more job openings each year. Occupations that meet this standard are included because they provide more opportunities for employment.

The 272 major job titles in Part II are listed in alphabetical order. This makes it easy to look up a job that you've identified in a list from Part I and want to learn more about. Note that the 500 descriptions are arranged under the 272 general job titles used by the Bureau of Labor Statistics. We did this so that we could include earnings data. Each description includes the following information:

- ▲ **Job Title.** The title commonly used to describe the occupation. This is followed by the related job titles.

- ▲ **Growth.** The projected percentage increase in the number of people employed in the occupation through 2008.

- ▲ **Annual Job Openings.** The number of openings projected per year, including openings from job growth and turnover.

- ▲ **Yearly Earnings.** The average annual pay received by all workers in this occupation.

- ▲ **Education Required.** The amount of training, education, or work experience typically required for entry into this occupation. The letters "O-J-T" stand for "on-the-job training."

- ▲ **Self-Employed.** The percentage of self-employed workers in the occupation.

- ▲ **Part-Time.** The percentage of part-time workers employed in the occupation.

Following this labor market information are descriptions for each related job. There may only be one job description, or there may be several. For example, the major job "accountants and auditors" has two job descriptions—one for "accountants" and another for "auditors." Each description contains the following information:

- ▲ **Summary Description and Tasks.** The first lines, in bold, give a summary description of the occupation. This is followed by a listing of tasks generally performed by people who work in the job.

- ▲ **Personality Type.** This is a description of the personality type that would find the job engaging or fulfilling. The six types include Artistic, Conventional, Enterprising, Investigative, Realistic, and Social. A summary of the personality type is included in the job description.

- ▲ **Abilities.** This section lists the mental, physical, and sensory abilities typically required to perform the job. We include abilities that have been rated as most critical for the job.

- ▲ **Skills.** The O*NET includes data on 10 basic skills that assist in learning new things and an additional 36 functional (or "transferable") skills that help you in a variety of job settings. We include only those skills, from among the 46, that are rated as the most important for that occupation.

- ▲ **Generalized Work Activities.** These are tasks common to many jobs. There are 42 generalized work activities in the O*NET. We include only those activities rated as most important for a job.

Sample Job Description

Job Title

Desktop ← ⌐ Publishing Specialists

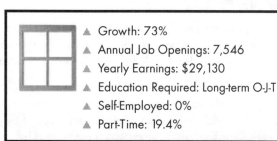

- ▲ Growth: 73%
- ▲ Annual Job Openings: 7,546
- ▲ Yearly Earnings: $29,130
- ▲ Education Required: Long-term O-J-T
- ▲ Self-Employed: 0%
- ▲ Part-Time: 19.4%

Summary Description

Related Job

Desktop Publishers ←⌐

Format typescript and graphic elements using computer software to produce publication-ready material. Activates options such as masking or text processing. Saves completed work on floppy disks or magnetic tape. Studies layout or other instructions to determine work to be done and sequence of operations. Loads floppy disks or tapes containing information into system. Creates special effects such as vignettes, mosaics, and image combining. Views monitors for visual representation of work in progress and for instructions and feedback throughout process. Enters data such as background color, shapes, and coordination of images. Enters digitized data into electronic prepress-system computer memory, using scanner, camera, keyboard, or mouse. Activates options such as masking, pixel (picture element) editing, airbrushing, or image retouching. Enters data such as coordinates of images and color specifications into system to retouch and make color corrections.

Personality Type: Realistic. Realistic occupations frequently involve work activities that include practical, hands-on problems and solutions. They often deal with plants, animals, and real-world materials like wood, tools, and machinery. Many of the occupations require working outside and do not involve a lot of paperwork or working closely with others.

Abilities: Near Vision—The ability to see details of objects at a close range. Wrist-Finger Speed—The ability to make fast, simple, repeated movements of the fingers, hands, and wrists. Visual Color Discrimination—The ability to match or detect differences between colors, including shades of color and brightness. Visualization—The ability to imagine how some-thing will look after it is moved around or when its parts are

moved or rearranged. Control Precision—The ability to quickly and repeatedly make precise adjustments in moving the controls of a machine or vehicle to exact positions. Information Ordering—The ability to correctly follow a given rule or set of rules in order to arrange things or actions in a certain order. The things or actions can include numbers, letters, words, pictures, proce-dures, sentences, and mathematical or logical operations. Written Comprehension—The ability to read and understand informa-tion and ideas presented in writing.

Abilities

Skills: Reading Comprehension—Understanding written infor-mation in work-related documents. Equipment Selection—Determining the kind of tools and equipment needed to do a job. Operation and Control—Controlling operations of equip-ment or systems. Operations Analysis—Analyzing needs and product requirements to create a design. Monitoring—Assessing how well one is doing when learning or doing something.

Skills

Generalized Work Activities: Interacting with Computers—Controlling computer functions by using programs, setting up functions, writing software, or otherwise communicating with computer systems. Getting Information Needed to Do the Job—Observing, receiving, and otherwise obtaining information from all relevant sources. Handling and Moving Objects—Using one's hands and arms in handling, installing, forming, positioning, and moving materials, or in manipulating things. Includes the use of keyboards. Identifying Objects, Actions, and Events—Identifying information received by making estimates or categorizations, recognizing differences or similarities, or sensing changes in circumstances or events. Thinking Creatively—Origi-nating, inventing, designing, or creating new applications, ideas, relationships, systems, or products, including artistic contributions.

Abilities

Personality Type

Tasks

Generalized Work Activities ←

Caveat Datum (or, Loosely Translated, Beware of Data)

A problem with data is that it is true on the average. But just as there is no precisely average person, there is no such thing as a statistically average example of a particular job. We say this because data, while helpful, can also be misleading.

Take, for example, the yearly earnings information in this book. This is highly reliable data obtained from a very large U.S. working population sample by the Bureau of Labor Statistics. It tells us the average annual pay received by people in various job titles (actually, it is the "median" annual pay, which means that half earned more and half less).

This sounds great, except that you have to realize that half of all people in that occupation earned less than that amount. For example, people entering the occupation or with a few years of work experience will often earn much less than the average. People who live in rural areas or who work for smaller employers typically earn less than those who do similar work in cities (where the cost of living is higher) or for bigger employers. People in certain areas of the country earn less than those in others. For example, lifeguards in northern states may only work two to three months out of the year. Thus, their earnings are much lower than the average earnings of $17,470 for all lifeguards per year. However, in southern states and Hawaii, lifeguards can work almost year-round and may earn more than $17,470.

So, in reviewing the information in Part II, please understand the limitations of data. You need to use common sense in career decision-making as in most other things in life. Even so, we hope that you find the information helpful and interesting.

We Wish You a Satisfying Career

Thanks for reading the introduction. You are surely a more thorough person than someone who jumped into the book without reading it. The truth is, one of the authors is the type of person who never reads documentation before trying to use software. That same type of person turns to a book's good parts and skips the introduction. This is an example of an important point: All of us are different, but there is always something for each us.

We wish you a satisfying career and, more importantly, a satisfying life.

Part I

Lists of the Best Jobs for the 21st Century

Many interesting lists appear in this part, and we suggest that this is where you start using this book. We think you will find the lists to be very helpful in exploring your career options. Here are some suggestions for using the lists, along with additional information points:

▲ The table of contents presents the titles of all lists. Use it to find the lists that interest you most, or simply browse through this part.

▲ We tried to create clear titles for each list and think most are easy to understand and require little explanation. We give comments as needed for each list to inform you of the selection criteria we used or other details we think you may want to know.

▲ The large variety of lists meets a variety of interests and needs. Some lists will help you identify jobs based on your interests or personality type. Others provide information on jobs with the highest pay, on education or training needed, and on many other criteria. These lists are in Section A.

▲ New in this edition are lists with job information for each state, plus the 30 largest metropolitan areas. These lists appear in Section B. There you will find lists of jobs employing the most workers and jobs with the highest pay for each region.

▲ As you review the lists, one or more occupations may appeal to you enough to seek additional information. Mark that occupation so that you can look up that job's description in Part II. If someone else will be using this book, write the appealing job titles on a separate sheet of paper. Note that the job titles used in Section B's lists may vary slightly from those used in the Part II descriptions. This is explained in more detail on Section B's opening page.

▲ Keep in mind that all jobs in the Section A lists met our basic criteria for high annual pay, fast growth through 2008, or large number of annual openings. These measures are easily quantified and are often presented in lists of best jobs in newspapers and

(continues)

(continued)

other media. While earnings, growth, and numerous openings are important, you need to consider other factors in your career planning. For example, being in a good location, liking your coworkers, serving others, and enjoying your work are a few of many factors that may define your ideal job. These measures are difficult or impossible to quantify and so are not used in this book. You need to consider the importance of these issues yourself.

▲ Data in this book comes from government sources, including the U.S. Department of Labor and the Census Bureau. The earnings figures are based on the average annual pay received by full-time workers. Since some occupations have high percentages of part-time workers, those workers would receive, of course, relatively less pay on a weekly or annual basis. The earnings also represent the national averages, and actual pay rates can vary greatly by location, amount of previous work experience, and other factors.

We hope you find these lists both interesting and helpful. Based on how well the lists were received in the previous edition, we include even more to help you explore your career options. There are a lot of lists, but don't be overwhelmed by them. We suggest you find the ones that are most helpful to you and focus your attention on them. Enjoy!

Best Jobs Lists Overall, for Different Groups of People, and by Various Criteria

This section contains lists designed to get you thinking about career options in a variety of ways. The jobs in the various lists were selected based on high annual earnings, rapid growth rates through 2008, or large numbers of annual openings. All are described in Part II. Among these jobs is an enormous variety of opportunity, and we hope you find one or more that meets your needs.

Best of the Best—Jobs with Highest Pay, Fastest Growth, and Largest Number of Openings

We consider the four lists that follow to be our premier lists. They are the ones most often mentioned in the media and that most readers want to see. The first list presents the jobs with the highest combined scores for pay, growth, and number of openings. This is a *very* popular list, since it represents jobs from our entire labor market with the highest quantifiable measures. Three additional lists present jobs with the highest numbers in each of three measures: annual earnings, projected percent growth through 2008, and largest number of annual openings.

50 Best Jobs for the 21st Century

This is our premier list—the one that most people want to know about. Here are some observations about it:

▲ A quick review of the best jobs for the 21st century reveals the importance of education. Over 75 percent of the best 50 jobs require a four-year college degree. Almost 50 percent of the top 15 jobs are in the computer field. Topping the list are systems analyst; computer engineer; and engineering, natural science, and computer and information systems manager.

▲ Many jobs in the top 20 require advanced technology skills and training. But among the top 50 are jobs in most major occupational groups and industries, including the arts, education, health care and other helping professions, business, and management.

▲ Many of these jobs are in the service and information industries. Contrary to what we often hear, these are not dead-end jobs with low pay and status.

▲ While pay is only one of three factors determining which jobs made this list, about 85 percent of the jobs pay more than the average for all workers, which is just above $29,000 a year, and 56 percent of the jobs on the list pay $40,000 or more annually.

The main point is that many opportunities exist for jobs with good pay in the 21st century, but to get them you may need to learn new skills and continually update them.

Details on the selection process: We began with a database of almost 1,000 jobs listed by the U.S. Department of Labor's O*NET database. Of these, approximately 500 jobs met our criteria for inclusion in this book based on high pay, fast growth, or large numbers of openings. We then arranged these jobs within 272 major job titles from another database system that contained earnings and other data. We sorted these 272 job titles into three lists in order of highest pay, fastest growth, and largest number of openings. The occupation with the highest pay was given a score of 272; the one with the next highest pay was given a score of 271. This ranking continued to the lowest-paying job, which was assigned a score of 1. The scoring procedure was then carried out for the two remaining lists.

The following list was created based on the combined score given to each occupation on all three measures. Systems analyst is the occupation with the highest combined score, and it appears on the top of the list. The other top 49 occupations follow, in descending order, based on their total scores.

50 Best Jobs for the 21st Century

Job	Annual Earnings	Percent Growth	Annual Openings
1. Systems Analysts	$52,180	94	154,157
2. Computer Engineers	$61,910	108	81,337
3. Engineering, Natural Science, and Computer and Information Systems Managers	$75,320	44	54,120
4. Securities, Commodities, and Financial Services Sales Agents	$48,090	41	61,084
5. Computer Support Specialists	$37,120	102	113,041
6. Advertising, Marketing, Promotions, Public Relations, and Sales Managers	$57,300	23	89,237
7. Computer Programmers	$47,550	30	74,773
8. Computer Scientists	$46,670	118	27,942
9. General Managers and Top Executives	$55,890	16	421,006
10. College and University Faculty	$46,600	23	139,101
11. Medical and Health Services Managers	$48,870	33	31,238
12. Electrical and Electronics Engineers	$62,260	26	29,636
13. Registered Nurses	$40,690	22	195,231
14. Database Administrators	$47,980	77	19,027
15. Physicians	$102,020	21	32,563
16. Management Analysts	$49,470	28	23,831
17. Secondary School Teachers	$37,890	23	133,585
18. Police Patrol Officers	$37,710	32	51,739
19. Lawyers	$78,170	17	38,182
20. Special Education Teachers	$37,850	34	36,540
21. Paralegals and Legal Assistants	$32,760	62	33,971
22. Physical Therapists	$56,600	34	10,602
23. Dental Hygienists	$45,890	40	15,372
24. Correctional Officers	$28,540	39	64,835
25. Human Resources Managers	$49,010	19	32,929
26. Financial Managers	$55,070	14	78,071

50 Best Jobs for the 21st Century

Job	Annual Earnings	Percent Growth	Annual Openings
27. Writers and Editors	$36,480	24	52,971
28. Artists and Commercial Artists	$31,690	26	58,769
29. Office and Administrative Support Supervisors	$31,090	19	238,168
30. Civil Engineers	$53,450	21	20,603
31. Communication, Transportation, and Utilities Operations Managers	$52,810	19	25,388
32. Administrative Services Managers	$44,370	18	46,558
33. Biological Scientists	$46,140	35	10,417
34. Education Administrators	$60,400	13	60,229
35. Designers	$29,190	27	57,787
36. Social Workers	$30,590	36	29,630
37. Adjustment Clerks	$22,040	34	141,670
38. Human Resources, Training, and Labor Relations Specialists	$37,710	18	82,760
39. Human Service Workers and Assistants	$21,360	53	91,824
40. Bill and Account Collectors	$22,540	35	106,068
41. Physician Assistants	$47,090	48	6,142
42. Speech-Language Pathologists and Audiologists	$43,080	38	9,862
43. Dental Assistants	$22,640	42	56,389
44. Counselors	$38,650	25	21,279
45. Occupational Therapists	$48,230	34	6,484
46. Personal Care and Home Health Aides	$15,800	58	249,694
47. Data Processing Equipment Repairers	$29,340	47	20,080
48. Loan Counselors and Officers	$35,340	21	39,836
49. Medical Assistants	$20,680	58	49,015
50. Sports and Physical Training Instructors and Coaches	$22,230	28	104,431

Best-Paying Jobs for the 21st Century

We know that many people will turn to this list first. We included all jobs that have average earnings of $40,000 or more annually. This resulted in 83 jobs. Like most people, you probably consider the amount of money you can earn to be important in selecting a career. That is one reason we provide this list. Keep in mind that the earnings reflect the national average for all workers in the occupations. This is an important consideration because starting pay in the job is usually a lot less than what can be earned with several years of experience. Earnings also vary significantly by region of the country, so pay in your area could be substantially different.

The highest-paying job is dentist, with average annual earnings of $110,160. The top 25 jobs each have average annual earnings greater than $55,800. The average annual earnings for all workers are slightly more than $29,000, so the top 25 jobs on this list pay just less than twice the national average.

Twenty-three of the top 25 best-paying jobs require four or more years of college. This isn't surprising, since the lifetime earnings of someone with a bachelor's degree is more than double that of a high school graduate. Five of the top 10 best-paying jobs require a professional degree, which normally means at least three years of education beyond a bachelor's degree. Workers with professional degrees have lifetime earnings four times greater than those of high school graduates.

Other lists later in this section present high-paying jobs at various levels of education and training. While it is clear that higher levels of education and training are often required for jobs with high earnings, opportunities exist for higher-than-average pay at all levels of education.

Best-Paying Jobs for the 21st Century

Job	Annual Earnings
1. Dentists	$110,160
2. Physicians	$102,020
3. Aircraft Pilots and Flight Engineers	$91,750
4. Podiatrists	$79,530
5. Lawyers	$78,170
6. Engineering, Natural Science, and Computer and Information Systems Managers	$75,320
7. Petroleum Engineers	$74,260
8. Physicists and Astronomers	$73,240
9. Nuclear Engineers	$71,310
10. Optometrists	$68,480

Best-Paying Jobs for the 21st Century

Job	Annual Earnings
11. Aerospace Engineers	$66,950
12. Pharmacists	$66,220
13. Actuaries	$65,560
14. Air Traffic Controllers	$64,880
15. Chemical Engineers	$64,760
16. Chiropractors	$63,930
17. Electrical and Electronics Engineers	$62,260
18. Computer Engineers	$61,910
19. Education Administrators	$60,400
20. Materials Engineers	$57,970
21. Advertising, Marketing, Promotions, Public Relations, and Sales Managers	$57,300
22. Physical Therapists	$56,600
23. Industrial Production Managers	$56,320
24. Mining Engineers	$56,090
25. General Managers and Top Executives	$55,890
26. Financial Managers	$55,070
27. Sales Engineers	$54,600
28. Atmospheric Scientists	$54,430
29. Geologists, Geophysicists, and Oceanographers	$53,890
30. Civil Engineers	$53,450
31. Mechanical Engineers	$53,290
32. Communication, Transportation, and Utilities Operations Managers	$52,810
33. Industrial Engineers	$52,610
34. Systems Analysts	$52,180
35. Veterinarians	$50,950
36. Medical Scientists	$50,410
37. Management Analysts	$49,470
38. Mathematicians	$49,100
39. Operations Research Analysts	$49,070
40. Human Resources Managers	$49,010
41. Medical and Health Services Managers	$48,870
42. Police and Detective Supervisors	$48,700
43. Statisticians	$48,540
44. Economists and Marketing Research Analysts	$48,330
45. Occupational Therapists	$48,230
46. Securities, Commodities, and Financial Services Sales Agents	$48,090

(continues)

(continued)

Best-Paying Jobs for the 21st Century

Job	Annual Earnings
47. Psychologists	$48,050
48. Database Administrators	$47,980
49. Elevator Installers and Repairers	$47,860
50. Architects	$47,710
51. Construction Managers	$47,610
52. Computer Programmers	$47,550
53. Physician Assistants	$47,090
54. Computer Scientists	$46,670
55. College and University Faculty	$46,600
56. Chemists	$46,220
57. Biological Scientists	$46,140
58. Dental Hygienists	$45,890
59. Power Distributors and Dispatchers	$45,690
60. Budget Analysts	$44,950
61. Fire Fighting and Prevention Supervisors	$44,830
62. Power Generating and Reactor Plant Operators	$44,800
63. Postmasters and Mail Superintendents	$44,730
64. Administrative Services Managers	$44,370
65. Gas and Petroleum Plant and System Occupations	$43,800
66. Central Office and PBX Installers and Repairers	$43,680
67. Subway and Streetcar Operators	$43,330
68. Speech-Language Pathologists and Audiologists	$43,080
69. Urban and Regional Planners	$42,860
70. Conservation Scientists and Foresters	$42,750
71. Electrical Powerline Installers and Repairers	$42,600
72. Agricultural and Food Scientists	$42,340
73. Purchasing Managers	$41,830
74. Fishing Vessel Captains and Officers	$41,200
75. Water Vessel Captains and Pilots	$41,200
76. Registered Nurses	$40,690
77. Cost Estimators	$40,590
78. Numerical Control Machine Tool Programmers	$40,490
79. Real Estate Appraisers	$40,290
80. Ship Engineers	$40,150
81. Property and Casualty Insurance Claims Examiners	$40,110
82. Auto Insurance Appraisers	$40,000
83. Fire Inspectors	$40,000

Fastest Growing Jobs for the 21st Century

The occupations in this list are projected to have the highest percentage increase in the numbers of people employed through 2008. We listed all jobs that will grow 20 percent or more; the average growth rate projected for all jobs is 14 percent. A total of 97 jobs are on this list.

The five fastest growing jobs are computer scientist, computer engineer, computer support specialist, systems analyst, and database administrator. All are projected to approximately double by 2008. It is not surprising to find that computer and technology-related jobs lead this list in this information age. Health-related professions also dominate the list, which is consistent with the increasing health needs of the aging baby-boom generation and the many new medical procedures now available. Eleven—almost 45 percent—of the 25 fastest growing jobs are in health-related occupations. Both computer- and health-related jobs will provide many opportunities for employment in the 21st century. But, as this list demonstrates, computer- and health-related jobs are not the only opportunities with potential for strong growth.

Fastest Growing Jobs for the 21st Century

Job	Percent Growth
1. Computer Scientists	118
2. Computer Engineers	108
3. Computer Support Specialists	102
4. Systems Analysts	94
5. Database Administrators	77
6. Desktop Publishing Specialists	73
7. Paralegals and Legal Assistants	62
8. Medical Assistants	58
9. Personal Care and Home Health Aides	58
10. Human Service Workers and Assistants	53
11. Physician Assistants	48
12. Data Processing Equipment Repairers	47
13. Residential Counselors	46
14. Electronic Semiconductor Processors	45
15. Engineering, Natural Science, and Computer and Information Systems Managers	44
16. Medical Records and Health Information Technicians	44
17. Physical Therapy Assistants and Aides	44
18. Respiratory Therapists	43
19. Dental Assistants	42
20. Surgical Technologists	42

(continues)

(continued)

Fastest Growing Jobs for the 21st Century

Job	Percent Growth
21. Securities, Commodities, and Financial Services Sales Agents	41
22. Dental Hygienists	40
23. Occupational Therapy Assistants and Aides	40
24. Cardiovascular Technologists and Technicians	39
25. Correctional Officers	39
26. Speech-Language Pathologists and Audiologists	38
27. Social Workers	36
28. Ambulance Drivers and Attendants	35
29. Bill and Account Collectors	35
30. Biological Scientists	35
31. Adjustment Clerks	34
32. Occupational Therapists	34
33. Physical Therapists	34
34. Sheriffs and Deputy Sheriffs	34
35. Special Education Teachers	34
36. Medical and Health Services Managers	33
37. Central Office and PBX Installers and Repairers	32
38. Emergency Medical Technicians	32
39. Models, Demonstrators, and Product Promoters	32
40. Police Patrol Officers	32
41. Teacher Assistants	32
42. Parking Lot Attendants	31
43. Amusement and Recreation Attendants	30
44. Computer Programmers	30
45. Flight Attendants	30
46. Telephone and Cable TV Line Installers and Repairers	30
47. Guards	29
48. Athletes, Coaches, and Umpires	28
49. Brokerage Clerks	28
50. Management Analysts	28
51. Sports and Physical Training Instructors and Coaches	28
52. Veterinary Assistants	28
53. Designers	27
54. Interior Designers	27
55. Artists and Commercial Artists	26
56. Child Care Workers	26
57. Electrical and Electronics Engineers	26
58. Manicurists	26
59. Preschool Teachers	26

Fastest Growing Jobs for the 21st Century

Job	Percent Growth
60. Cleaners of Vehicles and Equipment	25
61. Counselors	25
62. Directors of Religious Activities and Education	25
63. Medical Scientists	25
64. Pest Control Workers	25
65. Public Relations Specialists	25
66. Veterinarians	25
67. Actors, Directors, and Producers	24
68. Meat, Poultry, and Fish Cutters and Trimmers	24
69. Nursing Aides, Orderlies, and Attendants	24
70. Private Detectives and Investigators	24
71. Receptionists and Information Clerks	24
72. Sprayers and Applicators	24
73. Writers and Editors	24
74. Advertising, Marketing, Promotions, Public Relations, and Sales Managers	23
75. Bicycle Repairers	23
76. Chiropractors	23
77. College and University Faculty	23
78. Counter and Rental Clerks	23
79. Interviewing Clerks	23
80. Numerical Control Machine Tool Operators and Tenders	23
81. Secondary School Teachers	23
82. Animal Caretakers	22
83. Hand Packers and Packagers	22
84. Registered Nurses	22
85. Surveying and Mapping Technicians	22
86. Adult Education Instructors	21
87. Civil Engineers	21
88. Detectives and Criminal Investigators	21
89. Landscaping and Groundskeeping Workers	21
90. Loan Counselors and Officers	21
91. Physicians	21
92. Credit Analysts	20
93. Insurance Adjusters, Examiners, and Investigators	20
94. Lawn Service Managers	20
95. Licensed Practical Nurses	20
96. Radiologic Technologists and Technicians	20
97. Taxi Drivers and Chauffeurs	20

Jobs with the Most Annual Openings for the 21st Century

Jobs with large numbers of openings are typically in occupations that employ many people. While some of these occupations pay well, most do not require advanced skills, education, or training and therefore are not among those with high pay. For example, the top 25 occupations on this list pay an average of just over $20,000 a year—much less than the $29,000 a year average paid to all workers. And the average growth rate of these jobs is less than 17 percent, just a bit higher than the 14 percent average growth projected for all occupations through 2008.

While many of these jobs are not among the highest paying or fastest growing, they have advantages for many people. Many are relatively easy to obtain and can be learned quickly. They provide entry-level employment for new workers and flexibility for students and others. Such jobs are attractive to people reentering the labor market, part-time job seekers, and workers who want to move from one employer or location to another. People who want to supplement their incomes also use these occupations as second jobs. We included in this list all jobs that have 100,000 or more openings annually—a total of 51 jobs.

Jobs with the Most Annual Openings for the 21st Century

Job	Annual Openings
1. Retail Salespersons	1,305,317
2. Cashiers	1,290,302
3. Food Counter and Fountain Workers	944,970
4. General Office Clerks	745,378
5. Janitors, Cleaners, Maids, and Housekeeping Cleaners	735,967
6. Truck Drivers	535,419
7. Food Preparation Workers	529,498
8. General Managers and Top Executives	421,006
9. Marketing and Sales Worker Supervisors	410,550
10. Receptionists and Information Clerks	386,806
11. Secretaries	358,379
12. Nursing Aides, Orderlies, and Attendants	349,640
13. Teacher Assistants	343,831
14. Child Care Workers	328,786
15. Bookkeeping, Accounting, and Auditing Clerks	325,366
16. Freight, Stock, and Material Movers	306,549
17. Landscaping and Groundskeeping Workers	283,459

Jobs with the Most Annual Openings for the 21st Century

Job	Annual Openings
18. Restaurant Cooks	262,535
19. Guards	256,671
20. Personal Care and Home Health Aides	249,694
21. Hand Packers and Packagers	249,421
22. Shipping, Receiving, and Traffic Clerks	242,666
23. Office and Administrative Support Supervisors	238,168
24. Carpenters	236,108
25. Short Order and Fast Food Cooks	226,320
26. Blue-Collar Worker Supervisors	216,115
27. Elementary School Teachers	204,210
28. Counter and Rental Clerks	199,406
29. Registered Nurses	195,231
30. Dining Room and Cafeteria Attendants and Bar Helpers	181,922
31. General Utility Maintenance Repairers	180,704
32. Construction Helpers	167,103
33. Farm Workers	157,331
34. Systems Analysts	154,157
35. Amusement and Recreation Attendants	141,783
36. Adjustment Clerks	141,670
37. College and University Faculty	139,101
38. Food Service and Lodging Managers	138,826
39. Secondary School Teachers	133,585
40. Accountants and Auditors	129,566
41. Institution or Cafeteria Cooks	124,088
42. Automotive Mechanics and Service Technicians	119,161
43. File Clerks	117,451
44. Cleaners of Vehicles and Equipment	116,789
45. Computer Support Specialists	113,041
46. Restaurant Hosts and Hostesses	110,848
47. Data Entry Keyers	107,440
48. Bank Tellers	106,674
49. Vocational Education Teachers and Instructors	106,468
50. Bill and Account Collectors	106,068
51. Sports and Physical Training Instructors and Coaches	104,431

Best Jobs Lists for Different Types of Workers

We created a series of very interesting (and somewhat controversial) lists of the best jobs for younger workers, older workers, part-time workers, self-employed workers, and jobs employing high percentages of men or women. Five lists appear for each category. For example, the best jobs lists for younger workers include

▲ Jobs with the Highest Percentage of Workers 16–24

▲ Best Jobs for Workers 16–24

▲ Best-Paying Jobs for Workers 16–24

▲ Jobs with the Most Annual Openings for Workers 16–24

▲ Fastest Growing Jobs for Workers 16–24

The Potential Controversy

In this book's first edition, we considered excluding the best jobs lists for men and for women for fear of upsetting some readers. But we also knew that most people could handle and would appreciate the facts. This has proven to be true. Many readers have commented on how useful the lists for jobs held by high percentages of men and women are to them. So we again asked our computer to tell us which jobs employed the highest percentages of men and women. Our computer told us lots of things we knew, like the fact that most nurses are women and most bricklayers are men. Many of these facts should not surprise anyone who lives in the real world. We decided that if we get in trouble with some readers for presenting the obvious, we would simply say it is not our fault because the computer did it. The computer also found that most ski patrol officers and lifeguards are young and that most lawn service managers are over 55. Some findings will make sense, like the one about lifeguards, and others are simply interesting, like the one about lawn service managers.

So we think that you can learn some interesting information from these lists, including facts you can use to plan your career. As needed, we provide additional comments prior to each list to help you understand it.

Best Jobs Lists for Workers 16–24

We sorted through the jobs that met our criteria for this book to find those with the highest percentage of workers 16 through 24. While these young folks represent about 16 percent of the workforce, we included only those occupations that employ 30 percent or more of them—about twice the average for all occupations. This produced a list of 25 occupations. The occupations with the highest percentage of young workers tend to be in entry-level, part-time, seasonal, and service jobs. This makes sense in that many young workers have not settled into careers or are working while going to school. The jobs they get tend to be relatively easy to obtain but have relatively low wages. The average earnings for all 25 jobs with high percentages of young workers are just $15,624. These low-paying jobs are often referred to as entry-level jobs because they offer inexperienced workers an opportunity to enter the labor market. More than 70 percent of these jobs have over 100,000 annual job openings. Many young people work in them to earn some money and gain basic job skills.

Jobs with the Highest Percentage of Workers 16–24

Job	Percent Workers 16–24
1. Ski Patrol Workers and Life Guards	76
2. Dining Room and Cafeteria Attendants and Bar Helpers	56
3. Cashiers	52
4. Food Counter and Fountain Workers	51
5. Tire Repairers and Changers	47
6. Freight, Stock, and Material Movers	46
7. Amusement and Recreation Attendants	46
8. Ushers, Lobby Attendants, and Ticket Takers	46
9. Counter and Rental Clerks	45
10. Construction Helpers	44
11. Food Preparation Workers	40
12. File Clerks	39
13. Restaurant Hosts and Hostesses	39
14. Cleaners of Vehicles and Equipment	39
15. Library Assistants and Bookmobile Drivers	38
16. Bread and Pastry Bakers	38
17. Institution or Cafeteria Cooks	38
18. Restaurant Cooks	38
19. Short Order and Fast Food Cooks	38
20. Bank Tellers	34
21. Retail Salespersons	33
22. Animal Caretakers	31
23. Veterinary Assistants	31
24. Landscaping and Groundskeeping Workers	30
25. Sprayers and Applicators	30

Best Jobs for Workers 16–24

Job	Percent Workers 16–24	Annual Earnings	Annual Openings	Percent Growth
1. Landscaping and Groundskeeping Workers	30	$17,140	283,459	21
2. Restaurant Cooks	38	$16,250	262,535	19
3. Sprayers and Applicators	30	$21,650	5,167	24
4. Counter and Rental Clerks	45	$14,510	199,406	23
5. Retail Salespersons	33	$15,830	1,305,317	14
6. Freight, Stock, and Material Movers	46	$18,470	306,549	2
7. Amusement and Recreation Attendants	46	$12,860	141,783	30
8. Cleaners of Vehicles and Equipment	39	$14,540	116,789	25
9. Construction Helpers	44	$19,510	167,103	7
10. Cashiers	52	$13,690	1,290,302	17
11. Ski Patrol Workers and Life Guards	76	$17,470	23,282	19
12. Bread and Pastry Bakers	38	$16,990	56,526	17
13. Veterinary Assistants	31	$16,200	14,770	28
14. Animal Caretakers	31	$14,820	43,263	22
15. File Clerks	39	$16,830	117,451	10
16. Food Preparation Workers	40	$13,700	529,498	10
17. Short Order and Fast Food Cooks	38	$12,700	226,320	18
18. Food Counter and Fountain Workers	51	$12,600	944,970	12
19. Library Assistants and Bookmobile Drivers	38	$16,980	35,994	16
20. Restaurant Hosts and Hostesses	39	$13,400	110,848	18
21. Bank Tellers	34	$17,200	106,674	−6
22. Institution or Cafeteria Cooks	38	$16,090	124,088	3
23. Tire Repairers and Changers	47	$16,810	26,095	10
24. Dining Room and Cafeteria Attendants and Bar Helpers	56	$12,580	181,922	4
25. Ushers, Lobby Attendants, and Ticket Takers	46	$12,520	22,505	18

Best-Paying Jobs for Workers 16–24

Job	Percent Workers 16–24	Annual Earnings
1. Sprayers and Applicators	30	$21,650
2. Construction Helpers	44	$19,510
3. Freight, Stock, and Material Movers	46	$18,470
4. Ski Patrol Workers and Life Guards	76	$17,470
5. Bank Tellers	34	$17,200
6. Landscaping and Groundskeeping Workers	30	$17,140
7. Bread and Pastry Bakers	38	$16,990
8. Library Assistants and Bookmobile Drivers	38	$16,980
9. File Clerks	39	$16,830
10. Tire Repairers and Changers	47	$16,810
11. Restaurant Cooks	38	$16,250
12. Veterinary Assistants	31	$16,200
13. Institution or Cafeteria Cooks	38	$16,090
14. Retail Salespersons	33	$15,830
15. Animal Caretakers	31	$14,820
16. Cleaners of Vehicles and Equipment	39	$14,540
17. Counter and Rental Clerks	45	$14,510
18. Food Preparation Workers	40	$13,700
19. Cashiers	52	$13,690
20. Restaurant Hosts and Hostesses	39	$13,400
21. Amusement and Recreation Attendants	46	$12,860
22. Short Order and Fast Food Cooks	38	$12,700
23. Food Counter and Fountain Workers	51	$12,600
24. Dining Room and Cafeteria Attendants and Bar Helpers	56	$12,580
25. Ushers, Lobby Attendants, and Ticket Takers	46	$12,520

Jobs with the Most Annual Openings for Workers 16–24

Job	Percent Workers 16–24	Annual Openings
1. Retail Salespersons	33	1,305,317
2. Cashiers	52	1,290,302
3. Food Counter and Fountain Workers	51	944,970
4. Food Preparation Workers	40	529,498
5. Freight, Stock, and Material Movers	46	306,549
6. Landscaping and Groundskeeping Workers	30	283,459
7. Restaurant Cooks	38	262,535
8. Short Order and Fast Food Cooks	38	226,320
9. Counter and Rental Clerks	45	199,406
10. Dining Room and Cafeteria Attendants and Bar Helpers	56	181,922
11. Construction Helpers	44	167,103
12. Amusement and Recreation Attendants	46	141,783
13. Institution or Cafeteria Cooks	38	124,088
14. File Clerks	39	117,451
15. Cleaners of Vehicles and Equipment	39	116,789
16. Restaurant Hosts and Hostesses	39	110,848
17. Bank Tellers	34	106,674
18. Bread and Pastry Bakers	38	56,526
19. Animal Caretakers	31	43,263
20. Library Assistants and Bookmobile Drivers	38	35,994
21. Tire Repairers and Changers	47	26,095
22. Ski Patrol Workers and Life Guards	76	23,282
23. Ushers, Lobby Attendants, and Ticket Takers	46	22,505
24. Veterinary Assistants	31	14,770
25. Sprayers and Applicators	30	5,167

Fastest Growing Jobs for Workers 16–24

Job	Percent Workers 16–24	Percent Growth
1. Amusement and Recreation Attendants	46	30
2. Veterinary Assistants	31	28
3. Cleaners of Vehicles and Equipment	39	25
4. Sprayers and Applicators	30	24
5. Counter and Rental Clerks	45	23
6. Animal Caretakers	31	22
7. Landscaping and Groundskeeping Workers	30	21
8. Restaurant Cooks	38	19
9. Ski Patrol Workers and Life Guards	76	19
10. Restaurant Hosts and Hostesses	39	18
11. Short Order and Fast Food Cooks	38	18
12. Ushers, Lobby Attendants, and Ticket Takers	46	18
13. Bread and Pastry Bakers	38	17
14. Cashiers	52	17
15. Library Assistants and Bookmobile Drivers	38	16
16. Retail Salespersons	33	14
17. Food Counter and Fountain Workers	51	12
18. File Clerks	39	10
19. Food Preparation Workers	40	10
20. Tire Repairers and Changers	47	10
21. Construction Helpers	44	7
22. Dining Room and Cafeteria Attendants and Bar Helpers	56	4
23. Institution or Cafeteria Cooks	38	3
24. Freight, Stock, and Material Movers	46	2
25. Bank Tellers	34	–6

Best Jobs Lists for Workers 55 and Over

We sorted the occupations in this book to include those with 15 percent or more of workers who are 55 and older. These workers account for approximately 12.5 percent of the workforce. The participation in the workforce for people 55 and over is less than that of other age groups as workers begin to retire. This is also an age group that had been particularly affected by layoffs in the past.

One use of these lists is to help identify work that might be interesting as you decide to change careers or approach retirement. Some occupations are on the lists because they attract older workers who want part-time work to supplement their retirement income. For example, we think that lawn service manager is on the list because it pays pretty well, can be done less than full-time and on a flexible schedule, and lends itself to self-employment—all things that might appeal to an older worker.

Other occupations such as clergy, physician, and musician take many years of training and experience. Once a person is established in such a career, the person often works in that occupation until retirement.

Jobs with the Highest Percentage of Workers 55 and Over

Job	Percent Workers 55 and Over
1. Lawn Service Managers	35
2. Nursery and Greenhouse Managers	35
3. Clergy	31
4. Property, Real Estate, and Community Association Managers	27
5. Real Estate Appraisers	27
6. Bus Drivers	23
7. School Bus Drivers	23
8. Management Analysts	22
9. Guards	22
10. Human Service Workers and Assistants	22
11. Personal Care and Home Health Aides	22
12. Private Detectives and Investigators	22
13. Taxi Drivers and Chauffeurs	22
14. Institutional Cleaning Supervisors	20
15. Archivists, Curators, Museum Technicians, and Conservators	20
16. Musicians	19
17. College and University Faculty	19
18. Bookkeeping, Accounting, and Auditing Clerks	18
19. Physicians	18
20. Pest Control Workers	18
21. Janitors, Cleaners, Maids, and Housekeeping Cleaners	18
22. Chiropractors	17
23. Civil Engineers	17
24. Dentists	17
25. Directors of Religious Activities and Education	17
26. Optometrists	17
27. Podiatrists	17
28. Recreation Workers	17
29. Veterinarians	17
30. Library Assistants and Bookmobile Drivers	17
31. Subway and Streetcar Operators	16
32. Dietitians and Nutritionists	15
33. Education Administrators	15
34. Construction and Building Inspectors	15
35. Inspectors and Compliance Officers	15

Best Jobs for Workers 55 and Over

Job	Percent Workers 55 and Over	Annual Earnings	Annual Openings	Percent Growth
1. College and University Faculty	19	$46,600	139,101	23
2. Physicians	18	$102,020	32,563	21
3. Management Analysts	22	$49,470	23,831	28
4. Human Service Workers and Assistants	22	$21,360	91,824	53
5. Civil Engineers	17	$53,450	20,603	21
6. Guards	22	$16,240	256,671	29
7. Personal Care and Home Health Aides	22	$15,800	249,694	58
8. Education Administrators	15	$60,400	60,229	13
9. Chiropractors	17	$63,930	2,516	23
10. Veterinarians	17	$50,950	3,227	25
11. Directors of Religious Activities and Education	17	$24,970	13,292	25
12. Musicians	19	$30,020	44,774	15
13. Property, Real Estate, and Community Association Managers	27	$29,860	47,581	14
14. School Bus Drivers	23	$18,820	65,136	18
15. Dietitians and Nutritionists	15	$35,040	8,153	19
16. Private Detectives and Investigators	22	$21,020	14,675	24
17. Bus Drivers	23	$24,370	29,885	16
18. Lawn Service Managers	35	$25,410	10,385	20
19. Pest Control Workers	18	$22,490	7,983	25
20. Recreation Workers	17	$16,500	43,829	19
21. Construction and Building Inspectors	15	$37,540	3,515	16
22. Bookkeeping, Accounting, and Auditing Clerks	18	$23,190	325,366	-4
23. Inspectors and Compliance Officers	15	$36,820	19,910	10
24. Library Assistants and Bookmobile Drivers	17	$16,980	35,994	16
25. Janitors, Cleaners, Maids, and Housekeeping Cleaners	18	$15,300	735,967	12

Best-Paying Jobs for Workers 55 and Over

Job	Percent Workers 55 and Over	Annual Earnings
1. Dentists	17	$110,160
2. Physicians	18	$102,020
3. Podiatrists	17	$79,530
4. Optometrists	17	$68,480
5. Chiropractors	17	$63,930
6. Education Administrators	15	$60,400
7. Civil Engineers	17	$53,450
8. Veterinarians	17	$50,950
9. Management Analysts	22	$49,470
10. College and University Faculty	19	$46,600
11. Subway and Streetcar Operators	16	$43,330
12. Real Estate Appraisers	27	$40,290
13. Construction and Building Inspectors	15	$37,540
14. Inspectors and Compliance Officers	15	$36,820
15. Dietitians and Nutritionists	15	$35,040
16. Archivists, Curators, Museum Technicians, and Conservators	20	$31,750
17. Musicians	19	$30,020
18. Property, Real Estate, and Community Association Managers	27	$29,860
19. Clergy	31	$28,850
20. Lawn Service Managers	35	$25,410
21. Nursery and Greenhouse Managers	35	$25,360
22. Directors of Religious Activities and Education	17	$24,970
23. Bus Drivers	23	$24,370
24. Bookkeeping, Accounting, and Auditing Clerks	18	$23,190
25. Pest Control Workers	18	$22,490

Jobs with the Most Annual Openings for Workers 55 and Over

Job	Percent Workers 55 and Over	Annual Openings
1. Janitors, Cleaners, Maids, and Housekeeping Cleaners	18	735,967
2. Bookkeeping, Accounting, and Auditing Clerks	18	325,366
3. Guards	22	256,671
4. Personal Care and Home Health Aides	22	249,694
5. College and University Faculty	19	139,101
6. Human Service Workers and Assistants	22	91,824
7. School Bus Drivers	23	65,136
8. Education Administrators	15	60,229
9. Property, Real Estate, and Community Association Managers	27	47,581
10. Musicians	19	44,774
11. Recreation Workers	17	43,829
12. Library Assistants and Bookmobile Drivers	17	35,994
13. Physicians	18	32,563
14. Bus Drivers	23	29,885
15. Taxi Drivers and Chauffeurs	22	26,739
16. Management Analysts	22	23,831
17. Civil Engineers	17	20,603
18. Inspectors and Compliance Officers	15	19,910
19. Private Detectives and Investigators	22	14,675
20. Clergy	31	14,197
21. Directors of Religious Activities and Education	17	13,292
22. Lawn Service Managers	35	10,385
23. Institutional Cleaning Supervisors	20	9,030
24. Dietitians and Nutritionists	15	8,153
25. Pest Control Workers	18	7,983

Fastest Growing Jobs for Workers 55 and Over

Job	Percent Workers 55 and Over	Percent Growth
1. Personal Care and Home Health Aides	22	58
2. Human Service Workers and Assistants	22	53
3. Guards	22	29
4. Management Analysts	22	28
5. Directors of Religious Activities and Education	17	25
6. Pest Control Workers	18	25
7. Veterinarians	17	25
8. Private Detectives and Investigators	22	24
9. College and University Faculty	19	23
10. Chiropractors	17	23
11. Physicians	18	21
12. Civil Engineers	17	21
13. Taxi Drivers and Chauffeurs	22	20
14. Lawn Service Managers	35	20
15. Recreation Workers	17	19
16. Dietitians and Nutritionists	15	19
17. School Bus Drivers	23	18
18. Library Assistants and Bookmobile Drivers	17	16
19. Bus Drivers	23	16
20. Construction and Building Inspectors	15	16
21. Musicians	19	15
22. Nursery and Greenhouse Managers	35	15
23. Property, Real Estate, and Community Association Managers	27	14
24. Education Administrators	15	13
25. Clergy	31	13

Best Jobs Lists for Part-Time Workers

Many people work less than full-time or hold down more than one part-time job. For example, people who are going to school or who have young children may desire part-time work so that they can attend classes or spend more time with their families. Others work a second job to supplement their incomes or work two or more part-time jobs because one desirable full-time job is not available.

If you want to work part-time, these lists will be helpful in identifying where most others are finding opportunities for this kind of work. Many of the jobs, particularly those with lower pay, can be learned quickly, offer flexible work schedules, are easy to obtain, and offer other advantages.

While many people think that part-time jobs require low skill and offer low pay, this is not always the case. For example, 7 of the 10 best-paying, part-time jobs require professional credentials or substantial experience, such as university faculty and musician, and 7 of the 20 best jobs overall are in teaching and education.

The occupations chosen were those where 30 percent or more of the workers were part-time—a total of 49 jobs. Note that these are the only lists where earnings are reported as hourly earnings—we thought this made more sense for evaluating these jobs.

Jobs with the Highest Percentage of Part-Time Workers

Job	Percent Part-Time Workers
1. Food Counter and Fountain Workers	63
2. Library Assistants and Bookmobile Drivers	62
3. Teacher Assistants	62
4. Dining Room and Cafeteria Attendants and Bar Helpers	60
5. Food Preparation Workers	57
6. Cashiers	57
7. Musicians	54
8. Ski Patrol Workers and Life Guards	51
9. Counter and Rental Clerks	51
10. Amusement and Recreation Attendants	49
11. Ushers, Lobby Attendants, and Ticket Takers	49
12. Flight Attendants	46
13. Child Care Workers	43
14. Bus Drivers	43
15. School Bus Drivers	43

Jobs with the Highest Percentage of Part-Time Workers

Job	Percent Part-Time Workers
16. Adult Education Instructors	43
17. Sports and Physical Training Instructors and Coaches	43
18. Vocational Education Teachers and Instructors	43
19. Human Service Workers and Assistants	42
20. Personal Care and Home Health Aides	42
21. Baggage Porters and Bellhops	41
22. Retail Salespersons	40
23. Dental Assistants	40
24. Bread and Pastry Bakers	39
25. Institution or Cafeteria Cooks	39
26. Restaurant Cooks	39
27. Short Order and Fast Food Cooks	39
28. Freight, Stock, and Material Movers	38
29. Restaurant Hosts and Hostesses	38
30. Animal Caretakers	38
31. Veterinary Assistants	38
32. Hairdressers, Hairstylists, and Cosmetologists	37
33. Manicurists	37
34. File Clerks	36
35. Receptionists and Information Clerks	35
36. Bank Tellers	35
37. Ambulance Drivers and Attendants	35
38. Physical Therapy Assistants and Aides	35
39. Bookkeeping, Accounting, and Auditing Clerks	33
40. Banking New Accounts Clerks	33
41. Interviewing Clerks	33
42. Kindergarten Teachers	32
43. Preschool Teachers	32
44. College and University Faculty	32
45. Janitors, Cleaners, Maids, and Housekeeping Cleaners	32
46. Travel Agents	32
47. General Office Clerks	31
48. Pest Control Workers	30
49. Tire Repairers and Changers	30

Best Jobs for Part-Time Workers

Job	Percent Part-Time Workers	Hourly Earnings	Annual Openings	Percent Growth
1. College and University Faculty	32	$22	139,101	23
2. Receptionists and Information Clerks	35	$9	386,806	24
3. Human Service Workers and Assistants	42	$10	91,824	53
4. Dental Assistants	40	$11	56,389	42
5. Sports and Physical Training Instructors and Coaches	43	$11	104,431	28
6. Personal Care and Home Health Aides	42	$8	249,694	58
7. Teacher Assistants	62	$8	343,831	32
8. General Office Clerks	31	$9	745,378	15
9. Adult Education Instructors	43	$12	46,224	21
10. Flight Attendants	46	$18	5,376	30
11. Child Care Workers	43	$7	328,786	26
12. Physical Therapy Assistants and Aides	35	$11	14,195	44
13. Restaurant Cooks	39	$8	262,535	19
14. Bookkeeping, Accounting, and Auditing Clerks	33	$11	325,366	−4
15. Vocational Education Teachers and Instructors	43	$17	106,468	11
16. School Bus Drivers	43	$9	65,136	18
17. Amusement and Recreation Attendants	49	$6	141,783	30
18. Interviewing Clerks	33	$9	44,483	23
19. Preschool Teachers	32	$8	41,894	26
20. Retail Salespersons	40	$8	1,305,317	14
21. Counter and Rental Clerks	51	$7	199,406	23
22. Musicians	54	$14	44,774	15
23. Pest Control Workers	30	$11	7,983	25
24. Cashiers	57	$7	1,290,302	17
25. Bus Drivers	43	$12	29,885	16

Best-Paying Jobs for Part-Time Workers

Job	Percent Part-Time Workers	Hourly Earnings
1. College and University Faculty	32	$22
2. Flight Attendants	46	$18
3. Vocational Education Teachers and Instructors	43	$17
4. Kindergarten Teachers	32	$16
5. Musicians	54	$14
6. Adult Education Instructors	43	$12
7. Bus Drivers	43	$12
8. Bookkeeping, Accounting, and Auditing Clerks	33	$11
9. Travel Agents	32	$11
10. Dental Assistants	40	$11
11. Pest Control Workers	30	$11
12. Sports and Physical Training Instructors and Coaches	43	$11
13. Physical Therapy Assistants and Aides	35	$11
14. Human Service Workers and Assistants	42	$10
15. Banking New Accounts Clerks	33	$10
16. General Office Clerks	31	$9
17. School Bus Drivers	43	$9
18. Receptionists and Information Clerks	35	$9
19. Interviewing Clerks	33	$9
20. Freight, Stock, and Material Movers	38	$9
21. Ski Patrol Workers and Life Guards	51	$8
22. Preschool Teachers	32	$8
23. Bank Tellers	35	$8
24. Bread and Pastry Bakers	39	$8
25. Library Assistants and Bookmobile Drivers	62	$8

Jobs with the Most Annual Openings for Part-Time Workers

Job	Percent Part-Time Workers	Annual Openings
1. Retail Salespersons	40	1,305,317
2. Cashiers	57	1,290,302
3. Food Counter and Fountain Workers	63	944,970
4. General Office Clerks	31	745,378
5. Janitors, Cleaners, Maids, and Housekeeping Cleaners	32	735,967
6. Food Preparation Workers	57	529,498
7. Receptionists and Information Clerks	35	386,806
8. Teacher Assistants	62	343,831
9. Child Care Workers	43	328,786
10. Bookkeeping, Accounting, and Auditing Clerks	33	325,366
11. Freight, Stock, and Material Movers	38	306,549
12. Restaurant Cooks	39	262,535
13. Personal Care and Home Health Aides	42	249,694
14. Short Order and Fast Food Cooks	39	226,320
15. Counter and Rental Clerks	51	199,406
16. Dining Room and Cafeteria Attendants and Bar Helpers	60	181,922
17. Amusement and Recreation Attendants	49	141,783
18. College and University Faculty	32	139,101
19. Institution or Cafeteria Cooks	39	124,088
20. File Clerks	36	117,451
21. Restaurant Hosts and Hostesses	38	110,848
22. Bank Tellers	35	106,674
23. Vocational Education Teachers and Instructors	43	106,468
24. Sports and Physical Training Instructors and Coaches	43	104,431
25. Human Service Workers and Assistants	42	91,824

Fastest Growing Jobs for Part-Time Workers

Job	Percent Part-Time Workers	Percent Growth
1. Personal Care and Home Health Aides	42	58
2. Human Service Workers and Assistants	42	53
3. Physical Therapy Assistants and Aides	35	44
4. Dental Assistants	40	42
5. Ambulance Drivers and Attendants	35	35
6. Teacher Assistants	62	32
7. Amusement and Recreation Attendants	49	30
8. Flight Attendants	46	30
9. Sports and Physical Training Instructors and Coaches	43	28
10. Veterinary Assistants	38	28
11. Child Care Workers	43	26
12. Preschool Teachers	32	26
13. Manicurists	37	26
14. Pest Control Workers	30	25
15. Receptionists and Information Clerks	35	24
16. Counter and Rental Clerks	51	23
17. College and University Faculty	32	23
18. Interviewing Clerks	33	23
19. Animal Caretakers	38	22
20. Adult Education Instructors	43	21
21. Restaurant Cooks	39	19
22. Ski Patrol Workers and Life Guards	51	19
23. Short Order and Fast Food Cooks	39	18
24. Restaurant Hosts and Hostesses	38	18
25. School Bus Drivers	43	18

Best Jobs Lists for Self-Employed Workers

About 10 percent of all working people are self-employed or own their own businesses. This is a substantial part of our workforce, yet they get little mention in most career books. That is one reason we have included these lists. Many occupations in these lists, such as greenhouse manager and bicycle repairer, are held by people who operate one- or two-person businesses and who may also do this work part-time. Others, such as carpenter, will often work on a per-job basis.

While the lists do not show it, older workers and women make up a rapidly growing part of the self-employed. With the large-scale layoffs of the past decades, some highly experienced older workers had difficulty finding employment and set up consulting and other small businesses as a result. Large numbers of women are now forming small businesses or creating self-employment opportunities as an alternative to traditional employment.

We sorted our database of occupations and included in the lists that follow occupations where 20 percent or more of the workers are self-employed. A total of 42 jobs met this requirement. Thirteen of the 25 best jobs for self-employment require at least a bachelor's degree, and most of the remaining jobs require postsecondary education or long-term, on-the-job training.

The 25 best-paying jobs show that self-employed workers can have very high earnings—23 of the top 25 jobs pay above average. In addition, two-thirds of the jobs are growing faster than the national average. It would seem that self-employment can be a good career move for those with highly sought-after skills.

Jobs with the Highest Percentage of Self-Employed Workers

Job	Percent Self-Employed Workers
1. Nursery and Greenhouse Managers	85
2. Bicycle Repairers	70
3. Artists and Commercial Artists	61
4. Lawn Service Managers	59
5. Chiropractors	58
6. Child Care Workers	58
7. Adult Education Instructors	49
8. Dentists	49

Jobs with the Highest Percentage of Self-Employed Workers

Job	Percent Self-Employed Workers
9. Podiatrists	47
10. Management Analysts	46
11. Interior Designers	46
12. Hairdressers, Hairstylists, and Cosmetologists	46
13. Taxi Drivers and Chauffeurs	44
14. Psychologists	44
15. Property, Real Estate, and Community Association Managers	40
16. Veterinarians	40
17. Food Service and Lodging Managers	38
18. Optometrists	38
19. Manicurists	37
20. Marketing and Sales Worker Supervisors	37
21. Carpenters	37
22. Dancers and Choreographers	37
23. Lawyers	36
24. Designers	32
25. Athletes, Coaches, and Umpires	31
26. Writers and Editors	31
27. Roofers	31
28. Architects	31
29. Locksmiths and Safe Repairers	31
30. Bricklayers, Blockmasons, and Stonemasons	28
31. Landscaping and Groundskeeping Workers	28
32. Musicians	26
33. Animal Caretakers	24
34. Actors, Directors, and Producers	24
35. Securities, Commodities, and Financial Services Sales Agents	22
36. Automotive Mechanics and Service Technicians	22
37. Landscape Architects	22
38. Automotive Body Repairers	21
39. Real Estate Appraisers	21
40. Physicians	20
41. Plasterers and Stucco Masons	20
42. Private Detectives and Investigators	20

Best Jobs for Self-Employed Workers

Job	Percent Self-Employed Workers	Annual Earnings	Annual Openings	Percent Growth
1. Securities, Commodities, and Financial Services Sales Agents	22	$48,090	61,084	41
2. Artists and Commercial Artists	61	$31,690	58,769	26
3. Management Analysts	46	$49,470	23,831	28
4. Designers	32	$29,190	57,787	27
5. Writers and Editors	31	$36,480	52,971	24
6. Physicians	20	$102,020	32,563	21
7. Lawyers	36	$78,170	38,182	17
8. Interior Designers	46	$31,760	9,201	27
9. Child Care Workers	58	$13,750	328,786	26
10. Veterinarians	40	$50,950	3,227	25
11. Actors, Directors, and Producers	24	$27,370	31,279	24
12. Automotive Mechanics and Service Technicians	22	$27,360	119,161	17
13. Chiropractors	58	$63,930	2,516	23
14. Landscaping and Groundskeeping Workers	28	$17,140	283,459	21
15. Food Service and Lodging Managers	38	$26,700	138,826	16
16. Musicians	26	$30,020	44,774	15
17. Athletes, Coaches, and Umpires	31	$22,210	19,465	28
18. Marketing and Sales Worker Supervisors	37	$29,570	410,550	10
19. Adult Education Instructors	49	$24,790	46,224	21
20. Architects	31	$47,710	7,762	19
21. Property, Real Estate, and Community Association Managers	40	$29,860	47,581	14
22. Automotive Body Repairers	21	$27,400	33,051	16
23. Bricklayers, Blockmasons, and Stonemasons	28	$35,200	29,721	12
24. Carpenters	37	$28,700	236,108	7
25. Psychologists	44	$48,050	21,473	11

Best-Paying Jobs for Self-Employed Workers

Job	Percent Self-Employed Workers	Annual Earnings
1. Dentists	49	$110,160
2. Physicians	20	$102,020
3. Podiatrists	47	$79,530
4. Lawyers	36	$78,170
5. Optometrists	38	$68,480
6. Chiropractors	58	$63,930
7. Veterinarians	40	$50,950
8. Management Analysts	46	$49,470
9. Securities, Commodities, and Financial Services Sales Agents	22	$48,090
10. Psychologists	44	$48,050
11. Architects	31	$47,710
12. Real Estate Appraisers	21	$40,290
13. Landscape Architects	22	$37,930
14. Writers and Editors	31	$36,480
15. Bricklayers, Blockmasons, and Stonemasons	28	$35,200
16. Interior Designers	46	$31,760
17. Artists and Commercial Artists	61	$31,690
18. Musicians	26	$30,020
19. Property, Real Estate, and Community Association Managers	40	$29,860
20. Marketing and Sales Worker Supervisors	37	$29,570
21. Plasterers and Stucco Masons	20	$29,390
22. Designers	32	$29,190
23. Carpenters	37	$28,700
24. Automotive Body Repairers	21	$27,400
25. Actors, Directors, and Producers	24	$27,370

Jobs with the Most Annual Openings for Self-Employed Workers

Job	Percent Self-Employed Workers	Annual Openings
1. Marketing and Sales Worker Supervisors	37	410,550
2. Child Care Workers	58	328,786
3. Landscaping and Groundskeeping Workers	28	283,459
4. Carpenters	37	236,108
5. Food Service and Lodging Managers	38	138,826
6. Automotive Mechanics and Service Technicians	22	119,161
7. Hairdressers, Hairstylists, and Cosmetologists	46	73,177
8. Securities, Commodities, and Financial Services Sales Agents	22	61,084
9. Artists and Commercial Artists	61	58,769
10. Designers	32	57,787
11. Writers and Editors	31	52,971
12. Property, Real Estate, and Community Association Managers	40	47,581
13. Adult Education Instructors	49	46,224
14. Musicians	26	44,774
15. Animal Caretakers	24	43,263
16. Lawyers	36	38,182
17. Automotive Body Repairers	21	33,051
18. Physicians	20	32,563
19. Actors, Directors, and Producers	24	31,279
20. Bricklayers, Blockmasons, and Stonemasons	28	29,721
21. Roofers	31	28,797
22. Taxi Drivers and Chauffeurs	44	26,739
23. Management Analysts	46	23,831
24. Psychologists	44	21,473
25. Athletes, Coaches, and Umpires	31	19,465

Fastest Growing Jobs for Self-Employed Workers

Job	Percent Self-Employed Workers	Percent Growth
1. Securities, Commodities, and Financial Services Sales Agents	22	41
2. Athletes, Coaches, and Umpires	31	28
3. Management Analysts	46	28
4. Designers	32	27
5. Interior Designers	46	27
6. Artists and Commercial Artists	61	26
7. Child Care Workers	58	26
8. Manicurists	37	26
9. Veterinarians	40	25
10. Actors, Directors, and Producers	24	24
11. Private Detectives and Investigators	20	24
12. Writers and Editors	31	24
13. Bicycle Repairers	70	23
14. Chiropractors	58	23
15. Animal Caretakers	24	22
16. Adult Education Instructors	49	21
17. Landscaping and Groundskeeping Workers	28	21
18. Physicians	20	21
19. Lawn Service Managers	59	20
20. Taxi Drivers and Chauffeurs	44	20
21. Architects	31	19
22. Automotive Mechanics and Service Technicians	22	17
23. Lawyers	36	17
24. Plasterers and Stucco Masons	20	17
25. Automotive Body Repairers	21	16

Best Jobs Lists for Women

As stated earlier, this group of lists is not meant to restrict women from considering job options. Our reason for including these lists is exactly the opposite. Many readers have shared that these lists help them see possibilities that they might not otherwise have considered. For example, we suggest that women browse the lists that employ high percentages of men. Many of those occupations pay quite well and could be held by women who want to do them—and who get the necessary education and training.

We created the lists by sorting the database of occupations in this book to include jobs where 70 percent or more of the workers were women. That resulted in 66 jobs.

The lists that follow present occupations employing high percentages of women. In comparing these lists to those with a high percentage of men, it struck us that there were distinct differences beyond the obvious. For example, jobs employing high percentages of women are growing much faster than those on the similar lists for men. The average growth for the jobs for women is 23 percent, almost two-thirds more than the rate for men—15 percent. The number of annual job openings shows a similar pattern. Occupations with the highest percent of men average 46,890 openings a year, while those for women are more than double at 114,516 openings.

This might explain why men have had more problems than women in adapting to an economy dominated by service and information-based jobs. Many women may simply be better prepared, with more appropriate skills, for the jobs that are now growing rapidly. Economists have long noticed that men over 50 who are laid off find it very difficult to locate new jobs. Looking over our lists based on gender, you can see how this might be so. Older males, traditionally employed in manufacturing, trade, and other "male" jobs, may have developed few skills needed in booming occupations. When men lose jobs, fewer similar jobs are likely to be available. The result is longer lengths of unemployment, new employment in lower-paying jobs, forced withdrawal from the labor market, and other fates not suffered by many women who have skills that are more in demand.

Perhaps you can come to other conclusions, but evidence shows that women with good technical training and education are doing quite well. And it is increasingly true that people without these skills are less likely to find the best jobs.

Jobs with the Highest Percentage of Women

Job	Percent Women
1. Court Reporters, Medical Transcriptionists, and Stenographers	99
2. Legal Secretaries	99
3. Medical Secretaries	99
4. Secretaries	99
5. Kindergarten Teachers	98
6. Preschool Teachers	98
7. Dental Assistants	97
8. Child Care Workers	95
9. Licensed Practical Nurses	95
10. Receptionists and Information Clerks	94
11. Registered Nurses	94
12. Bookkeeping, Accounting, and Auditing Clerks	92
13. Dietitians and Nutritionists	92
14. Hairdressers, Hairstylists, and Cosmetologists	91
15. Manicurists	91
16. Bank Tellers	91
17. Nursing Aides, Orderlies, and Attendants	89
18. Psychiatric Technicians	89
19. Travel Agents	88
20. Hotel, Motel, and Resort Desk Clerks	87
21. Cost Estimators	87
22. Pharmacists	86
23. Physician Assistants	86
24. Elementary School Teachers	86
25. Human Service Workers and Assistants	85
26. Personal Care and Home Health Aides	85
27. Special Education Teachers	84
28. Data Entry Keyers	84
29. Billing, Cost, and Rate Clerks	82
30. Flight Attendants	82
31. Cardiovascular Technologists and Technicians	82
32. Dental Hygienists	82
33. Medical Assistants	82
34. Medical Records and Health Information Technicians	82
35. Pharmacy Technicians	82
36. Surgical Technologists	82
37. Archivists, Curators, Museum Technicians, and Conservators	81
38. Banking New Accounts Clerks	81

(continues)

(continued)

Jobs with the Highest Percentage of Women

Job	Percent Women
39. Interviewing Clerks	81
40. Occupational Therapy Assistants and Aides	81
41. General Office Clerks	80
42. Cashiers	80
43. Paralegals and Legal Assistants	80
44. File Clerks	79
45. Physical Therapy Assistants and Aides	79
46. Library Assistants and Bookmobile Drivers	78
47. Teacher Assistants	78
48. Brokerage Clerks	77
49. Clinical Laboratory Technologists and Technicians	77
50. Loan and Credit Clerks	76
51. Correspondence Clerks	76
52. Court Clerks	75
53. Insurance Adjusters, Examiners, and Investigators	75
54. Insurance Claims Clerks	75
55. Municipal Clerks	75
56. Property and Casualty Insurance Claims Examiners	75
57. Adjustment Clerks	75
58. Food Preparation Workers	74
59. Occupational Therapists	74
60. Physical Therapists	74
61. Recreational Therapists	74
62. Respiratory Therapists	74
63. Speech-Language Pathologists and Audiologists	74
64. Nuclear Medicine Technologists	74
65. Radiologic Technologists and Technicians	74
66. Food Counter and Fountain Workers	73

Best Jobs Employing 70 Percent or More Women

Job	Percent Women	Annual Earnings	Annual Openings	Percent Growth
1. Registered Nurses	94	$40,690	195,231	22
2. Paralegals and Legal Assistants	80	$32,760	33,971	62
3. Dental Hygienists	82	$45,890	15,372	40
4. Special Education Teachers	84	$37,850	36,540	34
5. Human Service Workers and Assistants	85	$21,360	91,824	53
6. Physician Assistants	86	$47,090	6,142	48
7. Dental Assistants	97	$22,640	56,389	42
8. Physical Therapists	74	$56,600	10,602	34
9. Adjustment Clerks	75	$22,040	141,670	34
10. Speech-Language Pathologists and Audiologists	74	$43,080	9,862	38
11. Medical Assistants	82	$20,680	49,015	58
12. Personal Care and Home Health Aides	85	$15,800	249,694	58
13. Elementary School Teachers	86	$36,110	204,210	12
14. Occupational Therapists	74	$48,230	6,484	34
15. Respiratory Therapists	74	$34,830	8,553	43
16. Insurance Adjusters, Examiners, and Investigators	75	$38,290	16,055	20
17. Receptionists and Information Clerks	94	$18,620	386,806	24
18. Brokerage Clerks	77	$27,920	17,895	28
19. Licensed Practical Nurses	95	$26,940	43,314	20
20. Cost Estimators	87	$40,590	27,649	13
21. Teacher Assistants	78	$15,800	343,831	32
22. Nursing Aides, Orderlies, and Attendants	89	$16,620	349,640	24
23. Surgical Technologists	82	$25,780	9,182	42
24. Cardiovascular Technologists and Technicians	82	$35,770	3,458	39
25. Clinical Laboratory Technologists and Technicians	77	$32,440	20,441	17

Best-Paying Jobs Employing 70 Percent or More Women

Job	Percent Women	Annual Earnings
1. Pharmacists	86	$66,220
2. Physical Therapists	74	$56,600
3. Occupational Therapists	74	$48,230
4. Physician Assistants	86	$47,090
5. Dental Hygienists	82	$45,890
6. Speech-Language Pathologists and Audiologists	74	$43,080
7. Registered Nurses	94	$40,690
8. Cost Estimators	87	$40,590
9. Property and Casualty Insurance Claims Examiners	75	$40,110
10. Nuclear Medicine Technologists	74	$39,610
11. Insurance Adjusters, Examiners, and Investigators	75	$38,290
12. Special Education Teachers	84	$37,850
13. Flight Attendants	82	$37,800
14. Elementary School Teachers	86	$36,110
15. Cardiovascular Technologists and Technicians	82	$35,770
16. Dietitians and Nutritionists	92	$35,040
17. Respiratory Therapists	74	$34,830
18. Kindergarten Teachers	98	$33,590
19. Radiologic Technologists and Technicians	74	$32,880
20. Paralegals and Legal Assistants	80	$32,760
21. Clinical Laboratory Technologists and Technicians	77	$32,440
22. Archivists, Curators, Museum Technicians, and Conservators	81	$31,750
23. Legal Secretaries	99	$30,050
24. Occupational Therapy Assistants and Aides	81	$28,690
25. Brokerage Clerks	77	$27,920

Jobs with the Most Annual Openings Employing 70 Percent or More Women

Job	Percent Women	Annual Openings
1. Cashiers	80	1,290,302
2. Food Counter and Fountain Workers	73	944,970
3. General Office Clerks	80	745,378
4. Food Preparation Workers	74	529,498
5. Receptionists and Information Clerks	94	386,806
6. Secretaries	99	358,379
7. Nursing Aides, Orderlies, and Attendants	89	349,640
8. Teacher Assistants	78	343,831
9. Child Care Workers	95	328,786
10. Bookkeeping, Accounting, and Auditing Clerks	92	325,366
11. Personal Care and Home Health Aides	85	249,694
12. Elementary School Teachers	86	204,210
13. Registered Nurses	94	195,231
14. Adjustment Clerks	75	141,670
15. File Clerks	79	117,451
16. Data Entry Keyers	84	107,440
17. Bank Tellers	91	106,674
18. Human Service Workers and Assistants	85	91,824
19. Hairdressers, Hairstylists, and Cosmetologists	91	73,177
20. Billing, Cost, and Rate Clerks	82	63,239
21. Hotel, Motel, and Resort Desk Clerks	87	60,382
22. Dental Assistants	97	56,389
23. Medical Assistants	82	49,015
24. Loan and Credit Clerks	76	46,537
25. Interviewing Clerks	81	44,483

Fastest Growing Jobs Employing 70 Percent or More Women

Job	Percent Women	Percent Growth
1. Paralegals and Legal Assistants	80	62
2. Medical Assistants	82	58
3. Personal Care and Home Health Aides	85	58
4. Human Service Workers and Assistants	85	53
5. Physician Assistants	86	48
6. Medical Records and Health Information Technicians	82	44
7. Physical Therapy Assistants and Aides	79	44
8. Respiratory Therapists	74	43
9. Dental Assistants	97	42
10. Surgical Technologists	82	42
11. Dental Hygienists	82	40
12. Occupational Therapy Assistants and Aides	81	40
13. Cardiovascular Technologists and Technicians	82	39
14. Speech-Language Pathologists and Audiologists	74	38
15. Adjustment Clerks	75	34
16. Occupational Therapists	74	34
17. Physical Therapists	74	34
18. Special Education Teachers	84	34
19. Teacher Assistants	78	32
20. Flight Attendants	82	30
21. Brokerage Clerks	77	28
22. Child Care Workers	95	26
23. Manicurists	91	26
24. Preschool Teachers	98	26
25. Nursing Aides, Orderlies, and Attendants	89	24

Best Jobs Lists for Men

We suggest you read the introductory material to "Best Job Lists for Different Types of Workers" and "Best Jobs Lists for Women" to better understand the purpose for including these lists. As stated earlier, as with the lists of best jobs for women, we are not suggesting that the best jobs lists for men include the only jobs that men should consider.

For example, male nurses and male elementary school teachers are in short supply, and the few available are highly recruited and often find jobs quickly. Just as many women should consider careers typically held by men, many men should consider career opportunities among occupations typically held by women. This is particularly true now, since occupations with high percentages of women workers are growing more rapidly than those on our lists for men.

We created the lists by sorting the database of occupations in this book to include jobs where 70 percent or more of the workers were men. That resulted in 98 jobs.

Note that 13 of the best jobs employing high percentages of men are in technical and mechanical fields, while 18 of the best jobs with a high percentage of women are in humanitarian fields—primarily in the rapidly growing health and education areas. This confirms the concern that many educators, counselors, and social advocates have about sexual stereotyping. In many cases, both men and women would be well advised to consider occupations typically held by the opposite gender.

Another thing we noticed is that the 25 best-paying jobs for men have earnings significantly higher than the women's best-paying jobs. The average for the top 25 best-paying jobs for men is $65,717, while for women it is $38,955. Twelve of the 25 highest-paying jobs for men are in the engineering field while 14 of the highest-paying jobs for women are in the health area. This indicates that women interested in improving their earnings might want to seriously consider jobs traditionally dominated by men.

Jobs with the Highest Percentage of Men

Job	Percent Men
1. Roofers	100
2. Excavation and Loading Machine Operators	100
3. Bus and Truck Mechanics and Diesel Engine Specialists	100
4. Heating, Air Conditioning, and Refrigeration Mechanics and Installers	99
5. Carpenters	99
6. Automotive Mechanics and Service Technicians	99
7. Automotive Body Repairers	99
8. Bricklayers, Blockmasons, and Stonemasons	99

(continues)

(continued)

Jobs with the Highest Percentage of Men

Job	Percent Men
9. Subway and Streetcar Operators	98
10. Electricians	98
11. Electrical Powerline Installers and Repairers	98
12. Fire Inspectors	98
13. Water Vessel Captains and Pilots	98
14. Ship Engineers	98
15. Fishing Vessel Captains and Officers	98
16. Plasterers and Stucco Masons	98
17. Paving, Surfacing, and Tamping Equipment Operators	98
18. Highway Maintenance Workers	97
19. Aircraft Pilots and Flight Engineers	97
20. Construction Helpers	97
21. Truck Drivers	96
22. Aircraft Mechanics and Service Technicians	95
23. Water and Liquid Waste Treatment Plant and System Operators	95
24. Power Generating and Reactor Plant Operators	95
25. Power Distributors and Dispatchers	95
26. Gas and Petroleum Plant and System Occupations	95
27. Chemical Plant and System Operators	95
28. Mechanical Engineers	95
29. Tire Repairers and Changers	95
30. Office Machine and Cash Register Servicers	94
31. Elevator Installers and Repairers	94
32. Locksmiths and Safe Repairers	94
33. Landscaping and Groundskeeping Workers	94
34. Sprayers and Applicators	94
35. Electrical and Electronics Engineers	94
36. Aircraft Assemblers	94
37. Sheet Metal Workers and Duct Installers	93
38. Medical Equipment Repairers	93
39. Bicycle Repairers	93
40. General Utility Maintenance Repairers	93
41. Coin, Vending, and Amusement Machine Servicers and Repairers	93
42. Commercial and Industrial Electronics Equipment Repairers	92
43. Civil Engineers	92
44. Chemical Engineers	92

Jobs with the Highest Percentage of Men

Job	Percent Men
45. Mining Engineers	92
46. Petroleum Engineers	92
47. Materials Engineers	92
48. Nuclear Engineers	92
49. Aerospace Engineers	92
50. Blue-Collar Worker Supervisors	91
51. Taxi Drivers and Chauffeurs	90
52. Chemical Equipment Controllers, Operators and Tenders	90
53. Pruners	89
54. Parking Lot Attendants	89
55. Clergy	89
56. Cleaners of Vehicles and Equipment	88
57. Police and Detective Supervisors	88
58. Fire Fighting and Prevention Supervisors	88
59. Police Patrol Officers	87
60. Detectives and Criminal Investigators	87
61. Telephone and Cable TV Line Installers and Repairers	85
62. Electrical and Electronic Technicians	85
63. Industrial Engineers	85
64. Combination Machine Tool Setters, Set-Up Operators, Operators, and Tenders	85
65. Numerical Control Machine Tool Operators and Tenders	85
66. Sheriffs and Deputy Sheriffs	84
67. Private Detectives and Investigators	84
68. Guards	84
69. Central Office and PBX Installers and Repairers	84
70. Architects	84
71. Landscape Architects	84
72. Farm Workers	84
73. Data Processing Equipment Repairers	82
74. Correctional Officers	81
75. Freight, Stock, and Material Movers	80
76. Dentists	79
77. Optometrists	79
78. Podiatrists	79
79. Veterinarians	79
80. Chiropractors	79

(continues)

(continued)

Jobs with the Highest Percentage of Men

Job	Percent Men
81. Physicians	78
82. Electrolytic Plating Machine Setters, Set-Up Operators, Operators, and Tenders	77
83. Lawn Service Managers	76
84. Nursery and Greenhouse Managers	76
85. Lawyers	75
86. Bindery Machine Operators and Set-Up Operators	75
87. Inspectors and Compliance Officers	72
88. Construction and Building Inspectors	72
89. General Managers and Top Executives	72
90. Administrative Services Managers	72
91. Communication, Transportation, and Utilities Operations Managers	72
92. Construction Managers	72
93. Industrial Production Managers	72
94. Engineering, Natural Science, and Computer and Information Systems Managers	72
95. Shipping, Receiving, and Traffic Clerks	72
96. Electronic Semiconductor Processors	72
97. Computer Programmers	71
98. Securities, Commodities, and Financial Services Sales Agents	70

Best Jobs Employing 70 Percent or More Men

Job	Percent Men	Annual Earnings	Annual Openings	Percent Growth
1. Engineering, Natural Science, and Computer and Information Systems Managers	72	$75,320	54,120	44
2. Securities, Commodities, and Financial Services Sales Agents	70	$48,090	61,084	41
3. Physicians	78	$102,020	32,563	21
4. Computer Programmers	71	$47,550	74,773	30
5. Electrical and Electronics Engineers	94	$62,260	29,636	26
6. General Managers and Top Executives	72	$55,890	421,006	16
7. Lawyers	75	$78,170	38,182	17
8. Police Patrol Officers	87	$37,710	51,739	32
9. Civil Engineers	92	$53,450	20,603	21
10. Communication, Transportation, and Utilities Operations Managers	72	$52,810	25,388	19
11. Administrative Services Managers	72	$44,370	46,558	18
12. Correctional Officers	81	$28,540	64,835	39
13. Construction Managers	72	$47,610	32,841	14
14. Data Processing Equipment Repairers	82	$29,340	20,080	47
15. Electrical and Electronic Technicians	85	$35,970	42,572	17
16. Central Office and PBX Installers and Repairers	84	$43,680	4,617	32
17. Telephone and Cable TV Line Installers and Repairers	85	$32,750	18,246	30
18. Chiropractors	79	$63,930	2,516	23
19. Guards	84	$16,240	256,671	29
20. Automotive Mechanics and Service Technicians	99	$27,360	119,161	17
21. Veterinarians	79	$50,950	3,227	25
22. Architects	84	$47,710	7,762	19
23. Truck Drivers	96	$24,300	535,419	17
24. Landscaping and Groundskeeping Workers	94	$17,140	283,459	21
25. Mechanical Engineers	95	$53,290	9,388	16

Best-Paying Jobs Employing 70 Percent or More Men

Job	Percent Men	Annual Earnings
1. Dentists	79	$110,160
2. Physicians	78	$102,020
3. Aircraft Pilots and Flight Engineers	97	$91,750
4. Podiatrists	79	$79,530
5. Lawyers	75	$78,170
6. Engineering, Natural Science, and Computer and Information Systems Managers	72	$75,320
7. Petroleum Engineers	92	$74,260
8. Nuclear Engineers	92	$71,310
9. Optometrists	79	$68,480
10. Aerospace Engineers	92	$66,950
11. Chemical Engineers	92	$64,760
12. Chiropractors	79	$63,930
13. Electrical and Electronics Engineers	94	$62,260
14. Materials Engineers	92	$57,970
15. Industrial Production Managers	72	$56,320
16. Mining Engineers	92	$56,090
17. General Managers and Top Executives	72	$55,890
18. Civil Engineers	92	$53,450
19. Mechanical Engineers	95	$53,290
20. Communication, Transportation, and Utilities Operations Managers	72	$52,810
21. Industrial Engineers	85	$52,610
22. Veterinarians	79	$50,950
23. Police and Detective Supervisors	88	$48,700
24. Securities, Commodities, and Financial Services Sales Agents	70	$48,090
25. Elevator Installers and Repairers	94	$47,860

Jobs with the Most Annual Openings Employing 70 Percent or More Men

Job	Percent Men	Annual Openings
1. Truck Drivers	96	535,419
2. General Managers and Top Executives	72	421,006
3. Freight, Stock, and Material Movers	80	306,549
4. Landscaping and Groundskeeping Workers	94	283,459
5. Guards	84	256,671
6. Shipping, Receiving, and Traffic Clerks	72	242,666
7. Carpenters	99	236,108
8. Blue-Collar Worker Supervisors	91	216,115
9. General Utility Maintenance Repairers	93	180,704
10. Construction Helpers	97	167,103
11. Farm Workers	84	157,331
12. Automotive Mechanics and Service Technicians	99	119,161
13. Cleaners of Vehicles and Equipment	88	116,789
14. Electricians	98	92,734
15. Computer Programmers	71	74,773
16. Correctional Officers	81	64,835
17. Securities, Commodities, and Financial Services Sales Agents	70	61,084
18. Engineering, Natural Science, and Computer and Information Systems Managers	72	54,120
19. Police Patrol Officers	87	51,739
20. Administrative Services Managers	72	46,558
21. Electrical and Electronic Technicians	85	42,572
22. Lawyers	75	38,182
23. Automotive Body Repairers	99	33,051
24. Construction Managers	72	32,841
25. Physicians	78	32,563

Fastest Growing Jobs Employing 70 Percent or More Men

Job	Percent Men	Percent Growth
1. Data Processing Equipment Repairers	82	47
2. Electronic Semiconductor Processors	72	45
3. Engineering, Natural Science, and Computer and Information Systems Managers	72	44
4. Securities, Commodities, and Financial Services Sales Agents	70	41
5. Correctional Officers	81	39
6. Sheriffs and Deputy Sheriffs	84	34
7. Police Patrol Officers	87	32
8. Central Office and PBX Installers and Repairers	84	32
9. Parking Lot Attendants	89	31
10. Computer Programmers	71	30
11. Telephone and Cable TV Line Installers and Repairers	85	30
12. Guards	84	29
13. Electrical and Electronics Engineers	94	26
14. Cleaners of Vehicles and Equipment	88	25
15. Veterinarians	79	25
16. Private Detectives and Investigators	84	24
17. Sprayers and Applicators	94	24
18. Numerical Control Machine Tool Operators and Tenders	85	23
19. Chiropractors	79	23
20. Bicycle Repairers	93	23
21. Landscaping and Groundskeeping Workers	94	21
22. Physicians	78	21
23. Civil Engineers	92	21
24. Detectives and Criminal Investigators	87	21
25. Taxi Drivers and Chauffeurs	90	20

Best Jobs Lists Based on Levels of Education, Training, and Experience

A very clear relationship exists between education and earnings—the more education you have, the more you are likely to earn. The lists that follow arrange all the jobs that met our criteria for inclusion in this book (see the introduction) by level of education, training, and work experience. The levels are typically required for a new entrant to begin work in the occupation.

Unlike many of the other lists, we did not include separate lists for highest pay, growth, or number of openings. Instead, we included on one list all the occupations in our database that fit into each education level. For example, one list includes all the jobs that require a bachelor's degree, rather than just the ones with the highest ratings. We then arranged these occupations based on their total scores for earnings, growth, and number of openings. We think this list will be more helpful than separate but limited lists.

Our lists use the U.S. Department of Labor categories for entry into various occupations. We provide comments that define the categories and offer other fascinating details.

Use the Lists to Locate Better Job Opportunities

On the back cover, we give the example of a real person who used these lists to identify a higher-paying job requiring an education level similar to her current job. Considering jobs with similar education and experience requirements may help you leverage your present skills and background into better-paying or more interesting opportunities. With a bit of effort, you could realize big pay advances for similar work.

You can also use these lists to explore career options if you obtain additional training, education, or work experience. For example, suppose you are a high school graduate interested in the field of medicine. You will find jobs related to this field at most training and education levels. After getting just one year of training and working at a medical job, you could obtain even more training for an even better-paying job. Or maybe you are considering a four-year college degree. Looking over the lists in this section will help you identify a possible area of study or eliminate one you were considering.

The lists can also help you decide which jobs to pursue. For example, a restaurant cook job requires long-term, on-the-job training and pays an average of $16,250 a year. A flight attendant job requires the same level of education but pays $37,800 a year. This looks like a good reason to be a flight attendant until you note that for every 49 restaurant cook openings there is only one flight attendant opening—and a flight attendant must be away from home often.

Caveat Datum, Revisited

We warn in the introduction to "beware the data," and we want to do it again here. The occupational data in this book is the most accurate available anywhere, but it has its limitations. For example, a four-year college degree in accounting, finance, or a related area is typically required for entry into the accounting profession. But some people working as accountants don't have such a degree, and others have much more education than the minimum required for entry.

In a similar way, people with a bachelor's degree will typically earn considerably more than high school dropouts, but some dropouts earn much more than the average for the highest paid occupation in this book. And, some college grads, particularly recent ones, work in jobs where the pay is much lower than the average for all college grads.

So, as you browse the lists that follow, please use them as a way to be encouraged rather than discouraged. Education and training are very important for success, but so is ability, drive, initiative and, yes, luck.

Having said this, we encourage you to get as much education and training as you can. It used to be that you got your schooling and never went back, but this is not a good attitude to have now. You will probably need to learn new things throughout your working life. This can be done by going to school, and this is a good thing for many people to do. But other ways to learn include workshops, certification programs, employer training, Internet learning programs, and reading related books and magazines. Upgrading your computer and other technical skills is particularly important in our rapidly changing workplace, and you avoid doing so at your peril.

As one of our grandfathers used to say, "The harder you work, the luckier you get." It was just as true then as it is now.

Best Jobs Requiring a Graduate or Professional Degree

Jobs requiring a degree beyond the bachelor's degree have been combined in the next list. The education levels include the following:

▲ **First professional degree.** This type of degree normally requires a minimum of two years of education beyond the bachelor's degree and frequently requires three years. Physician and attorney are two such occupations.

▲ **Doctor's degree.** This degree normally requires at least two years of full-time academic work beyond the master's degree. An example is medical scientist.

▲ **Master's degree.** Completion of a master's degree usually requires one to two years of full-time study beyond the bachelor's degree. An example is urban and regional planner.

This group includes 21 jobs. The average annual earnings for the group are $56,653. The average rate of growth through 2008 is 17 percent, and the average number of openings annually is 16,580.

Best Jobs Requiring a Graduate or Professional Degree

Job	Education Level	Annual Earnings	Annual Openings	Percent Growth
1. Physicians	First professional degree	$102,020	32,563	21
2. Lawyers	First professional degree	$78,170	38,182	17
3. Management Analysts	Master's degree	$49,470	23,831	28
4. College and University Faculty	Doctor's degree	$46,600	139,101	23
5. Biological Scientists	Doctor's degree	$46,140	10,417	35
6. Speech-Language Pathologists and Audiologists	Master's degree	$43,080	9,862	38
7. Veterinarians	First professional degree	$50,950	3,227	25
8. Counselors	Master's degree	$38,650	21,279	25
9. Medical Scientists	Doctor's degree	$50,410	3,214	25
10. Chiropractors	First professional degree	$63,930	2,516	23
11. Psychologists	Master's degree	$48,050	21,473	11
12. Dentists	First professional degree	$110,160	2,301	3
13. Optometrists	First professional degree	$68,480	1,532	11
14. Urban and Regional Planners	Master's degree	$42,860	5,057	17
15. Clergy	First professional degree	$28,850	14,197	13
16. Operations Research Analysts	Master's degree	$49,070	5,355	9
17. Podiatrists	First professional degree	$79,530	562	10
18. Social Scientists	Master's degree	$38,990	6,928	13
19. Archivists, Curators, Museum Technicians, and Conservators	Master's degree	$31,750	4,118	13
20. Physicists and Astronomers	Doctor's degree	$73,240	1,164	2
21. Mathematicians	Doctor's degree	$49,100	1,304	–6

Best Jobs Requiring a Bachelor's Degree, Plus Experience

Jobs in this category are often management-related and require some experience in a related nonmanagerial position. The average earnings for the 13 jobs in this group are $49,778. The average rate of growth is 19 percent, and the average number of openings annually is 71,317.

Best Jobs Requiring a Bachelor's Degree, Plus Experience

Job	Annual Earnings	Annual Openings	Percent Growth
1. Engineering, Natural Science, and Computer and Information Systems Managers	$75,320	54,120	44
2. Medical and Health Services Managers	$48,870	31,238	33
3. Artists and Commercial Artists	$31,690	58,769	26
4. Advertising, Marketing, Promotions, Public Relations, and Sales Managers	$57,300	89,237	23
5. Communication, Transportation, and Utilities Operations Managers	$52,810	25,388	19
6. Human Resources Managers	$49,010	32,929	19
7. Administrative Services Managers	$44,370	46,558	18
8. General Managers and Top Executives	$55,890	421,006	16
9. Financial Managers	$55,070	78,071	14
10. Education Administrators	$60,400	60,229	13
11. Assessors	$29,830	1,807	12
12. Purchasing Managers	$41,830	24,516	7
13. Postmasters and Mail Superintendents	$44,730	3,256	3

Best Jobs Requiring a Bachelor's Degree

The bachelor's degree normally requires four to five years of full-time academic work beyond high school. There are 59 jobs on our list that require a bachelor's degree. The average earnings for the group are $43,798. The average growth rate is 24 percent, and the average number of openings annually is 30,270.

Best Jobs Requiring a Bachelor's Degree

Job	Annual Earnings	Annual Openings	Percent Growth
1. Computer Engineers	$61,910	81,337	108
2. Systems Analysts	$52,180	154,157	94
3. Electrical and Electronics Engineers	$62,260	29,636	26
4. Computer Programmers	$47,550	74,773	30
5. Computer Scientists	$46,670	27,942	118
6. Computer Support Specialists	$37,120	113,041	102
7. Physical Therapists	$56,600	10,602	34
8. Database Administrators	$47,980	19,027	77
9. Secondary School Teachers	$37,890	133,585	23
10. Civil Engineers	$53,450	20,603	21
11. Special Education Teachers	$37,850	36,540	34
12. Occupational Therapists	$48,230	6,484	34
13. Writers and Editors	$36,480	52,971	24
14. Human Resources, Training, and Labor Relations Specialists	$37,710	82,760	18
15. Physician Assistants	$47,090	6,142	48
16. Designers	$29,190	57,787	27
17. Social Workers	$30,590	29,630	36
18. Construction Managers	$47,610	32,841	14
19. Economists and Marketing Research Analysts	$48,330	11,550	18
20. Loan Counselors and Officers	$35,340	39,836	21
21. Mechanical Engineers	$53,290	9,388	16
22. Residential Counselors	$18,840	27,865	46
23. Architects	$47,710	7,762	19
24. Public Relations Specialists	$34,550	25,334	25
25. Accountants and Auditors	$37,860	129,566	11
26. Elementary School Teachers	$36,110	204,210	12
27. Industrial Engineers	$52,610	13,125	13
28. Preschool Teachers	$17,310	41,894	26
29. Industrial Production Managers	$56,320	20,865	−1

(continues)

(continued)

Best Jobs Requiring a Bachelor's Degree

Job	Annual Earnings	Annual Openings	Percent Growth
30. Geologists, Geophysicists, and Oceanographers	$53,890	3,613	16
31. Purchasing Agents	$38,040	42,342	11
32. Budget Analysts	$44,950	9,617	14
33. Recreation Workers	$16,500	43,829	19
34. Interior Designers	$31,760	9,201	27
35. Pharmacists	$66,220	6,382	7
36. Chemical Engineers	$64,760	3,892	10
37. Chemists	$46,220	8,137	14
38. Directors of Religious Activities and Education	$24,970	13,292	25
39. Property, Real Estate, and Community Association Managers	$29,860	47,581	14
40. Clinical Laboratory Technologists and Technicians	$32,440	20,441	17
41. Conservation Scientists and Foresters	$42,750	3,328	18
42. Atmospheric Scientists	$54,430	683	15
43. Credit Analysts	$35,590	7,260	20
44. Aerospace Engineers	$66,950	1,606	9
45. Dietitians and Nutritionists	$35,040	8,153	19
46. Actuaries	$65,560	1,712	7
47. Nuclear Engineers	$71,310	882	6
48. Materials Engineers	$57,970	1,567	9
49. Kindergarten Teachers	$33,590	18,836	13
50. Petroleum Engineers	$74,260	802	−4
51. Employment Interviewers	$29,800	14,194	13
52. Radiation Therapists	$39,640	829	17
53. Property and Casualty Insurance Claims Examiners	$40,110	3,838	12
54. Landscape Architects	$37,930	1,605	14
55. Statisticians	$48,540	1,635	2
56. Agricultural and Food Scientists	$42,340	1,639	11
57. Mining Engineers	$56,090	282	−13
58. Merchandise Displayers and Window Dressers	$18,180	5,067	13
59. Recreational Therapists	$27,760	2,439	13

Best Jobs Requiring an Associate Degree

Two years of full-time academic work beyond high school are usually required to obtain this degree. There are 11 jobs on this list, and their average earnings are $32,705. The average growth rate through 2008 is 30 percent, and the average number of openings annually is 30,976.

Best Jobs Requiring an Associate Degree

Job	Annual Earnings	Annual Openings	Percent Growth
1. Dental Hygienists	$45,890	15,372	40
2. Registered Nurses	$40,690	195,231	22
3. Paralegals and Legal Assistants	$32,760	33,971	62
4. Electrical and Electronic Technicians	$35,970	42,572	17
5. Respiratory Therapists	$34,830	8,553	43
6. Medical Records and Health Information Technicians	$20,590	11,453	44
7. Cardiovascular Technologists and Technicians	$35,770	3,458	39
8. Radiologic Technologists and Technicians	$32,880	11,306	20
9. Nuclear Medicine Technologists	$39,610	833	12
10. Psychiatric Technicians	$20,890	15,167	11
11. Veterinary Technologists and Technicians	$19,870	2,822	16

Best Jobs Requiring Postsecondary Vocational Training

Training for these jobs varies from a few months to a year. In a few instances, as many as four years of combined classroom and on-the-job training may be required. There are 16 jobs on the list. Average earnings are $25,838, average growth rate through 2008 is 19 percent, and the average number of openings annually is 48,934.

Best Jobs Requiring Postsecondary Vocational Training

Job	Annual Earnings	Annual Openings	Percent Growth
1. Data Processing Equipment Repairers	$29,340	20,080	47
2. Licensed Practical Nurses	$26,940	43,314	20
3. Legal Secretaries	$30,050	44,130	13
4. Central Office and PBX Installers and Repairers	$43,680	4,617	32
5. Surgical Technologists	$25,780	9,182	42
6. Commercial and Industrial Electronics Equipment Repairers	$35,590	9,744	13
7. Emergency Medical Technicians	$20,290	23,138	32
8. Aircraft Mechanics and Service Technicians	$38,100	11,323	10
9. Secretaries	$23,550	358,379	0
10. Travel Agents	$23,010	17,019	18
11. Medical Secretaries	$22,390	33,608	12
12. Court Reporters, Medical Transcriptionists, and Stenographers	$25,430	15,612	10
13. Data Entry Keyers	$19,200	107,440	9
14. Hairdressers, Hairstylists, and Cosmetologists	$15,150	73,177	10
15. Dancers and Choreographers	$21,420	5,099	14
16. Manicurists	$13,480	7,081	26

Best Jobs Requiring Work Experience in a Related Job

This type of job requires a worker to have experience in a related occupation. An example is police detectives who are selected based on their experience as police patrol officers. Some of these jobs require special training or education (but not a bachelor's degree) to qualify for the related jobs. There are 23 jobs on the list for this group, and their average earnings are $34,203. The average growth rate through 2008 is 12 percent, and the average number of job openings annually is 57,061.

Best Jobs Requiring Work Experience in a Related Job

Job	Annual Earnings	Annual Openings	Percent Growth
1. Office and Administrative Support Supervisors	$31,090	238,168	19
2. Police and Detective Supervisors	$48,700	14,034	12
3. Cost Estimators	$40,590	27,649	13
4. Adult Education Instructors	$24,790	46,224	21
5. Fire Fighting and Prevention Supervisors	$44,830	9,147	11
6. Food Service and Lodging Managers	$26,700	138,826	16
7. Lawn Service Managers	$25,410	10,385	20
8. Aircraft Assemblers	$38,400	2,363	19
9. Blue-Collar Worker Supervisors	$37,180	216,115	9
10. Vocational Education Teachers and Instructors	$34,430	106,468	11
11. Construction and Building Inspectors	$37,540	3,515	16
12. Marketing and Sales Worker Supervisors	$29,570	410,550	10
13. Fire Inspectors	$40,000	900	17
14. Real Estate Appraisers	$40,290	6,383	11
15. Banking New Accounts Clerks	$21,340	36,231	15
16. Detectives and Criminal Investigators	$21,000	8,048	21
17. Inspectors and Compliance Officers	$36,820	19,910	10
18. Water Vessel Captains and Pilots	$41,200	3,581	3
19. Fishing Vessel Captains and Officers	$41,200	2,378	−19
20. Numerical Control Machine Tool Programmers	$40,490	706	6
21. Ship Engineers	$40,150	1,219	4
22. Nursery and Greenhouse Managers	$25,360	583	15
23. Institutional Cleaning Supervisors	$19,590	9,030	10

Best Jobs Requiring Long-Term, On-the-Job Training

These jobs require more than 12 months of on-the-job training or combined work experience and formal classroom instruction. Also included are occupations that use formal apprenticeships taking up to four years and intensive occupation-specific, employer-sponsored training like police academies. Furthermore, the list includes occupations that require natural talent that must be developed over many years. There are 37 jobs in this group. The average earnings are $34,878. The average growth rate is 17 percent through 2008, and the average number of job openings annually is 41,066.

Best Jobs Requiring Long-Term, On-the-Job Training

Job	Annual Earnings	Annual Openings	Percent Growth
1. Securities, Commodities, and Financial Services Sales Agents	$48,090	61,084	41
2. Police Patrol Officers	$37,710	51,739	32
3. Correctional Officers	$28,540	64,835	39
4. Insurance Adjusters, Examiners, and Investigators	$38,290	16,055	20
5. Flight Attendants	$37,800	5,376	30
6. Telephone and Cable TV Line Installers and Repairers	$32,750	18,246	30
7. Desktop Publishing Specialists	$29,130	7,546	73
8. Automotive Mechanics and Service Technicians	$27,360	119,161	17
9. Electricians	$35,310	92,734	10
10. Restaurant Cooks	$16,250	262,535	19
11. Musicians	$30,020	44,774	15
12. Heating, Air Conditioning, and Refrigeration Mechanics and Installers	$29,160	29,552	17
13. Actors, Directors, and Producers	$27,370	31,279	24
14. Bricklayers, Blockmasons, and Stonemasons	$35,200	29,721	12
15. Elevator Installers and Repairers	$47,860	5,088	12
16. Plasterers and Stucco Masons	$29,390	7,984	17
17. Automotive Body Repairers	$27,400	33,051	16
18. Carpenters	$28,700	236,108	7
19. Aircraft Pilots and Flight Engineers	$91,750	4,555	6
20. Athletes, Coaches, and Umpires	$22,210	19,465	28
21. Auto Insurance Appraisers	$40,000	871	16
22. Sheriffs and Deputy Sheriffs	$28,270	3,130	34

Best Jobs Requiring Long-Term, On-the-Job Training

Job	Annual Earnings	Annual Openings	Percent Growth
23. Funeral Directors and Morticians	$35,040	3,972	16
24. Water and Liquid Waste Treatment Plant and System Operators	$29,660	12,735	14
25. Bus and Truck Mechanics and Diesel Engine Specialists	$29,340	21,502	10
26. General Utility Maintenance Repairers	$23,290	180,704	8
27. Chemical Plant and System Operators	$39,030	3,484	11
28. Electrical Powerline Installers and Repairers	$42,600	5,616	1
29. Air Traffic Controllers	$64,880	2,321	2
30. Institution or Cafeteria Cooks	$16,090	124,088	3
31. Power Generating and Reactor Plant Operators	$44,800	2,216	3
32. Medical Equipment Repairers	$34,190	1,675	14
33. Gas and Petroleum Plant and System Occupations	$43,800	2,335	−13
34. Coin, Vending, and Amusement Machine Servicers and Repairers	$23,260	4,315	16
35. Dispensing Opticians	$22,440	5,799	14
36. Office Machine and Cash Register Servicers	$27,830	2,931	16
37. Power Distributors and Dispatchers	$45,690	855	−12

Best Jobs Requiring Moderate-Term, On-the-Job Training

Occupations that require this type of training can be performed adequately after a one month to one year of combined on-the-job and informal training. Typically workers observe experienced workers perform tasks and are gradually moved into progressively more difficult assignments. There are 33 jobs in this group. The average earnings for the group are $23,401. The average growth rate is 21 percent through 2008, and the average number of openings annually is 35,641.

Best Jobs Requiring Moderate-Term, On-the-Job Training

Job	Annual Earnings	Annual Openings	Percent Growth
1. Human Service Workers and Assistants	$21,360	91,824	53
2. Dental Assistants	$22,640	56,389	42
3. Sports and Physical Training Instructors and Coaches	$22,230	104,431	28
4. Medical Assistants	$20,680	49,015	58
5. Numerical Control Machine Tool Operators and Tenders	$27,110	18,908	23
6. Commercial Dispatchers	$26,370	32,141	14
7. Bus Drivers	$24,370	29,885	16
8. Electronic Semiconductor Processors	$24,810	10,615	45
9. Occupational Therapy Assistants and Aides	$28,690	3,106	40
10. Sheet Metal Workers and Duct Installers	$28,000	22,680	14
11. Tax Preparers	$27,960	13,654	19
12. Physical Therapy Assistants and Aides	$21,870	14,195	44
13. Chemical Equipment Controllers, Operators and Tenders	$32,200	19,720	11
14. Roofers	$25,340	28,797	12
15. Combination Machine Tool Setters, Set-Up Operators, Operators, and Tenders	$23,900	21,256	14
16. Bookkeeping, Accounting, and Auditing Clerks	$23,190	325,366	−4
17. Bread and Pastry Bakers	$16,990	56,526	17
18. Models, Demonstrators, and Product Promoters	$16,931	27,574	32

Best Jobs Requiring Moderate-Term, On-the-Job Training

Job	Annual Earnings	Annual Openings	Percent Growth
19. Excavation and Loading Machine Operators	$27,090	6,199	15
20. Pest Control Workers	$22,490	7,983	25
21. Private Detectives and Investigators	$21,020	14,675	24
22. Packaging and Filling Machine Operators	$20,060	88,131	13
23. Insurance Claims Clerks	$24,010	12,974	14
24. Sprayers and Applicators	$21,650	5,167	24
25. Paving, Surfacing, and Tamping Equipment Operators	$24,510	13,780	11
26. Plastic Molding Machine Setters, Set-Up Operators, Operators, and Tenders	$18,600	20,701	15
27. Subway and Streetcar Operators	$43,330	250	7
28. Pharmacy Technicians	$17,763	14,132	16
29. Bindery Machine Operators and Set-Up Operators	$20,600	16,466	12
30. Laundry and Dry-Cleaning Machine Operators	$14,670	38,082	10
31. Locksmiths and Safe Repairers	$24,890	4,557	10
32. Bicycle Repairers	$15,700	1,854	23
33. Electrolytic Plating Machine Setters, Set-Up Operators, Operators, and Tenders	$21,200	5,108	10

Best Jobs Requiring Short-Term, On-the-Job Training

It is possible to work in these occupations and achieve an average level of performance within a few days or weeks through on-the-job training. There are 56 jobs in this group. The average annual earnings are $17,605. The average growth rate is 18 percent through 2008, and the average number of openings annually is 205,842.

Best Jobs Requiring Short-Term, On-the-Job Training

Job	Annual Earnings	Annual Openings	Percent Growth
1. Truck Drivers	$24,300	535,419	17
2. Adjustment Clerks	$22,040	141,670	34
3. Bill and Account Collectors	$22,540	106,068	35
4. Receptionists and Information Clerks	$18,620	386,806	24
5. General Office Clerks	$19,580	745,378	15
6. Personal Care and Home Health Aides	$15,800	249,694	58
7. Teacher Assistants	$15,800	343,831	32
8. Brokerage Clerks	$27,920	17,895	28
9. Nursing Aides, Orderlies, and Attendants	$16,620	349,640	24
10. Guards	$16,240	256,671	29
11. Landscaping and Groundskeeping Workers	$17,140	283,459	21
12. Child Care Workers	$13,750	328,786	26
13. Billing, Cost, and Rate Clerks	$22,670	63,239	15
14. Interviewing Clerks	$18,540	44,483	23
15. Retail Salespersons	$15,830	1,305,317	14
16. School Bus Drivers	$18,820	65,136	18
17. Hand Packers and Packagers	$14,540	249,421	22
18. Cashiers	$13,690	1,290,302	17
19. Counter and Rental Clerks	$14,510	199,406	23
20. Cleaners of Vehicles and Equipment	$14,540	116,789	25
21. Shipping, Receiving, and Traffic Clerks	$22,500	242,666	3
22. Amusement and Recreation Attendants	$12,860	141,783	30
23. Meat, Poultry, and Fish Cutters and Trimmers	$16,270	33,193	24
24. Loan and Credit Clerks	$22,580	46,537	12
25. Janitors, Cleaners, Maids, and Housekeeping Cleaners	$15,300	735,967	12
26. Ambulance Drivers and Attendants	$16,960	4,191	35

Best Jobs Requiring Short-Term, On-the-Job Training

Job	Annual Earnings	Annual Openings	Percent Growth
27. Freight, Stock, and Material Movers	$18,470	306,549	2
28. Library Technicians	$21,730	9,478	18
29. Ski Patrol Workers and Life Guards	$17,470	23,282	19
30. Construction Helpers	$19,510	167,103	7
31. Veterinary Assistants	$16,200	14,770	28
32. Highway Maintenance Workers	$24,490	20,512	11
33. Painting, Coating, and Decorating Workers	$19,060	8,593	18
34. Animal Caretakers	$14,820	43,263	22
35. Library Assistants and Bookmobile Drivers	$16,980	35,994	16
36. Court Clerks	$22,960	13,394	11
37. Parking Lot Attendants	$13,930	17,725	31
38. Food Counter and Fountain Workers	$12,600	944,970	12
39. License Clerks	$22,900	6,424	13
40. Short Order and Fast Food Cooks	$12,700	226,320	18
41. Taxi Drivers and Chauffeurs	$15,540	26,739	20
42. File Clerks	$16,830	117,451	10
43. Restaurant Hosts and Hostesses	$13,400	110,848	18
44. Food Preparation Workers	$13,700	529,498	10
45. Municipal Clerks	$22,810	6,545	12
46. Pruners	$22,070	10,504	12
47. Correspondence Clerks	$22,270	4,276	12
48. Hotel, Motel, and Resort Desk Clerks	$15,160	60,382	14
49. Bank Tellers	$17,200	106,674	−6
50. Mail Clerks	$17,660	26,426	10
51. Solderers and Brazers	$17,600	7,519	14
52. Tire Repairers and Changers	$16,810	26,095	10
53. Ushers, Lobby Attendants, and Ticket Takers	$12,520	22,505	18
54. Dining Room and Cafeteria Attendants and Bar Helpers	$12,580	181,922	4
55. Farm Workers	$12,600	157,331	−7
56. Baggage Porters and Bellhops	$13,330	10,287	14

Best Jobs Based on Personality Types

A popular system used in many career assessment instruments and systems is based on six personality types developed by John Holland some time ago. All major jobs can be organized into one of these types, and the O*NET database we use for the information in this book gives each job's personality type. The six personality types are pretty easy to understand, and brief explanations appear before each list. We sorted all the major occupations in this book into one of the six lists that follow. Once you know what personality type you tend to be, refer to the corresponding list to review the jobs that met our criteria for pay, growth, and number of openings. All jobs are listed in order of their overall scores based on annual pay, growth through 2008, and number of annual openings.

Best Jobs for Artistic Personality Types

Artistic occupations frequently involve working with forms, designs, and patterns. They often require self-expression, and the work can be done without following a clear set of rules. There are 12 jobs included in the artistic category.

Best Jobs for Artistic Personality Types

Job	Annual Earnings	Annual Openings	Percent Growth
1. Artists and Commercial Artists	$31,690	58,769	26
2. Designers	$29,190	57,787	27
3. Writers and Editors	$36,480	52,971	24
4. Interior Designers	$31,760	9,201	27
5. Architects	$47,710	7,762	19
6. Actors, Directors, and Producers	$27,370	31,279	24
7. Models, Demonstrators, and Product Promoters	$16,931	27,574	32
8. Musicians	$30,020	44,774	15
9. Landscape Architects	$37,930	1,605	14
10. Archivists, Curators, Museum Technicians, and Conservators	$31,750	4,118	13
11. Dancers and Choreographers	$21,420	5,099	14
12. Merchandise Displayers and Window Dressers	$18,180	5,067	13

Best Jobs for Conventional Personality Types

Conventional occupations frequently involve following set procedures and routines. These occupations can include working with data and details more than with ideas. Usually the jobs have clear lines of authority to follow. There are 45 jobs in the conventional category.

Best Jobs for Conventional Personality Types

Job	Annual Earnings	Annual Openings	Percent Growth
1. Engineering, Natural Science, and Computer and Information Systems Managers	$75,320	54,120	44
2. Adjustment Clerks	$22,040	141,670	34
3. Bill and Account Collectors	$22,540	106,068	35
4. Receptionists and Information Clerks	$18,620	386,806	24
5. Brokerage Clerks	$27,920	17,895	28
6. Accountants and Auditors	$37,860	129,566	11
7. Tax Preparers	$27,960	13,654	19
8. Cost Estimators	$40,590	27,649	13
9. Credit Analysts	$35,590	7,260	20
10. General Office Clerks	$19,580	745,378	15
11. Billing, Cost, and Rate Clerks	$22,670	63,239	15
12. Legal Secretaries	$30,050	44,130	13
13. Budget Analysts	$44,950	9,617	14
14. Cashiers	$13,690	1,290,302	17
15. Counter and Rental Clerks	$14,510	199,406	23
16. Commercial Dispatchers	$26,370	32,141	14
17. Interviewing Clerks	$18,540	44,483	23
18. Construction and Building Inspectors	$37,540	3,515	16
19. Fire Inspectors	$40,000	900	17
20. Auto Insurance Appraisers	$40,000	871	16
21. Secretaries	$23,550	358,379	0
22. Medical Records and Health Information Technicians	$20,590	11,453	44
23. Bookkeeping, Accounting, and Auditing Clerks	$23,190	325,366	−4
24. Banking New Accounts Clerks	$21,340	36,231	15
25. Loan and Credit Clerks	$22,580	46,537	12
26. Insurance Claims Clerks	$24,010	12,974	14
27. Shipping, Receiving, and Traffic Clerks	$22,500	242,666	3
28. Library Technicians	$21,730	9,478	18

(continues)

(continued)

Best Jobs for Conventional Personality Types

Job	Annual Earnings	Annual Openings	Percent Growth
29. Library Assistants and Bookmobile Drivers	$16,980	35,994	16
30. Property and Casualty Insurance Claims Examiners	$40,110	3,838	12
31. Court Reporters, Medical Transcriptionists, and Stenographers	$25,430	15,612	10
32. Hotel, Motel, and Resort Desk Clerks	$15,160	60,382	14
33. Medical Secretaries	$22,390	33,608	12
34. Assessors	$29,830	1,807	12
35. Pharmacy Technicians	$17,763	14,132	16
36. Actuaries	$65,560	1,712	7
37. Data Entry Keyers	$19,200	107,440	9
38. Air Traffic Controllers	$64,880	2,321	2
39. Court Clerks	$22,960	13,394	11
40. License Clerks	$22,900	6,424	13
41. File Clerks	$16,830	117,451	10
42. Municipal Clerks	$22,810	6,545	12
43. Correspondence Clerks	$22,270	4,276	12
44. Bank Tellers	$17,200	106,674	–6
45. Mail Clerks	$17,660	26,426	10

Best Jobs for Enterprising Personality Types

Enterprising occupations frequently involve starting up and carrying out projects. These occupations can involve leading people and making many decisions. Sometimes they require risk taking and often deal with business. There are 46 jobs in the enterprising category.

Best Jobs for Enterprising Personality Types

Job	Annual Earnings	Annual Openings	Percent Growth
1. Advertising, Marketing, Promotions, Public Relations, and Sales Managers	$57,300	89,237	23
2. Securities, Commodities, and Financial Services Sales Agents	$48,090	61,084	41
3. General Managers and Top Executives	$55,890	421,006	16
4. Medical and Health Services Managers	$48,870	31,238	33
5. Lawyers	$78,170	38,182	17
6. Management Analysts	$49,470	23,831	28
7. Communication, Transportation, and Utilities Operations Managers	$52,810	25,388	19
8. Human Resources Managers	$49,010	32,929	19
9. Financial Managers	$55,070	78,071	14
10. Administrative Services Managers	$44,370	46,558	18
11. Education Administrators	$60,400	60,229	13
12. Paralegals and Legal Assistants	$32,760	33,971	62
13. Office and Administrative Support Supervisors	$31,090	238,168	19
14. Human Resources, Training, and Labor Relations Specialists	$37,710	82,760	18
15. Loan Counselors and Officers	$35,340	39,836	21
16. Public Relations Specialists	$34,550	25,334	25
17. Food Service and Lodging Managers	$26,700	138,826	16
18. Construction Managers	$47,610	32,841	14
19. Insurance Adjusters, Examiners, and Investigators	$38,290	16,055	20
20. Flight Attendants	$37,800	5,376	30
21. Athletes, Coaches, and Umpires	$22,210	19,465	28
22. Blue-Collar Worker Supervisors	$37,180	216,115	9
23. Restaurant Hosts and Hostesses	$13,400	110,848	18
24. Purchasing Agents	$38,040	42,342	11

(continues)

(continued)

Best Jobs for Enterprising Personality Types

Job	Annual Earnings	Annual Openings	Percent Growth
25. Marketing and Sales Worker Supervisors	$29,570	410,550	10
26. Industrial Production Managers	$56,320	20,865	−1
27. Retail Salespersons	$15,830	1,305,317	14
28. Property, Real Estate, and Community Association Managers	$29,860	47,581	14
29. Sales Engineers	$54,600	3,039	16
30. Police and Detective Supervisors	$48,700	14,034	12
31. Private Detectives and Investigators	$21,020	14,675	24
32. Lawn Service Managers	$25,410	10,385	20
33. Purchasing Managers	$41,830	24,516	7
34. Travel Agents	$23,010	17,019	18
35. Detectives and Criminal Investigators	$21,000	8,048	21
36. Manicurists	$13,480	7,081	26
37. Funeral Directors and Morticians	$35,040	3,972	16
38. Hairdressers, Hairstylists, and Cosmetologists	$15,150	73,177	10
39. Real Estate Appraisers	$40,290	6,383	11
40. Postmasters and Mail Superintendents	$44,730	3,256	3
41. Water Vessel Captains and Pilots	$41,200	3,581	3
42. Dispensing Opticians	$22,440	5,799	14
43. Baggage Porters and Bellhops	$13,330	10,287	14
44. Nursery and Greenhouse Managers	$25,360	583	15
45. Fishing Vessel Captains and Officers	$41,200	2,378	−19
46. Institutional Cleaning Supervisors	$19,590	9,030	10

Best Jobs for Investigative Personality Types

Investigative occupations frequently involve working with ideas and require an extensive amount of thinking. These occupations can involve searching for facts and figuring out problems mentally. There 42 jobs in the investigative category.

Best Jobs for Investigative Personality Types

Job	Annual Earnings	Annual Openings	Percent Growth
1. Computer Engineers	$61,910	81,337	108
2. Physicians	$102,020	32,563	21
3. Systems Analysts	$52,180	154,157	94
4. Electrical and Electronics Engineers	$62,260	29,636	26
5. Computer Scientists	$46,670	27,942	118
6. Computer Programmers	$47,550	74,773	30
7. Computer Support Specialists	$37,120	113,041	102
8. Database Administrators	$47,980	19,027	77
9. Chiropractors	$63,930	2,516	23
10. Industrial Engineers	$52,610	13,125	13
11. Biological Scientists	$46,140	10,417	35
12. Physician Assistants	$47,090	6,142	48
13. Economists and Marketing Research Analysts	$48,330	11,550	18
14. Veterinarians	$50,950	3,227	25
15. Medical Scientists	$50,410	3,214	25
16. Geologists, Geophysicists, and Oceanographers	$53,890	3,613	16
17. Chemical Engineers	$64,760	3,892	10
18. Psychologists	$48,050	21,473	11
19. Pharmacists	$66,220	6,382	7
20. Respiratory Therapists	$34,830	8,553	43
21. Dentists	$110,160	2,301	3
22. Optometrists	$68,480	1,532	11
23. Chemists	$46,220	8,137	14
24. Clinical Laboratory Technologists and Technicians	$32,440	20,441	17
25. Cardiovascular Technologists and Technicians	$35,770	3,458	39

(continues)

(continued)

Best Jobs for Investigative Personality Types

Job	Annual Earnings	Annual Openings	Percent Growth
26. Dietitians and Nutritionists	$35,040	8,153	19
27. Aerospace Engineers	$66,950	1,606	9
28. Urban and Regional Planners	$42,860	5,057	17
29. Conservation Scientists and Foresters	$42,750	3,328	18
30. Podiatrists	$79,530	562	10
31. Atmospheric Scientists	$54,430	683	15
32. Operations Research Analysts	$49,070	5,355	9
33. Inspectors and Compliance Officers	$36,820	19,910	10
34. Social Scientists	$38,990	6,928	13
35. Nuclear Engineers	$71,310	882	6
36. Physicists and Astronomers	$73,240	1,164	2
37. Materials Engineers	$57,970	1,567	9
38. Agricultural and Food Scientists	$42,340	1,639	11
39. Statisticians	$48,540	1,635	2
40. Mathematicians	$49,100	1,304	–6
41. Mining Engineers	$56,090	282	–13
42. Nuclear Medicine Technologists	$39,610	833	12

Best Jobs for Realistic Personality Types

Realistic occupations frequently involve work activities that include practical, hands-on problems and solutions. They often deal with plant, animals, and real-world materials like wood, tools, and machinery. Many of the occupations require working outside and do not involve a lot of paperwork or working closely with others. There are 86 jobs in the realistic category.

Best Jobs for Realistic Personality Types

Job	Annual Earnings	Annual Openings	Percent Growth
1. Correctional Officers	$28,540	64,835	39
2. Civil Engineers	$53,450	20,603	21
3. Data Processing Equipment Repairers	$29,340	20,080	47
4. Electrical and Electronic Technicians	$35,970	42,572	17
5. Telephone and Cable TV Line Installers and Repairers	$32,750	18,246	30
6. Automotive Mechanics and Service Technicians	$27,360	119,161	17
7. Central Office and PBX Installers and Repairers	$43,680	4,617	32
8. Truck Drivers	$24,300	535,419	17
9. Landscaping and Groundskeeping Workers	$17,140	283,459	21
10. Desktop Publishing Specialists	$29,130	7,546	73
11. Heating, Air Conditioning, and Refrigeration Mechanics and Installers	$29,160	29,552	17
12. Radiologic Technologists and Technicians	$32,880	11,306	20
13. Numerical Control Machine Tool Operators and Tenders	$27,110	18,908	23
14. Mechanical Engineers	$53,290	9,388	16
15. Automotive Body Repairers	$27,400	33,051	16
16. Electronic Semiconductor Processors	$24,810	10,615	45
17. Bricklayers, Blockmasons, and Stonemasons	$35,200	29,721	12
18. Electricians	$35,310	92,734	10
19. Restaurant Cooks	$16,250	262,535	19
20. Surgical Technologists	$25,780	9,182	42
21. Amusement and Recreation Attendants	$12,860	141,783	30
22. Hand Packers and Packagers	$14,540	249,421	22
23. Cleaners of Vehicles and Equipment	$14,540	116,789	25
24. Surveying and Mapping Technicians	$25,940	15,057	22
25. Meat, Poultry, and Fish Cutters and Trimmers	$16,270	33,193	24
26. School Bus Drivers	$18,820	65,136	18

(continues)

(continued)

Best Jobs for Realistic Personality Types

Job	Annual Earnings	Annual Openings	Percent Growth
27. Carpenters	$28,700	236,108	7
28. Bus Drivers	$24,370	29,885	16
29. Sheet Metal Workers and Duct Installers	$28,000	22,680	14
30. Aircraft Assemblers	$38,400	2,363	19
31. Animal Caretakers	$14,820	43,263	22
32. Bread and Pastry Bakers	$16,990	56,526	17
33. Plasterers and Stucco Masons	$29,390	7,984	17
34. Short Order and Fast Food Cooks	$12,700	226,320	18
35. Commercial and Industrial Electronics Equipment Repairers	$35,590	9,744	13
36. Chemical Equipment Controllers, Operators and Tenders	$32,200	19,720	11
37. Fire Fighting and Prevention Supervisors	$44,830	9,147	11
38. Water and Liquid Waste Treatment Plant and System Operators	$29,660	12,735	14
39. Pest Control Workers	$22,490	7,983	25
40. Hazardous Materials Removal Workers	$27,620	5,470	19
41. Ski Patrol Workers and Life Guards	$17,470	23,282	19
42. Bus and Truck Mechanics and Diesel Engine Specialists	$29,340	21,502	10
43. Elevator Installers and Repairers	$47,860	5,088	12
44. Packaging and Filling Machine Operators	$20,060	88,131	13
45. Taxi Drivers and Chauffeurs	$15,540	26,739	20
46. Veterinary Assistants	$16,200	14,770	28
47. Aircraft Mechanics and Service Technicians	$38,100	11,323	10
48. Roofers	$25,340	28,797	12
49. Combination Machine Tool Setters, Set-Up Operators, Operators, and Tenders	$23,900	21,256	14
50. Janitors, Cleaners, Maids, and Housekeeping Cleaners	$15,300	735,967	12
51. General Utility Maintenance Repairers	$23,290	180,704	8
52. Parking Lot Attendants	$13,930	17,725	31
53. Sprayers and Applicators	$21,650	5,167	24
54. Construction Helpers	$19,510	167,103	7
55. Plastic Molding Machine Setters, Set-Up Operators, Operators, and Tenders	$18,600	20,701	15
56. Excavation and Loading Machine Operators	$27,090	6,199	15

Best Jobs for Realistic Personality Types

Job	Annual Earnings	Annual Openings	Percent Growth
57. Aircraft Pilots and Flight Engineers	$91,750	4,555	6
58. Chemical Plant and System Operators	$39,030	3,484	11
59. Highway Maintenance Workers	$24,490	20,512	11
60. Painting, Coating, and Decorating Workers	$19,060	8,593	18
61. Freight, Stock, and Material Movers	$18,470	306,549	2
62. Medical Equipment Repairers	$34,190	1,675	14
63. Office Machine and Cash Register Servicers	$27,830	2,931	16
64. Food Preparation Workers	$13,700	529,498	10
65. Bindery Machine Operators and Set-Up Operators	$20,600	16,466	12
66. Paving, Surfacing, and Tamping Equipment Operators	$24,510	13,780	11
67. Electrical Powerline Installers and Repairers	$42,600	5,616	1
68. Coin, Vending, and Amusement Machine Servicers and Repairers	$23,260	4,315	16
69. Pruners	$22,070	10,504	12
70. Institution or Cafeteria Cooks	$16,090	124,088	3
71. Power Generating and Reactor Plant Operators	$44,800	2,216	3
72. Bicycle Repairers	$15,700	1,854	23
73. Petroleum Engineers	$74,260	802	−4
74. Laundry and Dry-Cleaning Machine Operators	$14,670	38,082	10
75. Subway and Streetcar Operators	$43,330	250	7
76. Tire Repairers and Changers	$16,810	26,095	10
77. Dining Room and Cafeteria Attendants and Bar Helpers	$12,580	181,922	4
78. Gas and Petroleum Plant and System Occupations	$43,800	2,335	−13
79. Numerical Control Machine Tool Programmers	$40,490	706	6
80. Power Distributors and Dispatchers	$45,690	855	−12
81. Ship Engineers	$40,150	1,219	4
82. Solderers and Brazers	$17,600	7,519	14
83. Veterinary Technologists and Technicians	$19,870	2,822	16
84. Farm Workers	$12,600	157,331	−7
85. Locksmiths and Safe Repairers	$24,890	4,557	10
86. Electrolytic Plating Machine Setters, Set-Up Operators, Operators, and Tenders	$21,200	5,108	10

Best Jobs for Social Personality Types

Social occupations frequently involve working with, communicating with, and teaching people. These occupations often involve helping or providing service to others. There are 40 jobs in the social category.

Best Jobs for Social Personality Types

Job	Annual Earnings	Annual Openings	Percent Growth
1. Dental Hygienists	$45,890	15,372	40
2. Registered Nurses	$40,690	195,231	22
3. Human Service Workers and Assistants	$21,360	91,824	53
4. Police Patrol Officers	$37,710	51,739	32
5. Dental Assistants	$22,640	56,389	42
6. Secondary School Teachers	$37,890	133,585	23
7. Medical Assistants	$20,680	49,015	58
8. Personal Care and Home Health Aides	$15,800	249,694	58
9. Special Education Teachers	$37,850	36,540	34
10. Social Workers	$30,590	29,630	36
11. Physical Therapists	$56,600	10,602	34
12. Speech-Language Pathologists and Audiologists	$43,080	9,862	38
13. Occupational Therapists	$48,230	6,484	34
14. Counselors	$38,650	21,279	25
15. Elementary School Teachers	$36,110	204,210	12
16. Sports and Physical Training Instructors and Coaches	$22,230	104,431	28
17. Residential Counselors	$18,840	27,865	46
18. Teacher Assistants	$15,800	343,831	32
19. Guards	$16,240	256,671	29
20. Nursing Aides, Orderlies, and Attendants	$16,620	349,640	24
21. Physical Therapy Assistants and Aides	$21,870	14,195	44
22. Vocational Education Teachers and Instructors	$34,430	106,468	11
23. Child Care Workers	$13,750	328,786	26
24. Occupational Therapy Assistants and Aides	$28,690	3,106	40
25. Adult Education Instructors	$24,790	46,224	21
26. Licensed Practical Nurses	$26,940	43,314	20
27. Emergency Medical Technicians	$20,290	23,138	32
28. Sheriffs and Deputy Sheriffs	$28,270	3,130	34
29. Preschool Teachers	$17,310	41,894	26

Best Jobs for Social Personality Types

Job	Annual Earnings	Annual Openings	Percent Growth
30. Kindergarten Teachers	$33,590	18,836	13
31. Directors of Religious Activities and Education	$24,970	13,292	25
32. Clergy	$28,850	14,197	13
33. Food Counter and Fountain Workers	$12,600	944,970	12
34. Radiation Therapists	$39,640	829	17
35. Ambulance Drivers and Attendants	$16,960	4,191	35
36. Employment Interviewers	$29,800	14,194	13
37. Recreation Workers	$16,500	43,829	19
38. Psychiatric Technicians	$20,890	15,167	11
39. Recreational Therapists	$27,760	2,439	13
40. Ushers, Lobby Attendants, and Ticket Takers	$12,520	22,505	18

Best Jobs Lists Based on Interests

The next lists organize occupations into 14 interest groupings. These "Interest Areas" are based on a system developed by the U.S. Department of Labor as an intuitive way to assist in career exploration. The system is called the *Guide for Occupational Exploration,* or *GOE,* and is named after a book first published by the Labor Department. A revised edition of the *Guide for Occupational Exploration* was published by JIST in 2001 (as the third edition). We use here the 14 new Interest Areas presented in that third edition.

Each list includes a brief description of the Interest Area. Occupations in each list are arranged in order of their total scores based on annual earnings, growth through 2008, and annual number of openings. An effective way to use these lists is to select one or more Interest Areas that appeal to you, and then review the jobs listed.

Since there are so many interest areas, here is a brief list to help you identify those that appeal to you most:

01   Arts, Entertainment, and Media

02   Science, Math, and Engineering

03   Plants and Animals

04   Law, Law Enforcement, and Public Safety

05 Mechanics, Installers, and Repairers

06 Construction, Mining, and Drilling

07 Transportation

08 Industrial Production

09 Business Detail

10 Sales and Marketing

11 Recreation, Travel, and Other Personal Services

12 Education and Social Service

13 General Management and Support

14 Medical and Health Services

Best Jobs for People Interested in Arts, Entertainment, and Media

An interest in creatively expressing feelings or ideas, in communicating news or information, or in performing. You can satisfy this interest in several creative, verbal, or performing activities. For example, if you enjoy literature, perhaps writing or editing would appeal to you. Do you prefer to work in the performing arts? If so, you could direct or perform in drama, music, or dance. If you especially enjoy the visual arts, you could become a critic in painting, sculpture, or ceramics. You may want to use your hands to create or decorate products. You may prefer to model clothes or develop sets for entertainment. Or you may want to participate in sports professionally, as an athlete or coach.

Best Jobs for People Interested in Arts, Entertainment, and Media

Job	Annual Earnings	Annual Openings	Percent Growth
1. Artists and Commercial Artists	$31,690	58,769	26
2. Sports and Physical Training Instructors and Coaches	$22,230	104,431	28
3. Designers	$29,190	57,787	27
4. Writers and Editors	$36,480	52,971	24
5. Public Relations Specialists	$34,550	25,334	25
6. Interior Designers	$31,760	9,201	27

Best Jobs for People Interested in Arts, Entertainment, and Media

Job	Annual Earnings	Annual Openings	Percent Growth
7. Athletes, Coaches, and Umpires	$22,210	19,465	28
8. Models, Demonstrators, and Product Promoters	$16,931	27,574	32
9. Musicians	$30,020	44,774	15
10. Actors, Directors, and Producers	$27,370	31,279	24
11. Dancers and Choreographers	$21,420	5,099	14
12. Merchandise Displayers and Window Dressers	$18,180	5,067	13

Best Jobs for People Interested in Science, Math, and Engineering

An interest in discovering, collecting, and analyzing information about the natural world; in applying scientific research findings to problems in medicine, the life sciences, and the natural sciences; in imagining and manipulating quantitative data; and in applying technology to manufacturing, transportation, mining, and other economic activities. You can satisfy this interest by working with the knowledge and processes of the sciences. You may enjoy researching and developing new knowledge in mathematics, or perhaps solving problems in the physical or life sciences would appeal to you. You may wish to study engineering and help create new machines, processes, and structures. If you want to work with scientific equipment and procedures, you could seek a job in a research or testing laboratory.

Best Jobs for People Interested in Science, Math, and Engineering

Job	Annual Earnings	Annual Openings	Percent Growth
1. Engineering, Natural Science, and Computer and Information Systems Managers	$75,320	54,120	44
2. Computer Engineers	$61,910	81,337	108
3. Systems Analysts	$52,180	154,157	94
4. Electrical and Electronics Engineers	$62,260	29,636	26
5. Civil Engineers	$53,450	20,603	21

(continues)

(continued)

Best Jobs for People Interested in Science, Math, and Engineering

Job	Annual Earnings	Annual Openings	Percent Growth
6. Computer Scientists	$46,670	27,942	118
7. Computer Programmers	$47,550	74,773	30
8. Database Administrators	$47,980	19,027	77
9. Computer Support Specialists	$37,120	113,041	102
10. Biological Scientists	$46,140	10,417	35
11. Economists and Marketing Research Analysts	$48,330	11,550	18
12. Mechanical Engineers	$53,290	9,388	16
13. Industrial Engineers	$52,610	13,125	13
14. Medical Scientists	$50,410	3,214	25
15. Geologists, Geophysicists, and Oceanographers	$53,890	3,613	16
16. Architects	$47,710	7,762	19
17. Chemical Engineers	$64,760	3,892	10
18. Electrical and Electronic Technicians	$35,970	42,572	17
19. Sales Engineers	$54,600	3,039	16
20. Psychologists	$48,050	21,473	11
21. Surveying and Mapping Technicians	$25,940	15,057	22
22. Aerospace Engineers	$66,950	1,606	9
23. Actuaries	$65,560	1,712	7
24. Chemists	$46,220	8,137	14
25. Urban and Regional Planners	$42,860	5,057	17
26. Conservation Scientists and Foresters	$42,750	3,328	18
27. Atmospheric Scientists	$54,430	683	15
28. Operations Research Analysts	$49,070	5,355	9
29. Physicists and Astronomers	$73,240	1,164	2
30. Materials Engineers	$57,970	1,567	9
31. Nuclear Engineers	$71,310	882	6
32. Petroleum Engineers	$74,260	802	−4
33. Construction and Building Inspectors	$37,540	3,515	16
34. Social Scientists	$38,990	6,928	13
35. Statisticians	$48,540	1,635	2
36. Agricultural and Food Scientists	$42,340	1,639	11
37. Mining Engineers	$56,090	282	−13
38. Landscape Architects	$37,930	1,605	14
39. Mathematicians	$49,100	1,304	−6

Best Jobs for People Interested in Plants and Animals

An interest in working with plants and animals, usually outdoors. You can satisfy this interest by working in farming, forestry, fishing, and related fields. You may like doing physical work outdoors, such as on a farm. You may enjoy animals; perhaps training or taking care of animals would appeal to you. If you have management ability, you could own, operate, or manage a farm or related business.

Best Jobs for People Interested in Plants and Animals

Job	Annual Earnings	Annual Openings	Percent Growth
1. Landscaping and Groundskeeping Workers	$17,140	283,459	21
2. Pest Control Workers	$22,490	7,983	25
3. Veterinary Assistants	$16,200	14,770	28
4. Lawn Service Managers	$25,410	10,385	20
5. Animal Caretakers	$14,820	43,263	22
6. Sprayers and Applicators	$21,650	5,167	24
7. Pruners	$22,070	10,504	12
8. Nursery and Greenhouse Managers	$25,360	583	15
9. Farm Workers	$12,600	157,331	–7

Best Jobs for People Interested in Law, Law Enforcement, and Public Safety

An interest in upholding people's rights, or in protecting people and property by using authority, inspecting, or monitoring. You can satisfy this interest by working in law, law enforcement, fire fighting, and related fields. For example, if you enjoy mental challenge and intrigue, you could investigate crimes or fires for a living. If you enjoy working with verbal skills, you may want to defend citizens in court or research deeds, wills, and other legal documents. You may prefer to fight fires and respond to other emergencies. Or, if you want more routine work, perhaps a job in guarding or patrolling would appeal to you; if you have management ability, you could seek a leadership position in law enforcement and the protective services. Work in the military gives you the chance to use technical and/or leadership skills while serving your country.

Best Jobs for People Interested in Law, Law Enforcement, and Public Safety

Job	Annual Earnings	Annual Openings	Percent Growth
1. Correctional Officers	$28,540	64,835	39
2. Police Patrol Officers	$37,710	51,739	32
3. Paralegals and Legal Assistants	$32,760	33,971	62
4. Lawyers	$78,170	38,182	17
5. Guards	$16,240	256,671	29
6. Police and Detective Supervisors	$48,700	14,034	12
7. Private Detectives and Investigators	$21,020	14,675	24
8. Sheriffs and Deputy Sheriffs	$28,270	3,130	34
9. Fire Fighting and Prevention Supervisors	$44,830	9,147	11
10. Fire Inspectors	$40,000	900	17
11. Inspectors and Compliance Officers	$36,820	19,910	10
12. Ski Patrol Workers and Life Guards	$17,470	23,282	19
13. Detectives and Criminal Investigators	$21,000	8,048	21

Best Jobs for People Interested in Mechanics, Installers, and Repairers

An interest in applying mechanical and electrical/electronic principles to practical situations by use of machines or hand tools. You can satisfy this interest working with a variety of tools, technologies, materials, and settings. If you enjoy making machines run efficiently or fixing them when they break down, you could seek a job installing or repairing such devices as copiers, aircraft engines, automobiles, or watches. You may instead prefer to deal directly with certain materials, and find work cutting and shaping metal or wood. Or if electricity and electronics interest you, you could install cables, troubleshoot telephone networks, or repair videocassette recorders. If you prefer routine or physical work in settings other than factories, perhaps work repairing tires or batteries would appeal to you.

Best Jobs for People Interested in Mechanics, Installers, and Repairers

Job	Annual Earnings	Annual Openings	Percent Growth
1. Central Office and PBX Installers and Repairers	$43,680	4,617	32
2. Data Processing Equipment Repairers	$29,340	20,080	47
3. Telephone and Cable TV Line Installers and Repairers	$32,750	18,246	30
4. Automotive Mechanics and Service Technicians	$27,360	119,161	17
5. Heating, Air Conditioning, and Refrigeration Mechanics and Installers	$29,160	29,552	17
6. Automotive Body Repairers	$27,400	33,051	16
7. Elevator Installers and Repairers	$47,860	5,088	12
8. Aircraft Mechanics and Service Technicians	$38,100	11,323	10
9. Commercial and Industrial Electronics Equipment Repairers	$35,590	9,744	13
10. Bus and Truck Mechanics and Diesel Engine Specialists	$29,340	21,502	10
11. Electrical Powerline Installers and Repairers	$42,600	5,616	1
12. General Utility Maintenance Repairers	$23,290	180,704	8
13. Medical Equipment Repairers	$34,190	1,675	14
14. Office Machine and Cash Register Servicers	$27,830	2,931	16
15. Tire Repairers and Changers	$16,810	26,095	10
16. Bicycle Repairers	$15,700	1,854	23
17. Coin, Vending, and Amusement Machine Servicers and Repairers	$23,260	4,315	16
18. Locksmiths and Safe Repairers	$24,890	4,557	10

Best Jobs for People Interested in Construction, Mining, and Drilling

An interest in assembling components of buildings and other structures, or in using mechanical devices to drill or excavate. If construction interests you, you can find fulfillment in the many building projects that are being undertaken at all times. If you like to organize and plan, you can find careers in management. On the other hand, you can play a more direct role in putting up and finishing buildings by doing jobs such as plumbing, carpentry, masonry, painting, or roofing. You may like working at a mine or oilfield, operating the powerful drilling or digging equipment. There are also several jobs that let you put your hands to the task.

Best Jobs for People Interested in Construction, Mining, and Drilling

Job	Annual Earnings	Annual Openings	Percent Growth
1. Construction Managers	$47,610	32,841	14
2. Blue-Collar Worker Supervisors	$37,180	216,115	9
3. Bricklayers, Blockmasons, and Stonemasons	$35,200	29,721	12
4. Electricians	$35,310	92,734	10
5. Carpenters	$28,700	236,108	7
6. Plasterers and Stucco Masons	$29,390	7,984	17
7. Sheet Metal Workers and Duct Installers	$28,000	22,680	14
8. Roofers	$25,340	28,797	12
9. Construction Helpers	$19,510	167,103	7
10. Highway Maintenance Workers	$24,490	20,512	11
11. Paving, Surfacing, and Tamping Equipment Operators	$24,510	13,780	11

Best Jobs for People Interested in Transportation

An interest in operations that move people or materials. You can satisfy this interest by managing a transportation service, by helping vehicles keep on their assigned schedules and routes, or by driving or piloting a vehicle. If you enjoy taking responsibility, perhaps managing a rail line would appeal to you. If you work well with details and can take pressure on the job, you might consider being an air traffic controller. Or would you rather get out on the highway, on the water, or up in the air? If so, then you could drive a truck from state to state, sail down the Mississippi on a barge, or fly a crop duster over a cornfield. If you prefer to stay closer to home, you could drive a delivery van, taxi, or school bus. You can use your physical strength to load freight and arrange it so it gets to its destination in one piece.

Best Jobs for People Interested in Transportation

Job	Annual Earnings	Annual Openings	Percent Growth
1. Communication, Transportation, and Utilities Operations Managers	$52,810	25,388	19
2. Aircraft Pilots and Flight Engineers	$91,750	4,555	6
3. Truck Drivers	$24,300	535,419	17
4. School Bus Drivers	$18,820	65,136	18
5. Bus Drivers	$24,370	29,885	16
6. Taxi Drivers and Chauffeurs	$15,540	26,739	20
7. Ambulance Drivers and Attendants	$16,960	4,191	35
8. Air Traffic Controllers	$64,880	2,321	2
9. Subway and Streetcar Operators	$43,330	250	7
10. Water Vessel Captains and Pilots	$41,200	3,581	3
11. Fishing Vessel Captains and Officers	$41,200	2,378	−19
12. Ship Engineers	$40,150	1,219	4

Best Jobs for People Interested in Industrial Production

An interest in repetitive, concrete, organized activities most often done in a factory setting. You can satisfy this interest by working in one of many industries that mass-produce goods, or for a utility that distributes electric power, gas, and so on. You may enjoy manual work, using your hands or hand tools. Perhaps you prefer to operate machines. You may like to inspect, sort, count, or weigh products. Using your training and experience to set up machines or supervise other workers may appeal to you.

Best Jobs for People Interested in Industrial Production

Job	Annual Earnings	Annual Openings	Percent Growth
1. Desktop Publishing Specialists	$29,130	7,546	73
2. Numerical Control Machine Tool Operators and Tenders	$27,110	18,908	23
3. Electronic Semiconductor Processors	$24,810	10,615	45
4. Industrial Production Managers	$56,320	20,865	−1
5. Meat, Poultry, and Fish Cutters and Trimmers	$16,270	33,193	24
6. Combination Machine Tool Setters, Set-Up Operators, Operators, and Tenders	$23,900	21,256	14
7. Hand Packers and Packagers	$14,540	249,421	22
8. Chemical Equipment Controllers, Operators and Tenders	$32,200	19,720	11
9. Aircraft Assemblers	$38,400	2,363	19
10. Water and Liquid Waste Treatment Plant and System Operators	$29,660	12,735	14
11. Packaging and Filling Machine Operators	$20,060	88,131	13
12. Hazardous Materials Removal Workers	$27,620	5,470	19
13. Plastic Molding Machine Setters, Set-Up Operators, Operators, and Tenders	$18,600	20,701	15
14. Excavation and Loading Machine Operators	$27,090	6,199	15
15. Painting, Coating, and Decorating Workers	$19,060	8,593	18
16. Bindery Machine Operators and Set-Up Operators	$20,600	16,466	12
17. Chemical Plant and System Operators	$39,030	3,484	11
18. Freight, Stock, and Material Movers	$18,470	306,549	2
19. Laundry and Dry-Cleaning Machine Operators	$14,670	38,082	10
20. Power Generating and Reactor Plant Operators	$44,800	2,216	3
21. Numerical Control Machine Tool Programmers	$40,490	706	6
22. Power Distributors and Dispatchers	$45,690	855	−12
23. Solderers and Brazers	$17,600	7,519	14
24. Gas and Petroleum Plant and System Occupations	$43,800	2,335	−13
25. Electrolytic Plating Machine Setters, Set-Up Operators, Operators, and Tenders	$21,200	5,108	10

Best Jobs for People Interested in Business Detail

An interest in organized, clearly defined activities requiring accuracy and attention to details, primarily in an office setting. You can satisfy this interest in a variety of jobs in which you attend to the details of a business operation. You may enjoy using your math skills; if so, perhaps a job in billing, computing, or financial record-keeping would satisfy you. If you prefer to deal with people, you may want a job in which you meet the public, talk on the telephone, or supervise other workers. You may like to do word processing on a computer, turn out copies on a duplicating machine, or work out sums on a calculator. Perhaps a job in filing or recording would satisfy you. Or you may wish to use your training and experience to manage an office.

Best Jobs for People Interested in Business Detail

Job	Annual Earnings	Annual Openings	Percent Growth
1. Office and Administrative Support Supervisors	$31,090	238,168	19
2. Administrative Services Managers	$44,370	46,558	18
3. Bill and Account Collectors	$22,540	106,068	35
4. Adjustment Clerks	$22,040	141,670	34
5. Brokerage Clerks	$27,920	17,895	28
6. Receptionists and Information Clerks	$18,620	386,806	24
7. General Office Clerks	$19,580	745,378	15
8. Legal Secretaries	$30,050	44,130	13
9. Tax Preparers	$27,960	13,654	19
10. Billing, Cost, and Rate Clerks	$22,670	63,239	15
11. Cashiers	$13,690	1,290,302	17
12. Commercial Dispatchers	$26,370	32,141	14
13. Secretaries	$23,550	358,379	0
14. Counter and Rental Clerks	$14,510	199,406	23
15. Bookkeeping, Accounting, and Auditing Clerks	$23,190	325,366	−4
16. Interviewing Clerks	$18,540	44,483	23
17. Insurance Claims Clerks	$24,010	12,974	14
18. Loan and Credit Clerks	$22,580	46,537	12
19. Shipping, Receiving, and Traffic Clerks	$22,500	242,666	3
20. Banking New Accounts Clerks	$21,340	36,231	15
21. Court Reporters, Medical Transcriptionists, and Stenographers	$25,430	15,612	10
22. License Clerks	$22,900	6,424	13

(continues)

(continued)

Best Jobs for People Interested in Business Detail

Job	Annual Earnings	Annual Openings	Percent Growth
23. Medical Secretaries	$22,390	33,608	12
24. Court Clerks	$22,960	13,394	11
25. Data Entry Keyers	$19,200	107,440	9
26. File Clerks	$16,830	117,451	10
27. Municipal Clerks	$22,810	6,545	12
28. Correspondence Clerks	$22,270	4,276	12
29. Bank Tellers	$17,200	106,674	−6
30. Mail Clerks	$17,660	26,426	10

Best Jobs for People Interested in Sales and Marketing

An interest in bringing others to a particular point of view by personal persuasion, using sales and promotional techniques. You can satisfy this interest in a variety of sales and marketing jobs. If you like using technical knowledge of science or agriculture, you may enjoy selling technical products or services. Or perhaps you are more interested in selling business-related services such as insurance coverage, advertising space, or investment opportunities. Real estate offers several kinds of sales jobs. Perhaps you'd rather work with something you can pick up and show to people. You may work in stores, sales offices, or customers' homes.

Best Jobs for People Interested in Sales and Marketing

Job	Annual Earnings	Annual Openings	Percent Growth
1. Advertising, Marketing, Promotions, Public Relations, and Sales Managers	$57,300	89,237	23
2. Securities, Commodities, and Financial Services Sales Agents	$48,090	61,084	41
3. Marketing and Sales Worker Supervisors	$29,570	410,550	10
4. Retail Salespersons	$15,830	1,305,317	14
5. Travel Agents	$23,010	17,019	18

Best Jobs for People Interested in Recreation, Travel, and Other Personal Services

An interest in catering to the personal wishes and needs of others, so that they may enjoy cleanliness, good food and drink, comfortable lodging away from home, and enjoyable recreation. You can satisfy this interest by providing services for the convenience, feeding, and pampering of others in hotels, restaurants, airplanes, and so on. If you enjoy improving the appearance of others, perhaps working in the hair and beauty care field would satisfy you. You may wish to provide personal services such as taking care of small children, tailoring garments, or ushering. Or you may use your knowledge of the field to manage workers who are providing these services.

Best Jobs for People Interested in Recreation, Travel, and Other Personal Services

Job	Annual Earnings	Annual Openings	Percent Growth
1. Personal Care and Home Health Aides	$15,800	249,694	58
2. Restaurant Cooks	$16,250	262,535	19
3. Food Service and Lodging Managers	$26,700	138,826	16
4. Flight Attendants	$37,800	5,376	30
5. Janitors, Cleaners, Maids, and Housekeeping Cleaners	$15,300	735,967	12
6. Recreation Workers	$16,500	43,829	19
7. Amusement and Recreation Attendants	$12,860	141,783	30
8. Cleaners of Vehicles and Equipment	$14,540	116,789	25
9. Bread and Pastry Bakers	$16,990	56,526	17
10. Parking Lot Attendants	$13,930	17,725	31
11. Food Preparation Workers	$13,700	529,498	10
12. Short Order and Fast Food Cooks	$12,700	226,320	18
13. Food Counter and Fountain Workers	$12,600	944,970	12
14. Restaurant Hosts and Hostesses	$13,400	110,848	18
15. Hotel, Motel, and Resort Desk Clerks	$15,160	60,382	14
16. Institution or Cafeteria Cooks	$16,090	124,088	3
17. Manicurists	$13,480	7,081	26
18. Hairdressers, Hairstylists, and Cosmetologists	$15,150	73,177	10
19. Institutional Cleaning Supervisors	$19,590	9,030	10
20. Dining Room and Cafeteria Attendants and Bar Helpers	$12,580	181,922	4
21. Baggage Porters and Bellhops	$13,330	10,287	14
22. Ushers, Lobby Attendants, and Ticket Takers	$12,520	22,505	18

Best Jobs for People Interested in Education and Social Service

An interest in teaching people or improving their social or spiritual well-being. You can satisfy this interest by teaching students, who may be preschoolers, retirees, or any age in between. Or if you are interested in helping people sort out their complicated lives, you may find fulfillment as a counselor, social worker, or religious worker. Working in a museum or library may give you opportunities to expand people's understanding of the world. If you also have an interest in business, you may find satisfaction in managerial work in this field.

Best Jobs for People Interested in Education and Social Service

Job	Annual Earnings	Annual Openings	Percent Growth
1. College and University Faculty	$46,600	139,101	23
2. Secondary School Teachers	$37,890	133,585	23
3. Special Education Teachers	$37,850	36,540	34
4. Human Service Workers and Assistants	$21,360	91,824	53
5. Teacher Assistants	$15,800	343,831	32
6. Counselors	$38,650	21,279	25
7. Education Administrators	$60,400	60,229	13
8. Social Workers	$30,590	29,630	36
9. Child Care Workers	$13,750	328,786	26
10. Elementary School Teachers	$36,110	204,210	12
11. Residential Counselors	$18,840	27,865	46
12. Vocational Education Teachers and Instructors	$34,430	106,468	11
13. Adult Education Instructors	$24,790	46,224	21
14. Preschool Teachers	$17,310	41,894	26
15. Directors of Religious Activities and Education	$24,970	13,292	25
16. Kindergarten Teachers	$33,590	18,836	13
17. Archivists, Curators, Museum Technicians, and Conservators	$31,750	4,118	13
18. Clergy	$28,850	14,197	13
19. Library Assistants and Bookmobile Drivers	$16,980	35,994	16
20. Library Technicians	$21,730	9,478	18

Best Jobs for People Interested in General Management and Support

An interest in making an organization run smoothly. You can satisfy this interest by working in a position of leadership, or by specializing in a function that contributes to the overall effort. The organization may be a profit-making business, a nonprofit, or a government agency. If you especially enjoy working with people, you may find fulfillment from working in human resources. An interest in numbers may cause you to consider accounting, finance, budgeting, or purchasing. Or perhaps you would enjoy managing the organization's physical resources (for example, land, buildings, equipment, and utilities).

Best Jobs for People Interested in General Management and Support

Job	Annual Earnings	Annual Openings	Percent Growth
1. General Managers and Top Executives	$55,890	421,006	16
2. Management Analysts	$49,470	23,831	28
3. Financial Managers	$55,070	78,071	14
4. Human Resources Managers	$49,010	32,929	19
5. Human Resources, Training, and Labor Relations Specialists	$37,710	82,760	18
6. Loan Counselors and Officers	$35,340	39,836	21
7. Insurance Adjusters, Examiners, and Investigators	$38,290	16,055	20
8. Budget Analysts	$44,950	9,617	14
9. Cost Estimators	$40,590	27,649	13
10. Accountants and Auditors	$37,860	129,566	11
11. Credit Analysts	$35,590	7,260	20
12. Property, Real Estate, and Community Association Managers	$29,860	47,581	14
13. Purchasing Agents	$38,040	42,342	11
14. Purchasing Managers	$41,830	24,516	7
15. Auto Insurance Appraisers	$40,000	871	16
16. Funeral Directors and Morticians	$35,040	3,972	16
17. Property and Casualty Insurance Claims Examiners	$40,110	3,838	12
18. Real Estate Appraisers	$40,290	6,383	11
19. Postmasters and Mail Superintendents	$44,730	3,256	3
20. Employment Interviewers	$29,800	14,194	13
21. Assessors	$29,830	1,807	12

Best Jobs for People Interested in Medical and Health Services

An interest in helping people be healthy. You can satisfy this interest by working in a health-care team as a doctor, therapist, or nurse. You might specialize in one of the many different parts of the body or types of care, or you might be a generalist who deals with the whole patient. If you like technology, you might find satisfaction working with X rays, one of the electronic means of diagnosis, or clinical laboratory testing. You might work with healthy people, helping them stay in condition through exercise and eating right. If you like to organize, analyze, and plan, a managerial role might be right for you.

Best Jobs for People Interested in Medical and Health Services

Job	Annual Earnings	Annual Openings	Percent Growth
1. Physicians	$102,020	32,563	21
2. Dental Hygienists	$45,890	15,372	40
3. Medical and Health Services Managers	$48,870	31,238	33
4. Dental Assistants	$22,640	56,389	42
5. Medical Assistants	$20,680	49,015	58
6. Registered Nurses	$40,690	195,231	22
7. Physical Therapists	$56,600	10,602	34
8. Physician Assistants	$47,090	6,142	48
9. Speech-Language Pathologists and Audiologists	$43,080	9,862	38
10. Occupational Therapists	$48,230	6,484	34
11. Respiratory Therapists	$34,830	8,553	43
12. Physical Therapy Assistants and Aides	$21,870	14,195	44
13. Medical Records and Health Information Technicians	$20,590	11,453	44
14. Licensed Practical Nurses	$26,940	43,314	20
15. Surgical Technologists	$25,780	9,182	42
16. Veterinarians	$50,950	3,227	25
17. Cardiovascular Technologists and Technicians	$35,770	3,458	39
18. Chiropractors	$63,930	2,516	23
19. Nursing Aides, Orderlies, and Attendants	$16,620	349,640	24
20. Clinical Laboratory Technologists and Technicians	$32,440	20,441	17
21. Emergency Medical Technicians	$20,290	23,138	32
22. Radiologic Technologists and Technicians	$32,880	11,306	20
23. Occupational Therapy Assistants and Aides	$28,690	3,106	40
24. Dietitians and Nutritionists	$35,040	8,153	19

Best Jobs for People Interested in Medical and Health Services

Job	Annual Earnings	Annual Openings	Percent Growth
25. Pharmacists	$66,220	6,382	7
26. Dentists	$110,160	2,301	3
27. Optometrists	$68,480	1,532	11
28. Podiatrists	$79,530	562	10
29. Psychiatric Technicians	$20,890	15,167	11
30. Pharmacy Technicians	$17,763	14,132	16
31. Radiation Therapists	$39,640	829	17
32. Dispensing Opticians	$22,440	5,799	14
33. Nuclear Medicine Technologists	$39,610	833	12
34. Recreational Therapists	$27,760	2,439	13
35. Veterinary Technologists and Technicians	$19,870	2,822	16

Best Jobs Lists for All States, Plus the 30 Largest Metropolitan Areas

Section A provides the best jobs lists based on national earnings, growth projections, and number of job openings. But some readers of the previous edition wanted information on jobs in their area—information that could be significantly different from a national average.

This section offers two lists for each geographic area. The first list shows you the 25 jobs that employ the most people in the area. For example, in Alabama, cashier and retail sales-person are the two jobs employing the most people. The second list includes the jobs with the highest average annual pay for that area. Using Alabama as our example again, its second list shows the two highest-paying jobs as dentist (at $110,380 annually) and physicians and surgeons (at $103,350 annually).

We provide the two lists for each of the 50 states and the District of Columbia in alphabetical order. Then, we give the same two lists for the 30 largest metropolitan areas in the United States. We provide the population of each area based on U.S. Census Bureau estimates.

Note: The state and metropolitan lists use data on jobs employing the most people. This is a bit different from the data employed in the lists in Section A, where we used data for jobs with the most annual openings. The data for annual openings includes turnover resulting from workers leaving their jobs as well as projected growth in the occupation. While the underlying data is a bit different, we think these lists will provide you with useful information.

Each state controls the collection of data for their state and the cities within the state. States may use job titles that are slightly different than those used by the federal government. For example, the following lists use "physicians and surgeons" rather than "physicians" and "atmospheric and space scientists" rather than "atmospheric scientists." In some cases, the state collects data on more specific occupations. For example, the federal government reports on the occupation titled "janitors, cleaners, maids, and housekeeping cleaners," but some states collect data for the occupation "janitors and cleaners" and for a separate occupation titled "maids and housekeeping cleaners." For this reason jobs appearing in Section A lists may not appear here and vice versa.

We ask that you stretch your mind in adjusting for these differences. When you look up job descriptions in Part II, you may need to search for jobs under more than one name or in some location that doesn't immediately come to mind. The table of contents has been designed to make this search a little easier. You can more quickly scan through the various job titles found in Section II using the table of contents. This sounds more difficult than it will be in practice. Despite these minor inconsistencies, we think these lists are valuable additions to the book.

Some Ways You Can Use These Lists

We think it is interesting to see the data for jobs in each area. You can look at the data for your area or for the areas you may want to move to in the future, with the following purposes in mind:

Career choice. We think the lists in Section A are more useful for exploring career options, since they list more jobs and do so in many more ways than in the geographic lists. Even so, the information on jobs by geographic area can give you some idea of the larger occupations and better-paying jobs in your area.

Cost of living information: You can use the lists to see what others are paid in different parts of the country. Typically, areas with lower wages also have lower costs of living, and you can get some sense of this from these lists. For example, pay for most jobs is higher in Southern California than in some other areas, but the cost of living is much higher. If considering relocation, you can compare data between states and metropolitan areas. For example, dental hygienists in the San Francisco-Oakland-San Jose area may be interested to find that while they don't make the list for the highest earnings in their region, their counterparts in the Seattle-Tacoma-Bremerton area hold the 16th highest paid job. This information may encourage dental hygienists in San Francisco to explore openings in Seattle.

Pay negotiation: If your job is on the list for your area or an area you are considering, it will give you some idea of average earnings. You can use this information to negotiate pay with a current or potential employer. But, as we explained in the introduction to this book, average earnings can be misleading. Those just entering an occupation, or with less than average experience, will typically earn less than average. Smaller employers often pay less, although they may offer more flexibility or other advantages over larger employers. If you have lots of experience and great credentials, you may earn more than average.

For employers, teachers, and counselors: Employers can determine how competitive their pay rates are in their area. Counselors and teachers can have students and clients compare jobs in their state or metropolitan area with those elsewhere.

Jobs Lists by State

ALABAMA
Population 4,351,037

Jobs Employing the Most Workers

Job	Number Employed
1. Cashiers	64,990
2. Retail Salespersons	56,970
3. General Managers and Top Executives	53,170
4. General Office Clerks	46,590
5. Secretaries	33,880
6. Truck Drivers—Heavy	33,690
7. Registered Nurses	28,130
8. Combined Food Preparation and Service Workers	25,970
9. Bookkeeping, Accounting, and Auditing Clerks	25,370
10. Janitors and Cleaners	24,730
11. Waiters and Waitresses	24,610
12. First-Line Supervisors and Managers— Sales Workers	21,830
13. Elementary School Teachers	19,900
14. Truck Drivers—Light	19,650
15. General Utility Maintenance Repairers	19,440
16. Secondary School Teachers	19,150
17. Assemblers and Fabricators	18,350
18. Nursing Aides, Orderlies, and Attendants	18,240
19. Stock Clerks—Sales Floor	17,700
20. Sales Representatives	17,280
21. Sewing Machine Operators	17,250
22. First-Line Supervisors and Managers— Clerical and Administrative Workers	16,580
23. Hand Packers and Packagers	16,310
24. Licensed Practical Nurses	15,400
25. Shipping, Receiving, and Traffic Clerks	15,130

Jobs with the Highest Earnings

Job	Annual Earnings
1. Dentists	$110,380
2. Physicians and Surgeons	$103,350
3. Optometrists	$79,080
4. Podiatrists	$75,770
5. Lawyers	$71,630
6. Medical Scientists	$70,330
7. Securities, Commodities, and Financial Services Sales Agents	$67,430
8. College and University Faculty (Engineering Teachers)	$66,830
9. Engineering, Mathematical, and Natural Sciences Managers	$64,640
10. Chiropractors	$63,550
11. Mining Engineers	$61,820
12. Mining, Quarrying, and Oil and Gas Well Drilling Managers	$61,700
13. Materials Engineers	$61,140
14. Air Traffic Controllers	$60,420
15. Electrical and Electronic Engineers	$59,470
16. College and University Faculty (Agricultural Sciences)	$59,040
17. Atmospheric and Space Scientists	$58,430
18. Chemical Engineers	$58,270
19. Physical Therapists	$57,810
20. Computer Engineers	$57,700
21. Pharmacists	$57,320
22. Criminal Investigators, Public Service	$57,320
23. Operations Research Analysts	$56,550
24. Education Administrators	$56,430
25. Mechanical Engineers	$55,390

ALASKA
Population 615,205

Jobs Employing the Most Workers

Job	Number Employed
1. Retail Salespersons	7,650
2. General Office Clerks	6,880
3. General Managers and Top Executives	6,420
4. Cashiers	6,340
5. Janitors and Cleaners	4,900
6. Bookkeeping, Accounting, and Auditing Clerks	4,820
7. Secretaries	4,800
8. Elementary School Teachers	4,120
9. Waiters and Waitresses	3,850
10. General Utility Maintenance Repairers	3,840
11. Registered Nurses	3,810
12. First-Line Supervisors and Managers—Administrative Workers	3,440
13. Receptionists and Information Clerks	3,300
14. First-Line Supervisors and Managers—Sales Workers	3,050
15. Combined Food Preparation and Service Workers	3,050
16. Teachers, Secondary School	2,970
17. Food Preparation Workers	2,870
18. Carpenters	2,560
19. Stock Clerks—Sales Floor	2,500
20. Teacher Assistants	2,430
21. Truck Drivers—Light	2,410
22. Truck Drivers—Heavy	2,220
23. Cannery Workers	2,060
24. Maids and Housekeeping Cleaners	2,000
25. Bartenders	1,970

Jobs with the Highest Earnings

Job	Annual Earnings
1. Dentists	$114,380
2. Physicians and Surgeons	$106,850
3. Optometrists	$101,700
4. Mining, Quarrying, and Oil and Gas Well Drilling Managers	$81,160
5. Lawyers	$80,490
6. Judges and Magistrates	$78,140
7. Aircraft Pilots and Flight Engineers	$74,870
8. Physician Assistants	$72,420
9. College and University Faculty (Education)	$70,110
10. Mining Engineers, Including Mine Safety	$68,450
11. College and University Faculty (Computer Science)	$67,940
12. Engineering, Mathematical, and Natural Sciences Managers	$66,360
13. Real Estate Brokers	$65,680
14. Pharmacists	$64,420
15. Dental Hygienists	$64,250
16. College and University Faculty (Mathematical Sciences)	$63,530
17. Rotary Drill Operators, Oil and Gas Extraction	$63,340
18. Petroleum Refinery and Control Panel Operators	$63,150
19. Central Office and PBX Installers and Repairers	$62,410
20. Fire Inspectors	$62,180
21. College and University Faculty (History Teachers)	$62,110
22. Electrical and Electronic Engineers	$61,790
23. College and University Faculty (Business Teachers)	$61,590
24. Cost Estimators	$61,440
25. Construction Managers	$61,070

ARIZONA
Population 4,667,277

Jobs Employing the Most Workers

Job	Number Employed
1. Cashiers	52,950
2. Retail Salespersons	51,790
3. General Office Clerks	45,270
4. General Managers and Top Executives	42,300
5. Secretaries	37,100
6. Waiters and Waitresses	35,910
7. Janitors and Cleaners	31,180
8. First-Line Supervisors and Managers—Sales Workers	29,030
9. Registered Nurses	28,740
10. First-Line Supervisors and Managers—Administrative Workers	28,200
11. Combined Food Preparation and Service Workers	27,150
12. Receptionists and Information Clerks	26,890
13. Elementary School Teachers	26,720
14. Bookkeeping, Accounting, and Auditing Clerks	26,720
15. Landscaping and Groundskeeping Laborers	24,310
16. Truck Drivers—Heavy	21,300
17. Truck Drivers—Light	20,770
18. Carpenters	20,760
19. General Utility Maintenance Repairers	19,910
20. Food Preparation Workers	19,620
21. Stock Clerks—Sales Floor	18,620
22. Secondary School Teachers	18,160
23. Adjustment Clerks	17,910
24. Guards and Watch Guards	16,440
25. Hand Packers and Packagers	15,970

Jobs with the Highest Earnings

Job	Annual Earnings
1. Physicians and Surgeons	$108,530
2. Dentists	$101,600
3. Optometrists	$85,000
4. Podiatrists	$77,990
5. Lawyers	$76,680
6. College and University Faculty (Law)	$72,660
7. Mining, Quarrying, and Oil and Gas Well Drilling Managers	$70,880
8. Engineering, Mathematical, and Natural Sciences Managers	$70,750
9. Judges and Magistrates	$68,060
10. Industrial Production Managers	$65,430
11. General Managers and Top Executives	$64,870
12. Veterinarians	$64,770
13. Electrical and Electronic Engineers	$64,010
14. Computer Engineers	$63,950
15. Pharmacists	$63,350
16. Sales Engineers	$59,700
17. Atmospheric and Space Scientists	$59,040
18. Operations Research Analysts	$58,740
19. Actuaries	$58,640
20. Marketing, Advertising, and Public Relations Managers	$58,590
21. Financial Managers	$57,950
22. College and University Faculty (Economics)	$57,650
23. Chiropractors	$56,770
24. Dental Hygienists	$56,400
25. Power Distributors and Dispatchers	$55,960

ARKANSAS
Population 2,551,373

Jobs Employing the Most Workers

Job	Number Employed
1. Retail Salespersons	38,950
2. Cashiers	33,460
3. Truck Drivers—Heavy	30,720
4. Assemblers and Fabricators	28,740
5. General Managers and Top Executives	25,760
6. General Office Clerks	24,290
7. Combined Food Preparation and Service Workers	19,590
8. Registered Nurses	19,020
9. Secretaries	19,000
10. Packaging and Filling Machine Operators and Tenders	16,680
11. First-Line Supervisors and Managers— Sales Workers	16,290
12. Nursing Aides, Orderlies, and Attendants	16,210
13. Waiters and Waitresses	15,980
14. Secondary School Teachers	14,740
15. Janitors and Cleaners	13,300
16. Elementary School Teachers	12,470
17. General Utility Maintenance Repairers	12,440
18. Licensed Practical Nurses	11,910
19. Bookkeeping, Accounting, and Auditing Clerks	11,770
20. First-Line Supervisors and Managers— Administrative Workers	11,400
21. Stock Clerks—Sales Floor	10,800
22. Food Preparation Workers	10,750
23. Hand Packers and Packagers	9,560
24. Meat, Poultry, and Fish Cutters and Trimmers, Hand	9,350
25. Sales Representatives	9,230

Jobs with the Highest Earnings

Job	Annual Earnings
1. Physicians and Surgeons	$93,020
2. Dentists	$92,810
3. Water Vessel Captains	$78,300
4. Securities, Commodities, and Financial Services Sales Agents	$67,800
5. Optometrists	$66,650
6. Petroleum Engineers	$64,710
7. Actuaries	$62,700
8. Engineering, Mathematical, and Natural Sciences Managers	$60,200
9. Chiropractors	$59,690
10. Medical Scientists	$59,180
11. Lawyers	$59,080
12. Physical Therapists	$57,780
13. Electrical and Electronic Engineers	$56,460
14. Chemical Engineers	$55,990
15. Pharmacists	$55,880
16. Financial Analysts	$55,520
17. College and University Faculty (Economics)	$54,850
18. Materials Engineers	$54,650
19. Occupational Therapists	$54,250
20. Civil Engineers	$52,860
21. Air Traffic Controllers	$52,750
22. Communication, Transportation, and Utilities Operations Managers	$52,720
23. Veterinarians	$52,470
24. Education Administrators	$52,380
25. Marketing, Advertising, and Public Relations Managers	$51,330

CALIFORNIA
Population 32,682,794

Jobs Employing the Most Workers

Job	Number Employed
1. Retail Salespersons	429,600
2. General Managers and Top Executives	370,340
3. General Office Clerks	354,630
4. Cashiers	308,440
5. Secretaries	240,760
6. Waiters and Waitresses	203,870
7. Bookkeeping, Accounting, and Auditing Clerks	199,480
8. Janitors and Cleaners	196,040
9. First-Line Supervisors and Managers— Administrative Workers	191,810
10. First-Line Supervisors and Managers— Sales Workers	186,900
11. Combined Food Preparation and Service Workers	180,740
12. Registered Nurses	172,210
13. Elementary School Teachers	169,070
14. Receptionists and Information Clerks	160,490
15. Truck Drivers—Light	143,680
16. Stock Clerks—Sales Floor	139,890
17. Food Preparation Workers	134,160
18. Landscaping and Groundskeeping Laborers	133,180
19. Shipping, Receiving, and Traffic Clerks	131,200
20. Farm Workers	129,050
21. Guards and Watch Guards	128,300
22. Sales Representatives	123,780
23. Secondary School Teachers	123,690
24. Assemblers and Fabricators	117,560
25. General Utility Maintenance Repairers	115,670

Jobs with the Highest Earnings

Job	Annual Earnings
1. Physicians and Surgeons	$100,040
2. Dentists	$92,510
3. Judges and Magistrates	$91,670
4. Aircraft Pilots and Flight Engineers	$85,830
5. Lawyers	$83,920
6. Engineering, Mathematical, and Natural Sciences Managers	$80,610
7. Nuclear Engineers	$78,290
8. Actuaries	$74,260
9. General Managers and Top Executives	$72,740
10. Physicists and Astronomers	$71,040
11. Aerospace Engineers	$68,440
12. College and University Faculty (Health Diagnostics)	$68,190
13. Mining, Quarrying, and Oil and Gas Well Drilling Managers	$68,080
14. Petroleum Engineers	$67,130
15. Securities, Commodities, and Financial Services Sales Agents	$66,920
16. Electrical and Electronic Engineers	$66,670
17. Chemical Engineers	$66,670
18. Broadcast News Analysts	$66,660
19. Financial Managers	$65,980
20. Marketing, Advertising, and Public Relations Managers	$65,770
21. Pharmacists	$65,280
22. Sales Engineers	$65,010
23. College and University Faculty (Engineering Teachers)	$64,420
24. Veterinarians	$64,050
25. Computer Engineers	$64,020

COLORADO
Population 3,968,967

Jobs Employing the Most Workers

Job	Number Employed
1. Retail Salespersons	73,680
2. General Office Clerks	52,730
3. Cashiers	45,370
4. General Managers and Top Executives	42,840
5. Waiters and Waitresses	39,940
6. First-Line Supervisors and Managers—Sales Workers	34,890
7. Bookkeeping, Accounting, and Auditing Clerks	34,040
8. Secretaries	33,960
9. First-Line Supervisors and Managers—Administrative Workers	30,710
10. Combined Food Preparation and Service Workers	30,380
11. Janitors and Cleaners	29,030
12. Registered Nurses	27,420
13. Receptionists and Information Clerks	24,990
14. Truck Drivers—Heavy	21,920
15. Sales Representatives	20,430
16. Secondary School Teachers	20,310
17. Elementary School Teachers	20,260
18. Truck Drivers—Light	19,590
19. Food Preparation Workers	18,950
20. Cooks, Restaurant	17,560
21. General Utility Maintenance Repairers	16,590
22. Accountants and Auditors	16,280
23. Stock Clerks—Sales Floor	16,200
24. Maids and Housekeeping Cleaners	15,770
25. Shipping, Receiving, and Traffic Clerks	14,730

Jobs with the Highest Earnings

Job	Annual Earnings
1. Physicians and Surgeons	$102,930
2. Dentists	$92,010
3. Podiatrists	$84,310
4. Real Estate Brokers	$80,330
5. Nuclear Engineers	$77,890
6. Petroleum Engineers	$76,560
7. Optometrists	$76,480
8. Engineering, Mathematical, and Natural Sciences Managers	$75,410
9. College and University Faculty (Law)	$73,670
10. Mining, Quarrying, and Oil and Gas Well Drilling Managers	$73,040
11. Chiropractors	$71,770
12. Physicists and Astronomers	$71,090
13. Lawyers	$69,790
14. General Managers and Top Executives	$69,280
15. College and University Faculty (Engineering Teachers)	$68,200
16. Economists	$68,080
17. Sales Engineers	$66,520
18. Judges and Magistrates	$65,270
19. College and University Faculty (Physics)	$64,980
20. Computer Engineers	$64,460
21. Geologists, Geophysicists, and Oceanographers	$63,970
22. Sales Representatives—Scientific Products	$63,280
23. Financial Managers	$62,210
24. Electrical and Electronic Engineers	$61,860
25. Pharmacists	$61,410

CONNECTICUT
Population 3,272,563

Jobs Employing the Most Workers

Job	Number Employed
1. General Managers and Top Executives	54,300
2. Retail Salespersons	50,860
3. Cashiers	49,700
4. Secretaries	41,870
5. General Office Clerks	32,180
6. Registered Nurses	29,470
7. Janitors and Cleaners	27,590
8. First-Line Supervisors and Managers— Administrative Workers	24,970
9. Bookkeeping, Accounting, and Auditing Clerks	24,660
10. Nursing Aides, Orderlies, and Attendants	24,540
11. Elementary School Teachers	23,030
12. Waiters and Waitresses	22,870
13. First-Line Supervisors and Managers— Sales Workers	22,760
14. Secondary School Teachers	19,900
15. Receptionists and Information Clerks	15,330
16. Sales Representatives	15,150
17. Accountants and Auditors	14,960
18. Food Preparation Workers	14,830
19. Truck Drivers—Light	14,550
20. Assemblers and Fabricators	14,480
21. Financial Managers	13,080
22. Guards and Watch Guards	12,770
23. Truck Drivers—Heavy	12,580
24. Adjustment Clerks	12,490
25. Shipping, Receiving, and Traffic Clerks	12,330

Jobs with the Highest Earnings

Job	Annual Earnings
1. Physicians and Surgeons	$104,140
2. Dentists	$102,890
3. College and University Faculty (Law)	$93,140
4. Chiropractors	$92,290
5. Judges and Magistrates	$91,030
6. Securities, Commodities, and Financial Services Sales Agents	$81,080
7. Lawyers	$79,100
8. Optometrists	$77,190
9. General Managers and Top Executives	$74,390
10. Actuaries	$74,250
11. Engineering, Mathematical, and Natural Sciences Managers	$73,640
12. Podiatrists	$73,600
13. College and University Faculty (Health Diagnostics)	$69,110
14. Financial Managers	$68,750
15. Marketing, Advertising, and Public Relations Managers	$67,500
16. Agricultural and Food Scientists	$67,420
17. Veterinarians	$67,290
18. Medicine and Health Services Managers	$66,620
19. College and University Faculty (Mathematics)	$65,420
20. Industrial Production Managers	$65,150
21. Personnel, Training, and Labor Relations Managers	$64,410
22. College and University Faculty (Engineering Teachers)	$64,310
23. Education Administrators	$63,450
24. Pharmacists	$63,200
25. College and University Faculty (Economics)	$62,960

DELAWARE
Population 744,066

Jobs Employing the Most Workers

Job	Number Employed
1. General Managers and Top Executives	12,950
2. Retail Salespersons	12,840
3. General Office Clerks	11,100
4. Cashiers	9,770
5. Secretaries	9,040
6. Janitors and Cleaners	6,720
7. First-Line Supervisors and Managers—Administrative Workers	6,430
8. Adjustment Clerks	6,290
9. Registered Nurses	6,190
10. Bookkeeping, Accounting, and Auditing Clerks	6,000
11. Waiters and Waitresses	5,930
12. First-Line Supervisors and Managers—Sales Workers	5,610
13. Sales Representatives	5,020
14. Combined Food Preparation and Service Workers	4,660
15. Receptionists and Information Clerks	4,550
16. Nursing Aides, Orderlies, and Attendants	4,010
17. Tellers	3,640
18. Truck Drivers—Light	3,600
19. Accountants and Auditors	3,590
20. Stock Clerks—Sales Floor	3,550
21. Truck Drivers—Heavy	3,450
22. Meat, Poultry, and Fish Cutters and Trimmers, Hand	3,430
23. General Utility Maintenance Repairers	3,400
24. Food Preparation Workers	3,270
25. Guards and Watch Guards	3,220

Jobs with the Highest Earnings

Job	Annual Earnings
1. Chiropractors	$108,190
2. Dentists	$97,150
3. Optometrists	$92,830
4. Physicians and Surgeons	$89,410
5. Lawyers	$77,150
6. Engineering, Mathematical, and Natural Sciences Managers	$72,120
7. Physician Assistants	$69,900
8. Industrial Production Managers	$69,410
9. Aircraft Pilots and Flight Engineers	$67,950
10. Marketing, Advertising, and Public Relations Managers	$67,230
11. Real Estate Brokers	$64,900
12. Chemical Engineers	$64,810
13. Physical Therapists	$64,140
14. Securities, Commodities, and Financial Services Sales Agents	$63,860
15. Pharmacists	$63,260
16. Computer Engineers	$62,120
17. Mathematical Scientists	$61,930
18. Electrical and Electronic Engineers	$61,730
19. Materials Engineers	$61,240
20. Chemists	$61,120
21. Personnel, Training, and Labor Relations Managers	$59,940
22. Financial Managers	$59,640
23. Education Administrators	$59,340
24. General Managers and Top Executives	$58,860
25. Actuaries	$58,590

DISTRICT OF COLUMBIA
Population 521,426

Jobs Employing the Most Workers

Job	Number Employed
1. Secretaries	23,590
2. Lawyers	21,550
3. General Managers and Top Executives	20,670
4. Janitors and Cleaners	16,320
5. First-Line Supervisors and Managers—Administrative Workers	10,600
6. Registered Nurses	9,700
7. Accountants and Auditors	9,150
8. Guards and Watch Guards	8,720
9. Bookkeeping, Accounting, and Auditing Clerks	7,400
10. Receptionists and Information Clerks	7,100
11. Legal Secretaries	6,890
12. Waiters and Waitresses	6,760
13. Retail Salespersons	5,160
14. General Utility Maintenance Repairers	4,590
15. Paralegal Personnel	4,460
16. Maids and Housekeeping Cleaners	4,450
17. First-Line Supervisors and Managers—Sales Workers	4,430
18. Food Preparation Workers	4,290
19. Typists, Including Word Processing	4,260
20. Financial Managers	4,110
21. Writers and Editors	4,020
22. Cashiers	3,660
23. Nursing Aides, Orderlies, and Attendants	3,400
24. Administrative Services Managers	3,230
25. Marketing, Advertising, and Public Relations Managers	3,010

Jobs with the Highest Earnings

Job	Annual Earnings
1. Physicians and Surgeons	$87,820
2. Lawyers	$85,330
3. College and University Faculty (Law)	$79,210
4. General Managers and Top Executives	$72,970
5. Industrial Production Managers	$70,860
6. Dentists	$68,890
7. Communication, Transportation, and Utilities Operations Managers	$68,180
8. Agricultural Engineers	$66,770
9. Computer Engineers	$66,040
10. Industrial Engineers	$64,650
11. Financial Managers	$63,430
12. Securities, Commodities, and Financial Services Sales Agents	$63,310
13. Veterinarians	$62,820
14. College and University Faculty (Engineering Teachers)	$62,200
15. Barbers	$62,200
16. Construction Managers	$61,670
17. Public Relations Specialists and Publicity Writers	$61,190
18. Marketing, Advertising, and Public Relations Managers	$59,680
19. Civil Engineers	$59,510
20. Speech-Language Pathologists and Audiologists	$59,380
21. Personnel, Training, and Labor Relations Managers	$59,340
22. Safety Engineers	$58,660
23. Pharmacists	$58,140
24. Geologists, Geophysicists, and Oceanographers	$57,710
25. Medicine and Health Services Managers	$57,520

FLORIDA
Population 14,908,230

Jobs Employing the Most Workers

Job	Number Employed
1. Retail Salespersons	239,940
2. General Managers and Top Executives	189,020
3. General Office Clerks	184,000
4. Cashiers	172,520
5. Secretaries	138,710
6. Waiters and Waitresses	125,710
7. Registered Nurses	116,900
8. Combined Food Preparation and Service Workers	115,140
9. Bookkeeping, Accounting, and Auditing Clerks	103,990
10. First-Line Supervisors and Managers— Sales Workers	102,200
11. Stock Clerks—Sales Floor	94,970
12. First-Line Supervisors and Managers— Administrative Workers	90,590
13. Receptionists and Information Clerks	87,730
14. Janitors and Cleaners	84,660
15. Truck Drivers—Light	78,000
16. Elementary School Teachers	71,260
17. Sales Representatives	66,850
18. Food Preparation Workers	65,500
19. Guards and Watch Guards	64,880
20. Landscaping and Groundskeeping Laborers	62,530
21. General Utility Maintenance Repairers	62,050
22. Maids and Housekeeping Cleaners	61,890
23. Secondary School Teachers	59,130
24. Nursing Aides, Orderlies, and Attendants	58,970
25. Truck Drivers—Heavy	58,000

Jobs with the Highest Earnings

Job	Annual Earnings
1. Physicians and Surgeons	$104,420
2. Dentists	$103,070
3. Judges and Magistrates	$100,910
4. Podiatrists	$99,670
5. Optometrists	$76,800
6. Lawyers	$74,900
7. Chiropractors	$71,890
8. College and University Faculty (Health Assessment and Treatment)	$69,110
9. Physicists and Astronomers	$68,970
10. Actuaries	$67,990
11. Nuclear Engineers	$66,970
12. Medical Scientists	$64,190
13. Engineering, Mathematical, and Natural Sciences Managers	$63,520
14. Pharmacists	$62,510
15. Marine Engineers	$61,700
16. Veterinarians	$61,490
17. Broadcast News Analysts	$61,060
18. Securities, Commodities, and Financial Services Sales Agents	$60,410
19. Air Traffic Controllers	$59,540
20. Computer Engineers	$59,250
21. College and University Faculty (Law)	$58,260
22. Chemical Engineers	$57,950
23. Aircraft Pilots and Flight Engineers	$57,820
24. Electrical and Electronic Engineers	$57,140
25. Materials Engineers	$57,100

GEORGIA
Population 7,636,522

Jobs Employing the Most Workers

Job	Number Employed
1. Retail Salespersons	114,920
2. Cashiers	109,930
3. General Managers and Top Executives	106,110
4. General Office Clerks	80,670
5. Secretaries	75,170
6. Waiters and Waitresses	54,840
7. Janitors and Cleaners	52,490
8. First-Line Supervisors and Managers— Sales Workers	51,280
9. Registered Nurses	50,640
10. Bookkeeping, Accounting, and Auditing Clerks	50,630
11. Truck Drivers—Heavy	50,250
12. Food Preparation Workers	48,450
13. Combined Food Preparation and Service Workers	46,150
14. Elementary School Teachers	44,480
15. First-Line Supervisors and Managers— Administrative Workers	41,060
16. Sales Representatives	40,980
17. Stock Clerks—Sales Floor	40,090
18. Assemblers and Fabricators	39,390
19. Receptionists and Information Clerks	37,210
20. Hand Packers and Packagers	36,690
21. Truck Drivers—Light	35,330
22. Textile Machine Operators and Tenders	33,820
23. General Utility Maintenance Repairers	32,800
24. Shipping, Receiving, and Traffic Clerks	32,210
25. Nursing Aides, Orderlies, and Attendants	31,870

Jobs with the Highest Earnings

Job	Annual Earnings
1. Physicians and Surgeons	$104,240
2. Dentists	$93,620
3. Podiatrists	$89,070
4. Aerospace Engineers	$80,100
5. Lawyers	$73,870
6. Engineering, Mathematical, and Natural Sciences Managers	$69,280
7. College and University Faculty (Law)	$69,110
8. Nuclear Engineers	$66,800
9. Judges and Magistrates	$65,770
10. College and University Faculty (Health Diagnostics)	$63,640
11. Securities, Commodities, and Financial Services Sales Agents	$63,230
12. Optometrists	$63,090
13. General Managers and Top Executives	$62,550
14. Sales Engineers	$60,590
15. Chiropractors	$60,390
16. Education Administrators	$60,370
17. Marketing, Advertising, and Public Relations Managers	$58,890
18. Financial Managers	$58,540
19. Veterinarians	$58,480
20. College and University Faculty (Engineering Teachers)	$58,180
21. Computer Engineers	$57,960
22. Medical Scientists	$57,580
23. Chemical Engineers	$57,370
24. Pharmacists	$57,270
25. College and University Faculty (Agricultural Sciences)	$56,370

HAWAII
Population 1,190,472

Jobs Employing the Most Workers

Job	Number Employed
1. Retail Salespersons	22,180
2. Janitors and Cleaners	13,250
3. Cashiers	12,730
4. General Office Clerks	12,540
5. Waiters and Waitresses	12,190
6. Combined Food Preparation and Service Workers	11,490
7. General Managers and Top Executives	10,670
8. Maids and Housekeeping Cleaners	10,010
9. First-Line Supervisors and Managers—Sales Workers	9,410
10. Secretaries	9,230
11. Registered Nurses	8,560
12. Guards and Watch Guards	8,110
13. Bookkeeping, Accounting, and Auditing Clerks	8,040
14. First-Line Supervisors and Managers—Administrative Workers	7,730
15. Food Preparation Workers	7,650
16. Maintenance Repairers, General Utility	6,440
17. Laborers, Landscaping and Groundskeeping	6,420
18. Truck Drivers, Light, Including Delivery and Route Workers	5,460
19. Restaurant Cooks	5,390
20. Secondary School Teachers	5,210
21. Stock Clerks—Sales Floor	5,170
22. Receptionists and Information Clerks	5,080
23. Accountants and Auditors	4,230
24. Nursing Aides, Orderlies, and Attendants	4,180
25. Carpenters	3,740

Jobs with the Highest Earnings

Job	Annual Earnings
1. Aircraft Pilots and Flight Engineers	$107,250
2. Physicians and Surgeons	$95,360
3. Dentists	$86,020
4. Lawyers	$76,140
5. Real Estate Brokers	$68,330
6. Engineering, Mathematical, and Natural Sciences Managers	$68,260
7. Real Estate Appraisers	$67,200
8. General Managers and Top Executives	$66,190
9. Pharmacists	$63,440
10. Medicine and Health Services Managers	$62,950
11. Construction Managers	$62,500
12. Financial Managers	$62,230
13. Tapers	$62,090
14. Electrical and Electronic Engineers	$61,620
15. Sales Engineers	$61,530
16. College and University Faculty (Agricultural Sciences)	$61,350
17. Grader, Bulldozer, and Scraper Operators	$60,100
18. College and University Faculty (Physics Teachers)	$59,840
19. Brickmasons	$59,560
20. Veterinarians and Veterinary Inspectors	$59,230
21. College and University Faculty (Business)	$59,100
22. Concrete and Terrazzo Finishers	$58,910
23. Industrial Engineers, Except Safety	$58,570
24. College and University Faculty (Nursing Instructors)	$58,530
25. Physical Therapists	$58,360

IDAHO
Population 1,230,923

Jobs Employing the Most Workers

Job	Number Employed
1. General Managers and Top Executives	19,130
2. Retail Salespersons	15,690
3. Cashiers	14,030
4. General Office Clerks	11,500
5. Secretaries	10,290
6. Truck Drivers—Heavy	10,120
7. Janitors and Cleaners	9,180
8. Secondary School Teachers	8,790
9. Elementary School Teachers	8,730
10. Waiters and Waitresses	8,600
11. Bookkeeping, Accounting, and Auditing Clerks	7,830
12. Registered Nurses	7,430
13. Combined Food Preparation and Service Workers	6,920
14. First-Line Supervisors and Managers— Sales Workers	6,340
15. Food Preparation Workers	6,310
16. Truck Drivers—Light	6,200
17. Nursing Aides, Orderlies, and Attendants	5,870
18. First-Line Supervisors and Managers— Administrative Workers	5,460
19. Receptionists and Information Clerks	5,390
20. Teacher Assistants	5,290
21. Carpenters	5,110
22. General Utility Maintenance Repairers	4,680
23. Stock Clerks—Sales Floor	4,250
24. Sales Representatives	4,080
25. Landscaping and Groundskeeping Laborers	3,880

Jobs with the Highest Earnings

Job	Annual Earnings
1. Physicians and Surgeons	$111,880
2. Dentists	$88,910
3. Podiatrists	$84,080
4. Judges and Magistrates	$83,980
5. Engineering, Mathematical, and Natural Sciences Managers	$65,720
6. Securities, Commodities, and Financial Services Sales Agents	$64,040
7. Optometrists	$62,950
8. Operations Research Analysts	$60,770
9. Chemical Engineers	$59,090
10. Dental Hygienists	$58,930
11. Power Distributors and Dispatchers	$58,750
12. Electrical and Electronic Engineers	$58,450
13. Pharmacists	$58,410
14. Education Administrators	$58,060
15. Mining, Quarrying, and Oil and Gas Well Drilling Managers	$57,920
16. Mining Engineers	$56,910
17. College and University Faculty (Engineering Teachers)	$55,440
18. Safety Engineers	$54,380
19. Mechanical Engineers	$53,930
20. Physical Therapists	$53,500
21. Psychologists	$53,450
22. Chiropractors	$53,190
23. Industrial Production Managers	$52,700
24. Powerhouse, Substation, and Relay Electricians	$52,530
25. Computer Engineers	$52,440

ILLINOIS
Population 12,069,774

Jobs Employing the Most Workers

Job	Number Employed
1. General Managers and Top Executives	184,490
2. Retail Salespersons	170,640
3. Cashiers	138,740
4. Secretaries	136,920
5. General Office Clerks	134,840
6. Janitors and Cleaners	101,950
7. Registered Nurses	98,300
8. Waiters and Waitresses	86,380
9. Elementary School Teachers	80,470
10. First-Line Supervisors and Managers—Administrative Workers	80,030
11. Bookkeeping, Accounting, and Auditing Clerks	78,060
12. Stock Clerks—Sales Floor	71,960
13. First-Line Supervisors and Managers—Sales Workers	68,170
14. Truck Drivers—Heavy	62,920
15. Assemblers and Fabricators	58,500
16. Hand Packers and Packagers	57,490
17. Truck Drivers—Light	56,340
18. Receptionists and Information Clerks	56,170
19. Food Preparation Workers	55,040
20. Combined Food Preparation and Service Workers	54,510
21. General Utility Maintenance Repairers	51,180
22. Shipping, Receiving, and Traffic Clerks	51,150
23. Sales Representatives	51,110
24. Nursing Aides, Orderlies, and Attendants	49,550
25. Landscaping and Groundskeeping Laborers	48,770

Jobs with the Highest Earnings

Job	Annual Earnings
1. Physicians and Surgeons	$104,050
2. Aircraft Pilots and Flight Engineers	$100,720
3. Judges and Magistrates	$97,010
4. Chiropractors	$84,950
5. Lawyers	$82,010
6. Dentists	$76,350
7. Engineering, Mathematical, and Natural Sciences Managers	$69,640
8. Podiatrists	$68,990
9. Actuaries	$68,730
10. Petroleum Engineers	$67,570
11. Real Estate Brokers	$66,080
12. Nuclear Engineers	$64,920
13. General Managers and Top Executives	$63,630
14. Financial Managers	$61,080
15. Mining Engineers	$60,520
16. Psychologists	$60,190
17. Pharmacists	$59,800
18. Physicists and Astronomers	$59,510
19. Chemical Engineers	$59,420
20. Aerospace Engineers	$59,060
21. Elevator Installers and Repairers	$58,920
22. Management Analysts	$58,910
23. Musicians, Instrumental	$58,350
24. Materials Engineers	$57,710
25. Marketing, Advertising, and Public Relations Managers	$57,480

INDIANA
Population 5,907,617

Jobs Employing the Most Workers

Job	Number Employed
1. Retail Salespersons	86,310
2. Cashiers	78,660
3. Assemblers and Fabricators	69,600
4. General Office Clerks	67,050
5. General Managers and Top Executives	57,310
6. Truck Drivers—Heavy	51,600
7. Secretaries	46,960
8. Combined Food Preparation and Service Workers	46,820
9. Registered Nurses	46,490
10. Janitors and Cleaners	45,740
11. Waiters and Waitresses	45,050
12. First-Line Supervisors and Managers—Sales Workers	39,050
13. Bookkeeping, Accounting, and Auditing Clerks	35,720
14. Elementary School Teachers	34,540
15. Stock Clerks—Sales Floor	31,880
16. Secondary School Teachers	30,150
17. Food Preparation Workers	29,490
18. Truck Drivers—Light	28,970
19. Sales Representatives	27,300
20. First-Line Supervisors and Managers—Administrative Workers	27,290
21. General Utility Maintenance Repairers	26,010
22. Nursing Aides, Orderlies, and Attendants	25,780
23. Hand Packers and Packagers	25,580
24. Receptionists and Information Clerks	23,980
25. Shipping, Receiving, and Traffic Clerks	23,720

Jobs with the Highest Earnings

Job	Annual Earnings
1. Physicians and Surgeons	$113,210
2. Podiatrists	$97,750
3. Dentists	$92,960
4. College and University Faculty (Law)	$71,810
5. Chiropractors	$69,810
6. Optometrists	$66,120
7. Engineering, Mathematical, and Natural Sciences Managers	$64,060
8. General Managers and Top Executives	$62,900
9. College and University Faculty (Economics)	$62,670
10. Lawyers	$61,420
11. Physicists and Astronomers	$61,290
12. Veterinarians	$61,280
13. Pharmacists	$60,730
14. College and University Faculty (Engineering Teachers)	$59,350
15. Management Analysts	$58,120
16. Actuaries	$57,990
17. Education Administrators	$57,550
18. Industrial Production Managers	$57,430
19. Marketing, Advertising, and Public Relations Managers	$57,400
20. Chemical Engineers	$57,130
21. Materials Engineers	$55,710
22. Physical Therapists	$55,700
23. College and University Faculty (Physics)	$55,170
24. Securities, Commodities, and Financial Services Sales Agents	$54,900
25. Elevator Installers and Repairers	$54,020

IOWA
Population 2,861,025

Jobs Employing the Most Workers

Job	Number Employed
1. Retail Salespersons	45,820
2. General Managers and Top Executives	43,140
3. Cashiers	36,000
4. General Office Clerks	30,950
5. Secretaries	27,280
6. Waiters and Waitresses	25,640
7. Registered Nurses	24,800
8. Assemblers and Fabricators	24,180
9. Bookkeeping, Accounting, and Auditing Clerks	23,590
10. Janitors and Cleaners	21,310
11. First-Line Supervisors and Managers— Sales Workers	21,270
12. Secondary School Teachers	20,630
13. Truck Drivers—Heavy	20,020
14. Combined Food Preparation and Service Workers	18,700
15. Elementary School Teachers	18,420
16. Truck Drivers—Light	18,200
17. Nursing Aides, Orderlies, and Attendants	18,040
18. First-Line Supervisors and Managers— Administrative Workers	16,800
19. Stock Clerks—Sales Floor	16,500
20. Food Preparation Workers	14,280
21. Receptionists and Information Clerks	13,430
22. Sales Representatives	12,800
23. General Utility Maintenance Repairers	12,400
24. Cooks, Institution or Cafeteria	10,720
25. Hand Packers and Packagers	10,580

Jobs with the Highest Earnings

Job	Annual Earnings
1. Physicians and Surgeons	$104,540
2. Dentists	$104,000
3. Securities, Commodities, and Financial Services Sales Agents	$76,460
4. Optometrists	$70,580
5. Actuaries	$68,310
6. Lawyers	$62,790
7. Engineering, Mathematical, and Natural Sciences Managers	$60,920
8. Locomotive Firers	$59,860
9. Judges and Magistrates	$58,560
10. Electrical and Electronic Engineers	$56,460
11. College and University Faculty (Physics)	$55,660
12. Pharmacists	$55,070
13. Education Administrators	$54,160
14. Agricultural Engineers	$53,280
15. Chemical Engineers	$53,120
16. College and University Faculty (Area Studies)	$52,680
17. General Managers and Top Executives	$52,340
18. College and University Faculty (Health Assessment and Treatment)	$52,260
19. Sales Engineers	$52,130
20. Physical Therapists	$52,120
21. Materials Engineers	$51,330
22. Industrial Production Managers	$51,320
23. Computer Engineers	$50,780
24. Mechanical Engineers	$50,720
25. College and University Faculty (Agricultural Sciences)	$50,590

KANSAS
Population 2,638,667

Jobs Employing the Most Workers

Job	Number Employed
1. Retail Salespersons	41,070
2. General Managers and Top Executives	40,030
3. Cashiers	35,770
4. General Office Clerks	31,530
5. Secretaries	23,300
6. Registered Nurses	22,740
7. Combined Food Preparation and Service Workers	21,830
8. Janitors and Cleaners	20,530
9. Waiters and Waitresses	20,440
10. Bookkeeping, Accounting, and Auditing Clerks	19,030
11. Elementary School Teachers	18,320
12. Secondary School Teachers	18,110
13. Truck Drivers—Heavy	18,000
14. First-Line Supervisors and Managers— Sales Workers	16,420
15. Assemblers and Fabricators	16,320
16. Food Preparation Workers	15,640
17. Nursing Aides, Orderlies, and Attendants	15,130
18. First-Line Supervisors and Managers— Administrative Workers	14,260
19. Receptionists and Information Clerks	12,770
20. Truck Drivers—Light	12,730
21. Stock Clerks—Sales Floor	12,260
22. Sales Representatives	11,880
23. General Utility Maintenance Repairers	11,470
24. Teacher Assistants	11,370
25. Shipping, Receiving, and Traffic Clerks	9,700

Jobs with the Highest Earnings

Job	Annual Earnings
1. Physicians and Surgeons	$104,660
2. Dentists	$93,200
3. Podiatrists	$87,420
4. Optometrists	$73,890
5. Actuaries	$65,610
6. Aerospace Engineers	$64,230
7. Engineering, Mathematical, and Natural Sciences Managers	$63,130
8. Petroleum Engineers	$62,740
9. College and University Faculty (Engineering Teachers)	$62,400
10. College and University Faculty (Agricultural Sciences)	$60,850
11. Pharmacists	$60,470
12. Lawyers	$59,610
13. Economists	$58,980
14. Sales Engineers	$57,740
15. Chiropractors	$57,120
16. Marketing, Advertising, and Public Relations Managers	$56,940
17. Securities, Commodities, and Financial Services Sales Agents	$56,340
18. Judges and Magistrates	$56,300
19. Physician Assistants	$56,150
20. Railroad Conductors and Yardmasters	$55,910
21. Industrial Production Managers	$55,890
22. Electrical and Electronic Engineers	$55,280
23. Sales Representatives—Scientific Products	$55,080
24. Communication, Transportation, and Utilities Operations Managers	$54,390
25. Education Administrators	$53,470

KENTUCKY
Population 3,934,310

Jobs Employing the Most Workers

Job	Number Employed
1. Cashiers	50,910
2. Retail Salespersons	45,980
3. General Managers and Top Executives	45,620
4. Combined Food Preparation and Service Workers	39,630
5. Assemblers and Fabricators	38,750
6. General Office Clerks	38,000
7. Registered Nurses	31,280
8. Secretaries	30,420
9. Truck Drivers—Heavy	25,300
10. Janitors and Cleaners	23,790
11. Stock Clerks—Sales Floor	23,330
12. Bookkeeping, Accounting, and Auditing Clerks	23,020
13. Waiters and Waitresses	22,200
14. First-Line Supervisors and Managers— Sales Workers	21,860
15. Elementary School Teachers	19,960
16. Nursing Aides, Orderlies, and Attendants	19,200
17. General Utility Maintenance Repairers	18,820
18. Truck Drivers—Light	18,800
19. Food Preparation Workers	17,960
20. Hand Packers and Packagers	15,910
21. First-Line Supervisors and Managers— Administrative Workers	15,580
22. Secondary School Teachers	14,310
23. Receptionists and Information Clerks	13,460
24. Maids and Housekeeping Cleaners	13,030
25. Shipping, Receiving, and Traffic Clerks	12,950

Jobs with the Highest Earnings

Job	Annual Earnings
1. Physicians and Surgeons	$107,790
2. Podiatrists	$107,360
3. Dentists	$83,330
4. College and University Faculty (Health Diagnostics)	$73,880
5. Judges and Magistrates	$72,160
6. College and University Faculty (Law)	$70,840
7. Petroleum Engineers	$66,590
8. Engineering, Mathematical, and Natural Sciences Managers	$65,580
9. Chiropractors	$63,160
10. College and University Faculty (Economics)	$60,980
11. Sales Engineers	$60,440
12. Optometrists	$60,340
13. Air Traffic Controllers	$59,480
14. Lawyers	$59,430
15. Pharmacists	$59,410
16. Physical Therapists	$58,490
17. Chemical Engineers	$58,010
18. Mining, Quarrying, and Oil and Gas Well Drilling Managers	$57,690
19. Criminal Investigators, Public Service	$57,410
20. Education Administrators	$55,790
21. Atmospheric and Space Scientists	$55,530
22. Marketing, Advertising, and Public Relations Managers	$54,900
23. Mining Engineers	$54,710
24. Industrial Production Managers	$54,400
25. College and University Faculty (Physics)	$54,340

LOUISIANA
Population 4,362,758

Jobs Employing the Most Workers

Job	Number Employed
1. Cashiers	58,180
2. Retail Salespersons	53,380
3. General Managers and Top Executives	51,960
4. General Office Clerks	49,300
5. Secretaries	34,350
6. Registered Nurses	32,180
7. Janitors and Cleaners	29,640
8. Elementary School Teachers	28,250
9. Waiters and Waitresses	24,370
10. First-Line Supervisors and Managers— Sales Workers	24,320
11. Combined Food Preparation and Service Workers	23,150
12. Nursing Aides, Orderlies, and Attendants	22,960
13. Truck Drivers—Heavy	22,600
14. Bookkeeping, Accounting, and Auditing Clerks	22,290
15. First-Line Supervisors and Managers— Administrative Workers	20,780
16. General Utility Maintenance Repairers	20,580
17. Stock Clerks—Sales Floor	19,790
18. Truck Drivers—Light	19,560
19. Food Preparation Workers	19,530
20. Welders and Cutters	17,520
21. Licensed Practical Nurses	16,940
22. Maids and Housekeeping Cleaners	15,910
23. Secondary School Teachers	15,650
24. Receptionists and Information Clerks	15,570
25. Sales Representatives	14,030

Jobs with the Highest Earnings

Job	Annual Earnings
1. Dentists	$98,830
2. Physicians and Surgeons	$92,960
3. Podiatrists	$86,420
4. Real Estate Brokers	$78,550
5. Mining, Quarrying, and Oil and Gas Well Drilling Managers	$75,910
6. College and University Faculty (Economics)	$71,190
7. Lawyers	$68,100
8. Petroleum Engineers	$67,600
9. Chemical Engineers	$64,700
10. Engineering, Mathematical, and Natural Sciences Managers	$63,350
11. Physical Therapists	$63,110
12. Geologists, Geophysicists, and Oceanographers	$62,420
13. Aerospace Engineers	$61,370
14. Optometrists	$59,640
15. Industrial Production Managers	$59,170
16. Civil Engineers	$57,420
17. Securities, Commodities, and Financial Services Sales Agents	$57,330
18. Criminal Investigators, Public Service	$56,160
19. Electrical and Electronic Engineers	$55,180
20. Veterinarians	$54,960
21. Air Traffic Controllers	$54,950
22. Marine Engineers	$54,890
23. Occupational Therapists	$54,570
24. Pharmacists	$54,250
25. Industrial Engineers	$53,420

MAINE
Population 1,247,554

Jobs Employing the Most Workers

Job	Number Employed
1. Cashiers	17,910
2. Retail Salespersons	17,830
3. General Managers and Top Executives	15,670
4. Registered Nurses	11,620
5. Elementary School Teachers	11,510
6. Waiters and Waitresses	10,450
7. General Office Clerks	10,260
8. Secretaries	9,560
9. Truck Drivers—Heavy	9,450
10. Nursing Aides, Orderlies, and Attendants	9,090
11. Bookkeeping, Accounting, and Auditing Clerks	8,960
12. Janitors and Cleaners	8,780
13. Food Preparation Workers	8,350
14. First-Line Supervisors and Managers— Sales Workers	8,190
15. Stock Clerks—Sales Floor	6,060
16. First-Line Supervisors and Managers— Administrative Workers	6,020
17. Combined Food Preparation and Service Workers	5,900
18. Maids and Housekeeping Cleaners	5,650
19. Truck Drivers—Light	5,340
20. Secondary School Teachers	5,240
21. General Utility Maintenance Repairers	5,000
22. Teacher Assistants	4,940
23. Carpenters	4,710
24. Receptionists and Information Clerks	4,460
25. Shipping, Receiving, and Traffic Clerks	4,460

Jobs with the Highest Earnings

Job	Annual Earnings
1. Physicians and Surgeons	$111,610
2. Dentists	$99,650
3. Judges and Magistrates	$85,950
4. College and University Faculty (Law)	$70,710
5. College and University Faculty (Health Diagnostics)	$70,020
6. Engineering, Mathematical, and Natural Sciences Managers	$64,770
7. Pharmacists	$64,250
8. Optometrists	$64,190
9. Lawyers	$62,240
10. Physician Assistants	$60,360
11. College and University Faculty (Physics)	$59,200
12. Chemical Engineers	$59,110
13. Psychologists	$57,960
14. Securities, Commodities, and Financial Services Sales Agents	$57,520
15. Real Estate Brokers	$56,350
16. Electrical and Electronic Engineers	$56,230
17. Sales Engineers	$55,110
18. College and University Faculty (Political Science)	$54,450
19. General Managers and Top Executives	$54,360
20. Geologists, Geophysicists, and Oceanographers	$53,860
21. Mechanical Engineers	$53,770
22. Management Analysts	$53,480
23. Computer Engineers	$53,470
24. College and University Faculty (Economics)	$53,290
25. Veterinarians	$52,970

MARYLAND
Population 5,130,072

Jobs Employing the Most Workers

Job	Number Employed
1. Retail Salespersons	83,900
2. General Managers and Top Executives	81,810
3. Cashiers	55,600
4. General Office Clerks	53,750
5. Secretaries	53,670
6. Registered Nurses	40,790
7. Janitors and Cleaners	38,450
8. Waiters and Waitresses	33,610
9. First-Line Supervisors and Managers— Sales Workers	33,460
10. Bookkeeping, Accounting, and Auditing Clerks	31,340
11. First-Line Supervisors and Managers— Administrative Workers	31,120
12. Elementary School Teachers	27,000
13. Combined Food Preparation and Service Workers	25,470
14. Receptionists and Information Clerks	24,690
15. Secondary School Teachers	24,140
16. Truck Drivers—Heavy	24,030
17. Guards and Watch Guards	22,820
18. Nursing Aides, Orderlies, and Attendants	22,560
19. Truck Drivers—Light	22,560
20. General Utility Maintenance Repairers	21,050
21. Sales Representatives	20,800
22. Food Preparation Workers	20,640
23. Systems Analysts	18,820
24. Stock Clerks—Sales Floor	18,720
25. Accountants and Auditors	17,220

Jobs with the Highest Earnings

Job	Annual Earnings
1. Physicians and Surgeons	$89,380
2. Judges and Magistrates	$83,650
3. Dentists	$83,540
4. Nuclear Engineers	$82,460
5. Podiatrists	$75,520
6. College and University Faculty (Law)	$73,040
7. Physicists and Astronomers	$70,910
8. College and University Faculty (Health Diagnostics)	$70,320
9. Lawyers	$70,140
10. Engineering, Mathematical, and Natural Sciences Managers	$69,350
11. Optometrists	$69,180
12. Actuaries	$67,440
13. Materials Engineers	$66,750
14. Aerospace Engineers	$64,350
15. Pharmacists	$62,500
16. Veterinarians	$62,420
17. Medical Scientists	$62,410
18. General Managers and Top Executives	$61,170
19. Economists	$60,690
20. Atmospheric and Space Scientists	$60,590
21. Chemical Engineers	$60,480
22. Chemists	$59,110
23. Electrical and Electronic Engineers	$59,100
24. Music Directors, Singers, Composers, and Related Workers	$59,000
25. Safety Engineers	$58,480

MASSACHUSETTS
Population 6,144,407

Jobs Employing the Most Workers

Job	Number Employed
1. Retail Salespersons	96,300
2. General Managers and Top Executives	93,010
3. Cashiers	75,000
4. Registered Nurses	72,050
5. General Office Clerks	71,140
6. Secretaries	69,200
7. Waiters and Waitresses	57,950
8. Janitors and Cleaners	52,500
9. Bookkeeping, Accounting, and Auditing Clerks	44,160
10. Elementary School Teachers	42,440
11. First-Line Supervisors and Managers— Administrative Workers	42,300
12. First-Line Supervisors and Managers— Sales Workers	42,090
13. Nursing Aides, Orderlies, and Attendants	38,620
14. Secondary School Teachers	37,280
15. Combined Food Preparation and Service Workers	36,000
16. Stock Clerks—Sales Floor	33,620
17. Truck Drivers—Light	28,170
18. Receptionists and Information Clerks	27,710
19. Shipping, Receiving, and Traffic Clerks	27,460
20. Sales Representatives	26,920
21. Accountants and Auditors	25,580
22. Truck Drivers—Heavy	24,620
23. Food Preparation Workers	24,540
24. Hand Packers and Packagers	24,180
25. Financial Managers	23,760

Jobs with the Highest Earnings

Job	Annual Earnings
1. Aircraft Pilots and Flight Engineers	$103,800
2. Physicians and Surgeons	$100,420
3. Dentists	$95,270
4. College and University Faculty (Law)	$87,960
5. Chiropractors	$86,180
6. Podiatrists	$85,660
7. College and University Faculty (Health Diagnostics)	$78,460
8. Engineering, Mathematical, and Natural Sciences Managers	$77,800
9. Medical Scientists	$77,380
10. Lawyers	$77,160
11. General Managers and Top Executives	$72,200
12. College and University Faculty (Business)	$70,870
13. College and University Faculty (Economics)	$68,960
14. Physicists and Astronomers	$68,330
15. Marketing, Advertising, and Public Relations Managers	$67,690
16. College and University Faculty (Political Science)	$67,320
17. Real Estate Brokers	$66,870
18. Actuaries	$66,830
19. Computer Engineers	$66,680
20. Management Analysts	$66,070
21. Securities, Commodities, and Financial Services Sales Agents	$65,370
22. Financial Managers	$65,140
23. College and University Faculty (Chemistry)	$63,590
24. Aerospace Engineers	$63,360
25. College and University Faculty (Physics)	$63,120

MICHIGAN
Population 9,820,231

Jobs Employing the Most Workers

Job	Number Employed
1. Retail Salespersons	142,220
2. Cashiers	103,800
3. General Managers and Top Executives	93,720
4. General Office Clerks	91,600
5. Secretaries	84,240
6. Waiters and Waitresses	76,730
7. Registered Nurses	70,010
8. Janitors and Cleaners	67,740
9. Combined Food Preparation and Service Workers	57,210
10. First-Line Supervisors and Managers— Sales Workers	54,520
11. Bookkeeping, Accounting, and Auditing Clerks	53,450
12. Stock Clerks—Sales Floor	53,290
13. Elementary School Teachers	48,670
14. Food Preparation Workers	44,530
15. Secondary School Teachers	44,190
16. Receptionists and Information Clerks	42,780
17. Nursing Aides, Orderlies, and Attendants	40,640
18. First-Line Supervisors and Managers— Administrative Workers	38,730
19. Sales Representatives	37,810
20. General Utility Maintenance Repairers	36,710
21. Shipping, Receiving, and Traffic Clerks	34,420
22. First-Line Supervisors and Managers— Production Workers	28,520
23. Electricians	28,360
24. Stock Clerks—Stockroom and Warehouse	28,340
25. Accountants and Auditors	27,800

Jobs with the Highest Earnings

Job	Annual Earnings
1. Physicians and Surgeons	$101,310
2. Podiatrists	$99,520
3. Dentists	$98,350
4. Lawyers	$75,370
5. College and University Faculty (Law)	$74,790
6. Chiropractors	$74,020
7. Engineering, Mathematical, and Natural Sciences Managers	$72,720
8. Judges and Magistrates	$71,720
9. Optometrists	$70,930
10. Real Estate Brokers	$69,690
11. College and University Faculty (Engineering Teachers)	$69,240
12. Aerospace Engineers	$66,700
13. Nuclear Engineers	$65,560
14. General Managers and Top Executives	$65,510
15. College and University Faculty (Economics)	$63,780
16. Actuaries	$63,680
17. Sales Engineers	$63,670
18. College and University Faculty (Physics)	$63,280
19. Physicists and Astronomers	$63,130
20. Petroleum Engineers	$62,720
21. Education Administrators	$62,680
22. College and University Faculty (Agricultural Sciences)	$62,260
23. Veterinarians	$62,250
24. Industrial Production Managers	$61,930
25. Pharmacists	$61,410

MINNESOTA
Population 4,726,411

Jobs Employing the Most Workers

Job	Number Employed
1. Retail Salespersons	83,040
2. Cashiers	64,350
3. General Managers and Top Executives	59,360
4. General Office Clerks	54,890
5. Waiters and Waitresses	47,480
6. Secretaries	40,320
7. Janitors and Cleaners	39,890
8. Registered Nurses	38,940
9. Bookkeeping, Accounting, and Auditing Clerks	36,480
10. First-Line Supervisors and Managers— Sales Workers	32,940
11. Combined Food Preparation and Service Workers	31,920
12. Secondary School Teachers	30,500
13. Truck Drivers—Heavy	29,710
14. Nursing Aides, Orderlies, and Attendants	29,350
15. Sales Representatives	28,450
16. Elementary School Teachers	27,930
17. First-Line Supervisors and Managers— Administrative Workers	27,510
18. Stock Clerks—Sales Floor	26,580
19. Assemblers and Fabricators	25,470
20. Receptionists and Information Clerks	25,470
21. Food Preparation Workers	22,700
22. Truck Drivers—Light	22,110
23. Shipping, Receiving, and Traffic Clerks	19,510
24. General Utility Maintenance Repairers	18,690
25. Accountants and Auditors	18,670

Jobs with the Highest Earnings

Job	Annual Earnings
1. Physicians and Surgeons	$108,540
2. Dentists	$86,900
3. Podiatrists	$75,890
4. College and University Faculty (Law)	$70,950
5. Lawyers	$70,900
6. Engineering, Mathematical, and Natural Sciences Managers	$70,750
7. Securities, Commodities, and Financial Services Sales Agents	$68,570
8. Physicists and Astronomers	$67,950
9. Chiropractors	$67,940
10. Nuclear Engineers	$64,570
11. Real Estate Brokers	$63,890
12. Marketing, Advertising, and Public Relations Managers	$63,850
13. General Managers and Top Executives	$63,310
14. Actuaries	$62,350
15. Optometrists	$61,900
16. Air Traffic Controllers	$61,800
17. Financial Managers	$61,450
18. Chemical Engineers	$60,090
19. Medical Scientists	$59,930
20. College and University Faculty (Political Science)	$59,710
21. Materials Engineers	$59,330
22. Education Administrators	$59,200
23. Pharmacists	$59,190
24. College and University Faculty (Physics)	$59,130
25. Industrial Production Managers	$58,700

MISSISSIPPI
Population 2,751,335

Jobs Employing the Most Workers

Job	Number Employed
1. Cashiers	38,030
2. Retail Salespersons	37,330
3. General Managers and Top Executives	23,460
4. Truck Drivers—Heavy	22,030
5. Registered Nurses	20,290
6. Assemblers and Fabricators	20,000
7. Secretaries	18,370
8. General Office Clerks	18,210
9. First-Line Supervisors and Managers— Sales Workers	16,380
10. Elementary School Teachers	16,000
11. Combined Food Preparation and Service Workers	14,330
12. Janitors and Cleaners	13,740
13. Bookkeeping, Accounting, and Auditing Clerks	13,640
14. Waiters and Waitresses	13,250
15. Nursing Aides, Orderlies, and Attendants	13,130
16. First-Line Supervisors and Managers— Administrative Workers	13,040
17. Secondary School Teachers	12,860
18. Stock Clerks—Sales Floor	11,290
19. Meat, Poultry, and Fish Cutters and Trimmers, Hand	11,260
20. Maids and Housekeeping Cleaners	10,910
21. General Utility Maintenance Repairers	9,970
22. Truck Drivers—Light	9,930
23. First-Line Supervisors and Managers— Production and Operating Workers	9,530
24. Guards and Watch Guards	9,380
25. Sewing Machine Operators	9,360

Jobs with the Highest Earnings

Job	Annual Earnings
1. Physicians and Surgeons	$94,230
2. Dentists	$84,890
3. Optometrists	$70,160
4. Securities, Commodities, and Financial Services Sales Agents	$67,960
5. Real Estate Brokers	$64,680
6. Petroleum Engineers	$64,110
7. Architects	$63,930
8. Physical Therapists	$62,750
9. Engineering, Mathematical, and Natural Sciences Managers	$61,810
10. Occupational Therapists	$59,730
11. Chemical Engineers	$59,680
12. Chiropractors	$59,660
13. Medical Scientists	$58,870
14. College and University Faculty (Law)	$58,580
15. College and University Faculty (Health Assessment and Treatment)	$58,370
16. Lawyers	$57,990
17. College and University Faculty (Engineering Teachers)	$57,150
18. Criminal Investigators, Public Service	$56,870
19. Water Vessel Captains	$56,220
20. Mining, Quarrying, and Oil and Gas Well Drilling Managers	$55,660
21. Physicists and Astronomers	$55,550
22. Pharmacists	$54,340
23. Civil Engineers	$53,720
24. Electrical and Electronic Engineers	$53,180
25. Industrial Production Managers	$52,680

MISSOURI
Population 5,437,562

Jobs Employing the Most Workers

Job	Number Employed
1. Retail Salespersons	80,770
2. Cashiers	62,730
3. First-Line Supervisors and Managers— Sales Workers	57,390
4. General Office Clerks	56,280
5. Secretaries	49,290
6. Registered Nurses	48,580
7. General Managers and Top Executives	45,700
8. Waiters and Waitresses	44,680
9. Combined Food Preparation and Service Workers	41,760
10. Truck Drivers—Heavy	41,360
11. Janitors and Cleaners	39,510
12. Elementary School Teachers	37,490
13. Nursing Aides, Orderlies, and Attendants	36,410
14. Assemblers and Fabricators	35,610
15. Bookkeeping, Accounting, and Auditing Clerks	35,580
16. First-Line Supervisors and Managers— Administrative Workers	33,140
17. Stock Clerks—Sales Floor	28,960
18. Secondary School Teachers	28,940
19. Sales Representatives	25,680
20. Truck Drivers—Light	24,180
21. Receptionists and Information Clerks	23,570
22. General Utility Maintenance Repairers	22,850
23. Maids and Housekeeping Cleaners	22,470
24. Food Preparation Workers	21,560
25. Carpenters	20,830

Jobs with the Highest Earnings

Job	Annual Earnings
1. Physicians and Surgeons	$107,390
2. Dentists	$93,160
3. College and University Faculty (Health Diagnostics)	$74,250
4. Optometrists	$72,080
5. Actuaries	$71,540
6. Engineering, Mathematical, and Natural Sciences Managers	$69,670
7. Lawyers	$68,210
8. Mining, Quarrying, and Oil and Gas Well Drilling Managers	$66,890
9. College and University Faculty (Law)	$66,150
10. Podiatrists	$65,490
11. Chiropractors	$64,150
12. Aerospace Engineers	$63,990
13. Industrial Engineers	$61,780
14. General Managers and Top Executives	$61,630
15. College and University Faculty (Engineering Teachers)	$60,560
16. Mining Engineers	$60,090
17. Air Traffic Controllers	$58,910
18. Pharmacists	$57,860
19. Mechanical Engineering Technicians and Technologists	$57,480
20. Chemical Engineers	$57,420
21. Atmospheric and Space Scientists	$56,900
22. Industrial Production Managers	$56,830
23. Marketing, Advertising, and Public Relations Managers	$55,840
24. Sales Engineers	$55,730
25. Materials Engineers	$55,590

MONTANA
Population 879,533

Jobs Employing the Most Workers

Job	Number Employed
1. Retail Salespersons	13,960
2. General Office Clerks	10,650
3. Cashiers	10,430
4. Combined Food Preparation and Service Workers	8,130
5. Waiters and Waitresses	7,900
6. Elementary School Teachers	7,280
7. Janitors and Cleaners	7,160
8. Secretaries	7,140
9. General Managers and Top Executives	6,970
10. Registered Nurses	6,850
11. Bookkeeping, Accounting, and Auditing Clerks	6,780
12. Truck Drivers—Heavy	6,440
13. First-Line Supervisors and Managers— Sales Workers	5,520
14. Bartenders	5,060
15. Secondary School Teachers	4,890
16. Nursing Aides, Orderlies, and Attendants	4,620
17. Truck Drivers—Light	4,260
18. Maids and Housekeeping Cleaners	4,230
19. First-Line Supervisors and Managers— Administrative Workers	3,830
20. Food Preparation Workers	3,630
21. Stock Clerks—Sales Floor	3,570
22. General Utility Maintenance Repairers	3,550
23. Receptionists and Information Clerks	3,540
24. Sales Representatives	2,990
25. Cooks, Restaurant	2,980

Jobs with the Highest Earnings

Job	Annual Earnings
1. Physicians and Surgeons	$112,130
2. Real Estate Brokers	$76,720
3. Securities, Commodities, and Financial Services Sales Agents	$62,780
4. Optometrists	$62,470
5. Dentists	$62,000
6. Mining, Quarrying, and Oil and Gas Well Drilling Managers	$61,470
7. Engineering, Mathematical, and Natural Sciences Managers	$59,450
8. Chemical Engineers	$59,300
9. Power Distributors and Dispatchers	$58,920
10. Management Analysts	$58,230
11. Criminal Investigators, Public Service	$57,270
12. Lawyers	$57,120
13. Atmospheric and Space Scientists	$56,270
14. Mining Engineers	$56,160
15. Physician Assistants	$55,890
16. Computer Engineers	$55,680
17. Petroleum Engineers	$55,660
18. Education Administrators	$54,790
19. General Managers and Top Executives	$53,940
20. Dental Hygienists	$53,900
21. Locomotive Engineers	$52,460
22. Funeral Directors and Morticians	$52,100
23. College and University Faculty (History)	$51,260
24. Physical Therapists	$50,750
25. College and University Faculty (Business)	$50,190

NEBRASKA
Population 1,660,772

Jobs Employing the Most Workers

Job	Number Employed
1. General Managers and Top Executives	27,760
2. Retail Salespersons	25,200
3. Cashiers	23,860
4. General Office Clerks	16,450
5. Secretaries	16,450
6. Registered Nurses	15,720
7. Waiters and Waitresses	14,890
8. Truck Drivers—Heavy	14,740
9. Janitors and Cleaners	13,900
10. Bookkeeping, Accounting, and Auditing Clerks	12,990
11. Combined Food Preparation and Service Workers	12,480
12. Nursing Aides, Orderlies, and Attendants	11,000
13. Elementary School Teachers	10,700
14. First-Line Supervisors and Managers—Sales Workers	10,560
15. Secondary School Teachers	10,450
16. Assemblers and Fabricators	10,330
17. First-Line Supervisors and Managers—Administrative Workers	9,430
18. Food Preparation Workers	7,710
19. Sales Representatives	7,510
20. Stock Clerks—Sales Floor	7,460
21. Truck Drivers—Light	7,450
22. General Utility Maintenance Repairers	6,930
23. Maids and Housekeeping Cleaners	6,800
24. Receptionists and Information Clerks	6,660
25. Licensed Practical Nurses	6,200

Jobs with the Highest Earnings

Job	Annual Earnings
1. Physicians and Surgeons	$99,630
2. Podiatrists	$96,780
3. Judges and Magistrates	$82,830
4. Dentists	$80,860
5. College and University Faculty (Engineering Teachers)	$75,660
6. Optometrists	$68,800
7. Lawyers	$67,350
8. College and University Faculty (Physics)	$66,310
9. College and University Faculty (Life Sciences)	$65,380
10. Engineering, Mathematical, and Natural Sciences Managers	$63,810
11. Railroad Conductors and Yardmasters	$62,500
12. College and University Faculty (Chemistry)	$61,720
13. College and University Faculty (Political Science)	$60,830
14. College and University Faculty (Anthropology and Sociology)	$59,260
15. Aerospace Engineers	$58,870
16. College and University Faculty (Psychology)	$58,620
17. Physician Assistants	$57,920
18. Education Administrators	$57,710
19. Actuaries	$57,290
20. College and University Faculty (Business)	$56,760
21. College and University Faculty (Health Assessment and Treatment)	$56,750
22. Electrical and Electronic Engineers	$56,370
23. Civil Engineers	$55,350
24. Computer Engineers	$54,940
25. College and University Faculty (Recreation and Fitness Studies)	$54,270

NEVADA
Population 1,743,772

Jobs Employing the Most Workers

Job	Number Employed
1. Cashiers	37,890
2. Amusement and Recreation Attendants	31,510
3. Retail Salespersons	29,240
4. Waiters and Waitresses	27,800
5. General Office Clerks	23,200
6. Janitors and Cleaners	22,320
7. Maids and Housekeeping Cleaners	19,330
8. General Managers and Top Executives	18,860
9. Guards and Watch Guards	15,450
10. Bookkeeping, Accounting, and Auditing Clerks	14,370
11. Combined Food Preparation and Service Workers	13,500
12. Carpenters	13,410
13. Cooks, Restaurant	12,630
14. First-Line Supervisors and Managers—Sales Workers	12,180
15. Food Preparation Workers	12,000
16. Secretaries	11,890
17. Dining Room and Cafeteria Attendants and Bartender Helpers	11,580
18. First-Line Supervisors and Managers—Administrative Workers	10,980
19. Bartenders	10,870
20. General Utility Maintenance Repairers	10,690
21. Landscaping and Groundskeeping Laborers	10,690
22. Elementary School Teachers	10,260
23. Registered Nurses	9,420
24. Receptionists and Information Clerks	9,330
25. Truck Drivers—Light	9,130

Jobs with the Highest Earnings

Job	Annual Earnings
1. Physicians and Surgeons	$116,760
2. Dentists	$114,940
3. Chiropractors	$93,870
4. Lawyers	$85,260
5. Mining, Quarrying, and Oil and Gas Well Drilling Managers	$80,670
6. Optometrists	$77,420
7. Engineering, Mathematical, and Natural Sciences Managers	$69,610
8. Physicists and Astronomers	$69,460
9. College and University Faculty (Engineering Teachers)	$65,240
10. General Managers and Top Executives	$64,810
11. Veterinarians	$64,800
12. Chemical Engineers	$64,510
13. Pharmacists	$64,080
14. Psychologists	$62,480
15. Physical Therapists	$62,250
16. Police and Detective Supervisors	$61,990
17. Financial Managers	$60,660
18. Education Administrators	$60,630
19. Judges and Magistrates	$60,080
20. Producers, Directors, Actors, and Other Entertainers	$59,600
21. Architects	$59,090
22. Computer Engineers	$59,020
23. Materials Engineers	$58,880
24. Occupational Therapists	$58,460
25. Civil Engineers	$58,300

NEW HAMPSHIRE
Population 1,185,823

Jobs Employing the Most Workers

Job	Number Employed
1. Retail Salespersons	25,940
2. General Managers and Top Executives	16,410
3. Cashiers	14,910
4. Secretaries	10,770
5. Registered Nurses	10,500
6. Waiters and Waitresses	10,120
7. General Office Clerks	10,060
8. First-Line Supervisors and Managers— Sales Workers	9,940
9. Bookkeeping, Accounting, and Auditing Clerks	8,830
10. Elementary School Teachers	8,320
11. Janitors and Cleaners	8,030
12. Combined Food Preparation and Service Workers	7,050
13. First-Line Supervisors and Managers— Administrative Workers	6,950
14. Stock Clerks—Sales Floor	6,890
15. Assemblers and Fabricators	6,590
16. Secondary School Teachers	6,360
17. Food Preparation Workers	6,290
18. Nursing Aides, Orderlies, and Attendants	5,980
19. Shipping, Receiving, and Traffic Clerks	5,770
20. Truck Drivers—Heavy	5,740
21. Receptionists and Information Clerks	5,680
22. Truck Drivers—Light	5,560
23. Sales Representatives	5,560
24. Teacher Assistants	5,140
25. Hand Packers and Packagers	4,320

Jobs with the Highest Earnings

Job	Annual Earnings
1. Physicians and Surgeons	$107,070
2. Podiatrists	$95,830
3. Dentists	$90,720
4. Insurance Special Agents	$87,750
5. College and University Faculty (Physics)	$74,290
6. College and University Faculty (Chemistry)	$73,260
7. Lawyers	$72,280
8. Optometrists	$69,210
9. Engineering, Mathematical, and Natural Sciences Managers	$69,160
10. College and University Faculty (Economics)	$66,420
11. College and University Faculty (Business)	$65,050
12. Pharmacists	$62,070
13. Actuaries	$61,840
14. Chemical Engineers	$60,860
15. General Managers and Top Executives	$60,310
16. College and University Faculty (Political Science)	$58,840
17. College and University Faculty (Computer Science)	$58,320
18. Electrical and Electronic Engineers	$57,700
19. Physicists and Astronomers	$57,250
20. College and University Faculty (Mathematics)	$56,880
21. Marketing, Advertising, and Public Relations Managers	$56,590
22. Industrial Production Managers	$56,550
23. College and University Faculty (Anthropology and Sociology)	$56,470
24. College and University Faculty (Psychology)	$55,530
25. College and University Faculty (History)	$55,260

NEW JERSEY
Population 8,095,542

Jobs Employing the Most Workers

Job	Number Employed
1. Retail Salespersons	113,890
2. Secretaries	93,340
3. General Office Clerks	90,440
4. Cashiers	89,180
5. Janitors and Cleaners	70,270
6. Registered Nurses	67,810
7. General Managers and Top Executives	60,200
8. Bookkeeping, Accounting, and Auditing Clerks	59,350
9. Elementary School Teachers	57,070
10. Waiters and Waitresses	57,020
11. First-Line Supervisors and Managers— Sales Workers	53,550
12. First-Line Supervisors and Managers— Administrative Workers	53,360
13. Sales Representatives	45,450
14. Secondary School Teachers	43,540
15. Receptionists and Information Clerks	43,480
16. Stock Clerks—Sales Floor	39,980
17. Nursing Aides, Orderlies, and Attendants	37,970
18. Food Preparation Workers	37,760
19. Shipping, Receiving, and Traffic Clerks	36,170
20. Combined Food Preparation and Service Workers	35,610
21. Guards and Watch Guards	32,350
22. Accountants and Auditors	28,020
23. Computer Programmers	26,770
24. Systems Analysts	26,110
25. General Utility Maintenance Repairers	24,330

Jobs with the Highest Earnings

Job	Annual Earnings
1. Physicians and Surgeons	$108,020
2. Dentists	$89,720
3. General Managers and Top Executives	$87,500
4. Podiatrists	$86,430
5. Engineering, Mathematical, and Natural Sciences Managers	$84,100
6. Judges and Magistrates	$82,640
7. Lawyers	$78,880
8. College and University Faculty (Health Diagnostics)	$78,210
9. Marketing, Advertising, and Public Relations Managers	$76,960
10. Broadcast News Analysts	$76,350
11. Petroleum Engineers	$75,190
12. Optometrists	$73,970
13. Education Administrators	$73,610
14. Industrial Production Managers	$73,180
15. Medical Scientists	$71,180
16. Construction Managers	$70,530
17. Physicists and Astronomers	$70,320
18. Communication, Transportation, and Utilities Operations Managers	$69,810
19. Mining, Quarrying, and Oil and Gas Well Drilling Managers	$69,570
20. Veterinarians	$69,510
21. Financial Managers	$68,570
22. College and University Faculty (Engineering Teachers)	$68,200
23. Personnel, Training, and Labor Relations Managers	$67,880
24. Police and Detective Supervisors	$66,540
25. Securities, Commodities, and Financial Services Sales Agents	$66,360

NEW MEXICO
Population 1,733,535

Jobs Employing the Most Workers

Job	Number Employed
1. Retail Salespersons	24,370
2. Cashiers	19,400
3. General Managers and Top Executives	18,640
4. Secretaries	14,470
5. General Office Clerks	14,470
6. Waiters and Waitresses	14,180
7. Janitors and Cleaners	10,890
8. Registered Nurses	10,490
9. Bookkeeping, Accounting, and Auditing Clerks	9,940
10. Elementary School Teachers	9,610
11. Combined Food Preparation and Service Workers	9,050
12. First-Line Supervisors and Managers— Sales Workers	8,980
13. Secondary School Teachers	8,710
14. Truck Drivers—Heavy	8,630
15. First-Line Supervisors and Managers— Administrative Workers	7,340
16. Receptionists and Information Clerks	7,300
17. Carpenters	6,990
18. General Utility Maintenance Repairers	6,930
19. Maids and Housekeeping Cleaners	6,700
20. Nursing Aides, Orderlies, and Attendants	6,540
21. Cooks, Restaurant	6,480
22. Truck Drivers—Light	6,370
23. Stock Clerks—Sales Floor	6,310
24. Farm Workers	6,160
25. Landscaping and Groundskeeping Laborers	5,720

Jobs with the Highest Earnings

Job	Annual Earnings
1. Physicians and Surgeons	$96,340
2. Optometrists	$86,490
3. Podiatrists	$78,710
4. Dentists	$76,320
5. Operations Research Analysts	$71,260
6. Engineering, Mathematical, and Natural Sciences Managers	$65,730
7. Petroleum Engineers	$65,160
8. Real Estate Brokers	$63,620
9. Mining, Quarrying, and Oil and Gas Well Drilling Managers	$63,310
10. Lawyers	$63,010
11. Electrical and Electronic Engineers	$61,210
12. Geologists, Geophysicists, and Oceanographers	$60,990
13. Securities, Commodities, and Financial Services Sales Agents	$60,540
14. Mechanical Engineers	$59,080
15. Pharmacists	$59,050
16. Statisticians	$57,590
17. Computer Engineers	$57,330
18. Aerospace Engineers	$56,270
19. Industrial Production Managers	$56,080
20. Atmospheric and Space Scientists	$55,610
21. Economists	$55,190
22. Physical Therapists	$54,970
23. Safety Engineers	$54,930
24. Mining Engineers	$53,600
25. Civil Engineers	$53,500

NEW YORK
Population 18,159,175

Jobs Employing the Most Workers

Job	Number Employed
1. Retail Salespersons	229,620
2. General Office Clerks	223,130
3. Secretaries	185,830
4. Cashiers	174,840
5. General Managers and Top Executives	169,930
6. Janitors and Cleaners	168,870
7. Registered Nurses	150,760
8. Bookkeeping, Accounting, and Auditing Clerks	123,400
9. First-Line Supervisors and Managers—Administrative Workers	122,370
10. First-Line Supervisors and Managers—Sales Workers	121,450
11. Waiters and Waitresses	111,110
12. Secondary School Teachers	108,230
13. Elementary School Teachers	104,150
14. Nursing Aides, Orderlies, and Attendants	101,050
15. Food Preparation Workers	95,210
16. Guards and Watch Guards	94,780
17. Sales Representatives	86,710
18. Receptionists and Information Clerks	82,460
19. Stock Clerks—Sales Floor	80,130
20. General Utility Maintenance Repairers	72,580
21. Accountants and Auditors	72,010
22. Truck Drivers—Light	63,900
23. Shipping, Receiving, and Traffic Clerks	63,670
24. Personal and Home Care Aides	60,560
25. Home Health Aides	60,070

Jobs with the Highest Earnings

Job	Annual Earnings
1. Physicians and Surgeons	$93,510
2. College and University Faculty (Health Diagnostics)	$89,070
3. Dentists	$87,730
4. Aircraft Pilots and Flight Engineers	$87,100
5. Lawyers	$82,180
6. Engineering, Mathematical, and Natural Sciences Managers	$77,250
7. Financial Managers	$75,880
8. General Managers and Top Executives	$75,770
9. Actuaries	$75,040
10. Physicists and Astronomers	$71,520
11. Nuclear Engineers	$70,690
12. College and University Faculty (Life Sciences)	$69,510
13. Construction Managers	$68,980
14. Marketing, Advertising, and Public Relations Managers	$68,860
15. Financial Analysts	$67,190
16. Securities, Commodities, and Financial Services Sales Agents	$66,930
17. Chiropractors	$66,590
18. Communication, Transportation, and Utilities Operations Managers	$64,900
19. Education Administrators	$64,410
20. Podiatrists	$64,230
21. Elevator Installers and Repairers	$64,180
22. Medicine and Health Services Managers	$63,800
23. Aerospace Engineers	$63,370
24. Veterinarians	$62,960
25. Chemical Engineers	$62,460

NORTH CAROLINA
Population 7,545,828

Jobs Employing the Most Workers

Job	Number Employed
1. Retail Salespersons	116,680
2. General Managers and Top Executives	105,770
3. Cashiers	103,600
4. General Office Clerks	76,750
5. Secretaries	60,160
6. Registered Nurses	59,900
7. Truck Drivers—Heavy	55,340
8. Waiters and Waitresses	53,710
9. Bookkeeping, Accounting, and Auditing Clerks	51,300
10. Janitors and Cleaners	50,950
11. Assemblers and Fabricators	49,600
12. Hand Packers and Packagers	49,020
13. First-Line Supervisors and Managers— Sales Workers	46,630
14. Elementary School Teachers	44,030
15. Textile Machine Operators and Tenders	43,990
16. Nursing Aides, Orderlies, and Attendants	42,060
17. Food Preparation Workers	40,350
18. General Utility Maintenance Repairers	37,220
19. Stock Clerks—Sales Floor	36,940
20. First-Line Supervisors and Managers— Administrative Workers	34,290
21. Truck Drivers—Light	32,530
22. Secondary School Teachers	31,610
23. Shipping, Receiving, and Traffic Clerks	31,000
24. Sales Representatives	30,690
25. Combined Food Preparation and Service Workers	30,240

Jobs with the Highest Earnings

Job	Annual Earnings
1. Physicians and Surgeons	$109,400
2. Dentists	$103,970
3. Optometrists	$85,500
4. Podiatrists	$81,300
5. College and University Faculty (Health Diagnostics)	$76,120
6. Engineering, Mathematical, and Natural Sciences Managers	$71,060
7. Actuaries	$70,810
8. Lawyers	$70,060
9. Chiropractors	$69,600
10. College and University Faculty (Law)	$66,670
11. Physicists and Astronomers	$62,090
12. Chemical Engineers	$61,600
13. College and University Faculty (Life Sciences)	$61,520
14. Medical Scientists	$59,920
15. Computer Engineers	$59,230
16. Pharmacists	$58,240
17. Physician Assistants	$57,590
18. General Managers and Top Executives	$57,530
19. Marketing, Advertising, and Public Relations Managers	$57,470
20. Air Traffic Controllers	$57,460
21. College and University Faculty (Physics)	$57,270
22. Atmospheric and Space Scientists	$57,230
23. Electrical and Electronic Engineers	$57,090
24. Financial Managers	$56,780
25. Sales Engineers	$56,510

NORTH DAKOTA
Population 637,808

Jobs Employing the Most Workers

Job	Number Employed
1. Retail Salespersons	12,140
2. Cashiers	7,250
3. Waiters and Waitresses	6,810
4. General Managers and Top Executives	6,630
5. Registered Nurses	6,440
6. Secretaries	6,090
7. Nursing Aides, Orderlies, and Attendants	6,070
8. Elementary School Teachers	6,010
9. Truck Drivers—Heavy	5,930
10. Janitors and Cleaners	5,870
11. General Office Clerks	5,720
12. Bookkeeping, Accounting, and Auditing Clerks	5,580
13. First-Line Supervisors and Managers— Sales Workers	4,670
14. Food Preparation Workers	3,950
15. Maids and Housekeeping Cleaners	3,450
16. Receptionists and Information Clerks	3,130
17. First-Line Supervisors and Managers— Administrative Workers	3,130
18. Truck Drivers—Light	3,120
19. Stock Clerks—Sales Floor	3,030
20. Computer Support Specialists	2,960
21. Secondary School Teachers	2,940
22. Teacher Assistants and Educational Assistants, Clerical	2,910
23. Licensed Practical Nurses	2,770
24. Bartenders	2,610
25. Amusement and Recreation Attendants	2,610

Jobs with the Highest Earnings

Job	Annual Earnings
1. Physicians and Surgeons	$109,170
2. Dentists	$90,330
3. Optometrists	$70,490
4. Chiropractors	$66,400
5. Engineering, Mathematical, and Natural Sciences Managers	$66,090
6. Securities, Commodities, and Financial Services Sales Agents	$63,560
7. Lawyers	$62,330
8. Petroleum Engineers	$59,600
9. Computer Engineers	$59,590
10. Physician Assistants	$57,040
11. Power Distributors and Dispatchers	$56,600
12. General Managers and Top Executives	$52,390
13. Financial Managers	$51,860
14. Industrial Production Managers	$51,730
15. College and University Faculty (Economics)	$51,000
16. Veterinarians	$51,000
17. Safety Engineers	$50,510
18. Elevator Installers and Repairers	$50,270
19. Railroad Conductors and Yardmasters	$50,130
20. Powerhouse, Substation, and Relay Electricians	$49,880
21. Criminal Investigators, Public Service	$49,870
22. Appraisers, Real Estate	$49,780
23. Geologists, Geophysicists, and Oceanographers	$49,700
24. Communication, Transportation, and Utilities Operations Managers	$49,700
25. College and University Faculty (Chemistry)	$48,830

OHIO
Population 11,237,752

Jobs Employing the Most Workers

Job	Number Employed
1. Retail Salespersons	165,290
2. General Managers and Top Executives	142,210
3. Cashiers	121,680
4. General Office Clerks	117,390
5. Secretaries	101,790
6. Registered Nurses	100,180
7. Assemblers and Fabricators	88,670
8. Waiters and Waitresses	88,660
9. Combined Food Preparation and Service Workers	86,970
10. Janitors and Cleaners	84,490
11. First-Line Supervisors and Managers—Sales Workers	74,970
12. Bookkeeping, Accounting, and Auditing Clerks	70,270
13. Truck Drivers—Heavy	68,430
14. Stock Clerks—Sales Floor	66,160
15. Elementary School Teachers	64,320
16. Nursing Aides, Orderlies, and Attendants	62,000
17. Food Preparation Workers	58,220
18. First-Line Supervisors and Managers—Administrative Workers	55,480
19. Truck Drivers—Light	55,420
20. Secondary School Teachers	53,470
21. General Utility Maintenance Repairers	53,230
22. Sales Representatives	51,450
23. Receptionists and Information Clerks	49,540
24. Hand Packers and Packagers	49,480
25. Shipping, Receiving, and Traffic Clerks	45,330

Jobs with the Highest Earnings

Job	Annual Earnings
1. Physicians and Surgeons	$104,770
2. Dentists	$93,230
3. Podiatrists	$87,490
4. Chiropractors	$76,460
5. College and University Faculty (Health Diagnostics)	$72,100
6. Lawyers	$70,220
7. Optometrists	$68,990
8. Physicists and Astronomers	$67,260
9. Engineering, Mathematical, and Natural Sciences Managers	$65,880
10. Real Estate Brokers	$65,550
11. Aerospace Engineers	$64,920
12. Nuclear Engineers	$63,680
13. Petroleum Engineers	$61,400
14. Aircraft Pilots and Flight Engineers	$61,140
15. College and University Faculty (Law)	$60,930
16. Chemical Engineers	$60,000
17. Pharmacists	$59,500
18. Atmospheric and Space Scientists	$59,020
19. General Managers and Top Executives	$58,640
20. Industrial Production Managers	$58,260
21. Medical Scientists	$57,890
22. Veterinarians	$57,490
23. College and University Faculty (Agricultural Sciences)	$57,430
24. Marketing, Advertising, and Public Relations Managers	$57,100
25. Physical Therapists	$57,010

OKLAHOMA
Population 3,339,478

Jobs Employing the Most Workers

Job	Number Employed
1. Retail Salespersons	45,860
2. General Office Clerks	43,580
3. General Managers and Top Executives	40,970
4. Cashiers	40,100
5. Secretaries	30,360
6. Waiters and Waitresses	24,320
7. Registered Nurses	23,140
8. Truck Drivers—Heavy	21,410
9. Elementary School Teachers	21,150
10. Bookkeeping, Accounting, and Auditing Clerks	19,820
11. Secondary School Teachers	19,790
12. Janitors and Cleaners	19,790
13. Nursing Aides, Orderlies, and Attendants	19,240
14. Stock Clerks—Sales Floor	17,280
15. First-Line Supervisors and Managers—Sales Workers	17,160
16. Combined Food Preparation and Service Workers	16,060
17. First-Line Supervisors and Managers—Administrative Workers	15,980
18. Assemblers and Fabricators	15,320
19. General Utility Maintenance Repairers	14,800
20. Truck Drivers—Light	12,750
21. Licensed Practical Nurses	12,460
22. Receptionists and Information Clerks	12,380
23. Stock Clerks—Stockroom and Warehouse	12,140
24. Food Preparation Workers	11,230
25. Sales Representatives	10,920

Jobs with the Highest Earnings

Job	Annual Earnings
1. Physicians and Surgeons	$110,260
2. Dentists	$86,720
3. College and University Faculty (Health Diagnostics)	$70,010
4. College and University Faculty (Law)	$68,660
5. Petroleum Engineers	$68,500
6. Chemical Engineers	$65,860
7. Real Estate Brokers	$63,910
8. College and University Faculty (Engineering Teachers)	$63,760
9. Lawyers	$63,490
10. Engineering, Mathematical, and Natural Sciences Managers	$63,330
11. Physicists and Astronomers	$63,290
12. Optometrists	$62,250
13. Aerospace Engineers	$60,830
14. Aircraft Pilots and Flight Engineers	$60,760
15. Geologists, Geophysicists, and Oceanographers	$60,030
16. Air Traffic Controllers	$59,730
17. Actuaries	$59,460
18. Sales Engineers	$57,580
19. Securities, Commodities, and Financial Services Sales Agents	$57,040
20. Electrical and Electronic Engineers	$56,780
21. Pharmacists	$55,580
22. Mechanical Engineers	$54,230
23. College and University Faculty (Economics)	$53,580
24. Civil Engineers	$53,520
25. Industrial Engineers	$53,240

OREGON
Population 3,282,055

Jobs Employing the Most Workers

Job	Number Employed
1. Retail Salespersons	53,300
2. General Office Clerks	39,180
3. Combined Food Preparation and Service Workers	31,490
4. Cashiers	29,510
5. General Managers and Top Executives	26,890
6. Bookkeeping, Accounting, and Auditing Clerks	25,910
7. First-Line Supervisors and Managers— Sales Workers	25,370
8. Waiters and Waitresses	23,680
9. Truck Drivers—Heavy	23,600
10. Secretaries	23,080
11. Janitors and Cleaners	21,880
12. Registered Nurses	20,990
13. Food Preparation Workers	17,360
14. First-Line Supervisors and Managers— Administrative Workers	17,200
15. Elementary School Teachers	17,030
16. Receptionists and Information Clerks	16,950
17. Assemblers and Fabricators	16,730
18. Secondary School Teachers	15,470
19. Truck Drivers—Light	15,100
20. Sales Representatives	13,990
21. Nursing Aides, Orderlies, and Attendants	13,440
22. Carpenters	13,280
23. Hand Packers and Packagers	12,810
24. Cooks, Restaurant	12,140
25. Shipping, Receiving, and Traffic Clerks	11,560

Jobs with the Highest Earnings

Job	Annual Earnings
1. Physicians and Surgeons	$105,250
2. Dentists	$104,830
3. Podiatrists	$94,540
4. College and University Faculty (Health Diagnostics)	$74,490
5. Engineering, Mathematical, and Natural Sciences Managers	$73,920
6. College and University Faculty (Law)	$71,560
7. Lawyers	$68,220
8. Securities, Commodities, and Financial Services Sales Agents	$67,910
9. Computer Engineers	$65,330
10. Sales Engineers	$64,820
11. General Managers and Top Executives	$64,250
12. Mining, Quarrying, and Oil and Gas Well Drilling Managers	$62,300
13. Dental Hygienists	$61,220
14. Actuaries	$60,920
15. Judges and Magistrates	$60,810
16. Pharmacists	$60,430
17. Elevator Installers and Repairers	$59,520
18. Mechanical Engineers	$58,770
19. Construction Managers	$58,760
20. Sales Representatives—Scientific Products	$58,460
21. Chemical Engineers	$57,800
22. Marketing, Advertising, and Public Relations Managers	$57,800
23. Materials Engineers	$57,180
24. Electric Meter Installers and Repairers	$56,990
25. Power Distributors and Dispatchers	$56,350

PENNSYLVANIA
Population 12,002,329

Jobs Employing the Most Workers

Job	Number Employed
1. Retail Salespersons	176,330
2. Cashiers	138,000
3. General Managers and Top Executives	137,540
4. General Office Clerks	125,080
5. Secretaries	123,320
6. Registered Nurses	103,680
7. Waiters and Waitresses	93,460
8. Janitors and Cleaners	88,770
9. First-Line Supervisors and Managers— Sales Workers	73,170
10. Elementary School Teachers	71,030
11. Nursing Aides, Orderlies, and Attendants	70,860
12. Bookkeeping, Accounting, and Auditing Clerks	66,320
13. Stock Clerks—Sales Floor	65,010
14. Truck Drivers—Heavy	64,240
15. Food Preparation Workers	62,210
16. Secondary School Teachers	61,580
17. First-Line Supervisors and Managers— Administrative Workers	58,430
18. Truck Drivers—Light	51,550
19. Assemblers and Fabricators	51,140
20. General Utility Maintenance Repairers	50,780
21. Receptionists and Information Clerks	50,100
22. Hand Packers and Packagers	48,180
23. Shipping, Receiving, and Traffic Clerks	45,630
24. Sales Representatives	45,390
25. Combined Food Preparation and Service Workers	44,590

Jobs with the Highest Earnings

Job	Annual Earnings
1. Physicians and Surgeons	$97,520
2. Dentists	$86,910
3. Judges and Magistrates	$83,450
4. Podiatrists	$74,830
5. Lawyers	$71,620
6. Marine Engineers	$71,580
7. College and University Faculty (Law)	$68,500
8. College and University Faculty (Engineering Teachers)	$68,310
9. Engineering, Mathematical, and Natural Sciences Managers	$67,500
10. Actuaries	$66,410
11. College and University Faculty (Architecture)	$64,970
12. General Managers and Top Executives	$63,220
13. Aerospace Engineers	$62,790
14. Petroleum Engineers	$61,860
15. Securities, Commodities, and Financial Services Sales Agents	$60,790
16. Air Traffic Controllers	$60,620
17. College and University Faculty (Economics)	$60,130
18. Physical Therapists	$59,720
19. Computer Engineers	$58,860
20. Optometrists	$58,850
21. Education Administrators	$58,710
22. Veterinarians	$58,580
23. College and University Faculty (History)	$58,160
24. Marketing, Advertising, and Public Relations Managers	$57,640
25. College and University Faculty (Business)	$57,470

RHODE ISLAND
Population 987,704

Jobs Employing the Most Workers

Job	Number Employed
1. Retail Salespersons	13,340
2. Cashiers	12,530
3. General Office Clerks	10,410
4. Registered Nurses	9,770
5. General Managers and Top Executives	9,510
6. Secretaries	8,840
7. Nursing Aides, Orderlies, and Attendants	8,710
8. Waiters and Waitresses	8,330
9. Assemblers and Fabricators	7,660
10. Janitors and Cleaners	7,540
11. Bookkeeping, Accounting, and Auditing Clerks	6,560
12. First-Line Supervisors and Managers—Sales Workers	6,520
13. First-Line Supervisors and Managers—Administrative Workers	6,180
14. Secondary School Teachers	6,170
15. Truck Drivers—Light	5,750
16. Elementary School Teachers	5,650
17. Hand Packers and Packagers	5,470
18. Sales Representatives	4,760
19. Receptionists and Information Clerks	4,230
20. Combined Food Preparation and Service Workers	4,120
21. General Utility Maintenance Repairers	4,110
22. Food Preparation Workers	3,850
23. Shipping, Receiving, and Traffic Clerks	3,740
24. Stock Clerks—Sales Floor	3,430
25. Carpenters	3,390

Jobs with the Highest Earnings

Job	Annual Earnings
1. Dentists	$106,110
2. Physicians and Surgeons	$93,910
3. Podiatrists	$88,070
4. Lawyers	$80,610
5. College and University Faculty (Physics)	$78,290
6. Engineering, Mathematical, and Natural Sciences Managers	$75,660
7. College and University Faculty (History)	$74,600
8. College and University Faculty (Mathematics)	$73,970
9. Financial Analysts	$73,830
10. Securities, Commodities, and Financial Services Sales Agents	$72,850
11. Optometrists	$71,350
12. College and University Faculty (Foreign Language)	$70,510
13. College and University Faculty (Chemistry)	$70,270
14. College and University Faculty (Life Sciences)	$68,330
15. Financial Managers	$68,230
16. College and University Faculty (Political Science)	$67,460
17. College and University Faculty (Philosophy and Religion)	$66,910
18. College and University Faculty (Anthropology and Sociology)	$66,890
19. College and University Faculty (Economics)	$66,850
20. College and University Faculty (Business)	$66,480
21. General Managers and Top Executives	$65,600
22. College and University Faculty (English Language and Literature)	$65,040
23. Veterinarians	$64,530
24. Marine Engineers	$63,450
25. Computer Engineers	$62,560

SOUTH CAROLINA
Population 3,839,578

Jobs Employing the Most Workers

Job	Number Employed
1. Retail Salespersons	59,230
2. Cashiers	55,890
3. General Managers and Top Executives	45,820
4. General Office Clerks	35,920
5. Waiters and Waitresses	32,120
6. Secretaries	31,710
7. Janitors and Cleaners	29,460
8. Registered Nurses	26,770
9. First-Line Supervisors and Managers—Sales Workers	26,440
10. Assemblers and Fabricators	25,010
11. Elementary School Teachers	24,550
12. Textile Machine Operators and Tenders	23,220
13. Truck Drivers—Heavy	22,680
14. Bookkeeping, Accounting, and Auditing Clerks	21,540
15. Combined Food Preparation and Service Workers	20,270
16. Secondary School Teachers	20,130
17. Hand Packers and Packagers	20,100
18. General Utility Maintenance Repairers	18,780
19. First-Line Supervisors and Managers—Administrative Workers	18,480
20. Food Preparation Workers	17,270
21. Truck Drivers—Light	16,580
22. Stock Clerks—Sales Floor	16,240
23. Landscaping and Groundskeeping Laborers	16,180
24. Maids and Housekeeping Cleaners	16,070
25. Nursing Aides, Orderlies, and Attendants	15,520

Jobs with the Highest Earnings

Job	Annual Earnings
1. Physicians and Surgeons	$103,420
2. Dentists	$91,660
3. Chiropractors	$71,890
4. Lawyers	$70,220
5. Optometrists	$68,610
6. College and University Faculty (Economics)	$66,440
7. College and University Faculty (Law)	$64,590
8. Engineering, Mathematical, and Natural Sciences Managers	$64,470
9. Chemical Engineers	$60,540
10. Physicists and Astronomers	$60,050
11. Real Estate Brokers	$58,530
12. College and University Faculty (Engineering Teachers)	$58,050
13. Education Administrators	$57,450
14. Atmospheric and Space Scientists	$57,150
15. Pharmacists	$56,860
16. College and University Faculty (Health Assessment and Treatment)	$56,460
17. Physical Therapists	$56,440
18. Air Traffic Controllers	$55,920
19. Electrical and Electronic Engineers	$55,910
20. Agricultural Engineers	$55,760
21. Actuaries	$55,550
22. Civil Engineers	$55,280
23. Stevedores, Except Equipment Operators	$55,170
24. College and University Faculty (Business)	$55,030
25. Industrial Production Managers	$54,470

SOUTH DAKOTA
Population 730,789

Jobs Employing the Most Workers

Job	Number Employed
1. Retail Salespersons	12,480
2. Cashiers	11,390
3. Waiters and Waitresses	8,340
4. General Office Clerks	8,130
5. Registered Nurses	7,620
6. Bookkeeping, Accounting, and Auditing Clerks	7,130
7. Janitors and Cleaners	7,080
8. Food Preparation Workers	6,520
9. Truck Drivers—Heavy	6,320
10. Secretaries	6,260
11. Nursing Aides, Orderlies, and Attendants	5,750
12. Combined Food Preparation and Service Workers	5,480
13. Elementary School Teachers	5,150
14. General Managers and Top Executives	4,980
15. Secondary School Teachers	4,640
16. Maids and Housekeeping Cleaners	4,400
17. First-Line Supervisors and Managers— Sales Workers	4,330
18. Stock Clerks—Sales Floor	4,120
19. Assemblers and Fabricators	4,010
20. Adjustment Clerks	3,430
21. Sales Representatives	3,160
22. Electrical and Electronic Equipment Assemblers, Precision	3,150
23. Receptionists and Information Clerks	2,980
24. First-Line Supervisors and Managers— Administrative Workers	2,960
25. Hand Packers and Packagers	2,880

Jobs with the Highest Earnings

Job	Annual Earnings
1. Physicians and Surgeons	$106,310
2. Dentists	$81,350
3. Securities, Commodities, and Financial Services Sales Agents	$73,140
4. General Managers and Top Executives	$65,910
5. Marketing, Advertising, and Public Relations Managers	$65,060
6. Engineering, Mathematical, and Natural Sciences Managers	$63,180
7. Physician Assistants	$61,220
8. Veterinarians	$60,850
9. Sales Engineers	$58,610
10. Financial Managers	$56,720
11. Psychologists	$54,940
12. Industrial Production Managers	$54,110
13. Physical Therapists	$52,130
14. Pharmacists	$51,860
15. Systems Analysts	$50,870
16. Geologists, Geophysicists, and Oceanographers	$50,610
17. Lawyers	$50,560
18. Medicine and Health Services Managers	$49,900
19. Atmospheric and Space Scientists	$49,750
20. Personnel, Training, and Labor Relations Managers	$49,730
21. Chiropractors	$49,510
22. Administrative Services Managers	$49,310
23. Purchasing Managers	$49,060
24. Education Administrators	$48,710
25. Construction Managers	$48,530

TENNESSEE
Population 5,432,679

Jobs Employing the Most Workers

Job	Number Employed
1. Retail Salespersons	77,760
2. Cashiers	71,700
3. General Managers and Top Executives	66,450
4. General Office Clerks	55,320
5. Secretaries	45,690
6. Registered Nurses	42,790
7. Combined Food Preparation and Service Workers	39,990
8. Waiters and Waitresses	39,240
9. Janitors and Cleaners	36,780
10. Bookkeeping, Accounting, and Auditing Clerks	33,490
11. Elementary School Teachers	32,710
12. First-Line Supervisors and Managers— Sales Workers	32,170
13. First-Line Supervisors and Managers— Administrative Workers	30,050
14. Stock Clerks—Sales Floor	26,730
15. General Utility Maintenance Repairers	25,400
16. Nursing Aides, Orderlies, and Attendants	25,230
17. Food Preparation Workers	23,400
18. Shipping, Receiving, and Traffic Clerks	21,530
19. Receptionists and Information Clerks	21,490
20. Sales Representatives	20,420
21. Maids and Housekeeping Cleaners	19,990
22. Guards and Watch Guards	19,310
23. Licensed Practical Nurses	19,280
24. Secondary School Teachers	19,240
25. Accountants and Auditors	18,660

Jobs with the Highest Earnings

Job	Annual Earnings
1. Podiatrists	$111,850
2. Physicians and Surgeons	$103,620
3. Dentists	$93,930
4. Securities, Commodities, and Financial Services Sales Agents	$74,460
5. Lawyers	$73,670
6. Real Estate Brokers	$70,710
7. College and University Faculty (Law)	$65,100
8. Chiropractors	$64,950
9. Actuaries	$64,020
10. Precision Instrument Makers	$62,990
11. Engineering, Mathematical, and Natural Sciences Managers	$62,830
12. Camera and Photographic Equipment Repairers	$61,630
13. Optometrists	$58,750
14. College and University Faculty (Engineering Teachers)	$58,690
15. General Managers and Top Executives	$58,310
16. Pharmacists	$57,890
17. Geologists, Geophysicists, and Oceanographers	$57,790
18. Veterinarians	$57,220
19. Materials Engineers	$57,150
20. Economists	$57,080
21. Criminal Investigators, Public Service	$56,550
22. Atmospheric and Space Scientists	$56,310
23. Agricultural Engineers	$56,240
24. Aerospace Engineers	$56,150
25. College and University Faculty (Economics)	$55,460

TEXAS
Population 19,712,389

Jobs Employing the Most Workers

Job	Number Employed
1. General Managers and Top Executives	288,290
2. Retail Salespersons	266,540
3. Cashiers	224,660
4. General Office Clerks	216,130
5. Secretaries	172,410
6. Combined Food Preparation and Service Workers	149,650
7. Waiters and Waitresses	132,090
8. Janitors and Cleaners	130,360
9. Elementary School Teachers	128,700
10. Secondary School Teachers	127,710
11. Registered Nurses	125,070
12. Bookkeeping, Accounting, and Auditing Clerks	114,330
13. Truck Drivers—Heavy	114,000
14. First-Line Supervisors and Managers—Sales Workers	107,830
15. First-Line Supervisors and Managers—Administrative Workers	104,640
16. Receptionists and Information Clerks	88,860
17. Nursing Aides, Orderlies, and Attendants	88,230
18. Sales Representatives	86,230
19. General Utility Maintenance Repairers	84,530
20. Truck Drivers—Light	76,920
21. Stock Clerks—Sales Floor	76,390
22. Food Preparation Workers	74,100
23. Guards and Watch Guards	71,400
24. Accountants and Auditors	70,670
25. Assemblers and Fabricators	67,550

Jobs with the Highest Earnings

Job	Annual Earnings
1. Physicians and Surgeons	$108,250
2. Dentists	$90,520
3. Lawyers	$78,810
4. Mining, Quarrying, and Oil and Gas Well Drilling Managers	$75,320
5. Geologists, Geophysicists, and Oceanographers	$75,160
6. Petroleum Engineers	$73,280
7. Engineering, Mathematical, and Natural Sciences Managers	$72,900
8. Optometrists	$71,330
9. Physicists and Astronomers	$71,140
10. College and University Faculty (Health Diagnostics)	$70,040
11. Podiatrists	$69,970
12. College and University Faculty (Law)	$66,610
13. Flight Attendants	$66,160
14. Nuclear Engineers	$66,080
15. Actuaries	$65,750
16. Chemical Engineers	$64,750
17. College and University Faculty (Life Sciences)	$64,630
18. Medical Scientists	$64,570
19. Air Traffic Controllers	$62,730
20. Electrical and Electronic Engineers	$61,460
21. Aerospace Engineers	$60,980
22. College and University Faculty (Engineering Teachers)	$60,770
23. Marketing, Advertising, and Public Relations Managers	$60,730
24. Physical Therapists	$60,460
25. Pharmacists	$60,390

UTAH
Population 2,100,562

Jobs Employing the Most Workers

Job	Number Employed
1. Retail Salespersons	35,310
2. Cashiers	30,080
3. General Managers and Top Executives	22,510
4. General Office Clerks	20,230
5. Secretaries	19,360
6. Truck Drivers—Heavy	18,190
7. Janitors and Cleaners	14,720
8. First-Line Supervisors and Managers— Sales Workers	14,530
9. Waiters and Waitresses	13,840
10. Bookkeeping, Accounting, and Auditing Clerks	13,090
11. Registered Nurses	13,080
12. Combined Food Preparation and Service Workers	12,170
13. Secondary School Teachers	11,510
14. First-Line Supervisors and Managers— Administrative Workers	11,300
15. Assemblers and Fabricators	10,280
16. Truck Drivers—Light	10,170
17. Food Preparation Workers	10,130
18. Sales Representatives	10,090
19. Receptionists and Information Clerks	10,070
20. Elementary School Teachers	9,800
21. Teacher Assistants	9,330
22. Landscaping and Groundskeeping Laborers	8,740
23. Carpenters	8,710
24. Stock Clerks—Sales Floor	8,630
25. Adjustment Clerks	8,480

Jobs with the Highest Earnings

Job	Annual Earnings
1. College and University Faculty (Health Diagnostics)	$101,310
2. Physicians and Surgeons	$97,240
3. Dentists	$90,610
4. College and University Faculty (Health Assessment and Treatment)	$82,110
5. Lawyers	$72,220
6. Engineering, Mathematical, and Natural Sciences Managers	$68,930
7. College and University Faculty (Law)	$68,090
8. Pharmacists	$63,470
9. College and University Faculty (Geography)	$62,900
10. College and University Faculty (Economics)	$62,840
11. Physicists and Astronomers	$62,050
12. Mining Engineers	$61,870
13. College and University Faculty (Engineering Teachers)	$61,850
14. Petroleum Engineers	$59,770
15. Veterinarians	$59,750
16. Physician Assistants	$59,020
17. Electrical and Electronic Engineers	$58,950
18. General Managers and Top Executives	$58,310
19. Transportation Inspectors	$57,790
20. Marketing, Advertising, and Public Relations Managers	$57,730
21. Computer Engineers	$57,180
22. College and University Faculty (Computer Science)	$57,060
23. College and University Faculty (Political Science)	$56,570
24. Mining, Quarrying, and Oil and Gas Well Drilling Managers	$55,900
25. Operations Research Analysts	$55,700

VERMONT
Population 590,579

Jobs Employing the Most Workers

Job	Number Employed
1. Retail Salespersons	8,630
2. Cashiers	7,660
3. Waiters and Waitresses	6,460
4. Secretaries	5,720
5. Registered Nurses	5,130
6. Bookkeeping, Accounting, and Auditing Clerks	4,980
7. General Office Clerks	4,900
8. Janitors and Cleaners	4,730
9. First-Line Supervisors and Managers— Sales Workers	4,430
10. Teacher Assistants	4,270
11. General Managers and Top Executives	4,190
12. Elementary School Teachers	4,110
13. Truck Drivers—Heavy	4,010
14. Food Preparation Workers	3,810
15. Secondary School Teachers	3,690
16. Carpenters	3,340
17. Maids and Housekeeping Cleaners	3,300
18. First-Line Supervisors and Managers— Administrative Workers	3,110
19. Truck Drivers—Light	3,050
20. Combined Food Preparation and Service Workers	2,930
21. Stock Clerks—Sales Floor	2,910
22. Assemblers and Fabricators	2,790
23. General Utility Maintenance Repairers	2,760
24. Nursing Aides, Orderlies, and Attendants	2,450
25. Human Services Workers and Assistants	2,440

Jobs with the Highest Earnings

Job	Annual Earnings
1. Dentists	$93,590
2. Physicians and Surgeons	$87,060
3. Optometrists	$76,560
4. Management Analysts	$68,080
5. Engineering, Mathematical, and Natural Sciences Managers	$67,930
6. Pharmacists	$64,360
7. College and University Faculty (Physics)	$63,090
8. General Managers and Top Executives	$62,840
9. Physician Assistants	$60,450
10. Industrial Production Managers	$58,950
11. Marketing, Advertising, and Public Relations Managers	$58,310
12. College and University Faculty (Computer Science)	$57,650
13. Sales Engineers	$57,150
14. College and University Faculty (Area Studies)	$56,530
15. Personnel, Training, and Labor Relations Managers	$56,450
16. Securities, Commodities, and Financial Services Sales Agents	$55,420
17. College and University Faculty (Anthropology and Sociology)	$55,010
18. College and University Faculty (Philosophy and Religion)	$54,880
19. Financial Managers	$54,680
20. Industrial Engineers	$54,470
21. Criminal Investigators, Public Service	$54,290
22. Computer Engineers	$54,240
23. Construction Managers	$53,690
24. College and University Faculty (Life Sciences)	$53,340
25. College and University Faculty (Business)	$53,300

VIRGINIA
Population 6,789,225

Jobs Employing the Most Workers

Job	Number Employed
1. Retail Salespersons	114,740
2. Cashiers	91,510
3. General Managers and Top Executives	91,470
4. General Office Clerks	75,140
5. Secretaries	65,010
6. Janitors and Cleaners	52,600
7. Waiters and Waitresses	49,090
8. Registered Nurses	45,780
9. First-Line Supervisors and Managers—Sales Workers	42,230
10. Bookkeeping, Accounting, and Auditing Clerks	41,410
11. First-Line Supervisors and Managers—Administrative Workers	41,260
12. Elementary School Teachers	39,000
13. Truck Drivers—Heavy	37,650
14. Combined Food Preparation and Service Workers	36,690
15. Secondary School Teachers	35,430
16. Receptionists and Information Clerks	34,740
17. Truck Drivers—Light	31,890
18. Systems Analysts	29,890
19. Nursing Aides, Orderlies, and Attendants	29,710
20. Food Preparation Workers	27,690
21. Computer Programmers	26,960
22. General Utility Maintenance Repairers	26,920
23. Maids and Housekeeping Cleaners	26,480
24. Hand Packers and Packagers	25,890
25. Stock Clerks—Sales Floor	25,770

Jobs with the Highest Earnings

Job	Annual Earnings
1. Physicians and Surgeons	$101,930
2. Dentists	$101,510
3. Judges and Magistrates	$94,940
4. Podiatrists	$90,310
5. Aircraft Pilots and Flight Engineers	$85,670
6. Chiropractors	$78,220
7. Lawyers	$77,390
8. College and University Faculty (Health Diagnostics)	$75,540
9. Actuaries	$74,350
10. Optometrists	$72,400
11. Engineering, Mathematical, and Natural Sciences Managers	$71,450
12. College and University Faculty (Law)	$70,900
13. Physicists and Astronomers	$68,540
14. Marine Architects	$67,630
15. College and University Faculty (Engineering Teachers)	$65,710
16. Aerospace Engineers	$64,220
17. Pharmacists	$61,930
18. Electrical and Electronic Engineers	$61,300
19. Medical Scientists	$60,790
20. General Managers and Top Executives	$60,650
21. Petroleum Engineers	$60,560
22. Securities, Commodities, and Financial Services Sales Agents	$60,470
23. Systems Analysts	$59,350
24. Marketing, Advertising, and Public Relations Managers	$59,140
25. Atmospheric and Space Scientists	$58,650

WASHINGTON
Population 5,687,832

Jobs Employing the Most Workers

Job	Number Employed
1. Retail Salespersons	90,760
2. General Managers and Top Executives	65,540
3. General Office Clerks	60,620
4. Cashiers	51,060
5. Combined Food Preparation and Service Workers	50,000
6. Bookkeeping, Accounting, and Auditing Clerks	41,530
7. Registered Nurses	39,620
8. Waiters and Waitresses	38,400
9. Janitors and Cleaners	37,050
10. Secretaries	36,680
11. First-Line Supervisors and Managers— Sales Workers	34,030
12. Elementary School Teachers	30,860
13. Receptionists and Information Clerks	30,030
14. Secondary School Teachers	29,520
15. Truck Drivers—Heavy	29,100
16. First-Line Supervisors and Managers— Administrative Workers	28,070
17. Truck Drivers—Light	24,330
18. Teacher Assistants	23,090
19. Food Preparation Workers	22,880
20. Nursing Aides, Orderlies, and Attendants	22,440
21. General Utility Maintenance Repairers	21,090
22. Carpenters	20,970
23. Sales Representatives	20,890
24. Stock Clerks—Sales Floor	19,620
25. Shipping, Receiving, and Traffic Clerks	19,160

Jobs with the Highest Earnings

Job	Annual Earnings
1. Dentists	$101,760
2. Physicians and Surgeons	$97,200
3. Podiatrists	$94,770
4. Optometrists	$87,570
5. Lawyers	$74,360
6. Judges and Magistrates	$72,230
7. Engineering, Mathematical, and Natural Sciences Managers	$69,910
8. College and University Faculty (Engineering Teachers)	$68,320
9. Actuaries	$68,000
10. Chemical Engineers	$66,490
11. College and University Faculty (Law)	$65,960
12. Chiropractors	$64,730
13. Longshore Equipment Operators	$63,990
14. Marine Architects	$62,920
15. Pharmacists	$62,660
16. Marine Engineers	$61,980
17. General Managers and Top Executives	$61,280
18. Dental Hygienists	$61,190
19. Real Estate Brokers	$61,030
20. Water Vessel Captains	$60,680
21. Computer Engineers	$60,540
22. Nuclear Engineers	$60,500
23. Securities, Commodities, and Financial Services Sales Agents	$60,230
24. Pilots, Ship	$59,280
25. Industrial Production Managers	$58,950

WEST VIRGINIA
Population 1,811,688

Jobs Employing the Most Workers

Job	Number Employed
1. Retail Salespersons	23,450
2. Cashiers	21,550
3. General Managers and Top Executives	18,230
4. General Office Clerks	15,710
5. Registered Nurses	14,840
6. Secretaries	13,580
7. Janitors and Cleaners	11,760
8. Truck Drivers—Heavy	10,490
9. Combined Food Preparation and Service Workers	9,740
10. Elementary School Teachers	9,400
11. Waiters and Waitresses	8,830
12. Bookkeeping, Accounting, and Auditing Clerks	8,790
13. Nursing Aides, Orderlies, and Attendants	8,610
14. General Utility Maintenance Repairers	8,490
15. First-Line Supervisors and Managers— Sales Workers	8,170
16. Secondary School Teachers	7,860
17. Food Preparation Workers	7,570
18. Stock Clerks—Sales Floor	7,220
19. Truck Drivers—Light	7,090
20. Licensed Practical Nurses	6,390
21. First-Line Supervisors and Managers— Administrative Workers	6,060
22. Maids and Housekeeping Cleaners	6,010
23. Guards and Watch Guards	5,780
24. Carpenters	5,440
25. Receptionists and Information Clerks	5,410

Jobs with the Highest Earnings

Job	Annual Earnings
1. Physicians and Surgeons	$109,600
2. Dentists	$97,360
3. Chiropractors	$89,700
4. Optometrists	$68,750
5. Petroleum Engineers	$65,420
6. Securities, Commodities, and Financial Services Sales Agents	$62,900
7. Chemical Engineers	$61,490
8. Pharmacists	$61,320
9. Architects	$61,170
10. Veterinarians	$60,390
11. Engineering, Mathematical, and Natural Sciences Managers	$60,120
12. Lawyers	$58,560
13. College and University Faculty (Engineering Teachers)	$58,380
14. Mining, Quarrying, and Oil and Gas Well Drilling Managers	$58,020
15. Water Vessel Captains	$57,750
16. Materials Engineers	$57,150
17. Criminal Investigators, Public Service	$57,110
18. College and University Faculty (Health Assessment and Treatment)	$56,830
19. Physicists and Astronomers	$56,440
20. Industrial Engineers	$56,370
21. Operations Research Analysts	$56,150
22. Agricultural and Food Scientists	$55,000
23. Physical Therapists	$54,790
24. Mining Engineers	$54,750
25. Safety Engineers	$54,610

WISCONSIN
Population 5,222,124

Jobs Employing the Most Workers

Job	Number Employed
1. Retail Salespersons	77,080
2. General Managers and Top Executives	70,350
3. General Office Clerks	65,400
4. Cashiers	63,310
5. Waiters and Waitresses	46,760
6. Assemblers and Fabricators	46,320
7. Truck Drivers—Heavy	45,560
8. Janitors and Cleaners	43,960
9. Secretaries	43,920
10. Registered Nurses	41,620
11. Nursing Aides, Orderlies, and Attendants	35,850
12. Bookkeeping, Accounting, and Auditing Clerks	32,820
13. Stock Clerks—Sales Floor	31,380
14. Combined Food Preparation and Service Workers	31,180
15. First-Line Supervisors and Managers—Sales Workers	31,010
16. Secondary School Teachers	29,680
17. Elementary School Teachers	28,620
18. Hand Packers and Packagers	27,600
19. Sales Representatives	26,660
20. Food Preparation Workers	25,800
21. Receptionists and Information Clerks	25,780
22. First-Line Supervisors and Managers—Administrative Workers	24,830
23. Truck Drivers—Light	24,740
24. General Utility Maintenance Repairers	24,630
25. Shipping, Receiving, and Traffic Clerks	23,830

Jobs with the Highest Earnings

Job	Annual Earnings
1. Physicians and Surgeons	$103,750
2. Podiatrists	$87,470
3. Dentists	$82,000
4. Lawyers	$66,670
5. Securities, Commodities, and Financial Services Sales Agents	$65,340
6. Engineering, Mathematical, and Natural Sciences Managers	$64,000
7. Chiropractors	$63,940
8. Pharmacists	$62,850
9. Optometrists	$62,280
10. Aerospace Engineers	$61,430
11. College and University Faculty (Computer Science)	$61,410
12. Education Administrators	$61,220
13. Actuaries	$60,790
14. Insurance Special Agents	$60,490
15. Chemical Engineers	$59,520
16. Nuclear Engineers	$58,270
17. General Managers and Top Executives	$56,110
18. Physical Therapists	$56,050
19. Psychologists	$55,640
20. Computer Engineers	$55,530
21. Sales Engineers	$54,300
22. Electrical and Electronic Engineers	$54,090
23. Financial Analysts	$53,180
24. Management Analysts	$52,980
25. Marketing, Advertising, and Public Relations Managers	$52,960

WYOMING
Population 480,045

Jobs Employing the Most Workers

Job	Number Employed
1. Retail Salespersons	7,170
2. General Managers and Top Executives	6,620
3. Waiters and Waitresses	5,680
4. Secretaries	5,150
5. Cashiers	4,720
6. Janitors and Cleaners	3,970
7. General Office Clerks	3,920
8. Bookkeeping, Accounting, and Auditing Clerks	3,880
9. Combined Food Preparation and Service Workers	3,760
10. Truck Drivers—Heavy	3,710
11. Registered Nurses	3,520
12. Maids and Housekeeping Cleaners	3,370
13. Secondary School Teachers	3,330
14. Elementary School Teachers	3,180
15. General Utility Maintenance Repairers	3,110
16. First-Line Supervisors and Managers—Administrative Workers	2,900
17. First-Line Supervisors and Managers—Sales Workers	2,770
18. Truck Drivers—Light	2,530
19. Food Preparation Workers	2,310
20. Stock Clerks—Sales Floor	2,280
21. Carpenters	2,050
22. Cooks, Restaurant	2,030
23. Teacher Assistants	2,030
24. Landscaping and Groundskeeping Laborers	2,030
25. Nursing Aides, Orderlies, and Attendants	1,940

Jobs with the Highest Earnings

Job	Annual Earnings
1. Physicians and Surgeons	$105,200
2. Dentists	$80,000
3. Mining, Quarrying, and Oil and Gas Well Drilling Managers	$66,810
4. Petroleum Engineers	$63,430
5. Safety Engineers	$61,460
6. Securities, Commodities, and Financial Services Sales Agents	$61,110
7. Engineering, Mathematical, and Natural Sciences Managers	$60,620
8. Chemical Engineers	$59,610
9. Optometrists	$58,940
10. Mining Engineers	$57,160
11. Physical Therapists	$55,110
12. Dragline Operators	$54,880
13. Geologists, Geophysicists, and Oceanographers	$54,000
14. Pharmacists	$53,670
15. Education Administrators	$53,600
16. Estimators and Drafters, Utilities	$52,900
17. Physician Assistants	$52,550
18. Blasters and Explosives Workers	$51,790
19. Sales Engineers	$51,310
20. Mechanical Engineers	$51,230
21. Landscape Architects	$50,180
22. Rotary Drill Operators, Oil and Gas Extraction	$50,150
23. Financial Managers	$49,720
24. Lawyers	$49,720
25. Electrical and Electronic Engineers	$49,560

Jobs Lists for the 30 Largest Metropolitan Areas

This section features information on jobs for the 30 largest metropolitan areas in the United States. As with the lists for the states, we list the 25 highest-paying jobs and the 25 jobs employing the most people.

We present the 30 metro areas in order of size, beginning with the largest, which is the metropolitan New York area. Notice that many areas include multiple cities and states. For example, the Chicago metropolitan area includes Gary, Indiana, and Kenosha, Wisconsin. The federal government collects data for Metropolitan Statistical Areas (MSA), and these areas are often made up of more than one city and county. An MSA can even cross state borders. Each MSA must include a city of at least 50,000 people, with outlying areas that increase the total population to more than 100,000. Outlying cities and counties are included in a metropolitan area when at least 25 percent of their workforce commutes to the central city or county. There are about 250 metropolitan statistical areas in the United States. The 30 largest ones are as follows:

Area	Population	Area	Population
1. New York City-Northern New Jersey-Long Island, NY-NJ	20,124,377	16. Minneapolis-St. Paul, MN	2,831,234
2. Los Angeles-Riverside-Orange County, CA	15,781,273	17. San Diego, CA	2,780,592
3. Chicago-Gary-Kenosha, IL-IN-WI	8,809,846	18. St. Louis, MO	2,563,801
4. Washington-Baltimore, DC-MD-VA-WV	7,285,206	19. Denver-Boulder-Greeley, CO	2,365,345
5. San Francisco-Oakland-San Jose, CA	6,816,047	20. Pittsburgh, PA	2,346,153
6. Philadelphia-Wilmington-Atlantic City, PA-NJ-DE-MD	5,988,348	21. Tampa-St. Petersburg-Clearwater, FL	2,256,559
7. Boston-Worcester-Lawrence, MA-NH-ME-CT	5,644,060	22. Portland-Salem, OR-WA	2,149,056
8. Detroit-Ann Arbor-Flint, MI	5,457,583	23. Cincinnati-Hamilton, OH-KY-IN	1,948,264
9. Dallas-Fort Worth, TX	4,802,463	24. Kansas City, MO-KS	1,737,025
10. Houston-Galveston-Brazoria, TX	4,407,579	25. Sacramento-Yolo, CA	1,685,812
11. Atlanta, GA	3,746,059	26. Milwaukee-Racine, WI	1,645,924
12. Miami-Fort Lauderdale, FL	3,655,844	27. Norfolk-Virginia Beach-Newport News, VA-NC	1,542,143
13. Seattle-Tacoma-Bremerton, WA	3,424,361	28. San Antonio, TX	1,538,338
14. Phoenix-Mesa, AZ	2,931,004	29. Indianapolis, IN	1,519,194
15. Cleveland-Akron, OH	2,911,683	30. Orlando, FL	1,504,569

1. NEW YORK CITY-NORTHERN NEW JERSEY-LONG ISLAND, NY-NJ
Population 20,124,377

Jobs Employing the Most Workers

Job	Number Employed
1. General Office Clerks	116,660
2. Janitors and Cleaners	99,280
3. Secretaries	97,750
4. Retail Salespersons	96,330
5. General Managers and Top Executives	90,550
6. Registered Nurses	72,310
7. First-Line Supervisors and Managers—Administrative Workers	68,660
8. Guards and Watch Guards	65,910
9. Cashiers	62,520
10. Bookkeeping, Accounting, and Auditing Clerks	58,330
11. First-Line Supervisors and Managers—Sales Workers	53,810
12. Nursing Aides, Orderlies, and Attendants	52,010
13. Elementary School Teachers	51,130
14. Waiters and Waitresses	45,750
15. Sales Representatives	44,450
16. Secondary School Teachers	43,760
17. Accountants and Auditors	43,470
18. Personal and Home Care Aides	42,810
19. Receptionists and Information Clerks	40,910
20. Securities, Commodities, and Financial Services Sales Agents	40,780
21. Home Health Aides	39,240
22. Food Preparation Workers	37,450
23. Financial Managers	33,340
24. General Utility Maintenance Repairers	33,150
25. Lawyers	32,870

Jobs with the Highest Earnings

Job	Annual Earnings
1. Aircraft Pilots and Flight Engineers	$94,970
2. Lawyers	$91,130
3. Physicians and Surgeons	$86,930
4. Financial Managers	$85,370
5. General Managers and Top Executives	$83,660
6. Dentists	$83,170
7. Engineering, Mathematical, and Natural Sciences Managers	$83,100
8. Construction Managers	$79,750
9. Actuaries	$75,650
10. Veterinarians	$75,540
11. College and University Faculty (Life Sciences Teachers)	$74,490
12. Nuclear Engineers	$74,050
13. Marketing, Advertising, and Public Relations Managers	$72,230
14. Communication, Transportation, and Utilities Operations Managers	$70,730
15. Insurance Special Agents	$69,500
16. Physicists and Astronomers	$69,450
17. Securities, Commodities, and Financial Services Sales Agents	$69,170
18. Financial Analysts	$69,150
19. Medicine and Health Services Managers	$68,180
20. Structural Metal Workers	$67,260
21. Personnel, Training, and Labor Relations Managers	$67,240
22. Elevator Installers and Repairers	$66,470
23. Economists	$66,000
24. Education Administrators	$65,660
25. Physical Therapists	$64,930

2. LOS ANGELES-RIVERSIDE-ORANGE COUNTY, CA
Population 15,781,273

Jobs Employing the Most Workers

Job	Number Employed
1. General Managers and Top Executives	109,500
2. Retail Salespersons	109,100
3. General Office Clerks	102,410
4. Cashiers	82,620
5. Secretaries	67,770
6. First-Line Supervisors and Managers—Administrative Workers	57,220
7. Janitors and Cleaners	54,430
8. Bookkeeping, Accounting, and Auditing Clerks	54,340
9. Guards and Watch Guards	53,240
10. Combination Food Preparation and Service Workers	52,630
11. Sewing Machine Operators	51,950
12. Waiters and Waitresses	51,270
13. First-Line Supervisors and Managers—Sales Workers	50,750
14. Registered Nurses	49,960
15. Receptionists and Information Clerks	49,420
16. Elementary School Teachers	49,250
17. Shipping, Receiving, and Traffic Clerks	48,020
18. Food Preparation Workers	40,880
19. Truck Drivers—Light	40,650
20. Assemblers and Fabricators	38,820
21. Sales Representatives	38,240
22. Stock Clerks—Sales Floor	38,240
23. Secondary School Teachers	34,780
24. Stock Clerks—Stockroom and Warehouse	33,800
25. Producers, Directors, Actors, and Other Entertainers	32,960

Jobs with the Highest Earnings

Job	Annual Earnings
1. Dentists	$88,190
2. Lawyers	$87,520
3. Physicians and Surgeons	$86,570
4. Broadcast News Analysts	$84,790
5. Engineering, Mathematical, and Natural Sciences Managers	$80,220
6. General Managers and Top Executives	$76,180
7. Veterinarians	$75,820
8. Physicists and Astronomers	$74,350
9. Aerospace Engineers	$72,080
10. Actuaries	$70,770
11. Petroleum Engineers	$69,550
12. Financial Managers	$69,060
13. Physical Therapists	$68,500
14. Insurance Special Agents	$67,900
15. College and University Faculty (Engineering Teachers)	$67,810
16. Securities, Commodities, and Financial Services Sales Agents	$66,870
17. Mining, Quarrying, and Oil and Gas Well Drilling Managers	$66,850
18. Optometrists	$66,610
19. Pharmacists	$66,290
20. Fire Fighting and Prevention Supervisors	$66,100
21. Police and Detective Supervisors	$65,220
22. Marketing, Advertising, and Public Relations Managers	$64,830
23. Occupational Therapists	$64,420
24. Pile-Driver Operators	$63,770
25. Real Estate Brokers	$64,670

3. CHICAGO-GARY-KENOSHA, IL-IN-WI
Population 8,809,846

Jobs Employing the Most Workers

Job	Number Employed
1. General Managers and Top Executives	130,470
2. Retail Salespersons	115,880
3. Secretaries	98,590
4. General Office Clerks	93,480
5. Cashiers	88,970
6. Janitors and Cleaners	69,960
7. Registered Nurses	66,140
8. First-Line Supervisors and Managers—Administrative Workers	58,560
9. Waiters and Waitresses	55,720
10. Bookkeeping, Accounting, and Auditing Clerks	52,840
11. Elementary School Teachers	52,090
12. Stock Clerks—Sales Floor	49,470
13. First-Line Supervisors and Managers—Sales Workers	47,970
14. Hand Packers and Packagers	42,680
15. Receptionists and Information Clerks	41,030
16. Truck Drivers—Light	39,640
17. Shipping, Receiving, and Traffic Clerks	39,450
18. Sales Representatives	37,760
19. Guards and Watch Guards	37,570
20. Truck Drivers—Heavy	36,430
21. Accountants and Auditors	36,060
22. Assemblers and Fabricators	35,630
23. Combination Food Preparation and Service Workers	34,230
24. Landscaping and Groundskeeping Laborers	34,190
25. General Utility Maintenance Repairers	33,650

Jobs with the Highest Earnings

Job	Annual Earnings
1. Aircraft Pilots and Flight Engineers	$101,980
2. Physicians and Surgeons	$100,670
3. Chiropractors	$86,790
4. Lawyers	$85,250
5. Podiatrists	$72,750
6. Dentists	$72,060
7. Actuaries	$71,740
8. Engineering, Mathematical, and Natural Sciences Managers	$70,530
9. General Managers and Top Executives	$68,020
10. Real Estate Brokers	$67,930
11. Psychologists	$65,820
12. Nuclear Engineers	$65,410
13. Financial Managers	$63,460
14. Mining, Quarrying, and Oil and Gas Well Drilling Managers	$62,560
15. Reinforcing Metal Workers	$61,970
16. Elevator Installers and Repairers	$60,120
17. Pharmacists	$60,030
18. Police and Detective Supervisors	$59,940
19. Stonemasons	$59,940
20. Marketing, Advertising, and Public Relations Managers	$59,750
21. College and University Faculty (Agricultural Sciences)	$59,440
22. Physicists and Astronomers	$59,340
23. Chemical Engineers	$59,270
24. Education Administrators	$58,910
25. Materials Engineers	$58,770

4. WASHINGTON-BALTIMORE, DC-MD-VA-WV
Population 7,285,206

Jobs Employing the Most Workers

Job	Number Employed
1. General Managers and Top Executives	84,400
2. Retail Salespersons	79,330
3. Secretaries	67,190
4. General Office Clerks	65,480
5. Cashiers	50,460
6. Janitors and Cleaners	48,600
7. Systems Analysts	42,730
8. First-Line Supervisors and Managers—Administrative Workers	39,200
9. Waiters and Waitresses	34,240
10. Registered Nurses	32,480
11. Bookkeeping, Accounting, and Auditing Clerks	31,770
12. First-Line Supervisors and Managers—Sales Workers	31,620
13. Receptionists and Information Clerks	31,250
14. Computer Programmers	30,130
15. Lawyers	28,620
16. Accountants and Auditors	25,230
17. Guards and Watch Guards	25,080
18. Elementary School Teachers	24,830
19. Combination Food Preparation and Service Workers	24,430
20. Management Analysts	24,090
21. Secondary School Teachers	23,320
22. General Utility Maintenance Repairers	20,620
23. Food Preparation Workers	19,410
24. Computer Engineers	19,110
25. Maids and Housekeeping Cleaners	18,430

Jobs with the Highest Earnings

Job	Annual Earnings
1. Dentists	$92,710
2. Physicians and Surgeons	$91,330
3. Aircraft Pilots and Flight Engineers	$88,190
4. Lawyers	$83,150
5. Podiatrists	$81,480
6. Chiropractors	$76,390
7. Optometrists	$75,780
8. Engineering, Mathematical, and Natural Sciences Managers	$72,950
9. Physicists and Astronomers	$72,210
10. Marine Architects	$70,490
11. General Managers and Top Executives	$69,960
12. Foresters and Conservation Scientists	$68,170
13. College and University Faculty (Law)	$66,380
14. Agricultural Engineers	$65,330
15. Aerospace Engineers	$65,110
16. Electrical and Electronic Engineers	$62,950
17. Medical Scientists	$62,950
18. Industrial Production Managers	$62,390
19. Financial Managers	$62,200
20. Chemists	$62,080
21. Veterinarians	$61,900
22. Atmospheric and Space Scientists	$61,820
23. Securities, Commodities, and Financial Services Sales Agents	$61,420
24. Systems Analysts	$61,140
25. Marketing, Advertising, and Public Relations Managers	$61,060

5. SAN FRANCISCO-OAKLAND-SAN JOSE, CA
Population 6,816,047

Jobs Employing the Most Workers

Job	Number Employed
1. General Managers and Top Executives	33,950
2. Retail Salespersons	33,470
3. General Office Clerks	30,520
4. Secretaries	21,770
5. Cashiers	18,690
6. Waiters and Waitresses	18,530
7. Bookkeeping, Accounting, and Auditing Clerks	17,860
8. First-Line Supervisors and Managers—Administrative Workers	16,750
9. Janitors and Cleaners	16,660
10. First-Line Supervisors and Managers—Sales Workers	14,220
11. Receptionists and Information Clerks	13,940
12. Combination Food Preparation and Service Workers	12,000
13. Accountants and Auditors	11,780
14. Registered Nurses	11,380
15. Guards and Watch Guards	9,970
16. Truck Drivers—Light	9,870
17. Elementary School Teachers	9,450
18. Shipping, Receiving, and Traffic Clerks	9,230
19. Food Preparation Workers	9,080
20. Lawyers	9,000
21. Computer Programmers	8,960
22. Sales Representatives	8,820
23. Financial Managers	8,780
24. Cooks, Restaurant	8,710
25. Maids and Housekeeping Cleaners	8,550

Jobs with the Highest Earnings

Job	Annual Earnings
1. Physicians and Surgeons	$107,320
2. Real Estate Brokers	$104,490
3. Judges and Magistrates	$99,780
4. Securities, Commodities, and Financial Services Sales Agents	$88,770
5. Lawyers	$87,210
6. Dentists	$83,470
7. Engineering, Mathematical, and Natural Sciences Managers	$82,740
8. Chemical Engineers	$82,490
9. General Managers and Top Executives	$79,680
10. Veterinarians	$77,710
11. Musicians, Instrumental	$77,360
12. Actuaries	$76,690
13. Financial Managers	$76,170
14. Financial Analysts	$74,730
15. Podiatrists	$73,440
16. Computer Engineers	$70,190
17. Sales Engineers	$68,230
18. Industrial Production Managers	$68,030
19. Construction Managers	$67,770
20. Marketing, Advertising, and Public Relations Managers	$67,150
21. Electrical and Electronic Engineers	$66,440
22. Police and Detective Supervisors	$66,290
23. Computer Programmers	$65,210
24. Civil Engineers	$64,750
25. Optometrists	$64,510

6. PHILADELPHIA-WILMINGTON-ATLANTIC CITY, PA-NJ-DE-MD
Population 5,988,348

Jobs Employing the Most Workers

Job	Number Employed
1. Retail Salespersons	75,290
2. General Managers and Top Executives	60,410
3. Cashiers	53,770
4. Secretaries	53,720
5. General Office Clerks	51,290
6. Registered Nurses	45,550
7. Janitors and Cleaners	38,200
8. Waiters and Waitresses	34,110
9. First-Line Supervisors and Managers—Administrative Workers	31,620
10. Bookkeeping, Accounting, and Auditing Clerks	30,320
11. First-Line Supervisors and Managers—Sales Workers	29,820
12. Elementary School Teachers	28,760
13. Nursing Aides, Orderlies, and Attendants	28,010
14. Receptionists and Information Clerks	25,570
15. Secondary School Teachers	24,620
16. Food Preparation Workers	23,590
17. Stock Clerks—Sales Floor	23,250
18. Truck Drivers—Light	22,590
19. Guards and Watch Guards	21,790
20. Shipping, Receiving, and Traffic Clerks	21,370
21. Combination Food Preparation and Service Workers	21,230
22. Accountants and Auditors	20,250
23. General Utility Maintenance Repairers	19,690
24. Sales Representatives	19,440
25. Truck Drivers—Heavy	18,970

Jobs with the Highest Earnings

Job	Annual Earnings
1. Dentists	$89,820
2. Lawyers	$75,910
3. Engineering, Mathematical, and Natural Sciences Managers	$69,950
4. General Managers and Top Executives	$69,000
5. Podiatrists	$67,790
6. Actuaries	$66,420
7. Mining, Quarrying, and Oil and Gas Well Drilling Managers	$64,540
8. College and University Faculty (Architecture)	$64,120
9. Physical Therapists	$62,260
10. Financial Managers	$61,940
11. Marketing, Advertising, and Public Relations Managers	$61,320
12. Aerospace Engineers	$60,700
13. College and University Faculty (Political Science)	$60,590
14. Architects	$60,250
15. Education Administrators	$59,380
16. Optometrists	$59,050
17. Industrial Production Managers	$59,020
18. College and University Faculty (Chemistry)	$58,840
19. Veterinarians	$58,460
20. Structural Metal Workers	$57,950
21. Pharmacists	$57,770
22. Financial Analysts	$57,740
23. Medical Scientists	$57,700
24. College and University Faculty (Physics)	$57,410
25. College and University Faculty (Anthropology and Sociology)	$57,370

7. BOSTON-WORCESTER-LAWRENCE, MA-NH-ME-CT Population 5,644,060

Jobs Employing the Most Workers

Job	Number Employed
1. General Managers and Top Executives	58,740
2. Retail Salespersons	55,950
3. Secretaries	45,200
4. General Office Clerks	44,680
5. Registered Nurses	42,900
6. Cashiers	40,400
7. Janitors and Cleaners	35,010
8. Waiters and Waitresses	32,770
9. First-Line Supervisors and Managers—Administrative Workers	26,820
10. Bookkeeping, Accounting, and Auditing Clerks	26,260
11. First-Line Supervisors and Managers—Sales Workers	25,610
12. Secondary School Teachers	22,450
13. Elementary School Teachers	21,960
14. Combination Food Preparation and Service Workers	19,640
15. Nursing Aides, Orderlies, and Attendants	18,630
16. Stock Clerks—Sales Floor	18,310
17. Accountants and Auditors	17,840
18. Receptionists and Information Clerks	17,200
19. Computer Engineers	17,060
20. Financial Managers	16,590
21. Sales Representatives	16,520
22. Guards and Watch Guards	15,770
23. Computer Programmers	15,490
24. Truck Drivers—Light	15,060
25. Computer Support Specialists	14,640

Jobs with the Highest Earnings

Job	Annual Earnings
1. Aircraft Pilots and Flight Engineers	$108,840
2. Physicians and Surgeons	$97,910
3. Dentists	$93,740
4. College and University Faculty (Law)	$91,050
5. Chiropractors	$88,450
6. Lawyers	$80,950
7. Medical Scientists	$80,510
8. Engineering, Mathematical, and Natural Sciences Managers	$79,610
9. College and University Faculty (Health Diagnostics)	$79,470
10. College and University Faculty (Business)	$79,420
11. General Managers and Top Executives	$78,360
12. Real Estate Brokers	$74,320
13. College and University Faculty (Economics)	$73,300
14. College and University Faculty (Political Science)	$71,720
15. Marketing, Advertising, and Public Relations Managers	$69,080
16. Financial Managers	$68,860
17. Management Analysts	$67,570
18. Computer Engineers	$66,770
19. College and University Faculty (Chemistry)	$66,180
20. Actuaries	$66,060
21. Securities, Commodities, and Financial Services Sales Agents	$65,670
22. College and University Faculty (Life Sciences)	$64,920
23. Personnel, Training, and Labor Relations Managers	$64,900
24. College and University Faculty (Physics)	$64,620
25. College and University Faculty (Engineering Teachers)	$64,410

8. DETROIT-ANN ARBOR-FLINT, MI
Population 5,457,583

Jobs Employing the Most Workers

Job	Number Employed
1. Retail Salespersons	62,560
2. Assemblers and Fabricators	46,030
3. General Office Clerks	44,390
4. Cashiers	43,770
5. General Managers and Top Executives	42,180
6. Secretaries	38,160
7. Registered Nurses	33,090
8. Janitors and Cleaners	30,140
9. Waiters and Waitresses	29,900
10. First-Line Supervisors and Managers— Sales Workers	24,250
11. Bookkeeping, Accounting, and Auditing Clerks	24,000
12. Combination Food Preparation and Service Workers	23,330
13. Hand Packers and Packagers	20,730
14. Sales Representatives	20,680
15. Elementary School Teachers	20,610
16. Stock Clerks—Sales Floor	20,510
17. Truck Drivers—Light	20,310
18. Receptionists and Information Clerks	19,840
19. First-Line Supervisors and Managers— Administrative Workers	18,650
20. Truck Drivers—Heavy	18,470
21. Food Preparation Workers	17,730
22. Nursing Aides, Orderlies, and Attendants	17,310
23. Secondary School Teachers	16,970
24. Shipping, Receiving, and Traffic Clerks	16,680
25. Guards and Watch Guards	16,040

Jobs with the Highest Earnings

Job	Annual Earnings
1. Podiatrists	$98,850
2. Physicians and Surgeons	$98,370
3. Dentists	$98,100
4. Broadcast News Analysts	$90,710
5. Chiropractors	$80,390
6. Judges and Magistrates	$79,970
7. Lawyers	$78,070
8. Engineering, Mathematical, and Natural Sciences Managers	$76,170
9. Optometrists	$72,110
10. Veterinarians	$71,220
11. General Managers and Top Executives	$71,070
12. Sales Agents, Real Estate	$70,470
13. Physicists and Astronomers	$69,720
14. College and University Faculty (Engineering Teachers)	$68,400
15. Industrial Production Managers	$65,840
16. Actuaries	$65,510
17. Sales Engineers	$64,700
18. Marketing, Advertising, and Public Relations Managers	$63,940
19. Construction Managers	$63,570
20. Pharmacists	$62,590
21. Financial Managers	$62,020
22. Real Estate Brokers	$61,820
23. Education Administrators	$61,730
24. Broadcast Technicians	$61,500
25. Communication, Transportation, and Utilities Operations Managers	$60,590

9. DALLAS-FORT WORTH, TX
Population 4,802,463

Jobs Employing the Most Workers

Job	Number Employed
1. General Managers and Top Executives	65,120
2. Retail Salespersons	52,340
3. General Office Clerks	49,410
4. Cashiers	41,440
5. Secretaries	34,980
6. First-Line Supervisors and Managers—Administrative Workers	27,100
7. Waiters and Waitresses	26,170
8. Bookkeeping, Accounting, and Auditing Clerks	25,520
9. Sales Representatives	24,980
10. Janitors and Cleaners	24,760
11. Elementary School Teachers	24,690
12. First-Line Supervisors and Managers—Sales Workers	23,760
13. Combination Food Preparation and Service Workers	23,730
14. Truck Drivers—Heavy	23,280
15. Receptionists and Information Clerks	20,830
16. Registered Nurses	20,660
17. Hand Packers and Packagers	19,430
18. Accountants and Auditors	19,360
19. Assemblers and Fabricators	19,280
20. Guards and Watch Guards	16,690
21. Shipping, Receiving, and Traffic Clerks	16,370
22. General Utility Maintenance Repairers	15,950
23. Truck Drivers—Light	15,310
24. Secondary School Teachers	15,170
25. Adjustment Clerks	14,680

Jobs with the Highest Earnings

Job	Annual Earnings
1. Physicians and Surgeons	$104,800
2. Dentists	$98,650
3. Lawyers	$79,020
4. Petroleum Engineers	$78,320
5. Mining, Quarrying, and Oil and Gas Well Drilling Managers	$75,870
6. Engineering, Mathematical, and Natural Sciences Managers	$75,090
7. Real Estate Brokers	$73,850
8. Actuaries	$70,320
9. Optometrists	$69,990
10. Geologists, Geophysicists, and Oceanographers	$69,320
11. Marketing, Advertising, and Public Relations Managers	$66,810
12. General Managers and Top Executives	$64,990
13. Electrical and Electronic Engineers	$64,990
14. Occupational Therapists	$64,720
15. Chemical Engineers	$64,070
16. Medical Scientists	$63,980
17. Aircraft Pilots and Flight Engineers	$63,400
18. Appraisers, Real Estate	$62,980
19. Aerospace Engineers	$61,950
20. Pharmacists	$61,900
21. Physical Therapists	$61,800
22. Industrial Production Managers	$61,460
23. Sales Engineers	$61,020
24. College and University Faculty (Business)	$60,580
25. Computer Engineers	$60,150

10. HOUSTON-GALVESTON-BRAZORIA, TX
Population 4,407,579

Jobs Employing the Most Workers

Job	Number Employed
1. General Managers and Top Executives	67,890
2. Retail Salespersons	52,890
3. Cashiers	46,980
4. General Office Clerks	46,860
5. Secretaries	40,600
6. Janitors and Cleaners	34,900
7. Combination Food Preparation and Service Workers	29,820
8. Waiters and Waitresses	27,230
9. Registered Nurses	26,220
10. Bookkeeping, Accounting, and Auditing Clerks	25,190
11. Secondary School Teachers	23,680
12. First-Line Supervisors and Managers— Sales Workers	23,580
13. Elementary School Teachers	23,070
14. Truck Drivers—Heavy	22,630
15. First-Line Supervisors and Managers— Administrative Workers	22,510
16. Receptionists and Information Clerks	21,770
17. Sales Representatives	20,800
18. Accountants and Auditors	19,670
19. General Utility Maintenance Repairers	17,530
20. Truck Drivers—Light	17,410
21. Guards and Watch Guards	17,340
22. Food Preparation Workers	16,140
23. Shipping, Receiving, and Traffic Clerks	15,230
24. Stock Clerks—Sales Floor	15,130
25. Landscaping and Groundskeeping Laborers	15,050

Jobs with the Highest Earnings

Job	Annual Earnings
1. Physicians and Surgeons	$107,120
2. Dentists	$92,120
3. Mining, Quarrying, and Oil and Gas Well Drilling Managers	$90,670
4. Lawyers	$87,120
5. Chiropractors	$82,510
6. Aircraft Pilots and Flight Engineers	$79,190
7. College and University Faculty (Law)	$79,080
8. Geologists, Geophysicists, and Oceanographers	$78,860
9. Petroleum Engineers	$76,570
10. Engineering, Mathematical, and Natural Sciences Managers	$74,980
11. Optometrists	$73,280
12. Judges and Magistrates	$72,530
13. Mining Engineers	$65,590
14. Chemical Engineers	$65,570
15. Medical Scientists	$64,950
16. Financial Managers	$64,740
17. Marketing, Advertising, and Public Relations Managers	$64,000
18. Financial Analysts	$63,590
19. General Managers and Top Executives	$63,220
20. College and University Faculty (Engineering Teachers)	$62,720
21. Broadcast News Analysts	$62,690
22. Physical Therapists	$62,560
23. Industrial Production Managers	$62,280
24. Mechanical Engineers	$62,070
25. Civil Engineers	$62,050

11. ATLANTA, GA
Population 3,746,059

Jobs Employing the Most Workers

Job	Number Employed
1. Retail Salespersons	35,380
2. General Managers and Top Executives	32,750
3. General Office Clerks	29,850
4. Cashiers	21,800
5. Registered Nurses	18,870
6. Secretaries	18,460
7. Combination Food Preparation and Service Workers	18,150
8. Bookkeeping, Accounting, and Auditing Clerks	16,150
9. First-Line Supervisors and Managers— Sales Workers	15,680
10. First-Line Supervisors and Managers— Administrative Workers	13,790
11. Waiters and Waitresses	13,420
12. Guards and Watch Guards	12,780
13. Sales Representatives	12,420
14. Janitors and Cleaners	12,270
15. Stock Clerks—Sales Floor	12,090
16. Receptionists and Information Clerks	11,930
17. Truck Drivers—Light	11,340
18. Shipping, Receiving, and Traffic Clerks	9,640
19. Stock Clerks—Stockroom and Warehouse	9,630
20. General Utility Maintenance Repairers	8,830
21. Nursing Aides, Orderlies, and Attendants	8,610
22. Accountants and Auditors	8,230
23. Maids and Housekeeping Cleaners	8,010
24. Food Preparation Workers	7,840
25. Truck Drivers—Heavy	7,380

Jobs with the Highest Earnings

Job	Annual Earnings
1. Dentists	$99,400
2. Physicians and Surgeons	$81,670
3. Actuaries	$80,830
4. Lawyers	$77,710
5. Broadcast News Analysts	$75,400
6. College and University Faculty (Business)	$70,680
7. Engineering, Mathematical, and Natural Sciences Managers	$65,750
8. College and University Faculty (Psychology)	$61,550
9. Police and Detective Supervisors	$61,470
10. Aircraft Pilots and Flight Engineers	$61,240
11. Veterinarians	$61,230
12. College and University Faculty (Communications)	$60,910
13. Interior Designers	$60,550
14. College and University Faculty (Life Sciences)	$60,310
15. Pharmacists	$60,230
16. Securities, Commodities, and Financial Services Sales Agents	$59,290
17. General Managers and Top Executives	$58,900
18. Medical Scientists	$58,160
19. College and University Faculty (Education)	$57,790
20. Optometrists	$57,760
21. Physical Therapists	$57,630
22. Physicists and Astronomers	$57,010
23. College and University Faculty (Foreign Language)	$56,550
24. Financial Managers	$56,440
25. Geologists, Geophysicists, and Oceanographers	$56,390

12. MIAMI-FORT LAUDERDALE, FL
Population 3,655,844

Jobs Employing the Most Workers

Job	Number Employed
1. Retail Salespersons	35,380
2. General Managers and Top Executives	32,750
3. General Office Clerks	29,850
4. Cashiers	21,800
5. Registered Nurses	18,870
6. Secretaries	18,460
7. Combination Food Preparation and Service Workers	18,150
8. Bookkeeping, Accounting, and Auditing Clerks	16,150
9. First-Line Supervisors and Managers—Sales Workers	15,680
10. First-Line Supervisors and Managers—Administrative Workers	13,790
11. Waiters and Waitresses	13,420
12. Guards and Watch Guards	12,780
13. Sales Representatives	12,420
14. Janitors and Cleaners	12,270
15. Stock Clerks—Sales Floor	12,090
16. Receptionists and Information Clerks	11,930
17. Truck Drivers—Light	11,340
18. Shipping, Receiving, and Traffic Clerks	9,640
19. Stock Clerks—Stockroom and Warehouse	9,630
20. General Utility Maintenance Repairers	8,830
21. Nursing Aides, Orderlies, and Attendants	8,610
22. Accountants and Auditors	8,230
23. Maids and Housekeeping Cleaners	8,010
24. Food Preparation Workers	7,840
25. Truck Drivers—Heavy	7,380

Jobs with the Highest Earnings

Job	Annual Earnings
1. Dentists	$99,400
2. Physicians and Surgeons	$81,670
3. Actuaries	$80,830
4. Lawyers	$77,710
5. Broadcast News Analysts	$75,400
6. College and University Faculty (Business)	$70,680
7. Engineering, Mathematical, and Natural Sciences Managers	$65,750
8. College and University Faculty (Psychology)	$61,550
9. Police and Detective Supervisors	$61,470
10. Aircraft Pilots and Flight Engineers	$61,240
11. Veterinarians	$61,230
12. College and University Faculty (Communications)	$60,910
13. Interior Designers	$60,550
14. College and University Faculty (Life Sciences)	$60,310
15. Pharmacists	$60,230
16. Securities, Commodities, and Financial Services Sales Agents	$59,290
17. General Managers and Top Executives	$58,900
18. Medical Scientists	$58,160
19. College and University Faculty (Education)	$57,790
20. Optometrists	$57,760
21. Physical Therapists	$57,630
22. Physicists and Astronomers	$57,010
23. College and University Faculty (Foreign Language)	$56,550
24. Financial Managers	$56,440
25. Geologists, Geophysicists, and Oceanographers	$56,390

13. SEATTLE-TACOMA-BREMERTON, WA
Population 3,424,361

Jobs Employing the Most Workers

Job	Number Employed
1. Retail Salespersons	47,150
2. General Managers and Top Executives	35,830
3. General Office Clerks	30,940
4. Cashiers	23,940
5. Combination Food Preparation and Service Workers	22,590
6. Bookkeeping, Accounting, and Auditing Clerks	20,430
7. Registered Nurses	18,930
8. Secretaries	18,900
9. First-Line Supervisors and Managers—Sales Workers	18,330
10. Waiters and Waitresses	17,610
11. Janitors and Cleaners	17,250
12. Receptionists and Information Clerks	16,240
13. First-Line Supervisors and Managers—Administrative Workers	15,480
14. Truck Drivers—Light	13,260
15. Sales Representatives	13,150
16. Computer Support Specialists	12,530
17. Truck Drivers—Heavy	12,250
18. Assemblers and Fabricators	11,330
19. Elementary School Teachers	11,210
20. Shipping, Receiving, and Traffic Clerks	11,190
21. Accountants and Auditors	10,800
22. Food Preparation Workers	10,780
23. Carpenters	10,300
24. Secondary School Teachers	10,290
25. Stock Clerks—Stockroom and Warehouse	9,720

Jobs with the Highest Earnings

Job	Annual Earnings
1. Dentists	$108,310
2. Physicists and Astronomers	$95,280
3. Optometrists	$93,990
4. Physicians and Surgeons	$87,880
5. Lawyers	$80,580
6. Judges and Magistrates	$73,790
7. Engineering, Mathematical, and Natural Sciences Managers	$71,070
8. Actuaries	$68,980
9. Marine Architects	$67,390
10. Real Estate Brokers	$68,970
11. General Managers and Top Executives	$67,060
12. Marine Engineers	$66,000
13. Fire Fighting and Prevention Supervisors	$65,380
14. Chemical Engineers	$65,310
15. Securities, Commodities, and Financial Services Sales Agents	$65,060
16. Dental Hygienists	$64,100
17. Water Vessel Captains	$62,740
18. Pharmacists	$62,310
19. Police and Detective Supervisors	$62,070
20. Computer Engineers	$61,310
21. Broadcast News Analysts	$59,890
22. Management Analysts	$59,760
23. Financial Managers	$59,460
24. Marketing, Advertising, and Public Relations Managers	$59,150
25. Music Directors, Singers, Composers, and Related Workers	$58,870

14. PHOENIX-MESA, AZ
Population 2,931,004

Jobs Employing the Most Workers

Job	Number Employed
1. Retail Salespersons	35,590
2. Cashiers	35,080
3. General Office Clerks	31,740
4. General Managers and Top Executives	30,210
5. Secretaries	26,690
6. Waiters and Waitresses	24,030
7. Janitors and Cleaners	22,070
8. First-Line Supervisors and Managers— Sales Workers	20,910
9. First-Line Supervisors and Managers— Administrative Workers	20,680
10. Receptionists and Information Clerks	19,560
11. Registered Nurses	18,990
12. Bookkeeping, Accounting, and Auditing Clerks	18,870
13. Combination Food Preparation and Service Workers	18,850
14. Landscaping and Groundskeeping Laborers	17,270
15. Elementary School Teachers	16,580
16. Truck Drivers—Heavy	15,600
17. Carpenters	15,230
18. Adjustment Clerks	15,040
19. Truck Drivers—Light	14,930
20. General Utility Maintenance Repairers	13,670
21. Sales Representatives	13,140
22. Stock Clerks—Sales Floor	12,570
23. Food Preparation Workers	12,230
24. Guards and Watch Guards	11,890
25. Secondary School Teachers	11,820

Jobs with the Highest Earnings

Job	Annual Earnings
1. Physicians and Surgeons	$110,930
2. Dentists	$102,450
3. Optometrists	$86,520
4. Podiatrists	$81,760
5. Lawyers	$78,330
6. Mining, Quarrying, and Oil and Gas Well Drilling Managers	$77,860
7. Engineering, Mathematical, and Natural Sciences Managers	$71,390
8. General Managers and Top Executives	$69,020
9. Industrial Production Managers	$68,410
10. Computer Engineers	$66,900
11. Electrical and Electronic Engineers	$65,860
12. Pharmacists	$63,870
13. Insurance Special Agents	$61,830
14. Sales Engineers	$61,750
15. Veterinarians	$61,270
16. Marketing, Advertising, and Public Relations Managers	$60,040
17. Financial Managers	$60,030
18. Actuaries	$59,410
19. Operations Research Analysts	$59,220
20. Dental Hygienists	$58,160
21. Chemical Engineers	$57,290
22. Industrial Engineers	$56,960
23. Computer Programmers	$56,790
24. Civil Engineers	$56,690
25. Architects	$56,650

15. CLEVELAND-AKRON, OH
Population 2,911,683

Jobs Employing the Most Workers

Job	Number Employed
1. Retail Salespersons	32,550
2. General Managers and Top Executives	31,940
3. General Office Clerks	26,410
4. Cashiers	25,430
5. Registered Nurses	23,720
6. Secretaries	21,850
7. Combination Food Preparation and Service Workers	19,010
8. Janitors and Cleaners	18,640
9. Assemblers and Fabricators	16,550
10. Waiters and Waitresses	16,360
11. First-Line Supervisors and Managers— Sales Workers	16,020
12. Bookkeeping, Accounting, and Auditing Clerks	15,900
13. Nursing Aides, Orderlies, and Attendants	12,500
14. Stock Clerks—Sales Floor	12,160
15. Sales Representatives	11,960
16. Shipping, Receiving, and Traffic Clerks	11,790
17. First-Line Supervisors and Managers— Administrative Workers	11,790
18. Truck Drivers—Light	11,220
19. Elementary School Teachers	11,210
20. Receptionists and Information Clerks	11,060
21. Truck Drivers—Heavy	10,810
22. General Utility Maintenance Repairers	10,630
23. Guards and Watch Guards	10,540
24. Secondary School Teachers	10,320
25. Hand Packers and Packagers	9,890

Jobs with the Highest Earnings

Job	Annual Earnings
1. Physicians and Surgeons	$102,540
2. Dentists	$93,610
3. Podiatrists	$80,050
4. Lawyers	$72,920
5. Real Estate Brokers	$70,840
6. Medical Scientists	$70,630
7. Engineering, Mathematical, and Natural Sciences Managers	$69,330
8. Physicists and Astronomers	$65,060
9. Nuclear Engineers	$64,100
10. Veterinarians	$64,000
11. Optometrists	$62,250
12. Pharmacists	$61,800
13. General Managers and Top Executives	$61,750
14. Marketing, Advertising, and Public Relations Managers	$60,350
15. Chemical Engineers	$59,910
16. Materials Engineers	$59,750
17. Chemists	$59,530
18. Industrial Production Managers	$58,920
19. Education Administrators	$58,820
20. Actuaries	$58,710
21. Safety Engineers	$57,710
22. Architects	$57,360
23. Financial Managers	$56,680
24. Chiropractors	$56,650
25. Computer Engineers	$56,620

16. MINNEAPOLIS-ST. PAUL, MN Population 2,831,234

Jobs Employing the Most Workers

Job	Number Employed
1. Retail Salespersons	53,450
2. General Managers and Top Executives	40,100
3. Cashiers	37,990
4. General Office Clerks	37,190
5. Waiters and Waitresses	29,970
6. Secretaries	27,160
7. Janitors and Cleaners	25,780
8. Registered Nurses	24,190
9. Bookkeeping, Accounting, and Auditing Clerks	22,590
10. First-Line Supervisors and Managers— Sales Workers	21,600
11. Sales Representatives	20,280
12. First-Line Supervisors and Managers— Administrative Workers	19,770
13. Secondary School Teachers	18,970
14. Receptionists and Information Clerks	18,330
15. Combination Food Preparation and Service Workers	17,840
16. Stock Clerks—Sales Floor	16,390
17. Elementary School Teachers	15,560
18. Assemblers and Fabricators	15,550
19. Truck Drivers—Heavy	15,000
20. Truck Drivers—Light	14,530
21. Nursing Aides, Orderlies, and Attendants	14,430
22. Systems Analysts	14,070
23. Accountants and Auditors	13,940
24. Shipping, Receiving, and Traffic Clerks	13,780
25. Food Preparation Workers	13,320

Jobs with the Highest Earnings

Job	Annual Earnings
1. Physicians and Surgeons	$104,580
2. Dentists	$85,970
3. College and University Faculty (Law)	$81,700
4. Lawyers	$74,350
5. Engineering, Mathematical, and Natural Sciences Managers	$72,220
6. General Managers and Top Executives	$69,710
7. Securities, Commodities, and Financial Services Sales Agents	$68,670
8. Chiropractors	$68,490
9. Real Estate Brokers	$67,620
10. Podiatrists	$67,260
11. Optometrists	$67,160
12. Physicists and Astronomers	$66,670
13. Marketing, Advertising, and Public Relations Managers	$66,570
14. Medical Scientists	$65,370
15. Financial Managers	$63,970
16. College and University Faculty (Economics)	$63,920
17. Actuaries	$62,560
18. Industrial Production Managers	$62,280
19. College and University Faculty (Life Sciences)	$62,110
20. Broadcast News Analysts	$61,300
21. Pharmacists	$61,130
22. Materials Engineers	$60,590
23. Chemical Engineers	$60,360
24. Education Administrators	$59,990
25. Computer Engineers	$59,970

17. SAN DIEGO, CA
Population 2,780,592

Jobs Employing the Most Workers

Job	Number Employed
1. Retail Salespersons	37,310
2. General Office Clerks	29,350
3. General Managers and Top Executives	28,350
4. Cashiers	24,760
5. Secretaries	20,880
6. Waiters and Waitresses	18,890
7. Janitors and Cleaners	17,420
8. Combination Food Preparation and Service Workers	17,310
9. Bookkeeping, Accounting, and Auditing Clerks	15,560
10. First-Line Supervisors and Managers— Administrative Workers	14,970
11. First-Line Supervisors and Managers— Sales Workers	14,950
12. Receptionists and Information Clerks	13,640
13. Elementary School Teachers	13,360
14. Landscaping and Groundskeeping Laborers	12,980
15. Food Preparation Workers	12,940
16. Registered Nurses	12,630
17. Stock Clerks—Sales Floor	12,530
18. Truck Drivers—Light	12,220
19. Carpenters	12,100
20. Guards and Watch Guards	11,260
21. Secondary School Teachers	10,670
22. Assemblers and Fabricators	10,440
23. General Utility Maintenance Repairers	9,720
24. Maids and Housekeeping Cleaners	9,000
25. Sales Representatives	8,300

Jobs with the Highest Earnings

Job	Annual Earnings
1. Physicians and Surgeons	$119,150
2. Dentists	$88,710
3. Engineering, Mathematical, and Natural Sciences Managers	$76,490
4. Lawyers	$75,050
5. Nuclear Engineers	$72,130
6. General Managers and Top Executives	$70,260
7. Broadcast News Analysts	$69,130
8. Psychologists	$69,110
9. Physicists and Astronomers	$68,150
10. Actuaries	$67,740
11. College and University Faculty (Geography)	$67,330
12. Pharmacists	$66,190
13. Chemical Engineers	$64,870
14. College and University Faculty (Life Sciences)	$64,300
15. Marketing, Advertising, and Public Relations Managers	$64,190
16. Aerospace Engineers	$63,570
17. Architects	$63,570
18. College and University Faculty (Economics)	$63,280
19. Materials Engineers	$61,870
20. Electrical and Electronic Engineers	$61,690
21. Optometrists	$61,690
22. Securities, Commodities, and Financial Services Sales Agents	$61,340
23. College and University Faculty (Recreation and Fitness Studies)	$61,180
24. College and University Faculty (Chemistry)	$61,180
25. Financial Managers	$61,120

18. ST. LOUIS, MO
Population 2,563,801

Jobs Employing the Most Workers

Job	Number Employed
1. General Managers and Top Executives	25,730
2. First-Line Supervisors and Managers—Sales Workers	24,700
3. Registered Nurses	23,550
4. Elementary School Teachers	17,160
5. Secondary School Teachers	11,890
6. Accountants and Auditors	9,790
7. Computer Programmers	7,050
8. Financial Managers	6,640
9. Physicians and Surgeons	5,840
10. Licensed Practical Nurses	5,680
11. Systems Analysts	5,560
12. Marketing, Advertising, and Public Relations Managers	4,970
13. Computer Support Specialists	4,450
14. Lawyers	4,280
15. Personnel, Training, and Labor Relations Specialists	4,010
16. Education Administrators	3,970
17. Vocational Education Teachers and Instructors	3,910
18. Preschool Teachers	3,880
19. Food Service and Lodging Managers	3,670
20. Teacher Assistants	3,660
21. Administrative Services Managers	3,600
22. Engineering, Mathematical, and Natural Sciences Managers	3,400
23. Special Education Teachers	3,250
24. Sports and Physical Training Instructors and Coaches	3,200
25. Emergency Medical Technicians	3,050

Jobs with the Highest Earnings

Job	Annual Earnings
1. Physicians and Surgeons	$108,060
2. Dentists	$102,350
3. Podiatrists	$101,210
4. Judges and Magistrates	$85,190
5. Dentists	$79,130
6. Engineering, Mathematical, and Natural Sciences Managers	$75,450
7. Lawyers	$73,500
8. Mining, Quarrying, and Oil and Gas Well Drilling Managers	$71,330
9. Optometrists	$69,490
10. Chiropractors	$68,810
11. Industrial Engineers	$67,530
12. General Managers and Top Executives	$64,440
13. Engineering, Mathematical, and Natural Sciences Managers	$64,120
14. Aerospace Engineers	$63,810
15. Industrial Production Managers	$62,140
16. Atmospheric and Space Scientists	$61,470
17. Pharmacists	$61,080
18. Chemical Engineers	$60,220
19. Architects	$60,210
20. College and University Faculty (Engineering Teachers)	$60,060
21. Financial Managers	$58,440
22. Construction Managers	$58,410
23. Systems Analysts	$58,370
24. Pharmacists	$58,280
25. Marketing, Advertising, and Public Relations Managers	$56,860

19. DENVER-BOULDER-GREELEY, CO
Population 2,365,345

Jobs Employing the Most Workers

Job	Number Employed
1. Retail Salespersons	39,180
2. General Office Clerks	30,390
3. General Managers and Top Executives	23,190
4. Cashiers	21,250
5. First-Line Supervisors and Managers—Sales Workers	19,010
6. First-Line Supervisors and Managers—Administrative Workers	18,100
7. Bookkeeping, Accounting, and Auditing Clerks	18,100
8. Waiters and Waitresses	17,950
9. Secretaries	17,910
10. Combination Food Preparation and Service Workers	16,220
11. Janitors and Cleaners	16,150
12. Registered Nurses	15,180
13. Receptionists and Information Clerks	14,270
14. Sales Representatives	14,030
15. Truck Drivers—Heavy	12,260
16. Truck Drivers—Light	11,230
17. Accountants and Auditors	11,130
18. Elementary School Teachers	9,670
19. Secondary School Teachers	9,420
20. Computer Programmers	9,070
21. Shipping, Receiving, and Traffic Clerks	8,540
22. General Utility Maintenance Repairers	8,330
23. Food Preparation Workers	8,110
24. Guards and Watch Guards	8,040
25. Cooks, Restaurant	7,850

Jobs with the Highest Earnings

Job	Annual Earnings
1. Physicians and Surgeons	$97,460
2. Optometrists	$90,330
3. Dentists	$88,690
4. Mining, Quarrying, and Oil and Gas Well Drilling Managers	$86,810
5. Real Estate Brokers	$86,430
6. Podiatrists	$82,890
7. Nuclear Engineers	$78,420
8. Petroleum Engineers	$77,100
9. General Managers and Top Executives	$75,270
10. Engineering, Mathematical, and Natural Sciences Managers	$74,750
11. Lawyers	$71,490
12. Economists	$70,950
13. Judges and Magistrates	$67,580
14. College and University Faculty (Physics)	$67,560
15. Psychologists	$67,460
16. Sales Engineers	$67,080
17. Financial Managers	$66,370
18. Geologists, Geophysicists, and Oceanographers	$66,090
19. College and University Faculty (Engineering Teachers)	$66,010
20. Physicists and Astronomers	$65,720
21. Insurance Special Agents	$64,650
22. Systems Analysts	$64,460
23. Mining Engineers	$63,060
24. Pharmacists	$62,970
25. Marketing, Advertising, and Public Relations Managers	$62,950

20. PITTSBURGH, PA
Population 2,346,153

Jobs Employing the Most Workers

Job	Number Employed
1. Retail Salespersons	33,930
2. Cashiers	28,450
3. General Managers and Top Executives	27,520
4. General Office Clerks	25,410
5. Secretaries	24,580
6. Registered Nurses	23,200
7. Waiters and Waitresses	20,780
8. Janitors and Cleaners	16,080
9. Elementary School Teachers	15,900
10. First-Line Supervisors and Managers— Sales Workers	14,350
11. Secondary School Teachers	14,290
12. Nursing Aides, Orderlies, and Attendants	12,960
13. First-Line Supervisors and Managers— Administrative Workers	12,890
14. Bookkeeping, Accounting, and Auditing Clerks	12,830
15. Food Preparation Workers	12,720
16. Stock Clerks—Sales Floor	12,410
17. General Utility Maintenance Repairers	10,560
18. Combination Food Preparation and Service Workers	10,520
19. Truck Drivers—Heavy	10,490
20. Receptionists and Information Clerks	10,290
21. Truck Drivers—Light	9,810
22. Assemblers and Fabricators	8,390
23. Guards and Watch Guards	8,280
24. Shipping, Receiving, and Traffic Clerks	8,170
25. Landscaping and Groundskeeping Laborers	7,980

Jobs with the Highest Earnings

Job	Annual Earnings
1. Physicians and Surgeons	$98,110
2. Actuaries	$79,260
3. Podiatrists	$78,180
4. Lawyers	$74,610
5. Dentists	$71,440
6. Judges and Magistrates	$70,090
7. Optometrists	$67,060
8. Engineering, Mathematical, and Natural Sciences Managers	$63,010
9. Nuclear Engineers	$62,460
10. General Managers and Top Executives	$60,760
11. Chiropractors	$60,040
12. Education Administrators	$59,810
13. College and University Faculty (Engineering Teachers)	$58,800
14. College and University Faculty (Computer Science)	$58,070
15. Management Analysts	$57,540
16. College and University Faculty (Physics)	$57,450
17. Veterinarians	$56,460
18. Securities, Commodities, and Financial Services Sales Agents	$56,340
19. College and University Faculty (History)	$54,890
20. College and University Faculty (Economics)	$54,740
21. College and University Faculty (Life Sciences)	$54,210
22. Marketing, Advertising, and Public Relations Managers	$53,990
23. Industrial Engineers	$53,650
24. College and University Faculty (Mathematics)	$53,510
25. Industrial Production Managers	$53,310

21. TAMPA-ST. PETERSBURG-CLEARWATER, FL
Population 2,256,559

Jobs Employing the Most Workers

Job	Number Employed
1. Retail Salespersons	32,100
2. General Office Clerks	29,320
3. General Managers and Top Executives	28,030
4. Cashiers	24,340
5. Secretaries	23,130
6. Registered Nurses	18,250
7. Waiters and Waitresses	17,880
8. First-Line Supervisors and Managers—Sales Workers	15,990
9. Combination Food Preparation and Service Workers	15,520
10. First-Line Supervisors and Managers—Administrative Workers	15,170
11. Receptionists and Information Clerks	14,680
12. Bookkeeping, Accounting, and Auditing Clerks	14,550
13. Janitors and Cleaners	12,570
14. Food Preparation Workers	11,320
15. Truck Drivers—Light	11,000
16. Sales Representatives	10,930
17. Nursing Aides, Orderlies, and Attendants	10,060
18. General Utility Maintenance Repairers	9,910
19. Elementary School Teachers	8,700
20. Shipping, Receiving, and Traffic Clerks	8,670
21. Secondary School Teachers	8,570
22. Accountants and Auditors	8,470
23. Hand Packers and Packagers	7,890
24. Truck Drivers—Heavy	7,880
25. Landscaping and Groundskeeping Laborers	7,180

Jobs with the Highest Earnings

Job	Annual Earnings
1. Physicians and Surgeons	$103,410
2. Chiropractors	$96,610
3. Podiatrists	$93,620
4. Dentists	$91,580
5. Lawyers	$74,170
6. College and University Faculty (Health Assessment and Treatment)	$68,530
7. Securities, Commodities, and Financial Services Sales Agents	$67,890
8. Engineering, Mathematical, and Natural Sciences Managers	$63,910
9. Aircraft Pilots and Flight Engineers	$62,910
10. Pharmacists	$62,720
11. Veterinarians	$61,350
12. General Managers and Top Executives	$60,700
13. Real Estate Brokers	$60,690
14. College and University Faculty (English Language and Literature)	$60,450
15. College and University Faculty (Engineering Teachers)	$60,350
16. Geologists, Geophysicists, and Oceanographers	$59,430
17. Actuaries	$59,180
18. Industrial Engineers	$58,680
19. Postmasters and Mail Superintendents	$57,950
20. Sales Engineers	$56,700
21. Computer Engineers	$56,420
22. Electrical and Electronic Engineers	$56,310
23. Financial Managers	$56,190
24. Police and Detective Supervisors	$56,040
25. College and University Faculty (Psychology)	$54,890

22. PORTLAND-SALEM, OR-WA
Population 2,149,056

Jobs Employing the Most Workers

Job	Number Employed
1. Retail Salespersons	31,110
2. General Office Clerks	22,670
3. Combination Food Preparation and Service Workers	18,720
4. General Managers and Top Executives	17,870
5. Cashiers	15,990
6. First-Line Supervisors and Managers— Sales Workers	15,420
7. Bookkeeping, Accounting, and Auditing Clerks	14,870
8. Secretaries	13,630
9. Janitors and Cleaners	12,910
10. Waiters and Waitresses	12,630
11. Truck Drivers—Heavy	12,470
12. Registered Nurses	12,060
13. Sales Representatives	10,530
14. Receptionists and Information Clerks	10,460
15. First-Line Supervisors and Managers— Administrative Workers	10,360
16. Elementary School Teachers	9,920
17. Assemblers and Fabricators	9,420
18. Secondary School Teachers	8,530
19. Food Preparation Workers	8,220
20. Shipping, Receiving, and Traffic Clerks	8,000
21. Carpenters	7,610
22. Nursing Aides, Orderlies, and Attendants	7,000
23. Cooks, Restaurant	6,650
24. Teacher Assistants	6,520
25. Stock Clerks—Sales Floor	6,500

Jobs with the Highest Earnings

Job	Annual Earnings
1. Physicians and Surgeons	$103,350
2. Dentists	$101,530
3. Engineering, Mathematical, and Natural Sciences Managers	$76,180
4. Lawyers	$70,440
5. College and University Faculty (Law)	$69,400
6. General Managers and Top Executives	$68,600
7. Securities, Commodities, and Financial Services Sales Agents	$67,150
8. Computer Engineers	$64,510
9. Sales Engineers	$63,900
10. Judges and Magistrates	$63,890
11. Dental Hygienists	$62,950
12. Actuaries	$62,120
13. Mechanical Engineers	$61,780
14. Police and Detective Supervisors	$61,320
15. Pharmacists	$61,310
16. College and University Faculty (Engineering Teachers)	$60,810
17. Marketing, Advertising, and Public Relations Managers	$60,590
18. Sales Representatives, Scientific and Related Products and Services	$60,470
19. Chemical Engineers	$60,140
20. Elevator Installers and Repairers	$59,690
21. Industrial Production Managers	$59,390
22. Electric Meter Installers and Repairers	$59,290
23. Communication, Transportation, and Utilities Operations Managers	$58,740
24. Computer Programmers	$58,400
25. Construction Managers	$58,320

23. CINCINNATI-HAMILTON, OH-KY-IN
Population 1,948,264

Jobs Employing the Most Workers

Job	Number Employed
1. Retail Salespersons	25,940
2. General Managers and Top Executives	23,000
3. Cashiers	19,820
4. General Office Clerks	19,420
5. Secretaries	16,130
6. Registered Nurses	13,810
7. Waiters and Waitresses	13,470
8. Combination Food Preparation and Service Workers	13,210
9. Janitors and Cleaners	12,650
10. First-Line Supervisors and Managers—Sales Workers	12,360
11. Food Preparation Workers	11,030
12. Hand Packers and Packagers	10,500
13. Bookkeeping, Accounting, and Auditing Clerks	10,330
14. Stock Clerks—Sales Floor	10,060
15. First-Line Supervisors and Managers—Administrative Workers	9,660
16. Truck Drivers—Light	9,230
17. Sales Representatives	8,860
18. Secondary School Teachers	8,680
19. Elementary School Teachers	8,680
20. Receptionists and Information Clerks	8,520
21. General Utility Maintenance Repairers	8,340
22. Truck Drivers—Heavy	8,230
23. Shipping, Receiving, and Traffic Clerks	7,970
24. Nursing Aides, Orderlies, and Attendants	7,670
25. Assemblers and Fabricators	6,630

Jobs with the Highest Earnings

Job	Annual Earnings
1. Podiatrists	$114,200
2. Physicians and Surgeons	$100,440
3. Dentists	$80,890
4. Lawyers	$76,370
5. Aerospace Engineers	$67,680
6. Chiropractors	$67,560
7. Musicians, Instrumental	$66,850
8. Engineering, Mathematical, and Natural Sciences Managers	$66,550
9. General Managers and Top Executives	$62,910
10. Optometrists	$62,150
11. Real Estate Brokers	$61,120
12. Pharmacists	$60,090
13. College and University Faculty (Life Sciences)	$59,700
14. Physical Therapists	$59,630
15. Marketing, Advertising, and Public Relations Managers	$59,200
16. Veterinarians	$58,760
17. Financial Managers	$58,410
18. Judges and Magistrates	$58,110
19. Operations Research Analysts	$58,030
20. Industrial Production Managers	$57,820
21. Chemical Engineers	$57,780
22. Industrial Engineers	$56,480
23. Civil Engineers	$56,030
24. Education Administrators	$55,820
25. Actuaries	$55,690

24. KANSAS CITY, MO-KS
Population 1,737,025

Jobs Employing the Most Workers

Job	Number Employed
1. Retail Salespersons	28,550
2. General Managers and Top Executives	22,630
3. General Office Clerks	22,330
4. Cashiers	19,780
5. Secretaries	17,780
6. First-Line Supervisors and Managers—Sales Workers	17,430
7. Registered Nurses	16,370
8. Waiters and Waitresses	15,010
9. Combination Food Preparation and Service Workers	13,940
10. Truck Drivers—Heavy	13,760
11. First-Line Supervisors and Managers—Administrative Workers	13,030
12. Janitors and Cleaners	12,960
13. Bookkeeping, Accounting, and Auditing Clerks	12,910
14. Receptionists and Information Clerks	10,070
15. Assemblers and Fabricators	10,050
16. Elementary School Teachers	9,870
17. Secondary School Teachers	9,500
18. Sales Representatives	9,460
19. Truck Drivers—Light	9,280
20. Hand Packers and Packagers	9,250
21. Stock Clerks—Sales Floor	9,220
22. Nursing Aides, Orderlies, and Attendants	8,500
23. Shipping, Receiving, and Traffic Clerks	8,190
24. General Utility Maintenance Repairers	8,130
25. Accountants and Auditors	7,990

Jobs with the Highest Earnings

Job	Annual Earnings
1. Physicians and Surgeons	$109,250
2. Dentists	$87,230
3. Optometrists	$68,670
4. Lawyers	$66,020
5. Engineering, Mathematical, and Natural Sciences Managers	$64,380
6. Aerospace Engineers	$64,200
7. Marketing, Advertising, and Public Relations Managers	$62,840
8. General Managers and Top Executives	$62,150
9. Purchasing Agents and Buyers, Farm Products	$61,300
10. Actuaries	$60,600
11. Sales Engineers	$60,180
12. Industrial Production Managers	$58,600
13. Communication, Transportation, and Utilities Operations Managers	$57,790
14. Pharmacists	$57,780
15. Financial Managers	$56,430
16. Economists	$56,420
17. Biological Scientists	$56,210
18. Education Administrators	$55,970
19. Sales Representatives, Scientific and Related Products	$55,460
20. Electrical and Electronic Engineers	$55,100
21. Industrial Engineers	$54,990
22. Judges and Magistrates	$54,940
23. Medicine and Health Services Managers	$54,190
24. Management Analysts	$54,090
25. Veterinarians	$53,860

25. SACRAMENTO-YOLO, CA Population 1,685,812

Jobs Employing the Most Workers

Job	Number Employed
1. General Office Clerks	19,880
2. Retail Salespersons	19,650
3. General Managers and Top Executives	16,270
4. Cashiers	15,160
5. Secretaries	11,310
6. Combination Food Preparation and Service Workers	10,520
7. Waiters and Waitresses	10,310
8. Bookkeeping, Accounting, and Auditing Clerks	10,110
9. Registered Nurses	10,000
10. First-Line Supervisors and Managers—Administrative Workers	9,720
11. First-Line Supervisors and Managers—Sales Workers	8,900
12. Elementary School Teachers	8,570
13. Janitors and Cleaners	7,680
14. Stock Clerks—Sales Floor	6,900
15. Landscaping and Groundskeeping Laborers	6,810
16. Secondary School Teachers	6,810
17. Receptionists and Information Clerks	6,670
18. Food Preparation Workers	6,330
19. Guards and Watch Guards	6,310
20. Carpenters	6,290
21. Truck Drivers—Light	5,990
22. General Utility Maintenance Repairers	5,300
23. Automotive Mechanics	4,820
24. Stock Clerks—Stockroom and Warehouse	4,780
25. Truck Drivers—Heavy	4,760

Jobs with the Highest Earnings

Job	Annual Earnings
1. Physicians and Surgeons	$116,820
2. Dentists	$107,520
3. Optometrists	$76,360
4. Lawyers	$73,750
5. Actuaries	$67,320
6. Real Estate Brokers	$65,520
7. Electrical and Electronic Engineers	$65,340
8. General Managers and Top Executives	$63,560
9. Psychologists	$63,190
10. Education Administrators	$62,730
11. Computer Engineers	$62,590
12. Pharmacists	$61,840
13. Marketing, Advertising, and Public Relations Managers	$60,700
14. Medicine and Health Services Managers	$60,390
15. Safety Engineers, Except Mining	$59,860
16. Police and Detective Supervisors	$59,850
17. Dental Hygienists	$59,420
18. Sales Engineers	$58,340
19. Chemical Engineers	$58,210
20. Physician Assistants	$57,950
21. Electrical Power-Line Installers and Repairers	$57,870
22. Construction Managers	$57,770
23. Foresters and Conservation Scientists	$57,630
24. Financial Managers	$57,400
25. Industrial Engineers	$56,860

26. MILWAUKEE-RACINE, WI
Population 1,645,924

Jobs Employing the Most Workers

Job	Number Employed
1. Retail Salespersons	24,210
2. General Managers and Top Executives	23,330
3. General Office Clerks	23,150
4. Cashiers	16,970
5. Secretaries	14,970
6. Janitors and Cleaners	14,350
7. Registered Nurses	13,690
8. Waiters and Waitresses	11,650
9. Nursing Aides, Orderlies, and Attendants	10,670
10. Sales Representatives	10,580
11. Combination Food Preparation and Service Workers	10,410
12. First-Line Supervisors and Managers— Sales Workers	10,160
13. Stock Clerks—Sales Floor	10,010
14. Bookkeeping, Accounting, and Auditing Clerks	9,830
15. Elementary School Teachers	9,070
16. First-Line Supervisors and Managers— Administrative Workers	8,950
17. Receptionists and Information Clerks	8,770
18. Shipping, Receiving, and Traffic Clerks	8,560
19. Food Preparation Workers	7,180
20. Secondary School Teachers	7,090
21. General Utility Maintenance Repairers	6,100
22. Accountants and Auditors	6,060
23. First-Line Supervisors and Managers/ Supervisors—Production and Operations	5,880
24. Guards and Watch Guards	5,380
25. Stock Clerks—Stockroom and Warehouse	5,320

Jobs with the Highest Earnings

Job	Annual Earnings
1. Physicians and Surgeons	$98,120
2. Insurance Special Agents	$75,270
3. Lawyers	$70,420
4. Securities, Commodities, and Financial Services Sales Agents	$69,780
5. Dentists	$69,370
6. College and University Faculty (Computer Science)	$68,000
7. Engineering, Mathematical, and Natural Sciences Managers	$66,010
8. Education Administrators	$64,700
9. Pharmacists	$63,420
10. Psychologists	$63,040
11. General Managers and Top Executives	$62,270
12. College and University Faculty (Physics)	$62,240
13. Actuaries	$62,030
14. Management Analysts	$59,410
15. Construction Managers	$58,310
16. Chemical Engineers	$57,740
17. Sales Agents and Placers, Insurance	$57,300
18. College and University Faculty (Chemistry)	$56,890
19. Postmasters and Mail Superintendents	$56,710
20. Physical Therapists	$56,700
21. Fire Fighting and Prevention Supervisors	$56,660
22. Electrical and Electronic Engineers	$56,360
23. Financial Managers	$56,260
24. Computer Engineers	$55,610
25. Sales Engineers	$54,810

27. NORFOLK-VIRGINIA BEACH-NEWPORT NEWS, VA-NC
Population 1,542,143

Jobs Employing the Most Workers

Job	Number Employed
1. Retail Salespersons	26,180
2. Cashiers	18,740
3. General Managers and Top Executives	16,670
4. General Office Clerks	13,710
5. Secretaries	13,200
6. Waiters and Waitresses	12,860
7. Registered Nurses	10,790
8. Janitors and Cleaners	10,460
9. Elementary School Teachers	10,410
10. Combination Food Preparation and Service Workers	9,710
11. First-Line Supervisors and Managers—Sales Workers	9,360
12. Bookkeeping, Accounting, and Auditing Clerks	9,000
13. First-Line Supervisors and Managers—Administrative Workers	8,430
14. Secondary School Teachers	8,210
15. Truck Drivers—Light	8,160
16. Receptionists and Information Clerks	7,190
17. Nursing Aides, Orderlies, and Attendants	7,130
18. Food Preparation Workers	6,340
19. General Utility Maintenance Repairers	6,240
20. Truck Drivers—Heavy	6,090
21. Maids and Housekeeping Cleaners	5,860
22. Guards and Watch Guards	5,560
23. Landscaping and Groundskeeping Laborers	5,170
24. Stock Clerks—Sales Floor	5,110
25. Cooks, Restaurant	4,590

Jobs with the Highest Earnings

Job	Annual Earnings
1. Podiatrists	$113,140
2. Dentists	$111,390
3. Physicians and Surgeons	$108,320
4. Lawyers	$73,080
5. College and University Faculty (Area Studies)	$72,740
6. College and University Faculty (Law)	$68,280
7. Physicists and Astronomers	$66,470
8. Optometrists	$65,680
9. Engineering, Mathematical, and Natural Sciences Managers	$64,430
10. College and University Faculty (Physics)	$63,920
11. Pharmacists	$63,410
12. Electrical and Electronic Engineers	$63,320
13. Chemical Engineers	$61,550
14. College and University Faculty (Engineering Teachers)	$60,360
15. College and University Faculty (Political Science)	$59,820
16. Architects	$59,240
17. Physical Therapists	$58,430
18. Water Vessel Captains	$57,500
19. Materials Engineers	$57,410
20. Pilots, Ship	$57,140
21. Medical Scientists	$56,980
22. Insurance Appraisers, Auto Damage	$56,760
23. Broadcast News Analysts	$55,660
24. Education Administrators	$55,240
25. Industrial Production Managers	$54,670

28. SAN ANTONIO, TX
Population 1,538,338

Jobs Employing the Most Workers

Job	Number Employed
1. Retail Salespersons	22,720
2. General Managers and Top Executives	18,960
3. Cashiers	16,800
4. Combination Food Preparation and Service Workers	16,010
5. General Office Clerks	15,510
6. Secretaries	13,290
7. Janitors and Cleaners	10,980
8. Registered Nurses	10,720
9. Guards and Watch Guards	10,490
10. Waiters and Waitresses	8,900
11. First-Line Supervisors and Managers— Sales Workers	8,680
12. First-Line Supervisors and Managers— Administrative Workers	8,310
13. Secondary School Teachers	8,300
14. Nursing Aides, Orderlies, and Attendants	8,250
15. Bookkeeping, Accounting, and Auditing Clerks	7,770
16. Elementary School Teachers	7,290
17. Truck Drivers—Heavy	7,030
18. Receptionists and Information Clerks	6,470
19. General Utility Maintenance Repairers	6,450
20. Truck Drivers—Light	5,810
21. Food Preparation Workers	5,670
22. Sales Representatives	5,500
23. Stock Clerks—Sales Floor	5,360
24. Licensed Practical Nurses	5,080
25. Maids and Housekeeping Cleaners	4,810

Jobs with the Highest Earnings

Job	Annual Earnings
1. Physicians and Surgeons	$107,260
2. Podiatrists	$98,150
3. Petroleum Engineers	$82,320
4. Optometrists	$80,400
5. Lawyers	$75,930
6. Dentists	$74,300
7. Judges and Magistrates	$71,450
8. Medical Scientists	$70,060
9. Mining, Quarrying, and Oil and Gas Well Drilling Managers	$68,540
10. Engineering, Mathematical, and Natural Sciences Managers	$67,540
11. Chemical Engineers	$60,710
12. Pharmacists	$59,540
13. College and University Faculty (Economics)	$59,460
14. Pharmacists	$59,380
15. Physical Therapists	$59,310
16. Education Administrators	$59,170
17. Veterinarians	$58,810
18. Geologists, Geophysicists, and Oceanographers	$57,710
19. Urban and Regional Planners	$57,580
20. Electrical and Electronic Engineers	$57,290
21. Mechanical Engineers	$56,980
22. College and University Faculty (Physics)	$56,630
23. Financial Managers	$56,610
24. Purchasing Agents and Buyers, Farm Products	$55,720
25. Industrial Engineers	$55,170

29. INDIANAPOLIS, IN
Population 1,519,194

Jobs Employing the Most Workers

Job	Number Employed
1. Retail Salespersons	26,600
2. General Office Clerks	22,910
3. Cashiers	21,170
4. General Managers and Top Executives	18,840
5. Waiters and Waitresses	14,290
6. Secretaries	14,210
7. Registered Nurses	13,950
8. Truck Drivers—Heavy	13,400
9. Combination Food Preparation and Service Workers	12,170
10. Janitors and Cleaners	12,040
11. First-Line Supervisors and Managers—Sales Workers	11,990
12. Bookkeeping, Accounting, and Auditing Clerks	11,190
13. Truck Drivers—Light	11,150
14. Sales Representatives	10,830
15. Stock Clerks—Sales Floor	9,610
16. Elementary School Teachers	9,210
17. First-Line Supervisors and Managers—Administrative Workers	8,850
18. Assemblers and Fabricators	8,410
19. Food Preparation Workers	7,810
20. Receptionists and Information Clerks	7,570
21. Shipping, Receiving, and Traffic Clerks	7,530
22. Secondary School Teachers	6,950
23. Nursing Aides, Orderlies, and Attendants	6,420
24. Accountants and Auditors	6,360
25. Guards and Watch Guards	6,250

Jobs with the Highest Earnings

Job	Annual Earnings
1. Physicians and Surgeons	$112,200
2. Podiatrists	$101,800
3. Dentists	$79,690
4. Optometrists	$73,670
5. General Managers and Top Executives	$68,250
6. Management Analysts	$67,310
7. Lawyers	$64,150
8. Engineering, Mathematical, and Natural Sciences Managers	$63,480
9. Veterinarians	$62,200
10. Marketing, Advertising, and Public Relations Managers	$61,480
11. Pharmacists	$60,540
12. Chiropractors	$60,230
13. Industrial Production Managers	$60,180
14. Physical Therapists	$58,350
15. Judges and Magistrates	$58,130
16. Materials Engineers	$57,890
17. Education Administrators	$57,550
18. Industrial Engineers	$57,480
19. Securities, Commodities, and Financial Services Sales Agents	$57,220
20. Sales Engineers	$56,520
21. Chemical Engineers	$55,950
22. Electrical and Electronic Engineers	$55,910
23. Actuaries	$55,740
24. Audio-Visual Specialists	$55,470
25. Financial Managers	$55,060

30. ORLANDO, FL
Population 1,504,569

Jobs Employing the Most Workers

Job	Number Employed
1. Retail Salespersons	30,850
2. General Office Clerks	21,260
3. Cashiers	20,970
4. General Managers and Top Executives	20,000
5. Waiters and Waitresses	19,750
6. Combination Food Preparation and Service Workers	19,550
7. Secretaries	15,980
8. Truck Drivers—Light	13,460
9. Maids and Housekeeping Cleaners	13,460
10. First-Line Supervisors and Managers—Sales Workers	12,620
11. Amusement and Recreation Attendants	12,400
12. Bookkeeping, Accounting, and Auditing Clerks	12,140
13. Janitors and Cleaners	11,170
14. Registered Nurses	11,120
15. Receptionists and Information Clerks	10,160
16. Guards and Watch Guards	10,050
17. First-Line Supervisors and Managers—Administrative Workers	9,890
18. Food Preparation Workers	8,800
19. Sales Representatives	8,200
20. Stock Clerks—Sales Floor	7,940
21. Cooks, Restaurant	7,770
22. Landscaping and Groundskeeping Laborers	7,570
23. General Utility Maintenance Repairers	7,300
24. Truck Drivers—Heavy	6,980
25. Hosts and Hostesses, Restaurant, Lounge, or Coffee Shop	6,530

Jobs with the Highest Earnings

Job	Annual Earnings
1. Dentists	$109,880
2. Physicians and Surgeons	$109,380
3. Chiropractors	$82,480
4. Lawyers	$82,430
5. Optometrists	$68,110
6. Veterinarians	$66,030
7. Pharmacists	$64,340
8. Computer Engineers	$63,990
9. Engineering, Mathematical, and Natural Sciences Managers	$63,590
10. College and University Faculty (Law)	$60,640
11. Real Estate Brokers	$60,400
12. College and University Faculty (History)	$58,370
13. College and University Faculty (Communications)	$58,270
14. General Managers and Top Executives	$57,750
15. College and University Faculty (Engineering Teachers)	$56,540
16. Civil Engineers	$55,940
17. Electrical and Electronic Engineers	$54,630
18. Sales Engineers	$54,520
19. College and University Faculty (Anthropology and Sociology)	$54,410
20. Occupational Therapists	$53,380
21. Physical Therapists	$53,340
22. Industrial Production Managers	$52,440
23. Education Administrators	$52,230
24. Architects	$52,000
25. Aerospace Engineers	$51,420

Part II

The Best Jobs Directory

Descriptions of the 500 Best Jobs for the 21st Century

This part provides descriptions for all the jobs included in one or more of the lists in Part I. While the book's introduction gives more details on how to use and interpret the job descriptions, here are the highlights, along with some additional information:

▲ The jobs described meet one of more of our criteria for inclusion in this book: average earnings of $40,000 or more a year, projected increase in the number of people employed in that occupation by 10 percent or more by 2008, and 100,000 or more job openings each year. Many good jobs do not meet one or more of these criteria, but we think the jobs that do are the best ones to consider in your career planning.

▲ The job descriptions are arranged in alphabetical order by job title. This approach allows you to quickly find a description if you know its correct title. If you are using this section to browse for interesting options, we suggest you begin with the table of contents. There you will find jobs listed within groupings of related jobs. This is a helpful way to quickly locate jobs most likely to interest you. Part I features many interesting lists that will also help you identify job titles to explore in more detail. If you have not browsed Part I's lists, consider spending some time there. The lists are interesting and will help you identify job titles you can find described in the material that follows.

▲ For the education information in this part, "O-J-T" stands for "on-the-job training." "Work experience, plus degree" means you need a bachelor's degree in addition to experience. See pages 64–76 for definitions of the various education requirements.

(continues)

(continued)

▲ When reviewing the descriptions, keep in mind that the jobs meet one or more of our criteria for pay, growth, and number of openings—but not necessarily all. For example, an occupation that has over 100,000 new openings a year would be included, even if its pay and growth rate are below average.

Well, you might ask, doesn't this mean that at least some "bad" jobs are described in this part. Our answer is yes and no. Some jobs with high scores for all measures, such as systems analyst—the job with the highest total for pay, growth, and number of openings—would be a very bad job for the people who dislike or are not good at that sort of work. On the other hand, many people love working as bread and pastry bakers, even though it has lower earnings, a lower projected growth rate, and fewer openings. Yet both jobs are described in the directory that follows.

Most likely, somewhere an ex-systems analyst works as a bread and pastry baker and loves it. Maybe this person likes the work better because of the physical activity and creating something you can see. Maybe the person likes the change of pace as a part-time job after doing the systems analyst gig as a day job. Maybe the person got tired of being a systems analyst and is making a transition to something else, such as owning a gourmet pastry shop. Or maybe the individual has found a way to make more money baking bread and pastries than as a systems analyst—some do.

So, the point is that each job is right for some people at the right time in their lives. We are all likely to change careers and jobs several times, and it's not always money that motivates us. So browse the job descriptions that follow and know that somewhere there is a good place for you. We hope you find it.

Accountants and Auditors

- ▲ Growth: 11%
- ▲ Annual Job Openings: 129,566
- ▲ Yearly Earnings: $37,860
- ▲ Education Required: Bachelor's degree
- ▲ Self-Employed: 10.6%
- ▲ Part-Time: 7.8%

Accountants

Analyze financial information and prepare financial reports to determine or maintain record of assets, liabilities, profit and loss, tax liability, or other financial activities within an organization. Prepares forms and manuals for workers performing accounting and bookkeeping tasks. Prepares balance sheet, profit and loss statement, amortization and depreciation schedules, and other financial reports, using calculator or computer. Reports finances of establishment to management. Advises management about resource utilization, tax strategies, and assumptions underlying budget forecasts. Analyzes records of financial transactions to determine accuracy and completeness of entries, using computer. Develops, maintains, and analyzes budgets. Prepares periodic reports comparing budgeted costs to actual costs. Develops, implements, modifies, and documents budgeting, cost, general, property, and tax accounting systems. Audits contracts and prepares reports to substantiate transactions prior to settlement. Predicts revenues and expenditures and submits reports to management. Appraises, evaluates, and inventories real property and equipment; records description, value, location, and other information. Adapts accounting and record keeping functions to current technology of computerized accounting systems. Directs activities of workers performing accounting and bookkeeping tasks. Computes taxes owed; ensures compliance with tax payment, reporting, and other tax requirements; and represents establishment before taxing authority. Surveys establishment operations to ascertain accounting needs. Uses computer to analyze operations, trends, costs, revenues, financial commitments, and obligations incurred, to project future revenues and expenses. Establishes table of accounts and assigns entries to proper accounts.

Personality Type: Conventional. Conventional occupations frequently involve following set procedures and routines. These occupations can include working with data and details more than with ideas. Usually there is a clear line of authority to follow.

Abilities: Number Facility—The ability to add, subtract, multiply, or divide quickly and correctly. Mathematical Reasoning—The ability to understand and organize a problem and then select a mathematical method or formula to solve the problem. Near Vision—The ability to see details of objects at a close range. Written Comprehension—The ability to read and understand information and ideas presented in writing. Written Expression—The ability to communicate information and ideas in writing so others will understand.

Skills: Mathematics—Using mathematics to solve problems. Information Gathering—Knowing how to find information and identifying essential information. Information Organization—Finding ways to structure or classify multiple pieces of information. Management of Financial Resources—Determining how money will be spent to get the work done, and accounting for these expenditures. Judgment and Decision Making—Weighing the relative costs and benefits of a potential action. Reading Comprehension—Understanding written information in work-related documents. Problem Identification—Identifying the nature of problems.

Generalized Work Activities: Analyzing Data or Information—Identifying underlying principles, reasons, or facts by breaking down information or data into separate parts. Getting Information Needed to Do the Job—Observing, receiving, and otherwise obtaining information from all relevant sources. Processing

Information—Compiling, coding, categorizing, calculating, tabulating, auditing, verifying, or processing information or data. Providing Consultation and Advice to Others—Providing consultation and expert advice to management or other groups on technical, systems-related, or process-related topics. Evaluating Information against Standards—Evaluating information against a set of standards and verifying that it is correct. Communicating with Other Workers—Providing information to supervisors, fellow workers, and subordinates. This information can be exchanged face-to-face, in writing, or via telephone/electronic transfer. Identifying Objects, Actions, and Events—Identifying information received by making estimates or categorizations, recognizing differences or similarities, or sensing changes in circumstances or events.

Auditors

Examine and analyze accounting records to determine financial status of establishment and prepare financial reports concerning operating procedures. Inspects account books and system for efficiency, effectiveness, and use of accepted accounting procedures to record transactions. Confers with company officials about financial and regulatory matters. Audits records to determine unemployment insurance premiums, liabilities, and compliance with tax laws. Reviews taxpayer accounts and conducts audits on-site, by correspondence, or by summoning taxpayer to office. Analyzes annual reports, financial statements, and other records, using accepted accounting and statistical procedures, to determine financial condition. Verifies journal and ledger entries by examining inventory. Evaluates taxpayer finances to determine tax liability, using knowledge of interest and discount, annuities, valuation of stocks and bonds, and amortization valuation of depletable assets. Inspects cash on hand, receivable and payable notes, negotiable securities, and canceled checks. Supervises auditing of establishments and determines scope of investigation required. Examines records, tax returns, and related documents pertaining to settlement of decedent's estate. Examines payroll and personnel records to determine worker's compensation coverage. Analyzes data for deficient controls, duplicated effort, extravagance, fraud, or noncompliance with laws, regulations, and management policies. Reports to management about asset utilization and audit results and recommends changes in operations and financial activities. Reviews data about material assets, net worth, liabilities, capital stock, surplus, income, and expenditures. Directs activities of personnel engaged in filing, recording, compiling, and transmitting financial records. Examines records and interviews workers to ensure recording of transactions and compliance with laws and regulations.

Personality Type: Conventional. Conventional occupations frequently involve following set procedures and routines. These occupations can include working with data and details more than with ideas. Usually there is a clear line of authority to follow.

Abilities: Number Facility—The ability to add, subtract, multiply, or divide quickly and correctly. Near Vision—The ability to see details of objects at a close range. Written Comprehension—The ability to read and understand information and ideas presented in writing. Problem Sensitivity—The ability to tell when something is wrong or is likely to go wrong. Does not involve solving the problem, only recognizing there is a problem. Mathematical Reasoning—The ability to understand and organize a problem and then select a mathematical method or formula to solve the problem.

Skills: Information Gathering—Knowing how to find information and identifying essential information. Mathematics—Using mathematics to solve problems. Problem Identification—Identifying the nature of problems. Information Organization—Finding ways to structure or classify multiple pieces of information. Critical Thinking—Using logic and analysis to identify the strengths and weaknesses of different approaches.

Generalized Work Activities: Getting Information Needed to Do the Job—Observing, receiving, and otherwise obtaining information from all relevant sources. Analyzing Data or Information—Identifying underlying principles, reasons, or facts by breaking down information or data into separate parts. Processing Information—Compiling, coding, categorizing, calculating, tabulating, auditing, verifying, or processing information or data. Providing Consultation and Advice

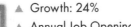

to Others—Providing consultation and expert advice to management or other groups on technical, systems-related, or process-related topics. Identifying Objects, Actions, and Events—Identifying information received by making estimates or categorizations, recognizing differences or similarities, or sensing changes in circumstances or events. Interpreting Meaning of Information to Others—Translating or explaining what information means and how it can be understood or used to support responses or feedback to others.

Actors, Directors, and Producers

- ▲ Growth: 24%
- ▲ Annual Job Openings: 31,279
- ▲ Yearly Earnings: $27,370
- ▲ Education Required: Long-term O-J-T
- ▲ Self-Employed: 23.7%
- ▲ Part-Time: 25.3%

Actors

Play parts in stage, television, radio, video, or motion picture productions for entertainment, information, or instruction. Interpret serious or comic role by speech, gesture, and body movement to entertain or inform audience. Dance and sing. Reads from script or book to narrate action, inform, or entertain audience, utilizing few or no stage props. Performs humorous and serious interpretations of emotions, actions, and situations, using only body movements, facial expressions, and gestures. Performs original and stock tricks of illusion to entertain and mystify audience, occasionally including audience members as participants. Tells jokes, performs comic dances and songs, impersonates mannerisms and voices of others, contorts face, and uses other devices to amuse audience. Prepares for and performs action stunts for motion picture, television, or stage production. Reads and rehearses role from script to learn lines, stunts, and cues as directed. Manipulates string, wire, rod, or fingers to animate puppet or dummy in synchronization to talking, singing, or recorded program. Portrays and interprets role—using speech, gestures, and body movements—to entertain radio, film, television, or live audience. Signals start and introduces performers to stimulate excitement and to coordinate smooth transition of acts during circus performance. Writes original or adapted material for drama, comedy, puppet show, narration, or other performance. Constructs puppets and ventriloquist dummies and sews accessory clothing using hand tools and machines. Sings or dances during dramatic or comedy performance. Dresses in comical clown costume and makeup and performs comedy routines to entertain audience.

Personality Type: Artistic. Artistic occupations frequently involve working with forms, designs, and patterns. They often require self-expression, and the work can be done without following a clear set of rules.

Abilities: Oral Expression—The ability to communicate information and ideas verbally so others will understand. Memorization—The ability to remember information such as words, numbers, pictures, and procedures. Originality—The ability to come up with unusual or clever ideas about a given topic or situation, or to develop creative ways to solve a problem. Speech Clarity—The ability to speak clearly so that what is said is understandable to a listener. Written Comprehension—The ability to read and understand information and ideas presented in writing.

Skills: Speaking—Talking to others to effectively convey information. Monitoring—Assessing how well one is doing when learning or doing something. Reading Comprehension—Understanding written information in work-related documents. Social Perceptiveness—Being aware of other people's reactions and understanding why people react the way they do. Active Learning—Working with new material or information to grasp its implications. Coordination—Adjusting actions in relation to others' actions.

Generalized Work Activities: Thinking Creatively—Originating, inventing, designing, or creating new applications, ideas, relationships, systems, or products, including artistic contributions. Performing for/Working with Public—Performing for people or dealing directly with the public, including serving persons in restaurants and stores and receiving clients or guests. Getting Information Needed to Do the Job—Observing, receiving, and otherwise obtaining information from all relevant sources. Performing General Physical Activities—Performing physical activities that require moving one's whole body, such as climbing, lifting, balancing, walking, and stooping. Performing activities that often also require considerable use of the arms and legs, such as in the physical handling of materials. Communicating with Persons Outside Organization—Communicating with persons outside the organization. Representing the organization to customers, the public, government, and other external sources. Exchanging information face-to-face, in writing, or via telephone/electronic transfer. Implementing Ideas and Programs—Conducting or carrying out work procedures and activities in accord with one's own ideas or information provided through directions/instructions for purposes of installing, modifying, preparing, delivering, constructing, integrating, finishing, or completing programs, systems, structures, or products. Communicating with Other Workers—Providing information to supervisors, fellow workers, and subordinates. This information can be exchanged face-to-face, in writing, or via telephone/electronic transfer.

Directors—Stage, Motion Pictures, Television, and Radio

Interpret script, conduct rehearsals, and direct activities of cast and technical crew for stage, motion pictures, television, or radio programs. Reviews educational material to gather information for scripts. Directs live broadcasts, films and recordings, or nonbroadcast programming for public entertainment or education. Directs cast, crew, and technicians during production or recording and filming in studio or on location. Establishes pace of program and sequences of scenes according to time requirements and cast and set accessibility. Cuts and edits film or tape to integrate component parts of film into desired sequence. Auditions and selects cast and technical staff. Approves equipment and elements required for production, such as scenery, lights, props, costumes, choreography, and music. Compiles cue words and phrases. Cues announcers, cast members, and technicians during performances. Interprets stage-set diagrams to determine stage layout. Supervises placement of equipment and scenery. Coaches performers in acting techniques to develop and improve performance and image. Confers with technical directors, managers, and writers to discuss details of production, such as photography, script, music, sets, and costumes. Reads and rehearses cast to develop performance based on script interpretations. Writes and compiles letters, memos, notes, scripts, and other program material, using computer.

Personality Type: Artistic. Artistic occupations frequently involve working with forms, designs, and patterns. They often require self-expression, and the work can be done without following a clear set of rules.

Abilities: Speech Clarity—The ability to speak clearly so that what is said is understandable to a listener. Oral Comprehension—The ability to listen to and understand information and ideas presented verbally. Written Comprehension—The ability to read and understand information and ideas presented in writing. Oral Expression—The ability to communicate information and ideas verbally so others will understand. Visualization—The ability to imagine how something will look after it is moved around or when its parts are moved or rearranged. Time Sharing—The ability to efficiently shift back and forth between two or more activities or sources of information such as speech, sounds, or touch.

Skills: Coordination—Adjusting actions in relation to others' actions. Speaking—Talking to others to effectively convey information. Reading Comprehension—Understanding written information in work-related documents. Management of Personnel Resources—Motivating, developing, and directing people as they work, identifying the best people for the job. Idea Evaluation—Evaluating the likely success of an idea in relation to the demands of the situation.

Generalized Work Activities: Communicating with Other Workers—Providing information to supervisors, fellow workers, and subordinates. This information can be exchanged face-to-face, in writing, or via telephone/electronic transfer. Scheduling Work and Activities—Scheduling events, programs, activities, and the work of others. Coordinating Work and Activities of Others—Coordinating members of a work group to accomplish tasks. Thinking Creatively—Originating, inventing, designing, or creating new applications, ideas, relationships, systems, or products, including artistic contributions. Making Decisions and Solving Problems—Combining, evaluating, and analyzing information and data to make decisions and solve problems. Involves making decisions about the relative importance of information and choosing the best solution. Staffing Organizational Units—Recruiting, interviewing, selecting, hiring, and promoting persons for the organization. Judging Qualities—Making judgments about or assessing the value, importance, or quality of things, services, or other people's work.

Producers

Plan and coordinate various aspects of radio, television, stage, or motion picture production, such as selecting script, coordinating writing, directing and editing, and arranging financing. Represents network or company in negotiations with independent producers. Conducts meetings with staff to discuss production progress and to ensure production objectives are attained. Reviews film, recordings, or rehearsals to ensure conformance to production and broadcast standards. Directs activities of one or more departments of motion picture studio. Prepares rehearsal call sheets and reports of activities and operating costs. Selects and hires cast and staff members and arbitrates personnel disputes. Produces shows for special occasions, such as holidays or testimonials. Obtains and distributes costumes, props, music, and studio equipment to complete production. Selects scenes from taped program to be used for promotional purposes. Distributes rehearsal call sheets and copies of script. Arranges for rehearsal quarters. Contacts cast members to verify readiness for rehearsal. Times scene and calculates program timing. Establishes management policies, production schedules, and operating budgets for production. Composes and edits script, or outlines story for screenwriter to write script. Coordinates various aspects of production, such as audio and camera work, music, timing, writing, and staging. Reads manuscript and selects play for stage performance.

Personality Type: Artistic. Artistic occupations frequently involve working with forms, designs, and patterns. They often require self-expression, and the work can be done without following a clear set of rules.

Abilities: Oral Expression—The ability to communicate information and ideas verbally so others will understand. Written Comprehension—The ability to read and understand information and ideas presented in writing. Written Expression—The ability to communicate information and ideas in writing so others will understand. Originality—The ability to come up with unusual or clever ideas about a given topic or situation, or to develop creative ways to solve a problem. Oral Comprehension—The ability to listen to and understand information and ideas presented verbally. Problem Sensitivity—The ability to tell when something is wrong or is likely to go wrong. Does not involve solving the problem, only recognizing there is a problem.

Skills: Coordination—Adjusting actions in relation to others' actions. Reading Comprehension—Understanding written information in work-related documents. Speaking—Talking to others to effectively convey information. Idea Generation—Generating a number of different approaches to problems.

Generalized Work Activities: Coordinating Work and Activities of Others—Coordinating members of a work group to accomplish tasks. Making Decisions and Solving Problems—Combining, evaluating, and analyzing information and data to make decisions and solve problems. Involves making decisions about the relative importance of information and choosing the best solution. Scheduling Work and Activities—Scheduling events, programs, activities, and the work of others. Communicating with Other Workers—Providing information to supervisors, fellow workers, and subordinates. This information can be exchanged face-to-face, in writing, or via telephone/electronic transfer. Staffing Organizational Units—Recruiting, interviewing, selecting, hiring, and promoting persons for the organization. Resolving Conflict, Negotiating with Others—Handling complaints, arbitrating disputes, resolving grievances, or otherwise negotiating with others. Getting Information Needed to Do the Job—Observing, receiving, and otherwise obtaining information from all relevant sources.

Program Directors

Direct and coordinate activities of personnel engaged in preparation of radio or television station program schedules and programs, such as sports or news. Coordinates activities between departments, such as news and programming. Plans and schedules programming and event coverage based on length of broadcast and available station or network time. Reviews, corrects, and advises member stations concerning programs and schedules. Confers with director and production staff to discuss issues, such as production and casting problems, budget, policy, and news coverage. Evaluates length, content, and suitability of programs for broadcast. Examines expenditures to ensure programming and broadcasting activities are within budget. Directs and coordinates activities of personnel engaged in broadcast news, sports, or programming. Writes news copy, notes, letters, and memos, using computer. Establishes work schedules and hires, assigns, and evaluates staff. Monitors and reviews news and programming copy and film, using audio or video equipment. Originates feature ideas and researches program topics for implementation. Directs setup of remote facilities and installs or cancels programs at remote stations.

Personality Type: Enterprising. Enterprising occupations frequently involve starting up and carrying out projects. These occupations can involve leading people

and making many decisions. They sometimes require risk taking and often deal with business.

Abilities: Oral Expression—The ability to communicate information and ideas verbally so others will understand. Near Vision—The ability to see details of objects at a close range. Written Expression—The ability to communicate information and ideas in writing so others will understand. Oral Comprehension—The ability to listen to and understand information and ideas presented verbally. Written Comprehension—The ability to read and understand information and ideas presented in writing.

Skills: Coordination—Adjusting actions in relation to others' actions. Management of Personnel Resources—Motivating, developing, and directing people as they work, identifying the best people for the job. Writing—Communicating effectively with others in writing as indicated by the needs of the audience. Reading Comprehension—Understanding written information in work-related documents. Implementation Planning—Developing approaches for implementing an idea.

Generalized Work Activities: Scheduling Work and Activities—Scheduling events, programs, activities, and the work of others. Identifying Objects, Actions, and Events—Identifying information received by making estimates or categorizations, recognizing differences or similarities, or sensing changes in circumstances or events. Making Decisions and Solving Problems—Combining, evaluating, and analyzing information and data to make decisions and solve problems. Involves making decisions about the relative importance of information and choosing the best solution. Guiding, Directing, and Motivating Subordinates—Providing guidance and direction to subordinates, including setting performance standards and monitoring subordinates. Organizing, Planning, and Prioritizing—Developing plans to accomplish work. Prioritizing and organizing one's own work. Judging Qualities—Making judgments about or assessing the value, importance, or quality of things, services, or other people's work. Monitoring and Controlling Resources—Monitoring and controlling resources and overseeing the spending of money.

Public Address System and Other Announcers

Make announcements over loud speaker at sporting or other public events. Act as master of ceremonies or disc jockey at weddings, parties, clubs, or other gathering places. Furnishes information concerning play to scoreboard operator. Speaks extemporaneously to audience on items of interest, such as background and history of event or past record of participants. Observes event to provide running commentary of activities, such as play-by-play description or explanation of official decisions. Provides information about event to cue operation of scoreboard or control board. Announces program and substitutions or other changes to patrons. Informs patrons of coming events or emergency calls. Reads prepared script to describe acts or tricks during performance.

Personality Type: Social. Social occupations frequently involve working with, communicating with, and teaching people. These occupations often involve helping or providing service to others.

Abilities: Speech Clarity—The ability to speak clearly so that what is said is understandable to a listener. Oral Expression—The ability to communicate information and ideas verbally so others will understand. Far Vision—The ability to see details at a distance. Selective Attention—The ability to concentrate and not be distracted while performing a task over a period of time. Written Comprehension—The ability to read and understand information and ideas presented in writing.

Skills: Speaking—Talking to others to effectively convey information. Reading Comprehension—Understanding written information in work-related documents. Social Perceptiveness—Being aware of other people's reactions and understanding why people react the way they do. Monitoring—Assessing how well one is doing when learning or doing something. Coordination—Adjusting actions in relation to others' actions.

Generalized Work Activities: Performing for/Working with Public—Performing for people or dealing directly with the public, including serving persons in restaurants and stores and receiving clients or guests. Getting Information Needed to Do the Job—Observing, receiving, and otherwise obtaining information from all relevant sources. Communicating with Persons Outside Organization—Communicating with persons outside the organization. Representing the organization to customers, the public, government, and other external sources. Exchanging information face-to-face, in writing, or via telephone/electronic transfer. Monitoring Processes, Materials, Surroundings—Monitoring and reviewing information from materials, events, or the environment, often to detect problems or to find out when things are finished. Identifying Objects, Actions, and Events—Identifying information received by making estimates or categorizations, recognizing differences or similarities, or sensing changes in circumstances or events.

Talent Directors

Audition and interview performers to select most appropriate talent for parts in stage, television, radio, or motion picture productions. Maintains talent file, including information about personalities, such as specialties, past performances, and availability. Selects performer or submits list of suitable performers to producer or director for final selection. Negotiates contract agreements with performers. Directs recording sessions for musical artists. Auditions and interviews performers to identify most suitable talent for broadcasting, stage, or musical production. Arranges for screen tests or auditions for new performers. Promotes record sales by personal appearances and contacts with broadcasting personalities.

Personality Type: Artistic. Artistic occupations frequently involve working with forms, designs, and patterns. They often require self-expression, and the work can be done without following a clear set of rules.

Abilities: Oral Expression—The ability to communicate information and ideas verbally so others will understand. Speech Clarity—The ability to speak clearly so that what is said is understandable to a listener. Memorization—The ability to remember information such as words, numbers, pictures, and procedures. Hearing

Sensitivity—The ability to detect or tell the difference between sounds that vary over broad ranges of pitch and loudness.

Skills: Speaking—Talking to others to effectively convey information. Negotiation—Bringing others together and trying to reconcile differences. Active Listening—Listening to what other people are saying; asking questions as appropriate. Writing—Communicating effectively with others in writing as indicated by the needs of the audience. Social Perceptiveness—Being aware of other people's reactions and understanding why people react the way they do. Reading Comprehension—Understanding written information in work-related documents.

Generalized Work Activities: Judging Qualities—Making judgments about or assessing the value, importance, or quality of things, services, or other people's work. Communicating with Persons Outside Organization—Communicating with persons outside the organization. Representing the organization to customers, the public, government, and other external sources. Exchanging information face-to-face, in writing, or via telephone/electronic transfer. Establishing and Maintaining Relationships—Developing constructive and cooperative working relationships with others. Resolving Conflict, Negotiating with Others—Handling complaints, arbitrating disputes, resolving grievances, or otherwise negotiating with others.

Technical Directors/ Managers

Coordinate activities of technical departments, such as taping, editing, engineering, and maintenance, to produce radio or television programs. Trains workers in use of equipment such as switcher, camera, monitor, microphones, and lights. Supervises and assigns duties to workers engaged in technical control and production of radio and television programs. Observes picture through monitor and directs camera and video staff concerning shading and composition. Monitors broadcast to ensure that programs conform with station or network policies and regulations. Directs personnel in auditioning talent and programs. Schedules use of studio and editing facilities for producers and engineering and maintenance staff. Coordinates activities of radio or television studio and control-room personnel to ensure technical quality of programs. Operates equipment to produce programs or to broadcast live programs from remote locations. Coordinates elements of program, such as audio, camera, special effects, timing, and script, to ensure production objectives are met.

Personality Type: Realistic. Realistic occupations frequently involve work activities that include practical, hands-on problems and solutions. They often deal with plants, animals, and real-world materials like wood, tools, and machinery. Many of the occupations require working outside and do not involve a lot of paperwork or working closely with others.

Abilities: Speech Clarity—The ability to speak clearly so that what is said is understandable to a listener. Oral Comprehension—The ability to listen to and understand information and ideas presented verbally. Oral Expression—The ability to communicate information and ideas verbally so others will understand. Selective Attention—The ability to concentrate and not be distracted while performing a task over a period of time. Time Sharing—The ability to efficiently shift back and forth between two or more activities or sources of information such as speech, sounds, or touch. Near Vision—The ability to see details of objects at a close range.

Skills: Coordination—Adjusting actions in relation to others' actions. Management of Personnel Resources—Motivating, developing, and directing people as they work, identifying the best people for the job. Speaking—Talking to others to effectively convey information. Operation Monitoring—Watching gauges, dials, or other indicators to make sure a machine is working properly. Operation and Control—Controlling operations of equipment or systems.

Generalized Work Activities: Scheduling Work and Activities—Scheduling events, programs, activities, and the work of others. Coordinating Work and Activities of Others—Coordinating members of a work group to accomplish tasks. Monitoring Processes, Materials, Surroundings—Monitoring and reviewing information from materials, events, or the environment, often to detect problems or to find out when things are finished. Guiding, Directing, and Motivating Subordinates— Providing guidance and direction to subordinates, including setting performance standards and monitoring subordinates. Communicating with Other Workers— Providing information to supervisors, fellow workers, and subordinates. This information can be exchanged face-to-face, in writing, or via telephone/electronic transfer. Judging Qualities—Making judgments about or assessing the value, importance, or quality of things, services, or other people's work. Making Decisions and Solving Problems—Combining, evaluating, and analyzing information and data to make decisions and solve problems. Involves making decisions about the relative importance of information and choosing the best solution.

Actuaries

- ▲ Growth: 7%
- ▲ Annual Job Openings: 1,712
- ▲ Yearly Earnings: $65,560
- ▲ Education Required: Bachelor's degree
- ▲ Self-Employed: 11.6%
- ▲ Part-Time: 5.2%

Actuaries

Analyze statistical data such as mortality, accident, sickness, disability, and retirement rates. Construct probability tables to forecast risk and liability for payment of future benefits. Ascertain premium rates required and cash reserves necessary to ensure payment of future benefits. Determines mortality, accident, sickness, disability, and retirement rates. Constructs probability tables regarding fire, natural disasters, and unemployment, based on analysis of statistical data and other pertinent information. Designs or reviews insurance and pension plans; calculates premiums. Ascertains premium rates required and cash reserves and liabilities necessary to ensure payment of future benefits. Determines equitable basis for distributing surplus earnings under participating insurance and annuity contracts in mutual companies.

Personality Type: Conventional. Conventional occupations frequently involve following set procedures and routines. These occupations can include working with data and details more than with ideas. Usually there is a clear line of authority to follow.

Abilities: Number Facility—The ability to add, subtract, multiply, or divide quickly and correctly. Mathematical Reasoning—The ability to understand and organize a problem and then select a mathematical method or formula to solve the problem. Deductive Reasoning— The ability to apply general rules to specific problems to come up with logical answers. Involves deciding if an answer makes sense. Written Comprehension—The ability to read and understand information and ideas presented in writing. Near Vision—The ability to see details of objects at a close range.

Skills: Mathematics—Using mathematics to solve problems. Information Organization—Finding ways to structure or classify multiple pieces of information. Information Gathering—Knowing how to find information and identifying essential information. Critical Thinking—Using logic and analysis to identify the strengths and weaknesses of different approaches.

Generalized Work Activities: Analyzing Data or Information—Identifying underlying principles, reasons, or facts by breaking down information or data into separate parts. Processing Information— Compiling, coding, categorizing, calculating, tabulating, auditing, verifying, or processing information or data.

Getting Information Needed to Do the Job—Observing, receiving, and otherwise obtaining information from all relevant sources. Evaluating Information against Standards—Evaluating information against a set of standards and verifying that it is correct. Judging Qualities—Making judgments about or assessing the value, importance, or quality of things, services, or other people's work. Making Decisions and Solving Problems—Combining, evaluating, and analyzing information and data to make decisions and solve problems. Involves making decisions about the relative importance of information and choosing the best solution.

Adjustment Clerks

- ▲ Growth: 34%
- ▲ Annual Job Openings: 141,670
- ▲ Yearly Earnings: $22,040
- ▲ Education Required: Short-term O-J-T
- ▲ Self-Employed: 0%
- ▲ Part-Time: 12.6%

Adjustment Clerks

Investigate and resolve customers' inquiries concerning merchandise, service, billing, or credit rating. Examine pertinent information to determine accuracy of customers' complaints and responsibility for errors. Notify customers and appropriate personnel of findings, adjustments, and recommendations such as exchange of merchandise, refund of money, credit to customers' accounts, or adjustment to customers' bills. Trains dealers or service personnel in construction of products, service operations, and customer service. Compares merchandise with original requisition and information on invoice and prepares invoice for returned goods. Prepares reports showing volume, types, and disposition of claims handled. Examines weather conditions and number of days in billing period; reviews meter accounts for errors which might explain high utility charges. Reviews claims adjustments with dealer, examines parts claimed to be defective, and approves or disapproves of dealer's claim. Notifies customer and designated personnel of findings and recommendations such as exchanging merchandise, refunding money, or adjusting bill. Orders tests to detect product malfunction and determines if defect resulted from faulty construction. Writes work order.

Personality Type: Conventional. Conventional occupations frequently involve following set procedures and routines. These occupations can include working with data and details more than with ideas. Usually there is a clear line of authority to follow.

Abilities: Oral Expression—The ability to communicate information and ideas verbally so others will understand. Oral Comprehension—The ability to listen to and understand information and ideas presented verbally. Written Comprehension—The ability to read and understand information and ideas presented in writing. Near Vision—The ability to see details of objects at a close range. Written Expression—The ability to communicate information and ideas in writing so others will understand. Deductive Reasoning—The ability to apply general rules to specific problems to come up with logical answers. Involves deciding if an answer makes sense.

Skills: Problem Identification—Identifying the nature of problems. Active Listening—Listening to what other people are saying; asking questions as appropriate. Information Gathering—Knowing how to find information and identifying essential information. Writing—Communicating effectively with others in writing as indicated by the needs of the audience. Reading Comprehension—Understanding written

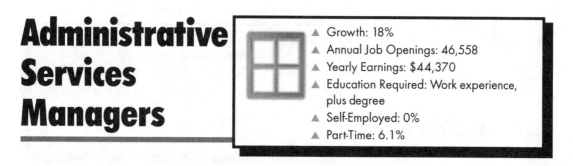

information in work-related documents. Speaking—Talking to others to effectively convey information.

Generalized Work Activities: Performing for/Working with Public—Performing for people or dealing directly with the public, including serving persons in restaurants and stores and receiving clients or guests. Getting Information Needed to Do the Job—Observing, receiving, and otherwise obtaining information from all relevant sources. Resolving Conflict, Negotiating with Others—Handling complaints, arbitrating disputes, resolving grievances, or otherwise negotiating with others. Communicating with Persons Outside Organization—Communicating with persons outside the organization. Representing the organization to customers, the public, government, and other external sources. Exchanging information face-to-face, in writing, or via telephone/electronic transfer. Documenting/Recording Information—Entering, transcribing, recording, storing, or maintaining information in either written form or by electronic/magnetic recording. Identifying Objects, Actions, and Events—Identifying information received by making estimates or categorizations, recognizing differences or similarities, or sensing changes in circumstances or events.

Administrative Services Managers

- ▲ Growth: 18%
- ▲ Annual Job Openings: 46,558
- ▲ Yearly Earnings: $44,370
- ▲ Education Required: Work experience, plus degree
- ▲ Self-Employed: 0%
- ▲ Part-Time: 6.1%

Administrative Services Managers

Plan, direct, or coordinate supportive services of an organization, such as recordkeeping, mail distribution, telephone operator/receptionist, and other office support services. Oversee facilities planning and maintenance and custodial operations. Prepares and reviews operational reports and schedules, to ensure accuracy and efficiency. Recommends cost saving methods such as supply changes and disposal of records to improve efficiency of department. Conducts classes to teach procedures to staff. Formulates budgetary reports. Analyzes internal processes and plans; implements procedural and policy changes to improve operations. Coordinates activities of clerical and administrative personnel in establishment or organization. Hires and terminates clerical and administrative personnel.

Personality Type: Enterprising. Enterprising occupations frequently involve starting up and carrying out projects. These occupations can involve leading people and making many decisions. They sometimes require risk taking and often deal with business.

Abilities: Oral Expression—The ability to communicate information and ideas verbally so others will understand. Speech Clarity—The ability to speak clearly so that what is said is understandable to a listener. Written Expression—The ability to communicate information and ideas in writing so others will understand. Oral Comprehension—The ability to listen to and understand information and ideas presented verbally. Written Comprehension—The ability to read and understand information and ideas presented in writing.

Skills: Writing—Communicating effectively with others in writing as indicated by the needs of the audience. Coordination—Adjusting actions in relation to others' actions. Judgment and Decision Making—Weighing the relative costs and benefits of a potential action. Management of Personnel Resources—Motivating, developing, and directing people as they work, identifying the best people for the job. Reading Comprehension—Understanding written information in work-related documents.

Generalized Work Activities: Communicating with Other Workers—Providing information to supervisors, fellow workers, and subordinates. This information can be exchanged face-to-face, in writing, or via telephone/electronic transfer. Getting Information Needed to Do the Job—Observing, receiving, and otherwise obtaining information from all relevant sources. Staffing

Organizational Units—Recruiting, interviewing, selecting, hiring, and promoting persons for the organization. Coordinating Work and Activities of Others—Coordinating members of a work group to accomplish tasks. Analyzing Data or Information—Identifying underlying principles, reasons, or facts by breaking down information or data into separate parts. Performing Administrative Activities—Approving requests, handling paperwork, and performing day-to-day administrative tasks. Providing Consultation and Advice to Others—Providing consultation and expert advice to management or other groups on technical, systems-related, or process-related topics.

Adult Education Instructors

- ▲ Growth: 21%
- ▲ Annual Job Openings: 46,224
- ▲ Yearly Earnings: $24,790
- ▲ Education Required: Work experience in a related occupation
- ▲ Self-Employed: 48.9%
- ▲ Part-Time: 42.5%

Adult Literacy, Remedial Education, and GED Teachers and Instructors

Teach or instruct out-of-school youths and adults in remedial education classes, preparatory classes for the General Educational Development test, literacy, or English as a second language. Teaching may or may not take place in a traditional educational institution. Plans course content and method of instruction. Administers oral, written, and performance tests and issues grades in accordance with performance. Prepares outline of instructional program, prepares lesson plans, and establishes course goals. Presents lectures and conducts discussions to increase students' knowledge and competence. Observes and evaluates students' work to determine progress and makes suggestions for

improvement. Adapts course of study and training methods to meet students' needs and abilities. Directs and supervises student project activities, performances, tournaments, exhibits, contests, or plays. Selects and assembles books, materials, and supplies for courses or projects. Confers with leaders of government and other groups to coordinate training or to assist students to fulfill required criteria. Maintains records such as student grades, attendance, and supply inventory. Writes instructional articles on designated subjects. Orders, stores, and inventories books, materials, and supplies. Evaluates success of instruction, based on number and enthusiasm of participants, and recommends retaining or eliminating course in future. Plans and conducts field trips to enrich instructional programs. Conducts classes, workshops, and demonstrations to teach principles, techniques, procedures, or methods of designated subject. Observes students to determine and evaluate qualifications, limitations, abilities, interests, aptitudes, temperament, and individual characteristics.

Personality Type: Social. Social occupations frequently involve working with, communicating with, and teaching people. These occupations often involve helping or providing service to others.

Abilities: Oral Expression—The ability to communicate information and ideas verbally so others will understand. Speech Clarity—The ability to speak clearly so that what is said is understandable to a listener. Written Expression—The ability to communicate information and ideas in writing so others will understand. Oral Comprehension—The ability to listen to and understand information and ideas presented verbally. Written Comprehension—The ability to read and understand information and ideas presented in writing.

Skills: Instructing—Teaching others how to do something. Speaking—Talking to others to effectively convey information. Learning Strategies—Using multiple approaches when learning or teaching new things. Active Listening—Listening to what other people are saying; asking questions as appropriate. Reading Comprehension—Understanding written information in work-related documents.

Generalized Work Activities: Teaching Others—Identifying educational needs, developing formal training programs or classes, and teaching or instructing others. Establishing and Maintaining Relationships—Developing constructive and cooperative working relationships with others. Communicating with Persons Outside Organization—Communicating with persons outside the organization. Representing the organization to customers, the public, government, and other external sources. Exchanging information face-to-face, in writing, or via telephone/electronic transfer. Coaching and Developing Others—Identifying developmental needs of others and coaching or otherwise helping others to improve their knowledge or skills. Getting Information Needed to Do the Job—Observing, receiving, and otherwise obtaining information from all relevant sources.

Self-Enrichment Education Teachers

Teach or instruct courses other than those that normally lead to an occupational objective or degree. Courses may include self-improvement, non-vocational, and nonacademic subjects. Teaching may or may not take place in a traditional educational institution. Directs and supervises student project activities, performances, tournaments, exhibits, contests, or plays. Confers with leaders of government and other groups to coordinate training or to assist students to fulfill required criteria. Administers oral, written, and performance tests and issues grades in accordance with performance. Prepares outline of instructional program, prepares lesson plans, and establishes course goals. Observes students to determine and evaluate qualifications, limitations, abilities, interests, aptitudes, temperament, and individual characteristics. Plans course content and method of instruction. Evaluates success of instruction, based on number and enthusiasm of participants, and recommends retaining or eliminating course in future. Writes instructional articles on designated subjects. Orders, stores, and inventories books, materials, and supplies. Plans and conducts field trips to enrich instructional programs. Selects and assembles books, materials, and supplies for courses or projects. Conducts classes, workshops, and demonstrations to teach principles, techniques, procedures, or methods of designated subject. Maintains records such as student grades, attendance, and supply inventory. Presents lectures and conducts discussions to increase students' knowledge and competence.

Personality Type: Social. Social occupations frequently involve working with, communicating with, and teaching people. These occupations often involve helping or providing service to others.

Abilities: Speech Clarity—The ability to speak clearly so that what is said is understandable to a listener. Oral Expression—The ability to communicate information and ideas verbally so others will understand. Written Expression—The ability to communicate information and ideas in writing so others will understand. Oral Comprehension—The ability to listen to and understand information and ideas presented verbally. Written Comprehension—The ability to read and understand information and ideas presented in writing.

Skills: Instructing—Teaching others how to do something. Speaking—Talking to others to effectively convey information. Learning Strategies—Using multiple approaches when learning or teaching new things. Active Listening—Listening to what other people are saying; asking questions as appropriate. Reading Comprehension—Understanding written information in work-related documents.

Generalized Work Activities: Teaching Others—Identifying educational needs, developing formal training programs or classes, and teaching or instructing others. Communicating with Persons Outside Organization—Communicating with persons outside the organization. Representing the organization to customers, the public, government, and other external sources. Exchanging information face-to-face, in writing, or via telephone/electronic transfer. Establishing and Maintaining Relationships—Developing constructive and cooperative working relationships with others. Coaching and Developing Others—Identifying developmental needs of others and coaching or otherwise helping others to improve their knowledge or skills. Getting Information Needed to Do the Job—Observing, receiving, and otherwise obtaining information from all relevant sources.

Advertising, Marketing, Promotions, Public Relations, and Sales Managers

- ▲ Growth: 23%
- ▲ Annual Job Openings: 89,237
- ▲ Yearly Earnings: $57,300
- ▲ Education Required: Work experience, plus degree
- ▲ Self-Employed: 2.4%
- ▲ Part-Time: 2.6%

Advertising and Promotions Managers

Plan and direct advertising policies and programs or produce collateral materials such as posters, contests, coupons, or giveaways, to create extra interest in the purchase of a product or service for a department, for an entire organization, or on an account basis. Contacts organizations to explain services and facilities offered or to secure props, audio visual materials, and sound effects. Inspects layouts and advertising copy and edits scripts, audio and video tapes, and other promotional material for adherence to specifications. Confers with department heads and/or staff to discuss topics such as contracts, selection of advertising media, or product to be advertised. Confers with clients to provide marketing or technical advice. Represents company at trade association meetings to promote products. Directs conversion of products from USA to foreign standards. Inspects premises of assigned stores for adequate security and compliance with safety codes and ordinances. Reads trade journals and professional literature to stay informed on trends, innovations, and changes that affect media planning. Coordinates activities of departments such as sales, graphic arts, media, finance, and research. Adjusts broadcasting schedules due to program cancellation. Plans and prepares advertising and promotional material. Formulates plans to extend business with established accounts and transacts business as agent for advertising accounts. Directs activities of workers engaged in developing and producing advertisements.

Monitors and analyzes sales promotion results to determine cost-effectiveness of promotion campaign. Supervises and trains service representatives. Consults publications to learn about conventions and social functions and organizes prospect files for promotional purposes. Directs product research and development. Plans and executes advertising policies of organization.

Personality Type: Artistic. Artistic occupations frequently involve working with forms, designs, and patterns. They often require self-expression, and the work can be done without following a clear set of rules.

Abilities: Oral Expression—The ability to communicate information and ideas verbally so others will understand. Originality—The ability to come up with unusual or clever ideas about a given topic or situation, or to develop creative ways to solve a problem. Fluency of Ideas—The ability to come up with a number of ideas about a given topic. Emphasis is on the number of ideas produced and not the quality, correctness, or creativity of the ideas. Written Expression—The ability to communicate information and ideas in writing so others will understand. Oral Comprehension—The ability to listen to and understand information and ideas presented verbally. Written Comprehension—The ability to read and understand information and ideas presented in writing.

Skills: Coordination—Adjusting actions in relation to others' actions. Idea Evaluation—Evaluating the likely success of an idea in relation to the demands of the situation. Time Management—Managing one's own time and the time of others. Implementation Planning —Developing approaches for implementing an idea. Idea Generation—Generating a number of different approaches to problems. Information Gathering—Knowing how to find information and identifying essential information. Reading Comprehension—Understanding written information in work-related documents.

Generalized Work Activities: Communicating with Other Workers—Providing information to supervisors, fellow workers, and subordinates. This information can be exchanged face-to-face, in writing, or via telephone/electronic transfer. Selling or Influencing Others—Convincing others to buy merchandise/goods, or otherwise changing their minds or actions. Making

Decisions and Solving Problems—Combining, evaluating, and analyzing information and data to make decisions and solve problems. Involves making decisions about the relative importance of information and choosing the best solution. Communicating with Persons Outside Organization—Communicating with persons outside the organization. Representing the organization to customers, the public, government, and other external sources. Exchanging information face-to-face, in writing, or via telephone/electronic transfer. Establishing and Maintaining Relationships—Developing constructive and cooperative working relationships with others. Organizing, Planning, and Prioritizing—Developing plans to accomplish work. Prioritizing and organizing one's own work. Coordinating Work and Activities of Others—Coordinating members of a work group to accomplish tasks.

Agents and Business Managers of Artists, Performers, and Athletes

Represent and promote artists, performers, and athletes to prospective employers. Handle contract negotiation and other business matters for clients. Schedules promotional or performance engagements for clients. Advises clients on financial and legal matters, such as investments and taxes. Manages business affairs for clients, such as obtaining travel and lodging accommodations, selling tickets, marketing and advertising, and paying expenses. Collects fees, commission, or other payment, according to contract terms. Hires trainer or coach to advise client on performance matters such as training techniques or presentation of act. Prepares periodic accounting statements for clients concerning financial affairs. Negotiates with manage-ment, promoters, union officials, and other persons to obtain contracts for clients such as entertainers, artists, and athletes. Obtains information and inspects facilities, equipment, and accommodations of potential performance venue. Conducts auditions or interviews new clients.

Personality Type: Enterprising. Enterprising occupations frequently involve starting up and carrying out projects. These occupations can involve leading people and making many decisions. They sometimes require risk taking and often deal with business.

Abilities: Oral Comprehension—The ability to listen to and understand information and ideas presented verbally. Oral Expression—The ability to communicate information and ideas verbally so others will understand. Speech Clarity—The ability to speak clearly so that what is said is understandable to a listener. Number Facility—The ability to add, subtract, multiply, or divide quickly and correctly. Written Comprehension—The ability to read and understand information and ideas presented in writing.

Skills: Negotiation—Bringing others together and trying to reconcile differences. Speaking—Talking to others to effectively convey information. Information Gathering—Knowing how to find information and identifying essential information. Coordination—Adjusting actions in relation to others' actions.

Generalized Work Activities: Resolving Conflict, Negotiating with Others—Handling complaints, arbitrating disputes, resolving grievances, or otherwise negotiating with others. Communicating with Persons Outside Organization—Communicating with persons outside the organization. Representing the organization to customers, the public, government, and other external sources. Exchanging information face-to-face, in writing, or via telephone/electronic transfer. Establishing and Maintaining Relationships—Developing constructive and cooperative working relationships with others. Organizing, Planning, and Prioritizing—Developing plans to accomplish work. Prioritizing and organizing one's own work. Scheduling Work and Activities—Scheduling events, programs, activities, and the work of others.

Marketing Managers

Determine the demand for products and services offered by a firm and its competitors and identify potential customers. Develop pricing strategies with the goal of maximizing the firm's profits or share of the market while ensuring that the firm's customers are satisfied. Oversee product development or monitor trends that indicate the need for new products and services. Confers with legal staff to resolve problems such as copyright infringement and royalty sharing with outside producers and distributors. Analyzes business developments and consults trade journals to monitor market trends and determine market opportunities for products. Coordinates promotional activities and shows to market products and services. Consults with buying personnel to gain advice regarding the types of products or services that are expected to be in demand. Advises business and other groups on local, national, and international factors affecting the buying and selling of products and services. Selects products and accessories to be displayed at trade or special production shows. Prepares report of marketing activities. Conducts economic and commercial surveys to identify potential markets for products and services. Coordinates and publicizes marketing activities to promote products and services. Develops marketing strategy based on knowledge of establishment policy, nature of market, and cost and markup factors. Compiles list describing product or service offerings and sets prices or fees.

Personality Type: Enterprising. Enterprising occupations frequently involve starting up and carrying out projects. These occupations can involve leading people and making many decisions. They sometimes require risk taking and often deal with business.

Abilities: Oral Expression—The ability to communicate information and ideas verbally so others will understand. Originality—The ability to come up with unusual or clever ideas about a given topic or situation, or to develop creative ways to solve a problem. Oral Comprehension—The ability to listen to and understand information and ideas presented verbally. Fluency of Ideas—The ability to come up with a number of ideas about a given topic. Emphasis is on the number of ideas produced and not the quality, correctness, or creativity of the ideas. Written Comprehension—The ability to read and understand information and ideas presented in writing.

Skills: Speaking—Talking to others to effectively convey information. Idea Generation—Generating a number of different approaches to problems. Visioning—Developing an image of how a system should work under ideal conditions. Active Listening—Listening to what other people are saying; asking questions as appropriate.

Generalized Work Activities: Getting Information Needed to Do the Job—Observing, receiving, and otherwise obtaining information from all relevant sources. Communicating with Other Workers— Providing information to supervisors, fellow workers, and subordinates. This information can be exchanged face-to-face, in writing, or via telephone/electronic transfer. Making Decisions and Solving Problems— Combining, evaluating, and analyzing information and data to make decisions and solve problems. Involves making decisions about the relative importance of information and choosing the best solution. Implementing Ideas and Programs—Conducting or carrying out work procedures and activities in accord with one's own ideas or information provided through directions/instructions for purposes of installing, modifying, preparing, delivering, constructing, integrating, finishing, or completing programs, systems, structures, or products. Communicating with Persons Outside Organization—Communicating with persons outside the organization. Representing the organization to customers, the public, government, and other external sources. Exchanging information face-to-face, in writing, or via telephone/electronic transfer. Providing Consultation and Advice to Others—Providing consultation and expert advice to management or other groups on technical, systems-related, or process-related topics. Analyzing Data or Information—Identifying underlying principles, reasons, or facts by breaking down information or data into separate parts.

Sales Managers

Direct the actual distribution or movement of a product or service to the customer. Coordinate sales distribution by establishing sales territories, quotas, and goals. Establish training programs for sales representatives. Analyze sales statistics gathered by staff to determine sales potential and inventory requirements and to monitor the preferences of customers. Inspects premises of assigned stores for adequate security exits and compliance with safety codes and ordinances. Plans and directs staffing, training, and

performance evaluations to develop and control sales and service programs. Reviews operational records and reports to project sales and determine profitability. Directs foreign sales and service outlets of organization. Directs clerical staff to maintain export correspondence, bid requests, credit collections, and current information on tariffs, licenses, and restrictions. Resolves customer complaints regarding sales and service. Directs, coordinates, and reviews activities in sales and service, accounting and record keeping, and receiving and shipping operations. Directs product research and development. Confers with potential customers regarding equipment needs and advises customers on types of equipment to purchase. Visits franchised dealers to stimulate interest in establishment or expansion of leasing programs. Advises dealers and distributors on policies and operating procedures to ensure functional effectiveness of business. Confers or consults with department heads to plan advertising services and to secure information on appliances, equipment, and customer-required specifications. Analyzes marketing potential of new and existing store locations, sales statistics, and expenditures to formulate policy. Directs and coordinates activities involving sales of manufactured goods, service outlets, technical services, operating retail chain, and advertising services for publication. Directs conversion of products from USA to foreign standards. Represents company at trade association meetings to promote products.

Personality Type: Enterprising. Enterprising occupations frequently involve starting up and carrying out projects. These occupations can involve leading people and making many decisions. They sometimes require risk taking and often deal with business.

Abilities: Oral Comprehension—The ability to listen to and understand information and ideas presented verbally. Written Comprehension—The ability to read and understand information and ideas presented in writing. Oral Expression—The ability to communicate information and ideas verbally so others will understand. Speech Clarity—The ability to speak clearly so that what is said is understandable to a listener. Mathematical Reasoning—The ability to understand and organize a problem and then select a mathematical method or formula to solve the problem.

Skills: Speaking—Talking to others to effectively convey information. Coordination—Adjusting actions in relation to others' actions. Problem Identification—Identifying the nature of problems. Time Management—Managing one's own time and the time of others. Critical Thinking—Using logic and analysis to identify the strengths and weaknesses of different approaches.

Generalized Work Activities: Selling or Influencing Others—Convincing others to buy merchandise/goods, or otherwise changing their minds or actions. Making Decisions and Solving Problems—Combining, evaluating, and analyzing information and data to make decisions and solve problems. Involves making decisions about the relative importance of information and choosing the best solution. Analyzing Data or

Information—Identifying underlying principles, reasons, or facts by breaking down information or data into separate parts. Getting Information Needed to Do the Job—Observing, receiving, and otherwise obtaining information from all relevant sources. Establishing and Maintaining Relationships—Developing constructive and cooperative working relationships with others. Communicating with Persons Outside Organization—Communicating with persons outside the organization. Representing the organization to customers, the public, government, and other external sources. Exchanging information face-to-face, in writing, or via telephone/electronic transfer. Staffing Organizational Units—Recruiting, interviewing, selecting, hiring, and promoting persons for the organization.

Aerospace Engineers

- ▲ Growth: 9%
- ▲ Annual Job Openings: 1,606
- ▲ Yearly Earnings: $66,950
- ▲ Education Required: Bachelor's degree
- ▲ Self-Employed: 1.8%
- ▲ Part-Time: 1.6%

Aerospace Engineers

Perform a variety of engineering work in designing, constructing, and testing aircraft, missiles, and spacecraft. Conduct basic and applied research to evaluate adaptability of materials and equipment to aircraft design and manufacture. Recommend improvements in testing equipment and techniques. Evaluates and approves selection of vendors by studying past performance and new advertisements. Evaluates product data and design from inspections and reports for conformance to engineering principles, customer requirements, and quality standards. Analyzes project requests and proposals and engineering data to determine feasibility, producibility, cost, and production time of aerospace or aeronautical product. Plans and coordinates activities concerned with investigating and resolving customers' reports of technical problems with aircraft or aerospace vehicles. Formulates mathematical

models or other methods of computer analysis to develop, evaluate, or modify design according to customer engineering requirements. Writes technical reports and other documentation such as handbooks and bulletins for use by engineering staff, management, and customers. Maintains records of performance reports for future reference. Reviews performance reports and documentation from customers and field engineers. Inspects malfunctioning or damaged products to determine problem. Directs and coordinates activities of engineering or technical personnel in designing, fabricating, modifying, or testing aircraft or aerospace products. Formulates conceptual design of aeronautical or aerospace products or systems to meet customer requirements. Develops design criteria for aeronautical or aerospace products or systems, including testing methods, production costs, quality standards, and completion dates. Directs research and development programs to improve production methods, parts, and equipment technology and to reduce costs. Plans and conducts experimental, environmental, operational, and stress tests on models and prototypes of aircraft and aerospace systems and equipment.

Personality Type: Investigative. Investigative occupations frequently involve working with ideas and require an extensive amount of thinking. These occupations can involve searching for facts and figuring out problems mentally.

Abilities: Written Comprehension—The ability to read and understand information and ideas presented in writing. Oral Expression—The ability to communicate information and ideas verbally so others will understand. Written Expression—The ability to communicate information and ideas in writing so others will understand. Number Facility—The ability to add, subtract, multiply, or divide quickly and correctly. Mathematical Reasoning—The ability to understand and organize a problem and then select a mathematical method or formula to solve the problem. Deductive Reasoning—The ability to apply general rules to specific problems to come up with logical answers. Involves deciding if an answer makes sense. Oral Comprehension—The ability to listen to and understand information and ideas presented verbally.

Skills: Science—Using scientific methods to solve problems. Mathematics—Using mathematics to solve problems. Active Learning—Working with new material or information to grasp its implications. Implementation Planning—Developing approaches for

implementing an idea. Technology Design—Generating or adapting equipment and technology to serve user needs. Reading Comprehension—Understanding written information in work-related documents. Testing—Conducting tests to determine whether equipment, software, or procedures are operating as expected.

Generalized Work Activities: Getting Information Needed to Do the Job—Observing, receiving, and otherwise obtaining information from all relevant sources. Identifying Objects, Actions, and Events—Identifying information received by making estimates or categorizations, recognizing differences or similarities, or sensing changes in circumstances or events. Monitoring Processes, Materials, Surroundings—Monitoring and reviewing information from materials, events, or the environment, often to detect problems or to find out when things are finished. Evaluating Information against Standards—Evaluating information against a set of standards and verifying that it is correct. Drafting and Specifying Technical Devices—Providing documentation, detailed instructions, drawings, or specifications to inform others about how devices, parts, equipment, or structures are to be fabricated, constructed, assembled, modified, maintained, or used. Updating and Using Job-Relevant Knowledge—Keeping up-to-date technically and knowing the functions of one's own job and related jobs. Thinking Creatively—Originating, inventing, designing, or creating new applications, ideas, relationships, systems, or products, including artistic contributions.

Agricultural and Food Scientists

▲ Growth: 11%

▲ Annual Job Openings: 1,639

▲ Yearly Earnings: $42,340

▲ Education Required: Bachelor's degree

▲ Self-Employed: 15.5%

▲ Part-Time: 6.6%

Animal Scientists

Conduct research in the genetics, nutrition, reproduction, growth, and development of domestic farm animals. Determines generic composition of animal population and heritability of traits, utilizing principles of genetics. Develops improved practices in feeding, housing, sanitation, and parasite and disease control of animals and poultry. Researches and controls selection and breeding practices to increase efficiency of production and improve quality of animals. Develops improved practices in incubation, brooding, and artificial insemination. Studies nutritional requirements of animals and nutritive value of feed materials for animals and poultry. Studies effects of management practices, processing methods, feed, and environmental conditions on quality and quantity of animal products such as eggs and milk. Crossbreeds animals with existing strains or crosses strains to obtain new combinations of desirable characteristics.

Personality Type: Investigative. Investigative occupations frequently involve working with ideas and require an extensive amount of thinking. These occupations can involve searching for facts and figuring out problems mentally.

Abilities: Deductive Reasoning—The ability to apply general rules to specific problems to come up with logical answers. Involves deciding if an answer makes sense. Inductive Reasoning—The ability to combine separate pieces of information, or specific answers to problems, to form general rules or conclusions. Includes coming up with a logical explanation for why a series of seemingly unrelated events occur together. Written Comprehension—The ability to read and understand information and ideas presented in writing. Oral Comprehension—The ability to listen to and understand information and ideas presented verbally. Written Expression—The ability to communicate information and ideas in writing so others will understand. Mathematical Reasoning—The ability to understand and organize a problem and then select a mathematical method or formula to solve the problem.

Skills: Science—Using scientific methods to solve problems. Information Gathering—Knowing how to find information and identifying essential information.

Active Learning—Working with new material or information to grasp its implications. Information Organization—Finding ways to structure or classify multiple pieces of information.

Generalized Work Activities: Making Decisions and Solving Problems—Combining, evaluating, and analyzing information and data to make decisions and solve problems. Involves making decisions about the relative importance of information and choosing the best solution. Getting Information Needed to Do the Job—Observing, receiving, and otherwise obtaining information from all relevant sources. Analyzing Data or Information—Identifying underlying principles, reasons, or facts by breaking down information or data into separate parts. Processing Information—Compiling, coding, categorizing, calculating, tabulating, auditing, verifying, or processing information or data. Identifying Objects, Actions, and Events—Identifying information received by making estimates or categorizations, recognizing differences or similarities, or sensing changes in circumstances or events.

Food Scientists and Technologists

Use chemistry, microbiology, engineering, and other sciences to study the principles underlying the processing and deterioration of foods. Analyze food content to determine levels of vitamins, fat, sugar, and protein. Discover new food sources. Research ways to make processed foods safe, palatable, and healthful. Apply food science knowledge to determine best ways to process, package, preserve, store, and distribute food. Confers with process engineers, flavor experts, and packaging and marketing specialists to resolve problems in product development. Tests new products in test kitchen. Develops new and improved methods and systems for food processing, production, quality control, packaging, and distribution. Develops food standards, safety and sanitary regulations, and waste management and water supply specifications. Studies methods to improve physical, chemical, and microbiological composition of foods. Conducts research on new products and development of foods, applying scientific and engineering principles. Studies methods to improve quality of foods, such as flavor, color, texture, nutritional value, and convenience.

Personality Type: Investigative. Investigative occupations frequently involve working with ideas and require an extensive amount of thinking. These occupations can involve searching for facts and figuring out problems mentally.

Abilities: Written Comprehension—The ability to read and understand information and ideas presented in writing. Oral Comprehension—The ability to listen to and understand information and ideas presented verbally. Deductive Reasoning—The ability to apply general rules to specific problems to come up with logical answers. Involves deciding if an answer makes sense. Inductive Reasoning—The ability to combine separate pieces of information, or specific answers to problems, to form general rules or conclusions. Includes coming up with a logical explanation for why a series of seemingly unrelated events occur together. Oral Expression—The ability to communicate information and ideas verbally so others will understand. Written Expression—The ability to communicate information and ideas in writing so others will understand. Number Facility—The ability to add, subtract, multiply, or divide quickly and correctly.

Skills: Science—Using scientific methods to solve problems. Product Inspection—Inspecting and evaluating the quality of products. Active Learning—Working with new material or information to grasp its implications.

Generalized Work Activities: Identifying Objects, Actions, and Events—Identifying information received by making estimates or categorizations, recognizing differences or similarities, or sensing changes in circumstances or events. Analyzing Data or Information—Identifying underlying principles, reasons, or facts by breaking down information or data into separate parts. Making Decisions and Solving Problems—Combining, evaluating, and analyzing information and data to make decisions and solve problems. Involves making decisions about the relative importance of information and choosing the best solution. Judging Qualities—Making judgments about or assessing the value, importance, or quality of things, services, or other people's work.

Getting Information Needed to Do the Job—Observing, receiving, and otherwise obtaining information from all relevant sources.

Plant Scientists

Conduct research in breeding, production, and yield of plants or crops and in control of pests. Studies insect distribution and habitat and recommends methods to prevent importation and spread of injurious species. Experiments to develop new or improved varieties of products having specific features such as higher yield, resistance to disease, size, or maturity. Studies crop production to discover effects of various climatic and soil conditions on crops. Aids in control and elimination of agricultural, structural, and forest pests by developing new and improved pesticides. Conducts experiments regarding causes of bee diseases and factors affecting yields of nectar pollen on various plants visited by bees. Conducts experiments and investigations to determine methods of storing, processing, and transporting horticultural products. Develops methods for control of noxious weeds, crop diseases, and insect pests. Identifies and classifies species of insects and allied forms such as mites and spiders. Conducts research to determine best methods of planting, spraying, cultivating, and harvesting horticultural products. Improves bee strains, utilizing selective breeding by artificial insemination.

Personality Type: Investigative. Investigative occupations frequently involve working with ideas and require an extensive amount of thinking. These occupations can involve searching for facts and figuring out problems mentally.

Abilities: Written Comprehension—The ability to read and understand information and ideas presented in writing. Oral Comprehension—The ability to listen to and understand information and ideas presented verbally. Deductive Reasoning—The ability to apply general rules to specific problems to come up with logical answers. Involves deciding if an answer makes sense. Inductive Reasoning—The ability to combine separate pieces of information, or specific answers to problems, to form general rules or conclusions. Includes coming up with a logical explanation for why a series of seemingly unrelated events occur together. Information Ordering—The ability to correctly follow a given rule or set of rules in order to arrange things or actions in a certain order. The things or actions can include numbers, letters, words, pictures, procedures, sentences, and mathematical or logical operations.

Skills: Science—Using scientific methods to solve problems. Information Gathering—Knowing how to find information and identifying essential information. Reading Comprehension—Understanding written information in work-related documents. Critical Thinking—Using logic and analysis to identify the strengths and weaknesses of different approaches. Information Organization—Finding ways to structure or classify multiple pieces of information. Writing—Communicating effectively with others in writing as indicated by the needs of the audience. Problem Identification—Identifying the nature of problems.

Generalized Work Activities: Identifying Objects, Actions, and Events—Identifying information received by making estimates or categorizations, recognizing differences or similarities, or sensing changes in circumstances or events. Analyzing Data or Information—Identifying underlying principles, reasons, or facts by breaking down information or data into separate parts. Processing Information—Compiling, coding, categorizing, calculating, tabulating, auditing, verifying, or processing information or data. Getting Information Needed to Do the Job—Observing, receiving, and otherwise obtaining information from all relevant sources. Updating and Using Job-Relevant Knowledge—Keeping up-to-date technically and knowing the functions of one's own job and related jobs. Making Decisions and Solving Problems—Combining, evaluating, and analyzing information and data to make decisions and solve problems. Involves making decisions about the relative importance of information and choosing the best solution.

Soil Scientists

Research or study soil characteristics, map soil types, and investigate responses of soils to known management practices to determine use capabilities of soils and effects of alternative practices on soil productivity. Performs chemical analysis on microorganism content of soil to determine microbial reactions and chemical mineralogical relationship to plant growth. Conducts experiments on farms or experimental stations to determine best soil types for different plants. Studies soil characteristics and classifies soils according to standard types. Investigates responses of specific soil types to soil management practices such as fertilization, crop rotation, and industrial waste control. Provides advice on rural or urban land use.

Personality Type: Investigative. Investigative occupations frequently involve working with ideas and require an extensive amount of thinking. These occupations can involve searching for facts and figuring out problems mentally.

Abilities: Deductive Reasoning—The ability to apply general rules to specific problems to come up with logical answers. Involves deciding if an answer makes sense. Inductive Reasoning—The ability to combine separate pieces of information, or specific answers to problems, to form general rules or conclusions. Includes coming up with a logical explanation for why a series of seemingly unrelated events occur together. Written Comprehension—The ability to read and understand information and ideas presented in writing. Category Flexibility—The ability to produce many rules so that each rule tells how to group or combine a set of things in a different way. Mathematical Reasoning—The ability to understand and organize a problem and then select a mathematical method or formula to solve the problem.

Skills: Science—Using scientific methods to solve problems. Information Gathering—Knowing how to find information and identifying essential information. Critical Thinking—Using logic and analysis to identify the strengths and weaknesses of different approaches. Reading Comprehension—Understanding written information in work-related documents. Information Organization—Finding ways to structure or classify multiple pieces of information.

Generalized Work Activities: Identifying Objects, Actions, and Events—Identifying information received by making estimates or categorizations, recognizing

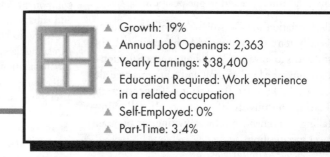

differences or similarities, or sensing changes in circumstances or events. Analyzing Data or Information—Identifying underlying principles, reasons, or facts by breaking down information or data into separate parts. Getting Information Needed to Do the Job—Observing, receiving, and otherwise obtaining information from all relevant sources. Making Decisions and Solving Problems—Combining, evaluating, and analyzing information and data to make decisions and solve problems. Involves making decisions about the relative importance of information and choosing the best solution. Processing Information—Compiling, coding, categorizing, calculating, tabulating, auditing, verifying, or processing information or data. Implementing Ideas and Programs—Conducting or carrying out work procedures and activities in accord with one's own ideas or information provided through directions/instructions for purposes of installing, modifying, preparing, delivering, constructing, integrating, finishing, or completing programs, systems, structures, or products. Monitoring Processes, Materials, Surroundings—Monitoring and reviewing information from materials, events, or the environment, often to detect problems or to find out when things are finished.

Aircraft Assemblers

- ▲ Growth: 19%
- ▲ Annual Job Openings: 2,363
- ▲ Yearly Earnings: $38,400
- ▲ Education Required: Work experience in a related occupation
- ▲ Self-Employed: 0%
- ▲ Part-Time: 3.4%

Aircraft Rigging Assemblers

Fabricate and assemble aircraft tubing or cable components or assemblies. Swages fittings onto cable, using swaging machine. Verifies dimensions of cable assembly and position of fittings, using measuring instruments. Repairs and reworks defective assemblies. Measures, cuts, and inspects cable and tubing, using master template, measuring instruments, and cable cutter or saw. Assembles and attaches fittings onto cable and tubing components, using hand tools. Welds tubing and fittings and solders cable ends, using tack-welder, induction brazing chamber, or other equipment. Forms loops or splices in cables, using clamps and fittings, or reweaves cable strands. Fabricates cable templates. Cleans, lubricates, and coats tubing and cable assemblies. Marks identifying information on tubing or cable assemblies, using electrochemical etching device, label, rubber stamp, or other methods. Tests tubing and cable assemblies for defects, using pressure testing equipment and proofloading machines. Selects and installs accessories in swaging machine, using hand tools. Marks location of cutouts, holes, and trim lines of parts and relationship of parts, using measuring instruments. Sets up and operates machines and systems to crimp, cut, bend, form, swage, flare, bead, burr, and straighten tubing according to specifications. Reads and interprets blueprints, work orders, data charts, and specifications to determine operations and to determine type, quantity, dimensions, configuration, and finish of tubing, cable, and fittings.

Personality Type: Realistic. Realistic occupations frequently involve work activities that include practical, hands-on problems and solutions. They often deal with plants, animals, and real-world materials like wood, tools, and machinery. Many of the occupations require working outside and do not involve a lot of paperwork or working closely with others.

Abilities: Manual Dexterity—The ability to quickly make coordinated movements of one hand, a hand together with its arm, or two hands, to grasp, manipulate, or assemble objects. Written Comprehension—The ability to read and understand information and ideas presented in writing. Near Vision—The ability to see details of objects at a close range. Control Precision—The ability to quickly and repeatedly make precise adjustments in moving the controls of a machine or vehicle to exact positions. Arm-Hand Steadiness—The ability to keep the hand and arm steady while making an arm movement or while holding the arm and hand in one position.

Skills: Operation and Control—Controlling operations of equipment or systems. Mathematics—Using mathematics to solve problems. Equipment Selection—Determining the kind of tools and equipment needed to do a job. Product Inspection—Inspecting and evaluating the quality of products. Installation—Installing equipment, machines, wiring, or programs to meet specifications.

Generalized Work Activities: Handling and Moving Objects—Using one's hands and arms in handling, installing, forming, positioning, and moving materials, or in manipulating things. Includes the use of keyboards. Inspecting Equipment, Structures, Materials—Inspecting or diagnosing equipment, structures, or materials to identify the causes of errors or other problems or defects. Controlling Machines and Processes—Using either control mechanisms or direct physical activity to operate machines or processes. Does not involve working with computers or vehicles. Implementing Ideas and Programs—Conducting or carrying out work procedures and activities in accord with one's own ideas or information provided through directions/instructions for purposes of installing, modifying, preparing, delivering, constructing, integrating, finishing, or completing programs, systems, structures, or products. Getting Information Needed to Do the Job—Observing, receiving, and otherwise obtaining information from all relevant sources.

Aircraft Structure Assemblers, Precision

Assemble tail, wing, fuselage, or other structural section of aircraft, space vehicles, and missiles from parts, subassemblies, and components. Install functional units, parts, or equipment, such as landing gear, control surfaces, doors, and floorboards. Inspects and tests installed units, parts, and equipment for fit, performance, and compliance with standards, using measuring instruments and test equipment. Bolts, screws, or rivets accessories to fasten, support, or hang components and subassemblies. Drills holes in structure and subassemblies. Attaches brackets, hinges, or clips to secure installation or to fasten subassemblies. Cuts, trims, and files parts. Verifies fitting tolerances to prepare for installation. Aligns structural assemblies. Installs units, parts, equipment, and components in structural assembly, according to blueprints and specifications, using hand tools and power tools. Locates and marks reference points and holes for installation of parts and components, using jigs, templates, and measuring instruments. Positions and aligns subassemblies in jigs or fixtures, using measuring instruments, following blueprint lines and index points.

Personality Type: Realistic. Realistic occupations frequently involve work activities that include practical, hands-on problems and solutions. They often deal with plants, animals, and real-world materials like wood, tools, and machinery. Many of the occupations require working outside and do not involve a lot of paperwork or working closely with others.

Abilities: Arm-Hand Steadiness—The ability to keep the hand and arm steady while making an arm movement or while holding the arm and hand in one position. Visualization—The ability to imagine how something will look after it is moved around or when its parts are moved or rearranged. Manual Dexterity—The ability to quickly make coordinated movements of one hand, a hand together with its arm, or two hands, to grasp, manipulate, or assemble objects. Extent Flexibility—The ability to bend, stretch, twist, or reach out with the body, arms, and/or legs. Information Ordering—The ability to correctly follow a given rule or set of rules in order to arrange things or actions in a certain order. The things or actions can include numbers, letters, words, pictures, procedures, sentences, and mathematical or logical operations. Finger Dexterity—The ability to make precisely coordinated movements of the fingers of one or both hands to grasp, manipulate, or assemble very small objects.

Skills: Installation—Installing equipment, machines, wiring, or programs to meet specifications. Equipment Selection—Determining the kind of tools and equipment needed to do a job. Mathematics—Using mathematics to solve problems. Product Inspection—Inspecting and evaluating the quality of products. Troubleshooting—Determining what is causing an operating error and deciding what to do about it.

Generalized Work Activities: Handling and Moving Objects—Using one's hands and arms in handling, installing, forming, positioning, and moving materials, or in manipulating things. Includes the use of keyboards. Inspecting Equipment, Structures, Materials—Inspecting or diagnosing equipment, structures, or materials to identify the causes of errors or other problems or defects. Implementing Ideas and Programs—Conducting or carrying out work procedures and activities in accord with one's own ideas or information provided through directions/instructions for purposes of installing, modifying, preparing, delivering, constructing, integrating, finishing, or completing programs, systems, structures, or products. Getting Information Needed to Do the Job—Observing, receiving, and otherwise obtaining information from all relevant sources. Controlling Machines and Processes—Using either control mechanisms or direct physical activity to operate machines or processes. Does not involve working with computers or vehicles. Identifying Objects, Actions, and Events—Identifying information received by making estimates or categorizations, recognizing differences or similarities, or sensing changes in circumstances or events.

Aircraft Systems Assemblers, Precision

Lay out, assemble, install, and test aircraft systems, such as armament, environmental control, plumbing, and hydraulic. Measures, drills, files, cuts, bends, and smoothes materials to ensure fit and clearance of parts. Assembles and installs parts, fittings, and assemblies on aircraft, using layout tools, hand tools, power tools, and fasteners. Lays out location of parts and assemblies according to specifications. Cleans, oils, assembles, and attaches system components to aircraft, using hand tools, power tools, and measuring instruments. Reads and interprets blueprints, illustrations, and specifications to determine layout, sequence of operations, or identity and relationship of parts. Reworks, replaces, realigns, and adjusts parts and assemblies according to specifications. Installs mechanical linkages and actuators. Verifies tension of cables, using tensiometer. Tests systems and assemblies for functional performance. Adjusts, repairs, or replaces malfunctioning units or parts. Aligns, fits, and assembles system components such as armament, structural, and mechanical components, using jigs, fixtures, measuring instruments, hand tools, and power tools. Examines parts for defects and for conformance to specifications, using precision measuring instruments.

Personality Type: Realistic. Realistic occupations frequently involve work activities that include practical, hands-on problems and solutions. They often deal with plants, animals, and real-world materials like wood, tools, and machinery. Many of the occupations require working outside and do not involve a lot of paperwork or working closely with others.

Abilities: Manual Dexterity—The ability to quickly make coordinated movements of one hand, a hand together with its arm, or two hands, to grasp, manipulate, or assemble objects. Arm-Hand Steadiness—The ability to keep the hand and arm steady while making an arm movement or while holding the arm and hand in one position. Written Comprehension—The ability to read and understand information and ideas presented in writing. Visualization—The ability to imagine how something will look after it is moved around or when its parts are moved or rearranged. Information Ordering—The ability to correctly follow a given rule or set of rules in order to arrange things or actions in a certain order. The things or actions can include numbers, letters, words, pictures, procedures, sentences, and mathematical or logical operations.

Skills: Product Inspection—Inspecting and evaluating the quality of products. Equipment Maintenance—Performing routine maintenance and determining when and what kind of maintenance is needed. Troubleshooting—Determining what is causing an operating error and deciding what to do about it. Installation—Installing equipment, machines, wiring, or programs to meet specifications. Equipment Selection—Determining the kind of tools and equipment needed to do a job. Testing—Conducting tests to determine whether equipment, software, or procedures are operating as expected.

Generalized Work Activities: Handling and Moving Objects—Using one's hands and arms in handling, installing, forming, positioning, and moving materials, or in manipulating things. Includes the use of keyboards.

Implementing Ideas and Programs—Conducting or carrying out work procedures and activities in accord with one's own ideas or information provided through directions/instructions for purposes of installing, modifying, preparing, delivering, constructing, integrating, finishing, or completing programs, systems, structures, or products. Performing General Physical Activities—Performing physical activities that require moving one's whole body, such as climbing, lifting, balancing, walking, and stooping. Performing activities that often also require considerable use of the arms and legs, such as in the physical handling of materials. Controlling Machines and Processes—Using either control mechanisms or direct physical activity to operate machines or processes. Does not involve working with computers or vehicles. Inspecting Equipment, Structures, Materials—Inspecting or diagnosing equipment, structures, or materials to identify the causes of errors or other problems or defects. Repairing and Maintaining Mechanical Equipment—Fixing, servicing, aligning, setting up, adjusting, and testing machines, devices, moving parts, and equipment that operate primarily on the basis of mechanical, not electronic, principles.

Aircraft Mechanics and Service Technicians

- ▲ Growth: 10%
- ▲ Annual Job Openings: 11,323
- ▲ Yearly Earnings: $38,100
- ▲ Education Required: Postsecondary vocational training
- ▲ Self-Employed: 0%
- ▲ Part-Time: 2.3%

Aircraft Body and Bonded Structure Repairers

Repair body or structure of aircraft according to specifications. Cleans, strips, primes, and sands structural surfaces and materials prior to bonding.

Communicates with other workers to fit and align heavy parts or expedite processing of repair parts. Repairs or fabricates defective section or part, using metal fabricating machines, saws, brakes, shears, and grinders. Reads work orders, blueprints, and specifications or examines sample or damaged part or structure to determine repair or fabrication procedures and sequence of operations. Removes or cuts out defective part or drills holes to gain access to internal defect or damage, using drill and punch. Cures bonded structure, using portable or stationary curing equipment. Reinstalls repaired or replacement parts for subsequent riveting or welding, using clamps and wrenches. Locates and marks dimension and reference lines on defective or replacement part, using templates, scribes, compass, and steel rule. Trims and shapes replacement section to specified size and fits and secures section in place, using adhesives, hand tools, and power tools. Spreads plastic film over area to be repaired to prevent damage to surrounding area.

Personality Type: Realistic. Realistic occupations frequently involve work activities that include practical, hands-on problems and solutions. They often deal with plants, animals, and real-world materials like wood, tools, and machinery. Many of the occupations require working outside and do not involve a lot of paperwork or working closely with others.

Abilities: Arm-Hand Steadiness—The ability to keep the hand and arm steady while making an arm movement or while holding the arm and hand in one position. Manual Dexterity—The ability to quickly make coordinated movements of one hand, a hand together with its arm, or two hands, to grasp, manipulate, or assemble objects. Information Ordering—The ability to correctly follow a given rule or set of rules in order to arrange things or actions in a certain order. The things or actions can include numbers, letters, words, pictures, procedures, sentences, and mathematical or logical operations. Extent Flexibility—The ability to bend, stretch, twist, or reach out with the body, arms, and/or legs. Control Precision—The ability to quickly and repeatedly make precise adjustments in moving the controls of a machine or vehicle to exact positions.

Skills: Installation—Installing equipment, machines, wiring, or programs to meet specifications. Equipment Selection—Determining the kind of tools and equipment needed to do a job. Problem Identification—Identifying the nature of problems. Repairing—Repairing machines or systems, using the needed tools.

Generalized Work Activities: Handling and Moving Objects—Using one's hands and arms in handling, installing, forming, positioning, and moving materials, or in manipulating things. Inspecting Equipment, Structures, Materials—Inspecting or diagnosing equipment, structures, or materials to identify the causes of errors or other problems or defects. Getting Information Needed to Do the Job—Observing, receiving, and otherwise obtaining information from all relevant sources. Implementing Ideas and Programs—Conducting or carrying out work proce-dures and activities in accord with one's own ideas or information provided through directions/instructions for purposes of installing, modifying, preparing, delivering, constructing, integrating, finishing, or completing programs, systems, structures, or products. Controlling Machines and Processes—Using either control mechanisms or direct physical activity to operate machines or processes. Does not involve working with computers or vehicles. Updating and Using Job-Relevant Knowledge—Keeping up-to-date technically and knowing the functions of one's own job and related jobs.

Aircraft Engine Specialists

Repair and maintain the operating condition of aircraft engines. Includes helicopter engine mechanics. Adjusts, repairs, or replaces electrical wiring system and aircraft accessories. Removes engine from aircraft, using hoist or forklift truck. Listens to operating engine to detect and diagnose malfunctions such as sticking or burned valves. Reads and interprets manufacturers' maintenance manuals, service bulletins, and other specifications to determine feasibility and methods of repair. Services, repairs, and rebuilds aircraft structures such as wings, fuselage, rigging, and surface and hydraulic controls, using hand or power tools and equipment. Services and maintains aircraft and related apparatus by performing activities such as flushing crankcase, cleaning screens, and lubricating moving parts. Tests engine operation, using test equipment such as ignition analyzer, compression checker, distributor timer, and ammeter to identify malfunction. Reassembles engine and installs engine in aircraft. Replaces or repairs worn, defective, or damaged components, using hand tools, gauges, and testing equipment. Disassembles and inspects engine parts, such as turbine blades and cylinders, for wear, warping, cracks, and leaks.

Personality Type: Realistic. Realistic occupations frequently involve work activities that include practical, hands-on problems and solutions. They often deal with plants, animals, and real-world materials like wood, tools, and machinery. Many of the occupations require working outside and do not involve a lot of paperwork or working closely with others.

Abilities: Problem Sensitivity—The ability to tell when something is wrong or is likely to go wrong. Does not involve solving the problem, only recognizing there is a problem. Deductive Reasoning—The ability to apply general rules to specific problems to come up with logical answers. Involves deciding if an answer makes sense. Manual Dexterity—The ability to quickly make coordinated movements of one hand, a hand together with its arm, or two hands, to grasp, manipulate, or assemble objects. Written Comprehension—The ability to read and understand information and ideas presented in writing. Inductive Reasoning—The ability to combine separate pieces of information, or specific answers to problems, to form general rules or conclusions. Includes coming up with a logical explanation for why a series of seemingly unrelated events occur together. Near Vision—The ability to see details of objects at a close range.

Skills: Repairing—Repairing machines or systems, using the needed tools. Equipment Maintenance—Performing routine maintenance and determining when and what kind of maintenance is needed. Testing—Conducting tests to determine whether equipment, software, or procedures are operating as expected. Operation Monitoring—Watching gauges, dials, or other indicators to make sure a machine is working properly. Troubleshooting—Determining what is causing an operating error and deciding what to do about it.

Generalized Work Activities: Repairing and Maintaining Mechanical Equipment—Fixing, servicing, aligning, setting up, adjusting, and testing machines, devices, moving parts, and equipment that operate primarily on the basis of mechanical, not electronic, principles. Getting Information Needed to Do the Job—Observing, receiving, and otherwise obtaining information from all relevant sources. Inspecting Equipment, Structures, Materials—Inspecting or diagnosing equipment, structures, or materials to identify the causes of errors or other problems or defects. Updating and Using Job-Relevant Knowledge—Keeping up-to-date technically and knowing the functions of one's own job and related jobs. Handling and Moving Objects—Using one's hands and arms in handling, installing, forming, positioning, and moving materials, or in manipulating things. Includes the use of keyboards.

Airframe-and-Power-Plant Mechanics

Inspect, test, repair, maintain, and service aircraft. Assembles and installs electrical, plumbing, mechanical, hydraulic, and structural components and accessories, using hand tools and power tools. Services and maintains aircraft systems by performing tasks such as flushing crankcase, cleaning screens, greasing moving parts, and checking brakes. Removes engine from aircraft or installs engine, using hoist or forklift truck. Reads and interprets aircraft maintenance manuals and specifications to determine feasibility and method of repairing or replacing malfunctioning or damaged components. Repairs, replaces, and rebuilds aircraft structures, functional components, and parts, such as wings and fuselage, rigging, and hydraulic units. Tests engine and system operations, using testing equipment, and listens to engine sounds to detect and diagnose malfunctions. Disassembles and inspects parts for wear, warping, or other defects. Examines and inspects engines or other components for cracks, breaks, or leaks. Adjusts, aligns, and calibrates aircraft systems, using hand tools, gauges, and test equipment. Modifies aircraft structures, space vehicles, systems, or components, following drawings, engineering orders and technical publications.

Personality Type: Realistic. Realistic occupations frequently involve work activities that include practical, hands-on problems and solutions. They often deal with plants, animals, and real-world materials like wood, tools, and machinery. Many of the occupations require working outside and do not involve a lot of paperwork or working closely with others.

Abilities: Manual Dexterity—The ability to quickly make coordinated movements of one hand, a hand together with its arm, or two hands, to grasp, manipulate, or assemble objects. Arm-Hand Steadiness—The ability to keep the hand and arm steady while making an arm movement or while holding the arm and hand in one position. Deductive Reasoning—The ability to apply general rules to specific problems to come up with logical answers. Involves deciding if an answer makes sense. Finger Dexterity—The ability to make precisely coordinated movements of the fingers of one or both hands to grasp, manipulate, or assemble very small objects. Information Ordering—The ability to correctly follow a given rule or set of rules in order to arrange things or actions in a certain order. The things or actions can include numbers, letters, words, pictures, procedures, sentences, and mathematical or logical operations. Near Vision—The ability to see details of objects at a close range. Control Precision—The ability to quickly and repeatedly make precise adjustments in moving the controls of a machine or vehicle to exact positions.

Skills: Testing—Conducting tests to determine whether equipment, software, or procedures are operating as expected. Repairing—Repairing machines or systems, using the needed tools. Equipment Selection—Determining the kind of tools and equipment needed to do a job. Equipment Maintenance—Performing routine maintenance and determining when and what kind of maintenance is needed. Troubleshooting—Determining what is causing an operating error and deciding what to do about it.

Generalized Work Activities: Repairing and Maintaining Mechanical Equipment—Fixing, servicing, aligning, setting up, adjusting, and testing machines, devices, moving parts, and equipment that operate primarily on the basis of mechanical, not electronic, principles. Handling and Moving Objects—Using one's hands and arms in handling, installing, forming, positioning, and moving materials, or in manipulating things. Includes the use of keyboards. Inspecting Equipment, Structures, Materials—Inspecting or diagnosing equipment, structures, or materials to identify the causes of errors or other problems or defects. Getting Information Needed to Do the Job—Observing, receiving, and otherwise obtaining information from all relevant sources.

Aircraft Pilots and Flight Engineers

- ▲ Growth: 6%
- ▲ Annual Job Openings: 4,555
- ▲ Yearly Earnings: $91,750
- ▲ Education Required: Long-term O-J-T
- ▲ Self-Employed: 2.2%
- ▲ Part-Time: 23.3%

Airline Pilots, Copilots, and Flight Engineers

Pilot and navigate the flight of multiengine aircraft in regularly scheduled service for the transport of passengers and cargo. Requires Federal Air Transport rating and certification in specific aircraft type used. Conducts in-flight tests and evaluations at specified altitudes and in all types of weather to determine receptivity and other characteristics of equipment and systems. Conducts preflight checks and reads gauges to verify that fluids and pressure are at prescribed levels. Obtains and reviews data such as load weight, fuel supply, weather conditions, and flight schedule. Orders changes in fuel supply, load, route, or schedule to ensure safety of flight. Coordinates flight activities with ground crew and air-traffic control, and informs crew members of flight and test procedures. Operates radio equipment and contacts control tower for takeoff, clearance, arrival instructions, and other information. Logs information such as flight time, altitude flown, and fuel consumption. Plans and formulates flight activities and test schedules and prepares flight evaluation reports. Starts engines, operates controls, and pilots airplane to transport passengers, mail, or freight, adhering to flight plan, regulations, and procedures. Holds commercial pilot's license issued by Federal Aviation Administration. Gives training and instruction in aircraft operations for students and other pilots. Plots flight pattern and files flight plan with appropriate officials.

Personality Type: Realistic. Realistic occupations frequently involve work activities that include practical, hands-on problems and solutions. They often deal with plants, animals, and real-world materials like wood, tools, and machinery. Many of the occupations require working outside and do not involve a lot of paperwork or working closely with others.

Abilities: Problem Sensitivity—The ability to tell when something is wrong or is likely to go wrong. Does not involve solving the problem, only recognizing there is a problem. Spatial Orientation—The ability to know one's location in relation to the environment or to know where other objects are in relation to one's self. Control Precision—The ability to quickly and repeatedly make precise adjustments in moving the controls of a machine or vehicle to exact positions. Oral Expression—The ability to communicate information and ideas verbally so others will understand. Near Vision—The ability to see details of objects at a close range.

Skills: Operation and Control—Controlling operations of equipment or systems. Coordination—Adjusting actions in relation to others' actions. Operation Monitoring—Watching gauges, dials, or other indicators to make sure a machine is working properly. Judgment and Decision Making—Weighing the relative costs and benefits of a potential action. Active Listening—Listening to what other people are saying; asking questions as appropriate.

Generalized Work Activities: Operating Vehicles or Equipment—Running, maneuvering, navigating, or driving vehicles or mechanized equipment such as forklifts, passenger vehicles, aircraft, or water craft. Getting Information Needed to Do the Job—Observing, receiving, and otherwise obtaining information from all relevant sources. Monitoring Processes, Materials, Surroundings—Monitoring and reviewing information from materials, events, or the environment, often to detect problems or to find out when things are finished. Inspecting Equipment, Structures, Materials—Inspecting or diagnosing equipment, structures, or materials to identify the causes of errors or other problems or defects. Identifying Objects, Actions, and Events—Identifying information received by making estimates or categorizations, recognizing differences or similarities, or sensing changes in circumstances or events. Documenting/Recording Information—Entering, transcribing, recording, storing, or maintaining information in either written form or by electronic/magnetic recording.

Commercial Pilots

Pilot and navigate the flight of small fixed or rotary winged aircraft, primarily for the transport of cargo and passengers. Requires Commercial Rating. Gives training and instruction in aircraft operations for students and other pilots. Plots flight pattern and files flight plan with appropriate officials. Obtains and reviews data such as load weight, fuel supply, weather conditions, and flight schedule. Conducts preflight checks and reads gauges to verify that fluids and pressure are at prescribed levels. Coordinates flight activities with ground crew and air-traffic control and informs crew members of flight and test procedures. Plans and formulates flight activities and test schedules and prepares flight evaluation reports. Logs information such as flight time, altitude flown, and fuel consumption. Holds commercial pilot's license issued by Federal Aviation Administration. Operates radio equipment and contacts control tower for takeoff, clearance, arrival instructions, and other information. Orders changes in fuel supply, load, route, or schedule to ensure safety of flight. Starts engines, operates controls, and pilots airplane to transport passengers, mail, or freight, adhering to flight plan, regulations, and procedures. Conducts in-flight tests and evaluations at specified altitudes and in all types of weather to determine receptivity and other characteristics of equipment and systems.

Personality Type: Realistic. Realistic occupations frequently involve work activities that include practical, hands-on problems and solutions. They often deal with plants, animals, and real-world materials like wood, tools, and machinery. Many of the occupations require working outside and do not involve a lot of paperwork or working closely with others.

Abilities: Control Precision—The ability to quickly and repeatedly make precise adjustments in moving the controls of a machine or vehicle to exact positions. Problem Sensitivity—The ability to tell when something is wrong or is likely to go wrong. Does not involve solving the problem, only recognizing there is a problem. Spatial Orientation—The ability to know one's location in relation to the environment or to know where other objects are in relation to one's self. Near Vision—The ability to see details of objects at a close range. Oral Expression—The ability to communicate information and ideas verbally so others will understand.

Skills: Operation and Control—Controlling operations of equipment or systems. Coordination—Adjusting actions in relation to others' actions. Judgment and

Decision Making—Weighing the relative costs and benefits of a potential action. Operation Monitoring—Watching gauges, dials, or other indicators to make sure a machine is working properly. Active Listening—Listening to what other people are saying; asking questions as appropriate.

Generalized Work Activities: Operating Vehicles or Equipment—Running, maneuvering, navigating, or driving vehicles or mechanized equipment such as forklifts, passenger vehicles, aircraft, or water craft. Getting Information Needed to Do the Job—Observing, receiving, and otherwise obtaining information from all relevant sources. Inspecting Equipment, Structures, Materials—Inspecting or diagnosing equipment, structures, or materials to identify the causes of errors or other problems or defects. Monitoring Processes, Materials, Surroundings—Monitoring and reviewing information from materials, events, or the environment, often to detect problems or to find out when things are finished. Documenting/Recording Information—Entering, transcribing, recording, storing, or maintaining information in either written form or by electronic/magnetic recording. Identifying Objects, Actions, and Events—Identifying information received by making estimates or categorizations, recognizing differences or similarities, or sensing changes in circumstances or events.

Air Traffic Controllers

- ▲ Growth: 2%
- ▲ Annual Job Openings: 2,321
- ▲ Yearly Earnings: $64,880
- ▲ Education Required: Long-term O-J-T
- ▲ Self-Employed: 0%
- ▲ Part-Time: 11.7%

Air Traffic Controllers

Control air traffic on and within vicinity of airport and movement of air traffic between altitude sectors and control centers according to established procedures and policies. Authorize, regulate, and control commercial airline flights according to government or company regulations to expedite and ensure flight safety. Controls air traffic at and within vicinity of airport. Determines timing of and procedure for flight vector changes in sector. Reviews records and reports for clarity and completeness and maintains records and reports. Relays air traffic information such as altitude, expected time of arrival, and course of aircraft to control centers. Analyzes factors such as weather reports, fuel requirements, and maps to determine flights and air routes. Inspects, adjusts, and controls radio equipment and airport lights. Directs radio searches for aircraft and alerts control-center emergency facilities of flight difficulties. Transfers control of departing flights to traffic control center and accepts control of arriving flights from air traffic control center. Recommends flight path changes to planes traveling in storms or fog or in emergency situations. Issues landing and take-off authorizations and instructions and communicates other information to aircraft. Communicates with, relays flight plans to, and coordinates movement of air traffic between control centers. Completes daily activity report and keeps record of messages from aircraft.

Personality Type: Conventional. Conventional occupations frequently involve following set procedures and routines. These occupations can include working with data and details more than with ideas. Usually there is a clear line of authority to follow.

Abilities: Speech Clarity—The ability to speak clearly so that what is said is understandable to a listener. Written Comprehension—The ability to read and understand information and ideas presented in writing. Oral Comprehension—The ability to listen to and understand information and ideas presented verbally. Selective Attention—The ability to concentrate and not be distracted while performing a task over a period of time. Oral Expression—The ability to communicate information and ideas verbally so others will understand. Near Vision—The ability to see details of objects at a close range.

Skills: Speaking—Talking to others to effectively convey information. Active Listening—Listening to what other people are saying; asking questions as appropriate. Operation and Control—Controlling operations of equipment or systems. Coordination—Adjusting actions in relation to others' actions. Operation Monitoring—Watching gauges, dials, or other indicators to make sure a machine is working properly.

Generalized Work Activities: Monitoring Processes, Materials, Surroundings—Monitoring and reviewing information from materials, events, or the environment, often to detect problems or to find out when things are finished. Getting Information Needed to Do the Job—Observing, receiving, and otherwise obtaining information from all relevant sources. Analyzing Data or Information—Identifying underlying principles, reasons, or facts by breaking down information or data into separate parts. Communicating with Other Workers—Providing information to supervisors, fellow workers, and subordinates. This information can be exchanged face-to-face, in writing, or via telephone/ electronic transfer. Identifying Objects, Actions, and Events—Identifying information received by making estimates or categorizations, recognizing differences or similarities, or sensing changes in circumstances or events. Making Decisions and Solving Problems—Combining, evaluating, and analyzing information and data to make decisions and solve problems. Involves making decisions about the relative importance of information and choosing the best solution.

Ambulance Drivers and Attendants

- ▲ Growth: 35%
- ▲ Annual Job Openings: 4,191
- ▲ Yearly Earnings: $16,960
- ▲ Education Required: Short-term O-J-T
- ▲ Self-Employed: 0%
- ▲ Part-Time: 34.5%

Ambulance Drivers and Attendants, Except Emergency Medical Technicians

Drive ambulance or assist ambulance driver in transporting sick, injured, or convalescent persons. Assist in lifting patients. Changes equipment to maintain sanitary conditions. Transports sick or injured persons to hospital or convalescents to destination, avoiding sudden motions detrimental to patients. Reports facts concerning accident or emergency to hospital personnel or law enforcement officials. Administers first aid as needed. Replaces supplies and disposable items on ambulance. Places patients on stretcher and loads stretcher into ambulance, usually with help of ambulance attendant.

Personality Type: Social. Social occupations frequently involve working with, communicating with, and teaching people. These occupations often involve helping or providing service to others.

Abilities: Reaction Time—The ability to quickly respond with the hand, finger, or foot to a signal such as a sound, a light, or a picture. Spatial Orientation—The ability to know one's location in relation to the environment or to know where other objects are in relation to one's self. Wrist-Finger Speed—The ability to make fast, simple, repeated movements of the fingers, hands, and wrists. Manual Dexterity—The ability to quickly make coordinated movements of one hand, a hand together with its arm, or two hands, to grasp, manipulate, or assemble objects. Response

Orientation—The ability to choose quickly and correctly between two or more movements in response to two or more signals (lights, sounds, pictures, etc.). Includes the speed with which the correct response is started with the hand, foot, or other body parts. Static Strength—The ability to exert maximum muscle force to lift, push, pull, or carry objects. Control Precision—The ability to quickly and repeatedly make precise adjustments in moving the controls of a machine or vehicle to exact positions.

Skills: Identification of Key Causes—Identifying the things that must be changed to achieve a goal. Judgment and Decision Making—Weighing the relative costs and benefits of a potential action. Active Listening—Listening to what other people are saying; asking questions as appropriate. Operation and Control—Controlling operations of equipment or systems. Coordination—Adjusting actions in relation to others' actions. Idea Evaluation—Evaluating the likely success of an idea in relation to the demands of the situation.

Generalized Work Activities: Operating Vehicles or Equipment—Running, maneuvering, navigating, or driving vehicles or mechanized equipment such as forklifts, passenger vehicles, aircraft, or water craft. Assisting and Caring for Others—Providing assistance or personal care to others. Performing General Physical Activities—Performing physical activities that require moving one's whole body, such as climbing, lifting, balancing, walking, and stooping. Performing activities that often also require considerable use of the arms and legs, such as in the physical handling of materials. Getting Information Needed to Do the Job—Observing, receiving, and otherwise obtaining information from all relevant sources. Monitoring

Processes, Materials, Surroundings—Monitoring and reviewing information from materials, events, or the environment, often to detect problems or to find out when things are finished.

Amusement and Recreation Attendants

▲ Growth: 30%
▲ Annual Job Openings: 141,783
▲ Yearly Earnings: $12,860
▲ Education Required: Short-term O-J-T
▲ Self-Employed: 0.7%
▲ Part-Time: 48.8%

Amusement and Recreation Attendants

Perform variety of attending duties at amusement or recreation facility. Schedule use of recreation facilities, maintain and provide equipment to participants of sporting events or recreational pursuits, or operate amusement concessions and rides. Rents, sells, and issues sports equipment and supplies such as bowling shoes, golf balls, swim suits, and beach chairs. Provides entertainment services such as guessing patrons' weight, conducting games, explaining use of arcade game machines, and photographing patrons. Sells tickets and collects fees from customers and collects or punches tickets. Monitors activities to ensure adherence to rules and safety procedures to protect environment and maintain order; ejects unruly patrons. Attends animals, performing such tasks as harnessing, saddling, feeding, watering, and grooming. Drives horse-drawn vehicle for entertainment or advertising purposes. Records details of attendance, sales, receipts, reservations, and repair activities. Operates, drives, or explains use of mechanical riding devices or other automatic equipment in amusement parks, carnivals, or recreation areas. Announces and describes amusement park attractions to patrons to entice customers to games and other entertainment. Directs patrons of establishment to rides, seats, or attractions. Escorts patrons on tours of points of interest. Attends amusement booth in parks, carnivals, or stadiums and awards prizes to winning players. Cleans sporting equipment, vehicles, rides, booths, facilities, and grounds. Inspects, repairs, adjusts, tests, fuels, and oils sporting and recreation equipment, game machines, and amusement rides. Provides information about facilities, entertainment options, and rules and regulations. Assists patrons in getting on and off amusement rides, boats, or ski lifts and in mounting and riding animals. Fastens, or directs patrons to fasten, safety devices. Receives, retrieves, replaces, and stores sports equipment and supplies, arranges items in designated areas, and erects or removes equipment. Schedules use of recreation facilities such as golf courses, tennis courts, bowling alleys, and softball diamonds. Sells and serves refreshments to customers.

Personality Type: Realistic. Realistic occupations frequently involve work activities that include practical, hands-on problems and solutions. They often deal with plants, animals, and real-world materials like wood, tools, and machinery. Many of the occupations require working outside and do not involve a lot of paperwork or working closely with others.

Abilities: Oral Expression—The ability to communicate information and ideas verbally so others will understand. Speech Clarity—The ability to speak clearly so that what is said is understandable to a listener. Rate Control—The ability to time the adjustments of a movement or equipment control in anticipation of changes in the speed and/or direction of a continuously moving object or scene. Control Precision—The ability to quickly and repeatedly make precise adjustments in moving the controls of a machine or vehicle to exact positions. Oral Comprehension—The ability to listen to and understand information and ideas presented verbally.

Skills: Speaking—Talking to others to effectively convey information. Service Orientation—Actively looking for ways to help people. Operation and Control—Controlling operations of equipment or systems. Social Perceptiveness—Being aware of other people's reactions and understanding why people react the way they do. Management of Material Resources—Obtaining and seeing to the appropriate use of equipment, facilities, and materials needed to do certain work.

Generalized Work Activities: Communicating with Persons Outside Organization—Communicating with persons outside the organization. Representing the organization to customers, the public, government, and other external sources. Exchanging information face-to-face, in writing, or via telephone/electronic transfer. Performing for/Working with Public—Performing for people or dealing directly with the public, including serving persons in restaurants and stores and receiving clients or guests. Establishing and Maintaining Relationships—Developing constructive and cooperative working relationships with others. Monitoring Processes, Materials, Surroundings—Monitoring and reviewing information from materials, events, or the environment, often to detect problems or to find out when things are finished. Inspecting Equipment, Structures, Materials—Inspecting or diagnosing equipment, structures, or materials to identify the causes of errors or other problems or defects. Controlling Machines and Processes—Using either control mechanisms or direct physical activity to operate machines or processes. Does not involve working with computers or vehicles.

Gaming and Sports Book Writers and Runners

Conduct games of chance such as dice, roulette, or cards. Perform a variety of tasks such as collecting bets or wagers, paying winnings, and explaining rules to customers. Conducts gambling table or games such as dice, roulette, cards, or keno. Ensures that game rules are followed. Verifies, computes, and pays out winnings. Participates in game for gambling establishment to provide minimum complement of players at table. Seats patrons at gaming tables. Sells food, beverages, and tobacco to players. Prepares collection report for submission to supervisor. Exchanges paper currency for playing chips or coin money and collects game fees or wagers.

Personality Type: Enterprising. Enterprising occupations frequently involve starting up and carrying out projects. These occupations can involve leading people and making many decisions. They sometimes require risk taking and often deal with business.

Abilities: Number Facility—The ability to add, subtract, multiply, or divide quickly and correctly. Speech Clarity—The ability to speak clearly so that what is said is understandable to a listener. Near Vision—The ability to see details of objects at a close range. Oral Expression—The ability to communicate information and ideas verbally so others will understand. Information Ordering—The ability to correctly follow a given rule or set of rules in order to arrange things or actions in a certain order. The things or actions can include numbers, letters, words, pictures, procedures, sentences, and mathematical or logical operations.

Skills: Mathematics—Using mathematics to solve problems. Social Perceptiveness—Being aware of other people's reactions and understanding why people react the way they do. Service Orientation—Actively looking for ways to help people. Speaking—Talking to others to effectively convey information. Active Listening—Listening to what other people are saying; asking questions as appropriate.

Generalized Work Activities: Performing for/Working with Public—Performing for people or dealing directly with the public, including serving persons in restaurants and stores and receiving clients or guests. Handling and Moving Objects—Using one's hands and arms in handling, installing, forming, positioning, and moving materials, or in manipulating things. Establishing and Maintaining Relationships—Developing constructive and cooperative working relationships with others.

Communicating with Persons Outside Organization—Communicating with persons outside the organization. Representing the organization to customers, the public, government, and other external sources. Exchanging information face-to-face, in writing, or via telephone/electronic transfer. Identifying Objects, Actions, and Events—Identifying information received by making estimates or categorizations, recognizing differences or similarities, or sensing changes in circumstances or events.

Gaming Dealers

Assist operators or customers in conducting games of chance. Seats patrons at gaming tables. Prepares collection report for submission to supervisor. Sells food, beverages, and tobacco to players. Verifies, computes, and pays out winnings. Exchanges paper currency for playing chips or coin money and collects game fees or wagers. Conducts gambling table or games such as dice, roulette, cards, or keno, and ensures that game rules are followed. Participates in game for gambling establishment to provide minimum complement of players at table.

Personality Type: Enterprising. Enterprising occupations frequently involve starting up and carrying out projects. These occupations can involve leading people and making many decisions. They sometimes require risk taking and often deal with business.

Abilities: Number Facility—The ability to add, subtract, multiply, or divide quickly and correctly. Near Vision—The ability to see details of objects at a close range. Speech Clarity—The ability to speak clearly so that what is said is understandable to a listener. Information

Ordering—The ability to correctly follow a given rule or set of rules in order to arrange things or actions in a certain order. The things or actions can include numbers, letters, words, pictures, procedures, sentences, and mathematical or logical operations. Oral Expression—The ability to communicate information and ideas verbally so others will understand.

Skills: Mathematics—Using mathematics to solve problems. Social Perceptiveness—Being aware of other people's reactions and understanding why people react the way they do. Service Orientation—Actively looking for ways to help people. Speaking—Talking to others to effectively convey information. Active Listening—Listening to what other people are saying; asking questions as appropriate.

Generalized Work Activities: Performing for/Working with Public—Performing for people or dealing directly with the public, including serving persons in restaurants and stores and receiving clients or guests. Handling and Moving Objects—Using one's hands and arms in handling, installing, forming, positioning, and moving materials, or in manipulating things. Establishing and Maintaining Relationships—Developing constructive and cooperative working relationships with others. Communicating with Persons Outside Organization—Communicating with persons outside the organization. Representing the organization to customers, the public, government, and other external sources. Exchanging information face-to-face, in writing, or via telephone/electronic transfer. Identifying Objects, Actions, and Events—Identifying information received by making estimates or categorizations, recognizing differences or similarities, or sensing changes in circumstances or events.

Animal Caretakers

▲ Growth: 22%
▲ Annual Job Openings: 43,263
▲ Yearly Earnings: $14,820
▲ Education Required: Short-term O-J-T
▲ Self-Employed: 24%
▲ Part-Time: 38.1%

Nonfarm Animal Caretakers

Feed, water, groom, bathe, exercise, or otherwise care for pets and other nonfarm animals such as dogs, cats, ornamental fish or birds, zoo animals, and mice. Work in settings such as kennels, animal shelters, zoos, circuses, and aquariums. Keep records of feedings, treatments, and animals received or discharged. Clean, disinfect, and repair cages, pens, or fish tanks. Records information about animals, such as weight, size, physical condition, diet, medications, and food intake. Transfers animals between enclosures for breeding, birthing, shipping, or rearranging exhibits. Examines and observes animals for signs of illness, disease, or injury; provides treatment or informs veterinarian. Mixes food, liquid formulas, medications, or food supplements according to instructions, prescriptions, and knowledge of animal species. Adjusts controls to regulate specified temperature and humidity of animal quarters, nursery, or exhibit area. Exercises animals to maintain their fitness and health. Trains animals to perform certain tasks. Washes, brushes, clips, trims, and grooms animals. Cleans and disinfects animal quarters such as pens, stables, cages, and yards. Cleans and disinfects surgical or other equipment such as saddles and bridles. Orders, unloads, and stores feed and supplies. Saddles and shoes animals. Responds to questions from patrons and provides information about animals, such as behavior, habitat, breeding habits, or facility activities. Observes and cautions children who are petting and feeding animals in designated area. Installs equipment in animal care facility, such as infrared lights, feeding devices, or cribs. Repairs fences, cages, or pens. Feeds and waters animal according to schedules and feeding instructions. Anesthetizes and inoculates animals according to instructions.

Personality Type: Realistic. Realistic occupations frequently involve work activities that include practical, hands-on problems and solutions. They often deal with plants, animals, and real-world materials like wood, tools, and machinery. Many of the occupations require working outside and do not involve a lot of paperwork or working closely with others.

Abilities: Oral Expression—The ability to communicate information and ideas verbally so others will understand. Problem Sensitivity—The ability to tell when something is wrong or is likely to go wrong. Does not involve solving the problem, only recognizing there is a problem. Oral Comprehension—The ability to listen to and understand information and ideas presented verbally. Information Ordering—The ability to correctly follow a given rule or set of rules in order to arrange things or actions in a certain order. The things or actions can include numbers, letters, words, pictures, procedures, sentences, and mathematical or logical operations. Written Expression—The ability to communicate information and ideas in writing so others will understand.

Skills: Problem Identification—Identifying the nature of problems. Reading Comprehension—Understanding written information in work-related documents. Speaking—Talking to others to effectively convey information. Writing—Communicating effectively with others in writing as indicated by the needs of the audience. Active Listening—Listening to what other people are saying; asking questions as appropriate. Service Orientation—Actively looking for ways to help people. Equipment Selection—Determining the kind of tools and equipment needed to do a job.

Generalized Work Activities: Performing General Physical Activities—Performing physical activities that require moving one's whole body, such as climbing, lifting, balancing, walking, and stooping. Performing activities that often also require considerable use of the arms and legs, such as in the physical handling of materials. Handling and Moving Objects—Using one's hands and arms in handling, installing, forming, positioning, and moving materials, or in manipulating things. Monitoring Processes, Materials, Surroundings—Monitoring and reviewing information from materials, events, or the environment, often to detect problems or to find out when things are finished. Documenting/Recording Information—Entering, transcribing, recording, storing, or maintaining information in either written form or by electronic/magnetic recording. Getting Information Needed to Do the Job—Observing, receiving, and otherwise obtaining information from all relevant sources. Identifying

Objects, Actions, and Events—Identifying information received by making estimates or categorizations, recognizing differences or similarities, or sensing changes in circumstances or events.

Architects

- ▲ Growth: 19%
- ▲ Annual Job Openings: 7,762
- ▲ Yearly Earnings: $47,710
- ▲ Education Required: Bachelor's degree
- ▲ Self-Employed: 30.8%
- ▲ Part-Time: 8%

Architects, Except Landscape and Naval

Plan and design structures such as private residences, office buildings, theaters, factories, and other structural property. Prepares operating and maintenance manuals, studies, and reports. Prepares contract documents for building contractors. Administers construction contracts. Conducts periodic on-site observation of work during construction to monitor compliance with plans. Directs activities of workers engaged in preparing drawings and specification documents. Consults with client to determine functional and spatial requirements of structure. Integrates engineering element into unified design. Plans layout of project. Prepares scale drawings. Prepares information regarding design, structure specifications, materials, color, equipment, estimated costs, and construction time. Represents client in obtaining bids and awarding construction contracts.

Personality Type: Artistic. Artistic occupations frequently involve working with forms, designs, and patterns. They often require self-expression, and the work can be done without following a clear set of rules.

Abilities: Visualization—The ability to imagine how something will look after it is moved around or when its parts are moved or rearranged. Written Expression— The ability to communicate information and ideas in writing so others will understand. Deductive

Reasoning—The ability to apply general rules to specific problems to come up with logical answers. Involves deciding if an answer makes sense. Fluency of Ideas— The ability to come up with a number of ideas about a given topic. Emphasis is on the number of ideas produced and not the quality, correctness, or creativity of the ideas.

Skills: Mathematics—Using mathematics to solve problems. Coordination—Adjusting actions in relation to others' actions. Implementation Planning— Developing approaches for implementing an idea. Idea Generation—Generating a number of different approaches to problems. Product Inspection— Inspecting and evaluating the quality of products. Speaking—Talking to others to effectively convey information.

Generalized Work Activities: Drafting and Specifying Technical Devices—Providing documentation, detailed instructions, drawings, or specifications to inform others about how devices, parts, equipment, or structures are to be fabricated, constructed, assembled, modified, maintained, or used. Thinking Creatively—Originating, inventing, designing, or creating new applications, ideas, relationships, systems, or products, including artistic contributions. Evaluating Information against Standards—Evaluating information against a set of standards and verifying that it is correct. Estimating Needed Characteristics—Estimating the characteristics of materials, products, events, or information; estimating sizes, distances, and quantities; determining time, costs, resources, or materials needed to perform a work activity. Getting Information Needed to Do the Job—Observing, receiving, and otherwise obtaining information from all relevant sources.

Marine Architects

Design and oversee construction and repair of marine craft and floating structures such as ships, barges, tugs, dredges, submarines, torpedoes, floats, and buoys. Confer with marine engineers. Oversees construction and testing of prototype in model basin. Develops sectional and waterline curves of hull to establish center of gravity, ideal hull form, and buoyancy and stability data. Designs layout of craft interior, including cargo space, passenger compartments, ladder wells, and elevators. Evaluates performance of craft during dock and sea trials to determine design changes and conformance with national and international standards. Studies design proposals and specifications to establish basic characteristics of craft, such as size, weight, speed, propulsion, displacement, and draft. Designs complete hull and superstructure according to specifications and test data, in conformity with standards of safety, efficiency, and economy. Confers with marine engineering personnel to establish arrangement of boiler room equipment and propulsion machinery, heating and ventilating systems, refrigeration equipment, piping, and other functional equipment.

Personality Type: Realistic. Realistic occupations frequently involve work activities that include practical, hands-on problems and solutions. They often deal with plants, animals, and real-world materials like wood, tools, and machinery. Many of the occupations require working outside and do not involve a lot of paperwork or working closely with others.

Abilities: Visualization—The ability to imagine how something will look after it is moved around or when its parts are moved or rearranged. Deductive Reasoning—The ability to apply general rules to specific problems to come up with logical answers. Involves deciding if an answer makes sense. Written Comprehension—The ability to read and understand information and ideas presented in writing. Oral Comprehension—The ability to listen to and understand information and ideas presented verbally. Information Ordering—The ability to correctly follow a given rule or set of rules in order to arrange things or actions in a certain order. The things or actions can include numbers, letters, words, pictures, procedures, sentences, and mathematical or logical operations. Originality—The ability to come up with unusual or clever ideas about a given topic or situation, or to develop creative ways to solve a problem.

Skills: Active Learning—Working with new material or information to grasp its implications. Reading Comprehension—Understanding written information in work-related documents. Critical Thinking—Using logic and analysis to identify the strengths and weaknesses of different approaches. Testing—Conducting tests to determine whether equipment, software, or procedures are operating as expected. Synthesis/Reorganization—Reorganizing information to get a better approach to problems or tasks. Mathematics—Using mathematics to solve problems. Idea Evaluation—Evaluating the likely success of an idea in relation to the demands of the situation.

Generalized Work Activities: Drafting and Specifying Technical Devices—Providing documentation, detailed instructions, drawings, or specifications to inform others about how devices, parts, equipment, or structures are to be fabricated, constructed, assembled, modified, maintained, or used. Getting Information Needed to Do the Job—Observing, receiving, and otherwise obtaining information from all relevant sources. Thinking Creatively—Originating, inventing, designing, or creating new applications, ideas, relationships, systems, or products, including artistic contributions. Making Decisions and Solving Problems—Combining, evaluating, and analyzing information and data to make decisions and solve problems. Involves making decisions about the relative importance of information and choosing the best solution. Inspecting Equipment, Structures, Materials—Inspecting or diagnosing equipment, structures, or materials to identify the causes of errors or other problems or defects.

Archivists, Curators, Museum Technicians, and Conservators

- ▲ Growth: 13%
- ▲ Annual Job Openings: 4,118
- ▲ Yearly Earnings: $31,750
- ▲ Education Required: Master's degree
- ▲ Self-Employed: 0%
- ▲ Part-Time: 21.9%

Archivists

Appraise, edit, and direct safekeeping of permanent records and historically valuable documents. Participate in research activities based on archival materials. Requests or recommends pertinent materials available in libraries, private collections, or other archives. Selects and edits documents for publication and display, according to knowledge of subject, literary expression, and techniques for presentation and display. Directs filing and cross indexing of selected documents in alphabetical and chronological order. Directs acquisition and physical arrangement of new materials. Advises government agencies, scholars, journalists, and others conducting research by supplying available materials and information. Establishes policy guidelines concerning public access and use of materials. Prepares document descriptions and reference aids for use of archives, such as accession lists, bibliographies, abstracts, and microfilmed documents. Directs activities of workers engaged in cataloging and safekeeping of valuable materials and disposition of worthless materials. Analyzes documents by ascertaining date of writing, author, or original recipient of letter to appraise value to posterity.

Personality Type: Investigative. Investigative occupations frequently involve working with ideas and require an extensive amount of thinking. These occupations can involve searching for facts and figuring out problems mentally.

Abilities: Written Comprehension—The ability to read and understand information and ideas presented in writing. Written Expression—The ability to communicate information and ideas in writing so others will understand. Near Vision—The ability to see details of objects at a close range. Oral Expression—The ability to communicate information and ideas verbally so others will understand. Speech Clarity—The ability to speak clearly so that what is said is understandable to a listener.

Skills: Information Gathering—Knowing how to find information and identifying essential information. Information Organization—Finding ways to structure or classify multiple pieces of information. Reading Comprehension—Understanding written information in work-related documents. Writing—Communicating effectively with others in writing as indicated by the needs of the audience. Product Inspection—Inspecting and evaluating the quality of products.

Generalized Work Activities: Judging Qualities—Making judgments about or assessing the value, importance, or quality of things, services, or other people's work. Getting Information Needed to Do the Job—Observing, receiving, and otherwise obtaining information from all relevant sources. Providing Consultation and Advice to Others—Providing consultation and expert advice to management or other groups on technical, systems-related, or process-related topics. Identifying Objects, Actions, and Events—Identifying information received by making estimates or categorizations, recognizing differences or similarities, or sensing changes in circumstances or events. Analyzing Data or Information—Identifying underlying principles, reasons, or facts by breaking down information or data into separate parts. Documenting/

Recording Information—Entering, transcribing, recording, storing, or maintaining information in either written form or by electronic/magnetic recording. Communicating with Other Workers—Providing information to supervisors, fellow workers, and subordinates. This information can be exchanged face-to-face, in writing, or via telephone/electronic transfer.

Curators

Administer affairs of museum and conduct research programs. Direct instructional, research, and public service activities of institution. Inspects premises for evidence of deterioration and need for repair. Develops and maintains institution's registration, cataloging, and basic recordkeeping systems. Arranges insurance coverage for objects on loan or special exhibits and recommends changes in coverage for entire collection. Negotiates and authorizes purchase, sale, exchange, or loan of collections. Directs and coordinates activities of curatorial, personnel, fiscal, technical, research, and clerical staff. Writes and reviews grant proposals, journal articles, institutional reports, and publicity materials. Conducts or organizes tours, workshops, and instructional sessions to acquaint individuals with use of institution's facilities and materials. Reserves facilities for group tours and social events and collects admission fees. Attends meetings, conventions, and civic events to promote use of institution's services, to seek financing, and to maintain community alliances. Plans and conducts special research projects. Confers with institution's board of directors to formulate and interpret policies, determine budget requirements, and plan overall operations. Plans and organizes acquisition, storage, and exhibition of collections and related educational materials. Schedules special events at facility and organizes details such as refreshments, entertainment, and decorations. Studies, examines, and tests acquisitions to authenticate their origin, composition, history, and current value.

Personality Type: Artistic. Artistic occupations frequently involve working with forms, designs, and patterns. They often require self-expression, and the work can be done without following a clear set of rules.

Abilities: Oral Expression—The ability to communicate information and ideas verbally so others will understand.

Written Expression—The ability to communicate information and ideas in writing so others will understand. Speech Clarity—The ability to speak clearly so that what is said is understandable to a listener. Oral Comprehension—The ability to listen to and understand information and ideas presented verbally. Written Comprehension—The ability to read and understand information and ideas presented in writing.

Skills: Speaking—Talking to others to effectively convey information. Active Listening—Listening to what other people are saying; asking questions as appropriate. Reading Comprehension—Understanding written information in work-related documents. Writing—Communicating effectively with others in writing as indicated by the needs of the audience. Judgment and Decision Making—Weighing the relative costs and benefits of a potential action. Coordination—Adjusting actions in relation to others' actions. Implementation Planning—Developing approaches for implementing an idea.

Generalized Work Activities: Judging Qualities—Making judgments about or assessing the value, importance, or quality of things, services, or other people's work. Establishing and Maintaining Relationships—Developing constructive and cooperative working relationships with others. Communicating with Persons Outside Organization—Communicating with persons outside the organization. Representing the organization to customers, the public, government, and other external sources. Exchanging information face-to-face, in writing, or via telephone/electronic transfer. Getting Information Needed to Do the Job—Observing, receiving, and otherwise obtaining information from all relevant sources. Monitoring and Controlling Resources—Monitoring and controlling resources and overseeing the spending of money.

Museum Technicians and Conservators

Prepare specimens such as fossils, skeletal parts, lace, and textiles for museum collection and exhibits. Restore documents or install, arrange, and exhibit materials. Prepares reports of activities. Documents methods of preservation and repair. Repairs and restores surfaces of artifacts to recover original appearance and to prevent deterioration, according to accepted procedures. Cleans objects such as paper, textiles, wood, metal, glass, rock, pottery, and furniture, using cleansers, solvents, soap solutions, and polishes. Studies descriptive information on object. Conducts standard chemical and physical tests to determine age, composition, and original appearance. Repairs or reassembles broken objects, using glue, solder, hand tools, power tools, and small machines. Constructs skeletal mounts of fossils, replicas of archaeological artifacts, or duplicate specimens, using variety of materials and hand tools. Evaluates need for repair and determines safest and most effective method of treating surface of object. Recommends preservation measures, such as control of temperature, humidity, and exposure to light, to curatorial and building maintenance staff. Designs and fabricates missing or broken parts. Installs, arranges, assembles, and prepares artifacts for exhibition. Cuts and welds metal sections in reconstruction or renovation of exterior structural sections and accessories of exhibits. Plans and conducts research to develop and improve methods of restoring and preserving specimens. Builds, repairs, and installs wooden steps, scaffolds, and walkways to permit access to or improved view of exhibited equipment. Estimates cost of restoration work. Directs curatorial and technical staff in handling, mounting, caring for, and storing art objects. Notifies superior when restoration of artifact requires outside experts. Preserves or directs preservation of objects, using plaster, resin, sealants, hardeners, and shellac.

Personality Type: Artistic. Artistic occupations frequently involve working with forms, designs, and patterns. They often require self-expression, and the work can be done without following a clear set of rules.

Abilities: Visualization—The ability to imagine how something will look after it is moved around or when its parts are moved or rearranged. Written Expression—The ability to communicate information and ideas in writing so others will understand. Near Vision—The ability to see details of objects at a close range. Visual Color Discrimination—The ability to match or detect differences between colors, including shades of color and brightness. Oral Expression—The ability to communicate information and ideas verbally so others will understand.

Skills: Product Inspection—Inspecting and evaluating the quality of products. Equipment Selection—Determining the kind of tools and equipment needed to do a job. Judgment and Decision Making—Weighing the relative costs and benefits of a potential action. Reading Comprehension—Understanding written information in work-related documents. Writing—Communicating effectively with others in writing as indicated by the needs of the audience. Information Gathering—Knowing how to find information and identifying essential information.

Generalized Work Activities: Handling and Moving Objects—Using one's hands and arms in handling, installing, forming, positioning, and moving materials, or in manipulating things. Includes the use of keyboards. Getting Information Needed to Do the Job—Observing, receiving, and otherwise obtaining information from all relevant sources. Making Decisions and Solving Problems—Combining, evaluating, and analyzing information and data to make decisions and solve problems. Involves making decisions about the relative importance of information and choosing the best solution. Communicating with Other Workers—Providing information to supervisors, fellow workers, and subordinates. This information can be exchanged face-to-face, in writing, or via telephone/electronic transfer. Implementing Ideas and Programs—Conducting or carrying out work procedures and activities in accord with one's own ideas or information provided through directions/instructions for purposes of installing, modifying, preparing, delivering, constructing, integrating, finishing, or completing programs, systems, structures, or products. Judging Qualities—Making judgments about or assessing the value, importance, or quality of things, services, or other people's work. Analyzing Data or Information—Identifying underlying principles, reasons, or facts by breaking down information or data into separate parts.

Artists and Commercial Artists

- ▲ Growth: 26%
- ▲ Annual Job Openings: 58,769
- ▲ Yearly Earnings: $31,690
- ▲ Education Required: Work experience, plus degree
- ▲ Self-Employed: 60.9%
- ▲ Part-Time: 24%

Cartoonists

Create original artwork using any of a wide variety of mediums and techniques, such as painting and sculpture. Creates and prepares sketches and model drawings of characters, providing details from memory, live models, manufactured products, or reference material. Renders sequential drawings of characters or other subject material which, when photographed and projected at a specific speed, becomes animated. Makes changes and corrections to cartoon, comic strip, or animation as necessary. Sketches and submits cartoon or animation for approval. Develops color patterns and moods. Paints background layouts to dramatize action for animated cartoon scenes. Labels each section with designated colors when colors are used. Discusses ideas for cartoons, comic strips, or animations with editor or publisher's representative. Develops personal ideas for cartoons, comic strips, or animations, or reads written material to develop ideas.

Personality Type: Artistic. Artistic occupations frequently involve working with forms, designs, and patterns. They often require self-expression, and the work can be done without following a clear set of rules.

Abilities: Originality—The ability to come up with unusual or clever ideas about a given topic or situation, or to develop creative ways to solve a problem. Fluency of Ideas—The ability to come up with a number of ideas about a given topic. Emphasis is on the number of ideas produced and not the quality, correctness, or creativity of the ideas. Visual Color Discrimination—The ability to match or detect differences between colors, including shades of color and brightness. Visualization—The ability to imagine how something will look after it is moved around or when its parts are moved or rearranged. Oral Comprehension—The ability to listen to and understand information and ideas presented verbally. Arm-Hand Steadiness—The ability to keep the hand and arm steady while making an arm movement or while holding the arm and hand in one position.

Skills: Idea Generation—Generating a number of different approaches to problems. Reading Comprehension—Understanding written information in work-related documents. Idea Evaluation—Evaluating the likely success of an idea in relation to the demands of the situation. Writing—Communicating effectively with others in writing as indicated by the needs of the audience. Active Listening—Listening to what other people are saying; asking questions as appropriate. Product Inspection—Inspecting and evaluating the quality of products.

Generalized Work Activities: Thinking Creatively—Originating, inventing, designing, or creating new applications, ideas, relationships, systems, or products, including artistic contributions. Handling and Moving Objects—Using one's hands and arms in handling, installing, forming, positioning, and moving materials, or in manipulating things. Includes the use of keyboards. Getting Information Needed to Do the Job—Observing, receiving, and otherwise obtaining information from all relevant sources. Implementing Ideas and Programs—Conducting or carrying out work procedures and activities in accord with one's own ideas or information provided through directions/instructions for purposes of installing, modifying, preparing, delivering, constructing, integrating, finishing, or completing programs, systems, structures, or products.

Making Decisions and Solving Problems—Combining, evaluating, and analyzing information and data to make decisions and solve problems. Involves making decisions about the relative importance of information and choosing the best solution.

Engravers/Carvers

Engrave or carve designs or lettering onto objects, using hand-held power tools. Dresses and shapes cutting wheels by holding dressing stone against rotating wheel. Prepares workpiece to be engraved or carved, such as glassware, rubber, or plastic product. Traces, sketches, or presses design or facsimile signature on workpiece by hand or by using artist equipment. Polishes engravings using felt and cork wheels. Suggests original designs to customer or management. Holds workpiece against outer edge of wheel and twists and turns workpiece to grind glass according to marked design. Selects and mounts wheel and miter on lathe. Equips lathe with water to cool wheel and prevent dust. Cuts outline of impression with graver and removes excess material with knife. Carves design on workpiece, using electric hand tool. Attaches engraved workpiece to mount, using cement.

Personality Type: Realistic. Realistic occupations frequently involve work activities that include practical, hands-on problems and solutions. They often deal with plants, animals, and real-world materials like wood, tools, and machinery. Many of the occupations require working outside and do not involve a lot of paperwork or working closely with others.

Abilities: Arm-Hand Steadiness—The ability to keep the hand and arm steady while making an arm movement or while holding the arm and hand in one position. Manual Dexterity—The ability to quickly make coordinated movements of one hand, a hand together with its arm, or two hands, to grasp, manipulate, or assemble objects. Near Vision—The ability to see details of objects at a close range. Visualization—The ability to imagine how something will look after it is moved around or when its parts are moved or rearranged. Control Precision—The ability to quickly and repeatedly make precise adjustments in moving the controls of a machine or vehicle to exact positions.

Skills: Product Inspection—Inspecting and evaluating the quality of products. Equipment Selection—Determining the kind of tools and equipment needed to do a job. Operation and Control—Controlling operations of equipment or systems. Judgment and Decision Making—Weighing the relative costs and benefits of a potential action. Monitoring—Assessing how well one is doing when learning or doing something.

Generalized Work Activities: Handling and Moving Objects—Using one's hands and arms in handling, installing, forming, positioning, and moving materials, or in manipulating things. Includes the use of keyboards. Controlling Machines and Processes—Using either control mechanisms or direct physical activity to operate machines or processes. Does not involve working with computers or vehicles. Monitoring Processes, Materials, Surroundings—Monitoring and reviewing information from materials, events, or the environment, often to detect problems or to find out when things are finished. Implementing Ideas and Programs—Conducting or carrying out work procedures and activities in accord with one's own ideas or information provided through directions/instructions for purposes of installing, modifying, preparing, delivering, constructing, integrating, finishing, or completing programs, systems, structures, or products. Thinking Creatively—Originating, inventing, designing, or creating new applications, ideas, relationships, systems, or products, including artistic contributions.

Etchers

Etch or cut artistic designs in glass articles, using acid solutions, sandblasting equipment, and design patterns. Removes wax or tape, using stylus or knife, to expose glassware surface to be etched. Positions pattern against waxed or taped ware and sprays ink through pattern to transfer design to wax or tape. Immerses ware in hot water to remove wax, or peels off tape. Sandblasts exposed area of glass, using spray gun, to cut design in surface. Immerses waxed ware in hydrofluoric acid to etch design on glass surface. Coats glass in molten wax or masks glassware with tape.

Personality Type: Realistic. Realistic occupations frequently involve work activities that include practical, hands-on problems and solutions. They often deal with plants, animals, and real-world materials like wood, tools, and machinery. Many of the occupations require working outside and do not involve a lot of paperwork or working closely with others.

Abilities: Manual Dexterity—The ability to quickly make coordinated movements of one hand, a hand together with its arm, or two hands, to grasp, manipulate, or assemble objects. Arm-Hand Steadiness—The ability to keep the hand and arm steady while making an arm movement or while holding the arm and hand in one position. Information Ordering—The ability to correctly follow a given rule or set of rules in order to arrange things or actions in a certain order. The things or actions can include numbers, letters, words, pictures, procedures, sentences, and mathematical or logical operations. Control Precision—The ability to quickly and repeatedly make precise adjustments in moving the controls of a machine or vehicle to exact positions. Near Vision—The ability to see details of objects at a close range. Visualization—The ability to imagine how something will look after it is moved around or when its parts are moved or rearranged.

Skills: Product Inspection—Inspecting and evaluating the quality of products. Operation and Control—Controlling operations of equipment or systems. Equipment Selection—Determining the kind of tools and equipment needed to do a job. Operation Monitoring—Watching gauges, dials, or other indicators to make sure a machine is working properly.

Generalized Work Activities: Handling and Moving Objects—Using one's hands and arms in handling, installing, forming, positioning, and moving materials, or in manipulating things. Includes the use of keyboards. Monitoring Processes, Materials, Surroundings—Monitoring and reviewing information from materials, events, or the environment, often to detect problems or to find out when things are finished. Controlling Machines and Processes—Using either control mechanisms or direct physical activity to operate machines or processes. Does not involve working with computers or vehicles. Implementing Ideas and Programs—Conducting or carrying out work procedures and activities in accord with one's own ideas or information provided through directions/instructions for purposes of installing, modifying, preparing, delivering, constructing, integrating, finishing, or completing programs, systems, structures, or products. Getting Information Needed to Do the Job—Observing, receiving, and otherwise obtaining information from all relevant sources.

Glass Blowers, Molders, Benders, and Finishers

Shape molten glass according to patterns. Inspects and measures product to verify conformance to specifications, using instruments such as micrometers, calipers, magnifiers, and rulers. Cuts length of tubing to specified size, using file or cutting wheel. Develops sketch of glass product into blueprint specifications, applying knowledge of glass technology and glass blowing. Adjusts press stroke length and pressure and regulates oven temperatures according to glass type processed. Determines type and quantity of glass required to fabricate product. Strikes neck of finished article to separate article from blowpipe. Heats glass to pliable stage, using gas flame or oven. Shapes, bends, or joins sections of glass, using paddles, pressing and flattening hand tools, or cork. Preheats or melts glass pieces or anneals or cools glass products and components, using ovens and refractory powder. Dips end of blowpipe into molten glass to collect gob on pipe head or cuts gob from molten glass, using sheers. Places glass into die or mold of press and controls press to form products such as glassware components or optical blanks. Blows tubing into specified shape, using compressed air or own breath. Examines gob of molten glass for imperfections, utilizing knowledge of molten glass characteristics.

Personality Type: Realistic. Realistic occupations frequently involve work activities that include practical, hands-on problems and solutions. They often deal with plants, animals, and real-world materials like wood,

tools, and machinery. Many of the occupations require working outside and do not involve a lot of paperwork or working closely with others.

Abilities: Visualization—The ability to imagine how something will look after it is moved around or when its parts are moved or rearranged. Manual Dexterity—The ability to quickly make coordinated movements of one hand, a hand together with its arm, or two hands, to grasp, manipulate, or assemble objects. Arm-Hand Steadiness—The ability to keep the hand and arm steady while making an arm movement or while holding the arm and hand in one position. Wrist-Finger Speed—The ability to make fast, simple, repeated movements of the fingers, hands, and wrists. Control Precision—The ability to quickly and repeatedly make precise adjustments in moving the controls of a machine or vehicle to exact positions.

Skills: Equipment Selection—Determining the kind of tools and equipment needed to do a job. Product Inspection—Inspecting and evaluating the quality of products. Monitoring—Assessing how well one is doing when learning or doing something. Operation and Control—Controlling operations of equipment or systems. Information Organization—Finding ways to structure or classify multiple pieces of information. Mathematics—Using mathematics to solve problems.

Generalized Work Activities: Handling and Moving Objects—Using one's hands and arms in handling, installing, forming, positioning, and moving materials, or in manipulating things. Includes the use of keyboards. Controlling Machines and Processes—Using either control mechanisms or direct physical activity to operate machines or processes. Does not involve working with computers or vehicles. Getting Information Needed to Do the Job—Observing, receiving, and otherwise obtaining information from all relevant sources. Evaluating Information against Standards—Evaluating information against a set of standards and verifying that it is correct. Performing General Physical Activities—Performing physical activities that require moving one's whole body, such as climbing, lifting, balancing, walking, and stooping. Performing activities that often also require considerable use of the arms and legs, such as in the physical handling of materials. Monitoring

Processes, Materials, Surroundings—Monitoring and reviewing information from materials, events, or the environment, often to detect problems or to find out when things are finished.

Graphic Designers

Design or create graphics to meet a client's specific commercial or promotional needs, such as packaging, displays, or logos. Use a variety of mediums to achieve artistic or decorative effects. Keys information into computer equipment to create layouts for client or supervisor. Prepares series of drawings to illustrate sequence and timing of story development for television production. Determines size and arrangement of illustrative material and copy and selects style and size of type. Marks up, pastes, and assembles final layouts to prepare them for printer. Draws and prints charts, graphs, illustrations, and other artwork, using computer. Studies illustrations and photographs to plan presentation of material, product, or service. Reviews final layout and suggests improvements as needed. Photographs layouts, using camera, to make layout prints for supervisor or client. Prepares notes and instructions for workers who assemble and prepare final layouts for printing. Develops negatives and prints, using negative and print developing equipment and tools and work aids to produce layout photographs. Prepares illustrations or rough sketches of material according to instructions of client or supervisor. Produces still and animated graphic formats for on-air and taped portions of television news broadcasts, using electronic video equipment. Draws sample of finished layout and presents sample to art director for approval. Arranges layout based upon available space, knowledge of layout principles, and aesthetic design concepts. Confers with client regarding layout design.

Personality Type: Artistic. Artistic occupations frequently involve working with forms, designs, and patterns. They often require self-expression, and the work can be done without following a clear set of rules.

Abilities: Originality—The ability to come up with unusual or clever ideas about a given topic or situation, or to develop creative ways to solve a problem. Fluency of Ideas—The ability to come up with a number of ideas about a given topic. Emphasis is on the number of ideas produced and not the quality, correctness, or creativity of the ideas. Visualization—The ability to imagine how something will look after it is moved around or when its parts are moved or rearranged. Visual Color Discrimination—The ability to match or detect differences between colors, including shades of color and brightness. Oral Expression—The ability to communicate information and ideas verbally so others will understand.

Skills: Operation and Control—Controlling operations of equipment or systems. Information Organization—Finding ways to structure or classify multiple pieces of information. Idea Generation—Generating a number of different approaches to problems. Idea Evaluation—Evaluating the likely success of an idea in relation to the demands of the situation. Equipment Selection—Determining the kind of tools and equipment needed to do a job. Writing—Communicating effectively with others in writing as indicated by the needs of the audience. Reading Comprehension—Understanding written information in work-related documents.

Generalized Work Activities: Drafting and Specifying Technical Devices—Providing documentation, detailed instructions, drawings, or specifications to inform others about how devices, parts, equipment, or structures are to be fabricated, constructed, assembled, modified, maintained, or used. Getting Information Needed to Do the Job—Observing, receiving, and otherwise obtaining information from all relevant sources. Thinking Creatively—Originating, inventing, designing, or creating new applications, ideas, relationships, systems, or products, including artistic contributions. Interacting with Computers—Controlling computer functions by using programs, setting up functions, writing software, or otherwise communicating with computer systems. Handling and Moving Objects—Using one's hands and arms in handling, installing, forming, positioning, and moving materials, or in manipulating things. Includes the use of keyboards. Communicating with Persons Outside Organization—Communicating with persons outside the organization. Representing the organization to customers, the public, government, and other external sources. Exchanging information face-to-face, in writing, or via telephone/electronic transfer. Identifying Objects, Actions, and Events—Identifying information received by making estimates or categorizations, recognizing differences or similarities, or sensing changes in circumstances or events.

Painters and Illustrators

Paint or draw subject material to produce original artwork or illustrations, using watercolors, oils, acrylics, tempera, or other paint mediums. Paints scenic backgrounds, murals, and portraiture for motion picture and television production sets, glass artworks, and exhibits. Installs finished stained glass in window or door frame. Integrates and develops visual elements such as line, space, mass, color, and perspective to produce desired effect. Brushes or sprays protective or decorative finish on completed background panels, informational legends, exhibit accessories, or finished painting. Studies style, techniques, colors, textures, and materials used by artist to maintain consistency in reconstruction or retouching procedures. Removes painting from frame or paint layer from canvas to restore artwork, following specified technique and equipment. Examines surfaces of paintings and proofs of artwork, using magnifying device, to determine method of restoration or needed corrections. Applies select solvents and cleaning agents to clean surface of painting and remove accretions, discolorations, and deteriorated varnish. Performs tests to determine factors such as age, structure, pigment stability, and probable reaction to various cleaning agents and solvents. Confers with professional personnel or client to discuss objectives of artwork, develop illustration ideas, and theme to be portrayed. Renders drawings, illustrations, and sketches of buildings, manufactured products, or models, working from sketches, blueprints, memory, or reference materials. Develops drawings, paintings, diagrams, and models of medical or biological subjects for use in publications, exhibits, consultations, research, and teaching. Etches, carves, paints, or draws artwork on material, such as stone, glass, canvas, wood, and linoleum. Assembles, leads, and solders finished glass to fabricate stained glass article.

Personality Type: Artistic. Artistic occupations frequently involve working with forms, designs, and patterns. They often require self-expression, and the work can be done without following a clear set of rules.

Abilities: Originality—The ability to come up with unusual or clever ideas about a given topic or situation, or to develop creative ways to solve a problem. Visualization—The ability to imagine how something will look after it is moved around or when its parts are moved or rearranged. Visual Color Discrimination—The ability to match or detect differences between colors, including shades of color and brightness. Fluency of Ideas—The ability to come up with a number of ideas about a given topic. Emphasis is on the number of ideas produced and not the quality, correctness, or creativity of the ideas.

Skills: Idea Generation—Generating a number of different approaches to problems. Product Inspection—Inspecting and evaluating the quality of products. Equipment Selection—Determining the kind of tools and equipment needed to do a job. Visioning—Developing an image of how a system should work under ideal conditions. Operations Analysis—Analyzing needs and product requirements to create a design.

Generalized Work Activities: Thinking Creatively—Originating, inventing, designing, or creating new applications, ideas, relationships, systems, or products, including artistic contributions. Getting Information Needed to Do the Job—Observing, receiving, and otherwise obtaining information from all relevant sources. Identifying Objects, Actions, and Events—Identifying information received by making estimates or categorizations, recognizing differences or similarities, or sensing changes in circumstances or events. Handling and Moving Objects—Using one's hands and arms in handling, installing, forming, positioning, and moving materials, or in manipulating things. Includes the use of keyboards. Implementing Ideas and Programs—Conducting or carrying out work procedures and activities in accord with one's own ideas or information provided through directions/instructions for purposes of installing, modifying, preparing, delivering, constructing, integrating, finishing, or completing programs, systems, structures, or products.

Potters

Mold clay into ware as clay revolves on potter's wheel. Adjusts speed of wheel according to feel of changing firmness of clay. Moves piece from wheel to dry. Verifies size and form, using calipers and templates. Pulls wire through base of article and wheel to separate finished piece. Positions ball of clay in center of potters wheel. Smoothes surfaces of finished piece, using rubber scrapers and wet sponge. Raises and shapes clay into ware such as vases, saggers, and pitchers, on revolving wheel, using hands, fingers, and thumbs. Starts motor or pumps treadle with foot to revolve wheel.

Personality Type: Realistic. Realistic occupations frequently involve work activities that include practical, hands-on problems and solutions. They often deal with plants, animals, and real-world materials like wood, tools, and machinery. Many of the occupations require working outside and do not involve a lot of paperwork or working closely with others.

Abilities: Arm-Hand Steadiness—The ability to keep the hand and arm steady while making an arm movement or while holding the arm and hand in one position. Visualization—The ability to imagine how something will look after it is moved around or when its parts are moved or rearranged. Manual Dexterity—The ability to quickly make coordinated movements of one hand, a hand together with its arm, or two hands, to grasp, manipulate, or assemble objects. Wrist-Finger Speed—The ability to make fast, simple, repeated movements of the fingers, hands, and wrists. Finger Dexterity—The ability to make precisely coordinated movements of the fingers of one or both hands to grasp, manipulate, or assemble very small objects.

Skills: Operation and Control—Controlling operations of equipment or systems. Product Inspection—Inspecting and evaluating the quality of products. Operations Analysis—Analyzing needs and product requirements to create a design. Monitoring—Assessing how well one is doing when learning or doing something. Technology Design—Generating or adapting equipment and technology to serve user needs. Equipment Selection—Determining the kind of tools and equipment needed to do a job.

Generalized Work Activities: Handling and Moving Objects—Using one's hands and arms in handling, installing, forming, positioning, and moving materials, or in manipulating things. Includes the use of keyboards. Thinking Creatively—Originating, inventing, designing, or creating new applications, ideas, relationships, systems, or products, including artistic contributions. Controlling Machines and Processes—Using either control mechanisms or direct physical activity to operate machines or processes. Does not involve working with computers or vehicles. Monitoring Processes, Materials, Surroundings—Monitoring and reviewing information from materials, events, or the environment, often to detect problems or to find out when things are finished. Getting Information Needed to Do the Job—Observing, receiving, and otherwise obtaining information from all relevant sources.

Sculptors

Design and construct three-dimensional art works, using materials such as stone, wood, plaster, and metal and employing various manual and tool techniques. Carves objects from stone, concrete, plaster, wood, or other material, using abrasives and tools such as chisels, gouges, and mall. Constructs artistic forms from metal or stone, using metalworking, welding, or masonry tools and equipment. Cuts, bends, laminates, arranges, and fastens individual or mixed raw and manufactured materials and products to form works of art. Models substances such as clay or wax, using fingers and small hand tools to form objects.

Personality Type: Artistic. Artistic occupations frequently involve working with forms, designs, and patterns. They often require self-expression, and the work can be done without following a clear set of rules.

Abilities: Visualization—The ability to imagine how something will look after it is moved around or when its parts are moved or rearranged. Originality—The ability to come up with unusual or clever ideas about a given topic or situation, or to develop creative ways to solve a problem. Manual Dexterity—The ability to quickly make coordinated movements of one hand, a hand together with its arm, or two hands, to grasp, manipulate, or assemble objects. Finger Dexterity—The ability to make precisely coordinated movements of the fingers of one or both hands to grasp, manipulate, or assemble very small objects. Fluency of Ideas—The ability to come up with a number of ideas about a given topic. Emphasis is on the number of ideas produced and not the quality, correctness, or creativity of the ideas.

Skills: Equipment Selection—Determining the kind of tools and equipment needed to do a job. Idea Generation—Generating a number of different approaches to problems. Implementation Planning—Developing approaches for implementing an idea. Idea Evaluation—Evaluating the likely success of an idea in relation to the demands of the situation. Monitoring—Assessing how well one is doing when learning or doing something. Operation and Control—Controlling operations of equipment or systems.

Generalized Work Activities: Thinking Creatively—Originating, inventing, designing, or creating new applications, ideas, relationships, systems, or products, including artistic contributions. Handling and Moving Objects—Using one's hands and arms in handling, installing, forming, positioning, and moving materials, or in manipulating things. Includes the use of keyboards. Implementing Ideas and Programs—Conducting or carrying out work procedures and activities in accord with one's own ideas or information provided through directions/instructions for purposes of installing, modifying, preparing, delivering, constructing, integrating, finishing, or completing programs, systems, structures, or products. Getting Information Needed to Do the Job—Observing, receiving, and otherwise obtaining information from all relevant sources. Performing General Physical Activities—Performing physical activities that require moving one's whole body, such as climbing, lifting, balancing, walking, and stooping. Performing activities that often also require considerable use of the arms and legs, such as in the physical handling of materials.

Sketch Artists

Sketch likenesses of subjects according to observation or descriptions to assist law enforcement agencies in identifying suspects, to depict court room scenes, or to entertain patrons, using mediums such as pencil,

charcoal, and pastels. Operates photocopy or similar machine to reproduce composite image. Interviews crime victims and witnesses to obtain descriptive information concerning physical build, sex, nationality, and facial features of unidentified suspect. Prepares series of simple line drawings conforming to description of suspect and presents drawings to informant for selection of sketch. Alters copy of composite image until witness or victim is satisfied that composite is best possible representation of suspect. Assembles and arranges outlines of features to form composite image, according to information provided by witness or victim. Poses subject to accentuate most pleasing features or profile. Measures distances and develops sketches of crime scene from photograph and measurements. Classifies and codes components of image, using established system, to help identify suspect. Draws sketch, profile, or likeness of posed subject or photograph, using pencil, charcoal, pastels, or other medium. Searches police photograph records, using classification and coding system to determine if existing photograph of suspects is available.

Personality Type: Artistic. Artistic occupations frequently involve working with forms, designs, and patterns. They often require self-expression, and the work can be done without following a clear set of rules.

Abilities: Visualization—The ability to imagine how something will look after it is moved around or when its parts are moved or rearranged. Oral Comprehension—The ability to listen to and understand information and ideas presented verbally. Arm-Hand Steadiness—The ability to keep the hand and arm steady while making an arm movement or while holding the arm and hand in one position. Finger Dexterity—The ability to make precisely coordinated movements of the fingers of one or both hands to grasp, manipulate, or assemble very small objects.

Skills: Active Listening—Listening to what other people are saying; asking questions as appropriate. Information Organization—Finding ways to structure or classify multiple pieces of information. Synthesis/Reorganization—Reorganizing information to get a better approach to problems or tasks. Speaking—Talking to others to effectively convey information. Information Gathering—Knowing how to find information and identifying essential information.

Generalized Work Activities: Getting Information Needed to Do the Job—Observing, receiving, and otherwise obtaining information from all relevant sources. Thinking Creatively—Originating, inventing, designing, or creating new applications, ideas, relationships, systems, or products, including artistic contributions. Identifying Objects, Actions, and Events—Identifying information received by making estimates or categorizations, recognizing differences or similarities, or sensing changes in circumstances or events. Handling and Moving Objects—Using one's hands and arms in handling, installing, forming, positioning, and moving materials, or in manipulating things. Includes the use of keyboards. Estimating Needed Characteristics—Estimating the characteristics of materials, products, events, or information; estimating sizes, distances, and quantities; determining time, costs, resources, or materials needed to perform a work activity.

Assessors

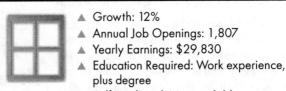

- ▲ Growth: 12%
- ▲ Annual Job Openings: 1,807
- ▲ Yearly Earnings: $29,830
- ▲ Education Required: Work experience, plus degree
- ▲ Self-Employed: Not available
- ▲ Part-Time: Not available

Assessors

Appraise real and personal property to determine its fair value. Assess taxes in accordance with prescribed schedules. Interprets property laws, formulates operational policies, and directs assessment office activities. Assesses and computes taxes according to prescribed tax tables and schedules. Writes and submits appraisal and tax reports for public record. Inspects property, considering factors such as market value, location, and building or replacement costs, to determine appraisal value. Appraises real and personal property such as aircraft, marine craft, buildings, and land to determine fair value.

Personality Type: Conventional. Conventional occupations frequently involve following set procedures and routines. These occupations can include working with data and details more than with ideas. Usually there is a clear line of authority to follow.

Abilities: Number Facility—The ability to add, subtract, multiply, or divide quickly and correctly. Written Expression—The ability to communicate information and ideas in writing so others will understand. Mathematical Reasoning—The ability to understand and organize a problem and then select a mathematical method or formula to solve the problem. Written Comprehension—The ability to read and understand information and ideas presented in writing. Inductive Reasoning—The ability to combine separate pieces of information, or specific answers to problems, to form general rules or conclusions. Includes coming up with a logical explanation for why a series of seemingly unrelated events occur together.

Skills: Information Gathering—Knowing how to find information and identifying essential information. Product Inspection—Inspecting and evaluating the quality of products. Writing—Communicating effectively with others in writing as indicated by the needs of the audience. Judgment and Decision Making—Weighing the relative costs and benefits of a potential action. Reading Comprehension—Understanding written information in work-related documents.

Generalized Work Activities: Processing Information—Compiling, coding, categorizing, calculating, tabulating, auditing, verifying, or processing information or data. Judging Qualities—Making judgments about or assessing the value, importance, or quality of things, services, or other people's work. Estimating Needed Characteristics—Estimating the characteristics of materials, products, events, or information; estimating sizes, distances, and quantities; determining time, costs, resources, or materials needed to perform a work activity. Getting Information Needed to Do the Job—Observing, receiving, and otherwise obtaining information from all relevant sources.

Athletes, Coaches, and Umpires

- ▲ Growth: 28%
- ▲ Annual Job Openings: 19,465
- ▲ Yearly Earnings: $22,210
- ▲ Education Required: Long-term O-J-T
- ▲ Self-Employed: 31.4%
- ▲ Part-Time: 25.3%

Athletes and Sports Competitors

Compete in athletic events. Participates in athletic events and competitive sports, according to established rules and regulations. Plays professional sport and is identified according to sport played, such as football, basketball, baseball, hockey, or boxing. Represents team or professional sports club, speaking to groups involved in activities such as sports clinics and fund raisers.

Exercises and practices under direction of athletic trainer or professional coach to prepare and train for competitive events.

Personality Type: Enterprising. Enterprising occupations frequently involve starting up and carrying out projects. These occupations can involve leading people and making many decisions. They sometimes require risk taking and often deal with business.

Abilities: Speed of Limb Movement—The ability to quickly move the arms or legs. Stamina—The ability to exert one's self physically over long periods of time without getting winded or out of breath. Gross Body Coordination—The ability to coordinate the movement of the arms, legs, and torso together in activities where the whole body is in motion. Explosive Strength—The ability to use short bursts of muscle force to propel oneself, as in jumping or sprinting, or to throw an object.

Skills: Monitoring—Assessing how well one is doing when learning or doing something. Active Listening— Listening to what other people are saying; asking questions as appropriate. Coordination—Adjusting actions in relation to others' actions. Active Learning— Working with new material or information to grasp its implications. Speaking—Talking to others to effectively convey information.

Generalized Work Activities: Performing General Physical Activities—Performing physical activities that require moving one's whole body, such as climbing, lifting, balancing, walking, and stooping. Performing activities that often also require considerable use of the arms and legs, such as in the physical handling of materials. Getting Information Needed to Do the Job— Observing, receiving, and otherwise obtaining information from all relevant sources. Communicating with Other Workers—Providing information to supervisors, fellow workers, and subordinates. This information can be exchanged face-to-face, in writing, or via telephone/electronic transfer. Handling and Moving Objects—Using one's hands and arms in handling, installing, forming, positioning, and moving materials, or in manipulating things. Establishing and Maintaining Relationships—Developing constructive and cooperative working relationships with others.

Athletic Trainers

Evaluate, advise, and treat athletes to assist them in recovering from injury, avoiding injury, or maintaining peak physical fitness. Evaluates physical condition of athletes and advises or prescribes routine and corrective exercises to strengthen muscles. Administers emergency first aid, treats minor chronic disabilities, or refers injured person to physician. Recommends special diets to improve health, increase stamina, and reduce weight of athletes. Wraps ankles, fingers, wrists or other body parts with synthetic skin, gauze, or adhesive tape to support muscles and ligaments. Massages body parts to relieve soreness, strains, and bruises.

Personality Type: Social. Social occupations frequently involve working with, communicating with, and teaching people. These occupations often involve helping or providing service to others.

Abilities: Oral Expression—The ability to communicate information and ideas verbally so others will understand. Problem Sensitivity—The ability to tell when something is wrong or is likely to go wrong. Does not involve solving the problem, only recognizing there is a problem. Speech Clarity—The ability to speak clearly so that what is said is understandable to a listener. Trunk Strength— The ability to use one's abdominal and lower back muscles to support part of the body repeatedly or continuously over time without giving out or fatiguing. Wrist-Finger Speed—The ability to make fast, simple, repeated movements of the fingers, hands, and wrists.

Skills: Active Listening—Listening to what other people are saying; asking questions as appropriate. Problem Identification—Identifying the nature of problems. Speaking—Talking to others to effectively convey information. Information Gathering—Knowing how to find information and identifying essential information. Social Perceptiveness—Being aware of other people's reactions and understanding why people react the way they do.

Generalized Work Activities: Assisting and Caring for Others—Providing assistance or personal care to others. Getting Information Needed to Do the Job— Observing, receiving, and otherwise obtaining information from all relevant sources. Identifying

Objects, Actions, and Events—Identifying information received by making estimates or categorizations, recognizing differences or similarities, or sensing changes in circumstances or events. Performing General Physical Activities—Performing physical activities that require moving one's whole body, such as climbing, lifting, balancing, walking, and stooping. Performing activities that often also require considerable use of the arms and legs, such as in the physical handling of materials. Making Decisions and Solving Problems—Combining, evaluating, and analyzing information and data to make decisions and solve problems. Involves making decisions about the relative importance of information and choosing the best solution. Establishing and Maintaining Relationships—Developing constructive and cooperative working relationships with others. Communicating with Other Workers—Providing information to supervisors, fellow workers, and subordinates. This information can be exchanged face-to-face, in writing, or via telephone/electronic transfer.

Coaches and Scouts

Instruct or coach groups or individuals in the fundamentals of sports. Demonstrate techniques and methods of participation. Evaluate athletes' strengths and weaknesses to identify possible recruits or to improve the athletes' technique and prepare them for competition. Evaluates team and opposition capabilities to develop and plan game strategy. Observes athletes to determine areas of deficiency and need for individual or team improvement. Plans and directs physical conditioning program for athletes to achieve maximum athletic performance. Instructs athletes, individually or in groups, demonstrating sport techniques and game strategies. Prepares scouting reports detailing information such as selection or rejection of athletes and locations identified for future recruitment. Evaluates athletes' skills and discusses or recommends acquisition, trade, or position assignment of players. Analyzes athletes' performance and reviews game statistics or records to determine fitness and potential for professional sports. Negotiates with professional athletes or representatives to obtain services and arrange contracts.

Personality Type: Enterprising. Enterprising occupations frequently involve starting up and carrying out projects. These occupations can involve leading people and making many decisions. They sometimes require risk taking and often deal with business.

Abilities: Oral Expression—The ability to communicate information and ideas verbally so others will understand. Far Vision—The ability to see details at a distance. Problem Sensitivity—The ability to tell when something is wrong or is likely to go wrong. Does not involve solving the problem, only recognizing there is a problem. Visualization—The ability to imagine how something will look after it is moved around or when its parts are moved or rearranged. Deductive Reasoning—The ability to apply general rules to specific problems to come up with logical answers. Involves deciding if an answer makes sense. Speech Clarity—The ability to speak clearly so that what is said is understandable to a listener.

Skills: Instructing—Teaching others how to do something. Management of Personnel Resources—Motivating, developing, and directing people as they work, identifying the best people for the job. Identification of Key Causes—Identifying the things that must be changed to achieve a goal. Idea Generation—Generating a number of different approaches to problems. Speaking—Talking to others to effectively convey information. Negotiation—Bringing others together and trying to reconcile differences. Judgment and Decision Making—Weighing the relative costs and benefits of a potential action.

Generalized Work Activities: Coaching and Developing Others—Identifying developmental needs of others and coaching or otherwise helping others to improve their knowledge or skills. Getting Information Needed to Do the Job—Observing, receiving, and otherwise obtaining information from all relevant sources. Communicating with Other Workers—Providing information to supervisors, fellow workers, and subordinates. This information can be exchanged face-to-face, in writing, or via telephone/electronic transfer. Judging Qualities—Making judgments about or assessing the value, importance, or quality of things, services, or other people's work. Making Decisions and Solving Problems—Combining, evaluating, and analyzing information and data to make decisions and solve problems. Involves making decisions about the relative importance of information and choosing the best solution.

Umpires, Referees, and Other Sports Officials

Officiate at competitive athletic or sporting events. Detect infractions of rules and decide penalties according to established regulations. Inspects sporting equipment or examines participants to ensure compliance to regulations and safety of participants and spectators. Signals participants or other officials to facilitate identification of infractions or otherwise regulate play or competition. Directs participants to assigned areas such as starting blocks or penalty areas. Resolves claims of rule infractions, or complaints lodged by participants, and assesses penalties based on established regulations. Clocks events according to established standards for play, to measure performance of participants. Prepares reports to regulating organization concerning sporting activities, complaints, and actions taken or needed, such as fines or other disciplinary actions. Records and maintains information regarding participants and sporting activities. Observes actions of participants at athletic and sporting events to regulate competition and detect infractions of rules. Makes qualifying determinations regarding participants, such as qualifying order or handicap. Confers with other sporting officials and facility managers to provide information, coordinate activities, and discuss problems.

Personality Type: Enterprising. Enterprising occupations frequently involve starting up and carrying out projects. These occupations can involve leading people and making many decisions. They sometimes require risk taking and often deal with business.

Abilities: Oral Expression—The ability to communicate information and ideas verbally so others will understand. Selective Attention—The ability to concentrate and not be distracted while performing a task over a period of time. Far Vision—The ability to see details at a distance. Near Vision—The ability to see details of objects at a close range.

Skills: Coordination—Adjusting actions in relation to others' actions. Speaking—Talking to others to effectively convey information. Active Listening—Listening to what other people are saying; asking questions as appropriate. Judgment and Decision Making—Weighing the relative costs and benefits of a potential action. Information Gathering—Knowing how to find information and identifying essential information.

Generalized Work Activities: Getting Information Needed to Do the Job—Observing, receiving, and otherwise obtaining information from all relevant sources. Monitoring Processes, Materials, Surroundings—Monitoring and reviewing information from materials, events, or the environment, often to detect problems or to find out when things are finished. Identifying Objects, Actions, and Events—Identifying information received by making estimates or categorizations, recognizing differences or similarities, or sensing changes in circumstances or events. Making Decisions and Solving Problems—Combining, evaluating, and analyzing information and data to make decisions and solve problems. Involves making decisions about the relative importance of information and choosing the best solution. Documenting/Recording Information—Entering, transcribing, recording, storing, or maintaining information in either written form or by electronic/magnetic recording.

Atmospheric Scientists

▲ Growth: 15%
▲ Annual Job Openings: 683
▲ Yearly Earnings: $54,430
▲ Education Required: Bachelor's degree
▲ Self-Employed: 0%
▲ Part-Time: 6.6%

Atmospheric and Space Scientists

Investigate atmospheric phenomena and interpret meteorological data gathered by surface and air stations, satellites, and radar to prepare reports and forecasts for public and other uses. Prepares special forecasts and briefings for air and sea transportation, agriculture, fire prevention, air-pollution control, and school groups. Operates computer graphic equipment to produce weather reports and maps for analysis, distribution, or use in televised weather broadcast. Directs forecasting services at weather station or at radio or television broadcasting facility. Issues hurricane and other severe weather warnings. Conducts basic or applied research in meteorology. Studies and interprets synoptic reports, maps, photographs, and prognostic charts to predict long- and short-range weather conditions. Analyzes and interprets meteorological data gathered by surface and upper-air stations, satellites, and radar to prepare reports and forecasts. Broadcasts weather forecast over television or radio.

Personality Type: Investigative. Investigative occupations frequently involve working with ideas and require an extensive amount of thinking. These occupations can involve searching for facts and figuring out problems mentally.

Abilities: Speech Clarity—The ability to speak clearly so that what is said is understandable to a listener. Oral Expression—The ability to communicate information and ideas verbally so others will understand. Written Comprehension—The ability to read and understand information and ideas presented in writing. Speed of Closure—The ability to quickly make sense of information that seems to be without meaning or organization. Involves quickly combining and organizing different pieces of information into a meaningful pattern. Near Vision—The ability to see details of objects at a close range. Inductive Reasoning—The ability to combine separate pieces of information, or specific answers to problems, to form general rules or conclusions. Includes coming up with a logical explanation for why a series of seemingly unrelated events occur together.

Skills: Information Gathering—Knowing how to find information and identifying essential information. Information Organization—Finding ways to structure or classify multiple pieces of information. Critical Thinking—Using logic and analysis to identify the strengths and weaknesses of different approaches. Speaking—Talking to others to effectively convey information. Reading Comprehension—Understanding written information in work-related documents. Active Learning—Working with new material or information to grasp its implications. Science—Using scientific methods to solve problems.

Generalized Work Activities: Getting Information Needed to Do the Job—Observing, receiving, and otherwise obtaining information from all relevant sources. Interpreting Meaning of Information to Others—Translating or explaining what information means and how it can be understood or used to support responses or feedback to others. Analyzing Data or Information—Identifying underlying principles, reasons, or facts by breaking down information or data into separate parts. Monitoring Processes, Materials, Surroundings—Monitoring and reviewing information from materials, events, or the environment, often to detect problems or to find out when things are finished.

Auto Insurance Appraisers

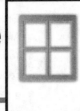

▲ Growth: 16%
▲ Annual Job Openings: 871
▲ Yearly Earnings: $40,000
▲ Education Required: Long-term O-J-T
▲ Self-Employed: Not available
▲ Part-Time: Not available

Insurance Appraisers, Auto Damage

Appraise automobile or other vehicle damage to determine cost of repair for insurance claim settlement. Seek agreement with automotive repair shop on cost of repair. Prepare insurance forms to indicate repair cost or cost estimates and recommendations. Evaluates practicality of repair as opposed to payment of market value of vehicle before accident. Examines damaged vehicle to determine extent of structural, body, mechanical, electrical, or interior damage. Reviews repair-cost estimates with automobile repair shop to secure agreement on cost of repairs. Arranges to have damage appraised by another appraiser to resolve disagreement with shop on repair cost. Prepares insurance forms to indicate repair-cost estimates and recommendations. Estimates parts and labor to repair damage, using standard automotive labor and parts-cost manuals and knowledge of automotive repair. Determines salvage value on total-loss vehicles.

Personality Type: Conventional. Conventional occupations frequently involve following set procedures and routines. These occupations can include working with data and details more than with ideas. Usually there is a clear line of authority to follow.

Abilities: Number Facility—The ability to add, subtract, multiply, or divide quickly and correctly. Mathematical Reasoning—The ability to understand and organize a problem and then select a mathematical method or formula to solve the problem. Written

Comprehension—The ability to read and understand information and ideas presented in writing. Oral Comprehension—The ability to listen to and understand information and ideas presented verbally. Written Expression—The ability to communicate information and ideas in writing so others will understand.

Skills: Judgment and Decision Making—Weighing the relative costs and benefits of a potential action. Mathematics—Using mathematics to solve problems. Information Gathering—Knowing how to find information and identifying essential information. Critical Thinking—Using logic and analysis to identify the strengths and weaknesses of different approaches. Active Listening—Listening to what other people are saying; asking questions as appropriate. Problem Identification—Identifying the nature of problems.

Generalized Work Activities: Getting Information Needed to Do the Job—Observing, receiving, and otherwise obtaining information from all relevant sources. Inspecting Equipment, Structures, Materials—Inspecting or diagnosing equipment, structures, or materials to identify the causes of errors or other problems or defects. Identifying Objects, Actions, and Events—Identifying information received by making estimates or categorizations, recognizing differences or similarities, or sensing changes in circumstances or events. Performing Administrative Activities—Approving requests, handling paperwork, and performing day-to-day administrative tasks. Documenting/Recording Information—Entering, transcribing, recording, storing, or maintaining information in either written form or by electronic/magnetic recording.

Automotive Body Repairers

▲ Growth: 16%
▲ Annual Job Openings: 33,051
▲ Yearly Earnings: $27,400
▲ Education Required: Long-term O-J-T
▲ Self-Employed: 21.1%
▲ Part-Time: 8.6%

Automotive Body and Related Repairers

Repair and refinish automotive vehicle bodies and straighten vehicle frames. Cuts and tapes plastic separating film to outside repair area to avoid damaging surrounding surfaces during repair procedure. Cuts opening in vehicle body for installation of customized windows, using templates and power shears or chisel. Fits and secures windows, vinyl roof, and metal trim to vehicle body, using caulking gun, adhesive brush, and mallet. Removes damaged fenders and panels, using wrenches and cutting torch. Installs replacement parts, using wrenches or welding equipment. Cuts away damaged fiberglass from automobile body, using air grinder. Mixes polyester resin and hardener to be used in restoring damaged area. Examines vehicle to determine extent and type of damage. Adjusts or aligns headlights, wheels, and brake system. Cleans work area, using air hose to remove damaged material and to remove discarded fiberglass strips used in repair procedures. Reads specifications or confers with customer to determine custom modifications to alter appearance of vehicle. Peels separating film from repair area and washes repaired surface with water. Soaks fiberglass matting in resin mixture and applies layers matting over repair area to specified thickness. Measures and marks vinyl material and cuts material to size for roof installation, using rule, straightedge, and hand shears. Paints and sands repaired surface, using paint spray gun and motorized sander. Fills depressions with body filler and files, grinds, and sands repaired surfaces, using power tools and hand tools. Straightens bent automobile or other vehicle frames, using pneumatic frame-straightening machine. Positions dolly block against surface of dented area and beats opposite surface to remove dents, using hammer. Removes upholstery, accessories, electrical window- and seat-operating equipment, and trim to gain access to vehicle body and fenders.

Personality Type: Realistic. Realistic occupations frequently involve work activities that include practical, hands-on problems and solutions. They often deal with plants, animals, and real-world materials like wood, tools, and machinery. Many of the occupations require working outside and do not involve a lot of paperwork or working closely with others.

Abilities: Manual Dexterity—The ability to quickly make coordinated movements of one hand, a hand together with its arm, or two hands, to grasp, manipulate, or assemble objects. Oral Comprehension —The ability to listen to and understand information and ideas presented verbally. Visualization—The ability to imagine how something will look after it is moved around or when its parts are moved or rearranged. Multilimb Coordination—The ability to coordinate movements of two or more limbs together (for example, two arms, two legs, or one leg and one arm) while sitting, standing, or lying down. Does not involve performing the activities while the body is in motion. Information Ordering—The ability to correctly follow a given rule or set of rules in order to arrange things or actions in a certain order. The things or actions can include numbers, letters, words, pictures, procedures, sentences, and mathematical or logical operations.

Skills: Product Inspection—Inspecting and evaluating the quality of products. Repairing—Repairing machines or systems, using the needed tools. Installation—Installing equipment, machines, wiring, or programs to meet specifications. Equipment Selection—Determining the kind of tools and equipment needed to do a job. Information Gathering—Knowing how to find information and identifying essential information. Information Organization—Finding ways to structure or classify multiple pieces of information.

Generalized Work Activities: Handling and Moving Objects—Using one's hands and arms in handling, installing, forming, positioning, and moving materials, or in manipulating things. Includes the use of keyboards. Performing General Physical Activities—Performing physical activities that require moving one's whole body, such as climbing, lifting, balancing, walking, and stooping. Performing activities that often also require considerable use of the arms and legs, such as in the physical handling of materials. Controlling Machines and Processes—Using either control mechanisms or direct physical activity to operate machines or processes. Does not involve working with computers or vehicles. Inspecting Equipment, Structures, Materials—Inspecting or diagnosing equipment, structures, or materials to identify the causes of errors or other problems or defects. Repairing and Maintaining Mechanical Equipment—Fixing, servicing, aligning, setting up, adjusting, and testing machines, devices, moving parts, and equipment that operate primarily on the basis of mechanical, not electronic, principles. Getting Information Needed to Do the Job—Observing, receiving, and otherwise obtaining information from all relevant sources.

Automotive Glass Installers and Repairers

Replace or repair broken windshields and window glass in motor vehicles. Obtains windshield for specific automobile make and model from stock and examines for defects prior to installation. Applies moisture-proofing compound along glass edges and installs glass into windshield or into glass frame in door or side panel

of vehicle. Cuts flat safety glass according to specified pattern, using glass cutter. Holds cut or uneven edge of glass against automated abrasive belt to shape or smooth edges. Installs rubber channeling strip around edge of glass or frame to weather proof or to prevent rattling. Installs precut replacement glass to replace curved or custom-shaped windows. Removes broken or damaged glass windshield or window glass from motor vehicles, using hand tools to remove screws from frame holding glass. Replaces or adjusts motorized or manual window-raising mechanisms.

Personality Type: Realistic. Realistic occupations frequently involve work activities that include practical, hands-on problems and solutions. They often deal with plants, animals, and real-world materials like wood, tools, and machinery. Many of the occupations require working outside and do not involve a lot of paperwork or working closely with others.

Abilities: Static Strength—The ability to exert maximum muscle force to lift, push, pull, or carry objects. Arm-Hand Steadiness—The ability to keep the hand and arm steady while making an arm movement or while holding the arm and hand in one position. Gross Body Coordination—The ability to coordinate the movement of the arms, legs, and torso together in activities where the whole body is in motion. Extent Flexibility—The ability to bend, stretch, twist, or reach out with the body, arms, and/or legs. Trunk Strength—The ability to use one's abdominal and lower back muscles to support part of the body repeatedly or continuously over time without giving out or fatiguing. Multilimb Coordination—The ability to coordinate movements of two or more limbs together (for example, two arms, two legs, or one leg and one arm) while sitting, standing, or lying down. Does not involve performing the activities while the body is in motion.

Skills: Installation—Installing equipment, machines, wiring, or programs to meet specifications. Product Inspection—Inspecting and evaluating the quality of products. Equipment Selection—Determining the kind of tools and equipment needed to do a job. Repairing—Repairing machines or systems, using the needed tools. Problem Identification—Identifying the nature of problems.

Generalized Work Activities: Handling and Moving Objects—Using one's hands and arms in handling, installing, forming, positioning, and moving materials, or in manipulating things. Includes the use of keyboards. Performing General Physical Activities—Performing physical activities that require moving one's whole body, such as climbing, lifting, balancing, walking, and stooping. Performing activities that often also require considerable use of the arms and legs, such as in the physical handling of materials. Inspecting Equipment, Structures, Materials—Inspecting or diagnosing equipment, structures, or materials to identify the causes of errors or other problems or defects. Repairing and Maintaining Mechanical Equipment—Fixing, servicing, aligning, setting up, adjusting, and testing machines, devices, moving parts, and equipment that operate primarily on the basis of mechanical, not electronic, principles. Controlling Machines and Processes—Using either control mechanisms or direct physical activity to operate machines or processes. Does not involve working with computers or vehicles. Getting Information Needed to Do the Job—Observing, receiving, and otherwise obtaining information from all relevant sources.

Automotive Mechanics and Service Technicians

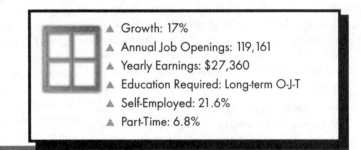

- ▲ Growth: 17%
- ▲ Annual Job Openings: 119,161
- ▲ Yearly Earnings: $27,360
- ▲ Education Required: Long-term O-J-T
- ▲ Self-Employed: 21.6%
- ▲ Part-Time: 6.8%

Automotive Master Mechanics

Repair automobiles, trucks, buses, and other vehicles. Repair virtually any part on the vehicle or specialize in the transmission system. Repairs damaged automobile bodies. Repairs, relines, replaces, and adjusts brakes. Rewires ignition system, lights, and instrument panel. Repairs or replaces shock absorbers. Repairs radiator leaks. Rebuilds parts such as crankshafts and cylinder blocks. Aligns front end. Replaces and adjusts headlights. Installs and repairs accessories such as radios, heaters, mirrors, and windshield wipers. Repairs manual and automatic transmissions. Overhauls or replaces carburetors, blowers, generators, distributors, starts, and pumps. Repairs or replaces parts such as pistons, rods, gears, valves, and bearings. Repairs and overhauls defective automotive units such as engines, transmissions, or differentials. Examines vehicles and discusses extent of damage or malfunction with customer.

Personality Type: Realistic. Realistic occupations frequently involve work activities that include practical, hands-on problems and solutions. They often deal with plants, animals, and real-world materials like wood, tools, and machinery. Many of the occupations require working outside and do not involve a lot of paperwork or working closely with others.

Abilities: Information Ordering—The ability to correctly follow a given rule or set of rules in order to arrange things or actions in a certain order. The things or actions can include numbers, letters, words, pictures, procedures, sentences, and mathematical or logical operations. Problem Sensitivity—The ability to tell when something is wrong or is likely to go wrong. Does not involve solving the problem, only recognizing there is a problem. Hearing Sensitivity—The ability to detect or tell the difference between sounds that vary over broad ranges of pitch and loudness. Visualization—The ability to imagine how something will look after it is moved around or when its parts are moved or rearranged. Extent Flexibility—The ability to bend, stretch, twist, or reach out with the body, arms, and/or legs. Manual Dexterity—The ability to quickly make coordinated movements of one hand, a hand together with its arm, or two hands, to grasp, manipulate, or assemble objects.

Skills: Repairing—Repairing machines or systems, using the needed tools. Troubleshooting—Determining what is causing an operating error and deciding what to do about it. Problem Identification—Identifying the nature of problems. Equipment Maintenance—Performing routine maintenance and determining when and what kind of maintenance is needed. Installation—Installing equipment, machines, wiring, or programs to meet specifications.

Generalized Work Activities: Repairing and Maintaining Mechanical Equipment—Fixing, servicing, aligning, setting up, adjusting, and testing machines, devices, moving parts, and equipment that operate primarily on the basis of mechanical, not electronic, principles. Inspecting Equipment, Structures, Materials—Inspecting or diagnosing equipment, structures, or materials to identify the causes of errors or other problems or defects. Updating and Using Job-Relevant Knowledge—Keeping up-to-date technically and knowing the functions of one's own job and related jobs. Repairing and Maintaining Electrical Equipment—Fixing, servicing, adjusting, regulating, calibrating, fine-tuning, or testing machines, devices, and equipment that operate primarily on the basis of electrical or electronic, not mechanical, principles. Controlling Machines and Processes—Using either control mechanisms or direct physical activity to operate machines or processes. Does not involve working with computers or vehicles. Handling and Moving Objects—Using one's hands and arms in handling, installing, forming, positioning, and moving materials, or in manipulating things. Includes the use of keyboards.

Automotive Specialty Technicians

Repair only one system or component on a vehicle, such as brakes, suspension, or radiator. Repairs and replaces defective balljoint suspension, brakeshoes, and wheelbearings. Repairs and replaces automobile leaf springs. Repairs and rebuilds clutch systems. Removes and replaces defective mufflers and tailpipes from automobiles. Repairs and aligns defective wheels of automobiles. Installs and repairs automotive air-conditioning units. Repairs, replaces, and adjusts defective carburetor parts and gasoline filters. Inspects, tests, repairs, and replaces automotive cooling systems and fuel tanks. Tunes automobile engines and tests electronic computer components. Examines vehicle, compiles estimate of repair costs, and secures customer approval to perform repairs. Repairs, overhauls, and adjusts automobile brake systems. Converts vehicle fuel systems from gasoline to butane gas operations. Repairs and services operating butane fuel units. Aligns and repairs wheels, axles, frames, torsion bars, and steering mechanisms of automobiles. Rebuilds, repairs, and tests automotive injection units. Repairs, installs, and adjusts hydraulic and electromagnetic automatic lift mechanisms used to raise and lower automobile windows, seats, and tops. Inspects and tests new vehicles for damage, records findings, and makes repairs.

Personality Type: Realistic. Realistic occupations frequently involve work activities that include practical, hands-on problems and solutions. They often deal with plants, animals, and real-world materials like wood, tools, and machinery. Many of the occupations require working outside and do not involve a lot of paperwork or working closely with others.

Abilities: Extent Flexibility—The ability to bend, stretch, twist, or reach out with the body, arms, and/or legs. Information Ordering—The ability to correctly follow a given rule or set of rules in order to arrange things or actions in a certain order. The things or actions can include numbers, letters, words, pictures, procedures, sentences, and mathematical or logical operations. Visualization—The ability to imagine how something will look after it is moved around or when its parts are moved or rearranged. Hearing Sensitivity— The ability to detect or tell the difference between sounds that vary over broad ranges of pitch and loudness. Manual Dexterity—The ability to quickly make coordinated movements of one hand, a hand together with its arm, or two hands, to grasp, manipulate, or assemble objects.

Skills: Repairing—Repairing machines or systems, using the needed tools. Installation—Installing equipment, machines, wiring, or programs to meet specifications. Troubleshooting—Determining what is causing an operating error and deciding what to do about it. Testing—Conducting tests to determine whether equipment, software, or procedures are operating as expected. Equipment Maintenance—Performing routine maintenance and determining when and what kind of maintenance is needed. Problem Identification— Identifying the nature of problems.

Generalized Work Activities: Repairing and Maintaining Mechanical Equipment—Fixing, servicing, aligning, setting up, adjusting, and testing machines, devices, moving parts, and equipment that operate primarily on the basis of mechanical, not electronic, principles. Inspecting Equipment, Structures, Materials—Inspecting or diagnosing equipment, structures, or materials to identify the causes of errors or other problems or defects. Identifying Objects, Actions, and Events—Identifying information received by making estimates or categorizations, recognizing differences or similarities, or sensing changes in circumstances or events. Handling and Moving Objects—Using one's hands and arms in handling, installing, forming, positioning, and moving materials, or in manipulating things. Includes the use of keyboards. Getting Information Needed to Do the Job— Observing, receiving, and otherwise obtaining information from all relevant sources.

Baggage Porters and Bellhops

- ▲ Growth: 14%
- ▲ Annual Job Openings: 10,287
- ▲ Yearly Earnings: $13,330
- ▲ Education Required: Short-term O-J-T
- ▲ Self-Employed: 0%
- ▲ Part-Time: 40.7%

Baggage Porters and Bellhops

Handle baggage for travelers at transportation terminals or for guests at hotels or similar establishments. Runs errands for guests. Delivers, carries, or transfers luggage, trunks, and packages to/ from rooms, loading areas, vehicles, or transportation terminals. Escorts incoming hotel guests to their rooms. Sets up display tables, racks, or shelves. Arranges merchandise display for sales personnel. Pages guests in hotel lobby, dining room, or other areas; delivers messages and room service orders. Arranges for clothing of hotel guests to be cleaned, laundered, or repaired.

Weighs and bills baggage and parcels for shipment. Arranges for freight to be shipped. Transports guests about premises and local area. Calls taxicabs. Computes and completes charge slips for services rendered; maintains records. Supplies guests or travelers with directions, travel information, and other information such as available services and points of interest. Inspects guest's room and explains features, such as night lock and operation of television. Completes and attaches baggage claim checks and completes baggage insurance forms.

Personality Type: Enterprising. Enterprising occupations frequently involve starting up and carrying out projects. These occupations can involve leading people and making many decisions. They sometimes require risk taking and often deal with business.

Abilities: Static Strength—The ability to exert maximum muscle force to lift, push, pull, or carry objects. Oral Expression—The ability to communicate information and ideas verbally so others will understand. Oral Comprehension—The ability to listen to and understand information and ideas presented verbally. Trunk Strength—The ability to use one's abdominal and lower back muscles to support part of the body repeatedly or continuously over time without giving out or fatiguing. Stamina—The ability to exert one's self physically over long periods of time without getting winded or out of breath.

Skills: Service Orientation—Actively looking for ways to help people. Active Listening—Listening to what other people are saying; asking questions as appropriate. Speaking—Talking to others to effectively convey information. Social Perceptiveness—Being aware of other people's reactions and understanding why people

react the way they do. Mathematics—Using mathematics to solve problems.

Generalized Work Activities: Assisting and Caring for Others—Providing assistance or personal care to others. Handling and Moving Objects—Using one's hands and arms in handling, installing, forming, positioning, and moving materials, or in manipulating things. Performing General Physical Activities—Performing physical activities that require moving one's whole body, such as in climbing, lifting, balancing, walking, and stooping. Performing activities that often also require considerable use of the arms and legs, such as in the physical handling of materials. Performing for/Working with Public—Performing for people or dealing directly with the public, including serving persons in restaurants and stores and receiving clients or guests. Communicating with Persons Outside Organization—Communicating with persons outside the organization. Representing the organization to customers, the public, government, and other external sources. Exchanging information face-to-face, in writing, or via telephone/electronic transfer.

Banking New Accounts Clerks

- ▲ Growth: 15%
- ▲ Annual Job Openings: 36,231
- ▲ Yearly Earnings: $21,340
- ▲ Education Required: Work experience in a related occupation
- ▲ Self-Employed: 0%
- ▲ Part-Time: 32.5%

New Accounts Clerks

Interview persons desiring to open bank accounts. Explain banking services available to prospective customers and assist them in preparing application form. Collects and records fees and funds for deposit from customer; issues receipt, using computer. Issues initial and replacement safe-deposit key to customer and admits customer to vault. Investigates and corrects errors upon customer request, according to customer and bank records, using calculator or computer. Executes wire transfers of funds. Obtains credit records from reporting

agency. Enters account information in computer and files forms or other documents. Answers customer questions and explains available services such as deposit accounts, bonds, and securities. Assists customer in completing application forms for loans, accounts, or safe-deposit boxes, using typewriter or computer; obtains customer signature. Interviews customer to obtain information needed to open account or rent safe-deposit box. Schedules repairs for locks on safe-deposit box.

Personality Type: Conventional. Conventional occupations frequently involve following set procedures and routines. These occupations can include working with data and details more than with ideas. Usually there is a clear line of authority to follow.

Abilities: Oral Expression—The ability to communicate information and ideas verbally so others will understand. Oral Comprehension—The ability to listen to and understand information and ideas presented verbally. Written Comprehension—The ability to read and understand information and ideas presented in writing. Number Facility—The ability to add, subtract, multiply, or divide quickly and correctly. Near Vision—The ability to see details of objects at a close range.

Skills: Speaking—Talking to others to effectively convey information. Active Listening—Listening to what other people are saying; asking questions as appropriate. Mathematics—Using mathematics to solve problems. Information Gathering—Knowing how to find information and identifying essential information. Instructing—Teaching others how to do something. Information Organization—Finding ways to structure or classify multiple pieces of information. Reading Comprehension—Understanding written information in work-related documents.

Generalized Work Activities: Communicating with Persons Outside Organization—Communicating with persons outside the organization. Representing the organization to customers, the public, government, and other external sources. Exchanging information face-to-face, in writing, or via telephone/electronic transfer. Documenting/Recording Information—Entering, transcribing, recording, storing, or maintaining information in either written form or by electronic/magnetic recording. Performing Administrative Activities—Approving requests, handling paperwork, and performing day-to-day administrative tasks. Interacting with Computers—Controlling computer functions by using programs, setting up functions, writing software, or otherwise communicating with computer systems. Performing for/Working with Public—Performing for people or dealing directly with the public, including serving persons in restaurants and stores and receiving clients or guests.

Bank Tellers

- ▲ Growth: –6%
- ▲ Annual Job Openings: 106,674
- ▲ Yearly Earnings: $17,200
- ▲ Education Required: Short-term O-J-T
- ▲ Self-Employed: 0%
- ▲ Part-Time: 34.8%

Tellers

Receive and pay out money. Keep records of money and negotiable instruments involved in a financial institution's various transactions. Quotes unit exchange rate, following daily international rate sheet or computer display. Cashes checks and pays out money after verification of signatures and customer balances. Gives information to customer about foreign currency regulations and computes exchange value and transaction fee for currency exchange. Explains, promotes, or sells products or services such as traveler's checks, savings bonds, money orders, and cashier's checks. Removes deposits from automated teller machines and night depository; counts and balances the cash. Composes, types, and mails correspondence relating to discrepancies, errors, and outstanding unpaid items. Balances currency, coin, and checks in cash drawer at end of shift and calculates daily transactions. Counts currency, coins, and checks received for deposit or for shipment to branch banks or Federal Reserve Bank, by hand or using currency-counting machine. Prepares daily inventory of currency, drafts, and traveler's checks. Examines coupons and bills presented for payment to verify issue, payment date, and amount due. Receives checks and cash for deposit, verifies amount, and examines checks for endorsements. Enters customers' transactions into computer to record transactions; issues computer-generated receipts. Issues checks to bond owners in settlement of transactions.

Personality Type: Conventional. Conventional occupations frequently involve following set procedures and routines. These occupations can include working with data and details more than with ideas. Usually there is a clear line of authority to follow.

Abilities: Number Facility—The ability to add, subtract, multiply, or divide quickly and correctly. Oral Expression—The ability to communicate information and ideas verbally so others will understand. Near Vision—The ability to see details of objects at a close range. Speech Clarity—The ability to speak clearly so that what is said is understandable to a listener. Oral Comprehension—The ability to listen to and understand information and ideas presented verbally. Perceptual Speed—The ability to quickly and accurately compare letters, numbers, objects, pictures, or patterns. The things to be compared may be presented at the same time or one after the other. Includes comparing a presented object with a remembered object. Information Ordering—The ability to correctly follow a given rule or set of rules in order to arrange things or actions in a certain order. The things or actions can include

numbers, letters, words, pictures, procedures, sentences, and mathematical or logical operations.

Skills: Mathematics—Using mathematics to solve problems. Service Orientation—Actively looking for ways to help people. Speaking—Talking to others to effectively convey information. Social Perceptiveness—Being aware of other people's reactions and understanding why people react the way they do. Active Listening—Listening to what other people are saying; asking questions as appropriate.

Generalized Work Activities: Documenting/Recording Information—Entering, transcribing, recording, storing, or maintaining information in either written form or by electronic/magnetic recording. Communicating with Persons Outside Organization—Communicating with persons outside the organization. Representing the organization to customers, the public, government, and other external sources. Exchanging information face-to-face, in writing, or via telephone/electronic transfer. Processing Information—Compiling, coding, categorizing, calculating, tabulating, auditing, verifying, or processing information or data. Monitoring and Controlling Resources—Monitoring and controlling resources and overseeing the spending of money. Performing for/Working with Public—Performing for people or dealing directly with the public, including serving persons in restaurants and stores and receiving clients or guests.

Bicycle Repairers

- ▲ Growth: 23%
- ▲ Annual Job Openings: 1,854
- ▲ Yearly Earnings: $15,700
- ▲ Education Required: Moderate-term O-J-T
- ▲ Self-Employed: 70.3%
- ▲ Part-Time: 9.3%

Bicycle Repairers

Repair and service bicycles. Assembles new bicycles. Installs, repairs, and replaces equipment or accessories such as handlebars, stands, lights, and seats. Aligns wheels. Installs and adjusts speed and gear mechanisms. Shapes replacement parts, using bench grinder. Paints bicycle frame, using spray gun or brush. Disassembles axle to repair, adjust, and replace defective parts, using hand tools. Welds broken or cracked frame together, using oxyacetylene torch and welding rods. Repairs holes in tire tubes, using scraper and patch.

Personality Type: Realistic. Realistic occupations frequently involve work activities that include practical, hands-on problems and solutions. They often deal with plants, animals, and real-world materials like wood, tools, and machinery. Many of the occupations require working outside and do not involve a lot of paperwork or working closely with others.

Abilities: Manual Dexterity—The ability to quickly make coordinated movements of one hand, a hand together with its arm, or two hands, to grasp, manipulate, or assemble objects. Finger Dexterity—The ability to make precisely coordinated movements of the fingers of one or both hands to grasp, manipulate, or assemble very small objects. Wrist-Finger Speed—The ability to make fast, simple, repeated movements of the fingers, hands, and wrists. Speech Clarity—The ability to speak clearly so that what is said is understandable to a listener. Near Vision—The ability to see details of objects at a close range. Visualization—The ability to imagine how something will look after it is moved around or when its parts are moved or rearranged. Arm-Hand Steadiness—The ability to keep the hand and arm steady while making an arm movement or while holding the arm and hand in one position.

Skills: Repairing—Repairing machines or systems, using the needed tools. Installation—Installing equipment, machines, wiring, or programs to meet specifications. Problem Identification—Identifying the nature of problems. Troubleshooting—Determining what is causing an operating error and deciding what to do about it. Equipment Selection—Determining the kind of tools and equipment needed to do a job.

Generalized Work Activities: Repairing and Maintaining Mechanical Equipment—Fixing, servicing, aligning, setting up, adjusting, and testing machines, devices, moving parts, and equipment that operate primarily on the basis of mechanical, not electronic, principles. Handling and Moving Objects—Using one's hands and arms in handling, installing, forming, positioning, and moving materials, or in manipulating things. Includes the use of keyboards. Getting Information Needed to Do the Job—Observing, receiving, and otherwise obtaining information from all relevant sources. Inspecting Equipment, Structures, Materials—Inspecting or diagnosing equipment, structures, or materials to identify the causes of errors or other problems or defects. Performing for/Working with Public—Performing for people or dealing directly with the public, including serving persons in restaurants and stores and receiving clients or guests. Selling or Influencing Others—Convincing others to buy merchandise/goods, or otherwise changing their minds or actions. Performing General Physical Activities—Performing physical activities that require moving one's whole body, such as in climbing, lifting, balancing, walking, and stooping. Performing activities that often also require considerable use of the arms and legs, such as in the physical handling of materials.

Bill and Account Collectors

- ▲ Growth: 35%
- ▲ Annual Job Openings: 106,068
- ▲ Yearly Earnings: $22,540
- ▲ Education Required: Short-term O-J-T
- ▲ Self-Employed: 1.2%
- ▲ Part-Time: 12.7%

Bill and Account Collectors

Locate and notify customers of delinquent accounts by mail, telephone, or personal visit, to solicit payment. Receive payment and post amount to customer's account. Prepare statements to credit department if customer fails to respond, initiating repossession proceedings or service disconnection. Keep records of collection and status of accounts. Mails form letters to customers to encourage payment of delinquent accounts. Receives payments and posts amount paid to customer account, using computer or paper records. Records information about financial status of customer and status of collection efforts. Traces delinquent customer to new address by inquiring at post office or questioning neighbors. Sorts and files correspondence and performs miscellaneous clerical duties. Drives vehicle to visit customer, return merchandise to creditor, or deliver bills. Confers with customer by telephone or in person to determine reason for overdue payment and to review terms of sales, service, or credit contract. Notifies credit department, orders merchandise repossession or service disconnection, or turns over account to attorney if customer fails to respond. Persuades customer to pay amount due on credit account, damage claim, or nonpayable check. Negotiates extension of credit.

Personality Type: Conventional. Conventional occupations frequently involve following set procedures and routines. These occupations can include working with data and details more than with ideas. Usually there is a clear line of authority to follow.

Abilities: Number Facility—The ability to add, subtract, multiply, or divide quickly and correctly. Oral Expression—The ability to communicate information and ideas verbally so others will understand. Oral Comprehension—The ability to listen to and understand information and ideas presented verbally. Speech Clarity—The ability to speak clearly so that what is said is understandable to a listener.

Skills: Speaking—Talking to others to effectively convey information. Information Gathering—Knowing how to find information and identifying essential information. Social Perceptiveness—Being aware of other people's reactions and understanding why people react the way they do. Active Listening—Listening to what other people are saying; asking questions as appropriate. Problem Identification—Identifying the nature of problems.

Generalized Work Activities: Getting Information Needed to Do the Job—Observing, receiving, and otherwise obtaining information from all relevant sources. Communicating with Persons Outside Organization—Communicating with persons outside the organization. Representing the organization to customers, the public, government, and other external sources. Exchanging information face-to-face, in writing, or via telephone/electronic transfer. Performing for/Working with Public—Performing for people or dealing directly with the public, including serving persons in restaurants and stores and receiving clients or guests. Resolving Conflict, Negotiating with Others—Handling complaints, arbitrating disputes, resolving grievances, or otherwise negotiating with others. Selling or Influencing Others—Convincing others to buy merchandise/goods, or otherwise changing their minds or actions.

Billing, Cost, and Rate Clerks

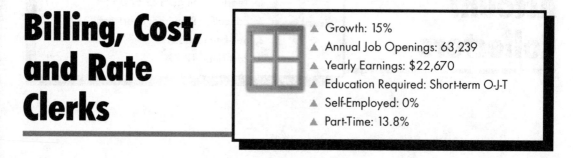

- ▲ Growth: 15%
- ▲ Annual Job Openings: 63,239
- ▲ Yearly Earnings: $22,670
- ▲ Education Required: Short-term O-J-T
- ▲ Self-Employed: 0%
- ▲ Part-Time: 13.8%

Billing, Cost, and Rate Clerks

Compile data, compute fees and charges, and prepare invoices for billing purposes. Compute costs and calculate rates for goods, services, and shipment of goods. Post data. Keeps records of invoices and support documents. Computes amounts due from such documents as purchase orders, sales tickets, and charge slips. Compiles and computes credit terms, discounts, and purchase prices for billing documents. Types billing documents, shipping labels, credit memorandums, and credit forms, using typewriter or computer. Resolves discrepancies on accounting records. Verifies compiled data from vendor invoices to ensure accuracy; revises billing data when errors are found. Consults manuals which include rates, rules, regulations, and government tax and tariff information. Answers mail and telephone inquiries regarding rates, routing, and procedures. Estimates market value of products or services. Updates manuals when rates, rules, or regulations are amended. Compiles cost-factor reports on labor, production, storage, and equipment.

Personality Type: Conventional. Conventional occupations frequently involve following set procedures and routines. These occupations can include working with data and details more than with ideas. Usually there is a clear line of authority to follow.

Abilities: Number Facility—The ability to add, subtract, multiply, or divide quickly and correctly. Mathematical Reasoning—The ability to understand and organize a problem and then select a mathematical method or formula to solve the problem. Written Expression—The ability to communicate information and ideas in writing so others will understand. Written Comprehension—The ability to read and understand information and ideas presented in writing. Near Vision—The ability to see details of objects at a close range.

Skills: Mathematics—Using mathematics to solve problems. Reading Comprehension—Understanding written information in work-related documents. Information Gathering—Knowing how to find information and identifying essential information. Problem Identification—Identifying the nature of problems. Active Listening—Listening to what other people are saying; asking questions as appropriate.

Generalized Work Activities: Processing Information—Compiling, coding, categorizing, calculating, tabulating, auditing, verifying, or processing information or data. Getting Information Needed to Do the Job—Observing, receiving, and otherwise obtaining information from all relevant sources. Documenting/Recording Information—Entering, transcribing, recording, storing, or maintaining information in either written form or by electronic/magnetic recording. Evaluating Information against Standards—Evaluating information against a set of standards and verifying that it is correct. Updating and Using Job-Relevant Knowledge—Keeping up-to-date technically and knowing the functions of one's own job and related jobs.

Bindery Machine Operators and Set-Up Operators

- ▲ Growth: 12%
- ▲ Annual Job Openings: 16,466
- ▲ Yearly Earnings: $20,600
- ▲ Education Required: Moderate-term O-J-T
- ▲ Self-Employed: 0%
- ▲ Part-Time: 6.3%

Bindery Machine Operators and Tenders

Operate or tend binding machines that round, back, case, line stitch, press, fold, or trim. Perform other binding operations on books and related articles. Rolls, bends, smoothes, and folds sheets, using hands; stacks sheets to be returned to binding machines. Inserts illustrated pages, extra sheets, and collated sets into catalogs, periodicals, directories, and other printed products. Applies labels to envelopes, using hands or machine. Removes broken wire pieces from machine and loads machine with spool of wire. Punches holes in paper sheets; fastens sheets, signatures, or other material, using hand or machine punch or stapler. Examines printed material and related products for defects and to ensure conformance to specifications. Creases or compresses signatures before affixing covers and places paper jackets on finished books. Applies materials on books or related articles, using machine. Removes printed material or finished products from machines or conveyor belts; stacks material on pallets or skids. Moves controls to adjust and activate bindery machine to meet specifications. Selects, loads, and adjusts workpieces and machine parts, using hand tools. Operates or tends machines that perform binding operations such as pressing, folding, and trimming books and related articles. Feeds books and related articles, such as periodicals and pamphlets, into binding machines, following specifications. Stitches or fastens endpapers or bindings and stitches signatures. Applies glue along binding edge of first and last signatures of books. Threads spirals in perforated holes of items to be bound, using spindle or rollers. Opens machine and removes and replaces damaged covers and book, using hand tools. Cleans work area and maintains equipment and work stations, using hand tools. Maintains records of daily production, using specified forms. Wraps product in plastic, using machine, and packs products in boxes.

Personality Type: Realistic. Realistic occupations frequently involve work activities that include practical, hands-on problems and solutions. They often deal with plants, animals, and real-world materials like wood, tools, and machinery. Many of the occupations require working outside and do not involve a lot of paperwork or working closely with others.

Abilities: Manual Dexterity—The ability to quickly make coordinated movements of one hand, a hand together with its arm, or two hands, to grasp, manipulate, or assemble objects. Control Precision—The ability to quickly and repeatedly make precise adjustments in moving the controls of a machine or vehicle to exact positions. Extent Flexibility—The ability to bend, stretch, twist, or reach out with the body, arms, and/or legs. Arm-Hand Steadiness—The ability to keep the hand and arm steady while making an arm movement or while holding the arm and hand in one position. Information Ordering—The ability to correctly follow a given rule or set of rules in order to arrange things or actions in a certain order. The things or actions can include numbers, letters, words, pictures, procedures, sentences, and mathematical or logical operations.

Skills: Product Inspection—Inspecting and evaluating the quality of products. Operation Monitoring—Watching gauges, dials, or other indicators to make sure a machine is working properly. Equipment Maintenance—Performing routine maintenance and determining when and what kind of maintenance is needed. Operation and Control—Controlling operations of equipment or systems. Equipment Selection—Determining the kind of tools and equipment needed to do a job. Problem Identification—Identifying the nature of problems.

Generalized Work Activities: Controlling Machines and Processes—Using either control mechanisms or direct physical activity to operate machines or processes. Does not involve working with computers or vehicles. Handling and Moving Objects—Using one's hands and arms in handling, installing, forming, positioning, and moving materials, or in manipulating things. Includes the use of keyboards. Monitoring Processes, Materials, Surroundings—Monitoring and reviewing information from materials, events, or the environment, often to detect problems or to find out when things are finished. Inspecting Equipment, Structures, Materials—

Inspecting or diagnosing equipment, structures, or materials to identify the causes of errors or other problems or defects. Implementing Ideas and Programs—Conducting or carrying out work procedures and activities in accord with one's own ideas or information provided through directions/instructions for purposes of installing, modifying, preparing, delivering, constructing, integrating, finishing, or completing programs, systems, structures, or products.

Bindery Machine Setters and Set-Up Operators

Set up, or set up and operate, machines that produce books, magazines, pamphlets, catalogs, and other printed materials by gathering, folding, cutting, stitching, rounding, backing, supering, casing-in, lining, pressing, and trimming. Records time spent on specific tasks and number of items produced, for daily production sheet. Sets machine controls to adjust length and thickness of folds, stitches, or cuts. Sets machine controls to adjust speed and pressure. Positions and clamps stitching heads on crossarms to space stitches to specified lengths. Threads wire into machine to load stitcher head for stapling. Reads work order to determine work instructions. Examines product samples for defects. Cleans and lubricates machinery parts and makes minor repairs. Mounts and secures rolls or reels of wire, cloth, paper, or other material onto machine spindles; fills paper feed. Trains workers to set up, operate, and use automatic bindery machines. Manually stocks supplies such as signatures, books, or paper. Observes and monitors machine operations to detect malfunctions and makes required adjustments. Fills glue pot and adjusts flow of glue and speed of conveyors. Starts machines and makes trial runs to verify accuracy of machine setup. Installs bindery machine devices such as knives, guides, and clamps, to accommodate sheets, signatures, or books of specified sizes. Removes books or products from machine and stacks them.

Personality Type: Realistic. Realistic occupations frequently involve work activities that include practical, hands-on problems and solutions. They often deal with plants, animals, and real-world materials like wood, tools, and machinery. Many of the occupations require working outside and do not involve a lot of paperwork or working closely with others.

Abilities: Control Precision—The ability to quickly and repeatedly make precise adjustments in moving the controls of a machine or vehicle to exact positions. Information Ordering—The ability to correctly follow a given rule or set of rules in order to arrange things or actions in a certain order. The things or actions can include numbers, letters, words, pictures, procedures, sentences, and mathematical or logical operations. Manual Dexterity—The ability to quickly make coordinated movements of one hand, a hand together with its arm, or two hands, to grasp, manipulate, or assemble objects. Written Comprehension—The ability to read and understand information and ideas presented in writing. Perceptual Speed—The ability to quickly and accurately compare letters, numbers, objects, pictures, or patterns. The things to be compared may be presented at the same time or one after the other. Includes comparing a presented object with a remembered object.

Skills: Operation and Control—Controlling operations of equipment or systems. Product Inspection—Inspecting and evaluating the quality of products. Reading Comprehension—Understanding written information in work-related documents. Operation Monitoring—Watching gauges, dials, or other indicators to make sure a machine is working properly.

Generalized Work Activities: Controlling Machines and Processes—Using either control mechanisms or direct physical activity to operate machines or processes. Does not involve working with computers or vehicles. Handling and Moving Objects—Using one's hands and arms in handling, installing, forming, positioning, and moving materials, or in manipulating things. Includes the use of keyboards. Getting Information Needed to Do the Job—Observing, receiving, and otherwise obtaining information from all relevant sources. Performing General Physical Activities—Performing physical activities that require moving one's whole body, such as in climbing, lifting, balancing, walking, and stooping. Performing activities that often also require considerable use of the arms and legs, such as in the physical handling of materials. Inspecting Equipment, Structures, Materials—Inspecting or diagnosing equipment, structures, or materials to identify the causes of errors or other problems or defects.

Biological Scientists

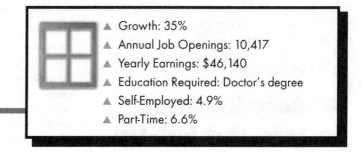

- ▲ Growth: 35%
- ▲ Annual Job Openings: 10,417
- ▲ Yearly Earnings: $46,140
- ▲ Education Required: Doctor's degree
- ▲ Self-Employed: 4.9%
- ▲ Part-Time: 6.6%

Biochemists

Research or study chemical composition and processes of living organisms that affect vital processes such as growth and aging. Determine chemical actions and their effects on organisms, such as the action of foods, drugs, or other substances on body functions and tissues. Prepares reports and recommendations based upon research outcomes. Examines chemical aspects of formation of antibodies; researches chemistry of cells and blood corpuscles. Isolates, analyzes, and identifies hormones, vitamins, allergens, minerals, and enzymes, and determines their effects on body functions. Develops methods to process, store, and use food, drugs, and chemical compounds. Researches methods of transferring characteristics, such as resistance to disease, from one organism to another. Develops and executes tests to detect disease, genetic disorders, or other abnormalities. Designs and builds laboratory equipment needed for special research projects. Cleans, purifies, refines, and otherwise prepares pharmaceutical compounds for commercial distribution. Develops and tests new drugs and medications for commercial distribution. Studies chemistry of living processes such as cell development, breathing, and digestion. Studies chemistry of living energy changes such as growth, aging, and death. Analyzes food to determine its nutritional value and how it is affected by cooking, canning, and processing. Researches and determines chemical action of substances such as drugs, serums, hormones, and food on tissues and vital processes.

Personality Type: Investigative. Investigative occupations frequently involve working with ideas and require an extensive amount of thinking. These occupations can involve searching for facts and figuring out problems mentally.

Abilities: Inductive Reasoning—The ability to combine separate pieces of information, or specific answers to problems, to form general rules or conclusions. Includes coming up with a logical explanation for why a series of seemingly unrelated events occur together. Deductive Reasoning—The ability to apply general rules to specific problems to come up with logical answers. Involves deciding if an answer makes sense. Written Comprehension—The ability to read and understand information and ideas presented in writing. Written Expression—The ability to communicate information and ideas in writing so others will understand. Information Ordering—The ability to correctly follow a given rule or set of rules in order to arrange things or actions in a certain order. The things or actions can include numbers, letters, words, pictures, procedures, sentences, and mathematical or logical operations.

Skills: Science—Using scientific methods to solve problems. Information Gathering—Knowing how to find information and identifying essential information. Active Learning—Working with new material or information to grasp its implications. Critical Thinking—Using logic and analysis to identify the strengths and weaknesses of different approaches. Reading Comprehension—Understanding written information in work-related documents. Writing—Communicating effectively with others in writing as indicated by the needs of the audience. Mathematics—Using mathematics to solve problems.

Generalized Work Activities: Getting Information Needed to Do the Job—Observing, receiving, and otherwise obtaining information from all relevant sources. Identifying Objects, Actions, and Events—Identifying information received by making estimates or categorizations, recognizing differences or similarities, or sensing changes in circumstances or events. Monitoring Processes, Materials, Surroundings—Monitoring and reviewing information from materials, events, or the environment, often to detect problems or to find out when things are finished. Documenting/Recording Information—Entering, transcribing, recording, storing, or maintaining information in either written form or by electronic/magnetic recording. Processing Information—Compiling, coding, categorizing, calculating, tabulating, auditing, verifying, or processing information or data. Analyzing Data or Information—Identifying underlying principles, reasons, or facts by breaking down information or data into separate parts.

Biologists

Research or study basic principles of plant and animal life, such as origin, relationship, development, anatomy, and functions. Communicates test results to state and federal representatives and general public. Identifies, classifies, and studies structure, behavior, ecology, physiology, nutrition, culture, and distribution of plant and animal species. Studies reactions of plants, animals, and marine species to parasites. Collects and analyzes biological data about relationship among and between organisms and their environment. Studies aquatic plants and animals and environmental conditions affecting them, such as radioactivity or pollution. Investigates and develops pest management and control measures. Prepares environmental-impact reports for industry, government, or publication. Cultivates, breeds, and grows aquatic life such as lobsters, clams, or fish farming. Plans and administers biological research programs for government, research firms,

medical industries, or manufacturing firms. Researches environmental effects of present and potential uses of land and water areas. Determines methods of improving environment or crop yields. Develops methods of extracting drugs from aquatic plants and animals. Measures salinity, acidity, light, oxygen content, and other physical conditions of water to determine their relationship to aquatic life. Studies and manages wild-animal populations. Studies basic principles of plant and animal life, such as origin, relationship, development, anatomy, and functions. Develops methods and apparatus for securing representative plant, animal, aquatic, or soil samples.

Personality Type: Investigative. Investigative occupations frequently involve working with ideas and require an extensive amount of thinking. These occupations can involve searching for facts and figuring out problems mentally.

Abilities: Information Ordering—The ability to correctly follow a given rule or set of rules in order to arrange things or actions in a certain order. The things or actions can include numbers, letters, words, pictures, procedures, sentences, and mathematical or logical operations. Inductive Reasoning—The ability to combine separate pieces of information, or specific answers to problems, to form general rules or conclusions. Includes coming up with a logical explanation for why a series of seemingly unrelated events occur together. Deductive Reasoning—The ability to apply general rules to specific problems to come up with logical answers. Involves deciding if an answer makes sense. Written Expression—The ability to communicate information and ideas in writing so others will understand. Written Comprehension—The ability to read and understand information and ideas presented in writing.

Skills: Science—Using scientific methods to solve problems. Writing—Communicating effectively with others in writing as indicated by the needs of the audience. Reading Comprehension—Understanding written information in work-related documents. Mathematics—Using mathematics to solve problems. Active Learning—Working with new material or information to grasp its implications. Critical

Thinking—Using logic and analysis to identify the strengths and weaknesses of different approaches. Information Organization—Finding ways to structure or classify multiple pieces of information.

Generalized Work Activities: Analyzing Data or Information—Identifying underlying principles, reasons, or facts by breaking down information or data into separate parts. Getting Information Needed to Do the Job—Observing, receiving, and otherwise obtaining information from all relevant sources. Identifying Objects, Actions, and Events—Identifying information received by making estimates or categorizations, recognizing differences or similarities, or sensing changes in circumstances or events. Providing Consultation and Advice to Others—Providing consultation and expert advice to management or other groups on technical, systems-related, or process-related topics. Processing Information—Compiling, coding, categorizing, calculating, tabulating, auditing, verifying, or processing information or data. Monitoring Processes, Materials, Surroundings—Monitoring and reviewing information from materials, events, or the environment, often to detect problems or to find out when things are finished. Documenting/Recording Information—Entering, transcribing, recording, storing, or maintaining information in either written form or by electronic/magnetic recording.

Biophysicists

Research or study physical principles of living cells and organisms, their electrical and mechanical energy, and related phenomena. Analyzes functions of electronic and human brains, such as learning, thinking, and memory. Researches transformation of substances in cells, using atomic isotopes. Researches manner in which characteristics of plants and animals are carried through successive generations. Studies spatial configuration of submicroscopic molecules such as proteins, using X rays and electron microscope. Investigates dynamics of seeing and hearing. Studies absorption of light by chlorophyll in photosynthesis or by pigments of eye involved in vision. Investigates transmission of electrical impulses along nerves and muscles. Investigates damage to cells and tissues caused by X rays and nuclear particles. Studies physical principles of living cells and organisms and their electrical and mechanical energy. Researches cancer treatment, using radiation and nuclear particles.

Personality Type: Investigative. Investigative occupations frequently involve working with ideas and require an extensive amount of thinking. These occupations can involve searching for facts and figuring out problems mentally.

Abilities: Written Comprehension—The ability to read and understand information and ideas presented in writing. Deductive Reasoning—The ability to apply general rules to specific problems to come up with logical answers. Involves deciding if an answer makes sense. Inductive Reasoning—The ability to combine separate pieces of information, or specific answers to problems, to form general rules or conclusions. Includes coming up with a logical explanation for why a series of seemingly unrelated events occur together. Near Vision—The ability to see details of objects at a close range. Information Ordering—The ability to correctly follow a given rule or set of rules in order to arrange things or actions in a certain order. The things or actions can include numbers, letters, words, pictures, procedures, sentences, and mathematical or logical operations.

Skills: Science—Using scientific methods to solve problems. Reading Comprehension—Understanding written information in work-related documents. Mathematics—Using mathematics to solve problems. Information Gathering—Knowing how to find information and identifying essential information. Idea Generation—Generating a number of different approaches to problems.

Generalized Work Activities: Analyzing Data or Information—Identifying underlying principles, reasons, or facts by breaking down information or data into separate parts. Monitoring Processes, Materials, Surroundings—Monitoring and reviewing information from materials, events, or the environment, often to detect problems or to find out when things are finished. Getting Information Needed to Do the Job—Observing, receiving, and otherwise obtaining information from all relevant sources. Identifying Objects, Actions, and Events—Identifying information received by making estimates or categorizations, recognizing differences or similarities, or sensing changes in circumstances or events. Documenting/Recording Information—Entering, transcribing, recording, storing, or maintaining information in either written form or by electronic/magnetic recording.

Microbiologists

Investigate the growth, structure, development, and other characteristics of microscopic organisms such as bacteria, algae, or fungi. Includes medical microbiologists who study the relationship between organisms and disease or the effects of antibiotics on microorganisms. Isolates and makes cultures of bacteria or other microorganisms in prescribed media, controlling moisture, aeration, temperature, and nutrition. Observes action of microorganisms upon living tissues of plants, higher animals, and other microorganisms. Observes action of microorganisms on dead organic matter. Studies growth structure and development of viruses and rickettsiae. Examines physiological, morphological, and cultural characteristics, using microscope, to identify microorganisms. Prepares technical reports and recommendations based upon research outcomes. Studies growth, structure, development, and general characteristics of bacteria and other microorganisms. Conducts chemical analyses of substances such as acids, alcohols, and enzymes. Researches use of bacteria and microorganisms to develop vitamins, antibiotics, amino acids, grain alcohol, sugars, and polymers.

Personality Type: Investigative. Investigative occupations frequently involve working with ideas and require an extensive amount of thinking. These occupations can involve searching for facts and figuring out problems mentally.

Abilities: Deductive Reasoning—The ability to apply general rules to specific problems to come up with logical answers. Involves deciding if an answer makes sense. Inductive Reasoning—The ability to combine separate pieces of information, or specific answers to problems, to form general rules or conclusions. Includes coming up with a logical explanation for why a series of seemingly unrelated events occur together. Near

Vision—The ability to see details of objects at a close range. Written Comprehension—The ability to read and understand information and ideas presented in writing. Written Expression—The ability to communicate information and ideas in writing so others will understand. Information Ordering—The ability to correctly follow a given rule or set of rules in order to arrange things or actions in a certain order. The things or actions can include numbers, letters, words, pictures, procedures, sentences, and mathematical or logical operations.

Skills: Science—Using scientific methods to solve problems. Writing—Communicating effectively with others in writing as indicated by the needs of the audience. Reading Comprehension—Understanding written information in work-related documents. Information Gathering—Knowing how to find information and identifying essential information. Critical Thinking—Using logic and analysis to identify the strengths and weaknesses of different approaches. Problem Identification—Identifying the nature of problems.

Generalized Work Activities: Getting Information Needed to Do the Job—Observing, receiving, and otherwise obtaining information from all relevant sources. Identifying Objects, Actions, and Events—Identifying information received by making estimates or categorizations, recognizing differences or similarities, or sensing changes in circumstances or events. Analyzing Data or Information—Identifying underlying principles, reasons, or facts by breaking down information or data into separate parts. Monitoring Processes, Materials, Surroundings—Monitoring and reviewing information from materials, events, or the environment, often to detect problems or to find out when things are finished. Processing Information—Compiling, coding, categorizing, calculating, tabulating, auditing, verifying, or processing information or data.

Zoologists and Wildlife Biologists

Study the origins, behavior, diseases, genetics, and life processes of animals and wildlife. Specialize in wildlife research and management, including the collection and analysis of biological data to determine the environmental effects of present and potential use of land and water areas. Prepares collections of preserved specimens or microscopic slides for species identification and for study of species development or animal disease. Studies origin, interrelationships, classification, life histories, diseases, development, genetics, and distribution of animals. Studies animals in their natural habitats; assesses effects of environment on animals. Analyzes characteristics of animals to identify and classify animals. Raises specimens for study and observation or for use in experiments. Conducts experimental studies, using chemicals and various types of scientific equipment. Collects and dissects animal specimens and examines specimens under microscope.

Personality Type: Investigative. Investigative occupations frequently involve working with ideas and require an extensive amount of thinking. These occupations can involve searching for facts and figuring out problems mentally.

Abilities: Deductive Reasoning—The ability to apply general rules to specific problems to come up with logical answers. Involves deciding if an answer makes sense. Inductive Reasoning—The ability to combine separate pieces of information, or specific answers to problems, to form general rules or conclusions. Includes coming up with a logical explanation for why a series of seemingly unrelated events occur together. Category Flexibility—The ability to produce many rules so that each rule tells how to group or combine a set of things in a different way. Near Vision—The ability to see details

of objects at a close range. Written Comprehension—The ability to read and understand information and ideas presented in writing.

Skills: Science—Using scientific methods to solve problems. Information Gathering—Knowing how to find information and identifying essential information. Reading Comprehension—Understanding written information in work-related documents. Active Learning—Working with new material or information to grasp its implications. Information Organization—Finding ways to structure or classify multiple pieces of information.

Generalized Work Activities: Identifying Objects, Actions, and Events—Identifying information received by making estimates or categorizations, recognizing differences or similarities, or sensing changes in circumstances or events. Getting Information Needed to Do the Job—Observing, receiving, and otherwise obtaining information from all relevant sources. Analyzing Data or Information—Identifying underlying principles, reasons, or facts by breaking down information or data into separate parts. Processing Information—Compiling, coding, categorizing, calculating, tabulating, auditing, verifying, or processing information or data. Monitoring Processes, Materials, Surroundings—Monitoring and reviewing information from materials, events, or the environment, often to detect problems or to find out when things are finished. Documenting/Recording Information—Entering, transcribing, recording, storing, or maintaining information in either written form or by electronic/magnetic recording.

Blue-Collar Worker Supervisors

- ▲ Growth: 9%
- ▲ Annual Job Openings: 216,115
- ▲ Yearly Earnings: $37,180
- ▲ Education Required: Work experience in a related occupation
- ▲ Self-Employed: 10.4%
- ▲ Part-Time: 2.3%

First-Line Supervisors and Manager/Supervisors—Construction Trades Workers

Directly supervise and coordinate activities of construction trades workers and their helpers. Manager/Supervisors are generally found in smaller establishments where they perform both supervisory and management functions such as accounting, marketing, and personnel work and may also engage in the same construction trades work as the workers they supervise. Trains workers in construction methods and operation of equipment. Confers with staff and worker to ensure production and personnel problems are resolved. Estimates material and worker requirements to complete job. Reads specifications such as blueprints and data, to determine construction requirements. Analyzes and plans installation and construction of equipment and structures. Directs and leads workers engaged in construction activities. Records information such as personnel, production, and operational data on specified forms and reports. Assists workers engaged in construction activities, using hand tools and equipment. Analyzes and resolves worker problems and recommends motivational plans. Examines and inspects work progress, equipment, and construction sites, to verify safety and ensure that specifications are met. Suggests and initiates personnel actions such as promotions, transfers, and hires. Assigns work to employees, using material and worker requirements data. Supervises and coordinates activities of construction trades workers. Locates, measures, and marks location and placement of structures and equipment. Recommends measures to improve production methods and equipment performance, to increase efficiency and safety.

Personality Type: Enterprising. Enterprising occupations frequently involve starting up and carrying out projects. These occupations can involve leading people and making many decisions. They sometimes require risk taking and often deal with business.

Abilities: Oral Expression—The ability to communicate information and ideas verbally so others will understand. Problem Sensitivity—The ability to tell when something is wrong or is likely to go wrong. Does not involve solving the problem, only recognizing there is a problem. Oral Comprehension—The ability to listen to and understand information and ideas presented verbally. Written Comprehension—The ability to read and understand information and ideas presented in writing. Information Ordering—The ability to correctly follow a given rule or set of rules in order to arrange things or actions in a certain order. The things or actions can include numbers, letters, words, pictures, procedures, sentences, and mathematical or logical operations.

Skills: Coordination—Adjusting actions in relation to others' actions. Product Inspection—Inspecting and evaluating the quality of products. Time Management—Managing one's own time and the time of others. Management of Personnel Resources—Motivating, developing, and directing people as they work, identifying the best people for the job.

Generalized Work Activities: Evaluating Information against Standards—Evaluating information against a set of standards and verifying that it is correct. Getting Information Needed to Do the Job—Observing, receiving, and otherwise obtaining information from all relevant sources. Inspecting Equipment, Structures, Materials—Inspecting or diagnosing equipment, structures, or materials to identify the causes of errors or other problems or defects. Guiding, Directing, and Motivating Subordinates—Providing guidance and direction to subordinates, including setting performance standards and monitoring subordinates. Coordinating Work and Activities of Others—Coordinating members of a work group to accomplish tasks. Communicating with Other Workers—Providing information to supervisors, fellow workers, and subordinates. This information can be exchanged face-to-face, in writing, or via telephone/electronic transfer.

First-Line Supervisors and Manager/Supervisors—Extractive Workers

Directly supervise and coordinate activities of extractive workers and their helpers. Manager/Supervisors are generally found in smaller establishments where they perform both supervisory and management functions such as accounting, marketing, and personnel work and may also engage in the same extractive work as the workers they supervise. Examines and inspects equipment, site, and materials, to verify that specifications are met. Confers with staff and workers to ensure that production personnel problems are resolved. Analyzes and plans extraction process of geological materials. Suggests and initiates personnel actions such as promotions, transfers, and hires. Records information such as personnel, production, and operational data on specified forms. Assists workers engaged in extraction activities, using hand tools and equipment. Orders materials, supplies, and repair of equipment and machinery. Recommends measures to improve production methods and equipment performance, to increase efficiency and safety. Trains workers in construction methods and operation of equipment. Analyzes and resolves worker problems and recommends motivational plans. Assigns work to employees, using material and worker requirements data. Directs and leads workers engaged in extraction of geological materials. Supervises and coordinates activities of workers engaged in the extraction of geological materials. Locates, measures, and marks materials and site location, using measuring and marking equipment.

Personality Type: Enterprising. Enterprising occupations frequently involve starting up and carrying out projects. These occupations can involve leading people and making many decisions. They sometimes require risk taking and often deal with business.

Abilities: Oral Expression—The ability to communicate information and ideas verbally so others will understand. Near Vision—The ability to see details of objects at a close range. Deductive Reasoning—The ability to apply general rules to specific problems to come up with logical answers. Involves deciding if an answer makes sense. Problem Sensitivity—The ability to tell when something is wrong or is likely to go wrong. Does not involve solving the problem, only recognizing there is a problem. Information Ordering—The ability to correctly follow a given rule or set of rules in order to arrange things or actions in a certain order. The things or actions can include numbers, letters, words, pictures, procedures, sentences, and mathematical or logical operations. Inductive Reasoning—The ability to combine separate pieces of information, or specific answers to problems, to form general rules or conclusions. Includes coming up with a logical explanation for why a series of seemingly unrelated events occur together.

Skills: Coordination—Adjusting actions in relation to others' actions. Management of Personnel Resources—Motivating, developing, and directing people as they work, identifying the best people for the job. Judgment and Decision Making—Weighing the relative costs and benefits of a potential action. Time Management—Managing one's own time and the time of others. Problem Identification—Identifying the nature of problems. Speaking—Talking to others to effectively convey information.

Generalized Work Activities: Monitoring Processes, Materials, Surroundings—Monitoring and reviewing information from materials, events, or the environment, often to detect problems or to find out when things are finished. Coordinating Work and Activities of Others—Coordinating members of a work group to accomplish tasks. Identifying Objects, Actions, and Events—Identifying information received by making estimates or categorizations, recognizing differences or similarities, or sensing changes in circumstances or events. Getting Information Needed to Do the Job—Observing, receiving, and otherwise obtaining information from all relevant sources. Communicating with Other Workers—Providing information to supervisors, fellow workers, and subordinates. This information can be exchanged face-to-face, in writing, or via telephone/electronic transfer.

First-Line Supervisors/ Managers of Helpers, Laborers, and Material Movers, Hand

Supervise and coordinate the activities of helpers, laborers, or material movers. Quotes prices to customers. Examines freight to determine sequence of loading. Examines equipment to determine compliance with specifications. Observes work procedures to ensure quality of work. Inspects equipment for wear. Inspects completed work for conformance to standards. Inventories and orders supplies. Informs designated employee or department of items loaded; reports loading deficiencies. Resolves customer complaints. Records information such as daily receipts, employee time and wage data, description of freight, and inspection results. Verifies materials loaded or unloaded against work order; schedules times of shipment and mode of transportation. Trains and instructs workers. Assigns duties and work schedules. Determines work sequence and equipment needed, according to work order, shipping records, and experience. Supervises and coordinates activities of workers performing assigned tasks.

Personality Type: Enterprising. Enterprising occupations frequently involve starting up and carrying out projects. These occupations can involve leading people and making many decisions. They sometimes require risk taking and often deal with business.

Abilities: Oral Expression—The ability to communicate information and ideas verbally so others will understand. Oral Comprehension—The ability to listen to and understand information and ideas presented verbally. Problem Sensitivity—The ability to tell when something is wrong or is likely to go wrong. Does not involve solving the problem, only recognizing there is a problem. Information Ordering—The ability to correctly follow a given rule or set of rules in order to arrange things or actions in a certain order. The things or actions can include numbers, letters, words, pictures, procedures, sentences, and mathematical or logical operations.

Speech Clarity—The ability to speak clearly so that what is said is understandable to a listener. Written Comprehension—The ability to read and understand information and ideas presented in writing.

Skills: Instructing—Teaching others how to do something. Problem Identification—Identifying the nature of problems. Management of Personnel Resources—Motivating, developing, and directing people as they work, identifying the best people for the job. Critical Thinking—Using logic and analysis to identify the strengths and weaknesses of different approaches. Systems Perception—Determining when important changes have occurred in a system or are likely to occur. Coordination—Adjusting actions in relation to others' actions.

Generalized Work Activities: Evaluating Information against Standards—Evaluating information against a set of standards and verifying that it is correct. Communicating with Other Workers—Providing information to supervisors, fellow workers, and subordinates. This information can be exchanged face-to-face, in writing, or via telephone/electronic transfer. Documenting/ Recording Information—Entering, transcribing, recording, storing, or maintaining information in either written form or by electronic/magnetic recording. Guiding, Directing, and Motivating Subordinates— Providing guidance and direction to subordinates, including setting performance standards and monitoring subordinates. Inspecting Equipment, Structures, Materials—Inspecting or diagnosing equipment, structures, or materials to identify the causes of errors or other problems or defects.

First-Line Supervisors/ Managers of Mechanics, Installers, and Repairers

Supervise and coordinate the activities of mechanics, installers, and repairers. Computes estimates and actual costs of factors such as materials, labor, and outside contractors; prepares budgets. Confers with personnel such as management, engineering, quality control, customers, and workers' representatives to coordinate work activities and resolve problems. Recommends or initiates personnel actions such as employment, performance evaluations, promotions, transfers, discharges, and disciplinary measures. Directs, coordinates, and assists in performance of workers' activities such as engine tune-up, hydroelectric-turbine repair, or circuit-breaker installation. Examines object, system, or facilities such as telephone, air-conditioning, or industrial plant; analyzes information to determine installation, service, or repair needed. Monitors operations. Inspects, tests, and measures completed work, using devices such as hand tools, gauges, and specifications to verify conformance to standards. Completes and maintains reports such as time and production records, inventories, and test results. Trains workers in methods, procedures, and use of equipment and work aids such as blueprints, hand tools, and test equipment. Patrols work area and examines tools and equipment to detect unsafe conditions or violations of safety rules. Requisitions materials and supplies, such as tools, equipment, and replacement parts, for work activities. Establishes or adjusts work methods and procedures to meet production schedules, using knowledge of capacities of machines, equipment, and personnel. Interprets specifications, blueprints, and job orders; constructs templates; lays out reference points for workers. Assigns workers to perform activities such as servicing appliances, repairing and maintaining vehicles, and installing machinery and equipment. Recommends measures such as procedural changes, service manual revisions, and equipment purchases, to improve work performance and minimize operating costs.

Personality Type: Enterprising. Enterprising occupations frequently involve starting up and carrying out projects. These occupations can involve leading people and making many decisions. They sometimes require risk taking and often deal with business.

Abilities: Oral Expression—The ability to communicate information and ideas verbally so others will understand. Near Vision—The ability to see details of objects at a close range. Information Ordering—The ability to correctly follow a given rule or set of rules in order to

arrange things or actions in a certain order. The things or actions can include numbers, letters, words, pictures, procedures, sentences, and mathematical or logical operations. Oral Comprehension—The ability to listen to and understand information and ideas presented verbally. Deductive Reasoning—The ability to apply general rules to specific problems to come up with logical answers. Involves deciding if an answer makes sense. Written Comprehension—The ability to read and understand information and ideas presented in writing.

Skills: Coordination—Adjusting actions in relation to others' actions. Management of Personnel Resources—Motivating, developing, and directing people as they work, identifying the best people for the job. Time Management—Managing one's own time and the time of others.

Generalized Work Activities: Getting Information Needed to Do the Job—Observing, receiving, and otherwise obtaining information from all relevant sources. Guiding, Directing, and Motivating Subordinates—Providing guidance and direction to subordinates, including setting performance standards and monitoring subordinates. Monitoring Processes, Materials, Surroundings—Monitoring and reviewing information from materials, events, or the environment, often to detect problems or to find out when things are finished. Coordinating Work and Activities of Others—Coordinating members of a work group to accomplish tasks. Identifying Objects, Actions, and Events—Identifying information received by making estimates or categorizations, recognizing differences or similarities, or sensing changes in circumstances or events.

First-Line Supervisors/ Managers of Production and Operating Workers

Supervise and coordinate the activities of production and operating workers such as inspectors, precision workers, machine setters and operators, assemblers, fabricators, and plant and system operators. Sets up and adjusts machines and equipment. Calculates labor and equipment requirements and production specifications, using standard formulas. Reviews operations and accounting records or reports to determine the feasibility of production estimates and to evaluate current production. Maintains operations data such as time, production, and cost records; prepares management reports. Recommends or implements measures to motivate employees and improve production methods, equipment performance, product quality, or efficiency. Requisitions materials, supplies, equipment parts, or repair services. Interprets specifications, blueprints, job orders, and company policies and procedures for workers. Inspects materials, products, or equipment to detect defects or malfunctions. Demonstrates equipment operations or work procedures to new employees or assigns employees to experienced workers for training. Monitors gauges, dials, and other indicators to ensure that operators conform to production or processing standards. Confers with other supervisors to coordinate operations and activities within departments or between departments. Reads and analyzes charts, work orders, or production schedules to determine production requirements. Confers with management or subordinates to resolve worker problems, complaints, or grievances. Determines standards, production, and rates based on company policy, equipment and labor availability, and workload. Plans and establishes work schedules, assignments, and production sequences to meet production goals. Directs and coordinates the activities of employees engaged in the production or processing of goods. Monitors or patrols work area and enforces safety or sanitation regulations.

Personality Type: Enterprising. Enterprising occupations frequently involve starting up and carrying out projects. These occupations can involve leading people and making many decisions. They sometimes require risk taking and often deal with business.

Abilities: Oral Expression—The ability to communicate information and ideas verbally so others will understand. Oral Comprehension—The ability to listen to and understand information and ideas presented verbally. Written Comprehension—The ability to read and understand information and ideas presented in writing. Mathematical Reasoning—The ability to understand and organize a problem and then select a mathematical method or formula to solve the problem. Speech Clarity—The ability to speak clearly so that what is said is understandable to a listener. Problem Sensitivity—The ability to tell when something is wrong or is likely to go wrong. Does not involve solving the problem, only recognizing there is a problem. Deductive Reasoning—The ability to apply general rules to specific problems to come up with logical answers. Involves deciding if an answer makes sense.

Skills: Coordination—Adjusting actions in relation to others' actions. Speaking—Talking to others to effectively convey information. Product Inspection—Inspecting and evaluating the quality of products. Critical Thinking—Using logic and analysis to identify the strengths and weaknesses of different approaches. Time Management—Managing one's own time and the time of others. Reading Comprehension—Understanding written information in work-related documents. Information Gathering—Knowing how to find information and identifying essential information.

Generalized Work Activities: Communicating with Other Workers—Providing information to supervisors, fellow workers, and subordinates. This information can be exchanged face-to-face, in writing, or via telephone/electronic transfer. Monitoring Processes, Materials, Surroundings—Monitoring and reviewing information from materials, events, or the environment, often to detect problems or to find out when things are finished. Guiding, Directing, and Motivating Subordinates—Providing guidance and direction to subordinates, including setting performance standards and monitoring subordinates. Getting Information Needed to Do the Job—Observing, receiving, and otherwise obtaining information from all relevant sources. Coordinating Work and Activities of Others—Coordinating members of a work group to accomplish tasks.

First-Line Supervisors/ Managers of Transportation and Material-Moving Machine and Vehicle Operators

Directly supervise and coordinate activities of transportation and material-moving machine and vehicle operators and helpers. Interprets transportation and tariff regulations, shipping orders, safety regulations, and company policies and procedures for workers. Requisitions needed personnel, supplies, equipment, parts, or repair services. Resolves worker problems or assists workers in solving problems. Directs workers in transportation or related services such as pumping, moving, storing, and loading/unloading materials or people. Plans and establishes transportation routes, work schedules, and assignments. Allocates equipment to meet transportation, operations, or production goals. Recommends or implements personnel actions such as hiring, firing, and performance evaluations. Maintains or verifies time, transportation, financial, inventory, and personnel records. Assists workers in performing tasks such as coupling railroad cars or loading vehicles. Explains and demonstrates work tasks to new workers or assigns workers to experienced workers for further training. Inspects or tests materials, stock, vehicles, equipment, and facilities to locate defects, meet maintenance or production specifications, and verify safety standards. Reviews orders, production schedules, and shipping/receiving notices to determine work sequence and material shipping dates, type, volume, and destinations. Receives telephone or radio reports of emergencies; dispatches personnel and vehicles in response to request. Recommends and implements measures to improve worker motivation, equipment performance, work methods, and customer services. Confers with customers, supervisors, contractors, and other personnel to exchange information and resolve problems. Prepares, compiles, and submits reports on work activities, operations, production, and work-related accidents. Drives vehicles or operates machines or equipment. Examines, measures, and weighs cargo or materials to determine specific handling requirements.

Personality Type: Enterprising. Enterprising occupations frequently involve starting up and carrying out projects. These occupations can involve leading people and making many decisions. They sometimes require risk taking and often deal with business.

Abilities: Oral Expression—The ability to communicate information and ideas verbally so others will understand. Written Comprehension—The ability to read and understand information and ideas presented in writing. Written Expression—The ability to communicate information and ideas in writing so others will understand. Information Ordering—The ability to correctly follow a given rule or set of rules in order to arrange things or actions in a certain order. The things or actions can include numbers, letters, words, pictures, procedures, sentences, and mathematical or logical operations. Oral Comprehension—The ability to listen to and understand information and ideas presented verbally.

Skills: Speaking—Talking to others to effectively convey information. Coordination—Adjusting actions in relation to others' actions. Mathematics—Using mathematics to solve problems. Active Listening—Listening to what other people are saying; asking questions as appropriate.

Generalized Work Activities: Communicating with Other Workers—Providing information to supervisors, fellow workers, and subordinates. This information can be exchanged face-to-face, in writing, or via telephone/electronic transfer. Guiding, Directing, and Motivating Subordinates—Providing guidance and direction to subordinates, including setting performance standards and monitoring subordinates. Coordinating Work and Activities of Others—Coordinating members of a work group to accomplish tasks. Inspecting Equipment, Structures, Materials—Inspecting or diagnosing equipment, structures, or materials to identify the causes of errors or other problems or defects.

Bookkeeping, Accounting, and Auditing Clerks

- ▲ Growth: –4%
- ▲ Annual Job Openings: 325,366
- ▲ Yearly Earnings: $23,190
- ▲ Education Required: Moderate-term O-J-T
- ▲ Self-Employed: 11%
- ▲ Part-Time: 32.8%

Bookkeeping, Accounting, and Auditing Clerks

Compute, classify, and record numerical data to keep financial records complete. Perform any combination of routine calculating, posting, and verifying duties to obtain primary financial data for use in maintaining accounting records. Check the accuracy of figures, calculations, and postings pertaining to business transactions recorded by other workers. Performs financial calculations such as amounts due, balances, discounts, equity, and principal. Verifies balances and entries, calculations, and postings recorded by other workers. Compiles reports and tables to show statistics related to cash receipts, expenditures, accounts payable and receivable, and profit and loss. Processes negotiable instruments such as checks and vouchers. Debits or credits accounts. Records financial transactions and other account information to update and maintain accounting records. Complies with federal, state, and company policies, procedures, and regulations. Evaluates records for accuracy of balances, postings, calculations, and other records pertaining to business or operating transactions; reconciles records or notes discrepancies.

Personality Type: Conventional. Conventional occupations frequently involve following set procedures and routines. These occupations can include working with data and details more than with ideas. Usually there is a clear line of authority to follow.

Abilities: Number Facility—The ability to add, subtract, multiply, or divide quickly and correctly. Mathematical Reasoning—The ability to understand and organize a problem and then select a mathematical method or formula to solve the problem. Near Vision—The ability to see details of objects at a close range. Written Comprehension—The ability to read and understand information and ideas presented in writing. Perceptual Speed—The ability to quickly and accurately compare letters, numbers, objects, pictures, or patterns. The things to be compared may be presented at the same time or one after the other. Includes comparing a presented object with a remembered object. Information Ordering—The ability to correctly follow a given rule or set of rules in order to arrange things or actions in a certain order. The things or actions can include numbers, letters, words, pictures, procedures, sentences, and mathematical or logical operations.

Skills: Mathematics—Using mathematics to solve problems. Information Gathering—Knowing how to find information and identifying essential information. Information Organization—Finding ways to structure or classify multiple pieces of information. Reading Comprehension—Understanding written information in work-related documents. Writing—Communicating effectively with others in writing as indicated by the needs of the audience.

Generalized Work Activities: Documenting/Recording Information—Entering, transcribing, recording, storing, or maintaining information in either written form or by electronic/magnetic recording. Getting Information Needed to Do the Job—Observing, receiving, and otherwise obtaining information from all relevant sources. Processing Information—Compiling, coding, categorizing, calculating, tabulating, auditing, verifying, or processing information or data. Analyzing Data or Information—Identifying underlying principles, reasons, or facts by breaking down information or data into separate parts. Identifying Objects, Actions, and Events—Identifying information received by making estimates or categorizations, recognizing differences or similarities, or sensing changes in circumstances or events. Communicating with Other Workers—Providing information to supervisors, fellow workers, and subordinates. This information can be exchanged face-to-face, in writing, or via telephone/electronic transfer. Performing Administrative Activities—Approving requests, handling paperwork, and performing day-to-day administrative tasks.

Bread and Pastry Bakers

- ▲ Growth: 17%
- ▲ Annual Job Openings: 56,526
- ▲ Yearly Earnings: $16,990
- ▲ Education Required: Moderate-term O-J-T
- ▲ Self-Employed: 8.2%
- ▲ Part-Time: 38.5%

Bakers, Bread and Pastry

Mix and bake ingredients according to recipes to produce small quantities of breads, pastries, and other baked goods for consumption on premises or for sale as specialty baked goods. Covers filling with top crust. Mixes ingredients to form dough or batter, by hand or using electric mixer. Rolls and shapes dough, using rolling pin; cuts dough in uniform portions with knife, divider, or cookie cutter. Checks production schedule to determine variety and quantity of goods to bake. Mixes ingredients to make icings; decorates cakes and pastries; blends colors for icings, shaped ornaments, and statuaries. Spreads or sprinkles toppings on loaves or specialties. Places dough in oven, using long-handled paddle (peel). Mixes and cooks pie fillings; pours fillings into pie shells; tops fillings with meringue or cream. Weighs and measures ingredients, using measuring cups and spoons. Cuts, peels, and prepares fruit for pie fillings. Molds dough into desired shapes, places dough in greased or floured pans, and trims overlapping edges with knife.

Personality Type: Realistic. Realistic occupations frequently involve work activities that include practical, hands-on problems and solutions. They often deal with plants, animals, and real-world materials like wood, tools, and machinery. Many of the occupations require working outside and do not involve a lot of paperwork or working closely with others.

Abilities: Written Comprehension—The ability to read and understand information and ideas presented in writing. Information Ordering—The ability to correctly follow a given rule or set of rules in order to arrange things or actions in a certain order. The things or actions can include numbers, letters, words, pictures, procedures, sentences, and mathematical or logical operations. Finger Dexterity—The ability to make precisely coordinated movements of the fingers of one or both hands to grasp, manipulate, or assemble very small objects. Manual Dexterity—The ability to quickly make coordinated movements of one hand, a hand together with its arm, or two hands, to grasp, manipulate, or assemble objects. Wrist-Finger Speed—The ability to make fast, simple, repeated movements of the fingers, hands, and wrists.

Skills: Operation and Control—Controlling operations of equipment or systems. Product Inspection—Inspecting and evaluating the quality of products. Information Organization—Finding ways to structure or classify multiple pieces of information. Reading Comprehension—Understanding written information in work-related documents. Mathematics—Using mathematics to solve problems.

Generalized Work Activities: Handling and Moving Objects—Using one's hands and arms in handling, installing, forming, positioning, and moving materials, or in manipulating things. Includes the use of keyboards. Monitoring Processes, Materials, Surroundings—Monitoring and reviewing information from materials, events, or the environment, often to detect problems or to find out when things are finished. Implementing Ideas and Programs—Conducting or carrying out work procedures and activities in accord with one's own ideas or information provided through directions/instructions for purposes of installing, modifying, preparing, delivering, constructing, integrating, finishing, or completing programs, systems, structures, or products. Getting Information Needed to Do the Job—Observing, receiving, and otherwise obtaining information from all relevant sources. Controlling Machines and Processes—Using either control mechanisms or direct physical activity to operate machines or processes. Does not involve working with computers or vehicles.

Bricklayers, Blockmasons, and Stonemasons

- ▲ Growth: 12%
- ▲ Annual Job Openings: 29,721
- ▲ Yearly Earnings: $35,200
- ▲ Education Required: Long-term O-J-T
- ▲ Self-Employed: 27.9%
- ▲ Part-Time: 8.7%

Brickmasons and Blockmasons

Lay and bind building materials such as brick, structural tile, concrete block, cinder block, glass block, and terra-cotta block, with mortar and other substances, to construct or repair walls, partitions, arches, sewers, and other structures. Fastens or fuses brick or other building material to structure with wire clamps, anchor holes, torch, or cement. Calculates angles and courses; determines vertical and horizontal alignment of courses. Mixes specified amount of sand, clay, dirt, or mortar powder with water to form refractory mixture. Breaks or cuts bricks, tiles, or blocks to size, using edge of trowel, hammer, or power saw. Removes burned or damaged brick or mortar, using sledgehammer, crowbar, chipping gun, or chisel. Cleans working surface to remove scale, dust, soot, or chips of brick and mortar, using broom, wire brush, or scrapper. Examines brickwork or structure to determine need for repair. Measures distance from reference points and marks guidelines to lay out work, using plumb bobs and levels. Applies and smoothes mortar or other mixture over work surface and removes excess, using trowel and hand tools. Lays and aligns bricks, blocks, or tiles to build or repair structures or high temperature equipment such as cupola, kilns, ovens, or furnaces. Sprays or spreads refractory material over brickwork to protect against deterioration.

Personality Type: Realistic. Realistic occupations frequently involve work activities that include practical, hands-on problems and solutions. They often deal with plants, animals, and real-world materials like wood, tools, and machinery. Many of the occupations require working outside and do not involve a lot of paperwork or working closely with others.

Abilities: Manual Dexterity—The ability to quickly make coordinated movements of one hand, a hand together with its arm, or two hands, to grasp, manipulate, or assemble objects. Information Ordering—The ability to correctly follow a given rule or set of rules in order to arrange things or actions in a certain order. The things or actions can include numbers, letters, words, pictures, procedures, sentences, and mathematical or logical operations. Visualization—The ability to imagine how something will look after it is moved around or when its parts are moved or rearranged. Dynamic Strength—The ability to exert muscle force repeatedly or continuously over time. This involves muscular endurance and resistance to muscle fatigue. Extent Flexibility—The ability to bend, stretch, twist, or reach out with the body, arms, and/or legs.

Skills: Mathematics—Using mathematics to solve problems. Equipment Selection—Determining the kind of tools and equipment needed to do a job. Monitoring—Assessing how well one is doing when learning or doing something. Product Inspection—Inspecting and evaluating the quality of products. Information Organization—Finding ways to structure or classify multiple pieces of information. Repairing—Repairing machines or systems, using the needed tools.

Generalized Work Activities: Handling and Moving Objects—Using one's hands and arms in handling, installing, forming, positioning, and moving materials, or in manipulating things. Performing General Physical Activities—Performing physical activities that require moving one's whole body, such as in climbing, lifting, balancing, walking, and stooping. Performing activities that often also require considerable use of the arms and legs, such as in the physical handling of materials. Controlling Machines and Processes—Using either control mechanisms or direct physical activity to operate machines or processes. Does not involve working with computers or vehicles. Inspecting Equipment, Structures, Materials—Inspecting or diagnosing equipment, structures, or materials to identify the causes

of errors or other problems or defects. Getting Information Needed to Do the Job—Observing, receiving, and otherwise obtaining information from all relevant sources.

Stone Cutters and Carvers

Cut or carve stone according to diagrams and patterns. Selects chisels, pneumatic or surfacing tools, or sandblasting nozzles; determines sequence of their use according to intricacy of design or figure. Moves fingers over surface of carving to ensure smoothness of finish. Verifies depth and dimensions of cut or carving, using measuring instruments, to ensure adherence to specifications. Guides nozzle over stone following stencil outline, or chips along marks to create design or to work a surface down to desired finish. Removes or adds stencil during blasting to create differences in depth of cuts, intricate designs, or rough, pitted finish. Lays out designs or dimensions on stone surface, by freehand or transfer from tracing paper, using scribe or chalk and measuring instruments. Studies artistic objects or graphic materials such as models, sketches, or blueprints; plans carving or cutting technique. Drills holes or cuts molding and grooves in stone. Loads sandblasting equipment with abrasive, attaches nozzle to hose, and turns valves to admit compressed air and activate jet.

Personality Type: Realistic. Realistic occupations frequently involve work activities that include practical, hands-on problems and solutions. They often deal with plants, animals, and real-world materials like wood, tools, and machinery. Many of the occupations require working outside and do not involve a lot of paperwork or working closely with others.

Abilities: Arm-Hand Steadiness—The ability to keep the hand and arm steady while making an arm movement or while holding the arm and hand in one position. Visualization—The ability to imagine how something will look after it is moved around or when its parts are moved or rearranged. Wrist-Finger Speed—The ability to make fast, simple, repeated movements of the fingers, hands, and wrists. Near Vision—The ability to see details of objects at a close range.

Information Ordering—The ability to correctly follow a given rule or set of rules in order to arrange things or actions in a certain order. The things or actions can include numbers, letters, words, pictures, procedures, sentences, and mathematical or logical operations. Manual Dexterity—The ability to quickly make coordinated movements of one hand, a hand together with its arm, or two hands, to grasp, manipulate, or assemble objects.

Skills: Equipment Selection—Determining the kind of tools and equipment needed to do a job. Product Inspection—Inspecting and evaluating the quality of products. Operation and Control—Controlling operations of equipment or systems. Mathematics—Using mathematics to solve problems. Information Gathering—Knowing how to find information and identifying essential information.

Generalized Work Activities: Handling and Moving Objects—Using one's hands and arms in handling, installing, forming, positioning, and moving materials, or in manipulating things. Controlling Machines and Processes—Using either control mechanisms or direct physical activity to operate machines or processes. Does not involve working with computers or vehicles. Thinking Creatively—Originating, inventing, designing, or creating new applications, ideas, relationships, systems, or products, including artistic contributions. Getting Information Needed to Do the Job—Observing, receiving, and otherwise obtaining information from all relevant sources. Performing General Physical Activities—Performing physical activities that require moving one's whole body, such as in climbing, lifting, balancing, walking, and stooping. Performing activities that often also require considerable use of the arms and legs, such as in the physical handling of materials.

Stonemasons

Build stone structures such as piers, walls, and abutments. Lay walks, curbstones, or special types of masonry for vats, tanks, and floors. Drills holes in marble or ornamental stone; anchors bracket. Removes sections of monument from truck bed and guides stone onto foundation, using skids, hoist, or truck crane. Sets stone or marble in place, according to layout or pattern. Aligns and levels stone or marble, using measuring devices such as rule, square, and plumbline. Mixes mortar or grout; pours or spreads mortar or grout on marble slabs, stone, or foundation. Cleans excess mortar or grout from surface of marble, stone, or monument, using sponge, brush, water, or acid. Lines interiors of molds with treated paper and fills molds with composition-stone mixture. Repairs cracked or chipped areas of ornamental stone or marble surface, using blowtorch and mastic. Shapes, trims, faces, and cuts marble or stone preparatory to setting, using power saws, cutting equipment, and hand tools. Positions mold along guidelines of wall, presses mold in place, and removes mold and paper from wall. Smoothes, polishes, and bevels surfaces, using hand tools and power tools. Finishes joints between stones, using trowel. Lays out wall pattern or foundation of monument, using straight edge, rule, or staked lines. Digs trench for foundation of monument, using pick and shovel.

Personality Type: Realistic. Realistic occupations frequently involve work activities that include practical, hands-on problems and solutions. They often deal with plants, animals, and real-world materials like wood, tools, and machinery. Many of the occupations require working outside and do not involve a lot of paperwork or working closely with others.

Abilities: Wrist-Finger Speed—The ability to make fast, simple, repeated movements of the fingers, hands, and wrists. Static Strength—The ability to exert maximum muscle force to lift, push, pull, or carry objects. Dynamic Strength—The ability to exert muscle force repeatedly or continuously over time. This involves muscular endurance and resistance to muscle fatigue. Visualization—The ability to imagine how something will look after it is moved around or when its parts are moved or rearranged. Speed of Limb Movement—The ability to quickly move the arms or legs. Explosive Strength—The ability to use short bursts of muscle force to propel oneself, as in jumping or sprinting, or to throw an object.

Skills: Product Inspection—Inspecting and evaluating the quality of products. Equipment Selection—Determining the kind of tools and equipment needed to do a job. Operation and Control—Controlling operations of equipment or systems. Monitoring—Assessing how well one is doing when learning or doing something. Repairing—Repairing machines or systems, using the needed tools.

Generalized Work Activities: Performing General Physical Activities—Performing physical activities that require moving one's whole body, such as in climbing, lifting, balancing, walking, and stooping. Performing activities that often also require considerable use of the arms and legs, such as in the physical handling of materials. Handling and Moving Objects—Using one's hands and arms in handling, installing, forming, positioning, and moving materials, or in manipulating things. Controlling Machines and Processes—Using either control mechanisms or direct physical activity to operate machines or processes. Does not involve working with computers or vehicles. Drafting and Specifying Technical Devices—Providing documentation, detailed instructions, drawings, or specifications to inform others about how devices, parts, equipment, or structures are to be fabricated, constructed, assembled, modified, maintained, or used. Getting Information Needed to Do the Job—Observing, receiving, and otherwise obtaining information from all relevant sources.

Brokerage Clerks

- ▲ Growth: 28%
- ▲ Annual Job Openings: 17,895
- ▲ Yearly Earnings: $27,920
- ▲ Education Required: Short-term O-J-T
- ▲ Self-Employed: 0%
- ▲ Part-Time: 19.1%

Brokerage Clerks

Perform clerical duties involving the purchase or sale of securities. Write orders for stock purchases and sales. Compute transfer taxes. Verify stock transactions. Accept and deliver securities. Track stock price fluctuations. Compute equity. Distribute dividends. Keep records of daily transactions and holdings. Verifies ownership and transaction information and dividend distribution instructions, to ensure conformance with governmental regulations, using stock records and reports. Prepares reports summarizing daily transactions and earnings for individual customer accounts. Computes total holdings, dividends, interest, transfer taxes, brokerage fees, and commissions; allocates appropriate payments to customers. Corresponds with customers and confers with coworkers to answer inquiries, discuss market fluctuations, and resolve account problems. Monitors daily stock prices and computes fluctuations to determine the need for additional collateral to secure loans. Schedules and coordinates transfer and delivery of security certificates between companies, departments, and customers. Prepares forms such as receipts, withdrawal orders, transmittal papers, and transfer confirmations, based on transaction requests from stockholders. Records and documents security transactions such as purchases, sales, conversions, redemptions, and payments, using computers, accounting ledgers, and certificate records. Files, types, and operates standard office machines.

Personality Type: Conventional. Conventional occupations frequently involve following set procedures and routines. These occupations can include working with data and details more than with ideas. Usually there is a clear line of authority to follow.

Abilities: Written Expression—The ability to communicate information and ideas in writing so others will understand. Number Facility—The ability to add, subtract, multiply, or divide quickly and correctly. Mathematical Reasoning—The ability to understand and organize a problem and then select a mathematical

method or formula to solve the problem. Written Comprehension—The ability to read and understand information and ideas presented in writing. Oral Expression—The ability to communicate information and ideas verbally so others will understand.

Skills: Mathematics—Using mathematics to solve problems. Writing—Communicating effectively with others in writing as indicated by the needs of the audience. Reading Comprehension—Understanding written information in work-related documents. Information Gathering—Knowing how to find information and identifying essential information. Active Listening—Listening to what other people are saying; asking questions as appropriate. Speaking—Talking to others to effectively convey information.

Generalized Work Activities: Getting Information Needed to Do the Job—Observing, receiving, and otherwise obtaining information from all relevant

sources. Processing Information—Compiling, coding, categorizing, calculating, tabulating, auditing, verifying, or processing information or data. Communicating with Persons Outside Organization—Communicating with persons outside the organization. Representing the organization to customers, the public, government, and other external sources. Exchanging information face-to-face, in writing, or via telephone/electronic transfer. Documenting/Recording Information—Entering, transcribing, recording, storing, or maintaining information in either written form or by electronic/magnetic recording. Updating and Using Job-Relevant Knowledge—Keeping up-to-date technically and knowing the functions of one's own job and related jobs. Identifying Objects, Actions, and Events—Identifying information received by making estimates or categorizations, recognizing differences or similarities, or sensing changes in circumstances or events.

Budget Analysts

▲ Growth: 14%

▲ Annual Job Openings: 9,617

▲ Yearly Earnings: $44,950

▲ Education Required: Bachelor's degree

▲ Self-Employed: 0%

▲ Part-Time: 7.2%

Budget Analysts

Examine budget estimates for completeness, accuracy, and conformance with procedures and regulations. Analyze budgeting and accounting reports for the purpose of maintaining expenditure controls. Directs compilation of data based on statistical studies and analyses of past and current years, to prepare budgets. Analyzes costs in relation to services performed during previous fiscal years to prepare comparative analyses of operating programs. Reviews operating budgets periodically to analyze trends affecting budget needs. Directs preparation of regular and special budget reports to interpret budget directives and to establish policies for carrying out directives. Consults with unit heads to

ensure adjustments are made in accordance with program changes to facilitate long-term planning. Correlates appropriations for specific programs with appropriations for divisional programs, including items for emergency funds. Recommends approval or disapproval of requests for funds. Analyzes accounting records to determine financial resources required to implement program and submits recommendations for budget allocations. Advises staff on cost analysis and fiscal allocations. Testifies regarding proposed budgets, before examining and fund-granting authorities, to clarify reports and gain support for estimated budget needs.

Personality Type: Conventional. Conventional occupations frequently involve following set procedures and routines. These occupations can include working with data and details more than with ideas. Usually there is a clear line of authority to follow.

Abilities: Number Facility—The ability to add, subtract, multiply, or divide quickly and correctly. Mathematical Reasoning—The ability to understand and organize a problem and then select a mathematical method or formula to solve the problem. Written Comprehension—The ability to read and understand information and ideas presented in writing. Oral Comprehension—The ability to listen to and understand information and ideas presented verbally.

Skills: Management of Financial Resources—Determining how money will be spent to get the work done, and accounting for these expenditures. Information Gathering—Knowing how to find information and identifying essential information. Problem Identification—Identifying the nature of problems. Mathematics—Using mathematics to solve

problems. Judgment and Decision Making—Weighing the relative costs and benefits of a potential action.

Generalized Work Activities: Monitoring and Controlling Resources—Monitoring and controlling resources and overseeing the spending of money. Getting Information Needed to Do the Job—Observing, receiving, and otherwise obtaining information from all relevant sources. Communicating with Other Workers—Providing information to supervisors, fellow workers, and subordinates. This information can be exchanged face-to-face, in writing, or via telephone/electronic transfer. Analyzing Data or Information—Identifying underlying principles, reasons, or facts by breaking down information or data into separate parts. Making Decisions and Solving Problems—Combining, evaluating, and analyzing information and data to make decisions and solve problems. Involves making decisions about the relative importance of information and choosing the best solution.

Bus and Truck Mechanics and Diesel Engine Specialists

- ▲ Growth: 10%
- ▲ Annual Job Openings: 21,502
- ▲ Yearly Earnings: $29,340
- ▲ Education Required: Long-term O-J-T
- ▲ Self-Employed: 4.8%
- ▲ Part-Time: 2.9%

Bus and Truck Mechanics and Diesel Engine Specialists

Inspect, repair, and maintain diesel engines used to power machines. Reads job orders and observes and listens to operating equipment to ensure conformance to specifications or to determine malfunctions. Inspects, repairs, and maintains automotive and mechanical equipment and machinery such as pumps and compressors. Disassembles and overhauls internal combustion

engines, pumps, generators, transmissions, clutches, and rear ends. Operates valve-grinding machine to grind and reset valves. Examines and adjusts protective guards, loose bolts, and specified safety devices. Changes oil, checks batteries, repairs tires and tubes, and lubricates equipment and machinery. Inspects defective equipment and diagnoses malfunctions, using test instruments such as motor analyzers, chassis charts, and pressure gauges. Attaches test instruments to equipment and reads dials and gauges to diagnose malfunctions. Reconditions and replaces parts, pistons, bearings, gears, and valves. Adjusts brakes, aligns wheels, tightens bolts and screws, and reassembles equipment. Inspects and verifies

dimensions and clearances of parts to ensure conformance to factory specifications.

Personality Type: Realistic. Realistic occupations frequently involve work activities that include practical, hands-on problems and solutions. They often deal with plants, animals, and real-world materials like wood, tools, and machinery. Many of the occupations require working outside and do not involve a lot of paperwork or working closely with others.

Abilities: Problem Sensitivity—The ability to tell when something is wrong or is likely to go wrong. Does not involve solving the problem, only recognizing there is a problem. Hearing Sensitivity—The ability to detect or tell the difference between sounds that vary over broad ranges of pitch and loudness. Written Comprehension—The ability to read and understand information and ideas presented in writing. Deductive Reasoning—The ability to apply general rules to specific problems to come up with logical answers. Involves deciding if an answer makes sense. Inductive Reasoning—The ability to combine separate pieces of information, or specific answers to problems, to form general rules or conclu-sions. Includes coming up with a logical explanation for why a series of seemingly unrelated events occur together.

Skills: Repairing—Repairing machines or systems, using the needed tools. Troubleshooting—Determining what

is causing an operating error and deciding what to do about it. Equipment Maintenance—Performing routine maintenance and determining when and what kind of maintenance is needed. Equipment Selection—Determining the kind of tools and equipment needed to do a job.

Generalized Work Activities: Repairing and Maintaining Mechanical Equipment—Fixing, servicing, aligning, setting up, adjusting, and testing machines, devices, moving parts, and equipment that operate primarily on the basis of mechanical, not electronic, principles. Handling and Moving Objects—Using one's hands and arms in handling, installing, forming, positioning, and moving materials, or in manipulating things. Includes the use of keyboards. Identifying Objects, Actions, and Events—Identifying information received by making estimates or categorizations, recognizing differences or similarities, or sensing changes in circumstances or events. Inspecting Equipment, Structures, Materials—Inspecting or diagnosing equipment, structures, or materials to identify the causes of errors or other problems or defects. Performing General Physical Activities—Performing physical activities that require moving one's whole body, such as in climbing, lifting, balancing, walking, and stooping. Performing activities that often also require considerable use of the arms and legs, such as in the physical handling of materials.

Bus Drivers

- ▲ Growth: 16%
- ▲ Annual Job Openings: 29,885
- ▲ Yearly Earnings: $24,370
- ▲ Education Required: Moderate-term O-J-T
- ▲ Self-Employed: 6.1%
- ▲ Part-Time: 43.3%

Bus Drivers, Transit and Intercity

Drive bus or motor coach, including regular route operations, charters, and private carriage. Assist passengers with baggage. Collect fares or tickets. Inspects vehicle; checks gas, oil, and water before departure. Assists passengers with baggage; collects tickets or cash fares. Loads and unloads baggage in baggage compartment. Advises passengers to be seated and orderly while on vehicle. Reports delays or accidents.

Records cash receipts and ticket fares. Regulates heating, lighting, and ventilating systems for passenger comfort. Parks vehicle at loading area for passengers to board. Drives vehicle over specified route or to specified destination according to time schedule, to transport passengers, complying with traffic regulations. Makes minor repairs to vehicle and changes tires.

Personality Type: Realistic. Realistic occupations frequently involve work activities that include practical, hands-on problems and solutions. They often deal with plants, animals, and real-world materials like wood, tools, and machinery. Many of the occupations require working outside and do not involve a lot of paperwork or working closely with others.

Abilities: Reaction Time—The ability to quickly respond with the hand, finger, or foot to a signal such as a sound, a light, or a picture. Far Vision—The ability to see details at a distance. Night Vision—The ability to see under low-light conditions. Control Precision—The ability to quickly and repeatedly make precise adjustments in moving the controls of a machine or vehicle to exact positions. Near Vision—The ability to see details of objects at a close range.

Skills: Operation and Control—Controlling operations of equipment or systems. Operation Monitoring—Watching gauges, dials, or other indicators to make sure a machine is working properly. Equipment Maintenance—Performing routine maintenance and determining when and what kind of maintenance is needed. Reading Comprehension—Understanding written information in work-related documents. Time Management—Managing one's own time and the time of others. Speaking—Talking to others to effectively convey information. Social Perceptiveness—Being aware of other people's reactions and understanding why people react the way they do.

Generalized Work Activities: Operating Vehicles or Equipment—Running, maneuvering, navigating, or driving vehicles or mechanized equipment such as forklifts, passenger vehicles, aircraft, or water craft. Inspecting Equipment, Structures, Materials—Inspecting or diagnosing equipment, structures, or materials to identify the causes of errors or other problems or defects. Performing for/Working with Public—Performing for people or dealing directly with the public, including serving persons in restaurants and stores and receiving clients or guests. Handling and Moving Objects—Using one's hands and arms in handling, installing, forming, positioning, and moving materials, or in manipulating things. Monitoring Processes, Materials, Surroundings—Monitoring and reviewing information from materials, events, or the environment, often to detect problems or to find out when things are finished. Communicating with Persons Outside Organization—Communicating with persons outside the organization. Representing the organization to customers, the public, government, and other external sources. Exchanging information face-to-face, in writing, or via telephone/electronic transfer. Repairing and Maintaining Mechanical Equipment—Fixing, servicing, aligning, setting up, adjusting, and testing machines, devices, moving parts, and equipment that operate primarily on the basis of mechanical, not electronic, principles.

Cardiovascular Technologists and Technicians

▲ Growth: 39%

▲ Annual Job Openings: 3,458

▲ Yearly Earnings: $35,770

▲ Education Required: Associate degree

▲ Self-Employed: 0%

▲ Part-Time: 22.9%

Cardiovascular Technologists and Technicians

Conduct tests on pulmonary or cardiovascular systems of patients for diagnostic purposes. Conduct or assist in electrocardiograms, cardiac catheterizations, pulmonary-functions, lung capacity, and similar tests. Prepares and positions patients for testing. Explains testing procedures to patient to obtain cooperation and reduce anxiety. Records test results and other data into patient's record. Reviews test results with physician. Adjusts equipment and controls according to physician's orders or established protocol. Compares measurements of heart-wall thickness and chamber sizes to standard norms, to identify abnormalities. Operates monitor to measure and record functions of cardiovascular and pulmonary systems, as part of cardiac catheterization team. Alerts physician to abnormalities or changes in patient responses. Records analyses of heart and related structures, using ultrasound equipment. Observes ultrasound display screen and listens to signals to acquire data for measurement of blood flow velocities. Records variations in action of heart muscle, using electrocardiograph. Observes gauges, recorder, and video screens of data analysis system, during imaging of cardiovascular system. Operates diagnostic imaging equipment to produce contrast-enhanced radiographs of heart and cardiovascular system. Conducts tests of pulmonary system, using spirometer and other respiratory testing equipment. Enters factors such as amount and quality of radiation beam and filming sequence into computer. Conducts electrocardiogram, phonocardiogram, echocardiogram, stress testing, and other cardiovascular tests, using specialized electronic test equipment, recording devices, and laboratory instruments. Injects contrast medium into blood vessels of patient. Activates fluoroscope and camera to produce images used to guide catheter through cardiovascular system. Assesses cardiac physiology and calculates valve areas from blood flow velocity measurements.

Personality Type: Investigative. Investigative occupations frequently involve working with ideas and require an extensive amount of thinking. These occupations can involve searching for facts and figuring out problems mentally.

Abilities: Written Comprehension—The ability to read and understand information and ideas presented in writing. Oral Comprehension—The ability to listen to and understand information and ideas presented verbally. Oral Expression—The ability to communicate information and ideas verbally so others will understand. Problem Sensitivity—The ability to tell when something is wrong or is likely to go wrong. Does not involve solving the problem, only recognizing there is a problem. Near Vision—The ability to see details of objects at a close range. Information Ordering—The ability to correctly follow a given rule or set of rules in order to arrange things or actions in a certain order. The things or actions can include numbers, letters, words, pictures, procedures, sentences, and mathematical or logical operations.

Skills: Operation and Control—Controlling operations of equipment or systems. Science—Using scientific methods to solve problems. Operation Monitoring—Watching gauges, dials, or other indicators to make sure a machine is working properly. Reading Comprehension—Understanding written information in work-related documents.

Generalized Work Activities: Monitoring Processes, Materials, Surroundings—Monitoring and reviewing information from materials, events, or the environment, often to detect problems or to find out when things are finished. Identifying Objects, Actions, and Events—Identifying information received by making estimates or categorizations, recognizing differences or similarities, or sensing changes in circumstances or events. Documenting/Recording Information—Entering, transcribing, recording, storing, or maintaining information in either written form or by electronic/magnetic recording. Communicating with Other Workers—Providing information to supervisors, fellow workers, and subordinates. This information can be exchanged face-to-face, in writing, or via telephone/electronic transfer. Making Decisions and Solving Problems—Combining, evaluating, and analyzing information and data to make decisions and solve problems. Involves making decisions about the relative importance of information and choosing the best solution. Updating and Using Job-Relevant Knowledge—Keeping up-to-date technically and knowing the functions of one's own job and related jobs. Assisting and Caring for Others—Providing assistance or personal care to others.

Carpenters

- ▲ Growth: 7%
- ▲ Annual Job Openings: 236,108
- ▲ Yearly Earnings: $28,700
- ▲ Education Required: Long-term O-J-T
- ▲ Self-Employed: 36.8%
- ▲ Part-Time: 8.1%

Boat Builders and Shipwrights

Construct and repair ships or boats according to blueprints. Marks outline of boat on building dock, shipway, or mold loft according to blueprint specifications, using measuring instruments and crayon. Constructs and shapes wooden frames, structures, and other parts according to blueprint specifications, using hand tools, power tools, and measuring instruments. Assembles and installs hull timbers and other structures in ship, using adhesive, measuring instruments, and hand tools or power tools. Cuts out defect, using power tools and hand tools; fits and secures replacement part, using caulking gun, adhesive, or hand tools. Inspects boat to determine location and extent of defect. Attaches hoist to sections of hull; directs hoist operator to align parts over blocks, according to layout of boat. Establishes dimensional reference points on layout and hull to make template of parts and locate machinery and equipment. Measures and marks dimensional lines on lumber, following template and using scriber. Smoothes and finishes ship surfaces, using power sander, broadax, adze, and paint; waxes and buffs surface to specified finish. Attaches metal parts such as fittings, plates, and bulkheads to ship, using brace and bits, augers, and wrenches. Cuts and forms parts such as keel, ribs, sidings, and support structures and blocks, using woodworking hand tools and power tools. Positions and secures support structures on construction area.

Consults with customer or supervisor and reads blueprint to determine necessary repairs.

Personality Type: Realistic. Realistic occupations frequently involve work activities that include practical, hands-on problems and solutions. They often deal with plants, animals, and real-world materials like wood, tools, and machinery. Many of the occupations require working outside and do not involve a lot of paperwork or working closely with others.

Abilities: Visualization—The ability to imagine how something will look after it is moved around or when its parts are moved or rearranged. Manual Dexterity—The ability to quickly make coordinated movements of one hand, a hand together with its arm, or two hands, to grasp, manipulate, or assemble objects. Information Ordering—The ability to correctly follow a given rule or set of rules in order to arrange things or actions in a certain order. The things or actions can include numbers, letters, words, pictures, procedures, sentences, and mathematical or logical operations. Extent Flexibility—The ability to bend, stretch, twist, or reach out with the body, arms, and/or legs. Arm-Hand Steadiness—The ability to keep the hand and arm steady while making an arm movement or while holding the arm and hand in one position.

Skills: Equipment Selection—Determining the kind of tools and equipment needed to do a job. Repairing—Repairing machines or systems, using the needed tools. Product Inspection—Inspecting and evaluating the quality of products. Operation and Control—Controlling operations of equipment or systems. Operations Analysis—Analyzing needs and product requirements to create a design. Installation—Installing equipment, machines, wiring, or programs to meet specifications. Active Listening—Listening to what other people are saying; asking questions as appropriate.

Generalized Work Activities: Performing General Physical Activities—Performing physical activities that require moving one's whole body, such as in climbing, lifting, balancing, walking, and stooping. Performing activities that often also require considerable use of the arms and legs, such as in the physical handling of materials. Getting Information Needed to Do the Job—Observing, receiving, and otherwise obtaining information from all relevant sources. Handling and Moving Objects—Using one's hands and arms in handling, installing, forming, positioning, and moving materials, or in manipulating things. Includes the use of keyboards. Inspecting Equipment, Structures, Materials—Inspecting or diagnosing equipment, structures, or materials to identify the causes of errors or other problems or defects. Estimating Needed Characteristics—Estimating the characteristics of materials, products, events, or information; estimating sizes, distances, and quantities; determining time, costs, resources, or materials needed to perform a work activity.

Brattice Builders

Build doors or brattices (ventilation walls or partitions) in underground passageways to control the proper circulation of air through the passageways and to the working places. Installs rigid and flexible air ducts to transport air to work areas. Erects partitions to support roof in areas unsuited to timbering or bolting. Drills and blasts obstructing boulders to reopen ventilation shafts.

Personality Type: Realistic. Realistic occupations frequently involve work activities that include practical, hands-on problems and solutions. They often deal with plants, animals, and real-world materials like wood, tools, and machinery. Many of the occupations require working outside and do not involve a lot of paperwork or working closely with others.

Abilities: Static Strength—The ability to exert maximum muscle force to lift, push, pull, or carry objects. Extent Flexibility—The ability to bend, stretch, twist, or reach out with the body, arms, and/or legs. Multilimb Coordination—The ability to coordinate movements of two or more limbs together (for example, two arms, two legs, or one leg and one arm) while sitting, standing, or lying down. Does not involve performing the activities while the body is in motion. Manual Dexterity—The ability to quickly make coordinated movements of one hand, a hand together with its arm, or two hands, to grasp, manipulate, or assemble objects. Control Precision—The ability to quickly and repeatedly make precise adjustments in moving the controls of a machine or vehicle to exact positions. Dynamic Strength—The ability to exert muscle force repeatedly or continuously over time. This involves muscular endurance and resistance to muscle fatigue. Wrist-Finger Speed—The ability to make fast, simple, repeated movements of the fingers, hands, and wrists.

Skills: Installation—Installing equipment, machines, wiring, or programs to meet specifications. Product Inspection—Inspecting and evaluating the quality of products. Equipment Selection—Determining the kind of tools and equipment needed to do a job. Solution Appraisal—Observing and evaluating the outcomes of a problem solution to identify lessons learned or to redirect efforts. Technology Design—Generating or adapting equipment and technology to serve user needs. Judgment and Decision Making—Weighing the relative costs and benefits of a potential action. Problem Identification—Identifying the nature of problems.

Generalized Work Activities: Performing General Physical Activities—Performing physical activities that require moving one's whole body, such as in climbing, lifting, balancing, walking, and stooping. Performing activities that often also require considerable use of the arms and legs, such as in the physical handling of materials. Handling and Moving Objects—Using one's hands and arms in handling, installing, forming, positioning, and moving materials, or in manipulating things. Includes the use of keyboards. Getting Information Needed to Do the Job—Observing, receiving, and otherwise obtaining information from all relevant sources. Controlling Machines and

Processes—Using either control mechanisms or direct physical activity to operate machines or processes. Does not involve working with computers or vehicles. Identifying Objects, Actions, and Events—Identifying information received by making estimates or categorizations, recognizing differences or similarities, or sensing changes in circumstances or events.

Carpenter Assemblers and Repairers

Perform a variety of tasks requiring a limited knowledge of carpentry, such as applying siding and weatherboard to building exteriors or assembling and erecting prefabricated buildings. Moves panel or roof section to other work stations or to storage or shipping area, using electric hoist. Aligns and fastens materials together, using hand tools and power tools, to form building or bracing. Cuts sidings and moldings, sections of weatherboard, openings in sheetrock, and lumber, using hand tools and power tools. Lays out and aligns materials on worktable or in assembly jig according to specified instructions. Repairs or replaces defective locks, hinges, cranks, and pieces of wood, using glue, hand tools, and power tools. Realigns windows and screens to fit casements; oils moving parts. Measures cut materials to determine conformance to specifications, using tape measure. Examines wood surfaces for defects such as nicks, cracks, or blisters. Studies blueprints, specification sheets, and drawings to determine style and type of window or wall panel required. Directs crane operator in positioning floor, wall, ceiling, and roof panel on house foundation. Applies stain, paint, or crayons to defects and filter to touch up the repaired area. Trims overlapping edges of wood or weatherboard, using portable router or power saw and hand tools. Removes surface defects, using knife, scraper, wet sponge, electric iron, and sanding tools. Installs prefabricated windows and doors, insulation, wall, ceiling and floor panels, or siding, using adhesives, hoists, hand tools, and power tools. Measures and marks location of studs, leaders, and receptacle openings, using tape measure, template, and marker. Fills cracks, seams, depressions, and nail holes with filler.

Personality Type: Realistic. Realistic occupations frequently involve work activities that include practical, hands-on problems and solutions. They often deal with plants, animals, and real-world materials like wood, tools, and machinery. Many of the occupations require working outside and do not involve a lot of paperwork or working closely with others.

Abilities: Manual Dexterity—The ability to quickly make coordinated movements of one hand, a hand together with its arm, or two hands, to grasp, manipulate, or assemble objects. Static Strength—The ability to exert maximum muscle force to lift, push, pull, or carry objects. Explosive Strength—The ability to use short bursts of muscle force to propel oneself, as in jumping or sprinting, or to throw an object. Extent Flexibility—The ability to bend, stretch, twist, or reach out with the body, arms, and/or legs. Arm-Hand Steadiness—The ability to keep the hand and arm steady while making an arm movement or while holding the arm and hand in one position.

Skills: Installation—Installing equipment, machines, wiring, or programs to meet specifications. Repairing—Repairing machines or systems, using the needed tools. Product Inspection—Inspecting and evaluating the quality of products. Operation and Control—Controlling operations of equipment or systems. Equipment Selection—Determining the kind of tools and equipment needed to do a job.

Generalized Work Activities: Performing General Physical Activities—Performing physical activities that require moving one's whole body, such as in climbing, lifting, balancing, walking, and stooping. Performing activities that often also require considerable use of the arms and legs, such as in the physical handling of materials. Handling and Moving Objects—Using one's hands and arms in handling, installing, forming, positioning, and moving materials, or in manipulating things. Getting Information Needed to Do the Job—Observing, receiving, and otherwise obtaining information from all relevant sources. Controlling Machines and Processes—Using either control mechanisms or direct physical activity to operate machines or processes. Does not involve working with computers or vehicles. Identifying Objects, Actions, and

Events—Identifying information received by making estimates or categorizations, recognizing differences or similarities, or sensing changes in circumstances or events.

Construction Carpenters

Construct, erect, install, and repair structures and fixtures of wood, plywood, and wallboard, using carpenter's hand tools and power tools. Fills cracks and other defects in plaster or plasterboard and sands patch, using patching plaster, trowel, and sanding tool. Finishes surfaces of woodworking or wallboard in houses and buildings, using paint, hand tools, and paneling. Measures and marks cutting lines on materials, using ruler, pencil, chalk, and marking gauge. Studies specifications in blueprints, sketches, or building plans to determine materials required and dimensions of structure to be fabricated. Inspects ceiling or floor tile, wall coverings, siding, glass, or woodwork to detect broken or damaged structures. Estimates amount and kind of lumber or other materials required; selects and orders the materials. Prepares layout according to blueprint or oral instructions, using rule, framing square, and calipers. Removes damaged or defective parts or sections of structure, and repairs or replaces, using hand tools. Builds or repairs cabinets, doors, frameworks, floors, and other wooden fixtures used in buildings, using woodworking machines, carpenter's hand tools, and power tools. Installs structures and fixtures such as windows, frames, floorings, trim, or hardware, using carpenter's hand tools and power tools. Assembles and fastens materials, using hand tools and wood screws, nails, dowel pins, or glue, to make framework or props. Shapes or cuts materials to specified measurements, using hand tools, machines, or power saw. Verifies trueness of structure, using plumb bob and level.

Personality Type: Realistic. Realistic occupations frequently involve work activities that include practical, hands-on problems and solutions. They often deal with plants, animals, and real-world materials like wood, tools, and machinery. Many of the occupations require working outside and do not involve a lot of paperwork or working closely with others.

Abilities: Visualization—The ability to imagine how something will look after it is moved around or when its parts are moved or rearranged. Manual Dexterity—The ability to quickly make coordinated movements of one hand, a hand together with its arm, or two hands, to grasp, manipulate, or assemble objects. Arm-Hand Steadiness—The ability to keep the hand and arm steady while making an arm movement or while holding the arm and hand in one position. Explosive Strength—The ability to use short bursts of muscle force to propel oneself, as in jumping or sprinting, or to throw an object. Extent Flexibility—The ability to bend, stretch, twist, or reach out with the body, arms, and/or legs.

Skills: Installation—Installing equipment, machines, wiring, or programs to meet specifications. Product Inspection—Inspecting and evaluating the quality of products. Equipment Selection—Determining the kind of tools and equipment needed to do a job. Repairing—Repairing machines or systems, using the needed tools.

Generalized Work Activities: Performing General Physical Activities—Performing physical activities that require moving one's whole body, such as in climbing, lifting, balancing, walking, and stooping. Performing activities that often also require considerable use of the arms and legs, such as in the physical handling of materials. Handling and Moving Objects—Using one's hands and arms in handling, installing, forming, positioning, and moving materials, or in manipulating things. Getting Information Needed to Do the Job—Observing, receiving, and otherwise obtaining information from all relevant sources. Inspecting Equipment, Structures, Materials—Inspecting or diagnosing equipment, structures, or materials to identify the causes of errors or other problems or defects. Controlling Machines and Processes—Using either control mechanisms or direct physical activity to operate machines or processes. Does not involve working with computers or vehicles. Estimating Needed Characteristics—Estimating the characteristics of materials, products, events, or information; estimating sizes, distances, and quantities; determining time, costs, resources, or materials needed to perform a work activity. Evaluating Information against Standards—Evaluating information against a set of standards and verifying that it is correct.

Rough Carpenters

Build rough wooden structures such as concrete forms; scaffolds; tunnel, bridge, or sewer supports; billboard signs; and temporary frame shelters, according to sketches, blueprints, or oral instructions. Digs or directs digging of post holes; sets poles to support structure. Studies blueprints and diagrams to determine dimensions of structure or form to be constructed or erected. Cuts or saws boards, timbers, or plywood to required size, using handsaw, power saw, or woodworking machine. Erects prefabricated forms, frameworks, scaffolds, hoists, roof supports, or chutes, using hand tools, plumb rule, and level. Anchors and braces forms and other structures in place, using nails, bolts, anchor rods, steel cables, planks, wedges, and timbers. Examines structural timbers and supports to detect decay; replaces timber, using hand tools, nuts, and bolts. Installs rough door and window frames, subflooring, fixtures, or temporary supports in structures undergoing construction or repair. Bores boltholes in timber with masonry or concrete walls, using power drill. Measures materials or distances, using square, measuring tape, or rule, to lay out work. Assembles and fastens material together to construct wood or metal framework of structure, using bolts, nails, or screws. Fabricates parts, using woodworking and metalworking machines.

Personality Type: Realistic. Realistic occupations frequently involve work activities that include practical, hands-on problems and solutions. They often deal with plants, animals, and real-world materials like wood, tools, and machinery. Many of the occupations require working outside and do not involve a lot of paperwork or working closely with others.

Abilities: Manual Dexterity—The ability to quickly make coordinated movements of one hand, a hand together with its arm, or two hands, to grasp, manipulate, or assemble objects. Visualization—The ability to imagine how something will look after it is moved around or when its parts are moved or rearranged. Information Ordering—The ability to correctly follow a given rule or set of rules in order to arrange things or actions in a certain order. The things or actions can include numbers, letters, words, pictures, procedures, sentences, and mathematical or logical operations. Near Vision—The ability to see details of objects at a close range. Static Strength—The ability to exert maximum muscle force to lift, push, pull, or carry objects. Trunk Strength—The ability to use one's abdominal and lower back muscles to support part of the body repeatedly or continuously over time without giving out or fatiguing.

Skills: Installation—Installing equipment, machines, wiring, or programs to meet specifications. Product Inspection—Inspecting and evaluating the quality of products. Mathematics—Using mathematics to solve problems. Operation and Control—Controlling operations of equipment or systems. Equipment Selection—Determining the kind of tools and equipment needed to do a job.

Generalized Work Activities: Performing General Physical Activities—Performing physical activities that require moving one's whole body, such as in climbing, lifting, balancing, walking, and stooping. Performing activities that often also require considerable use of the arms and legs, such as in the physical handling of materials. Inspecting Equipment, Structures, Materials—Inspecting or diagnosing equipment, structures, or materials to identify the causes of errors or other problems or defects. Getting Information Needed to Do the Job—Observing, receiving, and otherwise obtaining information from all relevant sources. Handling and Moving Objects—Using one's hands and arms in handling, installing, forming, positioning, and moving materials, or in manipulating things. Controlling Machines and Processes—Using either control mechanisms or direct physical activity to operate machines or processes. Does not involve working with computers or vehicles.

Ship Carpenters and Joiners

Fabricate, assemble, install, or repair wooden furnishings in ships or boats. Shapes irregular parts and trims excess material from bulkhead and furnishings to ensure fit meets specifications. Shapes and laminates wood to form parts of ship, using steam chambers, clamps, glue, and jigs. Repairs structural woodwork and replaces defective parts and equipment, using hand tools and power tools. Transfers dimensions or measurements of wood parts or bulkhead on plywood, using measuring instruments and marking devices. Cuts wood or glass to specified dimensions, using hand tools and power tools. Assembles and installs hardware, gaskets, floors, furnishings, or insulation, using adhesive, hand tools, and power tools. Reads blueprints to determine dimensions of furnishings in ships or boats. Greases gears and other moving parts of machines on ship. Constructs floors, doors, and partitions, using woodworking machines, hand tools, and power tools.

Personality Type: Realistic. Realistic occupations frequently involve work activities that include practical, hands-on problems and solutions. They often deal with plants, animals, and real-world materials like wood, tools, and machinery. Many of the occupations require working outside and do not involve a lot of paperwork or working closely with others.

Abilities: Manual Dexterity—The ability to quickly make coordinated movements of one hand, a hand together with its arm, or two hands, to grasp, manipulate, or assemble objects. Visualization—The ability to imagine how something will look after it is moved around or when its parts are moved or rearranged. Information Ordering—The ability to correctly follow a given rule or set of rules in order to arrange things or actions in a certain order. The things or actions can include numbers, letters, words, pictures, procedures, sentences, and mathematical or logical operations. Near Vision—The ability to see details of objects at a close range. Static Strength—The ability to exert maximum muscle force to lift, push, pull, or carry objects. Finger Dexterity—The ability to make precisely coordinated

movements of the fingers of one or both hands to grasp, manipulate, or assemble very small objects.

Skills: Operations Analysis—Analyzing needs and product requirements to create a design. Information Organization—Finding ways to structure or classify multiple pieces of information. Information Gathering—Knowing how to find information and identifying essential information. Installation—Installing equipment, machines, wiring, or programs to meet specifications. Repairing—Repairing machines or systems, using the needed tools. Mathematics—Using mathematics to solve problems.

Generalized Work Activities: Handling and Moving Objects—Using one's hands and arms in handling, installing, forming, positioning, and moving materials, or in manipulating things. Performing General Physical Activities—Performing physical activities that require moving one's whole body, such as in climbing, lifting, balancing, walking, and stooping. Performing activities that often also require considerable use of the arms and legs, such as in the physical handling of materials. Getting Information Needed to Do the Job—Observing, receiving, and otherwise obtaining information from all relevant sources. Controlling Machines and Processes—Using either control mechanisms or direct physical activity to operate machines or processes. Does not involve working with computers or vehicles. Making Decisions and Solving Problems—Combining, evaluating, and analyzing information and data to make decisions and solve problems. Involves making decisions about the relative importance of information and choosing the best solution. Monitoring Processes, Materials, Surroundings—Monitoring and reviewing information from materials, events, or the environment, often to detect problems or to find out when things are finished.

Cashiers

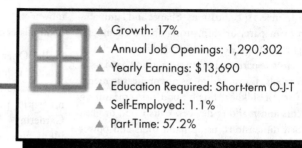

▲ Growth: 17%
▲ Annual Job Openings: 1,290,302
▲ Yearly Earnings: $13,690
▲ Education Required: Short-term O-J-T
▲ Self-Employed: 1.1%
▲ Part-Time: 57.2%

Cashiers

Receive and disburse money in establishments other than financial institutions. Use electronic scanners, cash registers, or related equipment. Process credit or debit card transactions and validate checks. Keeps periodic balance sheet of amount and number of transactions. Learns prices, stocks shelves, marks prices, weighs items, issues trading stamps, and redeems food stamps and coupons. Answers questions and provides information to customers. Bags, boxes, or wraps merchandise. Compiles and maintains nonmonetary reports and records. Resolves customer's complaints. Monitors checkout stations, issues and removes cash as needed, and assigns workers to reduce customer delay. Sorts, counts, and wraps currency and coins. Computes and records totals of transactions. Operates cash register or electronic scanner. Cashes checks. Receives sales slip, cash, check, voucher, or charge payments; issues receipts, refunds, credits, or change due to customer. Sells tickets and other items to customer.

Personality Type: Conventional. Conventional occupations frequently involve following set procedures and routines. These occupations can include working with data and details more than with ideas. Usually there is a clear line of authority to follow.

Abilities: Oral Expression—The ability to communicate information and ideas verbally so others will understand. Number Facility—The ability to add, subtract, multiply, or divide quickly and correctly. Near Vision—The ability to see details of objects at a close range. Finger Dexterity—The ability to make precisely coordinated movements of the fingers of one or both hands to grasp, manipulate, or assemble very small objects.

Speech Clarity—The ability to speak clearly so that what is said is understandable to a listener. Oral Comprehension—The ability to listen to and understand information and ideas presented verbally.

Skills: Mathematics—Using mathematics to solve problems. Service Orientation—Actively looking for ways to help people. Speaking—Talking to others to effectively convey information. Social Perceptiveness—Being aware of other people's reactions and understanding why people react the way they do. Active Listening—Listening to what other people are saying; asking questions as appropriate.

Generalized Work Activities: Controlling Machines and Processes—Using either control mechanisms or direct physical activity to operate machines or processes. Does not involve working with computers or vehicles. Communicating with Persons Outside Organization—Communicating with persons outside the organization. Representing the organization to customers, the public, government, and other external sources. Exchanging information face-to-face, in writing, or via telephone/electronic transfer. Performing for/Working with Public—Performing for people or dealing directly with the public, including serving persons in restaurants and stores and receiving clients or guests. Handling and Moving Objects—Using one's hands and arms in handling, installing, forming, positioning, and moving materials, or in manipulating things. Includes the use of keyboards. Establishing and Maintaining Relationships—Developing constructive and cooperative working relationships with others. Documenting/Recording Information—Entering, transcribing, recording, storing, or maintaining information in either written form or by electronic/magnetic recording.

Central Office and PBX Installers and Repairers

Central Office and PBX Installers and Repairers

Test, analyze, and repair telephone or telegraph circuits and equipment at a central office location using test meters and hand tools. Analyze and repair defects in communications equipment on customers' premises, using circuit diagrams, polarity probes, meters, and a telephone test set. Install equipment. Repairs or replaces defective components such as switches, relays, amplifiers, and circuit boards, using hand tools and soldering iron. Installs preassembled or partially assembled switching equipment, switchboards, wiring frames, and power apparatus according to floor plans. Connects wires to equipment, using hand tools, soldering iron, or wire wrap gun. Enters codes to correct programming of electronic switching systems. Routes cables and trunklines from entry points to specified equipment, following diagrams. Tests and adjusts installed equipment to ensure circuit continuity and operational performance, using test instruments. Retests repaired equipment to ensure that malfunction has been corrected. Analyzes test readings, computer printouts, and trouble reports to determine method of repair. Tests circuits and components of malfunctioning telecommunication equipment to isolate source of malfunction, using test instruments and circuit diagrams. Removes and remakes connections on wire distributing frame to change circuit layout, following diagrams.

Personality Type: Realistic. Realistic occupations frequently involve work activities that include practical, hands-on problems and solutions. They often deal with plants, animals, and real-world materials like wood, tools, and machinery. Many of the occupations require working outside and do not involve a lot of paperwork or working closely with others.

Abilities: Problem Sensitivity—The ability to tell when something is wrong or is likely to go wrong. Does not involve solving the problem, only recognizing there is a problem. Arm-Hand Steadiness—The ability to keep the hand and arm steady while making an arm movement or while holding the arm and hand in one position. Near Vision—The ability to see details of objects at a close range. Finger Dexterity—The ability to make precisely coordinated movements of the fingers of one or both hands to grasp, manipulate, or assemble very small objects. Inductive Reasoning—The ability to combine separate pieces of information, or specific answers to problems, to form general rules or conclusions. Includes coming up with a logical explanation for why a series of seemingly unrelated events occur together.

Skills: Repairing—Repairing machines or systems, using the needed tools. Installation—Installing equipment, machines, wiring, or programs to meet specifications. Troubleshooting—Determining what is causing an operating error and deciding what to do about it. Testing—Conducting tests to determine whether equipment, software, or procedures are operating as expected. Problem Identification—Identifying the nature of problems.

Generalized Work Activities: Repairing and Maintaining Electrical Equipment—Fixing, servicing, adjusting, regulating, calibrating, fine-tuning, or testing machines, devices, and equipment that operate primarily on the basis of electrical or electronic, not mechanical, principles. Getting Information Needed to Do the Job—Observing, receiving, and otherwise obtaining information from all relevant sources. Handling and Moving Objects—Using one's hands and arms in handling, installing, forming, positioning, and moving materials, or in manipulating things. Includes the use

of keyboards. Inspecting Equipment, Structures, Materials—Inspecting or diagnosing equipment, structures, or materials to identify the causes of errors or other problems or defects. Identifying Objects, Actions, and Events—Identifying information received by making estimates or categorizations, recognizing differences or similarities, or sensing changes in circumstances or events.

Chemical Engineers

- ▲ Growth: 10%
- ▲ Annual Job Openings: 3,892
- ▲ Yearly Earnings: $64,760
- ▲ Education Required: Bachelor's degree
- ▲ Self-Employed: 2%
- ▲ Part-Time: 1.6%

Chemical Engineers

Design chemical plant equipment. Devise processes for manufacturing chemicals and products such as gasoline, synthetic rubber, plastics, detergents, cement, paper, and pulp, by applying principles and technology of chemistry, physics, and engineering. Develops safety procedures to be employed by workers operating equipment or working in close proximity to ongoing chemical reactions. Conducts research to develop new and improved chemical manufacturing processes. Determines most effective arrangement of operations, such as mixing, crushing, heat transfer, distillation, and drying. Designs measurement and control systems for chemical plants based on data collected in laboratory experiments and in pilot plant operations. Develops processes to separate components of liquids or gases or to generate electrical currents, using controlled chemical processes. Directs activities of workers who operate, construct, and improve absorption, evaporation, or electromagnetic equipment. Prepares estimate of production costs. Prepares production progress reports for management. Performs laboratory studies of steps in manufacture of new product; tests proposed process in small scale operation (pilot plant). Performs tests

throughout stages of production to determine degree of control over variables, including temperature, density, specific gravity, and pressure. Designs and plans layout of equipment.

Personality Type: Investigative. Investigative occupations frequently involve working with ideas and require an extensive amount of thinking. These occupations can involve searching for facts and figuring out problems mentally.

Abilities: Deductive Reasoning—The ability to apply general rules to specific problems to come up with logical answers. Involves deciding if an answer makes sense. Written Comprehension—The ability to read and understand information and ideas presented in writing. Mathematical Reasoning—The ability to understand and organize a problem and then select a mathematical method or formula to solve the problem. Written Expression—The ability to communicate information and ideas in writing so others will understand. Originality—The ability to come up with unusual or clever ideas about a given topic or situation, or to develop creative ways to solve a problem. Inductive Reasoning—The ability to combine separate pieces of information, or specific answers to problems, to form general rules or conclusions. Includes coming up with a logical explanation for why a series of seemingly unrelated events occur together.

Skills: Science—Using scientific methods to solve problems. Operations Analysis—Analyzing needs and product requirements to create a design. Critical Thinking—Using logic and analysis to identify the strengths and weaknesses of different approaches. Operation Monitoring—Watching gauges, dials, or other indicators to make sure a machine is working properly.

Generalized Work Activities: Analyzing Data or Information—Identifying underlying principles, reasons, or facts by breaking down information or data into separate parts. Monitoring Processes, Materials, Surroundings—Monitoring and reviewing information from materials, events, or the environment, often to detect problems or to find out when things are finished. Getting Information Needed to Do the Job—Observing, receiving, and otherwise obtaining information from all relevant sources. Identifying Objects, Actions, and Events—Identifying information received by making estimates or categorizations, recognizing differences or similarities, or sensing changes in circumstances or events. Organizing, Planning, and Prioritizing—Developing plans to accomplish work. Prioritizing and organizing one's own work. Updating and Using Job-Relevant Knowledge—Keeping up-to-date technically and knowing the functions of one's own job and related jobs. Drafting and Specifying Technical Devices—Providing documentation, detailed instructions, drawings, or specifications to inform others about how devices, parts, equipment, or structures are to be fabricated, constructed, assembled, modified, maintained, or used.

Chemical Equipment Controllers, Operators and Tenders

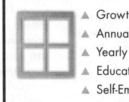

- ▲ Growth: 11%
- ▲ Annual Job Openings: 19,720
- ▲ Yearly Earnings: $32,200
- ▲ Education Required: Moderate-term O-J-T
- ▲ Self-Employed: 0%
- ▲ Part-Time: 0.3%

Chemical Equipment Controllers and Operators

Control or operate equipment to control chemical changes or reactions in the processing of industrial or consumer products, using reaction kettles, catalytic converters, continuous or batch treating equipment, saturator tanks, electrolytic cells, reactor vessels, recovery units, and fermentation chambers. Patrols and inspects equipment or unit to detect leaks and malfunctions. Weighs or measures specified amounts of materials. Reads plant specifications to ascertain product, ingredient, and prescribed modifications of plant procedures. Dumps or scoops prescribed solid, granular, or powdered materials into equipment. Adds treating or neutralizing agent to product and pumps product through filter or centrifuge to remove impurities or precipitate product. Mixes chemicals according to proportion tables or prescribed formulas. Moves controls to adjust feed and flow of liquids and gases through equipment in specified sequence. Opens valves or operates pumps to admit or drain specified amounts of materials, impurities, or treating agents to or from equipment. Adjusts controls to regulate temperature, pressure, and time of prescribed reaction, according to knowledge of equipment and process. Starts pumps, agitators, reactors, blowers, or automatic feed of materials. Operates or tends auxiliary equipment such as heaters, scrubbers, filters, or driers, to prepare or further process materials. Monitors gauges, recording instruments, flowmeters, or product to regulate or maintain specified conditions. Sets and adjusts indicating, controlling, or timing devices such as gauging instruments, thermostat, gas analyzers, or recording calorimeter. Directs activities of workers assisting in control or verification of process or in unloading materials. Makes minor repairs and lubricates and maintains equipment, using hand tools. Records operational data such as temperature, pressure, ingredients used, processing time, or test results, in operating log. Flushes or cleans equipment, using steamhose or mechanical reamer. Draws samples of product and sends to laboratory for analysis. Tests sample for specific gravity, chemical characteristics, pH level, concentration, or viscosity.

Personality Type: Realistic. Realistic occupations frequently involve work activities that include practical, hands-on problems and solutions. They often deal with plants, animals, and real-world materials like wood, tools, and machinery. Many of the occupations require working outside and do not involve a lot of paperwork or working closely with others.

Abilities: Information Ordering—The ability to correctly follow a given rule or set of rules in order to arrange things or actions in a certain order. The things or actions can include numbers, letters, words, pictures, procedures, sentences, and mathematical or logical operations. Written Comprehension—The ability to read and understand information and ideas presented in writing. Near Vision—The ability to see details of objects at a close range. Control Precision—The ability to quickly and repeatedly make precise adjustments in moving the controls of a machine or vehicle to exact positions. Oral Expression—The ability to communicate information and ideas verbally so others

will understand. Problem Sensitivity—The ability to tell when something is wrong or is likely to go wrong. Does not involve solving the problem, only recognizing there is a problem.

Skills: Operation and Control—Controlling operations of equipment or systems. Science—Using scientific methods to solve problems. Testing—Conducting tests to determine whether equipment, software, or procedures are operating as expected. Operation Monitoring—Watching gauges, dials, or other indicators to make sure a machine is working properly. Product Inspection—Inspecting and evaluating the quality of products. Reading Comprehension—Understanding written information in work-related documents.

Generalized Work Activities: Monitoring Processes, Materials, Surroundings—Monitoring and reviewing information from materials, events, or the environment, often to detect problems or to find out when things are finished. Controlling Machines and Processes—Using either control mechanisms or direct physical activity to operate machines or processes. Does not involve working with computers or vehicles. Handling and Moving Objects—Using one's hands and arms in handling, installing, forming, positioning, and moving materials, or in manipulating things. Includes the use of keyboards. Inspecting Equipment, Structures, Materials—Inspecting or diagnosing equipment, structures, or materials to identify the causes of errors or other problems or defects. Getting Information Needed to Do the Job—Observing, receiving, and otherwise obtaining information from all relevant sources.

Chemical Equipment Tenders

Tend equipment in which a chemical change or reaction takes place in the processing of industrial or consumer products, using devulcanizers, batch stills, fermenting tanks, steam-jacketed kettles, and reactor vessels. Assists other workers in preparing and maintaining equipment. Records data in log from instruments and gauges concerning temperature, pressure, materials used, treating time, and shift production. Adjusts valves or controls to maintain system within specified operating conditions. Observes gauges, meters, and panel lights to monitor operating conditions such as temperature or pressure. Patrols work area to detect leaks and equipment malfunctions and to monitor operating conditions. Replaces filtering media or makes minor repairs to equipment, using hand tools. Tests samples to determine specific gravity, composition, or acidity, using chemical test equipment such as hydrometer or pH meter. Loads specified amounts of chemicals into processing equipment. Notifies maintenance engineer of equipment malfunction. Starts pumps and agitators, turns valves, or moves controls of processing equipment to admit, transfer, filter, or mix chemicals. Observes safety precautions to prevent fires and explosions. Weighs, measures, or mixes prescribed quantities of materials. Draws sample of products for analysis to aid in process adjustments and to maintain production standards. Drains equipment and pumps water or other solution through to flush and clean tanks or equipment. Inventories supplies received and consumed.

Personality Type: Realistic. Realistic occupations frequently involve work activities that include practical, hands-on problems and solutions. They often deal with plants, animals, and real-world materials like wood, tools, and machinery. Many of the occupations require working outside and do not involve a lot of paperwork or working closely with others.

Abilities: Problem Sensitivity—The ability to tell when something is wrong or is likely to go wrong. Does not involve solving the problem, only recognizing there is a problem. Control Precision—The ability to quickly and repeatedly make precise adjustments in moving the controls of a machine or vehicle to exact positions. Reaction Time—The ability to quickly respond with the hand, finger, or foot to a signal such as a sound, a light, or a picture. Information Ordering—The ability

to correctly follow a given rule or set of rules in order to arrange things or actions in a certain order. The things or actions can include numbers, letters, words, pictures, procedures, sentences, and mathematical or logical operations. Oral Expression—The ability to communicate information and ideas verbally so others will understand. Written Expression—The ability to communicate information and ideas in writing so others will understand.

Skills: Operation and Control—Controlling operations of equipment or systems. Operation Monitoring— Watching gauges, dials, or other indicators to make sure a machine is working properly. Science—Using scientific methods to solve problems. Product Inspection— Inspecting and evaluating the quality of products. Equipment Selection—Determining the kind of tools and equipment needed to do a job. Testing— Conducting tests to determine whether equipment, software, or procedures are operating as expected.

Generalized Work Activities: Controlling Machines and Processes—Using either control mechanisms or direct physical activity to operate machines or processes. Does not involve working with computers or vehicles. Monitoring Processes, Materials, Surroundings— Monitoring and reviewing information from materials, events, or the environment, often to detect problems or to find out when things are finished. Inspecting Equipment, Structures, Materials—Inspecting or diagnosing equipment, structures, or materials to identify the causes of errors or other problems or defects. Handling and Moving Objects—Using one's hands and arms in handling, installing, forming, positioning, and moving materials, or in manipulating things. Includes the use of keyboards. Getting Information Needed to Do the Job—Observing, receiving, and otherwise obtaining information from all relevant sources. Identifying Objects, Actions, and Events—Identifying information received by making estimates or categorizations, recognizing differences or similarities, or sensing changes in circumstances or events.

Chemical Plant and System Operators

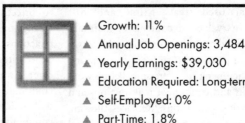

▲ Growth: 11%
▲ Annual Job Openings: 3,484
▲ Yearly Earnings: $39,030
▲ Education Required: Long-term O-J-T
▲ Self-Employed: 0%
▲ Part-Time: 1.8%

Chemical Plant and System Operators

Control or operate an entire chemical process or system of machines. Interprets chemical reactions visible through sight glasses or on television monitor and reviews laboratory test reports for process adjustments. Inspects equipment for potential and actual hazards, wear, leaks, and other conditions requiring maintenance shutdown. Defrosts frozen valves, using steam hose. Patrols work area to observe level of carbon in thickener tank and level of wash solutions in overflow troughs, to prevent spills. Gauges tank levels, using calibrated rod. Monitors recording instruments, flowmeters, panel lights, and other indicators, and listens for warning signals to verify conformity of process conditions. Notifies maintenance, stationary-engineering, and other auxiliary personnel to correct equipment malfunction and adjust power, steam, water, or air supply. Confers with technical and supervisory personnel to report or resolve conditions affecting safety, efficiency, and product quality. Draws samples of products and conducts quality control tests to monitor processing and to ensure that standards are met. Records operating data such as process conditions, test results, and instrument readings; calculates material requirements or yield according to formulas. Moves control settings to make control adjustments on equipment units affecting speed of chemical reactions and quality and yield. Turns valves to regulate flow of product or byproducts through agitator tanks, storage drums, or neutralizer tanks, according to process. Starts pumps to wash and rinse reactor vessels, to exhaust gases and vapors, and to mix product with water. Regulates or shuts down equipment manually during emergency situations, as directed by supervisory personnel.

Personality Type: Realistic. Realistic occupations frequently involve work activities that include practical, hands-on problems and solutions. They often deal with plants, animals, and real-world materials like wood, tools, and machinery. Many of the occupations require working outside and do not involve a lot of paperwork or working closely with others.

Abilities: Control Precision—The ability to quickly and repeatedly make precise adjustments in moving the controls of a machine or vehicle to exact positions. Information Ordering—The ability to correctly follow a given rule or set of rules in order to arrange things or actions in a certain order. The things or actions can include numbers, letters, words, pictures, procedures, sentences, and mathematical or logical operations. Problem Sensitivity—The ability to tell when something is wrong or is likely to go wrong. Does not involve solving the problem, only recognizing there is a problem. Oral Comprehension—The ability to listen to and understand information and ideas presented verbally. Written Comprehension—The ability to read and understand information and ideas presented in writing. Reaction Time—The ability to quickly respond with the hand, finger, or foot to a signal such as a sound, a light, or a picture.

Skills: Operation Monitoring—Watching gauges, dials, or other indicators to make sure a machine is working properly. Operation and Control—Controlling operations of equipment or systems. Problem Identification—Identifying the nature of problems. Science—Using scientific methods to solve problems.

Systems Perception—Determining when important changes have occurred in a system or are likely to occur. Information Gathering—Knowing how to find information and identifying essential information.

Generalized Work Activities: Controlling Machines and Processes—Using either control mechanisms or direct physical activity to operate machines or processes. Does not involve working with computers or vehicles. Monitoring Processes, Materials, Surroundings— Monitoring and reviewing information from materials, events, or the environment, often to detect problems or to find out when things are finished. Inspecting Equipment, Structures, Materials—Inspecting or diagnosing equipment, structures, or materials to identify the causes of errors or other problems or defects. Getting Information Needed to Do the Job— Observing, receiving, and otherwise obtaining information from all relevant sources. Handling and Moving Objects—Using one's hands and arms in handling, installing, forming, positioning, and moving materials, or in manipulating things. Includes the use of keyboards.

Chemists

- ▲ Growth: 14%
- ▲ Annual Job Openings: 8,137
- ▲ Yearly Earnings: $46,220
- ▲ Education Required: Bachelor's degree
- ▲ Self-Employed: 1%
- ▲ Part-Time: 3.3%

Chemists

Conduct qualitative and quantitative chemical analyses or chemical experiments in laboratories for quality or process control or to develop new products or knowledge. Directs, coordinates, and advises personnel in test procedures for analyzing components and physical properties of materials. Compiles and analyzes test information to determine process or equipment operating efficiency and to diagnose malfunctions. Induces changes in composition of substances by introducing heat, light, energy, and chemical catalysts for quantitative and qualitative analysis. Writes technical papers and reports and prepares standards and specifications for processes, facilities, products, and tests. Prepares test solutions, compounds, and reagents for laboratory personnel to conduct test. Confers with scientists and engineers to conduct analyses of research projects, interpret test results, or develop nonstandard tests. Studies effects of various methods of processing, preserving, and packaging on composition and properties of foods. Analyzes organic and inorganic compounds to determine chemical and physical properties, composition, structure, relationships, and reactions, utilizing chromatography, spectroscopy, and spectrophotometry techniques. Develops, improves, and customizes products, equipment, formulas, processes, and analytical methods.

Personality Type: Investigative. Investigative occupations frequently involve working with ideas and require an extensive amount of thinking. These occupations can involve searching for facts and figuring out problems mentally.

Abilities: Written Expression—The ability to communicate information and ideas in writing so others will understand. Written Comprehension—The ability to read and understand information and ideas presented in writing. Oral Expression—The ability to communicate information and ideas verbally so others will understand. Mathematical Reasoning—The ability to understand and organize a problem and then select a mathematical method or formula to solve the problem. Deductive Reasoning—The ability to apply general rules to specific problems to come up with logical answers. Involves deciding if an answer makes sense.

Skills: Science—Using scientific methods to solve problems. Information Gathering—Knowing how to find information and identifying essential information. Active Learning—Working with new material or information to grasp its implications. Critical Thinking—Using logic and analysis to identify the strengths and weaknesses of different approaches. Reading Comprehension—Understanding written information in work-related documents.

Generalized Work Activities: Analyzing Data or Information—Identifying underlying principles, reasons, or facts by breaking down information or data into separate parts. Processing Information—Compiling, coding, categorizing, calculating, tabulating, auditing, verifying, or processing information or data.

Updating and Using Job-Relevant Knowledge—Keeping up-to-date technically and knowing the functions of one's own job and related jobs. Controlling Machines and Processes—Using either control mechanisms or direct physical activity to operate machines or processes. Does not involve working with computers or vehicles. Documenting/Recording Information—Entering, transcribing, recording, storing, or maintaining information in either written form or by electronic/magnetic recording. Monitoring Processes, Materials, Surroundings—Monitoring and reviewing information from materials, events, or the environment, often to detect problems or to find out when things are finished. Getting Information Needed to Do the Job—Observing, receiving, and otherwise obtaining information from all relevant sources.

Child Care Workers

- ▲ Growth: 26%
- ▲ Annual Job Openings: 328,786
- ▲ Yearly Earnings: $13,750
- ▲ Education Required: Short-term O-J-T
- ▲ Self-Employed: 57.5%
- ▲ Part-Time: 43.4%

Child Care Workers

Attend to children in schools, businesses, private households, and child care institutions. Perform a variety of tasks such as dressing, feeding, bathing, and overseeing play. Organizes and participates in recreational activities such as games. Reads to children and teaches them simple painting, drawing, handwork, and singing. Places or lifts children into baths or pools. Instructs children regarding desirable health and personal habits related to eating, resting, and using the toilet. Wheels handicapped children to classes or other areas of facility. Secures children in equipment such as chairs and slings. Assists in preparing food for children; serves meals and refreshments to children. Regulates rest periods. Disciplines children and recommends or initiates other measures to control behavior. Teaches children such things as caring for their own clothing and picking up toys and books. Cares for children in institutional settings such as group homes, nursery schools, private businesses, or schools for the handicapped. Monitors children on life-support equipment to detect malfunctioning of equipment; calls for medical assistance when needed.

Personality Type: Social. Social occupations frequently involve working with, communicating with, and teaching people. These occupations often involve helping or providing service to others.

Abilities: Oral Expression—The ability to communicate information and ideas verbally so others will understand. Oral Comprehension—The ability to listen to and understand information and ideas presented verbally. Problem Sensitivity—The ability to tell when something is wrong or is likely to go wrong. Does not involve solving the problem, only recognizing there is a problem.

Written Comprehension—The ability to read and understand information and ideas presented in writing. Speech Clarity—The ability to speak clearly so that what is said is understandable to a listener. Time Sharing—The ability to efficiently shift back and forth between two or more activities or sources of information such as speech, sounds, or touch.

Skills: Social Perceptiveness—Being aware of other people's reactions and understanding why people react the way they do. Speaking—Talking to others to effectively convey information. Service Orientation—Actively looking for ways to help people. Active Listening—Listening to what other people are saying; asking questions as appropriate. Instructing—Teaching others how to do something.

Generalized Work Activities: Assisting and Caring for Others—Providing assistance or personal care to others. Performing General Physical Activities—Performing physical activities that require moving one's whole body,

such as in climbing, lifting, balancing, walking, and stooping. Performing activities that often also require considerable use of the arms and legs, such as in the physical handling of materials. Handling and Moving Objects—Using one's hands and arms in handling, installing, forming, positioning, and moving materials, or in manipulating things. Includes the use of keyboards. Monitoring Processes, Materials, Surroundings—Monitoring and reviewing information from materials, events, or the environment, often to detect problems or to find out when things are finished. Identifying Objects, Actions, and Events—Identifying information received by making estimates or categorizations, recognizing differences or similarities, or sensing changes in circumstances or events. Communicating with Other Workers—Providing information to supervisors, fellow workers, and subordinates. This information can be exchanged face-to-face, in writing, or via telephone/electronic transfer.

Chiropractors

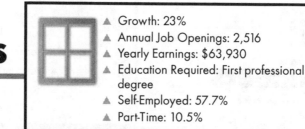

- ▲ Growth: 23%
- ▲ Annual Job Openings: 2,516
- ▲ Yearly Earnings: $63,930
- ▲ Education Required: First professional degree
- ▲ Self-Employed: 57.7%
- ▲ Part-Time: 10.5%

Chiropractors

Adjust spinal column and other articulations of the human body to correct abnormalities believed to be caused by interference with the nervous system. Examine patient to determine nature and extent of disorder. Manipulate spine or other involved area. Utilize supplementary measures such as exercise, rest, water, light, heat, and nutritional therapy. Performs diagnostic procedures including physical, neurologic, and orthopedic examinations and laboratory tests, using instruments and equipment such as X-ray machine and electrocardiograph. Utilizes supplementary measures, such as exercise, rest, water, light, heat, and nutritional

therapy. Examines patient to determine nature and extent of disorder. Manipulates spinal column and other extremities to adjust, align, or correct abnormalities caused by neurologic and kinetic articular dysfunction.

Personality Type: Investigative. Investigative occupations frequently involve working with ideas and require an extensive amount of thinking. These occupations can involve searching for facts and figuring out problems mentally.

Abilities: Problem Sensitivity—The ability to tell when something is wrong or is likely to go wrong. Does not involve solving the problem, only recognizing there is a problem. Manual Dexterity—The ability to quickly make coordinated movements of one hand, a hand together with its arm, or two hands, to grasp, manipulate, or assemble objects. Finger Dexterity—The ability to make precisely coordinated movements of the fingers of one or both hands to grasp, manipulate, or assemble very small objects. Multilimb Coordination—The ability to coordinate movements of two or more limbs together (for example, two arms, two legs, or one leg and one arm) while sitting, standing, or lying down. Does not involve performing the activities while the body is in motion.

Skills: Problem Identification—Identifying the nature of problems. Critical Thinking—Using logic and analysis to identify the strengths and weaknesses of different approaches. Judgment and Decision Making—Weighing the relative costs and benefits of a potential action. Active Listening—Listening to what other people are saying; asking questions as appropriate. Speaking—Talking to others to effectively convey information. Active Learning—Working with new material or information to grasp its implications.

Generalized Work Activities: Assisting and Caring for Others—Providing assistance or personal care to others. Identifying Objects, Actions, and Events—Identifying information received by making estimates or categorizations, recognizing differences or similarities, or sensing changes in circumstances or events. Getting Information Needed to Do the Job—Observing, receiving, and otherwise obtaining information from all relevant sources. Handling and Moving Objects—Using one's hands and arms in handling, installing, forming, positioning, and moving materials, or in manipulating things. Includes the use of keyboards. Making Decisions and Solving Problems—Combining, evaluating, and analyzing information and data to make decisions and solve problems. Involves making decisions about the relative importance of information and choosing the best solution.

Civil Engineers

- ▲ Growth: 21%
- ▲ Annual Job Openings: 20,603
- ▲ Yearly Earnings: $53,450
- ▲ Education Required: Bachelor's degree
- ▲ Self-Employed: 4.9%
- ▲ Part-Time: 5.4%

Civil Engineers

Perform engineering duties in planning, designing, and overseeing construction and maintenance of building structures and facilities such as roads, railroads, airports, bridges, harbors, channels, dams, irrigation projects, pipelines, power plants, water and sewage systems, and waste disposal units. Includes architectural, structural, traffic, ocean, and geo-technical engineers. Conducts studies of traffic patterns or environmental conditions to identify engineering problems and assess the potential impact of projects. Computes load and grade requirements, water flow rates, and material stress factors to determine design specifications. Directs or participates in surveying to lay out installations and establish reference points, grades, and elevations to guide construction. Directs construction, operations, and maintenance activities at project site. Estimates quantities and cost of materials, equipment, or labor to determine project feasibility. Inspects project sites to monitor progress and to ensure conformance to design specifications and safety or sanitation standards. Tests soils and materials to determine the adequacy and strength of foundations, concrete, asphalt, or steel. Provides technical advice regarding design, construction, or program modifications and structural repairs, to industrial and managerial personnel. Prepares or presents public reports such as bid proposals, deeds, environmental impact statements, and property and right-of-way descriptions. Analyzes survey reports, maps, drawings, blueprints, aerial photography, and other topographical or geologic data to plan projects. Plans and designs transportation or hydraulic systems and structures, following construction and government standards, using design software and drawing tools.

Personality Type: Realistic. Realistic occupations frequently involve work activities that include practical, hands-on problems and solutions. They often deal with plants, animals, and real-world materials like wood, tools, and machinery. Many of the occupations require working outside and do not involve a lot of paperwork or working closely with others.

Abilities: Deductive Reasoning—The ability to apply general rules to specific problems to come up with logical answers. Involves deciding if an answer makes sense. Oral Expression—The ability to communicate information and ideas verbally so others will understand. Written Comprehension—The ability to read and understand information and ideas presented in writing. Inductive Reasoning—The ability to combine separate pieces of information, or specific answers to problems, to form general rules or conclusions. Includes coming up with a logical explanation for why a series of seemingly unrelated events occur together. Oral Comprehension—The ability to listen to and understand information and ideas presented verbally.

Skills: Mathematics—Using mathematics to solve problems. Operations Analysis—Analyzing needs and product requirements to create a design. Reading Comprehension—Understanding written information in work-related documents. Implementation Planning—Developing approaches for implementing an idea. Information Gathering—Knowing how to find information and identifying essential information. Problem Identification—Identifying the nature of problems. Critical Thinking—Using logic and analysis to identify the strengths and weaknesses of different approaches.

Generalized Work Activities: Getting Information Needed to Do the Job—Observing, receiving, and otherwise obtaining information from all relevant sources. Analyzing Data or Information—Identifying underlying principles, reasons, or facts by breaking down information or data into separate parts. Making Decisions and Solving Problems—Combining, evaluating, and analyzing information and data to make decisions and solve problems. Involves making decisions about the relative importance of information and choosing the best solution. Inspecting Equipment, Structures, Materials—Inspecting or diagnosing equipment, structures, or materials to identify the causes of errors or other problems or defects. Processing Information—Compiling, coding, categorizing, calculating, tabulating, auditing, verifying, or processing information or data. Drafting and Specifying Technical Devices—Providing documentation, detailed instructions, drawings, or specifications to inform others about how devices, parts, equipment, or structures are to be fabricated, constructed, assembled, modified, maintained, or used.

Cleaners of Vehicles and Equipment

- ▲ Growth: 25%
- ▲ Annual Job Openings: 116,789
- ▲ Yearly Earnings: $14,540
- ▲ Education Required: Short-term O-J-T
- ▲ Self-Employed: 6.8%
- ▲ Part-Time: 22.9%

Cleaners of Vehicles and Equipment

Wash or otherwise clean vehicles, machinery, and other equipment. Use such materials as water, cleaning agents, brushes, cloths, and hoses. Transports materials, equipment, or supplies to and from work area, using carts or hoists. Connects hoses and lines to pumps and other equipment. Maintains inventory of supplies. Disassembles and reassembles machines or equipment, or removes and reattaches vehicle parts and trim, using hand tools. Places objects on drying racks or dye surfaces, using cloth, squeegees, or air compressors. Examines and inspects parts, equipment, and vehicles for cleanliness, damage, and compliance with standards or regulations. Turns valves or disconnects hoses to eliminate water, cleaning solutions, or vapors from machinery or tanks. Lubricates machinery, vehicles, and equipment, and performs minor repairs and adjustments, using hand tools. Applies paints, dyes, polishes, reconditioners, and masking materials to vehicles to preserve, protect, or restore color and condition. Records production and operational data on specified forms. Mixes cleaning solutions and abrasive compositions and other compounds according to formula. Monitors operation of cleaning machines; stops machine or notifies supervisor when malfunctions occur. Sweeps, shovels, or vacuums loose debris and salvageable scrap into containers and removes from work area. Turns valves or handles on equipment to regulate pressure and flow of water, air, steam, or abrasives from sprayer nozzles. Presses buttons to activate cleaning equipment or machines. Presoaks or rinses machine parts, equipment, or vehicles by immersing objects in cleaning solutions or water, manually or using hoists. Scrubs, scrapes, or sprays machine parts, equipment, or vehicles, using scrapers, brushes, cleaners, disinfectants, insecticides, acid, and abrasives. Collects and tests samples of cleaning solutions and vapors.

Personality Type: Realistic. Realistic occupations frequently involve work activities that include practical, hands-on problems and solutions. They often deal with plants, animals, and real-world materials like wood, tools, and machinery. Many of the occupations require

working outside and do not involve a lot of paperwork or working closely with others.

Abilities: Manual Dexterity—The ability to quickly make coordinated movements of one hand, a hand together with its arm, or two hands, to grasp, manipulate, or assemble objects. Extent Flexibility—The ability to bend, stretch, twist, or reach out with the body, arms, and/or legs. Trunk Strength—The ability to use one's abdominal and lower back muscles to support part of the body repeatedly or continuously over time without giving out or fatiguing. Near Vision—The ability to see details of objects at a close range. Multilimb Coordination—The ability to coordinate movements of two or more limbs together (for example, two arms, two legs, or one leg and one arm) while sitting, standing, or lying down. Does not involve performing the activities while the body is in motion. Wrist-Finger Speed—The ability to make fast, simple, repeated movements of the fingers, hands, and wrists.

Skills: Equipment Selection—Determining the kind of tools and equipment needed to do a job. Operation Monitoring—Watching gauges, dials, or other indicators to make sure a machine is working properly. Monitoring—Assessing how well one is doing when learning or doing something. Equipment Maintenance—Performing routine maintenance and determining when and what kind of maintenance is needed. Operation and Control—Controlling operations of equipment or systems. Repairing—Repairing machines or systems, using the needed tools.

Generalized Work Activities: Controlling Machines and Processes—Using either control mechanisms or direct physical activity to operate machines or processes. Does not involve working with computers or vehicles. Performing General Physical Activities—Performing physical activities that require moving one's whole body, such as in climbing, lifting, balancing, walking, and stooping. Performing activities that often also require considerable use of the arms and legs, such as in the physical handling of materials. Handling and Moving Objects—Using one's hands and arms in handling, installing, forming, positioning, and moving materials, or in manipulating things. Monitoring Processes, Materials, Surroundings—Monitoring and reviewing information from materials, events, or the environment, often to detect problems or to find out when things are finished. Inspecting Equipment, Structures, Materials—Inspecting or diagnosing equipment, structures, or materials to identify the causes of errors or other problems or defects. Documenting/Recording Information—Entering, transcribing, recording, storing, or maintaining information in either written form or by electronic/magnetic recording.

Clergy

- ▲ Growth: 13%
- ▲ Annual Job Openings: 14,197
- ▲ Yearly Earnings: $28,850
- ▲ Education Required: First professional degree
- ▲ Self-Employed: 0%
- ▲ Part-Time: 10.8%

Clergy

Conduct religious worship and perform other spiritual functions associated with beliefs and practices of religious faith or denomination. Provide spiritual and moral guidance and assistance to members. Engages in interfaith, community, civic, educational, and recreational activities sponsored by or related to interest of denomination. Administers religious rites or ordinances. Conducts weddings and funerals. Counsels those in spiritual need. Visits sick persons and shut-ins, and helps the poor. Instructs people who seek conversion to faith. Leads congregation in worship services. Interprets doctrine of religion. Prepares and delivers sermons and other talks. Writes articles for publication.

Personality Type: Social. Social occupations frequently involve working with, communicating with, and teaching people. These occupations often involve helping or providing service to others.

Abilities: Speech Clarity—The ability to speak clearly so that what is said is understandable to a listener. Oral Expression—The ability to communicate information and ideas verbally so others will understand. Written Expression—The ability to communicate information and ideas in writing so others will understand. Written Comprehension—The ability to read and understand information and ideas presented in writing. Problem Sensitivity—The ability to tell when something is wrong or is likely to go wrong. Does not involve solving the problem, only recognizing there is a problem. Oral Comprehension—The ability to listen to and understand information and ideas presented verbally.

Skills: Speaking—Talking to others to effectively convey information. Active Listening—Listening to what other people are saying; asking questions as appropriate. Service Orientation—Actively looking for ways to help people. Social Perceptiveness—Being aware of other people's reactions and understanding why people react the way they do. Reading Comprehension—Understanding written information in work-related documents. Writing—Communicating effectively with others in writing as indicated by the needs of the audience.

Generalized Work Activities: Establishing and Maintaining Relationships—Developing constructive and cooperative working relationships with others. Assisting and Caring for Others—Providing assistance or personal care to others. Interpreting Meaning of Information to Others—Translating or explaining what information means and how it can be understood or used to support responses or feedback to others. Organizing, Planning, and Prioritizing—Developing plans to accomplish work. Prioritizing and organizing one's own work. Performing for/Working with Public—Performing for people or dealing directly with the public, including serving persons in restaurants and stores and receiving clients or guests.

Clinical Laboratory Technologists and Technicians

- ▲ Growth: 17%
- ▲ Annual Job Openings: 20,441
- ▲ Yearly Earnings: $32,440
- ▲ Education Required: Bachelor's degree
- ▲ Self-Employed: 0.7%
- ▲ Part-Time: 19.5%

Medical and Clinical Laboratory Technicians

Perform routine medical laboratory tests for the diagnosis, treatment, and prevention of disease. Work under the supervision of a medical technologist. Conducts quantitative and qualitative chemical analyses of body fluids such as blood, urine, and spinal fluid. Inoculates fertilized eggs, broths, or other bacteriological media with organisms. Performs blood counts, using microscope. Incubates bacteria for specified period and prepares vaccines and serums by standard laboratory methods. Prepares standard volumetric solutions and reagents used in testing. Draws blood from patient, observing principles of asepsis to obtain blood sample. Conducts blood tests for transfusion purposes. Tests vaccines for sterility and virus inactivity.

Personality Type: Realistic. Realistic occupations frequently involve work activities that include practical, hands-on problems and solutions. They often deal with plants, animals, and real-world materials like wood, tools, and machinery. Many of the occupations require working outside and do not involve a lot of paperwork or working closely with others.

Abilities: Information Ordering—The ability to correctly follow a given rule or set of rules in order to arrange things or actions in a certain order. The things or actions can include numbers, letters, words, pictures, procedures, sentences, and mathematical or logical operations. Visual Color Discrimination—The ability to match or detect differences between colors, including shades of color and brightness. Near Vision—The ability to see details of objects at a close range. Arm-Hand Steadiness—The ability to keep the hand and arm steady while making an arm movement or while holding the arm and hand in one position.

Skills: Science—Using scientific methods to solve problems. Product Inspection—Inspecting and evaluating the quality of products. Information Gathering—Knowing how to find information and identifying essential information. Information Organization—Finding ways to structure or classify multiple pieces of information. Mathematics—Using mathematics to solve problems. Operation and Control—Controlling operations of equipment or systems.

Generalized Work Activities: Evaluating Information against Standards—Evaluating information against a set of standards and verifying that it is correct. Identifying Objects, Actions, and Events—Identifying information received by making estimates or categorizations, recognizing differences or similarities, or sensing changes in circumstances or events. Controlling Machines and Processes—Using either control mechanisms or direct physical activity to operate machines or processes. Does not involve working with computers or vehicles. Monitoring Processes, Materials, Surroundings— Monitoring and reviewing information from materials, events, or the environment, often to detect problems or to find out when things are finished. Documenting/Recording Information—Entering, transcribing, recording, storing, or maintaining information in either written form or by electronic/magnetic recording.

Medical and Clinical Laboratory Technologists

Perform complex medical laboratory tests for diagnosis, treatment, and prevention of disease. Train or supervise staff. Prepares slide of cell culture to identify chromosomes; views and photographs slide under photo- microscope; prints picture. Cuts, stains, and mounts biological material on slides for microscopic study and diagnosis, following standard laboratory procedures. Cultivates, isolates, and assists in identifying microbial organisms; performs various tests on these microorganisms. Performs tests to determine blood group, type, and compatibility for transfusion purposes. Harvests cell culture at optimum time sequence based on knowledge of cell cycle differences and culture conditions. Analyzes samples of biological material for chemical content or reaction. Examines slides under microscope to detect deviations from norm and to report abnormalities for further study. Selects and prepares specimen and media for cell culture, using aseptic techniques and knowledge of medium components and cell requirements. Conducts chemical analysis of body fluids including blood, urine, and spinal fluid, to determine presence of normal and abnormal components. Studies blood cells, number of blood cells, and morphology, using microscopic technique. Cuts images of chromosomes from photograph and identifies and arranges them in numbered pairs on karyotype chart, using standard practices. Conducts research under direction of microbiologist or biochemist. Communicates with physicians, family members, and researchers requesting technical information regarding test results. Calibrates and maintains equipment used in quantitative and qualitative analysis, such as spectrophotometers, calorimeters, flame photometers, and computer-controlled analyzers. Enters analysis of medical tests and clinical results into computer for storage. Sets up, cleans, and maintains laboratory equipment. Examines and tests human, animal, or other materials for microbial organisms.

Personality Type: Investigative. Investigative occupations frequently involve working with ideas and require an extensive amount of thinking. These occupations can involve searching for facts and figuring out problems mentally.

Abilities: Information Ordering—The ability to correctly follow a given rule or set of rules in order to arrange things or actions in a certain order. The things or actions can include numbers, letters, words, pictures, procedures, sentences, and mathematical or logical operations. Written Expression—The ability to communicate information and ideas in writing so others will understand. Oral Expression—The ability to communicate information and ideas verbally so others will understand. Oral Comprehension—The ability to listen to and understand information and ideas presented verbally. Written Comprehension—The ability to read and understand information and ideas presented in writing.

Skills: Science—Using scientific methods to solve problems. Reading Comprehension—Understanding written information in work-related documents. Information Gathering—Knowing how to find information and identifying essential information. Problem Identification—Identifying the nature of problems.

Generalized Work Activities: Identifying Objects, Actions, and Events—Identifying information received by making estimates or categorizations, recognizing differences or similarities, or sensing changes in circumstances or events. Monitoring Processes, Materials, Surroundings—Monitoring and reviewing information from materials, events, or the environment, often to detect problems or to find out when things are finished. Getting Information Needed to Do the Job—Observing, receiving, and otherwise obtaining information from all relevant sources. Updating and Using Job-Relevant Knowledge—Keeping up-to-date technically and knowing the functions of one's own job and related jobs. Evaluating Information against

Standards—Evaluating information against a set of standards and verifying that it is correct. Communicating with Other Workers—Providing information to supervisors, fellow workers, and subordinates. This information can be exchanged face-to-face, in writing, or via telephone/electronic transfer.

Coin, Vending, and Amusement Machine Servicers and Repairers

▲ Growth: 16%
▲ Annual Job Openings: 4,315
▲ Yearly Earnings: $23,260
▲ Education Required: Long-term O-J-T
▲ Self-Employed: 0%
▲ Part-Time: 9.3%

Coin, Vending, and Amusement Machine Servicers and Repairers

Install, service, adjust, or repair coin, vending, or amusement machines including video games, juke boxes, pinball machines, or slot machines. Collects coins from machine and makes settlements with concessionaires. Cleans and oils parts with soap and water, gasoline, kerosene, or carbon tetrachloride. Disassembles and assembles machines, following specifications and using hand tools and power tools. Tests dispensing, coin-handling, electrical, refrigeration, carbonation, or ice-making systems of machine. Keeps records of machine maintenance and repair. Replenishes vending machines with ingredients or products. Shellacs or paints dial markings or mechanism's exterior, using brush or spray gun. Adjusts and repairs vending machines and meters and replaces defective mechanical and electrical parts, using hand tools, soldering iron, and diagrams. Examines and inspects vending machines and meters to determine cause of malfunction.

Personality Type: Realistic. Realistic occupations frequently involve work activities that include practical, hands-on problems and solutions. They often deal with plants, animals, and real-world materials like wood, tools, and machinery. Many of the occupations require working outside and do not involve a lot of paperwork or working closely with others.

Abilities: Manual Dexterity—The ability to quickly make coordinated movements of one hand, a hand together with its arm, or two hands, to grasp, manipulate, or assemble objects. Finger Dexterity—The ability to make precisely coordinated movements of the fingers of one or both hands to grasp, manipulate, or assemble very small objects. Wrist-Finger Speed—The ability to make fast, simple, repeated movements of the fingers, hands, and wrists. Number Facility—The ability to add, subtract, multiply, or divide quickly and correctly. Control Precision—The ability to quickly and repeatedly make precise adjustments in moving the controls of a machine or vehicle to exact positions. Problem Sensitivity—The ability to tell when something is wrong or is likely to go wrong. Does not involve solving the problem, only recognizing there is a problem.

Skills: Repairing—Repairing machines or systems, using the needed tools. Equipment Maintenance—Performing routine maintenance and determining when and what kind of maintenance is needed. Troubleshooting—Determining what is causing an operating error and deciding what to do about it. Testing—Conducting tests to determine whether equipment, software, or procedures are operating as expected. Installation—Installing equipment, machines, wiring, or programs to meet specifications. Problem Identification—Identifying the nature of problems.

Generalized Work Activities: Repairing and Maintaining Mechanical Equipment—Fixing, servicing, aligning, setting up, adjusting, and testing machines, devices, moving parts, and equipment that operate primarily on the basis of mechanical, not electronic, principles. Inspecting Equipment, Structures, Materials—Inspecting or diagnosing equipment, structures, or materials to identify the causes of errors or other problems or defects. Handling and Moving Objects—Using one's hands and arms in handling, installing, forming, positioning, and moving materials, or in manipulating things. Getting Information Needed to Do the Job—Observing, receiving, and otherwise obtaining information from all relevant sources. Performing General Physical Activities—Performing physical activities that require moving one's whole body, such as in climbing, lifting, balancing, walking, and stooping. Performing activities that often also require considerable use of the arms and legs, such as in the physical handling of materials.

College and University Faculty

- ▲ Growth: 23%
- ▲ Annual Job Openings: 139,101
- ▲ Yearly Earnings: $46,600
- ▲ Education Required: Doctor's degree
- ▲ Self-Employed: 0%
- ▲ Part-Time: 32.3%

Agricultural Sciences Teachers, Postsecondary

Teach courses in the agricultural sciences. Includes teachers of agronomy, dairy sciences, fisheries management, horticultural sciences, poultry sciences, range management, and agricultural soil conservation. Conducts research in particular field of knowledge and publishes findings in professional journals. Stimulates class discussions. Directs research of other teachers or graduate students working for advanced academic degrees. Compiles bibliographies of specialized materials for outside reading assignments. Advises students on academic and vocational curricula. Compiles, administers, and grades examinations, or assigns this work to others. Prepares and delivers lectures to students. Acts as adviser to student organizations. Serves on faculty committee providing professional consulting services to government and industry.

Personality Type: Investigative. Investigative occupations frequently involve working with ideas and require an extensive amount of thinking. These occupations can involve searching for facts and figuring out problems mentally.

Abilities: Oral Expression—The ability to communicate information and ideas verbally so others will understand. Speech Clarity—The ability to speak clearly so that what is said is understandable to a listener. Written Expression—The ability to communicate information and ideas in writing so others will understand. Written Comprehension—The ability to read and understand information and ideas presented in writing. Oral Comprehension—The ability to listen to and understand information and ideas presented verbally.

Skills: Reading Comprehension—Understanding written information in work-related documents. Instructing—Teaching others how to do something. Speaking—Talking to others to effectively convey information. Science—Using scientific methods to solve problems. Active Learning—Working with new material or information to grasp its implications.

Generalized Work Activities: Teaching Others—Identifying educational needs, developing formal training programs or classes, and teaching or instructing others. Getting Information Needed to Do the Job—Observing, receiving, and otherwise obtaining information from all relevant sources. Coaching and Developing Others—Identifying developmental needs of others and coaching or otherwise helping others to improve their knowledge or skills. Communicating with Other Workers—Providing information to supervisors, fellow workers, and subordinates. This information can be exchanged face-to-face, in writing, or via telephone/electronic transfer. Communicating with Persons Outside Organization—Communicating with persons outside the organization. Representing the organization to customers, the public, government, and other external sources. Exchanging information face-to-face, in writing, or via telephone/electronic transfer.

Anthropology and Archeology Teachers, Postsecondary

Teach courses in anthropology or archeology. Advises students on academic and vocational curricula. Compiles, administers, and grades examinations, or assigns this work to others. Compiles bibliographies of specialized materials for outside reading assignments. Stimulates class discussions. Conducts research in particular field of knowledge and publishes findings in professional journals. Acts as adviser to student organizations. Serves on faculty committee providing professional consulting services to government and industry. Prepares and delivers lectures to students. Directs research of other teachers or graduate students working for advanced academic degrees.

Personality Type: Social. Social occupations frequently involve working with, communicating with, and teaching people. These occupations often involve helping or providing service to others.

Abilities: Oral Expression—The ability to communicate information and ideas verbally so others will understand. Speech Clarity—The ability to speak clearly so that what is said is understandable to a listener. Written Comprehension—The ability to read and understand information and ideas presented in writing. Written

Expression—The ability to communicate information and ideas in writing so others will understand. Oral Comprehension—The ability to listen to and understand information and ideas presented verbally.

Skills: Instructing—Teaching others how to do something. Speaking—Talking to others to effectively convey information. Reading Comprehension—Understanding written information in work-related documents. Critical Thinking—Using logic and analysis to identify the strengths and weaknesses of different approaches. Active Learning—Working with new material or information to grasp its implications. Learning Strategies—Using multiple approaches when learning or teaching new things. Writing—Communicating effectively with others in writing as indicated by the needs of the audience.

Generalized Work Activities: Teaching Others—Identifying educational needs, developing formal training programs or classes, and teaching or instructing others. Communicating with Other Workers—Providing information to supervisors, fellow workers, and subordinates. This information can be exchanged face-to-face, in writing, or via telephone/electronic transfer. Getting Information Needed to Do the Job—Observing, receiving, and otherwise obtaining information from all relevant sources. Coaching and Developing Others—Identifying developmental needs of others and coaching or otherwise helping others to improve their knowledge or skills. Judging Qualities—Making judgments about or assessing the value, importance, or quality of things, services, or other people's work.

Area, Ethnic, and Cultural Studies Teachers, Postsecondary

Teach courses pertaining to the culture and development of an area (for example, Latin America), an ethnic group, or any other group (for example, women's studies). Compiles bibliographies of specialized materials for outside reading assignments.

Serves on faculty committee providing professional consulting services to government and industry. Stimulates class discussions. Advises students on academic and vocational curricula. Prepares and delivers lectures to students. Compiles, administers, and grades examinations, or assigns this work to others. Acts as adviser to student organizations. Conducts research in particular field of knowledge and publishes findings in professional journals. Directs research of other teachers or graduate students working for advanced academic degrees.

Personality Type: Social. Social occupations frequently involve working with, communicating with, and teaching people. These occupations often involve helping or providing service to others.

Abilities: Oral Expression—The ability to communicate information and ideas verbally so others will understand. Speech Clarity—The ability to speak clearly so that what is said is understandable to a listener. Written Comprehension—The ability to read and understand information and ideas presented in writing. Written Expression—The ability to communicate information and ideas in writing so others will understand. Oral Comprehension—The ability to listen to and understand information and ideas presented verbally.

Skills: Instructing—Teaching others how to do something. Speaking—Talking to others to effectively convey information. Reading Comprehension—Understanding written information in work-related documents. Critical Thinking—Using logic and analysis to identify the strengths and weaknesses of different approaches. Learning Strategies—Using multiple approaches when learning or teaching new things. Active Learning—Working with new material or information to grasp its implications. Writing—Communicating effectively with others in writing as indicated by the needs of the audience.

Generalized Work Activities: Teaching Others—Identifying educational needs, developing formal training programs or classes, and teaching or instructing others. Communicating with Other Workers—Providing information to supervisors, fellow workers, and subordinates. This information can be exchanged face-to-face, in writing, or via telephone/electronic

transfer. Getting Information Needed to Do the Job—Observing, receiving, and otherwise obtaining information from all relevant sources. Coaching and Developing Others—Identifying developmental needs of others and coaching or otherwise helping others to improve their knowledge or skills. Judging Qualities—Making judgments about or assessing the value, importance, or quality of things, services, or other people's work.

Art, Drama, and Music Teachers, Postsecondary

Teach courses in drama, music, and the arts including fine and applied art, such as painting and sculpture, or design and crafts. Acts as adviser to student organizations. Advises students on academic and vocational curricula. Compiles, administers, and grades examinations, or assigns this work to others. Compiles bibliographies of specialized materials for outside reading assignments. Serves on faculty committee providing professional consulting services to government and industry. Directs research of other teachers or graduate students working for advanced academic degrees. Conducts research in particular field of knowledge and publishes findings in professional journals. Prepares and delivers lectures to students. Stimulates class discussions.

Personality Type: Artistic. Artistic occupations frequently involve working with forms, designs, and patterns. They often require self-expression, and the work can be done without following a clear set of rules.

Abilities: Oral Expression—The ability to communicate information and ideas verbally so others will understand. Written Comprehension—The ability to read and understand information and ideas presented in writing. Written Expression—The ability to communicate information and ideas in writing so others will understand. Oral Comprehension—The ability to listen to and understand information and ideas presented verbally. Speech Clarity—The ability to speak clearly so that what is said is understandable to a listener.

Skills: Instructing—Teaching others how to do something. Speaking—Talking to others to effectively convey information. Reading Comprehension—Understanding written information in work-related documents. Information Gathering—Knowing how to find information and identifying essential information.

Generalized Work Activities: Teaching Others—Identifying educational needs, developing formal training programs or classes, and teaching or instructing others. Communicating with Other Workers—Providing information to supervisors, fellow workers, and subordinates. This information can be exchanged face-to-face, in writing, or via telephone/electronic transfer. Coaching and Developing Others—Identifying developmental needs of others and coaching or otherwise helping others to improve their knowledge or skills. Communicating with Persons Outside Organization—Communicating with persons outside the organization. Representing the organization to customers, the public, government, and other external sources. Exchanging information face-to-face, in writing, or via telephone/electronic transfer. Getting Information Needed to Do the Job—Observing, receiving, and otherwise obtaining information from all relevant sources.

Biological Science Teachers, Postsecondary

Teach courses in biological sciences. Acts as adviser to student organizations. Stimulates class discussions. Advises students on academic and vocational curricula. Serves on faculty committee providing professional consulting services to government and industry. Compiles bibliographies of specialized materials for outside reading assignments. Directs research of other teachers or graduate students working for advanced academic degrees. Compiles, administers, and grades examinations, or assigns this work to others. Prepares and delivers lectures to students. Conducts research in particular field of knowledge and publishes findings in professional journals.

Personality Type: Investigative. Investigative occupations frequently involve working with ideas and require an extensive amount of thinking. These occupations can involve searching for facts and figuring out problems mentally.

Abilities: Oral Expression—The ability to communicate information and ideas verbally so others will understand. Written Expression—The ability to communicate information and ideas in writing so others will understand. Speech Clarity—The ability to speak clearly so that what is said is understandable to a listener. Written Comprehension—The ability to read and understand information and ideas presented in writing. Oral Comprehension—The ability to listen to and understand information and ideas presented verbally.

Skills: Reading Comprehension—Understanding written information in work-related documents. Speaking—Talking to others to effectively convey information. Instructing—Teaching others how to do something. Active Learning—Working with new material or information to grasp its implications. Science—Using scientific methods to solve problems.

Generalized Work Activities: Teaching Others—Identifying educational needs, developing formal training programs or classes, and teaching or instructing others. Getting Information Needed to Do the Job—Observing, receiving, and otherwise obtaining information from all relevant sources. Coaching and Developing Others—Identifying developmental needs of others and coaching or otherwise helping others to improve their knowledge or skills. Communicating with Other Workers—Providing information to supervisors, fellow workers, and subordinates. This information can be exchanged face-to-face, in writing, or via telephone/electronic transfer. Communicating with Persons Outside Organization—Communicating with persons outside the organization. Representing the organization to customers, the public, government, and other external sources. Exchanging information face-to-face, in writing, or via telephone/electronic transfer.

Chemistry Teachers, Postsecondary

Teach courses pertaining to the chemical and physical properties and compositional changes of substances. Provide instruction in the methods of qualitative and quantitative chemical analysis. Includes both teachers primarily engaged in teaching and those who do a combination of both teaching and research. Acts as adviser to student organizations. Directs research of other teachers or graduate students working for advanced academic degrees. Compiles, administers, and grades examinations, or assigns this work to others. Stimulates class discussions. Compiles bibliographies of specialized materials for outside reading assignments. Prepares and delivers lectures to students. Conducts research in particular field of knowledge and publishes findings in professional journals. Advises students on academic and vocational curricula. Serves on faculty committee providing professional consulting services to government and industry.

Personality Type: Investigative. Investigative occupations frequently involve working with ideas and require an extensive amount of thinking. These occupations can involve searching for facts and figuring out problems mentally.

Abilities: Speech Clarity—The ability to speak clearly so that what is said is understandable to a listener. Oral Expression—The ability to communicate information and ideas verbally so others will understand. Written Comprehension—The ability to read and understand information and ideas presented in writing. Oral Comprehension—The ability to listen to and understand information and ideas presented verbally. Written Expression—The ability to communicate information and ideas in writing so others will understand. Information Ordering—The ability to correctly follow a given rule or set of rules in order to arrange things or actions in a certain order. The things or actions can include numbers, letters, words, pictures, procedures, sentences, and mathematical or logical operations.

Skills: Instructing—Teaching others how to do something. Science—Using scientific methods to solve problems. Reading Comprehension—Understanding written information in work-related documents. Writing—Communicating effectively with others in writing as indicated by the needs of the audience. Speaking—Talking to others to effectively convey information. Critical Thinking—Using logic and analysis to identify the strengths and weaknesses of different approaches.

Generalized Work Activities: Teaching Others—Identifying educational needs, developing formal training programs or classes, and teaching or instructing others. Getting Information Needed to Do the Job—Observing, receiving, and otherwise obtaining information from all relevant sources. Analyzing Data or Information—Identifying underlying principles, reasons, or facts by breaking down information or data into separate parts. Interpreting Meaning of Information to Others—Translating or explaining what information means and how it can be understood or used to support responses or feedback to others. Communicating with Persons Outside Organization—Communicating with persons outside the organization. Representing the organization to customers, the public, government, and other external sources. Exchanging information face-to-face, in writing, or via telephone/electronic transfer.

Computer Science Teachers, Postsecondary

Teach courses in computer science. Specialize in a field of computer science, such as the design and function of computers, or operations and research analysis. Serves on faculty committee providing professional consulting services to government and industry. Acts as adviser to student organizations. Compiles bibliographies of specialized materials for outside reading assignments. Compiles, administers, and grades examinations, or assigns this work to others. Prepares and delivers lectures to students. Advises students on academic and vocational curricula. Stimulates class discussions. Directs research of other teachers or graduate students working for advanced academic degrees. Conducts research in particular field of knowledge and publishes findings in professional journals.

Personality Type: Investigative. Investigative occupations frequently involve working with ideas and require an extensive amount of thinking. These occupations can involve searching for facts and figuring out problems mentally.

Abilities: Speech Clarity—The ability to speak clearly so that what is said is understandable to a listener. Oral Expression—The ability to communicate information and ideas verbally so others will understand. Written Comprehension—The ability to read and understand information and ideas presented in writing. Written Expression—The ability to communicate information and ideas in writing so others will understand. Oral Comprehension—The ability to listen to and understand information and ideas presented verbally.

Skills: Instructing—Teaching others how to do something. Learning Strategies—Using multiple approaches when learning or teaching new things. Speaking—Talking to others to effectively convey information. Reading Comprehension—Understanding written information in work-related documents. Information Gathering—Knowing how to find information and identifying essential information. Mathematics—Using mathematics to solve problems. Information Organization—Finding ways to structure or classify multiple pieces of information.

Generalized Work Activities: Teaching Others—Identifying educational needs, developing formal training programs or classes, and teaching or instructing others. Getting Information Needed to Do the Job—Observing, receiving, and otherwise obtaining information from all relevant sources. Updating and Using Job-Relevant Knowledge—Keeping up-to-date technically and knowing the functions of one's own job and related jobs. Interacting with Computers—Controlling computer functions by using programs, setting up functions, writing software, or otherwise communicating with computer systems. Communicating with Persons Outside Organization—Communicating with persons outside the organization. Representing the organization to customers, the public,

government, and other external sources. Exchanging information face-to-face, in writing, or via telephone/electronic transfer.

Economics Teachers, Postsecondary

Teach courses in economics. Advises students on academic and vocational curricula. Stimulates class discussions. Directs research of other teachers or graduate students working for advanced academic degrees. Compiles bibliographies of specialized materials for outside reading assignments. Conducts research in particular field of knowledge and publishes findings in professional journals. Acts as adviser to student organizations. Serves on faculty committee providing professional consulting services to government and industry. Prepares and delivers lectures to students. Compiles, administers, and grades examinations, or assigns this work to others.

Personality Type: Social. Social occupations frequently involve working with, communicating with, and teaching people. These occupations often involve helping or providing service to others.

Abilities: Oral Expression—The ability to communicate information and ideas verbally so others will understand. Speech Clarity—The ability to speak clearly so that what is said is understandable to a listener. Written Comprehension—The ability to read and understand information and ideas presented in writing. Written Expression—The ability to communicate information and ideas in writing so others will understand. Oral Comprehension—The ability to listen to and understand information and ideas presented verbally.

Skills: Instructing—Teaching others how to do something. Speaking—Talking to others to effectively convey information. Reading Comprehension—Understanding written information in work-related documents. Critical Thinking—Using logic and analysis to identify the strengths and weaknesses of different approaches. Learning Strategies—Using multiple approaches when learning or teaching new things. Active Learning—Working with new material or information to grasp its implications. Writing—Communicating effectively with others in writing as indicated by the needs of the audience.

Generalized Work Activities: Teaching Others—Identifying educational needs, developing formal training programs or classes, and teaching or instructing others. Communicating with Other Workers—Providing information to supervisors, fellow workers, and subordinates. This information can be exchanged face-to-face, in writing, or via telephone/electronic transfer. Getting Information Needed to Do the Job—Observing, receiving, and otherwise obtaining information from all relevant sources. Coaching and Developing Others—Identifying developmental needs of others and coaching or otherwise helping others to improve their knowledge or skills. Judging Qualities—Making judgments about or assessing the value, importance, or quality of things, services, or other people's work.

Engineering Teachers, Postsecondary

Teach courses pertaining to the application of physical laws and principles of engineering for the development of machines, materials, instruments, processes, and services. Includes teachers of subjects such as chemical, civil, electrical, industrial, mechanical, mineral, and petroleum engineering. Includes both teachers primarily engaged in teaching and those who do a combination of both teaching and research. Directs research of other teachers or graduate students working for advanced academic degrees. Compiles bibliographies of specialized materials for outside reading assignments. Stimulates class discussions. Compiles, administers, and grades examinations, or assigns this work to others. Prepares and delivers lectures to students. Acts as adviser to student organizations. Conducts research in particular field of knowledge and publishes findings in professional journals. Advises students on academic and vocational curricula. Serves on faculty committee providing professional consulting services to government and industry.

Personality Type: Investigative. Investigative occupations frequently involve working with ideas and require an extensive amount of thinking. These occupations can involve searching for facts and figuring out problems mentally.

Abilities: Oral Comprehension—The ability to listen to and understand information and ideas presented verbally. Written Comprehension—The ability to read and understand information and ideas presented in writing. Speech Clarity—The ability to speak clearly so that what is said is understandable to a listener. Oral Expression—The ability to communicate information and ideas verbally so others will understand. Written Expression—The ability to communicate information and ideas in writing so others will understand.

Skills: Mathematics—Using mathematics to solve problems. Reading Comprehension—Understanding written information in work-related documents. Instructing—Teaching others how to do something.

Generalized Work Activities: Teaching Others—Identifying educational needs, developing formal training programs or classes, and teaching or instructing others. Getting Information Needed to Do the Job—Observing, receiving, and otherwise obtaining information from all relevant sources. Interpreting Meaning of Information to Others—Translating or explaining what information means and how it can be understood or used to support responses or feedback to others. Communicating with Other Workers—Providing information to supervisors, fellow workers, and subordinates. This information can be exchanged face-to-face, in writing, or via telephone/electronic transfer. Coaching and Developing Others—Identifying developmental needs of others and coaching or otherwise helping others to improve their knowledge or skills.

English Language and Literature Teachers, Postsecondary

Teach courses in English language and literature, including linguistics and comparative literature. Stimulates class discussions. Compiles, administers, and grades examinations, or assigns this work to others. Acts as adviser to student organizations. Directs research of other teachers or graduate students working for advanced academic degrees. Conducts research in particular field of knowledge and publishes findings in professional journals. Advises students on academic and vocational curricula. Prepares and delivers lectures to students. Compiles bibliographies of specialized materials for outside reading assignments. Serves on faculty committee providing professional consulting services to government and industry.

Personality Type: Artistic. Artistic occupations frequently involve working with forms, designs, and patterns. They often require self-expression, and the work can be done without following a clear set of rules.

Abilities: Speech Clarity—The ability to speak clearly so that what is said is understandable to a listener. Oral Expression—The ability to communicate information and ideas verbally so others will understand. Oral Comprehension—The ability to listen to and understand information and ideas presented verbally. Written Comprehension—The ability to read and understand information and ideas presented in writing. Written Expression—The ability to communicate information and ideas in writing so others will understand.

Skills: Speaking—Talking to others to effectively convey information. Reading Comprehension—Understanding written information in work-related documents. Instructing—Teaching others how to do something. Writing—Communicating effectively with others in writing as indicated by the needs of the audience. Learning Strategies—Using multiple approaches when learning or teaching new things.

Generalized Work Activities: Teaching Others—Identifying educational needs, developing formal training programs or classes, and teaching or instructing others. Communicating with Other Workers—Providing information to supervisors, fellow workers, and subordinates. This information can be exchanged face-to-face, in writing, or via telephone/electronic transfer. Getting Information Needed to Do the Job—Observing, receiving, and otherwise obtaining information from all relevant sources. Establishing and Maintaining Relationships—Developing constructive and cooperative working relationships with others. Interpreting Meaning of Information to Others—Translating or explaining what information means and how it can be understood or used to support responses or feedback to others.

Foreign Language and Literature Teachers, Postsecondary

Teach courses in foreign (that is, other than English) languages and literature. Stimulates class discussions. Compiles bibliographies of specialized materials for outside reading assignments. Compiles, administers, and grades examinations, or assigns this work to others. Advises students on academic and vocational curricula. Serves on faculty committee providing professional consulting services to government and industry. Acts as adviser to student organizations. Prepares and delivers lectures to students. Directs research of other teachers or graduate students working for advanced academic degrees. Conducts research in particular field of knowledge and publishes findings in professional journals.

Personality Type: Artistic. Artistic occupations frequently involve working with forms, designs, and patterns. They often require self-expression, and the work can be done without following a clear set of rules.

Abilities: Speech Clarity—The ability to speak clearly so that what is said is understandable to a listener. Oral

Expression—The ability to communicate information and ideas verbally so others will understand. Oral Comprehension—The ability to listen to and understand information and ideas presented verbally. Written Comprehension—The ability to read and understand information and ideas presented in writing. Written Expression—The ability to communicate information and ideas in writing so others will understand.

Skills: Reading Comprehension—Understanding written information in work-related documents. Speaking—Talking to others to effectively convey information. Writing—Communicating effectively with others in writing as indicated by the needs of the audience. Instructing—Teaching others how to do something. Learning Strategies—Using multiple approaches when learning or teaching new things.

Generalized Work Activities: Teaching Others—Identifying educational needs, developing formal training programs or classes, and teaching or instructing others. Communicating with Other Workers—Providing information to supervisors, fellow workers, and subordinates. This information can be exchanged face-to-face, in writing, or via telephone/electronic transfer. Getting Information Needed to Do the Job—Observing, receiving, and otherwise obtaining information from all relevant sources. Establishing and Maintaining Relationships—Developing constructive and cooperative working relationships with others. Interpreting Meaning of Information to Others—Translating or explaining what information means and how it can be understood or used to support responses or feedback to others.

Forestry and Conservation Science Teachers, Postsecondary

Teach courses in environmental and conservation science. Directs research of other teachers or graduate students working for advanced academic degrees.

Stimulates class discussions. Compiles bibliographies of specialized materials for outside reading assignments. Compiles, administers, and grades examinations, or assigns this work to others. Acts as adviser to student organizations. Serves on faculty committee providing professional consulting services to government and industry. Conducts research in particular field of knowledge and publishes findings in professional journals. Prepares and delivers lectures to students. Advises students on academic and vocational curricula.

Personality Type: Investigative. Investigative occupations frequently involve working with ideas and require an extensive amount of thinking. These occupations can involve searching for facts and figuring out problems mentally.

Abilities: Oral Expression—The ability to communicate information and ideas verbally so others will understand. Written Expression—The ability to communicate information and ideas in writing so others will understand. Speech Clarity—The ability to speak clearly so that what is said is understandable to a listener. Written Comprehension—The ability to read and understand information and ideas presented in writing. Oral Comprehension—The ability to listen to and understand information and ideas presented verbally.

Skills: Reading Comprehension—Understanding written information in work-related documents. Instructing—Teaching others how to do something. Speaking—Talking to others to effectively convey information. Active Learning—Working with new material or information to grasp its implications. Science—Using scientific methods to solve problems.

Generalized Work Activities: Teaching Others—Identifying educational needs, developing formal training programs or classes, and teaching or instructing others. Getting Information Needed to Do the Job—Observing, receiving, and otherwise obtaining information from all relevant sources. Coaching and Developing Others—Identifying developmental needs of others and coaching or otherwise helping others to improve their knowledge or skills. Communicating with Other Workers—Providing information to supervisors, fellow workers, and subordinates. This information can be exchanged face-to-face, in writing, or via telephone/

electronic transfer. Communicating with Persons Outside Organization—Communicating with persons outside the organization. Representing the organization to customers, the public, government, and other external sources. Exchanging information face-to-face, in writing, or via telephone/electronic transfer.

Graduate Teaching Assistants

Assist department chairperson, faculty members, or other professional staff members in college or university by performing teaching or teaching-related duties such as teaching lower-level courses, developing teaching materials, preparing and giving examinations, and grading examinations or papers. Graduate assistants must be enrolled in a graduate school program. Assists faculty member or staff with laboratory or field research. Assists faculty member or staff with student conferences. Grades examinations and papers. Prepares and gives examinations. Teaches lower-level courses. Develops teaching materials such as syllabi and visual aids. Assists library staff in maintaining library collection.

Personality Type: Social. Social occupations frequently involve working with, communicating with, and teaching people. These occupations often involve helping or providing service to others.

Abilities: Oral Expression—The ability to communicate information and ideas verbally so others will understand. Speech Clarity—The ability to speak clearly so that what is said is understandable to a listener. Written Comprehension—The ability to read and understand information and ideas presented in writing. Oral Comprehension—The ability to listen to and understand information and ideas presented verbally. Written Expression—The ability to communicate information and ideas in writing so others will understand.

Skills: Instructing—Teaching others how to do something. Speaking—Talking to others to effectively convey information. Critical Thinking—Using logic and analysis to identify the strengths and weaknesses of different approaches. Reading Comprehension—Understanding written information in work-related documents. Learning Strategies—Using multiple approaches when learning or teaching new things.

Generalized Work Activities: Teaching Others—Identifying educational needs, developing formal training programs or classes, and teaching or instructing others. Communicating with Other Workers—Providing information to supervisors, fellow workers, and subordinates. This information can be exchanged face-to-face, in writing, or via telephone/electronic transfer. Getting Information Needed to Do the Job—Observing, receiving, and otherwise obtaining information from all relevant sources. Establishing and Maintaining Relationships—Developing constructive and cooperative working relationships with others. Judging Qualities—Making judgments about or assessing the value, importance, or quality of things, services, or other people's work. Processing Information—Compiling, coding, categorizing, calculating, tabulating, auditing, verifying, or processing information or data.

Health Specialties Teachers, Postsecondary

Teach courses in health specialties such as veterinary medicine, dentistry, pharmacy, therapy, laboratory technology, and public health. Serves on faculty committee providing professional consulting services to government and industry. Compiles bibliographies of specialized materials for outside reading assignments. Compiles, administers, and grades examinations, or assigns this work to others. Acts as adviser to student organizations. Directs research of other teachers or graduate students working for advanced academic degrees. Conducts research in particular field of knowledge and publishes findings in professional journals. Prepares and delivers lectures to students. Stimulates class discussions. Advises students on academic and vocational curricula.

Personality Type: Investigative. Investigative occupations frequently involve working with ideas and require an extensive amount of thinking. These occupations can involve searching for facts and figuring out problems mentally.

Abilities: Oral Expression—The ability to communicate information and ideas verbally so others will understand. Written Expression—The ability to communicate information and ideas in writing so others will understand. Written Comprehension—The ability to read and understand information and ideas presented in writing. Speech Clarity—The ability to speak clearly so that what is said is understandable to a listener. Oral Comprehension—The ability to listen to and understand information and ideas presented verbally.

Skills: Instructing—Teaching others how to do something. Science—Using scientific methods to solve problems. Reading Comprehension—Understanding written information in work-related documents. Writing—Communicating effectively with others in writing as indicated by the needs of the audience.

Generalized Work Activities: Teaching Others—Identifying educational needs, developing formal training programs or classes, and teaching or instructing others. Communicating with Other Workers—Providing information to supervisors, fellow workers, and subordinates. This information can be exchanged face-to-face, in writing, or via telephone/electronic transfer. Getting Information Needed to Do the Job—Observing, receiving, and otherwise obtaining information from all relevant sources. Coaching and Developing Others—Identifying developmental needs of others and coaching or otherwise helping others to improve their knowledge or skills. Communicating with Persons Outside Organization—Communicating with persons outside the organization. Representing the organization to customers, the public, government, and other external sources. Exchanging information face-to-face, in writing, or via telephone/electronic transfer. Interpreting Meaning of Information to Others—Translating or explaining what information means and how it can be understood or used to support responses or feedback to others.

History Teachers, Postsecondary

Teach courses in human history and historiography. Conducts research in particular field of knowledge and publishes findings in professional journals. Stimulates class discussions. Compiles bibliographies of specialized materials for outside reading assignments. Serves on faculty committee providing professional consulting services to government and industry. Prepares and delivers lectures to students. Directs research of other teachers or graduate students working for advanced academic degrees. Advises students on academic and vocational curricula. Compiles, administers, and grades examinations, or assigns this work to others. Acts as adviser to student organizations.

Personality Type: Social. Social occupations frequently involve working with, communicating with, and teaching people. These occupations often involve helping or providing service to others.

Abilities: Oral Expression—The ability to communicate information and ideas verbally so others will understand. Written Comprehension—The ability to read and understand information and ideas presented in writing. Speech Clarity—The ability to speak clearly so that what is said is understandable to a listener. Written Expression—The ability to communicate information and ideas in writing so others will understand. Oral Comprehension—The ability to listen to and understand information and ideas presented verbally.

Skills: Instructing—Teaching others how to do something. Speaking—Talking to others to effectively convey information. Reading Comprehension—Understanding written information in work-related documents. Critical Thinking—Using logic and analysis to identify the strengths and weaknesses of different approaches. Learning Strategies—Using multiple approaches when learning or teaching new things. Active Learning—Working with new material or information to grasp its implications. Writing—Communicating effectively with others in writing as indicated by the needs of the audience.

Generalized Work Activities: Teaching Others—Identifying educational needs, developing formal training programs or classes, and teaching or instructing others. Communicating with Other Workers—Providing information to supervisors, fellow workers, and subordinates. This information can be exchanged face-to-face, in writing, or via telephone/electronic transfer. Getting Information Needed to Do the Job—Observing, receiving, and otherwise obtaining information from all relevant sources. Coaching and Developing Others—Identifying developmental needs of others and coaching or otherwise helping others to improve their knowledge or skills. Judging Qualities—Making judgments about or assessing the value, importance, or quality of things, services, or other people's work.

Mathematical Science Teachers, Postsecondary

Teach courses pertaining to mathematical concepts, statistics, and actuarial science and to the application of original and standardized mathematical techniques in solving specific problems and situations. Compiles, administers, and grades examinations, or assigns this work to others. Stimulates class discussions. Directs research of other teachers or graduate students working for advanced academic degrees. Acts as adviser to student organizations. Conducts research in particular field of knowledge and publishes findings in professional journals. Advises students on academic and vocational curricula. Compiles bibliographies of specialized materials for outside reading assignments. Prepares and delivers lectures to students. Serves on faculty committee providing professional consulting services to government and industry.

Personality Type: Investigative. Investigative occupations frequently involve working with ideas and require an extensive amount of thinking. These occupations can involve searching for facts and figuring out problems mentally.

Abilities: Written Comprehension—The ability to read and understand information and ideas presented in writing. Mathematical Reasoning—The ability to understand and organize a problem and then select a mathematical method or formula to solve the problem. Oral Expression—The ability to communicate information and ideas verbally so others will understand. Written Expression—The ability to communicate information and ideas in writing so others will understand. Speech Clarity—The ability to speak clearly so that what is said is understandable to a listener.

Skills: Mathematics—Using mathematics to solve problems. Instructing—Teaching others how to do something. Reading Comprehension—Understanding written information in work-related documents. Learning Strategies—Using multiple approaches when learning or teaching new things. Speaking—Talking to others to effectively convey information.

Generalized Work Activities: Teaching Others—Identifying educational needs, developing formal training programs or classes, and teaching or instructing others. Getting Information Needed to Do the Job—Observing, receiving, and otherwise obtaining information from all relevant sources. Interpreting Meaning of Information to Others—Translating or explaining what information means and how it can be understood or used to support responses or feedback to others. Communicating with Other Workers—Providing information to supervisors, fellow workers, and subordinates. This information can be exchanged face-to-face, in writing, or via telephone/electronic transfer. Implementing Ideas and Programs—Conducting or carrying out work procedures and activities in accord with one's own ideas or information provided through directions/instructions for purposes of installing, modifying, preparing, delivering, constructing, integrating, finishing, or completing programs, systems, structures, or products.

Nursing Instructors and Teachers, Postsecondary

Demonstrate and teach patient care in classroom and clinical units to nursing students. Includes both teachers primarily engaged in teaching and those who do a combination of both teaching and research. Evaluates student progress and maintains records of student classroom and clinical experience. Issues assignments to students. Conducts and supervises laboratory work. Cooperates with medical and nursing personnel in evaluating and improving teaching and nursing practices. Prepares and administers examinations to nursing students. Directs seminars and panels. Supervises student nurses and demonstrates patient care in clinical units of hospital. Instructs and lectures nursing students in principles and application of physical, biological, and psychological subjects related to nursing. Participates in planning curriculum, teaching schedule, and course outline with medical and nursing personnel. Conducts classes for patients in health practices and procedures.

Personality Type: Social. Social occupations frequently involve working with, communicating with, and teaching people. These occupations often involve helping or providing service to others.

Abilities: Oral Expression—The ability to communicate information and ideas verbally so others will understand. Speech Clarity—The ability to speak clearly so that what is said is understandable to a listener. Written Expression—The ability to communicate information and ideas in writing so others will understand. Written Comprehension—The ability to read and understand information and ideas presented in writing. Inductive Reasoning—The ability to combine separate pieces of information, or specific answers to problems, to form general rules or conclusions. Includes coming up with a logical explanation for why a series of seemingly unrelated events occur together. Oral Comprehension—The ability to listen to and understand information and ideas presented verbally. Deductive Reasoning—The ability to apply general rules to specific problems to come up with logical answers. Involves deciding if an answer makes sense.

Skills: Instructing—Teaching others how to do something. Learning Strategies—Using multiple approaches when learning or teaching new things. Speaking—Talking to others to effectively convey information. Management of Personnel Resources—Motivating, developing, and directing people as they work, identifying the best people for the job. Science—

Using scientific methods to solve problems. Reading Comprehension—Understanding written information in work-related documents.

Generalized Work Activities: Teaching Others—Identifying educational needs, developing formal training programs or classes, and teaching or instructing others. Getting Information Needed to Do the Job—Observing, receiving, and otherwise obtaining information from all relevant sources. Monitoring Processes, Materials, Surroundings—Monitoring and reviewing information from materials, events, or the environment, often to detect problems or to find out when things are finished. Updating and Using Job-Relevant Knowledge—Keeping up-to-date technically and knowing the functions of one's own job and related jobs. Interpreting Meaning of Information to Others—Translating or explaining what information means and how it can be understood or used to support responses or feedback to others. Coaching and Developing Others—Identifying developmental needs of others and coaching or otherwise helping others to improve their knowledge or skills.

Physics Teachers, Postsecondary

Teach courses pertaining to the laws of matter and energy. Includes both teachers primarily engaged in teaching and those who do a combination of both teaching and research. Directs research of other teachers or graduate students working for advanced academic degrees. Stimulates class discussions. Compiles bibliographies of specialized materials for outside reading assignments. Acts as adviser to student organizations. Compiles, administers, and grades examinations, or assigns this work to others. Conducts research in particular field of knowledge and publishes findings in professional journals. Advises students on academic and vocational curricula. Prepares and delivers lectures to students. Serves on faculty committee providing professional consulting services to government and industry.

Personality Type: Investigative. Investigative occupations frequently involve working with ideas and require an extensive amount of thinking. These occupations can involve searching for facts and figuring out problems mentally.

Abilities: Oral Expression—The ability to communicate information and ideas verbally so others will understand. Written Comprehension—The ability to read and understand information and ideas presented in writing. Speech Clarity—The ability to speak clearly so that what is said is understandable to a listener. Number Facility—The ability to add, subtract, multiply, or divide quickly and correctly. Deductive Reasoning—The ability to apply general rules to specific problems to come up with logical answers. Involves deciding if an answer makes sense. Oral Comprehension—The ability to listen to and understand information and ideas presented verbally. Mathematical Reasoning—The ability to understand and organize a problem and then select a mathematical method or formula to solve the problem.

Skills: Instructing—Teaching others how to do something. Reading Comprehension—Understanding written information in work-related documents. Writing—Communicating effectively with others in writing as indicated by the needs of the audience. Speaking—Talking to others to effectively convey information. Science—Using scientific methods to solve problems. Critical Thinking—Using logic and analysis to identify the strengths and weaknesses of different approaches. Mathematics—Using mathematics to solve problems.

Generalized Work Activities: Teaching Others—Identifying educational needs, developing formal training programs or classes, and teaching or instructing others. Getting Information Needed to Do the Job—Observing, receiving, and otherwise obtaining information from all relevant sources. Analyzing Data or Information—Identifying underlying principles, reasons, or facts by breaking down information or data into separate parts. Processing Information—Compiling, coding, categorizing, calculating, tabulating, auditing, verifying, or processing information or data. Interpreting Meaning of Information to Others—Translating or explaining what information means and how it can be understood or used to support responses or feedback to others.

Political Science Teachers, Postsecondary

Teach courses in political science, international affairs, and international relations. Directs research of other teachers or graduate students working for advanced academic degrees. Stimulates class discussions. Compiles, administers, and grades examinations, or assigns this work to others. Acts as adviser to student organizations. Advises students on academic and vocational curricula. Conducts research in particular field of knowledge and publishes findings in professional journals. Serves on faculty committee providing professional consulting services to government and industry. Prepares and delivers lectures to students. Compiles bibliographies of specialized materials for outside reading assignments.

Personality Type: Social. Social occupations frequently involve working with, communicating with, and teaching people. These occupations often involve helping or providing service to others.

Abilities: Oral Expression—The ability to communicate information and ideas verbally so others will understand. Speech Clarity—The ability to speak clearly so that what is said is understandable to a listener. Written Comprehension—The ability to read and understand information and ideas presented in writing. Written Expression—The ability to communicate information and ideas in writing so others will understand. Oral Comprehension—The ability to listen to and understand information and ideas presented verbally.

Skills: Instructing—Teaching others how to do something. Speaking—Talking to others to effectively convey information. Reading Comprehension—Understanding written information in work-related documents. Critical Thinking—Using logic and analysis to identify the strengths and weaknesses of different approaches. Active Learning—Working with new material or information to grasp its implications. Learning Strategies—Using multiple approaches when learning or teaching new things. Writing—

Communicating effectively with others in writing as indicated by the needs of the audience.

Generalized Work Activities: Teaching Others—Identifying educational needs, developing formal training programs or classes, and teaching or instructing others. Communicating with Other Workers—Providing information to supervisors, fellow workers, and subordinates. This information can be exchanged face-to-face, in writing, or via telephone/electronic transfer. Getting Information Needed to Do the Job—Observing, receiving, and otherwise obtaining information from all relevant sources. Coaching and Developing Others—Identifying developmental needs of others and coaching or otherwise helping others to improve their knowledge or skills. Judging Qualities—Making judgments about or assessing the value, importance, or quality of things, services, or other people's work.

Psychology Teachers, Postsecondary

Teach courses in psychology, such as child, clinical, and developmental psychology, and psychological counseling. Serves on faculty committee providing professional consulting services to government and industry. Stimulates class discussions. Compiles, administers, and grades examinations, or assigns this work to others. Directs research of other teachers or graduate students working for advanced academic degrees. Conducts research in particular field of knowledge and publishes findings in professional journals. Advises students on academic and vocational curricula. Prepares and delivers lectures to students. Compiles bibliographies of specialized materials for outside reading assignments. Acts as adviser to student organizations.

Personality Type: Social. Social occupations frequently involve working with, communicating with, and teaching people. These occupations often involve helping or providing service to others.

Abilities: Oral Expression—The ability to communicate information and ideas verbally so others will understand. Speech Clarity—The ability to speak clearly so that what is said is understandable to a listener. Written Comprehension—The ability to read and understand information and ideas presented in writing. Written Expression—The ability to communicate information and ideas in writing so others will understand. Oral Comprehension—The ability to listen to and understand information and ideas presented verbally.

Skills: Instructing—Teaching others how to do something. Speaking—Talking to others to effectively convey information. Reading Comprehension—Understanding written information in work-related documents. Critical Thinking—Using logic and analysis to identify the strengths and weaknesses of different approaches. Active Learning—Working with new material or information to grasp its implications. Writing—Communicating effectively with others in writing as indicated by the needs of the audience. Learning Strategies—Using multiple approaches when learning or teaching new things.

Generalized Work Activities: Teaching Others—Identifying educational needs, developing formal training programs or classes, and teaching or instructing others. Communicating with Other Workers—Providing information to supervisors, fellow workers, and subordinates. This information can be exchanged face-to-face, in writing, or via telephone/electronic transfer. Getting Information Needed to Do the Job—Observing, receiving, and otherwise obtaining information from all relevant sources. Coaching and Developing Others—Identifying developmental needs of others and coaching or otherwise helping others to improve their knowledge or skills. Judging Qualities—Making judgments about or assessing the value, importance, or quality of things, services, or other people's work.

Sociology Teachers, Postsecondary

Teach courses in sociology. Serves on faculty committee providing professional consulting services to government and industry. Stimulates class discussions. Advises students on academic and vocational curricula. Acts as adviser to student organizations. Compiles, administers, and grades examinations, or assigns this work to others. Directs research of other teachers or graduate students working for advanced academic degrees. Compiles bibliographies of specialized materials for outside reading assignments. Prepares and delivers lectures to students. Conducts research in particular field of knowledge and publishes findings in professional journals.

Personality Type: Social. Social occupations frequently involve working with, communicating with, and teaching people. These occupations often involve helping or providing service to others.

Abilities: Oral Expression—The ability to communicate information and ideas verbally so others will understand. Speech Clarity—The ability to speak clearly so that what is said is understandable to a listener. Written Comprehension—The ability to read and understand information and ideas presented in writing. Written Expression—The ability to communicate information and ideas in writing so others will understand. Oral Comprehension—The ability to listen to and understand information and ideas presented verbally.

Skills: Instructing—Teaching others how to do something. Speaking—Talking to others to effectively convey information. Reading Comprehension—Understanding written information in work-related documents. Critical Thinking—Using logic and analysis to identify the strengths and weaknesses of different approaches. Learning Strategies—Using multiple approaches when learning or teaching new things. Active Learning—Working with new material or information to grasp its implications. Writing—Communicating effectively with others in writing as indicated by the needs of the audience.

Generalized Work Activities: Teaching Others—Identifying educational needs, developing formal training programs or classes, and teaching or instructing others. Communicating with Other Workers—Providing information to supervisors, fellow workers, and subordinates. This information can be exchanged face-to-face, in writing, or via telephone/electronic transfer. Getting Information Needed to Do the Job—Observing, receiving, and otherwise obtaining information from all relevant sources. Coaching and Developing Others—Identifying developmental needs of others and coaching or otherwise helping others to improve their knowledge or skills. Judging Qualities—Making judgments about or assessing the value, importance, or quality of things, services, or other people's work.

Combination Machine Tool Setters, Set-Up Operators, Operators, and Tenders

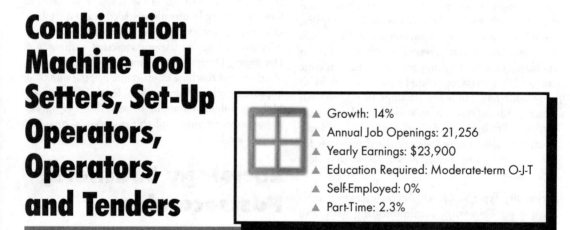

▲ Growth: 14%
▲ Annual Job Openings: 21,256
▲ Yearly Earnings: $23,900
▲ Education Required: Moderate-term O-J-T
▲ Self-Employed: 0%
▲ Part-Time: 2.3%

Combination Machine Tool Operators and Tenders, Metal and Plastic

Operate or tend more than one type of cutting or forming machine tool that has been previously set up. Includes such machine tools as band saws, press brakes, slitting machines, drills, lathes, and boring machines. Removes burrs, sharp edges, rust, or scale from workpiece, using file, hand grinder, wire brush, or power tools. Performs minor machine maintenance such as oiling or cleaning machines, dies, or workpieces, or adding coolant to machine reservoir. Inspects workpiece for defects and measures workpiece, using rule, template, or other measuring instruments to determine accuracy of machine operation. Installs machine components such as chucks, boring bars, or cutting tools, according to specifications, using hand tools. Sets machine stops or guides to specified length as indicated by scale, rule, or template. Adjusts machine components and changes worn accessories such as cutting tools and brushes, using hand tools. Aligns layout marks with die or blade. Reads job specifications to determine machine adjustments and material requirements. Positions, adjusts, and secures workpiece against stops, on arbor, or in chuck, fixture, or automatic feeding mechanism, manually or using hoist. Observes machine operation to detect workpiece defects or machine malfunction. Activates and tends or operates machines to cut, shape, thread, bore, drill, tap, bend, or mill metal or nonmetallic material. Extracts or lifts jammed pieces from machine, using fingers, wire hooks, or lift bar.

Personality Type: Realistic. Realistic occupations frequently involve work activities that include practical, hands-on problems and solutions. They often deal with plants, animals, and real-world materials like wood, tools, and machinery. Many of the occupations require working outside and do not involve a lot of paperwork or working closely with others.

Abilities: Manual Dexterity—The ability to quickly make coordinated movements of one hand, a hand together with its arm, or two hands, to grasp, manipulate, or assemble objects. Information Ordering—The ability to correctly follow a given rule or set of rules in order to arrange things or actions in a certain order. The things or actions can include numbers, letters, words, pictures, procedures, sentences, and mathematical or logical operations. Control Precision—The ability to quickly and repeatedly make precise adjustments in moving the controls of a machine or vehicle to exact positions. Problem Sensitivity—The ability to tell when something is wrong or is likely to go wrong. Does not involve solving the problem, only recognizing there is a problem. Written Comprehension—The ability to read and understand information and ideas presented in writing.

Skills: Operation and Control—Controlling operations of equipment or systems. Operation Monitoring—Watching gauges, dials, or other indicators to make sure a machine is working properly. Product Inspection—Inspecting and evaluating the quality of products. Equipment Maintenance—Performing routine maintenance and determining when and what kind of maintenance is needed. Reading Comprehension—Understanding written information in work-related documents.

Generalized Work Activities: Controlling Machines and Processes—Using either control mechanisms or direct physical activity to operate machines or processes. Does not involve working with computers or vehicles. Handling and Moving Objects—Using one's hands and arms in handling, installing, forming, positioning, and moving materials, or in manipulating things. Includes the use of keyboards. Monitoring Processes, Materials, Surroundings—Monitoring and reviewing information from materials, events, or the environment, often to detect problems or to find out when things are finished. Implementing Ideas and Programs—Conducting or carrying out work procedures and activities in accord with one's own ideas or information provided through directions/instructions for purposes of installing, modifying, preparing, delivering, constructing, integrating, finishing, or completing programs, systems, structures, or products. Inspecting Equipment, Structures, Materials—Inspecting or diagnosing equipment, structures, or materials to identify the causes of errors or other problems or defects. Performing General Physical Activities—Performing physical activities that require moving one's whole body, such as in climbing, lifting, balancing, walking, and stooping. Performing activities that often also require considerable use of the arms and legs, such as in the physical handling of materials. Getting Information Needed to Do the Job—Observing, receiving, and otherwise obtaining information from all relevant sources.

Combination Machine Tool Setters and Set-Up Operators, Metal and Plastic

Set up, or set up and operate, more than one type of cutting or forming machine tool, such as gear hobbers, lathes, press brakes, shearing, and boring machines. Measures and marks reference points and cutting lines on workpiece, using traced templates, compasses, and rules. Instructs operators or other workers in machine setup and operation. Records operational data such as pressure readings, length of stroke, feeds, and speeds. Makes minor electrical and mechanical repairs and adjustments to machines, and notifies supervisor when major service is required. Lifts, positions, and secures workpieces in holding devices, using hoists and hand tools. Computes data such as gear dimensions and machine settings, applying knowledge of shop mathematics. Reads blueprint or job order to determine product specifications and tooling instructions and to plan operational sequences. Starts machine and turns handwheels or valves to engage feeding, cooling, and lubricating mechanisms. Selects, installs, and adjusts alignment of drills, cutters, dies, guides, and holding devices, using template, measuring instruments, and hand tools. Monitors machine operation and moves controls to align and adjust position of workpieces and action of cutting tools. Moves controls or mounts gears, cams, or templates in machine to set feed rate and cutting speed, depth, and angle. Sets up and operates lathes, cutters, borers, millers, grinders, presses, drills, and auxiliary machines to make metallic and plastic workpieces. Inspects first-run workpieces and verifies conformance to specifications to check accuracy of machine setup.

Personality Type: Realistic. Realistic occupations frequently involve work activities that include practical, hands-on problems and solutions. They often deal with plants, animals, and real-world materials like wood, tools, and machinery. Many of the occupations require working outside and do not involve a lot of paperwork or working closely with others.

Abilities: Control Precision—The ability to quickly and repeatedly make precise adjustments in moving the controls of a machine or vehicle to exact positions. Written Comprehension—The ability to read and understand information and ideas presented in writing. Information Ordering—The ability to correctly follow a given rule or set of rules in order to arrange things or actions in a certain order. The things or actions can include numbers, letters, words, pictures, procedures, sentences, and mathematical or logical operations. Number Facility—The ability to add, subtract, multiply, or divide quickly and correctly. Oral Expression—The ability to communicate information and ideas verbally so others will understand. Mathematical Reasoning—The ability to understand and organize a problem and then select a mathematical method or formula to solve the problem. Manual Dexterity—The ability to quickly make coordinated movements of one hand, a hand together with its arm, or two hands, to grasp, manipulate, or assemble objects. Near Vision—The ability to see details of objects at a close range.

Skills: Operation and Control—Controlling operations of equipment or systems. Product Inspection—Inspecting and evaluating the quality of products. Operation Monitoring—Watching gauges, dials, or other indicators to make sure a machine is working properly. Testing—Conducting tests to determine whether equipment, software, or procedures are operating as expected. Mathematics—Using mathematics to solve problems.

Generalized Work Activities: Controlling Machines and Processes—Using either control mechanisms or direct physical activity to operate machines or processes. Does not involve working with computers or vehicles.

Monitoring Processes, Materials, Surroundings—Monitoring and reviewing information from materials, events, or the environment, often to detect problems or to find out when things are finished. Inspecting Equipment, Structures, Materials—Inspecting or diagnosing equipment, structures, or materials to identify the causes of errors or other problems or defects. Handling and Moving Objects—Using one's hands and arms in handling, installing, forming, positioning, and moving materials, or in manipulating things. Includes the use of keyboards. Repairing and Maintaining Mechanical Equipment—Fixing, servicing, aligning, setting up, adjusting, and testing machines, devices, moving parts, and equipment that operate primarily on the basis of mechanical, not electronic, principles. Getting Information Needed to Do the Job—Observing, receiving, and otherwise obtaining information from all relevant sources.

Commercial and Industrial Electronics Equipment Repairers

- ▲ Growth: 13%
- ▲ Annual Job Openings: 9,744
- ▲ Yearly Earnings: $35,590
- ▲ Education Required: Postsecondary vocational training
- ▲ Self-Employed: 12.1%
- ▲ Part-Time: 6.2%

Avionics Technicians

Install, inspect, test, adjust, or repair avionics equipment such as radar, radio, navigation, and missile control systems in aircraft or space vehicles. Interprets flight test data to diagnose malfunctions and systemic performance problems. Tests components or assemblies, using circuit tester, oscilloscope, and voltmeter. Connects components to assemblies such as radio systems, instruments, magnetos, inverters, and in-flight refueling systems, using hand tools and soldering iron. Installs electrical and electronic components, assemblies, and systems in aircraft, using hand tools, power tools, and soldering iron. Fabricates parts and test aids as required. Sets up and operates ground support and test equipment to perform functional flight test of electrical and electronic systems. Lays out installation of assemblies and systems in aircraft according to blueprints and wiring diagrams, using scribe, scale, and protractor. Assembles components such as switches, electrical controls, and junction boxes, using hand tools and soldering iron. Adjusts, repairs, or replaces malfunctioning components or assemblies, using hand tools and soldering iron.

Personality Type: Realistic. Realistic occupations frequently involve work activities that include practical, hands-on problems and solutions. They often deal with plants, animals, and real-world materials like wood, tools, and machinery. Many of the occupations require working outside and do not involve a lot of paperwork or working closely with others.

Abilities: Near Vision—The ability to see details of objects at a close range. Visualization—The ability to imagine how something will look after it is moved around or when its parts are moved or rearranged. Information Ordering—The ability to correctly follow a given rule or set of rules in order to arrange things or actions in a certain order. The things or actions can include numbers, letters, words, pictures, procedures, sentences, and mathematical or logical operations. Written Comprehension—The ability to read and understand information and ideas presented in writing. Finger Dexterity—The ability to make precisely coordinated movements of the fingers of one or both hands to grasp, manipulate, or assemble very small objects. Problem Sensitivity—The ability to tell when something is wrong or is likely to go wrong. Does not involve solving the problem, only recognizing there is a problem.

Skills: Troubleshooting—Determining what is causing an operating error and deciding what to do about it. Installation—Installing equipment, machines, wiring, or programs to meet specifications. Testing—Conducting tests to determine whether equipment, software, or procedures are operating as expected. Operation and Control—Controlling operations of equipment or systems.

Generalized Work Activities: Handling and Moving Objects—Using one's hands and arms in handling, installing, forming, positioning, and moving materials, or in manipulating things. Includes the use of keyboards. Repairing and Maintaining Electrical Equipment—Fixing, servicing, adjusting, regulating, calibrating, fine-tuning, or testing machines, devices, and equipment that operate primarily on the basis of electrical or electronic, not mechanical, principles. Monitoring Processes, Materials, Surroundings—Monitoring and reviewing information from materials, events, or the environment, often to detect problems or to find out when things are finished. Getting Information Needed to Do the Job—Observing, receiving, and otherwise obtaining information from all relevant sources. Inspecting Equipment, Structures, Materials—Inspecting or diagnosing equipment, structures, or materials to identify the causes of errors or other problems or defects.

Electrical and Electronics Installers and Repairers, Transportation Equipment

Install, adjust, or maintain mobile electronics communication equipment including sound, sonar, security, navigation, and surveillance systems on trains, watercraft, or other mobile equipment. Installs fixtures, outlets, terminal boards, switches, and wall boxes, using hand tools. Adjusts, repairs, or replaces defective wiring and relays in ignition, lighting, air-conditioning, and safety control systems, using electrician's tools. Splices wires with knife or cutting pliers; solders connections to fixtures, outlets, and equipment. Installs electrical equipment such as air-conditioning systems, heating systems, ignition systems, generator brushes, and commutators, using hand tools. Measures, cuts, and installs framework and conduit to support and connect wiring, control panels, and junction boxes, using hand tools. Repairs or rebuilds starters, generators, distributors, or door controls, using electrician's tools. Confers with customer to determine nature of malfunction. Estimates cost of repairs based on parts and labor charges. Cuts openings and drills holes for fixtures, outlet boxes, and fuse holders, using electric drill and router. Visually inspects and tests electrical system or equipment, using testing devices such as oscilloscope, voltmeter, and ammeter, to determine malfunctions.

Personality Type: Realistic. Realistic occupations frequently involve work activities that include practical, hands-on problems and solutions. They often deal with plants, animals, and real-world materials like wood, tools, and machinery. Many of the occupations require working outside and do not involve a lot of paperwork or working closely with others.

Abilities: Manual Dexterity—The ability to quickly make coordinated movements of one hand, a hand together with its arm, or two hands, to grasp, manipulate, or assemble objects. Finger Dexterity—The ability to make precisely coordinated movements of the fingers of one or both hands to grasp, manipulate, or assemble very small objects. Arm-Hand Steadiness—The ability to keep the hand and arm steady while making an arm movement or while holding the arm and hand in one position. Control Precision—The ability to quickly and repeatedly make precise adjustments in moving the controls of a machine or vehicle to exact positions. Near Vision—The ability to see details of objects at a close range.

Skills: Repairing—Repairing machines or systems, using the needed tools. Problem Identification—Identifying the nature of problems. Installation—Installing equipment, machines, wiring, or programs to meet specifications. Equipment Selection—Determining the kind of tools and equipment needed to do a job. Mathematics—Using mathematics to solve problems.

Generalized Work Activities: Repairing and Maintaining Electrical Equipment—Fixing, servicing, adjusting, regulating, calibrating, fine-tuning, or testing machines, devices, and equipment that operate primarily on the basis of electrical or electronic, not mechanical, principles. Handling and Moving Objects—Using one's hands and arms in handling, installing, forming, positioning, and moving materials, or in manipulating things. Includes the use of keyboards. Inspecting Equipment, Structures, Materials—Inspecting or diagnosing equipment, structures, or materials to identify the causes of errors or other problems or defects. Monitoring Processes, Materials, Surroundings—Monitoring and reviewing information from materials, events, or the environment, often to detect problems or to find out when things are finished. Implementing Ideas and Programs—Conducting or carrying out work procedures and activities in accord with one's own ideas or information provided through directions/instructions for purposes of installing, modifying, preparing, delivering, constructing, integrating, finishing, or completing programs, systems, structures, or products. Getting Information Needed to Do the Job—Observing, receiving, and otherwise obtaining information from all relevant sources.

Electrical and Electronics Repairers, Powerhouse, Substation, and Relay

Inspect, test, repair, or maintain electrical equipment in generating stations, substations, and in-service relays. Repairs or rebuilds circuit breakers, transformers, and lightning arresters by replacing worn parts. Inspects and tests equipment and circuits to identify malfunction or defect, using wiring diagrams and testing devices such as ohmmeters, voltmeters, or ammeters. Tests insulators and bushings of equipment by inducing voltage across insulation, using testing apparatus to calculate insulation loss. Notifies personnel of need for equipment shutdown requiring changes from normal operation to maintain service. Analyzes test data to diagnose malfunctions and evaluate effect of system modifications. Prepares reports of work performed. Repairs, replaces, and cleans equipment such as brushes, commutators, windings, bearings, relays, switches, controls, and instruments. Disconnects voltage regulators, bolts, and screws; connects replacement regulators to high-voltage lines. Paints, repairs, and maintains buildings. Sets forms and pours concrete footings for installation of heavy equipment. Tests oil in circuit breakers and transformers for dielectric strength; periodically refills.

Personality Type: Realistic. Realistic occupations frequently involve work activities that include practical, hands-on problems and solutions. They often deal with plants, animals, and real-world materials like wood, tools, and machinery. Many of the occupations require working outside and do not involve a lot of paperwork or working closely with others.

Abilities: Wrist-Finger Speed—The ability to make fast, simple, repeated movements of the fingers, hands, and wrists. Deductive Reasoning—The ability to apply general rules to specific problems to come up with logical answers. Involves deciding if an answer makes sense. Near Vision—The ability to see details of objects at a close range. Information Ordering—The ability to correctly follow a given rule or set of rules in order to arrange things or actions in a certain order. The things or actions can include numbers, letters, words, pictures, procedures, sentences, and mathematical or logical operations. Manual Dexterity—The ability to quickly make coordinated movements of one hand, a hand together with its arm, or two hands, to grasp, manipulate, or assemble objects. Finger Dexterity—The ability to make precisely coordinated movements of the fingers of one or both hands to grasp, manipulate, or assemble very small objects.

Skills: Testing—Conducting tests to determine whether equipment, software, or procedures are operating as expected. Equipment Maintenance—Performing routine maintenance and determining when and what kind of maintenance is needed. Repairing—Repairing machines or systems, using the needed tools. Troubleshooting—Determining what is causing an operating error and deciding what to do about it. Problem Identification—Identifying the nature of problems.

Generalized Work Activities: Inspecting Equipment, Structures, Materials—Inspecting or diagnosing equipment, structures, or materials to identify the causes of errors or other problems or defects. Repairing and Maintaining Electrical Equipment—Fixing, servicing, adjusting, regulating, calibrating, fine-tuning, or testing machines, devices, and equipment that operate primarily on the basis of electrical or electronic, not mechanical, principles. Monitoring Processes, Materials, Surroundings—Monitoring and reviewing information from materials, events, or the environment, often to detect problems or to find out when things are finished. Getting Information Needed to Do the Job—Observing, receiving, and otherwise obtaining information from all relevant sources. Analyzing Data or Information—Identifying underlying principles, reasons, or facts by breaking down information or data into separate parts.

Electrical Parts Reconditioners

Recondition and rebuild salvaged electrical parts of equipment. Wind new coils on armatures of used generators and motors. Solders ends of coils to commutator segments. Cuts insulating material to fit slots on armature core; places material in bottom of core slots. Winds new coils on armatures of generators and motors. Replaces broken and defective parts. Disassembles salvaged equipment used in electric power systems such as air circuit breakers and lightning arresters, using hand tools; discards nonrepairable parts. Cleans and polishes parts, using solvent and buffing wheel. Bolts porcelain insulators to wood parts to assemble hot stools. Solders, wraps, and coats wires to ensure proper insulation. Inserts and hammers ready-made coils in place. Tests armatures and motors to ensure proper operation.

Personality Type: Realistic. Realistic occupations frequently involve work activities that include practical, hands-on problems and solutions. They often deal with plants, animals, and real-world materials like wood, tools, and machinery. Many of the occupations require working outside and do not involve a lot of paperwork or working closely with others.

Abilities: Finger Dexterity—The ability to make precisely coordinated movements of the fingers of one or both hands to grasp, manipulate, or assemble very small objects. Arm-Hand Steadiness—The ability to keep the hand and arm steady while making an arm movement or while holding the arm and hand in one position. Problem Sensitivity—The ability to tell when something is wrong or is likely to go wrong. Does not involve solving the problem, only recognizing there is a problem. Explosive Strength—The ability to use short bursts of muscle force to propel oneself, as in jumping or sprinting, or to throw an object.

Skills: Repairing—Repairing machines or systems, using the needed tools. Equipment Selection—Determining the kind of tools and equipment needed to do a job. Installation—Installing equipment, machines, wiring, or programs to meet specifications. Testing—Conducting tests to determine whether equipment, software, or procedures are operating as expected. Product Inspection—Inspecting and evaluating the quality of products.

Generalized Work Activities: Handling and Moving Objects—Using one's hands and arms in handling, installing, forming, positioning, and moving materials, or in manipulating things. Includes the use of keyboards. Performing General Physical Activities—Performing physical activities that require moving one's whole body, such as in climbing, lifting, balancing, walking, and stooping. Performing activities that often also require considerable use of the arms and legs, such as in the physical handling of materials. Inspecting Equipment, Structures, Materials—Inspecting or diagnosing equipment, structures, or materials to identify the causes of errors or other problems or defects. Repairing and Maintaining Mechanical Equipment—Fixing, servicing, aligning, setting up, adjusting, and testing machines, devices, moving parts, and equipment that operate primarily on the basis of mechanical, not electronic, principles. Controlling Machines and Processes—Using either control mechanisms or direct physical activity to operate machines or processes. Does not involve working with computers or vehicles.

Commercial Dispatchers

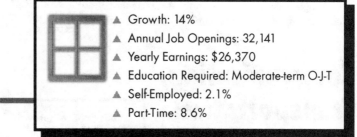

- ▲ Growth: 14%
- ▲ Annual Job Openings: 32,141
- ▲ Yearly Earnings: $26,370
- ▲ Education Required: Moderate-term O-J-T
- ▲ Self-Employed: 2.1%
- ▲ Part-Time: 8.6%

Dispatchers, Except Police, Fire, and Ambulance

Schedule and dispatch workers, work crews, equipment, or service vehicles for conveyance of materials, freight, or passengers, or for normal installation, service, or emergency repairs rendered outside the place of business. Use radio, telephone, or computer to transmit assignments. Compile statistics and reports on work progress. Determines types or amount of equipment, vehicles, materials or personnel required, according to work order or specifications. Routes or assigns workers or equipment to appropriate location, according to customer request, specifications, or needs. Relays work orders, messages, and information to or from work crews, supervisors, and field inspectors, using telephone or two-way radio. Receives or prepares work orders, according to customer request or specifications. Orders supplies and equipment; issues them to personnel. Confers with customer or supervising personnel regarding questions, problems, and requests for service or equipment. Maintains files and records regarding customer requests, work or services performed, charges, expenses, inventory, and other dispatch information.

Personality Type: Conventional. Conventional occupations frequently involve following set procedures and routines. These occupations can include working with data and details more than with ideas. Usually there is a clear line of authority to follow.

Abilities: Oral Expression—The ability to communicate information and ideas verbally so others will understand. Oral Comprehension—The ability to listen to and understand information and ideas presented verbally. Speech Clarity—The ability to speak clearly so that what is said is understandable to a listener. Written Comprehension—The ability to read and understand information and ideas presented in writing. Information Ordering—The ability to correctly follow a given rule or set of rules in order to arrange things or actions in a certain order. The things or actions can include numbers, letters, words, pictures, procedures, sentences, and mathematical or logical operations. Near Vision—The ability to see details of objects at a close range.

Skills: Active Listening—Listening to what other people are saying; asking questions as appropriate. Speaking—Talking to others to effectively convey information. Coordination—Adjusting actions in relation to others' actions. Writing—Communicating effectively with others in writing as indicated by the needs of the audience.

Generalized Work Activities: Communicating with Other Workers—Providing information to supervisors, fellow workers, and subordinates. This information can be exchanged face-to-face, in writing, or via telephone/electronic transfer. Coordinating Work and Activities of Others—Coordinating members of a work group to accomplish tasks. Getting Information Needed to Do the Job—Observing, receiving, and otherwise obtaining information from all relevant sources. Documenting/Recording Information—Entering, transcribing, recording, storing, or maintaining information in either written form or by electronic/magnetic recording. Communicating with Persons Outside Organization—Communicating with persons outside the organization. Representing the organization to customers, the public, government, and other external sources. Exchanging information face-to-face, in writing, or via telephone/electronic transfer.

Communication, Transportation, and Utilities Operations Managers

▲ Growth: 19%
▲ Annual Job Openings: 25,388
▲ Yearly Earnings: $52,810
▲ Education Required: Work experience, plus degree
▲ Self-Employed: 0%
▲ Part-Time: 6.1%

Storage and Distribution Managers

Plan, direct, and coordinate the storage and distribution operations within an organization. Plan, direct, and coordinate the activities of organizations that are engaged in storing and distributing materials and products. Develops and implements plans for facility modification or expansion, such as equipment purchases or changes in space allocation or structural design. Confers with department heads to coordinate warehouse activities such as production, sales, records control, and purchasing. Negotiates contracts, settlements, and freight-handling agreements to resolve problems between foreign and domestic shippers. Inspects physical condition of warehouse and equipment; prepares work orders for testing, maintenance, or repair. Supervises the activities of workers engaged in receiving, storing, testing, and shipping products or materials. Reviews invoices, work orders, consumption reports, and demand forecasts to estimate peak delivery periods and to issue work assignments. Interviews, selects, and trains warehouse and supervisory personnel. Schedules air or surface pickup, delivery, or distribution of products or materials. Prepares or directs preparation of correspondence, reports, and operations, maintenance, and safety manuals. Establishes standard and emergency operating procedures for receiving, handling, storing, shipping, or salvaging products or materials. Interacts with customers or shippers to solicit new business, to answer questions about services offered or required, and to investigate complaints. Examines products or materials to estimate quantities or weight and type of container required for storage or transport. Examines invoices and shipping manifests for conformity to tariff and customs regulations; contacts customs officials to effect release of shipments. Plans, develops, and implements warehouse safety and security programs and activities.

Personality Type: Enterprising. Enterprising occupations frequently involve starting up and carrying out projects. These occupations can involve leading people and making many decisions. They sometimes require risk taking and often deal with business.

Abilities: Oral Comprehension—The ability to listen to and understand information and ideas presented verbally. Written Comprehension—The ability to read and understand information and ideas presented in writing. Oral Expression—The ability to communicate information and ideas verbally so others will understand. Written Expression—The ability to communicate information and ideas in writing so others will understand. Problem Sensitivity—The ability to tell when something is wrong or is likely to go wrong. Does not involve solving the problem, only recognizing there is a problem.

Skills: Implementation Planning—Developing approaches for implementing an idea. Problem Identification—Identifying the nature of problems. Idea Generation—Generating a number of different approaches to problems. Speaking—Talking to others to effectively convey information. Management of Personnel Resources—Motivating, developing, and directing people as they work, identifying the best people for the job. Negotiation—Bringing others together and trying to reconcile differences.

Generalized Work Activities: Communicating with Other Workers—Providing information to supervisors, fellow workers, and subordinates. This information can be exchanged face-to-face, in writing, or via telephone/electronic transfer. Coordinating Work and Activities of Others—Coordinating members of a work group to accomplish tasks. Scheduling Work and Activities—Scheduling events, programs, activities, and the work of others. Estimating Needed Characteristics—Estimating the characteristics of materials, products, events, or information; estimating sizes, distances, and quantities; determining time, costs, resources, or

materials needed to perform a work activity. Guiding, Directing, and Motivating Subordinates—Providing guidance and direction to subordinates, including setting performance standards and monitoring subordinates.

Transportation Managers

Plan, direct, and coordinate the transportation operations within an organization or the activities of organizations that provide transportation services. Inspects or oversees repairs and maintenance to equipment, vehicles, and facilities to enforce standards for safety, efficiency, cleanliness, and appearance. Enforces compliance of operations personnel with administrative policies, procedures, safety rules, and government regulations. Confers and cooperates with management and other coworkers in formulating and implementing administrative, operational, and customer relations policies and procedures. Analyzes expenditures and other financial reports to develop plans, policies, and budgets for increasing profits and improving services. Oversees activities relating to dispatching, routing, and tracking transportation vehicles such as aircraft and railroad cars. Prepares management recommendations such as need for increasing fares or tariffs or need for expanding or changing existing schedules. Conducts investigations in cooperation with government agencies to determine causes of transportation accidents and to improve safety procedures. Reviews transportation schedules and worker assignments and routes to ensure compliance with standards for personnel selection, safety, and union contract terms. Oversees process of investigating and responding to customer or shipper complaints relating to operations department. Directs and coordinates, through subordinates, activities of operations department, to obtain use of equipment, facilities, and human resources. Acts as organization representative before commissions or regulatory bodies during hearings on matters such as increasing rates and changing routes and schedules. Oversees workers who assign tariff classifications and prepare billing according to mode of transportation and destination of shipment. Oversees procurement process, including research and testing of equipment, vendor contacts, and approval of requisitions. Negotiates and authorizes contracts with equipment and materials suppliers. Participates in union contract negotiations and settlement of grievances.

Personality Type: Enterprising. Enterprising occupations frequently involve starting up and carrying out projects. These occupations can involve leading people and making many decisions. They sometimes require risk taking and often deal with business.

Abilities: Oral Expression—The ability to communicate information and ideas verbally so others will understand. Problem Sensitivity—The ability to tell when something is wrong or is likely to go wrong. Does not involve solving the problem, only recognizing there is a problem. Oral Comprehension—The ability to listen to and understand information and ideas presented verbally. Written Comprehension—The ability to read and understand information and ideas presented in writing. Speech Clarity—The ability to speak clearly so that what is said is understandable to a listener.

Skills: Management of Material Resources—Obtaining and seeing to the appropriate use of equipment, facilities, and materials needed to do certain work. Speaking—Talking to others to effectively convey information.

Coordination—Adjusting actions in relation to others' actions. Critical Thinking—Using logic and analysis to identify the strengths and weaknesses of different approaches. Problem Identification—Identifying the nature of problems. Reading Comprehension—Understanding written information in work-related documents.

Generalized Work Activities: Getting Information Needed to Do the Job—Observing, receiving, and otherwise obtaining information from all relevant sources. Communicating with Other Workers—Providing information to supervisors, fellow workers, and subordinates. This information can be exchanged face-to-face, in writing, or via telephone/electronic transfer. Guiding, Directing, and Motivating Subordinates—Providing guidance and direction to subordinates, including setting performance standards and monitoring subordinates. Monitoring Processes, Materials, Surroundings—Monitoring and reviewing information from materials, events, or the environment, often to detect problems or to find out when things are finished. Evaluating Information against Standards—Evaluating information against a set of standards and verifying that it is correct. Monitoring and Controlling Resources—Monitoring and controlling resources and overseeing the spending of money.

Computer Engineers

- ▲ Growth: 108%
- ▲ Annual Job Openings: 81,337
- ▲ Yearly Earnings: $61,910
- ▲ Education Required: Bachelor's degree
- ▲ Self-Employed: 4.1%
- ▲ Part-Time: 5.7%

Computer Software Engineers, Applications

Develop, create, and modify general computer applications software or specialized utility programs.

Analyze user needs and develop software solutions. Design or customize software for client use with the aim of optimizing operational efficiency. Analyze and design databases within an application area, working individually or coordinating database development as part of a team. Develops and directs software-system testing procedures, programming, and documentation.

Consults with customer concerning maintenance of software system. Specifies power supply requirements and configuration. Enters data into computer terminal to store, retrieve, and manipulate data for analysis of system capabilities and requirements. Recommends purchase of equipment to control dust, temperature, and humidity in area of system installation. Trains customers to use new or modified equipment. Monitors functioning of equipment to ensure system operates in conformance with specifications. Consults with engineering staff to evaluate interface between hardware and software and operational and performance requirements of overall system. Evaluates factors such as reporting formats required, cost constraints, and need for security restrictions to determine hardware configuration. Confers with data processing and project managers to obtain information on limitations and capabilities for data processing projects. Formulates and designs software system, using scientific analysis and mathematical models to predict and measure outcome and consequences of design. Analyzes information to determine, recommend, and plan layout for type of computers and for peripheral equipment modifications to existing systems. Analyzes software requirements to determine feasibility of design within time and cost constraints. Coordinates installation of software system.

Personality Type: Investigative. Investigative occupations frequently involve working with ideas and require an extensive amount of thinking. These occupations can involve searching for facts and figuring out problems mentally.

Abilities: Written Comprehension—The ability to read and understand information and ideas presented in writing. Inductive Reasoning—The ability to combine separate pieces of information, or specific answers to problems, to form general rules or conclusions. Includes coming up with a logical explanation for why a series of seemingly unrelated events occur together. Oral Comprehension—The ability to listen to and understand information and ideas presented verbally. Oral Expression—The ability to communicate information and ideas verbally so others will understand. Written Expression—The ability to communicate information and ideas in writing so others will

understand. Mathematical Reasoning—The ability to understand and organize a problem and then select a mathematical method or formula to solve the problem.

Skills: Operations Analysis—Analyzing needs and product requirements to create a design. Mathematics—Using mathematics to solve problems. Information Organization—Finding ways to structure or classify multiple pieces of information. Programming—Writing computer programs for various purposes. Troubleshooting—Determining what is causing an operating error and deciding what to do about it. Science—Using scientific methods to solve problems.

Generalized Work Activities: Interacting with Computers—Controlling computer functions by using programs, setting up functions, writing software, or otherwise communicating with computer systems. Providing Consultation and Advice to Others—Providing consultation and expert advice to management or other groups on technical, systems-related, or process-related topics. Updating and Using Job-Relevant Knowledge—Keeping up-to-date technically and knowing the functions of one's own job and related jobs. Drafting and Specifying Technical Devices—Providing documentation, detailed instructions, drawings, or specifications to inform others about how devices, parts, equipment, or structures are to be fabricated, constructed, assembled, modified, maintained, or used. Thinking Creatively—Originating, inventing, designing, or creating new applications, ideas, relationships, systems, or products, including artistic contributions.

Computer Software Engineers, Systems Software

Research, design, develop, and test operating systems-level software, compilers, and network distribution software for medical, industrial, military, communications, aerospace, business, scientific, and general computing applications. Set operational specifications; formulate and analyze software requirements. Apply principles and techniques of

computer science, engineering, and mathematical analysis. Recommends purchase of equipment to control dust, temperature, and humidity in area of system installation. Consults with customer concerning maintenance of software system. Formulates and designs software system, using scientific analysis and mathematical models to predict and measure outcome and consequences of design. Confers with data processing and project managers to obtain information on limitations and capabilities for data processing projects. Develops and directs software-system testing procedures, programming, and documentation. Coordinates installation of software system. Monitors functioning of equipment to ensure system operates in conformance with specifications. Enters data into computer terminal to store, retrieve, and manipulate data for analysis of system capabilities and requirements. Analyzes software requirements to determine feasibility of design within time and cost constraints. Trains others to use new or modified equipment. Consults with engineering staff to evaluate interface between hardware and software. Consults with engineering staff to evaluate operational and performance requirements of overall system. Evaluates factors such as reporting formats required, cost constraints, and need for security restrictions, to determine hardware configuration. Analyzes information to determine, recommend, and plan layout for type of computers and peripheral equipment modifications to existing systems. Specifies power supply requirements and configuration.

Personality Type: Investigative. Investigative occupations frequently involve working with ideas and require an extensive amount of thinking. These occupations can involve searching for facts and figuring out problems mentally.

Abilities: Written Comprehension—The ability to read and understand information and ideas presented in writing. Inductive Reasoning—The ability to combine separate pieces of information, or specific answers to problems, to form general rules or conclusions. Includes coming up with a logical explanation for why a series of seemingly unrelated events occur together. Oral Comprehension—The ability to listen to and understand information and ideas presented verbally. Written Expression—The ability to communicate information and ideas in writing so others will understand. Mathematical Reasoning—The ability to understand and organize a problem and then select a mathematical method or formula to solve the problem. Oral Expression—The ability to communicate information and ideas verbally so others will understand.

Skills: Operations Analysis—Analyzing needs and product requirements to create a design. Mathematics—Using mathematics to solve problems. Programming—Writing computer programs for various purposes. Information Organization—Finding ways to structure or classify multiple pieces of information. Troubleshooting—Determining what is causing an operating error and deciding what to do about it. Science—Using scientific methods to solve problems.

Generalized Work Activities: Interacting with Computers—Controlling computer functions by using programs, setting up functions, writing software, or otherwise communicating with computer systems. Providing Consultation and Advice to Others—Providing consultation and expert advice to management or other groups on technical, systems-related, or process-related topics. Updating and Using Job-Relevant Knowledge—Keeping up-to-date technically and knowing the functions of one's own job and related jobs. Drafting and Specifying Technical Devices—Providing documentation, detailed instructions, drawings, or specifications to inform others about how devices, parts, equipment, or structures are to be fabricated, constructed, assembled, modified, maintained, or used. Thinking Creatively—Originating, inventing, designing, or creating new applications, ideas, relationships, systems, or products, including artistic contributions.

Computer Programmers

- ▲ Growth: 30%
- ▲ Annual Job Openings: 74,773
- ▲ Yearly Earnings: $47,550
- ▲ Education Required: Bachelor's degree
- ▲ Self-Employed: 4.8%
- ▲ Part-Time: 7.3%

Computer Programmers

Convert project specifications and statements of problems and procedures to detailed logical flow charts for coding into computer language. Develop and write computer programs to store, locate, and retrieve specific documents, data, and information. Program Web sites. Prepares or receives detailed workflow chart and diagram to illustrate sequence of steps to describe input, output, and logical operation. Collaborates with computer manufacturers and other users to develop new programming methods. Converts detailed, logical flow chart to language processible by computer. Develops programs from workflow charts or diagrams, considering computer storage capacity, speed, and intended use of output data. Consults with managerial and engineering and technical personnel to clarify program intent, identify problems, and suggest changes. Writes instructions to guide operating personnel during production runs. Prepares records and reports. Assigns, coordinates, and reviews work and activities of programming personnel. Trains subordinates in programming and program coding. Analyzes, reviews, and rewrites programs, using workflow chart and diagram, applying knowledge of computer capabilities, subject matter, and symbolic logic. Revises or directs revision of existing programs to increase operating efficiency or adapt to new requirements. Compiles and writes documentation of program development and subsequent revisions. Resolves symbolic formulations, prepares flow charts and block diagrams, and encodes resultant equations for processing. Assists computer operators or system analysts in resolving problems with running computer program.

Personality Type: Investigative. Investigative occupations frequently involve working with ideas and require an extensive amount of thinking. These occupations can involve searching for facts and figuring out problems mentally.

Abilities: Oral Expression—The ability to communicate information and ideas verbally so others will understand. Oral Comprehension—The ability to listen to and understand information and ideas presented verbally. Written Comprehension—The ability to read and understand information and ideas presented in writing. Written Expression—The ability to communicate information and ideas in writing so others will understand. Deductive Reasoning—The ability to apply general rules to specific problems to come up with logical answers. Involves deciding if an answer makes sense. Mathematical Reasoning—The ability to understand and organize a problem and then select a mathematical method or formula to solve the problem.

Skills: Programming—Writing computer programs for various purposes. Writing—Communicating effectively with others in writing as indicated by the needs of the audience. Critical Thinking—Using logic and analysis to identify the strengths and weaknesses of different approaches. Reading Comprehension—Understanding written information in work-related documents. Information Organization—Finding ways to structure or classify multiple pieces of information.

Generalized Work Activities: Interacting with Computers—Controlling computer functions by using programs, setting up functions, writing software, or otherwise communicating with computer systems. Providing Consultation and Advice to Others—Providing consultation and expert advice to management or other groups on technical, systems-related, or process-related topics. Getting Information Needed to Do the Job—Observing, receiving, and otherwise obtaining information from all relevant sources.

Communicating with Other Workers—Providing information to supervisors, fellow workers, and subordinates. This information can be exchanged face-to-face, in writing, or via telephone/electronic transfer.

Computer Scientists

- ▲ Growth: 118%
- ▲ Annual Job Openings: 27,942
- ▲ Yearly Earnings: $46,670
- ▲ Education Required: Bachelor's degree
- ▲ Self-Employed: 2.7%
- ▲ Part-Time: 5.7%

Network Systems and Data Communications Analysts

Analyze, design, test, and evaluate network systems such as local area networks (LAN), wide area networks (WAN), Internet, intranet, and other data communications systems. Perform network modeling, analysis, and planning. Research and recommend network and data communications hardware and software. Supervise computer programmers. Includes telecommunications specialists who deal with the interfacing of computer and communications equipment. Conducts survey to determine user needs. Visits vendors to learn about available products or services. Trains others in use of equipment. Develops and writes procedures for installation and use of communications hardware and software; solves related problems. Monitors system performance. Tests and evaluates hardware and software to determine efficiency, reliability, and compatibility with existing system. Identifies areas of operation which need upgraded equipment such as modems, fiber optic cables, and telephone wires. Reads technical manuals and brochures to determine equipment which meets establishment requirements. Analyzes test data and recommends

hardware or software for purchase. Assists users in identifying and solving data communication problems.

Personality Type: Investigative. Investigative occupations frequently involve working with ideas and require an extensive amount of thinking. These occupations can involve searching for facts and figuring out problems mentally.

Abilities: Written Comprehension—The ability to read and understand information and ideas presented in writing. Oral Expression—The ability to communicate information and ideas verbally so others will understand. Near Vision—The ability to see details of objects at a close range. Speech Clarity—The ability to speak clearly so that what is said is understandable to a listener. Oral Comprehension—The ability to listen to and understand information and ideas presented verbally. Written Expression—The ability to communicate information and ideas in writing so others will understand.

Skills: Active Learning—Working with new material or information to grasp its implications. Operations Analysis—Analyzing needs and product requirements to create a design. Testing—Conducting tests to determine whether equipment, software, or procedures are operating as expected.

Generalized Work Activities: Interacting with Computers—Controlling computer functions by using programs, setting up functions, writing software, or otherwise communicating with computer systems. Updating and Using Job-Relevant Knowledge—Keeping up-to-date technically and knowing the functions of one's own job and related jobs. Providing Consultation and Advice to Others—Providing consultation and expert advice to management or other groups on technical, systems-related, or process-related topics. Getting Information Needed to Do the Job—Observing, receiving, and otherwise obtaining information from all relevant sources. Analyzing Data or Information—Identifying underlying principles, reasons, or facts by breaking down information or data into separate parts.

Computer Support Specialists

- ▲ Growth: 102%
- ▲ Annual Job Openings: 113,041
- ▲ Yearly Earnings: $37,120
- ▲ Education Required: Bachelor's degree
- ▲ Self-Employed: Not available
- ▲ Part-Time: Not available

Computer Support Specialists

Provide technical assistance to computer-system users. Answer questions or resolve computer problems for clients, in person, via telephone, or from remote location. Provide assistance concerning the use of computer hardware and software, including printing, installation, word processing, electronic mail, and operating systems. Inspects equipment and reads order sheets to prepare for delivery to users. Confers with staff, users, and management to determine requirements for new systems or modifications. Develops training materials and procedures; conducts training programs. Refers major hardware or software problems or defective products to vendors or technicians for service. Maintains record of daily data communication transactions, problems and remedial action taken, and installation activities. Conducts office-automation feasibility studies, including workflow analysis, space design, and cost comparison analysis. Supervises and coordinates workers engaged in solving problems and in monitoring and installing data-communication equipment and software. Tests and monitors software, hardware, and peripheral equipment to evaluate use, effectiveness, and adequacy of product for user. Prepares evaluations of software and hardware; submits recommendations to management for review. Enters commands and observes system functioning to verify correct operations and detect errors. Reads technical manuals, confers with users, and conducts computer diagnostics to determine nature of problems and provide technical assistance. Installs and performs minor repairs to hardware, software, and peripheral equipment, following design or installation specifications. Reads trade magazines and technical manuals and attends conferences and seminars to maintain knowledge of hardware and software.

Personality Type: Investigative. Investigative occupations frequently involve working with ideas and require an extensive amount of thinking. These occupations can involve searching for facts and figuring out problems mentally.

Abilities: Written Comprehension—The ability to read and understand information and ideas presented in writing. Oral Expression—The ability to communicate information and ideas verbally so others will understand. Oral Comprehension—The ability to listen to and understand information and ideas presented verbally. Problem Sensitivity—The ability to tell when something is wrong or is likely to go wrong. Does not involve solving the problem, only recognizing there is a problem. Near Vision—The ability to see details of objects at a close range. Speech Clarity—The ability to speak clearly so that what is said is understandable to a listener.

Skills: Testing—Conducting tests to determine whether equipment, software, or procedures are operating as expected. Operations Analysis—Analyzing needs and product requirements to create a design. Troubleshooting—Determining what is causing an operating error and deciding what to do about it. Instructing—Teaching others how to do something. Problem Identification—Identifying the nature of problems.

Generalized Work Activities: Interacting with Computers—Controlling computer functions by using programs, setting up functions, writing software, or otherwise communicating with computer systems. Getting Information Needed to Do the Job—Observing, receiving, and otherwise obtaining infor-

mation from all relevant sources. Updating and Using Job-Relevant Knowledge—Keeping up-to-date technically and knowing the functions of one's own job and related jobs. Repairing and Maintaining Electrical Equipment—Fixing, servicing, adjusting, regulating, calibrating, fine-tuning, or testing machines, devices, and equipment that operate primarily on the basis of electrical or electronic, not mechanical, principles. Making Decisions and Solving Problems—Combining, evaluating, and analyzing information and data to make decisions and solve problems. Involves making decisions about the relative importance of information and choosing the best solution. Identifying Objects, Actions, and Events—Identifying information received by making estimates or categorizations, recognizing differences or similarities, or sensing changes in circumstances or events.

Conservation Scientists and Foresters

▲ Growth: 18%
▲ Annual Job Openings: 3,328
▲ Yearly Earnings: $42,750
▲ Education Required: Bachelor's degree
▲ Self-Employed: 2.4%
▲ Part-Time: 6.6%

Foresters

Manage forested lands for economic, recreational, and conservation purposes. Inventory the type, amount, and location of standing timber, appraise the timber's worth, negotiate the purchase, and draw up contracts for procurement. Determine how to conserve wildlife habitats, creek beds, water quality, and soil stability, and how best to comply with environmental regulations. Devise plans for planting and growing new trees, monitor trees for healthy growth, and determine the best time for harvesting. Develop forest management plans for public and privately owned forested lands. Supervises activities of other forestry workers. Researches forest propagation and culture affecting growth rates, yield, duration, seed production,

growth viability, and germination of different tree species. Analyzes forest conditions to determine reason for prevalence of different variety of trees. Maps forest areas and estimates standing timber and future growth. Participates in environmental studies and prepares environmental reports. Plans and directs construction and maintenance of recreation facilities, fire towers, trails, roads, and fire breaks. Plans cutting programs to ensure continuous production or to assist timber companies in achieving production goals. Suggests methods of processing wood for various uses. Investigates adaptability of different tree species to new environmental conditions such as soil type, climate, and altitude. Conducts public educational programs on forest care and conservation. Directs suppression of forest fires; fights forest fires. Plans and directs forestation and reforestation projects. Determines methods of cutting and removing timber with minimum waste and environmental damage. Studies classification, life history, light and soil requirements, and resistance to disease and insects of different tree species. Manages tree nurseries; thins forest to encourage natural growth of sprouts or seedlings of desired varieties. Assists in planning and implementing projects for control of floods, soil erosion, tree diseases, infestation, and forest fire. Develops techniques for measuring and identifying trees. Advises landowners on forestry management techniques.

Personality Type: Realistic. Realistic occupations frequently involve work activities that include practical, hands-on problems and solutions. They often deal with plants, animals, and real-world materials like wood, tools, and machinery. Many of the occupations require working outside and do not involve a lot of paperwork or working closely with others.

Abilities: Oral Expression—The ability to communicate information and ideas verbally so others will understand. Speech Clarity—The ability to speak clearly so that what is said is understandable to a listener. Deductive Reasoning—The ability to apply general rules to specific problems to come up with logical answers. Involves deciding if an answer makes sense.

Skills: Reading Comprehension—Understanding written information in work-related documents. Solution Appraisal—Observing and evaluating the outcomes of a problem solution to identify lessons learned or to redirect efforts. Systems Perception—Determining when important changes have occurred in a system or are likely to occur. Implementation Planning—Developing approaches for implementing an idea.

Generalized Work Activities: Getting Information Needed to Do the Job—Observing, receiving, and otherwise obtaining information from all relevant sources. Analyzing Data or Information—Identifying underlying principles, reasons, or facts by breaking down information or data into separate parts. Identifying Objects, Actions, and Events—Identifying information received by making estimates or categorizations, recognizing differences or similarities, or sensing changes

in circumstances or events. Monitoring Processes, Materials, Surroundings—Monitoring and reviewing information from materials, events, or the environment, often to detect problems or to find out when things are finished. Developing Objectives and Strategies—Establishing long-range objectives and specifying the strategies and actions to achieve these objectives.

Park Naturalists

Plan, develop, and conduct programs to inform public of historical, natural, and scientific features of national, state, or local park. Takes photographs and motion pictures to illustrate lectures and publications and to develop displays. Conducts field trips to point out scientific, historic, and natural features of park. Interviews specialists in desired fields to obtain and develop data for park information programs. Confers with park staff to determine subjects to be presented to public. Prepares and presents illustrated lectures of park features. Surveys park to determine distribution and abundance of fauna and flora. Maintains official park photographic and information files. Performs emergency duties to protect human life, government property, and natural features of park. Plans and organizes activities of seasonal staff members. Surveys park to determine forest conditions. Constructs historical, scientific, and nature displays for visitor center. Plans and develops audiovisual devices for public programs.

Personality Type: Social. Social occupations frequently involve working with, communicating with, and teaching people. These occupations often involve helping or providing service to others.

Abilities: Speech Clarity—The ability to speak clearly so that what is said is understandable to a listener. Oral Comprehension—The ability to listen to and understand information and ideas presented verbally. Oral Expression—The ability to communicate information and ideas verbally so others will understand. Written Expression—The ability to communicate information and ideas in writing so others will understand.

Skills: Speaking—Talking to others to effectively convey information. Information Gathering—Knowing how to find information and identifying essential information. Service Orientation—Actively looking for ways to help people. Active Listening—Listening to what other people are saying; asking questions as appropriate. Implementation Planning—Developing approaches for implementing an idea. Reading Comprehension—Understanding written information in work-related documents. Problem Identification—Identifying the nature of problems.

Generalized Work Activities: Getting Information Needed to Do the Job—Observing, receiving, and otherwise obtaining information from all relevant sources. Communicating with Persons Outside Organization—Communicating with persons outside the organization. Representing the organization to customers, the public, government, and other external sources. Exchanging information face-to-face, in writing, or via telephone/electronic transfer. Teaching Others—Identifying educational needs, developing formal training programs or classes, and teaching or instructing others. Performing for/Working with Public—Performing for people or dealing directly with the public, including serving persons in restaurants and stores and receiving clients or guests. Processing Information—Compiling, coding, categorizing, calculating, tabulating, auditing, verifying, or processing information or data. Analyzing Data or Information—Identifying underlying principles, reasons, or facts by breaking down information or data into separate parts. Identifying Objects, Actions, and Events—Identifying information received by making estimates or categorizations, recognizing differences or similarities, or sensing changes in circumstances or events.

Range Managers

Research or study range-land management practices to provide sustained production of forage, livestock, and wildlife. Develops methods for controlling poisonous plants in range lands. Develops improved practices for range reseeding. Studies forage plants and their growth requirements to determine varieties best suited to particular range. Studies range lands to determine number and kind of livestock that can be most profitably grazed. Plans and directs construction

of range improvements such as fencing, corrals, stock-watering reservoirs and soil-erosion control structures. Develops methods for protecting range from fire and rodent damage. Studies range lands to determine best grazing seasons. Plans and directs maintenance of range improvements.

Personality Type: Investigative. Investigative occupations frequently involve working with ideas and require an extensive amount of thinking. These occupations can involve searching for facts and figuring out problems mentally.

Abilities: Oral Expression—The ability to communicate information and ideas verbally so others will understand. Inductive Reasoning—The ability to combine separate pieces of information, or specific answers to problems, to form general rules or conclusions. Includes coming up with a logical explanation for why a series of seemingly unrelated events occur together. Problem Sensitivity—The ability to tell when something is wrong or is likely to go wrong. Does not involve solving the problem, only recognizing there is a problem. Speech Clarity—The ability to speak clearly so that what is said is understandable to a listener. Deductive Reasoning—The ability to apply general rules to specific problems to come up with logical answers. Involves deciding if an answer makes sense.

Skills: Judgment and Decision Making—Weighing the relative costs and benefits of a potential action. Implementation Planning—Developing approaches for implementing an idea. Idea Evaluation—Evaluating the likely success of an idea in relation to the demands of the situation. Information Gathering—Knowing how to find information and identifying essential information. Critical Thinking—Using logic and analysis to identify the strengths and weaknesses of different approaches. Identifying Downstream Consequences—Determining the long-term outcomes of a change in operations. Identification of Key Causes—Identifying the things that must be changed to achieve a goal.

Generalized Work Activities: Making Decisions and Solving Problems—Combining, evaluating, and analyzing information and data to make decisions and solve problems. Involves making decisions about the relative importance of information and choosing the best solution. Analyzing Data or Information—Identifying underlying principles, reasons, or facts by breaking down information or data into separate parts. Getting Information Needed to Do the Job—Observing, receiving, and otherwise obtaining information from all relevant sources. Estimating Needed Characteristics—Estimating the characteristics of materials, products, events, or information; estimating sizes, distances, and quantities; determining time, costs, resources, or materials needed to perform a work activity. Developing Objectives and Strategies—Establishing long-range objectives and specifying the strategies and actions to achieve these objectives.

Soil Conservationists

Plan and develop coordinated practices for soil erosion control, soil and water conservation, and sound land use. Develops plans for conservation, such as conservation cropping systems, woodlands management, pasture planning and engineering systems. Discusses conservation plans, problems, and alternative solutions with land users, applying knowledge of agronomy, soil science, forestry, or agricultural sciences. Computes design specification for implementation of conservation practices, using survey and field information, technical guides, engineering manuals, and calculator. Develops or participates in environmental studies. Conducts surveys and investigations of various land uses such as agriculture, construction, forestry, or mining. Computes cost estimates of different conservation practices based on needs of land users, maintenance requirements, and life expectancy of practices. Revisits land users to view implemented land-use practices and plans. Surveys property to mark locations and measurements, using surveying instruments. Analyzes results of investigations to determine measures needed to maintain or restore proper soil management. Plans soil management practices such as crop rotation, reforestation, permanent vegetation, contour plowing, or terracing, to maintain soil and conserve water. Monitors projects during and after construction to ensure that projects conform to design specifications.

Personality Type: Investigative. Investigative occupations frequently involve working with ideas and require

an extensive amount of thinking. These occupations can involve searching for facts and figuring out problems mentally.

Abilities: Deductive Reasoning—The ability to apply general rules to specific problems to come up with logical answers. Involves deciding if an answer makes sense. Oral Expression—The ability to communicate information and ideas verbally so others will understand. Problem Sensitivity—The ability to tell when something is wrong or is likely to go wrong. Does not involve solving the problem, only recognizing there is a problem. Oral Comprehension—The ability to listen to and understand information and ideas presented verbally. Inductive Reasoning—The ability to combine separate pieces of information, or specific answers to problems, to form general rules or conclusions. Includes coming up with a logical explanation for why a series of seemingly unrelated events occur together.

Skills: Implementation Planning—Developing approaches for implementing an idea. Solution Appraisal—Observing and evaluating the outcomes of a problem solution to identify lessons learned or to redirect efforts. Science—Using scientific methods to solve problems.

Generalized Work Activities: Getting Information Needed to Do the Job—Observing, receiving, and otherwise obtaining information from all relevant sources. Providing Consultation and Advice to Others—Providing consultation and expert advice to management or other groups on technical, systems-related, or process-related topics. Implementing Ideas and Programs—Conducting or carrying out work procedures and activities in accord with one's own ideas or information provided through directions/instructions for purposes of installing, modifying, preparing, delivering, constructing, integrating, finishing, or completing programs, systems, structures, or products. Making Decisions and Solving Problems—Combining, evaluating, and analyzing information and data to make decisions and solve problems. Involves making decisions about the relative importance of information and choosing the best solution. Analyzing Data or Information—Identifying underlying principles, reasons, or facts by breaking down information or data into separate parts.

Construction and Building Inspectors

- ▲ Growth: 16%
- ▲ Annual Job Openings: 3,515
- ▲ Yearly Earnings: $37,540
- ▲ Education Required: Work experience in a related occupation
- ▲ Self-Employed: 1.6%
- ▲ Part-Time: 2.9%

Construction and Building Inspectors

Inspect structures, using engineering skills to determine structural soundness and compliance with specifications, building codes, and other regulations. Inspections may be general in nature or may be limited to a specific area, such as electrical systems or plumbing. Issues violation notices, stop-work orders, and permits for construction and occupancy. Computes estimates of work completed and approves payment for contractors. Evaluates premises for cleanliness, including garbage disposal and lack of vermin infestation. Maintains daily logs, inventory, and inspection and construction records; prepares reports. Confers with owners, violators, and authorities to explain regulations and recommend alterations in construction or specifications. Records and notifies owners, violators, and authorities of violations of construction specifications and building codes. Approves and signs plans that meet required specifications. Measures dimensions and verifies level, alignment, and elevation of structures and fixtures to ensure compliance to building plans and codes. Reviews and interprets plans, blueprints, specifications, and construction methods to ensure compliance to legal requirements. Inspects bridges, dams, highways, building, wiring, plumbing, electrical circuits, sewer, heating system, and foundation for conformance to specifications and codes. Reviews complaints, obtains evidence, and testifies in court that construction does not conform to code.

Personality Type: Conventional. Conventional occupations frequently involve following set procedures and routines. These occupations can include working with data and details more than with ideas. Usually there is a clear line of authority to follow.

Abilities: Problem Sensitivity—The ability to tell when something is wrong or is likely to go wrong. Does not involve solving the problem, only recognizing there is a problem. Oral Expression—The ability to communicate information and ideas verbally so others will understand. Written Expression—The ability to communicate information and ideas in writing so others will understand. Written Comprehension—The ability to read and understand information and ideas presented in writing. Near Vision—The ability to see details of objects at a close range. Deductive Reasoning—The ability to apply general rules to specific problems to come up with logical answers. Involves deciding if an answer makes sense.

Skills: Product Inspection—Inspecting and evaluating the quality of products. Problem Identification—Identifying the nature of problems. Judgment and Decision Making—Weighing the relative costs and benefits of a potential action. Writing—Communicating effectively with others in writing as indicated by the needs of the audience. Identification of Key Causes—Identifying the things that must be changed to achieve a goal.

Generalized Work Activities: Inspecting Equipment, Structures, Materials—Inspecting or diagnosing equipment, structures, or materials to identify the causes of errors or other problems or defects. Getting Information Needed to Do the Job—Observing, receiving, and otherwise obtaining information from all relevant sources. Evaluating Information against Standards—Evaluating information against a set of standards and verifying that it is correct. Judging

Qualities—Making judgments about or assessing the value, importance, or quality of things, services, or other people's work. Communicating with Persons Outside Organization—Communicating with persons outside the organization. Representing the organization to customers, the public, government, and other external sources. Exchanging information face-to-face, in writing, or via telephone/electronic transfer. Identifying Objects, Actions, and Events—Identifying information received by making estimates or categorizations, recognizing differences or similarities, or sensing changes in circumstances or events.

Construction Helpers

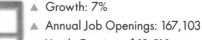

- ▲ Growth: 7%
- ▲ Annual Job Openings: 167,103
- ▲ Yearly Earnings: $19,510
- ▲ Education Required: Short-term O-J-T
- ▲ Self-Employed: 0.8%
- ▲ Part-Time: 16%

Floor Sanders and Finishers

Scrape and sand wooden floors to smooth surfaces, using floor scraper and floor sanding machine. Apply coats of finish. Applies filler compound to floor to seal wood. Scrapes and sands floor edges and areas inaccessible to floor sander, using scraper and disk-type sander. Guides machine over surface of floor until surface is smooth. Attaches sandpaper to roller of sanding machine.

Personality Type: Realistic. Realistic occupations frequently involve work activities that include practical, hands-on problems and solutions. They often deal with plants, animals, and real-world materials like wood, tools, and machinery. Many of the occupations require working outside and do not involve a lot of paperwork or working closely with others.

Abilities: Trunk Strength—The ability to use one's abdominal and lower back muscles to support part of the body repeatedly or continuously over time without giving out or fatiguing. Manual Dexterity—The ability to quickly make coordinated movements of one hand, a hand together with its arm, or two hands, to grasp, manipulate, or assemble objects. Dynamic Flexibility—The ability to quickly and repeatedly bend, stretch, twist, or reach out with the body, arms, and/or legs. Stamina—The ability to exert one's self physically over long periods of time without getting winded or out of breath. Dynamic Strength—The ability to exert muscle force repeatedly or continuously over time. This involves muscular endurance and resistance to muscle fatigue. Control Precision—The ability to quickly and repeatedly make precise adjustments in moving the controls of a machine or vehicle to exact positions.

Skills: Operation and Control—Controlling operations of equipment or systems. Product Inspection—Inspecting and evaluating the quality of products. Equipment Selection—Determining the kind of tools and equipment needed to do a job. Operation Monitoring—Watching gauges, dials, or other indicators to make sure a machine is working properly. Equipment Maintenance—Performing routine maintenance and determining when and what kind of maintenance is needed.

Generalized Work Activities: Performing General Physical Activities—Performing physical activities that require moving one's whole body, such as in climbing, lifting, balancing, walking, and stooping. Performing activities that often also require considerable use of the arms and legs, such as in the physical handling of materials. Controlling Machines and Processes—Using either control mechanisms or direct physical activity to operate machines or processes. Does not involve working with computers or vehicles. Handling and Moving Objects—Using one's hands and arms in handling, installing, forming, positioning, and moving materials, or in manipulating things. Monitoring Processes, Materials, Surroundings—Monitoring and reviewing information from materials, events, or the environment, often to detect problems or to find out when things are finished. Implementing Ideas and Programs—Conducting or carrying out work procedures and activities in accord with one's own ideas or information provided through directions/instructions for purposes of installing, modifying, preparing, delivering, constructing, integrating, finishing, or completing programs, systems, structures, or products.

Helpers—Brickmasons, Blockmasons, Stone-masons, and Tile and Marble Setters

Help brickmasons, blockmasons, stonemasons, or tile and marble setters by performing duties of lesser skill. Use, supply, or hold materials or tools. Clean work area and equipment. Erects scaffolding or other installation structures. Transports materials, tools, and machines to installation site, manually or using conveyance equipment. Mixes mortar, plaster, and grout, according to standard formulas, manually or with a machine. Selects materials for installation, following numbered sequence or drawings. Cuts materials to specified size for installation, using power saw or tile cutter. Applies caulk, sealants, or other agents to installed surface. Arranges and stores materials, machines, tools, and equipment. Modifies material-moving, mixing, grouting, grinding, polishing, or cleaning procedures according to the type of installation or materials required. Cleans installation surfaces, equipment, tools, work site, and storage areas, using water, chemical solutions, oxygen lance, or polishing machines. Removes excess grout and residue from tile or brick joints with wet sponge or trowel. Applies grout between joints of bricks or tiles, using grouting trowel. Removes damaged tile, brick, or mortar. Prepares installation surfaces, using

pliers, chipping hammers, chisels, drills, and metal wire anchors. Assists in the preparation, installation, repair, or rebuilding of tile, brick, or stone surfaces. Moves or positions marble slabs and ingot covers, using crane, hoist, or dolly. Corrects surface imperfections or fills chipped, cracked, or broken bricks or tiles, using fillers, adhesives, and grouting materials.

Personality Type: Realistic. Realistic occupations frequently involve work activities that include practical, hands-on problems and solutions. They often deal with plants, animals, and real-world materials like wood, tools, and machinery. Many of the occupations require working outside and do not involve a lot of paperwork or working closely with others.

Abilities: Static Strength—The ability to exert maximum muscle force to lift, push, pull, or carry objects. Dynamic Strength—The ability to exert muscle force repeatedly or continuously over time. This involves muscular endurance and resistance to muscle fatigue. Wrist-Finger Speed—The ability to make fast, simple, repeated movements of the fingers, hands, and wrists. Extent Flexibility—The ability to bend, stretch, twist, or reach out with the body, arms, and/or legs. Speed of Limb Movement—The ability to quickly move the arms or legs. Arm-Hand Steadiness—The ability to keep the hand and arm steady while making an arm movement or while holding the arm and hand in one position. Manual Dexterity—The ability to quickly make coordinated movements of one hand, a hand together with its arm, or two hands, to grasp, manipulate, or assemble objects.

Skills: Equipment Selection—Determining the kind of tools and equipment needed to do a job. Installation—Installing equipment, machines, wiring, or programs to meet specifications. Equipment Maintenance—Performing routine maintenance and determining when and what kind of maintenance is needed. Product Inspection—Inspecting and evaluating the quality of products. Operation and Control—Controlling operations of equipment or systems. Active Listening—Listening to what other people are saying; asking questions as appropriate.

Generalized Work Activities: Handling and Moving Objects—Using one's hands and arms in handling, installing, forming, positioning, and moving materials, or in manipulating things. Performing General Physical Activities—Performing physical activities that require moving one's whole body, such as in climbing, lifting, balancing, walking, and stooping. Performing activities that often also require considerable use of the arms and legs, such as in the physical handling of materials. Assisting and Caring for Others—Providing assistance or personal care to others. Controlling Machines and Processes—Using either control mechanisms or direct physical activity to operate machines or processes. Does not involve working with computers or vehicles. Getting Information Needed to Do the Job—Observing, receiving, and otherwise obtaining information from all relevant sources.

Helpers—Carpenters

Help carpenters by performing duties of lesser skill. Use, supply, or hold materials or tools. Cleaning work area and equipment. Drills holes in timbers or lumber. Cuts and installs insulating or sound-absorbing material. Glues and clamps edges or joints of assembled parts. Smoothes and sands surfaces to remove ridges, tool marks, glue, or caulking. Spreads adhesives on flooring to install tile or linoleum. Fastens timbers and/or lumber with glue, screws, pegs, or nails. Cuts tile or linoleum to fit. Covers surfaces with laminated plastic covering material. Selects needed tools, equipment, and materials from storage and transports items to work site. Erects scaffolding, shoring, and braces. Hews timbers. Positions and holds timbers, lumber, and paneling in place for fastening or cutting. Holds plumb bobs, sighting rods, and other equipment to aid in establishing reference points and lines. Cuts timbers, lumber, and/or paneling to specified dimensions.

Personality Type: Realistic. Realistic occupations frequently involve work activities that include practical, hands-on problems and solutions. They often deal with plants, animals, and real-world materials like wood, tools, and machinery. Many of the occupations require working outside and do not involve a lot of paperwork or working closely with others.

Abilities: Static Strength—The ability to exert maximum muscle force to lift, push, pull, or carry objects. Explosive Strength—The ability to use short bursts of muscle force to propel oneself, as in jumping or sprinting, or to throw an object. Dynamic Strength—The ability to exert muscle force repeatedly or continuously over time. This involves muscular endurance and resistance to muscle fatigue. Extent Flexibility—The ability to bend, stretch, twist, or reach out with the body, arms, and/or legs.

Skills: Equipment Selection—Determining the kind of tools and equipment needed to do a job. Installation—Installing equipment, machines, wiring, or programs to meet specifications. Coordination—Adjusting actions in relation to others' actions. Information Organization—Finding ways to structure or classify multiple pieces of information.

Generalized Work Activities: Performing General Physical Activities—Performing physical activities that require moving one's whole body, such as in climbing, lifting, balancing, walking, and stooping. Performing activities that often also require considerable use of the arms and legs, such as in the physical handling of materials. Handling and Moving Objects—Using one's hands and arms in handling, installing, forming, positioning, and moving materials, or in manipulating things. Communicating with Other Workers—Providing information to supervisors, fellow workers, and subordinates. This information can be exchanged face-to-face, in writing, or via telephone/electronic transfer. Controlling Machines and Processes—Using either control mechanisms or direct physical activity to operate machines or processes. Does not involve working with computers or vehicles. Establishing and Maintaining Relationships—Developing constructive and cooperative working relationships with others.

Helpers—Electricians

Help electricians by performing duties of lesser skill. Use, supply, or hold materials or tools. Clean work area and equipment. Raises, lowers, or positions equipment, tools, and materials for installation or use, using hoist, handline, or block and tackle. Rigs scaffolds, hoists, and shoring; erects barricades; digs trenches. Transports tools, materials, equipment, and supplies to work site, manually or using truck or handtruck. Strips insulation from wire ends, using wire-stripping pliers; attaches wires to terminals for subsequent soldering. Measures, cuts, and bends wire and conduit, using measuring instruments and hand tools. Drills holes for wiring, using power drill; pulls or pushes wiring through opening. Bolts component parts together to form tower assemblies, using hand tools. Solders electrical connections, using soldering iron. Examines electrical units for loose connections and broken insulation; tightens connections, using hand tools. Strings transmission lines or cables through ducts or conduits, underground, through equipment, or to towers. Disassembles defective electrical equipment, replaces defective or worn parts, and reassembles equipment, using hand tools. Threads conduit ends, connects couplings, and fabricates and secures conduit support brackets, using hand tools. Maintains tools and equipment, washes parts, and keeps supplies and parts in order. Trims trees and clears undergrowth along right-of-way. Traces out short circuits in wiring, using test meter. Breaks up concrete to facilitate installation or repair of equipment, using airhammer.

Personality Type: Realistic. Realistic occupations frequently involve work activities that include practical, hands-on problems and solutions. They often deal with plants, animals, and real-world materials like wood, tools, and machinery. Many of the occupations require working outside and do not involve a lot of paperwork or working closely with others.

Abilities: Manual Dexterity—The ability to quickly make coordinated movements of one hand, a hand together with its arm, or two hands, to grasp, manipulate, or assemble objects. Arm-Hand Steadiness—The ability to keep the hand and arm steady while making an arm movement or while holding the arm and hand in one position. Static Strength—The ability to exert maximum muscle force to lift, push, pull, or carry objects. Spatial Orientation—The ability to know one's location in relation to the environment, or to know where other objects are in relation to one's self. Trunk Strength—The ability to use one's abdominal and lower back muscles to support part of the body repeatedly or continuously over time without giving out or fatiguing. Near Vision—The ability to see details of objects at a close range. Information Ordering—The ability to correctly follow a given rule or set of rules in order to arrange things or actions in a certain order. The things or actions can include numbers, letters, words, pictures, procedures, sentences, and mathematical or logical operations. Explosive Strength—The ability to use short bursts of muscle force to propel oneself, as in jumping or sprinting, or to throw an object.

Skills: Equipment Selection—Determining the kind of tools and equipment needed to do a job. Equipment Maintenance—Performing routine maintenance and determining when and what kind of maintenance is needed. Installation—Installing equipment, machines, wiring, or programs to meet specifications. Mathematics—Using mathematics to solve problems.

Generalized Work Activities: Handling and Moving Objects—Using one's hands and arms in handling, installing, forming, positioning, and moving materials, or in manipulating things. Performing General Physical Activities—Performing physical activities that require moving one's whole body, such as in climbing, lifting, balancing, walking, and stooping. Performing activities that often also require considerable use of the arms and legs, such as in the physical handling of materials. Repairing and Maintaining Electrical Equipment—Fixing, servicing, adjusting, regulating, calibrating, fine-tuning, or testing machines, devices, and equipment that operate primarily on the basis of electrical or electronic, not mechanical, principles. Assisting and Caring for Others—Providing assistance or personal care to others. Identifying Objects, Actions, and Events—Identifying information received by making estimates or categorizations, recognizing differences or similarities, or sensing changes in circumstances or events. Getting Information Needed to Do the Job—Observing, receiving, and otherwise obtaining information from all relevant sources. Implementing Ideas and Programs—Conducting or carrying out work procedures and activities in accord with one's own ideas or information provided through directions/instructions for purposes of installing, modifying, preparing, delivering, constructing, integrating, finishing, or completing programs, systems, structures, or products.

Helpers—Painters, Paperhangers, Plasterers, and Stucco Masons

Help painters, paperhangers, plasterers, or stucco masons by performing duties of lesser skill. Use, supply, or hold materials or tools. Clean work area and equipment. Performs any combination of support duties to assist painter, paperhanger, plasterer, or mason. Uses masking tape prior to painting, to cover surfaces of articles not to be painted. Smoothes surfaces of articles to be painted, using sanding and buffing tools and equipment. Fills cracks or breaks in surfaces of plaster articles with putty or epoxy compounds. Removes articles such as cabinets, metal furniture, and paint containers from stripping tanks after prescribed period of time. Pours specified amounts of chemical solutions into stripping tanks. Places articles to be stripped into stripping tanks.

Personality Type: Realistic. Realistic occupations frequently involve work activities that include practical, hands-on problems and solutions. They often deal with plants, animals, and real-world materials like wood, tools, and machinery. Many of the occupations require working outside and do not involve a lot of paperwork or working closely with others.

Abilities: Static Strength—The ability to exert maximum muscle force to lift, push, pull, or carry objects. Visual Color Discrimination—The ability to match or detect differences between colors, including shades of color and brightness. Manual Dexterity—The ability to quickly make coordinated movements of one hand, a hand together with its arm, or two hands, to grasp, manipulate, or assemble objects. Dynamic Strength—The ability to exert muscle force repeatedly or continuously over time. This involves muscular endurance and resistance to muscle fatigue. Oral Comprehension—The ability to listen to and understand information and ideas presented verbally. Trunk Strength—The ability to use one's abdominal and lower back muscles to support part of the body repeatedly or continuously over time without giving out or fatiguing.

Skills: Equipment Selection—Determining the kind of tools and equipment needed to do a job. Coordination—Adjusting actions in relation to others' actions. Active Listening—Listening to what other people are saying; asking questions as appropriate. Speaking—Talking to others to effectively convey information. Product Inspection—Inspecting and evaluating the quality of products.

Generalized Work Activities: Handling and Moving Objects—Using one's hands and arms in handling, installing, forming, positioning, and moving materials, or in manipulating things. Performing General Physical Activities—Performing physical activities that require moving one's whole body, such as in climbing, lifting, balancing, walking, and stooping. Performing activities that often also require considerable use of the arms and legs, such as in the physical handling of materials. Controlling Machines and Processes—Using either control mechanisms or direct physical activity to operate machines or processes. Does not involve working with computers or vehicles. Getting Information Needed to Do the Job—Observing, receiving, and otherwise obtaining information from all relevant sources. Assisting and Caring for Others—Providing assistance or personal care to others. Communicating with Other Workers—Providing information to supervisors, fellow workers, and subordinates. This information can be exchanged face-to-face, in writing, or via telephone/electronic transfer. Inspecting Equipment, Structures, Materials—Inspecting or diagnosing equipment, structures, or materials to identify the causes of errors or other problems or defects.

Helpers—Pipelayers, Plumbers, Pipefitters, and Steamfitters

Help plumbers, pipefitters, steamfitters, or pipelayers by performing duties of lesser skill. Use, supply, or hold materials or tools. Clean work area and equipment. Mounts brackets and hangers on walls and ceilings to hold pipes. Cleans shop, work area, and machines, using solvent and rags. Immerses pipe in chemical solution to remove dirt, oil, and scale. Cuts or drills holes in walls to accommodate passage of pipes, using pneumatic drill. Disassembles and removes damaged or worn pipe. Assists in installing gas burners to convert furnaces from wood, coal, or oil. Fits or assists in fitting valves, couplings, or assemblies to tanks, pumps, or systems, using hand tools. Requisitions tools and equipment; selects type and size of pipe. Fills pipe with sand or resin to prevent distortion. Holds pipes during bending and installation.

Personality Type: Realistic. Realistic occupations frequently involve work activities that include practical, hands-on problems and solutions. They often deal with plants, animals, and real-world materials like wood, tools, and machinery. Many of the occupations require working outside and do not involve a lot of paperwork or working closely with others.

Abilities: Manual Dexterity—The ability to quickly make coordinated movements of one hand, a hand together with its arm, or two hands, to grasp, manipulate, or assemble objects. Extent Flexibility—The ability to bend, stretch, twist, or reach out with the body, arms, and/or legs. Arm-Hand Steadiness—The ability to keep the hand and arm steady while making an arm movement or while holding the arm and hand in one position. Trunk Strength—The ability to use one's abdominal and lower back muscles to support part of the body repeatedly or continuously over time without giving out or fatiguing. Static

Strength—The ability to exert maximum muscle force to lift, push, pull, or carry objects.

Skills: Equipment Maintenance—Performing routine maintenance and determining when and what kind of maintenance is needed. Equipment Selection—Determining the kind of tools and equipment needed to do a job. Repairing—Repairing machines or systems, using the needed tools. Installation—Installing equipment, machines, wiring, or programs to meet specifications. Product Inspection—Inspecting and evaluating the quality of products. Coordination—Adjusting actions in relation to others' actions.

Generalized Work Activities: Handling and Moving Objects—Using one's hands and arms in handling, installing, forming, positioning, and moving materials, or in manipulating things. Controlling Machines and Processes—Using either control mechanisms or direct physical activity to operate machines or processes. Does not involve working with computers or vehicles. Performing General Physical Activities—Performing physical activities that require moving one's whole body, such as in climbing, lifting, balancing, walking, and stooping. Performing activities that often also require considerable use of the arms and legs, such as in the physical handling of materials. Assisting and Caring for Others—Providing assistance or personal care to others. Communicating with Other Workers—Providing information to supervisors, fellow workers, and subordinates. This information can be exchanged face-to-face, in writing, or via telephone/electronic transfer.

Construction Managers

- ▲ Growth: 14%
- ▲ Annual Job Openings: 32,841
- ▲ Yearly Earnings: $47,610
- ▲ Education Required: Bachelor's degree
- ▲ Self-Employed: 1%
- ▲ Part-Time: 6.1%

Construction Managers

Plan, direct, coordinate, or budget, usually through subordinate supervisory personnel, activities concerned with the construction and maintenance of structures, facilities, and systems. Participate in the conceptual development of a construction project and oversee its organization, scheduling, and implementation. Studies job specifications to plan and approve construction of project. Confers with supervisory personnel to discuss such matters as work procedures, complaints, and construction problems. Inspects and reviews construction work, repair projects, and reports, to ensure that work conforms to specifications. Requisitions supplies and materials to complete construction project. Interprets and explains plans and contract terms to administrative staff, workers, and clients. Directs and supervises workers on construction site to ensure that project meets specifications. Formulates reports concerning such areas as work progress, costs, and scheduling. Dispatches workers to construction sites to work on specified project. Investigates reports of damage at construction sites to ensure that proper procedures are being carried out. Plans, organizes, and directs activities concerned with construction and maintenance of structures, facilities, and systems. Contracts workers to perform construction work in accordance with specifications.

Personality Type: Enterprising. Enterprising occupations frequently involve starting up and carrying out projects. These occupations can involve leading people and making many decisions. They sometimes require risk taking and often deal with business.

Abilities: Oral Comprehension—The ability to listen to and understand information and ideas presented verbally. Oral Expression—The ability to communicate information and ideas verbally so others will understand. Written Comprehension—The ability to read and understand information and ideas presented in writing. Written Expression—The ability to communicate information and ideas in writing so others will understand. Problem Sensitivity—The ability to tell when something is wrong or is likely to go wrong. Does not involve solving the problem, only recognizing there is a problem.

Skills: Coordination—Adjusting actions in relation to others' actions. Management of Personnel Resources—Motivating, developing, and directing people as they work, identifying the best people for the job. Judgment and Decision Making—Weighing the relative costs and benefits of a potential action. Product Inspection—Inspecting and evaluating the quality of products. Problem Identification—Identifying the nature of problems.

Generalized Work Activities: Monitoring Processes, Materials, Surroundings—Monitoring and reviewing information from materials, events, or the environment, often to detect problems or to find out when things are finished. Coordinating Work and Activities of Others—Coordinating members of a work group to accomplish tasks. Getting Information Needed to Do the Job—Observing, receiving, and otherwise obtaining information from all relevant sources. Making Decisions and Solving Problems—Combining, evaluating, and analyzing information and data to make decisions and solve problems. Involves making decisions about the relative importance of information and choosing the best solution. Guiding, Directing, and Motivating Subordinates—Providing guidance and direction to subordinates, including setting performance standards and monitoring subordinates. Inspecting Equipment, Structures, Materials—Inspecting or diagnosing equipment, structures, or materials to identify the causes of errors or other problems or defects. Implementing Ideas and Programs—Conducting or carrying out work procedures and activities in accord with one's own ideas or information provided through directions/instructions for purposes of installing, modifying, preparing, delivering, constructing, integrating, finishing, or completing programs, systems, structures, or products.

Correctional Officers

▲ Growth: 39%
▲ Annual Job Openings: 64,835
▲ Yearly Earnings: $28,540
▲ Education Required: Long-term O-J-T
▲ Self-Employed: 0%
▲ Part-Time: 1.5%

Correctional Officers and Jailers

Guard inmates in penal or rehabilitative institution in accordance with established regulations and procedures. Guard prisoners in transit between jail, courtroom, prison, or other point. Includes deputy sheriffs and police who spend the majority of their time guarding prisoners in correctional institutions. Serves meals and distributes commissary items to prisoners. Uses weapons, handcuffs, and physical force to maintain discipline and order among prisoners. Takes prisoner into custody and escorts to locations inside and outside facility, such as visiting room, courtroom, or airport. Guards facility entrance to screen visitors. Records information such as prisoner identification, charges, and incidences of inmate disturbance. Monitors conduct of prisoners, according to established policies, regulations, and procedures, to prevent escape or violence. Searches prisoners, cells, and vehicles for weapons, valuables, or drugs. Inspects locks, window bars, grills, doors, and gates at correctional facility, to prevent escape.

Personality Type: Realistic. Realistic occupations frequently involve work activities that include practical, hands-on problems and solutions. They often deal with plants, animals, and real-world materials like wood, tools, and machinery. Many of the occupations require working outside and do not involve a lot of paperwork or working closely with others.

Abilities: Problem Sensitivity—The ability to tell when something is wrong or is likely to go wrong. Does not involve solving the problem, only recognizing there is a problem. Explosive Strength—The ability to use short bursts of muscle force to propel oneself, as in jumping or sprinting, or to throw an object. Selective Attention—The ability to concentrate and not be distracted while performing a task over a period of time. Oral Expression—The ability to communicate information and ideas verbally so others will understand. Reaction Time—The ability to quickly respond with the hand, finger, or foot to a signal such as a sound, a light, or a picture. Far Vision—The ability to see details at a distance.

Skills: Social Perceptiveness—Being aware of other people's reactions and understanding why people react the way they do. Speaking—Talking to others to effectively convey information. Problem Identification—Identifying the nature of problems. Information Gathering—Knowing how to find information and identifying essential information.

Generalized Work Activities: Monitoring Processes, Materials, Surroundings—Monitoring and reviewing information from materials, events, or the environment, often to detect problems or to find out when things are finished. Inspecting Equipment, Structures, Materials—Inspecting or diagnosing equipment, structures, or materials to identify the causes of errors or other problems or defects. Assisting and Caring for Others—Providing assistance or personal care to others. Performing General Physical Activities—Performing physical activities that require moving one's whole body, such as in climbing, lifting, balancing, walking, and stooping. Performing activities that often also require considerable use of the arms and legs, such as in the physical handling of materials. Handling and Moving Objects—Using one's hands and arms in handling, installing, forming, positioning, and moving materials, or in manipulating things. Includes the use of keyboards.

Correspondence Clerks

- ▲ Growth: 12%
- ▲ Annual Job Openings: 4,276
- ▲ Yearly Earnings: $22,270
- ▲ Education Required: Short-term O-J-T
- ▲ Self-Employed: 0%
- ▲ Part-Time: 12.8%

Correspondence Clerks

Compose letters in reply to merchandise requests, damage claims, delinquent accounts, incorrect billings, unsatisfactory services, or requests for credit and other information. Gather data to formulate reply; type correspondence. Routes correspondence to other departments for reply. Reads incoming correspondence to ascertain nature of writer's concern and to determine disposition of correspondence. Investigates discrepancies in reports and records; confers with personnel in affected departments to ensure accuracy and compliance with procedures. Compiles data pertinent to manufacture of special products for customers. Maintains files and control records to show status of action in processing correspondence. Confers with company personnel regarding feasibility of complying with writer's request. Reviews records pertinent to resolution of problem for completeness and accuracy; attaches records to correspondence for reply by others. Processes orders for goods requested in correspondence. Completes form letters in response to request or problem identified by correspondence. Types acknowledgment letter to person sending correspondence. Gathers data to formulate reply. Composes letter in response to request or problem identified by correspondence. Compiles data from records to prepare periodic reports.

Personality Type: Conventional. Conventional occupations frequently involve following set procedures and routines. These occupations can include working with data and details more than with ideas. Usually there is a clear line of authority to follow.

Abilities: Written Expression—The ability to communicate information and ideas in writing so others will understand. Written Comprehension—The ability to read and understand information and ideas presented in writing. Wrist-Finger Speed—The ability to make fast, simple, repeated movements of the fingers, hands, and wrists. Oral Comprehension—The ability to listen to and understand information and ideas presented verbally. Near Vision—The ability to see details of objects at a close range.

Skills: Reading Comprehension—Understanding written information in work-related documents. Information Gathering—Knowing how to find information and identifying essential information. Writing—Communicating effectively with others in writing as indicated by the needs of the audience. Problem Identification—Identifying the nature of problems. Information Organization—Finding ways to structure or classify multiple pieces of information.

Generalized Work Activities: Getting Information Needed to Do the Job—Observing, receiving, and otherwise obtaining information from all relevant sources. Performing Administrative Activities—Approving requests, handling paperwork, and performing day-to-day administrative tasks. Communicating with Persons Outside Organization—Communicating with persons outside the organization. Representing the organization to customers, the public, government, and other external sources. Exchanging information face-to-face, in writing, or via telephone/electronic transfer. Processing Information—Compiling, coding, categorizing, calculating, tabulating, auditing, verifying, or processing information or data. Communicating with

Other Workers—Providing information to supervisors, fellow workers, and subordinates. This information can be exchanged face-to-face, in writing, or via telephone/electronic transfer. Evaluating Information against Standards—Evaluating information against a set of standards and verifying that it is correct.

Cost Estimators

▲ Growth: 13%
▲ Annual Job Openings: 27,649
▲ Yearly Earnings: $40,590
▲ Education Required: Work experience in a related occupation
▲ Self-Employed: 0%
▲ Part-Time: 9.4%

Cost Estimators

Prepare cost estimates for product manufacturing, construction projects, or services to aid management in bidding on or determining price of product or service. Specialize according to particular service performed or type of product manufactured. Prepares estimates used for management purposes such as planning, organizing, and scheduling work. Computes cost factors used for preparing estimates for management and determining cost effectiveness. Consults with clients, vendors, or other individuals to discuss and formulate estimates and resolve issues. Conducts special studies to develop and establish standard hour and related cost data or to effect cost reduction. Prepares estimates for selecting vendors or subcontractors and for determining cost effectiveness. Analyzes blueprints, specifications, proposals, and other documentation, to prepare time, cost, and labor estimates. Reviews data to determine material and labor requirements; prepares itemized list. Prepares time, cost, and labor estimates for products, projects, or services, applying specialized methodologies, techniques, or processes.

Personality Type: Conventional. Conventional occupations frequently involve following set procedures and routines. These occupations can include working with data and details more than with ideas. Usually there is a clear line of authority to follow.

Abilities: Mathematical Reasoning—The ability to understand and organize a problem and then select a mathematical method or formula to solve the problem. Number Facility—The ability to add, subtract, multiply, or divide quickly and correctly. Written Comprehension—The ability to read and understand information and ideas presented in writing. Oral Expression—The ability to communicate information and ideas verbally so others will understand. Oral Comprehension—The ability to listen to and understand information and ideas presented verbally.

Skills: Information Gathering—Knowing how to find information and identifying essential information. Mathematics—Using mathematics to solve problems. Reading Comprehension—Understanding written information in work-related documents. Active Learning—Working with new material or information to grasp its implications. Writing—Communicating effectively with others in writing as indicated by the needs of the audience. Information Organization—Finding ways to structure or classify multiple pieces of information.

Generalized Work Activities: Estimating Needed Characteristics—Estimating the characteristics of materials, products, events, or information; estimating sizes, distances, and quantities; determining time, costs, resources, or materials needed to perform a work activity. Getting Information Needed to Do the Job—Observing, receiving, and otherwise obtaining information from all relevant sources. Processing Information—Compiling, coding, categorizing, calculating, tabulating, auditing, verifying, or processing information or data. Providing Consultation and Advice

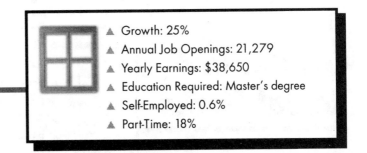

to Others—Providing consultation and expert advice to management or other groups on technical, systems-related, or process-related topics. Analyzing Data or Information—Identifying underlying principles, reasons, or facts by breaking down information or data into separate parts.

Counselors

- ▲ Growth: 25%
- ▲ Annual Job Openings: 21,279
- ▲ Yearly Earnings: $38,650
- ▲ Education Required: Master's degree
- ▲ Self-Employed: 0.6%
- ▲ Part-Time: 18%

Educational, Vocational, and School Counselors

Counsel individuals and provide group educational and vocational guidance services. Establishes and maintains relationships with employers and personnel from supportive service agencies to develop opportunities for counselees. Addresses community groups and faculty members to explain counseling services. Interprets program regulations or benefit requirements and assists counselees in obtaining needed supportive services. Compiles and studies occupational, educational, and economic information to assist counselees in making and carrying out vocational and educational objectives. Collects and evaluates information about counselees' abilities, interests, and personality characteristics, using records, tests, and interviews. Advises counselees in understanding and overcoming personal and social problems. Teaches vocational and educational guidance classes. Advises counselees in developing educational and vocational objectives. Refers qualified counselees to employer or employment service for placement. Conducts follow-up interviews with counselees and maintains case records. Plans and conducts orientation programs and group conferences to promote adjustment of individuals to new life experiences.

Personality Type: Social. Social occupations frequently involve working with, communicating with, and teaching people. These occupations often involve helping or providing service to others.

Abilities: Oral Expression—The ability to communicate information and ideas verbally so others will understand. Oral Comprehension—The ability to listen to and understand information and ideas presented verbally. Written Expression—The ability to communicate information and ideas in writing so others will understand. Problem Sensitivity—The ability to tell when something is wrong or is likely to go wrong. Does not involve solving the problem, only recognizing there is a problem. Written Comprehension—The ability to read and understand information and ideas presented in writing.

Skills: Speaking—Talking to others to effectively convey information. Problem Identification—Identifying the nature of problems. Social Perceptiveness—Being aware of other people's reactions and understanding why people react the way they do. Active Listening—Listening to what other people are saying; asking questions as appropriate. Service Orientation—Actively looking for ways to help people.

Generalized Work Activities: Assisting and Caring for Others—Providing assistance or personal care to others. Getting Information Needed to Do the Job—Observing, receiving, and otherwise obtaining information from all relevant sources. Establishing and Maintaining Relationships—Developing constructive and cooperative working relationships with others. Making Decisions and Solving Problems—Combining, evaluating, and analyzing information and data to make decisions and solve problems. Involves making decisions about the relative importance of information and choosing the best solution.

Counter and Rental Clerks

- ▲ Growth: 23%
- ▲ Annual Job Openings: 199,406
- ▲ Yearly Earnings: $14,510
- ▲ Education Required: Short-term O-J-T
- ▲ Self-Employed: 1.2%
- ▲ Part-Time: 50.8%

Counter and Rental Clerks

Receive orders for repairs, rentals, and services. Describe available options, compute cost, and accept payment. Answers telephone and receives orders by phone. Inspects and adjusts rental items to meet needs of customer. Recommends to customer items offered by rental facility that meet customer needs. Greets customers of agency that rents items such as apparel, tools, and conveyances, or that provide services such as rug cleaning. Collects deposit or payment; records credit charges. Computes charges based on rental rate. Rents item or arranges for provision of service to customer. Prepares rental forms, obtaining customer signature and other information such as required licenses. Receives, examines, and tags articles to be altered, cleaned, stored, or repaired. Reserves items for requested time. Keeps record of items rented. Explains rental fees. Provides information about rented items, such as operation or description.

Personality Type: Conventional. Conventional occupations frequently involve following set procedures and routines. These occupations can include working with data and details more than with ideas. Usually there is a clear line of authority to follow.

Abilities: Oral Comprehension—The ability to listen to and understand information and ideas presented verbally. Oral Expression—The ability to communicate information and ideas verbally so others will understand. Number Facility—The ability to add, subtract, multiply, or divide quickly and correctly. Information Ordering—The ability to correctly follow a given rule or set of rules in order to arrange things or actions in a certain order. The things or actions can include numbers, letters, words, pictures, procedures, sentences, and mathematical or logical operations. Speech Clarity—The ability to speak clearly so that what is said is understandable to a listener. Written Comprehension—The ability to read and understand information and ideas presented in writing.

Skills: Service Orientation—Actively looking for ways to help people. Speaking—Talking to others to effectively convey information. Mathematics—Using mathematics to solve problems. Active Listening—Listening to what other people are saying; asking questions as appropriate. Writing—Communicating effectively with others in writing as indicated by the needs of the audience.

Generalized Work Activities: Communicating with Persons Outside Organization—Communicating with persons outside the organization. Representing the organization to customers, the public, government, and other external sources. Exchanging information face-to-face, in writing, or via telephone/electronic transfer. Performing for/Working with Public—Performing for people or dealing directly with the public, including

serving persons in restaurants and stores and receiving clients or guests. Establishing and Maintaining Relationships—Developing constructive and cooperative working relationships with others. Selling or Influencing Others—Convincing others to buy merchandise/goods, or otherwise changing their minds or actions. Getting Information Needed to Do the Job—Observing, receiving, and otherwise obtaining information from all relevant sources. Processing Information—Compiling, coding, categorizing, calculating, tabulating, auditing, verifying, or processing information or data.

Court Clerks

- ▲ Growth: 11%
- ▲ Annual Job Openings: 13,394
- ▲ Yearly Earnings: $22,960
- ▲ Education Required: Short-term O-J-T
- ▲ Self-Employed: 0%
- ▲ Part-Time: 16%

Court Clerks

Perform clerical duties in court of law. Prepare docket of cases to be called. Explains procedures or forms to parties in case. Secures information for judges. Contacts witnesses, attorneys, and litigants to obtain information for court. Prepares case folders; posts, files, or routes documents. Examines legal documents submitted to court for adherence to law or court procedures. Records case disposition, court orders, and arrangement for payment of court fees. Collects court fees or fines; records amounts collected. Administers oath to witnesses. Records minutes of court proceedings, using stenotype machine or shorthand; transcribes testimony, using typewriter or computer. Instructs parties when to appear in court. Prepares docket or calendar of cases to be called, using typewriter or computer. Notifies district attorney's office of cases prosecuted by district attorney.

Personality Type: Conventional. Conventional occupations frequently involve following set procedures and routines. These occupations can include working with data and details more than with ideas. Usually there is a clear line of authority to follow.

Abilities: Oral Comprehension—The ability to listen to and understand information and ideas presented verbally. Written Expression—The ability to communicate information and ideas in writing so others will understand. Wrist-Finger Speed—The ability to make fast, simple, repeated movements of the fingers, hands, and wrists. Near Vision—The ability to see details of objects at a close range. Written Comprehension—The ability to read and understand information and ideas presented in writing. Oral Expression—The ability to communicate information and ideas verbally so others will understand.

Skills: Information Organization—Finding ways to structure or classify multiple pieces of information. Reading Comprehension—Understanding written information in work-related documents. Information Gathering—Knowing how to find information and identifying essential information. Active Listening—Listening to what other people are saying; asking questions as appropriate. Coordination—Adjusting actions in relation to others' actions. Speaking—Talking to others to effectively convey information.

Generalized Work Activities: Documenting/Recording Information—Entering, transcribing, recording, storing, or maintaining information in either written form or by electronic/magnetic recording. Performing Administrative Activities—Approving requests, handling paperwork, and performing day-to-day administrative tasks. Handling and Moving Objects—Using one's hands and arms in handling, installing, forming, positioning, and moving materials, or in manipulating things. Includes the use of keyboards. Getting Information Needed to Do the Job—Observing, receiving, and otherwise obtaining information from all relevant sources. Communicating with Persons Outside Organization—Communicating with persons outside the organization. Representing the organization to customers, the public, government, and other external sources. Exchanging information face-to-face, in writing, or via telephone/electronic transfer.

Court Reporters, Medical Transcriptionists, and Stenographers

- ▲ Growth: 10%
- ▲ Annual Job Openings: 15,612
- ▲ Yearly Earnings: $25,430
- ▲ Education Required: Postsecondary vocational training
- ▲ Self-Employed: 19.9%
- ▲ Part-Time: 19.8%

Court Reporters

Use verbatim methods and equipment to capture, store, retrieve, and transcribe pretrial and trial proceedings or other information.

Includes stenocaptioners who operate computerized stenographic captioning equipment to provide captions of live or prerecorded broadcasts for hearing-impaired viewers.

Note: The Department of Labor has not collected some data for this job, so it has fewer details than the other descriptions.

Medical Transcriptionists

Use transcribing machines with headset and foot pedal to listen to recordings by physicians and other healthcare professionals dictating a variety of medical reports on emergency room visits, diagnostic imaging studies, operations, chart reviews, and final summaries. Transcribe dictated reports; translate medical jargon and abbreviations into their expanded forms. Edit as necessary; return reports in either printed or electronic form to the healthcare professional for review and signature or for correction.

Note: The Department of Labor has not collected some data for this job, so it has fewer details than the other descriptions.

Credit Analysts

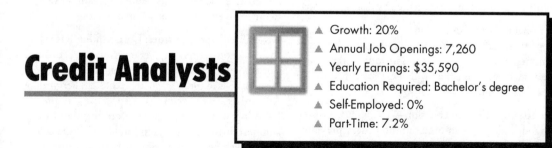

- ▲ Growth: 20%
- ▲ Annual Job Openings: 7,260
- ▲ Yearly Earnings: $35,590
- ▲ Education Required: Bachelor's degree
- ▲ Self-Employed: 0%
- ▲ Part-Time: 7.2%

Credit Analysts

Analyze current credit data and financial statements of individuals or firms to determine the degree of risk involved in extending credit or lending money. Prepare reports with this credit information for use in decision-making. Completes loan application, including credit analysis and summary of loan request; submits application to loan committee for approval. Evaluates customer records and recommends payment plan based on earnings, savings data, payment history, and purchase activity. Compares liquidity, profitability, and credit history with similar establishments of same industry and geographic location. Generates financial ratios, using computer program, to evaluate customer's financial status. Consults with customers to resolve complaints, to verify financial and credit transactions, and to adjust accounts as needed. Analyzes credit data and financial statements to determine degree of risk involved in extending credit or lending money. Reviews individual or commercial customer files to identify and select delinquent accounts for collection. Analyzes financial data such as income growth, quality of management, and market share, to determine profitability of loan. Confers with credit association and other business representatives to exchange credit information.

Personality Type: Conventional. Conventional occupations frequently involve following set procedures and routines. These occupations can include working with data and details more than with ideas. Usually there is a clear line of authority to follow.

Abilities: Mathematical Reasoning—The ability to understand and organize a problem and then select a mathematical method or formula to solve the problem. Near Vision—The ability to see details of objects at a close range. Written Comprehension—The ability to read and understand information and ideas presented in writing. Problem Sensitivity—The ability to tell when something is wrong or is likely to go wrong. Does not involve solving the problem, only recognizing there is a problem. Number Facility—The ability to add, subtract, multiply, or divide quickly and correctly.

Skills: Judgment and Decision Making—Weighing the relative costs and benefits of a potential action. Active Listening—Listening to what other people are saying; asking questions as appropriate. Speaking—Talking to others to effectively convey information. Problem Identification—Identifying the nature of problems. Information Gathering—Knowing how to find information and identifying essential information.

Generalized Work Activities: Getting Information Needed to Do the Job—Observing, receiving, and otherwise obtaining information from all relevant sources. Analyzing Data or Information—Identifying underlying principles, reasons, or facts by breaking down information or data into separate parts. Processing Information—Compiling, coding, categorizing, calculating, tabulating, auditing, verifying, or processing information or data. Interacting with Computers—Controlling computer functions by using programs, setting up functions, writing software, or otherwise communicating with computer systems. Communicating with Persons Outside Organization—Communicating with persons outside the organization. Representing the organization to customers, the public, government, and other external sources. Exchanging information face-to-face, in writing, or via telephone/electronic transfer. Evaluating Information against Standards—Evaluating information against a set of standards and verifying that it is correct.

Dancers and Choreographers

▲ Growth: 14%
▲ Annual Job Openings: 5,099
▲ Yearly Earnings: $21,420
▲ Education Required: Postsecondary vocational training
▲ Self-Employed: 36.8%
▲ Part-Time: 25.3%

Choreographers

Create and teach dance. Direct and stage presentations. Determines dance movements designed to suggest story, interpret emotion, or enliven show. Studies story line and music to envision and devise dance movements. Directs and stages dance presentations for various forms of entertainment. Auditions performers for one or more dance parts. Instructs cast in dance movements at rehearsals to achieve desired effect. Creates original dance routines for ballets, musicals, or other forms of entertainment.

Personality Type: Artistic. Artistic occupations frequently involve working with forms, designs, and patterns. They often require self-expression, and the work can be done without following a clear set of rules.

Abilities: Originality—The ability to come up with unusual or clever ideas about a given topic or situation, or to develop creative ways to solve a problem. Fluency of Ideas—The ability to come up with a number of ideas about a given topic. Emphasis is on the number of ideas produced and not the quality, correctness, or creativity of the ideas. Oral Expression—The ability to communicate information and ideas verbally so others will understand. Gross Body Coordination—The ability to coordinate the movement of the arms, legs, and torso together in activities where the whole body is in motion. Spatial Orientation—The ability to know one's location in relation to the environment or to know where other objects are in relation to one's self.

Skills: Instructing—Teaching others how to do something. Coordination—Adjusting actions in relation to others' actions. Idea Generation—Generating a number of different approaches to problems. Reading

Comprehension—Understanding written information in work-related documents. Speaking—Talking to others to effectively convey information.

Generalized Work Activities: Thinking Creatively— Originating, inventing, designing, or creating new applications, ideas, relationships, systems, or products, including artistic contributions. Coordinating Work and Activities of Others—Coordinating members of a work group to accomplish tasks. Teaching Others— Identifying educational needs, developing formal training programs or classes, and teaching or instructing others. Getting Information Needed to Do the Job— Observing, receiving, and otherwise obtaining information from all relevant sources. Judging Qualities—Making judgments about or assessing the value, importance, or quality of things, services, or other people's work. Implementing Ideas and Programs— Conducting or carrying out work procedures and activities in accord with one's own ideas or information provided through directions/instructions for purposes of installing, modifying, preparing, delivering, constructing, integrating, finishing, or completing programs, systems, structures, or products.

Dancers

Perform dances. Sing or act. Devises and choreographs dance for self or others. Studies and practices dance moves required in role. Auditions for parts in production. Works with choreographer to refine or modify dance steps. Coordinates dancing with that of partner or dance ensemble. Rehearses alone or with partners or troupe members. Performs classical, modern, or acrobatic dances in productions. Harmonizes body movements to rhythm of musical accompaniment.

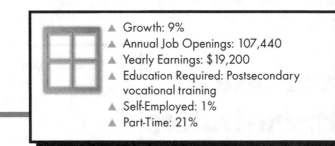

Personality Type: Artistic. Artistic occupations frequently involve working with forms, designs, and patterns. They often require self-expression, and the work can be done without following a clear set of rules.

Abilities: Speed of Limb Movement—The ability to quickly move the arms or legs. Gross Body Coordination—The ability to coordinate the movement of the arms, legs, and torso together in activities where the whole body is in motion. Stamina—The ability to exert one's self physically over long periods of time without getting winded or out of breath. Dynamic Strength—The ability to exert muscle force repeatedly or continuously over time. This involves muscular endurance and resistance to muscle fatigue.

Skills: Active Learning—Working with new material or information to grasp its implications. Active Listening—Listening to what other people are saying; asking questions as appropriate. Speaking—Talking to others to effectively convey information. Idea Generation—Generating a number of different approaches to problems. Monitoring—Assessing how well one is doing when learning or doing something.

Generalized Work Activities: Performing General Physical Activities—Performing physical activities that require moving one's whole body, such as in climbing, lifting, balancing, walking, and stooping. Performing activities that often also require considerable use of the arms and legs, such as in the physical handling of materials. Performing for/Working with Public—Performing for people or dealing directly with the public, including serving persons in restaurants and stores and receiving clients or guests. Thinking Creatively—Originating, inventing, designing, or creating new applications, ideas, relationships, systems, or products, including artistic contributions. Coordinating Work and Activities of Others—Coordinating members of a work group to accomplish tasks. Communicating with Other Workers—Providing information to supervisors, fellow workers, and subordinates. This information can be exchanged face-to-face, in writing, or via telephone/electronic transfer.

Data Entry Keyers

- ▲ Growth: 9%
- ▲ Annual Job Openings: 107,440
- ▲ Yearly Earnings: $19,200
- ▲ Education Required: Postsecondary vocational training
- ▲ Self-Employed: 1%
- ▲ Part-Time: 21%

Data Entry Keyers

Operate data entry device such as keyboard or photo-composing perforator. Verify data and prepare materials for printing. Enters data from source documents into computer or onto tape or disk for subsequent entry, using keyboard or scanning device. Compares data entered with source documents. Compiles, sorts, and verifies accuracy of data to be entered. Deletes incorrectly entered data. Keeps record of completed work. Loads machine with required input or output media such as paper, cards, disk, tape, or Braille media. Files completed documents. Resolves garbled or indecipherable messages, using cryptographic procedures and equipment. Selects materials needed to complete work assignment. Reenters data in verification format to detect errors.

Personality Type: Conventional. Conventional occupations frequently involve following set procedures and routines. These occupations can include working with data and details more than with ideas. Usually there is a clear line of authority to follow.

Abilities: Wrist-Finger Speed—The ability to make fast, simple, repeated movements of the fingers, hands, and wrists. Written Comprehension—The ability to read and understand information and ideas presented in writing. Near Vision—The ability to see details of objects at a close range. Category Flexibility—The ability to produce many rules so that each rule tells how to group or combine a set of things in a different way. Problem Sensitivity—The ability to tell when something is wrong or is likely to go wrong. Information Ordering—The ability to correctly follow a given rule or set of rules in order to arrange things or actions in a certain order. The things or actions can include numbers, letters, words, pictures, procedures, sentences, and mathematical or logical operations.

Skills: Product Inspection—Inspecting and evaluating the quality of products. Problem Identification—Identifying the nature of problems. Monitoring—Assessing how well one is doing when learning or doing something. Information Organization—Finding ways to structure or classify multiple pieces of information.

Generalized Work Activities: Interacting with Computers—Controlling computer functions by using programs, setting up functions, writing software, or otherwise communicating with computer systems. Evaluating Information against Standards—Evaluating information against a set of standards and verifying that it is correct. Handling and Moving Objects—Using one's hands and arms in handling, installing, forming, positioning, and moving materials, or in manipulating things. Includes the use of keyboards. Processing Information—Compiling, coding, categorizing, calculating, tabulating, auditing, verifying, or processing information or data. Documenting/Recording Information—Entering, transcribing, recording, storing, or maintaining information in either written form or by electronic/magnetic recording. Identifying Objects, Actions, and Events—Identifying information received by making estimates or categorizations, recognizing differences or similarities, or sensing changes in circumstances or events. Getting Information Needed to Do the Job—Observing, receiving, and otherwise obtaining information from all relevant sources. Implementing Ideas and Programs—Conducting or carrying out work procedures and activities in accord with one's own ideas or information provided through directions/instructions for purposes of installing, modifying, preparing, delivering, constructing, integrating, finishing, or completing programs, systems, structures, or products.

Database Administrators

▲ Growth: 77%

▲ Annual Job Openings: 19,027

▲ Yearly Earnings: $47,980

▲ Education Required: Bachelor's degree

▲ Self-Employed: Not available

▲ Part-Time: Not available

Database Administrators

Coordinate changes to computer databases. Test and implement the database, applying knowledge of database management systems. Plan, coordinate, and implement security measures to safeguard computer databases. Establishes and calculates optimum values for database parameters, using manuals and calculator.

Reviews workflow charts developed by programmer analyst to understand tasks computer will perform, such as updating records. Reviews procedures in database management system manuals for making changes to database. Confers with coworkers to determine scope and limitations of project. Revises company definition of data as defined in data dictionary. Specifies user and user access levels for each segment of database. Trains users and answers questions. Selects and enters codes to monitor database performance and to create production database. Reviews project request describing database user needs, estimating time and cost required to accomplish project. Develops data model describing data elements and how they are used, following procedures using pen, template, or computer software. Tests, corrects errors, and modifies changes to programs or to database. Codes database descriptions and specifies database identifiers to management system, or directs others in coding descriptions. Writes logical and physical database descriptions including location, space, access method, and security. Directs programmers and analysts to make changes to database management system.

Personality Type: Investigative. Investigative occupations frequently involve working with ideas and require an extensive amount of thinking. These occupations can involve searching for facts and figuring out problems mentally.

Abilities: Oral Expression—The ability to communicate information and ideas verbally so others will understand. Written Comprehension—The ability to read and understand information and ideas presented in writing. Information Ordering—The ability to correctly follow a given rule or set of rules in order to arrange things or actions in a certain order. The things or actions can include numbers, letters, words, pictures, procedures, sentences, and mathematical or logical operations. Mathematical Reasoning—The ability to understand and organize a problem and then select a mathematical method or formula to solve the problem. Deductive Reasoning—The ability to apply general rules to specific problems to come up with logical answers. Involves deciding if an answer makes sense.

Skills: Programming—Writing computer programs for various purposes. Mathematics—Using mathematics to solve problems. Reading Comprehension—Understanding written information in work-related documents. Operations Analysis—Analyzing needs and product requirements to create a design.

Generalized Work Activities: Interacting with Computers—Controlling computer functions by using programs, setting up functions, writing software, or otherwise communicating with computer systems. Getting Information Needed to Do the Job—Observing, receiving, and otherwise obtaining information from all relevant sources. Monitoring Processes, Materials, Surroundings—Monitoring and reviewing information from materials, events, or the environment, often to detect problems or to find out when things are finished. Analyzing Data or Information—Identifying underlying principles, reasons, or facts by breaking down information or data into separate parts. Updating and Using Job-Relevant Knowledge—Keeping up-to-date technically and knowing the functions of one's own job and related jobs.

Data Processing Equipment Repairers

- ▲ Growth: 47%
- ▲ Annual Job Openings: 20,080
- ▲ Yearly Earnings: $29,340
- ▲ Education Required: Postsecondary vocational training
- ▲ Self-Employed: 10.6%
- ▲ Part-Time: 6.9%

Data Processing Equipment Repairers

Repair, maintain, and install computer hardware such as peripheral equipment and word processing systems.

Tests electronic components and circuits to locate defects, using oscilloscopes, signal generators, ammeters, and voltmeters. Replaces defective components and wiring. Enters information into computer to copy program from one electronic component to another, or to draw, modify, or store schematics. Adjusts mechanical parts, using hand tools and soldering iron. Calibrates testing instruments. Converses with equipment operators to ascertain problems with equipment before breakdown, or to ascertain cause of breakdown. Aligns, adjusts, and calibrates equipment according to specifications. Tests faulty equipment; applies knowledge of functional operation of electronic units and systems to diagnose cause of malfunction. Maintains records of repairs, calibrations, and tests.

Personality Type: Realistic. Realistic occupations frequently involve work activities that include practical, hands-on problems and solutions. They often deal with plants, animals, and real-world materials like wood, tools, and machinery. Many of the occupations require working outside and do not involve a lot of paperwork or working closely with others.

Abilities: Near Vision—The ability to see details of objects at a close range. Inductive Reasoning—The ability to combine separate pieces of information, or specific answers to problems, to form general rules or conclusions. Includes coming up with a logical explanation for why a series of seemingly unrelated events occur together. Problem Sensitivity—The ability to tell when something is wrong or is likely to go wrong. Does not involve solving the problem, only recognizing there is a problem. Visual Color Discrimination—The ability to match or detect differences between colors, including shades of color and brightness. Written Comprehension—The ability to read and understand information and ideas presented in writing. Oral Comprehension—The ability to listen to and understand information and ideas presented verbally. Information Ordering—The ability to correctly follow

a given rule or set of rules in order to arrange things or actions in a certain order. The things or actions can include numbers, letters, words, pictures, procedures, sentences, and mathematical or logical operations. Deductive Reasoning—The ability to apply general rules to specific problems to come up with logical answers. Involves deciding if an answer makes sense.

Skills: Testing—Conducting tests to determine whether equipment, software, or procedures are operating as expected. Repairing—Repairing machines or systems, using the needed tools. Troubleshooting—Determining what is causing an operating error and deciding what to do about it. Operation Monitoring—Watching gauges, dials, or other indicators to make sure a machine is working properly. Science—Using scientific methods to solve problems. Problem Identification—Identifying the nature of problems.

Generalized Work Activities: Inspecting Equipment, Structures, Materials—Inspecting or diagnosing equipment, structures, or materials to identify the causes of errors or other problems or defects. Interacting with Computers—Controlling computer functions by using programs, setting up functions, writing software, or otherwise communicating with computer systems. Repairing and Maintaining Electrical Equipment—Fixing, servicing, adjusting, regulating, calibrating, fine-tuning, or testing machines, devices, and equipment that operate primarily on the basis of electrical or electronic, not mechanical, principles. Getting Information Needed to Do the Job—Observing, receiving, and otherwise obtaining information from all relevant sources. Updating and Using Job-Relevant Knowledge—Keeping up-to-date technically and knowing the functions of one's own job and related jobs.

Dental Assistants

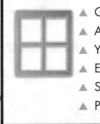

- ▲ Growth: 42%
- ▲ Annual Job Openings: 56,389
- ▲ Yearly Earnings: $22,640
- ▲ Education Required: Moderate-term O-J-T
- ▲ Self-Employed: 0%
- ▲ Part-Time: 39.7%

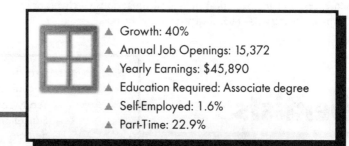

Dental Assistants

Assist dentist, prepare patient, set up equipment, and keep records. Exposes dental diagnostic X rays. Pours, trims, and polishes study casts. Makes preliminary impressions for study casts; makes occlusal registrations for mounting study casts. Cleans and polishes removable appliances. Schedules appointments, prepares bills, and receives payment for dental services; completes insurance forms; maintains records, manually or using computer. Fabricates temporary restorations and custom impressions from preliminary impressions. Applies protective coating of fluoride to teeth. Instructs patients in oral hygiene and plaque-control programs. Provides postoperative instructions prescribed by dentist. Records treatment information in patient records. Assists dentist in management of medical and dental emergencies. Takes and records medical and dental histories and vital signs of patients. Prepares patient, sterilizes and disinfects instruments, sets up instrument trays, prepares materials, and assists dentist during dental procedures. Cleans patient's teeth, using dental instruments.

Personality Type: Social. Social occupations frequently involve working with, communicating with, and teaching people. These occupations often involve helping or providing service to others.

Abilities: Arm-Hand Steadiness—The ability to keep the hand and arm steady while making an arm movement or while holding the arm and hand in one position. Near Vision—The ability to see details of objects at a close range. Control Precision—The ability to quickly and repeatedly make precise adjustments in moving the controls of a machine or vehicle to exact positions. Oral Comprehension—The ability to listen to and understand information and ideas presented verbally. Finger Dexterity—The ability to make precisely coordinated movements of the fingers of one or both hands to grasp, manipulate, or assemble very small objects.

Skills: Coordination—Adjusting actions in relation to others' actions. Speaking—Talking to others to effectively convey information. Time Management—Managing one's own time and the time of others. Active Listening—Listening to what other people are saying; asking questions as appropriate.

Generalized Work Activities: Handling and Moving Objects—Using one's hands and arms in handling, installing, forming, positioning, and moving materials, or in manipulating things. Includes the use of keyboards. Assisting and Caring for Others—Providing assistance or personal care to others. Communicating with Other Workers—Providing information to supervisors, fellow workers, and subordinates. This information can be exchanged face-to-face, in writing, or via telephone/electronic transfer. Documenting/Recording Information—Entering, transcribing, recording, storing, or maintaining information in either written form or by electronic/magnetic recording. Communicating with Persons Outside Organization—Communicating with persons outside the organization. Representing the organization to customers, the public, government, and other external sources. Exchanging information face-to-face, in writing, or via telephone/electronic transfer.

Dental Hygienists

- ▲ Growth: 40%
- ▲ Annual Job Openings: 15,372
- ▲ Yearly Earnings: $45,890
- ▲ Education Required: Associate degree
- ▲ Self-Employed: 1.6%
- ▲ Part-Time: 22.9%

Dental Hygienists

Clean teeth and examine oral areas, head, and neck for signs of oral disease. Educate patients on oral hygiene. Take and develop X rays. Apply fluoride or sealants. Removes sutures and dressings. Cleans calcareous deposits, accretions, and stains from teeth and beneath margins of gums, using dental instruments. Applies fluorides and other cavity-preventing agents to arrest dental decay. Conducts dental health clinics for community groups to augment services of dentist. Charts conditions of decay and disease for diagnosis and treatment by dentist. Feels and visually examines gums for sores and signs of disease. Places, carves, and finishes amalgam restorations. Makes impressions for study casts. Administers local anesthetic agents. Examines gums, using probes, to locate periodontal recessed gums and signs of gum disease. Feels lymph nodes under patient's chin to detect swelling or tenderness that could indicate presence of oral cancer. Places and removes rubber dams, matrices, and temporary restorations. Provides clinical services and health education to improve and maintain oral health of school children. Exposes and develops X-ray film. Removes excess cement from coronal surfaces of teeth.

Personality Type: Social. Social occupations frequently involve working with, communicating with, and teaching people. These occupations often involve helping or providing service to others.

Abilities: Arm-Hand Steadiness—The ability to keep the hand and arm steady while making an arm movement or while holding the arm and hand in one position. Oral Expression—The ability to communicate information and ideas verbally so others will understand. Information Ordering—The ability to correctly follow a given rule or set of rules in order to arrange things or actions in a certain order. The things or actions can include numbers, letters, words, pictures, procedures, sentences, and mathematical or logical operations. Manual Dexterity—The ability to quickly make coordinated movements of one hand, a hand together with its arm, or two hands, to grasp, manipulate, or assemble objects. Near Vision—The ability to see details of objects at a close range.

Skills: Reading Comprehension—Understanding written information in work-related documents. Problem Identification—Identifying the nature of problems. Science—Using scientific methods to solve problems. Information Organization—Finding ways to structure or classify multiple pieces of information. Equipment Selection—Determining the kind of tools and equipment needed to do a job. Judgment and Decision Making—Weighing the relative costs and benefits of a potential action. Critical Thinking—Using logic and analysis to identify the strengths and weaknesses of different approaches.

Generalized Work Activities: Handling and Moving Objects—Using one's hands and arms in handling, installing, forming, positioning, and moving materials, or in manipulating things. Assisting and Caring for Others—Providing assistance or personal care to others. Communicating with Other Workers—Providing information to supervisors, fellow workers, and subordinates. This information can be exchanged face-to-face, in writing, or via telephone/electronic transfer. Identifying Objects, Actions, and Events—Identifying information received by making estimates or categorizations, recognizing differences or similarities, or sensing changes in circumstances or events. Performing for/Working with Public—Performing for people or dealing directly with the public, including serving persons in restaurants and stores and receiving clients or guests.

Dentists

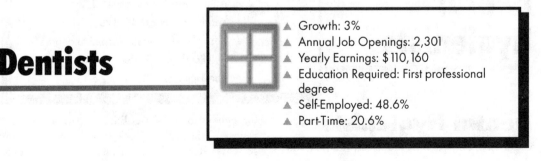

▲ Growth: 3%
▲ Annual Job Openings: 2,301
▲ Yearly Earnings: $110,160
▲ Education Required: First professional degree
▲ Self-Employed: 48.6%
▲ Part-Time: 20.6%

Dentists, General

Diagnose and treat diseases, injuries, and mal-formations of teeth, gums, and related oral structures. Treat diseases of nerve, pulp, and other dental tissues affecting vitality of teeth. Fabricates prosthodontic appliances such as space maintainers, bridges, dentures, and obturating appliances. Formulates plan of treatment for patient's teeth and mouth tissue. Removes pathologic tissue or diseased tissue using surgical instruments. Treats exposure of pulp by pulp capping, removal of pulp from pulp chamber, or root canal, using dental instruments. Restores natural color of teeth by bleaching, cleaning, and polishing. Treats infected root canal and related tissues. Analyzes and evaluates dental needs to determine changes and trends in patterns of dental disease. Counsels and advises patients about growth and development of dental problems and preventive, oral healthcare services. Produces and evaluates dental-health educational materials. Plans, organizes, and maintains dental-health programs. Eliminates irritating margins of fillings and corrects occlusions, using dental instruments. Fills pulp chamber and canal with endodontic materials. Applies fluoride and sealants to teeth. Fills, extracts, and replaces teeth, using rotary and hand instruments, dental appliances, medications, and surgical implements. Examines teeth, gums, and related tissues to determine condition, using dental instruments, X ray, and other diagnostic equipment. Fits and adjusts prosthodontic appliances in patient's mouth.

Personality Type: Investigative. Investigative occupations frequently involve working with ideas and require an extensive amount of thinking. These occupations can involve searching for facts and figuring out problems mentally.

Abilities: Control Precision—The ability to quickly and repeatedly make precise adjustments in moving the controls of a machine or vehicle to exact positions. Arm-Hand Steadiness—The ability to keep the hand and arm steady while making an arm movement or while holding the arm and hand in one position. Problem Sensitivity—The ability to tell when something is wrong or is likely to go wrong. Does not involve solving the problem, only recognizing there is a problem. Oral

Comprehension—The ability to listen to and understand information and ideas presented verbally. Finger Dexterity—The ability to make precisely coordinated movements of the fingers of one or both hands to grasp, manipulate, or assemble very small objects.

Skills: Reading Comprehension—Understanding written information in work-related documents. Problem Identification—Identifying the nature of problems. Critical Thinking—Using logic and analysis to identify the strengths and weaknesses of different approaches. Science—Using scientific methods to solve problems. Judgment and Decision Making—Weighing the relative costs and benefits of a potential action.

Generalized Work Activities: Assisting and Caring for Others—Providing assistance or personal care to others. Handling and Moving Objects—Using one's hands and arms in handling, installing, forming, positioning, and moving materials, or in manipulating things. Includes the use of keyboards. Making Decisions and Solving Problems—Combining, evaluating, and analyzing information and data to make decisions and solve problems. Involves making decisions about the relative importance of information and choosing the best solution. Getting Information Needed to Do the Job—Observing, receiving, and otherwise obtaining information from all relevant sources. Identifying Objects, Actions, and Events—Identifying information received by making estimates or categorizations, recognizing differences or similarities, or sensing changes in circumstances or events.

Oral and Maxillo-facial Surgeons

Perform surgery on mouth, jaws, and related head and neck structure to execute difficult and multiple extractions of teeth, to remove tumors and other abnormal growths, to correct abnormal jaw relations by mandibular or maxillary revision, to prepare mouth for insertion of dental prosthesis, or to treat fractured jaws. Performs preprosthetic surgery to prepare mouth for insertion of dental prosthesis. Treats fractures of jaws. Corrects abnormal jaw relations by mandibular or maxillary revision. Removes tumors and other abnormal growths, using surgical instruments. Executes difficult and multiple extraction of teeth. Administers general and local anesthetics.

Personality Type: Investigative. Investigative occupations frequently involve working with ideas and require an extensive amount of thinking. These occupations can involve searching for facts and figuring out problems mentally.

Abilities: Arm-Hand Steadiness—The ability to keep the hand and arm steady while making an arm movement or while holding the arm and hand in one position. Near Vision—The ability to see details of objects at a close range. Manual Dexterity—The ability to quickly make coordinated movements of one hand, a hand together with its arm, or two hands, to grasp, manipulate, or assemble objects. Finger Dexterity—The ability to make precisely coordinated movements of the fingers of one or both hands to grasp, manipulate, or assemble very small objects. Problem Sensitivity—The ability to tell when something is wrong or is likely to go wrong. Does not involve solving the problem, only recognizing there is a problem.

Skills: Reading Comprehension—Understanding written information in work-related documents. Problem Identification—Identifying the nature of problems. Critical Thinking—Using logic and analysis to identify the strengths and weaknesses of different approaches. Judgment and Decision Making—Weighing the relative costs and benefits of a potential action. Science—Using scientific methods to solve problems.

Generalized Work Activities: Making Decisions and Solving Problems—Combining, evaluating, and analyzing information and data to make decisions and solve problems. Involves making decisions about the relative importance of information and choosing the best solution. Handling and Moving Objects—Using one's hands and arms in handling, installing, forming, positioning, and moving materials, or in manipulating things. Includes the use of keyboards. Judging Qualities—Making judgments about or assessing the value, importance, or quality of things, services, or other people's work. Assisting and Caring for Others—

Providing assistance or personal care to others. Monitoring Processes, Materials, Surroundings—Monitoring and reviewing information from materials, events, or the environment, often to detect problems or to find out when things are finished. Implementing Ideas and Programs—Conducting or carrying out work procedures and activities in accord with one's own ideas or information provided through directions/instructions for purposes of installing, modifying, preparing, delivering, constructing, integrating, finishing, or completing programs, systems, structures, or products.

Orthodontists

Examine, diagnose, and treat dental malocclusions and oral-cavity anomalies. Design and fabricate appliances to realign teeth and jaws, to produce and maintain normal function and to improve appearance. Diagnoses teeth and jaw or other dental-facial abnormalities. Plans treatment, using cephalometric, height, and weight records, dental X rays and front and lateral dental photographs. Examines patient's mouth to determine position of teeth and jaw development. Fits dental appliances in patient's mouth to alter position and relationship of teeth and jaws and to realign teeth. Designs and fabricates appliances such as space maintainers, retainers, and labial and lingual arch wires. Adjusts dental appliances periodically to produce and maintain normal function.

Personality Type: Investigative. Investigative occupations frequently involve working with ideas and require an extensive amount of thinking. These occupations can involve searching for facts and figuring out problems mentally.

Abilities: Arm-Hand Steadiness—The ability to keep the hand and arm steady while making an arm movement or while holding the arm and hand in one position. Manual Dexterity—The ability to quickly make coordinated movements of one hand, a hand together with its arm, or two hands, to grasp, manipulate, or assemble objects. Control Precision—The ability to quickly and repeatedly make precise adjustments in moving the controls of a machine or vehicle to exact positions. Problem Sensitivity—The ability to tell when something is wrong or is likely to go wrong. Does not involve solving the problem, only recognizing there is a problem. Oral Comprehension—The ability to listen to and understand information and ideas presented verbally. Oral Expression—The ability to communicate information and ideas verbally so others will understand.

Skills: Reading Comprehension—Understanding written information in work-related documents. Problem Identification—Identifying the nature of problems. Science—Using scientific methods to solve problems. Judgment and Decision Making—Weighing the relative costs and benefits of a potential action. Critical Thinking—Using logic and analysis to identify the strengths and weaknesses of different approaches.

Generalized Work Activities: Getting Information Needed to Do the Job—Observing, receiving, and otherwise obtaining information from all relevant sources. Handling and Moving Objects—Using one's hands and arms in handling, installing, forming, positioning, and moving materials, or in manipulating things. Includes the use of keyboards. Assisting and Caring for Others—Providing assistance or personal care to others. Identifying Objects, Actions, and Events—Identifying information received by making estimates or categorizations, recognizing differences or similarities, or sensing changes in circumstances or events. Making Decisions and Solving Problems—Combining, evaluating, and analyzing information and data to make decisions and solve problems. Involves making decisions about the relative importance of information and choosing the best solution.

Prosthodontists

Construct oral prostheses to replace missing teeth. Construct other oral structures to correct natural and acquired deformation of mouth and jaws, to restore and maintain oral functions such as chewing and speaking, and to improve appearance. Adjusts prostheses to fit patient. Records physiologic position of jaws to determine shape and size of dental prostheses, using face bows, dental articulators, and recording devices. Corrects natural and acquired deformation of mouth and jaws through use of prosthetic appliances. Designs and fabricates dental prostheses. Replaces missing teeth and associated oral structures with artificial teeth, to improve chewing, speech, and appearance.

Personality Type: Investigative. Investigative occupations frequently involve working with ideas and require an extensive amount of thinking. These occupations can involve searching for facts and figuring out problems mentally.

Abilities: Arm-Hand Steadiness—The ability to keep the hand and arm steady while making an arm movement or while holding the arm and hand in one position. Near Vision—The ability to see details of objects at a close range. Visualization—The ability to imagine how something will look after it is moved around or when its parts are moved or rearranged. Finger Dexterity—The ability to make precisely coordinated movements of the fingers of one or both hands to grasp, manipulate, or assemble very small objects. Information Ordering—The ability to correctly follow a given rule or set of rules in order to arrange things or actions in a certain order. The things or actions can include numbers, letters, words, pictures, procedures, sentences, and mathematical or logical operations.

Skills: Problem Identification—Identifying the nature of problems. Reading Comprehension—Understanding written information in work-related documents. Judgment and Decision Making—Weighing the relative costs and benefits of a potential action. Science—Using scientific methods to solve problems. Technology Design—Generating or adapting equipment and technology to serve user needs. Equipment Selection—Determining the kind of tools and equipment needed to do a job. Product Inspection—Inspecting and evaluating the quality of products.

Generalized Work Activities: Getting Information Needed to Do the Job—Observing, receiving, and otherwise obtaining information from all relevant sources. Making Decisions and Solving Problems—Combining, evaluating, and analyzing information and data to make decisions and solve problems. Involves making decisions about the relative importance of information and choosing the best solution. Handling and Moving Objects—Using one's hands and arms in handling, installing, forming, positioning, and moving materials, or in manipulating things. Includes the use of keyboards. Assisting and Caring for Others—Providing assistance or personal care to others. Updating and Using Job-Relevant Knowledge—Keeping up-to-date technically and knowing the functions of one's own job and related jobs. Judging Qualities—Making judgments about or assessing the value, importance, or quality of things, services, or other people's work. Analyzing Data or Information—Identifying underlying principles, reasons, or facts by breaking down information or data into separate parts.

Designers

- ▲ Growth: 27%
- ▲ Annual Job Openings: 57,787
- ▲ Yearly Earnings: $29,190
- ▲ Education Required: Bachelor's degree
- ▲ Self-Employed: 31.9%
- ▲ Part-Time: 20%

Art Directors

Formulate design concepts and presentation approaches. Direct workers engaged in art work, layout design, and copy writing for visual communications media such as magazines, books, newspapers, and packaging. Draws custom illustrations for project. Presents final layouts to client for approval. Confers with creative, art, copy writing, or production department heads to discuss client requirements, outline presentation concepts, and coordinate creative activities. Prepares detailed storyboard showing sequence and timing of story development for television production. Marks up, pastes, and completes layouts to prepare for printing. Writes typography instructions such as margin widths and type sizes; submits for typesetting or printing. Reviews illustrative material and confers with client concerning objectives, budget, background information, and presentation approaches, styles, and techniques. Reviews and approves art and copy materials developed by staff. Reviews and approves proofs of printed copy. Assigns and directs staff members to develop design concepts into art layouts or to prepare layouts for printing. Formulates basic layout design or presentation approach; conceives material details such as style and size of type, photographs, graphics, and arrangement.

Personality Type: Artistic. Artistic occupations frequently involve working with forms, designs, and patterns. They often require self-expression, and the work can be done without following a clear set of rules.

Abilities: Originality—The ability to come up with unusual or clever ideas about a given topic or situation, or to develop creative ways to solve a problem. Speech Clarity—The ability to speak clearly so that what is said is understandable to a listener. Fluency of Ideas—The ability to come up with a number of ideas about a given topic. Emphasis is on the number of ideas produced and not the quality, correctness, or creativity of the ideas. Visualization—The ability to imagine how something will look after it is moved around or when its parts are moved or rearranged. Oral Expression—The ability to communicate information and ideas verbally so others will understand.

Skills: Management of Personnel Resources—Motivating, developing, and directing people as they work, identifying the best people for the job. Product Inspection—Inspecting and evaluating the quality of products. Operations Analysis—Analyzing needs and product requirements to create a design. Coordination—Adjusting actions in relation to others' actions.

Generalized Work Activities: Thinking Creatively—Originating, inventing, designing, or creating new applications, ideas, relationships, systems, or products, including artistic contributions. Getting Information Needed to Do the Job—Observing, receiving, and otherwise obtaining information from all relevant sources. Communicating with Other Workers—Providing information to supervisors, fellow workers, and subordinates. This information can be exchanged face-to-face, in writing, or via telephone/electronic transfer. Communicating with Persons Outside Organization—Communicating with persons outside the organization. Representing the organization to customers, the public, government, and other external sources. Exchanging information face-to-face, in writing, or via telephone/electronic transfer. Organizing, Planning, and Prioritizing—Developing plans to accomplish work. Prioritizing and organizing one's own work.

Commercial and Industrial Designers

Develop and design manufactured products such as cars, home appliances, and children's toys. Combine artistic talent with research on product use, marketing, and materials, to create the most functional and appealing product design. Integrates findings and concepts and sketches design ideas. Evaluates design ideas for feasibility, based on factors such as appearance, function, serviceability, budget, production costs/methods, and market characteristics. Presents design to customer or design committee for approval and discusses need for modification. Fabricates model or sample in paper, wood, glass, fabric, plastic, or metal, using hand and power tools. Prepares itemized production requirements to produce item. Reads publications, attends showings, and studies traditional, period, and contemporary design styles and motifs, to obtain perspective and design concepts. Directs and coordinates preparation of detailed drawings from sketches or fabrication of models or samples. Modifies design to conform with customer specifications, production limitations, or changes in design trends. Designs packaging and containers for products such as foods, beverages, toiletries, or medicines. Prepares detailed drawings, illustrations, artwork, or blueprints, using drawing instruments or paints and brushes. Confers with engineering, marketing, production, or sales department, or with customer, to establish design

concepts for manufactured products. Creates and designs graphic material for use as ornamentation, illustration, or advertising on manufactured materials and packaging.

Personality Type: Artistic. Artistic occupations frequently involve working with forms, designs, and patterns. They often require self-expression, and the work can be done without following a clear set of rules.

Abilities: Originality—The ability to come up with unusual or clever ideas about a given topic or situation, or to develop creative ways to solve a problem. Written Comprehension—The ability to read and understand information and ideas presented in writing. Visualization—The ability to imagine how something will look after it is moved around or when its parts are moved or rearranged. Oral Expression—The ability to communicate information and ideas verbally so others will understand. Fluency of Ideas—The ability to come up with a number of ideas about a given topic. Emphasis is on the number of ideas produced and not the quality, correctness, or creativity of the ideas. Oral Comprehension—The ability to listen to and understand information and ideas presented verbally.

Skills: Operations Analysis—Analyzing needs and product requirements to create a design. Identification of Key Causes—Identifying the things that must be changed to achieve a goal. Idea Evaluation—Evaluating the likely success of an idea in relation to the demands of the situation. Active Listening—Listening to what other people are saying; asking questions as appropriate. Idea Generation—Generating a number of different approaches to problems.

Generalized Work Activities: Thinking Creatively—Originating, inventing, designing, or creating new applications, ideas, relationships, systems, or products, including artistic contributions. Getting Information Needed to Do the Job—Observing, receiving, and otherwise obtaining information from all relevant sources. Communicating with Persons Outside Organization—Communicating with persons outside the organization. Representing the organization to customers, the public, government, and other external sources. Exchanging information face-to-face, in writing, or via telephone/electronic transfer. Drafting and Specifying Technical Devices—Providing documentation, detailed instructions, drawings, or specifications to inform others about how devices, parts, equipment, or structures are to be fabricated, constructed, assembled, modified, maintained, or used. Communicating with Other Workers—Providing information to supervisors, fellow workers, and subordinates. This information can be exchanged face-to-face, in writing, or via telephone/electronic transfer. Implementing Ideas and Programs—Conducting or carrying out work procedures and activities in accord with one's own ideas or information provided through directions/instructions for purposes of installing, modifying, preparing, delivering, constructing, integrating, finishing, or completing programs, systems, structures, or products.

Exhibit Designers

Plan, design, and oversee construction and installation of permanent and temporary exhibits and displays. Oversees preparation of artwork, construction of exhibit components, and placement of collection, to ensure intended interpretation of concepts and conformance to specifications. Designs display to decorate streets, fairgrounds, buildings, or other places for celebrations, using paper, cloth, plastic, or other materials. Submits plans for approval; adapts plan to serve intended purpose or to conform to budget or fabrication restrictions. Confers with client or staff regarding theme, interpretative or informational purpose, planned location, budget, materials, or promotion. Designs, draws, paints, or sketches backgrounds and fixtures for use in windows or interior displays. Inspects installed exhibit for conformance to specifications and satisfactory operation of special effects components. Prepares preliminary drawings of proposed exhibit, including detailed construction, layout, material specifications, or special effects diagrams. Arranges for acquisition of specimens or graphics. Arranges for the building of exhibit structures by outside contractors to complete exhibit.

Personality Type: Artistic. Artistic occupations frequently involve working with forms, designs, and patterns. They often require self-expression, and the work can be done without following a clear set of rules.

Abilities: Originality—The ability to come up with unusual or clever ideas about a given topic or situation, or to develop creative ways to solve a problem. Visualization—The ability to imagine how something will look after it is moved around or when its parts are moved or rearranged. Oral Expression—The ability to communicate information and ideas verbally so others will understand. Wrist-Finger Speed—The ability to make fast, simple, repeated movements of the fingers, hands, and wrists. Oral Comprehension—The ability to listen to and understand information and ideas presented verbally. Fluency of Ideas—The ability to come up with a number of ideas about a given topic. Emphasis is on the number of ideas produced and not the quality, correctness, or creativity of the ideas.

Skills: Operations Analysis—Analyzing needs and product requirements to create a design. Idea Generation—Generating a number of different approaches to problems. Coordination—Adjusting actions in relation to others' actions.

Generalized Work Activities: Thinking Creatively—Originating, inventing, designing, or creating new applications, ideas, relationships, systems, or products, including artistic contributions. Getting Information Needed to Do the Job—Observing, receiving, and otherwise obtaining information from all relevant sources. Drafting and Specifying Technical Devices—Providing documentation, detailed instructions, drawings, or specifications to inform others about how devices, parts, equipment, or structures are to be fabricated, constructed, assembled, modified, maintained, or used. Implementing Ideas and Programs—Conducting or carrying out work procedures and activities in accord with one's own ideas or information provided through directions/instructions for purposes of installing, modifying, preparing, delivering, constructing, integrating, finishing, or completing programs, systems, structures, or products. Handling and Moving Objects—Using one's hands and arms in handling, installing, forming, positioning, and moving materials, or in manipulating things. Includes the use of keyboards. Coordinating Work and Activities of Others—Coordinating members of a work group to accomplish tasks.

Fashion Designers

Design clothing and accessories. Create original garments, or design garments that follow well-established fashion trends. Develop the line of color and kinds of materials. Directs and coordinates workers who draw and cut patterns and who construct sample or finished garment. Examines sample garment on and off model; modifies design to achieve desired effect. Confers with sales and management executives or with clients, regarding design ideas. Arranges for showing of sample garments at sales meetings or fashion shows. Attends fashion shows and reviews garment magazines and manuals to analyze fashion trends, predictions, and consumer preferences. Draws pattern for article designed, cuts pattern, and cuts material according to pattern, using scissors and measuring and drawing instruments. Integrates findings of analysis and discussion with personal tastes and knowledge of design to originate design ideas. Designs custom garments for clients. Sketches rough and detailed drawings of apparel or accessories; writes specifications such as color scheme, construction, or material type. Sews together sections to form mockup or sample of garment or article, using sewing equipment.

Personality Type: Artistic. Artistic occupations frequently involve working with forms, designs, and patterns. They often require self-expression, and the work can be done without following a clear set of rules.

Abilities: Originality—The ability to come up with unusual or clever ideas about a given topic or situation, or to develop creative ways to solve a problem. Fluency of Ideas—The ability to come up with a number of ideas about a given topic. Emphasis is on the number of ideas produced and not the quality, correctness, or creativity of the ideas. Visual Color Discrimination—The ability to match or detect differences between colors, including shades of color and brightness. Visualization—The ability to imagine how something will look after it is moved around or when its parts are moved or rearranged.

Skills: Idea Generation—Generating a number of different approaches to problems. Active Learning—Working with new material or information to grasp its implications. Operations Analysis—Analyzing needs and product requirements to create a design. Identification of Key Causes—Identifying the things that must be changed to achieve a goal. Visioning—Developing an image of how a system should work under ideal conditions. Information Gathering—Knowing how to find information and identifying essential information. Coordination—Adjusting actions in relation to others' actions.

Generalized Work Activities: Thinking Creatively—Originating, inventing, designing, or creating new applications, ideas, relationships, systems, or products, including artistic contributions. Getting Information Needed to Do the Job—Observing, receiving, and otherwise obtaining information from all relevant sources. Implementing Ideas and Programs—Conducting or carrying out work procedures and activities in accord with one's own ideas or information provided through directions/instructions for purposes of installing, modifying, preparing, delivering, constructing, integrating, finishing, or completing programs, systems, structures, or products. Judging Qualities—Making judgments about or assessing the value, importance, or quality of things, services, or other people's work. Updating and Using Job-Relevant Knowledge—Keeping up-to-date technically and knowing the functions of one's own job and related jobs.

Floral Designers

Design, cut, and arrange live, dried, or artificial flowers and foliage. Estimates costs; prices arrangements. Confers with client regarding price and type of arrangement desired. Trims material and arranges bouquets, wreaths, terrariums, and other items using trimmers, shapers, wire, pin, floral tape, foam, and other materials. Decorates buildings, halls, churches, or other facilities where events are planned. Conducts classes and demonstrations; trains other workers. Packs and wraps completed arrangements. Plans arrangement according to client's requirements, utilizing knowledge of design and properties of materials, or selects appropriate standard design pattern. Selects flora and foliage for arrangement.

Personality Type: Artistic. Artistic occupations frequently involve working with forms, designs, and patterns. They often require self-expression, and the work can be done without following a clear set of rules.

Abilities: Originality—The ability to come up with unusual or clever ideas about a given topic or situation, or to develop creative ways to solve a problem. Visualization—The ability to imagine how something will look after it is moved around or when its parts are moved or rearranged. Visual Color Discrimination—The ability to match or detect differences between colors, including shades of color and brightness. Oral Comprehension—The ability to listen to and understand information and ideas presented verbally. Fluency of Ideas—The ability to come up with a number of ideas about a given topic. Emphasis is on the number of ideas produced and not the quality, correctness, or creativity of the ideas.

Skills: Active Listening—Listening to what other people are saying; asking questions as appropriate. Service Orientation—Actively looking for ways to help people. Speaking—Talking to others to effectively convey information. Mathematics—Using mathematics to solve problems. Idea Generation—Generating a number of different approaches to problems. Operations Analysis—Analyzing needs and product requirements to create a design. Product Inspection—Inspecting and evalu-ating the quality of products.

Generalized Work Activities: Thinking Creatively—Originating, inventing, designing, or creating new applications, ideas, relationships, systems, or products, including artistic contributions. Communicating with Persons Outside Organization—Communicating with persons outside the organization. Representing the organization to customers, the public, government, and other external sources. Exchanging information face-to-face, in writing, or via telephone/electronic transfer. Handling and Moving Objects—Using one's hands and arms in handling, installing, forming, positioning, and moving materials, or in manipulating things. Includes the use of keyboards. Estimating Needed Characteristics—Estimating the characteristics of materials, products, events, or information; estimating sizes, distances, and quantities; determining time, costs, resources, or materials needed to perform a work activity. Getting Information Needed to Do the Job—Observing, receiving, and otherwise obtaining information from all relevant sources. Implementing Ideas and Programs—Conducting or carrying out work

procedures and activities in accord with one's own ideas or information provided through directions/instructions for purposes of installing, modifying, preparing, delivering, constructing, integrating, finishing, or completing programs, systems, structures, or products.

Set Designers

Design sets for theatrical, motion picture, and television productions. Integrates requirements, including script, research, budget, and available locations, to develop design. Designs and builds scale models of set design or miniature sets used in filming backgrounds or special effects. Presents drawings for approval and makes changes and corrections as directed. Confers with heads of production and direction, to establish budget, schedules, and discuss design ideas. Prepares rough draft and scale working drawings of sets, including floor plans, scenery, and properties to be constructed. Selects furniture, draperies, pictures, lamps, and rugs for decorative quality and appearance. Assigns staff to complete design ideas and prepare sketches, illustrations, and detailed drawings of sets, graphics, and animation. Directs and coordinates set construction, erection, or decoration activities to ensure conformance to design, budget, and schedule requirements. Reads script to determine location, set, or decoration require-ments. Researches and consults experts to determine architectural and furnishing styles, to depict given periods or locations. Estimates costs of design materials and construction. Estimates costs of renting location or props. Examines dressed set to ensure props and scenery do not interfere with movements of cast or view of camera.

Personality Type: Artistic. Artistic occupations frequently involve working with forms, designs, and patterns. They often require self-expression, and the work can be done without following a clear set of rules.

Abilities: Visualization—The ability to imagine how something will look after it is moved around or when its parts are moved or rearranged. Oral Expression—The ability to communicate information and ideas verbally so others will understand. Originality—The ability to come up with unusual or clever ideas about a given topic or situation, or to develop creative ways to

solve a problem. Oral Comprehension—The ability to listen to and understand information and ideas presented verbally. Written Comprehension—The ability to read and understand information and ideas presented in writing.

Skills: Management of Material Resources—Obtaining and seeing to the appropriate use of equipment, facilities, and materials needed to do certain work. Implementation Planning—Developing approaches for implementing an idea. Coordination—Adjusting actions in relation to others' actions. Operations Analysis—Analyzing needs and product requirements to create a design. Product Inspection—Inspecting and evaluating the quality of products. Management of Financial Resources—Determining how money will be spent to get the work done, and accounting for these expenditures. Time Management—Managing one's own time and the time of others.

Generalized Work Activities: Thinking Creatively—Originating, inventing, designing, or creating new applications, ideas, relationships, systems, or products, including artistic contributions. Getting Information Needed to Do the Job—Observing, receiving, and otherwise obtaining information from all relevant sources. Estimating Needed Characteristics—Estimating the characteristics of materials, products, events, or information; estimating sizes, distances, and quantities; determining time, costs, resources, or materials needed to perform a work activity. Implementing Ideas and Programs—Conducting or carrying out work procedures and activities in accord with one's own ideas or information provided through directions/instructions for purposes of installing, modifying, preparing, delivering, constructing, integrating, finishing, or completing programs, systems, structures, or products. Organizing, Planning, and Prioritizing—Developing plans to accomplish work. Prioritizing and organizing one's own work. Drafting and Specifying Technical Devices—Providing documentation, detailed instructions, drawings, or specifications to inform others about how devices, parts, equipment, or structures are to be fabricated, constructed, assembled, modified, maintained, or used.

Desktop Publishing Specialists

- ▲ Growth: 73%
- ▲ Annual Job Openings: 7,546
- ▲ Yearly Earnings: $29,130
- ▲ Education Required: Long-term O-J-T
- ▲ Self-Employed: 0%
- ▲ Part-Time: 19.4%

Desktop Publishers

Format typescript and graphic elements using computer software to produce publication-ready material. Activates options such as masking or text processing. Saves completed work on floppy disks or magnetic tape. Studies layout or other instructions to determine work to be done and sequence of operations. Loads floppy disks or tapes containing information into system. Creates special effects such as vignettes, mosaics, and image combining. Views monitors for visual representation of work in progress and for instructions and feedback throughout process. Enters data such as background color, shapes, and coordination of images. Enters digitized data into electronic prepress-system computer memory, using scanner, camera, keyboard, or mouse. Activates options such as masking, pixel (picture element) editing, airbrushing, or image retouching. Enters data such as coordinates of images and color specifications into system to retouch and make color corrections.

Personality Type: Realistic. Realistic occupations frequently involve work activities that include practical, hands-on problems and solutions. They often deal with plants, animals, and real-world materials like wood,

tools, and machinery. Many of the occupations require working outside and do not involve a lot of paperwork or working closely with others.

Abilities: Near Vision—The ability to see details of objects at a close range. Wrist-Finger Speed—The ability to make fast, simple, repeated movements of the fingers, hands, and wrists. Visual Color Discrimination—The ability to match or detect differences between colors, including shades of color and brightness. Visualization—The ability to imagine how something will look after it is moved around or when its parts are moved or rearranged. Control Precision—The ability to quickly and repeatedly make precise adjustments in moving the controls of a machine or vehicle to exact positions. Information Ordering—The ability to correctly follow a given rule or set of rules in order to arrange things or actions in a certain order. The things or actions can include numbers, letters, words, pictures, procedures, sentences, and mathematical or logical operations. Written Comprehension—The ability to read and understand information and ideas presented in writing.

Skills: Reading Comprehension—Understanding written information in work-related documents.

Equipment Selection—Determining the kind of tools and equipment needed to do a job. Operation and Control—Controlling operations of equipment or systems. Operations Analysis—Analyzing needs and product requirements to create a design. Monitoring—Assessing how well one is doing when learning or doing something.

Generalized Work Activities: Interacting with Computers—Controlling computer functions by using programs, setting up functions, writing software, or otherwise communicating with computer systems. Getting Information Needed to Do the Job—Observing, receiving, and otherwise obtaining information from all relevant sources. Handling and Moving Objects—Using one's hands and arms in handling, installing, forming, positioning, and moving materials, or in manipulating things. Includes the use of keyboards. Identifying Objects, Actions, and Events—Identifying information received by making estimates or categorizations, recognizing differences or similarities, or sensing changes in circumstances or events. Thinking Creatively—Originating, inventing, designing, or creating new applications, ideas, relationships, systems, or products, including artistic contributions.

Detectives and Criminal Investigators

- ▲ Growth: 21%
- ▲ Annual Job Openings: 8,048
- ▲ Yearly Earnings: $21,000
- ▲ Education Required: Work experience in a related occupation
- ▲ Self-Employed: 0%
- ▲ Part-Time: 1.5%

Criminal Investigators and Special Agents

Investigate alleged or suspected criminal violations of federal, state, or local laws, to determine if evidence is sufficient to recommend prosecution. Develops and uses informants to get leads to information. Assists in determining scope, timing, and direction of

investigation. Analyzes charge, complaint, or allegation of law violation to identify issues involved and types of evidence needed. Examines records to detect links in chain of evidence or information. Searches for evidence, dusts surfaces to reveal latent fingerprints, and collects and records evidence and documents, using cameras and investigative equipment. Obtains and uses search and arrest warrants. Compares crime scene fingerprints with those of suspect or fingerprint files to identify perpetrator, using computer. Presents findings in reports. Reports critical information to and coordinates activities with other offices or agencies when applicable. Photographs, fingerprints, and measures height and weight of arrested suspects, noting physical characteristics; posts data on record for filing. Serves subpoenas or other official papers. Obtains and verifies evidence or establishes facts by interviewing, observing, and interrogating suspects and witnesses and analyzing records. Testifies before grand juries. Maintains surveillance and performs undercover assignments.

Personality Type: Enterprising. Enterprising occupations frequently involve starting up and carrying out projects. These occupations can involve leading people and making many decisions. They sometimes require risk taking and often deal with business.

Abilities: Oral Comprehension—The ability to listen to and understand information and ideas presented verbally. Inductive Reasoning—The ability to combine separate pieces of information, or specific answers to problems, to form general rules or conclusions. Includes coming up with a logical explanation for why a series of seemingly unrelated events occur together. Oral Expression—The ability to communicate information and ideas verbally so others will understand. Written Expression—The ability to communicate information and ideas in writing so others will understand. Flexibility of Closure—The ability to identify or detect a known pattern (a figure, object, word, or sound) that is hidden in other distracting material.

Skills: Information Gathering—Knowing how to find information and identifying essential information. Active Listening—Listening to what other people are saying; asking questions as appropriate. Speaking— Talking to others to effectively convey information. Critical Thinking—Using logic and analysis to identify the strengths and weaknesses of different approaches. Information Organization—Finding ways to structure or classify multiple pieces of information.

Generalized Work Activities: Getting Information Needed to Do the Job—Observing, receiving, and otherwise obtaining information from all relevant sources. Documenting/Recording Information— Entering, transcribing, recording, storing, or main-

taining information in either written form or by electronic/magnetic recording. Analyzing Data or Information—Identifying underlying principles, reasons, or facts by breaking down information or data into separate parts. Identifying Objects, Actions, and Events—Identifying information received by making estimates or categorizations, recognizing differences or similarities, or sensing changes in circumstances or events. Communicating with Other Workers— Providing information to supervisors, fellow workers, and subordinates. This information can be exchanged face-to-face, in writing, or via telephone/electronic transfer. Judging Qualities—Making judgments about or assessing the value, importance, or quality of things, services, or other people's work.

Police Detectives

Conduct investigations to prevent crimes or solve criminal cases. Reviews governmental agency files to obtain identifying data pertaining to suspects or establishments suspected of violating laws. Maintains surveillance of establishments to attain identifying information on suspects. Arrests or assists in arrest of criminals or suspects. Records progress of investigation, maintains informational files on suspects, and submits reports to commanding officer or magistrate to authorize warrants. Observes and photographs narcotic purchase transactions to compile evidence and protect undercover investigators. Testifies before court and grand jury; appears in court as witness. Schedules polygraph tests for consenting parties; records results of test interpretations for presentation with findings. Interviews complainant, witnesses, and accused persons to obtain facts or statements. Examines scene of crime to obtain clues and gather evidence. Investigates establishments or persons to verify facts supporting complainant or accused, using supportive information from witnesses or tangible evidence. Prepares assigned cases for court and charges or responses to charges, according to formalized procedures.

Personality Type: Enterprising. Enterprising occupations frequently involve starting up and carrying out projects. These occupations can involve leading people and making many decisions. They sometimes require risk taking and often deal with business.

Abilities: Inductive Reasoning—The ability to combine separate pieces of information, or specific answers to problems, to form general rules or conclusions. Includes coming up with a logical explanation for why a series of seemingly unrelated events occur together. Oral Comprehension—The ability to listen to and understand information and ideas presented verbally. Oral Expression—The ability to communicate information and ideas verbally so others will understand. Written Expression—The ability to communicate information and ideas in writing so others will understand. Deductive Reasoning—The ability to apply general rules to specific problems to come up with logical answers. Involves deciding if an answer makes sense.

Skills: Information Gathering—Knowing how to find information and identifying essential information. Speaking—Talking to others to effectively convey information. Active Listening—Listening to what other people are saying; asking questions as appropriate. Critical Thinking—Using logic and analysis to identify the strengths and weaknesses of different approaches. Active Learning—Working with new material or information to grasp its implications.

Generalized Work Activities: Getting Information Needed to Do the Job—Observing, receiving, and otherwise obtaining information from all relevant sources. Identifying Objects, Actions, and Events—Identifying information received by making estimates or categorizations, recognizing differences or similarities, or sensing changes in circumstances or events. Documenting/Recording Information—Entering, transcribing, recording, storing, or maintaining information in either written form or by electronic/magnetic recording. Analyzing Data or Information—Identifying underlying principles, reasons, or facts by breaking down information or data into separate parts. Making Decisions and Solving Problems—Combining, evaluating, and analyzing information and data to make decisions and solve problems. Involves making decisions about the relative importance of information and choosing the best solution.

Police Identification and Records Officers

Collect evidence at crime scene, classify and identify fingerprints, and photograph evidence for use in criminal and civil cases. Develops film and prints, using photographic developing equipment. Submits evidence to supervisor. Takes photographs and fingerprints, and records physical description, of homicide victims and suspects for identification. Classifies and files fingerprints. Lifts prints from crime site, using special tape. Dusts selected areas of crime scene to locate and reveal latent fingerprints. Photographs crime or accident scene to obtain record of evidence.

Personality Type: Conventional. Conventional occupations frequently involve following set procedures and routines. These occupations can include working with data and details more than with ideas. Usually there is a clear line of authority to follow.

Abilities: Category Flexibility—The ability to produce many rules so that each rule tells how to group or combine a set of things in a different way. Near Vision—The ability to see details of objects at a close range. Information Ordering—The ability to correctly follow a given rule or set of rules in order to arrange things or actions in a certain order. The things or actions can include numbers, letters, words, pictures, procedures, sentences, and mathematical or logical operations. Arm-Hand Steadiness—The ability to keep the hand and arm steady while making an arm movement or while holding the arm and hand in one position.

Skills: Information Gathering—Knowing how to find information and identifying essential information. Information Organization—Finding ways to structure or classify multiple pieces of information. Writing—Communicating effectively with others in writing as indicated by the needs of the audience. Operation and Control—Controlling operations of equipment or systems. Product Inspection—Inspecting and evaluating the quality of products.

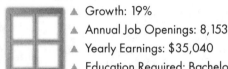

Generalized Work Activities: Getting Information Needed to Do the Job—Observing, receiving, and otherwise obtaining information from all relevant sources. Documenting/Recording Information—Entering, transcribing, recording, storing, or maintaining information in either written form or by electronic/magnetic recording. Communicating with Other Workers—Providing information to supervisors, fellow workers, and subordinates. This information can be exchanged face-to-face, in writing, or via telephone/electronic transfer. Identifying Objects, Actions, and Events—Identifying information received by making estimates or categorizations, recognizing differences or similarities, or sensing changes in circumstances or events. Processing Information—Compiling, coding, categorizing, calculating, tabulating, auditing, verifying, or processing information or data.

Dietitians and Nutritionists

- ▲ Growth: 19%
- ▲ Annual Job Openings: 8,153
- ▲ Yearly Earnings: $35,040
- ▲ Education Required: Bachelor's degree
- ▲ Self-Employed: 13.2%
- ▲ Part-Time: 29.1%

Dietitians and Nutritionists

Plan and conduct food service or nutritional programs to assist in the promotion of health and the control of disease. Supervise activities of a department providing quantity food services. Counsel individuals. Conduct nutritional research. Plans, organizes, and conducts training programs in dietetics, nutrition, and institutional management and administration for medical students and hospital personnel. Monitors food service operations and ensures conformance to nutritional and quality standards. Develops and implements dietary-care plans based on assessments of nutritional needs, diet restrictions, and other current health plans. Consults with physicians and healthcare personnel to determine nutritional needs and diet restrictions of patient or client. Inspects meals served for conformance to prescribed diets and standards of palatability and appearance. Develops curriculum and prepares manuals, visual aids, course outlines, and other materials used in teaching. Plans and prepares grant proposals to request program funding. Confers with design, building, and equipment personnel to plan for construction and remodeling of food service units. Evaluates nutritional care plans and provides follow-up on continuity of care. Plans, conducts, and evaluates dietary, nutritional, and epidemiological research; analyzes findings for practical applications. Supervises activities of workers engaged in planning, preparing, and serving meals. Writes research reports and other publications to document and communicate research findings. Instructs patients and their families in nutritional principles, dietary plans, and food selection and preparation.

Personality Type: Investigative. Investigative occupations frequently involve working with ideas and require an extensive amount of thinking. These occupations can involve searching for facts and figuring out problems mentally.

Abilities: Oral Expression—The ability to communicate information and ideas verbally so others will understand. Written Expression—The ability to communicate information and ideas in writing so others will understand. Speech Clarity—The ability to speak clearly so that what is said is understandable to a listener. Written Comprehension—The ability to read and understand information and ideas presented in writing. Near Vision—The ability to see details of objects at a close range. Inductive Reasoning—The ability to combine separate pieces of information, or specific answers to problems, to form general rules or conclusions. Includes coming up with a logical explanation for why a series of seemingly unrelated events occur together. Information Ordering—The ability to correctly follow a given rule or set of rules in order to arrange things or actions in a certain order. The things or actions can include numbers, letters, words, pictures, procedures, sentences, and mathematical or logical operations. Oral Comprehension—The ability to listen to and understand information and ideas presented verbally.

Skills: Judgment and Decision Making—Weighing the relative costs and benefits of a potential action. Writing—Communicating effectively with others in writing as indicated by the needs of the audience. Instructing—Teaching others how to do something. Speaking—Talking to others to effectively convey information.

Generalized Work Activities: Getting Information Needed to Do the Job—Observing, receiving, and otherwise obtaining information from all relevant sources. Communicating with Persons Outside Organization—Communicating with persons outside the organization. Representing the organization to customers, the public, government, and other external sources. Exchanging information face-to-face, in writing, or via telephone/electronic transfer. Making Decisions and Solving Problems—Combining, evaluating, and analyzing information and data to make decisions and solve problems. Involves making decisions about the relative importance of information and choosing the best solution. Identifying Objects, Actions, and Events—Identifying information received by making estimates or categorizations, recognizing differences or similarities, or sensing changes in circumstances or events. Communicating with Other Workers—Providing information to supervisors, fellow workers, and subordinates. This information can be exchanged face-to-face, in writing, or via telephone/ electronic transfer. Analyzing Data or Information— Identifying underlying principles, reasons, or facts by breaking down information or data into separate parts.

Dining Room and Cafeteria Attendants and Bar Helpers

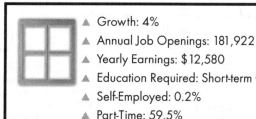

- ▲ Growth: 4%
- ▲ Annual Job Openings: 181,922
- ▲ Yearly Earnings: $12,580
- ▲ Education Required: Short-term O-J-T
- ▲ Self-Employed: 0.2%
- ▲ Part-Time: 59.5%

Dining Room and Cafeteria Attendants and Bar Helpers

Facilitate food service. Clean tables. Carry dirty dishes. Replace soiled table linens. Set tables. Replenish supply of clean linens, silverware, glassware, and dishes. Supply service bar with food. Serve water, butter, and coffee to patrons. Mixes and prepares flavors for mixed drinks. Carries food, dishes, trays, and silverware from kitchen and supply departments to serving counters. Replenishes supply of clean linens, silverware, glassware, and dishes in dining room. Carries trays from food counters to tables for cafeteria patrons. Serves ice water and butter to patrons. Keeps assigned area and equipment clean. Makes coffee. Fills fruit juice dispensers. Stocks vending machines with food in automat. Stocks refrigerating units with wines and bottled beer; replaces empty beer kegs; slices and pits fruit used to garnish drinks. Washes glasses, bar, and equipment; polishes bar fixtures; mops floors; removes empty bottles and trash. Garnishes and positions foods on table to ensure visibility to patrons and convenience in serving. Sets tables with clean linens, sugar bowls, and condiments. Cleans bar and equipment. Replenishes bar supplies such as liquor, fruit, ice, and dishes. Replenishes food and equipment at steam tables and serving counters of cafeteria to facilitate service to patrons. Carries dirty dishes to kitchen; wipes tables and seats with dampened cloth. Circulates among diners and serves coffee.

Personality Type: Realistic. Realistic occupations frequently involve work activities that include practical, hands-on problems and solutions. They often deal with plants, animals, and real-world materials like wood, tools, and machinery. Many of the occupations require working outside and do not involve a lot of paperwork or working closely with others.

Abilities: Wrist-Finger Speed—The ability to make fast, simple, repeated movements of the fingers, hands, and wrists. Static Strength—The ability to exert maximum muscle force to lift, push, pull, or carry objects. Oral Comprehension—The ability to listen to and understand information and ideas presented verbally. Manual Dexterity—The ability to quickly make coordinated movements of one hand, a hand together with its arm, or two hands, to grasp, manipulate, or assemble objects. Time Sharing—The ability to efficiently shift back and forth between two or more activities or sources of information such as speech, sounds, or touch.

Skills: Service Orientation—Actively looking for ways to help people. Social Perceptiveness—Being aware of other people's reactions and understanding why people react the way they do. Active Listening—Listening to what other people are saying; asking questions as appropriate. Coordination—Adjusting actions in relation to others' actions.

Generalized Work Activities: Handling and Moving Objects—Using one's hands and arms in handling, installing, forming, positioning, and moving materials, or in manipulating things. Performing General Physical Activities—Performing physical activities that require moving one's whole body, such as in climbing, lifting, balancing, walking, and stooping. Performing activities that often also require considerable use of the arms and legs, such as in the physical handling of materials. Monitoring Processes, Materials, Surroundings—Monitoring and reviewing information from materials, events, or the environment, often to detect problems or to find out when things are finished. Performing for/Working with Public—Performing for people or dealing directly with the public, including serving persons in restaurants and stores and receiving clients or guests. Implementing Ideas and Programs—Conducting or carrying out work procedures and activities in accord with one's own ideas or information provided through directions/instructions for purposes of installing, modifying, preparing, delivering, constructing, integrating, finishing, or completing programs, systems, structures, or products.

Directors of Religious Activities and Education

- ▲ Growth: 25%
- ▲ Annual Job Openings: 13,292
- ▲ Yearly Earnings: $24,970
- ▲ Education Required: Bachelor's degree
- ▲ Self-Employed: 1.2%
- ▲ Part-Time: 14%

Directors, Religious Activities and Education

Direct and coordinate activities of a denominational group to meet religious needs of students. Plan, direct, or coordinate church-school programs designed to promote religious education among church membership. Provide counseling and guidance relative to marital, health, financial, and religious problems. Analyzes member participation and changes in congregation emphasis to determine needs for religious education. Counsels individuals regarding marital, health, financial, and religious problems. Plans congregational activities and projects to encourage participation in religious education programs. Assists and advises groups in promoting interfaith understanding. Solicits support of, participation in, and interest in religious education programs from congregation members, organizations, officials, and clergy. Interprets policies of university to community religious workers. Analyzes revenue and program cost data to determine budget priorities. Orders and distributes school supplies. Supervises instructional staff in religious education program. Promotes student participation in extracurricular congregational activities. Develops, organizes, and directs study courses and religious education programs within congregation. Coordinates activities with religious advisers, councils, and university officials to meet religious needs of students. Interprets religious education to public through speaking, leading discussions, and writing articles for local and national publications. Plans and conducts conferences dealing with interpretation of religious ideas and convictions.

Personality Type: Social. Social occupations frequently involve working with, communicating with, and teaching people. These occupations often involve helping or providing service to others.

Abilities: Oral Expression—The ability to communicate information and ideas verbally so others will understand. Oral Comprehension—The ability to listen to and understand information and ideas presented verbally. Speech Clarity—The ability to speak clearly so that what is said is understandable to a listener. Written Expression—The ability to communicate information and ideas in writing so others will understand. Problem Sensitivity—The ability to tell when something is wrong or is likely to go wrong. Does not involve solving the problem, only recognizing there is a problem.

Skills: Speaking—Talking to others to effectively convey information. Active Listening—Listening to what other people are saying; asking questions as appropriate. Information Gathering—Knowing how to find information and identifying essential information. Service Orientation—Actively looking for ways to help people. Reading Comprehension—Understanding written information in work-related documents. Social Perceptiveness—Being aware of other people's reactions and understanding why people react the way they do. Implementation Planning—Developing approaches for implementing an idea.

Generalized Work Activities: Communicating with Persons Outside Organization—Communicating with persons outside the organization. Representing the organization to customers, the public, government, and other external sources. Exchanging information face-to-face, in writing, or via telephone/electronic transfer. Communicating with Other Workers—Providing information to supervisors, fellow workers, and subordinates. This information can be exchanged face-to-face, in writing, or via telephone/electronic transfer. Establishing and Maintaining Relationships—Developing constructive and cooperative working relationships with others. Providing Consultation and Advice to Others—Providing consultation and expert advice to management or other groups on technical, systems-related, or process-related topics. Teaching Others—Identifying educational needs, developing formal training programs or classes, and teaching or instructing others. Assisting and Caring for Others—Providing assistance or personal care to others. Getting Information Needed to Do the Job—Observing, receiving, and otherwise obtaining information from all relevant sources.

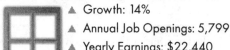

Dispensing Opticians

- ▲ Growth: 14%
- ▲ Annual Job Openings: 5,799
- ▲ Yearly Earnings: $22,440
- ▲ Education Required: Long-term O-J-T
- ▲ Self-Employed: 6.4%
- ▲ Part-Time: 10.6%

Opticians, Dispensing

Design, measure, fit, and adapt lenses and frames for client according to written optical prescription or specification. Assist client with selecting frames. Measure customer for size of eyeglasses; coordinate frames with facial and eye measurements and optical prescription. Prepare work order for optical laboratory, including instructions for grinding and mounting lenses in frames. Verify exactness of finished lens spectacles. Adjust frame and lens position to fit client. Shape or reshape frames. Heats, shapes, or bends plastic or metal frames to adjust eyeglasses to fit client, using pliers and hands. Determines client's current lens prescription, using lensometer or lens analyzer and client's eyeglasses. Evaluates prescription in conjunction with client's vocational and avocational visual requirements. Repairs damaged frames. Prepares work order and instructions for grinding lenses and fabricating eyeglasses. Fabricates lenses to prescription specifications. Assists client in selecting frames according to style and color, coordinating frames with facial and eye measurements and optical prescription. Recommends specific lenses, lens coatings, and frames to suit client needs. Verifies that finished lenses are ground to specification. Measures client's bridge and eye size, temple length, vertex distance, pupillary distance, and optical centers of eyes, using measuring devices. Instructs clients in adapting to wearing and caring for eyeglasses. Grinds lens edges or applies coating to lenses.

Personality Type: Enterprising. Enterprising occupations frequently involve starting up and carrying out projects. These occupations can involve leading people and making many decisions. They sometimes require risk taking and often deal with business.

Abilities: Oral Expression—The ability to communicate information and ideas verbally so others will understand. Arm-Hand Steadiness—The ability to keep the hand and arm steady while making an arm movement or while holding the arm and hand in one position. Oral Comprehension—The ability to listen to and understand information and ideas presented verbally. Near Vision—The ability to see details of objects at a close range. Written Comprehension—The ability to read and understand information and ideas presented in writing.

Skills: Product Inspection—Inspecting and evaluating the quality of products. Problem Identification—Identifying the nature of problems. Active Listening—Listening to what other people are saying; asking questions as appropriate. Service Orientation—Actively looking for ways to help people. Technology Design—Generating or adapting equipment and technology to serve user needs. Mathematics—Using mathematics to solve problems.

Generalized Work Activities: Getting Information Needed to Do the Job—Observing, receiving, and otherwise obtaining information from all relevant sources. Performing for/Working with Public—Performing for people or dealing directly with the public, including serving persons in restaurants and stores and receiving clients or guests. Evaluating Information against Standards—Evaluating information against a set of standards and verifying that it is correct. Implementing Ideas and Programs—Conducting or carrying out work procedures and activities in accord with one's own ideas or information provided through directions/instructions for purposes of installing, modifying, preparing, delivering, constructing, integrating, finishing, or completing programs, systems, structures, or products. Assisting and Caring for Others—Providing assistance or personal care to others. Communicating with Persons Outside Organization—Communicating with persons outside the organization. Representing the organization to customers, the public, government, and other external sources. Exchanging information face-to-face, in writing, or via telephone/electronic transfer. Handling and Moving Objects—Using one's hands and arms in handling, installing, forming, positioning, and moving materials, or in manipulating things. Includes the use of keyboards.

Economists and Marketing Research Analysts

- ▲ Growth: 18%
- ▲ Annual Job Openings: 11,550
- ▲ Yearly Earnings: $48,330
- ▲ Education Required: Bachelor's degree
- ▲ Self-Employed: 18.9%
- ▲ Part-Time: 8.8%

Economists

Conduct research, prepare reports, and formulate plans to aid in solution of economic problems arising from production and distribution of goods and services. Collect and process economic and statistical data using econometric and sampling techniques. Provides advice and consultation to business and public and private agencies. Reviews and analyzes data to prepare reports, to forecast future marketing trends, and to stay abreast of economic changes. Compiles data relating to research areas such as employment, productivity, and wages and hours. Develops economic guidelines and standards and prepares points of view used in forecasting trends and in formulating economic policy. Supervises research projects and students' study projects. Organizes research data into report format, including graphic illustrations of research findings. Teaches theories, principles, and methods of economics. Devises methods and procedures for collecting and processing data, using various econometric and sampling techniques. Formulates recommendations, policies, or plans to interpret markets or solve economic problems. Studies economic and statistical data in area of specialization, such as finance, labor, or agriculture. Assigns work to staff. Testifies at regulatory or legislative hearings to present recommendations.

Personality Type: Investigative. Investigative occupations frequently involve working with ideas and require an extensive amount of thinking. These occupations can involve searching for facts and figuring out problems mentally.

Abilities: Written Comprehension—The ability to read and understand information and ideas presented in writing. Mathematical Reasoning—The ability to understand and organize a problem and then select a mathematical method or formula to solve the problem. Written Expression—The ability to communicate information and ideas in writing so others will understand. Number Facility—The ability to add, subtract, multiply, or divide quickly and correctly. Oral Expression—The ability to communicate information and ideas verbally so others will understand.

Skills: Problem Identification—Identifying the nature of problems. Information Gathering—Knowing how to find information and identifying essential information. Monitoring—Assessing how well one is doing when learning or doing something. Writing—Communicating effectively with others in writing as indicated by the needs of the audience. Reading Comprehension—Understanding written information in work-related documents. Visioning—Developing an image of how a system should work under ideal conditions. Systems Perception—Determining when important changes have occurred in a system or are likely to occur.

Generalized Work Activities: Updating and Using Job-Relevant Knowledge—Keeping up-to-date technically and knowing the functions of one's own job and related jobs. Getting Information Needed to Do the Job—Observing, receiving, and otherwise obtaining information from all relevant sources. Processing Information—Compiling, coding, categorizing, calculating, tabulating, auditing, verifying, or processing information or data. Analyzing Data or Information—Identifying underlying principles, reasons, or facts by breaking down information or data into separate parts. Making Decisions and Solving Problems—Combining, evaluating, and analyzing information and data to make decisions and solve problems. Involves making decisions about the relative importance of information and choosing the best solution. Identifying Objects, Actions, and Events—Identifying information received by making estimates or categorizations, recognizing differences or similarities, or sensing changes in circumstances or events. Handling and Moving Objects—Using one's hands and arms in handling, installing, forming, positioning, and moving materials, or in manipulating things. Includes the use of keyboards.

Market Research Analysts

Research market conditions in local, regional, or national areas to determine potential sales of a product or service. Gather information on competitors, prices, sales, and methods of marketing and distribution. Use survey results to create a marketing campaign based on regional preferences and buying habits. Collects data on customer preferences and buying habits. Checks consumer reaction to new or improved products or services. Attends staff conferences to submit findings and proposals to management for consideration. Prepares reports and graphic illustrations of findings. Gathers data on competitors and analyzes prices, sales, and method of marketing and distribution. Establishes research methodology and designs format for gathering data, such as surveys, opinion polls, or questionnaires.

Examines and analyzes statistical data to forecast future marketing trends and to identify potential markets. Translates complex numerical data into nontechnical, written text.

Personality Type: Investigative. Investigative occupations frequently involve working with ideas and require an extensive amount of thinking. These occupations can involve searching for facts and figuring out problems mentally.

Abilities: Mathematical Reasoning—The ability to understand and organize a problem and then select a mathematical method or formula to solve the problem. Number Facility—The ability to add, subtract, multiply, or divide quickly and correctly. Written Expression—The ability to communicate information and ideas in writing so others will understand. Written Comprehension—The ability to read and understand information and ideas presented in writing. Oral Expression—The ability to communicate information and ideas verbally so others will understand. Near Vision—The ability to see details of objects at a close range.

Skills: Information Gathering—Knowing how to find information and identifying essential information. Identification of Key Causes—Identifying the things that must be changed to achieve a goal. Mathematics—Using mathematics to solve problems. Critical Thinking—Using logic and analysis to identify the strengths and weaknesses of different approaches. Writing—Communicating effectively with others in writing as indicated by the needs of the audience.

Generalized Work Activities: Getting Information Needed to Do the Job—Observing, receiving, and otherwise obtaining information from all relevant sources. Analyzing Data or Information—Identifying underlying principles, reasons, or facts by breaking down information or data into separate parts. Interpreting Meaning of Information to Others—Translating or explaining what information means and how it can be understood or used to support responses or feedback to others. Processing Information—Compiling, coding, categorizing, calculating, tabulating, auditing, verifying, or processing information or data. Communicating with Other Workers—Providing information to supervisors, fellow workers, and subordinates. This information can be exchanged face-to-face, in writing, or via telephone/ electronic transfer. Identifying Objects, Actions, and Events—Identifying information received by making estimates or categorizations, recognizing differences or similarities, or sensing changes in circumstances or events. Handling and Moving Objects—Using one's hands and arms in handling, installing, forming, positioning, and moving materials, or in manipulating things. Includes the use of keyboards.

Education Administrators

▲ Growth: 13%
▲ Annual Job Openings: 60,229
▲ Yearly Earnings: $60,400
▲ Education Required: Work experience, plus degree
▲ Self-Employed: 13.8%
▲ Part-Time: 9.8%

Education Administrators, Elementary and Secondary School

Plan, direct, and coordinate the academic, clerical, or auxiliary activities of public or private elementary or secondary level schools. Collects and analyzes survey data, regulatory information, and demographic and employment trends to forecast enrollment patterns and curriculum changes. Completes, maintains, or assigns preparation of attendance, activity, planning, or personnel reports and records for officials and agencies. Coordinates outreach activities with businesses, communities, and other institutions or organizations to identify educational needs and to establish and coordinate programs. Determines scope of educational programs; prepares drafts of course schedules and descriptions to estimate staffing and facility requirements. Prepares and submits budget requests or grant proposals to solicit program funding. Evaluates programs to determine effectiveness, efficiency, and utilization and to ensure that activities comply with federal, state, and local regulations. Counsels and provides guidance to students regarding personal, academic, or behavioral problems. Reviews and interprets government codes; develops programs to ensure facility safety, security, and maintenance. Plans, directs, and monitors instructional methods and content for educational, vocational, or student activity programs. Confers with parents and staff to discuss educational activities, policies, and student behavioral or learning problems. Reviews and approves new programs or recommends modifications to existing programs. Teaches classes or courses to students. Establishes program philosophy plans, policies, and academic codes of ethics to maintain educational standards for student screening, placement, and training. Writes articles, manuals, and other publications; assists in the distribution of promotional literature. Contacts and addresses commercial, community, or political groups to promote educational programs and services or to lobby for legislative changes. Recruits, hires, trains, and evaluates primary and supplemental staff. Recommends personnel actions for programs and services.

Personality Type: Social. Social occupations frequently involve working with, communicating with, and teaching people. These occupations often involve helping or providing service to others.

Abilities: Written Expression—The ability to communicate information and ideas in writing so others will understand. Oral Expression—The ability to communicate information and ideas verbally so others will understand. Written Comprehension—The ability to read and understand information and ideas presented in writing. Oral Comprehension—The ability to listen to and understand information and ideas presented verbally. Speech Clarity—The ability to speak clearly so that what is said is understandable to a listener.

Skills: Coordination—Adjusting actions in relation to others' actions. Speaking—Talking to others to effectively convey information. Reading Comprehension—Understanding written information in work-related documents. Writing—Communicating effectively with others in writing as indicated by the needs of the audience. Social Perceptiveness—Being aware of other people's reactions and understanding why people react the way they do.

Generalized Work Activities: Communicating with Persons Outside Organization—Communicating with persons outside the organization. Representing the organization to customers, the public, government, and other external sources. Exchanging information face-to-face, in writing, or via telephone/electronic transfer. Communicating with Other Workers—Providing information to supervisors, fellow workers, and subordinates. This information can be exchanged face-to-face, in writing, or via telephone/electronic transfer. Providing Consultation and Advice to Others—Providing consultation and expert advice to management or other groups on technical, systems-related, or process-related topics. Getting Information Needed to Do the Job—Observing, receiving, and otherwise obtaining information from all relevant sources. Coordinating Work and Activities of Others—Coordinating members of a work group to accomplish tasks. Teaching Others—Identifying educational needs, developing formal training programs or classes, and teaching or instructing others. Handling and Moving Objects—Using one's hands and arms in handling, installing, forming, positioning, and moving materials, or in manipulating things. Includes the use of keyboards.

Education Administrators, Postsecondary

Plan, direct, and coordinate research, instruction, student administration and services, and other educational activities at postsecondary institutions, including universities, colleges, and junior and community colleges. Directs work activities of personnel engaged in administration of academic institutions, departments, and alumni organizations. Coordinates alumni functions and encourages alumni endorsement of recruiting and fund-raising activities. Determines course schedules and correlates room assignments to ensure optimum use of buildings and equipment. Completes and submits operating budget for approval, controls expenditures, and maintains financial reports and records. Consults with staff, students, alumni, and subject experts to determine needs/feasibility and to formulate admission policies and educational programs. Estimates and allocates department funding based on financial success of previous courses and other pertinent factors. Advises staff and students on problems relating to policies, program administration, and financial and personal matters; recommends solutions. Evaluates personnel and physical plant operations, student programs, and statistical and research data to implement procedures or modifications to administrative policies. Represents college/university as liaison officer with accrediting agencies; facilitates exchange of information between academic institutions and community. Meets with academic and administrative personnel to disseminate information, identify problems, monitor progress reports, and ensure adherence to goals/objectives. Confers with other academic staff to explain requirements for admission and policies for transfer of credits; compares course equivalencies to university/college curriculum. Negotiates with foundation and industry representatives to secure loans for university and to identify costs and materials for building construction. Reviews reports on student misconduct requiring disciplinary action; counsels students to ensure conformance to university policies. Plans and promotes athletic policies, sports events, ticket sales, and student participation in social, cultural, and recreational activities.

Personality Type: Enterprising. Enterprising occupations frequently involve starting up and carrying out projects. These occupations can involve leading people and making many decisions. They sometimes require risk taking and often deal with business.

Abilities: Written Expression—The ability to communicate information and ideas in writing so others will understand. Oral Comprehension—The ability to listen to and understand information and ideas presented verbally. Deductive Reasoning—The ability to apply general rules to specific problems to come up with logical answers. Involves deciding if an answer makes sense. Written Comprehension—The ability to read and understand information and ideas presented in writing. Oral Expression—The ability to communicate information and ideas verbally so others will understand.

Skills: Management of Financial Resources— Determining how money will be spent to get the work done, and accounting for these expenditures. Coordination—Adjusting actions in relation to others' actions. Judgment and Decision Making—Weighing the relative costs and benefits of a potential action. Management of Personnel Resources—Motivating, developing, and directing people as they work, identifying the best people for the job. Speaking— Talking to others to effectively convey information.

Generalized Work Activities: Performing Administrative Activities—Approving requests, handling paperwork, and performing day-to-day administrative tasks. Making Decisions and Solving Problems—Combining, evaluating, and analyzing information and data to make decisions and solve problems. Involves making decisions about the relative importance of information and choosing the best solution. Communicating with Persons Outside Organization—Communicating with persons outside the organization. Representing the organization to customers, the public, government, and other external sources. Exchanging information face-to-face, in writing, or via telephone/electronic transfer. Establishing and Maintaining Relationships—Developing constructive and cooperative working relationships with others. Getting Information Needed to Do the Job— Observing, receiving, and otherwise obtaining information from all relevant sources. Monitoring and Controlling Resources—Monitoring and controlling resources and overseeing the spending of money. Handling and Moving Objects—Using one's hands and arms in handling, installing, forming, positioning, and moving materials, or in manipulating things. Includes the use of keyboards.

Education Administrators, Preschool and Child Care Center/Program

Plan, direct, or coordinate the academic and non-academic activities of preschool and child-care centers or programs. Counsels and provides guidance to students regarding personal, academic, or behavioral problems. Plans, directs, and monitors instructional methods and content for educational, vocational, or student activity programs. Evaluates programs to determine effectiveness, efficiency, and utilization. Evaluates programs to ensure that activities comply with federal, state, and local regulations. Determines scope of educational programs and prepares drafts of course schedules and descriptions to estimate staffing and facility requirements. Collects and analyzes survey data, regulatory information, and demographic and employment trends to forecast enrollment patterns and curriculum changes. Determines allocations of funds for staff, supplies, materials, and equipment; authorizes purchases. Contacts and addresses commercial, community, or political groups to promote educational programs and services or to lobby for legislative changes. Writes articles, manuals, and other publications; assists in the distribution of promotional literature. Confers with parents and staff to discuss educational activities, policies, and student behavioral or learning problems. Establishes program philosophy, plans, policies, and academic codes of ethics to maintain educational standards for student screening, placement, and training. Reviews and interprets government codes; develops programs to ensure facility safety, security, and maintenance. Reviews and approves new programs or recommends modifications to existing programs. Prepares and submits budget requests or grant proposals to solicit program funding. Coordinates outreach activities with businesses, communities, and other institutions or organizations to identify educational needs and to establish and coordinate programs. Directs and coordinates activities of teachers or administrators at daycare centers, schools, public agencies, and institutions. Teaches classes or courses to students.

Personality Type: Social. Social occupations frequently involve working with, communicating with, and teaching people. These occupations often involve helping or providing service to others.

Abilities: Oral Expression—The ability to communicate information and ideas verbally so others will understand. Written Expression—The ability to communicate information and ideas in writing so others will understand. Written Comprehension—The ability to read and understand information and ideas presented in writing. Oral Comprehension—The ability to listen to and understand information and ideas presented verbally. Speech Clarity—The ability to speak clearly so that what is said is understandable to a listener.

Skills: Coordination—Adjusting actions in relation to others' actions. Speaking—Talking to others to effectively convey information. Reading Comprehension—Understanding written information in work-related documents. Writing—Communicating effectively with others in writing as indicated by the needs of the audience. Social Perceptiveness—Being aware of other people's reactions and understanding why people react the way they do.

Generalized Work Activities: Communicating with Persons Outside Organization—Communicating with persons outside the organization. Representing the organization to customers, the public, government, and other external sources. Exchanging information face-to-face, in writing, or via telephone/electronic transfer. Communicating with Other Workers—Providing information to supervisors, fellow workers, and subordinates. This information can be exchanged face-to-face, in writing, or via telephone/electronic transfer. Getting Information Needed to Do the Job—Observing, receiving, and otherwise obtaining information from all relevant sources. Providing Consultation and Advice to Others—Providing consultation and expert advice to management or other groups on technical, systems-related, or process-related topics.

Teaching Others—Identifying educational needs, developing formal training programs or classes, and teaching or instructing others. Coordinating Work and Activities of Others—Coordinating members of a work group to accomplish tasks. Handling and Moving Objects—Using one's hands and arms in handling, installing, forming, positioning, and moving materials, or in manipulating things. Includes the use of keyboards.

Instructional Coordinators

Develop instructional material, coordinate educational content, and incorporate current technology in specialized fields that provide guidelines to educators and instructors for developing curricula and for conducting courses. Conducts or participates in workshops, committees, and conferences designed to promote intellectual, social, and physical welfare of students. Addresses public audiences to explain and elicit support for program objectives. Confers with school officials, teachers, and administrative staff to plan and develop curricula and establish guidelines for educational programs. Advises school officials on implementation of state and federal programs and procedures. Prepares or approves manuals, guidelines, and reports on state educational policies and practices, for distribution to school districts. Coordinates activities of workers engaged in cataloging, distributing, and maintaining educational materials and equipment in curriculum library and laboratory. Interprets and enforces provisions of state education codes. Interprets and enforces rules and regulations of state board of education. Prepares or assists in preparation of grant proposals, budgets, and program policies and goals. Inspects and authorizes repair of instructional equipment such as musical instruments. Advises teaching and administrative staff in assessment, curriculum development, management of student behavior, and use of materials and equipment. Observes, evaluates, and recommends changes in work of teaching staff to strengthen teaching skills in classroom. Confers with educational committees and advisory groups to gather information on instructional methods and materials related to specific academic subjects. Orders or authorizes purchase of instructional materials, supplies, equipment, and visual aids designed to meet educational needs of students. Develops tests, questionnaires, and procedures to measure effectiveness of curriculum and to determine if program objectives are being met. Researches, evaluates, and prepares recommendations on curricula, instructional methods, and materials for school system.

Personality Type: Social. Social occupations frequently involve working with, communicating with, and teaching people. These occupations often involve helping or providing service to others.

Abilities: Oral Expression—The ability to communicate information and ideas verbally so others will understand. Written Expression—The ability to communicate information and ideas in writing so others will understand. Written Comprehension—The ability to read and understand information and ideas presented in writing. Oral Comprehension—The ability to listen to and understand information and ideas presented verbally. Deductive Reasoning—The ability to apply general rules to specific problems to come up with logical answers. Involves deciding if an answer makes sense.

Skills: Learning Strategies—Using multiple approaches when learning or teaching new things. Speaking—Talking to others to effectively convey information. Writing—Communicating effectively with others in writing as indicated by the needs of the audience. Reading Comprehension—Understanding written information in work-related documents. Instructing—Teaching others how to do something.

Generalized Work Activities: Getting Information Needed to Do the Job—Observing, receiving, and otherwise obtaining information from all relevant sources. Communicating with Persons Outside Organization—Communicating with persons outside the organization. Representing the organization to customers, the public, government, and other external sources. Exchanging information face-to-face, in writing, or via telephone/electronic transfer. Providing Consultation and Advice to Others—Providing consultation and expert advice to management or other groups on technical, systems-related, or process-related topics. Teaching Others—Identifying educational needs, developing formal training programs or classes, and teaching or instructing others. Analyzing Data or Information—Identifying underlying principles, reasons, or facts by breaking down information or data into separate parts. Communicating with Other Workers—Providing information to supervisors, fellow workers, and subordinates. This information can be exchanged face-to-face, in writing, or via telephone/electronic transfer. Handling and Moving Objects—Using one's hands and arms in handling, installing, forming, positioning, and moving materials, or in manipulating things. Includes the use of keyboards.

Electrical and Electronics Engineers

- ▲ Growth: 26%
- ▲ Annual Job Openings: 29,636
- ▲ Yearly Earnings: $62,260
- ▲ Education Required: Bachelor's degree
- ▲ Self-Employed: 2.9%
- ▲ Part-Time: 2.6%

Computer Hardware Engineers

Research, design, develop, and test computer or computer-related equipment for commercial, industrial, military, or scientific use. Supervise the manufacturing and installation of computer or computer-related equipment and components. Trains users to use new or modified equipment. Coordinates installation of software system. Consults with engineering staff to evaluate interface between hardware and software. Consults with engineering staff to evaluate operational and performance requirements of overall system. Confers with data processing and project managers to obtain information on limitations and capabilities for data-processing projects. Consults with customer concerning maintenance of software system. Enters data into computer terminal to store, retrieve, and manipulate data for analysis of system capabilities and requirements. Evaluates factors such as reporting formats required, cost constraints, and need for security restrictions, to determine hardware configuration. Specifies power-supply requirements and configuration. Monitors functioning of equipment to ensure that system operates in conformance with specifications. Develops and directs software system testing procedures, programming, and documentation. Analyzes software requirements to determine feasibility of design within time and cost constraints. Formulates and designs software system, using scientific analysis and mathematical models to predict and measure outcome and consequences of design. Analyzes information to determine, recommend, and plan layout for type of computers and for peripheral equipment modifications to existing systems. Recommends purchase of equipment to control dust, temperature, and humidity in area of system installation.

Personality Type: Investigative. Investigative occupations frequently involve working with ideas and require an extensive amount of thinking. These occupations can involve searching for facts and figuring out problems mentally.

Abilities: Written Comprehension—The ability to read and understand information and ideas presented in writing. Inductive Reasoning—The ability to combine separate pieces of information, or specific answers to problems, to form general rules or conclusions. Includes coming up with a logical explanation for why a series of seemingly unrelated events occur together. Oral Comprehension—The ability to listen to and understand information and ideas presented verbally. Mathematical Reasoning—The ability to understand and organize a problem and then select a mathematical method or formula to solve the problem. Oral Expression—The ability to communicate information and ideas verbally so others will understand. Written

Expression—The ability to communicate information and ideas in writing so others will understand.

Skills: Operations Analysis—Analyzing needs and product requirements to create a design. Mathematics—Using mathematics to solve problems. Information Organization—Finding ways to structure or classify multiple pieces of information. Programming—Writing computer programs for various purposes. Troubleshooting—Determining what is causing an operating error and deciding what to do about it. Science—Using scientific methods to solve problems.

Generalized Work Activities: Interacting with Computers—Controlling computer functions by using programs, setting up functions, writing software, or otherwise communicating with computer systems. Providing Consultation and Advice to Others—Providing consultation and expert advice to management or other groups on technical, systems-related, or process-related topics. Updating and Using Job-Relevant Knowledge—Keeping up-to-date technically and knowing the functions of one's own job and related jobs. Drafting and Specifying Technical Devices—Providing documentation, detailed instructions, drawings, or specifications to inform others about how devices, parts, equipment, or structures are to be fabricated, constructed, assembled, modified, maintained, or used. Thinking Creatively—Originating, inventing, designing, or creating new applications, ideas, relationships, systems, or products, including artistic contributions. Handling and Moving Objects—Using one's hands and arms in handling, installing, forming, positioning, and moving materials, or in manipulating things. Includes the use of keyboards.

Electrical Engineers

Design, develop, test, or supervise the manufacturing and installation of electrical equipment, components, or systems for commercial, industrial, military, or scientific use. Operates computer-assisted engineering and design software and equipment to perform engineering tasks. Collects data relating to commercial and residential development, population, and power-system interconnection to determine operating efficiency of electrical systems. Estimates labor, material, and construction costs; prepares specifications for purchase of materials and equipment. Performs detailed calculations to compute and establish manufacturing, construction, and installation standards and specifications. Develops applications of controls, instruments, and systems for new commercial, domestic, and industrial uses. Investigates customer or public complaints, determines nature and extent of problem, and recommends remedial measures. Plans and implements research methodology and procedures to apply principles of electrical theory to engineering projects. Plans layout of electric power generating plants and distribution lines and stations. Evaluates and analyzes data regarding electric power systems and stations; recommends changes to improve operating efficiency. Confers with engineers, customers, and others to discuss existing or potential engineering projects and products. Conducts field surveys and studies maps, graphs, diagrams, and other data to identify and correct power-system problems. Directs operations and coordinates manufacturing, construction, installation, maintenance, and testing activities to ensure compliance with specifications, codes, and customer requirements. Prepares and studies technical drawings, specifications of electrical systems, and topographical maps to ensure that installation and operations conform to standards and customer requirements. Designs electrical instruments, equipment, facilities, components, products, and systems for commercial, industrial, and domestic purposes. Compiles data and writes reports regarding existing and potential engineering studies and projects.

Personality Type: Investigative. Investigative occupations frequently involve working with ideas and require an extensive amount of thinking. These occupations can involve searching for facts and figuring out problems mentally.

Abilities: Written Comprehension—The ability to read and understand information and ideas presented in writing. Oral Expression—The ability to communicate information and ideas verbally so others will understand. Number Facility—The ability to add, subtract, multiply, or divide quickly and correctly. Oral Comprehension—The ability to listen to and understand information and ideas presented verbally. Deductive Reasoning—The ability to apply general rules to specific problems to

come up with logical answers. Involves deciding if an answer makes sense. Mathematical Reasoning—The ability to understand and organize a problem and then select a mathematical method or formula to solve the problem.

Skills: Mathematics—Using mathematics to solve problems. Science—Using scientific methods to solve problems. Reading Comprehension—Understanding written information in work-related documents. Judgment and Decision Making—Weighing the relative costs and benefits of a potential action. Technology Design—Generating or adapting equipment and technology to serve user needs. Critical Thinking—Using logic and analysis to identify the strengths and weaknesses of different approaches. Idea Generation—Generating a number of different approaches to problems.

Generalized Work Activities: Getting Information Needed to Do the Job—Observing, receiving, and otherwise obtaining information from all relevant sources. Analyzing Data or Information—Identifying underlying principles, reasons, or facts by breaking down information or data into separate parts. Drafting and Specifying Technical Devices—Providing documentation, detailed instructions, drawings, or specifications to inform others about how devices, parts, equipment, or structures are to be fabricated, constructed, assembled, modified, maintained, or used. Making Decisions and Solving Problems—Combining, evaluating, and analyzing information and data to make decisions and solve problems. Involves making decisions about the relative importance of information and choosing the best solution. Implementing Ideas and Programs—Conducting or carrying out work procedures and activities in accord with one's own ideas or information provided through directions/instructions for purposes of installing, modifying, preparing, delivering, constructing, integrating, finishing, or completing programs, systems, structures, or products. Identifying Objects, Actions, and Events—Identifying information received by making estimates or categorizations, recognizing differences or similarities, or sensing changes in circumstances or events. Handling and Moving Objects—Using one's hands and arms in handling, installing, forming, positioning, and moving materials, or in manipulating things. Includes the use of keyboards.

Electronics Engineers, Except Computer

Research, design, develop, and test electronic components and systems for commercial, industrial, military, or scientific use, utilizing knowledge of electronic theory and materials properties. Design electronic circuits and components for use in fields such as telecommunications, aerospace guidance and propulsion control, acoustics, or instruments and controls. Determines material and equipment needs and orders supplies. Reviews or prepares budget and cost estimates for equipment, construction, and installation projects; controls expenditures. Prepares, reviews, and maintains maintenance schedules and operational reports and charts. Provides technical assistance to field and laboratory staff regarding equipment standards and problems and regarding applications of transmitting and receiving methods. Inspects electronic equipment, instruments, products, and systems to ensure conformance to specifications, safety standards, and applicable codes and regulations. Analyzes system requirements, capacity, cost, and customer needs to determine feasibility of project and to develop system plan. Directs and coordinates activities concerned with manufacture, construction, installation, maintenance, operation, and modification of electronic equipment, products, and systems. Plans and implements research, methodology, and procedures to apply principles of electronic theory to engineering projects. Plans and develops applications and modifications for electronic properties used in components, products, and systems, to improve technical performance. Confers with engineers, customers, and others to discuss existing and potential engineering projects or products. Operates computer-assisted engineering and design software and equipment to perform engineering tasks. Prepares engineering sketches and specifications for construction, relocation, and installation of transmitting and receiving equipment, facilities, products, and systems. Designs electronic components, products, and systems for commercial, industrial, medical, military, and scientific applications. Evaluates operational systems; recommends repair or design modifications based on factors such as environment, service, cost, and system capabilities. Develops operational, maintenance, and testing procedures for electronic products, components, equipment, and systems.

Personality Type: Investigative. Investigative occupations frequently involve working with ideas and require an extensive amount of thinking. These occupations can involve searching for facts and figuring out problems mentally.

Abilities: Mathematical Reasoning—The ability to understand and organize a problem and then select a mathematical method or formula to solve the problem. Oral Expression—The ability to communicate information and ideas verbally so others will understand. Oral Comprehension—The ability to listen to and understand information and ideas presented verbally. Written Comprehension—The ability to read and understand information and ideas presented in writing. Deductive Reasoning—The ability to apply general rules to specific problems to come up with logical answers. Involves deciding if an answer makes sense. Number Facility—The ability to add, subtract, multiply, or divide quickly and correctly.

Skills: Judgment and Decision Making—Weighing the relative costs and benefits of a potential action. Mathematics—Using mathematics to solve problems. Reading Comprehension—Understanding written information in work-related documents. Science—Using scientific methods to solve problems. Critical Thinking—Using logic and analysis to identify the strengths and weaknesses of different approaches. Idea Generation—Generating a number of different approaches to problems. Writing—Communicating effectively with others in writing as indicated by the needs of the audience.

Generalized Work Activities: Getting Information Needed to Do the Job—Observing, receiving, and otherwise obtaining information from all relevant sources. Analyzing Data or Information—Identifying underlying principles, reasons, or facts by breaking down information or data into separate parts. Drafting and Specifying Technical Devices—Providing documentation, detailed instructions, drawings, or specifications to inform others about how devices, parts, equipment, or structures are to be fabricated, constructed, assembled, modified, maintained, or used. Inspecting Equipment, Structures, Materials—Inspecting or diagnosing equipment, structures, or materials to identify the causes of errors or other problems or defects. Implementing Ideas and Programs—Conducting or carrying out work procedures and activities in accord with one's own ideas or information provided through directions/instructions for purposes of installing, modifying, preparing, delivering, constructing, integrating, finishing, or completing programs, systems, structures, or products. Making Decisions and Solving Problems—Combining, evaluating, and analyzing information and data to make decisions and solve problems. Involves making decisions about the relative importance of information and choosing the best solution. Handling and Moving Objects—Using one's hands and arms in handling, installing, forming, positioning, and moving materials, or in manipulating things. Includes the use of keyboards.

Electrical and Electronic Technicians

- ▲ Growth: 17%
- ▲ Annual Job Openings: 42,572
- ▲ Yearly Earnings: $35,970
- ▲ Education Required: Associate degree
- ▲ Self-Employed: 2.2%
- ▲ Part-Time: 3.1%

Calibration and Instrumentation Technicians

Develop, test, calibrate, operate, and repair electrical, mechanical, electromechanical, electrohydraulic, or electronic measuring and recording instruments, apparatus, and equipment. Sets up test equipment; conducts tests on performance and reliability of mechanical, structural, or electromechanical equipment. Performs preventive and corrective maintenance of test apparatus and peripheral equipment. Confers with engineers, supervisor, and other technical workers to assist with equipment installation, maintenance, and repair techniques. Sketches plans for developing jigs, fixtures, instruments, and related nonstandard apparatus. Selects sensing, telemetering, and recording instrumentation and circuitry. Modifies performance and operation of component parts and circuitry to specifications, using test equipment and precision instruments. Plans sequence of testing and calibration program for instruments and equipment according to blueprints, schematics, technical manuals, and other specifications. Analyzes and converts test data, using mathematical formulas; reports results and proposed modifications. Disassembles and reassembles instruments and equipment, using hand tools. Inspects instruments and equipment for defects.

Personality Type: Realistic. Realistic occupations frequently involve work activities that include practical, hands-on problems and solutions. They often deal with plants, animals, and real-world materials like wood, tools, and machinery. Many of the occupations require working outside and do not involve a lot of paperwork or working closely with others.

Abilities: Mathematical Reasoning—The ability to understand and organize a problem and then select a mathematical method or formula to solve the problem. Deductive Reasoning—The ability to apply general rules to specific problems to come up with logical answers. Involves deciding if an answer makes sense. Problem Sensitivity—The ability to tell when something is wrong or is likely to go wrong. Does not involve solving the problem, only recognizing there is a problem. Information Ordering—The ability to correctly follow a given rule or set of rules in order to arrange things or actions in a certain order. The things or actions can include numbers, letters, words, pictures, procedures, sentences, and mathematical or logical operations. Written Comprehension—The ability to read and understand information and ideas presented in writing.

Skills: Information Gathering—Knowing how to find information and identifying essential information. Equipment Selection—Determining the kind of tools and equipment needed to do a job. Testing—Conducting tests to determine whether equipment, software, or procedures are operating as expected. Mathematics—Using mathematics to solve problems. Equipment Maintenance—Performing routine maintenance and determining when and what kind of maintenance is needed.

Generalized Work Activities: Getting Information Needed to Do the Job—Observing, receiving, and otherwise obtaining information from all relevant sources. Analyzing Data or Information—Identifying underlying principles, reasons, or facts by breaking down information or data into separate parts. Monitoring Processes, Materials, Surroundings—Monitoring and reviewing information from materials, events, or the environment, often to detect problems or to find out when things are finished. Repairing and Maintaining Mechanical Equipment—Fixing, servicing, aligning, setting up, adjusting, and testing machines, devices, moving parts, and equipment that operate primarily on the basis of mechanical, not electronic, principles. Inspecting Equipment, Structures, Materials—Inspecting or diagnosing equipment, structures, or materials to identify the causes of errors or other problems or defects. Handling and Moving Objects—Using one's hands and arms in handling, installing, forming, positioning, and moving materials, or in manipulating things. Includes the use of keyboards.

Electrical Engineering Technicians

Apply electrical theory and related knowledge to test and modify developmental or operational electrical machinery and electrical control equipment and circuitry in industrial or commercial plants and laboratories. Work under direction of engineering staff. Assembles electrical and electronic systems and prototypes according to engineering data and knowledge of electrical principles, using hand tools and measuring instruments. Analyzes and interprets test information. Collaborates with electrical engineer and other personnel to solve developmental problems. Draws diagrams and writes engineering specifications to clarify design details and functional criteria of experimental electronics units. Modifies electrical prototypes, parts, assemblies, and systems to correct functional deviations. Plans method and sequence of operations for testing and developing experimental electronic and electrical equipment. Sets up and operates test equipment to evaluate performance of developmental parts, assemblies, or systems under simulated operating conditions. Maintains and repairs testing equipment.

Personality Type: Realistic. Realistic occupations frequently involve work activities that include practical, hands-on problems and solutions. They often deal with plants, animals, and real-world materials like wood, tools, and machinery. Many of the occupations require working outside and do not involve a lot of paperwork or working closely with others.

Abilities: Written Comprehension—The ability to read and understand information and ideas presented in writing. Oral Comprehension—The ability to listen to and understand information and ideas presented verbally. Deductive Reasoning—The ability to apply general rules to specific problems to come up with logical answers. Involves deciding if an answer makes sense. Information Ordering—The ability to correctly follow a given rule or set of rules in order to arrange things or actions in a certain order. The things or actions can include numbers, letters, words, pictures, procedures, sentences, and mathematical or logical operations.

Skills: Technology Design—Generating or adapting equipment and technology to serve user needs. Troubleshooting—Determining what is causing an operating error and deciding what to do about it. Information Gathering—Knowing how to find information and identifying essential information. Active Learning—Working with new material or information to grasp its implications. Problem Identification—Identifying the nature of problems.

Generalized Work Activities: Repairing and Maintaining Electrical Equipment—Fixing, servicing, adjusting, regulating, calibrating, fine-tuning, or testing machines, devices, and equipment that operate primarily on the basis of electrical or electronic, not mechanical, principles. Inspecting Equipment, Structures, Materials—Inspecting or diagnosing equipment, structures, or materials to identify the causes of errors or other problems or defects. Analyzing Data or Information—Identifying underlying principles, reasons, or facts by breaking down information or data into separate parts. Getting Information Needed to Do the Job—Observing, receiving, and otherwise obtaining information from all relevant sources. Updating and Using Job-Relevant Knowledge—Keeping up-to-date technically and knowing the functions of one's own job and related jobs. Handling and Moving Objects—Using one's hands and arms in handling, installing, forming, positioning, and moving materials, or in manipulating things. Includes the use of keyboards.

Electronics Engineering Technicians

Lay out, build, test, troubleshoot, repair, and modify developmental and production electronic components, parts, equipment, and systems, such as computer equipment, missile control instrumentation, electron tubes, test equipment, and machine-tool numerical controls, applying principles and theories of electronics, electrical circuitry, engineering mathematics, electronic and electrical testing, and physics. Work under direction of engineering staff. Assembles circuitry or electronic components according to engineering instructions, technical manuals, and knowledge of electronics, using hand tools and power tools. Reads blueprints, wiring diagrams, schematic drawings, and engineering instructions for assembling electronics units, applying knowledge of electronic theory and components. Adjusts and replaces defective or improperly functioning circuitry and electronics components, using hand tools and soldering iron. Assists engineers in development of testing techniques,

laboratory equipment, and circuitry or installation specifications, by writing reports and recording data. Designs basic circuitry and sketches for design documentation as directed by engineers, using drafting instruments and computer-aided design equipment. Fabricates parts such as coils, terminal boards, and chassis, using bench lathes, drills, or other machine tools. Tests electronics unit, using standard test equipment, to evaluate performance and determine needs for adjustments.

Personality Type: Realistic. Realistic occupations frequently involve work activities that include practical, hands-on problems and solutions. They often deal with plants, animals, and real-world materials like wood, tools, and machinery. Many of the occupations require working outside and do not involve a lot of paperwork or working closely with others.

Abilities: Visualization—The ability to imagine how something will look after it is moved around or when its parts are moved or rearranged. Written Comprehension—The ability to read and understand information and ideas presented in writing. Problem Sensitivity—The ability to tell when something is wrong or is likely to go wrong. Does not involve solving the problem, only recognizing there is a problem. Deductive Reasoning—The ability to apply general rules to specific problems to come up with logical answers. Involves deciding if an answer makes sense. Written Expression—The ability to communicate information and ideas in writing so others will understand. Oral Comprehension—The ability to listen to and understand information and ideas presented verbally.

Skills: Troubleshooting—Determining what is causing an operating error and deciding what to do about it. Mathematics—Using mathematics to solve problems. Testing—Conducting tests to determine whether equipment, software, or procedures are operating as expected. Problem Identification—Identifying the nature of problems. Active Learning—Working with new material or information to grasp its implications.

Generalized Work Activities: Repairing and Maintaining Electrical Equipment—Fixing, servicing, adjusting, regulating, calibrating, fine-tuning, or testing machines, devices, and equipment that operate primarily on the basis of electrical or electronic, not mechanical, principles. Getting Information Needed to Do the Job—Observing, receiving, and otherwise obtaining information from all relevant sources. Inspecting Equipment, Structures, Materials—Inspecting or diagnosing equipment, structures, or materials to identify the causes of errors or other problems or defects. Updating and Using Job-Relevant Knowledge— Keeping up-to-date technically and knowing the functions of one's own job and related jobs. Drafting and Specifying Technical Devices—Providing documentation, detailed instructions, drawings, or specifications to inform others about how devices, parts, equipment, or structures are to be fabricated, constructed, assembled, modified, maintained, or used. Handling and Moving Objects—Using one's hands and arms in handling, installing, forming, positioning, and moving materials, or in manipulating things. Includes the use of keyboards.

Radio Operators

Receive and transmit communications using radiotelegraph or radiotelephone equipment in accordance with government regulations. Repair equipment. Examines and operates new equipment prior to installation in airport radio stations. Monitors emergency frequency for distress calls and dispatches emergency equipment. Establishes and maintains standards of operation by periodic inspections of equipment and routine tests. Maintains station log of messages transmitted and received regarding flight testing, fire locations, and other matters. Reviews company and Federal Aviation Authority regulations regarding radio communications; reports violations. Determines and obtains bearings of source from which signal originated, using direction-finding procedures and equipment. Communicates with receiving operator to give and receive instruction for transmission. Coordinates radio searches for overdue or lost airplanes. Repairs transmitting equipment, using electronic testing equipment, hand tools, and power tools, to maintain communication system in operative condition. Turns controls or throws switches to activate power, adjust voice volume and modulation, and set transmitter on specified frequency. Communicates by radio with test

pilot, engineering personnel, and others during flight testing, to relay information. Operates sound-recording equipment to record signals and preserve broadcast for analysis by intelligence personnel.

Personality Type: Realistic. Realistic occupations frequently involve work activities that include practical, hands-on problems and solutions. They often deal with plants, animals, and real-world materials like wood, tools, and machinery. Many of the occupations require working outside and do not involve a lot of paperwork or working closely with others.

Abilities: Oral Comprehension—The ability to listen to and understand information and ideas presented verbally. Oral Expression—The ability to communicate information and ideas verbally so others will understand. Control Precision—The ability to quickly and repeatedly make precise adjustments in moving the controls of a machine or vehicle to exact positions. Speech Clarity—The ability to speak clearly so that what is said is understandable to a listener. Auditory Attention—The ability to focus on a single source of sound in the presence of other distracting sounds.

Skills: Operation Monitoring—Watching gauges, dials, or other indicators to make sure a machine is working properly. Active Listening—Listening to what other people are saying; asking questions as appropriate. Operation and Control—Controlling operations of equipment or systems. Speaking—Talking to others to effectively convey information. Information Gathering—Knowing how to find information and identifying essential information.

Generalized Work Activities: Monitoring Processes, Materials, Surroundings—Monitoring and reviewing information from materials, events, or the environment, often to detect problems or to find out when things are finished. Getting Information Needed to Do the Job— Observing, receiving, and otherwise obtaining information from all relevant sources. Identifying Objects, Actions, and Events—Identifying information received by making estimates or categorizations, recognizing differences or similarities, or sensing changes in circumstances or events. Repairing and Maintaining Electrical Equipment—Fixing, servicing, adjusting, regulating, calibrating, fine-tuning, or testing machines, devices, and equipment that operate primarily on the basis of electrical or electronic, not mechanical, principles. Documenting/Recording Information—Entering, transcribing, recording, storing, or maintaining information in either written form or by electronic/magnetic recording. Handling and Moving Objects—Using one's hands and arms in handling, installing, forming, positioning, and moving materials, or in manipulating things. Includes the use of keyboards.

Electrical Powerline Installers and Repairers

- ▲ Growth: 1%
- ▲ Annual Job Openings: 5,616
- ▲ Yearly Earnings: $42,600
- ▲ Education Required: Long-term O-J-T
- ▲ Self-Employed: 0.9%
- ▲ Part-Time: 1%

Electrical Powerline Installers and Repairers

Install or repair cables or wires used in electrical power or distribution systems. Erect poles and light- or heavy-duty transmission towers. Installs watt-hour meters and connects service drops between powerline and consumer. Cuts and peels lead sheath and insulation from defective or newly installed cables and conducts prior to splicing. Tests electric powerlines and auxiliary equipment, using direct reading and testing instruments, to identify cause of disturbances. Splices, solders, and insulates conductors and wiring to join sections of powerline and to connect transformers and electrical accessories. Splices cables together; splices cables to overhead transmission line, customer service line, or streetlight line. Installs and repairs conduits, cables, wires, and auxiliary equipment, following blueprints. Opens switches, or clamps grounding device, to deenergize disturbed or fallen lines, to facilitate repairs or to remove electrical hazards. Replaces and straightens poles; attaches crossarms, insulators, and auxiliary equipment to wood poles before erecting them. Tests conductors to identify corresponding conductors and to prevent incorrect connections, according to electrical diagrams and specifications. Covers conductors with insulating or fireproofing materials. Works on energized lines to avoid interruption of service. Drives conveyance equipped with tools and materials to job site. Strings wire conductors and cable between erected poles; adjusts slack, using winch. Climbs poles and removes and installs hardware, wires, and other equipment. Repairs electrical power cables and auxiliary equipment for electrical powerlines. Cleans, tins, and splices corresponding conductors by twisting ends together or by joining ends with metal clamps and soldering connection.

Personality Type: Realistic. Realistic occupations frequently involve work activities that include practical, hands-on problems and solutions. They often deal with plants, animals, and real-world materials like wood, tools, and machinery. Many of the occupations require working outside and do not involve a lot of paperwork or working closely with others.

Abilities: Multilimb Coordination—The ability to coordinate movements of two or more limbs together (for example, two arms, two legs, or one leg and one arm) while sitting, standing, or lying down. Does not involve performing the activities while the body is in motion. Manual Dexterity—The ability to quickly make coordinated movements of one hand, a hand together with its arm, or two hands, to grasp, manipulate, or assemble objects. Visualization—The ability to imagine how something will look after it is moved around or when its parts are moved or rearranged. Information Ordering—The ability to correctly follow a given rule or set of rules in order to arrange things or actions in a certain order. The things or actions can include numbers, letters, words, pictures, procedures, sentences, and mathematical or logical operations. Finger Dexterity—The ability to make precisely coordinated movements of the fingers of one or both hands to grasp, manipulate, or assemble very small objects.

Skills: Installation—Installing equipment, machines, wiring, or programs to meet specifications. Troubleshooting—Determining what is causing an operating error and deciding what to do about it. Repairing—Repairing machines or systems, using the needed tools. Equipment Maintenance—Performing routine maintenance and determining when and what kind of maintenance is needed. Testing—Conducting tests to determine whether equipment, software, or procedures are operating as expected.

Generalized Work Activities: Performing General Physical Activities—Performing physical activities that require moving one's whole body, such as in climbing, lifting, balancing, walking, and stooping. Performing activities that often also require considerable use of the arms and legs, such as in the physical handling of materials. Repairing and Maintaining Electrical Equipment—Fixing, servicing, adjusting, regulating, calibrating, fine-tuning, or testing machines, devices, and equipment that operate primarily on the basis of electrical or electronic, not mechanical, principles. Handling and Moving Objects—Using one's hands and arms in handling, installing, forming, positioning, and moving materials, or in manipulating things. Includes the use of keyboards. Inspecting Equipment, Structures, Materials—Inspecting or diagnosing equipment, structures, or materials to identify the causes of errors or other problems or defects. Operating Vehicles or Equipment—Running, maneuvering, navigating, or driving vehicles or mechanized equipment such as forklifts, passenger vehicles, aircraft, or water craft. Monitoring Processes, Materials, Surroundings—Monitoring and reviewing information from materials, events, or the environment, often to detect problems or to find out when things are finished. Handling and Moving Objects—Using one's hands and arms in handling, installing, forming, positioning, and moving materials, or in manipulating things. Includes the use of keyboards.

Electricians

- ▲ Growth: 10%
- ▲ Annual Job Openings: 92,734
- ▲ Yearly Earnings: $35,310
- ▲ Education Required: Long-term O-J-T
- ▲ Self-Employed: 9.8%
- ▲ Part-Time: 4.4%

Electricians

Install, maintain, and repair electrical wiring, equipment, and fixtures. Ensure that work is in accordance with relevant codes. Install or service street lights, intercom systems, or electrical control systems. Maintains and repairs or replaces wiring, equipment and fixtures, using hand tools. Constructs and fabricates parts, using hand tools and specifications. Inspects systems and electrical parts to detect hazards, defects, and need for adjustments or repair. Readies and assembles electrical wiring, equipment, and fixtures, using specifications and hand tools. Prepares sketches of location of wiring and equipment. Follows blueprints to determine location of equipment and conformance to safety codes. Climbs ladder to install, maintain, or repair electrical wiring, equipment, and fixtures. Directs and trains workers to install, maintain, or repair electrical wiring, equipment, and fixtures. Drives vehicle, operates flood lights, and places flares during power failure or emergency. Tests electrical systems and continuity of circuits in electrical wiring, equipment, and fixtures, using testing devices such as ohmmeter, voltmeter, and oscilloscope. Installs electrical wiring, equipment, apparatus, and fixtures, using hand tools and power tools. Diagnoses malfunctioning systems, apparatus, and components, using test equipment and hand tools. Plans layout and installation of electrical wiring, equipment, and fixtures consistent with specifications and local codes. Possesses electrician's license or identification card to meet governmental regulations.

Personality Type: Realistic. Realistic occupations frequently involve work activities that include practical, hands-on problems and solutions. They often deal with plants, animals, and real-world materials like wood, tools, and machinery. Many of the occupations require working outside and do not involve a lot of paperwork or working closely with others.

Abilities: Manual Dexterity—The ability to quickly make coordinated movements of one hand, a hand together with its arm, or two hands, to grasp, manipulate, or assemble objects. Near Vision—The ability to see details of objects at a close range. Finger Dexterity—The ability to make precisely coordinated movements of the fingers of one or both hands to grasp, manipulate, or assemble very small objects. Arm-Hand Steadiness—The ability to keep the hand and arm steady while making an arm movement or while holding the arm and hand in one position. Problem Sensitivity—The ability to tell when something is wrong or is likely to go wrong. Does not involve solving the problem, only recognizing there is a problem. Visual Color Discrimination—The ability to match or detect differences between colors, including shades of color and brightness. Wrist-Finger Speed—The ability to make fast, simple, repeated movements of the fingers, hands, and wrists.

Skills: Troubleshooting—Determining what is causing an operating error and deciding what to do about it. Installation—Installing equipment, machines, wiring, or programs to meet specifications. Repairing—Repairing machines or systems, using the needed tools. Equipment Maintenance—Performing routine maintenance and determining when and what kind of maintenance is needed.

Generalized Work Activities: Handling and Moving Objects—Using one's hands and arms in handling, installing, forming, positioning, and moving materials, or in manipulating things. Includes the use of keyboards. Repairing and Maintaining Electrical Equipment—Fixing, servicing, adjusting, regulating, calibrating, fine-tuning, or testing machines, devices, and equipment that operate primarily on the basis of electrical or electronic, not mechanical, principles. Implementing Ideas and Programs—Conducting or carrying out work procedures and activities in accord with one's own ideas or information provided through directions/instructions for purposes of installing, modifying, preparing, delivering, constructing, integrating, finishing, or completing programs, systems, structures, or products. Monitoring Processes, Materials, Surroundings—Monitoring and reviewing information from materials, events, or the environment, often to detect problems or to find out when things are finished. Inspecting Equipment, Structures, Materials—Inspecting or diagnosing equipment, structures, or materials to identify the causes of errors or other problems or defects. Getting Information Needed to Do the Job—Observing, receiving, and otherwise obtaining information from all relevant sources. Handling and Moving Objects—Using one's hands and arms in handling, installing, forming, positioning, and moving materials, or in manipulating things. Includes the use of keyboards.

Electrolytic Plating Machine Setters, Set-Up Operators, Operators, and Tenders

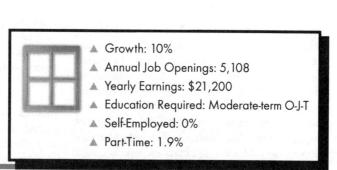

- ▲ Growth: 10%
- ▲ Annual Job Openings: 5,108
- ▲ Yearly Earnings: $21,200
- ▲ Education Required: Moderate-term O-J-T
- ▲ Self-Employed: 0%
- ▲ Part-Time: 1.9%

Electrolytic Plating and Coating Machine Operators and Tenders, Metal and Plastic

Operate or tend electrolytic plating or coating machines such as zinc-plating machines and anodizing machines, to coat metal or plastic products electrolytically with chromium, zinc, copper, cadmium, or other metal to provide protective or decorative surfaces or to build up worn surfaces. Mixes and tests plating solution to specified formula and turns valves to fill tank with solution. Measures or estimates amounts of electric current needed and time required to coat objects. Lubricates moving parts of plating conveyor and cleans plating and cleaning solution tanks. Rinses coated object in cleansing liquids and dries with cloth, centrifugal driers, or by tumbling in sawdust-filled barrels. Immerses objects to be coated or plated into cleaning solutions or sprays with conductive solution to prepare object for plating. Monitors and measures thickness of electroplating on component part to verify conformance to specifications, using micrometer. Removes objects from plating solution after specified time or when desired thickness of metal is deposited on them. Positions objects to be plated in frame or suspends them from positive or negative terminals of power supply. Adjusts dials to regulate flow of current and voltage supplied to terminals, to control plating process. Mixes forming acid solution, treats battery plates, and removes and rinses formed plates.

Personality Type: Realistic. Realistic occupations frequently involve work activities that include practical, hands-on problems and solutions. They often deal with plants, animals, and real-world materials like wood, tools, and machinery. Many of the occupations require working outside and do not involve a lot of paperwork or working closely with others.

Abilities: Control Precision—The ability to quickly and repeatedly make precise adjustments in moving the controls of a machine or vehicle to exact positions. Information Ordering—The ability to correctly follow a given rule or set of rules in order to arrange things or actions in a certain order. The things or actions can include numbers, letters, words, pictures, procedures, sentences, and mathematical or logical operations. Manual Dexterity—The ability to quickly make coordinated movements of one hand, a hand together with its arm, or two hands, to grasp, manipulate, or assemble objects. Problem Sensitivity—The ability to tell when something is wrong or is likely to go wrong. Does not involve solving the problem, only recognizing there is a problem.

Skills: Operation and Control—Controlling operations of equipment or systems. Operation Monitoring—Watching gauges, dials, or other indicators to make sure a machine is working properly. Testing—Conducting tests to determine whether equipment, software, or procedures are operating as expected. Product

Inspection—Inspecting and evaluating the quality of products. Equipment Maintenance—Performing routine maintenance and determining when and what kind of maintenance is needed.

Generalized Work Activities: Handling and Moving Objects—Using one's hands and arms in handling, installing, forming, positioning, and moving materials, or in manipulating things. Includes the use of keyboards. Controlling Machines and Processes—Using either control mechanisms or direct physical activity to operate machines or processes. Does not involve working with computers or vehicles. Monitoring Processes, Materials, Surroundings—Monitoring and reviewing information from materials, events, or the environment, often to detect problems or to find out when things are finished. Inspecting Equipment, Structures, Materials—Inspecting or diagnosing equipment, structures, or materials to identify the causes of errors or other problems or defects. Estimating Needed Characteristics—Estimating the characteristics of materials, products, events, or information; estimating sizes, distances, and quantities; determining time, costs, resources, or materials needed to perform a work activity. Handling and Moving Objects—Using one's hands and arms in handling, installing, forming, positioning, and moving materials, or in manipulating things. Includes the use of keyboards.

Electrolytic Plating and Coating Machine Setters and Set-Up Operators, Metal and Plastic

Set up, or set up and operate, electrolytic plating or coating machines such as continuous multistrand electrogalvanizing machines, to coat metal or plastic products electrolytically with chromium, copper, cadmium, or other metal to provide protective or decorative surfaces or to build up worn surfaces. Removes plated object from solution at periodic intervals and observes object to ensure conformance to specifications. Measures, marks, and masks areas excluded from plating. Grinds, polishes, or rinses object in water and dries object to maintain clean, even surface. Examines object at end of process to determine thickness of metal deposit; measures thickness, using instruments such as micrometers. Immerses object in cleaning and rinsing baths to complete plating process. Plates small objects such as nuts or bolts, using motor-driven barrel. Suspends stick or piece of plating metal from anode (positive terminal) and immerses metal in plating solution. Suspends object, such as part or mold, from cathode rod (negative terminal) and immerses object in plating solution. Determines size and composition of object to be plated and amount of electrical current and time required, following work order. Adjusts voltage and amperage, based on observations. Moves controls to permit electrodeposition of metal on object or to regulate movement of wire strand to obtain specified thickness. Mixes chemical solutions, fills tanks, and charges furnaces.

Personality Type: Realistic. Realistic occupations frequently involve work activities that include practical, hands-on problems and solutions. They often deal with plants, animals, and real-world materials like wood, tools, and machinery. Many of the occupations require working outside and do not involve a lot of paperwork or working closely with others.

Abilities: Control Precision—The ability to quickly and repeatedly make precise adjustments in moving the controls of a machine or vehicle to exact positions. Wrist-Finger Speed—The ability to make fast, simple, repeated movements of the fingers, hands, and wrists. Static Strength—The ability to exert maximum muscle force to lift, push, pull, or carry objects. Manual Dexterity—The ability to quickly make coordinated movements of one hand, a hand together with its arm, or two hands, to grasp, manipulate, or assemble objects. Multilimb Coordination—The ability to coordinate movements of two or more limbs together (for example, two arms, two legs, or one leg and one arm) while sitting, standing, or lying down. Does not involve performing the activities while the body is in motion.

Skills: Operation and Control—Controlling operations of equipment or systems. Product Inspection—

Inspecting and evaluating the quality of products. Operation Monitoring—Watching gauges, dials, or other indicators to make sure a machine is working properly. Mathematics—Using mathematics to solve problems. Testing—Conducting tests to determine whether equipment, software, or procedures are operating as expected. Monitoring—Assessing how well one is doing when learning or doing something.

Generalized Work Activities: Controlling Machines and Processes—Using either control mechanisms or direct physical activity to operate machines or processes. Does not involve working with computers or vehicles. Monitoring Processes, Materials, Surroundings—Monitoring and reviewing information from materials,

events, or the environment, often to detect problems or to find out when things are finished. Handling and Moving Objects—Using one's hands and arms in handling, installing, forming, positioning, and moving materials, or in manipulating things. Includes the use of keyboards. Inspecting Equipment, Structures, Materials—Inspecting or diagnosing equipment, structures, or materials to identify the causes of errors or other problems or defects. Performing General Physical Activities—Performing physical activities that require moving one's whole body, such as in climbing, lifting, balancing, walking, and stooping. Performing activities that often also require considerable use of the arms and legs, such as in the physical handling of materials.

Electronic Semiconductor Processors

- ▲ Growth: 45%
- ▲ Annual Job Openings: 10,615
- ▲ Yearly Earnings: $24,810
- ▲ Education Required: Moderate-term O-J-T
- ▲ Self-Employed: 0%
- ▲ Part-Time: 2.7%

Semiconductor Processors

Load semiconductor material into furnace. Saw formed ingots into segments. Load individual segment into crystal-growing chamber. Monitor controls. Locate crystal axis in ingot, using X-ray equipment. Saw ingots into wafers. Clean, polish, and load wafers into series of special-purpose furnaces, chemical baths, and equipment used to form circuitry and to change conductive properties. Aligns photomask pattern on photoresist layer; exposes pattern to ultraviolet light; develops pattern, using specialized equipment. Operates saw to cut remelt into sections of specified size or to cut ingots into wafers. Stamps or etches identifying information on finished component. Counts, sorts, and weighs processed items. Inspects materials, components, or products for surface defects. Measures circuitry, using electronic test equipment, precision measuring

instruments, and standard procedures. Loads and unloads equipment chambers. Transports finished product to storage or to area for further processing. Studies work order, instructions, formulas, and processing charts to determine specifications and sequence of operations. Cleans and dries materials and equipment, using solvent, etching or sandblasting equipment, and drying equipment, to remove contaminants or photoresist. Etches, laps, polishes, or grinds wafers or ingots, using etching, lapping, polishing, or grinding equipment. Manipulates valves, switches, and buttons; keys commands into control panels to start semiconductor processing cycles. Monitors operation and adjusts controls of processing machines and equipment, to produce compositions with specific electronic properties. Attaches ampoule to diffusion pump to remove air from ampoule; seals ampoule, using blowtorch. Maintains processing, production, and inspection information and reports. Forms seed crystal for crystal growing; locates crystal axis of ingot, using X-ray equipment, drill, and sanding machine. Measures and weighs amounts of crystal-growing materials, mixes and grinds materials, and loads materials into container, following procedures. Places semiconductor wafers in processing containers or equipment holders, using vacuum wand or tweezers.

Personality Type: Realistic. Realistic occupations frequently involve work activities that include practical, hands-on problems and solutions. They often deal with plants, animals, and real-world materials like wood, tools, and machinery. Many of the occupations require working outside and do not involve a lot of paperwork or working closely with others.

Abilities: Control Precision—The ability to quickly and repeatedly make precise adjustments in moving the controls of a machine or vehicle to exact positions. Near Vision—The ability to see details of objects at a close range. Information Ordering—The ability to correctly follow a given rule or set of rules in order to arrange things or actions in a certain order. The things or actions can include numbers, letters, words, pictures, proce-dures, sentences, and mathematical or logical operations. Written Comprehension—The ability to read and understand information and ideas presented in writing. Wrist-Finger Speed—The ability to make fast, simple, repeated movements of the fingers, hands, and wrists.

Skills: Operation and Control—Controlling operations of equipment or systems. Operation Monitoring—Watching gauges, dials, or other indicators to make sure a machine is working properly. Science—Using scientific methods to solve problems. Equipment Selection—Determining the kind of tools and equipment needed to do a job. Product Inspection—Inspecting and evaluating the quality of products.

Generalized Work Activities: Controlling Machines and Processes—Using either control mechanisms or direct physical activity to operate machines or processes. Does not involve working with computers or vehicles. Monitoring Processes, Materials, Surroundings—Monitoring and reviewing information from materials, events, or the environment, often to detect problems or to find out when things are finished. Inspecting Equipment, Structures, Materials—Inspecting or diagnosing equipment, structures, or materials to identify the causes of errors or other problems or defects. Getting Information Needed to Do the Job—Observing, receiving, and otherwise obtaining information from all relevant sources. Handling and Moving Objects—Using one's hands and arms in handling, installing, forming, positioning, and moving materials, or in manipulating things. Includes the use of keyboards.

Elementary School Teachers

- ▲ Growth: 12%
- ▲ Annual Job Openings: 204,210
- ▲ Yearly Earnings: $36,110
- ▲ Education Required: Bachelor's degree
- ▲ Self-Employed: 0%
- ▲ Part-Time: 11.7%

Elementary School Teachers, Except Special Education

Teach elementary-level pupils in public or private schools basic academic, social, and other formative skills. Assigns lessons, corrects papers, and hears oral presentations. Teaches combined-grade classes. Teaches subjects such as math, science, or social studies. Prepares, administers, and corrects tests; records results. Keeps attendance and grade records; prepares reports as required by school. Counsels pupils when adjustment and academic problems arise. Supervises outdoor and indoor play activities. Attends staff meetings, serves on committees, and attends workshops or in-service training activities. Coordinates class field trips. Prepares bulletin boards. Evaluates student performance and discusses pupil academic and behavioral attitudes and achievements with parents. Prepares course objectives and outline for course of study, following curriculum guidelines or requirements of state and school. Lectures, demonstrates, and uses audiovisual aids and computers to present academic, social, and motor-skill subject matter to class. Teaches rules of conduct; maintains discipline and suitable learning environment in classroom and on playground.

Personality Type: Social. Social occupations frequently involve working with, communicating with, and teaching people. These occupations often involve helping or providing service to others.

Abilities: Oral Expression—The ability to communicate information and ideas verbally so others will understand. Written Comprehension—The ability to read and understand information and ideas presented in writing. Speech Clarity—The ability to speak clearly so that what is said is understandable to a listener. Written Expression—The ability to communicate information and ideas in writing so others will understand. Oral Comprehension—The ability to listen to and understand information and ideas presented verbally.

Skills: Instructing—Teaching others how to do something. Speaking—Talking to others to effectively convey information. Learning Strategies—Using multiple approaches when learning or teaching new things. Reading Comprehension—Understanding written information in work-related documents.

Generalized Work Activities: Teaching Others—Identifying educational needs, developing formal training programs or classes, and teaching or instructing others. Establishing and Maintaining Relationships—Developing constructive and cooperative working relationships with others. Thinking Creatively—Originating, inventing, designing, or creating new applications, ideas, relationships, systems, or products, including artistic contributions. Interpreting Meaning of Information to Others—Translating or explaining what information means and how it can be understood or used to support responses or feedback to others. Developing Objectives and Strategies—Establishing long-range objectives and specifying the strategies and actions to achieve these objectives. Updating and Using Job-Relevant Knowledge—Keeping up-to-date technically and knowing the functions of one's own job and related jobs. Getting Information Needed to Do the Job—Observing, receiving, and otherwise obtaining information from all relevant sources.

Elevator Installers and Repairers

- ▲ Growth: 12%
- ▲ Annual Job Openings: 5,088
- ▲ Yearly Earnings: $47,860
- ▲ Education Required: Long-term O-J-T
- ▲ Self-Employed: 0%
- ▲ Part-Time: 7.5%

Elevator Installers and Repairers

Assemble, install, repair, or maintain electric or hydraulic freight or passenger elevators, escalators, or dumbwaiters. Cuts prefabricated sections of framework, rails, and other components to specified dimensions. Lubricates bearings and other parts to minimize friction. Disassembles defective unit; repairs or replaces parts such as locks, gears, cables, and electric wiring. Installs safety and control devices, cables, drives, rails, motors, and elevator cars. Connects electrical wiring to control panels and electric motors. Adjusts safety controls, counter weights, and mechanism of doors. Operates elevator to determine power demand; tests power consumption to detect overload factors. Inspects wiring connections, control panel hookups, door installation, and alignment and clearance of car hoistway. Completes service reports to verify conformance to prescribed standards. Studies blueprints to determine layout of framework and foundations. Locates malfunction in brakes, motor, switches, and signal and control systems, using test equipment.

Personality Type: Realistic. Realistic occupations frequently involve work activities that include practical, hands-on problems and solutions. They often deal with plants, animals, and real-world materials like wood, tools, and machinery. Many of the occupations require working outside and do not involve a lot of paperwork or working closely with others.

Abilities: Wrist-Finger Speed—The ability to make fast, simple, repeated movements of the fingers, hands, and wrists. Problem Sensitivity—The ability to tell when something is wrong or is likely to go wrong. Does not involve solving the problem, only recognizing there is a problem. Deductive Reasoning—The ability to apply general rules to specific problems to come up with logical answers. Involves deciding if an answer makes sense. Information Ordering—The ability to correctly follow a given rule or set of rules in order to arrange things or actions in a certain order. The things or actions can include numbers, letters, words, pictures, procedures, sentences, and mathematical or logical operations.

Manual Dexterity—The ability to quickly make coordinated movements of one hand, a hand together with its arm, or two hands, to grasp, manipulate, or assemble objects. Near Vision—The ability to see details of objects at a close range.

Skills: Product Inspection—Inspecting and evaluating the quality of products. Repairing—Repairing machines or systems, using the needed tools. Installation—Installing equipment, machines, wiring, or programs to meet specifications. Equipment Maintenance—Performing routine maintenance and determining when and what kind of maintenance is needed.

Generalized Work Activities: Repairing and Maintaining Mechanical Equipment—Fixing, servicing, aligning, setting up, adjusting, and testing machines, devices, moving parts, and equipment that operate primarily on the basis of mechanical, not electronic, principles. Inspecting Equipment, Structures, Materials—Inspecting or diagnosing equipment, structures, or materials to identify the causes of errors or other problems or defects. Getting Information Needed to Do the Job—Observing, receiving, and otherwise obtaining information from all relevant sources. Handling and Moving Objects—Using one's hands and arms in handling, installing, forming, positioning, and moving materials, or in manipulating things. Includes the use of keyboards. Repairing and Maintaining Electrical Equipment—Fixing, servicing, adjusting, regulating, calibrating, fine-tuning, or testing machines, devices, and equipment that operate primarily on the basis of electrical or electronic, not mechanical, principles.

Emergency Medical Technicians

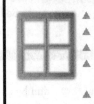

▲ Growth: 32%
▲ Annual Job Openings: 23,138
▲ Yearly Earnings: $20,290
▲ Education Required: Postsecondary vocational training
▲ Self-Employed: 0%
▲ Part-Time: 22.9%

Emergency Medical Technicians and Paramedics

Assess injuries, administer emergency medical care, and extricate trapped individuals. Transport injured or sick persons to medical facilities. Maintains vehicles and medical and communication equipment; replenishes first-aid equipment and supplies. Assists in removal and transport of victims to treatment center. Observes, records, and reports to the physician the patient's condition and the patient's reactions to drugs and treatment. Assesses nature and extent of illness or injury, to establish and prioritize medical procedures. Drives mobile intensive-care unit to specified location, following instructions from emergency medical dispatcher. Assists treatment-center personnel in obtaining and recording victim's vital statistics and in administering emergency treatment. Monitors patient's condition, using electrocardiograph. Administers first-aid treatment and life-support care to sick or injured persons in prehospital setting. Communicates with treatment-center personnel to arrange reception of victims and to receive instructions for further treatment. Assists treatment-center personnel in obtaining information relating to circumstances of emergency.

Personality Type: Social. Social occupations frequently involve working with, communicating with, and teaching people. These occupations often involve helping or providing service to others.

Abilities: Problem Sensitivity—The ability to tell when something is wrong or is likely to go wrong. Does not involve solving the problem, only recognizing there is a problem. Oral Expression—The ability to communicate information and ideas verbally so others will understand. Oral Comprehension—The ability to listen to and understand information and ideas presented verbally. Deductive Reasoning—The ability to apply general rules to specific problems to come up with logical answers. Involves deciding if an answer makes sense. Speed of Closure—The ability to quickly make sense of information that seems to be without meaning or organization. Involves quickly combining and organizing different pieces of information into a meaningful pattern.

Skills: Problem Identification—Identifying the nature of problems. Coordination—Adjusting actions in relation to others' actions. Speaking—Talking to others to effectively convey information. Operation Monitoring—Watching gauges, dials, or other indicators to make sure a machine is working properly. Service Orientation—Actively looking for ways to help people. Judgment and Decision Making—Weighing the relative costs and benefits of a potential action.

Generalized Work Activities: Assisting and Caring for Others—Providing assistance or personal care to others. Monitoring Processes, Materials, Surroundings—Monitoring and reviewing information from materials, events, or the environment, often to detect problems or to find out when things are finished. Updating and Using Job-Relevant Knowledge—Keeping up-to-date technically and knowing the functions of one's own job and related jobs. Identifying Objects, Actions, and Events—Identifying information received by making estimates or categorizations, recognizing differences or similarities, or sensing changes in circumstances or events. Getting Information Needed to Do the Job—Observing, receiving, and otherwise obtaining information from all relevant sources.

Employment Interviewers

- ▲ Growth: 13%
- ▲ Annual Job Openings: 14,194
- ▲ Yearly Earnings: $29,800
- ▲ Education Required: Bachelor's degree
- ▲ Self-Employed: 0%
- ▲ Part-Time: 6.9%

Employment Interviewers, Private or Public Employment Service

Interview job applicants in employment office and refer them to prospective employers for consideration. Search application files, notify selected applicants of job openings, and refer qualified applicants to prospective employers. Contact employers to verify referral results. Record and evaluate various pertinent data. Refers applicants to vocational counseling services. Reviews employment applications and evaluates work history, education and training, job skills, compensation needs, and other qualifications of applicants. Reviews job orders and matches applicants with job requirements, utilizing manual or computerized file search. Keeps records of applicants not selected for employment. Contacts employers to solicit orders for job vacancies; records information on forms to describe duties, hiring requirements, and related data. Conducts or arranges for skills, intelligence, or psychological testing of applicants. Performs reference and background checks on applicants. Searches for and recruits applicants for open positions. Informs applicants of job duties and responsibilities, compensation and benefits, work schedules, working conditions, promotional opportunities, and other related information. Records additional knowledge, skills, abilities, interests, test results, and other data pertinent to selection and referral of applicants. Refers selected applicants to person placing job order, according to policy of organization. Interviews job applicants to select people meeting employer qualifications. Evaluates selection and testing techniques by conducting research or follow-up activities and conferring with management and supervisory personnel.

Personality Type: Social. Social occupations frequently involve working with, communicating with, and teaching people. These occupations often involve helping or providing service to others.

Abilities: Oral Expression—The ability to communicate information and ideas verbally so others will understand. Oral Comprehension—The ability to listen to and understand information and ideas presented verbally. Written Comprehension—The ability to read and understand information and ideas presented in writing. Speech Clarity—The ability to speak clearly so that what is said is understandable to a listener.

Skills: Speaking—Talking to others to effectively convey information. Information Gathering—Knowing how to find information and identifying essential information. Judgment and Decision Making—Weighing the relative costs and benefits of a potential action. Reading Comprehension—Understanding written information in work-related documents. Active Listening—Listening to what other people are saying; asking questions as appropriate.

Generalized Work Activities: Communicating with Persons Outside Organization—Communicating with persons outside the organization. Representing the organization to customers, the public, government, and other external sources. Exchanging information face-to-face, in writing, or via telephone/electronic transfer. Judging Qualities—Making judgments about or assessing the value, importance, or quality of things, services, or other people's work. Getting Information Needed to Do the Job—Observing, receiving, and otherwise obtaining information from all relevant sources. Establishing and Maintaining Relationships—Developing constructive and cooperative working relationships with others. Documenting/Recording Information—Entering, transcribing, recording, storing, or maintaining information in either written form or by electronic/magnetic recording. Identifying Objects, Actions, and Events—Identifying information received by making estimates or categorizations, recognizing differences or similarities, or sensing changes in circumstances or events.

Engineering, Natural Science, and Computer and Information Systems Managers

- ▲ Growth: 44%
- ▲ Annual Job Openings: 54,120
- ▲ Yearly Earnings: $75,320
- ▲ Education Required: Work experience, plus degree
- ▲ Self-Employed: 0%
- ▲ Part-Time: 6.1%

Computer and Information Systems Managers

Plan, direct, or coordinate activities in such fields as electronic data processing, information systems, systems analysis, and computer programming. Analyzes workflow and assigns or schedules work to meet priorities and goals. Consults with users, management, vendors, and technicians to determine computing needs and system requirements. Prepares and reviews operational reports or project progress reports. Approves, prepares, monitors, and adjusts operational budget. Meets with department heads, managers, supervisors, vendors, and others to solicit cooperation and resolve problems. Develops performance standards and evaluates work in light of established standards. Participates in staffing decisions. Directs training of subordinates. Develops and interprets organizational goals, policies, and procedures; reviews project plans. Evaluates data-processing project proposals and assesses project feasibility. Directs daily operations of department and coordinates project activities with other departments.

Personality Type: Enterprising. Enterprising occupations frequently involve starting up and carrying out projects. These occupations can involve leading people and making many decisions. They sometimes require risk taking and often deal with business.

Abilities: Oral Expression—The ability to communicate information and ideas verbally so others will understand.

Oral Comprehension—The ability to listen to and understand information and ideas presented verbally. Written Comprehension—The ability to read and understand information and ideas presented in writing. Written Expression—The ability to communicate information and ideas in writing so others will understand. Mathematical Reasoning—The ability to understand and organize a problem and then select a mathematical method or formula to solve the problem. Number Facility—The ability to add, subtract, multiply, or divide quickly and correctly.

Skills: Problem Identification—Identifying the nature of problems. Coordination—Adjusting actions in relation to others' actions. Writing—Communicating effectively with others in writing as indicated by the needs of the audience. Implementation Planning—Developing approaches for implementing an idea. Judgment and Decision Making—Weighing the relative costs and benefits of a potential action. Active Learning—Working with new material or information to grasp its implications. Speaking—Talking to others to effectively convey information.

Generalized Work Activities: Getting Information Needed to Do the Job—Observing, receiving, and otherwise obtaining information from all relevant sources. Updating and Using Job-Relevant Knowledge—Keeping up-to-date technically and knowing the functions of one's own job and related jobs. Making Decisions and Solving Problems—Combining, evaluating, and analyzing information and data to make decisions and solve problems. Involves making decisions about the relative importance of information and choosing the best solution. Guiding, Directing, and

Motivating Subordinates—Providing guidance and direction to subordinates, including setting performance standards and monitoring subordinates. Coordinating Work and Activities of Others—Coordinating members of a work group to accomplish tasks. Establishing and Maintaining Relationships—Developing constructive and cooperative working relationships with others.

Engineering Managers

Plan, direct, or coordinate activities in such fields as architecture and engineering; manage research and development in these fields. Plans, coordinates, and directs engineering project, organizes and assigns staff, and directs integration of technical activities with products. Directs engineering of water control, treatment, and distribution projects. Administers highway planning, construction, and maintenance. Reviews and recommends or approves contracts and cost estimates. Plans, directs, and coordinates survey work with activities of other staff; certifies survey work; writes legal descriptions of land. Confers with and prepares reports for officials. Speaks to public to solicit support. Directs, reviews, and approves product design and changes. Directs testing. Plans and directs installation, maintenance, testing, and repair of facilities and equipment. Evaluates contract proposals, directs negotiation of research contracts, and prepares bids and contracts. Establishes procedures; directs testing, operation, maintenance, and repair of transmitter equipment. Plans and directs oil-field development, gas and oil production, and geothermal drilling. Analyzes technology, resource needs, and market demand; confers with management, production, and marketing staff to plan and assess feasibility of project.

Personality Type: Enterprising. Enterprising occupations frequently involve starting up and carrying out projects. These occupations can involve leading people and making many decisions. They sometimes require risk taking and often deal with business.

Abilities: Oral Comprehension—The ability to listen to and understand information and ideas presented verbally. Written Expression—The ability to communicate information and ideas in writing so others will understand. Written Comprehension—The ability to read and understand information and ideas presented

in writing. Oral Expression—The ability to communicate information and ideas verbally so others will understand. Deductive Reasoning—The ability to apply general rules to specific problems to come up with logical answers. Involves deciding if an answer makes sense.

Skills: Coordination—Adjusting actions in relation to others' actions. Implementation Planning—Developing approaches for implementing an idea. Reading Comprehension—Understanding written information in work-related documents. Speaking—Talking to others to effectively convey information. Operations Analysis—Analyzing needs and product requirements to create a design.

Generalized Work Activities: Guiding, Directing, and Motivating Subordinates—Providing guidance and direction to subordinates, including setting performance standards and monitoring subordinates. Getting Information Needed to Do the Job—Observing, receiv-ing, and otherwise obtaining information from all relevant sources. Providing Consultation and Advice to Others—Providing consultation and expert advice to management or other groups on technical, systems-related, or process-related topics. Organizing, Planning, and Prioritizing—Developing plans to accomplish work. Prioritizing and organizing one's own work. Coordinating Work and Activities of Others—Coordinating members of a work group to accomplish tasks.

Natural Sciences Managers

Plan, direct, or coordinate activities in such fields as life sciences, physical sciences, mathematics, statistics; manage research and development in these fields. Coordinates successive phases of problem analysis, solution proposals, and testing. Provides technical assistance to agencies conducting environmental studies. Advises and assists in obtaining patents or fulfilling other legal requirements. Confers with scientists, engineers, regulators, and others to plan and review projects and to provide technical assistance. Prepares and administers budget, approves and reviews expenditures, and prepares financial reports. Plans and directs research, development, and production activities of chemical plant. Schedules, directs, and assigns duties to engineers, technicians, researchers, and other staff. Reviews project activities; prepares and reviews research, testing, and operational reports.

Personality Type: Investigative. Investigative occupations frequently involve working with ideas and require an extensive amount of thinking. These occupations can involve searching for facts and figuring out problems mentally.

Abilities: Written Comprehension—The ability to read and understand information and ideas presented in writing. Oral Comprehension—The ability to listen to and understand information and ideas presented verbally. Oral Expression—The ability to communicate information and ideas verbally so others will understand. Written Expression—The ability to communicate information and ideas in writing so others will understand. Number Facility—The ability to add, subtract, multiply, or divide quickly and correctly. Fluency of Ideas—The ability to come up with a number of ideas about a given topic. Emphasis is on the number of ideas produced and not the quality, correctness, or creativity of the ideas.

Skills: Coordination—Adjusting actions in relation to others' actions. Reading Comprehension—Understanding written information in work-related documents. Critical Thinking—Using logic and analysis to identify the strengths and weaknesses of different approaches. Implementation Planning—Developing approaches for implementing an idea. Speaking—Talking to others to effectively convey information. Judgment and Decision Making—Weighing the relative costs and benefits of a potential action. Time Management—Managing one's own time and the time of others.

Generalized Work Activities: Documenting/Recording Information—Entering, transcribing, recording, storing, or maintaining information in either written form or by electronic/magnetic recording. Communicating with Other Workers—Providing information to supervisors, fellow workers, and subordinates. This information can be exchanged face-to-face, in writing, or via telephone/electronic transfer. Getting Information Needed to Do the Job—Observing, receiving, and otherwise obtaining information from all relevant sources. Providing Consultation and Advice to Others—Providing consultation and expert advice to management or other groups on technical, systems-related, or process-related topics. Developing and Building Teams—Encouraging and building mutual trust, respect, and cooperation among team members. Analyzing Data or Information—Identifying underlying principles, reasons, or facts by breaking down information or data into separate parts.

Excavation and Loading Machine Operators

- ▲ Growth: 15%
- ▲ Annual Job Openings: 6,199
- ▲ Yearly Earnings: $27,090
- ▲ Education Required: Moderate-term O-J-T
- ▲ Self-Employed: 14.7%
- ▲ Part-Time: 4.9%

Excavating and Loading Machine Operators

Operate machinery equipped with scoops, shovels, or buckets to excavate and load loose materials. Receives written or oral instructions to move or excavate material. Observes hand signals, grade stakes, and other markings when operating machines. Directs ground workers engaged in activities such as moving stakes or markers. Operates power machinery such as powered shovel, stripping shovel, scraper loader (mucking machine), or backhoe (trench excavating machine) to excavate and load material. Measures and verifies levels of rock or gravel, base, and other excavated material. Lubricates and repairs machinery; replaces parts such as gears, bearings, and bucket teeth.

Personality Type: Realistic. Realistic occupations frequently involve work activities that include practical, hands-on problems and solutions. They often deal with plants, animals, and real-world materials like wood, tools, and machinery. Many of the occupations require working outside and do not involve a lot of paperwork or working closely with others.

Abilities: Oral Comprehension—The ability to listen to and understand information and ideas presented verbally. Control Precision—The ability to quickly and repeatedly make precise adjustments in moving the controls of a machine or vehicle to exact positions. Written Comprehension—The ability to read and understand information and ideas presented in writing. Multilimb Coordination—The ability to coordinate movements of two or more limbs together (for example, two arms, two legs, or one leg and one arm) while sitting, standing, or lying down. Does not involve performing the activities while the body is in motion.

Skills: Operation and Control—Controlling operations of equipment or systems. Coordination—Adjusting actions in relation to others' actions. Operation Monitoring—Watching gauges, dials, or other indicators to make sure a machine is working properly. Reading Comprehension—Understanding written information in work-related documents. Active

Listening—Listening to what other people are saying; asking questions as appropriate. Equipment Maintenance—Performing routine maintenance and determining when and what kind of maintenance is needed.

Generalized Work Activities: Operating Vehicles or Equipment—Running, maneuvering, navigating, or driving vehicles or mechanized equipment such as forklifts, passenger vehicles, aircraft, or water craft. Controlling Machines and Processes—Using either control mechanisms or direct physical activity to operate machines or processes. Does not involve working with computers or vehicles. Handling and Moving Objects— Using one's hands and arms in handling, installing, forming, positioning, and moving materials, or in manipulating things. Repairing and Maintaining Mechanical Equipment—Fixing, servicing, aligning, setting up, adjusting, and testing machines, devices, moving parts, and equipment that operate primarily on the basis of mechanical, not electronic, principles. Monitoring Processes, Materials, Surroundings— Monitoring and reviewing information from materials, events, or the environment, often to detect problems or to find out when things are finished. Performing General Physical Activities—Performing physical activities that require moving one's whole body, such as in climbing, lifting, balancing, walking, and stooping. Performing activities that often also require considerable use of the arms and legs, such as in the physical handling of materials. Getting Information Needed to Do the Job—Observing, receiving, and otherwise obtaining information from all relevant sources.

Farm Workers

- ▲ Growth: –7%
- ▲ Annual Job Openings: 157,331
- ▲ Yearly Earnings: $12,600
- ▲ Education Required: Short-term O-J-T
- ▲ Self-Employed: 3.3%
- ▲ Part-Time: 21.7%

Agricultural Equipment Operators

Drive and control farm equipment to till soil and to plant, cultivate, and harvest crops. Perform tasks such as crop baling or hay bucking. Operate stationary equipment to perform post-harvest tasks such as husking, shelling, threshing, and ginning. Irrigates soil, using portable pipe or ditch system, and maintains ditch or pipe and pumps. Drives truck to haul harvested crops, supplies, tools, or farm workers. Sprays fertilizer or pesticide solutions, using hand sprayer, to control insects, fungus and weed growth, and diseases. Positions boxes or attaches bags at discharge end of machinery to catch products, places lids on boxes, and closes sacks. Hand picks fruit, such as apples, oranges, or strawberries. Oversees work crew engaged in planting, weeding, or harvesting activities. Thins, hoes, weeds, or prunes row crops, fruit trees, or vines, using hand implements. Loads hoppers, containers, or conveyor to feed machine with products, using suction gates, shovel, or pitchfork. Walks beside or rides on planting machine while inserting plants in planter mechanism at specified intervals. Drives truck, or tractor with trailer attached, alongside crew loading crop or adjacent to harvesting machine. Adjusts, repairs, lubricates, and services farm machinery, and notifies supervisor or appropriate personnel when machinery malfunctions. Manipulates controls to set, activate, and regulate mechanisms on machinery such as self-propelled machines, conveyors, separators, cleaners, and dryers. Observes and listens to machinery operation to detect equipment malfunction, and removes obstruction to avoid damage to product or machinery. Discards diseased or rotting product, and guides product on conveyor to regulate flow through machine. Attaches farm implements, such as plow, disc, sprayer, or harvester, to tractor, using bolts and mechanic's hand tools. Weighs crop-filled containers and records weights and other identifying information. Loads and unloads crops or containers of materials, manually or using conveyors, hand truck, forklift, or transfer auger. Mixes specified materials or chemicals and dumps solutions, powders, or seeds into planter or sprayer machinery.

Personality Type: Realistic. Realistic occupations frequently involve work activities that include practical, hands-on problems and solutions. They often deal with plants, animals, and real-world materials like wood, tools, and machinery. Many of the occupations require working outside and do not involve a lot of paperwork or working closely with others.

Abilities: Control Precision—The ability to quickly and repeatedly make precise adjustments in moving the controls of a machine or vehicle to exact positions. Multilimb Coordination—The ability to coordinate movements of two or more limbs together (for example, two arms, two legs, or one leg and one arm) while sitting, standing, or lying down. Does not involve performing the activities while the body is in motion. Static Strength—The ability to exert maximum muscle force to lift, push, pull, or carry objects. Far Vision—The ability to see details at a distance. Manual Dexterity—The ability to quickly make coordinated movements of one hand, a hand together with its arm, or two hands, to grasp, manipulate, or assemble objects.

Skills: Operation and Control—Controlling operations of equipment or systems. Equipment Maintenance—Performing routine maintenance and determining when and what kind of maintenance is needed. Product Inspection—Inspecting and evaluating the quality of products. Equipment Selection—Determining the kind of tools and equipment needed to do a job. Repairing—Repairing machines or systems, using the needed tools. Operation Monitoring—Watching gauges, dials, or other indicators to make sure a machine is working properly.

Generalized Work Activities: Operating Vehicles or Equipment—Running, maneuvering, navigating, or driving vehicles or mechanized equipment, such as forklifts, passenger vehicles, aircraft, or water craft. Performing General Physical Activities—Performing physical activities that require moving one's whole body, such as in climbing, lifting, balancing, walking, and stooping. Performing activities that often also require considerable use of the arms and legs, such as in the physical handling of materials. Controlling Machines and Processes—Using either control mechanisms or direct physical activity to operate machines or processes.

Does not involve working with computers or vehicles. Monitoring Processes, Materials, Surroundings—Monitoring and reviewing information from materials, events, or the environment, often to detect problems or to find out when things are finished. Handling and Moving Objects—Using one's hands and arms in handling, installing, forming, positioning, and moving materials, or in manipulating things.

Farmworkers, Farm and Ranch Animals

Attend to live farm, ranch, or aquacultural animals that may include cattle, sheep, swine, goats, horses and other equines, poultry, finfish, shellfish, and bees. Attend to animals produced for animal products, such as meat, fur, skins, feathers, eggs, milk, and honey. Duties may include feeding, watering, herding, grazing, castrating, branding, debeaking, weighing, catching, and loading animals. Maintain records on animals; examine animals to detect diseases and injuries; assist in birth deliveries; and administer medications, vaccinations, or insecticides as appropriate. Clean and maintain animal housing areas. Sprays livestock with disinfectants and insecticides. Collects, inspects, packs, or places eggs in incubator. Milks farm animals, such as cows and goats, by hand or using milking machine. Herds livestock to pasture for grazing, or to scales, trucks, or other enclosures. Marks livestock to identify ownership and grade, using brands, tags, paint, or tattoos. Cleans stalls, pens, and equipment, using disinfectant solutions, brushes, shovels and water hoses. Applies or administers medications and vaccinates animals. Mixes feed, additives, and medicines in prescribed portions. Debeaks and trims wings of poultry. Examines animals to detect disease and injuries. Waters livestock. Inspects and repairs fences, stalls, and pens. Moves equipment, poultry, or livestock manually or using truck or cart, from one location to another. Grooms, clips, and trims animals. Maintains equipment and machinery. Fills feed troughs with feed. Assists with birthing of animals. Castrates or docks ears and tails of animals. Maintains growth, feeding, production, and cost records. Segregates animals according to weight, age, color, and physical condition.

Personality Type: Realistic. Realistic occupations frequently involve work activities that include practical, hands-on problems and solutions. They often deal with plants, animals, and real-world materials like wood, tools, and machinery. Many of the occupations require working outside and do not involve a lot of paperwork or working closely with others.

Abilities: Static Strength—The ability to exert maximum muscle force to lift, push, pull, or carry objects. Manual Dexterity—The ability to quickly make coordinated movements of one hand, a hand together with its arm, or two hands, to grasp, manipulate, or assemble objects. Arm-Hand Steadiness—The ability to keep the hand and arm steady while making an arm movement or while holding the arm and hand in one position. Problem Sensitivity—The ability to tell when something is wrong or is likely to go wrong. Does not involve solving the problem, only recognizing there is a problem. Dynamic Strength—The ability to exert muscle force repeatedly or continuously over time. This involves muscular endurance and resistance to muscle fatigue.

Skills: Problem Identification—Identifying the nature of problems. Equipment Maintenance—Performing routine maintenance and determining when and what kind of maintenance is needed. Equipment Selection—Determining the kind of tools and equipment needed to do a job. Repairing—Repairing machines or systems, using the needed tools. Product Inspection—Inspecting and evaluating the quality of products. Writing—Communicating effectively with others in writing as indicated by the needs of the audience. Information Gathering—Knowing how to find information and identifying essential information.

Generalized Work Activities: Performing General Physical Activities—Performing physical activities that require moving one's whole body, such as in climbing, lifting, balancing, walking, and stooping. Performing activities that often also require considerable use of the arms and legs, such as in the physical handling of materials. Handling and Moving Objects—Using one's hands and arms in handling, installing, forming, positioning, and moving materials, or in manipulating things. Monitoring Processes, Materials, Surroundings

—Monitoring and reviewing information from materials, events, or the environment, often to detect problems or to find out when things are finished. Controlling Machines and Processes—Using either control mechanisms or direct physical activity to operate machines or processes. Does not involve working with computers or vehicles. Inspecting Equipment, Structures, Materials—Inspecting or diagnosing equipment, structures, or materials to identify the causes of errors or other problems or defects. Judging Qualities—Making judgments about or assessing the value, importance, or quality of things, services, or other people's work. Getting Information Needed to Do the Job—Observing, receiving, and otherwise obtaining information from all relevant sources.

General Farmworkers

Apply pesticides, herbicides, and fertilizer to crops and care for livestock; plant, maintain, and harvest food crops. Repairs farm buildings, fences, and other structures. Feeds, waters, grooms, and otherwise cares for livestock and poultry. Harvests fruits and vegetables by hand. Clears and maintains irrigation ditches. Sets up and operates irrigation equipment. Digs and transplants seedlings by hand. Cleans barns, stables, pens, and kennels. Administers simple medications to animals and fowls. Repairs and maintains farm vehicles, implements, and mechanical equipment. Oversees casual and seasonal help during planting and harvesting. Loads agricultural products into trucks for transport. Operates truck to haul livestock and products to market. Operates tractors, tractor-drawn machinery, and self-propelled machinery to plow, harrow and fertilize soil, and plant, cultivate, spray, and harvest crops.

Personality Type: Realistic. Realistic occupations frequently involve work activities that include practical, hands-on problems and solutions. They often deal with plants, animals, and real-world materials like wood, tools, and machinery. Many of the occupations require working outside and do not involve a lot of paperwork or working closely with others.

Abilities: Multilimb Coordination—The ability to coordinate movements of two or more limbs together (for example, two arms, two legs, or one leg and one arm) while sitting, standing, or lying down. Does not involve performing the activities while the body is in motion. Static Strength—The ability to exert maximum muscle force to lift, push, pull, or carry objects. Control Precision—The ability to quickly and repeatedly make precise adjustments in moving the controls of a machine or vehicle to exact positions. Dynamic Strength—The ability to exert muscle force repeatedly or continuously over time. This involves muscular endurance and resistance to muscle fatigue. Manual Dexterity—The ability to quickly make coordinated movements of one hand, a hand together with its arm, or two hands, to grasp, manipulate, or assemble objects. Trunk Strength—The ability to use one's abdominal and lower back muscles to support part of the body repeatedly or continuously over time without giving out or fatiguing. Gross Body Coordination—The ability to coordinate the movement of the arms, legs, and torso together in activities where the whole body is in motion.

Skills: Operation and Control—Controlling operations of equipment or systems. Equipment Maintenance—Performing routine maintenance and determining when and what kind of maintenance is needed. Equipment Selection—Determining the kind of tools and equipment needed to do a job. Repairing—Repairing machines or systems, using the needed tools. Operation Monitoring—Watching gauges, dials, or other indicators to make sure a machine is working properly.

Generalized Work Activities: Performing General Physical Activities—Performing physical activities that require moving one's whole body, such as in climbing, lifting, balancing, walking, and stooping. Performing activities that often also require considerable use of the arms and legs, such as in the physical handling of materials. Handling and Moving Objects—Using one's hands and arms in handling, installing, forming, positioning, and moving materials, or in manipulating things. Repairing and Maintaining Mechanical Equipment—Fixing, servicing, aligning, setting up, adjusting, and testing machines, devices, moving parts, and equipment that operate primarily on the basis of mechanical, not electronic, principles. Operating Vehicles or Equipment—Running, maneuvering, navigating, or driving vehicles or mechanized equipment such as forklifts, passenger vehicles, aircraft, or watercraft. Controlling Machines and Processes—Using either control mechanisms or direct physical activity to operate machines or processes. Does not involve working with computers or vehicles.

File Clerks

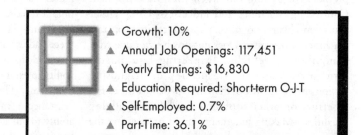

- ▲ Growth: 10%
- ▲ Annual Job Openings: 117,451
- ▲ Yearly Earnings: $16,830
- ▲ Education Required: Short-term O-J-T
- ▲ Self-Employed: 0.7%
- ▲ Part-Time: 36.1%

File Clerks

File correspondence, cards, invoices, receipts, and other records in alphabetical or numerical order or according to the filing system used. Locate and remove material from file when requested. Inserts additional data on file records. Places materials into storage receptacles, such as file cabinets, boxes, bins, or drawers, according to classification and identification information. Removes or destroys outdated materials in accordance with file maintenance schedules or legal requirements. Authorizes or documents materials movement, using logbook or computer, and traces missing files. Assigns and records or stamps identification numbers or codes to index materials for filing. Inspects or examines materials or files for accuracy, legibility, or damage. Scans or reads incoming materials to determine filing order or location. Sorts or classifies information, according to content, purpose, or user criteria, or chronological, alphabetical, or numerical order. Photographs or makes copies of data and records, using photocopying or microfilming equipment. Locates and retrieves files on request from authorized users.

Personality Type: Conventional. Conventional occupations frequently involve following set procedures and routines. These occupations can include working with data and details more than with ideas. Usually there is a clear line of authority to follow.

Abilities: Written Comprehension—The ability to read and understand information and ideas presented in writing. Information Ordering—The ability to correctly follow a given rule or set of rules in order to arrange things or actions in a certain order. The things or actions can include numbers, letters, words, pictures, procedures, sentences, and mathematical or logical operations. Near Vision—The ability to see details of objects at a close range. Category Flexibility—The ability to produce many rules so that each rule tells how to group or combine a set of things in a different way. Oral Comprehension—The ability to listen to and understand information and ideas presented verbally.

Skills: Information Organization—Finding ways to structure or classify multiple pieces of information. Synthesis/Reorganization—Reorganizing information to get a better approach to problems or tasks. Information Gathering—Knowing how to find information and identifying essential information. Reading Comprehension—Understanding written information in work-related documents. Problem Identification—Identifying the nature of problems.

Generalized Work Activities: Documenting/Recording Information—Entering, transcribing, recording, storing, or maintaining information in either written form or by electronic/magnetic recording. Processing Information—Compiling, coding, categorizing, calculating, tabulating, auditing, verifying, or processing information or data. Identifying Objects, Actions, and Events—Identifying information received by making estimates or categorizations, recognizing differences or similarities, or sensing changes in circumstances or events. Performing Administrative Activities—Approving requests, handling paperwork, and performing day-to-day administrative tasks. Handling

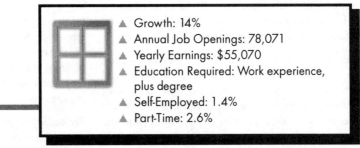

and Moving Objects—Using one's hands and arms in handling, installing, forming, positioning, and moving materials, or in manipulating things. Includes the use of keyboards. Getting Information Needed to Do the Job—Observing, receiving, and otherwise obtaining information from all relevant sources.

Financial Managers

- ▲ Growth: 14%
- ▲ Annual Job Openings: 78,071
- ▲ Yearly Earnings: $55,070
- ▲ Education Required: Work experience, plus degree
- ▲ Self-Employed: 1.4%
- ▲ Part-Time: 2.6%

Financial Managers, Branch or Department

Direct and coordinate financial activities of workers in a branch, office, or department of an establishment, such as branch bank, brokerage firm, risk and insurance department, or credit department. Directs insurance negotiations, selects insurance brokers and carriers, and places insurance. Submits delinquent accounts to attorney or outside agency for collection. Examines, evaluates, and processes loan applications. Establishes credit limitations on customer account. Reviews reports of securities transactions and price lists to analyze market conditions. Monitors order flow and transactions that brokerage firm executes on floor of exchange. Evaluates data pertaining to costs to plan budget. Evaluates effectiveness of current collection policies and procedures. Establishes procedures for custody and control of assets, records, loan collateral, and securities to ensure safekeeping. Plans, directs, and coordinates risk and insurance programs of establishment to control risks and losses. Prepares operational and risk reports for management analysis. Selects appropriate technique to minimize loss, such as avoidance and loss prevention and reduction. Analyzes and classifies risks as to frequency and financial impact of risk on company. Prepares financial and regulatory reports required by law, regulations, and board of directors. Directs and coordinates activities to implement institution policies, procedures, and practices concerning granting or extending lines of credit and loans. Manages branch or office of financial institution. Directs floor operations of brokerage firm engaged in buying and selling securities at exchange. Reviews collection reports to ascertain status of collections and balances outstanding. Directs and coordinates activities of workers engaged in conducting credit investigations and collecting delinquent accounts of customers.

Personality Type: Enterprising. Enterprising occupations frequently involve starting up and carrying out projects. These occupations can involve leading people and making many decisions. They sometimes require risk taking and often deal with business.

Abilities: Written Expression—The ability to communicate information and ideas in writing so others will understand. Mathematical Reasoning—The ability to understand and organize a problem and then select a mathematical method or formula to solve the problem. Oral Comprehension—The ability to listen to and understand information and ideas presented verbally. Written Comprehension—The ability to read and understand information and ideas presented in writing. Oral Expression—The ability to communicate information and ideas verbally so others will understand.

Skills: Judgment and Decision Making—Weighing the relative costs and benefits of a potential action. Critical Thinking—Using logic and analysis to identify the strengths and weaknesses of different approaches. Reading Comprehension—Understanding written information in work-related documents. Coordination—Adjusting actions in relation to others' actions. Management of Financial Resources—Determining how money will be spent to get the work done, and accounting for these expenditures. Information Gathering—Knowing how to find information and identifying essential information.

Generalized Work Activities: Getting Information Needed to Do the Job—Observing, receiving, and otherwise obtaining information from all relevant sources. Identifying Objects, Actions, and Events—Identifying information received by making estimates or categorizations, recognizing differences or similarities, or sensing changes in circumstances or events. Performing Administrative Activities—Approving requests, handling paperwork, and performing day-to-day administrative tasks. Estimating Needed Characteristics—Estimating the characteristics of materials, products, events, or information; estimating sizes, distances, and quantities; determining time, costs, resources, or materials needed to perform a work activity. Analyzing Data or Information—Identifying underlying principles, reasons, or facts by breaking down information or data into separate parts. Communicating with Other Workers—Providing information to supervisors, fellow workers, and subordinates. This information can be exchanged face-to-face, in writing, or via telephone/electronic transfer.

Treasurers, Controllers, and Chief Financial Officers

Plan, direct, and coordinate the financial activities of an organization at the highest level of management. Includes financial reserve officers. Arranges audits of company accounts. Analyzes past, present, and expected operations. Evaluates need for procurement of funds and investment of surplus. Advises management on economic objectives and policies, investments, and loans for short- and long-range financial plans. Coordinates and directs financial planning, budgeting, procurement, and investment activities of organization. Interprets current policies and practices and plans and implements new operating procedures to improve efficiency and reduce costs. Delegates authority for receipt, disbursement, banking, protection and custody of funds, securities, and financial instruments. Prepares reports or directs preparation of reports summarizing organization's current and forecasted financial position, business activity, and reports required by regulatory agencies. Ensures that institution reserves meet legal requirements.

Personality Type: Enterprising. Enterprising occupations frequently involve starting up and carrying out projects. These occupations can involve leading people and making many decisions. They sometimes require risk taking and often deal with business.

Abilities: Oral Comprehension—The ability to listen to and understand information and ideas presented verbally. Mathematical Reasoning—The ability to understand and organize a problem and then select a mathematical method or formula to solve the problem. Deductive Reasoning—The ability to apply general rules to specific problems to come up with logical answers. Involves deciding if an answer makes sense. Written Comprehension—The ability to read and understand information and ideas presented in writing. Written Expression—The ability to communicate information and ideas in writing so others will understand. Number Facility—The ability to add, subtract, multiply, or divide quickly and correctly.

Skills: Management of Financial Resources—Determining how money will be spent to get the work done, and accounting for these expenditures. Mathematics—Using mathematics to solve problems. Information Gathering—Knowing how to find information and identifying essential information. Problem Identification—Identifying the nature of problems. Critical Thinking—Using logic and analysis to identify the strengths and weaknesses of different approaches. Judgment and Decision Making—Weighing the relative costs and benefits of a potential action. Systems Evaluation—Looking at many indicators of system performance, taking into account their accuracy.

Generalized Work Activities: Analyzing Data or Information—Identifying underlying principles, reasons, or facts by breaking down information or data into separate parts. Making Decisions and Solving Problems—Combining, evaluating, and analyzing information and data to make decisions and solve problems. Involves making decisions about the relative importance of information and choosing the best solution. Communicating with Other Workers—Providing information to supervisors, fellow workers, and subordinates. This information can be exchanged face-to-face, in writing, or via telephone/electronic transfer. Getting Information Needed to Do the Job—Observing, receiving, and otherwise obtaining information from all relevant sources. Estimating Needed Characteristics—Estimating the characteristics of materials, products, events, or information; estimating sizes, distances, and quantities; determining time, costs, resources, or materials needed to perform a work activity. Providing Consultation and Advice to Others—Providing consultation and expert advice to management or other groups on technical, systems-related, or process-related topics. Documenting/Recording Information—Entering, transcribing, recording, storing, or maintaining information in either written form or by electronic/magnetic recording.

Fire Fighting and Prevention Supervisors

- ▲ Growth: 11%
- ▲ Annual Job Openings: 9,147
- ▲ Yearly Earnings: $44,830
- ▲ Education Required: Work experience in a related occupation
- ▲ Self-Employed: 0%
- ▲ Part-Time: 2.1%

Forest Fire Fighting and Prevention Supervisors

Supervise fire fighters who control and suppress fires in forests or vacant public land. Parachutes to major fire locations and directs fire containment and suppression activities. Observes fire and crews from air to determine force requirements and note changing conditions. Directs loading of fire suppression equipment into aircraft and parachuting of equipment to crews on ground. Trains workers in parachute jumping, fire suppression, aerial observation, and radio communication. Dispatches crews according to reported size, location, and condition of forest fires. Maintains radio communication with crews at fire scene to inform crew and base of changing conditions and learn of casualties.

Personality Type: Realistic. Realistic occupations frequently involve work activities that include practical, hands-on problems and solutions. They often deal with plants, animals, and real-world materials like wood, tools, and machinery. Many of the occupations require working outside and do not involve a lot of paperwork or working closely with others.

Abilities: Oral Expression—The ability to communicate information and ideas verbally so others will understand. Problem Sensitivity—The ability to tell when something is wrong or is likely to go wrong. Does not involve solving the problem, only recognizing there is a problem. Speech Clarity—The ability to speak clearly so that what is said is understandable to a listener. Far Vision—The ability to see details at a distance.

Skills: Judgment and Decision Making—Weighing the relative costs and benefits of a potential action. Coordination—Adjusting actions in relation to others' actions. Implementation Planning—Developing approaches for implementing an idea. Instructing—Teaching others how to do something.

Generalized Work Activities: Coordinating Work and Activities of Others—Coordinating members of a work group to accomplish tasks. Getting Information Needed to Do the Job—Observing, receiving, and otherwise obtaining information from all relevant sources. Communicating with Other Workers—Providing information to supervisors, fellow workers, and subordinates. This information can be exchanged face-to-face, in writing, or via telephone/electronic transfer. Estimating Needed Characteristics—Estimating the characteristics of materials, products, events, or information; estimating sizes, distances, and quantities; determining time, costs, resources, or materials needed to perform a work activity. Identifying Objects, Actions, and Events—Identifying information received by making estimates or categorizations, recognizing differences or similarities, or sensing changes in circumstances or events. Monitoring Processes, Materials, Surroundings—Monitoring and reviewing information from materials, events, or the environment, often to detect problems or to find out when things are finished.

Municipal Fire Fighting and Prevention Supervisors

Supervise fire fighters who control and extinguish municipal fires, protect life and property, and conduct rescue efforts. Writes and submits proposal for new equipment or modification of existing equipment. Orders and directs fire drills for occupants of buildings. Confers with civic representatives, and plans talks and demonstrations of fire safety to direct fire prevention information program. Trains subordinates in use of equipment, methods of extinguishing fires, and rescue operations. Studies and interprets fire safety codes to establish procedures for issuing permits regulating storage or use of hazardous or flammable substances. Compiles report of fire call, listing location, type, probable cause, estimated damage, and disposition. Keeps equipment and personnel records. Directs building inspections to ensure compliance with fire and safety regulations. Evaluates efficiency and performance of employees, and recommends awards for service. Directs investigation of cases of suspected arson, hazards, and false alarms. Assesses nature and extent of fire, condition of building, danger to adjacent buildings, and water supply to determine crew or company requirements. Coordinates and supervises fire fighting and rescue activities, and reports events to supervisor, using two-way radio. Inspects fire stations, equipment, and records to ensure efficiency and enforcement of departmental regulations. Oversees review of new building plans to ensure compliance with laws, ordinances, and administrative rules for public fire safety.

Personality Type: Realistic. Realistic occupations frequently involve work activities that include practical, hands-on problems and solutions. They often deal with plants, animals, and real-world materials like wood, tools, and machinery. Many of the occupations require working outside and do not involve a lot of paperwork or working closely with others.

Abilities: Oral Expression—The ability to communicate information and ideas verbally so others will understand. Time Sharing—The ability to efficiently shift back and forth between two or more activities or sources of information such as speech, sounds, or touch. Problem Sensitivity—The ability to tell when something is wrong or is likely to go wrong. Does not involve solving the problem, only recognizing there is a problem. Speech Clarity—The ability to speak clearly so that what is said is understandable to a listener. Deductive Reasoning—The ability to apply general rules to specific problems to come up with logical answers. Involves deciding if an answer makes sense. Oral Comprehension—The ability to listen to and understand information and ideas presented verbally.

Skills: Management of Personnel Resources—Motivating, developing, and directing people as they work, identifying the best people for the job. Writing—Communicating effectively with others in writing as indicated by the needs of the audience. Coordination—Adjusting actions in relation to others' actions. Implementation Planning—Developing approaches for implementing an idea. Instructing—Teaching others how to do something. Speaking—Talking to others to effectively convey information.

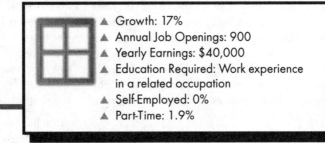
Generalized Work Activities: Getting Information Needed to Do the Job—Observing, receiving, and otherwise obtaining information from all relevant sources. Inspecting Equipment, Structures, Materials—Inspecting or diagnosing equipment, structures, or materials to identify the causes of errors or other problems or defects. Communicating with Other Workers—Providing information to supervisors, fellow workers, and subordinates. This information can be exchanged face-to-face, in writing, or via telephone/ electronic transfer. Documenting/Recording Information—Entering, transcribing, recording, storing, or maintaining information in either written form or by electronic/magnetic recording. Coordinating Work and Activities of Others—Coordinating members of a work group to accomplish tasks. Judging Qualities—Making judgments about or assessing the value, importance, or quality of things, services, or other people's work.

Fire Inspectors

- ▲ Growth: 17%
- ▲ Annual Job Openings: 900
- ▲ Yearly Earnings: $40,000
- ▲ Education Required: Work experience in a related occupation
- ▲ Self-Employed: 0%
- ▲ Part-Time: 1.9%

Fire Inspectors

Inspect buildings and equipment to detect fire hazards and enforce state and local regulations. Discusses violations and unsafe conditions with facility representative, makes recommendations, and instructs in fire safety practices. Collects fees for permits and licenses. Prepares reports, such as inspections performed, code violations, and recommendations for eliminating fire hazards. Tests equipment, such as gasoline storage tanks, air compressors, and fire-extinguishing and fire protection equipment to ensure conformance to fire and safety codes. Issues permits and summons, and enforces fire codes. Inspects interiors and exteriors of buildings to detect hazardous conditions or violations of fire codes. Gives first aid in emergencies.

Personality Type: Conventional. Conventional occupations frequently involve following set procedures and routines. These occupations can include working with data and details more than with ideas. Usually there is a clear line of authority to follow.

Abilities: Oral Expression—The ability to communicate information and ideas verbally so others will understand. Problem Sensitivity—The ability to tell when something is wrong or is likely to go wrong. Does not involve solving the problem, only recognizing there is a problem. Speech Clarity—The ability to speak clearly so that what is said is understandable to a listener. Inductive Reasoning—The ability to combine separate pieces of information, or specific answers to problems, to form general rules or conclusions. Includes coming up with a logical explanation for why a series of seemingly unrelated events occur together. Written Expression— The ability to communicate information and ideas in writing so others will understand.

Skills: Testing—Conducting tests to determine whether equipment, software, or procedures are operating as expected. Problem Identification—Identifying the nature of problems. Information Gathering—Knowing how to find information and identifying essential information. Writing—Communicating effectively with others in writing as indicated by the needs of the audience. Troubleshooting—Determining what is causing an operating error and deciding what to do about it.

Generalized Work Activities: Inspecting Equipment, Structures, Materials—Inspecting or diagnosing equipment, structures, or materials to identify the causes of errors or other problems or defects. Evaluating Information against Standards—Evaluating information against a set of standards and verifying that it is correct. Identifying Objects, Actions, and Events—Identifying information received by making estimates or categorizations, recognizing differences or similarities, or sensing changes in circumstances or events. Communicating with Persons Outside Organization—Communicating with persons outside the organization. Representing the organization to customers, the public, government, and other external sources. Exchanging information face-to-face, in writing, or via telephone/electronic transfer. Getting Information Needed to Do the Job—Observing, receiving, and otherwise obtaining information from all relevant sources. Providing Consultation and Advice to Others—Providing consultation and expert advice to management or other groups on technical, systems-related, or process-related topics.

Fire Investigators

Conduct investigations to determine causes of fires and explosions. Photographs damage and evidence relating to cause of fire or explosion, for future reference. Prepares and maintains reports of investigation results, and records of convicted arsonists and arson suspects. Testifies in court for cases involving fires, suspected arson, and false alarms. Swears out warrants and arrests, logs, fingerprints, and detains suspected arsonists. Instructs children about dangers of fire. Tests site and materials to establish facts, such as burn patterns and flash points of materials, using test equipment. Analyzes evidence and other information to determine probable cause of fire or explosion. Subpoenas and interviews witnesses, property owners, and building occupants to obtain information and sworn testimony. Examines site and collects evidence to gather information relating to cause of fire, explosion, or false alarm. Conducts internal investigation to determine negligence and violation of laws and regulations by fire department employees.

Personality Type: Investigative. Investigative occupations frequently involve working with ideas and require an extensive amount of thinking. These occupations can involve searching for facts and figuring out problems mentally.

Abilities: Inductive Reasoning—The ability to combine separate pieces of information, or specific answers to problems, to form general rules or conclusions. Includes coming up with a logical explanation for why a series of seemingly unrelated events occur together. Problem Sensitivity—The ability to tell when something is wrong or is likely to go wrong. Does not involve solving the problem, only recognizing there is a problem. Written Expression—The ability to communicate information and ideas in writing so others will understand. Oral Expression—The ability to communicate information and ideas verbally so others will understand. Speech Clarity—The ability to speak clearly so that what is said is understandable to a listener.

Skills: Judgment and Decision Making—Weighing the relative costs and benefits of a potential action. Active Listening—Listening to what other people are saying; asking questions as appropriate. Writing—Communicating effectively with others in writing as indicated by the needs of the audience. Speaking—Talking to others to effectively convey information.

Generalized Work Activities: Getting Information Needed to Do the Job—Observing, receiving, and otherwise obtaining information from all relevant sources. Documenting/Recording Information—Entering, transcribing, recording, storing, or maintaining information in either written form or by electronic/magnetic recording. Analyzing Data or Information—Identifying underlying principles, reasons, or facts by breaking down information or data into separate parts. Identifying Objects, Actions, and Events—Identifying information received by making estimates or categorizations, recognizing differences or similarities, or sensing changes in circumstances or events. Inspecting Equipment, Structures, Materials—Inspecting or diagnosing equipment, structures, or materials to identify the causes of errors or other problems or defects.

Forest Fire Inspectors and Prevention Specialists

Enforce fire regulations and inspect for forest fire hazards. Report forest fires and weather conditions. Extinguishes smaller fires with portable extinguisher, shovel, and ax. Examines and inventories firefighting equipment, such as axes, firehoses, shovels, pumps, buckets, and fire extinguishers to determine amount and condition. Observes instruments and reports meteorological data, such as temperature, relative humidity, wind direction and velocity, and types of cloud formations. Restricts public access and recreational use of forest lands during critical fire season. Maintains records and logbooks. Gives directions to crew on fireline during forest fire. Estimates size and characteristics of fire and reports findings to base camp by radio or telephone. Inspects camp sites to ensure camper compliance with forest use regulations. Inspects forest tracts and logging areas for fire hazards, such as accumulated wastes, mishandling of combustibles, or defective exhaust systems. Patrols and maintains surveillance, looking for forest fires, hazardous conditions, and weather phenomena. Gives directives and instructions regarding sanitation, fire prevention, violation corrections, and related forest regulations. Relays messages relative to emergencies, accidents, location of crew and personnel, weather forecasts, and fire hazard conditions. Locates forest fires on area map, using azimuth sighter and known landmarks. Directs maintenance and repair of firefighting equipment and requisitions new equipment.

Personality Type: Realistic. Realistic occupations frequently involve work activities that include practical, hands-on problems and solutions. They often deal with plants, animals, and real-world materials like wood, tools, and machinery. Many of the occupations require working outside and do not involve a lot of paperwork or working closely with others.

Abilities: Far Vision—The ability to see details at a distance. Problem Sensitivity—The ability to tell when something is wrong or is likely to go wrong. Does not involve solving the problem, only recognizing there is a problem. Speech Clarity—The ability to speak clearly so that what is said is understandable to a listener. Oral Expression—The ability to communicate information and ideas verbally so others will understand.

Skills: Information Gathering—Knowing how to find information and identifying essential information. Speaking—Talking to others to effectively convey information. Monitoring—Assessing how well one is doing when learning or doing something. Critical Thinking—Using logic and analysis to identify the strengths and weaknesses of different approaches. Judgment and Decision Making—Weighing the relative costs and benefits of a potential action.

Generalized Work Activities: Getting Information Needed to Do the Job—Observing, receiving, and otherwise obtaining information from all relevant sources. Performing General Physical Activities— Performing physical activities that require moving one's whole body, such as in climbing, lifting, balancing, walking, and stooping. Performing activities that often also require considerable use of the arms and legs, such as in the physical handling of materials. Monitoring Processes, Materials, Surroundings—Monitoring and reviewing information from materials, events, or the environment, often to detect problems or to find out when things are finished. Inspecting Equipment, Structures, Materials—Inspecting or diagnosing equipment, structures, or materials to identify the causes of errors or other problems or defects. Estimating Needed Characteristics—Estimating the characteristics of materials, products, events, or information; estimating sizes, distances, and quantities; determining time, costs, resources, or materials needed to perform a work activity.

Fishing Vessel Captains and Officers

- ▲ Growth: -19%
- ▲ Annual Job Openings: 2,378
- ▲ Yearly Earnings: $41,200
- ▲ Education Required: Work experience in a related occupation
- ▲ Self-Employed: 7.9%
- ▲ Part-Time: 3%

First-Line Supervisors and Manager/ Supervisors— Fishery Workers

Directly supervise and coordinate activities of fishery workers. Manager/Supervisors are generally found in smaller establishments where they perform both supervisory and management functions such as accounting, marketing, and personnel work and may also engage in the same fishery work as the workers they supervise. Confers with manager to determine time and place of seed planting, and cultivating, feeding, or harvesting of fish or shellfish. Plans work schedules according to availability of personnel and equipment, tidal levels, feeding schedules, or need for transfer or harvest. Oversees worker activities, such as treatment and rearing of fingerlings, maintenance of equipment, and harvesting of fish or shellfish. Records number and type of fish or shellfish reared and harvested, and keeps workers' time records. Directs workers to correct deviations or problems, such as disease, quality of seed distribution, or adequacy of cultivation. Assigns workers to duties, such as fertilizing and incubating spawn, feeding and transferring fish, and planting, cultivating, and harvesting shellfish beds. Trains workers in spawning, rearing, cultivating, and harvesting methods, and use of equipment. Observes fish and beds or ponds to detect diseases, determine quality of fish, or determine completeness of harvesting.

Personality Type: Realistic. Realistic occupations frequently involve work activities that include practical, hands-on problems and solutions. They often deal with plants, animals, and real-world materials like wood, tools, and machinery. Many of the occupations require working outside and do not involve a lot of paperwork or working closely with others.

Abilities: Oral Expression—The ability to communicate information and ideas verbally so others will understand. Problem Sensitivity—The ability to tell when something is wrong or is likely to go wrong. Does not involve solving the problem, only recognizing there is a problem. Oral Comprehension—The ability to listen to and understand information and ideas presented verbally. Deductive Reasoning—The ability to apply general rules to specific problems to come up with logical answers. Involves deciding if an answer makes sense. Near Vision—The ability to see details of objects at a close range. Information Ordering—The ability to correctly follow a given rule or set of rules in order to arrange things or actions in a certain order. The things or actions can include numbers, letters, words, pictures, procedures, sentences, and mathematical or logical operations.

Skills: Management of Personnel Resources— Motivating, developing, and directing people as they work, identifying the best people for the job. Coordination—Adjusting actions in relation to others' actions. Time Management—Managing one's own time and the time of others. Implementation Planning— Developing approaches for implementing an idea. Active Listening—Listening to what other people are saying; asking questions as appropriate.

Generalized Work Activities: Scheduling Work and Activities—Scheduling events, programs, activities, and the work of others. Monitoring Processes, Materials, Surroundings—Monitoring and reviewing information from materials, events, or the environment, often to detect problems or to find out when things are finished. Coordinating Work and Activities of Others—Coordinating members of a work group to accomplish tasks. Communicating with Other Workers—Providing information to supervisors, fellow workers, and subordinates. This information can be exchanged face-to-face, in writing, or via telephone/electronic transfer.

Getting Information Needed to Do the Job—Observing, receiving, and otherwise obtaining information from all relevant sources. Identifying Objects, Actions, and Events—Identifying information received by making estimates or categorizations, recognizing differences or similarities, or sensing changes in circumstances or events.

Flight Attendants

- ▲ Growth: 30%
- ▲ Annual Job Openings: 5,376
- ▲ Yearly Earnings: $37,800
- ▲ Education Required: Long-term O-J-T
- ▲ Self-Employed: 1%
- ▲ Part-Time: 45.7%

Flight Attendants

Provide personal services to ensure the safety and comfort of airline passengers during flight. Greet passengers, verify tickets, explain use of safety equipment, and serve food or beverages. Prepares reports showing place of departure and destination, passenger ticket numbers, meal and beverages inventories, and lost and found articles. Walks aisle of plane to verify that passengers have complied with federal regulations prior to takeoff. Assists passengers to store carry-on luggage in overhead, garment, or under-seat storage. Explains use of safety equipment to passengers. Administers first aid to passengers in distress. Collects money for meals and beverages. Greets passengers, verifies tickets, records destinations, and directs passengers to assigned seats. Serves prepared meals and beverages.

Personality Type: Enterprising. Enterprising occupations frequently involve starting up and carrying out projects. These occupations can involve leading people and making many decisions. They sometimes require risk taking and often deal with business.

Abilities: Oral Expression—The ability to communicate information and ideas verbally so others will understand. Speech Clarity—The ability to speak clearly so that what is said is understandable to a listener. Oral

Comprehension—The ability to listen to and understand information and ideas presented verbally. Problem Sensitivity—The ability to tell when something is wrong or is likely to go wrong. Does not involve solving the problem, only recognizing there is a problem. Speech Recognition—The ability to identify and understand the speech of another person.

Skills: Service Orientation—Actively looking for ways to help people. Speaking—Talking to others to effectively convey information. Social Perceptiveness—Being aware of other people's reactions and understanding why people react the way they do. Active Listening—Listening to what other people are saying; asking questions as appropriate. Coordination—Adjusting actions in relation to others' actions.

Generalized Work Activities: Performing for/Working with Public—Performing for people or dealing directly with the public, including serving persons and receiving clients or guests. Assisting and Caring for Others—Providing assistance or personal care to others. Handling and Moving Objects—Using one's hands and arms in handling, installing, forming, positioning, and moving materials, or in manipulating things. Communicating with Persons Outside Organization—Communicating with persons outside the organization. Representing the organization to customers, the public, government, and other external sources. Exchanging information face-to-face, in writing, or via telephone/electronic transfer. Monitoring Processes, Materials, Surroundings—

Monitoring and reviewing information from materials, events, or the environment, often to detect problems or to find out when things are finished.

Food Counter and Fountain Workers

- ▲ Growth: 12%
- ▲ Annual Job Openings: 944,970
- ▲ Yearly Earnings: $12,600
- ▲ Education Required: Short-term O-J-T
- ▲ Self-Employed: 0.1%
- ▲ Part-Time: 62.9%

Counter Attendants, Cafeteria, Food Concession, and Coffee Shop

Serve food to diners at counter or from a steam table. Does not include counter attendants who also wait tables. Adds relishes and garnishes according to instructions. Serves salads, vegetables, meat, breads, and cocktails, ladles soups and sauces, portions desserts, and fills beverage cups and glasses. Writes items ordered on tickets, totals orders, passes orders to cook, and gives ticket stubs to customers to identify filled orders. Prepares sandwiches, salads, and other short-order items. Wraps menu items, such as sandwiches, hot entrees, and desserts. Prepares and serves soft drinks and ice cream dishes, such as sundaes, using memorized formulas and directions. Orders items to replace stock. Scrubs and polishes counters, steamtables, and other equipment, and cleans glasses, dishes, and fountain equipment and polishes metalwork on fountain. Serves sandwiches, salads, beverages, desserts, and candies to employees in industrial establishment. Serves food, beverages, or desserts to customers in variety of settings, such as take out counter of restaurant or lunchroom. Calls order to kitchen and picks up and serves order when it is ready. Replenishes foods at serving stations. Brews coffee and tea and fills containers with requested

beverages. Accepts payment for food, using cash register or adding machine to total check. Carves meat.

Personality Type: Social. Social occupations frequently involve working with, communicating with, and teaching people. These occupations often involve helping or providing service to others.

Abilities: Wrist-Finger Speed—The ability to make fast, simple, repeated movements of the fingers, hands, and wrists. Oral Comprehension—The ability to listen to and understand information and ideas presented verbally. Number Facility—The ability to add, subtract, multiply, or divide quickly and correctly. Manual Dexterity—The ability to quickly make coordinated movements of one hand, a hand together with its arm, or two hands, to grasp, manipulate, or assemble objects.

Skills: Service Orientation—Actively looking for ways to help people. Active Listening—Listening to what other people are saying; asking questions as appropriate. Mathematics—Using mathematics to solve problems. Social Perceptiveness—Being aware of other people's reactions and understanding why people react the way they do. Writing—Communicating effectively with others in writing as indicated by the needs of the audience. Speaking—Talking to others to effectively convey information.

Generalized Work Activities: Performing for/Working with Public—Performing for people or dealing directly with the public, including serving persons in restaurants and stores and receiving clients or guests. Handling and Moving Objects—Using one's hands and arms in handling, installing, forming, positioning, and moving materials, or in manipulating things. Communicating with Persons Outside Organization—Communicating with persons outside the organization. Representing the organization to customers, the public, government, and other external sources. Exchanging information face-to-face, in writing, or via telephone/electronic transfer. Performing General Physical Activities—Performing physical activities that require moving one's whole body, such as in climbing, lifting, balancing, walking, and stooping. Performing activities that often also require considerable use of the arms and legs, such as in the physical handling of materials. Implementing Ideas and Programs—Conducting or carrying out work procedures and activities in accord with one's own ideas or information provided through directions/instructions for purposes of installing, modifying, preparing, delivering, constructing, integrating, finishing, or completing programs, systems, structures, or products. Communicating with Other Workers—Providing information to supervisors, fellow workers, and subordinates. This information can be exchanged face-to-face, in writing, or via telephone/electronic transfer. Getting Information Needed to Do the Job—Observing, receiving, and otherwise obtaining information from all relevant sources.

Food Preparation Workers

- ▲ Growth: 10%
- ▲ Annual Job Openings: 529,498
- ▲ Yearly Earnings: $13,700
- ▲ Education Required: Short-term O-J-T
- ▲ Self-Employed: 0.3%
- ▲ Part-Time: 57.4%

Combined Food Preparation and Serving Workers, Including Fast Food

Perform duties that combine both food preparation and food service, with no more than 80 percent of time being spent in either job area. Notifies kitchen personnel of shortages or special orders. Selects food items from serving or storage areas and places food and beverage items on serving tray or in take-out bag. Requests and records customer order and computes bill. Receives payment. Cooks or reheats food items, such as french fries. Makes and serves hot and cold beverages or desserts.

Personality Type: Realistic. Realistic occupations frequently involve work activities that include practical, hands-on problems and solutions. They often deal with plants, animals, and real-world materials like wood, tools, and machinery. Many of the occupations require working outside and do not involve a lot of paperwork or working closely with others.

Abilities: Wrist-Finger Speed—The ability to make fast, simple, repeated movements of the fingers, hands, and wrists. Manual Dexterity—The ability to quickly make coordinated movements of one hand, a hand together with its arm, or two hands, to grasp, manipulate, or assemble objects. Information Ordering—The ability to correctly follow a given rule or set of rules in order to arrange things or actions in a certain order. The things or actions can include numbers, letters, words, pictures, procedures, sentences, and mathematical or logical operations. Arm-Hand Steadiness—The ability to keep the hand and arm steady while making an arm movement or while holding the arm and hand in one position. Number Facility—The ability to add, subtract, multiply, or divide quickly and correctly. Oral Comprehension—The ability to listen to and understand information and ideas presented verbally.

Skills: Service Orientation—Actively looking for ways to help people. Active Listening—Listening to what other people are saying; asking questions as appropriate. Speaking—Talking to others to effectively convey information. Writing—Communicating effectively with others in writing as indicated by the needs of the audience. Mathematics—Using mathematics to solve problems.

Generalized Work Activities: Communicating with Persons Outside Organization—Communicating with persons outside the organization. Representing the organization to customers, the public, government, and other external sources. Exchanging information face-to-face, in writing, or via telephone/electronic transfer. Performing General Physical Activities—Performing physical activities that require moving one's whole body, such as in climbing, lifting, balancing, walking, and stooping. Performing activities that often also require considerable use of the arms and legs, such as in the physical handling of materials. Handling and Moving Objects—Using one's hands and arms in handling, installing, forming, positioning, and moving materials, or in manipulating things. Performing for/Working with Public—Performing for people or dealing directly with the public, including serving persons in restaurants and stores and receiving clients or guests. Getting Information Needed to Do the Job—Observing, receiving, and otherwise obtaining information from all relevant sources. Controlling Machines and Processes—Using either control mechanisms or direct physical activity to operate machines or processes. Does not involve working with computers or vehicles.

Dishwashers

Clean dishes, kitchen, food preparation equipment, or utensils. Carries or transfers by hand truck supplies and equipment between storage and work areas. Cleans and prepares various foods for cooking or serving. Prepares and packages individual place settings. Sets up banquet tables. Stocks serving stations with food and utensils. Removes garbage and trash and places refuse in designated pick up area. Cleans and maintains work areas, equipment, and utensils. Loads or unloads trucks used in delivering or picking up food and supplies.

Personality Type: Realistic. Realistic occupations frequently involve work activities that include practical, hands-on problems and solutions. They often deal with plants, animals, and real-world materials like wood, tools, and machinery. Many of the occupations require working outside and do not involve a lot of paperwork or working closely with others.

Abilities: Information Ordering—The ability to correctly follow a given rule or set of rules in order to arrange things or actions in a certain order. The things or actions can include numbers, letters, words, pictures, procedures, sentences, and mathematical or logical operations. Trunk Strength—The ability to use one's abdominal and lower back muscles to support part of the body repeatedly or continuously over time without giving out or fatiguing. Wrist-Finger Speed—The ability to make fast, simple, repeated movements of the fingers, hands, and wrists. Manual Dexterity—The ability to quickly make coordinated movements of one hand, a hand together with its arm, or two hands, to grasp, manipulate, or assemble objects. Extent Flexibility—The ability to bend, stretch, twist, or reach out with the body, arms, and/or legs. Static Strength—The ability to exert maximum muscle force to lift, push, pull, or carry objects.

Skills: Equipment Maintenance—Performing routine maintenance and determining when and what kind of maintenance is needed. Service Orientation—Actively looking for ways to help people. Information Organization—Finding ways to structure or classify multiple pieces of information. Equipment Selection—Determining the kind of tools and equipment needed to do a job. Active Listening—Listening to what other people are saying; asking questions as appropriate.

Generalized Work Activities: Handling and Moving Objects—Using one's hands and arms in handling, installing, forming, positioning, and moving materials, or in manipulating things. Performing General Physical Activities—Performing physical activities that require moving one's whole body, such as in climbing, lifting, balancing, walking, and stooping. Performing activities that often also require considerable use of the arms and legs, such as in the physical handling of materials. Getting Information Needed to Do the Job—

Observing, receiving, and otherwise obtaining information from all relevant sources. Monitoring Processes, Materials, Surroundings—Monitoring and reviewing information from materials, events, or the environment, often to detect problems or to find out when things are finished. Controlling Machines and Processes—Using either control mechanisms or direct physical activity to operate machines or processes. Does not involve working with computers or vehicles.

Food Preparation Workers

Perform a variety of food preparation duties other than cooking, such as preparing cold foods and shellfish, slicing meat, and brewing coffee or tea. Distributes food to waiters and waitresses to serve to customers. Cleans and maintains work areas, equipment, and utensils. Requisitions, stores, and distributes food supplies, equipment, and utensils. Butchers and cleans fowl, fish, poultry, and shellfish to prepare for cooking or serving. Stores food in designated containers and storage areas to prevent spoilage. Prepares variety of foods according to customers' orders or instructions of superior, following approved procedures. Portions and arranges food on serving dishes, trays, carts, or conveyor belts. Prepares and serves variety of beverages, such as coffee, tea, and soft drinks. Cleans, cuts, slices, or disjoints meats and poultry to prepare for cooking. Cleans and portions, and cuts or peels various foods to prepare for cooking or serving. Carries food supplies, equipment, and utensils to and from storage and work areas.

Personality Type: Realistic. Realistic occupations frequently involve work activities that include practical, hands-on problems and solutions. They often deal with plants, animals, and real-world materials like wood, tools, and machinery. Many of the occupations require working outside and do not involve a lot of paperwork or working closely with others.

Abilities: Wrist-Finger Speed—The ability to make fast, simple, repeated movements of the fingers, hands, and wrists. Manual Dexterity—The ability to quickly make coordinated movements of one hand, a hand together with its arm, or two hands, to grasp, manipulate, or assemble objects. Information Ordering—The ability to correctly follow a given rule or set of rules in order to arrange things or actions in a certain order. The things or actions can include numbers, letters, words, pictures, procedures, sentences, and mathematical or logical operations. Arm-Hand Steadiness—The ability to keep the hand and arm steady while making an arm movement or while holding the arm and hand in one position. Static Strength—The ability to exert maximum muscle force to lift, push, pull, or carry objects. Memorization—The ability to remember information such as words, numbers, pictures, and procedures. Oral Comprehension—The ability to listen to and understand information and ideas presented verbally.

Skills: Service Orientation—Actively looking for ways to help people. Active Listening—Listening to what other people are saying; asking questions as appropriate. Equipment Selection—Determining the kind of tools and equipment needed to do a job. Social Perceptiveness—Being aware of other people's reactions and understanding why people react the way they do. Reading Comprehension—Understanding written information in work-related documents.

Generalized Work Activities: Handling and Moving Objects—Using one's hands and arms in handling, installing, forming, positioning, and moving materials, or in manipulating things. Includes the use of keyboards. Performing General Physical Activities—Performing physical activities that require moving one's whole body, such as in climbing, lifting, balancing, walking, and stooping. Performing activities that often also require considerable use of the arms and legs, such as in the physical handling of materials. Monitoring Processes, Materials, Surroundings—Monitoring and reviewing information from materials, events, or the environment, often to detect problems or to find out when things are finished. Communicating with Other Workers—Providing information to supervisors, fellow workers, and subordinates. This information can be exchanged face-to-face, in writing, or via telephone/electronic transfer. Estimating Needed Characteristics—Estimating the characteristics of materials, products, events, or information; estimating sizes, distances, and quantities; determining time, costs, resources, or materials needed to perform a work activity.

Food Service and Lodging Managers

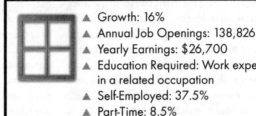

- ▲ Growth: 16%
- ▲ Annual Job Openings: 138,826
- ▲ Yearly Earnings: $26,700
- ▲ Education Required: Work experience in a related occupation
- ▲ Self-Employed: 37.5%
- ▲ Part-Time: 8.5%

Chefs and Head Cooks

Direct the preparation, seasoning, and cooking of salads, soups, fish, meats, vegetables, desserts, or other foods. Plan and price menu items, order supplies, and keep records and accounts. Participate in cooking. Collaborates with specified personnel and plans and develops recipes and menus. Inspects supplies, equipment, and work areas to ensure conformance to established standards. Records production and operational data on specified forms. Determines production schedules and worker-time requirements to ensure timely delivery of services. Estimates amounts and costs and requisitions supplies and equipment to ensure efficient operation. Trains and otherwise instructs cooks and workers in proper food preparation procedures. Observes workers and work procedures to ensure compliance with established standards. Helps cooks and workers cook and prepare food on demand. Supervises and coordinates activities of cooks and workers engaged in food preparation. Evaluates and solves procedural problems to ensure safe and efficient operations.

Personality Type: Enterprising. Enterprising occupations frequently involve starting up and carrying out projects. These occupations can involve leading people and making many decisions. They sometimes require risk taking and often deal with business.

Abilities: Oral Expression—The ability to communicate information and ideas verbally so others will understand. Problem Sensitivity—The ability to tell when something is wrong or is likely to go wrong. Does not involve solving the problem, only recognizing there is a problem.

Information Ordering—The ability to correctly follow a given rule or set of rules in order to arrange things or actions in a certain order. The things or actions can include numbers, letters, words, pictures, procedures, sentences, and mathematical or logical operations. Deductive Reasoning—The ability to apply general rules to specific problems to come up with logical answers. Involves deciding if an answer makes sense. Wrist-Finger Speed—The ability to make fast, simple, repeated movements of the fingers, hands, and wrists.

Skills: Coordination—Adjusting actions in relation to others' actions. Management of Material Resources—Obtaining and seeing to the appropriate use of equipment, facilities, and materials needed to do certain work. Speaking—Talking to others to effectively convey information. Time Management—Managing one's own time and the time of others. Management of Personnel Resources—Motivating, developing, and directing people as they work, identifying the best people for the job. Implementation Planning—Developing approaches for implementing an idea.

Generalized Work Activities: Communicating with Other Workers—Providing information to supervisors, fellow workers, and subordinates. This information can be exchanged face-to-face, in writing, or via telephone/ electronic transfer. Monitoring Processes, Materials, Surroundings—Monitoring and reviewing information from materials, events, or the environment, often to detect problems or to find out when things are finished. Identifying Objects, Actions, and Events—Identifying information received by making estimates or categorizations, recognizing differences or similarities, or sensing changes in circumstances or events. Judging Qualities—Making judgments about or assessing the value, importance, or quality of things, services, or other people's work. Getting Information Needed to Do the Job—Observing, receiving, and otherwise obtaining information from all relevant sources. Scheduling Work and Activities—Scheduling events, programs, activities, and the work of others.

First-Line Supervisors/Managers of Food Preparation and Serving Workers

Supervise workers engaged in preparing and serving food. Purchases or requisitions supplies and equipment to ensure quality and timely delivery of services. Analyzes operational problems, such as theft and wastage, and establishes controls. Trains workers in proper food preparation and service procedures. Records production and operational data on specified forms. Resolves customer complaints regarding food service. Initiates personnel actions, such as hires and discharges, to ensure proper staffing. Receives, issues, and takes inventory of supplies and equipment, and reports shortages to designated personnel. Specifies food portions and courses, production and time sequences, and work station and equipment arrangements. Inspects supplies, equipment, and work areas, to ensure efficient service and conformance to standards. Collaborates with specified personnel to plan menus, serving arrangements, and other related details. Supervises and coordinates activities of workers engaged in preparing and serving food and other related duties. Assigns duties, responsibilities, and work stations to employees, following work requirements. Recommends measures to improve work procedures and worker performance to increase quality of services and job safety. Observes and evaluates workers and work procedures to ensure quality standards and service. Schedules parties and reservations, and greets and escorts guests to seating arrangements.

Personality Type: Enterprising. Enterprising occupations frequently involve starting up and carrying out projects. These occupations can involve leading people

and making many decisions. They sometimes require risk taking and often deal with business.

Abilities: Oral Expression—The ability to communicate information and ideas verbally so others will understand. Oral Comprehension—The ability to listen to and understand information and ideas presented verbally. Written Comprehension—The ability to read and understand information and ideas presented in writing. Number Facility—The ability to add, subtract, multiply, or divide quickly and correctly. Speech Clarity—The ability to speak clearly so that what is said is understandable to a listener. Written Expression—The ability to communicate information and ideas in writing so others will understand.

Skills: Time Management—Managing one's own time and the time of others. Coordination—Adjusting actions in relation to others' actions. Management of Personnel Resources—Motivating, developing, and directing people as they work, identifying the best people for the job. Speaking—Talking to others to effectively convey information. Systems Perception—Determining when important changes have occurred in a system or are likely to occur. Implementation Planning—Developing approaches for implementing an idea. Judgment and Decision Making—Weighing the relative costs and benefits of a potential action.

Generalized Work Activities: Monitoring Processes, Materials, Surroundings—Monitoring and reviewing information from materials, events, or the environment, often to detect problems or to find out when things are finished. Coordinating Work and Activities of Others—Coordinating members of a work group to accomplish tasks. Communicating with Other Workers—Providing information to supervisors, fellow workers, and subordinates. This information can be exchanged face-to-face, in writing, or via telephone/electronic transfer. Getting Information Needed to Do the Job—Observing, receiving, and otherwise obtaining information from all relevant sources. Scheduling Work and Activities—Scheduling events, programs, activities, and the work of others. Identifying Objects, Actions, and Events—Identifying information received by making estimates or categorizations, recognizing differences or similarities, or sensing changes in circumstances or events.

First-Line Supervisors/Managers of Personal Service Workers

Supervise and coordinate activities of personal service workers, such as supervisors of flight attendants, hairdressers, or caddies. Requisitions supplies, equipment, and designated services, to ensure quality and timely service and efficient operations. Furnishes customers with information on events and activities. Observes and evaluates workers' appearance and performance to ensure quality service and compliance with specifications. Assigns work schedules, following work requirements, to ensure quality and timely delivery of services. Analyzes and records personnel and operational data and writes activity reports. Supervises and coordinates activities of workers engaged in lodging and personal services. Inspects work areas and operating equipment to ensure conformance to established standards. Resolves customer complaints regarding worker performance and services rendered. Collaborates with personnel to plan and develop programs of events, schedules of activities, and menus. Trains workers in proper operational procedures and functions, and explains company policy. Informs workers about interests of specific groups.

Personality Type: Enterprising. Enterprising occupations frequently involve starting up and carrying out projects. These occupations can involve leading people and making many decisions. They sometimes require risk taking and often deal with business.

Abilities: Oral Expression—The ability to communicate information and ideas verbally so others will understand. Near Vision—The ability to see details of objects at a close range. Oral Comprehension—The ability to listen to and understand information and ideas presented verbally. Information Ordering—The ability to correctly follow a given rule or set of rules in order to arrange things or actions in a certain order. The things or actions can include numbers, letters, words, pictures, procedures, sentences, and mathematical or logical operations.

Skills: Time Management—Managing one's own time and the time of others. Problem Identification—Identifying the nature of problems. Coordination—Adjusting actions in relation to others' actions. Management of Personnel Resources—Motivating, developing, and directing people as they work, identifying the best people for the job.

Generalized Work Activities: Scheduling Work and Activities—Scheduling events, programs, activities, and the work of others. Coordinating Work and Activities of Others—Coordinating members of a work group to accomplish tasks. Organizing, Planning, and Prioritizing—Developing plans to accomplish work. Prioritizing and organizing one's own work. Communicating with Other Workers—Providing information to supervisors, fellow workers, and subordinates. This information can be exchanged face-to-face, in writing, or via telephone/electronic transfer. Getting Information Needed to Do the Job—Observing, receiving, and otherwise obtaining information from all relevant sources.

Food Service Managers

Plan, direct, or coordinate activities of an organization or department that serves food and beverages. Keeps records required by government agencies regarding sanitation and food subsidies. Coordinates assignments of cooking personnel to ensure economical use of food and timely preparation. Investigates and resolves complaints regarding food quality, service, or accommodations. Establishes and enforces nutrition standards for dining establishment based on accepted industry standards. Tests cooked food by tasting and smelling to ensure palatability and flavor conformity. Creates specialty dishes and develops recipes to be used in dining facility. Monitors budget, payroll records, and reviews financial transactions to ensure expenditures are authorized and budgeted. Estimates food, liquor, wine, and other beverage consumption to anticipate amount to be purchased or requisitioned. Organizes and directs worker training programs, resolves personnel problems, hires new staff, and evaluates employee performance in dining and lodging facilities. Plans menus and food utilization based on anticipated number of guests, nutritional value, palatability, popularity, and costs. Monitors compliance with health and fire regulations regarding food preparation and serving and building maintenance in lodging and dining facility. Monitors food preparation and methods, size of portions, and garnishing and presentation of food to ensure food is prepared and presented in accepted manner. Reviews menus and analyzes recipes to determine labor and overhead costs, and assigns prices to menu items.

Personality Type: Enterprising. Enterprising occupations frequently involve starting up and carrying out projects. These occupations can involve leading people and making many decisions. They sometimes require risk taking and often deal with business.

Abilities: Oral Expression—The ability to communicate information and ideas verbally so others will understand. Oral Comprehension—The ability to listen to and understand information and ideas presented verbally. Near Vision—The ability to see details of objects at a close range. Written Comprehension—The ability to read and understand information and ideas presented in writing.

Skills: Time Management—Managing one's own time and the time of others. Coordination—Adjusting actions in relation to others' actions. Problem Identification—Identifying the nature of problems. Management of Personnel Resources—Motivating, developing, and directing people as they work, identifying the best people for the job. Implementation Planning—Developing approaches for implementing an idea. Service Orientation—Actively looking for ways to help people.

Generalized Work Activities: Monitoring and Controlling Resources—Monitoring and controlling resources and overseeing the spending of money. Communicating with Other Workers—Providing information to supervisors, fellow workers, and subordinates. This information can be exchanged face-to-face, in writing, or via telephone/electronic transfer. Guiding, Directing, and Motivating Subordinates— Providing guidance and direction to subordinates, including setting performance standards and monitoring subordinates. Identifying Objects, Actions, and

Events—Identifying information received by making estimates or categorizations, recognizing differences or similarities, or sensing changes in circumstances or events. Monitoring Processes, Materials, Surroundings—Monitoring and reviewing information from materials, events, or the environment, often to detect problems or to find out when things are finished.

Lodging Managers

Plan, direct, or coordinate activities of an organization or department that provides lodging and other accommodations. Observes and monitors performance to ensure efficient operations and adherence to facility's policies and procedures. Confers and cooperates with other department heads to ensure coordination of hotel activities. Receives and processes advance registration payments, sends out letters of confirmation, and returns checks when registration cannot be accepted. Shows, rents, or assigns accommodations. Collects payment and records data pertaining to funds and expenditures. Arranges telephone answering service, delivers mail and packages, and answers questions regarding locations for eating and entertainment. Inspects guest rooms, public areas, and grounds for cleanliness and appearance. Assigns duties to workers and schedules shifts. Purchases supplies and arranges for outside services, such as deliveries, laundry, maintenance and repair, and trash collection. Interviews and hires applicants. Answers inquiries pertaining to hotel policies and services and resolves occupants' complaints. Manages and maintains temporary or permanent lodging facilities. Coordinates front-office activities of hotel or motel and resolves problems. Greets and registers guests.

Personality Type: Enterprising. Enterprising occupations frequently involve starting up and carrying out projects. These occupations can involve leading people and making many decisions. They sometimes require risk taking and often deal with business.

Abilities: Oral Expression—The ability to communicate information and ideas verbally so others will understand. Number Facility—The ability to add, subtract, multiply, or divide quickly and correctly. Speech Clarity—The ability to speak clearly so that what is said is understandable to a listener. Oral Comprehension—

The ability to listen to and understand information and ideas presented verbally. Speech Recognition—The ability to identify and understand the speech of another person.

Skills: Service Orientation—Actively looking for ways to help people. Speaking—Talking to others to effectively convey information. Coordination—Adjusting actions in relation to others' actions. Management of Personnel Resources—Motivating, developing, and directing people as they work, identifying the best people for the job. Social Perceptiveness—Being aware of other people's reactions and understanding why people react the way they do. Problem Identification—Identifying the nature of problems.

Generalized Work Activities: Scheduling Work and Activities—Scheduling events, programs, activities, and the work of others. Monitoring and Controlling Resources—Monitoring and controlling resources and overseeing the spending of money. Performing for/Working with Public—Performing for people or dealing directly with the public, including serving persons in restaurants and stores and receiving clients or guests. Establishing and Maintaining Relationships—Developing constructive and cooperative working relationships with others. Communicating with Persons Outside Organization—Communicating with persons outside the organization. Representing the organization to customers, the public, government, and other external sources. Exchanging information face-to-face, in writing, or via telephone/electronic transfer. Communicating with Other Workers—Providing information to supervisors, fellow workers, and subordinates. This information can be exchanged face-to-face, in writing, or via telephone/electronic transfer.

Freight, Stock, and Material Movers

- ▲ Growth: 2%
- ▲ Annual Job Openings: 306,549
- ▲ Yearly Earnings: $18,470
- ▲ Education Required: Short-term O-J-T
- ▲ Self-Employed: 2.1%
- ▲ Part-Time: 38.4%

Freight, Stock, and Material Movers, Hand

Load, unload, and move materials at plant, yard, or other work site. Assembles product containers and crates, using hand tools and precut lumber. Shovels materials, such as gravel, ice, or spilled concrete, into containers or bins or onto conveyors. Sorts and stores items according to specifications. Installs protective devices, such as bracing, padding, or strapping, to prevent shifting or damage to items being transported. Cleans work area, using brooms, rags, and cleaning compounds. Attaches identifying tags or marks information on containers. Records number of units handled and moved, using daily production sheet or work tickets. Adjusts or replaces equipment parts, such as rollers, belts, plugs, and caps, using hand tools. Reads work orders or receives and listens to oral instructions to determine work assignment. Loads and unloads materials to and from designated storage areas, such as racks and shelves, or vehicles, such as trucks. Transports receptacles to and from designated areas by hand or using dollies, hand trucks, and wheelbarrows. Secures lifting attachments to materials and conveys load to destination, using crane or hoist. Stacks or piles materials, such as lumber, boards, or pallets. Directs spouts and positions receptacles, such as bins, carts, and containers, to receive loads. Bundles and bands material, such as fodder and tobacco leaves, using banding machines.

Personality Type: Realistic. Realistic occupations frequently involve work activities that include practical, hands-on problems and solutions. They often deal with plants, animals, and real-world materials like wood, tools, and machinery. Many of the occupations require working outside and do not involve a lot of paperwork or working closely with others.

Abilities: Static Strength—The ability to exert maximum muscle force to lift, push, pull, or carry objects. Extent Flexibility—The ability to bend, stretch, twist, or reach out with the body, arms, and/or legs. Oral Comprehension—The ability to listen to and understand information and ideas presented verbally. Written Comprehension—The ability to read and understand information and ideas presented in writing.

Skills: Equipment Selection—Determining the kind of tools and equipment needed to do a job. Installation—Installing equipment, machines, wiring, or programs to meet specifications. Reading Comprehension—Understanding written information in work-related documents. Active Listening—Listening to what other people are saying; asking questions as appropriate. Writing—Communicating effectively with others in

writing as indicated by the needs of the audience. Operation and Control—Controlling operations of equipment or systems. Mathematics—Using mathematics to solve problems.

Generalized Work Activities: Handling and Moving Objects—Using one's hands and arms in handling, installing, forming, positioning, and moving materials, or in manipulating things. Performing General Physical Activities—Performing physical activities that require moving one's whole body, such as in climbing, lifting, balancing, walking, and stooping. Performing activities that often also require considerable use of the arms and legs, such as in the physical handling of materials. Documenting/Recording Information—Entering, transcribing, recording, storing, or maintaining information in either written form or by electronic/magnetic recording. Performing Administrative Activities—Approving requests, handling paperwork, and performing day-to-day administrative tasks. Controlling Machines and Processes—Using either control mechanisms or direct physical activity to operate machines or processes. Does not involve working with computers or vehicles.

Funeral Directors and Morticians

- ▲ Growth: 16%
- ▲ Annual Job Openings: 3,972
- ▲ Yearly Earnings: $35,040
- ▲ Education Required: Long-term O-J-T
- ▲ Self-Employed: 11.6%
- ▲ Part-Time: 7.4%

Embalmers

Prepare bodies for interment in conformity with legal requirements. Dresses and places body in casket. Attaches trocar to pump-tube, starts pump, and repeats probing to force embalming fluid into organs. Incises stomach and abdominal walls and probes internal organs, using trocar, to withdraw blood and waste matter from organs. Makes incision in arm or thigh and drains blood from circulatory system and replaces blood with embalming fluid, using pump. Presses diaphragm to

evacuate air from lungs. Joins lips, using needle and thread or wire. Washes and dries body, using germicidal soap and towels or hot air drier. Maintains records, such as itemized list of clothing or valuables delivered with body and names of persons embalmed. Closes incisions, using needle and suture. Reshapes or reconstructs disfigured or maimed bodies, using materials such as clay, cotton, plaster of paris, and wax. Applies cosmetics to impart lifelike appearance. Packs body orifices with cotton saturated with embalming fluid to prevent escape of gases or waste matter. Inserts convex celluloid or cotton between eyeball and eyelid to prevent slipping and sinking of eyelid.

Personality Type: Realistic. Realistic occupations frequently involve work activities that include practical, hands-on problems and solutions. They often deal with plants, animals, and real-world materials like wood, tools, and machinery. Many of the occupations require working outside and do not involve a lot of paperwork or working closely with others.

Abilities: Finger Dexterity—The ability to make precisely coordinated movements of the fingers of one or both hands to grasp, manipulate, or assemble very small objects. Manual Dexterity—The ability to quickly make coordinated movements of one hand, a hand together with its arm, or two hands, to grasp, manipulate, or assemble objects. Arm-Hand Steadiness—The ability to keep the hand and arm steady while making an arm movement or while holding the arm and hand in one position. Wrist-Finger Speed—The ability to make fast, simple, repeated movements of the fingers, hands, and wrists. Near Vision—The ability to see details of objects at a close range.

Skills: Equipment Selection—Determining the kind of tools and equipment needed to do a job. Identification of Key Causes—Identifying the things that must be changed to achieve a goal. Monitoring—Assessing how well one is doing when learning or doing something. Time Management—Managing one's own time and the time of others. Solution Appraisal—Observing and evaluating the outcomes of a problem solution to identify lessons learned or to redirect efforts.

Generalized Work Activities: Handling and Moving Objects—Using one's hands and arms in handling, installing, forming, positioning, and moving materials, or in manipulating things. Includes the use of keyboards. Assisting and Caring for Others—Providing assistance or personal care to others. Documenting/Recording Information—Entering, transcribing, recording, storing, or maintaining information in either written form or by electronic/magnetic recording. Performing General Physical Activities—Performing physical activities that require moving one's whole body, such as in climbing, lifting, balancing, walking, and stooping.

Performing activities that often also require considerable use of the arms and legs, such as in the physical handling of materials. Getting Information Needed to Do the Job—Observing, receiving, and otherwise obtaining information from all relevant sources.

Funeral Directors

Perform various tasks to arrange and direct funeral services, such as coordinating transportation of body to mortuary for embalming, interviewing family or other authorized person to arrange details, selecting pallbearers, procuring official for religious rites, and providing transportation for mourners. Interviews family or other authorized person to arrange details, such as selection of casket and location and time of burial. Directs preparations and shipment of body for out-of-state burial. Plans placement of casket in parlor or chapel and adjusts lights, fixtures, and floral displays. Closes casket and leads funeral cortege to church or burial site. Arranges and directs funeral services. Directs placement and removal of casket from hearse.

Personality Type: Enterprising. Enterprising occupations frequently involve starting up and carrying out projects. These occupations can involve leading people and making many decisions. They sometimes require risk taking and often deal with business.

Abilities: Oral Expression—The ability to communicate information and ideas verbally so others will understand. Oral Comprehension—The ability to listen to and understand information and ideas presented verbally. Problem Sensitivity—The ability to tell when something is wrong or is likely to go wrong. Does not involve solving the problem, only recognizing there is a problem. Written Expression—The ability to communicate information and ideas in writing so others will understand. Written Comprehension—The ability to read and understand information and ideas presented in writing.

Skills: Coordination—Adjusting actions in relation to others' actions. Active Listening—Listening to what other people are saying; asking questions as appropriate. Social Perceptiveness—Being aware of other people's reactions and understanding why people react the way they do. Service Orientation—Actively looking for ways to help people. Speaking—Talking to others to effectively convey information.

Generalized Work Activities: Getting Information Needed to Do the Job—Observing, receiving, and otherwise obtaining information from all relevant sources. Making Decisions and Solving Problems—Combining, evaluating, and analyzing information and data to make decisions and solve problems. Involves making decisions about the relative importance of information and choosing the best solution.

Communicating with Persons Outside Organization—Communicating with persons outside the organization. Representing the organization to customers, the public, government, and other external sources. Exchanging information face-to-face, in writing, or via telephone/electronic transfer. Coordinating Work and Activities of Others—Coordinating members of a work group to accomplish tasks. Organizing, Planning, and Prioritizing—Developing plans to accomplish work. Prioritizing and organizing one's own work.

Gas and Petroleum Plant and System Occupations

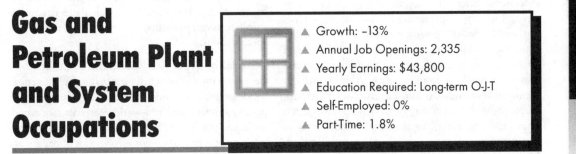

- ▲ Growth: –13%
- ▲ Annual Job Openings: 2,335
- ▲ Yearly Earnings: $43,800
- ▲ Education Required: Long-term O-J-T
- ▲ Self-Employed: 0%
- ▲ Part-Time: 1.8%

Gas Distribution Plant Operators

Control equipment to regulate flow and pressure of gas for utility companies and industrial use. Control distribution of gas for a municipal or industrial plant or a single process in an industrial plant. Adjusts governors to maintain specified gas pressure and volume. Controls equipment to regulate flow and pressure of gas to feedlines of boilers, furnaces, and related steam-generating or heating equipment. Determines causes of abnormal pressure variances and makes corrective recommendations, such as installation of pipe to relieve overloading. Changes charts in recording meters. Observes, records, and reports flow and pressure gauge readings on gas mains and fuel feedlines. Determines required governor adjustments, according to customer-demand estimates.

Personality Type: Realistic. Realistic occupations frequently involve work activities that include practical, hands-on problems and solutions. They often deal with

plants, animals, and real-world materials like wood, tools, and machinery. Many of the occupations require working outside and do not involve a lot of paperwork or working closely with others.

Abilities: Control Precision—The ability to quickly and repeatedly make precise adjustments in moving the controls of a machine or vehicle to exact positions. Number Facility—The ability to add, subtract, multiply, or divide quickly and correctly. Information Ordering—The ability to correctly follow a given rule or set of rules in order to arrange things or actions in a certain order. The things or actions can include numbers, letters, words, pictures, procedures, sentences, and mathematical or logical operations. Written Comprehension—The ability to read and understand information and ideas presented in writing. Inductive Reasoning—The ability to combine separate pieces of information, or specific answers to problems, to form general rules or conclusions. Includes coming up with a logical explanation for why a series of seemingly unrelated events occur together. Near Vision—The ability to see details of objects at a close range.

Skills: Operation and Control—Controlling operations of equipment or systems. Operation Monitoring—Watching gauges, dials, or other indicators to make sure a machine is working properly. Equipment Maintenance—Performing routine maintenance and determining when and what kind of maintenance is needed. Troubleshooting—Determining what is causing an operating error and deciding what to do about it. Problem Identification—Identifying the nature of problems.

Generalized Work Activities: Controlling Machines and Processes—Using either control mechanisms or direct physical activity to operate machines or processes. Does not involve working with computers or vehicles. Handling and Moving Objects—Using one's hands and arms in handling, installing, forming, positioning, and moving materials, or in manipulating things. Includes the use of keyboards. Monitoring Processes, Materials, Surroundings—Monitoring and reviewing information from materials, events, or the environment, often to detect problems or to find out when things are finished. Making Decisions and Solving Problems—Combining, evaluating, and analyzing information and data to make decisions and solve problems. Involves making decisions about the relative importance of information and choosing the best solution. Documenting/Recording Information—Entering, transcribing, recording, storing, or maintaining information in either written form or by electronic/magnetic recording. Identifying Objects, Actions, and Events—Identifying information received by making estimates or categorizations, recognizing differences or similarities, or sensing changes in circumstances or events.

Gas Processing Plant Operators

Control equipment, such as compressors, evaporators, heat exchangers, and refrigeration equipment to process gas for utility companies and for industrial use. Signals or directs workers tending auxiliary equipment. Controls operation of compressors, scrubbers, evaporators, and refrigeration equipment to liquefy, compress, or regasify natural gas. Adjusts

temperature, pressure, vacuum, level, flow rate, or transfer of gas, according to test results and knowledge of process and equipment. Tests oxygen for purity and moisture content at various stages of process, using burette and moisture meter. Cleans and repairs equipment, using hand tools. Records gauge readings and test results. Reads logsheet to ascertain demand and disposition of product or to detect equipment malfunctions. Controls fractioning columns, compressors, purifying towers, heat exchangers, and related equipment to extract nitrogen and oxygen from air. Observes pressure, temperature, level, and flow gauges to ensure standard operation. Calculates gas ratios, using testing apparatus, to detect deviations from specifications.

Personality Type: Realistic. Realistic occupations frequently involve work activities that include practical, hands-on problems and solutions. They often deal with plants, animals, and real-world materials like wood, tools, and machinery. Many of the occupations require working outside and do not involve a lot of paperwork or working closely with others.

Abilities: Control Precision—The ability to quickly and repeatedly make precise adjustments in moving the controls of a machine or vehicle to exact positions. Near Vision—The ability to see details of objects at a close range. Problem Sensitivity—The ability to tell when something is wrong or is likely to go wrong. Does not involve solving the problem, only recognizing there is a problem. Deductive Reasoning—The ability to apply general rules to specific problems to come up with logical answers. Involves deciding if an answer makes sense.

Skills: Operation and Control—Controlling operations of equipment or systems. Operation Monitoring—Watching gauges, dials, or other indicators to make sure a machine is working properly. Mathematics—Using mathematics to solve problems. Information Gathering—Knowing how to find information and identifying essential information. Testing—Conducting tests to determine whether equipment, software, or procedures are operating as expected.

Generalized Work Activities: Getting Information Needed to Do the Job—Observing, receiving, and otherwise obtaining information from all relevant sources. Controlling Machines and Processes—Using either control mechanisms or direct physical activity to operate machines or processes. Does not involve working with computers or vehicles. Monitoring Processes, Materials, Surroundings—Monitoring and reviewing information from materials, events, or the environment, often to detect problems or to find out when things are finished. Identifying Objects, Actions, and Events—Identifying information received by making estimates or categorizations, recognizing differences or similarities, or sensing changes in circumstances or events. Documenting/Recording Information—Entering, transcribing, recording, storing, or maintaining information in either written form or by electronic/magnetic recording.

Gaugers

Gauge and test oil in storage tanks. Regulate flow of oil into pipelines at wells, tank farms, refineries, and marine and rail terminals, following prescribed standards and regulations. Reports leaks or defective valves to maintenance. Tests oil to determine amount of bottom sediment, water, and foreign materials, using centrifugal tester. Starts pumps and opens valves to regulate flow of oil into and out of tanks, according to delivery schedules. Gauges tank containing petroleum and natural gas byproducts, such as condensate or natural gasoline. Records readings and test results. Gauges quality of oil in storage tanks before and after delivery, using calibrated steel tape and conversion. Records meter and pressure readings at gas well. Clamps seal around valves to secure tanks. Tightens connections with wrenches and greases and oils valves, using grease gum and oil can. Calculates test results, using standard formulas. Turns bleeder valves or lowers sample container into tank to obtain oil sample. Operates pumps, teletype, and mobile radio. Reads automatic gauges at specified intervals to determine flow rate of oil into or from tanks and amount of oil in tanks. Regulates flow of products into pipelines, using automated pumping equipment. Inspects pipelines, valves, and flanges to detect malfunctions, such as loose connections and leaks. Lowers thermometer into tanks to obtain temperature reading.

Personality Type: Realistic. Realistic occupations frequently involve work activities that include practical, hands-on problems and solutions. They often deal with plants, animals, and real-world materials like wood, tools, and machinery. Many of the occupations require working outside and do not involve a lot of paperwork or working closely with others.

Abilities: Near Vision—The ability to see details of objects at a close range. Manual Dexterity—The ability to quickly make coordinated movements of one hand, a hand together with its arm, or two hands, to grasp, manipulate, or assemble objects. Control Precision—The ability to quickly and repeatedly make precise adjustments in moving the controls of a machine or vehicle to exact positions. Problem Sensitivity—The ability to tell when something is wrong or is likely to go wrong. Does not involve solving the problem, only recognizing there is a problem. Wrist-Finger Speed—The ability to make fast, simple, repeated movements of the fingers, hands, and wrists.

Skills: Operation and Control—Controlling operations of equipment or systems. Operation Monitoring—Watching gauges, dials, or other indicators to make sure a machine is working properly. Mathematics—Using mathematics to solve problems. Science—Using scientific methods to solve problems. Equipment Maintenance—Performing routine maintenance and determining when and what kind of maintenance is needed.

Generalized Work Activities: Getting Information Needed to Do the Job—Observing, receiving, and otherwise obtaining information from all relevant sources. Monitoring Processes, Materials, Surroundings—Monitoring and reviewing information from materials, events, or the environment, often to detect problems or to find out when things are finished. Inspecting Equipment, Structures, Materials—Inspecting or diagnosing equipment, structures, or materials to identify the causes of errors or other problems or defects. Identifying Objects, Actions, and Events—Identifying information received by making estimates or categorizations, recognizing differences or similarities, or sensing changes in circumstances or events. Evaluating Information against Standards—

Evaluating information against a set of standards and verifying that it is correct. Controlling Machines and Processes—Using either control mechanisms or direct physical activity to operate machines or processes. Does not involve working with computers or vehicles.

Petroleum Pump System Operators

Control or operate manifold and pumping systems to circulate liquids through a petroleum refinery. Turns handwheels to open line valves and direct flow of product. Plans movement of products through lines to processing, storage, and shipping units, utilizing knowledge of interconnections and capacities system. Signals other workers by telephone or radio to operate pumps, open and close valves, and check temperatures. Records operating data, such as products and quantities pumped, stocks used, gauging results, and operating time. Reads operating schedules or instructions from dispatcher. Starts battery of pumps, observes pressure meters and flowmeters, and turns valves to regulate pumping speeds according to schedules. Synchronizes activities with other pumphouses to ensure continuous flow of products and minimum of contamination between products.

Personality Type: Realistic. Realistic occupations frequently involve work activities that include practical, hands-on problems and solutions. They often deal with plants, animals, and real-world materials like wood, tools, and machinery. Many of the occupations require working outside and do not involve a lot of paperwork or working closely with others.

Abilities: Oral Expression—The ability to communicate information and ideas verbally so others will understand. Control Precision—The ability to quickly and repeatedly make precise adjustments in moving the controls of a machine or vehicle to exact positions. Information Ordering—The ability to correctly follow a given rule or set of rules in order to arrange things or actions in a certain order. The things or actions can include numbers, letters, words, pictures, procedures, sentences, and mathematical or logical operations. Written Comprehension—The ability to read and understand information and ideas presented in writing.

Skills: Operation and Control—Controlling operations of equipment or systems. Operation Monitoring—Watching gauges, dials, or other indicators to make sure a machine is working properly. Coordination—Adjusting actions in relation to others' actions. Implementation Planning—Developing approaches for implementing an idea. Repairing—Repairing machines or systems, using the needed tools.

Generalized Work Activities: Controlling Machines and Processes—Using either control mechanisms or direct physical activity to operate machines or processes. Does not involve working with computers or vehicles. Handling and Moving Objects—Using one's hands and arms in handling, installing, forming, positioning, and moving materials, or in manipulating things. Includes the use of keyboards. Getting Information Needed to Do the Job—Observing, receiving, and otherwise obtaining information from all relevant sources. Monitoring Processes, Materials, Surroundings—Monitoring and reviewing information from materials, events, or the environment, often to detect problems or to find out when things are finished. Making Decisions and Solving Problems—Combining, evaluating, and analyzing information and data to make decisions and solve problems. Involves making decisions about the relative importance of information and choosing the best solution. Repairing and Maintaining Mechanical Equipment—Fixing, servicing, aligning, setting up, adjusting, and testing machines, devices, moving parts, and equipment that operate primarily on the basis of mechanical, not electronic, principles.

Petroleum Refinery and Control Panel Operators

Analyze specifications and control continuous operation of petroleum refining and processing units. Operate control panel to regulate temperature, pressure, rate of flow, and tank level in petroleum refining unit, according to process schedules. Compiles and records operating data, instrument readings, documents, and results of laboratory analyses. Monitors and adjusts unit controls to ensure safe and efficient operating conditions. Operates auxiliary equipment and controls multiple processing units during distilling or treating operations. Samples and tests liquids and gases for chemical characteristics and color of products, or sends products to laboratory for analysis. Cleans interior of processing units by circulating chemicals and solvents within unit. Inspects equipment and listens for automated warning signals to determine location and nature of malfunction, such as leaks and breakage. Observes instruments, gauges, and meters to verify conformance to specified quality and quantity of product. Operates control panel to coordinate and regulate process variables and to direct product flow rate, according to prescribed schedules. Reads and analyzes specifications, schedules, logs, and test results to determine changes to equipment controls required to produce specified product. Repairs, lubricates, and maintains equipment or reports malfunctioning equipment to supervisor to schedule needed repairs.

Personality Type: Realistic. Realistic occupations frequently involve work activities that include practical, hands-on problems and solutions. They often deal with plants, animals, and real-world materials like wood, tools, and machinery. Many of the occupations require working outside and do not involve a lot of paperwork or working closely with others.

Abilities: Problem Sensitivity—The ability to tell when something is wrong or is likely to go wrong. Does not involve solving the problem, only recognizing there is a problem. Written Comprehension—The ability to read and understand information and ideas presented in writing. Number Facility—The ability to add, subtract, multiply, or divide quickly and correctly. Information Ordering—The ability to correctly follow a given rule or set of rules in order to arrange things or actions in a certain order. The things or actions can include numbers, letters, words, pictures, procedures, sentences, and mathematical or logical operations. Near Vision—The ability to see details of objects at a close range.

Skills: Operation Monitoring—Watching gauges, dials, or other indicators to make sure a machine is working properly. Operation and Control—Controlling operations of equipment or systems. Reading Comprehension—Understanding written information in work-related documents. Product Inspection—Inspecting and evaluating the quality of products. Equipment Maintenance—Performing routine maintenance and determining when and what kind of maintenance is needed. Troubleshooting—Determining what is causing an operating error and deciding what to do about it.

Generalized Work Activities: Controlling Machines and Processes—Using either control mechanisms or direct physical activity to operate machines or processes. Does not involve working with computers or vehicles. Monitoring Processes, Materials, Surroundings—Monitoring and reviewing information from materials, events, or the environment, often to detect problems or to find out when things are finished. Inspecting Equipment, Structures, Materials—Inspecting or diagnosing equipment, structures, or materials to identify the causes of errors or other problems or defects. Getting Information Needed to Do the Job—Observing, receiving, and otherwise obtaining information from all relevant sources. Analyzing Data or Information—Identifying underlying principles, reasons, or facts by breaking down information or data into separate parts. Processing Information—Compiling, coding, categorizing, calculating, tabulating, auditing, verifying, or processing information or data. Repairing and Maintaining Mechanical Equipment—Fixing, servicing, aligning, setting up, adjusting, and testing machines, devices, moving parts, and equipment that operate primarily on the basis of mechanical, not electronic, principles.

General Managers and Top Executives

- ▲ Growth: 16%
- ▲ Annual Job Openings: 421,006
- ▲ Yearly Earnings: $55,890
- ▲ Education Required: Work experience, plus degree
- ▲ Self-Employed: 0%
- ▲ Part-Time: 6.1%

Private Sector Executives

Determine and formulate policies and business strategies and provide overall direction of private sector organizations. Plan, direct, and coordinate operational activities at the highest level of management with the help of subordinate managers. Promotes objectives of institution or business before associations, public, government agencies, or community groups. Directs and coordinates organization's financial and budget activities to fund operations, maximize investments, and increase efficiency. Directs activities of organization to plan procedures, establish responsibilities, and coordinate functions among departments and sites. Confers with board members, organization officials, and staff members to establish policies and formulate plans. Reviews financial statements and sales and activity reports to ensure that organization's objectives are achieved. Assigns or delegates responsibilities to subordinates. Directs and coordinates activities of business involved with buying and selling investment products and financial services. Presides over or serves on board of directors, management committees, or other governing boards. Negotiates or approves contracts with suppliers and distributors, and with maintenance, janitorial, and security providers. Analyzes operations to evaluate performance of company and staff and to determine areas of cost reduction and program improvement. Directs non-merchandising departments of business, such as advertising, purchasing, credit, and accounting. Directs, plans, and implements policies and objectives of organization or business in accordance with charter and board of directors. Screens, selects, hires, transfers, and discharges employees. Directs and coordinates activities of business or department concerned with production, pricing, sales, and/or distribution of products. Prepares reports and budgets. Establishes internal control procedures. Directs in-service training of staff. Administers program for selection of sites, construction of buildings, and provision of equipment and supplies.

Personality Type: Enterprising. Enterprising occupations frequently involve starting up and carrying out projects. These occupations can involve leading people and making many decisions. They sometimes require risk taking and often deal with business.

Abilities: Written Comprehension—The ability to read and understand information and ideas presented in writing. Oral Expression—The ability to communicate information and ideas verbally so others will understand. Oral Comprehension—The ability to listen to and understand information and ideas presented verbally. Written Expression—The ability to communicate information and ideas in writing so others will understand. Speech Clarity—The ability to speak clearly so that what is said is understandable to a listener.

Skills: Coordination—Adjusting actions in relation to others' actions. Judgment and Decision Making—Weighing the relative costs and benefits of a potential action. Identification of Key Causes—Identifying the things that must be changed to achieve a goal. Management of Financial Resources—Determining how money will be spent to get the work done, and accounting for these expenditures. Systems Evaluation—Looking at many indicators of system performance, taking into account their accuracy. Identifying Downstream Consequences—Determining the long-term outcomes of a change in operations.

Systems Perception—Determining when important changes have occurred in a system or are likely to occur.

Generalized Work Activities: Getting Information Needed to Do the Job—Observing, receiving, and otherwise obtaining information from all relevant sources. Monitoring and Controlling Resources—Monitoring and controlling resources and overseeing the spending of money. Making Decisions and Solving Problems—Combining, evaluating, and analyzing information and data to make decisions and solve problems. Involves making decisions about the relative importance of information and choosing the best solution. Developing Objectives and Strategies—Establishing long-range objectives and specifying the strategies and actions to achieve these objectives. Communicating with Other Workers—Providing information to supervisors, fellow workers, and subordinates. This information can be exchanged face-to-face, in writing, or via telephone/electronic transfer. Performing Administrative Activities—Approving requests, handling paperwork, and performing day-to-day administrative tasks.

General Office Clerks

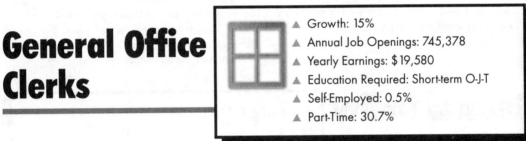

- ▲ Growth: 15%
- ▲ Annual Job Openings: 745,378
- ▲ Yearly Earnings: $19,580
- ▲ Education Required: Short-term O-J-T
- ▲ Self-Employed: 0.5%
- ▲ Part-Time: 30.7%

Office Clerks, General

Perform duties too varied and diverse to be classified in any specific office clerical occupation, requiring limited knowledge of office management systems and procedures. Perform clerical duties as assigned in accordance with the office procedures of individual establishments, including answering telephones, bookkeeping, typing or word processing, stenography, office machine operation, and filing. Compiles, copies, sorts, and files records of office activities, business transactions, and other activities. Computes, records, and proofreads data and other information, such as records or reports. Completes and mails bills, contracts, policies, invoices, or checks. Completes work schedules and arranges appointments for staff and students. Answers telephone, responds to requests, delivers messages, and runs errands. Reviews files, records, and other documents to obtain information to respond to requests. Communicates with customers, employees, and other individuals to disseminate or explain information. Transcribes dictation and composes and types letters and other correspondence, using typewriter or computer. Orders materials, supplies, and services, and completes records and reports. Operates office machines, such as photocopier, telecopier, and personal computer. Stuffs envelopes and addresses, stamps, sorts, and distributes mail, packages, and other materials. Collects, counts, and disburses money, completes banking transactions, and processes payroll.

Personality Type: Conventional. Conventional occupations frequently involve following set procedures and routines. These occupations can include working with data and details more than with ideas. Usually there is a clear line of authority to follow.

Abilities: Oral Comprehension—The ability to listen to and understand information and ideas presented verbally. Oral Expression—The ability to communicate information and ideas verbally so others will understand. Number Facility—The ability to add, subtract, multiply, or divide quickly and correctly. Information Ordering—The ability to correctly follow a given rule or set of rules in order to arrange things or actions in a certain order. The things or actions can include numbers, letters, words, pictures, procedures, sentences, and mathematical or logical operations. Speech Clarity—The ability to speak clearly so that what is said is understandable to a listener.

Skills: Reading Comprehension—Understanding written information in work-related documents. Writing—Communicating effectively with others in writing as indicated by the needs of the audience. Speaking—Talking to others to effectively convey information. Information Organization—Finding ways to structure or classify multiple pieces of information. Active Listening—Listening to what other people are saying; asking questions as appropriate.

Generalized Work Activities: Documenting/Recording Information—Entering, transcribing, recording, storing, or maintaining information in either written form or by electronic/magnetic recording. Processing Information—Compiling, coding, categorizing, calculating, tabulating, auditing, verifying, or processing information or data. Communicating with Persons Outside Organization—Communicating with persons outside the organization. Representing the organization to customers, the public, government, and other external sources. Exchanging information face-to-face, in writing, or via telephone/electronic transfer. Performing Administrative Activities—Approving requests, handling paperwork, and performing day-to-day administrative tasks. Getting Information Needed to Do the Job—Observing, receiving, and otherwise obtaining information from all relevant sources.

General Utility Maintenance Repairers

- ▲ Growth: 8%
- ▲ Annual Job Openings: 180,704
- ▲ Yearly Earnings: $23,290
- ▲ Education Required: Long-term O-J-T
- ▲ Self-Employed: 2.2%
- ▲ Part-Time: 9.3%

Maintenance and Repair Workers, General

Perform work involving the skills of two or more maintenance or craft occupations to keep machines, mechanical equipment, or the structure of an establishment in repair. Perform pipe fitting, boiler making, insulating, welding, machining, and carpentry. Repair electrical or mechanical equipment. Install, align, and balance new equipment. Repair buildings, floors, or stairs. Estimates costs of repairs. Assembles, installs, and/or repairs plumbing. Paints and repairs woodwork and plaster. Lays brick to repair and maintain physical structure of establishment. Sets up and operates machine tools to repair or fabricate machine parts, jigs and fixtures, and tools. Operates cutting torch or welding equipment to cut or join metal parts. Cleans and lubricates shafts, bearings, gears, and other parts of machinery. Fabricates and repairs counters, benches, partitions, and other wooden structures, such as sheds and outbuildings. Records repairs made and costs. Inspects and tests machinery and equipment to diagnose machine malfunctions. Dismantles and reassembles defective machines and equipment. Installs new or repaired parts. Installs and/or repairs wiring and electrical and electronic components. Installs machinery and equipment. Assembles, installs, and/or repairs pipe systems and hydraulic and pneumatic equipment.

Personality Type: Realistic. Realistic occupations frequently involve work activities that include practical, hands-on problems and solutions. They often deal with plants, animals, and real-world materials like wood,

tools, and machinery. Many of the occupations require working outside and do not involve a lot of paperwork or working closely with others.

Abilities: Information Ordering—The ability to correctly follow a given rule or set of rules in order to arrange things or actions in a certain order. The things or actions can include numbers, letters, words, pictures, procedures, sentences, and mathematical or logical operations. Visualization—The ability to imagine how something will look after it is moved around or when its parts are moved or rearranged. Finger Dexterity—The ability to make precisely coordinated movements of the fingers of one or both hands to grasp, manipulate, or assemble very small objects. Manual Dexterity—The ability to quickly make coordinated movements of one hand, a hand together with its arm, or two hands, to grasp, manipulate, or assemble objects. Control Precision—The ability to quickly and repeatedly make precise adjustments in moving the controls of a machine or vehicle to exact positions.

Skills: Installation—Installing equipment, machines, wiring, or programs to meet specifications. Repairing—Repairing machines or systems, using the needed tools. Equipment Maintenance—Performing routine

maintenance and determining when and what kind of maintenance is needed. Problem Identification—Identifying the nature of problems. Troubleshooting—Determining what is causing an operating error and deciding what to do about it.

Generalized Work Activities: Inspecting Equipment, Structures, Materials—Inspecting or diagnosing equipment, structures, or materials to identify the causes of errors or other problems or defects. Repairing and Maintaining Mechanical Equipment—Fixing, servicing, aligning, setting up, adjusting, and testing machines, devices, moving parts, and equipment that operate primarily on the basis of mechanical, not electronic, principles. Getting Information Needed to Do the Job—Observing, receiving, and otherwise obtaining information from all relevant sources. Handling and Moving Objects—Using one's hands and arms in handling, installing, forming, positioning, and moving materials, or in manipulating things. Includes the use of keyboards. Performing General Physical Activities—Performing physical activities that require moving one's whole body, such as in climbing, lifting, balancing, walking, and stooping. Performing activities that often also require considerable use of the arms and legs, such as in the physical handling of materials.

Geologists, Geophysicists, and Ocean- ographers

▲ Growth: 16%

▲ Annual Job Openings: 3,613

▲ Yearly Earnings: $53,890

▲ Education Required: Bachelor's degree

▲ Self-Employed: 15.1%

▲ Part-Time: 6.3%

Geologists

Study composition, structure, and history of the earth's crust. Examine rocks, minerals, and fossil remains to identify and determine the sequence of processes affecting the development of the earth. Develops instruments for geological work, such as diamond tool and dies, jeweled bearings, and grinding laps and wheels.

Prepares geological reports, maps, charts, and diagrams. Inspects proposed construction site and sets up test equipment and drilling machinery. Recommends and prepares reports on foundation design, acquisition, retention, or release of property leases, or areas of further research. Identifies and determines sequence of processes affecting development of earth. Analyzes engineering problems at construction projects, such as dams, tunnels, and large buildings, applying geological knowledge. Tests industrial diamonds and abrasives, soil, or rocks to determine geological characteristics, using optical, x-ray, heat, acid, and precision instruments. Interprets research data and recommends further study or action. Locates and estimates probable gas and oil deposits, using aerial photographs, charts, and research and survey results. Studies, examines, measures, and classifies composition, structure, and history of earth's crust, including rocks, minerals, fossils, soil, and ocean floor. Measures characteristics of earth, using seismograph, gravimeter, torsion balance, magnetometer, pendulum devices, and electrical resistivity apparatus.

Personality Type: Investigative. Investigative occupations frequently involve working with ideas and require an extensive amount of thinking. These occupations can involve searching for facts and figuring out problems mentally.

Abilities: Written Expression—The ability to communicate information and ideas in writing so others will understand. Written Comprehension—The ability to read and understand information and ideas presented in writing. Inductive Reasoning—The ability to combine separate pieces of information, or specific answers to problems, to form general rules or conclusions. Includes coming up with a logical explanation for why a series of seemingly unrelated events occur together. Deductive Reasoning—The ability to apply general rules to specific problems to come up with logical answers. Involves deciding if an answer makes sense. Number Facility—The ability to add, subtract, multiply, or divide quickly and correctly. Mathematical Reasoning—The ability to understand and organize a problem and then select a mathematical method or formula to solve the problem. Oral Expression—The ability to communicate information and ideas verbally so others will understand.

Skills: Science—Using scientific methods to solve problems. Critical Thinking—Using logic and analysis to identify the strengths and weaknesses of different approaches. Mathematics—Using mathematics to solve problems.

Generalized Work Activities: Getting Information Needed to Do the Job—Observing, receiving, and

otherwise obtaining information from all relevant sources. Identifying Objects, Actions, and Events—Identifying information received by making estimates or categorizations, recognizing differences or similarities, or sensing changes in circumstances or events. Processing Information—Compiling, coding, categorizing, calculating, tabulating, auditing, verifying, or processing information or data. Analyzing Data or Information—Identifying underlying principles, reasons, or facts by breaking down information or data into separate parts. Monitoring Processes, Materials, Surroundings—Monitoring and reviewing information from materials, events, or the environment, often to detect problems or to find out when things are finished.

Hydrologists

Research the distribution, circulation, and physical properties of underground and surface waters. Study the form and intensity of precipitation, its rate of infiltration into the soil, its movement through the earth, and its return to the ocean and atmosphere. Evaluates data in reference to project planning, such as flood and drought control, water power and supply, drainage, irrigation, and inland navigation. Studies, maps, and charts distribution, disposition, and development of waters of land areas, including form and intensity of precipitation. Studies, measures, and interprets seismic, gravitational, electrical, thermal, and magnetic forces and data affecting the earth. Compiles and evaluates data to prepare navigational charts and maps, predict atmospheric conditions, and prepare environmental reports. Prepares and issues maps and reports indicating areas of seismic risk to existing or proposed construction or development. Studies waters of land areas to determine modes of return to ocean and atmosphere. Studies and analyzes physical aspects of earth, including atmosphere and hydrosphere, and interior structure. Investigates origin and activity of glaciers, volcanoes, and earthquakes.

Personality Type: Investigative. Investigative occupations frequently involve working with ideas and require an extensive amount of thinking. These occupations can involve searching for facts and figuring out problems mentally.

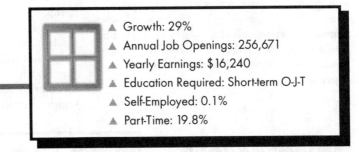

Abilities: Written Comprehension—The ability to read and understand information and ideas presented in writing. Deductive Reasoning—The ability to apply general rules to specific problems to come up with logical answers. Involves deciding if an answer makes sense. Mathematical Reasoning—The ability to understand and organize a problem and then select a mathematical method or formula to solve the problem. Number Facility—The ability to add, subtract, multiply, or divide quickly and correctly. Inductive Reasoning—The ability to combine separate pieces of information, or specific answers to problems, to form general rules or conclusions. Includes coming up with a logical explanation for why a series of seemingly unrelated events occur together. Oral Comprehension—The ability to listen to and understand information and ideas presented verbally.

Skills: Mathematics—Using mathematics to solve problems. Critical Thinking—Using logic and analysis to identify the strengths and weaknesses of different approaches. Information Gathering—Knowing how to find information and identifying essential information. Science—Using scientific methods to solve problems.

Generalized Work Activities: Analyzing Data or Information—Identifying underlying principles, reasons, or facts by breaking down information or data into separate parts. Processing Information—Compiling, coding, categorizing, calculating, tabulating, auditing, verifying, or processing information or data. Getting Information Needed to Do the Job—Observing, receiving, and otherwise obtaining information from all relevant sources. Identifying Objects, Actions, and Events—Identifying information received by making estimates or categorizations, recognizing differences or similarities, or sensing changes in circumstances or events. Monitoring Processes, Materials, Surroundings—Monitoring and reviewing information from materials, events, or the environment, often to detect problems or to find out when things are finished. Making Decisions and Solving Problems—Combining, evaluating, and analyzing information and data to make decisions and solve problems. Involves making decisions about the relative importance of information and choosing the best solution.

Guards

- ▲ Growth: 29%
- ▲ Annual Job Openings: 256,671
- ▲ Yearly Earnings: $16,240
- ▲ Education Required: Short-term O-J-T
- ▲ Self-Employed: 0.1%
- ▲ Part-Time: 19.8%

Security Guards

Guard, patrol, or monitor premises to prevent theft, violence, or infractions of rules. Operates detecting devices to screen individuals and prevent passage of prohibited articles into restricted areas. Writes reports of daily activities and irregularities, such as equipment or property damage, theft, presence of unauthorized persons, or unusual occurrences. Monitors and authorizes entrance and departure of employees, visitors, and other persons to guard against theft and maintain security of premises. Answers alarms and investigates disturbances. Circulates among visitors, patrons, and employees to preserve order and protect property. Drives and guards armored vehicle to transport money and valuables to prevent theft and ensure safe delivery. Inspects and adjusts security systems, equipment, and machinery to ensure operational use and to detect evidence of tampering. Answers telephone calls to take messages, answer questions, and provide information during nonbusiness hours or when switchboard is closed. Calls police or fire departments in cases of emergency, such as fire or presence of unauthorized persons. Warns persons of rule infractions or violations, and apprehends or evicts violators from premises, using force when necessary. Patrols industrial and commercial premises to prevent and detect signs of intrusion and ensure security of doors, windows, and gates. Escorts or drives motor vehicle to transport individuals to specified locations and to provide personal protection. Monitors and adjusts controls that regulate building systems, such as air conditioning, furnace, or boiler.

Personality Type: Social. Social occupations frequently involve working with, communicating with, and teaching people. These occupations often involve helping or providing service to others.

Abilities: Oral Expression—The ability to communicate information and ideas verbally so others will understand. Oral Comprehension—The ability to listen to and understand information and ideas presented verbally. Night Vision—The ability to see under low light conditions. Time Sharing—The ability to efficiently shift back and forth between two or more activities or sources of information such as speech, sounds, or touch. Selective Attention—The ability to concentrate and not be distracted while performing a task over a period of time. Problem Sensitivity—The ability to tell when something is wrong or is likely to go wrong. Does not involve solving the problem, only recognizing there is a problem. Near Vision—The ability to see details of objects at a close range.

Skills: Problem Identification—Identifying the nature of problems. Speaking—Talking to others to effectively convey information. Social Perceptiveness—Being aware of other people's reactions and understanding why people react the way they do. Active Listening—Listening to what other people are saying; asking questions as appropriate. Critical Thinking—Using logic and analysis to identify the strengths and weaknesses of different approaches. Judgment and Decision Making—Weighing the relative costs and benefits of a potential action.

Generalized Work Activities: Monitoring Processes, Materials, Surroundings—Monitoring and reviewing information from materials, events, or the environment, often to detect problems or to find out when things are finished. Performing General Physical Activities—Performing physical activities that require moving one's whole body, such as in climbing, lifting, balancing, walking, and stooping. Performing activities that often also require considerable use of the arms and legs, such as in the physical handling of materials. Getting Information Needed to Do the Job—Observing, receiving, and otherwise obtaining information from all relevant sources. Identifying Objects, Actions, and Events—Identifying information received by making estimates or categorizations, recognizing differences or similarities, or sensing changes in circumstances or events. Operating Vehicles or Equipment—Running, maneuvering, navigating, or driving vehicles or mechanized equipment such as forklifts, passenger vehicles, aircraft, or water craft.

Hairdressers, Hairstylists, and Cosmetologists

- ▲ Growth: 10%
- ▲ Annual Job Openings: 73,177
- ▲ Yearly Earnings: $15,150
- ▲ Education Required: Postsecondary vocational training
- ▲ Self-Employed: 46%
- ▲ Part-Time: 36.5%

Hairdressers, Hairstylists, and Cosmetologists

Provide beauty services, such as shampooing, cutting, coloring, and styling hair, and massaging and treating scalp. Apply makeup, dress wigs, perform hair removal, and provide nail and skin care services. Recommends and applies cosmetics, lotions, and creams to patron to soften and lubricate skin and enhance and restore natural appearance. Bleaches, dyes, or tints hair, using applicator or brush. Applies water, setting or waving solutions to hair and winds hair on curlers or rollers. Shampoos, rinses, and dries hair and scalp or hair pieces with water, liquid soap, or other solutions. Combs, brushes, and sprays hair or wigs to set style. Administers therapeutic medication and advises patron to seek medical treatment for chronic or contagious scalp conditions. Cleans, shapes, and polishes fingernails and toenails, using files and nail polish. Updates and maintains customer information records, such as beauty services provided. Analyzes patron's hair and other physical features or reads makeup instructions to determine and recommend beauty treatment. Massages and treats scalp for hygienic and remedial purposes, using hands, fingers, or vibrating equipment. Cuts, trims and shapes hair or hair pieces, using clippers, scissors, trimmers, and razors. Attaches wig or hairpiece to model head and dresses wigs and hairpieces according to instructions, samples, sketches or photographs. Shapes and colors eyebrows or eyelashes and removes facial hair, using depilatory cream and tweezers.

Personality Type: Enterprising. Enterprising occupations frequently involve starting up and carrying out projects. These occupations can involve leading people and making many decisions. They sometimes require risk taking and often deal with business.

Abilities: Manual Dexterity—The ability to quickly make coordinated movements of one hand, a hand together with its arm, or two hands, to grasp, manipulate, or assemble objects. Arm-Hand Steadiness—The ability to keep the hand and arm steady while making an arm movement or while holding the arm and hand in one position. Oral Expression—The ability to communicate information and ideas verbally so others will understand. Visualization—The ability to imagine how something will look after it is moved around or when its parts are moved or rearranged. Originality—The ability to come up with unusual or clever ideas about a given topic or situation, or to develop creative ways to solve a problem. Oral Comprehension—The ability to listen to and understand information and ideas presented verbally.

Skills: Service Orientation—Actively looking for ways to help people. Active Listening—Listening to what other people are saying; asking questions as appropriate. Speaking—Talking to others to effectively convey information. Social Perceptiveness—Being aware of other people's reactions and understanding why people react the way they do.

Generalized Work Activities: Handling and Moving Objects—Using one's hands and arms in handling, installing, forming, positioning, and moving materials, or in manipulating things. Includes the use of keyboards. Communicating with Persons Outside Organization—Communicating with persons outside the organization. Representing the organization to customers, the public, government, and other external sources. Exchanging information face-to-face, in writing, or via telephone/electronic transfer. Performing for/Working with Public—Performing for people or dealing directly with the public, including serving persons in restaurants and stores and receiving clients or guests. Establishing and Maintaining Relationships—Developing constructive and cooperative working relationships with others. Assisting and Caring for Others—Providing assistance or personal care to others.

Makeup Artists, Theatrical and Performance

Apply makeup to performers to reflect period, setting, and situation of their role. Designs rubber or plastic prostheses and requisitions materials, such as wigs, beards, and special cosmetics. Attaches prostheses to performer and applies makeup to change physical features and depict desired character. Studies production information, such as character, period settings and situations to determine makeup requirements. Examines sketches, photographs, and plaster models to obtain desired character image depiction. Confers with stage or motion picture officials and performers to determine dress or makeup alterations. Selects desired makeup shades from stock or mixes oil, grease, and coloring to achieve special color effects. Applies makeup to performers to alter their appearance to accord with their roles. Creates character drawings or models, based upon independent research to augment period production files.

Personality Type: Artistic. Artistic occupations frequently involve working with forms, designs, and patterns. They often require self-expression, and the work can be done without following a clear set of rules.

Abilities: Visual Color Discrimination—The ability to match or detect differences between colors, including shades of color and brightness. Originality—The ability to come up with unusual or clever ideas about a given topic or situation, or to develop creative ways to solve a problem. Arm-Hand Steadiness—The ability to keep the hand and arm steady while making an arm movement or while holding the arm and hand in one position. Visualization—The ability to imagine how something will look after it is moved around or when its parts are moved or rearranged. Near Vision—The ability to see details of objects at a close range. Manual Dexterity—The ability to quickly make coordinated movements of one hand, a hand together with its arm, or two hands, to grasp, manipulate, or assemble objects.

Skills: Information Gathering—Knowing how to find information and identifying essential information. Equipment Selection—Determining the kind of tools and equipment needed to do a job. Coordination—Adjusting actions in relation to others' actions. Reading Comprehension—Understanding written information in work-related documents.

Generalized Work Activities: Handling and Moving Objects—Using one's hands and arms in handling, installing, forming, positioning, and moving materials, or in manipulating things. Thinking Creatively—Originating, inventing, designing, or creating new applications, ideas, relationships, systems, or products, including artistic contributions. Getting Information Needed to Do the Job—Observing, receiving, and otherwise obtaining information from all relevant sources. Implementing Ideas and Programs—Conducting or carrying out work procedures and activities in accord with one's own ideas or information provided through directions/instructions for purposes of installing, modifying, preparing, delivering, constructing, integrating, finishing, or completing programs, systems, structures, or products. Making Decisions and Solving Problems—Combining, evaluating, and analyzing information and data to make decisions and solve problems. Involves making decisions about the relative importance of information and choosing the best solution.

Hand Packers and Packagers

- ▲ Growth: 22%
- ▲ Annual Job Openings: 249,421
- ▲ Yearly Earnings: $14,540
- ▲ Education Required: Short-term O-J-T
- ▲ Self-Employed: 0.1%
- ▲ Part-Time: 16.1%

Packers and Packagers, Hand

Pack or package by hand a wide variety of products and materials. Removes and places completed or defective product or materials on moving equipment or specified area. Seals containers or materials, using glues, fasteners, and hand tools. Places or pours products or materials into containers, using hand tools and equipment. Obtains and sorts products, materials, and orders, using hand tools. Assembles and lines cartons, crates and containers, using hand tools. Examines and inspects containers, materials, and products to ensure packaging process meets specifications. Records product and packaging information on specified forms and records. Tends packing machines and equipment that prepare and package materials and products. Measures, weighs, and counts products and materials, using equipment. Marks and labels containers or products, using marking instruments. Fastens and wraps products and materials, using hand tools. Cleans containers, materials, or work area, using cleaning solutions and hand tools. Loads materials and products into package processing equipment.

Personality Type: Realistic. Realistic occupations frequently involve work activities that include practical, hands-on problems and solutions. They often deal with plants, animals, and real-world materials like wood, tools, and machinery. Many of the occupations require working outside and do not involve a lot of paperwork or working closely with others.

Abilities: Manual Dexterity—The ability to quickly make coordinated movements of one hand, a hand together with its arm, or two hands, to grasp, manipulate, or assemble objects. Information Ordering—The ability to correctly follow a given rule or set of rules in order to arrange things or actions in a certain order. The things or actions can include numbers, letters, words, pictures, procedures, sentences, and mathematical or logical operations. Multilimb Coordination—The ability to coordinate movements of two or more limbs together (for example, two arms, two legs, or one leg and one arm) while sitting, standing, or lying down. Does not involve performing the activities while the body is in motion. Extent Flexibility—The ability to bend, stretch, twist, or reach out with the body, arms, and/or legs. Wrist-Finger Speed—The ability to make fast, simple, repeated movements of the fingers, hands, and wrists. Near Vision—The ability to see details of objects at a close range. Finger Dexterity—The ability to make precisely coordinated movements of the fingers of one or both hands to grasp, manipulate, or assemble very small objects.

Skills: Product Inspection—Inspecting and evaluating the quality of products. Operation and Control—Controlling operations of equipment or systems. Writing—Communicating effectively with others in writing as indicated by the needs of the audience. Reading Comprehension—Understanding written information in work-related documents. Monitoring—Assessing how well one is doing when learning or doing something. Equipment Selection—Determining the kind of tools and equipment needed to do a job. Problem Identification—Identifying the nature of problems.

Generalized Work Activities: Handling and Moving Objects—Using one's hands and arms in handling, installing, forming, positioning, and moving materials, or in manipulating things. Performing General Physical Activities—Performing physical activities that require moving one's whole body, such as in climbing, lifting, balancing, walking, and stooping. Performing activities that often also require considerable use of the arms and legs, such as in the physical handling of materials. Documenting/Recording Information—Entering, transcribing, recording, storing, or maintaining information in either written form or by electronic/magnetic recording. Controlling Machines and Processes—Using either control mechanisms or direct physical activity to operate machines or processes. Does not involve working with computers or vehicles. Inspecting Equipment, Structures, Materials—Inspecting or diagnosing equipment, structures, or materials to identify the causes of errors or other problems or defects. Getting Information Needed to Do the Job—Observing, receiving, and otherwise obtaining information from all relevant sources.

Hazardous Materials Removal Workers

▲ Growth: 19%
▲ Annual Job Openings: 5,470
▲ Yearly Earnings: $27,620
▲ Education Required: Not available
▲ Self-Employed: Not available
▲ Part-Time: Not available

Irradiated-Fuel Handlers

Package, store, and convey irradiated fuels and wastes, using hoists, mechanical arms, shovels, and industrial truck. Operates machines and equipment to package, store, or transport loads of waste materials. Follows prescribed safety procedures and complies with federal laws regulating waste disposal methods. Cleans contaminated equipment for reuse, using detergents and solvents, sandblasters, filter pumps and steam cleaners. Records number of containers stored at disposal site, and specifies amount and type of equipment and waste disposed. Mixes and pours concrete into forms to encase waste material for disposal. Loads and unloads materials into containers and onto trucks, using hoists or forklift. Drives truck to convey contaminated waste to designated sea or ground location.

Personality Type: Realistic. Realistic occupations frequently involve work activities that include practical, hands-on problems and solutions. They often deal with plants, animals, and real-world materials like wood, tools, and machinery. Many of the occupations require working outside and do not involve a lot of paperwork or working closely with others.

Abilities: Control Precision—The ability to quickly and repeatedly make precise adjustments in moving the controls of a machine or vehicle to exact positions. Information Ordering—The ability to correctly follow a given rule or set of rules in order to arrange things or actions in a certain order. The things or actions can include numbers, letters, words, pictures, procedures, sentences, and mathematical or logical operations. Static

Strength—The ability to exert maximum muscle force to lift, push, pull, or carry objects. Number Facility—The ability to add, subtract, multiply, or divide quickly and correctly. Multilimb Coordination—The ability to coordinate movements of two or more limbs together (for example, two arms, two legs, or one leg and one arm) while sitting, standing, or lying down. Does not involve performing the activities while the body is in motion.

Skills: Reading Comprehension—Understanding written information in work-related documents. Writing—Communicating effectively with others in writing as indicated by the needs of the audience. Mathematics—Using mathematics to solve problems. Operation and Control—Controlling operations of equipment or systems. Equipment Selection—Determining the kind of tools and equipment needed to do a job.

Generalized Work Activities: Handling and Moving Objects—Using one's hands and arms in handling, installing, forming, positioning, and moving materials, or in manipulating things. Includes the use of keyboards. Evaluating Information against Standards—Evaluating information against a set of standards and verifying that it is correct. Performing General Physical Activities—Performing physical activities that require moving one's whole body, such as in climbing, lifting, balancing, walking, and stooping. Performing activities that often also require considerable use of the arms and legs, such as in the physical handling of materials. Controlling Machines and Processes—Using either control mechanisms or direct physical activity to operate machines or processes. Does not involve working with computers or vehicles. Documenting/Recording Information—Entering, transcribing, recording, storing, or maintaining information in either written form or by electronic/magnetic recording.

Heating, Air Conditioning, and Refrigeration Mechanics and Installers

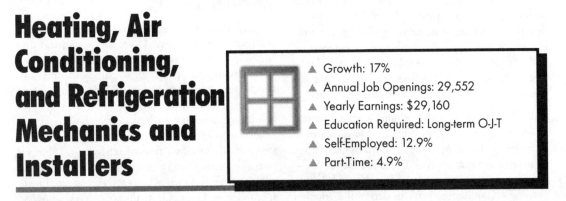

- ▲ Growth: 17%
- ▲ Annual Job Openings: 29,552
- ▲ Yearly Earnings: $29,160
- ▲ Education Required: Long-term O-J-T
- ▲ Self-Employed: 12.9%
- ▲ Part-Time: 4.9%

Heating and Air Conditioning Mechanics

Install, service, and repair heating and air conditioning systems in residences and commercial establishments. Tests pipe or tubing joints and connections for leaks, using pressure gauge or soap-and-water solution. Inspects inoperative equipment to locate source of trouble. Disassembles system and cleans and oils parts. Discusses heating-cooling system malfunctions with users to isolate problems or to verify malfunctions have been corrected. Cuts and drills holes in floors, walls, and roof to install equipment, using power saws and drills. Inspects and tests system to verify system compliance with plans and specifications and to detect malfunctions. Installs auxiliary components to heating-cooling equipment, such as expansion and discharge valves, air ducts, pipes, blowers, dampers, flues and stokers, following blueprints. Assembles, positions, and mounts heating or cooling equipment, following blueprints. Studies blueprints to determine configuration of heating or cooling equipment components. Adjusts system controls to setting recommended by manufacturer to balance system, using hand tools. Installs, connects, and adjusts thermostats, humidistats, and timers, using hand tools. Wraps pipes in insulation and secures it in place with cement or wire bands. Reassembles equipment and starts unit to test operation. Repairs or replaces defective equipment, components, or wiring. Joins pipes or tubing to equipment and to fuel, water, or refrigerant source to form complete circuit. Tests electrical circuits and components for continuity, using electrical test equipment. Fabricates, assembles, and installs duct work and chassis parts, using portable metal-working tools and welding equipment. Measures, cuts, threads, and bends pipe or tubing, using pipefitter's tools. Lays out and connects electrical wiring between controls and equipment according to wiring diagram, using electrician's hand tools.

Personality Type: Realistic. Realistic occupations frequently involve work activities that include practical, hands-on problems and solutions. They often deal with plants, animals, and real-world materials like wood, tools, and machinery. Many of the occupations require working outside and do not involve a lot of paperwork or working closely with others.

Abilities: Deductive Reasoning—The ability to apply general rules to specific problems to come up with logical answers. Involves deciding if an answer makes sense. Written Comprehension—The ability to read and understand information and ideas presented in writing. Manual Dexterity—The ability to quickly make coordinated movements of one hand, a hand together with its arm, or two hands, to grasp, manipulate, or assemble objects. Arm-Hand Steadiness—The ability to keep the hand and arm steady while making an arm movement or while holding the arm and hand in one position. Problem Sensitivity—The ability to tell when something is wrong or is likely to go wrong. Does not involve solving the problem, only recognizing there is a problem. Control Precision—The ability to quickly and repeatedly make precise adjustments in moving the controls of a machine or vehicle to exact positions.

Skills: Troubleshooting—Determining what is causing an operating error and deciding what to do about it. Installation—Installing equipment, machines, wiring, or programs to meet specifications. Repairing— Repairing machines or systems, using the needed tools. Testing —Conducting tests to determine whether equipment, software, or procedures are operating as expected. Equipment Maintenance—Performing routine maintenance and determining when and what kind of maintenance is needed. Equipment Selection— Determining the kind of tools and equipment needed to do a job.

Generalized Work Activities: Handling and Moving Objects—Using one's hands and arms in handling, installing, forming, positioning, and moving materials, or in manipulating things. Repairing and Maintaining Mechanical Equipment—Fixing, servicing, aligning, setting up, adjusting, and testing machines, devices, moving parts, and equipment that operate primarily on the basis of mechanical, not electronic, principles. Monitoring Processes, Materials, Surroundings— Monitoring and reviewing information from materials, events, or the environment, often to detect problems or to find out when things are finished. Performing General Physical Activities—Performing physical activities that require moving one's whole body, such as in climbing, lifting, balancing, walking, and stooping. Performing activities that often also require considerable use of the arms and legs, such as in the physical handling of materials. Inspecting Equipment, Structures, Materials—Inspecting or diagnosing equipment, structures, or materials to identify the causes of errors or other problems or defects.

Refrigeration Mechanics

Install and repair industrial and commercial refrigerating systems. Assembles structural and functional components, such as controls, switches, gauges, wiring harnesses, valves, pumps, compressors, condensers, cores, and pipes. Reads blueprints to determine location, size, capacity, and type of components needed to build refrigeration system. Adjusts valves according to specifications and charges system with specified type of refrigerant. Observes system operation, using gauges and instruments, and adjusts or replaces mechanisms and parts, according to specifications. Dismantles malfunctioning systems and tests components, using electrical, mechanical, and pneumatic testing equipment. Lays out reference points for installation of structural and functional components, using measuring instruments. Tests lines, components, and connections for leaks. Lifts and aligns components into position, using hoist or block and tackle. Keeps records of repairs and replacements made and causes of malfunctions. Fabricates and assembles components and structural portions of refrigeration system, using hand tools, powered tools, and welding equipment. Brazes or solders parts to repair defective joints and leaks. Installs expansion and control valves, using acetylene torch and wrenches. Cuts, bends, threads, and connects pipe to functional components and water, power, or refrigeration system. Replaces or adjusts defective or worn parts to repair system and reassembles system. Mounts compressor, condenser, and other components in specified location on frame, using hand tools and acetylene welding equipment. Drills holes and installs mounting brackets and hangers into floor and walls of building.

Personality Type: Realistic. Realistic occupations frequently involve work activities that include practical, hands-on problems and solutions. They often deal with plants, animals, and real-world materials like wood, tools, and machinery. Many of the occupations require working outside and do not involve a lot of paperwork or working closely with others.

Abilities: Deductive Reasoning—The ability to apply general rules to specific problems to come up with logical answers. Involves deciding if an answer makes sense. Manual Dexterity—The ability to quickly make coordinated movements of one hand, a hand together with its arm, or two hands, to grasp, manipulate, or assemble objects. Information Ordering—The ability to correctly follow a given rule or set of rules in order to arrange things or actions in a certain order. The things or actions can include numbers, letters, words, pictures, procedures, sentences, and mathematical or logical operations. Control Precision—The ability to quickly and repeatedly make precise adjustments in moving the controls of a machine or vehicle to exact positions. Extent Flexibility—The ability to bend, stretch, twist, or reach out with the body, arms, and/or legs.

Skills: Installation—Installing equipment, machines, wiring, or programs to meet specifications. Repairing—Repairing machines or systems, using the needed tools. Troubleshooting—Determining what is causing an operating error and deciding what to do about it. Testing—Conducting tests to determine whether equipment, software, or procedures are operating as expected. Problem Identification—Identifying the nature of problems.

Generalized Work Activities: Repairing and Maintaining Mechanical Equipment—Fixing, servicing, aligning, setting up, adjusting, and testing machines, devices, moving parts, and equipment that operate primarily on the basis of mechanical, not electronic, principles. Getting Information Needed to Do the Job—Observing, receiving, and otherwise obtaining information from all relevant sources. Handling and Moving Objects—Using one's hands and arms in handling, installing, forming, positioning, and moving materials, or in manipulating things. Performing General Physical Activities—Performing physical activities that require moving one's whole body, such as in climbing, lifting, balancing, walking, and stooping. Performing activities that often also require considerable use of the arms and legs, such as in the physical handling of materials. Monitoring Processes, Materials, Surroundings—Monitoring and reviewing information from materials, events, or the environment, often to detect problems or to find out when things are finished.

Highway Maintenance Workers

- ▲ Growth: 11%
- ▲ Annual Job Openings: 20,512
- ▲ Yearly Earnings: $24,490
- ▲ Education Required: Short-term O-J-T
- ▲ Self-Employed: 0%
- ▲ Part-Time: 8.5%

Highway Maintenance Workers

Maintain highways, municipal and rural roads, airport runways, and rights-of-way. Duties include patching broken or eroded pavement, repairing guardrails, highway markers, and snow fences. Mow or clear brush from along road or plow snow from roadway. Verifies alignment of markers by sight. Drives truck or tractor equipped with adjustable snow plow and blower unit. Dumps, spreads, and tamps asphalt, using pneumatic tamper to patch broken pavement. Measures and marks locations for installation of markers, using tape, string, or chalk. Blends compounds to form adhesive mixture, using spoon. Drives tractor with mower attachment to cut grass. Erects, installs, and repairs guardrails, highway markers, button-type lane markers, and snow fences, using hand tools and power tools. Drives truck to transport crew and equipment to work site. Sets signs and cones around work area to divert traffic.

Personality Type: Realistic. Realistic occupations frequently involve work activities that include practical, hands-on problems and solutions. They often deal with plants, animals, and real-world materials like wood, tools, and machinery. Many of the occupations require working outside and do not involve a lot of paperwork or working closely with others.

Abilities: Trunk Strength—The ability to use one's abdominal and lower back muscles to support part of the body repeatedly or continuously over time without giving out or fatiguing. Multilimb Coordination—The ability to coordinate movements of two or more limbs together (for example, two arms, two legs, or one leg and one arm) while sitting, standing, or lying down. Does not involve performing the activities while the body is in motion. Reaction Time—The ability to quickly respond with the hand, finger, or foot to a signal such as a sound, a light, or a picture. Gross Body Coordination—The ability to coordinate the movement of the arms, legs, and torso together in activities where the whole body is in motion. Spatial Orientation—The ability to know one's location in relation to the environment or to know where other objects are in relation to one's self.

Skills: Repairing—Repairing machines or systems, using the needed tools. Equipment Selection—Determining the kind of tools and equipment needed to do a job. Operation and Control—Controlling operations of equipment or systems. Installation—Installing equipment, machines, wiring, or programs to meet specifications. Equipment Maintenance—Performing routine maintenance and determining when and what kind of maintenance is needed.

Generalized Work Activities: Performing General Physical Activities—Performing physical activities that require moving one's whole body, such as in climbing, lifting, balancing, walking, and stooping. Performing activities that often also require considerable use of the arms and legs, such as in the physical handling of materials. Operating Vehicles or Equipment—Running, maneuvering, navigating, or driving vehicles or mechanized equipment such as forklifts, passenger vehicles, aircraft, or water craft. Handling and Moving Objects—Using one's hands and arms in handling, installing, forming, positioning, and moving materials, or in manipulating things. Controlling Machines and Processes—Using either control mechanisms or direct physical activity to operate machines or processes. Does not involve working with computers or vehicles. Implementing Ideas and Programs—Conducting or carrying out work procedures and activities in accord with one's own ideas or information provided through directions/instructions for purposes of installing, modifying, preparing, delivering, constructing, integrating, finishing, or completing programs, systems, structures, or products. Getting Information Needed to Do the Job—Observing, receiving, and otherwise obtaining information from all relevant sources.

Hotel, Motel, and Resort Desk Clerks

- ▲ Growth: 14%
- ▲ Annual Job Openings: 60,382
- ▲ Yearly Earnings: $15,160
- ▲ Education Required: Short-term O-J-T
- ▲ Self-Employed: 1.5%
- ▲ Part-Time: 25.8%

Hotel, Motel, and Resort Desk Clerks

Accommodate hotel, motel, and resort patrons by registering and assigning rooms to guests, issuing room keys, transmitting and receiving messages, keeping records of occupied rooms and guests' accounts, making and confirming reservations, and presenting statements to and collecting payments from departing guests. Deposits guests' valuables in hotel safe or safe-deposit box. Keeps records of room availability and guests' accounts, manually or using computer. Posts charges, such as room, food, liquor, or telephone, to ledger, manually or using computer. Transmits and receives messages, using telephone or telephone switchboard. Makes and confirms reservations. Computes bill, collects payment, and makes change for guests. Answers inquiries pertaining to hotel services Date-stamps, sorts, and racks incoming mail and messages. Greets, registers, and assigns rooms to guests of hotel or motel. Issues room key and escort instructions to bellhop.

Personality Type: Conventional. Conventional occupations frequently involve following set procedures and routines. These occupations can include working with data and details more than with ideas. Usually there is a clear line of authority to follow.

Abilities: Oral Expression—The ability to communicate information and ideas verbally so others will understand. Oral Comprehension—The ability to listen to and understand information and ideas presented verbally. Number Facility—The ability to add, subtract, multiply, or divide quickly and correctly. Speech Clarity—The ability to speak clearly so that what is said is understandable to a listener. Written Comprehension—The ability to read and understand information and ideas presented in writing.

Skills: Service Orientation—Actively looking for ways to help people. Speaking—Talking to others to effectively convey information. Active Listening—Listening to what other people are saying; asking questions as appropriate. Coordination—Adjusting actions in relation to others' actions. Mathematics—Using mathematics to solve problems.

Generalized Work Activities: Communicating with Persons Outside Organization—Communicating with persons outside the organization. Representing the organization to customers, the public, government, and other external sources. Exchanging information face-to-face, in writing, or via telephone/electronic transfer. Assisting and Caring for Others—Providing assistance or personal care to others. Performing for/Working with Public—Performing for people or dealing directly with the public, including serving persons in restaurants and stores and receiving clients or guests. Documenting/Recording Information—Entering, transcribing, recording, storing, or maintaining information in either written form or by electronic/magnetic recording. Communicating with Other Workers—Providing information to supervisors, fellow workers, and subordinates. This information can be exchanged face-to-face, in writing, or via telephone/electronic transfer.

Human Resources Managers

▲ Growth: 19%
▲ Annual Job Openings: 32,929
▲ Yearly Earnings: $49,010
▲ Education Required: Work experience, plus degree
▲ Self-Employed: 0.5%
▲ Part-Time: 3.6%

Compensation and Benefits Managers

Plan, direct, or coordinate compensation and benefits activities and staff of an organization. Contracts with vendors to provide employee services, such as canteen, transportation, or relocation service. Analyzes compensation policies, government regulations, and prevailing wage rates to develop competitive compensation plan. Represents organization at personnel-related hearings and investigations. Analyzes statistical data and reports to identify and determine causes of personnel problems and develop recommendations for improvement of organization's personnel policies and practices. Plans and conducts new employee orientation to foster positive attitude toward organizational objectives. Meets with shop stewards and supervisors to resolve grievances. Prepares and delivers presentations and reports to corporate officers or other management regarding human resource management policies and practices and recommendations for change. Develops methods to improve employment policies, processes, and practices and recommends changes to management. Writes directives advising department managers of organization policy in personnel matters such as equal employment opportunity, sexual harassment, and discrimination. Prepares personnel forecast to project employment needs. Plans, directs, supervises, and coordinates work activities of subordinates and staff relating to employment, compensation, labor relations, and employee relations. Investigates industrial accidents and prepares reports for insurance carrier. Formulates policies and procedures for recruitment, testing, placement, classification, orientation, benefits, and labor and industrial relations. Directs preparation and distribution of written and verbal information to inform employees of benefits, compensation, and personnel policies. Evaluates and modifies benefits policies to establish competitive programs and to ensure compliance with legal requirements. Prepares budget for personnel operations. Negotiates bargaining agreements and resolves labor disputes.

Personality Type: Enterprising. Enterprising occupations frequently involve starting up and carrying out projects. These occupations can involve leading people and making many decisions. They sometimes require risk taking and often deal with business.

Abilities: Written Comprehension—The ability to read and understand information and ideas presented in writing. Oral Expression—The ability to communicate information and ideas verbally so others will understand. Speech Clarity—The ability to speak clearly so that what is said is understandable to a listener. Oral Comprehension—The ability to listen to and understand information and ideas presented verbally. Written Expression—The ability to communicate information and ideas in writing so others will understand.

Skills: Management of Personnel Resources—Motivating, developing, and directing people as they work, identifying the best people for the job. Writing—Communicating effectively with others in writing as indicated by the needs of the audience. Speaking—Talking to others to effectively convey information. Reading Comprehension—Understanding written information in work-related documents. Problem Identification—Identifying the nature of problems.

Generalized Work Activities: Performing Administrative Activities—Approving requests, handling paperwork, and performing day-to-day administrative tasks. Communicating with Other Workers—Providing information to supervisors, fellow workers, and subordinates. This information can be exchanged face-to-face, in writing, or via telephone/electronic transfer. Resolving Conflict, Negotiating with Others—Handling complaints, arbitrating disputes, resolving grievances, or otherwise negotiating with others. Judging Qualities—Making judgments about or assessing the value, importance, or quality of things, services, or other people's work. Staffing Organizational Units—Recruiting, interviewing, selecting, hiring, and promoting persons for the organization. Getting Information Needed to Do the Job—Observing, receiving, and otherwise obtaining information from all relevant sources. Developing Objectives and Strategies—Establishing long range objectives and specifying the strategies and actions to achieve these objectives.

Human Resources Managers

Plan, direct, and coordinate human resource management activities of an organization to maximize the strategic use of human resources and maintain functions such as employee compensation,

recruitment, personnel policies, and regulatory compliance. Plans and conducts new employee orientation to foster positive attitude toward organizational objectives. Writes directives advising department managers of organization policy in personnel matters such as equal employment opportunity, sexual harassment, and discrimination. Studies legislation, arbitration decisions, and collective bargaining contracts to assess industry trends. Maintains records and compiles statistical reports concerning personnel-related data such as hires, transfers, performance appraisals, and absenteeism rates. Analyzes statistical data and reports to identify and determine causes of personnel problems and develop recommendations for improvement of organization's personnel policies and practices. Represents organization at personnel-related hearings and investigations. Investigates industrial accidents and prepares reports for insurance carrier. Conducts exit interviews to identify reasons for employee termination and writes separation notices. Directs preparation and distribution of written and verbal information to inform employees of benefits, compensation, and personnel policies. Contracts with vendors to provide employee services, such as canteen, transportation, or relocation service. Formulates policies and procedures for recruitment, testing, placement, classification, orientation, benefits, and labor and industrial relations. Negotiates bargaining agreements and resolves labor disputes. Prepares and delivers presentations and reports to corporate officers or other management regarding human resource management policies and practices and recommendations for change. Prepares budget for personnel operations. Prepares personnel forecast to project employment needs. Develops methods to improve employment policies, processes, and practices and recommends changes to management. Evaluates and modifies benefits policies to establish competitive programs and to ensure compliance with legal requirements.

Personality Type: Enterprising. Enterprising occupations frequently involve starting up and carrying out projects. These occupations can involve leading people and making many decisions. They sometimes require risk taking and often deal with business.

Abilities: Written Comprehension—The ability to read and understand information and ideas presented in writing. Written Expression—The ability to communicate information and ideas in writing so others will understand. Speech Clarity—The ability to speak clearly so that what is said is understandable to a listener. Oral Expression—The ability to communicate information and ideas verbally so others will understand. Oral Comprehension—The ability to listen to and understand information and ideas presented verbally.

Skills: Management of Personnel Resources—Motivating, developing, and directing people as they work, identifying the best people for the job. Writing—Communicating effectively with others in writing as indicated by the needs of the audience. Speaking—Talking to others to effectively convey information. Reading Comprehension—Understanding written information in work-related documents. Problem Identification—Identifying the nature of problems.

Generalized Work Activities: Performing Administrative Activities—Approving requests, handling paperwork, and performing day-to-day administrative tasks. Communicating with Other Workers—Providing information to supervisors, fellow workers, and subordinates. This information can be exchanged face-to-face, in writing, or via telephone/electronic transfer. Developing Objectives and Strategies—Establishing long range objectives and specifying the strategies and actions to achieve these objectives. Staffing Organizational Units—Recruiting, interviewing, selecting, hiring, and promoting persons for the organization. Resolving Conflict, Negotiating with Others—Handling complaints, arbitrating disputes, resolving grievances, or otherwise negotiating with others. Getting Information Needed to Do the Job—Observing, receiving, and otherwise obtaining information from all relevant sources. Judging Qualities—Making judgments about or assessing the value, importance, or quality of things, services, or other people's work.

H

Training and Development Managers

Plan, direct, or coordinate the training and development activities and staff of an organization. Evaluates effectiveness of training programs and instructor performance. Confers with management and supervisory personnel to identify training needs based on projected production processes, changes, and other factors. Interprets and clarifies regulatory policies governing apprenticeship training programs, and provides information and assistance to trainees and labor and management representatives. Trains instructors and supervisors in effective training techniques. Prepares training budget for department or organization. Reviews and evaluates training and apprenticeship programs for compliance with government standards. Develops testing and evaluation procedures. Develops and organizes training manuals, multimedia visual aids, and other educational materials. Formulates training policies and schedules, utilizing knowledge of identified training needs. Plans and develops training procedures utilizing knowledge of relative effectiveness of individual training, classroom training, demonstrations, on-the-job training, meetings, conferences, and workshops. Analyzes training needs to develop new training programs or modify and improve existing programs. Coordinates established courses with technical and professional courses provided by community schools and designates training procedures.

Personality Type: Enterprising. Enterprising occupations frequently involve starting up and carrying out projects. These occupations can involve leading people and making many decisions. They sometimes require risk taking and often deal with business.

Abilities: Speech Clarity—The ability to speak clearly so that what is said is understandable to a listener. Deductive Reasoning—The ability to apply general rules to specific problems to come up with logical answers. Involves deciding if an answer makes sense. Oral Comprehension—The ability to listen to and understand information and ideas presented verbally. Oral Expression—The ability to communicate information and ideas verbally so others will understand. Inductive Reasoning—The ability to combine separate pieces of information, or specific answers to problems, to form general rules or conclusions. Includes coming up with a logical explanation for why a series of seemingly unrelated events occur together.

Skills: Learning Strategies—Using multiple approaches when learning or teaching new things. Instructing—Teaching others how to do something. Speaking—Talking to others to effectively convey information. Reading Comprehension—Understanding written information in work-related documents. Implementation Planning—Developing approaches for implementing an idea. Critical Thinking—Using logic and analysis to identify the strengths and weaknesses of different approaches. Idea Evaluation—Evaluating the likely success of an idea in relation to the demands of the situation.

Generalized Work Activities: Teaching Others—Identifying educational needs, developing formal training programs or classes, and teaching or instructing others. Coaching and Developing Others—Identifying developmental needs of others and coaching or otherwise helping others to improve their knowledge or skills. Judging Qualities—Making judgments about or assessing the value, importance, or quality of things, services, or other people's work. Implementing Ideas and Programs—Conducting or carrying out work procedures and activities in accord with one's own ideas or information provided through directions/instructions for purposes of installing, modifying, preparing, delivering, constructing, integrating, finishing, or completing programs, systems, structures, or products. Developing Objectives and Strategies—Establishing long range objectives and specifying the strategies and actions to achieve these objectives. Getting Information Needed to Do the Job—Observing, receiving, and otherwise obtaining information from all relevant sources.

Human Resources, Training, and Labor Relations Specialists

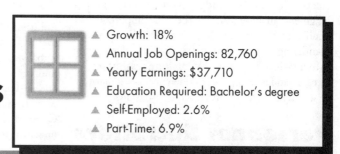

- ▲ Growth: 18%
- ▲ Annual Job Openings: 82,760
- ▲ Yearly Earnings: $37,710
- ▲ Education Required: Bachelor's degree
- ▲ Self-Employed: 2.6%
- ▲ Part-Time: 6.9%

Compensation, Benefits, and Job Analysis Specialists

Conduct programs of compensation and benefits and job analysis for employer. Specialize in specific areas, such as position classification and pension programs. Plans and develops curricula and materials for training programs and conducts training. Observes and interviews employees to collect job, organizational, and occupational information. Prepares reports, such as job descriptions, organization and flow charts, and career path reports to summarize job analysis information. Researches job and worker requirements, structural and functional relationships among jobs and occupations, and occupational trends. Evaluates and improves methods and techniques for selecting, promoting, evaluating, and training workers. Consults with business, industry, government, and union officials to arrange for, plan, and design occupational studies and surveys. Prepares research results for publication in form of journals, books, manuals, and film. Analyzes organizational, occupational, and industrial data to facilitate organizational functions and provide technical information to business, industry, and government. Determines need for and develops job analysis instruments and materials.

Personality Type: Investigative. Investigative occupations frequently involve working with ideas and require an extensive amount of thinking. These occupations can involve searching for facts and figuring out problems mentally.

Abilities: Oral Comprehension—The ability to listen to and understand information and ideas presented verbally. Written Expression—The ability to communicate information and ideas in writing so others will understand. Oral Expression—The ability to communicate information and ideas verbally so others will understand. Near Vision—The ability to see details of objects at a close range. Speech Clarity—The ability to speak clearly so that what is said is understandable to a listener.

Skills: Systems Evaluation—Looking at many indicators of system performance, taking into account their accuracy. Information Gathering—Knowing how to find information and identifying essential information. Speaking—Talking to others to effectively convey information. Information Organization—Finding ways to structure or classify multiple pieces of information.

Generalized Work Activities: Getting Information Needed to Do the Job—Observing, receiving, and otherwise obtaining information from all relevant sources. Analyzing Data or Information—Identifying underlying principles, reasons, or facts by breaking down information or data into separate parts. Documenting/Recording Information—Entering, transcribing, recording, storing, or maintaining information in either written form or by electronic/magnetic recording. Communicating with Persons Outside Organization—Communicating with persons outside the organization. Representing the organization to customers, the public, government, and other external sources. Exchanging information face-to-face, in writing, or via telephone/electronic transfer. Judging Qualities—Making judgments about or assessing the value, importance, or quality of things, services, or other people's work. Identifying Objects, Actions, and Events—Identifying information received by making estimates or categorizations, recognizing differences or similarities, or sensing changes in circumstances or events.

Personnel Recruiters

Seek out, interview, and screen applicants to fill existing and future job openings and promote career opportunities within an organization. Evaluates recruitment and selection criteria to ensure conformance to professional, statistical, and testing standards, and recommends revision as needed. Contacts college representatives to arrange for and schedule on-campus interviews with students. Conducts reference and background checks on applicants. Provides potential applicants with information regarding facilities, operations, benefits, and job or career opportunities in organization. Projects yearly recruitment expenditures for budgetary consideration and control. Arranges for interviews and travel and lodging for selected applicants at company expense. Reviews and evaluates applicant qualifications or eligibility for specified licensing, according to established guidelines and designated licensing codes. Speaks to civic, social, and other groups to provide information concerning job possibilities and career opportunities. Corrects and scores portions of examinations used to screen and select applicants. Notifies applicants by mail or telephone to inform them of employment possibilities, consideration, and selection. Hires or refers applicant to other hiring personnel in organization. Interviews applicants to obtain work history, training, education, job skills, and other background information. Prepares and maintains employment records and authorizes paperwork assigning applicant to positions. Assists and advises establishment management in organizing, preparing, and implementing recruiting and retention programs.

Personality Type: Enterprising. Enterprising occupations frequently involve starting up and carrying out projects. These occupations can involve leading people and making many decisions. They sometimes require risk taking and often deal with business.

Abilities: Oral Comprehension—The ability to listen to and understand information and ideas presented verbally. Oral Expression—The ability to communicate information and ideas verbally so others will understand. Speech Clarity—The ability to speak clearly so that what is said is understandable to a listener. Written Comprehension—The ability to read and understand information and ideas presented in writing. Written Expression—The ability to communicate information and ideas in writing so others will understand.

Skills: Speaking—Talking to others to effectively convey information. Active Listening—Listening to what other people are saying; asking questions as appropriate. Idea Generation—Generating a number of different approaches to problems. Judgment and Decision Making—Weighing the relative costs and benefits of a potential action. Management of Personnel Resources—Motivating, developing, and directing people as they work, identifying the best people for the job. Reading Comprehension—Understanding written information in work-related documents. Information Gathering—Knowing how to find information and identifying essential information.

Generalized Work Activities: Staffing Organizational Units—Recruiting, interviewing, selecting, hiring, and promoting persons for the organization. Judging Qualities—Making judgments about or assessing the value, importance, or quality of things, services, or other people's work. Communicating with Persons Outside Organization—Communicating with persons outside the organization. Representing the organization to customers, the public, government, and other external sources. Exchanging information face-to-face, in writing, or via telephone/electronic transfer. Getting Information Needed to Do the Job—Observing, receiving, and otherwise obtaining information from all relevant sources. Communicating with Other Workers—Providing information to supervisors, fellow workers, and subordinates. This information can be exchanged face-to-face, in writing, or via telephone/electronic transfer.

Training and Development Specialists

Conduct training and development programs for employees. Attends meetings and seminars to obtain information useful to train staff and to inform management of training programs and goals. Monitors training costs to ensure budget is not exceeded, and prepares budget report to justify expenditures. Evaluates training materials, such as outlines, text, and handouts, prepared by instructors. Assigns instructors to conduct training and assists them in obtaining required training materials. Confers with managers, instructors, or customer representatives of industrial or commercial establishment to determine training needs. Organizes and develops training procedure manuals and guides. Develops and conducts orientation and training for employees or customers of industrial or commercial establishment. Refers trainees with social problems to appropriate service agency. Screens, hires, and assigns workers to positions based on qualifications. Schedules classes based on availability of classrooms, equipment, and instructors. Coordinates recruitment and placement of participants in skill training. Supervises instructors, monitors and evaluates instructor performance, and refers instructors to classes for skill development. Maintains records and writes reports to monitor and evaluate training activities and program effectiveness.

Personality Type: Social. Social occupations frequently involve working with, communicating with, and teaching people. These occupations often involve helping or providing service to others.

Abilities: Speech Clarity—The ability to speak clearly so that what is said is understandable to a listener. Oral Expression—The ability to communicate information and ideas verbally so others will understand. Written Expression—The ability to communicate information and ideas in writing so others will understand. Oral Comprehension—The ability to listen to and understand information and ideas presented verbally. Written Comprehension—The ability to read and understand information and ideas presented in writing. Near Vision—The ability to see details of objects at a close range.

Skills: Time Management—Managing one's own time and the time of others. Learning Strategies—Using multiple approaches when learning or teaching new things. Reading Comprehension—Understanding written information in work-related documents.

Generalized Work Activities: Staffing Organizational Units—Recruiting, interviewing, selecting, hiring, and promoting persons for the organization. Coaching and Developing Others—Identifying developmental needs of others and coaching or otherwise helping others to improve their knowledge or skills. Communicating with Other Workers—Providing information to supervisors, fellow workers, and subordinates. This information can be exchanged face-to-face, in writing, or via telephone/electronic transfer. Getting Information Needed to Do the Job—Observing, receiving, and otherwise obtaining information from all relevant sources. Communicating with Persons Outside Organization—Communicating with persons outside the organization. Representing the organization to customers, the public, government, and other external sources. Exchanging information face-to-face, in writing, or via telephone/electronic transfer.

Human Service Workers and Assistants

- ▲ Growth: 53%
- ▲ Annual Job Openings: 91,824
- ▲ Yearly Earnings: $21,360
- ▲ Education Required: Moderate-term O-J-T
- ▲ Self-Employed: 0%
- ▲ Part-Time: 42.4%

Social and Human Service Assistants

Assist professionals from a wide variety of fields, such as psychology, rehabilitation, or social work, to provide client services as well as support for families. Assist clients in identifying available benefits and social and community services and help clients obtain them. Assist social workers with developing, organizing, and conducting programs to prevent and resolve problems relevant to substance abuse, human relationships, rehabilitation, or adult daycare. Explains rules established by owner or management, such as sanitation and maintenance requirements and parking regulations. Transports and accompanies clients to shopping areas and to appointments, using automobile. Oversees day-to-day group activities of residents in institution. Consults with supervisor concerning programs for individual families. Cares for children in client's home during client's appointments. Observes and discusses meal preparation and suggests alternate methods of food preparation. Demonstrates use and care of equipment for tenant use. Assists clients with preparation of forms, such as tax or rent forms. Meets with youth groups to acquaint them with consequences of delinquent acts. Assists in planning of food budget, utilizing charts and sample budgets. Informs tenants of facilities, such as laundries and playgrounds. Keeps records and prepares reports for owner or management concerning visits with clients. Observes clients' food selections and recommends alternate economical and nutritional food choices. Monitors free, supplementary meal program to ensure cleanliness of facility and that eligibility guidelines are met for persons receiving meals. Assists in locating housing for displaced individuals. Provides information on and refers individuals to public or private agencies and community services for assistance. Advises clients regarding food stamps, child care, food, money management, sanitation, and housekeeping. Interviews individuals and family members to compile information on social, educational, criminal, institutional, or drug history. Visits individuals in homes or attends group meetings to provide information on agency services, requirements and procedures. Submits to and reviews reports and problems with superior.

Personality Type: Social. Social occupations frequently involve working with, communicating with, and teaching people. These occupations often involve helping or providing service to others.

Abilities: Oral Expression—The ability to communicate information and ideas verbally so others will understand. Oral Comprehension—The ability to listen to and understand information and ideas presented verbally. Written Expression—The ability to communicate information and ideas in writing so others will understand. Written Comprehension—The ability to read and understand information and ideas presented in writing. Problem Sensitivity—The ability to tell when something is wrong or is likely to go wrong. Does not involve solving the problem, only recognizing there is a problem.

Skills: Social Perceptiveness—Being aware of other people's reactions and understanding why people react the way they do. Speaking—Talking to others to effectively convey information. Active Listening—Listening to what other people are saying; asking questions as appropriate. Service Orientation—Actively looking for ways to help people. Problem Identification—Identifying the nature of problems.

Generalized Work Activities: Assisting and Caring for Others—Providing assistance or personal care to others. Getting Information Needed to Do the Job—Observing, receiving, and otherwise obtaining information from all relevant sources. Communicating with Persons Outside Organization—Communicating with persons outside the organization. Representing the organization to customers, the public, government, and other external sources. Exchanging information face-to-face, in writing, or via telephone/electronic transfer. Providing Consultation and Advice to Others—Providing consultation and expert advice to management or other groups on technical, systems-related, or process-related topics. Establishing and Maintaining Relationships—Developing constructive and cooperative working relationships with others. Making Decisions and Solving Problems—Combining, evaluating, and analyzing information and data to make decisions and solve problems. Involves making decisions about the relative importance of information and choosing the best solution. Documenting/Recording Information—Entering, transcribing, recording, storing, or maintaining information in either written form or by electronic/magnetic recording.

Industrial Engineers

- ▲ Growth: 13%
- ▲ Annual Job Openings: 13,125
- ▲ Yearly Earnings: $52,610
- ▲ Education Required: Bachelor's degree
- ▲ Self-Employed: 0.9%
- ▲ Part-Time: 2.4%

Industrial Engineers

Design, develop, test, and evaluate integrated systems for managing industrial production processes, including human work factors, quality control, inventory control, logistics and material flow, cost analysis, and production coordination. Implements methods and procedures for disposition of discrepant material and defective or damaged parts and assesses cost and responsibility. Formulates sampling procedures and designs and develops forms and instructions for recording, evaluating, and reporting quality and reliability data. Coordinates quality control objectives and activities to resolve production problems, maximize product reliability, and minimize cost. Completes production reports, purchase orders, and material, tool, and equipment lists. Directs workers engaged in product measurement, inspection, and testing activities to ensure quality control and reliability. Evaluates precision and accuracy of production and testing equipment and engineering drawings to formulate corrective action plan. Regulates and alters workflow schedules according to established manufacturing sequences and lead times to expedite production operations. Drafts and designs layout of equipment, materials, and workspace to illustrate maximum efficiency, using drafting tools and computer. Reviews production schedules, engineering specifications, orders, and related information to obtain knowledge of manufacturing methods, procedures, and activities. Develops manufacturing methods, labor utilization standards, and cost analysis systems to promote efficient staff and facility utilization. Confers with vendors, staff, and management personnel regarding purchases, procedures, product specifications, manufacturing capabilities, and project status. Analyzes statistical data and product specifications to determine standards and establish quality and reliability objectives of finished product. Plans and establishes sequence of operations to fabricate and assemble parts or products and to promote efficient utilization of resources. Studies operations sequence, material flow, functional statements, organization charts, and project information to determine worker functions and responsibilities.

Personality Type: Enterprising. Enterprising occupations frequently involve starting up and carrying out projects. These occupations can involve leading people and making many decisions. They sometimes require risk taking and often deal with business.

Abilities: Written Comprehension—The ability to read and understand information and ideas presented in writing. Written Expression—The ability to communicate information and ideas in writing so others will understand. Oral Comprehension—The ability to listen to and understand information and ideas presented verbally. Oral Expression—The ability to communicate information and ideas verbally so others will understand.

Skills: Mathematics—Using mathematics to solve problems. Information Gathering—Knowing how to find information and identifying essential information. Reading Comprehension—Understanding written information in work-related documents. Judgment and Decision Making—Weighing the relative costs and benefits of a potential action.

Generalized Work Activities: Processing Information—Compiling, coding, categorizing, calculating, tabulating, auditing, verifying, or processing information or data. Communicating with Other Workers—Providing information to supervisors, fellow workers, and subordinates. This information can be exchanged face-to-face, in writing, or via telephone/electronic transfer. Getting Information Needed to Do the Job—Observing, receiving, and otherwise obtaining information from all relevant sources. Providing Consultation and Advice to Others—Providing consultation and expert advice to management or other groups on technical, systems-related, or process-related

topics. Making Decisions and Solving Problems—Combining, evaluating, and analyzing information and data to make decisions and solve problems. Involves making decisions about the relative importance of information and choosing the best solution. Identifying Objects, Actions, and Events—Identifying information received by making estimates or categorizations, recognizing differences or similarities, or sensing changes in circumstances or events. Monitoring Processes, Materials, Surroundings—Monitoring and reviewing information from materials, events, or the environment, often to detect problems or to find out when things are finished.

Industrial Production Managers

▲ Growth: -1%

▲ Annual Job Openings: 20,865

▲ Yearly Earnings: $56,320

▲ Education Required: Bachelor's degree

▲ Self-Employed: 0%

▲ Part-Time: 6.1%

Industrial Production Managers

Plan, direct, or coordinate the work activities and resources necessary for manufacturing products in accordance with cost, quality, and quantity specifications. Reviews plans and confers with research and support staff to develop new products and processes or the quality of existing products. Develops budgets and approves expenditures for supplies, materials, and human resources. Initiates and coordinates inventory and cost control programs. Negotiates materials prices with suppliers. Reviews operations and confers with technical or administrative staff to resolve production or processing problems. Reviews processing schedules and production orders to determine staffing requirements, work procedures, and duty assignments. Analyzes production, quality control, maintenance, and other operational reports to detect production problems. Prepares and maintains production reports and personnel records. Resolves personnel grievances.

Coordinates and recommends procedures for facility and equipment maintenance or modification. Directs and coordinates production, processing, distribution, and marketing activities of industrial organization. Hires, trains, evaluates, and discharges staff. Examines samples of raw products or directs testing during processing to ensure finished products conform to prescribed quality standards.

Personality Type: Enterprising. Enterprising occupations frequently involve starting up and carrying out projects. These occupations can involve leading people and making many decisions. They sometimes require risk taking and often deal with business.

Abilities: Oral Expression—The ability to communicate information and ideas verbally so others will understand. Oral Comprehension—The ability to listen to and understand information and ideas presented verbally. Written Comprehension—The ability to read and understand information and ideas presented in writing. Inductive Reasoning—The ability to combine separate pieces of information, or specific answers to problems, to form general rules or conclusion. Includes coming up with a logical explanation for why a series of seemingly unrelated events occur together. Written Expression—The ability to communicate information and ideas in writing so others will understand.

Skills: Coordination—Adjusting actions in relation to others' actions. Product Inspection—Inspecting and evaluating the quality of products. Judgment and Decision Making—Weighing the relative costs and benefits of a potential action. Problem Identification—Identifying the nature of problems. Implementation Planning—Developing approaches for implementing an idea.

Generalized Work Activities: Making Decisions and Solving Problems—Combining, evaluating, and analyzing information and data to make decisions and solve problems. Involves making decisions about the relative importance of information and choosing the best solution. Getting Information Needed to Do the Job—Observing, receiving, and otherwise obtaining information from all relevant sources. Implementing Ideas and Programs—Conducting or carrying out work procedures and activities in accord with one's own ideas or information provided through directions/instructions for purposes of installing, modifying, preparing, delivering, constructing, integrating, finishing, or completing programs, systems, structures, or products. Coordinating Work and Activities of Others—Coordinating members of a work group to accomplish tasks. Analyzing Data or Information—Identifying underlying principles, reasons, or facts by breaking down information or data into separate parts.

Inspectors and Compliance Officers

- ▲ Growth: 10%
- ▲ Annual Job Openings: 19,910
- ▲ Yearly Earnings: $36,820
- ▲ Education Required: Work experience in a related occupation
- ▲ Self-Employed: 1.3%
- ▲ Part-Time: 2.9%

Agricultural Inspectors

Inspect agricultural commodities, processing equipment, and facilities, and fish and logging operations, to ensure compliance with regulations and laws governing health, quality, and safety. Testifies in legal proceedings. Inspects horticultural products or livestock to detect harmful disease, infestation, or growth rate. Collects sample of pests or suspected diseased animals or materials and routes to laboratory for identification and analysis. Advises farmers and growers of development programs or new equipment and techniques to aid in quality production, applying agricultural knowledge. Writes reports of findings and recommendations and advises farmer, grower, or processor of corrective action to be taken. Examines, weighs, and measures commodities, such as poultry, eggs, meat, and seafood to certify wholesomeness, grade, and weight. Inspects facilities and equipment for adequacy, sanitation, and compliance with regulations. Inspects livestock to determine effectiveness of medication and feeding programs.

Personality Type: Realistic. Realistic occupations frequently involve work activities that include practical, hands-on problems and solutions. They often deal with plants, animals, and real-world materials like wood, tools, and machinery. Many of the occupations require working outside and do not involve a lot of paperwork or working closely with others.

Abilities: Problem Sensitivity—The ability to tell when something is wrong or is likely to go wrong. Does not involve solving the problem, only recognizing there is a problem. Oral Expression—The ability to communicate information and ideas verbally so others will understand. Written Expression—The ability to communicate information and ideas in writing so others will understand. Written Comprehension—The ability to read and understand information and ideas presented in writing. Deductive Reasoning—The ability to apply general rules to specific problems to come up with logical answers. Involves deciding if an answer makes sense.

Skills: Product Inspection—Inspecting and evaluating the quality of products. Reading Comprehension—Understanding written information in work-related documents. Speaking—Talking to others to effectively convey information. Writing—Communicating effectively with others in writing as indicated by the needs of the audience. Problem Identification—Identifying the nature of problems.

Generalized Work Activities: Getting Information Needed to Do the Job—Observing, receiving, and otherwise obtaining information from all relevant sources. Identifying Objects, Actions, and Events—Identifying information received by making estimates or categorizations, recognizing differences or similarities, or sensing changes in circumstances or events. Inspecting Equipment, Structures, Materials—Inspecting or diagnosing equipment, structures, or materials to identify the causes of errors or other problems or defects. Evaluating Information against Standards—Evaluating information against a set of standards and verifying that it is correct. Communicating with Persons Outside Organization—Communicating with persons outside the organization. Representing the organization to customers, the public, government, and other external sources. Exchanging information face-to-face, in writing, or via telephone/electronic transfer. Judging Qualities—Making judgments about or assessing the value, importance, or quality of things, services, or other people's work. Providing Consultation and Advice to Others—Providing consultation and expert advice to management or other groups on technical, systems-related, or process-related topics.

Aviation Inspectors

Inspect aircraft, maintenance procedures, air navigational aids, air traffic controls, and communications equipment to ensure conformance with federal safety regulations. Recommends purchase, repair, or modification of equipment. Investigates air accidents to determine cause. Approves or disapproves issuance of certificate of airworthiness. Schedules and coordinates in-flight testing program with ground crews and air traffic control to assure ground tracking, equipment monitoring, and related services. Analyzes training program and conducts examinations to assure competency of persons operating, installing, and repairing equipment. Conducts flight test program to test equipment, instruments, and systems under various conditions, including adverse weather, using both manual and automatic controls. Starts aircraft and observes gauges, meters, and other instruments to detect evidence of malfunction. Examines access plates and doors for security. Examines maintenance record and flight log to determine if service and maintenance checks and overhauls were performed at prescribed intervals. Inspects aircraft and components to identify damage or defects and to determine structural and mechanical airworthiness, using hand tools and test instruments. Prepares reports to document flight activities and inspection findings.

Personality Type: Realistic. Realistic occupations frequently involve work activities that include practical, hands-on problems and solutions. They often deal with plants, animals, and real-world materials like wood, tools, and machinery. Many of the occupations require working outside and do not involve a lot of paperwork or working closely with others.

Abilities: Problem Sensitivity—The ability to tell when something is wrong or is likely to go wrong. Does not involve solving the problem, only recognizing there is a problem. Written Expression—The ability to communicate information and ideas in writing so others will understand. Information Ordering—The ability to correctly follow a given rule or set of rules in order to arrange things or actions in a certain order. The things or actions can include numbers, letters, words, pictures, procedures, sentences, and mathematical or logical operations. Written Comprehension—The ability to read and understand information and ideas presented in writing. Near Vision—The ability to see details of objects at a close range.

Skills: Product Inspection—Inspecting and evaluating the quality of products. Testing—Conducting tests to determine whether equipment, software, or procedures are operating as expected. Information Gathering—Knowing how to find information and identifying essential information. Problem Identification—Identifying the nature of problems. Operation Monitoring—Watching gauges, dials, or other indicators to make sure a machine is working properly. Reading Comprehension—Understanding written information in work-related documents. Critical Thinking—Using logic and analysis to identify the strengths and weaknesses of different approaches.

Generalized Work Activities: Inspecting Equipment, Structures, Materials—Inspecting or diagnosing equipment, structures, or materials to identify the causes of errors or other problems or defects. Monitoring Processes, Materials, Surroundings—Monitoring and reviewing information from materials, events, or the environment, often to detect problems or to find out when things are finished. Getting Information Needed to Do the Job—Observing, receiving, and otherwise obtaining information from all relevant sources. Updating and Using Job-Relevant Knowledge—Keeping up-to-date technically and knowing the functions of one's own job and related jobs. Identifying Objects, Actions, and Events—Identifying information received by making estimates or categorizations, recognizing differences or similarities, or sensing changes in circumstances or events.

Coroners

Direct activities such as autopsies, pathological and toxicological analyses, and inquests relating to the investigation of deaths occurring within a legal jurisdiction to determine cause of death or to fix responsibility for accidental, violent, or unexplained deaths. Directs investigations into circumstances of deaths to fix responsibility for accidental, violent, or unexplained death. Provides information concerning death circumstance to relatives of deceased. Testifies at inquests, hearings, and court trials. Coordinates activities for disposition of unclaimed corpse and personal effects of deceased. Confers with officials of public health and law enforcement agencies to coordinate interdepartmental activities. Directs activities of physicians and technologists conducting autopsies and pathological and toxicological analyses to determine cause of death. Directs activities of workers involved in preparing documents for permanent records.

Personality Type: Investigative. Investigative occupations frequently involve working with ideas and require an extensive amount of thinking. These occupations can involve searching for facts and figuring out problems mentally.

Abilities: Inductive Reasoning—The ability to combine separate pieces of information, or specific answers to problems, to form general rules or conclusion. Includes coming up with a logical explanation for why a series of seemingly unrelated events occur together. Oral Expression—The ability to communicate information and ideas verbally so others will understand. Problem Sensitivity—The ability to tell when something is wrong or is likely to go wrong. Does not involve solving the problem, only recognizing there is a problem. Oral Comprehension—The ability to listen to and understand information and ideas presented verbally. Written Expression—The ability to communicate information and ideas in writing so others will understand. Near Vision—The ability to see details of objects at a close range.

Skills: Information Gathering—Knowing how to find information and identifying essential information. Science—Using scientific methods to solve problems. Active Listening—Listening to what other people are saying; asking questions as appropriate. Reading Comprehension—Understanding written information in work-related documents. Critical Thinking—Using logic and analysis to identify the strengths and weaknesses of different approaches. Writing—Communicating effectively with others in writing as indicated by the needs of the audience. Coordination—Adjusting actions in relation to others' actions.

Generalized Work Activities: Getting Information Needed to Do the Job—Observing, receiving, and otherwise obtaining information from all relevant sources. Analyzing Data or Information—Identifying underlying principles, reasons, or facts by breaking down information or data into separate parts. Identifying Objects, Actions, and Events—Identifying information received by making estimates or categorizations, recognizing differences or similarities, or sensing changes in circumstances or events. Implementing Ideas and Programs—Conducting or carrying out work procedures and activities in accord with one's own ideas or information provided through directions/instructions for purposes of installing, modifying, preparing, delivering, constructing, integrating, finishing, or completing programs, systems, structures, or products. Communicating with Other Workers—Providing information to supervisors, fellow workers, and subordinates. This information can be exchanged face-to-face, in writing, or via telephone/electronic transfer.

Environmental Compliance Inspectors

Inspect and investigate sources of pollution to protect the public and environment and ensure conformance with Federal, State, and local regulations and ordinances. Assists in development of spill prevention programs and hazardous waste rules and regulations, and recommends corrective action in event of hazardous spill. Advises individuals and groups concerning pollution control regulations, inspection, and investigation findings, and encourages voluntary action to correct problems or issues citations for violations. Reviews and evaluates applications for registration of products containing dangerous materials or pollution control discharge permits. Studies laws and statutes to determine nature of code violation and type of action to be taken. Evaluates label information for accuracy and conformance to regulatory requirements. Prepares, organizes, and maintains records to document activities, recommend action, provide reference materials, and prepare technical and evidentiary reports. Conducts research on hazardous waste management projects to determine magnitude of disposal problem, treatment, and disposal alternatives and costs. Interviews individuals to determine nature of suspected violations and to obtain evidence of violation. Investigates complaints and suspected violations concerning illegal dumping, pollution, pesticides, product quality, or labeling laws. Inspects establishments to ensure that handling, storage, and disposal of fertilizers, pesticides, and other hazardous chemicals conform with regulations. Conducts field tests and collects samples for laboratory analysis. Inspects solid waste disposal and treatment facilities, wastewater treatment facilities, or other water courses or sites for conformance with regulations. Examines permits, licenses, applications, and records to ensure compliance with licensing requirements.

Personality Type: Investigative. Investigative occupations frequently involve working with ideas and require an extensive amount of thinking. These occupations can involve searching for facts and figuring out problems mentally.

Abilities: Written Comprehension—The ability to read and understand information and ideas presented in writing. Problem Sensitivity—The ability to tell when something is wrong or is likely to go wrong. Does not involve solving the problem, only recognizing there is a problem. Oral Expression—The ability to communicate information and ideas verbally so others will understand. Written Expression—The ability to communicate information and ideas in writing so others will understand. Oral Comprehension—The ability to listen to and understand information and ideas presented verbally. Near Vision—The ability to see details of objects at a close range.

Skills: Reading Comprehension—Understanding written information in work-related documents. Information Gathering—Knowing how to find information and identifying essential information. Science—Using scientific methods to solve problems. Critical Thinking—Using logic and analysis to identify the strengths and weaknesses of different approaches. Judgment and Decision Making—Weighing the relative costs and benefits of a potential action. Speaking—

Talking to others to effectively convey information. Identifying Downstream Consequences—Determining the long-term outcomes of a change in operations.

Generalized Work Activities: Getting Information Needed to Do the Job—Observing, receiving, and otherwise obtaining information from all relevant sources. Identifying Objects, Actions, and Events—Identifying information received by making estimates or categorizations, recognizing differences or similarities, or sensing changes in circumstances or events. Evaluating Information against Standards—Evaluating information against a set of standards and verifying that it is correct. Inspecting Equipment, Structures, Materials—Inspecting or diagnosing equipment, structures, or materials to identify the causes of errors or other problems or defects. Documenting/Recording Information—Entering, transcribing, recording, storing, or maintaining information in either written form or by electronic/magnetic recording.

Equal Opportunity Representatives and Officers

Monitor and evaluate compliance with equal opportunity laws, guidelines, and policies to ensure that employment practices and contracting arrangements give equal opportunity without regard to race, religion, color, national origin, sex, age, or disability. Conducts surveys and evaluates findings to determine existence of systematic discrimination. Develops guidelines for nondiscriminatory employment practices for use by employers. Confers with management or other personnel to resolve or settle equal opportunity issues and disputes. Acts as representative between minority placement agencies and employers. Reviews contracts to determine company actions required to meet governmental equal opportunity provisions. Prepares report of findings and recommendations for corrective action. Consults with community representatives to develop technical assistance agreements in accordance with governmental regulations. Investigates employment practices and alleged violations of law to document and correct discriminatory factors. Interprets civil rights laws and equal opportunity governmental regulations for individuals and employers. Studies equal opportunity complaints to clarify issues.

Personality Type: Social. Social occupations frequently involve working with, communicating with, and teaching people. These occupations often involve helping or providing service to others.

Abilities: Written Comprehension—The ability to read and understand information and ideas presented in writing. Oral Comprehension—The ability to listen to and understand information and ideas presented verbally. Oral Expression—The ability to communicate information and ideas verbally so others will understand. Written Expression—The ability to communicate information and ideas in writing so others will understand. Problem Sensitivity—The ability to tell when something is wrong or is likely to go wrong. Does not involve solving the problem, only recognizing there is a problem.

Skills: Speaking—Talking to others to effectively convey information. Reading Comprehension—Understanding written information in work-related documents. Information Gathering—Knowing how to find information and identifying essential information. Implementation Planning—Developing approaches for implementing an idea. Problem Identification—Identifying the nature of problems. Active Listening—Listening to what other people are saying; asking questions as appropriate. Writing—Communicating effectively with others in writing as indicated by the needs of the audience.

Generalized Work Activities: Evaluating Information against Standards—Evaluating information against a set of standards and verifying that it is correct. Getting Information Needed to Do the Job—Observing, receiving, and otherwise obtaining information from all relevant sources. Interpreting Meaning of Information to Others—Translating or explaining what information means and how it can be understood or used to support responses or feedback to others. Processing Information—Compiling, coding, categorizing, calculating, tabulating, auditing, verifying, or processing information or data. Analyzing Data or

Information—Identifying underlying principles, reasons, or facts by breaking down information or data into separate parts. Communicating with Persons Outside Organization—Communicating with persons outside the organization. Representing the organization to customers, the public, government, and other external sources. Exchanging information face-to-face, in writing, or via telephone/electronic transfer.

Financial Examiners

Enforce or ensure compliance with laws and regulations governing financial and securities institutions and financial and real estate transactions. Examine, verify correctness of, or establish authenticity of records. Recommends action to ensure compliance with laws and regulations or to protect solvency of institution. Investigates activities of institutions to enforce laws and regulations and to ensure legality of transactions and operations or financial solvency. Determines if application action is in public interest and in accordance with regulations, and recommends acceptance or rejection of application. Establishes guidelines for and directs implementation of procedures and policies to comply with new and revised regulations. Reviews applications for merger, acquisition, establishment of new institution, acceptance in Federal Reserve System, or registration of securities sales. Reviews, analyzes, and interprets new, proposed, or revised laws, regulations, policies, and procedures. Directs workers engaged in designing, writing, and publishing guidelines, manuals, bulletins, and reports. Conducts or arranges for educational classes and training programs. Confers with officials of real estate, securities, or financial institution industries to exchange views and discuss issues or pending cases. Schedules audits and examines records and reports to determine regulatory compliance.

Personality Type: Enterprising. Enterprising occupations frequently involve starting up and carrying out projects. These occupations can involve leading people and making many decisions. They sometimes require risk taking and often deal with business.

Abilities: Written Comprehension—The ability to read and understand information and ideas presented in writing. Problem Sensitivity—The ability to tell when something is wrong or is likely to go wrong. Does not involve solving the problem, only recognizing there is a problem. Oral Expression—The ability to communicate information and ideas verbally so others will understand. Number Facility—The ability to add, subtract, multiply, or divide quickly and correctly. Near Vision—The ability to see details of objects at a close range. Mathematical Reasoning—The ability to understand and organize a problem and then select a mathematical method or formula to solve the problem.

Skills: Reading Comprehension—Understanding written information in work-related documents. Speaking—Talking to others to effectively convey information. Active Listening—Listening to what other people are saying; asking questions as appropriate. Writing—Communicating effectively with others in writing as indicated by the needs of the audience. Judgment and Decision Making—Weighing the relative costs and benefits of a potential action.

Generalized Work Activities: Getting Information Needed to Do the Job—Observing, receiving, and otherwise obtaining information from all relevant sources. Evaluating Information against Standards—Evaluating information against a set of standards and verifying that it is correct. Identifying Objects, Actions, and Events—Identifying information received by making estimates or categorizations, recognizing differences or similarities, or sensing changes in circumstances or events. Making Decisions and Solving Problems—Combining, evaluating, and analyzing information and data to make decisions and solve problems. Involves making decisions about the relative importance of information and choosing the best solution. Judging Qualities—Making judgments about or assessing the value, importance, or quality of things, services, or other people's work.

Government Property Inspectors and Investigators

Investigate or inspect government property to ensure compliance with contract agreements and government

regulations. Locates and interviews plaintiffs, witnesses, or representatives of business or government to gather facts relevant to inspection or alleged violation. Testifies in court or at administrative proceedings concerning findings of investigation. Submits samples of product to government laboratory for testing as indicated by departmental procedures. Prepares correspondence, reports of inspections or investigations, and recommendations for administrative or legal authorities. Inspects manufactured or processed products to ensure compliance with contract specifications and legal requirements. Examines records, reports, and documents to establish facts and detect discrepancies. Inspects government-owned equipment and materials in hands of private contractors to prevent waste, damage, theft, and other irregularities. Investigates regulated activities to detect violation of law relating to such activities as revenue collection, employment practices, or fraudulent benefit claims. Investigates character of applicant for special license or permit and misuses of license or permit.

Personality Type: Enterprising. Enterprising occupations frequently involve starting up and carrying out projects. These occupations can involve leading people and making many decisions. They sometimes require risk taking and often deal with business.

Abilities: Problem Sensitivity—The ability to tell when something is wrong or is likely to go wrong. Does not involve solving the problem, only recognizing there is a problem. Written Expression—The ability to communicate information and ideas in writing so others will understand. Written Comprehension—The ability to read and understand information and ideas presented in writing. Oral Expression—The ability to communicate information and ideas verbally so others will understand. Near Vision—The ability to see details of objects at a close range.

Skills: Judgment and Decision Making—Weighing the relative costs and benefits of a potential action. Reading Comprehension—Understanding written information in work-related documents. Information Gathering—Knowing how to find information and identifying essential information. Critical Thinking—Using logic and analysis to identify the strengths and weaknesses of

different approaches. Speaking—Talking to others to effectively convey information.

Generalized Work Activities: Getting Information Needed to Do the Job—Observing, receiving, and otherwise obtaining information from all relevant sources. Identifying Objects, Actions, and Events—Identifying information received by making estimates or categorizations, recognizing differences or similarities, or sensing changes in circumstances or events. Inspecting Equipment, Structures, Materials—Inspecting or diagnosing equipment, structures, or materials to identify the causes of errors or other problems or defects. Evaluating Information against Standards—Evaluating information against a set of standards and verifying that it is correct. Documenting/Recording Information—Entering, transcribing, recording, storing, or maintaining information in either written form or by electronic/magnetic recording. Communicating with Persons Outside Organization—Communicating with persons outside the organization. Representing the organization to customers, the public, government, and other external sources. Exchanging information face-to-face, in writing, or via telephone/electronic transfer. Monitoring Processes, Materials, Surroundings—Monitoring and reviewing information from materials, events, or the environment, often to detect problems or to find out when things are finished.

Immigration and Customs Inspectors

Investigate and inspect persons, common carriers, goods, and merchandise, arriving in or departing from the United States or between states to detect violations of immigration and customs laws and regulations. Collects samples of merchandise for examination, appraising, or testing and requests laboratory analyses. Keeps records and writes reports of activities, findings, transactions, violations, discrepancies, and decisions. Arrests, detains, paroles, or arranges for deportation of persons in violation of customs or immigration laws. Examines, classifies, weighs, measures, and appraises merchandise to enforce regulations of U.S. Customs Service and prevent illegal importing and exporting. Examines visas and passports and interviews persons to determine eligibility for admission, residence, and travel in U.S. Determines duty and taxes to be paid, investigates applications for duty refunds, or petitions for remission or mitigation of penalties. Issues or denies permits. Institutes civil and criminal prosecutions and assists other governmental agencies with regulation violation issues. Interprets and explains laws and regulations to others. Reviews private and public records and documents to establish, assemble, and verify facts and secure legal evidence. Inspects cargo, baggage, personal articles, and common carriers entering or leaving U.S. for compliance with revenue laws and U.S. Customs Service regulations. Determines investigative and seizure techniques to be used, and seizes contraband, undeclared merchandise, vehicles, and air or sea craft carrying smuggled merchandise. Testifies in administrative and judicial proceedings.

Personality Type: Conventional. Conventional occupations frequently involve following set procedures and routines. These occupations can include working with data and details more than with ideas. Usually there is a clear line of authority to follow.

Abilities: Oral Expression—The ability to communicate information and ideas verbally so others will understand. Problem Sensitivity—The ability to tell when something is wrong or is likely to go wrong. Does not involve solving the problem, only recognizing there is a problem. Oral Comprehension—The ability to listen to and understand information and ideas presented verbally. Written Comprehension—The ability to read and understand information and ideas presented in writing. Near Vision—The ability to see details of objects at a close range. Written Expression—The ability to communicate information and ideas in writing so others will understand.

Skills: Information Gathering—Knowing how to find information and identifying essential information. Problem Identification—Identifying the nature of problems. Reading Comprehension—Understanding written information in work-related documents. Judgment and Decision Making—Weighing the relative costs and benefits of a potential action.

Generalized Work Activities: Evaluating Information against Standards—Evaluating information against a set of standards and verifying that it is correct. Getting Information Needed to Do the Job—Observing, receiving, and otherwise obtaining information from all relevant sources. Communicating with Persons Outside Organization—Communicating with persons outside the organization. Representing the organization to customers, the public, government, and other external sources. Exchanging information face-to-face, in writing, or via telephone/electronic transfer. Identifying Objects, Actions, and Events—Identifying information received by making estimates or categorizations, recognizing differences or similarities, or sensing changes in circumstances or events. Judging Qualities—Making judgments about or assessing the value, importance, or quality of things, services, or other people's work. Interpreting Meaning of Information to Others—Translating or explaining what information means and how it can be understood or used to support responses or feedback to others. Documenting/Recording Information—Entering, transcribing, recording, storing, or maintaining information in either written form or by electronic/magnetic recording.

Licensing Examiners and Inspectors

Examine, evaluate, and investigate eligibility for, conformity with, or liability under licenses or permits. Issues licenses to individuals meeting standards. Evaluates applications, records, and documents to determine relevant eligibility information or liability incurred. Visits establishments to determine that valid licenses and permits are displayed and that licensing standards are being upheld. Confers with officials, technical, or professional specialists and interviews individuals to obtain information or clarify facts. Prepares reports of activities, evaluations, recommendations, and decisions. Warns violators of infractions or penalties. Provides information and answers questions of individuals or groups concerning licensing, permit, or passport regulations. Determines eligibility or liability and approves or disallows application or license. Administers oral, written, road, or flight test to determine applicant's eligibility for licensing. Prepares correspondence to inform concerned parties of decisions made and appeal rights. Scores tests and rates ability of applicant through observation of equipment operation and control.

Personality Type: Conventional. Conventional occupations frequently involve following set procedures and routines. These occupations can include working with data and details more than with ideas. Usually there is a clear line of authority to follow.

Abilities: Oral Expression—The ability to communicate information and ideas verbally so others will understand. Written Comprehension—The ability to read and understand information and ideas presented in writing. Written Expression—The ability to communicate information and ideas in writing so others will understand. Speech Clarity—The ability to speak clearly so that what is said is understandable to a listener. Oral Comprehension—The ability to listen to and understand information and ideas presented verbally.

Skills: Speaking—Talking to others to effectively convey information. Information Gathering—Knowing how to find information and identifying essential information. Monitoring—Assessing how well one is doing when learning or doing something. Reading Comprehension—Understanding written information in work-related documents. Critical Thinking—Using logic and analysis to identify the strengths and weaknesses of different approaches. Active Listening— Listening to what other people are saying; asking questions as appropriate. Writing—Communicating effectively with others in writing as indicated by the needs of the audience.

Generalized Work Activities: Getting Information Needed to Do the Job—Observing, receiving, and otherwise obtaining information from all relevant sources. Communicating with Persons Outside Organization—Communicating with persons outside the organization. Representing the organization to customers, the public, government, and other external sources. Exchanging information face-to-face, in writing, or via telephone/electronic transfer. Judging Qualities—Making judgments about or assessing the value, importance, or quality of things, services, or other people's work. Making Decisions and Solving Problems—Combining, evaluating, and analyzing

information and data to make decisions and solve problems. Involves making decisions about the relative importance of information and choosing the best solution. Evaluating Information against Standards— Evaluating information against a set of standards and verifying that it is correct.

Marine Cargo Inspectors

Inspect cargoes of seagoing vessels to certify compliance with health and safety regulations in cargo handling and stowage. Determines type of license and safety equipment required, and computes applicable tolls and wharfage fees. Analyzes data, formulates recommendations, and writes reports of findings. Times roll of ship, using stopwatch. Issues certificate of compliance when violations are not detected or recommends remedial procedures to correct deficiencies. Advises crew in techniques of stowing dangerous and heavy cargo, according to knowledge of hazardous cargo. Calculates gross and net tonnage, hold capacities, volume of stored fuel and water, cargo weight, and ship stability factors, using mathematical formulas. Reads vessel documents to ascertain cargo capabilities according to design and cargo regulations. Inspects loaded cargo in holds and cargo handling devices to determine compliance with regulations and need for maintenance. Writes certificates of admeasurement, listing details, such as design, length, depth, and breadth of vessel, and method of propulsion. Examines blueprints of ship and takes physical measurements to determine capacity and depth of vessel in water, using measuring instruments.

Personality Type: Conventional. Conventional occupations frequently involve following set procedures and routines. These occupations can include working with data and details more than with ideas. Usually there is a clear line of authority to follow.

Abilities: Problem Sensitivity—The ability to tell when something is wrong or is likely to go wrong. Does not involve solving the problem, only recognizing there is a problem. Number Facility—The ability to add, subtract, multiply, or divide quickly and correctly. Written

Comprehension—The ability to read and understand information and ideas presented in writing. Oral Expression—The ability to communicate information and ideas verbally so others will understand. Near Vision—The ability to see details of objects at a close range. Mathematical Reasoning—The ability to understand and organize a problem and then select a mathematical method or formula to solve the problem. Deductive Reasoning—The ability to apply general rules to specific problems to come up with logical answers. Involves deciding if an answer makes sense. Written Expression—The ability to communicate information and ideas in writing so others will understand.

Skills: Mathematics—Using mathematics to solve problems. Judgment and Decision Making—Weighing the relative costs and benefits of a potential action. Reading Comprehension—Understanding written information in work-related documents. Information Gathering—Knowing how to find information and identifying essential information. Product Inspection—Inspecting and evaluating the quality of products. Critical Thinking—Using logic and analysis to identify the strengths and weaknesses of different approaches.

Generalized Work Activities: Inspecting Equipment, Structures, Materials—Inspecting or diagnosing equipment, structures, or materials to identify the causes of errors or other problems or defects. Getting Information Needed to Do the Job—Observing, receiving, and otherwise obtaining information from all relevant sources. Identifying Objects, Actions, and Events—Identifying information received by making estimates or categorizations, recognizing differences or similarities, or sensing changes in circumstances or events. Documenting/Recording Information—Entering, transcribing, recording, storing, or maintaining information in either written form or by electronic/magnetic recording. Making Decisions and Solving Problems—Combining, evaluating, and analyzing information and data to make decisions and solve problems. Involves making decisions about the relative importance of information and choosing the best solution. Processing Information—Compiling, coding, categorizing, calculating, tabulating, auditing, verifying, or processing information or data. Evaluating

Information against Standards—Evaluating information against a set of standards and verifying that it is correct.

Pressure Vessel Inspectors

Inspect pressure vessel equipment for conformance with safety laws and standards regulating their design, fabrication, installation, repair, and operation. Examines permits and inspection records to determine that inspection schedule and remedial actions conform to procedures and regulations. Keeps records and prepares reports of inspections and investigations for administrative or legal authorities. Investigates accidents to determine causes and to develop methods of preventing recurrences. Witnesses acceptance and installation tests. Recommends or orders actions to correct violations of legal requirements or to eliminate unsafe conditions. Performs standard tests to verify condition of equipment and calibration of meters and gauges, using test equipment and hand tools. Calculates allowable limits of pressure, strength, and stresses. Inspects gas mains to determine that rate of flow, pressure, location, construction, or installation conform to standards. Inspects drawings, designs, and specifications for piping, boilers and other vessels. Evaluates factors, such as materials used, safety devices, regulators, construction quality, riveting, welding, pitting, corrosion, cracking, and safety valve operation. Confers with engineers, manufacturers, contractors, owners, and operators concerning problems in construction, operation, and repair.

Personality Type: Realistic. Realistic occupations frequently involve work activities that include practical, hands-on problems and solutions. They often deal with plants, animals, and real-world materials like wood, tools, and machinery. Many of the occupations require working outside and do not involve a lot of paperwork or working closely with others.

Abilities: Problem Sensitivity—The ability to tell when something is wrong or is likely to go wrong. Does not involve solving the problem, only recognizing there is a problem. Oral Expression—The ability to communicate information and ideas verbally so others will understand.

Written Expression—The ability to communicate information and ideas in writing so others will understand. Oral Comprehension—The ability to listen to and understand information and ideas presented verbally. Written Comprehension—The ability to read and understand information and ideas presented in writing.

Skills: Mathematics—Using mathematics to solve problems. Product Inspection—Inspecting and evaluating the quality of products. Testing—Conducting tests to determine whether equipment, software, or procedures are operating as expected. Identification of Key Causes—Identifying the things that must be changed to achieve a goal. Speaking—Talking to others to effectively convey information. Active Listening—Listening to what other people are saying; asking questions as appropriate.

Generalized Work Activities: Inspecting Equipment, Structures, Materials—Inspecting or diagnosing equipment, structures, or materials to identify the causes of errors or other problems or defects. Evaluating Information against Standards—Evaluating information against a set of standards and verifying that it is correct. Getting Information Needed to Do the Job—Observing, receiving, and otherwise obtaining information from all relevant sources. Documenting/Recording Information—Entering, transcribing, recording, storing, or maintaining information in either written form or by electronic/magnetic recording. Monitoring Processes, Materials, Surroundings—Monitoring and reviewing information from materials, events, or the environment, often to detect problems or to find out when things are finished. Communicating with Other Workers—Providing information to supervisors, fellow workers, and subordinates. This information can be exchanged face-to-face, in writing, or via telephone/electronic transfer.

Public Transportation Inspectors

Monitor operation of public transportation systems to ensure good service and compliance with regulations. Investigate accidents, equipment failures, **and complaints.** Drives automobile along route to detect conditions hazardous to equipment and passengers and negotiates with local governments to eliminate hazards. Assists in dispatching equipment when necessary. Recommends promotions and disciplinary actions involving transportation personnel. Reports disruptions to service. Submits written reports to management with recommendations for improving service. Determines need for changes in service, such as additional vehicles, route changes, and revised schedules to improve service and efficiency. Inspects company vehicles and other property for evidence of abuse, damage, and mechanical malfunction and directs repair. Investigates schedule delays, accidents, and complaints. Observes employees performing assigned duties to note their deportment, treatment of passengers, and adherence to company regulations and schedules. Observes and records time required to load and unload passengers or freight volume of traffic on vehicle and at stops.

Personality Type: Enterprising. Enterprising occupations frequently involve starting up and carrying out projects. These occupations can involve leading people and making many decisions. They sometimes require risk taking and often deal with business.

Abilities: Oral Expression—The ability to communicate information and ideas verbally so others will understand. Problem Sensitivity—The ability to tell when something is wrong or is likely to go wrong. Does not involve solving the problem, only recognizing there is a problem. Written Expression—The ability to communicate information and ideas in writing so others will understand. Oral Comprehension—The ability to listen to and understand information and ideas presented verbally.

Skills: Identification of Key Causes—Identifying the things that must be changed to achieve a goal. Information Gathering—Knowing how to find information and identifying essential information. Writing—Communicating effectively with others in writing as indicated by the needs of the audience. Product Inspection—Inspecting and evaluating the quality of products. Operations Analysis—Analyzing needs and product requirements to create a design.

Generalized Work Activities: Getting Information Needed to Do the Job—Observing, receiving, and otherwise obtaining information from all relevant sources. Inspecting Equipment, Structures, Materials—Inspecting or diagnosing equipment, structures, or materials to identify the causes of errors or other problems or defects. Monitoring Processes, Materials, Surroundings—Monitoring and reviewing information from materials, events, or the environment, often to detect problems or to find out when things are finished. Documenting/Recording Information—Entering, transcribing, recording, storing, or maintaining information in either written form or by electronic/ magnetic recording. Evaluating Information against Standards—Evaluating information against a set of standards and verifying that it is correct.

Institutional Cleaning Supervisors

- ▲ Growth: 10%
- ▲ Annual Job Openings: 9,030
- ▲ Yearly Earnings: $19,590
- ▲ Education Required: Work experience in a related occupation
- ▲ Self-Employed: 1.6%
- ▲ Part-Time: 6.4%

Housekeeping Supervisors

Supervise work activities of cleaning personnel to ensure clean, orderly, and attractive rooms in hotels, hospitals, educational institutions, and similar establishments. Assign duties, inspect work, and investigate complaints regarding housekeeping service and equipment and take corrective action. Purchase housekeeping supplies and equipment, take periodic inventories, screen applicants, train new employees, and recommend dismissals. Conducts orientation training and in-service training to explain policies, work procedures, and to demonstrate use and maintenance of equipment. Prepares reports concerning room occupancy, payroll, and department expenses. Records data regarding work assignments, personnel actions, and time cards, and prepares periodic reports. Investigates complaints regarding housekeeping service and equipment, and takes corrective action. Evaluates records to forecast department personnel requirements. Attends staff meetings to discuss company policies and patrons' complaints. Makes recommendations to improve service and ensure more efficient operation. Examines building to determine need for repairs or replacement of furniture or equipment, and makes recommendations to management. Selects and purchases new furnishings. Inventories stock to ensure adequate supplies. Issues supplies and equipment to workers. Establishes standards and procedures for work of housekeeping staff. Advises manager, desk clerk, or admitting personnel of rooms ready for occupancy. Screens job applicants, hires new employees, and recommends promotions, transfers, and dismissals. Obtains list of rooms to be cleaned immediately and list of prospective check-outs or discharges to prepare work assignments. Assigns workers their duties and inspects work for conformance to prescribed standards of cleanliness. Coordinates work activities among departments. Performs cleaning duties in cases of emergency or staff shortage.

Personality Type: Enterprising. Enterprising occupations frequently involve starting up and carrying out projects. These occupations can involve leading people and making many decisions. They sometimes require risk taking and often deal with business.

Abilities: Oral Expression—The ability to communicate information and ideas verbally so others will understand. Oral Comprehension—The ability to listen to and understand information and ideas presented verbally. Written Comprehension—The ability to read and understand information and ideas presented in writing.

Written Expression—The ability to communicate information and ideas in writing so others will understand.

Skills: Management of Personnel Resources—Motivating, developing, and directing people as they work, identifying the best people for the job. Coordination—Adjusting actions in relation to others' actions. Visioning—Developing an image of how a system should work under ideal conditions. Time Management—Managing one's own time and the time of others.

Generalized Work Activities: Coordinating Work and Activities of Others—Coordinating members of a work group to accomplish tasks. Monitoring and Controlling Resources—Monitoring and controlling resources and overseeing the spending of money. Guiding, Directing, and Motivating Subordinates—Providing guidance and direction to subordinates, including setting performance standards and monitoring subordinates. Communicating with Other Workers—Providing information to supervisors, fellow workers, and subordinates. This information can be exchanged face-to-face, in writing, or via telephone/electronic transfer. Making Decisions and Solving Problems—Combining, evaluating, and analyzing information and data to make decisions and solve problems. Involves making decisions about the relative importance of information and choosing the best solution.

Janitorial Supervisors

Supervise work activities of janitorial personnel in commercial and industrial establishments. Assign duties, inspect work, and investigate complaints regarding janitorial services and take corrective action. Purchase janitorial supplies and equipment, take periodic inventories, screen applicants, train new employees, and recommend dismissals. Recommends personnel actions, such as hires and discharges, to ensure proper staffing. Issues janitorial supplies and equipment to workers to ensure quality and timely delivery of services. Records personnel data on specified forms. Trains workers in janitorial methods and procedures and

proper operation of equipment. Assigns janitorial work to employees, following material and work requirements. Supervises and coordinates activities of workers engaged in janitorial services. Inspects work performed to ensure conformance to specifications and established standards. Confers with staff to resolve production and personnel problems.

Personality Type: Enterprising. Enterprising occupations frequently involve starting up and carrying out projects. These occupations can involve leading people and making many decisions. They sometimes require risk taking and often deal with business.

Abilities: Oral Expression—The ability to communicate information and ideas verbally so others will understand. Oral Comprehension—The ability to listen to and understand information and ideas presented verbally. Problem Sensitivity—The ability to tell when something is wrong or is likely to go wrong. Does not involve solving the problem, only recognizing there is a problem. Speech Clarity—The ability to speak clearly so that what is said is understandable to a listener. Near Vision—The ability to see details of objects at a close range.

Skills: Management of Personnel Resources—Motivating, developing, and directing people as they work, identifying the best people for the job. Coordination—Adjusting actions in relation to others' actions. Time Management—Managing one's own time and the time of others. Speaking—Talking to others to effectively convey information. Instructing—Teaching others how to do something.

Generalized Work Activities: Coordinating Work and Activities of Others—Coordinating members of a work group to accomplish tasks. Scheduling Work and Activities—Scheduling events, programs, activities, and the work of others. Communicating with Other Workers—Providing information to supervisors, fellow workers, and subordinates. This information can be exchanged face-to-face, in writing, or via telephone/electronic transfer. Getting Information Needed to Do the Job—Observing, receiving, and otherwise obtaining information from all relevant sources. Inspecting Equipment, Structures, Materials—Inspecting or diagnosing equipment, structures, or materials to identify the causes of errors or other problems or defects.

Institution or Cafeteria Cooks

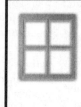

▲ Growth: 3%
▲ Annual Job Openings: 124,088
▲ Yearly Earnings: $16,090
▲ Education Required: Long-term O-J-T
▲ Self-Employed: 0%
▲ Part-Time: 38.5%

Cooks, Institution and Cafeteria

Prepare and cook large quantities of food for institutions, such as schools, hospitals, or cafeterias. Directs activities of one or more workers who assist in preparing and serving meals. Bakes breads, rolls, and other pastries. Prepares and cooks vegetables, salads, dressings, and desserts. Plans menus, taking advantage of foods in season and local availability. Compiles and maintains food cost records and accounts. Washes pots, pans, dishes, utensils, and other cooking equipment. Apportions and serves food to residents, employees, or patrons. Requisitions food supplies, kitchen equipment and appliances, and other supplies and receives deliveries. Cooks foodstuffs according to menu, special dietary or nutritional restrictions, and number of persons to be served. Cleans and inspects galley equipment, kitchen appliances, and work areas for cleanliness and functional operation. Cleans, cuts, and cooks meat, fish, and poultry.

Personality Type: Realistic. Realistic occupations frequently involve work activities that include practical, hands-on problems and solutions. They often deal with plants, animals, and real-world materials like wood, tools, and machinery. Many of the occupations require working outside and do not involve a lot of paperwork or working closely with others.

Abilities: Wrist-Finger Speed—The ability to make fast, simple, repeated movements of the fingers, hands, and wrists. Information Ordering—The ability to correctly follow a given rule or set of rules in order to arrange things or actions in a certain order. The things or actions can include numbers, letters, words, pictures, procedures, sentences, and mathematical or logical operations. Manual Dexterity—The ability to quickly make coordinated movements of one hand, a hand together with its arm, or two hands, to grasp, manipulate, or assemble objects. Oral Expression—The ability to communicate information and ideas verbally so others will understand.

Skills: Service Orientation—Actively looking for ways to help people. Mathematics—Using mathematics to solve problems. Product Inspection—Inspecting and evaluating the quality of products. Coordination—Adjusting actions in relation to others' actions. Reading Comprehension—Understanding written information in work-related documents. Operation and Control—Controlling operations of equipment or systems. Problem Identification—Identifying the nature of problems.

Generalized Work Activities: Monitoring Processes, Materials, Surroundings—Monitoring and reviewing information from materials, events, or the environment, often to detect problems or to find out when things are finished. Handling and Moving Objects—Using one's hands and arms in handling, installing, forming, positioning, and moving materials, or in manipulating things. Estimating Needed Characteristics—Estimating the characteristics of materials, products, events, or information; estimating sizes, distances, and quantities; determining time, costs, resources, or materials needed to perform a work activity. Implementing Ideas and Programs—Conducting or carrying out work procedures and activities in accord with one's own ideas or information provided through directions/instructions for purposes of installing, modifying, preparing, delivering, constructing, integrating, finishing, or completing programs, systems, structures, or products.

Monitoring and Controlling Resources—Monitoring and controlling resources and overseeing the spending of money. Making Decisions and Solving Problems—Combining, evaluating, and analyzing information and data to make decisions and solve problems. Involves making decisions about the relative importance of information and choosing the best solution. Performing

General Physical Activities—Performing physical activities that require moving one's whole body, such as in climbing, lifting, balancing, walking, and stooping. Performing activities that often also require considerable use of the arms and legs, such as in the physical handling of materials.

Insurance Adjusters, Examiners, and Investigators

- ▲ Growth: 20%
- ▲ Annual Job Openings: 16,055
- ▲ Yearly Earnings: $38,290
- ▲ Education Required: Long-term O-J-T
- ▲ Self-Employed: 3.7%
- ▲ Part-Time: 7.3%

Insurance Adjusters, Examiners, and Investigators

Investigate, analyze, and determine the extent of insurance company's liability concerning personal, casualty, or property loss or damages, and attempt to effect settlement with claimants. Correspond with or interview medical specialists, agents, witnesses, or claimants to compile information. Calculate benefit payments and approve payment of claims within a certain monetary limit. Interviews or corresponds with claimant and witnesses, consults police and hospital records, and inspects property damage to determine extent of liability. Obtains credit information from banks and other credit services. Interviews or corresponds with agents and claimants to correct errors or omissions and to investigate questionable entries. Negotiates claim settlements and recommends litigation when settlement cannot be negotiated. Examines titles to property to determine validity and acts as company agent in transactions with property owners. Analyzes information gathered by investigation and reports findings and recommendations. Refers questionable claims to investigator or claims adjuster for investigation

or settlement. Investigates and assesses damage to property. Prepares report of findings of investigation. Communicates with former associates to verify employment record and to obtain background information regarding persons or businesses applying for credit. Collects evidence to support contested claims in court. Examines claims form and other records to determine insurance coverage.

Personality Type: Enterprising. Enterprising occupations frequently involve starting up and carrying out projects. These occupations can involve leading people and making many decisions. They sometimes require risk taking and often deal with business.

Abilities: Written Comprehension—The ability to read and understand information and ideas presented in writing. Written Expression—The ability to communicate information and ideas in writing so others will understand. Oral Expression—The ability to communicate information and ideas verbally so others will understand. Oral Comprehension—The ability to listen to and understand information and ideas presented verbally. Near Vision—The ability to see details of objects at a close range. Inductive Reasoning—The ability to combine separate pieces of information, or specific answers to problems, to form general rules or conclusion. Includes coming up with a logical explanation for why a series of seemingly unrelated events occur together.

Skills: Speaking—Talking to others to effectively convey information. Judgment and Decision Making—Weighing the relative costs and benefits of a potential action. Active Listening—Listening to what other people are saying; asking questions as appropriate. Writing—Communicating effectively with others in writing as indicated by the needs of the audience. Identification of Key Causes—Identifying the things that must be changed to achieve a goal. Reading Comprehension—Understanding written information in work-related documents.

Generalized Work Activities: Documenting/Recording Information—Entering, transcribing, recording, storing, or maintaining information in either written form or by electronic/magnetic recording. Getting Information Needed to Do the Job—Observing, receiving, and otherwise obtaining information from all relevant sources. Communicating with Persons Outside Organization—Communicating with persons outside the organization. Representing the organization to customers, the public, government, and other external sources. Exchanging information face-to-face, in writing, or via telephone/electronic transfer. Analyzing Data or Information—Identifying underlying principles, reasons, or facts by breaking down information or data into separate parts. Judging Qualities—Making judgments about or assessing the value, importance, or quality of things, services, or other people's work. Evaluating Information against Standards—Evaluating information against a set of standards and verifying that it is correct.

Insurance Claims Clerks

- ▲ Growth: 14%
- ▲ Annual Job Openings: 12,974
- ▲ Yearly Earnings: $24,010
- ▲ Education Required: Moderate-term O-J-T
- ▲ Self-Employed: 0%
- ▲ Part-Time: 7.3%

Insurance Claims Clerks

Obtain information from insured or designated persons for purpose of settling claim with insurance carrier. Transmits claims for payment or further investigation. Posts or attaches information to claim file. Prepares and reviews insurance-claim forms and related documents for completeness. Calculates amount of claim. Contacts insured or other involved persons for missing information. Reviews insurance policy to determine coverage.

Personality Type: Conventional. Conventional occupations frequently involve following set procedures and routines. These occupations can include working with data and details more than with ideas. Usually there is a clear line of authority to follow.

Abilities: Number Facility—The ability to add, subtract, multiply, or divide quickly and correctly. Written Comprehension—The ability to read and understand information and ideas presented in writing. Near Vision—The ability to see details of objects at a close range. Oral Comprehension—The ability to listen to and understand information and ideas presented verbally. Information Ordering—The ability to correctly follow a given rule or set of rules in order to arrange things or actions in a certain order. The things or actions can include numbers, letters, words, pictures, procedures, sentences, and mathematical or logical operations.

Skills: Speaking—Talking to others to effectively convey information. Information Gathering—Knowing how to find information and identifying essential information. Active Listening—Listening to what other

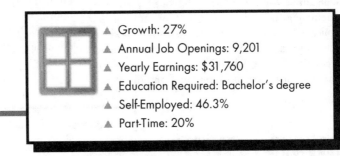

people are saying; asking questions as appropriate. Reading Comprehension—Understanding written information in work-related documents. Mathematics—Using mathematics to solve problems.

Generalized Work Activities: Getting Information Needed to Do the Job—Observing, receiving, and otherwise obtaining information from all relevant sources. Evaluating Information against Standards—Evaluating information against a set of standards and verifying that it is correct. Processing Information—Compiling, coding, categorizing, calculating, tabulating, auditing, verifying, or processing information or data.

Communicating with Persons Outside Organization—Communicating with persons outside the organization. Representing the organization to customers, the public, government, and other external sources. Exchanging information face-to-face, in writing, or via telephone/ electronic transfer. Performing Administrative Activities—Approving requests, handling paperwork, and performing day-to-day administrative tasks. Making Decisions and Solving Problems—Combining, evaluating, and analyzing information and data to make decisions and solve problems. Involves making decisions about the relative importance of information and choosing the best solution.

Interior Designers

- ▲ Growth: 27%
- ▲ Annual Job Openings: 9,201
- ▲ Yearly Earnings: $31,760
- ▲ Education Required: Bachelor's degree
- ▲ Self-Employed: 46.3%
- ▲ Part-Time: 20%

Interior Designers

Plan, design, and furnish interiors of residential, commercial, or industrial buildings. Formulate design that is practical, aesthetic, and conducive to intended purposes, such as raising productivity, selling merchandise, or improving lifestyle. Specialize in a particular field, style, or phase of interior design. Confers with client to determine factors affecting planning interior environments, such as budget, architectural preferences, and purpose and function. Plans and designs interior environments for boats, planes, buses, trains, and other enclosed spaces. Subcontracts fabrication, installation, and arrangement of carpeting, fixtures, accessories, draperies, paint and wall coverings, artwork, furniture, and related items. Renders design ideas in form of pasteups or drawings. Advises client on interior design factors, such as space planning, layout and utilization of furnishings and equipment, and color coordination. Selects or designs and purchases furnishings, art works, and accessories.

Formulates environmental plan to be practical, esthetic, and conducive to intended purposes, such as raising productivity or selling merchandise. Estimates material requirements and costs, and presents design to client for approval.

Personality Type: Artistic. Artistic occupations frequently involve working with forms, designs, and patterns. They often require self-expression, and the work can be done without following a clear set of rules.

Abilities: Visualization—The ability to imagine how something will look after it is moved around or when its parts are moved or rearranged. Fluency of Ideas— The ability to come up with a number of ideas about a given topic. Emphasis is on the number of ideas produced and not the quality, correctness, or creativity of the ideas. Originality—The ability to come up with unusual or clever ideas about a given topic or situation, or to develop creative ways to solve a problem. Oral Expression—The ability to communicate information and ideas verbally so others will understand. Oral

Comprehension—The ability to listen to and understand information and ideas presented verbally.

Skills: Coordination—Adjusting actions in relation to others' actions. Speaking—Talking to others to effectively convey information. Idea Generation—Generating a number of different approaches to problems. Judgment and Decision Making—Weighing the relative costs and benefits of a potential action. Active Listening—Listening to what other people are saying; asking questions as appropriate. Operations Analysis—Analyzing needs and product requirements to create a design.

Generalized Work Activities: Thinking Creatively—Originating, inventing, designing, or creating new applications, ideas, relationships, systems, or products, including artistic contributions. Getting Information Needed to Do the Job—Observing, receiving, and otherwise obtaining information from all relevant sources. Drafting and Specifying Technical Devices—Providing documentation, detailed instructions, drawings, or specifications to inform others about how devices, parts, equipment, or structures are to be fabricated, constructed, assembled, modified, maintained, or used. Estimating Needed Characteristics—Estimating the characteristics of materials, products, events, or information; estimating sizes, distances, and quantities; determining time, costs, resources, or materials needed to perform a work activity. Establishing and Maintaining Relationships—Developing constructive and cooperative working relationships with others. Making Decisions and Solving Problems—Combining, evaluating, and analyzing information and data to make decisions and solve problems. Involves making decisions about the relative importance of information and choosing the best solution.

Interviewing Clerks

- ▲ Growth: 23%
- ▲ Annual Job Openings: 44,483
- ▲ Yearly Earnings: $18,540
- ▲ Education Required: Short-term O-J-T
- ▲ Self-Employed: 0%
- ▲ Part-Time: 32.5%

Interviewers, Except Eligibility and Loan

Interview persons by telephone, mail, in person, or by other means for the purpose of completing forms, applications, or questionnaires. Ask specific questions, record answers, and assist persons with completing form. Sort, classify, and file forms. Assists person in filling out application or questionnaire. Records results and data from interview or survey, using computer or specified form. Contacts persons at home, place of business, or field location, by telephone, mail, or in person. Explains reason for questioning and other specified information. Compiles and sorts data from interview and reviews to correct errors. Asks questions to obtain various specified information, such as person's name, address, age, religion, and state of residency.

Personality Type: Conventional. Conventional occupations frequently involve following set procedures and routines. These occupations can include working with data and details more than with ideas. Usually there is a clear line of authority to follow.

Abilities: Oral Expression—The ability to communicate information and ideas verbally so others will understand. Oral Comprehension—The ability to listen to and understand information and ideas presented verbally. Speech Clarity—The ability to speak clearly so that what is said is understandable to a listener. Written

Expression—The ability to communicate information and ideas in writing so others will understand. Written Comprehension—The ability to read and understand information and ideas presented in writing.

Skills: Active Listening—Listening to what other people are saying; asking questions as appropriate. Speaking—Talking to others to effectively convey information. Reading Comprehension—Understanding written information in work-related documents. Information Gathering—Knowing how to find information and identifying essential information. Social Perceptiveness—Being aware of other people's reactions and understanding why people react the way they do. Writing—Communicating effectively with others in writing as indicated by the needs of the audience.

Generalized Work Activities: Documenting/Recording Information—Entering, transcribing, recording, stor-ing, or maintaining information in either written form or by electronic/magnetic recording. Communicating with Persons Outside Organization—Communicating with persons outside the organization. Representing the organization to customers, the public, government, and other external sources. Exchanging information face-to-face, in writing, or via telephone/electronic transfer. Getting Information Needed to Do the Job—Observing, receiving, and otherwise obtaining information from all relevant sources. Processing Information—Compiling, coding, categorizing, calculating, tabulating, auditing, verifying, or processing information or data. Interacting with Computers—Controlling computer functions by using programs, setting up functions, writing software, or otherwise communicating with computer systems.

Janitors, Cleaners, Maids and Housekeeping Cleaners

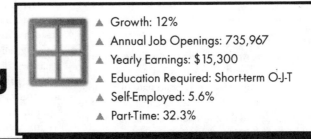

▲ Growth: 12%

▲ Annual Job Openings: 735,967

▲ Yearly Earnings: $15,300

▲ Education Required: Short-term O-J-T

▲ Self-Employed: 5.6%

▲ Part-Time: 32.3%

Janitors and Cleaners, Except Maids and Housekeeping Cleaners

Keep buildings in clean and orderly condition. Perform heavy cleaning duties, such as cleaning floors, shampooing rugs, washing walls and glass, and removing rubbish. Tend furnace and boiler, perform routine maintenance activities, notify management of need for repairs, and clean snow or debris from sidewalk. Drives vehicles, such as van, industrial truck or industrial vacuum cleaner. Dusts furniture, walls, machines, and equipment. Requisitions supplies and equipment used in cleaning and maintenance duties. Sets up, arranges, and removes decorations, tables, chairs, ladders, and scaffolding for events such as banquets and social functions. Moves items between departments, manually or using handtruck. Services and repairs cleaning and maintenance equipment and machinery and performs minor routine painting, plumbing, electrical, and related activities. Cleans chimneys, flues, and connecting pipes, using power and hand tools. Mixes water and detergents or acids in container to prepare cleaning solutions, according to specifications. Mows and trims lawns and shrubbery, using mowers and hand and power trimmers, and clears debris from grounds. Gathers and empties trash. Cleans and restores building interiors damaged by fire, smoke, or water, using commercial cleaning equipment. Sweeps, mops, scrubs, and vacuums floors of buildings, using cleaning solutions, tools and equipment. Cleans laboratory equipment, such as glassware and metal instruments, using solvents, brushes, rags, and power cleaning equipment. Cleans or polishes walls, ceilings, windows, plant equipment and building fixtures, using steam cleaning equipment, scrapers, brooms and variety of hand and power tools. Applies waxes or sealers to wood or concrete floors. Tends, cleans, adjusts and services furnaces, air conditioners, boilers and other building heating and cooling systems. Removes snow from sidewalks, driveways, and parking areas, using snowplow, snowblower, and snow shovel, and spreads snow melting chemicals. Notifies management personnel concerning need for major repairs or additions to building operating systems. Sprays insecticides and fumigants to prevent insect and rodent infestation.

Personality Type: Realistic. Realistic occupations frequently involve work activities that include practical, hands-on problems and solutions. They often deal with plants, animals, and real-world materials like wood, tools, and machinery. Many of the occupations require working outside and do not involve a lot of paperwork or working closely with others.

Abilities: Static Strength—The ability to exert maximum muscle force to lift, push, pull, or carry objects. Trunk Strength—The ability to use one's abdominal and lower back muscles to support part of the body repeatedly or continuously over time without giving out or fatiguing. Stamina—The ability to exert one's self physically over long periods of time without getting winded or out of breath. Multilimb Coordination—The ability to coordinate movements of two or more limbs together (for example, two arms, two legs, or one leg and one arm) while sitting, standing, or lying down. Does not involve performing the activities while the body is in motion. Manual

Dexterity—The ability to quickly make coordinated movements of one hand, a hand together with its arm, or two hands, to grasp, manipulate, or assemble objects.

Skills: Equipment Maintenance—Performing routine maintenance and determining when and what kind of maintenance is needed. Repairing—Repairing machines or systems, using the needed tools. Troubleshooting—Determining what is causing an operating error and deciding what to do about it. Equipment Selection—Determining the kind of tools and equipment needed to do a job. Operation and Control—Controlling operations of equipment or systems. Installation—Installing equipment, machines, wiring, or programs to meet specifications.

Generalized Work Activities: Handling and Moving Objects—Using one's hands and arms in handling, installing, forming, positioning, and moving materials, or in manipulating things. Includes the use of keyboards. Performing General Physical Activities—Performing physical activities that require moving one's whole body, such as in climbing, lifting, balancing, walking, and stooping. Performing activities that often also require considerable use of the arms and legs, such as in the physical handling of materials. Repairing and Maintaining Mechanical Equipment—Fixing, servicing, aligning, setting up, adjusting, and testing machines, devices, moving parts, and equipment that operate primarily on the basis of mechanical, not electronic, principles. Operating Vehicles or Equipment—Running, maneuvering, navigating, or driving vehicles or mechanized equipment such as forklifts, passenger vehicles, aircraft, or water craft. Controlling Machines and Processes—Using either control mechanisms or direct physical activity to operate machines or processes. Does not involve working with computers or vehicles.

Maids and House-keeping Cleaners

Perform any combination of light cleaning duties to maintain private households or commercial establishments, such as hotels, restaurants, and hospitals, in a clean and orderly manner. Duties

include making beds, replenishing linens, cleaning rooms and halls, and vacuuming. Replaces light bulbs. Cleans rooms, hallways, lobbies, lounges, restrooms, corridors, elevators, stairways, and locker rooms and other work areas. Washes windows, door panels, and sills. Delivers television sets, ironing boards, baby cribs, and rollaway beds to guests rooms. Cleans swimming pool with vacuum. Transports trash and waste to disposal area. Replenishes supplies, such as drinking glasses, writing supplies, and bathroom items. Moves and arranges furniture, turns mattresses, hangs draperies, dusts venetian blinds, and polishes metalwork to ready hotel facilities for occupancy. Washes beds and mattresses, and remakes beds after dismissal of hospital patients. Sweeps, scrubs, waxes, and polishes floors, using brooms and mops and powered scrubbing and waxing machines. Cleans rugs, carpets, upholstered furniture, and draperies, using vacuum cleaner. Cleans and removes debris from driveway and garage areas. Prepares sample rooms for sales meetings. Polishes metalwork, such as fixtures and fittings. Washes walls, ceiling, and woodwork. Collects soiled linens for laundering, and receives and stores linen supplies in linen closet. Empties wastebaskets and empties and cleans ashtrays. Arranges decorations, apparatus, or furniture for banquets and social functions. Dusts furniture and equipment.

Personality Type: Realistic. Realistic occupations frequently involve work activities that include practical, hands-on problems and solutions. They often deal with plants, animals, and real-world materials like wood, tools, and machinery. Many of the occupations require working outside and do not involve a lot of paperwork or working closely with others.

Abilities: Trunk Strength—The ability to use one's abdominal and lower back muscles to support part of the body repeatedly or continuously over time without giving out or fatiguing. Wrist-Finger Speed—The ability to make fast, simple, repeated movements of the fingers, hands, and wrists. Manual Dexterity—The ability to quickly make coordinated movements of one hand, a hand together with its arm, or two hands, to grasp, manipulate, or assemble objects. Static Strength—The ability to exert maximum muscle force to lift, push, pull, or carry objects. Problem Sensitivity—The ability to tell when something is wrong or is likely to go wrong. Does not involve solving the problem, only recognizing there is a problem. Stamina—The ability to exert one's self physically over long periods of time without getting winded or out of breath.

Skills: Service Orientation—Actively looking for ways to help people. Product Inspection—Inspecting and evaluating the quality of products. Equipment Selection—Determining the kind of tools and equipment needed to do a job. Information Organization—Finding ways to structure or classify multiple pieces of information. Active Listening—Listening to what other people are saying; asking questions as appropriate.

Generalized Work Activities: Handling and Moving Objects—Using one's hands and arms in handling, installing, forming, positioning, and moving materials, or in manipulating things. Includes the use of keyboards. Performing General Physical Activities—Performing physical activities that require moving one's whole body, such as in climbing, lifting, balancing, walking, and stooping. Performing activities that often also require considerable use of the arms and legs, such as in the physical handling of materials. Controlling Machines and Processes—Using either control mechanisms or direct physical activity to operate machines or processes. Does not involve working with computers or vehicles. Inspecting Equipment, Structures, Materials—Inspecting or diagnosing equipment, structures, or materials to identify the causes of errors or other problems or defects. Implementing Ideas and Programs—Conducting or carrying out work procedures and activities in accord with one's own ideas or information provided through directions/instructions for purposes of installing, modifying, preparing, delivering, constructing, integrating, finishing, or completing programs, systems, structures, or products.

Kindergarten Teachers

▲ Growth: 13%

▲ Annual Job Openings: 18,836

▲ Yearly Earnings: $33,590

▲ Education Required: Bachelor's degree

▲ Self-Employed: 1.5%

▲ Part-Time: 32.4%

Kindergarten Teachers, Except Special Education

Teach elemental natural and social sciences, personal hygiene, music, art, and literature to children from 4 to 6 years old. Promote physical, mental, and social development. Hold required state certification. Instructs children in practices of personal cleanliness and self-care. Supervises student activities, such as field visits, to stimulate student interest and broaden understanding of physical and social environment. Organizes and conducts games and group projects to develop cooperative behavior and assist children in forming satisfying relationships. Alternates periods of strenuous activity with periods of rest or light activity to avoid overstimulation and fatigue. Observes children to detect signs of ill health or emotional disturbance and to evaluate progress. Encourages students in activities, such as singing, dancing, and rhythmic activities, to promote self-expression and appreciation of esthetic experience. Teaches elemental science, personal hygiene, and humanities to children to promote physical, mental, and social development. Discusses student problems and progress with parents.

Personality Type: Social. Social occupations frequently involve working with, communicating with, and teaching people. These occupations often involve helping or providing service to others.

Abilities: Oral Expression—The ability to communicate information and ideas verbally so others will understand. Problem Sensitivity—The ability to tell when something is wrong or is likely to go wrong. Does not involve solving the problem, only recognizing there is a problem. Written Comprehension—The ability to read and understand information and ideas presented in writing. Oral Comprehension—The ability to listen to and understand information and ideas presented verbally.

Skills: Instructing—Teaching others how to do something. Learning Strategies—Using multiple approaches when learning or teaching new things. Speaking—Talking to others to effectively convey information. Active Listening—Listening to what other people are saying; asking questions as appropriate. Social Perceptiveness—Being aware of other people's reactions and understanding why people react the way they do. Service Orientation—Actively looking for ways to help people. Monitoring—Assessing how well one is doing when learning or doing something.

Generalized Work Activities: Teaching Others—Identifying educational needs, developing formal training programs or classes, and teaching or instructing others. Getting Information Needed to Do the Job—Observing, receiving, and otherwise obtaining information from all relevant sources. Assisting and Caring for Others—Providing assistance or personal care to others. Thinking Creatively—Originating, inventing, designing, or creating new applications, ideas, relationships, systems, or products, including artistic contributions. Documenting/Recording Information—Entering, transcribing, recording, storing, or maintaining information in either written form or by electronic/magnetic recording. Establishing and Maintaining Relationships—Developing constructive and cooperative working relationships with others. Organizing, Planning, and Prioritizing—Developing plans to accomplish work. Prioritizing and organizing one's own work.

Landscape Architects

- ▲ Growth: 14%
- ▲ Annual Job Openings: 1,605
- ▲ Yearly Earnings: $37,930
- ▲ Education Required: Bachelor's degree
- ▲ Self-Employed: 21.6%
- ▲ Part-Time: 8%

Landscape Architects

Plan and design land areas for such projects as parks and other recreational facilities, airports, highways, hospitals, schools, land subdivisions, and commercial, industrial, and residential sites. Prepares site plans, specifications, and cost estimates for land development, coordinating arrangement of existing and proposed land features and structures. Compiles and analyzes data on conditions, such as location, drainage, and location of structures for environmental reports and landscaping plans. Inspects landscape work to ensure compliance with specifications, approve quality of materials and work, and advise client and construction personnel. Confers with clients, engineering personnel, and architects on overall program.

Personality Type: Artistic. Artistic occupations frequently involve working with forms, designs, and patterns. They often require self-expression, and the work can be done without following a clear set of rules.

Abilities: Visualization—The ability to imagine how something will look after it is moved around or when its parts are moved or rearranged. Oral Comprehension—The ability to listen to and understand information and ideas presented verbally. Written Expression—The ability to communicate information and ideas in writing so others will understand. Speech Clarity—The ability to speak clearly so that what is said is understandable to a listener. Originality—The ability to come up with unusual or clever ideas about a given topic or situation, or to develop creative ways to solve a problem. Oral Expression—The ability to communicate information and ideas verbally so others will understand.

Skills: Mathematics—Using mathematics to solve problems. Idea Generation—Generating a number of different approaches to problems. Active Listening—Listening to what other people are saying; asking questions as appropriate. Synthesis/Reorganization—Reorganizing information to get a better approach to problems or tasks. Visioning—Developing an image of how a system should work under ideal conditions. Idea Evaluation—Evaluating the likely success of an idea in relation to the demands of the situation.

Generalized Work Activities: Thinking Creatively—Originating, inventing, designing, or creating new applications, ideas, relationships, systems, or products, including artistic contributions. Getting Information Needed to Do the Job—Observing, receiving, and otherwise obtaining information from all relevant sources. Providing Consultation and Advice to Others—Providing consultation and expert advice to management or other groups on technical, systems-related, or process-related topics. Drafting and Specifying Technical Devices—Providing documentation, detailed instructions, drawings, or specifications to inform others about how devices, parts, equipment, or structures are to be fabricated, constructed, assembled, modified, maintained, or used. Making Decisions and Solving Problems—Combining, evaluating, and analyzing information and data to make decisions and solve problems. Involves making decisions about the relative importance of information and choosing the best solution.

Landscaping and Groundskeeping Workers

▲ Growth: 21%
▲ Annual Job Openings: 283,459
▲ Yearly Earnings: $17,140
▲ Education Required: Short-term O-J-T
▲ Self-Employed: 27.9%
▲ Part-Time: 28.5%

Landscaping and Groundskeeping Workers

Landscape or maintain grounds of property using hand or power tools or equipment. Workers typically perform a variety of tasks, including laying sod, mowing, trimming, planting, watering, fertilizing, digging, raking, installing sprinklers, and installing mortarless segmental concrete masonry wall units. Hauls or spreads topsoil, and spreads straw over seeded soil to hold soil in place. Waters lawns, trees, and plants using portable sprinkler system, hose, or watering can. Applies herbicides, fungicides, fertilizers, and pesticides using spreaders or spray equipment. Builds forms and mixes and pours cement to form garden borders. Shovels snow from walks and driveways. Seeds and fertilizes lawns. Maintains tools and equipment. Decorates garden with stones and plants. Trims and picks flowers and cleans flower beds. Digs holes for plants, mixes fertilizer or lime with dirt in holes, inserts plants, and fills holes with dirt. Mows lawns using power mower. Attaches wires from planted trees to support stakes.

Personality Type: Realistic. Realistic occupations frequently involve work activities that include practical, hands-on problems and solutions. They often deal with plants, animals, and real-world materials like wood, tools, and machinery. Many of the occupations require working outside and do not involve a lot of paperwork or working closely with others.

Abilities: Manual Dexterity—The ability to quickly make coordinated movements of one hand, a hand together with its arm, or two hands, to grasp, manipulate, or assemble objects. Static Strength—The ability to exert maximum muscle force to lift, push, pull, or carry objects. Stamina—The ability to exert one's self physically over long periods of time without getting winded or out of breath. Trunk Strength—The ability to use one's abdominal and lower back muscles to support part of the body repeatedly or continuously over time without giving out or fatiguing. Dynamic Strength—The ability to exert muscle force repeatedly or continuously over time. This involves muscular endurance and resistance to muscle fatigue.

Skills: Equipment Selection—Determining the kind of tools and equipment needed to do a job. Operation and Control—Controlling operations of equipment or systems. Equipment Maintenance—Performing routine maintenance and determining when and what kind of maintenance is needed. Service Orientation—Actively looking for ways to help people. Installation—Installing equipment, machines, wiring, or programs to meet specifications.

Generalized Work Activities: Performing General Physical Activities—Performing physical activities that require moving one's whole body, such as in climbing, lifting, balancing, walking, and stooping. Performing activities that often also require considerable use of the arms and legs, such as in the physical handling of materials. Handling and Moving Objects—Using one's hands and arms in handling, installing, forming, positioning, and moving materials, or in manipulating things. Operating Vehicles or Equipment—Running, maneuvering, navigating, or driving vehicles or mechanized equipment such as forklifts, passenger vehicles, aircraft, or water craft. Implementing Ideas and Programs—Conducting or carrying out work procedures and activities in accord with one's own ideas or information provided through directions/instructions for purposes of installing, modifying, preparing, delivering, constructing, integrating, finishing, or completing programs, systems, structures, or products.

Repairing and Maintaining Mechanical Equipment—Fixing, servicing, aligning, setting up, adjusting, and testing machines, devices, moving parts, and equipment that operate primarily on the basis of mechanical, not electronic, principles.

Laundry and Dry-Cleaning Machine Operators

- ▲ Growth: 10%
- ▲ Annual Job Openings: 38,082
- ▲ Yearly Earnings: $14,670
- ▲ Education Required: Moderate-term O-J-T
- ▲ Self-Employed: 11.4%
- ▲ Part-Time: 26.3%

Laundry and Dry-Cleaning Machine Operators and Tenders, Except Pressing

Operate or tend washing or dry-cleaning machines to wash or dry-clean commercial, industrial, or household articles, such as cloth garments, suede, leather, furs, blankets, draperies, fine linens, rugs, and carpets. Cleans machine filters and lubricates equipment. Sorts and counts articles removed from dryer and folds, wraps, or hangs items for airing out, pickup, or delivery. Mixes and adds detergents, dyes, bleach, starch, and other solutions and chemicals to clean, color, dry, or stiffen articles. Starts pumps to operate distilling system that drains and reclaims dry-cleaning solvents. Washes, dry cleans, or glazes delicate articles or fur garment linings by hand, using mild detergent or dry cleaning solutions. Presoaks, sterilizes, scrubs, spot-cleans, and dries contaminated or stained articles, using neutralizer solutions and portable machines. Examines and sorts articles to be cleaned into lots, according to color, fabric, dirt content, and cleaning technique required. Irons or presses articles, fabrics, and furs using hand iron or pressing machine. Hangs curtains, drapes, blankets, pants, and other garments on stretch frames to dry and transports items between specified locations. Mends and sews articles, using hand stitching, adhesive patch, or power sewing machine. Adjusts switches to tend and regulate equipment that fumigates and removes foreign matter from furs. Starts washer, dry cleaner, drier, or extractor, and turns valves or levers to regulate and monitor cleaning or drying operations. Removes or directs other workers to remove items from washer or dry-cleaning machine and into extractor or tumbler. Loads or directs other workers to load articles into washer or dry-cleaning machine. Tends variety of automatic machines that comb and polish furs Receives and marks articles for laundry or dry cleaning with identifying code number or name, using hand or machine marker.

Personality Type: Realistic. Realistic occupations frequently involve work activities that include practical, hands-on problems and solutions. They often deal with plants, animals, and real-world materials like wood, tools, and machinery. Many of the occupations require working outside and do not involve a lot of paperwork or working closely with others.

Abilities: Visual Color Discrimination—The ability to match or detect differences between colors, including shades of color and brightness. Manual Dexterity—The ability to quickly make coordinated movements of one hand, a hand together with its arm, or two hands, to grasp, manipulate, or assemble objects. Trunk Strength—The ability to use one's abdominal and lower back muscles to support part of the body repeatedly or continuously over time without giving out or fatiguing. Information Ordering—The ability to correctly follow a given rule or set of rules in order to arrange things or actions in a certain order. The things or actions can include numbers, letters, words, pictures, procedures, sentences, and mathematical or logical operations. Category Flexibility—The ability to produce many rules so that each rule tells how to group or combine a set of things in a different way. Extent Flexibility—The ability to bend, stretch, twist, or reach out with the body, arms, and/or legs.

Skills: Operation and Control—Controlling operations of equipment or systems. Product Inspection—Inspecting and evaluating the quality of products. Operation Monitoring—Watching gauges, dials, or other indicators to make sure a machine is working properly. Equipment Maintenance—Performing routine maintenance and determining when and what kind of maintenance is needed. Information Organization—Finding ways to structure or classify multiple pieces of information.

Generalized Work Activities: Controlling Machines and Processes—Using either control mechanisms or direct physical activity to operate machines or processes. Does not involve working with computers or vehicles. Monitoring Processes, Materials, Surroundings—Monitoring and reviewing information from materials, events, or the environment, often to detect problems or to find out when things are finished. Handling and Moving Objects—Using one's hands and arms in handling, installing, forming, positioning, and moving materials, or in manipulating things. Performing General Physical Activities—Performing physical activities that require moving one's whole body, such as in climbing, lifting, balancing, walking, and stooping. Performing activities that often also require considerable use of the arms and legs, such as in the physical handling of materials. Identifying Objects, Actions, and Events—Identifying information received by making estimates or categorizations, recognizing differences or similarities, or sensing changes in circumstances or events. Communicating with Other Workers—Providing information to supervisors, fellow workers, and subordinates. Exchanging information face-to-face, in writing, or via telephone/electronic transfer.

Spotters, Dry Cleaning

Identify stains in wool, synthetic, and silk garments and household fabrics and apply chemical solutions to remove stain. Determine spotting procedures on basis of type of fabric and nature of stain. Inspects spots to ascertain composition and select solvent. Sprays steam, water, or air over spot to flush out chemicals, dry material, raise nap, or brighten color. Mixes bleaching agent with hot water in vats and soaks material until it is bleached. Cleans fabric using vacuum or airhose. Operates dry-cleaning machine. Sprinkles chemical solvents over stain and pats area with brush or sponge until stain is removed. Spreads article on worktable and positions stain over vacuum head or on marble slab. Applies bleaching powder to spot and sprays with steam to remove stains from certain fabrics that do not respond to other cleaning solvents. Applies chemicals to neutralize effect of solvents.

Personality Type: Realistic. Realistic occupations frequently involve work activities that include practical, hands-on problems and solutions. They often deal with plants, animals, and real-world materials like wood, tools, and machinery. Many of the occupations require working outside and do not involve a lot of paperwork or working closely with others.

Abilities: Wrist-Finger Speed—The ability to make fast, simple, repeated movements of the fingers, hands, and wrists. Manual Dexterity—The ability to quickly make coordinated movements of one hand, a hand together with its arm, or two hands, to grasp, manipulate, or assemble objects. Visual Color Discrimination—The ability to match or detect differences between colors, including shades of color and brightness. Near Vision—The ability to see details of objects at a close range. Deductive Reasoning—The ability to apply general rules to specific problems to come up with logical answers. Involves deciding if an answer makes sense.

Skills: Product Inspection—Inspecting and evaluating the quality of products. Problem Identification—Identifying the nature of problems. Equipment Selection—Determining the kind of tools and equipment needed to do a job. Operation and Control—Controlling operations of equipment or systems. Monitoring—Assessing how well one is doing when learning or doing something. Solution Appraisal—Observing and evaluating the outcomes of a problem solution to identify lessons learned or to redirect efforts.

Generalized Work Activities: Getting Information Needed to Do the Job—Observing, receiving, and otherwise obtaining information from all relevant sources. Handling and Moving Objects—Using one's hands and arms in handling, installing, forming, positioning, and moving materials, or in manipulating things. Identifying Objects, Actions, and Events—Identifying information received by making estimates or categorizations, recognizing differences or similarities, or sensing changes in circumstances or events. Controlling Machines and Processes—Using either control mechanisms or direct physical activity to operate machines or processes. Does not involve working with computers or vehicles. Performing General Physical Activities—Performing physical activities that require moving one's whole body, such as in climbing, lifting, balancing, walking, and stooping. Performing activities that often also require considerable use of the arms and legs, such as in the physical handling of materials.

Lawn Service Managers

- ▲ Growth: 20%
- ▲ Annual Job Openings: 10,385
- ▲ Yearly Earnings: $25,410
- ▲ Education Required: Work experience in a related occupation
- ▲ Self-Employed: 58.8%
- ▲ Part-Time: 24.5%

Lawn Service Managers

Plan, direct, and coordinate activities of workers engaged in pruning trees and shrubs, cultivating lawns, and applying pesticides and other chemicals according to service contract specifications. Schedules work for crew according to weather conditions, availability of equipment, and seasonal limitations. Prepares work activity and personnel reports. Suggests changes in work procedures and orders corrective work done. Investigates customer complaints. Prepares service cost estimates for customers. Answers customers' questions about groundskeeping care requirements. Reviews contracts to ascertain service, machine, and workforce requirements for job. Supervises workers who provide groundskeeping services on a contract basis. Spot-checks completed work to improve quality of service and to ensure contract compliance.

Personality Type: Enterprising. Enterprising occupations frequently involve starting up and carrying out projects. These occupations can involve leading people and making many decisions. They sometimes require risk taking and often deal with business.

Abilities: Oral Expression—The ability to communicate information and ideas verbally so others will understand. Oral Comprehension—The ability to listen to and understand information and ideas presented verbally. Written Comprehension—The ability to read and understand information and ideas presented in writing. Information Ordering—The ability to correctly follow a given rule or set of rules in order to arrange things or actions in a certain order. The things or actions can include numbers, letters, words, pictures, procedures, sentences, and mathematical or logical operations. Written Expression—The ability to communicate information and ideas in writing so others will understand. Number Facility—The ability to add, subtract, multiply, or divide quickly and correctly. Speech Clarity—The ability to speak clearly so that what is said is understandable to a listener.

Skills: Management of Personnel Resources—Motivating, developing, and directing people as they work, identifying the best people for the job. Time Management—Managing one's own time and the time of others. Active Listening—Listening to what other people are saying; asking questions as appropriate. Implementation Planning—Developing approaches for implementing an idea. Problem Identification—Identifying the nature of problems.

Generalized Work Activities: Guiding, Directing, and Motivating Subordinates—Providing guidance and direction to subordinates, including setting performance standards and monitoring subordinates. Coordinating Work and Activities of Others—Coordinating members of a work group to accomplish tasks. Making Decisions and Solving Problems—Combining, evaluating, and analyzing information and data to make decisions and solve problems. Involves making decisions about the relative importance of information and choosing the best solution. Estimating Needed Characteristics—Estimating the characteristics of materials, products, events, or information; estimating sizes, distances, and quantities; determining time, costs, resources, or materials needed to perform a work activity. Establishing and Maintaining Relationships—Developing constructive and cooperative working relationships with others.

Lawyers

- ▲ Growth: 17%
- ▲ Annual Job Openings: 38,182
- ▲ Yearly Earnings: $78,170
- ▲ Education Required: First professional degree
- ▲ Self-Employed: 36%
- ▲ Part-Time: 7%

Lawyers

Represent clients in criminal and civil litigation and other legal proceedings, draw up legal documents, and manage or advise clients on legal transactions. Specialize in a single area or practice broadly in many areas of law. Conducts case, examining and cross examining witnesses, and summarizes case to judge or jury. Prepares opinions on legal issues. Prepares and drafts legal documents, such as wills, deeds, patent applications, mortgages, leases, and contracts. Prepares and files legal briefs. Interprets laws, rulings, and regulations for individuals and business. Presents evidence to defend client in civil or criminal litigation. Confers with colleagues with specialty in area of legal issue to establish and verify basis for legal proceeding. Probates wills and represents and advises executors and administrators of estates. Presents evidence to prosecute defendant in civil or criminal litigation. Gathers evidence to formulate defense or to initiate legal actions. Acts as agent, trustee, guardian, or executor for business or individuals. Advises clients concerning business transactions, claim liability, advisability of prosecuting or defending lawsuits, or legal rights and obligations. Interviews clients and witnesses to ascertain facts of case. Examines legal data to determine advisability of defending or prosecuting lawsuit. Studies Constitution, statutes, decisions, regulations, and ordinances of quasi-judicial bodies. Evaluates findings and develops strategy and arguments in preparation for presentation of case. Represents client in court or before government agency. Searches for and examines public and other legal records to write opinions or establish ownership.

Personality Type: Enterprising. Enterprising occupations frequently involve starting up and carrying out projects. These occupations can involve leading people and making many decisions. They sometimes require risk taking and often deal with business.

Abilities: Oral Comprehension—The ability to listen to and understand information and ideas presented verbally. Written Comprehension—The ability to read and understand information and ideas presented in writing. Oral Expression—The ability to communicate information and ideas verbally so others will understand. Written Expression—The ability to communicate information and ideas in writing so others will understand. Speech Clarity—The ability to speak clearly so that what is said is understandable to a listener.

Skills: Persuasion—Persuading others to approach things differently. Critical Thinking—Using logic and analysis to identify the strengths and weaknesses of different approaches. Speaking—Talking to others to effectively convey information. Reading Comprehension—Understanding written information in work-related documents.

Generalized Work Activities: Getting Information Needed to Do the Job—Observing, receiving, and otherwise obtaining information from all relevant sources. Updating and Using Job-Relevant Knowledge—Keeping up-to-date technically and knowing the functions of one's own job and related jobs. Interpreting Meaning of Information to Others—Translating or explaining what information means and how it can be understood or used to support responses or feedback to others. Making Decisions and Solving Problems—Combining, evaluating, and analyzing information and data to make decisions and solve problems. Involves making decisions about the relative importance of information and choosing the best solution. Communicating with Persons Outside Organization—Communicating with persons outside the organization. Representing the organization to customers, the public, government, and other external sources. Exchanging information face-to-face, in writing, or via telephone/electronic transfer. Evaluating Information against Standards—Evaluating information against a set of standards and verifying that it is correct. Identifying Objects, Actions, and Events—Identifying information received by making estimates or categorizations, recognizing differences or similarities, or sensing changes in circumstances or events.

Legal Secretaries

- ▲ Growth: 13%
- ▲ Annual Job Openings: 44,130
- ▲ Yearly Earnings: $30,050
- ▲ Education Required: Postsecondary vocational training
- ▲ Self-Employed: 0%
- ▲ Part-Time: 19.8%

Legal Secretaries

Perform secretarial duties utilizing legal terminology, procedures, and documents. Prepare legal papers and correspondence, such as summonses, complaints, motions, and subpoenas. Assist with legal research. Schedules and makes appointments. Submits articles and information from searches to attorneys for review and approval for use. Reviews legal publications and performs database searches to identify laws and court decisions relevant to pending cases. Organizes and maintains law libraries and document and case files. Assists attorneys in collecting information such as employment, medical, and other records. Receives and places telephone calls. Mails, faxes, or arranges for delivery of legal correspondence to clients, witnesses, and court officials. Attends legal meetings, such as client interviews, hearings, or depositions, and takes notes.

Completes various forms, such as accident reports, trial and courtroom requests, and applications for clients. Prepares and processes legal documents and papers, such as summonses, subpoenas, complaints, appeals, motions, and pretrial agreements. Drafts and types office memos. Makes photocopies of correspondence, document, and other printed matter.

Personality Type: Conventional. Conventional occupations frequently involve following set procedures and routines. These occupations can include working with data and details more than with ideas. Usually there is a clear line of authority to follow.

Abilities: Written Comprehension—The ability to read and understand information and ideas presented in writing. Oral Comprehension—The ability to listen to and understand information and ideas presented verbally. Written Expression—The ability to communicate information and ideas in writing so others will understand. Near Vision—The ability to see details of objects at a close range. Wrist-Finger Speed—The ability to make fast, simple, repeated movements of the fingers, hands, and wrists. Oral Expression—The ability to communicate information and ideas verbally so others will understand.

Skills: Information Organization—Finding ways to structure or classify multiple pieces of information. Coordination—Adjusting actions in relation to others' actions. Information Gathering—Knowing how to find information and identifying essential information. Reading Comprehension—Understanding written information in work-related documents. Time Management—Managing one's own time and the time of others.

Generalized Work Activities: Communicating with Other Workers—Providing information to supervisors, fellow workers, and subordinates. Exchanging information face-to-face, in writing, or via telephone/electronic transfer. Getting Information Needed to Do the Job—Observing, receiving, and otherwise obtaining information from all relevant sources. Communicating with Persons Outside Organization—Communicating with persons outside the organization. Representing the organization to customers, the public, government, and other external sources. Exchanging information face-to-face, in writing, or via telephone/electronic transfer. Documenting/Recording Information—Entering, transcribing, recording, storing, or maintaining information in either written form or by electronic/magnetic recording. Performing Administrative Activities—Approving requests, handling paperwork, and performing day-to-day administrative tasks. Identifying Objects, Actions, and Events—Identifying information received by making estimates or categorizations, recognizing differences or similarities, or sensing changes in circumstances or events.

Library Assistants and Bookmobile Drivers

- ▲ Growth: 16%
- ▲ Annual Job Openings: 35,994
- ▲ Yearly Earnings: $16,980
- ▲ Education Required: Short-term O-J-T
- ▲ Self-Employed: 0%
- ▲ Part-Time: 61.7%

Library Assistants, Clerical

Compile records, sort and shelve books, and issue and receive library materials, such as pictures, cards, slides, and microfilm. Locate library materials for loan and replace material in shelving area, stacks, or files according to identification number and title. Register patrons to permit them to borrow books, periodicals, and other library materials. Prepares, stores, and retrieves classification and catalog information, lecture notes, or other documents related to document stored, using computer. Drives bookmobile to specified locations following library services schedule and to garage for preventive maintenance and repairs. Sorts books, publications, and other items according to procedure and returns them to shelves, files, or other designated storage area. Maintains records of items received, stored, issued, and returned and files catalog cards according to system used. Classifies and catalogs items according to contents and purpose. Issues books to patrons and records or scans information on borrower's card. Reviews records, such as microfilm and issue cards, to determine title of overdue materials and to identify borrower. Inspects returned books for damage, verifies due date, and computes and receives overdue fines. Delivers and retrieves items to and from departments by hand or push cart. Locates library materials for patrons, such as books, periodicals, tape cassettes, Braille volumes, and pictures. Issues borrower's identification card according to established procedures. Selects substitute titles, following criteria such as age, education, and interest when requested materials are unavailable. Answers routine inquiries and refers patrons who need professional assistance to librarian. Repairs books, using mending tape and paste and brush, and places plastic covers on new books. Prepares address labels for books to be mailed, overdue notices, and duty schedules, using computer or typewriter. Operates and maintains audiovisual equipment and explains use of reference equipment to patrons. Places books in mailing container, affixes address label, and secures container with straps for mailing to blind library patrons.

Personality Type: Conventional. Conventional occupations frequently involve following set procedures and routines. These occupations can include working with data and details more than with ideas. Usually there is a clear line of authority to follow.

Abilities: Information Ordering—The ability to correctly follow a given rule or set of rules in order to arrange things or actions in a certain order. The things or actions can include numbers, letters, words, pictures, procedures, sentences, and mathematical or logical operations. Category Flexibility—The ability to produce many rules so that each rule tells how to group or combine a set of things in a different way. Oral Expression—The ability to communicate information and ideas verbally so others will understand. Oral Comprehension—The ability to listen to and understand information and ideas presented verbally. Near Vision—The ability to see details of objects at a close range. Written Comprehension—The ability to read and understand information and ideas presented in writing.

Skills: Information Organization—Finding ways to structure or classify multiple pieces of information. Reading Comprehension—Understanding written information in work-related documents. Service Orientation—Actively looking for ways to help people. Speaking—Talking to others to effectively convey information. Active Listening—Listening to what other people are saying; asking questions as appropriate.

Generalized Work Activities: Communicating with Persons Outside Organization—Communicating with persons outside the organization. Representing the organization to customers, the public, government, and other external sources. Exchanging information face-to-face, in writing, or via telephone/electronic transfer. Handling and Moving Objects—Using one's hands and arms in handling, installing, forming, positioning, and moving materials, or in manipulating things. Includes the use of keyboards. Documenting/Recording Information—Entering, transcribing, recording, storing, or maintaining information in either written form or by electronic/magnetic recording. Performing for/Working with Public—Performing for people or dealing directly with the public, including serving persons in restaurants and stores and receiving clients or guests. Assisting and Caring for Others—Providing assistance or personal care to others.

L

Library Technicians

- ▲ Growth: 18%
- ▲ Annual Job Openings: 9,478
- ▲ Yearly Earnings: $21,730
- ▲ Education Required: Short-term O-J-T
- ▲ Self-Employed: 0%
- ▲ Part-Time: 11.7%

Audio-Visual Collections Specialists

Prepare, plan, and operate audio-visual teaching aids for use in education. Record, catalogue, and file audio-visual materials. Develops manuals, texts, workbooks, or related materials for use in conjunction with production materials. Directs and coordinates activities of assistants and other personnel during production. Locates and secures settings, properties, effects, and other production necessities. Develops production ideas based on assignment or generates own ideas based on objectives and interest. Executes, or directs assistants to execute, rough and finished graphics and graphic designs. Plans and develops preproduction ideas into outlines, scripts, continuity, story boards, and graphics, or directs assistants to develop ideas. Performs narration or presents announcements. Constructs and positions properties, sets, lighting equipment, and other equipment. Determines format, approach, content, level, and medium to meet objectives most effectively within budgetary constraints, utilizing research, knowledge, and training. Sets up, adjusts, and operates equipment, such as cameras, sound mixers, and recorders during production. Conducts training sessions on selection, use, and design of audiovisual materials, and operation of presentation equipment.

Personality Type: Conventional. Conventional occupations frequently involve following set procedures and routines. These occupations can include working with data and details more than with ideas. Usually there is a clear line of authority to follow.

Abilities: Speech Clarity—The ability to speak clearly so that what is said is understandable to a listener. Oral Expression—The ability to communicate information and ideas verbally so others will understand. Visualization—The ability to imagine how something will look after it is moved around or when its parts are moved or rearranged. Originality—The ability to come up with unusual or clever ideas about a given topic or situation, or to develop creative ways to solve a problem. Written Expression—The ability to communicate information and ideas in writing so others will understand.

Skills: Idea Generation—Generating a number of different approaches to problems. Implementation Planning—Developing approaches for implementing an idea. Synthesis/Reorganization—Reorganizing information to get a better approach to problems or tasks. Speaking—Talking to others to effectively convey information. Writing—Communicating effectively with others in writing as indicated by the needs of the audience.

Generalized Work Activities: Thinking Creatively—Originating, inventing, designing, or creating new applications, ideas, relationships, systems, or products, including artistic contributions. Implementing Ideas and Programs—Conducting or carrying out work procedures and activities in accord with one's own ideas or information provided through directions/instructions for purposes of installing, modifying, preparing, delivering, constructing, integrating, finishing, or completing programs, systems, structures, or products. Getting Information Needed to Do the Job—Observing, receiving, and otherwise obtaining information from all relevant sources. Monitoring Processes, Materials, Surroundings—Monitoring and reviewing information from materials, events, or the environment, often to detect problems or to find out when things are finished. Teaching Others—Identifying educational needs, developing formal training programs or classes, and teaching or instructing others. Establishing and Maintaining Relationships—Developing constructive and cooperative working relationships with others.

Library Technicians

Assist librarians by helping readers in the use of library catalogs, databases, and indexes to locate books and other materials and by answering questions that require only brief consultation of standard reference. Compile records sort and shelve books remove or repair damaged books register patrons check materials in and out of the circulation process. Replace materials in shelving area (stacks) or files. Includes bookmobile drivers who operate bookmobiles or light trucks that pull trailers to specific locations on a predetermined schedule and assist with providing services in mobile libraries. Designs posters and special displays to promote use of library facilities or specific reading program at library. Processes print and nonprint library materials, and classifies and catalogs materials. Reviews subject matter of materials to be classified and selects classification numbers and headings according to classification system. Issues identification card to borrowers and checks materials in and out. Directs activities of library clerks and aides. Compiles and maintains records relating to circulation, materials, and equipment. Composes explanatory summaries of contents of books or other reference materials. Files catalog cards according to system used. Verifies bibliographical data, including author, title, publisher, publication date, and edition on computer terminal. Assists patrons in operating equipment, obtaining library materials and services, and explains use of reference tools. Prepares order slips for materials, follows up on orders, and compiles lists of materials acquired or withdrawn.

Personality Type: Conventional. Conventional occupations frequently involve following set procedures and routines. These occupations can include working with data and details more than with ideas. Usually there is a clear line of authority to follow.

Abilities: Speech Clarity—The ability to speak clearly so that what is said is understandable to a listener. Category Flexibility—The ability to produce many rules so that each rule tells how to group or combine a set of things in a different way. Information Ordering—The ability to correctly follow a given rule or set of rules in order to arrange things or actions in a certain order. The things or actions can include numbers, letters, words, pictures, procedures, sentences, and mathematical or logical operations. Oral Expression—The ability to communicate information and ideas verbally so others will understand. Written Expression—The ability to communicate information and ideas in writing so others will understand. Written Comprehension—The ability to read and understand information and ideas presented in writing.

Skills: Reading Comprehension—Understanding written information in work-related documents. Information Organization—Finding ways to structure or classify multiple pieces of information. Information Gathering—Knowing how to find information and identifying essential information. Service Orientation—Actively looking for ways to help people. Active Listening—Listening to what other people are saying; asking questions as appropriate.

Generalized Work Activities: Communicating with Persons Outside Organization—Communicating with persons outside the organization. Representing the organization to customers, the public, government, and other external sources. Exchanging information face-to-face, in writing, or via telephone/electronic transfer. Performing for/Working with Public—Performing for people or dealing directly with the public, including serving persons in restaurants and stores and receiving clients or guests. Handling and Moving Objects—Using one's hands and arms in handling, installing, forming, positioning, and moving materials, or in manipulating things. Includes the use of keyboards. Communicating with Other Workers—Providing information to supervisors, fellow workers, and subordinates. Exchanging information face-to-face, in writing, or via telephone/electronic transfer. Documenting/Recording Information—Entering, transcribing, recording, storing, or maintaining information in either written form or by electronic/magnetic recording.

License Clerks

▲ Growth: 13%
▲ Annual Job Openings: 6,424
▲ Yearly Earnings: $22,900
▲ Education Required: Short-term O-J-T
▲ Self-Employed: Not available
▲ Part-Time: Not available

License Clerks

Issue licenses or permits to qualified applicants. Obtain necessary information; record data. Evaluates information obtained to determine applicant qualification for licensure. Conducts oral, visual, written, or performance test to determine applicant qualifications. Submits fees and reports to government for record. Counts collected fees and applications. Collects prescribed fee. Issues driver, automobile, marriage, dog, or other license. Questions applicant to obtain information, such as name, address, and age, and records data on prescribed forms.

Personality Type: Conventional. Conventional occupations frequently involve following set procedures and routines. These occupations can include working with data and details more than with ideas. Usually there is a clear line of authority to follow.

Abilities: Speech Clarity—The ability to speak clearly so that what is said is understandable to a listener. Near Vision—The ability to see details of objects at a close range. Oral Expression—The ability to communicate information and ideas verbally so others will understand. Written Expression—The ability to communicate information and ideas in writing so others will understand. Oral Comprehension—The ability to listen to and understand information and ideas presented verbally.

Skills: Active Listening—Listening to what other people are saying; asking questions as appropriate. Speaking—Talking to others to effectively convey information. Information Gathering—Knowing how to find information and identifying essential information. Reading Comprehension—Understanding written information in work-related documents. Mathematics—Using mathematics to solve problems.

Generalized Work Activities: Getting Information Needed to Do the Job—Observing, receiving, and otherwise obtaining information from all relevant sources. Evaluating Information against Standards—Evaluating information against a set of standards and verifying that it is correct. Performing for/Working with Public—Performing for people or dealing directly with the public, including serving persons in restaurants and stores and receiving clients or guests. Documenting/Recording Information—Entering, transcribing, recording, storing, or maintaining information in either written form or by electronic/magnetic recording. Communicating with Persons Outside Organization—Communicating with persons outside the organization. Representing the organization to customers, the public, government, and other external sources. Exchanging information face-to-face, in writing, or via telephone/electronic transfer.

Licensed Practical Nurses

- ▲ Growth: 20%
- ▲ Annual Job Openings: 43,314
- ▲ Yearly Earnings: $26,940
- ▲ Education Required: Postsecondary vocational training
- ▲ Self-Employed: 0.6%
- ▲ Part-Time: 22.1%

Licensed Practical and Licensed Vocational Nurses

Care for ill, injured, convalescent, or disabled persons in hospitals, nursing homes, clinics, private homes, group homes, and similar institutions. Work under the supervision of a registered nurse. Licensing required. Sterilizes equipment and supplies, using germicides, sterilizer, or autoclave. Observes patients and reports adverse reactions to medication or treatment to medical personnel in charge. Provides medical treatment and personal care to patients in private home settings. Takes and records patients' vital signs. Bathes, dresses, and assists patients in walking and turning. Inventories and requisitions supplies. Assembles and uses such equipment as catheters, tracheotomy tubes, and oxygen suppliers. Collects samples, such as urine, blood, and sputum, from patients for testing and performs routine laboratory tests on samples. Prepares or examines food trays for prescribed diet and feeds patients. Assists in delivery, care, and feeding of infants. Cleans rooms, makes beds, and answers patients' calls. Applies compresses, ice bags, and hot water bottles. Dresses wounds, gives enemas, douches, alcohol rubs, and massages. Administers specified medication, orally or by subcutaneous or intramuscular injection, and notes time and amount on patients' charts. Records food and fluid intake and output. Washes and dresses bodies of deceased persons.

Personality Type: Social. Social occupations frequently involve working with, communicating with, and teaching people. These occupations often involve helping or providing service to others.

Abilities: Oral Expression—The ability to communicate information and ideas verbally so others will understand. Oral Comprehension—The ability to listen to and understand information and ideas presented verbally. Problem Sensitivity—The ability to tell when something is wrong or is likely to go wrong. Does not involve solving the problem, only recognizing there is a problem. Arm-Hand Steadiness—The ability to keep the hand and arm steady while making an arm movement or while holding the arm and hand in one position. Near Vision—The ability to see details of objects at a close range.

Skills: Service Orientation—Actively looking for ways to help people. Active Listening—Listening to what other people are saying; asking questions as appropriate. Information Gathering—Knowing how to find information and identifying essential information. Reading Comprehension—Understanding written information in work-related documents. Problem Identification—Identifying the nature of problems.

Generalized Work Activities: Assisting and Caring for Others—Providing assistance or personal care to others. Performing General Physical Activities—Performing physical activities that require moving one's whole body, such as in climbing, lifting, balancing, walking, and stooping. Performing activities that often also require considerable use of the arms and legs, such as in the physical handling of materials. Monitoring Processes, Materials, Surroundings—Monitoring and reviewing information from materials, events, or the environment, often to detect problems or to find out when things are finished. Handling and Moving Objects—Using one's hands and arms in handling, installing, forming, positioning, and moving materials, or in manipulating things. Includes the use of keyboards. Documenting/

Recording Information—Entering, transcribing, recording, storing, or maintaining information in either written form or by electronic/magnetic recording. Communicating with Other Workers—Providing information to supervisors, fellow workers, and subordinates. Exchanging information face-to-face, in writing, or via telephone/electronic transfer.

Loan and Credit Clerks

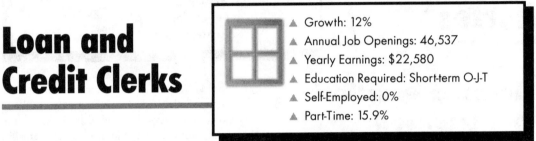

▲ Growth: 12%
▲ Annual Job Openings: 46,537
▲ Yearly Earnings: $22,580
▲ Education Required: Short-term O-J-T
▲ Self-Employed: 0%
▲ Part-Time: 15.9%

Loan Interviewers and Clerks

Interview loan applicants to elicit information, investigate applicants' backgrounds and verify references, prepare loan request papers and forward findings, reports, and documents to appraisal department. Review loan papers to ensure completeness, and complete transactions between loan establishment, borrowers, and sellers upon approval of loan. Accepts payment on accounts. Checks value of customer collateral to be held as loan security. Contacts credit bureaus, employers, and other sources to check applicant credit and personal references. Schedules and conducts closing of mortgage transaction. Presents loan and repayment schedule to customer. Establishes credit limit and grants extension of credit on overdue accounts. Files and maintains loan records. Orders property insurance or mortgage insurance policies to ensure protection against loss on mortgaged property. Submits loan application with recommendation for underwriting approval. Verifies and examines information and accuracy of loan application and closing documents. Answers questions and advises customer regarding loans and transactions. Contacts customer by mail, telephone, or in person concerning acceptance or rejection of application. Records applications for loan and credit, loan information, and disbursement of funds, using computer. Prepares and types loan applications, closing documents, legal documents, letters, forms, government notices, and checks, using computer. Assembles and compiles documents for closing, such as title abstract, insurance form, loan form, and tax receipt. Interviews loan applicant to obtain personal and financial data and to assist in filling out application. Reviews customer accounts to determine whether payments are made on time and that other loan terms are being followed. Calculates, reviews, and corrects errors on interest, principal, payment, and closing costs, using computer or calculator.

Personality Type: Conventional. Conventional occupations frequently involve following set procedures and routines. These occupations can include working with data and details more than with ideas. Usually there is a clear line of authority to follow.

Abilities: Number Facility—The ability to add, subtract, multiply, or divide quickly and correctly. Information Ordering—The ability to correctly follow a given rule or set of rules in order to arrange things or actions in a certain order. The things or actions can include numbers, letters, words, pictures, procedures, sentences, and mathematical or logical operations. Oral Expression—The ability to communicate information and ideas verbally so others will understand. Near Vision—The ability to see details of objects at a close range. Written Comprehension—The ability to read and understand information and ideas presented in writing.

Skills: Mathematics—Using mathematics to solve problems. Information Gathering—Knowing how to find information and identifying essential information. Reading Comprehension—Understanding written information in work-related documents. Active Listening—Listening to what other people are saying; asking questions as appropriate. Information Organization—Finding ways to structure or classify multiple pieces of information. Writing—Communicating effectively with others in writing as indicated by the needs of the audience.

Generalized Work Activities: Getting Information Needed to Do the Job—Observing, receiving, and otherwise obtaining information from all relevant sources. Evaluating Information against Standards—Evaluating information against a set of standards and verifying that it is correct. Processing Information—Compiling, coding, categorizing, calculating, tabulating, auditing, verifying, or processing information or data. Communicating with Persons Outside Organization—Communicating with persons outside the organization. Representing the organization to customers, the public, government, and other external sources. Exchanging information face-to-face, in writing, or via telephone/electronic transfer. Documenting/Recording Information—Entering, transcribing, recording, storing, or maintaining information in either written form or by electronic/magnetic recording. Performing Administrative Activities—Approving requests, handling paperwork, and performing day-to-day administrative tasks.

Loan Counselors and Officers

- ▲ Growth: 21%
- ▲ Annual Job Openings: 39,836
- ▲ Yearly Earnings: $35,340
- ▲ Education Required: Bachelor's degree
- ▲ Self-Employed: 0%
- ▲ Part-Time: 7.2%

Loan Counselors

Provide guidance to prospective loan applicants who have problems qualifying for traditional loans. Determine best type of loan for applicant and explain loan requirements or restrictions. Refers loan to loan committee for approval. Analyzes applicant's financial status, credit, and property evaluation to determine feasibility of granting loan. Interviews applicant and requests specified information for loan application. Approves loan within specified limits. Computes payment schedule. Ensures loan agreements are complete and accurate according to policy. Contacts applicant or creditors to resolve questions regarding application information. Analyzes potential loan markets to develop prospects for loans. Arranges for maintenance and liquidation of delinquent property. Negotiates payment arrangements with customers for delinquent loan balance. Supervises loan personnel. Petitions court to transfer title and deeds of collateral to bank. Submits application to credit analyst for verification and recommendation. Confers with underwriters to aid in resolving mortgage application problems.

Personality Type: Enterprising. Enterprising occupations frequently involve starting up and carrying out projects. These occupations can involve leading people and making many decisions. They sometimes require risk taking and often deal with business.

Abilities: Number Facility—The ability to add, subtract, multiply, or divide quickly and correctly. Written Comprehension—The ability to read and understand information and ideas presented in writing. Oral Expression—The ability to communicate information and ideas verbally so others will understand. Oral Comprehension—The ability to listen to and understand information and ideas presented verbally. Written Expression—The ability to communicate information and ideas in writing so others will understand.

Skills: Judgment and Decision Making—Weighing the relative costs and benefits of a potential action. Mathematics—Using mathematics to solve problems. Information Gathering—Knowing how to find information and identifying essential information. Speaking—Talking to others to effectively convey information. Active Listening—Listening to what other people are saying; asking questions as appropriate.

Generalized Work Activities: Analyzing Data or Information—Identifying underlying principles, reasons, or facts by breaking down information or data into separate parts. Evaluating Information against Standards—Evaluating information against a set of standards and verifying that it is correct. Getting Information Needed to Do the Job—Observing, receiving, and otherwise obtaining information from all relevant sources. Communicating with Other Workers—Providing information to supervisors, fellow workers, and subordinates. Exchanging information face-to-face, in writing, or via telephone/electronic transfer. Performing Administrative Activities—Approving requests, handling paperwork, and performing day-to-day administrative tasks.

Loan Officers

Evaluate, authorize, or recommend approval of commercial, real estate, or credit loans. Advise borrowers on financial status and methods of payments. Includes mortgage loan officers and agents, collection analysts, loan servicing officers, and loan underwriters. Analyzes potential loan markets to develop prospects for loans. Refers loan to loan committee for approval. Interviews applicant and requests specified information for loan application. Approves loan within specified limits. Contacts applicant or creditors to resolve questions regarding application information. Computes payment schedule. Petitions court to transfer title and deeds of collateral to bank. Supervises loan personnel. Arranges for maintenance and liquidation of delinquent property. Confers with underwriters to aid in resolving mortgage application problems. Submits application to credit analyst for verification and recommendation. Ensures loan agreements are complete and accurate according to policy. Analyzes applicant's financial status, credit, and property evaluation to determine feasibility of granting loan. Negotiates payment arrangements with customers for delinquent loan balance.

Personality Type: Enterprising. Enterprising occupations frequently involve starting up and carrying out projects. These occupations can involve leading people and making many decisions. They sometimes require risk taking and often deal with business.

Abilities: Written Comprehension—The ability to read and understand information and ideas presented in writing. Number Facility—The ability to add, subtract, multiply, or divide quickly and correctly. Oral Expres-sion—The ability to communicate information and ideas verbally so others will understand. Oral Comprehension—The ability to listen to and understand information and ideas presented verbally. Written Expression—The ability to communicate information and ideas in writing so others will understand.

Skills: Judgment and Decision Making—Weighing the relative costs and benefits of a potential action. Mathematics—Using mathematics to solve problems. Speaking—Talking to others to effectively convey information. Information Gathering—Knowing how to find information and identifying essential information. Active Listening—Listening to what other people are saying; asking questions as appropriate.

Generalized Work Activities: Analyzing Data or Information—Identifying underlying principles, reasons, or facts by breaking down information or data into separate parts. Evaluating Information against Standards—Evaluating information against a set of standards and verifying that it is correct. Getting Information Needed to Do the Job—Observing, receiving, and otherwise obtaining information from all relevant sources. Performing Administrative Activities—Approving requests, handling paperwork, and performing day-to-day administrative tasks. Communicating with Other Workers—Providing information to supervisors, fellow workers, and subordinates. Exchanging information face-to-face, in writing, or via telephone/electronic transfer.

Locksmiths and Safe Repairers

- ▲ Growth: 10%
- ▲ Annual Job Openings: 4,557
- ▲ Yearly Earnings: $24,890
- ▲ Education Required: Moderate-term O-J-T
- ▲ Self-Employed: 30.8%
- ▲ Part-Time: 7.5%

Locksmiths and Safe Repairers

Repair and open locks, make keys, change locks and safe combinations, and install and repair safes. Keeps record of company locks and keys. Installs safes, vault doors, and deposit boxes according to blueprints, using equipment such as powered drills, taps, dies, truck crane, and dolly. Cuts new or duplicate keys, using keycutting machine. Repairs and adjusts safes, vault doors, and vault components, using hand tools, lathes, drill presses, and welding and acetylene cutting apparatus. Removes interior and exterior finishes on safes and vaults and sprays on new finishes. Opens safe locks by drilling. Moves picklock in cylinder to open door locks without keys. Disassembles mechanical or electrical locking devices and repairs or replaces worn tumblers, springs, and other parts, using hand tools. Inserts new or repaired tumblers into lock to change combination.

Personality Type: Realistic. Realistic occupations frequently involve work activities that include practical, hands-on problems and solutions. They often deal with plants, animals, and real-world materials like wood, tools, and machinery. Many of the occupations require working outside and do not involve a lot of paperwork or working closely with others.

Abilities: Arm-Hand Steadiness—The ability to keep the hand and arm steady while making an arm movement or while holding the arm and hand in one position. Wrist-Finger Speed—The ability to make fast, simple, repeated movements of the fingers, hands, and wrists. Manual Dexterity—The ability to quickly make coordinated movements of one hand, a hand together with its arm, or two hands, to grasp, manipulate, or assemble objects. Finger Dexterity—The ability to make precisely coordinated movements of the fingers of one or both hands to grasp, manipulate, or assemble very small objects. Information Ordering—The ability to correctly follow a given rule or set of rules in order to arrange things or actions in a certain order. The things or actions can include numbers, letters, words, pictures, procedures, sentences, and mathematical or logical operations. Written Comprehension—The ability to read and understand information and ideas presented in writing.

Skills: Installation—Installing equipment, machines, wiring, or programs to meet specifications. Repairing—Repairing machines or systems, using the needed tools. Equipment Selection—Determining the kind of tools and equipment needed to do a job. Troubleshooting—Determining what is causing an operating error and deciding what to do about it. Problem Identification—Identifying the nature of problems.

Generalized Work Activities: Repairing and Maintaining Mechanical Equipment—Fixing, servicing, aligning, setting up, adjusting, and testing machines, devices, moving parts, and equipment that operate primarily on the basis of mechanical, not electronic, principles. Handling and Moving Objects—Using one's hands and arms in handling, installing, forming, positioning, and moving materials, or in manipulating things. Inspecting Equipment, Structures, Materials—Inspecting or diagnosing equipment, structures, or materials to identify the causes of errors or other problems or defects. Getting Information Needed to Do the Job—Observing, receiving, and otherwise obtaining information from all relevant sources. Performing General Physical Activities—Performing physical activities that require moving one's whole body, such as in climbing, lifting, balancing, walking, and stooping. Performing activities that often also require considerable use of the arms and legs, such as in the physical handling of materials.

Mail Clerks

- ▲ Growth: 10%
- ▲ Annual Job Openings: 26,426
- ▲ Yearly Earnings: $17,660
- ▲ Education Required: Short-term O-J-T
- ▲ Self-Employed: 0.8%
- ▲ Part-Time: 24.3%

Mail Clerks, Except Mail Machine Operators and Postal Service

Prepare incoming and outgoing mail for distribution. Duties include time stamping, opening, reading, sorting, and routing incoming mail; sealing, stamping, and affixing postage to outgoing mail or packages. Weighs packages or letters, computes charges, and accepts payment, using weight scale and rate chart. Wraps packages or bundles by hand or using tying machine. Inspects wrapping, address, and appearance of outgoing package or letter for conformance to standards, and accuracy. Receives request for merchandise samples or promotional literature, prepares shipping slips, and mails samples or literature. Answers inquiries regarding shipping or mailing policies. Stacks bundles of bulk printed matter for shipment, and loads and unloads from trucks and conveyors. Addresses packages or letters by hand, or using addressing machine, label, or stamp. Records and maintains records of information such as charges and destination of insured, registered or c.o.d. packages. Affixes postage to packages or letter by hand, or stamps with postage meter, and dispatches mail. Seals or opens envelopes by hand or machine. Stamps date and time of receipt of incoming mail, and distributes and collects mail. Sorts letters or packages into sacks or bins, and places identifying tag on sack or bin, according to destination and type.

Releases packages or letters to customer upon presentation of written notice or other identification.

Personality Type: Conventional. Conventional occupations frequently involve following set procedures and routines. These occupations can include working with data and details more than with ideas. Usually there is a clear line of authority to follow.

Abilities: Perceptual Speed—The ability to quickly and accurately compare letters, numbers, objects, pictures, or patterns. The things to be compared may be presented at the same time or one after the other. Includes comparing a presented object with a remembered object. Near Vision—The ability to see details of objects at a close range. Wrist-Finger Speed—The ability to make fast, simple, repeated movements of the fingers, hands, and wrists. Number Facility—The ability to add, subtract, multiply, or divide quickly and correctly. Written Comprehension—The ability to read and understand information and ideas presented in writing.

Skills: Writing—Communicating effectively with others in writing as indicated by the needs of the audience. Product Inspection—Inspecting and evaluating the quality of products. Information Organization—Finding ways to structure or classify multiple pieces of information. Mathematics—Using mathematics to solve problems. Problem Identification—Identifying the nature of problems.

Generalized Work Activities: Handling and Moving Objects—Using one's hands and arms in handling, installing, forming, positioning, and moving materials, or in manipulating things. Includes the use of keyboards. Performing General Physical Activities—Performing physical activities that require moving one's whole body, such as in climbing, lifting, balancing, walking, and stooping. Performing activities that often also require considerable use of the arms and legs, such as in the physical handling of materials. Documenting/Recording Information—Entering, transcribing, recording, storing, or maintaining information in either written form or by electronic/magnetic recording. Processing Information—Compiling, coding, categorizing, calculating, tabulating, auditing, verifying, or processing information or data. Evaluating Information against Standards—Evaluating information against a set of standards and verifying that it is correct. Getting Information Needed to Do the Job—Observing, receiving, and otherwise obtaining information from all relevant sources.

Management Analysts

▲ Growth: 28%

▲ Annual Job Openings: 23,831

▲ Yearly Earnings: $49,470

▲ Education Required: Master's degree

▲ Self-Employed: 46.4%

▲ Part-Time: 19.5%

Management Analysts

Conduct organizational studies and evaluations, design systems and procedures, conduct work simplifications and measurement studies, and prepare operations and procedures manuals to assist management in operating more efficiently and effectively. Includes program analysts and management consultants. Recommends purchase of storage equipment and designs area layout to locate equipment in space available. Interviews personnel and conducts on-site observation to ascertain unit functions, work performed, and methods, equipment, and personnel used. Designs, evaluates, recommends, and approves changes of forms and reports. Plans study of work problems and procedures, such as organizational change, communications, information flow, integrated production methods, inventory control, or cost analysis. Confers with personnel concerned to ensure successful functioning of newly implemented systems or procedures. Analyzes data gathered and develops solutions or alternative methods of proceeding. Gathers and organizes information on problems or procedures. Prepares manuals and trains workers in use of new forms, reports, procedures or equipment, according to organizational policy. Develops and implements records management program for filing, protection, and retrieval of records, and assures compliance with program. Reviews forms and reports, and confers with management and users about format, distribution, and purpose, to identify problems and improvements. Documents findings of study and prepares recommendations for implementation of new systems, procedures, or organizational changes.

Personality Type: Enterprising. Enterprising occupations frequently involve starting up and carrying out projects. These occupations can involve leading people and making many decisions. They sometimes require risk taking and often deal with business.

Abilities: Oral Expression—The ability to communicate information and ideas verbally so others will understand. Speech Clarity—The ability to speak clearly so that what is said is understandable to a listener. Written Expression—The ability to communicate information and ideas in writing so others will understand. Problem Sensitivity—The ability to tell when something is wrong or is likely to go wrong. Does not involve solving the problem, only recognizing there is a problem. Oral Comprehension—The ability to listen to and understand information and ideas presented verbally. Written Comprehension—The ability to read and understand information and ideas presented in writing.

Skills: Writing—Communicating effectively with others in writing as indicated by the needs of the audience. Reading Comprehension—Understanding written information in work-related documents. Identification of Key Causes—Identifying the things that must be changed to achieve a goal. Speaking—Talking to others to effectively convey information. Information Gathering—Knowing how to find information and identifying essential information.

Generalized Work Activities: Providing Consultation and Advice to Others—Providing consultation and expert advice to management or other groups on technical, systems-related, or process-related topics.

Getting Information Needed to Do the Job—Observing, receiving, and otherwise obtaining information from all relevant sources. Communicating with Other Workers—Providing information to supervisors, fellow workers, and subordinates. Exchanging information face-to-face, in writing, or via telephone/electronic transfer. Implementing Ideas and Programs—Conducting or carrying out work procedures and activities in accord with one's own ideas or information provided through directions/instructions for purposes of installing, modifying, preparing, delivering, constructing, integrating, finishing, or completing programs, systems, structures, or products. Analyzing Data or Information—Identifying underlying principles, reasons, or facts by breaking down information or data into separate parts.

Manicurists

- ▲ Growth: 26%
- ▲ Annual Job Openings: 7,081
- ▲ Yearly Earnings: $13,480
- ▲ Education Required: Postsecondary vocational training
- ▲ Self-Employed: 37.3%
- ▲ Part-Time: 36.5%

Manicurists and Pedicurists

Clean and shape customers' fingernails and toenails. Polish or decorate nails. Removes paper forms and shapes and smoothes edges of nails, using rotary abrasive wheel. Removes previously applied nail polish using liquid remover and swabs. Cleans customers' nails in soapy water, using swabs, files, and orange sticks. Forms artificial fingernails on customer's fingers. Polishes nails using powdered polish and buffer. Brushes coats of powder and solvent onto nails and paper forms with handbrush to maintain nail appearance and to extend nails to desired length. Whitens underside of nails with white paste or pencil. Softens nail cuticles with water and oil, pushes back cuticles using cuticle knife, and trims cuticles using scissors or nippers. Attaches paper forms to tips of customer's fingers to support and shape artificial nails. Roughens surfaces of fingernails using abrasive wheel. Shapes and smoothes ends of nails using scissors, files, and emery boards. Applies clear or colored liquid polish onto nails with brush.

Personality Type: Enterprising. Enterprising occupations frequently involve starting up and carrying out projects. These occupations can involve leading people and making many decisions. They sometimes require risk taking and often deal with business.

Abilities: Wrist-Finger Speed—The ability to make fast, simple, repeated movements of the fingers, hands, and wrists. Finger Dexterity—The ability to make precisely coordinated movements of the fingers of one or both hands to grasp, manipulate, or assemble very small objects. Near Vision—The ability to see details of objects at a close range. Arm-Hand Steadiness—The ability to keep the hand and arm steady while making an arm movement or while holding the arm and hand in one position. Manual Dexterity—The ability to quickly make coordinated movements of one hand, a hand together with its arm, or two hands, to grasp, manipulate, or assemble objects. Visual Color Discrimination—The ability to match or detect differences between colors, including shades of color and brightness.

Skills: Equipment Selection—Determining the kind of tools and equipment needed to do a job. Product Inspection—Inspecting and evaluating the quality of products. Time Management—Managing one's own time and the time of others. Active Listening—Listening to what other people are saying; asking questions as appropriate. Speaking—Talking to others to effectively convey information. Social Perceptiveness—Being aware of other people's reactions and understanding why people react the way they do.

Generalized Work Activities: Performing for/Working with Public—Performing for people or dealing directly with the public, including serving persons in restaurants and stores and receiving clients or guests. Handling and Moving Objects—Using one's hands and arms in handling, installing, forming, positioning, and moving materials, or in manipulating things. Establishing and Maintaining Relationships—Developing constructive and cooperative working relationships with others. Getting Information Needed to Do the Job— Observing, receiving, and otherwise obtaining information from all relevant sources. Assisting and Caring for Others—Providing assistance or personal care to others.

Marketing and Sales Worker Supervisors

- ▲ Growth: 10%
- ▲ Annual Job Openings: 410,550
- ▲ Yearly Earnings: $29,570
- ▲ Education Required: Work experience in a related occupation
- ▲ Self-Employed: 36.9%
- ▲ Part-Time: 8.2%

First-Line Supervisors/ Managers of Non-Retail Sales Workers

Directly supervise and coordinate activities of sales workers other than retail sales workers. Perform duties such as budgeting, accounting, and personnel work, in addition to supervisory duties. Examines merchandise to ensure that it is correctly priced, displayed, or functions as advertised. Plans and prepares work schedules and assigns employees to specific duties. Coordinates sales promotion activities and prepares merchandise displays and advertising copy. Prepares sales and inventory reports for management and budget departments. Keeps records pertaining to purchases, sales, and requisitions. Listens to and resolves customer complaints regarding service, product, or personnel. Hires, trains, and evaluates personnel in sales or marketing establishment. Inventories stock and reorders when inventories drop to specified level. Formulates pricing policies on merchandise according to requirements for profitability of store operations. Assists sales staff in completing complicated and difficult sales. Confers with company officials to develop methods and procedures to increase sales, expand markets, and promote business. Directs and supervises employees engaged in sales, inventory-taking, reconciling cash receipts, or performing specific service such as pumping gasoline for customers. Prepares rental or lease agreement, specifying charges and payment procedures, for use of machinery, tools, or other such items. Examines products purchased for resale or received for storage to determine condition of product or item.

Personality Type: Enterprising. Enterprising occupations frequently involve starting up and carrying out projects. These occupations can involve leading people and making many decisions. They sometimes require risk taking and often deal with business.

Abilities: Oral Expression—The ability to communicate information and ideas verbally so others will understand. Oral Comprehension—The ability to listen to and understand information and ideas presented verbally. Written Comprehension—The ability to read and understand information and ideas presented in writing. Written Expression—The ability to communicate information and ideas in writing so others will understand. Originality—The ability to come up with unusual or clever ideas about a given topic or situation, or to develop creative ways to solve a problem. Deductive Reasoning—The ability to apply general rules to specific problems to come up with logical answers. Involves deciding if an answer makes sense.

Skills: Critical Thinking—Using logic and analysis to identify the strengths and weaknesses of different approaches. Information Gathering—Knowing how to find information and identifying essential information. Speaking—Talking to others to effectively convey information. Coordination—Adjusting actions in relation to others' actions. Judgment and Decision Making—Weighing the relative costs and benefits of a potential action. Identification of Key Causes—Identifying the things that must be changed to achieve a goal.

Generalized Work Activities: Scheduling Work and Activities—Scheduling events, programs, activities, and the work of others. Monitoring and Controlling Resources—Monitoring and controlling resources and overseeing the spending of money. Communicating with Other Workers—Providing information to supervisors, fellow workers, and subordinates. Exchanging information face-to-face, in writing, or via telephone/electronic transfer. Staffing Organizational Units—Recruiting, interviewing, selecting, hiring, and promoting persons for the organization. Analyzing Data or Information—Identifying underlying principles, reasons, or facts by breaking down information or data into separate parts. Coordinating Work and Activities of Others—Coordinating members of a work group to accomplish tasks.

First-Line Supervisors/ Managers of Retail Sales Workers

Directly supervise sales workers in a retail establishment or department. Perform management functions such as purchasing, budgeting, accounting, and personnel work, in addition to supervisory duties. Examines products purchased for resale or received for storage to determine condition of product or item. Keeps records of employees' work schedules and time cards. Listens to and resolves customer complaints regarding service, product, or personnel. Keeps records pertaining to purchases, sales, and requisitions. Examines merchandise to ensure that it is correctly priced, displayed or functions as advertised. Formulates pricing policies on merchandise according to requirements for profitability of store operations. Prepares rental or lease agreement, specifying charges and payment procedures, for use of machinery, tools, or other such items. Prepares sales and inventory reports for management and budget departments. Assists sales staff in completing complicated and difficult sales. Confers with company officials to develop methods and procedures to increase sales, expand markets, and promote business. Hires, trains, and evaluates personnel in sales or marketing establishment. Plans and prepares work schedules and assigns employees to specific duties. Coordinates sales promotion activities and prepares merchandise displays and advertising copy. Directs and supervises employees engaged in sales, inventory-taking, reconciling cash receipts, or performing specific service such as pumping gasoline for customers. Inventories stock and reorders when inventories drop to specified level.

Personality Type: Enterprising. Enterprising occupations frequently involve starting up and carrying out projects. These occupations can involve leading people and making many decisions. They sometimes require risk taking and often deal with business.

Abilities: Oral Expression—The ability to communicate information and ideas verbally so others will understand. Oral Comprehension—The ability to listen to and understand information and ideas presented verbally.

Written Comprehension—The ability to read and understand information and ideas presented in writing. Written Expression—The ability to communicate information and ideas in writing so others will understand. Originality—The ability to come up with unusual or clever ideas about a given topic or situation, or to develop creative ways to solve a problem. Deductive Reasoning—The ability to apply general rules to specific problems to come up with logical answers. Involves deciding if an answer makes sense.

Skills: Critical Thinking—Using logic and analysis to identify the strengths and weaknesses of different approaches. Information Gathering—Knowing how to find information and identifying essential information. Speaking—Talking to others to effectively convey information. Judgment and Decision Making—Weighing the relative costs and benefits of a potential action. Identification of Key Causes—Identifying the

things that must be changed to achieve a goal. Coordination—Adjusting actions in relation to others' actions.

Generalized Work Activities: Scheduling Work and Activities—Scheduling events, programs, activities, and the work of others. Monitoring and Controlling Resources—Monitoring and controlling resources and overseeing the spending of money. Staffing Organizational Units—Recruiting, interviewing, selecting, hiring, and promoting persons for the organization. Communicating with Other Workers—Providing information to supervisors, fellow workers, and subordinates. Exchanging information face-to-face, in writing, or via telephone/electronic transfer. Analyzing Data or Information—Identifying underlying principles, reasons, or facts by breaking down information or data into separate parts. Coordinating Work and Activities of Others—Coordinating members of a work group to accomplish tasks.

Materials Engineers

- ▲ Growth: 9%
- ▲ Annual Job Openings: 1,567
- ▲ Yearly Earnings: $57,970
- ▲ Education Required: Bachelor's degree
- ▲ Self-Employed: 5.4%
- ▲ Part-Time: 3.1%

Materials Engineers

Evaluate materials and develop machinery and processes to manufacture materials for use in products that must meet specialized design and performance specifications. Develop new uses for known materials. Includes those working with composite materials or specializing in one type of material, such as graphite, metal and metal alloys, ceramics and glass, plastics and polymers, and naturally occurring materials. Evaluates technical and economic factors relating to process or product design objectives. Confers with producers of material during investigation and evaluation of material for product applications. Reviews product failure data and interprets laboratory test results to determine material or process causes. Plans and

implements laboratory operations to develop material and fabrication procedures that maintain cost and performance standards. Reviews new product plans and makes recommendations for material selection based on design objectives and cost.

Personality Type: Investigative. Investigative occupations frequently involve working with ideas and require an extensive amount of thinking. These occupations can involve searching for facts and figuring out problems mentally.

Abilities: Oral Expression—The ability to communicate information and ideas verbally so others will understand. Deductive Reasoning—The ability to apply general rules to specific problems to come up with logical answers. Involves deciding if an answer makes sense.

Problem Sensitivity—The ability to tell when something is wrong or is likely to go wrong. Does not involve solving the problem, only recognizing there is a problem. Written Comprehension—The ability to read and understand information and ideas presented in writing. Written Expression—The ability to communicate information and ideas in writing so others will understand. Inductive Reasoning—The ability to combine separate pieces of information, or specific answers to problems, to form general rules or conclusions. Includes coming up with a logical explanation for why a series of seemingly unrelated events occur together.

Skills: Judgment and Decision Making—Weighing the relative costs and benefits of a potential action. Operations Analysis—Analyzing needs and product requirements to create a design. Science—Using scientific methods to solve problems. Mathematics—Using mathematics to solve problems. Critical Thinking—Using logic and analysis to identify the strengths and weaknesses of different approaches. Information Gathering—Knowing how to find information and identifying essential information. Technology Design—Generating or adapting equipment and technology to serve user needs.

Generalized Work Activities: Getting Information Needed to Do the Job—Observing, receiving, and otherwise obtaining information from all relevant sources. Identifying Objects, Actions, and Events—Identifying information received by making estimates or categorizations, recognizing differences or similarities, or sensing changes in circumstances or events. Making Decisions and Solving Problems—Combining, evaluating, and analyzing information and data to make decisions and solve problems. Involves making decisions about the relative importance of information and choosing the best solution. Implementing Ideas and Programs—Conducting or carrying out work procedures and activities in accord with one's own ideas or information provided through directions/instructions for purposes of installing, modifying, preparing, delivering, constructing, integrating, finishing, or completing programs, systems, structures, or products.

Mathematicians

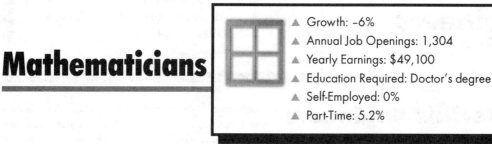

- ▲ Growth: –6%
- ▲ Annual Job Openings: 1,304
- ▲ Yearly Earnings: $49,100
- ▲ Education Required: Doctor's degree
- ▲ Self-Employed: 0%
- ▲ Part-Time: 5.2%

Mathematicians

Conduct research in fundamental mathematics or in application of mathematical techniques to science, management, and other fields. Solve or direct solutions to problems in various fields by mathematical methods. Conducts research in such branches of mathematics as algebra, geometry, number theory, logic and topology. Applies mathematics or mathematical methods of numerical analysis, and operates or directs operation of desk calculators and mechanical and other functional areas. Utilizes knowledge of such subjects or

fields as physics, engineering, astronomy, biology, economics, business and industrial management, or cryptography. Acts as advisor or consultant to research personnel concerning mathematical methods and applications. Performs computations and applies methods of numerical analysis. Conducts research in fundamental mathematics and in application of mathematical techniques to science, management and other fields. Studies and test hypotheses and alternative theories. Conceives or directs ideas for application of mathematics to wide variety of fields, including science, engineering, military planning, electronic data processing, and management. Operates or directs operation of desk calculators and mechanical and electronic computation machines, analyzers, and plotters in solving problem support of mathematical, scientific or industrial research.

Personality Type: Investigative. Investigative occupations frequently involve working with ideas and require an extensive amount of thinking. These occupations can involve searching for facts and figuring out problems mentally.

Abilities: Number Facility—The ability to add, subtract, multiply, or divide quickly and correctly. Mathematical Reasoning—The ability to understand and organize a problem and then select a mathematical method or formula to solve the problem. Deductive Reasoning—The ability to apply general rules to specific problems to come up with logical answers. Involves deciding if an answer makes sense. Written Comprehension—The ability to read and understand information and ideas presented in writing. Inductive Reasoning—The ability to combine separate pieces of information, or specific answers to problems, to form general rules or conclusions. Includes coming up with a logical explanation for why a series of seemingly unrelated events occur together. Oral Comprehension—The ability to listen to and understand information and ideas presented verbally.

Skills: Mathematics—Using mathematics to solve problems. Active Learning—Working with new material or information to grasp its implications. Learning Strategies—Using multiple approaches when learning or teaching new things. Reading Comprehension—Understanding written information in work-related documents.

Generalized Work Activities: Processing Information—Compiling, coding, categorizing, calculating, tabulating, auditing, verifying, or processing information or data. Analyzing Data or Information—Identifying underlying principles, reasons, or facts by breaking down information or data into separate parts. Getting Information Needed to Do the Job—Observing, receiving, and otherwise obtaining information from all relevant sources. Identifying Objects, Actions, and Events—Identifying information received by making estimates or categorizations, recognizing differences or similarities, or sensing changes in circumstances or events. Interacting with Computers—Controlling computer functions by using programs, setting up functions, writing software, or otherwise communicating with computer systems.

Meat, Poultry, and Fish Cutters and Trimmers

- ▲ Growth: 24%
- ▲ Annual Job Openings: 33,193
- ▲ Yearly Earnings: $16,270
- ▲ Education Required: Short-term O-J-T
- ▲ Self-Employed: 0%
- ▲ Part-Time: 8.6%

Meat, Poultry, and Fish Cutters and Trimmers

Use hand tools to perform routine cutting and trimming of meat, poultry, and fish. Weighs meats and tags containers for weight and contents. Seals containers of meat. Removes parts such as skin, feathers, scales or bones from carcass. Cuts and trims meat to prepare for packing. Inspects meat products for defects or blemishes. Trims, slices, and sections carcasses for future processing. Obtains and distributes specified meat or carcass. Slaughters live animals. Cleans carcasses and removes waste products or defective portions. Separates meats and byproducts into specified containers.

Personality Type: Realistic. Realistic occupations frequently involve work activities that include practical, hands-on problems and solutions. They often deal with plants, animals, and real-world materials like wood, tools, and machinery. Many of the occupations require working outside and do not involve a lot of paperwork or working closely with others.

Abilities: Information Ordering—The ability to correctly follow a given rule or set of rules in order to arrange things or actions in a certain order. The things or actions can include numbers, letters, words, pictures, procedures, sentences, and mathematical or logical operations. Wrist-Finger Speed—The ability to make fast, simple, repeated movements of the fingers, hands, and wrists. Static Strength—The ability to exert maximum muscle force to lift, push, pull, or carry objects. Manual Dexterity—The ability to quickly make coordinated movements of one hand, a hand together with its arm, or two hands, to grasp, manipulate, or assemble objects. Arm-Hand Steadiness—The ability to keep the hand and arm steady while making an arm movement or while holding the arm and hand in one position.

Skills: Product Inspection—Inspecting and evaluating the quality of products. Equipment Selection—Determining the kind of tools and equipment needed to do a job. Problem Identification—Identifying the

nature of problems. Operation and Control—Controlling operations of equipment or systems.

Generalized Work Activities: Handling and Moving Objects—Using one's hands and arms in handling, installing, forming, positioning, and moving materials, or in manipulating things. Judging Qualities—Making judgments about or assessing the value, importance, or quality of things, services, or other people's work. Performing General Physical Activities—Performing physical activities that require moving one's whole body, such as in climbing, lifting, balancing, walking, and stooping. Performing activities that often also require considerable use of the arms and legs, such as in the physical handling of materials. Monitoring Processes, Materials, Surroundings—Monitoring and reviewing information from materials, events, or the environment, often to detect problems or to find out when things are finished. Documenting/Recording Information—Entering, transcribing, recording, storing, or maintaining information in either written form or by electronic/magnetic recording. Inspecting Equipment, Structures, Materials—Inspecting or diagnosing equipment, structures, or materials to identify the causes of errors or other problems or defects. Identifying Objects, Actions, and Events—Identifying information received by making estimates or categorizations, recognizing differences or similarities, or sensing changes in circumstances or events.

Mechanical Engineers

- ▲ Growth: 16%
- ▲ Annual Job Openings: 9,388
- ▲ Yearly Earnings: $53,290
- ▲ Education Required: Bachelor's degree
- ▲ Self-Employed: 3.5%
- ▲ Part-Time: 2.1%

Mechanical Engineers

Perform engineering duties in planning and designing tools, engines, machines, and other mechanically functioning equipment. Oversee installation, operation, maintenance, and repair of such equipment

as centralized heat, gas, water, and steam systems. Selects or designs tools to meet specifications, using manuals, drafting tools, computer, and specialized software programs. Tests ability of machines to perform tasks. Develops models of alternate processing methods to test feasibility or new applications of system components, and recommends implementation of procedures. Confers with establishment personnel and engineers to implement operating procedures and resolve system malfunctions, and to provide technical information. Plans and directs engineering personnel in fabrication of test control apparatus and equipment, and develops procedures for testing products. Determines parts supply, maintenance tasks, safety procedures, and service schedule required to maintain machines and equipment in prescribed condition. Assists drafter in developing structural design of product, using drafting tools or computer-assisted design/drafting equipment and software. Researches and analyzes data, such as customer design proposal, specifications, and manuals to determine feasibility of design or application. Designs products and systems to meet process requirements, applying knowledge of engineering principles. Studies industrial processes to determine where and how application of equipment can be made. Specifies system components or directs modification of products to ensure conformance with engineering design and performance specifications. Oversees installation to ensure machines and equipment are installed and functioning according to specifications. Coordinates building, fabrication, and installation of product design and operation, maintenance, and repair activities to utilize machines and equipment. Inspects, evaluates, and arranges field installations and recommends design modifications to eliminate machine or system malfunctions. Investigates equipment failures and difficulties, diagnoses faulty operation, and makes recommendations to maintenance crew.

Personality Type: Realistic. Realistic occupations frequently involve work activities that include practical, hands-on problems and solutions. They often deal with plants, animals, and real-world materials like wood, tools, and machinery. Many of the occupations require working outside and do not involve a lot of paperwork or working closely with others.

Abilities: Mathematical Reasoning—The ability to understand and organize a problem and then select a mathematical method or formula to solve the problem. Deductive Reasoning—The ability to apply general rules to specific problems to come up with logical answers. Involves deciding if an answer makes sense. Written Comprehension—The ability to read and understand information and ideas presented in writing. Number Facility—The ability to add, subtract, multiply, or divide quickly and correctly. Near Vision—The ability to see details of objects at a close range.

Skills: Mathematics—Using mathematics to solve problems. Technology Design—Generating or adapting equipment and technology to serve user needs. Science—Using scientific methods to solve problems. Operations Analysis—Analyzing needs and product requirements to create a design.

Generalized Work Activities: Drafting and Specifying Technical Devices—Providing documentation, detailed instructions, drawings, or specifications to inform others about how devices, parts, equipment, or structures are to be fabricated, constructed, assembled, modified, maintained, or used. Getting Information Needed to Do the Job—Observing, receiving, and otherwise obtaining information from all relevant sources. Analyzing Data or Information—Identifying underlying principles, reasons, or facts by breaking down information or data into separate parts. Thinking Creatively—Originating, inventing, designing, or creating new applications, ideas, relationships, systems, or products, including artistic contributions. Inspecting Equipment, Structures, Materials—Inspecting or diagnosing equipment, structures, or materials to identify the causes of errors or other problems or defects. Interacting with Computers—Controlling computer functions by using programs, setting up functions, writing software, or otherwise communicating with computer systems.

Medical and Health Services Managers

- ▲ Growth: 33%
- ▲ Annual Job Openings: 31,238
- ▲ Yearly Earnings: $48,870
- ▲ Education Required: Work experience, plus degree
- ▲ Self-Employed: Not available
- ▲ Part-Time: Not available

Medical and Health Services Managers

Plan, direct, or coordinate medicine and health services in hospitals, clinics, managed care organizations, public health agencies, or similar organizations. Implements and administers programs and services for health care or medical facility. Inspects facilities for emergency readiness and compliance of access, safety, and sanitation regulations and recommends building or equipment modifications. Directs and coordinates activities of medical, nursing, technical, clerical, service, and maintenance personnel of health care facility or mobile unit. Develops organizational policies and procedures and establishes evaluative or operational criteria for facility or medical unit. Establishes work schedules and assignments for staff, according to workload, space, and equipment availability. Consults with medical, business, and community groups to discuss service problems, coordinate activities and plans, and promote health programs. Develops instructional materials and conducts in-service and community-based educational programs. Recruits, hires, and evaluates the performance of medical staff and auxiliary personnel. Administers fiscal operations, such as planning budgets, authorizing expenditures, and coordinating financial reporting. Prepares activity reports to inform management of the status and implementation plans of programs, services, and quality initiatives. Reviews and analyzes facility activities and data to aid planning and cash and risk management and to improve service utilization. Develops or expands medical programs or health services for research, rehabilitation, and community health promotion. Develops and maintains computerized records management system to store or process personnel, activity, or personnel data.

Personality Type: Enterprising. Enterprising occupations frequently involve starting up and carrying out projects. These occupations can involve leading people and making many decisions. They sometimes require risk taking and often deal with business.

Abilities: Oral Expression—The ability to communicate information and ideas verbally so others will understand. Oral Comprehension—The ability to listen to and understand information and ideas presented verbally. Written Expression—The ability to communicate information and ideas in writing so others will understand. Written Comprehension—The ability to read and understand information and ideas presented in writing. Speech Clarity—The ability to speak clearly so that what is said is understandable to a listener.

Skills: Management of Personnel Resources—Motivating, developing, and directing people as they work, identifying the best people for the job. Judgment and Decision Making—Weighing the relative costs and benefits of a potential action. Reading Comprehension—Understanding written information in work-related documents. Coordination—Adjusting actions in relation to others' actions. Management of Financial Resources—Determining how money will be spent to get the work done, and accounting for these expenditures. Speaking—Talking to others to effectively convey information. Writing—Communicating effectively with others in writing as indicated by the needs of the audience.

Generalized Work Activities: Communicating with Other Workers—Providing information to supervisors, fellow workers, and subordinates. Exchanging information face-to-face, in writing, or via telephone/electronic transfer. Guiding, Directing, and Motivating Subordinates—Providing guidance and direction to subordinates, including setting performance standards and monitoring subordinates. Staffing Organizational Units—Recruiting, interviewing, selecting, hiring, and promoting persons for the organization. Communicating with Persons Outside Organization—Communicating with persons outside the organization. Representing the organization to customers, the public, government, and other external sources. Exchanging information face-to-face, in writing, or via telephone/electronic transfer.

Medical Assistants

- ▲ Growth: 58%
- ▲ Annual Job Openings: 49,015
- ▲ Yearly Earnings: $20,680
- ▲ Education Required: Moderate-term O-J-T
- ▲ Self-Employed: 0%
- ▲ Part-Time: 22.9%

Medical Assistants

Perform administrative and certain clinical duties under the direction of physician. Schedule appointments, maintain medical records, prepare billing, and code for insurance purposes. Take and record vital signs and medical histories, prepare patients for examination, draw blood, and administer medications as directed by physician. Schedules appointments. Interviews patients, measures vital signs, weight, and height, and records information. Gives physiotherapy treatments, such as diathermy, galvanics, and hydrotherapy. Hands instruments and materials to physician. Inventories and orders medical supplies and materials. Lifts and turns patients. Completes insurance forms. Operates x ray, electrocardiograph (EKG), and other equipment to administer routine diagnostic tests. Receives payment for bills. Gives injections or treatments to patients. Performs routine laboratory tests. Contacts medical facility or department to schedule patients for tests. Computes and mails monthly statements to patients and records transactions. Cleans and sterilizes instruments. Prepares treatment rooms for examination of patients. Maintains medical records.

Personality Type: Social. Social occupations frequently involve working with, communicating with, and teaching people. These occupations often involve helping or providing service to others.

Abilities: Near Vision—The ability to see details of objects at a close range. Oral Comprehension—The ability to listen to and understand information and ideas presented verbally. Arm-Hand Steadiness—The ability to keep the hand and arm steady while making an arm movement or while holding the arm and hand in one position. Information Ordering—The ability to correctly follow a given rule or set of rules in order to arrange things or actions in a certain order. The things or actions can include numbers, letters, words, pictures, procedures, sentences, and mathematical or logical operations. Control Precision—The ability to quickly and repeatedly make precise adjustments in moving the controls of a machine or vehicle to exact positions.

Skills: Service Orientation—Actively looking for ways to help people. Writing—Communicating effectively with others·in writing as indicated by the needs of the audience. Active Listening—Listening to what other people are saying; asking questions as appropriate. Speaking—Talking to others to effectively convey information. Information Organization—Finding ways to structure or classify multiple pieces of information.

Generalized Work Activities: Assisting and Caring for Others—Providing assistance or personal care to others.

M

Evaluating Information against Standards—Evaluating information against a set of standards and verifying that it is correct. Communicating with Other Workers—Providing information to supervisors, fellow workers, and subordinates. Exchanging information face-to-face, in writing, or via telephone/electronic transfer. Performing General Physical Activities—Performing physical activities that require moving one's whole body, such as in climbing, lifting, balancing, walking, and stooping. Performing activities that often also require considerable use of the arms and legs, such as in the physical handling of materials. Processing Information—Compiling, coding, categorizing, calculating, tabulating, auditing, verifying, or processing information or data. Getting Information Needed to Do the Job—Observing, receiving, and otherwise obtaining information from all relevant sources.

Medical Equipment Repairers

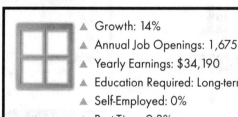

- ▲ Growth: 14%
- ▲ Annual Job Openings: 1,675
- ▲ Yearly Earnings: $34,190
- ▲ Education Required: Long-term O-J-T
- ▲ Self-Employed: 0%
- ▲ Part-Time: 9.3%

Medical Equipment Repairers

Test, adjust, or repair biomedical or electromedical equipment. Consults with medical or research staff to ensure that equipment functions properly and safely. Logs records of maintenance and repair work and approved updates of equipment as required by manufacturer. Repairs and replaces defective parts, such as motors, clutches, tubes, transformers, resistors, condensers, and switches, using hand tools. Disassembles malfunctioning equipment and removes defective components. Solders loose connections using soldering iron. Installs medical, dental, and related technical equipment in medical and research facilities. Inspects and tests malfunctioning medical and related equipment, using test and analysis instruments and following manufacturers' specifications. Cleans and lubricates equipment, using solvents, rags, and lubricants. Maintains various equipment and apparatus, such as patient monitors, electrocardiographs, x-ray units, defibrillators, electrosurgical units, anesthesia apparatus, pacemakers, and sterilizers. Safety-tests medical equipment and facility's structural environment to ensure patient and staff safety from electrical or mechanical hazards. Calibrates and adjusts components and equipment, using hand tools, power tools, measuring devices, and following manufacturers' manuals and troubleshooting techniques. Demonstrates and explains correct operation of equipment to medical personnel.

Personality Type: Realistic. Realistic occupations frequently involve work activities that include practical, hands-on problems and solutions. They often deal with plants, animals, and real-world materials like wood, tools, and machinery. Many of the occupations require working outside and do not involve a lot of paperwork or working closely with others.

Abilities: Deductive Reasoning—The ability to apply general rules to specific problems to come up with logical answers. Involves deciding if an answer makes sense. Problem Sensitivity—The ability to tell when something is wrong or is likely to go wrong. Does not involve solving the problem, only recognizing there is a problem. Near Vision—The ability to see details of objects at a close range. Oral Expression—The ability to communicate information and ideas verbally so others will understand. Control Precision—The ability to quickly and repeatedly make precise adjustments in moving the controls of a machine or vehicle to exact positions. Finger Dexterity—The ability to make precisely coordinated movements of the fingers of one or both hands to grasp, manipulate, or assemble very small objects. Speech Clarity—The ability to speak clearly so that what is said is understandable to a listener. Manual Dexterity—The ability to quickly make coordinated movements of one hand, a hand together with its arm, or two hands, to grasp, manipulate, or assemble objects.

Skills: Repairing—Repairing machines or systems, using the needed tools. Equipment Maintenance—Performing routine maintenance and determining when and what kind of maintenance is needed. Testing—Conducting tests to determine whether equipment, software, or procedures are operating as expected. Troubleshooting—Determining what is causing an operating error and deciding what to do about it.

Generalized Work Activities: Repairing and Maintaining Electrical Equipment—Fixing, servicing, adjusting, regulating, calibrating, fine-tuning, or testing machines, devices, and equipment that operate primarily on the basis of electrical or electronic, not mechanical, principles. Inspecting Equipment, Structures, Materials—Inspecting or diagnosing equipment, structures, or materials to identify the causes of errors or other problems or defects. Getting Information Needed to Do the Job—Observing, receiving, and otherwise obtaining information from all relevant sources. Repairing and Maintaining Mechanical Equipment—Fixing, servicing, aligning, setting up, adjusting, and testing machines, devices, moving parts, and equipment that operate primarily on the basis of mechanical, not electronic, principles. Handling and Moving Objects—Using one's hands and arms in handling, installing, forming, positioning, and moving materials, or in manipulating things. Includes the use of keyboards. Monitoring Processes, Materials, Surroundings—Monitoring and reviewing information from materials, events, or the environment, often to detect problems or to find out when things are finished.

Medical Records and Health Information Technicians

- ▲ Growth: 44%
- ▲ Annual Job Openings: 11,453
- ▲ Yearly Earnings: $20,590
- ▲ Education Required: Associate degree
- ▲ Self-Employed: 0%
- ▲ Part-Time: 22.9%

Medical Records and Health Information Technicians

Compile, process, and maintain medical records of hospital and clinic patients in a manner consistent with medical, administrative, ethical, legal, and regulatory requirements of the health care system. Process, maintain, compile, and report patient information for health requirements and standards. Enters data, such as demographic characteristics, history and extent of disease, diagnostic procedures and treatment into computer. Compiles medical care and census data for statistical reports on diseases treated, surgery performed, and use of hospital beds. Reviews records for completeness and to abstract and code data, using standard classification systems, and to identify and compile patient data. Assists in special studies or research as needed. Prepares statistical reports, narrative reports, and graphic presentations of tumor registry data for use by hospital staff, researchers, and others. Maintains variety of health record indexes and storage and retrieval systems. Compiles and maintains medical records of patients to document condition and treatment and to provide data for research studies. Contacts discharged patients, their families, and physicians to maintain registry with follow-up information, such as quality of life and length of survival of cancer patients.

Personality Type: Conventional. Conventional occupations frequently involve following set procedures and routines. These occupations can include working with data and details more than with ideas. Usually there is a clear line of authority to follow.

Abilities: Written Comprehension—The ability to read and understand information and ideas presented in writing. Written Expression—The ability to communicate information and ideas in writing so others will understand. Oral Comprehension—The ability to listen to and understand information and ideas presented verbally. Near Vision—The ability to see details of objects at a close range. Information Ordering—The ability to correctly follow a given rule or set of rules in order to arrange things or actions in a certain order. The things or actions can include numbers, letters, words, pictures, procedures, sentences, and mathematical or logical operations. Mathematical Reasoning—The ability to understand and organize a problem and then select a mathematical method or formula to solve the problem.

Skills: Information Organization—Finding ways to structure or classify multiple pieces of information.

Information Gathering—Knowing how to find information and identifying essential information. Reading Comprehension—Understanding written information in work-related documents. Synthesis/Reorganization—Reorganizing information to get a better approach to problems or tasks. Writing—Communicating effectively with others in writing as indicated by the needs of the audience.

Generalized Work Activities: Documenting/Recording Information—Entering, transcribing, recording, storing, or maintaining information in either written form or by electronic/magnetic recording. Processing Information—Compiling, coding, categorizing, calculating, tabulating, auditing, verifying, or processing information or data. Interacting with Computers—Controlling computer functions by using programs, setting up functions, writing software, or otherwise communicating with computer systems. Getting Information Needed to Do the Job—Observing, receiving, and otherwise obtaining information from all relevant sources. Evaluating Information against Standards—Evaluating information against a set of standards and verifying that it is correct. Identifying Objects, Actions, and Events—Identifying information received by making estimates or categorizations, recognizing differences or similarities, or sensing changes in circumstances or events.

Medical Scientists

- ▲ Growth: 25%
- ▲ Annual Job Openings: 3,214
- ▲ Yearly Earnings: $50,410
- ▲ Education Required: Doctor's degree
- ▲ Self-Employed: 2.8%
- ▲ Part-Time: 6.6%

Epidemiologists

Investigate and describe the determinants and distribution of disease, disability, and other health outcomes, and develop the means for prevention and control. Plans methodological design of research study and arranges for data collection. Supervises activities of clerical and statistical or laboratory personnel. Conducts research to develop methodologies, instrumentation, or identification, diagnosing, and treatment procedures for medical application. Examines organs, tissues, cell structures, or microorganisms by systematic observation or using microscope. Prepares and analyzes samples for toxicity, bacteria, or microorganisms or to study cell structure and properties. Standardizes drug dosages, methods of immunization, and procedures for manufacture of drugs and medicinal compounds. Studies effects of drugs, gases, pesticides, parasites, or microorganisms, or health and physiological processes of animals and humans. Teaches principles of medicine and medical and laboratory procedures to physicians, residents, students, and technicians. Consults with and advises physicians, educators, researchers, and others regarding medical applications of sciences, such as physics, biology, and chemistry. Analyzes data, applying statistical techniques and scientific knowledge, prepares reports, and presents findings. Investigates cause, progress, life cycle, or mode of transmission of diseases or parasites. Plans and directs studies to investigate human or animal disease, preventive methods, and treatments for disease. Confers with health department, industry personnel, physicians, and others to develop health safety standards and programs to improve public health.

Personality Type: Investigative. Investigative occupations frequently involve working with ideas and require an extensive amount of thinking. These occupations can involve searching for facts and figuring out problems mentally.

Abilities: Oral Expression—The ability to communicate information and ideas verbally so others will understand. Speech Clarity—The ability to speak clearly so that what is said is understandable to a listener. Inductive Reasoning—The ability to combine separate pieces of information, or specific answers to problems, to form general rules or conclusions. Includes coming up with a logical explanation for why a series of seemingly unrelated events occur together. Oral Comprehension—The ability to listen to and understand information and ideas presented verbally. Written Expression—The ability to communicate information and ideas in writing so others will understand.

Skills: Active Learning—Working with new material or information to grasp its implications. Science—Using

scientific methods to solve problems. Idea Evaluation—Evaluating the likely success of an idea in relation to the demands of the situation. Information Gathering—Knowing how to find information and identifying essential information. Critical Thinking—Using logic and analysis to identify the strengths and weaknesses of different approaches. Instructing—Teaching others how to do something. Speaking—Talking to others to effectively convey information.

Generalized Work Activities: Getting Information Needed to Do the Job—Observing, receiving, and otherwise obtaining information from all relevant sources. Identifying Objects, Actions, and Events—Identifying information received by making estimates or categorizations, recognizing differences or similarities, or sensing changes in circumstances or events. Analyzing Data or Information—Identifying underlying principles, reasons, or facts by breaking down information or data into separate parts. Making Decisions and Solving Problems—Combining, evaluating, and analyzing information and data to make decisions and solve problems. Involves making decisions about the relative importance of information and choosing the best solution. Updating and Using Job-Relevant Knowledge—Keeping up-to-date technically and knowing the functions of one's own job and related jobs. Processing Information—Compiling, coding, categorizing, calculating, tabulating, auditing, verifying, or processing information or data. Monitoring Processes, Materials, Surroundings—Monitoring and reviewing information from materials, events, or the environment, often to detect problems or to find out when things are finished.

Medical Scientists, Except Epidemiologists

Conduct research dealing with the understanding of human diseases and the improvement of human health. Engage in clinical investigation or other research, production, technical writing, or related activities. Teaches principles of medicine and medical and laboratory procedures to physicians, residents, students, and technicians. Conducts research to develop methodologies, instrumentation, or identification, diagnosing, and treatment procedures for medical application. Investigates cause, progress, life cycle, or mode of transmission of diseases or parasites. Analyzes data, applying statistical techniques and scientific knowledge, prepares reports, and presents findings. Plans methodological design of research study and arranges for data collection. Studies effects of drugs, gases, pesticides, parasites, or microorganisms, or health and physiological processes of animals and humans. Supervises activities of clerical and statistical or laboratory personnel. Consults with and advises physicians, educators, researchers, and others regarding medical applications of sciences, such as physics, biology, and chemistry. Prepares and analyzes samples for toxicity, bacteria, or microorganisms or to study cell structure and properties. Examines organs, tissues, cell structures, or microorganisms by systematic observation or using microscope. Plans and directs studies to investigate human or animal disease, preventive methods, and treatments for disease. Standardizes drug dosages, methods of immunization, and procedures for manufacture of drugs and medicinal compounds. Confers with health department, industry personnel, physicians, and others to develop health safety standards and programs to improve public health.

Personality Type: Investigative. Investigative occupations frequently involve working with ideas and require an extensive amount of thinking. These occupations can involve searching for facts and figuring out problems mentally.

Abilities: Oral Expression—The ability to communicate information and ideas verbally so others will understand. Speech Clarity—The ability to speak clearly so that what is said is understandable to a listener. Inductive Reasoning—The ability to combine separate pieces of information, or specific answers to problems, to form general rules or conclusions. Includes coming up with a logical explanation for why a series of seemingly unrelated events occur together. Oral Comprehension—The ability to listen to and understand information and ideas presented verbally. Written Expression—The ability to communicate information and ideas in writing so others will understand.

Skills: Active Learning—Working with new material or information to grasp its implications. Instructing—Teaching others how to do something. Information Gathering—Knowing how to find information and identifying essential information. Science—Using scientific methods to solve problems. Critical Thinking—Using logic and analysis to identify the strengths and weaknesses of different approaches. Idea Evaluation—Evaluating the likely success of an idea in relation to the demands of the situation. Speaking—Talking to others to effectively convey information.

Generalized Work Activities: Getting Information Needed to Do the Job—Observing, receiving, and otherwise obtaining information from all relevant sources. Identifying Objects, Actions, and Events—Identifying information received by making estimates or categorizations, recognizing differences or similarities, or sensing changes in circumstances or events. Analyzing Data or Information—Identifying underlying principles, reasons, or facts by breaking down information or data into separate parts. Updating and Using Job-Relevant Knowledge—Keeping up-to-date technically and knowing the functions of one's own job and related jobs. Processing Information—Compiling, coding, categorizing, calculating, tabulating, auditing, verifying, or processing information or data. Making Decisions and Solving Problems—Combining, evaluating, and analyzing information and data to make decisions and solve problems. Involves making decisions about the relative importance of information and choosing the best solution. Monitoring Processes, Materials, Surroundings—Monitoring and reviewing information from materials, events, or the environment, often to detect problems or to find out when things are finished.

Medical Secretaries

▲ Growth: 12%
▲ Annual Job Openings: 33,608
▲ Yearly Earnings: $22,390
▲ Education Required: Postsecondary vocational training
▲ Self-Employed: 0%
▲ Part-Time: 19.8%

Medical Secretaries

Perform secretarial duties utilizing specific knowledge of medical terminology and hospital, clinic, or laboratory procedures. Duties include scheduling appointments, billing patients, and compiling and recording medical charts, reports, and correspondence. Routes messages and documents such as laboratory results to appropriate staff. Transcribes recorded messages and practitioner's diagnosis and recommendations into patient's medical record. Answers telephone and directs call to appropriate staff. Prepares and transmits patients' bills. Greets visitors, ascertains purpose of visits, and directs to appropriate staff. Transmits correspondence and medical records by mail, e-mail, or fax. Takes dictation in shorthand. Schedules patient diagnostic appointments and medical consultations. Compiles and records medical charts, reports, and correspondence, using typewriter or personal computer. Maintains medical records and correspondence files.

Personality Type: Conventional. Conventional occupations frequently involve following set procedures and routines. These occupations can include working with data and details more than with ideas. Usually there is a clear line of authority to follow.

Abilities: Oral Comprehension—The ability to listen to and understand information and ideas presented verbally. Oral Expression—The ability to communicate information and ideas verbally so others will understand. Wrist-Finger Speed—The ability to make fast, simple, repeated movements of the fingers, hands, and wrists. Written Comprehension—The ability to read and understand information and ideas presented in writing. Speech Clarity—The ability to speak clearly so that what is said is understandable to a listener.

Skills: Coordination—Adjusting actions in relation to others' actions. Synthesis/Reorganization—Reorganizing information to get a better approach to problems or tasks. Writing—Communicating effectively with others in writing as indicated by the needs of the audience. Reading Comprehension—Understanding written information in work-related documents. Active Listening—Listening to what other people are saying; asking questions as appropriate.

Generalized Work Activities: Documenting/Recording Information—Entering, transcribing, recording, storing, or maintaining information in either written form or by electronic/magnetic recording. Processing Information—Compiling, coding, categorizing, calculating, tabulating, auditing, verifying, or processing information or data. Performing Administrative Activities—Approving requests, handling paperwork, and performing day-to-day administrative tasks. Communicating with Other Workers—Providing information to supervisors, fellow workers, and subordinates. Exchanging information face-to-face, in writing, or via telephone/electronic transfer. Interacting with Computers—Controlling computer functions by using programs, setting up functions, writing software, or otherwise communicating with computer systems.

Merchandise Displayers and Window Dressers

- ▲ Growth: 13%
- ▲ Annual Job Openings: 5,067
- ▲ Yearly Earnings: $18,180
- ▲ Education Required: Bachelor's degree
- ▲ Self-Employed: Not available
- ▲ Part-Time: Not available

Merchandise Displayers and Window Trimmers

Plan and erect commercial displays, such as those in windows and interiors of retail stores and at trade exhibitions. Dresses mannequins for use in displays. Installs booths, exhibits, displays, carpets, and drapes, as guided by floor plan of building and specifications. Develops layout and selects theme, lighting, colors, and props to be used. Installs decorations, such as flags, banners, festive lights, and bunting, on or in building, street, exhibit hall, or booth. Places price and descriptive signs on backdrop, fixtures, merchandise, or floor. Cuts out designs on cardboard, hard board, and plywood according to motif of event. Arranges properties, furniture, merchandise, backdrop, and other accessories as shown in prepared sketch. Consults with advertising and sales staff to determine type of merchandise to be featured and time and place for each display. Prepares sketches or floor plans of proposed displays. Constructs or assembles prefabricated display properties from fabric, glass, paper, and plastic using hand tools and woodworking power tools, according to specifications. Originates ideas for merchandise display or window decoration.

Personality Type: Artistic. Artistic occupations frequently involve working with forms, designs, and patterns. They often require self-expression, and the work can be done without following a clear set of rules.

Abilities: Visualization—The ability to imagine how something will look after it is moved around or when its parts are moved or rearranged. Originality—The ability to come up with unusual or clever ideas about a given topic or situation, or to develop creative ways to solve a problem. Manual Dexterity—The ability to quickly make coordinated movements of one hand, a hand together with its arm, or two hands, to grasp, manipulate, or assemble objects. Near Vision—The ability to see details of objects at a close range. Fluency of Ideas—The ability to come up with a number of ideas about a given topic. Emphasis is on the number of ideas produced and not the quality, correctness, or creativity of the ideas.

Skills: Idea Generation—Generating a number of different approaches to problems. Installation—Installing equipment, machines, wiring, or programs to meet specifications. Idea Evaluation—Evaluating the likely success of an idea in relation to the demands of the situation. Product Inspection—Inspecting and evaluating the quality of products. Implementation Planning—Developing approaches for implementing an idea.

Generalized Work Activities: Implementing Ideas and Programs—Conducting or carrying out work procedures and activities in accord with one's own ideas or information provided through directions/instructions for purposes of installing, modifying, preparing, delivering, constructing, integrating, finishing, or completing programs, systems, structures, or products. Handling and Moving Objects—Using one's hands and arms in handling, installing, forming, positioning, and moving materials, or in manipulating things. Thinking Creatively—Originating, inventing, designing, or creating new applications, ideas, relationships, systems, or products, including artistic contributions. Getting Information Needed to Do the Job—Observing, receiving, and otherwise obtaining information from all relevant sources. Performing General Physical Activities—Performing physical activities that require moving one's whole body, such as in climbing, lifting, balancing, walking, and stooping. Performing activities that often also require considerable use of the arms and legs, such as in the physical handling of materials.

Mining Engineers

- ▲ Growth: -13%
- ▲ Annual Job Openings: 282
- ▲ Yearly Earnings: $56,090
- ▲ Education Required: Bachelor's degree
- ▲ Self-Employed: 0%
- ▲ Part-Time: 3.1%

Mining and Geological Engineers, Including Mining Safety Engineers

Determine the location and plan the extraction of coal, metallic ores, nonmetallic minerals, and building materials, such as stone and gravel. Work involves conducting preliminary surveys of deposits or undeveloped mines and planning their development; examining deposits or mines to determine whether they can be worked at a profit; making geological and topographical surveys; evolving methods of mining best suited to character, type, and size of deposits; and supervising mining operations. Prepares technical reports for use by mining, engineering, and management personnel. Monitors production rate of gas, oil, or minerals from wells or mines. Evaluates data to develop new mining products, equipment, or processes. Designs, implements, and monitors facility projects, such as water, communication, ventilation, drainage, power supply, and conveyor systems. Conducts or collaborates in geological exploration and reviews maps and drilling logs to determine location, size, accessibility, and value of mineral deposits, or optimal oil and gas reservoir locations. Determines methods to extract minerals, considering factors, such as safety, optimal costs, and deposit characteristics. Provides technical consultation during drilling operations. Plans and coordinates mining processes and labor utilization. Designs and maintains protective and rescue equipment and safety devices. Inspects mining areas for unsafe structures, equipment, and working conditions. Devises methods to solve environmental problems and reclaim mine sites. Plans, conducts, or directs others in performing mining experiments to test or prove research findings. Trains mine personnel in safe working practices and first aid. Lays out and directs mine construction operations. Tests air to detect toxic gases and recommends alterations or installation of ventilation shafts, partitions, or equipment, to remedy problem.

Personality Type: Investigative. Investigative occupations frequently involve working with ideas and require an extensive amount of thinking. These occupations can involve searching for facts and figuring out problems mentally.

Abilities: Oral Expression—The ability to communicate information and ideas verbally so others will understand. Deductive Reasoning—The ability to apply general rules to specific problems to come up with logical answers. Involves deciding if an answer makes sense. Speech Clarity—The ability to speak clearly so that what is said is understandable to a listener. Oral Comprehension—The ability to listen to and understand information and ideas presented verbally.

Visualization—The ability to imagine how something will look after it is moved around or when its parts are moved or rearranged.

Skills: Mathematics—Using mathematics to solve problems. Science—Using scientific methods to solve problems. Information Gathering—Knowing how to find information and identifying essential information. Operations Analysis—Analyzing needs and product requirements to create a design. Critical Thinking—Using logic and analysis to identify the strengths and weaknesses of different approaches.

Generalized Work Activities: Getting Information Needed to Do the Job—Observing, receiving, and otherwise obtaining information from all relevant sources. Making Decisions and Solving Problems—Combining, evaluating, and analyzing information and data to make decisions and solve problems. Involves making decisions about the relative importance of information and choosing the best solution. Inspecting Equipment, Structures, Materials—Inspecting or diagnosing equipment, structures, or materials to identify the causes of errors or other problems or defects. Drafting and Specifying Technical Devices—Providing documentation, detailed instructions, drawings, or specifications to inform others about how devices, parts, equipment, or structures are to be fabricated, constructed, assembled, modified, maintained, or used. Updating and Using Job-Relevant Knowledge—Keeping up-to-date technically and knowing the functions of one's own job and related jobs. Analyzing Data or Information—Identifying underlying principles, reasons, or facts by breaking down information or data into separate parts.

Models, Demonstrators, and Product Promoters

- ▲ Growth: 32%
- ▲ Annual Job Openings: 27,574
- ▲ Yearly Earnings: $16,931
- ▲ Education Required: Moderate-term O-J-T
- ▲ Self-Employed: Not available
- ▲ Part-Time: Not available

Demonstrators and Product Promoters

Demonstrate merchandise and answer questions for the purpose of creating public interest in buying the product. Sell demonstrated merchandise. Visits homes, community organizations, stores, and schools to demonstrate products or services. Lectures and shows slides to users of company product. Collects fees or accepts donations. Drives truck and trailer to transport exhibit. Prepares reports of services rendered and visits made. Conducts guided tours of plant where product is made. Advises customers on homemaking problems related to products or services offered by company. Attends trade, traveling, promotional, educational, or amusement exhibit to answer visitors' questions and to protect exhibit against theft or damage. Solicits new organization membership. Answers telephone and written requests from customers for information about product use and writes articles and pamphlets on product. Wears costume or sign boards and walks in public to attract attention to advertise merchandise, services, or belief. Contacts businesses and civic establishments and arranges to exhibit and sell merchandise made by disadvantaged persons. Develops list of prospective clients from sources, such as newspaper items, company records, local merchants, and customers. Trains demonstrators to present company's products or services. Suggests product improvements to employer and product to purchase to customer. Gives product samples or token gifts to customers and distributes handbills, brochures, or gift certificates to passers-by. Sets up and arranges display to attract attention of prospective customers. Demonstrates and explains products, methods, or services to persuade customers to purchase products or utilize services available, and answers questions. Instructs customers in alteration of products.

Personality Type: Enterprising. Enterprising occupations frequently involve starting up and carrying out projects. These occupations can involve leading people and making many decisions. They sometimes require risk taking and often deal with business.

Abilities: Speech Clarity—The ability to speak clearly so that what is said is understandable to a listener. Oral Expression—The ability to communicate information and ideas verbally so others will understand. Oral Comprehension—The ability to listen to and understand information and ideas presented verbally. Written Expression—The ability to communicate information and ideas in writing so others will understand.

Skills: Speaking—Talking to others to effectively convey information. Persuasion—Persuading others to approach things differently. Social Perceptiveness—Being aware of other people's reactions and understanding why people react the way they do. Active Listening—Listening to what other people are saying; asking questions as appropriate. Instructing—Teaching others how to do something.

Generalized Work Activities: Performing for/Working with Public—Performing for people or dealing directly with the public, including serving persons in restaurants and stores and receiving clients or guests. Selling or Influencing Others—Convincing others to buy merchandise/goods, or otherwise changing their minds or actions. Communicating with Persons Outside Organization—Communicating with persons outside the organization. Representing the organization to customers, the public, government, and other external sources. Exchanging information face-to-face, in writing, or via telephone/electronic transfer. Establishing and Maintaining Relationships—Developing constructive and cooperative working relationships with others. Interpreting Meaning of Information to Others—Translating or explaining what information means and how it can be understood or used to support responses or feedback to others.

Models

Model garments and other apparel to display clothing before photographers or prospective buyers at fashion shows, private showings, or retail establishments. Pose for photos to be used for advertising purposes. Pose as subject for paintings, sculptures, and other types of artistic expression. Poses as directed or strikes suitable interpretive poses for promoting and selling merchandise or fashions during photo session. Stands, turns, and walks to demonstrate features of garment to observers at fashion shows, private showings, and retail establishments. Hands out samples or presents, demonstrates toys, and converses with children and adults while dressed in costume. Applies makeup to face and styles hair to enhance appearance, considering such factors as color, camera techniques, and facial features. Informs prospective purchasers as to model, number, and price of garments and department where garment can be purchased. Poses as subject for paintings, sculptures, and other types of art for translation into plastic or pictorial values. Wears character costumes and impersonates characters portrayed to amuse children and adults. Dresses in sample or completed garments and selects own accessories.

Personality Type: Artistic. Artistic occupations frequently involve working with forms, designs, and patterns. They often require self-expression, and the work can be done without following a clear set of rules.

Abilities: Oral Comprehension—The ability to listen to and understand information and ideas presented verbally. Speech Clarity—The ability to speak clearly so that what is said is understandable to a listener. Gross Body Coordination—The ability to coordinate the movement of the arms, legs, and torso together in activities where the whole body is in motion. Selective Attention—The ability to concentrate and not be distracted while performing a task over a period of time. Oral Expression—The ability to communicate information and ideas verbally so others will understand.

Skills: Social Perceptiveness—Being aware of other people's reactions and understanding why people react the way they do. Speaking—Talking to others to effectively convey information. Coordination—Adjusting actions in relation to others' actions.

Persuasion—Persuading others to approach things differently. Active Listening—Listening to what other people are saying; asking questions as appropriate. Monitoring—Assessing how well one is doing when learning or doing something.

Generalized Work Activities: Performing for/Working with Public—Performing for people or dealing directly with the public, including serving persons in restaurants and stores and receiving clients or guests. Performing General Physical Activities—Performing physical activities that require moving one's whole body, such as in climbing, lifting, balancing, walking, and stooping.

Performing activities that often also require considerable use of the arms and legs, such as in the physical handling of materials. Communicating with Persons Outside Organization—Communicating with persons outside the organization. Representing the organization to customers, the public, government, and other external sources. Exchanging information face-to-face, in writing, or via telephone/electronic transfer. Establishing and Maintaining Relationships—Developing constructive and cooperative working relationships with others. Selling or Influencing Others—Convincing others to buy merchandise/goods, or otherwise changing their minds or actions.

Municipal Clerks

- ▲ Growth: 12%
- ▲ Annual Job Openings: 6,545
- ▲ Yearly Earnings: $22,810
- ▲ Education Required: Short-term O-J-T
- ▲ Self-Employed: 0%
- ▲ Part-Time: 16%

Municipal Clerks

Draft agendas and bylaws for town or city council; record minutes of council meetings. Answers official correspondence. Keeps fiscal records and accounts. Prepares agendas and bylaws for town council. Prepares reports on civic needs. Records minutes of council meetings.

Personality Type: Conventional. Conventional occupations frequently involve following set procedures and routines. These occupations can include working with data and details more than with ideas. Usually there is a clear line of authority to follow.

Abilities: Written Expression—The ability to communicate information and ideas in writing so others will understand. Oral Comprehension—The ability to listen to and understand information and ideas presented verbally. Number Facility—The ability to add, subtract, multiply, or divide quickly and correctly. Auditory Attention—The ability to focus on a single source of sound in the presence of other distracting sounds.

Written Comprehension—The ability to read and understand information and ideas presented in writing.

Skills: Writing—Communicating effectively with others in writing as indicated by the needs of the audience. Reading Comprehension—Understanding written information in work-related documents. Active Listening—Listening to what other people are saying; asking questions as appropriate. Information Gathering—Knowing how to find information and identifying essential information. Information Organization—Finding ways to structure or classify multiple pieces of information. Critical Thinking—Using logic and analysis to identify the strengths and weaknesses of different approaches. Mathematics—Using mathematics to solve problems.

Generalized Work Activities: Documenting/Recording Information—Entering, transcribing, recording, storing, or maintaining information in either written form or by electronic/magnetic recording. Processing Information—Compiling, coding, categorizing, calculating, tabulating, auditing, verifying, or processing information or data. Communicating with Persons Outside Organization—Communicating with persons outside the organization. Representing the organization to customers, the public, government, and other external sources. Exchanging information face-to-face, in writing, or via telephone/electronic transfer. Getting Information Needed to Do the Job—Observing, receiving, and otherwise obtaining information from

all relevant sources. Communicating with Other Workers—Providing information to supervisors, fellow workers, and subordinates. Exchanging information face-to-face, in writing, or via telephone/electronic transfer. Performing Administrative Activities—Approving requests, handling paperwork, and performing day-to-day administrative tasks.

Musicians

- ▲ Growth: 15%
- ▲ Annual Job Openings: 44,774
- ▲ Yearly Earnings: $30,020
- ▲ Education Required: Long-term O-J-T
- ▲ Self-Employed: 25.8%
- ▲ Part-Time: 53.5%

Composers

Compose music for orchestra, choral group, or band. Develops pattern of harmony, applying knowledge of music theory. Synthesizes ideas for melody of musical scores for choral group, or band. Creates musical and tonal structure, applying elements of music theory, such as instrumental and vocal capabilities. Transcribes or records musical ideas into notes on scored music paper. Creates original musical form or writes within circumscribed musical form, such as sonata, symphony, or opera. Determines basic pattern of melody, applying knowledge of music theory.

Personality Type: Artistic. Artistic occupations frequently involve working with forms, designs, and patterns. They often require self-expression, and the work can be done without following a clear set of rules.

Abilities: Hearing Sensitivity—The ability to detect or tell the difference between sounds that vary over broad ranges of pitch and loudness. Originality—The ability to come up with unusual or clever ideas about a given topic or situation, or to develop creative ways to solve a problem. Fluency of Ideas—The ability to come up with a number of ideas about a given topic. Emphasis is on the number of ideas produced and not the quality, correctness, or creativity of the ideas. Auditory

Attention—The ability to focus on a single source of sound in the presence of other distracting sounds.

Skills: Idea Generation—Generating a number of different approaches to problems. Idea Evaluation—Evaluating the likely success of an idea in relation to the demands of the situation. Synthesis/Reorganization—Reorganizing information to get a better approach to problems or tasks. Visioning—Developing an image of how a system should work under ideal conditions. Solution Appraisal—Observing and evaluating the outcomes of a problem solution to identify lessons learned or to redirect efforts. Implementation Planning—Developing approaches for implementing an idea.

Generalized Work Activities: Thinking Creatively—Originating, inventing, designing, or creating new applications, ideas, relationships, systems, or products, including artistic contributions. Implementing Ideas and Programs—Conducting or carrying out work procedures and activities in accord with one's own ideas or information provided through directions/instructions for purposes of installing, modifying, preparing, delivering, constructing, integrating, finishing, or completing programs, systems, structures, or products. Getting Information Needed to Do the Job—Observing, receiving, and otherwise obtaining

M

information from all relevant sources. Documenting/ Recording Information—Entering, transcribing, recording, storing, or maintaining information in either written form or by electronic/magnetic recording. Making Decisions and Solving Problems—Combining, evaluating, and analyzing information and data to make decisions and solve problems. Involves making decisions about the relative importance of information and choosing the best solution.

Music Arrangers and Orchestrators

Write and transcribe musical scores. Composes musical scores for orchestra, band, choral group, or individual instrumentalist or vocalist, using knowledge of music theory and instrumental and vocal capabilities. Transposes music from one voice or instrument to another to accommodate particular musician in musical group. Transcribes musical parts from score written by arranger or orchestrator for each instrument or voice, using knowledge of music composition. Copies parts from score for individual performers. Determines voice, instrument, harmonic structure, rhythm, tempo, and tone balance to achieve desired effect. Adapts musical composition for orchestra, band, choral group, or individual to style for which it was not originally written.

Personality Type: Artistic. Artistic occupations frequently involve working with forms, designs, and patterns. They often require self-expression, and the work can be done without following a clear set of rules.

Abilities: Originality—The ability to come up with unusual or clever ideas about a given topic or situation, or to develop creative ways to solve a problem. Hearing Sensitivity—The ability to detect or tell the difference between sounds that vary over broad ranges of pitch and loudness. Fluency of Ideas—The ability to come up with a number of ideas about a given topic. Emphasis is on the number of ideas produced and not the quality, correctness, or creativity of the ideas. Auditory Attention —The ability to focus on a single source of sound in the presence of other distracting sounds. Written Expression—The ability to communicate information and ideas in writing so others will understand.

Skills: Idea Generation—Generating a number of different approaches to problems. Synthesis/ Reorganization—Reorganizing information to get a better approach to problems or tasks. Writing— Communicating effectively with others in writing as indicated by the needs of the audience. Coordination— Adjusting actions in relation to others' actions. Idea Evaluation—Evaluating the likely success of an idea in relation to the demands of the situation.

Generalized Work Activities: Thinking Creatively— Originating, inventing, designing, or creating new applications, ideas, relationships, systems, or products, including artistic contributions. Identifying Objects, Actions, and Events—Identifying information received by making estimates or categorizations, recognizing differences or similarities, or sensing changes in circumstances or events. Getting Information Needed to Do the Job—Observing, receiving, and otherwise obtaining information from all relevant sources. Implementing Ideas and Programs—Conducting or carrying out work procedures and activities in accord with one's own ideas or information provided through directions/instructions for purposes of installing, modifying, preparing, delivering, constructing, integrating, finishing, or completing programs, systems, structures, or products. Interpreting Meaning of Information to Others—Translating or explaining what information means and how it can be understood or used to support responses or feedback to others.

Music Directors

Direct and conduct instrumental or vocal performances by musical groups, such as orchestras or choirs. Engages services of composer to write score. Auditions and selects vocal and instrumental groups for musical presentations. Transcribes musical compositions and melodic lines to adapt them to or create particular style for group. Issues assignments and reviews work of staff in such areas as scoring, arranging, and copying music, lyric and vocal coaching. Directs group at rehearsals and live or recorded performances to achieve desired effects, such as tonal and harmonic balance dynamics, rhythm, and tempo. Selects vocal, instrumental, and recorded music suitable to type of performance requirements to accommodate ability of group. Positions members within group to obtain balance among instrumental sections.

Personality Type: Artistic. Artistic occupations frequently involve working with forms, designs, and patterns. They often require self-expression, and the work can be done without following a clear set of rules.

Abilities: Oral Expression—The ability to communicate information and ideas verbally so others will understand. Oral Comprehension—The ability to listen to and understand information and ideas presented verbally. Written Comprehension—The ability to read and understand information and ideas presented in writing. Hearing Sensitivity—The ability to detect or tell the difference between sounds that vary over broad ranges of pitch and loudness. Originality—The ability to come up with unusual or clever ideas about a given topic or situation, or to develop creative ways to solve a problem. Auditory Attention—The ability to focus on a single source of sound in the presence of other distracting sounds.

Skills: Coordination—Adjusting actions in relation to others' actions. Monitoring—Assessing how well one is doing when learning or doing something. Management of Personnel Resources—Motivating, developing, and directing people as they work, identifying the best people for the job. Instructing—Teaching others how to do something. Speaking—Talking to others to effectively convey information. Implementation Planning—Developing approaches for implementing an idea.

Generalized Work Activities: Thinking Creatively—Originating, inventing, designing, or creating new applications, ideas, relationships, systems, or products, including artistic contributions. Coordinating Work and Activities of Others—Coordinating members of a work group to accomplish tasks. Judging Qualities—Making judgments about or assessing the value, importance, or quality of things, services, or other people's work. Scheduling Work and Activities—Scheduling events, programs, activities, and the work of others. Getting Information Needed to Do the Job—Observing, receiving, and otherwise obtaining information from all relevant sources.

Musicians, Instrumental

Play one or more musical instruments in recital, in accompaniment, or as members of an orchestra, band, or other musical group. Memorizes musical scores. Practices performance on musical instrument to maintain and improve skills. Improvises music during performance. Plays from memory or by following score. Composes new musical scores. Teaches music for specific instruments. Transposes music to play in alternate key, or to fit individual style or purposes. Plays musical instrument as soloist or as member of musical group, such as orchestra or band, to entertain audience. Studies and rehearses music to learn and interpret score. Directs band/orchestra.

Personality Type: Artistic. Artistic occupations frequently involve working with forms, designs, and patterns. They often require self-expression, and the work can be done without following a clear set of rules.

Abilities: Hearing Sensitivity—The ability to detect or tell the difference between sounds that vary over broad ranges of pitch and loudness. Auditory Attention—The ability to focus on a single source of sound in the presence of other distracting sounds. Memorization—The ability to remember information such as words, numbers, pictures, and procedures. Wrist-Finger Speed—The ability to make fast, simple, repeated movements of the fingers, hands, and wrists. Speed of Closure—The ability to quickly make sense of information that seems to be without meaning or organization. Involves quickly combining and organizing different pieces of information into a meaningful pattern.

Skills: Coordination—Adjusting actions in relation to others' actions. Active Learning—Working with new material or information to grasp its implications. Monitoring—Assessing how well one is doing when learning or doing something. Visioning—Developing an image of how a system should work under ideal conditions. Learning Strategies—Using multiple approaches when learning or teaching new things.

M

Generalized Work Activities: Thinking Creatively—Originating, inventing, designing, or creating new applications, ideas, relationships, systems, or products, including artistic contributions. Performing for/Working with Public—Performing for people or dealing directly with the public, including serving persons in restaurants and stores and receiving clients or guests. Developing and Building Teams—Encouraging and building mutual trust, respect, and cooperation among team members. Teaching Others—Identifying educational needs, developing formal training programs or classes, and teaching or instructing others. Handling and Moving Objects—Using one's hands and arms in handling, installing, forming, positioning, and moving materials, or in manipulating things.

Singers

Sing songs on stage, radio, television, or motion pictures. Sings before audience or recipient of message as soloist, or in group as member of vocal ensemble. Practices songs and routines to maintain and improve vocal skills. Observes choral leader or prompter for cues or directions in vocal presentation. Sings a cappella or with musical accompaniment. Memorizes musical selections and routines, or sings following printed text, musical notation, or customer instructions. Interprets or modifies music, applying knowledge of harmony, melody, rhythm, and voice production, to individualize presentation and maintain audience interest.

Personality Type: Artistic. Artistic occupations frequently involve working with forms, designs, and patterns. They often require self-expression, and the work can be done without following a clear set of rules.

Abilities: Hearing Sensitivity—The ability to detect or tell the difference between sounds that vary over broad ranges of pitch and loudness. Memorization—The ability to remember information such as words, numbers, pictures, and procedures. Oral Comprehension—The ability to listen to and understand information and ideas presented verbally. Written Comprehension—The ability to read and understand information and ideas presented in writing. Speech Clarity—The ability to speak clearly so that what is said is understandable to a listener. Auditory Attention—The ability to focus on a single source of sound in the presence of other distracting sounds. Oral Expression—The ability to communicate information and ideas verbally so others will understand. Originality—The ability to come up with unusual or clever ideas about a given topic or situation, or to develop creative ways to solve a problem.

Skills: Coordination—Adjusting actions in relation to others' actions. Active Learning—Working with new material or information to grasp its implications. Monitoring—Assessing how well one is doing when learning or doing something. Active Listening—Listening to what other people are saying; asking questions as appropriate. Speaking—Talking to others to effectively convey information.

Generalized Work Activities: Performing for/Working with Public—Performing for people or dealing directly with the public, including serving persons in restaurants and stores and receiving clients or guests. Thinking Creatively—Originating, inventing, designing, or creating new applications, ideas, relationships, systems, or products, including artistic contributions. Communicating with Persons Outside Organization—Communicating with persons outside the organization. Representing the organization to customers, the public, government, and other external sources. Exchanging information face-to-face, in writing, or via telephone/electronic transfer. Communicating with Other Workers—Providing information to supervisors, fellow workers, and subordinates. Exchanging information face-to-face, in writing, or via telephone/electronic transfer. Getting Information Needed to Do the Job—Observing, receiving, and otherwise obtaining information from all relevant sources. Establishing and Maintaining Relationships—Developing constructive and cooperative working relationships with others.

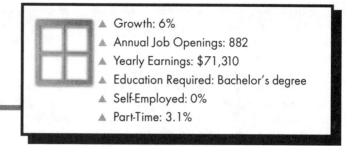

Nuclear Engineers

- ▲ Growth: 6%
- ▲ Annual Job Openings: 882
- ▲ Yearly Earnings: $71,310
- ▲ Education Required: Bachelor's degree
- ▲ Self-Employed: 0%
- ▲ Part-Time: 3.1%

Nuclear Engineers

Conduct research on nuclear engineering problems or apply principles and theory of nuclear science to problems concerned with release, control, and utilization of nuclear energy and nuclear waste disposal. Analyzes available data and consults with other scientists to determine parameters of experimentation and suitability of analytical models. Maintains reports to summarize work and document plant operations. Designs and develops nuclear machinery and equipment, such as reactor cores, radiation shielding, and associated instrumentation and control mechanisms. Inspects nuclear fuels, waste, equipment, test-reactor vessel and related systems, and control instrumentation to identify potential problems or hazards. Evaluates research findings to develop new concepts of thermonuclear analysis and new uses of radioactive models. Plans and designs nuclear research to discover facts, or to test, prove, or modify known nuclear theories. Monitors nuclear operations to identify potential or inherent design, construction, or operational problems to ensure safe operations. Writes operational instructions relative to nuclear plant operation and nuclear fuel and waste handling and disposal. Conducts tests to research nuclear fuel behavior and nuclear machinery and equipment performance. Determines potential hazard and accident conditions that may exist in fuel handling and storage and recommends preventive measures. Computes cost estimates of construction projects, prepares project proposals, and discusses projects with vendors, contractors, and nuclear facility's review board. Designs and oversees construction and operation of nuclear fuels reprocessing systems and reclamation systems. Synthesizes analyses of tests results and prepares technical reports of findings and recommendations. Examines accidents and obtains data to formulate preventive measures. Formulates equations that describe phenomena occurring during fission of nuclear fuels and develops analytical models for research. Performs experiments to determine acceptable methods of nuclear material usage, nuclear fuel reclamation, and waste disposal.

Personality Type: Investigative. Investigative occupations frequently involve working with ideas and require an extensive amount of thinking. These occupations can involve searching for facts and figuring out problems mentally.

Abilities: Mathematical Reasoning—The ability to understand and organize a problem and then select a mathematical method or formula to solve the problem. Written Expression—The ability to communicate information and ideas in writing so others will understand. Deductive Reasoning—The ability to apply general rules to specific problems to come up with logical answers. Involves deciding if an answer makes sense. Speech Clarity—The ability to speak clearly to that what is said is understandable to a listener. Problem Sensitivity—The ability to tell when something is wrong or is likely to go wrong. Does not involve solving the problem, only recognizing there is a problem.

Skills: Science—Using scientific methods to solve problems. Critical Thinking—Using logic and analysis to identify the strengths and weaknesses of different approaches. Judgment and Decision Making—Weighing the relative costs and benefits of a potential action. Problem Identification—Identifying the nature of problems. Information Gathering—Knowing how to find information and identifying essential information.

Generalized Work Activities: Getting Information Needed to Do the Job—Observing, receiving, and otherwise obtaining information from all relevant sources. Monitoring Processes, Materials, Surroundings—Monitoring and reviewing information from materials, events, or the environment, often to detect problems or to find out when things are finished. Inspecting Equipment, Structures, Materials—Inspecting or diagnosing equipment, structures, or materials to identify the causes of errors or other problems or defects. Analyzing Data or Information—Identifying underlying principles, reasons, or facts by breaking down information or data into separate parts. Making Decisions and Solving Problems—Combining, evaluating, and analyzing information and data to make decisions and solve problems. Involves making decisions about the relative importance of information and choosing the best solution. Identifying Objects, Actions, and Events—Identifying information received by making estimates or categorizations, recognizing differences or similarities, or sensing changes in circumstances or events.

Nuclear Medicine Technologists

▲ Growth: 12%

▲ Annual Job Openings: 833

▲ Yearly Earnings: $39,610

▲ Education Required: Associate degree

▲ Self-Employed: 0%

▲ Part-Time: 17.5%

Nuclear Medicine Technologists

Prepare, administer, and measure radioactive isotopes in therapeutic, diagnostic, and tracer studies utilizing a variety of radioisotope equipment. Prepare stock solutions of radioactive materials and calculate doses to be administered by radiologists. Subject patients to radiation. Execute blood volume, red cell survival, and fat absorption studies following standard laboratory techniques. Administers radiopharmaceuticals or radiation to patient to detect or treat diseases, using radioisotope equipment, under direction of physician. Positions radiation fields, radiation beams, and patient to develop most effective treatment of patient's disease, using computer. Develops treatment procedures for nuclear medicine treatment programs. Disposes of radioactive materials and stores radiopharmaceuticals following radiation safety procedures. Maintains and calibrates radioisotope and laboratory equipment. Calculates, measures, prepares, and records radiation dosage or radiopharmaceuticals, using computer and following physician's prescription and X rays. Measures glandular activity, blood volume, red cell survival, and radioactivity of patient, using scanners, Geiger counters, scintillometers, and other laboratory equipment.

Personality Type: Investigative. Investigative occupations frequently involve working with ideas and require an extensive amount of thinking. These occupations can involve searching for facts and figuring out problems mentally.

Abilities: Oral Comprehension—The ability to listen to and understand information and ideas presented verbally. Written Comprehension—The ability to read and understand information and ideas presented in writing. Oral Expression—The ability to communicate information and ideas verbally so others will understand. Problem Sensitivity—The ability to tell when something is wrong or is likely to go wrong. Does not involve solving the problem, only recognizing there is a problem. Written Expression—The ability to communicate information and ideas in writing so others will understand.

Skills: Mathematics—Using mathematics to solve problems. Operation and Control—Controlling operations of equipment or systems. Operation Monitoring—Watching gauges, dials, or other indicators to make sure a machine is working properly. Reading Comprehension—Understanding written information in work-related documents. Science—Using scientific methods to solve problems.

Generalized Work Activities: Getting Information Needed to Do the Job—Observing, receiving, and otherwise obtaining information from all relevant sources. Monitoring Processes, Materials, Surroundings—Monitoring and reviewing information from materials, events, or the environment, often to detect problems or to find out when things are finished. Analyzing Data or Information—Identifying underlying principles, reasons, or facts by breaking down information or data into separate parts. Identifying Objects, Actions, and Events—Identifying information received by making estimates or categorizations, recognizing differences or similarities, or sensing changes in circumstances or events. Processing Information—Compiling, coding, categorizing, calculating, tabulating, auditing, verifying, or processing information or data.

Numerical Control Machine Tool Operators and Tenders

⊞ ▲ Growth: 23%
▲ Annual Job Openings: 18,908
▲ Yearly Earnings: $27,110
▲ Education Required: Moderate-term O-J-T
▲ Self-Employed: 0%
▲ Part-Time: 2.3%

Numerical Control Machine Tool Operators and Tenders, Metal and Plastic

Set up and operate numerical control (magnetic- or punched-tape-controlled) machine tools that automatically mill, drill, broach, and ream metal and plastic parts. Adjust machine feed and speed, change cutting tools, or adjust machine controls when automatic programming is faulty or if machine malfunctions. Starts automatic operation of numerical control machine to machine parts or test setup, workpiece dimensions, or programming. Confers with supervisor or programmer to resolve machine malfunctions and production errors and obtains approval to continue production. Maintains machines and removes and replaces broken or worn machine tools using hand tools. Lifts workpiece to machine manually, with hoist or crane, or with tweezers. Stops machine to remove finished workpiece or change tooling, setup, or workpiece placement, according to required machining sequence. Lays out and marks areas of part to be shot-peened, and fills hopper with shot. Loads control media, such as tape, card, or disk, in machine controller or enters commands to retrieve programmed instructions. Measures dimensions of finished workpiece to ensure conformance to specifications, using precision measuring instruments, templates, and fixtures. Positions and secures workpiece on machine bed, indexing table, fixture, or dispensing or holding device. Cleans machine, tooling, and parts, using solvent or solution and rag. Examines electronic components for defects and completeness of laser-beam trimming, using microscope. Enters commands or manually adjusts machine controls to correct malfunctions or tolerances. Monitors machine operation and control panel displays to detect malfunctions and compare readings to specifications. Calculates and sets machine controls to position tools, synchronize tape and tool, or regulate cutting depth, speed, feed, or coolant flow. Determines specifications or procedures for tooling set-up, machine operation, workpiece dimensions, or numerical control sequences, using blueprints, instructions, and machine knowledge. Mounts, installs, aligns, and secures tools, attachments, fixtures, and workpiece on machine, using hand tools and precision measuring instruments. Operates lathe, drill-press, jig-boring machine, or other machines manually or semiautomatically.

Personality Type: Realistic. Realistic occupations frequently involve work activities that include practical, hands-on problems and solutions. They often deal with plants, animals, and real-world materials like wood, tools, and machinery. Many of the occupations require working outside and do not involve a lot of paperwork or working closely with others.

Abilities: Problem Sensitivity—The ability to tell when something is wrong or is likely to go wrong. Does not involve solving the problem, only recognizing there is a problem. Control Precision—The ability to quickly and repeatedly make precise adjustments in moving the controls of a machine or vehicle to exact positions. Reaction Time—The ability to quickly respond with the hand, finger, or foot to a signal such as a sound, a light, or a picture. Wrist-Finger Speed—The ability to make fast, simple, repeated movements of the fingers, hands, and wrists. Number Facility—The ability to add, subtract, multiply, or divide quickly and correctly.

Skills: Operation and Control—Controlling operations of equipment or systems. Operation Monitoring—Watching gauges, dials, or other indicators to make sure a machine is working properly. Equipment Selection—Determining the kind of tools and equipment needed to do a job. Product Inspection—Inspecting and evaluating the quality of products. Equipment Maintenance—Performing routine maintenance and determining when and what kind of maintenance is needed.

Generalized Work Activities: Handling and Moving Objects—Using one's hands and arms in handling, installing, forming, positioning, and moving materials, or in manipulating things. Controlling Machines and Processes—Using either control mechanisms or direct physical activity to operate machines or processes. Does not involve working with computers or vehicles. Repairing and Maintaining Mechanical Equipment—Fixing, servicing, aligning, setting up, adjusting, and testing machines, devices, moving parts, and equipment that operate primarily on the basis of mechanical, not electronic, principles. Monitoring Processes, Materials, Surroundings—Monitoring and reviewing information from materials, events, or the environment, often to detect problems or to find out when things are finished. Inspecting Equipment, Structures, Materials—Inspecting or diagnosing equipment, structures, or materials to identify the causes of errors or other problems or defects.

Numerical Control Machine Tool Programmers

▲ Growth: 6%
▲ Annual Job Openings: 706
▲ Yearly Earnings: $40,490
▲ Education Required: Work experience in a related occupation
▲ Self-Employed: 0%
▲ Part-Time: 11.7%

Numerical Tool and Process Control Programmers

Develop programs to control machining or processing of parts by automatic machine tools, equipment, or systems. Determines reference points, machine cutting paths, or hole locations and computes angular and linear dimensions, radii, and curvatures. Revises numerical control machine tape programs to eliminate instruction errors and omissions. Analyzes drawings, specifications, printed circuit board pattern film, and design data to calculate dimensions, tool selection, machine speeds, and feed rates. Enters computer commands to store or retrieve parts patterns, graphic displays, or programs to transfer data to other media. Draws machine tool paths on pattern film, using colored markers and following guidelines for tool speed and efficiency. Compares encoded tape or computer printout with original program sheet to verify accuracy of instructions. Moves reference table to align pattern film over circuit board holes with reference marks on enlarger scope. Depresses pedal or button of programmer to enter coordinates of each hole location into program memory. Loads and unloads disks or tapes and observes operation of machine on trial run to test taped or programmed instructions. Reviews shop orders to determine job specifications and requirements. Aligns and secures pattern film on reference table of optical programmer and observes enlarger scope view of printed circuit board. Sorts shop orders into groups to maximize materials utilization and minimize machine setup. Prepares geometric layout from graphic displays, using computer-assisted drafting software or drafting instruments and graph paper. Writes instruction sheets, cutter lists, and machine instructions programs to guide setup and encode numerical control tape.

Personality Type: Realistic. Realistic occupations frequently involve work activities that include practical, hands-on problems and solutions. They often deal with plants, animals, and real-world materials like wood, tools, and machinery. Many of the occupations require working outside and do not involve a lot of paperwork or working closely with others.

Abilities: Mathematical Reasoning—The ability to understand and organize a problem and then select a mathematical method or formula to solve the problem. Information Ordering—The ability to correctly follow a given rule or set of rules in order to arrange things or actions in a certain order. The things or actions can include numbers, letters, words, pictures, procedures, sentences, and mathematical or logical operations. Written Comprehension—The ability to read and understand information and ideas presented in writing. Number Facility—The ability to add, subtract, multiply, or divide quickly and correctly. Near Vision—The ability to see details of objects at a close range.

Skills: Programming—Writing computer programs for various purposes. Operations Analysis—Analyzing needs and product requirements to create a design. Information Gathering—Knowing how to find information and identifying essential information. Mathematics—Using mathematics to solve problems. Information Organization—Finding ways to structure or classify multiple pieces of information.

Generalized Work Activities: Drafting and Specifying Technical Devices—Providing documentation, detailed instructions, drawings, or specifications to inform others about how devices, parts, equipment, or structures are to be fabricated, constructed, assembled, modified, maintained, or used. Getting Information Needed to Do the Job—Observing, receiving, and otherwise obtaining information from all relevant sources. Analyzing Data or Information—Identifying underlying principles, reasons, or facts by breaking down information or data into separate parts. Making Decisions and Solving Problems—Combining, evaluating, and analyzing information and data to make decisions and solve problems. Involves making decisions about the relative importance of information and choosing the best solution. Identifying Objects, Actions, and Events—Identifying information received by making estimates or categorizations, recognizing differences or similarities, or sensing changes in circumstances or events. Handling and Moving Objects—Using one's hands and arms in handling, installing, forming, positioning, and moving materials, or in manipulating things. Includes the use of keyboards.

Nursery and Greenhouse Managers

- ▲ Growth: 15%
- ▲ Annual Job Openings: 583
- ▲ Yearly Earnings: $25,360
- ▲ Education Required: Work experience in a related occupation
- ▲ Self-Employed: 84.6%
- ▲ Part-Time: 24.5%

Nursery and Greenhouse Managers

Plan, organize, direct, control, and coordinate activities of workers engaged in propagating, cultivating, and harvesting horticultural specialties, such as trees, shrubs, flowers, mushrooms, and other plants. Coordinates clerical, record keeping, inventory, requisition, and marketing activities. Hires workers and directs supervisors and workers planting seeds, controlling plant growth and disease, potting, or cutting plants for marketing. Considers such factors as whether plants need hothouse/greenhouse or natural weather growing conditions. Selects and purchases seed, plant nutrients, and disease control chemicals. Grows horticultural plants under controlled conditions hydroponically. Tours work areas to observe work being done, to inspect crops, and to evaluate plant and soil conditions. Negotiates contracts for lease of lands or trucks or for purchase of trees. Confers with horticultural personnel in planning facility renovations or additions. Manages nursery to grow horticultural plants for sale to trade or retail customers, for display or exhibition, or for research. Determines type and quantity of horticultural plants to be grown, such as trees, shrubs, flowers, ornamental plants, or vegetables, based on budget, projected sales volume, or executive directive.

Personality Type: Enterprising. Enterprising occupations frequently involve starting up and carrying out projects. These occupations can involve leading people and making many decisions. They sometimes require risk taking and often deal with business.

Abilities: Oral Expression—The ability to communicate information and ideas verbally so others will understand. Written Comprehension—The ability to read and understand information and ideas presented in writing. Oral Comprehension—The ability to listen to and understand information and ideas presented verbally. Written Expression—The ability to communicate information and ideas in writing so others will understand.

Skills: Management of Personnel Resources—Motivating, developing, and directing people as they work, identifying the best people for the job. Implementation Planning—Developing approaches for implementing an idea. Time Management—Managing one's own time and the time of others. Judgment and Decision Making—Weighing the relative costs and benefits of a potential action. Management of Financial Resources—Determining how money will be spent to get the work done, and accounting for these expenditures.

Generalized Work Activities: Guiding, Directing, and Motivating Subordinates—Providing guidance and direction to subordinates, including setting performance standards and monitoring subordinates. Communicating with Persons Outside Organization—Communicating with persons outside the organization. Representing the organization to customers, the public, government, and other external sources. Exchanging information face-to-face, in writing, or via telephone/electronic transfer. Communicating with Other Workers—Providing information to supervisors, fellow workers, and subordinates. Exchanging information face-to-face, in writing, or via telephone/electronic transfer. Coordinating Work and Activities of Others—Coordinating members of a work group to accomplish

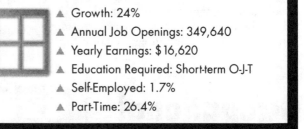

tasks. Staffing Organizational Units—Recruiting, interviewing, selecting, hiring, and promoting persons for the organization. Getting Information Needed to Do the Job—Observing, receiving, and otherwise obtaining information from all relevant sources. Making Decisions and Solving Problems—Combining, evaluating, and analyzing information and data to make decisions and solve problems. Involves making decisions about the relative importance of information and choosing the best solution.

Nursing Aides, Orderlies, and Attendants

- ▲ Growth: 24%
- ▲ Annual Job Openings: 349,640
- ▲ Yearly Earnings: $16,620
- ▲ Education Required: Short-term O-J-T
- ▲ Self-Employed: 1.7%
- ▲ Part-Time: 26.4%

Nursing Aides, Orderlies, and Attendants

Provide basic patient care under direction of nursing staff. Perform duties, such as feed, bathe, dress, groom, or move patients, or change linens. Bathes, grooms, and dresses patients. Stores, prepares, and issues dressing packs, treatment trays, and other supplies. Assists patient to walk. Turns and repositions bedfast patients, alone or with assistance, to prevent bedsores. Transports patient to areas, such as operating and X-ray rooms. Administers massages and alcohol rubs. Sterilizes equipment and supplies. Administers catheterizations, bladder irrigations, enemas, and douches. Administers medication as directed by physician or nurse. Feeds patients unable to feed themselves. Measures and records food and liquid intake and output. Measures and records vital signs. Prepares food trays. Sets up equipment, such as oxygen tents, portable X-ray machines, and overhead irrigation bottles. Cleans room and changes linen.

Personality Type: Social. Social occupations frequently involve working with, communicating with, and teaching people. These occupations often involve helping or providing service to others.

Abilities: Static Strength—The ability to exert maximum muscle force to lift, push, pull, or carry objects. Oral Comprehension—The ability to listen to and understand information and ideas presented verbally. Oral Expression—The ability to communicate information and ideas verbally so others will understand. Arm-Hand Steadiness—The ability to keep the hand and arm steady while making an arm movement or while holding the arm and hand in one position. Written Comprehension—The ability to read and understand information and ideas presented in writing. Near Vision—The ability to see details of objects at a close range. Information Ordering—The ability to correctly follow a given rule or set of rules in order to arrange things or actions in a certain order. The things or actions can include numbers, letters, words, pictures, procedures, sentences, and mathematical or logical operations.

Skills: Service Orientation—Actively looking for ways to help people. Social Perceptiveness—Being aware of other people's reactions and understanding why people react the way they do. Active Listening—Listening to what other people are saying; asking questions as appropriate. Coordination—Adjusting actions in relation to others' actions. Speaking—Talking to others to effectively convey information. Technology Design—Generating or adapting equipment and technology to serve user needs.

Generalized Work Activities: Performing General Physical Activities—Performing physical activities that require moving one's whole body, such as in climbing, lifting, balancing, walking, and stooping. Performing activities that often also require considerable use of the arms and legs, such as in the physical handling of materials. Assisting and Caring for Others—Providing assistance or personal care to others. Documenting/Recording Information—Entering, transcribing, recording, storing, or maintaining information in either written form or by electronic/magnetic recording. Establishing and Maintaining Relationships—

Developing constructive and cooperative working relationships with others. Identifying Objects, Actions, and Events—Identifying information received by making estimates or categorizations, recognizing differences or similarities, or sensing changes in circumstances or events. Handling and Moving Objects—Using one's hands and arms in handling, installing, forming, positioning, and moving materials, or in manipulating things. Includes the use of keyboards.

Occupational Therapists

▲ Growth: 34%

▲ Annual Job Openings: 6,484

▲ Yearly Earnings: $48,230

▲ Education Required: Bachelor's degree

▲ Self-Employed: 5.6%

▲ Part-Time: 20.8%

Occupational Therapists

Assess, plan, organize, and participate in rehabilitative programs that help restore vocational, homemaking, and daily living skills, as well as general independence, to disabled persons. Recommends changes in individual's work or living environment, consistent with needs and capabilities. Teaches individuals skills and techniques required for participation in activities and evaluates individual's progress. Requisitions supplies and equipment. Designs and constructs special equipment, such as splints and braces. Trains nurses and other medical staff in therapy techniques and objectives. Completes and maintains necessary records. Selects activities which will help individual learn work skills within limits of individual's mental and physical capabilities. Plans programs and social activities to help patients learn work skills and adjust to handicaps. Plans, organizes, and conducts occupational therapy program in hospital, institutional, or community setting. Lays out materials for individual's use and cleans and repairs tools after therapy sessions. Consults with rehabilitation

team to select activity programs and coordinate occupational therapy with other therapeutic activities.

Personality Type: Social. Social occupations frequently involve working with, communicating with, and teaching people. These occupations often involve helping or providing service to others.

Abilities: Oral Expression—The ability to communicate information and ideas verbally so others will understand. Oral Comprehension—The ability to listen to and understand information and ideas presented verbally. Written Comprehension—The ability to read and understand information and ideas presented in writing. Deductive Reasoning—The ability to apply general rules to specific problems to come up with logical answers. Involves deciding if an answer makes sense. Problem Sensitivity—The ability to tell when something is wrong or is likely to go wrong. Does not involve solving the problem, only recognizing there is a problem. Written Expression—The ability to communicate information and ideas in writing so others will understand.

Skills: Instructing—Teaching others how to do something. Implementation Planning—Developing approaches for implementing an idea. Social Perceptiveness—Being aware of other people's reactions and understanding why people react the way they do. Speaking—Talking to others to effectively convey information. Solution Appraisal—Observing and evaluating the outcomes of a problem solution to identify lessons learned or to redirect efforts.

Generalized Work Activities: Assisting and Caring for Others—Providing assistance or personal care to others. Providing Consultation and Advice to Others—Providing consultation and expert advice to management or other groups on technical, systems-related, or process-related topics. Getting Information Needed to Do the Job—Observing, receiving, and otherwise obtaining information from all relevant sources. Teaching Others—Identifying educational needs, developing formal training programs or classes, and teaching or instructing others. Analyzing Data or Information—Identifying underlying principles, reasons, or facts by breaking down information or data into separate parts. Updating and Using Job-Relevant Knowledge—Keeping up-to-date technically and knowing the functions of one's own job and related jobs.

Occupational Therapy Assistants and Aides

- ▲ Growth: 40%
- ▲ Annual Job Openings: 3,106
- ▲ Yearly Earnings: $28,690
- ▲ Education Required: Moderate-term O-J-T
- ▲ Self-Employed: 0%
- ▲ Part-Time: 24.9%

Occupational Therapist Aides

Under close supervision of an occupational therapist or occupational therapy assistant, perform only delegated, selected, or routine tasks in specific situations. These duties include preparing patient and treatment room. Maintains observed information in client records and prepares written reports. Helps professional staff demonstrate therapy techniques, such as manual and creative arts, and games. Assists educational specialist or clinical psychologist in administering situational or diagnostic tests to measure client's abilities or progress. Fabricates splints and other assistant devices. Designs and adapts equipment and working-living environment. Transports patient to and from occupational therapy work area. Reports information and observations to supervisor verbally. Instructs or assists in instructing patient and family in home programs and basic living skills as well as care and use of adaptive equipment. Assists in evaluation of physically, developmentally, mentally retarded, or emotionally disabled client's daily living skills and capacities. Assists occupational therapist to plan, implement, and administer educational, vocational, and recreational activities to restore, reinforce, and enhance task performances. Prepares work material, assembles and maintains equipment, and orders supplies.

Personality Type: Social. Social occupations frequently involve working with, communicating with, and teaching people. These occupations often involve helping or providing service to others.

Abilities: Problem Sensitivity—The ability to tell when something is wrong or is likely to go wrong. Does not involve solving the problem, only recognizing there is a problem. Oral Comprehension—The ability to listen to and understand information and ideas presented verbally. Oral Expression—The ability to communicate information and ideas verbally so others will understand. Written Comprehension—The ability to read and understand information and ideas presented in writing.

Skills: Instructing—Teaching others how to do something. Social Perceptiveness—Being aware of other people's reactions and understanding why people react the way they do. Active Listening—Listening to what other people are saying; asking questions as appropriate. Service Orientation—Actively looking for ways to help people. Speaking—Talking to others to effectively convey information.

Generalized Work Activities: Assisting and Caring for Others—Providing assistance or personal care to others. Communicating with Other Workers—Providing information to supervisors, fellow workers, and subordinates. Exchanging information face-to-face, in writing, or via telephone/electronic transfer. Getting Information Needed to Do the Job—Observing, receiving, and otherwise obtaining information from all relevant sources. Teaching Others—Identifying educational needs, developing formal training programs or classes, and teaching or instructing others. Identifying Objects, Actions, and Events—Identifying information received by making estimates or categorizations, recognizing differences or similarities, or sensing changes in circumstances or events. Establishing and Maintaining Relationships—Developing constructive and cooperative working relationships with others.

Occupational Therapist Assistants

Assist occupational therapists in providing occupational therapy treatments and procedures. In accordance with state laws, assist in development of treatment plans, carry out routine functions, direct activity programs, and document the progress of treatments. Generally requires formal training. Designs and adapts equipment and working-living environment. Transports patient to and from occupational therapy work area. Maintains observed information in client records and prepares written reports. Assists educational specialist or clinical psychologist in administering situational or diagnostic tests to measure client's abilities or progress. Prepares work material, assembles and maintains equipment, and orders supplies. Assists occupational therapist to plan, implement, and administer educational, vocational, and recreational activities to restore, reinforce, and enhance task performances. Instructs or assists in instructing patient and family in home programs and basic living skills as well as care and use of adaptive equipment. Assists in evaluation of physically, developmentally, mentally retarded, or emotionally disabled client's daily living skills and capacities. Reports information and observations to supervisor verbally. Fabricates splints and other assistant devices. Helps professional staff demonstrate therapy techniques, such as manual and creative arts, and games.

Personality Type: Social. Social occupations frequently involve working with, communicating with, and teaching people. These occupations often involve helping or providing service to others.

Abilities: Problem Sensitivity—The ability to tell when something is wrong or is likely to go wrong. Does not involve solving the problem, only recognizing there is a problem. Oral Comprehension—The ability to listen to and understand information and ideas presented verbally. Oral Expression—The ability to communicate information and ideas verbally so others will understand. Written Comprehension—The ability to read and understand information and ideas presented in writing.

Skills: Active Listening—Listening to what other people are saying; asking questions as appropriate. Social Perceptiveness—Being aware of other people's reactions and understanding why people react the way they do. Service Orientation—Actively looking for ways to help people. Instructing—Teaching others how to do something. Speaking—Talking to others to effectively convey information.

Generalized Work Activities: Assisting and Caring for Others—Providing assistance or personal care to others. Communicating with Other Workers—Providing information to supervisors, fellow workers, and subordinates. Exchanging information face-to-face, in writing, or via telephone/electronic transfer. Teaching Others—Identifying educational needs, developing formal training programs or classes, and teaching or instructing others. Getting Information Needed to Do the Job—Observing, receiving, and otherwise obtaining information from all relevant sources. Establishing and Maintaining Relationships—Developing constructive and cooperative working relationships with others. Identifying Objects, Actions, and Events—Identifying information received by making estimates or categorizations, recognizing differences or similarities, or sensing changes in circumstances or events.

Office and Administrative Support Supervisors

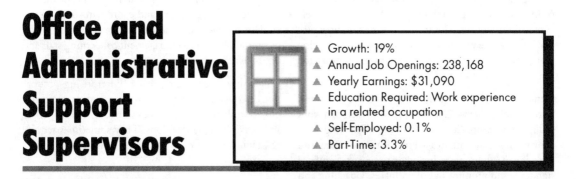

- ▲ Growth: 19%
- ▲ Annual Job Openings: 238,168
- ▲ Yearly Earnings: $31,090
- ▲ Education Required: Work experience in a related occupation
- ▲ Self-Employed: 0.1%
- ▲ Part-Time: 3.3%

First-Line Supervisors, Administrative Support

Supervise and coordinate activities of workers involved in providing administrative support. Oversees, coordinates, or performs activities associated with shipping, receiving, distribution, and transportation. Requisitions supplies. Computes figures, such as balances, totals, and commissions. Analyzes financial activities of establishment or department and assists in planning budget. Inspects equipment for defects and notifies maintenance personnel or outside service contractors for repairs. Plans layout of stockroom, warehouse, or other storage areas, considering turnover, size, weight, and related factors pertaining to items stored. Identifies and resolves discrepancies or errors. Verifies completeness and accuracy of subordinates' work, computations, and records. Examines procedures and recommends changes to save time, labor, and other costs and to improve quality control and operating efficiency. Compiles reports and information required by management or governmental agencies. Consults with supervisor and other personnel to resolve problems, such as equipment performance, output quality, and work schedules. Reviews records and reports pertaining to such activities as production, operation, pay roll, customer accounts, and shipping. Participates in work of subordinates to facilitate productivity or overcome difficult aspects of work. Maintains records of such matters as inventory, personnel, orders, supplies, and machine maintenance. Plans, prepares, and revises work schedules and duty assignments according to budget allotments, customer needs, problems, workloads, and statistical forecasts. Evaluates subordinate job performance and conformance to regulations, and recommends appropriate personnel action. Supervises and coordinates activities of workers engaged in clerical or administrative support activities. Interviews, selects, and discharges employees. Trains employees in work and safety procedures and company policies.

Personality Type: Enterprising. Enterprising occupations frequently involve starting up and carrying out projects. These occupations can involve leading people and making many decisions. They sometimes require risk taking and often deal with business.

Abilities: Oral Expression—The ability to communicate information and ideas verbally so others will understand. Oral Comprehension—The ability to listen to and understand information and ideas presented verbally. Written Expression—The ability to communicate information and ideas in writing so others will understand. Written Comprehension—The ability to read and understand information and ideas presented in writing. Near Vision—The ability to see details of objects at a close range.

Skills: Management of Personnel Resources—Motivating, developing, and directing people as they work, identifying the best people for the job. Time Management—Managing one's own time and the time of others. Speaking—Talking to others to effectively convey information. Monitoring—Assessing how well one is doing when learning or doing something. Reading Comprehension—Understanding written information in work-related documents.

Generalized Work Activities: Coordinating Work and Activities of Others—Coordinating members of a work group to accomplish tasks. Guiding, Directing, and Motivating Subordinates—Providing guidance and direction to subordinates, including setting performance standards and monitoring subordinates. Coaching and Developing Others—Identifying developmental needs of others and coaching or otherwise helping others to improve their knowledge or skills. Getting Information Needed to Do the Job—Observing, receiving, and otherwise obtaining information from all relevant sources. Performing Administrative Activities—Approving requests, handling paperwork, and performing day-to-day administrative tasks. Establishing and Maintaining Relationships—Developing constructive and cooperative working relationships with others.

First-Line Supervisors, Customer Service

Supervise and coordinate activities of workers involved in providing customer service. Requisitions or purchases supplies. Resolves complaints and answers questions of customers regarding services and procedures. Reviews and checks work of subordinates such as reports, records, and applications for accuracy and content, and corrects errors. Prepares, maintains, and submits reports and records, such as budgets and operational and personnel reports. Plans and develops improved procedures. Interprets and communicates work procedures and company policies to staff. Helps workers in resolving problems and completing work. Observes and evaluates workers' performance. Issues instructions and assigns duties to workers. Hires and

discharges workers. Trains and instructs employees. Plans, prepares, and devises work schedules, according to budgets and workloads. Communicates with other departments and management to resolve problems and expedite work. Supervises and coordinates activities of workers engaged in customer service activities. Makes recommendations to management concerning staff and improvement of procedures.

Personality Type: Enterprising. Enterprising occupations frequently involve starting up and carrying out projects. These occupations can involve leading people and making many decisions. They sometimes require risk taking and often deal with business.

Abilities: Oral Expression—The ability to communicate information and ideas verbally so others will understand. Oral Comprehension—The ability to listen to and understand information and ideas presented verbally. Near Vision—The ability to see details of objects at a close range. Written Expression—The ability to communicate information and ideas in writing so others will understand. Written Comprehension—The ability to read and understand information and ideas presented in writing.

Skills: Management of Personnel Resources—Motivating, developing, and directing people as they work, identifying the best people for the job. Speaking—Talking to others to effectively convey information. Coordination—Adjusting actions in relation to others' actions. Critical Thinking—Using logic and analysis to identify the strengths and weaknesses of different approaches. Time Management—Managing one's own time and the time of others. Active Listening—Listening to what other people are saying; asking questions as appropriate.

Generalized Work Activities: Staffing Organizational Units—Recruiting, interviewing, selecting, hiring, and promoting persons for the organization. Guiding, Directing, and Motivating Subordinates—Providing guidance and direction to subordinates, including setting performance standards and monitoring subordinates. Establishing and Maintaining Relationships—Developing constructive and cooperative working relationships with others. Communicating with Other Workers—Providing information to supervisors, fellow workers, and subordinates. Exchanging information face-to-face, in writing, or via telephone/electronic transfer. Resolving Conflict, Negotiating with Others—Handling complaints, arbitrating disputes, resolving grievances, or otherwise negotiating with others.

Documenting/Recording Information—Entering, transcribing, recording, storing, or maintaining information in either written form or by electronic/magnetic recording. Scheduling Work and Activities—Scheduling events, programs, activities, and the work of others.

Office Machine and Cash Register Servicers

- ▲ Growth: 16%
- ▲ Annual Job Openings: 2,931
- ▲ Yearly Earnings: $27,830
- ▲ Education Required: Long-term O-J-T
- ▲ Self-Employed: 6.8%
- ▲ Part-Time: 1.8%

Office Machine and Cash Register Servicers

Repair and service office machines, such as adding, accounting, calculating, duplicating, and typewriting machines. Includes the repair of manual, electrical, and electronic office machines. Reads specifications, such as blueprints, charts, and schematics to determine machine settings and adjustments. Instructs operators and servicers in operation, maintenance, and repair of machine. Cleans and oils mechanical parts to maintain machine. Assembles and installs machine according to specifications using hand tools, power tools, and measuring devices. Disassembles machine and examines parts, such as wires, gears, and bearings for wear and defects, using hand tools, power tools, and measuring devices. Operates machine, such as typewriter, cash register, or adding machine to test functioning of parts and mechanisms. Tests machine to locate cause of electrical problems, using testing devices, such as voltmeter, ohmmeter, and circuit test equipment. Repairs, adjusts, or replaces electrical and mechanical components and parts, using hand tools, power tools, and soldering or welding equipment.

Personality Type: Realistic. Realistic occupations frequently involve work activities that include practical, hands-on problems and solutions. They often deal with plants, animals, and real-world materials like wood, tools, and machinery. Many of the occupations require working outside and do not involve a lot of paperwork or working closely with others.

Abilities: Finger Dexterity—The ability to make precisely coordinated movements of the fingers of one or both hands to grasp, manipulate, or assemble very small objects. Written Comprehension—The ability to read and understand information and ideas presented in writing. Near Vision—The ability to see details of objects at a close range. Control Precision—The ability to quickly and repeatedly make precise adjustments in moving the controls of a machine or vehicle to exact positions. Manual Dexterity—The ability to quickly make coordinated movements of one hand, a hand together with its arm, or two hands, to grasp, manipulate, or assemble objects.

Skills: Repairing—Repairing machines or systems, using the needed tools. Testing—Conducting tests to determine whether equipment, software, or procedures are operating as expected. Operation and Control—Controlling operations of equipment or systems. Troubleshooting—Determining what is causing an operating error and deciding what to do about it. Reading Comprehension—Understanding written information in work-related documents. Installation—Installing equipment, machines, wiring, or programs to meet specifications.

Generalized Work Activities: Repairing and Maintaining Electrical Equipment—Fixing, servicing, adjusting, regulating, calibrating, fine-tuning, or testing machines, devices, and equipment that operate primarily on the basis of electrical or electronic, not mechanical, principles. Repairing and Maintaining Mechanical Equipment—Fixing, servicing, aligning, setting up, adjusting, and testing machines, devices, moving parts, and equipment that operate primarily on the basis of mechanical, not electronic, principles. Getting Information Needed to Do the Job—Observing,

receiving, and otherwise obtaining information from all relevant sources. Inspecting Equipment, Structures, Materials—Inspecting or diagnosing equipment, structures, or materials to identify the causes of errors or other problems or defects. Identifying Objects, Actions, and Events—Identifying information received by making estimates or categorizations, recognizing differences or similarities, or sensing changes in circumstances or events. Controlling Machines and Processes—Using either control mechanisms or direct physical activity to operate machines or processes. Does not involve working with computers or vehicles. Handling and Moving Objects—Using one's hands and arms in handling, installing, forming, positioning, and moving materials, or in manipulating things. Includes the use of keyboards.

Operations Research Analysts

- ▲ Growth: 9%
- ▲ Annual Job Openings: 5,355
- ▲ Yearly Earnings: $49,070
- ▲ Education Required: Master's degree
- ▲ Self-Employed: 0%
- ▲ Part-Time: 2.8%

Operations Research Analysts

Formulate and apply mathematical modeling and other optimizing methods using a computer to develop and interpret information that assists management with decision making, policy formulation, or other managerial functions. Develop related software, service, or products. Collect and analyze data and develop decision support software. Develop and supply optimal time, cost, or logistics networks for program evaluation, review, or implementation. Designs, conducts, and evaluates experimental operational models where insufficient data exists to formulate model. Defines data requirements and gathers and validates information, applying judgment and statistical tests. Studies information and selects plan from

competitive proposals that afford maximum probability of profit or effectiveness relating to cost or risk. Evaluates implementation and effectiveness of research. Develops and applies time and cost networks to plan and control large projects. Performs validation and testing of model to ensure adequacy, or determines need for reformulation. Specifies manipulative or computational methods to be applied to model. Prepares model of problem in form of one or several equations that relates constants and variables, restrictions, alternatives, conflicting objectives and their numerical parameters. Analyzes problem in terms of management information and conceptualizes and defines problem. Prepares for management reports defining problem, evaluation, and possible solution.

Personality Type: Investigative. Investigative occupations frequently involve working with ideas and require an extensive amount of thinking. These occupations can involve searching for facts and figuring out problems mentally.

Abilities: Mathematical Reasoning—The ability to understand and organize a problem and then select a mathematical method or formula to solve the problem. Written Comprehension—The ability to read and understand information and ideas presented in writing. Oral Comprehension—The ability to listen to and understand information and ideas presented verbally. Written Expression—The ability to communicate information and ideas in writing so others will understand. Deductive Reasoning—The ability to apply general rules to specific problems to come up with logical answers. Involves deciding if an answer makes sense.

Skills: Problem Identification—Identifying the nature of problems. Critical Thinking—Using logic and analysis to identify the strengths and weaknesses of different approaches. Mathematics—Using mathematics to solve problems. Systems Evaluation—Looking at many indicators of system performance, taking into

account their accuracy. Judgment and Decision Making—Weighing the relative costs and benefits of a potential action.

Generalized Work Activities: Making Decisions and Solving Problems—Combining, evaluating, and analyzing information and data to make decisions and solve problems. Involves making decisions about the relative importance of information and choosing the best solution. Providing Consultation and Advice to Others—Providing consultation and expert advice to management or other groups on technical, systems-related, or process-related topics. Getting Information Needed to Do the Job—Observing, receiving, and otherwise obtaining information from all relevant sources. Analyzing Data or Information—Identifying underlying principles, reasons, or facts by breaking down information or data into separate parts. Communicating with Other Workers—Providing information to supervisors, fellow workers, and subordinates. Exchanging information face-to-face, in writing, or via telephone/electronic transfer.

Optometrists

- ▲ Growth: 11%
- ▲ Annual Job Openings: 1,532
- ▲ Yearly Earnings: $68,480
- ▲ Education Required: First professional degree
- ▲ Self-Employed: 37.5%
- ▲ Part-Time: 10.5%

Optometrists

Diagnose, manage, and treat conditions and diseases of the human eye and visual system. Examine eyes and visual system, diagnose problems or impairments, prescribe corrective lenses, and provide treatment. Prescribe therapeutic drugs to treat specific eye conditions. Prescribes eyeglasses, contact lenses, and other vision aids or therapeutic procedures to correct or conserve vision. Examines eyes to determine visual acuity and perception and to diagnose diseases and other abnormalities, such as glaucoma and color blindness. Consults with and refers patients to ophthalmologist

or other health care practitioner if additional medical treatment is determined necessary. Prescribes medications to treat eye diseases if state laws permit.

Personality Type: Investigative. Investigative occupations frequently involve working with ideas and require an extensive amount of thinking. These occupations can involve searching for facts and figuring out problems mentally.

Abilities: Oral Expression—The ability to communicate information and ideas verbally so others will understand. Written Comprehension—The ability to read and understand information and ideas presented in writing.

Written Expression—The ability to communicate information and ideas in writing so others will understand. Problem Sensitivity—The ability to tell when something is wrong or is likely to go wrong. Does not involve solving the problem, only recognizing there is a problem. Near Vision—The ability to see details of objects at a close range. Oral Comprehension—The ability to listen to and understand information and ideas presented verbally.

Skills: Science—Using scientific methods to solve problems. Reading Comprehension—Understanding written information in work-related documents. Problem Identification—Identifying the nature of problems. Speaking—Talking to others to effectively convey information. Active Listening—Listening to what other people are saying; asking questions as appropriate.

Generalized Work Activities: Assisting and Caring for Others—Providing assistance or personal care to others. Updating and Using Job-Relevant Knowledge—Keeping up-to-date technically and knowing the functions of one's own job and related jobs. Getting Information Needed to Do the Job—Observing, receiving, and otherwise obtaining information from all relevant sources. Identifying Objects, Actions, and Events—Identifying information received by making estimates or categorizations, recognizing differences or similarities, or sensing changes in circumstances or events. Making Decisions and Solving Problems—Combining, evaluating, and analyzing information and data to make decisions and solve problems. Involves making decisions about the relative importance of information and choosing the best solution.

Packaging and Filling Machine Operators

- ▲ Growth: 13%
- ▲ Annual Job Openings: 88,131
- ▲ Yearly Earnings: $20,060
- ▲ Education Required: Moderate-term O-J-T
- ▲ Self-Employed: 0%
- ▲ Part-Time: 7.1%

Packaging and Filling Machine Operators and Tenders

Operate or tend machines to prepare industrial or consumer products for storage or shipment. Includes cannery workers who pack food products. Observes machine operations to ensure quality and conformity of filled or packaged products to standards. Inspects and removes defective product and packaging material. Stocks product for packaging or filling machine operation. Stocks packaging material for machine processing. Tests and evaluates product and verifies product weight or measurement to ensure quality standards. Secures finished packaged items by hand tying, sewing, or attaching fastener. Cleans, oils, and makes minor repairs to machinery and equipment. Counts and records finished and rejected packaged items. Attaches identification labels to finished packaged items. Removes finished packaged items from machine and separates rejected items. Adjusts machine tension and pressure and machine components according to size or processing angle of product. Operates mechanism to cut filler product or packaging material. Regulates machine flow, speed, or temperature. Stops or resets machine when malfunction occurs and clears machine jams. Starts machine, by engaging controls. Tends or operates machine that packages product. Stacks finished packaged items or packs items in cartons or containers.

Personality Type: Realistic. Realistic occupations frequently involve work activities that include practical, hands-on problems and solutions. They often deal with plants, animals, and real-world materials like wood, tools, and machinery. Many of the occupations require working outside and do not involve a lot of paperwork or working closely with others.

Abilities: Manual Dexterity—The ability to quickly make coordinated movements of one hand, a hand together with its arm, or two hands, to grasp, manipulate, or assemble objects. Perceptual Speed—The ability to quickly and accurately compare letters, numbers, objects, pictures, or patterns. The things to be compared may be presented at the same time or one after the other. Includes comparing a presented object with a remembered object. Information Ordering—The ability to correctly follow a given rule or set of rules in order to arrange things or actions in a certain order. The things or actions can include numbers, letters, words, pictures, procedures, sentences, and mathematical or logical operations. Near Vision—The ability to see details of objects at a close range. Control Precision—The ability to quickly and repeatedly make precise adjustments in moving the controls of a machine or vehicle to exact positions. Extent Flexibility—The ability to bend, stretch, twist, or reach out with the body, arms, and/or legs.

Skills: Operation Monitoring—Watching gauges, dials, or other indicators to make sure a machine is working properly. Operation and Control—Controlling operations of equipment or systems. Product Inspection—Inspecting and evaluating the quality of products. Equipment Maintenance—Performing routine maintenance and determining when and what kind of maintenance is needed. Testing—Conducting tests to determine whether equipment, software, or procedures are operating as expected. Troubleshooting—Determining what is causing an operating error and deciding what to do about it. Repairing—Repairing machines or systems, using the needed tools.

Generalized Work Activities: Controlling Machines and Processes—Using either control mechanisms or direct physical activity to operate machines or processes. Does not involve working with computers or vehicles. Handling and Moving Objects—Using one's hands and arms in handling, installing, forming, positioning, and moving materials, or in manipulating things. Includes the use of keyboards. Monitoring Processes, Materials, Surroundings—Monitoring and reviewing information from materials, events, or the environment, often to detect problems or to find out when things are finished. Repairing and Maintaining Mechanical Equipment—Fixing, servicing, aligning, setting up, adjusting, and testing machines, devices, moving parts, and equipment that operate primarily on the basis of mechanical, not electronic, principles. Inspecting Equipment, Structures, Materials—Inspecting or diagnosing equipment, structures, or materials to identify the causes of errors or other problems or defects.

Painting, Coating, and Decorating Workers

- ▲ Growth: 18%
- ▲ Annual Job Openings: 8,593
- ▲ Yearly Earnings: $19,060
- ▲ Education Required: Short-term O-J-T
- ▲ Self-Employed: 18.4%
- ▲ Part-Time: 8.6%

Painting, Coating, and Decorating Workers

Paint, coat, or decorate articles, such as furniture, glass, plateware, pottery, jewelry, cakes, toys, books, or leather. Cleans and maintains tools and equipment using solvent, brushes, and rags. Immerses workpiece into coating material for specified time. Positions and glues decorative pieces in cutout section, following pattern. Conceals blemishes in workpiece, such as nicks and dents, using filler, such as putty. Cleans surface of workpiece in preparation for coating, using cleaning fluid, solvent, brushes, scraper, steam, sandpaper, or cloth. Cuts out sections in surface of material to be inlaid with decorative pieces, using pattern and knife or scissors. Places coated workpiece in oven or dryer for specified time to dry or harden finish. Selects and mixes ingredients to prepare coating substance according to specifications using paddle or mechanical mixer. Drains or wipes workpieces to remove excess coating material or to facilitate setting of finish coat on workpiece. Examines finished surface of workpiece to verify conformance to specifications and retouches defective areas of surface. Rinses coated workpiece to remove excess coating material or to facilitate setting of finish coat on workpiece. Reads job order and inspects workpiece to determine work procedure and materials required. Applies coating, such as paint, ink, or lacquer, to protect or decorate workpiece surface, using spray gum, pen, or brush. Melts or heats coating material to specified temperature.

Personality Type: Realistic. Realistic occupations frequently involve work activities that include practical, hands-on problems and solutions. They often deal with plants, animals, and real-world materials like wood, tools, and machinery. Many of the occupations require working outside and do not involve a lot of paperwork or working closely with others.

Abilities: Manual Dexterity—The ability to quickly make coordinated movements of one hand, a hand together with its arm, or two hands, to grasp, manipulate, or assemble objects. Information Ordering—The ability to correctly follow a given rule or set of rules in order to arrange things or actions in a certain order. The things or actions can include numbers, letters, words, pictures, procedures, sentences, and mathematical or logical operations. Visual Color Discrimination—The ability to match or detect differences between colors, including shades of color and brightness. Near Vision—The ability to see details of objects at a close range. Arm-Hand Steadiness—The ability to keep the hand and arm steady while making an arm movement or while holding the arm and hand in one position. Finger Dexterity—The ability to make precisely coordinated movements of the fingers of one or both hands to grasp, manipulate, or assemble very small objects.

Skills: Product Inspection—Inspecting and evaluating the quality of products. Equipment Selection—Determining the kind of tools and equipment needed to do a job. Monitoring—Assessing how well one is doing when learning or doing something. Information Organization—Finding ways to structure or classify multiple pieces of information. Operations Analysis—Analyzing needs and product requirements to create a design. Operation and Control—Controlling operations of equipment or systems. Problem Identification—Identifying the nature of problems.

Generalized Work Activities: Handling and Moving Objects—Using one's hands and arms in handling, installing, forming, positioning, and moving materials, or in manipulating things. Includes the use of keyboards. Getting Information Needed to Do the Job—Observing, receiving, and otherwise obtaining information from all relevant sources. Performing General Physical Activities—Performing physical activities that require moving one's whole body, such as in climbing, lifting, balancing, walking, and stooping. Performing activities that often also require considerable use of the arms and legs, such as in the physical handling of materials. Evaluation Information against Standards—Evaluating information against a set of standards and verifying that it is correct. Controlling Machines and Processes—Using either control mechanisms or direct physical activity to operate machines or processes. Does not involve working with computers or vehicles.

Monitoring Processes, Materials, Surroundings—Monitoring and reviewing information from materials, events, or the environment, often to detect problems or to find out when things are finished.

Paralegals and Legal Assistants

- ▲ Growth: 62%
- ▲ Annual Job Openings: 33,971
- ▲ Yearly Earnings: $32,760
- ▲ Education Required: Associate degree
- ▲ Self-Employed: 0.9%
- ▲ Part-Time: 12.5%

Paralegals and Legal Assistants

Assist lawyers by researching legal precedent, investigating facts, or preparing legal documents. Conduct research to support a legal proceeding, to formulate a defense, or to initiate legal action. Appraises and inventories real and personal property for estate planning. Prepares affidavits or other documents, maintains document file, and files pleadings with court clerk. Answers questions regarding legal issues pertaining to civil service hearings. Directs and coordinates law office activity, including delivery of subpoenas. Keeps and monitors legal volumes to ensure that law library is up-to-date. Presents arguments and evidence to support appeal at appeal hearing. Calls upon witnesses to testify at hearing. Investigates facts and law of cases to determine causes of action and to prepare cases. Prepares legal documents, including briefs, pleadings, appeals, wills, contracts, and real estate closing statements. Gathers and analyzes research data, such as statutes, decisions, and legal articles, codes, and documents. Arbitrates disputes between parties and assists in real estate closing process.

Personality Type: Enterprising. Enterprising occupations frequently involve starting up and carrying out projects. These occupations can involve leading people and making many decisions. They sometimes require risk taking and often deal with business.

Abilities: Written Comprehension—The ability to read and understand information and ideas presented in writing. Written Expression—The ability to communicate information and ideas in writing so others will understand. Oral Comprehension—The ability to listen to and understand information and ideas presented verbally. Oral Expression—The ability to communicate information and ideas verbally so others will understand. Deductive Reasoning—The ability to apply general rules to specific problems to come up with logical answers. Involves deciding if an answer makes sense.

Skills: Information Gathering—Knowing how to find information and identifying essential information. Writing—Communicating effectively with others in writing as indicated by the needs of the audience. Reading Comprehension—Understanding written information in work-related documents. Critical Thinking—Using logic and analysis to identify the strengths and weaknesses of different approaches.

Generalized Work Activities: Getting Information Needed to Do the Job—Observing, receiving, and otherwise obtaining information from all relevant sources. Identifying Objects, Actions, and Events—Identifying information received by making estimates or categorizations, recognizing differences or similarities, or sensing changes in circumstances or events. Analyzing Data or Information—Identifying underlying principles, reasons, or facts by breaking down information or data into separate parts. Evaluation Information against Standards—Evaluating information against a set of standards and verifying that it is correct. Communicating with Other Workers—Providing information to supervisors, fellow workers, and subordinates. Exchanging information face-to-face, in writing, or via telephone/electronic transfer.

Parking Lot Attendants

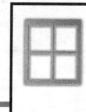

▲ Growth: 31%
▲ Annual Job Openings: 17,725
▲ Yearly Earnings: $13,930
▲ Education Required: Short-term O-J-T
▲ Self-Employed: 0%
▲ Part-Time: 15.4%

Parking Lot Attendants

Park automobiles or issue tickets for customers in a parking lot or garage. Collect fee. Services cars in storage to protect tires, battery, and finish against deterioration. Keeps new car lot in order and maximizes use of space. Inspects vehicles to detect damage. Services vehicles with gas, oil, and water. Lifts, positions, and removes barricades to open or close parking areas. Collects parking fee from customer based on charges for time automobile is parked. Takes numbered tag from customer, locates car, and delivers it to customer, or directs customer to parked car. Patrols area to prevent thefts of parked automobiles or items in automobiles. Parks automobiles in parking lot, storage garage, or new car lot. Places numbered tag on windshield of automobile to be parked, and hands customer similar tag to be used in locating parked automobile. Signals or directs vehicle drivers with hands or flashlight to parking area.

Personality Type: Realistic. Realistic occupations frequently involve work activities that include practical, hands-on problems and solutions. They often deal with plants, animals, and real-world materials like wood, tools, and machinery. Many of the occupations require working outside and do not involve a lot of paperwork or working closely with others.

Abilities: Oral Expression—The ability to communicate information and ideas verbally so others will understand. Control Precision—The ability to quickly and repeatedly make precise adjustments in moving the controls of a machine or vehicle to exact positions. Near Vision—The ability to see details of objects at a close range. Information Ordering—The ability to correctly follow a given rule or set of rules in order to arrange things or actions in a certain order. The things or actions can include numbers, letters, words, pictures, procedures, sentences, and mathematical or logical operations. Spatial Orientation—The ability to know one's location in relation to the environment or to know where other objects are in relation to one's self. Problem Sensitivity—The ability to tell when something is wrong or is likely to go wrong. Does not involve solving the problem, only recognizing there is a problem. Far Vision—The ability to see details at a distance. Written Comprehension—The ability to read and understand information and ideas presented in writing.

Skills: Mathematics—Using mathematics to solve problems. Service Orientation—Actively looking for ways to help people. Equipment Maintenance—Performing routine maintenance and determining when and what kind of maintenance is needed. Active Listening—Listening to what other people are saying; asking questions as appropriate. Social Perceptiveness—Being aware of other people's reactions and understanding why people react the way they do.

Generalized Work Activities: Operating Vehicles or Equipment—Running, maneuvering, navigating, or driving vehicles or mechanized equipment such as forklifts, passenger vehicles, aircraft, or water craft. Performing for/Working with Public—Performing for people or dealing directly with the public, including serving persons in restaurants and stores and receiving clients or guests. Communicating with Persons Outside Organization—Communicating with persons outside the organization. Representing the organization to customers, the public, government, and other external sources. Exchanging information face-to-face, in writing, or via telephone/electronic transfer. Monitoring Processes, Materials, Surroundings—Monitoring and reviewing information from materials, events, or the environment, often to detect problems or to find out when things are finished. Handling and Moving Objects—Using one's hands and arms in handling, installing, forming, positioning, and moving materials, or in manipulating things. Includes the use of keyboards. Identifying Objects, Actions, and Events—Identifying information received by making estimates or categorizations, recognizing differences or similarities, or sensing changes in circumstances or events. Performing General Physical Activities—Performing physical activities that require moving one's whole body, such as in climbing, lifting, balancing, walking, and stooping. Performing activities that often also require considerable use of the arms and legs, such as in the physical handling of materials.

Paving, Surfacing, and Tamping Equipment Operators

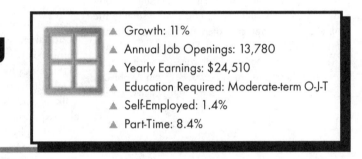

- ▲ Growth: 11%
- ▲ Annual Job Openings: 13,780
- ▲ Yearly Earnings: $24,510
- ▲ Education Required: Moderate-term O-J-T
- ▲ Self-Employed: 1.4%
- ▲ Part-Time: 8.4%

Paving, Surfacing, and Tamping Equipment Operators

Operate equipment used for applying concrete, asphalt, or other materials to road beds, parking lots, or airport runways and taxiways, or equipment used for tamping gravel, dirt, or other materials. Includes concrete and asphalt paving machine operators, form tampers, tamping machine operators, and stone spreader operators. Sets up forms and lays out guidelines for curbs, according to written specifications using string, spray paint, and concrete/water mix. Monitors machine operation and observes distribution of paving material to adjust machine settings or material flow. Starts machine, engages clutch, pushes and moves levers, and turns wheels to control and guide machine along forms or guidelines. Operates machine to clean or cut expansion joints in concrete or asphalt and to rout out cracks in pavement. Operate machine to mix and spray binding, waterproofing, and curing compounds. Operate machine to spread, smooth, or steel-reinforce stone, concrete, or asphalt. Drives and operates curbing machine to extrude concrete or asphalt curbing. Lights burner or starts heating unit of machine and regulates temperature. Drives machine onto truck trailer and drives truck to transport machine to and from job site. Installs dies, cutters, and extensions to screed onto machine, using hand tools. Cleans, maintains, and repairs equipment, according to specifications, using mechanics' hand tools, or reports malfunction to supervisor. Operates machine or manually rolls surfaces to compact earth fills, foundation forms, and finished road materials according to grade specifications. Fill tank, hopper, or machine with paving materials.

Personality Type: Realistic. Realistic occupations frequently involve work activities that include practical, hands-on problems and solutions. They often deal with plants, animals, and real-world materials like wood, tools, and machinery. Many of the occupations require working outside and do not involve a lot of paperwork or working closely with others.

Abilities: Control Precision—The ability to quickly and repeatedly make precise adjustments in moving the controls of a machine or vehicle to exact positions. Multilimb Coordination—The ability to coordinate movements of two or more limbs together (for example, two arms, two legs, or one leg and one arm) while sitting, standing, or lying down. Does not involve performing the activities while the body is in motion. Information Ordering—The ability to correctly follow a given rule or set of rules in order to arrange things or actions in a certain order. The things or actions can include numbers, letters, words, pictures, procedures, sentences, and mathematical or logical operations. Problem Sensitivity—The ability to tell when something is wrong or is likely to go wrong. Does not involve solving the problem, only recognizing there is a problem. Manual Dexterity—The ability to quickly make coordinated movements of one hand, a hand together with its arm, or two hands, to grasp, manipulate, or assemble objects. Depth Perception—The ability to judge which of several objects is closer or farther away from the observer, or to judge the distance between an object and the observer.

Skills: Operation and Control—Controlling operations of equipment or systems. Equipment Selection—Determining the kind of tools and equipment needed to do a job. Product Inspection—Inspecting and evaluating the quality of products. Operation Monitoring—Watching gauges, dials, or other indicators to make sure a machine is working properly. Equipment Maintenance—Performing routine maintenance and determining when and what kind of maintenance is needed.

Generalized Work Activities: Controlling Machines and Processes—Using either control mechanisms or direct physical activity to operate machines or processes. Does not involve working with computers or vehicles. Operating Vehicles or Equipment—Running, maneuvering, navigating, or driving vehicles or mechanized equipment such as forklifts, passenger vehicles, aircraft, or water craft. Handling and Moving Objects—Using one's hands and arms in handling, installing, forming, positioning, and moving materials, or in manipulating things. Performing General Physical Activities—Performing physical activities that require moving one's whole body, such as in climbing, lifting, balancing, walking, and stooping. Performing activities that often also require considerable use of the arms and legs, such as in the physical handling of materials. Monitoring Processes, Materials, Surroundings—Monitoring and reviewing information from materials, events, or the environment, often to detect problems or to find out when things are finished.

Personal Care and Home Health Aides

- ▲ Growth: 58%
- ▲ Annual Job Openings: 249,694
- ▲ Yearly Earnings: $15,800
- ▲ Education Required: Short-term O-J-T
- ▲ Self-Employed: 0%
- ▲ Part-Time: 42.4%

Home Health Aides

Provide routine, personal healthcare, such as bathing, dressing, or grooming, to elderly, convalescent, or disabled persons in the home of patients or in a residential care facility. Assists patients into and out of bed, automobiles, or wheelchair, to lavatory, and up and down stairs. Purchases, prepares, and serves food for patient and other members of family following special prescribed diets. Maintains records of services performed and of apparent condition of patient. Entertains patient, reads aloud, and plays cards and other games with patient. Performs variety of miscellaneous duties as requested, such as obtaining household supplies and running errands. Administers prescribed oral medication under written direction of physician or as directed by home care nurse and aide. Changes bed linens, washes and irons patient's laundry, and cleans patient's quarters. Massages patient and applies preparations and treatment, such as liniment or alcohol rubs and heat-lamp stimulation.

Personality Type: Social. Social occupations frequently involve working with, communicating with, and teaching people. These occupations often involve helping or providing service to others.

Abilities: Oral Comprehension—The ability to listen to and understand information and ideas presented verbally. Oral Expression—The ability to communicate information and ideas verbally so others will understand. Static Strength—The ability to exert maximum muscle force to lift, push, pull, or carry objects. Problem Sensitivity—The ability to tell when something is wrong or is likely to go wrong. Does not involve solving the problem, only recognizing there is a problem. Manual Dexterity—The ability to quickly make coordinated movements of one hand, a hand together with its arm, or two hands, to grasp, manipulate, or assemble objects. Written Comprehension—The ability to read and understand information and ideas presented in writing.

Skills: Service Orientation—Actively looking for ways to help people. Social Perceptiveness—Being aware of other people's reactions and understanding why people react the way they do. Active Listening—Listening to what other people are saying; asking questions as appropriate. Speaking—Talking to others to effectively convey information.

Generalized Work Activities: Assisting and Caring for Others—Providing assistance or personal care to others. Performing General Physical Activities—Performing physical activities that require moving one's whole body, such as in climbing, lifting, balancing, walking, and stooping. Performing activities that often also require considerable use of the arms and legs, such as in the physical handling of materials. Handling and Moving Objects—Using one's hands and arms in handling, installing, forming, positioning, and moving materials, or in manipulating things. Establishing and Maintaining Relationships—Developing constructive and cooperative working relationships with others. Documenting/Recording Information—Entering, transcribing, recording, storing, or maintaining information in either written form or by electronic/magnetic recording.

Personal and Home Care Aides

Assist elderly or disabled adults with daily living activities at the person's home or in a daytime nonresidential facility. Keep house, make beds, do laundry, wash dishes, and prepare meals at a place of residence. Provide meals and supervised activities at nonresidential care facilities. Advise families, the elderly, and the disabled on such things as nutrition, cleanliness, and household utilities. Assigns housekeeping duties according to children's capabilities. Evaluates needs of individuals served and plans for continuing services. Prepares and maintains records of assistance rendered. Assists client with dressing, undressing, and toilet activities. Assists parents in establishing good study habits for children. Drives motor vehicle to transport client to specified locations. Advises and assists family members in planning nutritious meals, purchasing and preparing foods, and utilizing commodities from surplus food programs. Obtains information for client, for personal and business purposes. Gives bedside care to incapacitated individuals and trains family members to provide bedside care. Assists in training children. Explains fundamental hygiene principles. Types correspondence and reports.

Personality Type: Social. Social occupations frequently involve working with, communicating with, and teaching people. These occupations often involve helping or providing service to others.

Abilities: Oral Expression—The ability to communicate information and ideas verbally so others will understand. Oral Comprehension—The ability to listen to and understand information and ideas presented verbally. Problem Sensitivity—The ability to tell when something is wrong or is likely to go wrong. Does not involve solving the problem, only recognizing there is a problem. Speech Clarity—The ability to speak clearly to that what is said is understandable to a listener. Written Expression—The ability to communicate information and ideas in writing so others will understand. Fluency of Ideas—The ability to come up with a number of ideas about a given topic. Emphasis is on the number of ideas produced and not the quality, correctness, or creativity of the ideas.

Skills: Speaking—Talking to others to effectively convey information. Service Orientation—Actively looking for ways to help people. Social Perceptiveness—Being aware of other people's reactions and understanding why people react the way they do. Active Listening—Listening to what other people are saying; asking questions as appropriate. Instructing—Teaching others how to do something.

Generalized Work Activities: Assisting and Caring for Others—Providing assistance or personal care to others.

Establishing and Maintaining Relationships—Developing constructive and cooperative working relationships with others. Performing General Physical Activities—Performing physical activities that require moving one's whole body, such as in climbing, lifting, balancing, walking, and stooping. Performing activities that often also require considerable use of the arms and legs, such as in the physical handling of materials. Teaching Others—Identifying educational needs, developing formal training programs or classes, and teaching or instructing others. Handling and Moving Objects—Using one's hands and arms in handling, installing, forming, positioning, and moving materials, or in manipulating things.

Pest Control Workers

- ▲ Growth: 25%
- ▲ Annual Job Openings: 7,983
- ▲ Yearly Earnings: $22,490
- ▲ Education Required: Moderate-term O-J-T
- ▲ Self-Employed: 7.1%
- ▲ Part-Time: 30.4%

Pest Control Workers

Spray or release chemical solutions or toxic gases and set traps to kill pests and vermin such as mice, termites, and roaches, that infest buildings and surrounding areas. Posts warning signs and locks building doors to secure area to be fumigated. Positions and fastens edges of tarpaulins over building and tapes vents to ensure air-tight environment and checks for leaks. Cleans and removes blockages from infested areas to facilitate spraying procedure and provide drainage, using broom, mop, shovel, and rake. Measures area dimensions requiring treatment, using rule, calculates fumigant requirements, and estimates cost for service. Inspects premises to identify infestation source and extent of damage to property, wall, and roof porosity, and access to infested locations. Drives truck equipped with power spraying equipment. Digs up and burns or sprays weeds

with herbicides. Cleans work site after completion of job. Sprays or dusts chemical solutions, powders, or gases into rooms, onto clothing, furnishings or wood, and over marshlands, ditches, catch-basins. Studies preliminary reports and diagrams of infested area and determines treatment type required to eliminate and prevent recurrence of infestation. Directs and/or assists other workers in treatment and extermination processes to eliminate and control rodents, insects, and weeds. Cuts or bores openings in building or surrounding concrete, accesses infested areas, inserts nozzle, and injects pesticide to impregnate ground. Sets mechanical traps and places poisonous paste or bait in sewers, burrows, and ditches. Records work activities performed.

Personality Type: Realistic. Realistic occupations frequently involve work activities that include practical, hands-on problems and solutions. They often deal with plants, animals, and real-world materials like wood, tools, and machinery. Many of the occupations require working outside and do not involve a lot of paperwork or working closely with others.

Abilities: Information Ordering—The ability to correctly follow a given rule or set of rules in order to arrange things or actions in a certain order. The things or actions can include numbers, letters, words, pictures, procedures, sentences, and mathematical or logical operations. Problem Sensitivity—The ability to tell when something is wrong or is likely to go wrong. Does not involve solving the problem, only recognizing there is a problem. Extent Flexibility—The ability to bend, stretch, twist, or reach out with the body, arms, and/or legs. Oral Comprehension—The ability to listen to and understand information and ideas presented verbally. Number Facility—The ability to add, subtract, multiply, or divide quickly and correctly.

Skills: Problem Identification—Identifying the nature of problems. Operation and Control—Controlling operations of equipment or systems. Mathematics— Using mathematics to solve problems. Equipment Selection—Determining the kind of tools and equipment needed to do a job. Implementation

Planning—Developing approaches for implementing an idea. Judgment and Decision Making—Weighing the relative costs and benefits of a potential action.

Generalized Work Activities: Performing General Physical Activities—Performing physical activities that require moving one's whole body, such as in climbing, lifting, balancing, walking, and stooping. Performing activities that often also require considerable use of the arms and legs, such as in the physical handling of materials. Handling and Moving Objects—Using one's hands and arms in handling, installing, forming, positioning, and moving materials, or in manipulating things. Inspecting Equipment, Structures, Materials— Inspecting or diagnosing equipment, structures, or materials to identify the causes of errors or other problems or defects. Estimating Needed Characteristics—Estimating the characteristics of materials, products, events, or information; estimating sizes, distances, and quantities; determining time, costs, resources, or materials needed to perform a work activity. Getting Information Needed to Do the Job— Observing, receiving, and otherwise obtaining information from all relevant sources.

Petroleum Engineers

- ▲ Growth: –4%
- ▲ Annual Job Openings: 802
- ▲ Yearly Earnings: $74,260
- ▲ Education Required: Bachelor's degree
- ▲ Self-Employed: 0%
- ▲ Part-Time: 3.1%

Petroleum Engineers

Devise methods to improve oil and gas well production and determine the need for new or modified tool designs. Oversee drilling and offer technical advice to achieve economical and satisfactory progress. Inspects oil and gas wells to determine that installations are completed. Writes technical reports for engineering and management personnel. Tests machinery and equipment to ensure conformance to performance specifications and to ensure safety. Interprets drilling and testing information for personnel. Monitors production rates and plans rework processes to improve production. Evaluates findings to develop, design, or test equipment or processes. Assists engineering and other personnel to solve operating problems. Assigns work to staff to obtain maximum utilization of personnel. Analyzes data to recommend placement of wells and supplementary processes to enhance production. Conducts engineering research experiments to improve or modify mining and oil machinery and operations. Confers with scientific, engineering, and technical personnel to resolve design, research and testing problems. Develops plans for oil and gas field drilling, and for product recovery and treatment. Designs or modifies mining and oil field machinery and tools, applying engineering principles. Coordinates activities of workers engaged in research, planning, and development.

Personality Type: Realistic. Realistic occupations frequently involve work activities that include practical, hands-on problems and solutions. They often deal with plants, animals, and real-world materials like wood, tools, and machinery. Many of the occupations require working outside and do not involve a lot of paperwork or working closely with others.

Abilities: Inductive Reasoning—The ability to combine separate pieces of information, or specific answers to problems, to form general rules or conclusions. Includes coming up with a logical explanation for why a series of seemingly unrelated events occur together. Oral Expression—The ability to communicate information and ideas verbally so others will understand. Written Comprehension—The ability to read and understand information and ideas presented in writing.

Skills: Mathematics—Using mathematics to solve problems. Writing—Communicating effectively with others in writing as indicated by the needs of the audience. Science—Using scientific methods to solve problems. Critical Thinking—Using logic and analysis to identify the strengths and weaknesses of different approaches. Reading Comprehension—Understanding written information in work-related documents.

Generalized Work Activities: Analyzing Data or Information—Identifying underlying principles, reasons, or facts by breaking down information or data into separate parts. Getting Information Needed to Do the Job—Observing, receiving, and otherwise obtaining information from all relevant sources. Making Decisions and Solving Problems—Combining, evaluating, and analyzing information and data to make decisions and solve problems. Involves making decisions about the relative importance of information and choosing the best solution. Processing Information—Compiling, coding, categorizing, calculating, tabulating, auditing, verifying, or processing information or data. Implementing Ideas and Programs—Conducting or carrying out work procedures and activities in accord with one's own ideas or information provided through directions/instructions for purposes of installing, modifying, preparing, delivering, constructing, integrating, finishing, or completing programs, systems, structures, or products. Identifying Objects, Actions, and Events—Identifying information received by making estimates or categorizations, recognizing differences or similarities, or sensing changes in circumstances or events. Updating and Using Job-Relevant Knowledge—Keeping up-to-date technically and knowing the functions of one's own job and related jobs.

Pharmacists

- ▲ Growth: 7%
- ▲ Annual Job Openings: 6,382
- ▲ Yearly Earnings: $66,220
- ▲ Education Required: Bachelor's degree
- ▲ Self-Employed: 4.2%
- ▲ Part-Time: 24.6%

Pharmacists

Compound and dispense medications following prescriptions issued by physicians, dentists, or other authorized medical practitioners. Maintains established procedures concerning quality assurance, security of controlled substances, and disposal of hazardous waste. Maintains records, such as pharmacy files, charge system, inventory, and control records for radioactive nuclei.

Oversees preparation and dispensation of experimental drugs. Verifies that specified radioactive substance and reagent will give desired results in examination or treatment procedures. Assays prepared radiopharmaceutical, using instruments and equipment to verify rate of drug disintegration and ensure patient receives required dose. Consults medical staff to advise on drug applications and characteristics and to review and evaluate quality and effectiveness of radiopharmaceuticals. Answers questions and provides information to pharmacy customers on drug interactions, side effects, dosage, and storage of pharmaceuticals. Compounds radioactive substances and reagents to prepare radiopharmaceutical, following radiopharmacy laboratory procedures. Plans and implements procedures in pharmacy, such as mixing, packaging, and labeling pharmaceuticals according to policies and legal requirements. Reviews prescription to assure accuracy and determine ingredients needed and suitability of radiopharmaceutical prescriptions. Compounds medications, using standard formulas and processes, such as weighing, measuring, and mixing ingredients. Analyzes records to indicate prescribing trends and excessive usage. Calculates volume of radioactive pharmaceutical required to provide patient desired level of radioactivity at prescribed time.

Personality Type: Investigative. Investigative occupations frequently involve working with ideas and require an extensive amount of thinking. These occupations can involve searching for facts and figuring out problems mentally.

Abilities: Written Comprehension—The ability to read and understand information and ideas presented in writing. Information Ordering—The ability to correctly follow a given rule or set of rules in order to arrange things or actions in a certain order. The things or actions can include numbers, letters, words, pictures, procedures, sentences, and mathematical or logical operations. Oral Comprehension—The ability to listen to and understand information and ideas presented verbally. Oral Expression—The ability to communicate information and ideas verbally so others will understand.

Skills: Science—Using scientific methods to solve problems. Reading Comprehension—Understanding written information in work-related documents. Mathematics—Using mathematics to solve problems. Product Inspection—Inspecting and evaluating the quality of products. Information Gathering—Knowing how to find information and identifying essential information.

Generalized Work Activities: Getting Information Needed to Do the Job—Observing, receiving, and otherwise obtaining information from all relevant sources. Updating and Using Job-Relevant Knowledge—Keeping up-to-date technically and knowing the functions of one's own job and related jobs. Evaluation Information against Standards—Evaluating information against a set of standards and verifying that it is correct. Identifying Objects, Actions, and Events—Identifying information received by making estimates or categorizations, recognizing differences or similarities, or sensing changes in circumstances or events. Communicating with Other Workers—Providing information to supervisors, fellow workers, and subordinates. Exchanging information face-to-face, in writing, or via telephone/electronic transfer.

Pharmacy Technicians

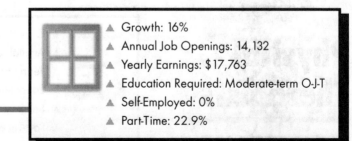

▲ Growth: 16%

▲ Annual Job Openings: 14,132

▲ Yearly Earnings: $17,763

▲ Education Required: Moderate-term O-J-T

▲ Self-Employed: 0%

▲ Part-Time: 22.9%

Pharmacy Technicians

Prepare medications under the direction of a pharmacist. Measure, mix, count out, label, and record amounts and dosages of medications. Receives and stores incoming supplies. Counts stock and enters data in computer to maintain inventory records. Processes records of medication and equipment dispensed to hospital patient, computes charges, and enters data in computer. Assists pharmacist to prepare and dispense medication. Cleans equipment and sterilizes glassware according to prescribed methods. Prepares intravenous (IV) packs, using sterile technique, under supervision of hospital pharmacist. Mixes pharmaceutical preparations, fills bottles with prescribed tablets and capsules, and types labels for bottles.

Personality Type: Conventional. Conventional occupations frequently involve following set procedures and routines. These occupations can include working with data and details more than with ideas. Usually there is a clear line of authority to follow.

Abilities: Information Ordering—The ability to correctly follow a given rule or set of rules in order to arrange things or actions in a certain order. The things or actions can include numbers, letters, words, pictures, procedures, sentences, and mathematical or logical operations. Number Facility—The ability to add, subtract, multiply, or divide quickly and correctly. Oral Comprehension—The ability to listen to and understand information and ideas presented verbally. Near Vision—The ability to see details of objects at a close range. Written Comprehension—The ability to read and understand information and ideas presented in writing.

Skills: Mathematics—Using mathematics to solve problems. Reading Comprehension—Understanding written information in work-related documents. Science—Using scientific methods to solve problems. Active Listening—Listening to what other people are saying; asking questions as appropriate. Information Gathering—Knowing how to find information and identifying essential information.

Generalized Work Activities: Getting Information Needed to Do the Job—Observing, receiving, and otherwise obtaining information from all relevant sources. Processing Information—Compiling, coding, categorizing, calculating, tabulating, auditing, verifying, or processing information or data. Handling and Moving Objects—Using one's hands and arms in handling, installing, forming, positioning, and moving materials, or in manipulating things. Includes the use of keyboards. Communicating with Other Workers—Providing information to supervisors, fellow workers, and subordinates. Exchanging information face-to-face, in writing, or via telephone/electronic transfer. Identifying Objects, Actions, and Events—Identifying information received by making estimates or categorizations, recognizing differences or similarities, or sensing changes in circumstances or events. Performing Administrative Activities—Approving requests, handling paperwork, and performing day-to-day administrative tasks. Documenting/Recording Information—Entering, transcribing, recording, storing, or maintaining information in either written form or by electronic/magnetic recording.

Physical Therapists

- ▲ Growth: 34%
- ▲ Annual Job Openings: 10,602
- ▲ Yearly Earnings: $56,600
- ▲ Education Required: Bachelor's degree
- ▲ Self-Employed: 5.9%
- ▲ Part-Time: 20.8%

Physical Therapists

Assess, plan, organize, and participate in rehabilitative programs that improve mobility, relieve pain, increase strength, and decrease or prevent deformity of patients suffering from disease or injury. Records treatment, response, and progress in patient's chart or enters information into computer. Administers treatment involving application of physical agents, using equipment, moist packs, ultraviolet and infrared lamps, and ultrasound machines. Evaluates effects of treatment at various stages and adjusts treatments to achieve maximum benefit. Tests and measures patient's strength, motor development, sensory perception, functional capacity, and respiratory and circulatory efficiency and records data. Reviews physician's referral and patient's condition and medical records to determine physical therapy treatment required. Plans and prepares written treatment program based on evaluation of patient data. Instructs patient and family in treatment procedures to be continued at home. Confers with medical practitioners to obtain additional information, suggest revisions in treatment, and integrate physical therapy into patient's care. Administers traction to relieve pain, using traction equipment. Instructs, motivates, and assists patient to perform various physical activities and use supportive devices, such as crutches, canes, and prostheses. Administers massage, applying knowledge of massage techniques and body physiology. Administers manual exercises to improve and maintain function. Evaluates, fits, and adjusts prosthetic and orthotic devices and recommends modification to orthotist.

Personality Type: Social. Social occupations frequently involve working with, communicating with, and teaching people. These occupations often involve helping or providing service to others.

Abilities: Oral Expression—The ability to communicate information and ideas verbally so others will understand. Problem Sensitivity—The ability to tell when something is wrong or is likely to go wrong. Does not involve solving the problem, only recognizing there is a problem. Written Expression—The ability to communicate information and ideas in writing so others will understand. Oral Comprehension—The ability to listen to and understand information and ideas presented verbally. Manual Dexterity—The ability to quickly make coordinated movements of one hand, a hand together with its arm, or two hands, to grasp, manipulate, or assemble objects. Speech Clarity—The ability to speak clearly to that what is said is understandable to a listener.

Skills: Reading Comprehension—Understanding written information in work-related documents. Judgment and Decision Making—Weighing the relative costs and benefits of a potential action. Critical Thinking—Using logic and analysis to identify the strengths and weaknesses of different approaches. Science—Using scientific methods to solve problems. Service Orientation—Actively looking for ways to help people. Speaking—Talking to others to effectively convey information. Active Listening—Listening to what other people are saying; asking questions as appropriate.

Generalized Work Activities: Assisting and Caring for Others—Providing assistance or personal care to others. Establishing and Maintaining Relationships—Developing constructive and cooperative working relationships with others. Getting Information Needed to Do the Job—Observing, receiving, and otherwise obtaining information from all relevant sources. Handling and Moving Objects—Using one's hands and arms in handling, installing, forming, positioning, and moving materials, or in manipulating things. Includes the use of keyboards. Identifying Objects, Actions, and Events—Identifying information received by making estimates or categorizations, recognizing differences or similarities, or sensing changes in circumstances or events. Making Decisions and Solving Problems—Combining, evaluating, and analyzing information and data to make decisions and solve problems. Involves making decisions about the relative importance of information and choosing the best solution. Monitoring Processes, Materials, Surroundings—Monitoring and reviewing information from materials, events, or the environment, often to detect problems or to find out when things are finished.

Physical Therapy Assistants and Aides

▲ Growth: 44%
▲ Annual Job Openings: 14,195
▲ Yearly Earnings: $21,870
▲ Education Required: Moderate-term O-J-T
▲ Self-Employed: 0%
▲ Part-Time: 34.5%

Physical Therapist Aides

Under close supervision of a physical therapist or physical therapy assistant, perform only delegated, selected, or routine tasks in specific situations. These duties include preparing the patient and the treatment area. Assists patients to dress, undress, and put on and remove supportive devices, such as braces, splints, and slings. Performs clerical duties, such as taking inventory, ordering supplies, answering telephone, taking messages, and filling out forms. Measures patient's range-of-joint motion, body parts, and vital signs to determine effects of treatments or for patient evaluations. Records treatment given and equipment used. Fits patients for orthopedic braces, prostheses, and supportive devices, such as crutches. Transports patients to and from treatment area. Cleans work area and equipment after treatment. Secures patients into or onto therapy equipment. Administers active and passive manual therapeutic exercises, therapeutic massage, and heat, light, sound, water, and electrical modality treatments, such as ultrasound. Provides routine treatments, such as hydrotherapy, hot and cold packs, and paraffin bath. Confers with physical therapy staff and others to discuss and evaluate patient information for planning, modifying, and coordinating treatment. Observes patients during treatment and compiles and evaluates data on patients' responses to treatments and progress, and reports to physical therapist. Administers traction to relieve neck and back pain, using intermittent and static traction equipment. Instructs, motivates, and assists patients to learn and improve functional activities, such as perambulation, transfer, ambulation, and daily-living activities. Safeguards, motivates, and assists patients practicing exercises and functional activities under direction of professional staff. Trains patients in use and care of orthopedic braces, prostheses, and supportive devices, such as crutches. Adjusts fit of supportive devices for patients, as instructed.

Personality Type: Social. Social occupations frequently involve working with, communicating with, and teaching people. These occupations often involve helping or providing service to others.

Abilities: Oral Expression—The ability to communicate information and ideas verbally so others will understand. Oral Comprehension—The ability to listen to and understand information and ideas presented verbally. Problem Sensitivity—The ability to tell when something is wrong or is likely to go wrong. Does not involve solving the problem, only recognizing there is a problem. Speech Clarity—The ability to speak clearly to that what is said is understandable to a listener. Written Comprehension—The ability to read and understand information and ideas presented in writing.

Skills: Speaking—Talking to others to effectively convey information. Instructing—Teaching others how to do something. Reading Comprehension—Understanding written information in work-related documents. Active Listening—Listening to what other people are saying; asking questions as appropriate. Service Orientation—Actively looking for ways to help people. Social Perceptiveness—Being aware of other people's reactions and understanding why people react the way they do. Monitoring—Assessing how well one is doing when learning or doing something.

Generalized Work Activities: Assisting and Caring for Others—Providing assistance or personal care to others. Performing General Physical Activities—Performing physical activities that require moving one's whole body, such as in climbing, lifting, balancing, walking, and stooping. Performing activities that often also require considerable use of the arms and legs, such as in the physical handling of materials. Monitoring Processes, Materials, Surroundings—Monitoring and reviewing information from materials, events, or the environment, often to detect problems or to find out when things are finished. Handling and Moving Objects—Using one's hands and arms in handling, installing, forming, positioning, and moving materials, or in manipulating things. Includes the use of keyboards. Communicating with Other Workers—Providing information to supervisors, fellow workers, and subordinates. Exchanging information face-to-face, in writing, or via telephone/electronic transfer. Establishing and Maintaining Relationships—Developing constructive and cooperative working relationships with others.

Physical Therapist Assistants

Assist physical therapists in providing physical therapy treatments and procedures. In accordance with state laws, assist in the development of treatment plans, carry out routine functions, document the progress of treatment, and modify specific treatments in accordance with patient status and within the scope of treatment plans established by a physical therapist. Generally requires formal training. Trains patients in use and care of orthopedic braces, prostheses, and supportive devices, such as crutches. Safeguards, motivates, and assists patients practicing exercises and functional activities under direction of professional staff. Assists patients to dress, undress, and put on and remove supportive devices, such as braces, splints, and slings. Measures patient's range-of-joint motion, body parts, and vital signs to determine effects of treatments or for patient evaluations. Observes patients during treatments and compiles and evaluates data on patients' responses to treatments and progress, and reports to physical therapist. Secures patients into or onto therapy equipment. Confers with physical therapy staff and others to discuss and evaluate patient information for planning, modifying, and coordinating treatment.

Provides routine treatments, such as hydrotherapy, hot and cold packs, and paraffin bath. Cleans work area and equipment after treatment. Adjusts fit of supportive devices for patients, as instructed. Performs clerical duties, such as taking inventory, ordering supplies, answering telephone, taking messages, and filling out forms. Transports patients to and from treatment area. Records treatment given and equipment used. Administers active and passive manual therapeutic exercises, therapeutic massage, and heat, light, sound, water, and electrical modality treatments, such as ultrasound. Administers traction to relieve neck and back pain, using intermittent and static traction equipment. Fits patients for orthopedic braces, prostheses, and supportive devices, such as crutches. Instructs, motivates, and assists patients to learn and improve functional activities, such as perambulation, transfer, ambulation, and daily-living activities.

Personality Type: Social. Social occupations frequently involve working with, communicating with, and teaching people. These occupations often involve helping or providing service to others.

Abilities: Oral Expression—The ability to communicate information and ideas verbally so others will understand. Oral Comprehension—The ability to listen to and understand information and ideas presented verbally. Problem Sensitivity—The ability to tell when something is wrong or is likely to go wrong. Does not involve solving the problem, only recognizing there is a problem. Speech Clarity—The ability to speak clearly to that what is said is understandable to a listener. Written Comprehension—The ability to read and understand information and ideas presented in writing.

Skills: Speaking—Talking to others to effectively convey information. Instructing—Teaching others how to do something. Reading Comprehension—Understanding written information in work-related documents. Social Perceptiveness—Being aware of other people's reactions and understanding why people react the way they do. Monitoring—Assessing how well one is doing when learning or doing something. Service Orientation—Actively looking for ways to help people. Active Listening—Listening to what other people are saying; asking questions as appropriate.

Generalized Work Activities: Assisting and Caring for Others—Providing assistance or personal care to others. Performing General Physical Activities—Performing physical activities that require moving one's whole body, such as in climbing, lifting, balancing, walking, and stooping. Performing activities that often also require considerable use of the arms and legs, such as in the physical handling of materials. Handling and Moving Objects—Using one's hands and arms in handling, installing, forming, positioning, and moving materials, or in manipulating things. Monitoring Processes, Materials, Surroundings—Monitoring and reviewing information from materials, events, or the environment, often to detect problems or to find out when things are finished. Communicating with Other Workers—Providing information to supervisors, fellow workers, and subordinates. Exchanging information face-to-face, in writing, or via telephone/electronic transfer. Establishing and Maintaining Relationships—Developing constructive and cooperative working relationships with others.

Physician Assistants

- ▲ Growth: 48%
- ▲ Annual Job Openings: 6,142
- ▲ Yearly Earnings: $47,090
- ▲ Education Required: Bachelor's degree
- ▲ Self-Employed: 0%
- ▲ Part-Time: 24.6%

Physician Assistants

Provide healthcare services typically performed by a physician, under the supervision of a physician. Conduct complete physicals, provide treatment, and counsel patients. In some cases, prescribe medication. Must graduate from an accredited educational program for physician assistants. Counsels patients regarding prescribed therapeutic regimens, normal growth and development, family planning, emotional problems of daily living, and health maintenance. Administers or orders diagnostic tests, such as X ray, electrocardiogram, and laboratory tests. Develops and implements patient management plans, records progress notes, and assists in provision of continuity of care. Compiles patient medical data, including health history and results of physical examination. Examines patient. Interprets diagnostic test results for deviations from normal. Performs therapeutic procedures, such as injections, immunizations, suturing and wound care, and managing infection.

Personality Type: Investigative. Investigative occupations frequently involve working with ideas and require an extensive amount of thinking. These occupations can involve searching for facts and figuring out problems mentally.

Abilities: Problem Sensitivity—The ability to tell when something is wrong or is likely to go wrong. Does not involve solving the problem, only recognizing there is a problem. Oral Comprehension—The ability to listen to and understand information and ideas presented verbally. Oral Expression—The ability to communicate information and ideas verbally so others will understand. Information Ordering—The ability to correctly follow a given rule or set of rules in order to arrange things or actions in a certain order. The things or actions can include numbers, letters, words, pictures, procedures, sentences, and mathematical or logical operations. Written Expression—The ability to communicate information and ideas in writing so others will understand. Near Vision—The ability to see details of objects at a close range.

Skills: Active Listening—Listening to what other people are saying; asking questions as appropriate. Problem Identification—Identifying the nature of problems.

Speaking—Talking to others to effectively convey information. Reading Comprehension—Understanding written information in work-related documents.

Generalized Work Activities: Assisting and Caring for Others—Providing assistance or personal care to others. Getting Information Needed to Do the Job—Observing, receiving, and otherwise obtaining information from all relevant sources. Identifying Objects, Actions, and Events—Identifying information received

by making estimates or categorizations, recognizing differences or similarities, or sensing changes in circumstances or events. Communicating with Other Workers—Providing information to supervisors, fellow workers, and subordinates. Exchanging information face-to-face, in writing, or via telephone/electronic transfer. Handling and Moving Objects—Using one's hands and arms in handling, installing, forming, positioning, and moving materials, or in manipulating things.

Physicians

- ▲ Growth: 21%
- ▲ Annual Job Openings: 32,563
- ▲ Yearly Earnings: $102,020
- ▲ Education Required: First professional degree
- ▲ Self-Employed: 20.4%
- ▲ Part-Time: 7.2%

Anesthesiologists

Administer anesthetics during surgery or other medical procedures. Examines patient to determine risk during surgical, obstetrical, and other medical procedures. Confers with medical professional to determine type and method of anesthetic or sedation to render patient insensible to pain. Positions patient on operating table to maximize patient comfort and surgical accessibility. Records type and amount of anesthesia and patient condition throughout procedure. Monitors patient before, during, and after anesthesia and counteracts adverse reactions or complications. Administers anesthetic or sedation during medical procedures, using local, intravenous, spinal, or caudal methods. Informs students and staff of types and methods of anesthesia administration, signs of complications, and emergency methods to counteract reactions.

Personality Type: Investigative. Investigative occupations frequently involve working with ideas and require an extensive amount of thinking. These occupations can involve searching for facts and figuring out problems mentally.

Abilities: Problem Sensitivity—The ability to tell when something is wrong or is likely to go wrong. Does not involve solving the problem, only recognizing there is a problem. Control Precision—The ability to quickly and repeatedly make precise adjustments in moving the controls of a machine or vehicle to exact positions. Speech Clarity—The ability to speak clearly to that what is said is understandable to a listener. Near Vision—The ability to see details of objects at a close range.

Skills: Judgment and Decision Making—Weighing the relative costs and benefits of a potential action. Active Listening—Listening to what other people are saying; asking questions as appropriate. Speaking—Talking to others to effectively convey information. Critical Thinking—Using logic and analysis to identify the strengths and weaknesses of different approaches. Monitoring—Assessing how well one is doing when learning or doing something.

Generalized Work Activities: Monitoring Processes, Materials, Surroundings—Monitoring and reviewing information from materials, events, or the environment, often to detect problems or to find out when things are finished. Updating and Using Job-Relevant Knowledge—Keeping up-to-date technically and knowing the functions of one's own job and related jobs. Controlling Machines and Processes—Using either control mechanisms or direct physical activity to operate machines or processes. Does not involve working with computers or vehicles. Assisting and Caring for Others—Providing assistance or personal care to others. Making Decisions and Solving Problems—Combining, evaluating, and analyzing information and data to make decisions and solve problems. Involves making decisions about the relative importance of information and choosing the best solution. Getting Information Needed to Do the Job—Observing, receiving, and otherwise obtaining information from all relevant sources.

Family and General Practitioners

Diagnose, treat, and help prevent diseases and injuries that commonly occur in the general population. Analyzes records, reports, test results, or examination information to diagnose medical condition of patient. Advises patients and community concerning diet, activity, hygiene, and disease prevention. Prescribes or administers treatment, therapy, medication, vaccination, and other specialized medical care to treat or prevent illness, disease, or injury. Collects, records, and maintains patient information, such as medical history, reports, and examination results. Operates on patients to remove, repair, or improve functioning of diseased or injured body parts and systems and delivers babies. Explains procedures and discusses test results on prescribed treatments with patients. Plans, implements, or administers health programs or standards in hospital, business, or community for information, prevention, or treatment of injury or illness. Directs and coordinates activities of nurses, students, assistants, specialists, therapists, and other medical staff. Prepares reports for government or management of birth, death, and disease statistics, workforce evaluations, or medical status of individuals. Refers patient to medical specialist or other practitioner when necessary. Examines or conducts tests on patient to provide information on medical condition. Conducts research to study anatomy and develop or test medications, treatments, or procedures to prevent, or control disease or injury.

Personality Type: Investigative. Investigative occupations frequently involve working with ideas and require an extensive amount of thinking. These occupations can involve searching for facts and figuring out problems mentally.

Abilities: Inductive Reasoning—The ability to combine separate pieces of information, or specific answers to problems, to form general rules or conclusions. Includes coming up with a logical explanation for why a series of seemingly unrelated events occur together. Oral Expression—The ability to communicate information and ideas verbally so others will understand. Arm-Hand Steadiness—The ability to keep the hand and arm steady while making an arm movement or while holding the arm and hand in one position. Manual Dexterity—The ability to quickly make coordinated movements of one hand, a hand together with its arm, or two hands, to grasp, manipulate, or assemble objects. Near Vision—The ability to see details of objects at a close range. Problem Sensitivity—The ability to tell when something is wrong or is likely to go wrong. Does not involve solving the problem, only recognizing there is a problem.

Skills: Reading Comprehension—Understanding written information in work-related documents. Identification of Key Causes—Identifying the things that must be changed to achieve a goal. Problem Identification—Identifying the nature of problems. Science—Using scientific methods to solve problems. Judgment and Decision Making—Weighing the relative costs and benefits of a potential action.

Generalized Work Activities: Monitoring Processes, Materials, Surroundings—Monitoring and reviewing information from materials, events, or the environment, often to detect problems or to find out when things are finished. Assisting and Caring for Others—Providing assistance or personal care to others. Making Decisions and Solving Problems—Combining, evaluating, and analyzing information and data to make decisions and solve problems. Involves making decisions about the relative importance of information and choosing the best solution. Getting Information Needed to Do the Job—Observing, receiving, and otherwise obtaining information from all relevant sources. Analyzing Data or Information—Identifying underlying principles, reasons, or facts by breaking down information or data into separate parts. Identifying Objects, Actions, and Events—Identifying information received by making estimates or categorizations, recognizing differences or similarities, or sensing changes in circumstances or events. Documenting/Recording Information—Entering, transcribing, recording, storing, or maintaining information in either written form or by electronic/magnetic recording.

Internists, General

Diagnose and provide nonsurgical treatment of diseases and injuries of internal organ systems. Provide care mainly for adults who have a wide range of problems associated with the internal organs. Directs and coordinates activities of nurses, students, assistants, specialists, therapists, and other medical staff. Operates on patients to remove, repair, or improve functioning of diseased or injured body parts and systems and delivers babies. Monitors patients' condition and progress and reevaluates treatments as necessary. Analyzes records, reports, test results, or examination information to diagnose medical condition of patient. Explains procedures and discusses test results on prescribed treatments with patients. Collects, records, and maintains patient information, such as medical history, reports, and examination results. Advises patients and community concerning diet, activity, hygiene, and disease prevention. Prepares reports for government or management of birth, death, and disease statistics, workforce evaluations, or medical status of individuals. Examines or conducts tests on patient to provide information on medical condition. Refers patient to medical specialist or other practitioner when necessary. Prescribes or administers treatment, therapy, medication, vaccination, and other specialized medical care to treat or prevent illness, disease, or injury. Plans, implements, or administers health programs or standards in hospital, business, or community for information, prevention, or treatment of injury or illness. Conducts research to study anatomy and develop or test medications, treatments, or procedures to prevent, or control disease or injury.

Personality Type: Investigative. Investigative occupations frequently involve working with ideas and require

an extensive amount of thinking. These occupations can involve searching for facts and figuring out problems mentally.

Abilities: Inductive Reasoning—The ability to combine separate pieces of information, or specific answers to problems, to form general rules or conclusions. Includes coming up with a logical explanation for why a series of seemingly unrelated events occur together. Problem Sensitivity—The ability to tell when something is wrong or is likely to go wrong. Does not involve solving the problem, only recognizing there is a problem. Near Vision—The ability to see details of objects at a close range. Oral Expression—The ability to communicate information and ideas verbally so others will understand. Arm-Hand Steadiness—The ability to keep the hand and arm steady while making an arm movement or while holding the arm and hand in one position. Manual Dexterity—The ability to quickly make coordinated movements of one hand, a hand together with its arm, or two hands, to grasp, manipulate, or assemble objects.

Skills: Reading Comprehension—Understanding written information in work-related documents. Identification of Key Causes—Identifying the things that must be changed to achieve a goal. Science—Using scientific methods to solve problems. Problem Identification—Identifying the nature of problems. Judgment and Decision Making—Weighing the relative costs and benefits of a potential action.

Generalized Work Activities: Monitoring Processes, Materials, Surroundings—Monitoring and reviewing information from materials, events, or the environment, often to detect problems or to find out when things are finished. Making Decisions and Solving Problems—Combining, evaluating, and analyzing information and data to make decisions and solve problems. Involves making decisions about the relative importance of information and choosing the best solution. Analyzing Data or Information—Identifying underlying principles, reasons, or facts by breaking down information or data into separate parts. Assisting and Caring for Others—Providing assistance or personal care to others. Getting Information Needed to Do the Job—Observing, receiving, and otherwise obtaining information from all relevant sources. Identifying Objects, Actions, and Events—Identifying information received by making estimates or categorizations, recognizing differences or similarities, or sensing changes in circumstances or events. Documenting/Recording Information—Entering, transcribing, recording, storing, or maintaining information in either written form or by electronic/magnetic recording.

Obstetricians and Gynecologists

Diagnose, treat, and help prevent diseases of women, especially those affecting the reproductive system and the process of childbirth. Prepares reports for government or management of birth, death, and disease statistics, workforce evaluations, or medical status of individuals. Explains procedures and discusses test results on prescribed treatments with patients. Operates on patients to remove, repair, or improve functioning of diseased or injured body parts and systems and delivers babies. Prescribes or administers treatment, therapy, medication, vaccination, and other specialized medical care to treat or prevent illness, disease, or injury. Analyzes records, reports, test results, or examination information to diagnose medical condition of patient. Directs and coordinates activities of nurses, students, assistants, specialists, therapists, and other medical staff. Conducts research to study anatomy and develop or test medications, treatments, or procedures to prevent, or control disease or injury. Advises patients and community concerning diet, activity, hygiene, and disease prevention. Plans, implements, or administers health programs or standards in hospital, business, or community for information, prevention, or treatment of injury or illness. Refers patient to medical specialist or other practitioner when necessary. Examines or conducts tests on patient to provide information on medical condition. Monitors patients' condition and progress and reevaluates treatments as necessary. Collects, records, and maintains patient information, such as medical history, reports, and examination results.

Personality Type: Investigative. Investigative occupations frequently involve working with ideas and require an extensive amount of thinking. These occupations can involve searching for facts and figuring out problems mentally.

Abilities: Inductive Reasoning—The ability to combine separate pieces of information, or specific answers to problems, to form general rules or conclusions. Includes coming up with a logical explanation for why a series of seemingly unrelated events occur together. Near Vision—The ability to see details of objects at a close range. Manual Dexterity—The ability to quickly make coordinated movements of one hand, a hand together with its arm, or two hands, to grasp, manipulate, or assemble objects. Problem Sensitivity—The ability to tell when something is wrong or is likely to go wrong. Does not involve solving the problem, only recognizing there is a problem. Oral Expression—The ability to communicate information and ideas verbally so others will understand. Arm-Hand Steadiness—The ability to keep the hand and arm steady while making an arm movement or while holding the arm and hand in one position.

Skills: Reading Comprehension—Understanding written information in work-related documents. Identification of Key Causes—Identifying the things that must be changed to achieve a goal. Science—Using scientific methods to solve problems. Problem Identification—Identifying the nature of problems. Judgment and Decision Making—Weighing the relative costs and benefits of a potential action.

Generalized Work Activities: Monitoring Processes, Materials, Surroundings—Monitoring and reviewing information from materials, events, or the environment, often to detect problems or to find out when things are finished. Identifying Objects, Actions, and Events—Identifying information received by making estimates or categorizations, recognizing differences or similarities, or sensing changes in circumstances or events. Assisting and Caring for Others—Providing assistance or personal care to others. Analyzing Data or Information—Identifying underlying principles, reasons, or facts by breaking down information or data into separate parts. Making Decisions and Solving Problems—Combining, evaluating, and analyzing information and data to make decisions and solve problems. Involves making decisions about the relative importance of information and choosing the best solution. Getting Information Needed to Do the Job—Observing, receiving, and otherwise obtaining information from all relevant sources.

Documenting/Recording Information—Entering, transcribing, recording, storing, or maintaining information in either written form or by electronic/ magnetic recording.

Pediatricians, General

Diagnose, treat, and help prevent children's diseases and injuries. Prescribes or administers treatment, therapy, medication, vaccination, and other specialized medical care to treat or prevent illness, disease, or injury. Prepares reports for government or management of birth, death, and disease statistics, workforce evaluations, or medical status of individuals. Monitors patients' condition and progress and reevaluates treatments as necessary. Analyzes records, reports, test results, or examination information to diagnose medical condition of patient. Operates on patients to remove, repair, or improve functioning of diseased or injured body parts and systems and delivers babies. Refers patient to medical specialist or other practitioner when necessary. Plans, implements, or administers health programs or standards in hospital, business, or community for information, prevention, or treatment of injury or illness. Directs and coordinates activities of nurses, students, assistants, specialists, therapists, and other medical staff. Advises patients and community concerning diet, activity, hygiene, and disease prevention. Examines or conducts tests on patient to provide information on medical condition. Explains procedures and discusses test results on prescribed treatments with patients. Collects, records, and maintains patient information, such as medical history, reports, and examination results. Conducts research to study anatomy and develop or test medications, treatments, or procedures to prevent, or control disease or injury.

Personality Type: Investigative. Investigative occupations frequently involve working with ideas and require an extensive amount of thinking. These occupations can involve searching for facts and figuring out problems mentally.

Abilities: Inductive Reasoning—The ability to combine separate pieces of information, or specific answers to problems, to form general rules or conclusions. Includes coming up with a logical explanation for why a series of seemingly unrelated events occur together. Near Vision—The ability to see details of objects at a close range. Problem Sensitivity—The ability to tell when something is wrong or is likely to go wrong. Does not involve solving the problem, only recognizing there is a problem. Oral Expression—The ability to communicate information and ideas verbally so others will understand. Arm-Hand Steadiness—The ability to keep the hand and arm steady while making an arm movement or while holding the arm and hand in one position. Manual Dexterity—The ability to quickly make coordinated movements of one hand, a hand together with its arm, or two hands, to grasp, manipulate, or assemble objects.

Skills: Reading Comprehension—Understanding written information in work-related documents. Identification of Key Causes—Identifying the things that must be changed to achieve a goal. Judgment and Decision Making—Weighing the relative costs and benefits of a potential action. Problem Identification— Identifying the nature of problems. Science—Using scientific methods to solve problems.

Generalized Work Activities: Monitoring Processes, Materials, Surroundings—Monitoring and reviewing information from materials, events, or the environment, often to detect problems or to find out when things are finished. Making Decisions and Solving Problems— Combining, evaluating, and analyzing information and data to make decisions and solve problems. Involves making decisions about the relative importance of information and choosing the best solution. Getting Information Needed to Do the Job—Observing, receiving, and otherwise obtaining information from all relevant sources. Identifying Objects, Actions, and Events—Identifying information received by making estimates or categorizations, recognizing differences or similarities, or sensing changes in circumstances or events. Assisting and Caring for Others—Providing assistance or personal care to others. Analyzing Data or Information—Identifying underlying principles, reasons, or facts by breaking down information or data into separate parts. Documenting/Recording

Information—Entering, transcribing, recording, storing, or maintaining information in either written form or by electronic/magnetic recording.

Psychiatrists

Diagnose, treat, and help prevent disorders of the mind. Prepares case reports and summaries for government agencies. Reviews and evaluates treatment procedures and outcomes of other psychiatrists and medical professionals. Teaches, conducts research, and publishes findings to increase understanding of mental, emotional, behavioral states and disorders. Advises and informs guardians, relatives, and significant others of patient's condition and treatment. Gathers and maintains patient information and records, including social and medical history obtained from patient, relatives, and other professionals. Prescribes, directs, and administers psychotherapeutic treatments or medications to treat mental, emotional, or behavioral disorders. Analyzes and evaluates patient data and test or examination findings to diagnose nature and extent of mental disorder. Examines or conducts laboratory or diagnostic tests on patient to provide information on general physical condition and mental disorder.

Personality Type: Investigative. Investigative occupations frequently involve working with ideas and require an extensive amount of thinking. These occupations can involve searching for facts and figuring out problems mentally.

Abilities: Oral Comprehension—The ability to listen to and understand information and ideas presented verbally. Written Comprehension—The ability to read and understand information and ideas presented in writing. Written Expression—The ability to communicate information and ideas in writing so others will understand. Problem Sensitivity—The ability to tell when something is wrong or is likely to go wrong. Does not involve solving the problem, only recognizing there is a problem. Speech Clarity—The ability to speak clearly to that what is said is understandable to a listener. Oral Expression—The ability to communicate information and ideas verbally so others will understand.

Skills: Speaking—Talking to others to effectively convey information. Social Perceptiveness—Being aware of other people's reactions and understanding why people react the way they do. Active Listening—Listening to what other people are saying; asking questions as appropriate. Information Gathering—Knowing how to find information and identifying essential information. Problem Identification—Identifying the nature of problems. Judgment and Decision Making—Weighing the relative costs and benefits of a potential action.

Generalized Work Activities: Getting Information Needed to Do the Job—Observing, receiving, and otherwise obtaining information from all relevant sources. Assisting and Caring for Others—Providing assistance or personal care to others. Establishing and Maintaining Relationships—Developing constructive and cooperative working relationships with others. Analyzing Data or Information—Identifying underlying principles, reasons, or facts by breaking down information or data into separate parts. Identifying Objects, Actions, and Events—Identifying information received by making estimates or categorizations, recognizing differences or similarities, or sensing changes in circumstances or events.

Surgeons

Treat diseases, injuries, and deformities by invasive methods, such as manual manipulation or by using instruments and appliances. Operates on patient to correct deformities, repair injuries, prevent diseases, or improve or restore patient's functions. Analyzes patient's medical history, medication allergies, physical condition, and examination results to verify operation's necessity and to determine best procedure. Examines patient to provide information on medical condition and patient's surgical risk. Conducts research to develop and test surgical techniques to improve operating procedures and outcomes. Directs and coordinates activities of nurses, assistants, specialists, and other medical staff. Examines instruments, equipment, and operating room to ensure sterility. Refers patient to medical specialist or other practitioners when necessary.

Personality Type: Investigative. Investigative occupations frequently involve working with ideas and require an extensive amount of thinking. These occupations can involve searching for facts and figuring out problems mentally.

Abilities: Manual Dexterity—The ability to quickly make coordinated movements of one hand, a hand together with its arm, or two hands, to grasp, manipulate, or assemble objects. Arm-Hand Steadiness—The ability to keep the hand and arm steady while making an arm movement or while holding the arm and hand in one position. Written Comprehension—The ability to read and understand information and ideas presented in writing. Problem Sensitivity—The ability to tell when something is wrong or is likely to go wrong. Does not involve solving the problem, only recognizing there is a problem. Oral Expression—The ability to communicate information and ideas verbally so others will understand.

Skills: Reading Comprehension—Understanding written information in work-related documents. Critical Thinking—Using logic and analysis to identify the strengths and weaknesses of different approaches. Judgment and Decision Making—Weighing the relative costs and benefits of a potential action. Identification of Key Causes—Identifying the things that must be changed to achieve a goal. Problem Identification—Identifying the nature of problems.

Generalized Work Activities: Getting Information Needed to Do the Job—Observing, receiving, and otherwise obtaining information from all relevant sources. Making Decisions and Solving Problems—Combining, evaluating, and analyzing information and data to make decisions and solve problems. Involves making decisions about the relative importance of information and choosing the best solution. Analyzing Data or Information—Identifying underlying principles, reasons, or facts by breaking down information or data into separate parts. Identifying Objects, Actions, and Events—Identifying information received by making estimates or categorizations, recognizing differences or similarities, or sensing changes in circumstances or events. Assisting and Caring for Others—Providing assistance or personal care to others.

Physicists and Astronomers

- ▲ Growth: 2%
- ▲ Annual Job Openings: 1,164
- ▲ Yearly Earnings: $73,240
- ▲ Education Required: Doctor's degree
- ▲ Self-Employed: 5%
- ▲ Part-Time: 6.6%

Astronomers

Observe, research, and interpret celestial and astronomical phenomena to increase basic knowledge and apply such information to practical problems. Calculates orbits and determines sizes, shapes, brightness, and motions of different celestial bodies. Computes positions of sun, moon, planets, stars, nebulae, and galaxies. Determines exact time by celestial observations and conducts research into relationships between time and space. Analyzes wave lengths of radiation from celestial bodies as observed in all ranges of spectrum. Develops mathematical tables giving positions of sun, moon, planets, and stars at given times for use by air and sea navigators. Studies history, structure, extent, and evolution of stars, stellar systems, and universe. Studies celestial phenomena from ground or above atmosphere, using various optical devices, such as telescopes situated on ground or attached to satellites. Designs optical, mechanical, and electronic instruments for astronomical research.

Personality Type: Investigative. Investigative occupations frequently involve working with ideas and require an extensive amount of thinking. These occupations can involve searching for facts and figuring out problems mentally.

Abilities: Mathematical Reasoning—The ability to understand and organize a problem and then select a mathematical method or formula to solve the problem. Written Comprehension—The ability to read and understand information and ideas presented in writing. Inductive Reasoning—The ability to combine separate pieces of information, or specific answers to problems, to form general rules or conclusions. Includes coming up with a logical explanation for why a series of seemingly unrelated events occur together. Deductive Reasoning—The ability to apply general rules to specific problems to come up with logical answers. Involves deciding if an answer makes sense. Number Facility—The ability to add, subtract, multiply, or divide quickly and correctly.

Skills: Mathematics—Using mathematics to solve problems. Science—Using scientific methods to solve problems. Information Gathering—Knowing how to find information and identifying essential information.

Generalized Work Activities: Identifying Objects, Actions, and Events—Identifying information received by making estimates or categorizations, recognizing differences or similarities, or sensing changes in circumstances or events. Processing Information—Compiling, coding, categorizing, calculating, tabulating, auditing, verifying, or processing information or data. Analyzing Data or Information—Identifying underlying principles, reasons, or facts by breaking down information or data into separate parts. Getting Information Needed to Do the Job—Observing, receiving, and otherwise obtaining information from all relevant sources. Monitoring Processes, Materials, Surroundings—Monitoring and reviewing information from materials, events, or the environment, often to detect problems or to find out when things are finished.

Physicists

Conduct research into the phases of physical phenomena, develop theories and laws on the basis of observation and experiments, and devise methods to apply laws and theories to industry and other fields. Conducts research pertaining to potential environmental impact of proposed atomic energy-related industrial development to determine qualifications for licensing. Advises authorities in procedures to be followed in radiation incidents or hazards, and assists in civil defense planning. Assists in developing standards of permissible concentrations of radioisotopes in liquids and gases. Incorporates methods for maintenance and repair of components and designs, and develops test instrumentation and test procedures. Directs testing and monitoring of contamination of radioactive equipment and recording of personnel and plant area radiation exposure data. Consults other scientists regarding innovations to ensure equipment or plant design conforms to health physics standards for protection of personnel. Conducts application analysis to determine commercial, industrial, scientific, medical, military, or other uses for electro-optical devices. Analyzes results of experiments designed to detect and measure previously unobserved physical phenomena. Assists with development of manufacturing, assembly, and fabrication processes of lasers, masers, infrared, and other light-emitting and light-sensitive devices. Describes and expresses observations and conclusions in mathematical terms. Conducts instrumental analyses to determine physical properties of materials. Observes structure and properties of matter and transformation and propagation of energy, using masers, lasers, telescopes and other equipment. Designs electronic circuitry and optical components with scientific characteristics to fit within specified mechanical limits and perform according to specifications.

Personality Type: Investigative. Investigative occupations frequently involve working with ideas and require an extensive amount of thinking. These occupations can involve searching for facts and figuring out problems mentally.

Abilities: Written Comprehension—The ability to read and understand information and ideas presented in writing. Written Expression—The ability to communicate information and ideas in writing so others will understand. Oral Comprehension—The ability to listen to and understand information and ideas presented verbally. Oral Expression—The ability to communicate information and ideas verbally so others will understand. Mathematical Reasoning—The ability to understand and organize a problem and then select a mathematical method or formula to solve the problem. Deductive Reasoning—The ability to apply general

rules to specific problems to come up with logical answers. Involves deciding if an answer makes sense. Inductive Reasoning—The ability to combine separate pieces of information, or specific answers to problems, to form general rules or conclusions. Includes coming up with a logical explanation for why a series of seemingly unrelated events occur together.

Skills: Science—Using scientific methods to solve problems. Active Learning—Working with new material or information to grasp its implications. Mathematics—Using mathematics to solve problems. Writing—Communicating effectively with others in writing as indicated by the needs of the audience. Critical Thinking—Using logic and analysis to identify the strengths and weaknesses of different approaches. Reading Comprehension—Understanding written information in work-related documents.

Generalized Work Activities: Analyzing Data or Information—Identifying underlying principles, reasons, or facts by breaking down information or data into separate parts. Getting Information Needed to Do the Job—Observing, receiving, and otherwise obtaining information from all relevant sources. Processing Information—Compiling, coding, categorizing, calculating, tabulating, auditing, verifying, or processing information or data. Identifying Objects, Actions, and Events—Identifying information received by making estimates or categorizations, recognizing differences or similarities, or sensing changes in circumstances or events. Monitoring Processes, Materials, Surroundings—Monitoring and reviewing information from materials, events, or the environment, often to detect problems or to find out when things are finished.

Plasterers and Stucco Masons

- ▲ Growth: 17%
- ▲ Annual Job Openings: 7,984
- ▲ Yearly Earnings: $29,390
- ▲ Education Required: Long-term O-J-T
- ▲ Self-Employed: 20.1%
- ▲ Part-Time: 8.4%

Plasterers and Stucco Masons

Apply interior or exterior plaster, cement, stucco, or similar materials. Set ornamental plaster. Mixes mortar to desired consistency and puts up scaffolds. Creates decorative textures in finish coat, using sand, pebbles, or stones. Applies weatherproof, decorative covering to exterior surfaces of building. Molds and installs ornamental plaster pieces, panels, and trim. Installs guidewires on exterior surface of buildings to indicate thickness of plaster or stucco. Applies coats of plaster or stucco to walls, ceilings, or partitions of buildings, using trowel, brush, or spray gun. Directs workers to mix plaster to desired consistency and to erect scaffolds.

Personality Type: Realistic. Realistic occupations frequently involve work activities that include practical, hands-on problems and solutions. They often deal with plants, animals, and real-world materials like wood, tools, and machinery. Many of the occupations require working outside and do not involve a lot of paperwork or working closely with others.

Abilities: Manual Dexterity—The ability to quickly make coordinated movements of one hand, a hand together with its arm, or two hands, to grasp, manipulate, or assemble objects. Wrist-Finger Speed—The ability to make fast, simple, repeated movements of the fingers, hands, and wrists. Arm-Hand Steadiness—The ability to keep the hand and arm steady while making an arm movement or while holding the arm and hand in one position. Finger Dexterity—The ability to make precisely coordinated movements of the fingers of one or both hands to grasp, manipulate, or assemble very small objects.

Skills: Product Inspection—Inspecting and evaluating the quality of products. Equipment Selection—Determining the kind of tools and equipment needed to do a job. Installation—Installing equipment, machines, wiring, or programs to meet specifications. Monitoring—Assessing how well one is doing when learning or doing something. Identification of Key Causes—Identifying the things that must be changed to achieve a goal. Active Listening—Listening to what other people are saying; asking questions as appropriate.

Generalized Work Activities: Handling and Moving Objects—Using one's hands and arms in handling, installing, forming, positioning, and moving materials, or in manipulating things. Includes the use of keyboards. Performing General Physical Activities—Performing physical activities that require moving one's whole body, such as in climbing, lifting, balancing, walking, and stooping. Performing activities that often also require considerable use of the arms and legs, such as in the physical handling of materials. Getting Information Needed to Do the Job—Observing, receiving, and otherwise obtaining information from all relevant sources. Implementing Ideas and Programs—Conducting or carrying out work procedures and activities in accord with one's own ideas or information provided through directions/instructions for purposes of installing, modifying, preparing, delivering, constructing, integrating, finishing, or completing programs, systems, structures, or products. Monitoring Processes, Materials, Surroundings—Monitoring and reviewing information from materials, events, or the environment, often to detect problems or to find out when things are finished.

Plastic Molding Machine Setters, Set-Up Operators, Operators, and Tenders

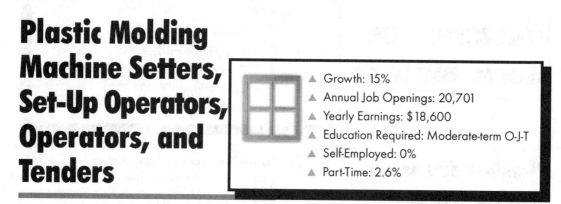

- ▲ Growth: 15%
- ▲ Annual Job Openings: 20,701
- ▲ Yearly Earnings: $18,600
- ▲ Education Required: Moderate-term O-J-T
- ▲ Self-Employed: 0%
- ▲ Part-Time: 2.6%

Plastic Molding and Casting Machine Operators and Tenders

Operate or tend plastic molding machines, such as compression or injection molding machines, to mold, form, or cast thermoplastic materials to specified shape. Mixes and pours liquid plastic into rotating drum of machine that spreads, hardens, and shapes mixture.

Positions mold frame to correct alignment and tubs containing mixture on top of mold to facilitate loading of molds. Fills tubs, molds, or cavities of machine with plastic material in solid or liquid form prior to activating machine. Trims flashing from product. Signals coworker to synchronize feed of materials into molding process. Throws flash and rejected parts into grinder machine to be recycled. Stacks molded parts in boxes or on conveyor for subsequent processing or leaves parts in mold to cool. Removes product from mold or conveyor, and cleans and reloads mold. Observes meters and gauges to verify specified temperatures, pressures, and press-cycle times. Reports defect in molds to supervisor.

Turns valves and dials of machines to regulate pressure and temperature, to set press-cycle time, and to close press. Examines molded product for surface defects, such as dents, bubbles, thin areas, and cracks. Starts machine that automatically liquefies plastic material in heating chamber, injects liquefied material into mold, and ejects molded product. Weighs prescribed amounts of material for molded part and finished product to ensure specifications are maintained. Observes continuous operation of automatic machine and width and alignment of plastic sheeting to ensure side flanges. Pulls level and toggle latches to fill mold and regulate tension on sheeting and to release mold covers. Dumps plastic powder, preformed plastic pellets, or preformed rubber slugs into hopper of molding machine. Feels stiffness and consistency of molded sheeting to detect machinery malfunction. Breaks seals that hold plastic product in molds, using hand tool, and removes product from mold. Heats plastic material prior to forming product or cools product after processing to prevent distortion.

Personality Type: Realistic. Realistic occupations frequently involve work activities that include practical, hands-on problems and solutions. They often deal with plants, animals, and real-world materials like wood, tools, and machinery. Many of the occupations require working outside and do not involve a lot of paperwork or working closely with others.

Abilities: Control Precision—The ability to quickly and repeatedly make precise adjustments in moving the controls of a machine or vehicle to exact positions. Manual Dexterity—The ability to quickly make coordinated movements of one hand, a hand together with its arm, or two hands, to grasp, manipulate, or assemble objects. Problem Sensitivity—The ability to tell when something is wrong or is likely to go wrong. Does not involve solving the problem, only recognizing there is a problem. Rate Control—The ability to time the adjustments of a movement or equipment control in anticipation of changes in the speed and/or direction of a continuously moving object or scene. Reaction Time—The ability to quickly respond with the hand, finger, or foot to a signal such as a sound, a light, or a picture. Information Ordering—The ability to correctly follow a given rule or set of rules in order to arrange things or actions in a certain order. The things or actions can include numbers, letters, words, pictures, procedures, sentences, and mathematical or logical operations. Near Vision—The ability to see details of objects at a close range. Perceptual Speed—The ability to quickly and accurately compare letters, numbers, objects, pictures, or patterns. The things to be compared may be presented at the same time or one after the other. Includes comparing a presented object with a remembered object.

Skills: Operation and Control—Controlling operations of equipment or systems. Product Inspection—Inspecting and evaluating the quality of products. Operation Monitoring—Watching gauges, dials, or other indicators to make sure a machine is working properly. Problem Identification—Identifying the nature of problems. Mathematics—Using mathematics to solve problems.

Generalized Work Activities: Controlling Machines and Processes—Using either control mechanisms or direct physical activity to operate machines or processes. Does not involve working with computers or vehicles. Handling and Moving Objects—Using one's hands and arms in handling, installing, forming, positioning, and moving materials, or in manipulating things. Monitoring Processes, Materials, Surroundings—Monitoring and reviewing information from materials, events, or the environment, often to detect problems or to find out when things are finished. Performing General Physical Activities—Performing physical activities that require moving one's whole body, such as in climbing, lifting, balancing, walking, and stooping. Performing activities that often also require considerable use of the arms and legs, such as in the physical handling of materials. Inspecting Equipment, Structures, Materials—Inspecting or diagnosing equipment, structures, or materials to identify the causes of errors or other problems or defects.

Plastic Molding and Casting Machine Setters and Set-Up Operators

Set up or set up and operate plastic molding machines, such as compression or injection molding machines,

to mold, form, or cast thermoplastic materials to specified shape. Measures and visually inspects products for surface and dimension defects, using precision measuring instruments, to ensure conformance to specifications. Trims excess material from part, using knife, and grinds scrap plastic into powder for reuse. Removes finished or cured product from dies or mold, using hand tools and airhose. Repairs and maintains machines and auxiliary equipment, using hand tools and power tools. Mixes catalysts, thermoplastic materials, and coloring pigments according to formula, using paddle and mixing machine. Reads specifications to determine setup and prescribed temperature and time settings to mold, form, or cast plastic materials. Installs dies onto machine or press and coats dies with parting agent, according to work order specifications. Sets machine controls to regulate molding temperature, volume, pressure, and time, according to knowledge of plastics and molding procedures. Positions, aligns, and secures assembled mold, mold components, and machine accessories onto machine press bed, and attaches connecting lines. Presses button or pulls lever to activate machine to inject dies and compress compounds to form and cure specified products. Weighs premixed compounds and dumps compound into die well or fills hoppers of machines that automatically supply compound to die. Observes and adjusts machine set up and operations to eliminate production of defective parts and products.

Personality Type: Realistic. Realistic occupations frequently involve work activities that include practical, hands-on problems and solutions. They often deal with plants, animals, and real-world materials like wood, tools, and machinery. Many of the occupations require working outside and do not involve a lot of paperwork or working closely with others.

Abilities: Manual Dexterity—The ability to quickly make coordinated movements of one hand, a hand together with its arm, or two hands, to grasp, manipulate, or assemble objects. Control Precision—The ability to quickly and repeatedly make precise adjustments in moving the controls of a machine or vehicle to exact positions. Static Strength—The ability to exert maximum muscle force to lift, push, pull, or carry objects. Explosive Strength—The ability to use short bursts of muscle force to propel oneself, as in jumping or sprinting, or to throw an object. Near Vision—The ability to see details of objects at a close range. Problem Sensitivity—The ability to tell when something is wrong or is likely to go wrong. Does not involve solving the problem, only recognizing there is a problem. Written Comprehension—The ability to read and understand information and ideas presented in writing.

Skills: Operation and Control—Controlling operations of equipment or systems. Product Inspection—Inspecting and evaluating the quality of products. Operation Monitoring—Watching gauges, dials, or other indicators to make sure a machine is working properly. Equipment Selection—Determining the kind of tools and equipment needed to do a job. Equipment Maintenance—Performing routine maintenance and determining when and what kind of maintenance is needed.

Generalized Work Activities: Handling and Moving Objects—Using one's hands and arms in handling, installing, forming, positioning, and moving materials, or in manipulating things. Includes the use of keyboards. Controlling Machines and Processes—Using either control mechanisms or direct physical activity to operate machines or processes. Does not involve working with computers or vehicles. Monitoring Processes, Materials, Surroundings—Monitoring and reviewing information from materials, events, or the environment, often to detect problems or to find out when things are finished. Performing General Physical Activities—Performing physical activities that require moving one's whole body, such as in climbing, lifting, balancing, walking, and stooping. Performing activities that often also require considerable use of the arms and legs, such as in the physical handling of materials. Getting Information Needed to Do the Job—Observing, receiving, and otherwise obtaining information from all relevant sources.

Podiatrists

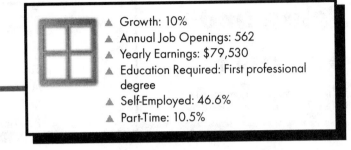

- ▲ Growth: 10%
- ▲ Annual Job Openings: 562
- ▲ Yearly Earnings: $79,530
- ▲ Education Required: First professional degree
- ▲ Self-Employed: 46.6%
- ▲ Part-Time: 10.5%

Podiatrists

Diagnose and treat diseases and deformities of the human foot. Performs surgery. Treats deformities by mechanical and electrical methods, such as whirlpool or paraffin baths and short wave and low voltage currents. Refers patients to physician when symptoms indicative of systemic disorders, such as arthritis or diabetes, are observed in feet and legs. Advises patients concerning continued treatment of disorders and foot care to prevent recurrence of disorders. Makes and fits prosthetic appliances. Treats bone, muscle, and joint disorders. Treats conditions, such as corns, calluses, ingrown nails, tumors, shortened tendons, bunions, cysts, and abscesses by surgical methods. Corrects deformities by means of plaster casts and strapping. Diagnoses ailments, such as tumors, ulcers, fractures, skin or nail diseases, and deformities, utilizing urinalysis, blood tests, and X rays. Prescribes corrective footwear. Prescribes drugs.

Personality Type: Social. Social occupations frequently involve working with, communicating with, and teaching people. These occupations often involve helping or providing service to others.

Abilities: Deductive Reasoning—The ability to apply general rules to specific problems to come up with logical answers. Involves deciding if an answer makes sense. Finger Dexterity—The ability to make precisely coordinated movements of the fingers of one or both hands to grasp, manipulate, or assemble very small objects. Problem Sensitivity—The ability to tell when something is wrong or is likely to go wrong. Does not involve solving the problem, only recognizing there is a problem. Oral Expression—The ability to communicate information and ideas verbally so others will understand.

Skills: Active Listening—Listening to what other people are saying; asking questions as appropriate. Reading Comprehension—Understanding written information in work-related documents. Critical Thinking—Using logic and analysis to identify the strengths and weaknesses of different approaches.

Generalized Work Activities: Assisting and Caring for Others—Providing assistance or personal care to others. Getting Information Needed to Do the Job—Observing, receiving, and otherwise obtaining information from all relevant sources. Analyzing Data or Information—Identifying underlying principles, reasons, or facts by breaking down information or data into separate parts. Identifying Objects, Actions, and Events—Identifying information received by making estimates or categorizations, recognizing differences or similarities, or sensing changes in circumstances or events. Communicating with Persons Outside Organization—Communicating with persons outside the organization. Representing the organization to customers, the public, government, and other external sources. Exchanging information face-to-face, in writing, or via telephone/electronic transfer. Making Decisions and Solving Problems—Combining, evaluating, and analyzing information and data to make decisions and solve problems. Involves making decisions about the relative importance of information and choosing the best solution.

Police and Detective Supervisors

▲ Growth: 12%
▲ Annual Job Openings: 14,034
▲ Yearly Earnings: $48,700
▲ Education Required: Work experience in a related occupation
▲ Self-Employed: 0%
▲ Part-Time: 0%

First-Line Supervisors/ Managers of Police and Detectives

Supervise and coordinate activities of members of police force. Meets with civic, educational, and community groups to develop community programs and events and addresses groups concerning law enforcement subjects. Prepares work schedules, assigns duties, and develops and revises departmental procedures. Directs collection, preparation, and handling of evidence and personal property of prisoners. Assists subordinates in performing job duties. Investigates charges of misconduct against staff. Trains staff. Inspects facilities, supplies, vehicles, and equipment to ensure conformance to standards. Prepares news releases and responds to police correspondence. Cooperates with court personnel and officials from other law enforcement agencies and testifies in court. Conducts raids and orders detention of witnesses and suspects for questioning. Directs release or transfer of prisoners. Reviews contents of written orders to ensure adherence to legal requirements. Requisitions and issues department equipment and supplies. Prepares budgets and manages expenditures of department funds. Prepares reports and directs preparation, handling, and maintenance of departmental records. Investigates and resolves personnel problems within organization. Monitors and evaluates job performance of subordinates. Supervises and coordinates investigation of criminal cases. Disciplines staff for violation of department rules and regulations.

Personality Type: Enterprising. Enterprising occupations frequently involve starting up and carrying out projects. These occupations can involve leading people and making many decisions. They sometimes require risk taking and often deal with business.

Abilities: Oral Expression—The ability to communicate information and ideas verbally so others will understand. Inductive Reasoning—The ability to combine separate pieces of information, or specific answers to problems, to form general rules or conclusions. Includes coming up with a logical explanation for why a series of seemingly unrelated events occur together. Oral Comprehension—The ability to listen to and understand information and ideas presented verbally. Written Expression—The ability to communicate information and ideas in writing so others will understand. Near Vision—The ability to see details of objects at a close range.

Skills: Coordination—Adjusting actions in relation to others' actions. Management of Personnel Resources—Motivating, developing, and directing people as they work, identifying the best people for the job. Judgment and Decision Making—Weighing the relative costs and benefits of a potential action. Speaking—Talking to others to effectively convey information. Critical Thinking—Using logic and analysis to identify the strengths and weaknesses of different approaches.

Generalized Work Activities: Organizing, Planning, and Prioritizing—Developing plans to accomplish work. Prioritizing and organizing one's own work. Getting Information Needed to Do the Job—Observing, receiving, and otherwise obtaining information from all relevant sources. Performing for/Working with Public—Performing for people or dealing directly with the public, including serving persons in restaurants and stores and receiving clients or guests. Resolving Conflict,

Negotiating with Others—Handling complaints, arbitrating disputes, resolving grievances, or otherwise negotiating with others. Analyzing Data or Information—Identifying underlying principles, reasons, or facts by breaking down information or data into separate parts. Communicating with Persons Outside Organization—Communicating with persons outside the organization. Representing the organization to customers, the public, government, and other external sources. Exchanging information face-to-face, in writing, or via telephone/electronic transfer. Documenting/Recording Information—Entering, transcribing, recording, storing, or maintaining information in either written form or by electronic/magnetic recording.

Police Patrol Officers

- ▲ Growth: 32%
- ▲ Annual Job Openings: 51,739
- ▲ Yearly Earnings: $37,710
- ▲ Education Required: Long-term O-J-T
- ▲ Self-Employed: 0%
- ▲ Part-Time: 1.5%

Highway Patrol Pilots

Pilot aircraft to patrol highway and enforce traffic laws. Arrests perpetrator of criminal act or submits citation or warning to violator of motor vehicle ordinance. Renders aid to accident victims and other persons requiring first aid for physical injuries. Evaluates complaint and emergency request information to determine response requirements. Relays complaint and emergency request information to appropriate agency dispatcher. Prepares reports to document activities. Expedites processing of prisoners, prepares and maintains records of prisoner bookings, and maintains record of prisoner status during booking and pre-trial process. Testifies in court to present evidence or act as witness in traffic and criminal cases. Informs ground personnel where to reroute traffic in case of emergencies. Reviews facts to determine if criminal act or statute violation involved. Investigates traffic accidents and other accidents to determine causes and to determine if crime was committed. Informs ground personnel of traffic congestion or unsafe driving conditions to ensure traffic flow and reduce incidence of accidents. Pilots airplane to maintain order, respond to emergencies, to enforce traffic and criminal laws, and apprehend criminals. Records facts, photographs and diagrams crime or accident scene, and interviews witnesses to gather information for possible use in legal action or safety programs.

Personality Type: Realistic. Realistic occupations frequently involve work activities that include practical, hands-on problems and solutions. They often deal with plants, animals, and real-world materials like wood, tools, and machinery. Many of the occupations require working outside and do not involve a lot of paperwork or working closely with others.

Abilities: Far Vision—The ability to see details at a distance. Rate Control—The ability to time the adjustments of a movement or equipment control in anticipation of changes in the speed and/or direction of a continuously moving object or scene. Spatial Orientation—The ability to know one's location in relation to the environment or to know where other objects are in relation to one's self. Oral Comprehension—The ability to listen to and understand information and ideas presented verbally. Oral Expression—The ability to communicate information and ideas verbally so others will understand.

Skills: Operation and Control—Controlling operations of equipment or systems. Speaking—Talking to others to effectively convey information. Social Perceptiveness—Being aware of other people's reactions and understanding why people react the way they do. Problem Identification—Identifying the nature of problems. Active Listening—Listening to what other people are saying; asking questions as appropriate.

Generalized Work Activities: Documenting/Recording Information—Entering, transcribing, recording, storing, or maintaining information in either written form or by electronic/magnetic recording. Getting Information Needed to Do the Job—Observing, receiving, and otherwise obtaining information from all relevant sources. Operating Vehicles or Equipment—Running, maneuvering, navigating, or driving vehicles or mechanized equipment such as forklifts, passenger vehicles, aircraft, or water craft. Performing for/Working with Public—Performing for people or dealing directly with the public, including serving persons in restaurants and stores and receiving clients or guests. Communicating with Persons Outside Organization—Communicating with persons outside the organization. Representing the organization to customers, the public, government, and other external sources. Exchanging information face-to-face, in writing, or via telephone/electronic transfer. Assisting and Caring for Others—Providing assistance or personal care to others.

Police Patrol Officers

Patrol assigned area to enforce laws and ordinances, regulate traffic, control crowds, prevent crime, and arrest violators. Maintains order, responds to emergencies, protects people and property, and enforces motor vehicle and criminal law. Expedites processing of prisoners, and prepares and maintains records of prisoner bookings and prisoner status during booking and pre-trial process. Draws diagram of crime or accident scene. Testifies in court to present evidence or act as witness in traffic and criminal cases. Records facts and prepares reports to document activities. Renders aid to accident victims and other persons requiring first aid for physical injuries. Interviews principal and eye witnesses. Photographs crime or accident scene. Patrols specific area on foot, horseback, or motorized convey-

ance. Arrests perpetrator of criminal act or submits citation or warning to violator of motor vehicle ordinance. Provides road information to assist motorists. Investigates traffic accidents and other accidents to determine causes and to determine if crime has been committed. Evaluates complaint and emergency-request information to determine response requirements. Reviews facts to determine if criminal act or statute violation is involved. Directs traffic flow and reroutes traffic in case of emergencies. Monitors traffic to ensure motorists observe traffic regulations and exhibit safe driving procedures. Relays complaint and emergency-request information to appropriate agency dispatcher.

Personality Type: Social. Social occupations frequently involve working with, communicating with, and teaching people. These occupations often involve helping or providing service to others.

Abilities: Oral Expression—The ability to communicate information and ideas verbally so others will understand. Reaction Time—The ability to quickly respond with the hand, finger, or foot to a signal such as a sound, a light, or a picture. Inductive Reasoning—The ability to combine separate pieces of information, or specific answers to problems, to form general rules or conclusions. Includes coming up with a logical explanation for why a series of seemingly unrelated events occur together. Written Expression—The ability to communicate information and ideas in writing so others will understand. Far Vision—The ability to see details at a distance.

Skills: Social Perceptiveness—Being aware of other people's reactions and understanding why people react the way they do. Problem Identification—Identifying the nature of problems. Critical Thinking—Using logic and analysis to identify the strengths and weaknesses of different approaches. Speaking—Talking to others to effectively convey information.

Generalized Work Activities: Performing for/Working with Public—Performing for people or dealing directly with the public, including serving persons in restaurants and stores and receiving clients or guests. Documenting/Recording Information—Entering, transcribing, recording, storing, or maintaining information in either written form or by electronic/magnetic recording. Assisting and Caring for Others—Providing assistance or personal care to others. Getting Information Needed to Do the Job—Observing, receiving, and otherwise obtaining information from all relevant sources.

Resolving Conflict, Negotiating with Others—Handling complaints, arbitrating disputes, resolving grievances, or otherwise negotiating with others.

Postmasters and Mail Superintendents

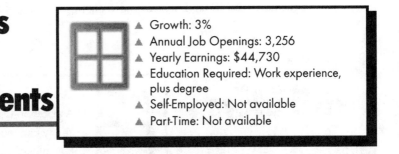

- ▲ Growth: 3%
- ▲ Annual Job Openings: 3,256
- ▲ Yearly Earnings: $44,730
- ▲ Education Required: Work experience, plus degree
- ▲ Self-Employed: Not available
- ▲ Part-Time: Not available

Postmasters and Mail Superintendents

Direct and coordinate operational, administrative, management, and supportive services of a U.S. post office or coordinate activities of workers engaged in postal and related work in assigned post office. Selects, trains, and evaluates performance of employees and prepares work schedules. Organizes and supervises directly, or through subordinates, such activities as processing incoming and outgoing mail to ensure efficient service to patrons. Selects, trains, and terminates postmasters and managers of associate postal units. Negotiates labor disputes. Confers with suppliers to obtain bids for proposed purchases, requisitions supplies, and disburses funds as specified by law. Prepares and submits detailed and summary reports of post office activities to designated supervisors. Directs and coordinates operational, management, and supportive services of associate post offices within district area known as sectional center. Resolves customer complaints and informs public of postal laws and regulations. Directs and coordinates operations of several sectional centers within district.

Personality Type: Enterprising. Enterprising occupations frequently involve starting up and carrying out projects. These occupations can involve leading people

and making many decisions. They sometimes require risk taking and often deal with business.

Abilities: Oral Expression—The ability to communicate information and ideas verbally so others will understand. Written Expression—The ability to communicate information and ideas in writing so others will understand. Oral Comprehension—The ability to listen to and understand information and ideas presented verbally. Written Comprehension—The ability to read and understand information and ideas presented in writing. Speech Clarity—The ability to speak clearly to that what is said is understandable to a listener.

Skills: Problem Identification—Identifying the nature of problems. Critical Thinking—Using logic and analysis to identify the strengths and weaknesses of different approaches. Judgment and Decision Making—Weighing the relative costs and benefits of a potential action. Negotiation—Bringing others together and trying to reconcile differences. Systems Evaluation—Looking at many indicators of system performance, taking into account their accuracy. Coordination—Adjusting actions in relation to others' actions. Management of Personnel Resources—Motivating, developing, and directing people as they work, identifying the best people for the job.

Generalized Work Activities: Communicating with Other Workers—Providing information to supervisors, fellow workers, and subordinates. Exchanging information face-to-face, in writing, or via telephone/

electronic transfer. Coordinating Work and Activities of Others—Coordinating members of a work group to accomplish tasks. Guiding, Directing, and Motivating Subordinates—Providing guidance and direction to subordinates, including setting performance standards and monitoring subordinates. Making Decisions and Solving Problems—Combining, evaluating, and analyzing information and data to make decisions and solve problems. Involves making decisions about the relative importance of information and choosing the best solution. Getting Information Needed to Do the Job—Observing, receiving, and otherwise obtaining information from all relevant sources.

Power Distributors and Dispatchers

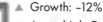

- ▲ Growth: –12%
- ▲ Annual Job Openings: 855
- ▲ Yearly Earnings: $45,690
- ▲ Education Required: Long-term O-J-T
- ▲ Self-Employed: 0%
- ▲ Part-Time: 1.8%

Power Distributors and Dispatchers

Coordinate, regulate, or distribute electricity or steam. Notifies workers or utilities of electrical and steam distribution process changes. Adjusts controls to regulate the flow of power between generating stations, substations, and distribution lines. Calculates and determines load estimates or equipment requirements to control electrical distribution equipment or stations. Directs activities of personnel engaged in the controlling and operating of electrical distribution equipment and machinery. Turns and moves controls to adjust and activate power distribution equipment and machines. Inspects equipment to ensure specifications are met and to detect defects. Compiles and records operational data, such as chart and meter readings, power demands, and usage and operating time. Monitors switchboard and control board to ensure equipment operation and electrical and steam distribution. Controls and operates equipment to regulate or distribute electricity or steam, according to data provided by recording or indicating instruments or computers. Repairs, maintains, and cleans equipment and machines, using hand tools. Tends auxiliary equipment used in the power distribution process.

Personality Type: Realistic. Realistic occupations frequently involve work activities that include practical, hands-on problems and solutions. They often deal with plants, animals, and real-world materials like wood, tools, and machinery. Many of the occupations require working outside and do not involve a lot of paperwork or working closely with others.

Abilities: Information Ordering—The ability to correctly follow a given rule or set of rules in order to arrange things or actions in a certain order. The things or actions can include numbers, letters, words, pictures, procedures, sentences, and mathematical or logical operations. Written Comprehension—The ability to read and understand information and ideas presented in writing. Near Vision—The ability to see details of objects at a close range. Problem Sensitivity—The ability to tell when something is wrong or is likely to go wrong. Does not involve solving the problem, only recognizing there is a problem. Wrist-Finger Speed—The ability to make fast, simple, repeated movements of the fingers, hands, and wrists. Manual Dexterity—The ability to quickly make coordinated movements of one hand, a hand together with its arm, or two hands, to grasp, manipulate, or assemble objects. Reaction Time—The ability to quickly respond with the hand, finger, or foot to a signal such as a sound, a light, or a picture. Time

Sharing—The ability to efficiently shift back and forth between two or more activities or sources of information such as speech, sounds, or touch.

Skills: Operation and Control—Controlling operations of equipment or systems. Operation Monitoring—Watching gauges, dials, or other indicators to make sure a machine is working properly. Repairing—Repairing machines or systems, using the needed tools. Equipment Maintenance—Performing routine maintenance and determining when and what kind of maintenance is needed. Management of Personnel Resources—Motivating, developing, and directing people as they work, identifying the best people for the job.

Generalized Work Activities: Monitoring Processes, Materials, Surroundings—Monitoring and reviewing information from materials, events, or the environment, often to detect problems or to find out when things are finished. Controlling Machines and Processes—Using either control mechanisms or direct physical activity to operate machines or processes. Does not involve working with computers or vehicles. Processing Information—Compiling, coding, categorizing, calculating, tabulating, auditing, verifying, or processing information or data. Inspecting Equipment, Structures, Materials—Inspecting or diagnosing equipment, structures, or materials to identify the causes of errors or other problems or defects. Coordinating Work and Activities of Others—Coordinating members of a work group to accomplish tasks. Getting Information Needed to Do the Job—Observing, receiving, and otherwise obtaining information from all relevant sources. Identifying Objects, Actions, and Events—Identifying information received by making estimates or categorizations, recognizing differences or similarities, or sensing changes in circumstances or events.

Power Generating and Reactor Plant Operators

- ▲ Growth: 3%
- ▲ Annual Job Openings: 2,216
- ▲ Yearly Earnings: $44,800
- ▲ Education Required: Long-term O-J-T
- ▲ Self-Employed: 0%
- ▲ Part-Time: 1.8%

Auxiliary Equipment Operators, Power

Control and maintain auxiliary equipment, such as pumps, fans, compressors, condensers, feedwater heaters, filters, and chlorinators, that supply water, fuel, lubricants, air, and auxiliary power for turbines, generators, boilers, and other power-generating plant facilities. Assists in making electrical repairs. Opens and closes valves and switches in sequence upon signal from other worker to start or shut down auxiliary units. Cleans and lubricates equipment and collects oil, water, and electrolyte samples for laboratory analysis to prevent equipment failure or deterioration. Reads gauges to verify that units are operating at specified capacity, and listens for sounds warning of mechanical malfunction. Tends portable or stationary high pressure boilers that supply heat or power for engines, turbines, and steam-powered equipment. Replenishes electrolyte in batteries and oil in voltage transformers and resets tripped electric relays. Tightens leaking gland and pipe joints and reports need for major equipment repairs.

Personality Type: Realistic. Realistic occupations frequently involve work activities that include practical, hands-on problems and solutions. They often deal with plants, animals, and real-world materials like wood, tools, and machinery. Many of the occupations require working outside and do not involve a lot of paperwork or working closely with others.

Abilities: Control Precision—The ability to quickly and repeatedly make precise adjustments in moving the controls of a machine or vehicle to exact positions. Problem Sensitivity—The ability to tell when something is wrong or is likely to go wrong. Does not involve solving the problem, only recognizing there is a problem. Near Vision—The ability to see details of objects at a close range. Finger Dexterity—The ability to make precisely coordinated movements of the fingers of one or both hands to grasp, manipulate, or assemble very small objects. Inductive Reasoning—The ability to combine separate pieces of information, or specific answers to problems, to form general rules or conclusions. Includes coming up with a logical explanation for why a series of seemingly unrelated events occur together.

Skills: Operation Monitoring—Watching gauges, dials, or other indicators to make sure a machine is working properly. Operation and Control—Controlling operations of equipment or systems. Equipment Maintenance—Performing routine maintenance and determining when and what kind of maintenance is needed. Equipment Selection—Determining the kind of tools and equipment needed to do a job. Troubleshooting—Determining what is causing an operating error and deciding what to do about it. Problem Identification—Identifying the nature of problems.

Generalized Work Activities: Monitoring Processes, Materials, Surroundings—Monitoring and reviewing information from materials, events, or the environment, often to detect problems or to find out when things are finished. Getting Information Needed to Do the Job—Observing, receiving, and otherwise obtaining information from all relevant sources. Identifying Objects, Actions, and Events—Identifying information received by making estimates or categorizations, recognizing differences or similarities, or sensing changes in circumstances or events. Controlling Machines and Processes—Using either control mechanisms or direct physical activity to operate machines or processes. Does not involve working with computers or vehicles. Evaluation Information against Standards—Evaluating information against a set of standards and verifying that it is correct.

Nuclear Power Reactor Operators

Control nuclear reactors. Dispatches orders and instructions to personnel through radiotelephone or intercommunication system to coordinate operation of auxiliary equipment. Adjusts controls to regulate flow of power between generating and substations. Monitors computer-operated equipment. Monitors gauges to determine effects of generator loading on other power equipment. Monitors and operates boilers, turbines, wells, and auxiliary power plant equipment. Corrects abnormal conditions following standard practices. Regulates equipment according to data provided by recording and indicating instruments or computers. Notes malfunctions of equipment, instruments, or controls.

Personality Type: Realistic. Realistic occupations frequently involve work activities that include practical, hands-on problems and solutions. They often deal with plants, animals, and real-world materials like wood, tools, and machinery. Many of the occupations require working outside and do not involve a lot of paperwork or working closely with others.

Abilities: Oral Expression—The ability to communicate information and ideas verbally so others will understand. Written Comprehension—The ability to read and understand information and ideas presented in writing. Oral Comprehension—The ability to listen to and understand information and ideas presented verbally. Control Precision—The ability to quickly and repeatedly make precise adjustments in moving the controls of a machine or vehicle to exact positions. Speech Clarity—The ability to speak clearly to that what is said is understandable to a listener.

Skills: Operation Monitoring—Watching gauges, dials, or other indicators to make sure a machine is working properly. Operation and Control—Controlling operations of equipment or systems. Coordination—Adjusting actions in relation to others' actions. Problem Identification—Identifying the nature of problems. Speaking—Talking to others to effectively convey information.

Generalized Work Activities: Controlling Machines and Processes—Using either control mechanisms or direct physical activity to operate machines or processes. Does not involve working with computers or vehicles. Monitoring Processes, Materials, Surroundings—Monitoring and reviewing information from materials, events, or the environment, often to detect problems or to find out when things are finished. Handling and Moving Objects—Using one's hands and arms in handling, installing, forming, positioning, and moving materials, or in manipulating things. Includes the use of keyboards. Getting Information Needed to Do the Job—Observing, receiving, and otherwise obtaining information from all relevant sources. Communicating with Other Workers—Providing information to supervisors, fellow workers, and subordinates. Exchanging information face-to-face, in writing, or via telephone/electronic transfer.

Power Generating Plant Operators, Except Auxiliary Equipment Operators

Control or operate machinery, such as steam-driven turbogenerators, to generate electric power, often through the use of panelboards, control boards, or semiautomatic equipment. Operates or controls machinery that generates electric power, using control boards or semiautomatic equipment. Examines and tests electrical power distribution machinery and equipment, using testing devices. Maintains and repairs electrical power distribution machinery and equipment, using hand tools. Compiles and records operational data on specified forms. Adjusts controls on equipment to generate specified electrical power. Monitors control and switchboard gauges to determine electrical power distribution meets specifications.

Personality Type: Realistic. Realistic occupations frequently involve work activities that include practical, hands-on problems and solutions. They often deal with plants, animals, and real-world materials like wood, tools, and machinery. Many of the occupations require

working outside and do not involve a lot of paperwork or working closely with others.

Abilities: Selective Attention—The ability to concentrate and not be distracted while performing a task over a period of time. Perceptual Speed—The ability to quickly and accurately compare letters, numbers, objects, pictures, or patterns. The things to be compared may be presented at the same time or one after the other. Includes comparing a presented object with a remembered object. Wrist-Finger Speed—The ability to make fast, simple, repeated movements of the fingers, hands, and wrists. Control Precision—The ability to quickly and repeatedly make precise adjustments in moving the controls of a machine or vehicle to exact positions. Deductive Reasoning—The ability to apply general rules to specific problems to come up with logical answers. Involves deciding if an answer makes sense.

Skills: Operation Monitoring—Watching gauges, dials, or other indicators to make sure a machine is working properly. Operation and Control—Controlling operations of equipment or systems. Testing—Conducting tests to determine whether equipment, software, or procedures are operating as expected. Repairing—Repairing machines or systems, using the needed tools.

Generalized Work Activities: Monitoring Processes, Materials, Surroundings—Monitoring and reviewing information from materials, events, or the environment, often to detect problems or to find out when things are finished. Controlling Machines and Processes—Using either control mechanisms or direct physical activity to operate machines or processes. Does not involve working with computers or vehicles. Repairing and Maintaining Electrical Equipment—Fixing, servicing, adjusting, regulating, calibrating, fine-tuning, or testing machines, devices, and equipment that operate primarily on the basis of electrical or electronic, not mechanical, principles. Getting Information Needed to Do the Job—Observing, receiving, and otherwise obtaining information from all relevant sources. Identifying Objects, Actions, and Events—Identifying information received by making estimates or categorizations, recognizing differences or similarities, or sensing changes in circumstances or events.

Preschool Teachers

- ▲ Growth: 26%
- ▲ Annual Job Openings: 41,894
- ▲ Yearly Earnings: $17,310
- ▲ Education Required: Bachelor's degree
- ▲ Self-Employed: 1.5%
- ▲ Part-Time: 32.4%

Preschool Teachers, Except Special Education

Instruct children (usually up to 5 years of age) in activities designed to promote social, physical, and intellectual growth needed for primary school in preschool, day care center, or other child development facility. Hold state certification. Attends staff meetings. Plans instructional activities for teacher aide. Structures play activities to instill concepts of respect and concern for others. Administers tests to determine each child's level of development according to design of test. Confers with parents to explain preschool program and to discuss ways they can develop their child's interests. Monitors individual and/or group activities to prevent accidents and promote social skills. Instructs children in activities designed to promote social, physical, and intellectual growth. Demonstrates activity. Plans individual and group activities for children, such as learning to listen to instructions, playing with others, and using play equipment. Reads books to entire class or to small groups.

Personality Type: Social. Social occupations frequently involve working with, communicating with, and teaching people. These occupations often involve helping or providing service to others.

Abilities: Oral Expression—The ability to communicate information and ideas verbally so others will understand. Oral Comprehension—The ability to listen to and understand information and ideas presented verbally. Speech Clarity—The ability to speak clearly to that what is said is understandable to a listener. Time Sharing—The ability to efficiently shift back and forth between two or more activities or sources of information such as speech, sounds, or touch. Problem Sensitivity—The ability to tell when something is wrong or is likely to go wrong. Does not involve solving the problem, only recognizing there is a problem.

Skills: Instructing—Teaching others how to do something. Learning Strategies—Using multiple approaches when learning or teaching new things. Speaking—Talking to others to effectively convey information. Social Perceptiveness—Being aware of other people's reactions and understanding why people react the way they do. Active Listening—Listening to what other people are saying; asking questions as appropriate.

Generalized Work Activities: Teaching Others—Identifying educational needs, developing formal training programs or classes, and teaching or instructing others. Assisting and Caring for Others—Providing assistance or personal care to others. Establishing and Maintaining Relationships—Developing constructive and cooperative working relationships with others. Organizing, Planning, and Prioritizing—Developing plans to accomplish work. Prioritizing and organizing one's own work. Thinking Creatively—Originating, inventing, designing, or creating new applications, ideas, relationships, systems, or products, including artistic contributions.

Private Detectives and Investigators

▲ Growth: 24%

▲ Annual Job Openings: 14,675

▲ Yearly Earnings: $21,020

▲ Education Required: Moderate-term O-J-T

▲ Self-Employed: 20.1%

▲ Part-Time: 19.8%

Private Detectives and Investigators

Detect occurrences of unlawful acts or infractions of rules in private establishment, or seek, examine, and compile information for client. Writes reports and case summaries to document investigations or inform supervisors. Examines crime scene for clues or fingerprints and submits evidence to laboratory for analysis. Warns and ejects troublemakers from premises and apprehends and releases suspects to authorities or security personnel. Obtains and analyzes information on suspects, crimes, and disturbances to solve cases, identify criminal activity, and maintain public peace and order. Counts cash and reviews transactions, sales checks, and register tapes to verify amount of cash and shortages. Alerts staff and superiors of presence of suspect in establishment. Testifies at hearings and court trials to present evidence. Locates persons using phone or mail directories to collect money owed or to serve legal papers. Evaluates performance and honesty of employees by posing as customer or employee and comparing employee to standards. Assists victims, police, fire department, and others during emergencies. Observes employees or customers and patrols premises to detect violations and obtain evidence, using binoculars, cameras, and television. Questions persons to obtain evidence for cases of divorce, child custody, or missing persons, or individuals character or financial status. Enforces conformance to establishment rules and protects persons or property. Confers with establishment officials, security department, police, or postal officials to identify problems, provide information, and receive instructions.

Personality Type: Enterprising. Enterprising occupations frequently involve starting up and carrying out projects. These occupations can involve leading people and making many decisions. They sometimes require risk taking and often deal with business.

Abilities: Inductive Reasoning—The ability to combine separate pieces of information, or specific answers to problems, to form general rules or conclusions. Includes coming up with a logical explanation for why a series of seemingly unrelated events occur together. Oral Comprehension—The ability to listen to and understand information and ideas presented verbally. Oral Expression—The ability to communicate information and ideas verbally so others will understand. Problem Sensitivity—The ability to tell when something is wrong or is likely to go wrong. Does not involve solving the problem, only recognizing there is a problem. Written Expression—The ability to communicate information and ideas in writing so others will understand.

Skills: Speaking—Talking to others to effectively convey information. Critical Thinking—Using logic and analysis to identify the strengths and weaknesses of different approaches. Information Gathering—Knowing how to find information and identifying essential information. Problem Identification—Identifying the nature of problems. Active Listening—Listening to what other people are saying; asking questions as appropriate.

Generalized Work Activities: Getting Information Needed to Do the Job—Observing, receiving, and otherwise obtaining information from all relevant sources. Analyzing Data or Information—Identifying underlying principles, reasons, or facts by breaking down information or data into separate parts. Communicating with Other Workers—Providing information to supervisors, fellow workers, and subordinates. Exchanging information face-to-face, in writing, or via telephone/electronic transfer. Documenting/Recording Information—Entering, transcribing, recording, storing, or maintaining information in either written form or by electronic/magnetic recording. Monitoring Processes, Materials, Surroundings—Monitoring and reviewing information from materials, events, or the environment, often to detect problems or to find out when things are finished. Communicating with Persons Outside Organization—Communicating with persons outside the organization. Representing the organization to customers, the public, government, and other external sources. Exchanging information face-to-face, in writing, or via telephone/electronic transfer.

Property and Casualty Insurance Claims Examiners

- ▲ Growth: 12%
- ▲ Annual Job Openings: 3,838
- ▲ Yearly Earnings: $40,110
- ▲ Education Required: Bachelor's degree
- ▲ Self-Employed: 0%
- ▲ Part-Time: 7.3%

Claims Examiners, Property and Casualty Insurance

Review settled insurance claims to determine that payments and settlements have been made in accordance with company practices and procedures. Report overpayments, underpayments, and other irregularities. Confer with legal counsel on claims requiring litigation. Analyzes data used in settling claim to determine its validity in payment of claims. Reports overpayments, underpayments, and other irregularities. Confers with legal counsel on claims requiring litigation.

Personality Type: Conventional. Conventional occupations frequently involve following set procedures and routines. These occupations can include working with data and details more than with ideas. Usually there is a clear line of authority to follow.

Abilities: Written Comprehension—The ability to read and understand information and ideas presented in writing. Mathematical Reasoning—The ability to understand and organize a problem and then select a mathematical method or formula to solve the problem. Number Facility—The ability to add, subtract, multiply, or divide quickly and correctly. Problem Sensitivity—The ability to tell when something is wrong or is likely to go wrong. Does not involve solving the problem, only recognizing there is a problem. Written Expression—The ability to communicate information and ideas in writing so others will understand. Oral Comprehension—The ability to listen to and understand information and ideas presented verbally.

Skills: Problem Identification—Identifying the nature of problems. Reading Comprehension—Understanding written information in work-related documents. Mathematics—Using mathematics to solve problems. Information Gathering—Knowing how to find information and identifying essential information. Solution Appraisal—Observing and evaluating the outcomes of a problem solution to identify lessons learned or to redirect efforts. Speaking—Talking to others to effectively convey information.

Generalized Work Activities: Evaluation Information against Standards—Evaluating information against a set of standards and verifying that it is correct. Analyzing Data or Information—Identifying underlying principles, reasons, or facts by breaking down information or data into separate parts. Judging Qualities—Making judgments about or assessing the value, importance, or quality of things, services, or other people's work. Getting Information Needed to Do the Job—Observing, receiving, and otherwise obtaining information from all relevant sources. Making Decisions and Solving Problems—Combining, evaluating, and analyzing information and data to make decisions and solve problems. Involves making decisions about the relative importance of information and choosing the best solution.

Property, Real Estate, and Community Association Managers

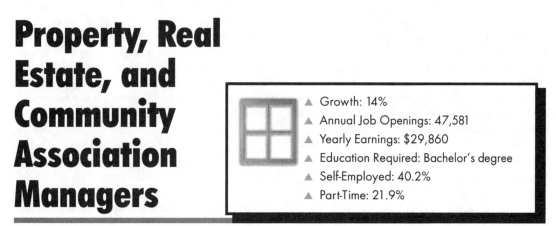

- ▲ Growth: 14%
- ▲ Annual Job Openings: 47,581
- ▲ Yearly Earnings: $29,860
- ▲ Education Required: Bachelor's degree
- ▲ Self-Employed: 40.2%
- ▲ Part-Time: 21.9%

Property, Real Estate, and Community Association Managers

Plan, direct, or coordinate selling, buying, leasing, or governance activities of commercial, industrial, or residential real estate properties. Develops and administers annual operating budget. Meets with prospective leasers to show property, explain terms of occupancy, and provide information about local area. Prepares reports summarizing financial and operational status of property or facility. Maintains contact with insurance carrier, fire and police departments, and other agencies to ensure protection and compliance with codes and regulations. Confers with legal authority to ensure transactions and terminations of contracts and agreements are in accordance with court orders, laws, and regulations. Assembles and analyzes construction and vendor service contract bids. Inspects facilities and equipment and inventories building contents to document damage and determine repair needs. Negotiates for sale, lease, or development of property, and completes or reviews appropriate documents and forms. Purchases building and maintenance supplies, equipment, or furniture. Maintains records of sales, rental or usage activity, special permits issued, maintenance and operating costs, or property availability. Directs and coordinates the activities of staff and contract personnel and evaluates performance. Recruits, hires, and trains managerial, clerical, and maintenance staff, or contracts with vendors for security, maintenance, extermination, or groundskeeping personnel. Investigates complaints, disturbances, and violations and resolves problems following management rules and regulations. Plans, schedules, and coordinates general maintenance, major repairs, and remodeling or construction projects for commercial or residential property. Meets with clients to negotiate management and service contracts, determine priorities, and discuss financial and operational status of property. Manages and oversees operations, maintenance, and administrative functions for commercial, industrial, or residential properties.

Personality Type: Enterprising. Enterprising occupations frequently involve starting up and carrying out projects. These occupations can involve leading people and making many decisions. They sometimes require risk taking and often deal with business.

Abilities: Number Facility—The ability to add, subtract, multiply, or divide quickly and correctly. Oral Comprehension—The ability to listen to and understand information and ideas presented verbally. Written Comprehension—The ability to read and understand information and ideas presented in writing. Oral Expression—The ability to communicate information and ideas verbally so others will understand. Mathematical Reasoning—The ability to understand and organize a problem and then select a mathematical method or formula to solve the problem.

Skills: Speaking—Talking to others to effectively convey information. Judgment and Decision Making—Weighing the relative costs and benefits of a potential action. Management of Personnel Resources—

Motivating, developing, and directing people as they work, identifying the best people for the job. Active Listening—Listening to what other people are saying; asking questions as appropriate. Coordination—Adjusting actions in relation to others' actions. Information Gathering—Knowing how to find information and identifying essential information. Reading Comprehension—Understanding written information in work-related documents.

Generalized Work Activities: Communicating with Other Workers—Providing information to supervisors, fellow workers, and subordinates. Exchanging information face-to-face, in writing, or via telephone/electronic transfer. Getting Information Needed to Do the Job—Observing, receiving, and otherwise obtaining information from all relevant sources. Communicating with Persons Outside Organization—Communicating with persons outside the organization. Representing the organization to customers, the public, government, and other external sources. Exchanging information face-to-face, in writing, or via telephone/electronic transfer. Evaluation Information against Standards—Evaluating information against a set of standards and verifying that it is correct.

Pruners

▲ Growth: 12%
▲ Annual Job Openings: 10,504
▲ Yearly Earnings: $22,070
▲ Education Required: Short-term O-J-T
▲ Self-Employed: 0%
▲ Part-Time: 25.4%

Tree Trimmers and Pruners

Cut away dead or excess branches from trees or shrubs to maintain right-of-way for roads, sidewalks, or utilities, or to improve appearance, health, and value of tree. Prune or treat trees or shrubs using handsaws, pruning hooks, sheers, and clippers. Use truck-

mounted lifts and power pruners. Fill cavities in trees to promote healing and prevent deterioration. Scrapes decayed matter from cavities in trees and fills holes with cement to promote healing and to prevent further deterioration. Climbs trees, using climbing hooks and belts, or climbs ladders to gain access to work area. Uses truck-mounted hydraulic lifts and pruners and power pruners. Applies tar or other protective substances to cut surfaces to seal surfaces against insects. Cuts away dead and excess branches from trees using handsaws, pruning hooks, shears, and clippers. Prunes, cuts down, fertilizes, and sprays trees as directed by tree surgeon.

Personality Type: Realistic. Realistic occupations frequently involve work activities that include practical, hands-on problems and solutions. They often deal with plants, animals, and real-world materials like wood, tools, and machinery. Many of the occupations require working outside and do not involve a lot of paperwork or working closely with others.

Abilities: Multilimb Coordination—The ability to coordinate movements of two or more limbs together (for example, two arms, two legs, or one leg and one arm) while sitting, standing, or lying down. Does not involve performing the activities while the body is in motion. Extent Flexibility—The ability to bend, stretch, twist, or reach out with the body, arms, and/or legs. Dynamic Strength—The ability to exert muscle force repeatedly or continuously over time. This involves muscular endurance and resistance to muscle fatigue. Static Strength—The ability to exert maximum muscle force to lift, push, pull, or carry objects. Manual Dexterity—The ability to quickly make coordinated movements of one hand, a hand together with its arm, or two hands, to grasp, manipulate, or assemble objects.

Skills: Operation and Control—Controlling operations of equipment or systems. Equipment Selection—Determining the kind of tools and equipment needed to do a job. Implementation Planning—Developing

approaches for implementing an idea. Problem Identification—Identifying the nature of problems. Product Inspection—Inspecting and evaluating the quality of products.

Generalized Work Activities: Performing General Physical Activities—Performing physical activities that require moving one's whole body, such as in climbing, lifting, balancing, walking, and stooping. Performing activities that often also require considerable use of the arms and legs, such as in the physical handling of materials. Handling and Moving Objects—Using one's hands and arms in handling, installing, forming, positioning, and moving materials, or in manipulating things. Controlling Machines and Processes—Using either control mechanisms or direct physical activity to operate machines or processes. Does not involve working with computers or vehicles. Judging Qualities—Making judgments about or assessing the value, importance, or quality of things, services, or other people's work. Getting Information Needed to Do the Job—Observing, receiving, and otherwise obtaining information from all relevant sources. Identifying Objects, Actions, and Events—Identifying information received by making estimates or categorizations, recognizing differences or similarities, or sensing changes in circumstances or events. Operating Vehicles or Equipment—Running, maneuvering, navigating, or driving vehicles or mechanized equipment such as forklifts, passenger vehicles, aircraft, or water craft.

Psychiatric Technicians

- ▲ Growth: 11%
- ▲ Annual Job Openings: 15,167
- ▲ Yearly Earnings: $20,890
- ▲ Education Required: Associate degree
- ▲ Self-Employed: 0%
- ▲ Part-Time: 26.4%

Psychiatric Technicians

Care for mentally impaired or emotionally disturbed individuals, following physician instructions and hospital procedures. Monitor patients' physical and emotional well-being and report to medical staff. Participate in rehabilitation and treatment programs, help with personal hygiene, and administer oral medications and hypodermic injections. Contacts patient's relatives by telephone to arrange family conferences. Issues medications from dispensary and maintains records in accordance with specified procedures. Observes patients to detect behavior patterns and reports observations to medical staff. Administers oral medications and hypodermic injections, following physician's prescriptions and hospital procedures. Completes initial admittance forms for new patients. Leads prescribed individual or group therapy sessions as part of specific therapeutic procedures. Intervenes to restrain violent or potentially violent or suicidal patients by verbal or physical means as required. Helps patients with their personal hygiene, such as bathing and keeping beds, clothing, and living areas clean. Takes and records measures of patient's general physical condition, such as pulse, temperature, and respiration, to provide daily information.

Personality Type: Social. Social occupations frequently involve working with, communicating with, and teaching people. These occupations often involve helping or providing service to others.

Abilities: Problem Sensitivity—The ability to tell when something is wrong or is likely to go wrong. Does not involve solving the problem, only recognizing there is a problem. Oral Comprehension—The ability to listen to and understand information and ideas presented verbally. Oral Expression—The ability to communicate information and ideas verbally so others will understand. Written Comprehension—The ability to read and understand information and ideas presented in writing. Speech Clarity—The ability to speak clearly to that what is said is understandable to a listener.

Skills: Social Perceptiveness—Being aware of other people's reactions and understanding why people react the way they do. Active Listening—Listening to what other people are saying; asking questions as appropriate. Service Orientation—Actively looking for ways to help people. Problem Identification—Identifying the nature of problems. Speaking—Talking to others to effectively convey information. Reading Comprehension—Understanding written information in work-related documents.

Generalized Work Activities: Assisting and Caring for Others—Providing assistance or personal care to others. Performing General Physical Activities—Performing physical activities that require moving one's whole body, such as in climbing, lifting, balancing, walking, and stooping. Performing activities that often also require considerable use of the arms and legs, such as in the physical handling of materials. Getting Information Needed to Do the Job—Observing, receiving, and otherwise obtaining information from all relevant sources. Communicating with Other Workers—Providing information to supervisors, fellow workers, and subordinates. Exchanging information face-to-face, in writing, or via telephone/electronic transfer. Documenting/Recording Information—Entering, transcribing, recording, storing, or maintaining information in either written form or by electronic/magnetic recording.

Psychologists

- ▲ Growth: 11%
- ▲ Annual Job Openings: 21,473
- ▲ Yearly Earnings: $48,050
- ▲ Education Required: Master's degree
- ▲ Self-Employed: 43.7%
- ▲ Part-Time: 23.4%

Clinical Psychologists

Diagnose or evaluate mental and emotional disorders of individuals through observation, interview, and psychological tests, and formulate and administer programs of treatment. Directs, coordinates, and evaluates activities of psychological staff and student interns engaged in patient evaluation and treatment in psychiatric facility. Assists clients to gain insight, define goals, and plan action to achieve effective personal, social, educational, and vocational development and adjustment. Interviews individuals, couples, or families, and reviews records to obtain information on medical, psychological, emotional, relationship, or other problems. Selects, administers, scores, and interprets psychological tests to obtain information on individual's intelligence, achievement, interest, and personality. Utilizes treatment methods, such as psychotherapy, hypnosis, behavior modification, stress reduction therapy, psychodrama, and play therapy. Plans and develops accredited psychological service programs in psychiatric center or hospital, in collaboration with psychiatrists and other professional staff. Consults reference material, such as textbooks, manuals, and journals, to identify symptoms, make diagnoses, and develop approach to treatment. Responds to client reactions, evaluates effectiveness of counseling or treatment, and modifies plan as needed. Plans, supervises, and conducts psychological research in fields such as personality development, and diagnosis, treatment, and prevention of mental disorders. Conducts individual and group counseling sessions regarding psychological or emotional problems, such as stress, substance abuse, and family situations. Provides psychological services and advice to private firms and community agencies on individual cases or mental health programs. Develops, directs, and participates in staff training programs. Develops treatment plan, including type, frequency, intensity, and duration of therapy, in collaboration with psychiatrist and other specialists. Provides occupational, educational, and other information to enable individual to formulate realistic educational and vocational plans.

Personality Type: Investigative. Investigative occupations frequently involve working with ideas and require an extensive amount of thinking. These occupations can involve searching for facts and figuring out problems mentally.

Abilities: Oral Comprehension—The ability to listen to and understand information and ideas presented verbally. Written Comprehension—The ability to read and understand information and ideas presented in writing. Oral Expression—The ability to communicate information and ideas verbally so others will understand. Problem Sensitivity—The ability to tell when something is wrong or is likely to go wrong. Does not involve solving the problem, only recognizing there is a problem. Inductive Reasoning—The ability to combine separate pieces of information, or specific answers to problems, to form general rules or conclusions. Includes coming up with a logical explanation for why a series of seemingly unrelated events occur together.

Skills: Active Listening—Listening to what other people are saying; asking questions as appropriate. Problem Identification—Identifying the nature of problems. Social Perceptiveness—Being aware of other people's reactions and understanding why people react the way they do. Reading Comprehension—Understanding written information in work-related documents. Identification of Key Causes—Identifying the things that must be changed to achieve a goal.

Generalized Work Activities: Making Decisions and Solving Problems—Combining, evaluating, and analyzing information and data to make decisions and solve problems. Involves making decisions about the relative importance of information and choosing the best solution. Getting Information Needed to Do the Job—Observing, receiving, and otherwise obtaining information from all relevant sources. Identifying Objects, Actions, and Events—Identifying information received by making estimates or categorizations, recognizing differences or similarities, or sensing changes in circumstances or events. Analyzing Data or Information—Identifying underlying principles, reasons, or facts by breaking down information or data into separate parts. Communicating with Persons Outside Organization—Communicating with persons outside the organization. Representing the organization to customers, the public, government, and other external sources. Exchanging information face-to-face, in writing, or via telephone/electronic transfer. Updating and Using Job-Relevant Knowledge—Keeping up-to-date technically and knowing the functions of one's own job and related jobs.

Counseling Psychologists

Assess and evaluate individuals' problems through the use of case history, interview, and observation and provide individual or group counseling services to assist individuals in achieving more effective personal, social, educational, and vocational development and adjustment. Analyzes data, such as interview notes, test results, and reference manuals and texts to identify symptoms and diagnose the nature of client's problems. Conducts research to develop or improve diagnostic or therapeutic counseling techniques. Evaluates results of counseling methods to determine the reliability and validity of treatments. Consults with other professionals to discuss therapy or treatment, counseling resources or techniques, and to share occupational information. Develops therapeutic and treatment plans based on individual interests, abilities, or needs of clients. Advises clients on the potential benefits of counseling or makes referrals to specialists or other institutions for non-counseling problems. Counsels clients to assist them in understanding personal or interactive problems, defining goals, and developing realistic action plans. Selects, administers, or interprets psychological tests to assess intelligence, aptitude, ability, or interests. Collects information about individuals or clients, using interviews, case histories, observational techniques, and other assessment methods.

Personality Type: Social. Social occupations frequently involve working with, communicating with, and teaching people. These occupations often involve helping or providing service to others.

Abilities: Oral Comprehension—The ability to listen to and understand information and ideas presented verbally. Problem Sensitivity—The ability to tell when something is wrong or is likely to go wrong. Does not involve solving the problem, only recognizing there is a problem. Inductive Reasoning—The ability to combine separate pieces of information, or specific answers to problems, to form general rules or conclusions. Includes coming up with a logical explanation for why a series of seemingly unrelated events occur together. Oral Expression—The ability to communicate information and ideas verbally so others will understand. Written Comprehension—The ability to read and understand information and ideas presented in writing. Written Expression—The ability to communicate information and ideas in writing so others will understand.

Skills: Active Listening—Listening to what other people are saying; asking questions as appropriate. Social Perceptiveness—Being aware of other people's reactions and understanding why people react the way they do. Reading Comprehension—Understanding written information in work-related documents. Critical Thinking—Using logic and analysis to identify the strengths and weaknesses of different approaches. Active Learning—Working with new material or information to grasp its implications.

Generalized Work Activities: Getting Information Needed to Do the Job—Observing, receiving, and otherwise obtaining information from all relevant sources. Assisting and Caring for Others—Providing assistance or personal care to others. Making Decisions and Solving Problems—Combining, evaluating, and analyzing information and data to make decisions and solve problems. Involves making decisions about the relative importance of information and choosing the best solution. Establishing and Maintaining Relationships—Developing constructive and cooperative working relationships with others. Analyzing Data or Information—Identifying underlying principles, reasons, or facts by breaking down information or data into separate parts.

Educational Psychologists

Investigate processes of learning and teaching and develop psychological principles and techniques applicable to educational problems. Advises teachers and other school personnel on methods to enhance school and classroom atmosphere to maximize student learning and motivation. Refers individuals to community agencies to obtain medical, vocational, or social services for child or family. Administers standardized tests to evaluate intelligence, achievement, and personality and to diagnose disabilities and difficulties among students. Collaborates with education specialists in developing curriculum content and methods of organizing and conducting classroom work. Recommends placement of students in classes and treatment programs based on individual needs. Counsels pupils individually and in groups, to assist pupils to achieve personal, social, and emotional adjustment. Advises school board, superintendent, administrative committees, and parent-teacher groups regarding provision of psychological services within educational system or school. Conducts research to aid introduction of programs in schools to meet current psychological, educational, and sociological needs of children. Evaluates needs, limitations, and potentials of child, through observation, review of school records, and consultation with parents and school personnel. Interprets and explains test results, in terms of norms, reliability, and validity, to teachers, counselors, students, and other entitled parties. Plans remedial classes and testing programs designed to meet needs of special students. Formulates achievement, diagnostic, and predictive tests to aid teachers in planning methods and content of instruction. Investigates traits, attitudes, and feelings of teachers to predict conditions that affect teacher's mental health and success with students. Analyzes characteristics and adjustment needs of students having various mental abilities and recommends educational program to promote maximum adjustment.

Personality Type: Investigative. Investigative occupations frequently involve working with ideas and require an extensive amount of thinking. These occupations can involve searching for facts and figuring out problems mentally.

Abilities: Oral Expression—The ability to communicate information and ideas verbally so others will understand. Written Comprehension—The ability to read and understand information and ideas presented in writing. Inductive Reasoning—The ability to combine separate pieces of information, or specific answers to problems, to form general rules or conclusions. Includes coming up with a logical explanation for why a series of seemingly unrelated events occur together. Problem Sensitivity—The ability to tell when something is wrong or is likely to go wrong. Does not involve solving the problem, only recognizing there is a problem. Written Expression—The ability to communicate information and ideas in writing so others will understand.

Skills: Reading Comprehension—Understanding written information in work-related documents. Writing—Communicating effectively with others in writing as indicated by the needs of the audience. Active Listening—Listening to what other people are saying; asking questions as appropriate. Information Gathering—Knowing how to find information and identifying essential information. Social Perceptiveness—Being aware of other people's reactions and understanding why people react the way they do. Systems Evaluation—Looking at many indicators of system performance, taking into account their accuracy. Mathematics—Using mathematics to solve problems.

Generalized Work Activities: Judging Qualities—Making judgments about or assessing the value, importance, or quality of things, services, or other people's work. Getting Information Needed to Do the Job—Observing, receiving, and otherwise obtaining information from all relevant sources. Making Decisions and Solving Problems—Combining, evaluating, and analyzing information and data to make decisions and solve problems. Involves making decisions about the relative importance of information and choosing the best solution. Implementing Ideas and Programs—Conducting or carrying out work procedures and activities in accord with one's own ideas or information provided through directions/instructions for purposes of installing, modifying, preparing, delivering, constructing, integrating, finishing, or completing programs, systems, structures, or products. Communicating with Other Workers—Providing information to supervisors, fellow workers, and subordinates. Exchanging information face-to-face, in writing, or via telephone/electronic transfer. Analyzing Data or Information—Identifying underlying principles, reasons, or facts by breaking down information or data into separate parts.

Industrial-Organizational Psychologists

Apply principles of psychology to personnel, administration, management, sales, and marketing problems. Activities include policy planning, employee screening, training and development, and organizational development and analysis. **Work with management to reorganize the work setting to improve worker productivity.** Conducts research studies of physical work environments, organizational structure, communication systems, group interaction, morale, and motivation to assess organizational functioning. Analyzes job requirements to establish criteria for classification, selection, training, and other related personnel functions. Plans, develops, and organizes training programs, applying principles of learning and individual differences. Analyzes data, using statistical methods and applications, to evaluate and measure the effectiveness of program implementation or training. Studies consumer reaction to new products and package designs, using surveys and tests, and measures the effectiveness of advertising media. Advises management in strategic changes to personnel, managerial, and marketing policies and practices to improve organizational effectiveness and efficiency. Develops interview techniques, rating scales, and psychological tests to assess skills, abilities, and interests as aids in selection, placement and promotion. Observes and interviews workers to identify the physical, mental, and educational requirements of job.

Personality Type: Investigative. Investigative occupations frequently involve working with ideas and require an extensive amount of thinking. These occupations can involve searching for facts and figuring out problems mentally.

Abilities: Oral Comprehension—The ability to listen to and understand information and ideas presented verbally. Written Comprehension—The ability to read and understand information and ideas presented in writing. Oral Expression—The ability to communicate information and ideas verbally so others will understand. Written Expression—The ability to communicate information and ideas in writing so others will understand. Originality—The ability to come up with unusual or clever ideas about a given topic or situation, or to develop creative ways to solve a problem. Mathematical Reasoning—The ability to understand and organize a problem and then select a mathematical method or formula to solve the problem.

Skills: Information Gathering—Knowing how to find information and identifying essential information. Active Learning—Working with new material or information to grasp its implications. Identification of Key Causes—Identifying the things that must be changed to achieve a goal. Problem Identification—Identifying the nature of problems. Critical Thinking—Using logic and analysis to identify the strengths and weaknesses of different approaches. Speaking—Talking to others to effectively convey information.

Generalized Work Activities: Providing Consultation and Advice to Others—Providing consultation and expert advice to management or other groups on technical, systems-related, or process-related topics. Getting Information Needed to Do the Job—Observing, receiving, and otherwise obtaining information from all relevant sources. Analyzing Data or Information—Identifying underlying principles, reasons, or facts by breaking down information or data into separate parts. Processing Information—Compiling, coding, categorizing, calculating, tabulating, auditing, verifying, or processing information or data. Communicating with Other Workers—Providing information to supervisors, fellow workers, and subordinates. Exchanging information face-to-face, in writing, or via telephone/electronic transfer. Making Decisions and Solving Problems—Combining, evaluating, and analyzing information and data to make decisions and solve problems. Involves making decisions about the relative importance of information and choosing the best solution.

Public Relations Specialists

▲ Growth: 25%
▲ Annual Job Openings: 25,334
▲ Yearly Earnings: $34,550
▲ Education Required: Bachelor's degree
▲ Self-Employed: 5.6%
▲ Part-Time: 25.3%

P

Public Relations Specialists

Engage in promoting or creating goodwill for individuals, groups, or organizations by writing or selecting favorable publicity material and releasing it through various communications media. Prepare and arrange displays and make speeches. Consults with advertising agencies or staff to arrange promotional campaigns in all types of media for products, organizations, or individuals. Conducts market and public opinion research to introduce or test specific products or measure public opinion. Counsels clients in effective ways of communicating with public. Purchases advertising space and time as required to promote client's product or agenda. Confers with production and support personnel to coordinate production of advertisements and promotions. Studies needs, objectives, and policies of organization or individual seeking to influence public opinion or promote specific products. Prepares or edits organizational publications, such as newsletters to employees or public or stockholders' reports to favorably present client's viewpoint. Promotes sales and/or creates goodwill for client's products, services, or persona by coordinating exhibits, lectures, contests, or public appearances. Prepares and distributes fact sheets, news releases, photographs, scripts, motion pictures, or tape recordings to media representatives and others. Plans and directs development and communication of informational programs designed to keep public informed of client's products, accomplishments, or agenda. Represents client during community projects and at public, social, and business gatherings. Arranges for and conducts public-contact programs designed to meet client's objectives.

Personality Type: Enterprising. Enterprising occupations frequently involve starting up and carrying out projects. These occupations can involve leading people and making many decisions. They sometimes require risk taking and often deal with business.

Abilities: Oral Expression—The ability to communicate information and ideas verbally so others will understand. Written Expression—The ability to communicate information and ideas in writing so others will understand. Oral Comprehension—The ability to listen to and understand information and ideas presented verbally. Speech Clarity—The ability to speak clearly to that what is said is understandable to a listener. Fluency of Ideas—The ability to come up with a number of ideas about a given topic. Emphasis is on the number of ideas produced and not the quality, correctness, or creativity of the ideas.

Skills: Writing—Communicating effectively with others in writing as indicated by the needs of the audience. Speaking—Talking to others to effectively convey information. Identification of Key Causes—Identifying the things that must be changed to achieve a goal. Persuasion—Persuading others to approach things differently. Information Gathering—Knowing how to find information and identifying essential information.

Generalized Work Activities: Communicating with Persons Outside Organization—Communicating with persons outside the organization. Representing the organization to customers, the public, government, and other external sources. Exchanging information face-to-face, in writing, or via telephone/electronic transfer.

Getting Information Needed to Do the Job—Observing, receiving, and otherwise obtaining information from all relevant sources. Judging Qualities—Making judgments about or assessing the value, importance, or quality of things, services, or other people's work. Making Decisions and Solving Problems—Combining, evaluating, and analyzing information and data to make decisions and solve problems. Involves making decisions about the relative importance of information and choosing the best solution. Organizing, Planning, and Prioritizing—Developing plans to accomplish work. Prioritizing and organizing one's own work. Establishing and Maintaining Relationships—Developing constructive and cooperative working relationships with others.

Purchasing Agents

- ▲ Growth: 11%
- ▲ Annual Job Openings: 42,342
- ▲ Yearly Earnings: $38,040
- ▲ Education Required: Bachelor's degree
- ▲ Self-Employed: 0%
- ▲ Part-Time: 2.3%

Purchasing Agents, Except Wholesale, Retail, and Farm Products

Purchase farm products either for further processing or resale. Arbitrates claims and resolves complaints generated during performance of contract. Prepares purchase orders or bid proposals and reviews requisitions for goods and services. Evaluates and monitors contract performance to determine need for changes and to ensure compliance with contractual obligations. Confers with personnel, users, and vendors to discuss defective or unacceptable goods or services and determines corrective action. Directs and coordinates workers' activities involving bid proposals and procurement of goods and services. Analyzes price proposals, financial reports, and other data and information to determine reasonable prices. Locates and arranges for purchase of goods and services necessary for efficient operation of organization. Formulates policies and procedures for bid proposals and procurement of goods and services. Negotiates or renegotiates, and administers contracts with suppliers, vendors, and other representatives. Maintains and reviews computerized or manual records of items purchased, costs, delivery, product performance, and inventories.

Personality Type: Enterprising. Enterprising occupations frequently involve starting up and carrying out projects. These occupations can involve leading people and making many decisions. They sometimes require risk taking and often deal with business.

Abilities: Oral Expression—The ability to communicate information and ideas verbally so others will understand. Oral Comprehension—The ability to listen to and understand information and ideas presented verbally. Written Comprehension—The ability to read and understand information and ideas presented in writing. Mathematical Reasoning—The ability to understand and organize a problem and then select a mathematical method or formula to solve the problem. Written Expression—The ability to communicate information and ideas in writing so others will understand.

Skills: Negotiation—Bringing others together and trying to reconcile differences. Critical Thinking—Using logic and analysis to identify the strengths and weaknesses of different approaches. Active Listening—Listening to what other people are saying; asking questions as appropriate. Management of Financial

Resources—Determining how money will be spent to get the work done, and accounting for these expenditures. Judgment and Decision Making—Weighing the relative costs and benefits of a potential action. Persuasion—Persuading others to approach things differently.

Generalized Work Activities: Judging Qualities—Making judgments about or assessing the value, importance, or quality of things, services, or other people's work. Making Decisions and Solving Problems—Combining, evaluating, and analyzing information and data to make decisions and solve problems. Involves making decisions about the relative importance of information and choosing the best solution. Resolving Conflict, Negotiating with Others—Handling complaints, arbitrating disputes, resolving grievances, or otherwise negotiating with others. Analyzing Data or Information—Identifying underlying principles, reasons, or facts by breaking down information or data into separate parts.

Purchasing Agents, Farm Products

Purchase machinery, equipment, tools, parts, supplies, or services necessary for the operation of an establishment. Purchase raw or semifinished materials for manufacturing. Negotiates contracts with farmers for production or purchase of agricultural products, such as milk, grains, and Christmas trees. Inspects and tests crops or other farm products to determine quality and to detect evidence of disease or insect damage. Maintains records of business transactions. Estimates production possibilities by surveying property and studying factors such as history of crop rotation, soil fertility, and irrigation facilities. Writes articles for publication. Coordinates and directs activities or workers engaged in cutting, transporting, storing, or milling products and in maintaining records. Advises farm groups and growers on land preparation and livestock care to maximize quantity and quality of production. Plans and arranges for transportation for crops, milk, or other products to dairy or processing facility. Arranges sales, loans, or financing for supplies, such as equipment, seed, feed, fertilizer, and chemicals. Reviews orders and determines product types and quantities required to meet demand.

Personality Type: Enterprising. Enterprising occupations frequently involve starting up and carrying out projects. These occupations can involve leading people and making many decisions. They sometimes require risk taking and often deal with business.

Abilities: Oral Expression—The ability to communicate information and ideas verbally so others will understand. Oral Comprehension—The ability to listen to and understand information and ideas presented verbally. Written Expression—The ability to communicate information and ideas in writing so others will understand. Number Facility—The ability to add, subtract, multiply, or divide quickly and correctly. Written Comprehension—The ability to read and understand information and ideas presented in writing.

Skills: Negotiation—Bringing others together and trying to reconcile differences. Judgment and Decision Making—Weighing the relative costs and benefits of a potential action. Reading Comprehension—Understanding written information in work-related documents. Speaking—Talking to others to effectively convey information. Writing—Communicating effectively with others in writing as indicated by the needs of the audience.

Generalized Work Activities: Identifying Objects, Actions, and Events—Identifying information received by making estimates or categorizations, recognizing differences or similarities, or sensing changes in circumstances or events. Monitoring and Controlling Resources—Monitoring and controlling resources and overseeing the spending of money. Judging Qualities—Making judgments about or assessing the value, importance, or quality of things, services, or other people's work. Inspecting Equipment, Structures, Materials—Inspecting or diagnosing equipment, structures, or materials to identify the causes of errors or other problems or defects. Getting Information Needed to Do the Job—Observing, receiving, and otherwise obtaining information from all relevant sources. Establishing and Maintaining Relationships—Developing constructive and cooperative working relationships with others.

Wholesale and Retail Buyers, Except Farm Products

Buy merchandise or commodities, other than farm products, for resale to consumers at the wholesale or retail level, including both durable and nondurable goods. Analyze past buying trends, sales records, price, and quality of merchandise to determine value and yield. Select, order, and authorize payment for merchandise according to contractual agreements. Conduct meetings with sales personnel and introduce new products. Examines, selects, orders, and purchases merchandise from suppliers or other merchants. Inspects, grades, or approves merchandise or products to determine value or yield. Authorizes payment of invoices or return of merchandise. Conducts staff meetings with sales personnel to introduce new merchandise. Approves advertising materials. Provides clerks with information, such as price, mark-ups or mark-downs, manufacturer number, season code, and style number to print on price tags. Trains purchasing or sales personnel. Arranges for transportation of purchases. Sets or recommends mark-up rates, mark-down rates, and selling prices for merchandise. Analyzes sales records and trends to determine current or expected demand and minimum inventory required. Confers with sales and purchasing personnel to obtain information about customer needs and preferences. Consults with store or merchandise managers about budget and goods to be purchased.

Personality Type: Enterprising. Enterprising occupations frequently involve starting up and carrying out projects. These occupations can involve leading people and making many decisions. They sometimes require risk taking and often deal with business.

Abilities: Oral Expression—The ability to communicate information and ideas verbally so others will understand. Oral Comprehension—The ability to listen to and understand information and ideas presented verbally. Near Vision—The ability to see details of objects at a close range. Written Comprehension—The ability to read and understand information and ideas presented in writing. Speech Clarity—The ability to speak clearly to that what is said is understandable to a listener. Deductive Reasoning—The ability to apply general rules to specific problems to come up with logical answers. Involves deciding if an answer makes sense.

Skills: Product Inspection—Inspecting and evaluating the quality of products. Critical Thinking—Using logic and analysis to identify the strengths and weaknesses of different approaches. Judgment and Decision Making—Weighing the relative costs and benefits of a potential action. Information Gathering—Knowing how to find information and identifying essential information. Social Perceptiveness—Being aware of other people's reactions and understanding why people react the way they do. Active Learning—Working with new material or information to grasp its implications. Speaking—Talking to others to effectively convey information.

Generalized Work Activities: Communicating with Other Workers—Providing information to supervisors, fellow workers, and subordinates. Exchanging information face-to-face, in writing, or via telephone/electronic transfer. Getting Information Needed to Do the Job—Observing, receiving, and otherwise obtaining information from all relevant sources. Identifying Objects, Actions, and Events—Identifying information received by making estimates or categorizations, recognizing differences or similarities, or sensing changes in circumstances or events. Monitoring and Controlling Resources—Monitoring and controlling resources and overseeing the spending of money. Analyzing Data or Information—Identifying underlying principles, reasons, or facts by breaking down information or data into separate parts.

Purchasing Managers

Purchasing Managers

Plan, direct, or coordinate the activities of buyers, purchasing officers, and related workers involved in purchasing materials, products, and services. Represents company in formulating policies and negotiating contracts with suppliers. Prepares report regarding market conditions and merchandise costs. Prepares, reviews, and processes requisitions and purchase orders for supplies and equipment. Determines merchandise costs and formulates and coordinates merchandising policies and activities to ensure profit. Conducts inventory and directs buyers in purchase of products, materials, and supplies. Develops and implements office, operations, and systems instructions, policies, and procedures. Directs and coordinates activities of personnel engaged in buying, selling, and distributing materials, equipment, machinery, and supplies. Analyzes market and delivery systems to determine present and future material availability.

Personality Type: Enterprising. Enterprising occupations frequently involve starting up and carrying out projects. These occupations can involve leading people and making many decisions. They sometimes require risk taking and often deal with business.

Abilities: Speech Clarity—The ability to speak clearly to that what is said is understandable to a listener. Mathematical Reasoning—The ability to understand and organize a problem and then select a mathematical method or formula to solve the problem. Oral Expression—The ability to communicate information and ideas verbally so others will understand.

Skills: Information Gathering—Knowing how to find information and identifying essential information. Speaking—Talking to others to effectively convey information. Management of Personnel Resources—Motivating, developing, and directing people as they work, identifying the best people for the job. Critical Thinking—Using logic and analysis to identify the strengths and weaknesses of different approaches. Judgment and Decision Making—Weighing the relative costs and benefits of a potential action.

Generalized Work Activities: Monitoring and Controlling Resources—Monitoring and controlling resources and overseeing the spending of money. Getting Information Needed to Do the Job—Observing, receiving, and otherwise obtaining information from all relevant sources. Making Decisions and Solving Problems—Combining, evaluating, and analyzing information and data to make decisions and solve problems. Involves making decisions about the relative importance of information and choosing the best solution. Communicating with Persons Outside Organization—Communicating with persons outside the organization. Representing the organization to customers, the public, government, and other external sources. Exchanging information face-to-face, in writing, or via telephone/electronic transfer. Communicating with Other Workers—Providing information to supervisors, fellow workers, and subordinates. Exchanging information face-to-face, in writing, or via telephone/electronic transfer. Analyzing Data or Information—Identifying underlying principles, reasons, or facts by breaking down information or data into separate parts.

Radiation Therapists

▲ Growth: 17%

▲ Annual Job Openings: 829

▲ Yearly Earnings: $39,640

▲ Education Required: Bachelor's degree

▲ Self-Employed: Not available

▲ Part-Time: Not available

Radiation Therapists

Provide radiation therapy to patients as prescribed by a radiologist according to established practices and standards. Review prescription and diagnosis. Act as liaison with physician and supportive care personnel. Prepare equipment such as immobilization, treatment, and protection devices. Maintain records, reports, and files. Assist in dosimetry procedures and tumor localization. Enters data into computer and sets controls to operate and adjust equipment and regulate dosage. Observes and reassures patient during treatment and reports unusual reactions to physician. Prepares equipment such as immobilization, treatment, and protection devices; positions patient according to prescription. Follows principles of radiation protection for patient, self, and others. Maintains records, reports, and files as required. Reviews prescription, diagnosis, patient chart, and identification. Photographs treated area of patient and processes film. Acts as liaison with physician and supportive care personnel.

Personality Type: Social. Social occupations frequently involve working with, communicating with, and teaching people. These occupations often involve helping or providing service to others.

Abilities: Written Comprehension—The ability to read and understand information and ideas presented in writing. Problem Sensitivity—The ability to tell when something is wrong or is likely to go wrong. Does not involve solving the problem, only recognizing there is a problem. Wrist-Finger Speed—The ability to make fast, simple, repeated movements of the fingers, hands, and wrists. Deductive Reasoning—The ability to apply general rules to specific problems to come up with logical answers. Involves deciding if an answer makes sense.

Oral Comprehension—The ability to listen to and understand information and ideas presented verbally.

Skills: Reading Comprehension—Understanding written information in work-related documents. Operation Monitoring—Watching gauges, dials, or other indicators to make sure a machine is working properly. Operation and Control—Controlling operations of equipment or systems. Science—Using scientific methods to solve problems. Writing—Communicating effectively with others in writing as indicated by the needs of the audience. Coordination—Adjusting actions in relation to others' actions.

Generalized Work Activities: Monitoring Processes, Materials, Surroundings—Monitoring and reviewing information from materials, events, or the environment, often to detect problems or to find out when things are finished. Assisting and Caring for Others—Providing assistance or personal care to others. Interacting with Computers—Controlling computer functions by using programs, setting up functions, writing software, or otherwise communicating with computer systems. Getting Information Needed to Do the Job—Observing, receiving, and otherwise obtaining information from all relevant sources. Communicating with Other Workers—Providing information to supervisors, fellow workers, and subordinates. This information can be exchanged face-to-face, in writing, or via telephone/electronic transfer. Documenting/ Recording Information—Entering, transcribing, recording, storing, or maintaining information in either written form or by electronic/magnetic recording. Controlling Machines and Processes—Using either control mechanisms or direct physical activity to operate machines or processes. Does not involve working with computers or vehicles.

Radiologic Technologists and Technicians

- ▲ Growth: 20%
- ▲ Annual Job Openings: 11,306
- ▲ Yearly Earnings: $32,880
- ▲ Education Required: Associate degree
- ▲ Self-Employed: 0%
- ▲ Part-Time: 17.5%

Radiologic Technicians

Maintain and use equipment and supplies necessary to demonstrate portions the human body on X-ray film or fluoroscopic screen for diagnostic purposes. Uses beam-restrictive devices and patient-shielding skills to minimize radiation exposure to patient and staff. Moves X-ray equipment into position and adjusts controls to set exposure factors such as time and distance. Operates mobile X-ray equipment in operating room, emergency room, or at patient's bedside. Positions patient on examining table and adjusts equipment to obtain optimum view of specific body area requested by physician. Explains procedures to patient to reduce anxieties and obtain patient cooperation.

Personality Type: Realistic. Realistic occupations frequently involve work activities that include practical, hands-on problems and solutions. They often deal with plants, animals, and real-world materials like wood, tools, and machinery. Many of the occupations require working outside and do not involve a lot of paperwork or working closely with others.

Abilities: Oral Expression—The ability to communicate information and ideas verbally so others will understand. Written Comprehension—The ability to read and understand information and ideas presented in writing. Oral Comprehension—The ability to listen to and understand information and ideas presented verbally. Information Ordering—The ability to correctly follow a given rule or set of rules in order to arrange things or actions in a certain order. The things or actions can include numbers, letters, words, pictures, procedures, sentences, and mathematical or logical operations. Speech Clarity—The ability to speak clearly so that what is said is understandable to a listener.

Skills: Operation and Control—Controlling operations of equipment or systems. Operation Monitoring—Watching gauges, dials, or other indicators to make sure a machine is working properly. Speaking—Talking to others to effectively convey information. Reading Comprehension—Understanding written information in work-related documents. Social Perceptiveness—Being aware of other people's reactions and understanding why people react the way they do. Active Listening—Listening to what other people are saying; asking questions as appropriate.

Generalized Work Activities: Controlling Machines and Processes—Using either control mechanisms or direct physical activity to operate machines or processes. Does not involve working with computers or vehicles. Handling and Moving Objects—Using one's hands and arms in handling, installing, forming, positioning, and moving materials, or in manipulating things. Includes the use of keyboards. Getting Information Needed to Do the Job—Observing, receiving, and otherwise obtaining information from all relevant sources. Assisting and Caring for Others—Providing assistance or personal care to others. Monitoring Processes, Materials, Surroundings—Monitoring and reviewing information from materials, events, or the environment, often to detect problems or to find out when things are finished. Communicating with Other Workers—Providing information to supervisors, fellow workers, and subordinates. This information can be exchanged face-to-face, in writing, or via telephone/electronic transfer. Interpreting Meaning of Information to Others—Translating or explaining what information means and how it can be understood or used to support responses or feedback to others.

Radiologic Technologists

Take X rays and CAT scans; administer nonradioactive materials into patient's blood stream for diagnostic purposes. Includes technologists who specialize in other modalities such as computed tomography, ultrasound, and magnetic resonance. Explains procedures and observes patients to ensure safety and comfort during scan. Monitors use of radiation safety measures to comply with government regulations and to ensure safety of patients and staff. Reviews and evaluates developed X rays, video tape, or computer-generated information for technical quality. Develops departmental operating budget and coordinates purchase of supplies and equipment. Demonstrates new equipment, procedures, and techniques; provides technical assistance to staff. Assigns duties to radiologic staff to maintain patient flows and achieve production goals. Monitors video display of area being scanned and adjusts density or contrast to improve picture quality. Positions imaging equipment and adjusts controls to set exposure time and distance, according to specification of examination. Administers oral or injected contrast media to patients. Operates fluoroscope to aid physician to view and guide wire or catheter through blood vessels to area of interest. Operates or oversees operation of radiologic and magnetic imaging equipment to produce photographs of the body for diagnostic purposes. Keys commands and data into computer to document and specify scan sequences, adjust transmitters and receivers, or photograph certain images. Positions and immobilizes patient on examining table.

Personality Type: Realistic. Realistic occupations frequently involve work activities that include practical, hands-on problems and solutions. They often deal with plants, animals, and real-world materials like wood, tools, and machinery. Many of the occupations require working outside and do not involve a lot of paperwork or working closely with others.

Abilities: Oral Expression—The ability to communicate information and ideas verbally so others will understand. Control Precision—The ability to quickly and repeatedly make precise adjustments in moving the controls of a machine or vehicle to exact positions. Speech Clarity—The ability to speak clearly so that what is said is understandable to a listener. Written Comprehension—The ability to read and understand information and ideas presented in writing. Oral Comprehension—The ability to listen to and understand information and ideas presented verbally. Near Vision—The ability to see details of objects at a close range.

Skills: Operation and Control—Controlling operations of equipment or systems. Operation Monitoring—Watching gauges, dials, or other indicators to make sure a machine is working properly. Reading Comprehension—Understanding written information in work-related documents. Product Inspection—Inspecting and evaluating the quality of products. Monitoring—Assessing how well one is doing when learning or doing something. Information Gathering—Knowing how to find information and identifying essential information.

Generalized Work Activities: Controlling Machines and Processes—Using either control mechanisms or direct physical activity to operate machines or processes. Does not involve working with computers or vehicles. Handling and Moving Objects—Using one's hands and arms in handling, installing, forming, positioning, and moving materials, or in manipulating things. Includes the use of keyboards. Monitoring Processes, Materials, Surroundings—Monitoring and reviewing information from materials, events, or the environment, often to detect problems or to find out when things are finished. Documenting/Recording Information—Entering, transcribing, recording, storing, or maintaining information in either written form or by electronic/magnetic recording. Assisting and Caring for Others—Providing assistance or personal care to others. Performing General Physical Activities—Performing physical activities that require moving one's whole body, such as in climbing, lifting, balancing, walking, and stooping. Performing activities that often also require considerable use of the arms and legs, such as in the physical handling of materials.

Real Estate Appraisers

▲ Growth: 11%
▲ Annual Job Openings: 6,383
▲ Yearly Earnings: $40,290
▲ Education Required: Work experience in a related occupation
▲ Self-Employed: 21.1%
▲ Part-Time: 16.6%

Appraisers, Real Estate

Appraise real property to determine its value for purchase, sales, investment, mortgage, or loan purposes. Photographs interiors and exteriors of property to assist in estimating property value, to substantiate finding, and to complete appraisal report. Inspects property for construction, condition, and functional design and takes property measurements. Interviews persons familiar with property and immediate surroundings, such as contractors, home owners, and other realtors to obtain pertinent information. Searches public records for transactions such as sales, leases, and assessments. Prepares written report, utilizing data collected; submits report to corroborate value established. Considers location and trends or impending changes that could influence future value of property. Considers such factors as depreciation, value comparison of similar property, and income potential, when computing final estimation of property value.

Personality Type: Enterprising. Enterprising occupations frequently involve starting up and carrying out projects. These occupations can involve leading people and making many decisions. They sometimes require risk taking and often deal with business.

Abilities: Oral Comprehension—The ability to listen to and understand information and ideas presented verbally. Oral Expression—The ability to communicate information and ideas verbally so others will understand. Written Expression—The ability to communicate information and ideas in writing so others will understand. Deductive Reasoning—The ability to apply general rules to specific problems to come up with logical answers. Involves deciding if an answer makes sense. Written Comprehension—The ability to read and understand information and ideas presented in writing.

Skills: Information Gathering—Knowing how to find information and identifying essential information. Mathematics—Using mathematics to solve problems. Active Listening—Listening to what other people are saying; asking questions as appropriate. Speaking—Talking to others to effectively convey information. Problem Identification—Identifying the nature of problems. Judgment and Decision Making—Weighing the relative costs and benefits of a potential action. Reading Comprehension—Understanding written information in work-related documents.

Generalized Work Activities: Judging Qualities—Making judgments about or assessing the value, importance, or quality of things, services, or other people's work. Getting Information Needed to Do the Job—Observing, receiving, and otherwise obtaining information from all relevant sources. Identifying Objects, Actions, and Events—Identifying information received by making estimates or categorizations, recognizing differences or similarities, or sensing changes in circumstances or events. Updating and Using Job-Relevant Knowledge—Keeping up-to-date technically and knowing the functions of one's own job and related jobs. Documenting/Recording Information—Entering, transcribing, recording, storing, or maintaining information in either written form or by electronic/magnetic recording. Making Decisions and Solving Problems—Combining, evaluating, and analyzing information and data to make decisions and solve problems. Involves making decisions about the relative importance of information and choosing the best solution.

Receptionists and Information Clerks

- ▲ Growth: 24%
- ▲ Annual Job Openings: 386,806
- ▲ Yearly Earnings: $18,620
- ▲ Education Required: Short-term O-J-T
- ▲ Self-Employed: 3.1%
- ▲ Part-Time: 35.1%

Receptionists and Information Clerks

Answer inquiries and obtain information for general public, customers, visitors, and other interested parties. Provide information regarding activities conducted at establishment and regarding location of departments, offices, and employees within organization. Enrolls individuals to participate in programs; prepares lists; notifies individuals of acceptance in programs; arranges and schedules space and equipment for participants. Types memos, correspondence, travel vouchers, or other documents. Calculates and quotes rates for tours, stocks, insurance policies, and other products and services. Collects and distributes messages for employees of organization. Records, compiles, enters, and retrieves information, by hand or using computer. Provides information to public concerning available land leases, land classification, or mineral resources. Provides information to public regarding tours, classes, workshops, and other programs. Greets persons entering establishment, determines nature and purpose of visit, directs visitors to specific destinations, answers questions, and provides information. Files and maintains records. Answers telephone to schedule future appointments, provide information, or forward call. Hears and resolves complaints from customers and public. Conducts tours or delivers talks describing features of public facility such as historic site or national park. Receives payment and records receipts for services. Monitors facility to ensure compliance with regulations. Performs duties such as taking care of plants and straightening magazines to maintain lobby or reception area. Operates telephone switchboard to receive incoming calls. Transmits information or documents to customer, using computer, mail, or facsimile. Registers visitors at public facility such as a national park or military base. Collects fees, explains regulations, and assigns sites. Analyzes data to determine answer to customer or public inquiry.

Personality Type: Conventional. Conventional occupations frequently involve following set procedures and routines. These occupations can include working with data and details more than with ideas. Usually there is a clear line of authority to follow.

Abilities: Oral Expression—The ability to communicate information and ideas verbally so others will understand. Speech Clarity—The ability to speak clearly so that what is said is understandable to a listener. Oral Comprehension—The ability to listen to and understand information and ideas presented verbally. Written Comprehension—The ability to read and understand information and ideas presented in writing. Speech Recognition—The ability to identify and understand the speech of another person.

Skills: Speaking—Talking to others to effectively convey information. Active Listening—Listening to what other people are saying; asking questions as appropriate. Service Orientation—Actively looking for ways to help people. Coordination—Adjusting actions in relation to others' actions. Social Perceptiveness—Being aware of other people's reactions and understanding why people react the way they do.

Generalized Work Activities: Performing for/Working with Public—Performing for people or dealing directly with the public, including serving persons in restaurants and stores and receiving clients or guests. Communicating with Persons Outside Organization— Communicating with persons outside the organization.

Representing the organization to customers, the public, government, and other external sources. Exchanging information face-to-face, in writing, or via telephone/electronic transfer. Establishing and Maintaining Relationships—Developing constructive and cooperative working relationships with others.

Documenting/Recording Information—Entering, transcribing, recording, storing, or maintaining information in either written form or by electronic/magnetic recording. Getting Information Needed to Do the Job—Observing, receiving, and otherwise obtaining information from all relevant sources.

Recreational Therapists

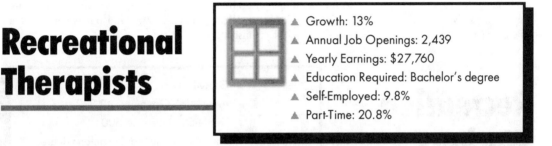

- ▲ Growth: 13%
- ▲ Annual Job Openings: 2,439
- ▲ Yearly Earnings: $27,760
- ▲ Education Required: Bachelor's degree
- ▲ Self-Employed: 9.8%
- ▲ Part-Time: 20.8%

Recreational Therapists

Plan, direct, or coordinate medically approved recreation programs for patients in hospitals, nursing homes, or other institutions. Programs may include sports, trips, dramatics, social activities, and arts and crafts. Assess patient's condition and recommend appropriate recreational activity. Evaluates patient's reactions to treatment experiences, to assess progress or regression and effectiveness of treatment plan. Modifies content of patient's treatment program based on observation and evaluation of progress. Conducts therapy sessions to improve patient's mental and physical well-being. Counsels and encourages patient to develop leisure activities. Confers with members of treatment team to determine patient's needs, capabilities, and interests, and to determine objectives of therapy. Instructs patient in activities and techniques, such as sports, dance, gardening, music, or art, designed to meet their specific physical or psychological needs. Observes and confers with patient to assess patient's needs, capabilities, and interests, and to devise a treatment plan. Develops treatment plan to meet needs of patient, based on needs assessment and objectives of therapy. Plans, organizes, and participates in treatment programs and activities to facilitate the physical, mental, or emotional rehabilitation or health of patient. Prepares and submits reports and charts to treatment team to reflect patient's reactions and evidence of progress or regression.

Personality Type: Social. Social occupations frequently involve working with, communicating with, and teaching people. These occupations often involve helping or providing service to others.

Abilities: Speech Clarity—The ability to speak clearly so that what is said is understandable to a listener. Oral Comprehension—The ability to listen to and understand information and ideas presented verbally. Oral Expression—The ability to communicate information and ideas verbally so others will understand. Written Expression—The ability to communicate information and ideas in writing so others will understand. Inductive Reasoning—The ability to combine separate pieces of information, or specific answers to problems, to form general rules or conclusions. Includes coming up with a logical explanation for why a series of seemingly unrelated events occur together.

Skills: Active Listening—Listening to what other people are saying; asking questions as appropriate. Speaking—Talking to others to effectively convey information. Learning Strategies—Using multiple approaches when learning or teaching new things.

Generalized Work Activities: Assisting and Caring for Others—Providing assistance or personal care to others. Getting Information Needed to Do the Job—Observing, receiving, and otherwise obtaining information from all relevant sources. Performing General Physical Activities—Performing physical activities that require moving one's whole body, such as in climbing, lifting, balancing, walking, and stooping. Performing activities that often also require considerable use of the arms and legs, such as in the physical handling of materials. Establishing and Maintaining Relationships—Developing constructive and cooperative working relationships with others. Teaching Others—Identifying educational needs, developing formal training programs or classes, and teaching or instructing others. Monitoring Processes, Materials, Surroundings—Monitoring and reviewing information from materials, events, or the environment, often to detect problems or to find out when things are finished.

Recreation Workers

- ▲ Growth: 19%
- ▲ Annual Job Openings: 43,829
- ▲ Yearly Earnings: $16,500
- ▲ Education Required: Bachelor's degree
- ▲ Self-Employed: 0%
- ▲ Part-Time: 14%

Recreation Workers

Conduct recreation activities with groups in public, private, or volunteer agencies or recreation facilities. Organize and promote activities such as arts and crafts, sports, games, music, dramatics, social recreation, camping, and hobbies, taking into account the needs and interests of individual members. Administers first aid according to prescribed procedures; notifies emergency medical personnel when necessary. Schedules facility activities and maintains record of programs. Enforces rules and regulations of facility; maintains discipline; ensures safety. Greets and introduces new arrivals to other guests; acquaints arrivals with facilities; encourages group participation. Tests and documents content of swimming pool water; schedules maintenance and use of facilities. Supervises and coordinates work activities of personnel; trains staff; assigns duties. Schedules maintenance and use of facilities. Evaluates staff performance and records reflective information on performance evaluation forms. Meets with staff to discuss rules, regulations, and work-related problems. Assists management to resolve complaints. Ascertains and interprets group interests, evaluates equipment and facilities, and adapts activities to meet participant needs. Meets and collaborates with agency personnel, community organizations, and other professional personnel to plan balanced recreational programs for participants. Explains principles, techniques, and safety procedures of facility activities to participants; demonstrates use of material and equipment. Arranges for activity requirements such as entertainment and setting up equipment and decorations. Conducts recreational activities and instructs participants in developing skills for participating in provided activities. Organizes, leads, and promotes interest in facility activities such as arts and crafts, sports, games, camping, and hobbies. Completes and maintains time and attendance forms and inventory lists.

Personality Type: Social. Social occupations frequently involve working with, communicating with, and teaching people. These occupations often involve helping or providing service to others.

Abilities: Oral Expression—The ability to communicate informa-tion and ideas verbally so others will understand. Speech Clarity—The ability to speak clearly so that what is said is understandable to a listener. Oral Comprehension—The ability to listen to and understand information and ideas presented verbally.

Fluency of Ideas—The ability to come up with a number of ideas about a given topic. Emphasis is on the number of ideas produced and not the quality, correctness, or creativity of the ideas. Written Expression—The ability to communicate information and ideas in writing so others will understand.

Skills: Coordination—Adjusting actions in relation to others' actions. Speaking—Talking to others to effectively convey information. Service Orientation—Actively looking for ways to help people. Social Perceptiveness—Being aware of other people's reactions and understanding why people react the way they do. Implementation Planning—Developing approaches for implementing an idea.

Generalized Work Activities: Coordinating Work and Activities of Others—Coordinating members of a work group to accomplish tasks. Establishing and

Maintaining Relationships—Developing constructive and cooperative working relationships with others. Communicating with Persons Outside Organization—Communicating with persons outside the organization. Representing the organization to customers, the public, government, and other external sources. Exchanging information face-to-face, in writing, or via telephone/electronic transfer. Organizing, Planning, and Prioritizing—Developing plans to accomplish work. Prioritizing and organizing one's own work. Thinking Creatively—Originating, inventing, designing, or creating new applications, ideas, relationships, systems, or products, including artistic contributions. Communicating with Other Workers—Providing information to supervisors, fellow workers, and subordinates. This information can be exchanged face-to-face, in writing, or via telephone/electronic transfer.

Registered Nurses

- ▲ Growth: 22%
- ▲ Annual Job Openings: 195,231
- ▲ Yearly Earnings: $40,690
- ▲ Education Required: Associate degree
- ▲ Self-Employed: 0.9%
- ▲ Part-Time: 26.3%

Registered Nurses

Assess patient health problems and needs; develop and implement nursing care plans; maintain medical records. Administer nursing care to ill, injured, convalescent, or disabled patients. Advise patients on health maintenance and disease prevention; provide case management. Licensing or registration required. Includes advance-practice nurses such as nurse practitioners, clinical nurse specialists, certified nurse midwives, and certified registered nurse anesthetists. Advanced practice nursing is practiced by RNs who have specialized formal, postbasic education and who function in highly autonomous and specialized roles. Refers students or patients to community agencies furnishing assistance; cooperates with agencies. Provides prenatal and postnatal care to obstetrical patients under supervision of obstetrician. Contracts independently to render nursing care, usually to one patient, in hospital or private home. Directs and coordinates infection-control program in hospital. Administers local, inhalation, intravenous, and other anesthetics. Maintains stock of supplies. Conducts specified laboratory tests. Prescribes or recommends drugs or other forms of treatment such as physical therapy, inhalation therapy, or related therapeutic procedures. Prepares patients for and assists with examinations. Discusses cases with physician or obstetrician. Administers stipulated emergency measures, and contacts obstetrician when deviations from standard are encountered during pregnancy or delivery. Advises and consults with specified personnel concerning necessary precautions to be taken to prevent possible contamination or infection. Instructs on topics such as health education, disease prevention, child birth, and home nursing; develops health-improvement programs. Delivers infants and performs postpartum examinations and treatment. Prepares rooms, sterile instruments, equipment, and supplies; hands items to surgeon. Records patient's medical information and vital signs. Observes patient's skin color, dilation of pupils, and computerized equipment, to monitor vital signs. Provides health care, first aid, and immunization in facilities such as schools, hospitals, and industry. Orders, interprets, and evaluates diagnostic tests to identify and assess patient's condition. Informs physician of patient's condition during anesthesia.

Personality Type: Social. Social occupations frequently involve working with, communicating with, and teaching people. These occupations often involve helping or providing service to others.

Abilities: Oral Expression—The ability to communicate information and ideas verbally so others will understand. Oral Comprehension—The ability to listen to and understand information and ideas presented verbally. Problem Sensitivity—The ability to tell when something is wrong or is likely to go wrong. Does not involve solving the problem, only recognizing there is a problem. Written Comprehension—The ability to read and understand information and ideas presented in writing. Written Expression—The ability to communicate information and ideas in writing so others will understand.

Skills: Service Orientation—Actively looking for ways to help people. Speaking—Talking to others to effectively convey information. Reading Comprehension—Understanding written information in work-related documents. Judgment and Decision Making—Weighing the relative costs and benefits of a potential action. Social Perceptiveness—Being aware of other people's reactions and understanding why people react the way they do.

Generalized Work Activities: Monitoring Processes, Materials, Surroundings—Monitoring and reviewing information from materials, events, or the environment, often to detect problems or to find out when things are finished. Documenting/Recording Information—Entering, transcribing, recording, storing, or maintaining information in either written form or by electronic/magnetic recording. Communicating with Other Workers—Providing information to supervisors, fellow workers, and subordinates. This information can be exchanged face-to-face, in writing, or via telephone/electronic transfer. Getting Information Needed to Do the Job—Observing, receiving, and otherwise obtaining information from all relevant sources. Updating and Using Job-Relevant Knowledge—Keeping up-to-date technically and knowing the functions of one's own job and related jobs. Assisting and Caring for Others—Providing assistance or personal care to others.

Residential Counselors

- ▲ Growth: 46%
- ▲ Annual Job Openings: 27,865
- ▲ Yearly Earnings: $18,840
- ▲ Education Required: Bachelor's degree
- ▲ Self-Employed: 0%
- ▲ Part-Time: 18%

Residential Advisors

Coordinate activities for residents of boarding schools, college fraternities or sororities, college dormitories, or similar establishments. Order supplies and determine need for maintenance, repairs, and furnishings. **Maintain household records and assign rooms. Refer residents to counseling resources if needed.** Plans menus of meals for residents of establishment. Compiles records of daily activities of residents. Escorts individuals on trips outside establishment for shopping or for obtaining medical or dental services. Answers telephone. Counsels residents in identifying and resolving social and other problems. Chaperons group-sponsored trips and social functions. Ascertains need for and secures service of physician. Orders supplies. Determines need for maintenance, repairs, and furnishings. Assigns rooms; assists in planning recreational activities; supervises work and study programs. Sorts and distributes mail. Hires and supervises activities of housekeeping personnel.

Personality Type: Social. Social occupations frequently involve working with, communicating with, and teaching people. These occupations often involve helping or providing service to others.

Abilities: Oral Expression—The ability to communicate information and ideas verbally so others will understand. Problem Sensitivity—The ability to tell when something is wrong or is likely to go wrong. Does not involve solving the problem, only recognizing there is a problem. Speech Clarity—The ability to speak clearly so that what is said is understandable to a listener. Oral Comprehension—The ability to listen to and understand information and ideas presented verbally. Near Vision—The ability to see details of objects at a close range.

Skills: Social Perceptiveness—Being aware of other people's reactions and understanding why people react the way they do. Active Listening—Listening to what other people are saying; asking questions as appropriate. Problem Identification—Identifying the nature of problems. Critical Thinking—Using logic and analysis to identify the strengths and weaknesses of different approaches.

Generalized Work Activities: Establishing and Maintaining Relationships—Developing constructive and cooperative working relationships with others. Assisting and Caring for Others—Providing assistance or personal care to others. Providing Consultation and Advice to Others—Providing consultation and expert advice to management or other groups on technical, systems-related, or process-related topics. Making Decisions and Solving Problems—Combining, evaluating, and analyzing information and data to make decisions and solve problems. Involves making decisions about the relative importance of information and choosing the best solution. Resolving Conflict, Negotiating With Others—Handling complaints, arbitrating disputes, resolving grievances, or otherwise negotiating with others.

Respiratory Therapists

- ▲ Growth: 43%
- ▲ Annual Job Openings: 8,553
- ▲ Yearly Earnings: $34,830
- ▲ Education Required: Associate degree
- ▲ Self-Employed: 0%
- ▲ Part-Time: 20.8%

Respiratory Therapists

Assess, treat, and care for patients with breathing disorders. Assume primary responsibility for all respiratory care modalities, including the supervision of respiratory therapy technicians. Initiate and conduct therapeutic procedures; maintain patient records; select, assemble, check, and operate equipment. Consults with physician in event of adverse reactions. Demonstrates respiratory care procedures to trainees and other health care personnel. Performs broncho-pulmonary drainage and assists patient in performing breathing exercises. Monitors patient's physiological responses to therapy, such as vital signs, arterial blood gases, and blood chemistry changes. Maintains patient's chart containing pertinent identification and therapy information. Orders repairs when necessary. Determines requirements for treatment, such as type and duration of therapy and medication and dosages. Performs pulmonary function and adjusts equipment to obtain optimum results to therapy. Reads prescription; measures arterial blood gases; reviews patient information to assess patient condition. Operates equipment to administer medicinal gases and aerosol drugs to patients following specified parameters of treatment. Sets up and operates devices such as mechanical ventilators, therapeutic gas-administration apparatus, environmental control systems, and aerosol generators. Determines most suitable method of administering inhalants, precautions to be observed, and potential modifications needed, compatible with physician's orders. Inspects and tests respiratory therapy equipment to ensure equipment is functioning safely and efficiently.

Personality Type: Investigative. Investigative occupations frequently involve working with ideas and require an extensive amount of thinking. These occupations can involve searching for facts and figuring out problems mentally.

Abilities: Written Comprehension—The ability to read and understand information and ideas presented in writing. Oral Comprehension—The ability to listen to and understand information and ideas presented verbally. Oral Expression—The ability to communicate information and ideas verbally so others will understand. Problem Sensitivity—The ability to tell when something is wrong or is likely to go wrong. Does not involve solving the problem, only recognizing there is a problem. Near Vision—The ability to see details of objects at a close range.

Skills: Operation and Control—Controlling operations of equipment or systems. Reading Comprehension—Understanding written information in work-related documents. Monitoring—Assessing how well one is doing when learning or doing something. Active Listening—Listening to what other people are saying; asking questions as appropriate. Operation Monitoring—Watching gauges, dials, or other indicators to make sure a machine is working properly. Problem Identification—Identifying the nature of problems. Critical Thinking—Using logic and analysis to identify the strengths and weaknesses of different approaches.

Generalized Work Activities: Assisting and Caring for Others—Providing assistance or personal care to others. Monitoring Processes, Materials, Surroundings—Monitoring and reviewing information from materials, events, or the environment, often to detect problems or to find out when things are finished. Getting Information Needed to Do the Job—Observing, receiving, and otherwise obtaining information from all relevant sources. Identifying Objects, Actions, and Events—Identifying information received by making estimates or categorizations, recognizing differences or similarities, or sensing changes in circumstances or events. Controlling Machines and Processes—Using either control mechanisms or direct physical activity to operate machines or processes. Does not involve working with computers or vehicles. Documenting/Recording Information—Entering, transcribing, recording, storing, or maintaining information in either written form or by electronic/magnetic recording. Handling and Moving Objects—Using one's hands and arms in handling, installing, forming, positioning, and moving materials, or in manipulating things.

Restaurant Cooks

- ▲ Growth: 19%
- ▲ Annual Job Openings: 262,535
- ▲ Yearly Earnings: $16,250
- ▲ Education Required: Long-term O-J-T
- ▲ Self-Employed: 5.7%
- ▲ Part-Time: 38.5%

Cooks, Restaurant

Prepare, season, and cook soups, meats, vegetables, desserts, or other foodstuffs in restaurants. Order supplies; keep records and accounts. Price items on menu. Plan menu. Inspects food preparation and serving areas to ensure observance of safe, sanitary food-handling practices. Portions, arranges, and garnishes food; serves food to waiter or patron. Plans items on menu. Carves and trims meats such as beef, veal, ham, pork, and lamb, for hot or cold service or for sandwiches. Butchers and dresses animals, fowl, or shellfish; cuts and bones meat prior to cooking. Estimates food consumption; requisitions or purchases supplies or procures food from storage. Bakes bread, rolls, cakes, and pastry. Bakes, roasts, broils, and steams meats, fish, vegetables, and other foods. Observes and tests food to determine that it is cooked, by tasting, smelling, or piercing; turns or stirs food if necessary. Regulates temperature of ovens, broilers, grills, and roasters. Seasons and cooks food according to recipes or personal judgment and experience. Weighs, measures, and mixes ingredients according to recipe or personal judgment, using various kitchen utensils and equipment. Washes, peels, cuts, and seeds fruits and vegetables to prepare them for use.

Personality Type: Realistic. Realistic occupations frequently involve work activities that include practical, hands-on problems and solutions. They often deal with plants, animals, and real-world materials like wood, tools, and machinery. Many of the occupations require working outside and do not involve a lot of paperwork or working closely with others.

Abilities: Information Ordering—The ability to correctly follow a given rule or set of rules in order to arrange things or actions in a certain order. The things or actions can include numbers, letters, words, pictures, procedures, sentences, and mathematical or logical operations. Memorization—The ability to remember information such as words, numbers, pictures, and procedures. Written Comprehension—The ability to read and understand information and ideas presented in writing. Manual Dexterity—The ability to quickly make coordinated movements of one hand, a hand together with its arm, or two hands, to grasp, manipulate, or assemble objects. Wrist-Finger Speed—The ability to make fast, simple, repeated movements of the fingers, hands, and wrists.

Skills: Equipment Selection—Determining the kind of tools and equipment needed to do a job. Product Inspection—Inspecting and evaluating the quality of products. Monitoring—Assessing how well one is doing when learning or doing something. Coordination—Adjusting actions in relation to others' actions. Information Organization—Finding ways to structure or classify multiple pieces of information. Speaking—Talking to others to effectively convey information.

Generalized Work Activities: Monitoring and Controlling Resources—Monitoring and controlling resources and overseeing the spending of money. Identifying Objects, Actions, and Events—Identifying information received by making estimates or categorizations, recognizing differences or similarities, or sensing changes in circumstances or events. Estimating Needed Characteristics—Estimating the characteristics of materials, products, events, or information; estimating sizes, distances, and quantities; determining time, costs, resources, or materials needed to perform a work activity. Handling and Moving Objects—Using one's hands and arms in handling, installing, forming, positioning, and moving materials, or in manipulating things. Monitoring Processes, Materials, Surroundings—Monitoring and reviewing information from materials, events, or the environment, often to detect problems or to find out when things are finished.

Restaurant Hosts and Hostesses

▲ Growth: 18%
▲ Annual Job Openings: 110,848
▲ Yearly Earnings: $13,400
▲ Education Required: Short-term O-J-T
▲ Self-Employed: 2%
▲ Part-Time: 38.3%

Hosts and Hostesses, Restaurant, Lounge, and Coffee Shop

Welcome patrons and seat them at tables or in lounge. Help ensure quality of facilities and service. Adjusts complaints of patrons. Schedules dining reservations and arranges parties or special service for diners. Requisitions table linens and other supplies for tables and serving stations. Inspects dining room serving stations for neatness and cleanliness. Greets and escorts guests to tables; provides menus. Assigns work tasks and coordinates activities of dining room personnel to ensure prompt and courteous service to patrons.

Personality Type: Enterprising. Enterprising occupations frequently involve starting up and carrying out projects. These occupations can involve leading people and making many decisions. They sometimes require risk taking and often deal with business.

Abilities: Oral Expression—The ability to communicate information and ideas verbally so others will understand. Oral Comprehension—The ability to listen to and understand information and ideas presented verbally. Number Facility—The ability to add, subtract, multiply, or divide quickly and correctly. Speech Clarity—The ability to speak clearly so that what is said is understandable to a listener. Problem Sensitivity—The ability to tell when something is wrong or is likely to go wrong. Does not involve solving the problem, only recognizing there is a problem.

Skills: Service Orientation—Actively looking for ways to help people. Coordination—Adjusting actions in relation to others' actions. Mathematics—Using mathematics to solve problems. Time Management—Managing one's own time and the time of others.

Generalized Work Activities: Communicating with Other Workers—Providing information to supervisors, fellow workers, and subordinates. This information can be exchanged face-to-face, in writing, or via telephone/electronic transfer. Performing for/Working with Public—Performing for people or dealing directly with the public, including serving persons in restaurants and stores and receiving clients or guests. Establishing and Maintaining Relationships—Developing constructive and cooperative working relationships with others. Scheduling Work and Activities—Scheduling events, programs, activities, and the work of others. Coordinating Work and Activities of Others—Coordinating members of a work group to accomplish tasks.

Retail Salespersons

- ▲ Growth: 14%
- ▲ Annual Job Openings: 1,305,317
- ▲ Yearly Earnings: $15,830
- ▲ Education Required: Short-term O-J-T
- ▲ Self-Employed: 4%
- ▲ Part-Time: 40.2%

Retail Salespersons

Sell merchandise such as furniture, motor vehicles, appliances, or apparel, in a retail establishment. Computes sales price of merchandise. Wraps merchandise. Estimates cost of repair or alteration of merchandise. Estimates and quotes trade-in allowances. Maintains records related to sales. Tickets, arranges, and displays merchandise to promote sales. Estimates quantity and cost of merchandise required, such as paint or floor covering. Greets customer. Rents merchandise to customers. Fits or assists customers in trying on merchandise. Sells or arranges for delivery, insurance, financing, or service contracts for merchandise. Requisitions new stock. Cleans shelves, counters, and tables. Recommends, selects, and obtains merchandise based on customer needs and desires. Demonstrates use or operation of merchandise. Prepares sales slip or sales contract. Describes merchandise and explains use, operation, and care of merchandise to customers. Inventories stock. Totals purchases, receives payment, makes change, or processes credit transaction.

Personality Type: Enterprising. Enterprising occupations frequently involve starting up and carrying out projects. These occupations can involve leading people and making many decisions. They sometimes require risk taking and often deal with business.

Abilities: Oral Expression—The ability to communicate information and ideas verbally so others will understand. Oral Comprehension—The ability to listen to and understand information and ideas presented verbally. Speech Clarity—The ability to speak clearly so that what is said is understandable to a listener. Number Facility—The ability to add, subtract, multiply, or divide quickly and correctly. Information Ordering—The ability to correctly follow a given rule or set of rules in order to arrange things or actions in a certain order. The things or actions can include numbers, letters, words, pictures, procedures, sentences, and mathematical or logical operations.

Skills: Service Orientation—Actively looking for ways to help people. Speaking—Talking to others to effectively convey information. Social Perceptiveness—Being aware of other people's reactions and understanding why people react the way they do. Active Listening—Listening to what other people are saying; asking questions as appropriate. Mathematics—Using mathematics to solve problems.

Generalized Work Activities: Selling or Influencing Others—Convincing others to buy merchandise/goods, or otherwise changing their minds or actions. Performing for/Working with Public—Performing for people or dealing directly with the public, including serving persons in restaurants and stores and receiving clients or guests. Communicating with Persons Outside Organization—Communicating with persons outside the organization. Representing the organization to customers, the public, government, and other external sources. Exchanging information face-to-face, in writing, or via telephone/electronic transfer. Establishing and Maintaining Relationships—Developing constructive and cooperative working relationships with others. Documenting/Recording Information—Entering, transcribing, recording, storing, or maintaining information in either written form or by electronic/magnetic recording.

Roofers

▲ Growth: 12%
▲ Annual Job Openings: 28,797
▲ Yearly Earnings: $25,340
▲ Education Required: Moderate-term O-J-T
▲ Self-Employed: 30.9%
▲ Part-Time: 13.8%

Roofers

Cover roofs of structures with shingles, slate, asphalt, aluminum, wood, and related materials. Spray roofs, sidings, and walls with material to bind, seal, insulate, or soundproof sections of structures. Mops or pours hot asphalt or tar onto roof base when applying asphalt or tar and gravel to roof. Insulates, soundproofs, and seals buildings with foam, using spray gun, air compressor, and heater. Applies alternate layers of hot asphalt or tar and roofing paper until roof covering is completed as specified. Aligns roofing material with edge of roof. Cuts strips of flashing and fits them into angles formed by walls, vents, and intersecting roof surfaces. Punches holes in slate, tile, terra cotta, or wooden shingles, using punch and hammer. Removes snow, water, or debris from roofs prior to applying roofing materials. Cleans and maintains equipment. Cuts roofing paper to size and nails or staples paper to roof in overlapping strips to form base for roofing materials. Overlaps successive layers of roofing material, determining distance of overlap, using chalkline, gauge on shingling hatchet, or lines on shingles. Fastens composition shingles or sheets to roof with asphalt, cement, or nails. Applies gravel or pebbles over top layer, using rake or stiff-bristled broom.

Personality Type: Realistic. Realistic occupations frequently involve work activities that include practical, hands-on problems and solutions. They often deal with plants, animals, and real-world materials like wood, tools, and machinery. Many of the occupations require working outside and do not involve a lot of paperwork or working closely with others.

Abilities: Gross Body Equilibrium—The ability to keep or regain one's body balance or stay upright when in an unstable position. Static Strength—The ability to exert maximum muscle force to lift, push, pull, or carry objects. Extent Flexibility—The ability to bend, stretch, twist, or reach out with the body, arms, and/or legs. Stamina—The ability to exert one's self physically over long periods of time without getting winded or out of breath. Manual Dexterity—The ability to quickly make coordinated movements of one hand, a hand together with its arm, or two hands, to grasp, manipulate, or assemble objects. Explosive Strength—The ability to use short bursts of muscle force to propel oneself, as in jumping or sprinting, or to throw an object.

Skills: Equipment Selection—Determining the kind of tools and equipment needed to do a job. Operation and Control—Controlling operations of equipment or systems. Installation—Installing equipment, machines, wiring, or programs to meet specifications. Coordination—Adjusting actions in relation to others' actions. Product Inspection—Inspecting and evaluating the quality of products.

Generalized Work Activities: Performing General Physical Activities—Performing physical activities that require moving one's whole body, such as in climbing, lifting, balancing, walking, and stooping. Performing activities that often also require considerable use of the arms and legs, such as in the physical handling of materials. Handling and Moving Objects—Using one's hands and arms in handling, installing, forming, positioning, and moving materials, or in manipulating things. Includes the use of keyboards. Getting Information Needed to Do the Job—Observing, receiving, and otherwise obtaining information from all relevant sources. Estimating Needed Characteristics—Estimating the characteristics of materials, products, events, or information; estimating sizes, distances, and

quantities; determining time, costs, resources, or materials needed to perform a work activity. Implementing Ideas and Programs—Conducting or carrying out work procedures and activities in accord with one's own ideas or information provided through directions/instructions for purposes of installing, modifying, preparing, delivering, constructing, integrating, finishing, or completing programs, systems, structures, or products. Identifying Objects, Actions, and Events—Identifying information received by making estimates or categorizations, recognizing differences or similarities, or sensing changes in circumstances or events.

Sales Engineers

▲ Growth: 16%
▲ Annual Job Openings: 3,039
▲ Yearly Earnings: $54,600
▲ Education Required: Not available
▲ Self-Employed: Not available
▲ Part-Time: Not available

Sales Engineers

Sell business goods or services, the selling of which requires a technical background equivalent to a baccalaureate degree in engineering. Arranges for trial installations of equipment. Draws up or proposes changes in equipment, processes, materials, or services, resulting in cost reduction or improvement in customer operations. Draws up sales or service contract for products or services. Demonstrates and explains product or service to customer representatives such as engineers, architects, and other professionals. Assists sales force in sale of company products. Provides technical services to clients relating to use, operation, and maintenance of equipment. Diagnoses problems with installed equipment. Provides technical training to employees of client. Calls on management representatives at commercial, industrial, and other establishments to convince prospective client to buy products or services offered. Reviews customer documents to develop and prepare cost estimates or projected production increases from use of proposed equipment or services. Assists in development of custom-made machinery. Designs and drafts variations of standard products in order to meet customer needs.

Personality Type: Enterprising. Enterprising occupations frequently involve starting up and carrying out projects. These occupations can involve leading people and making many decisions. They sometimes require risk taking and often deal with business.

Abilities: Oral Comprehension—The ability to listen to and understand information and ideas presented verbally. Oral Expression—The ability to communicate information and ideas verbally so others will understand. Speech Clarity—The ability to speak clearly so that what is said is understandable to a listener. Written Expression—The ability to communicate information and ideas in writing so others will understand. Written Comprehension—The ability to read and understand information and ideas presented in writing.

Skills: Persuasion—Persuading others to approach things differently. Speaking—Talking to others to effectively convey information. Service Orientation—Actively looking for ways to help people. Active Listening—Listening to what other people are saying; asking questions as appropriate. Social Perceptiveness—Being aware of other people's reactions and understanding why people react the way they do.

Generalized Work Activities: Drafting and Specifying Technical Devices—Providing documentation, detailed instructions, drawings, or specifications to inform others about how devices, parts, equipment, or structures are to be fabricated, constructed, assembled, modified, maintained, or used. Selling or Influencing Others—Convincing others to buy merchandise/goods, or otherwise changing their minds or actions. Communicating with Persons Outside Organization—Communicating with persons outside the organization. Representing the organization to customers, the public, government, and other external sources. Exchanging information face-to-face, in writing, or via telephone/electronic transfer. Updating and Using Job-Relevant

Knowledge—Keeping up-to-date technically and knowing the functions of one's own job and related jobs. Communicating with Other Workers—Providing information to supervisors, fellow workers, and subordinates. This information can be exchanged face-to-face, in writing, or via telephone/electronic transfer.

School Bus Drivers

- ▲ Growth: 18%
- ▲ Annual Job Openings: 65,136
- ▲ Yearly Earnings: $18,820
- ▲ Education Required: Short-term O-J-T
- ▲ Self-Employed: 0%
- ▲ Part-Time: 43.3%

Bus Drivers, School

Transport students or special clients such as the elderly or persons with disabilities. Ensure adherence to safety rules. Assist passengers in boarding or exiting. Makes minor repairs to bus. Maintains order among passengers during trip. Regulates heating, lighting, and ventilating systems for passenger comfort. Inspects bus and checks gas, oil, and water levels. Reports delays or accidents. Drives bus to transport passengers over specified routes. Complies with local traffic regulations.

Personality Type: Realistic. Realistic occupations frequently involve work activities that include practical, hands-on problems and solutions. They often deal with plants, animals, and real-world materials like wood, tools, and machinery. Many of the occupations require working outside and do not involve a lot of paperwork or working closely with others.

Abilities: Response Orientation—The ability to choose quickly and correctly between two or more movements in response to two or more signals, such as lights, sounds, or pictures. Includes the speed with which the correct response is started with the hand, foot, or other body parts. Reaction Time—The ability to quickly respond with the hand, finger, or foot to a signal such as a sound, a light, or a picture. Peripheral Vision—The ability to see objects or movement of objects to one's side when

the eyes are focused forward. Depth Perception—The ability to judge which of several objects is closer or farther away from the observer, or to judge the distance between an object and the observer. Night Vision—The ability to see under low light conditions. Multilimb Coordination—The ability to coordinate movements of two or more limbs together (for example, two arms, two legs, or one leg and one arm) while sitting, standing, or lying down. Does not involve performing the activities while the body is in motion. Far Vision—The ability to see details at a distance. Time Sharing—The ability to efficiently shift back and forth between two or more activities or sources of information such as speech, sounds, or touch.

Skills: Operation and Control—Controlling operations of equipment or systems. Operation Monitoring—Watching gauges, dials, or other indicators to make sure a machine is working properly. Social Perceptiveness—Being aware of other people's reactions and understanding why people react the way they do. Equipment Maintenance—Performing routine maintenance and determining when and what kind of maintenance is needed. Speaking—Talking to others to effectively convey information.

Generalized Work Activities: Operating Vehicles or Equipment—Running, maneuvering, navigating, or driving vehicles or mechanized equipment such as forklifts, passenger vehicles, aircraft, or water craft. Monitoring Processes, Materials, Surroundings— Monitoring and reviewing information from materials, events, or the environment, often to detect problems or to find out when things are finished. Getting Information Needed to Do the Job—Observing, receiving, and otherwise obtaining information from all relevant sources. Making Decisions and Solving Problems—Combining, evaluating, and analyzing information and data to make decisions and solve problems. Involves making decisions about the relative importance of information and choosing the best solution. Inspecting Equipment, Structures, Materials— Inspecting or diagnosing equipment, structures, or materials to identify the causes of errors or other problems or defects.

Secondary School Teachers

- ▲ Growth: 23%
- ▲ Annual Job Openings: 133,585
- ▲ Yearly Earnings: $37,890
- ▲ Education Required: Bachelor's degree
- ▲ Self-Employed: 0%
- ▲ Part-Time: 10.6%

Middle School Teachers, Except Special and Vocational Education

Teach students in public or private schools in one or more subjects at the middle, intermediate, or junior high level, which falls between elementary and senior high school as defined by applicable state laws and regulations. Evaluates, records, and reports student progress. Instructs students, using various teaching methods such as lecture and demonstration. Uses audiovisual aids and other materials to supplement presentations. Assigns lessons and corrects homework. Prepares course outlines and objectives according to curriculum guidelines or state and local requirements. Develops and administers tests. Performs advisory duties such as sponsoring student organizations or clubs, helping students select courses, and counseling students with problems. Selects, stores, orders, issues, and inventories classroom equipment, materials, and supplies. Keeps attendance records. Confers with students, parents, and school counselors to resolve behavioral and academic problems. Participates in faculty and professional meetings, educational conferences, and teacher-training workshops. Maintains discipline in classroom.

Personality Type: Social. Social occupations frequently involve working with, communicating with, and teaching people. These occupations often involve helping or providing service to others.

Abilities: Oral Expression—The ability to communicate information and ideas verbally so others will understand. Oral Comprehension—The ability to listen to and understand information and ideas presented verbally. Written Comprehension—The ability to read and understand information and ideas presented in writing. Written Expression—The ability to communicate information and ideas in writing so others will understand. Speech Clarity—The ability to speak clearly so that what is said is understandable to a listener.

Skills: Speaking—Talking to others to effectively convey information. Instructing—Teaching others how to do something. Learning Strategies—Using multiple approaches when learning or teaching new things. Reading Comprehension—Understanding written information in work-related documents. Social Perceptiveness—Being aware of other people's reactions and understanding why people react the way they do.

Active Listening—Listening to what other people are saying; asking questions as appropriate.

Generalized Work Activities: Teaching Others—Identifying educational needs, developing formal training programs or classes, and teaching or instructing others. Communicating with Persons Outside Organization—Communicating with persons outside the organization. Representing the organization to customers, the public, government, and other external sources. Exchanging information face-to-face, in writing, or via telephone/electronic transfer. Getting Information Needed to Do the Job—Observing, receiving, and otherwise obtaining information from all relevant sources. Updating and Using Job-Relevant Knowledge—Keeping up-to-date technically and knowing the functions of one's own job and related jobs. Documenting/Recording Information—Entering, transcribing, recording, storing, or maintaining information in either written form or by electronic/magnetic recording. Interpreting Meaning of Information to Others—Translating or explaining what information means and how it can be understood or used to support responses or feedback to others. Processing Information—Compiling, coding, categorizing, calculating, tabulating, auditing, verifying, or processing information or data.

Secondary School Teachers, Except Special and Vocational Education

Instruct students in secondary public or private schools in one or more subjects at the secondary level, such as English, mathematics, or social studies. Teach a designated subject matter specialty such as typing, commerce, or English. Evaluates, records, and reports student progress. Develops and administers tests. Confers with students, parents, and school counselors to resolve behavioral and academic problems. Keeps attendance records. Maintains discipline in classroom. Assigns lessons and corrects homework. Prepares course outlines and objectives according to curriculum guidelines or state and local requirements. Selects, stores, orders, issues, and inventories classroom equipment, materials, and supplies. Performs advisory duties such as sponsoring student organizations or clubs, helping students select courses, and counseling students with problems. Instructs students, using various teaching methods such as lecture and demonstration. Participates in faculty and professional meetings, educational conferences, and teacher training workshops. Uses audiovisual aids and other materials to supplement presentations.

Personality Type: Social. Social occupations frequently involve working with, communicating with, and teaching people. These occupations often involve helping or providing service to others.

Abilities: Oral Expression—The ability to communicate information and ideas verbally so others will understand. Written Expression—The ability to communicate information and ideas in writing so others will understand. Written Comprehension—The ability to read and understand information and ideas presented in writing. Oral Comprehension—The ability to listen to and understand information and ideas presented verbally. Speech Clarity—The ability to speak clearly so that what is said is understandable to a listener.

Skills: Speaking—Talking to others to effectively convey information. Instructing—Teaching others how to do something. Learning Strategies—Using multiple approaches when learning or teaching new things. Reading Comprehension—Understanding written information in work-related documents. Active Listening—Listening to what other people are saying; asking questions as appropriate. Social Perceptiveness—Being aware of other people's reactions and understanding why people react the way they do.

Generalized Work Activities: Teaching Others—Identifying educational needs, developing formal training programs or classes, and teaching or instructing others. Communicating with Persons Outside Organization—Communicating with persons outside the organization. Representing the organization to customers, the public, government, and other external sources. Exchanging information face-to-face, in writing, or via telephone/electronic transfer. Getting

Information Needed to Do the Job—Observing, receiving, and otherwise obtaining information from all relevant sources. Updating and Using Job-Relevant Knowledge—Keeping up-to-date technically and knowing the functions of one's own job and related jobs. Interpreting Meaning of Information to Others—Translating or explaining what information means and how it can be understood or used to support responses or feedback to others. Processing Information—Compiling, coding, categorizing, calculating, tabulating, auditing, verifying, or processing information or data. Documenting/Recording Information—Entering, transcribing, recording, storing, or maintaining information in either written form or by electronic/magnetic recording.

Secretaries

- ▲ Growth: 0%
- ▲ Annual Job Openings: 358,379
- ▲ Yearly Earnings: $23,550
- ▲ Education Required: Postsecondary vocational training
- ▲ Self-Employed: 2.8%
- ▲ Part-Time: 19.8%

Executive Secretaries and Administrative Assistants

Provide high-level administrative support by conducting research, preparing statistical reports, handling information requests, and performing clerical functions such as preparing correspondence, receiving visitors, arranging conference calls, and scheduling meetings. Train and supervise lower-level clerical staff. Coordinates and directs office services such as records and budget preparation, personnel, and housekeeping, to aid executives. Files and retrieves corporation documents, records, and reports. Interprets administrative and operating policies and procedures for employees. Plans conferences. Reads and answers correspondence. Studies management methods to improve workflow, to simplify reporting procedures, or to implement cost reductions. Analyzes operating practices and procedures to create new methods or to revise existing methods. Prepares records and reports such as recommendations for solutions of administrative problems and annual reports.

Personality Type: Conventional. Conventional occupations frequently involve following set procedures and routines. These occupations can include working with data and details more than with ideas. Usually there is a clear line of authority to follow.

Abilities: Written Comprehension—The ability to read and understand information and ideas presented in writing. Near Vision—The ability to see details of objects at a close range. Information Ordering—The ability to correctly follow a given rule or set of rules in order to arrange things or actions in a certain order. The things or actions can include numbers, letters, words, pictures, procedures, sentences, and mathematical or logical operations. Oral Comprehension—The ability to listen to and understand information and ideas presented verbally. Written Expression—The ability to communicate information and ideas in writing so others will understand.

Skills: Reading Comprehension—Understanding written information in work-related documents. Writing—Communicating effectively with others in writing as indicated by the needs of the audience. Coordination—Adjusting actions in relation to others' actions. Synthesis/Reorganization—Reorganizing information to get a better approach to problems or tasks. Time Management—Managing one's own time and the time of others. Speaking—Talking to others to effectively convey information.

Generalized Work Activities: Performing Administrative Activities—Approving requests, handling paperwork, and performing day-to-day administrative tasks. Communicating with Other Workers—Providing information to supervisors, fellow workers, and subordinates. This information can be exchanged face-to-face, in writing, or via telephone/electronic transfer. Analyzing Data or Information—Identifying underlying principles, reasons, or facts by breaking down information or data into separate parts. Monitoring and Controlling Resources—Monitoring and controlling resources and overseeing the spending of money. Processing Information—Compiling, coding, categorizing, calculating, tabulating, auditing, verifying, or processing information or data. Interpreting Meaning of Information to Others—Translating or explaining what information means and how it can be understood or used to support responses or feedback to others. Coordinating Work and Activities of Others—Coordinating members of a work group to accomplish tasks.

Secretaries, Except Legal, Medical, and Executive

Perform routine clerical and administrative functions such as drafting correspondence, scheduling appointments, organizing and maintaining paper and electronic files, or providing information to callers. Orders and dispenses supplies. Compiles and types statistical reports, using typewriter or computer. Opens incoming mail and routes mail to appropriate individuals. Composes and distributes meeting notes, correspondence, and reports. Maintains calendar; coordinates conferences and meetings. Locates and attaches appropriate file to incoming correspondence requiring reply. Greets and welcomes visitors, determines nature of business, and conducts visitors to employer or appropriate person. Records and types minutes of meetings, using typewriter or computer. Mails newsletters, promotional material, and other information. Files correspondence and other records. Prepares and mails checks. Answers routine correspondence. Takes dictation in shorthand or by machine; transcribes

information. Arranges travel schedules and reservations. Compiles and maintains lists and records, using typewriter or computer. Makes copies of correspondence and other printed matter. Answers telephone; gives information to callers; takes messages; transfers calls to appropriate individuals. Provides customer services such as placing orders and furnishing account information. Collects and disburses funds from cash account; keeps records. Schedules appointments.

Personality Type: Conventional. Conventional occupations frequently involve following set procedures and routines. These occupations can include working with data and details more than with ideas. Usually there is a clear line of authority to follow.

Abilities: Oral Expression—The ability to communicate information and ideas verbally so others will understand. Oral Comprehension—The ability to listen to and understand information and ideas presented verbally. Written Comprehension—The ability to read and understand information and ideas presented in writing. Wrist-Finger Speed—The ability to make fast, simple, repeated movements of the fingers, hands, and wrists. Speech Recognition—The ability to identify and understand the speech of another person. Speech Clarity—The ability to speak clearly so that what is said is understandable to a listener.

Skills: Coordination—Adjusting actions in relation to others' actions. Active Listening—Listening to what other people are saying; asking questions as appropriate. Reading Comprehension—Understanding written information in work-related documents. Writing—Communicating effectively with others in writing as indicated by the needs of the audience. Information Organization—Finding ways to structure or classify multiple pieces of information.

Generalized Work Activities: Communicating with Persons Outside Organization—Communicating with persons outside the organization. Representing the organization to customers, the public, government, and other external sources. Exchanging information face-to-face, in writing, or via telephone/electronic transfer. Communicating with Other Workers—Providing information to supervisors, fellow workers, and subordinates. This information can be exchanged

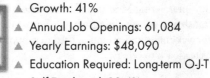

face-to-face, in writing, or via telephone/electronic transfer. Interacting with Computers—Controlling computer functions by using programs, setting up functions, writing software, or otherwise communicating with computer systems. Processing Information—Compiling, coding, categorizing, calculating, tabulating, auditing, verifying, or processing information or data. Establishing and Maintaining Relationships—Developing constructive and cooperative working relationships with others.

Securities, Commodities, and Financial Services Sales Agents

- ▲ Growth: 41%
- ▲ Annual Job Openings: 61,084
- ▲ Yearly Earnings: $48,090
- ▲ Education Required: Long-term O-J-T
- ▲ Self-Employed: 22.4%
- ▲ Part-Time: 8.6%

Sales Agents, Financial Services

Sell financial services such as loan, tax, and securities counseling, to customers of financial institutions and business establishments. Prepares forms or agreements to complete sale. Evaluates costs and revenue of agreements to determine continued profitability. Reviews business trends and advises customers regarding expected fluctuations. Determines customers' financial services needs; prepares proposals to sell services. Sells services and equipment such as trust, investment, and check-processing services. Contacts prospective customers to present information and to explain available services. Makes group presentations regarding financial services, to attract new clients. Develops prospects from current commercial customers, referral leads, and sales and trade meetings.

Personality Type: Enterprising. Enterprising occupations frequently involve starting up and carrying out projects. These occupations can involve leading people and making many decisions. They sometimes require risk taking and often deal with business.

Abilities: Oral Expression—The ability to communicate information and ideas verbally so others will understand. Number Facility—The ability to add, subtract, multiply, or divide quickly and correctly. Deductive Reasoning—The ability to apply general rules to specific problems to come up with logical answers. Involves deciding if an answer makes sense. Speech Clarity—The ability to speak clearly so that what is said is understandable to a listener. Written Comprehension—The ability to read and understand information and ideas presented in writing. Mathematical Reasoning—The ability to understand and organize a problem and then select a mathematical method or formula to solve the problem.

Skills: Persuasion—Persuading others to approach things differently. Information Gathering—Knowing how to find information and identifying essential information. Judgment and Decision Making—Weighing the relative costs and benefits of a potential action. Speaking—Talking to others to effectively convey information.

Generalized Work Activities: Communicating with Persons Outside Organization—Communicating with persons outside the organization. Representing the organization to customers, the public, government, and other external sources. Exchanging information face-to-face, in writing, or via telephone/electronic transfer. Selling or Influencing Others—Convincing others to buy merchandise/goods, or otherwise changing their minds or actions. Getting Information Needed to Do the Job—Observing, receiving, and otherwise obtaining information from all relevant sources. Making Decisions and Solving Problems—Combining, evaluating, and analyzing information and data to make decisions and solve problems. Involves making decisions about the relative importance of information and choosing the best solution. Interpreting Meaning of Information to Others—Translating or explaining what information means and how it can be understood or used to support responses or feedback to others.

Sales Agents, Securities and Commodities

Buy and sell securities in investment and trading firms. Develop and implement financial plans for individuals, businesses, and organizations. Prepares financial reports to monitor client or corporate finances. Informs and advises concerned parties regarding fluctuations and securities transactions affecting plan or account. Contacts exchange or brokerage firm to execute order; buys and sells securities based on market quotation and competition. Analyzes market conditions to determine optimum time to execute securities transactions. Reviews all securities transactions to ensure that information is accurate and that trades conform to regulations of governing agencies. Prepares documents to implement plan selected by client. Identifies potential clients, using advertising campaigns, mailing lists, and personal contacts; solicits business. Develops financial plan based on analysis of client's financial status; discusses financial options with client. Reads corporate reports and calculates ratios to determine best prospects for profit on stock purchase and to monitor client account. Interviews client to determine client's assets, liabilities, cash flow, insurance coverage, tax status, and financial objectives. Keeps informed about political and economic trends that influence stock prices. Records transactions accurately and keeps client informed about

transactions. Completes sales order tickets and submits tickets for processing of client-requested transaction.

Personality Type: Enterprising. Enterprising occupations frequently involve starting up and carrying out projects. These occupations can involve leading people and making many decisions. They sometimes require risk taking and often deal with business.

Abilities: Deductive Reasoning—The ability to apply general rules to specific problems to come up with logical answers. Involves deciding if an answer makes sense. Oral Comprehension—The ability to listen to and understand information and ideas presented verbally. Written Expression—The ability to communicate information and ideas in writing so others will understand. Written Comprehension—The ability to read and understand information and ideas presented in writing. Oral Expression—The ability to communicate information and ideas verbally so others will understand. Number Facility—The ability to add, subtract, multiply, or divide quickly and correctly. Mathematical Reasoning—The ability to understand and organize a problem and then select a mathematical method or formula to solve the problem.

Skills: Identifying Downstream Consequences—Determining the long-term outcomes of a change in operations. Systems Perception—Determining when important changes have occurred in a system or are likely to occur. Information Gathering—Knowing how to find information and identifying essential information. Judgment and Decision Making—Weighing the relative costs and benefits of a potential action. Management of Financial Resources—Determining how money will be spent to get the work done, and accounting for these expenditures. Systems Evaluation—Looking at many indicators of system performance, taking into account their accuracy. Visioning—Developing an image of how a system should work under ideal conditions.

Generalized Work Activities: Updating and Using Job-Relevant Knowledge—Keeping up-to-date technically and knowing the functions of one's own job and related jobs. Getting Information Needed to Do the Job—Observing, receiving, and otherwise obtaining information from all relevant sources. Analyzing Data or Information—Identifying underlying principles, reasons, or facts by breaking down information or data into separate parts. Providing Consultation and Advice to Others—Providing consultation and expert advice to management or other groups on technical, systems-related, or process-related topics. Documenting/ Recording Information—Entering, transcribing, recording, storing, or maintaining information in either written form or by electronic/magnetic recording.

Sheet Metal Workers and Duct Installers

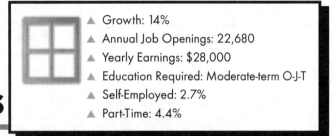

- ▲ Growth: 14%
- ▲ Annual Job Openings: 22,680
- ▲ Yearly Earnings: $28,000
- ▲ Education Required: Moderate-term O-J-T
- ▲ Self-Employed: 2.7%
- ▲ Part-Time: 4.4%

Sheet Metal Workers

Fabricate, assemble, install, and repair sheet metal products and equipment such as ducts, control boxes, drainpipes, and furnace casings. Set up and operate fabricating machines to cut, bend, and straighten sheet metal. Shape metal over anvils, blocks, or forms, using hammer. Operate soldering and welding equipment to join sheet-metal parts. Inspect, assemble, and smooth seams and joints of burred surfaces. Lays out and marks dimensions and reference lines on material, using scribes, dividers, squares, and rulers. Shapes metal material over anvil, block, or other form, using hand tools. Installs assemblies in supportive framework according to blueprints, using hand tools, power tools, and lifting and handling devices. Trims, files, grinds, deburrs, buffs, and smoothes surfaces, using hand tools and portable power tools. Determines sequence and methods of fabricating, assembling, and installing sheet metal products, using blueprints, sketches, or product specifications. Welds, solders, bolts, rivets, screws, clips, caulks, or bonds component parts to assemble products, using hand tools, power tools, and equipment. Sets up and operates fabricating machines such as shears, brakes, presses, and routers, to cut, bend, block, and form materials. Inspects assemblies and installation for conformance to specifications, using measuring instruments such as calipers, scales, dial indicators, gauges, and micrometers. Selects gauge and type of sheet metal or nonmetallic material according to product specifications.

Personality Type: Realistic. Realistic occupations frequently involve work activities that include practical, hands-on problems and solutions. They often deal with plants, animals, and real-world materials like wood, tools, and machinery. Many of the occupations require working outside and do not involve a lot of paperwork or working closely with others.

Abilities: Information Ordering—The ability to correctly follow a given rule or set of rules in order to arrange things or actions in a certain order. The things or actions can include numbers, letters, words, pictures, procedures, sentences, and mathematical or logical operations. Static Strength—The ability to exert maximum muscle force to lift, push, pull, or carry objects. Visualization—The ability to imagine how something will look after it is moved around or when its parts are moved or rearranged. Manual Dexterity—The ability to quickly make coordinated movements of one hand, a hand together with its arm, or two hands, to grasp, manipulate, or assemble objects. Written Comprehension—The ability to read and understand information and ideas presented in writing. Control Precision—The ability to quickly and repeatedly make precise adjustments in moving the controls of a machine or vehicle to exact positions.

Skills: Installation—Installing equipment, machines, wiring, or programs to meet specifications. Operation and Control—Controlling operations of equipment or systems. Product Inspection—Inspecting and evaluating the quality of products. Equipment Selection—

Determining the kind of tools and equipment needed to do a job. Mathematics—Using mathematics to solve problems.

Generalized Work Activities: Handling and Moving Objects—Using one's hands and arms in handling, installing, forming, positioning, and moving materials, or in manipulating things. Controlling Machines and Processes—Using either control mechanisms or direct physical activity to operate machines or processes. Does not involve working with computers or vehicles. Performing General Physical Activities—Performing physical activities that require moving one's whole body, such as in climbing, lifting, balancing, walking, and stooping. Performing activities that often also require considerable use of the arms and legs, such as in the physical handling of materials. Getting Information

Needed to Do the Job—Observing, receiving, and otherwise obtaining information from all relevant sources. Implementing Ideas and Programs—Conducting or carrying out work procedures and activities in accord with one's own ideas or information provided through directions/instructions for purposes of installing, modifying, preparing, delivering, constructing, integrating, finishing, or completing programs, systems, structures, or products. Inspecting Equipment, Structures, Materials—Inspecting or diagnosing equipment, structures, or materials to identify the causes of errors or other problems or defects. Identifying Objects, Actions, and Events—Identifying information received by making estimates or categorizations, recognizing differences or similarities, or sensing changes in circumstances or events.

Sheriffs and Deputy Sheriffs

- ▲ Growth: 34%
- ▲ Annual Job Openings: 3,130
- ▲ Yearly Earnings: $28,270
- ▲ Education Required: Long-term O-J-T
- ▲ Self-Employed: 0%
- ▲ Part-Time: 2.7%

Sheriffs and Deputy Sheriffs

Enforce law and order in rural or unincorporated districts; serve legal processes of courts. Patrol courthouse; guard court or grand jury; escort defendants. Arranges delivery of prisoner's arrest records from criminal investigation unit, at District Attorney's request. Transports or escorts prisoners or defendants between courtroom, prison or jail, District Attorney's offices, or medical facilities. Takes control of accident scene to maintain traffic flow, assist accident victims, and investigate causes. Confiscates real or personal property by court order; posts notices in public places. Questions individuals entering secured areas, to determine purpose of business; directs or reroutes individuals to destinations. Notifies patrol units to take

violators into custody or to provide needed assistance or medical aid. Investigates illegal or suspicious activities of persons. Executes arrest warrants, locating and taking persons into custody; issues citations. Serves subpoenas and summonses. Patrols and guards courthouse, grand-jury room, or assigned areas, to provide security, enforce laws, maintain order, and arrest violators. Maintains records and submits reports of dispositions; logs daily activities.

Personality Type: Social. Social occupations frequently involve working with, communicating with, and teaching people. These occupations often involve helping or providing service to others.

Abilities: Oral Expression—The ability to communicate information and ideas verbally so others will understand. Inductive Reasoning—The ability to combine separate pieces of information, or specific answers to problems, to form general rules or conclusions. Includes coming up with a logical explanation for why a series of seemingly unrelated events occur together. Oral Comprehension—The ability to listen to and understand information and ideas presented verbally. Written Comprehension—The ability to read and understand information and ideas presented in writing. Information Ordering—The ability to correctly follow a given rule or set of rules in order to arrange things or actions in a certain order. The things or actions can include numbers, letters, words, pictures, procedures, sentences, and mathematical or logical operations. Reaction Time—The ability to quickly respond with the hand, finger, or foot to a signal such as a sound, a light, or a picture. Near Vision—The ability to see details of objects at a close range. Deductive Reasoning—The ability to apply general rules to specific problems to come up with logical answers. Involves deciding if an answer makes sense.

Skills: Active Listening—Listening to what other people are saying; asking questions as appropriate. Judgment and Decision Making—Weighing the relative costs and benefits of a potential action. Information Gathering— Knowing how to find information and identifying essential information. Problem Identification— Identifying the nature of problems. Speaking—Talking to others to effectively convey information.

Generalized Work Activities: Performing for/Working with Public—Performing for people or dealing directly with the public, including serving persons in restaurants and stores and receiving clients or guests. Getting Information Needed to Do the Job—Observing, receiving, and otherwise obtaining information from all relevant sources. Documenting/Recording Information—Entering, transcribing, recording, storing, or maintaining information in either written form or by electronic/magnetic recording. Communicating with Persons Outside Organization—Communicating with persons outside the organization. Representing the organization to customers, the public, government, and other external sources. Exchanging information face-to-face, in writing, or via telephone/electronic transfer. Performing General Physical Activities—Performing physical activities that require moving one's whole body, such as in climbing, lifting, balancing, walking, and stooping. Performing activities that often also require considerable use of the arms and legs, such as in the physical handling of materials.

Ship Engineers

- ▲ Growth: 4%
- ▲ Annual Job Openings: 1,219
- ▲ Yearly Earnings: $40,150
- ▲ Education Required: Work experience in a related occupation
- ▲ Self-Employed: 0%
- ▲ Part-Time: 3%

Ship Engineers

Supervise and coordinate activities of crew engaged in operating and maintaining engines, boilers, deck machinery, and electrical, sanitary, and refrigeration equipment aboard ship. Maintains engineering log and bellbook (orders of changes in speed and direction of ship). Orders crew to repair or replace defective parts of engines and other equipment. Repairs machinery, using hand tools and power tools. Starts engines to propel ship and regulates engines and power transmission to control speed of ship. Stands watch in engine room, ensuring that lubricants and water levels are maintained in machinery and that load on generators is within limits. Inspects engines and other equipment.

Personality Type: Realistic. Realistic occupations frequently involve work activities that include practical, hands-on problems and solutions. They often deal with plants, animals, and real-world materials like wood, tools, and machinery. Many of the occupations require working outside and do not involve a lot of paperwork or working closely with others.

Abilities: Problem Sensitivity—The ability to tell when something is wrong or is likely to go wrong. Does not involve solving the problem, only recognizing there is a problem. Oral Expression—The ability to communicate information and ideas verbally so others will understand. Control Precision—The ability to quickly and repeatedly make precise adjustments in moving the controls of a machine or vehicle to exact positions. Written Comprehension—The ability to read and understand information and ideas presented in writing.

Skills: Operation and Control—Controlling operations of equipment or systems. Operation Monitoring—Watching gauges, dials, or other indicators to make sure a machine is working properly. Repairing—Repairing machines or systems, using the needed tools.

Generalized Work Activities: Inspecting Equipment, Structures, Materials—Inspecting or diagnosing equipment, structures, or materials to identify the causes of errors or other problems or defects. Monitoring Processes, Materials, Surroundings—Monitoring and reviewing information from materials, events, or the environment, often to detect problems or to find out when things are finished. Controlling Machines and Processes—Using either control mechanisms or direct physical activity to operate machines or processes. Does not involve working with computers or vehicles. Getting Information Needed to Do the Job—Observing, receiving, and otherwise obtaining information from all relevant sources. Making Decisions and Solving Problems—Combining, evaluating, and analyzing information and data to make decisions and solve problems. Involves making decisions about the relative importance of information and choosing the best solution. Coordinating Work and Activities of Others—Coordinating members of a work group to accomplish tasks.

Shipping, Receiving, and Traffic Clerks

- ▲ Growth: 3%
- ▲ Annual Job Openings: 242,666
- ▲ Yearly Earnings: $22,500
- ▲ Education Required: Short-term O-J-T
- ▲ Self-Employed: 0%
- ▲ Part-Time: 9.6%

Shipping, Receiving, and Traffic Clerks

Verify and keep records on incoming and outgoing shipments. Prepare items for shipment. Assemble, address, stamp, and ship merchandise or material. Receive, unpack, verify, and record incoming merchandise or material. Arrange for the transportation of products. Requisitions and stores shipping materials and supplies to maintain inventory of stock. Prepares documents such as work orders, bills of lading, and shipping orders to route materials. Computes amounts such as space available, shipping charges, storage charges, and demurrage charges, using calculator or price list.

Delivers or routes materials to departments, using work devices such as handtruck, conveyor, or sorting bins. Contacts carrier representative to make arrangements and to issue instructions for shipping and delivery of materials. Determines shipping method for materials, using knowledge of shipping procedures, routes, and rates. Records shipment data such as weight, charges, space availability, damages, and discrepancies, for reporting, accounting, and record keeping purposes. Examines contents and compares with records such as manifests, invoices, or orders, to verify accuracy of incoming or outgoing shipment. Packs, seals, labels, and affixes postage to materials in preparation for shipping, using work devices such as hand tools, power tools, and postage meter. Confers and corresponds with establishment representatives to rectify problems such as damages, shortages, and nonconformance to specifications.

Personality Type: Conventional. Conventional occupations frequently involve following set procedures and routines. These occupations can include working with data and details more than with ideas. Usually there is a clear line of authority to follow.

Abilities: Written Comprehension—The ability to read and understand information and ideas presented in writing. Written Expression—The ability to communicate information and ideas in writing so others will understand. Near Vision—The ability to see details of objects at a close range. Oral Expression—The ability to communicate information and ideas verbally so others will understand.

Skills: Problem Identification—Identifying the nature of problems. Mathematics—Using mathematics to solve problems. Information Gathering—Knowing how to find information and identifying essential information. Writing—Communicating effectively with others in writing as indicated by the needs of the audience. Implementation Planning—Developing approaches for implementing an idea.

Generalized Work Activities: Documenting/Recording Information—Entering, transcribing, recording, storing, or maintaining information in either written form or by electronic/magnetic recording. Handling and Moving Objects—Using one's hands and arms in handling, installing, forming, positioning, and moving materials, or in manipulating things. Includes the use of keyboards. Evaluating Information against Standards—Evaluating information against a set of standards and verifying that it is correct. Getting Information Needed to Do the Job—Observing, receiving, and otherwise obtaining information from all relevant sources. Communicating with Persons Outside Organization—Communicating with persons outside the organization. Representing the organization to customers, the public, government, and other external sources. Exchanging information face-to-face, in writing, or via telephone/electronic transfer. Making Decisions and Solving Problems—Combining, evaluating, and analyzing information and data to make decisions and solve problems. Involves making decisions about the relative importance of information and choosing the best solution.

Short Order and Fast Food Cooks

- ▲ Growth: 18%
- ▲ Annual Job Openings: 226,320
- ▲ Yearly Earnings: $12,700
- ▲ Education Required: Short-term O-J-T
- ▲ Self-Employed: 1.2%
- ▲ Part-Time: 38.5%

Cooks, Fast Food

Prepare and cook food in a fast-food restaurant with a limited menu. Prepare a few basic items and operate large-volume, single-purpose cooking equipment. Reads food order slip or receives verbal instructions as to food requested by patron; prepares and cooks food according to instructions. Cleans work area and food preparation equipment. Serves orders to customers at window or counter. Prepares and serves beverages such as coffee and fountain drinks. Measures required ingredients needed for specific food item being prepared. Slices meats, cheeses, and vegetables, using knives and food-slicing machines. Prepares specialty foods such as pizzas, fish and chips, sandwiches, and tacos, following specific methods, usually requiring short preparation time. Prepares dough, following recipe.

Personality Type: Realistic. Realistic occupations frequently involve work activities that include practical, hands-on problems and solutions. They often deal with plants, animals, and real-world materials like wood, tools, and machinery. Many of the occupations require working outside and do not involve a lot of paperwork or working closely with others.

Abilities: Oral Comprehension—The ability to listen to and understand information and ideas presented verbally. Wrist-Finger Speed—The ability to make fast, simple, repeated movements of the fingers, hands, and wrists. Manual Dexterity—The ability to quickly make coordinated movements of one hand, a hand together with its arm, or two hands, to grasp, manipulate, or assemble objects. Written Comprehension—The ability to read and understand information and ideas presented in writing. Information Ordering—The ability to correctly follow a given rule or set of rules in order to arrange things or actions in a certain order. The things or actions can include numbers, letters, words, pictures, procedures, sentences, and mathematical or logical operations.

Skills: Active Listening—Listening to what other people are saying; asking questions as appropriate. Operation and Control—Controlling operations of equipment or systems. Equipment Selection—Determining the kind of tools and equipment needed to do a job. Service Orientation—Actively looking for ways to help people. Mathematics—Using mathematics to solve problems. Product Inspection—Inspecting and evaluating the quality of products. Reading Comprehension—Understanding written information in work-related documents.

Generalized Work Activities: Handling and Moving Objects—Using one's hands and arms in handling, installing, forming, positioning, and moving materials, or in manipulating things. Includes the use of keyboards. Monitoring Processes, Materials, Surroundings—Monitoring and reviewing information from materials, events, or the environment, often to detect problems or to find out when things are finished. Performing for/Working with Public—Performing for people or dealing directly with the public, including serving persons in restaurants and stores and receiving clients or guests. Getting Information Needed to Do the Job—

Observing, receiving, and otherwise obtaining information from all relevant sources. Controlling Machines and Processes—Using either control mechanisms or direct physical activity to operate machines or processes. Does not involve working with computers or vehicles. Communicating with Persons Outside Organization—Communicating with persons outside the organization. Representing the organization to customers, the public, government, and other external sources. Exchanging information face-to-face, in writing, or via telephone/electronic transfer.

Cooks, Short Order

Prepare and cook to order a variety of foods that require only a short preparation time. Take customers' orders and serve patrons at counters or tables. Takes order from customer. Cooks foods requiring short preparation time, according to customer requirements. Accepts payment, makes change, or writes charge slip. Carves meats, makes sandwiches, and brews coffee. Completes order from steamtable; serves customer at table or counter. Cleans food preparation equipment, work area, and counter or tables.

Personality Type: Realistic. Realistic occupations frequently involve work activities that include practical, hands-on problems and solutions. They often deal with plants, animals, and real-world materials like wood, tools, and machinery. Many of the occupations require working outside and do not involve a lot of paperwork or working closely with others.

Abilities: Oral Comprehension—The ability to listen to and understand information and ideas presented verbally. Wrist-Finger Speed—The ability to make fast, simple, repeated movements of the fingers, hands, and wrists. Number Facility—The ability to add, subtract, multiply, or divide quickly and correctly. Manual Dexterity—The ability to quickly make coordinated movements of one hand, a hand together with its arm, or two hands, to grasp, manipulate, or assemble objects. Time Sharing—The ability to efficiently shift back and forth between two or more activities or sources of information such as speech, sounds, or touch.

Skills: Active Listening—Listening to what other people are saying; asking questions as appropriate. Service

Orientation—Actively looking for ways to help people. Mathematics—Using mathematics to solve problems. Writing—Communicating effectively with others in writing as indicated by the needs of the audience. Social Perceptiveness—Being aware of other people's reactions and understanding why people react the way they do.

Generalized Work Activities: Handling and Moving Objects—Using one's hands and arms in handling, installing, forming, positioning, and moving materials, or in manipulating things. Includes the use of keyboards. Performing for/Working with Public—Performing for

people or dealing directly with the public, including serving persons in restaurants and stores and receiving clients or guests. Getting Information Needed to Do the Job—Observing, receiving, and otherwise obtaining information from all relevant sources. Monitoring Processes, Materials, Surroundings—Monitoring and reviewing information from materials, events, or the environment, often to detect problems or to find out when things are finished. Controlling Machines and Processes—Using either control mechanisms or direct physical activity to operate machines or processes. Does not involve working with computers or vehicles.

Ski Patrol Workers and Life Guards

- ▲ Growth: 19%
- ▲ Annual Job Openings: 23,282
- ▲ Yearly Earnings: $17,470
- ▲ Education Required: Short-term O-J-T
- ▲ Self-Employed: 0%
- ▲ Part-Time: 51.4%

Lifeguards, Ski Patrol, and Other Recreational Protective Service Workers

Monitor recreational areas such as pools, beaches, or ski slopes, to provide assistance and protection to participants. Includes lifeguards and ski patrollers. Rescues distressed persons, using rescue techniques and equipment. Instructs participants in skiing, swimming, or other recreational activities. Participates in recreational demonstrations to entertain resort guests. Inspects facilities for cleanliness. Maintains order in recreational areas. Maintains information on emergency medical treatment and weather and beach conditions, using report forms. Inspects recreational equipment such as rope tows, T-bar, J-bar, and chair lifts, for safety hazards, damage, or wear. Contacts emergency medical services

in case of serious injury. Observes activities in assigned area with binoculars, to detect hazards, disturbances, or safety infractions. Patrols or monitors recreational areas such as trails, slopes, and swimming areas, on foot, in vehicle, or from tower. Cautions recreational participant regarding inclement weather, unsafe areas, or illegal conduct. Examines injured persons and administers first aid or cardiopulmonary resuscitation, utilizing training and medical supplies and equipment.

Personality Type: Realistic. Realistic occupations frequently involve work activities that include practical, hands-on problems and solutions. They often deal with plants, animals, and real-world materials like wood, tools, and machinery. Many of the occupations require working outside and do not involve a lot of paperwork or working closely with others.

Abilities: Far Vision—The ability to see details at a distance. Oral Expression—The ability to communicate information and ideas verbally so others will understand. Stamina—The ability to exert one's self physically over long periods of time without getting winded or out of breath. Problem Sensitivity—The ability to tell when something is wrong or is likely to go wrong. Does not involve solving the problem, only recognizing there is a problem. Gross Body Coordination—The ability to coordinate the movement of the arms, legs, and torso together in activities where the whole body is in motion.

Skills: Instructing—Teaching others how to do something. Service Orientation—Actively looking for ways to help people. Problem Identification—Identifying the nature of problems. Judgment and Decision Making—Weighing the relative costs and benefits of a potential action. Social Perceptiveness—Being aware of other people's reactions and understanding why people react the way they do.

Generalized Work Activities: Monitoring Processes, Materials, Surroundings—Monitoring and reviewing information from materials, events, or the environment, often to detect problems or to find out when things are finished. Assisting and Caring for Others—Providing assistance or personal care to others. Performing General Physical Activities—Performing physical activities that require moving one's whole body, such as in climbing, lifting, balancing, walking, and stooping. Performing activities that often also require considerable use of the arms and legs, such as in the physical handling of materials. Inspecting Equipment, Structures, Materials—Inspecting or diagnosing equipment, structures, or materials to identify the causes of errors or other problems or defects. Getting Information Needed to Do the Job—Observing, receiving, and otherwise obtaining information from all relevant sources. Making Decisions and Solving Problems—Combining, evaluating, and analyzing information and data to make decisions and solve problems. Involves making decisions about the relative importance of information and choosing the best solution.

Social Scientists

- ▲ Growth: 13%
- ▲ Annual Job Openings: 6,928
- ▲ Yearly Earnings: $38,990
- ▲ Education Required: Master's degree
- ▲ Self-Employed: 5.2%
- ▲ Part-Time: 18.1%

Anthropologists

Research or study the origins and physical, social, and cultural development and behavior of humans and of the cultures and organizations they have created. Applies anthropological concepts to current problems. Studies cultures, particularly preindustrial and non-Western societies, including religious, economic, mythological, traditional, intellectual, and artistic life. Studies physical and physiological adaptations to differing environments and hereditary characteristics of living populations. Applies anthropological data and techniques to solution of problems in human relations. Formulates general laws of cultural development, general rules of social and cultural behavior, or general value orientations. Observes and measures bodily variations and physical attributes of existing human types. Studies growth patterns, sexual differences, and aging phenomena of current and past human groups. Gathers, analyzes, and reports data on human physique, social customs, and artifacts such as weapons, tools, pottery, and clothing. Studies museum collections of skeletal remains and human fossils to determine their meaning in terms of long-range human evolution. Studies relationships between language and culture and socialinguistic studies, relationship between individual personality and culture, or complex industrialized societies.

Personality Type: Investigative. Investigative occupations frequently involve working with ideas and require an extensive amount of thinking. These occupations can involve searching for facts and figuring out problems mentally.

Abilities: Oral Comprehension—The ability to listen to and understand information and ideas presented verbally. Written Expression—The ability to communicate information and ideas in writing so others will understand. Inductive Reasoning—The ability to combine separate pieces of information, or specific answers to problems, to form general rules or conclusions. Includes coming up with a logical explanation for why a series of seemingly unrelated events occur together. Written Comprehension—The ability to read and understand information and ideas presented in writing. Fluency of Ideas—The ability to come up with a number of ideas about a given topic. Emphasis is on the number of ideas produced and not the quality, correctness, or creativity of the ideas.

Skills: Active Learning—Working with new material or information to grasp its implications. Writing—Communicating effectively with others in writing as indicated by the needs of the audience. Information Gathering—Knowing how to find information and identifying essential information. Reading Comprehension—Understanding written information in work-related documents. Information Organization—Finding ways to structure or classify multiple pieces of information. Science—Using scientific methods to solve problems.

Generalized Work Activities: Analyzing Data or Information—Identifying underlying principles, reasons, or facts by breaking down information or data into separate parts. Getting Information Needed to Do the Job—Observing, receiving, and otherwise obtaining information from all relevant sources. Processing Information—Compiling, coding, categorizing, calculating, tabulating, auditing, verifying, or processing information or data. Identifying Objects, Actions, and Events—Identifying information received by making estimates or categorizations, recognizing differences or similarities, or sensing changes in circumstances or events. Judging Qualities—Making judgments about or assessing the value, importance, or quality of things, services, or other people's work.

Archeologists

Conduct research to reconstruct record of past human life and culture from human remains, artifacts, architectural features, and structures recovered through excavation, underwater recovery, or other means of discovery. Studies, classifies, and interprets artifacts, architectural features, and types of structures recovered by excavation, to determine age and cultural identity. Establishes chronological sequence of development of each culture from simpler to more advanced levels.

Personality Type: Investigative. Investigative occupations frequently involve working with ideas and require an extensive amount of thinking. These occupations can involve searching for facts and figuring out problems mentally.

Abilities: Category Flexibility—The ability to produce many rules so that each rule tells how to group or combine a set of things in a different way. Inductive Reasoning—The ability to combine separate pieces of information, or specific answers to problems, to form general rules or conclusions. Includes coming up with a logical explanation for why a series of seemingly unrelated events occur together. Written Comprehension—The ability to read and understand information and ideas presented in writing. Deductive Reasoning—The ability to apply general rules to specific problems to come up with logical answers. Involves deciding if an answer makes sense. Information Ordering—The ability to correctly follow a given rule or set of rules in order to arrange things or actions in a certain order. The things or actions can include numbers, letters, words, pictures, procedures, sentences, and mathematical or logical operations.

Skills: Synthesis/Reorganization—Reorganizing information to get a better approach to problems or tasks. Information Gathering—Knowing how to find information and identifying essential information. Information Organization—Finding ways to structure or classify multiple pieces of information. Active Learning—Working with new material or information to grasp its implications. Critical Thinking—Using logic and analysis to identify the strengths and weaknesses of different approaches. Science—Using scientific methods to solve problems.

Generalized Work Activities: Identifying Objects, Actions, and Events—Identifying information received by making estimates or categorizations, recognizing differences or similarities, or sensing changes in circumstances or events. Getting Information Needed to Do the Job—Observing, receiving, and otherwise obtaining information from all relevant sources. Processing Information—Compiling, coding, categorizing, calculating, tabulating, auditing, verifying, or processing information or data. Judging Qualities—Making judgments about or assessing the value, importance, or quality of things, services, or other people's work. Analyzing Data or Information—Identifying underlying principles, reasons, or facts by breaking down information or data into separate parts. Interpreting Meaning of Information to Others—Translating or explaining what information means and how it can be understood or used to support responses or feedback to others. Documenting/Recording Information—Entering, transcribing, recording, storing, or maintaining information in either written form or by electronic/magnetic recording.

Historians

Research, analyze, record, and interpret the past as recorded in sources such as government and institutional records, newspapers, and other periodicals, photographs, interviews, films, and unpublished manuscripts such as personal diaries and letters. Coordinates activities of workers engaged in cataloging and filing materials. Consults experts or witnesses of historical events. Organizes and evaluates data on basis of authenticity and relative significance. Translates or requests translation of reference materials. Speaks before various groups, organizations, and clubs to promote societal aims and activities. Edits society publications. Reviews publications and exhibits prepared by others prior to public release, to ensure historical accuracy of presentations. Advises or consults with individuals, institutions, and commercial organizations on technological evolution or customs peculiar to certain historical period. Consults with or advises other individuals on historical authenticity of various materials. Reviews and collects data such as books, pamphlets, periodicals, and rare newspapers, to provide source material for research. Traces historical development in fields, such as economics, sociology, or philosophy. Conducts historical research on subjects of import to society; presents findings and theories in textbooks, journals, and other publications. Assembles historical data by consulting sources such as archives, court records, diaries, news files, and miscellaneous published and unpublished materials.

Personality Type: Investigative. Investigative occupations frequently involve working with ideas and require an extensive amount of thinking. These occupations can involve searching for facts and figuring out problems mentally.

Abilities: Written Comprehension—The ability to read and understand information and ideas presented in writing. Written Expression—The ability to communicate information and ideas in writing so others will understand. Oral Expression—The ability to communicate information and ideas verbally so others will understand. Oral Comprehension—The ability to listen to and understand information and ideas presented verbally. Memorization—The ability to remember information such as words, numbers, pictures, and procedures. Speech Clarity—The ability to speak clearly so that what is said is understandable to a listener.

Skills: Reading Comprehension—Understanding written information in work-related documents. Writing—Communicating effectively with others in writing as indicated by the needs of the audience. Information Gathering—Knowing how to find information and identifying essential information. Information Organization—Finding ways to structure or classify multiple pieces of information. Speaking—Talking to others to effectively convey information.

Generalized Work Activities: Getting Information Needed to Do the Job—Observing, receiving, and otherwise obtaining information from all relevant sources. Analyzing Data or Information—Identifying underlying principles, reasons, or facts by breaking down information or data into separate parts. Interpreting Meaning of Information to Others—Translating or explaining what information means and how it can be understood or used to support responses or feedback to others. Processing Information—Compiling, coding, categorizing, calculating, tabulating, auditing, verifying, or processing information or data. Documenting/Recording Information—Entering, transcribing, recording, storing, or maintaining information in either written form or by electronic/magnetic recording. Judging Qualities—Making judgments about or assessing the value, importance, or quality of things, services, or other people's work.

Political Scientists

Study the origin, development, and operation of political systems. Research a wide range of subjects such as relations between the United States and foreign countries, the beliefs and institutions of foreign nations, or the politics of a small town or major metropolis. Study topics such as public opinion, political decision making, and ideology. Analyze the structure and operation of governments and various other political entities. Conduct public opinion surveys; analyze election results and public documents. Consults with government officials, civic bodies, research agencies, and political parties. Recommends programs and policies to institutions and organizations. Prepares reports detailing findings and conclusions. Conducts research into political philosophy and theories of political systems, such as governmental institutions, public laws, and international law. Organizes and conducts public opinion surveys and interprets results. Analyzes and interprets results of studies; prepares reports detailing findings, recommendations, or conclusions.

Personality Type: Investigative. Investigative occupations frequently involve working with ideas and require an extensive amount of thinking. These occupations can involve searching for facts and figuring out problems mentally.

Abilities: Written Comprehension—The ability to read and understand information and ideas presented in writing. Oral Comprehension—The ability to listen to and understand information and ideas presented verbally. Oral Expression—The ability to communicate information and ideas verbally so others will understand. Written Expression—The ability to communicate information and ideas in writing so others will understand. Deductive Reasoning—The ability to apply general rules to specific problems to come up with logical answers. Involves deciding if an answer makes sense. Inductive Reasoning—The ability to combine separate pieces of information, or specific answers to problems, to form general rules or conclusions. Includes coming up with a logical explanation for why a series of seemingly unrelated events occur together.

Skills: Writing—Communicating effectively with others in writing as indicated by the needs of the audience. Information Gathering—Knowing how to find information and identifying essential information. Reading Comprehension—Understanding written information in work-related documents. Critical Thinking—Using logic and analysis to identify the strengths and weaknesses of different approaches. Speaking—Talking to others to effectively convey information.

Generalized Work Activities: Analyzing Data or Information—Identifying underlying principles, reasons, or facts by breaking down information or data into separate parts. Providing Consultation and Advice to Others—Providing consultation and expert advice to management or other groups on technical, systems-related, or process-related topics. Processing Information—Compiling, coding, categorizing, calculating, tabulating, auditing, verifying, or processing information or data. Communicating with Persons Outside Organization—Communicating with persons outside the organization. Representing the organization to customers, the public, government, and other external sources. Exchanging information face-to-face, in writing, or via telephone/electronic transfer. Getting Information Needed to Do the Job—Observing, receiving, and otherwise obtaining information from all relevant sources. Identifying Objects, Actions, and Events —Identifying information received by making estimates or categorizations, recognizing differences or similarities, or sensing changes in circumstances or events.

Sociologists

Study human society and social behavior by examining the groups and social institutions that people form, as well as various social, religious, political, and business

organizations. **Study the behavior and interaction of groups, trace their origin and growth, and analyze the influence of group activities on individual members.** Develops intervention procedures, utilizing techniques such as interviews, consultations, role playing, and participant observation of group interaction, to facilitate solution. Directs work of statistical clerks, statisticians, and others. Monitors group interaction and role affiliations to evaluate progress and to determine need for additional change. Consults with lawmakers, administrators, and other officials who deal with problems of social change. Interprets methods and findings to individuals within agency and community. Collaborates with research workers in other disciplines. Analyzes and evaluates data. Observes group interaction and interviews group members to identify problems and collect data related to factors such as group organization and authority relationships. Collects and analyzes scientific data concerning social phenomena such as community associations, social institutions, ethnic minorities, and social change. Develops research designs on basis of existing knowledge and evolving theory. Prepares publications and reports on subjects such as social factors affecting health, demographic characteristics, and social and racial discrimination in society. Constructs and tests methods of data collection. Develops approaches to solving group problems, based on findings, and incorporating sociological research and study in related disciplines. Plans and directs research on crime and prevention, group relations in industrial organization, urban communities, and physical environment and technology. Collects information and makes judgments, through observation, interview, and review of documents.

Personality Type: Investigative. Investigative occupations frequently involve working with ideas and require an extensive amount of thinking. These occupations can involve searching for facts and figuring out problems mentally.

Abilities: Written Expression—The ability to communicate information and ideas in writing so others will understand. Oral Comprehension—The ability to listen to and understand information and ideas presented verbally. Written Comprehension—The ability to read and understand information and ideas presented in writing. Oral Expression—The ability to communicate information and ideas verbally so others will understand. Deductive Reasoning—The ability to apply general rules to specific problems to come up with logical answers. Involves deciding if an answer makes sense.

Skills: Information Gathering—Knowing how to find information and identifying essential information. Reading Comprehension—Understanding written information in work-related documents. Critical Thinking—Using logic and analysis to identify the strengths and weaknesses of different approaches. Writing—Communicating effectively with others in writing as indicated by the needs of the audience.

Generalized Work Activities: Analyzing Data or Information—Identifying underlying principles, reasons, or facts by breaking down information or data into separate parts. Processing Information—Compiling, coding, categorizing, calculating, tabulating, auditing, verifying, or processing information or data. Getting Information Needed to Do the Job—Observing, receiving, and otherwise obtaining information from all relevant sources. Identifying Objects, Actions, and Events—Identifying information received by making estimates or categorizations, recognizing differences or similarities, or sensing changes in circumstances or events. Making Decisions and Solving Problems—Combining, evaluating, and analyzing information and data to make decisions and solve problems. Involves making decisions about the relative importance of information and choosing the best solution.

Social Workers

- ▲ Growth: 36%
- ▲ Annual Job Openings: 29,630
- ▲ Yearly Earnings: $30,590
- ▲ Education Required: Bachelor's degree
- ▲ Self-Employed: 3.1%
- ▲ Part-Time: 11.9%

Child, Family, and School Social Workers

Provide social services and assistance to improve the social and psychological functioning of children and their families and to maximize the family well-being and the academic functioning of children. Assist single parents, arrange adoptions, and find foster homes for abandoned or abused children. In schools, address such problems as teenage pregnancy, misbehavior, and truancy. Advise teachers on how to deal with problem children. Interviews individuals to assess social and emotional capabilities, physical and mental impairments, and financial needs. Investigates home conditions to determine suitability of foster or adoptive home or to protect children from harmful environment. Serves as liaison between student, home, school, family service agencies, child guidance clinics, courts, protective services, doctors, and clergy members. Consults with parents, teachers, and other school personnel to determine causes of problems and effect solutions. Arranges for medical, psychiatric, and other tests that may disclose cause of difficulties and indicate remedial measures. Counsels students whose behavior, school progress, or mental or physical impairment indicates need for assistance. Counsels parents with child-rearing problems. Counsels children and youth with difficulties in social adjustments. Assists travelers, including runaways, migrants, transients, refugees, repatriated Americans, and problem families. Develops program content; organizes and leads activities planned to enhance social development of individual members and accomplishment of group goals. Leads group counseling sessions to provide support in such areas as grief, stress, or chemical dependency. Reviews service plan and performs follow-up to determine quantity and quality of service provided to client. Places children in foster or adoptive homes, institutions, or medical treatment centers. Evaluates personal characteristics of foster home or adoption applicants. Counsels individuals or family members regarding behavior modifications, rehabilitation, social adjustments, financial assistance, vocational training, child care, or medical care. Collects supplementary information, such as employment, medical records, or school reports. Maintains case history records and prepares reports. Refers client to community resources for needed assistance. Determines client's eligibility for financial assistance.

Personality Type: Social. Social occupations frequently involve working with, communicating with, and teaching people. These occupations often involve helping or providing service to others.

Abilities: Oral Expression—The ability to communicate information and ideas verbally so others will understand. Oral Comprehension—The ability to listen to and understand information and ideas presented verbally. Written Expression—The ability to communicate information and ideas in writing so others will understand. Problem Sensitivity—The ability to tell when something is wrong or is likely to go wrong. Does not involve solving the problem, only recognizing there is a problem. Written Comprehension—The ability to read and understand information and ideas presented in writing.

Skills: Social Perceptiveness—Being aware of other people's reactions and understanding why people react the way they do. Service Orientation—Actively looking for ways to help people. Speaking—Talking to others to effectively convey information. Active Listening— Listening to what other people are saying; asking questions as appropriate. Problem Identification— Identifying the nature of problems.

Generalized Work Activities: Establishing and Maintaining Relationships—Developing constructive and cooperative working relationships with others. Assisting and Caring for Others—Providing assistance or personal care to others. Getting Information Needed to Do the Job—Observing, receiving, and otherwise obtaining information from all relevant sources. Communicating with Persons Outside Organization— Communicating with persons outside the organization. Representing the organization to customers, the public, government, and other external sources. Exchanging information face-to-face, in writing, or via telephone/ electronic transfer. Judging Qualities—Making judgments about or assessing the value, importance, or quality of things, services, or other people's work.

Medical and Public Health Social Workers

Provide persons, families, or vulnerable populations with the psychosocial support needed to cope with chronic, acute, or terminal illnesses such as Alzheimer's, cancer, or AIDS. Services include advising family care givers, providing patient education and counseling, and making necessary referrals for other social services. Counsels clients and patients, individually and in group sessions, to assist in overcoming dependencies, adjusting to life, and making changes. Formulates or coordinates program plan for treatment, care, and rehabilitation of client or patient, based on social work experience and knowledge. Monitors, evaluates, and records client progress according to measurable goals described in treatment and care plan. Interviews clients, reviews records, and confers with other professionals to evaluate mental or physical condition of client or patient. Counsels family members to assist in understanding, dealing with, and supporting client or patient. Modifies treatment plan

to comply with changes in client's status. Intervenes as advocate for client or patient to resolve emergency problems in crisis situation. Refers patient, client, or family to community resources to assist in recovery from mental or physical illness. Supervises and directs other workers providing services to client or patient. Plans and conducts programs to prevent substance abuse or improve health and counseling services in community.

Personality Type: Social. Social occupations frequently involve working with, communicating with, and teaching people. These occupations often involve helping or providing service to others.

Abilities: Oral Comprehension—The ability to listen to and understand information and ideas presented verbally. Problem Sensitivity—The ability to tell when something is wrong or is likely to go wrong. Does not involve solving the problem, only recognizing there is a problem. Oral Expression—The ability to communicate information and ideas verbally so others will understand. Speech Clarity—The ability to speak clearly so that what is said is understandable to a listener. Written Comprehension—The ability to read and understand information and ideas presented in writing.

Skills: Judgment and Decision Making—Weighing the relative costs and benefits of a potential action. Social Perceptiveness—Being aware of other people's reactions and understanding why people react the way they do. Speaking—Talking to others to effectively convey information. Service Orientation—Actively looking for ways to help people. Active Learning—Working with new material or information to grasp its implications.

Generalized Work Activities: Communicating with Persons Outside Organization—Communicating with persons outside the organization. Representing the organization to customers, the public, government, and other external sources. Exchanging information face-to-face, in writing, or via telephone/electronic transfer. Getting Information Needed to Do the Job—Observing, receiving, and otherwise obtaining information from all relevant sources. Establishing and Maintaining Relationships—Developing constructive and cooperative working relationships with others. Assisting and Caring for Others—Providing assistance or personal care to others. Identifying Objects, Actions, and

Events—Identifying information received by making estimates or categorizations, recognizing differences or similarities, or sensing changes in circumstances or events.

Mental Health and Substance Abuse Social Workers

Assess and treat individuals with mental, emotional, or substance abuse problems, including abuse of alcohol, tobacco, and/or other drugs. Participate in individual and group therapy, crisis intervention, case management, client advocacy, prevention, and education. Counsels clients and patients, individually and in group sessions, to assist in overcoming dependencies, adjusting to life, and making changes. Formulates or coordinates program plan for treatment, care, and rehabilitation of client or patient, based on social work experience and knowledge. Counsels family members to assist in understanding, dealing with, and supporting client or patient. Interviews clients, reviews records, and confers with other professionals to evaluate mental or physical condition of client or patient. Monitors, evaluates, and records client progress according to measurable goals described in treatment and care plan. Refers patient, client, or family to community resources to assist in recovery from mental or physical illness. Modifies treatment plan to comply with changes in client's status. Supervises and directs other workers providing services to client or patient. Plans and conducts programs to prevent substance abuse or improve health and counseling services in community. Intervenes as advocate for client or patient to resolve emergency problems in crisis situation.

Personality Type: Social. Social occupations frequently involve working with, communicating with, and teaching people. These occupations often involve helping or providing service to others.

Abilities: Oral Comprehension—The ability to listen to and understand information and ideas presented verbally. Oral Expression—The ability to communicate information and ideas verbally so others will understand. Speech Clarity—The ability to speak clearly so that what is said is understandable to a listener. Problem Sensitivity—The ability to tell when something is wrong or is likely to go wrong. Does not involve solving the problem, only recognizing there is a problem. Written Comprehension—The ability to read and understand information and ideas presented in writing.

Skills: Social Perceptiveness—Being aware of other people's reactions and understanding why people react the way they do. Judgment and Decision Making—Weighing the relative costs and benefits of a potential action. Active Learning—Working with new material or information to grasp its implications. Speaking—Talking to others to effectively convey information. Service Orientation—Actively looking for ways to help people.

Generalized Work Activities: Communicating with Persons Outside Organization—Communicating with persons outside the organization. Representing the organization to customers, the public, government, and other external sources. Exchanging information face-to-face, in writing, or via telephone/electronic transfer. Getting Information Needed to Do the Job—Observing, receiving, and otherwise obtaining information from all relevant sources. Establishing and Maintaining Relationships—Developing constructive and cooperative working relationships with others. Assisting and Caring for Others—Providing assistance or personal care to others. Identifying Objects, Actions, and Events—Identifying information received by making estimates or categorizations, recognizing differences or similarities, or sensing changes in circumstances or events.

Solderers and Brazers

▲ Growth: 14%
▲ Annual Job Openings: 7,519
▲ Yearly Earnings: $17,600
▲ Education Required: Short-term O-J-T
▲ Self-Employed: 3.7%
▲ Part-Time: 8.6%

Brazers

Braze together components to assemble fabricated metal parts, using torch or welding machine and flux. Removes workpiece from fixture, using tongs; cools workpiece, using air or water. Adjusts electric current and timing cycle of resistance welding machine to heat metal to bonding temperature. Connects hoses from torch to regulator valves and cylinders of oxygen and specified fuel gas, acetylene or natural. Brushes flux onto joint of workpiece or dips braze rod into flux to prevent oxidation of metal. Cleans joints of workpieces, by using wire brush or by dipping joints into cleaning solution. Cuts carbon electrodes to specified size and shape, using cutoff saw. Aligns and secures workpieces in fixtures, jigs, or vise, using rule, square, or template. Examines seam and rebrazes defective joints or broken parts. Melts and separates brazed joints to remove and straighten damaged or misaligned components, using hand torch or furnace. Guides torch and rod along joint of workpieces to heat to brazing temperature, melt braze alloy, and bond workpieces together. Selects torch tip, flux, and brazing alloy from data charts or work order. Turns valves to start flow of gases; lights flame; adjusts valves to obtain desired color and size of flame.

Personality Type: Realistic. Realistic occupations frequently involve work activities that include practical, hands-on problems and solutions. They often deal with plants, animals, and real-world materials like wood, tools, and machinery. Many of the occupations require working outside and do not involve a lot of paperwork or working closely with others.

Abilities: Near Vision—The ability to see details of objects at a close range. Manual Dexterity—The ability to quickly make coordinated movements of one hand, a hand together with its arm, or two hands, to grasp, manipulate, or assemble objects. Visualization—The ability to imagine how something will look after it is moved around or when its parts are moved or rearranged. Arm-Hand Steadiness—The ability to keep the hand and arm steady while making an arm movement or while holding the arm and hand in one position. Information Ordering—The ability to correctly follow a given rule or set of rules in order to arrange things or actions in a certain order. The things or actions can include numbers, letters, words, pictures, procedures, sentences, and mathematical or logical operations.

Skills: Operation and Control—Controlling operations of equipment or systems. Product Inspection—Inspecting and evaluating the quality of products. Operation Monitoring—Watching gauges, dials, or other indicators to make sure a machine is working properly. Equipment Selection—Determining the kind of tools and equipment needed to do a job. Monitoring—Assessing how well one is doing when learning or doing something.

Generalized Work Activities: Handling and Moving Objects—Using one's hands and arms in handling, installing, forming, positioning, and moving materials, or in manipulating things. Includes the use of keyboards. Controlling Machines and Processes—Using either control mechanisms or direct physical activity to operate machines or processes. Does not involve working with computers or vehicles. Monitoring Processes, Materials, Surroundings—Monitoring and reviewing information from materials, events, or the environment, often to detect problems or to find out when things are finished.

Inspecting Equipment, Structures, Materials—Inspecting or diagnosing equipment, structures, or materials to identify the causes of errors or other problems or defects. Getting Information Needed to Do the Job—Observing, receiving, and otherwise obtaining information from all relevant sources.

Solderers

Solder together components to assemble fabricated metal products, using soldering iron. Grinds, cuts, buffs, or bends edges of workpieces to be joined to ensure snug fit, using power grinder and hand tools. Dips workpieces into molten solder or places solder strip between seams and heats seam with iron to band items together. Applies flux to workpiece surfaces in preparation for soldering. Melts and separates soldered joints to repair misaligned or damaged assemblies, using soldering equipment. Cleans tip of soldering iron, using chemical solution or cleaning compound. Removes workpieces from molten solder and holds parts together until color indicates that solder has set. Melts and applies solder to fill holes, indentations, and seams of fabricated metal products, using soldering equipment. Aligns and clamps workpieces together, using rule, square, or hand tools; positions items in fixtures, jigs, or vise. Heats soldering iron or workpiece to specified temperature for soldering, using gas flame or electric current. Melts and applies solder along adjoining edges of workpieces to solder joints, using soldering iron, gas torch, or electric-ultrasonic equipment. Cleans workpieces, using chemical solution, file, wire brush, or grinder.

Personality Type: Realistic. Realistic occupations frequently involve work activities that include practical, hands-on problems and solutions. They often deal with plants, animals, and real-world materials like wood, tools, and machinery. Many of the occupations require working outside and do not involve a lot of paperwork or working closely with others.

Abilities: Manual Dexterity—The ability to quickly make coordinated movements of one hand, a hand together with its arm, or two hands, to grasp, manipulate, or assemble objects. Arm-Hand Steadiness—The ability to keep the hand and arm steady while making an arm movement or while holding the arm and hand in one position. Wrist-Finger Speed—The ability to make fast, simple, repeated movements of the fingers, hands, and wrists. Near Vision—The ability to see details of objects at a close range. Finger Dexterity—The ability to make precisely coordinated movements of the fingers of one or both hands to grasp, manipulate, or assemble very small objects.

Skills: Equipment Selection—Determining the kind of tools and equipment needed to do a job. Operation and Control—Controlling operations of equipment or systems. Monitoring—Assessing how well one is doing when learning or doing something. Product Inspection—Inspecting and evaluating the quality of products. Equipment Maintenance—Performing routine maintenance and determining when and what kind of maintenance is needed. Operation Monitoring—Watching gauges, dials, or other indicators to make sure a machine is working properly.

Generalized Work Activities: Handling and Moving Objects—Using one's hands and arms in handling, installing, forming, positioning, and moving materials, or in manipulating things. Includes the use of keyboards. Controlling Machines and Processes—Using either control mechanisms or direct physical activity to operate machines or processes. Does not involve working with computers or vehicles. Monitoring Processes, Materials, Surroundings—Monitoring and reviewing information from materials, events, or the environment, often to detect problems or to find out when things are finished. Getting Information Needed to Do the Job—Observing, receiving, and otherwise obtaining information from all relevant sources. Performing General Physical Activities—Performing physical activities that require moving one's whole body, such as in climbing, lifting, balancing, walking, and stooping. Performing activities that often also require considerable use of the arms and legs, such as in the physical handling of materials.

Special Education Teachers

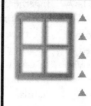

- ▲ Growth: 34%
- ▲ Annual Job Openings: 36,540
- ▲ Yearly Earnings: $37,850
- ▲ Education Required: Bachelor's degree
- ▲ Self-Employed: 0%
- ▲ Part-Time: 12.9%

Special Education Teachers, Middle School

Teach middle school subjects to educationally and physically handicapped students. Includes teachers who specialize and work with audibly and visually handicapped students and those who teach basic academic and life processes skills to the mentally impaired. Provides consistent learning reinforcement and continuous feedback to students. Instructs students, using special educational strategies and techniques to improve sensory-motor and perceptual-motor development, memory, language, and cognition. Instructs students in daily living skills required for independent maintenance and economic self-sufficiency, such as hygiene, safety, and food preparation. Selects and teaches reading material and math problems related to everyday life of individual students. Confers with parents, administrators, testing specialists, social workers, and others to develop individual educational plan for students. Observes, evaluates, and prepares reports on progress of students. Works with students to increase motivation. Confers with other staff members to plan programs designed to promote educational, physical, and social development of students. Administers and interprets results of ability and achievement tests. Plans curriculum and other instructional materials to meet students' needs, considering such factors as physical, emotional, and educational abilities. Instructs students in academic subjects, utilizing various teaching techniques such as phonetics, multisensory learning, and repetition, to reinforce learning. Teaches socially acceptable behavior, employing techniques such as behavior modification and positive reinforcement. Meets with parents to provide support, to guide them in using community resources, and to help them develop skills in dealing with students' learning impairment.

Personality Type: Social. Social occupations frequently involve working with, communicating with, and teaching people. These occupations often involve helping or providing service to others.

Abilities: Oral Expression—The ability to communicate information and ideas verbally so others will understand. Written Comprehension—The ability to read and understand information and ideas presented in writing. Problem Sensitivity—The ability to tell when something is wrong or is likely to go wrong. Does not involve solving the problem, only recognizing there is a problem. Speech Clarity—The ability to speak clearly so that what is said is understandable to a listener. Written Expression—The ability to communicate information and ideas in writing so others will understand. Oral Comprehension—The ability to listen to and understand information and ideas presented verbally.

Skills: Instructing—Teaching others how to do something. Learning Strategies—Using multiple approaches when learning or teaching new things. Social Perceptiveness—Being aware of other people's reactions and understanding why people react the way they do. Speaking—Talking to others to effectively convey information. Implementation Planning—Developing approaches for implementing an idea.

Generalized Work Activities: Teaching Others—Identifying educational needs, developing formal training programs or classes, and teaching or instructing others. Making Decisions and Solving Problems—

Combining, evaluating, and analyzing information and data to make decisions and solve problems. Involves making decisions about the relative importance of information and choosing the best solution. Interpreting Meaning of Information to Others—Translating or explaining what information means and how it can be understood or used to support responses or feedback to others. Establishing and Maintaining Relationships—Developing constructive and cooperative working relationships with others. Communicating with Persons Outside Organization—Communicating with persons outside the organization. Representing the organization to customers, the public, government, and other external sources. Exchanging information face-to-face, in writing, or via telephone/electronic transfer. Getting Information Needed to Do the Job—Observing, receiving, and otherwise obtaining information from all relevant sources.

Special Education Teachers, Preschool, Kindergarten, and Elementary School

Teach elementary school and preschool subjects to educationally and physically handicapped students. Includes teachers who specialize and work with audibly and visually handicapped students and those who teach basic academic and life processes skills to the mentally impaired. Works with students to increase motivation. Confers with other staff members to plan programs designed to promote educational, physical, and social development of students. Plans curriculum and other instructional materials to meet students' needs, considering such factors as physical, emotional, and educational abilities. Instructs students in daily living skills required for independent maintenance and economic self-sufficiency, such as hygiene, safety, and food preparation. Instructs students in academic subjects, utilizing various teaching techniques such as phonetics, multisensory learning, and repetition, to reinforce learning. Instructs students, using special educational strategies and techniques to improve sensory-motor and perceptual-motor development,

memory, language, and cognition. Provides consistent learning reinforcement and continuous feedback to students. Observes, evaluates, and prepares reports on progress of students. Meets with parents to provide support, to guide them in using community resources, and to help them develop skills in dealing with students' learning impairment. Selects and teaches reading material and math problems related to everyday life of individual students. Administers and interprets results of ability and achievement tests. Teaches socially acceptable behavior, employing techniques such as behavior modification and positive reinforcement. Confers with parents, administrators, testing specialists, social workers, and others to develop individual educational plan for students.

Personality Type: Social. Social occupations frequently involve working with, communicating with, and teaching people. These occupations often involve helping or providing service to others.

Abilities: Oral Expression—The ability to communicate information and ideas verbally so others will understand. Written Comprehension—The ability to read and understand information and ideas presented in writing. Problem Sensitivity—The ability to tell when something is wrong or is likely to go wrong. Does not involve solving the problem, only recognizing there is a problem. Written Expression—The ability to communicate information and ideas in writing so others will understand. Speech Clarity—The ability to speak clearly so that what is said is understandable to a listener. Oral Comprehension—The ability to listen to and understand information and ideas presented verbally.

Skills: Instructing—Teaching others how to do something. Learning Strategies—Using multiple approaches when learning or teaching new things. Social Perceptiveness—Being aware of other people's reactions and understanding why people react the way they do. Speaking—Talking to others to effectively convey information. Implementation Planning—Developing approaches for implementing an idea.

Generalized Work Activities: Teaching Others—Identifying educational needs, developing formal training programs or classes, and teaching or instructing others. Establishing and Maintaining Relationships—

Developing constructive and cooperative working relationships with others. Making Decisions and Solving Problems—Combining, evaluating, and analyzing information and data to make decisions and solve problems. Involves making decisions about the relative importance of information and choosing the best solution. Interpreting Meaning of Information to Others—Translating or explaining what information means and how it can be understood or used to support responses or feedback to others. Communicating with Persons Outside Organization—Communicating with persons outside the organization. Representing the organization to customers, the public, government, and other external sources. Exchanging information face-to-face, in writing, or via telephone/electronic transfer. Getting Information Needed to Do the Job—Observing, receiving, and otherwise obtaining information from all relevant sources.

Special Education Teachers, Secondary School

Teach secondary school subjects to educationally and physically handicapped students. Includes teachers who specialize and work with audibly and visually handicapped students and those who teach basic academic and life processes skills to the mentally impaired. Works with students to increase motivation. Instructs students in daily living skills required for independent maintenance and economic self-sufficiency, such as hygiene, safety, and food preparation. Instructs students in academic subjects, utilizing various teaching techniques such as phonetics, multisensory learning, and repetition, to reinforce learning. Instructs students, using special educational strategies and techniques to improve sensory-motor and perceptual-motor development, memory, language, and cognition. Plans curriculum and other instructional materials to meet students' needs, considering such factors as physical, emotional, and educational abilities. Confers with other staff members to plan programs designed to promote educational, physical, and social development of students. Observes, evaluates, and prepares reports on progress of students. Meets with parents to provide support, to guide them in using community resources, and to help them develop skills in dealing with students' learning impairment. Selects and teaches reading material and math problems related to everyday life of individual students. Administers and interprets results of ability and achievement tests. Teaches socially acceptable behavior, employing techniques such as behavior modification and positive reinforcement. Confers with parents, administrators, testing specialists, social workers, and others to develop individual educational plan for students. Provides consistent learning reinforcement and continuous feedback to students.

Personality Type: Social. Social occupations frequently involve working with, communicating with, and teaching people. These occupations often involve helping or providing service to others.

Abilities: Oral Expression—The ability to communicate information and ideas verbally so others will understand. Written Comprehension—The ability to read and understand information and ideas presented in writing. Problem Sensitivity—The ability to tell when something is wrong or is likely to go wrong. Does not involve solving the problem, only recognizing there is a problem. Speech Clarity—The ability to speak clearly so that what is said is understandable to a listener. Written Expression—The ability to communicate information and ideas in writing so others will understand. Oral Comprehension—The ability to listen to and understand information and ideas presented verbally.

Skills: Instructing—Teaching others how to do something. Learning Strategies—Using multiple approaches when learning or teaching new things. Speaking—Talking to others to effectively convey information. Social Perceptiveness—Being aware of other people's reactions and understanding why people react the way they do. Implementation Planning—Developing approaches for implementing an idea.

Generalized Work Activities: Teaching Others—Identifying educational needs, developing formal training programs or classes, and teaching or instructing others. Making Decisions and Solving Problems—Combining, evaluating, and analyzing information and data to make decisions and solve problems. Involves making decisions about the relative importance of information and choosing the best solution. Interpreting Meaning of Information to Others—Translating or explaining what information means and how it can be understood or used to support responses or feedback to others. Establishing and Maintaining Relationships—Developing constructive and cooperative working relationships with others. Communicating with Persons Outside Organization—Communicating with persons outside the organization. Representing the organization to customers, the public, government, and other external sources. Exchanging information face-to-face, in writing, or via telephone/electronic transfer. Getting Information Needed to Do the Job—Observing, receiving, and otherwise obtaining information from all relevant sources.

Speech-Language Pathologists and Audiologists

- ▲ Growth: 38%
- ▲ Annual Job Openings: 9,862
- ▲ Yearly Earnings: $43,080
- ▲ Education Required: Master's degree
- ▲ Self-Employed: 10.5%
- ▲ Part-Time: 20.8%

Audiologists

Assess and treat persons with hearing and related disorders. Fit hearing aids and provide auditory training. Perform research related to hearing problems. Advises educators or other medical staff on speech or hearing topics. Administers hearing or speech/language evaluations, tests, or examinations to patients, to collect information on type and degree of impairment. Counsels and instructs clients in techniques to improve speech or hearing impairment, including sign language or lipreading. Evaluates hearing and speech/language test results and medical or background information, to determine hearing or speech impairment and treatment. Conducts or directs research; reports findings on speech or hearing topics to develop procedures, technology, or treatments. Records and maintains reports of speech or hearing research or treatments. Participates in conferences or training to update or share knowledge of new hearing- or speech-disorder treatment methods or technology. Refers clients to additional medical or educational services if needed. Plans and conducts prevention and treatment programs for clients' hearing or speech problems.

Personality Type: Social. Social occupations frequently involve working with, communicating with, and teaching people. These occupations often involve helping or providing service to others.

Abilities: Oral Expression—The ability to communicate information and ideas verbally so others will understand. Oral Comprehension—The ability to listen to and understand information and ideas presented verbally. Written Comprehension—The ability to read and understand information and ideas presented in writing. Speech Clarity—The ability to speak clearly so that what is said is understandable to a listener. Written Expression—The ability to communicate information and ideas in writing so others will understand.

Skills: Instructing—Teaching others how to do something. Speaking—Talking to others to effectively convey information. Writing—Communicating effectively with others in writing as indicated by the needs of the audience. Reading Comprehension—Understanding written information in work-related documents. Active Learning—Working with new material or information to grasp its implications. Learning Strategies—Using multiple approaches when learning or teaching new things.

Generalized Work Activities: Getting Information Needed to Do the Job—Observing, receiving, and otherwise obtaining information from all relevant sources. Updating and Using Job-Relevant Knowledge—Keeping up-to-date technically and knowing the functions of one's own job and related jobs. Making Decisions and Solving Problems—Combining, evaluating, and analyzing information and data to make decisions and solve problems. Involves making decisions about the relative importance of information and choosing the best solution. Processing Information—Compiling, coding, categorizing, calculating, tabulating, auditing, verifying, or processing information or data. Identifying Objects, Actions, and Events—Identifying information received by making estimates or categorizations, recognizing differences or similarities, or sensing changes in circumstances or events.

Speech-Language Pathologists

Assess and treat persons with speech, language, voice, and fluency disorders. Select alternative communication systems and teach their use. Perform research related to speech and language problems. Evaluates hearing and speech/language test results and medical or background information, to determine hearing or speech impairment and treatment. Conducts or directs research and reports findings on speech or hearing topics, to develop procedures, technology, or treatments. Counsels and instructs clients in techniques to improve speech or hearing impairment, including sign language or lipreading. Refers clients to additional medical or educational services if needed. Advises educators or other medical staff on speech or hearing topics. Records and maintains reports of speech or hearing research or treatments. Administers hearing or speech/language evaluations, tests, or examinations to patients, to collect information on type and degree of impairment. Participates in conferences or training to update or share knowledge of new hearing- or speech-disorder treatment methods or technology.

Personality Type: Social. Social occupations frequently involve working with, communicating with, and teaching people. These occupations often involve helping or providing service to others.

Abilities: Oral Expression—The ability to communicate information and ideas verbally so others will understand. Oral Comprehension—The ability to listen to and understand information and ideas presented verbally. Written Comprehension—The ability to read and understand information and ideas presented in writing. Speech Clarity—The ability to speak clearly so that what is said is understandable to a listener. Written Expression—The ability to communicate information and ideas in writing so others will understand.

Skills: Speaking—Talking to others to effectively convey information. Instructing—Teaching others how to do something. Learning Strategies—Using multiple approaches when learning or teaching new things. Active Learning—Working with new material or information to grasp its implications. Writing—Communicating effectively with others in writing as indicated by the needs of the audience. Reading Comprehension—Understanding written information in work-related documents.

Generalized Work Activities: Getting Information Needed to Do the Job—Observing, receiving, and otherwise obtaining information from all relevant sources. Making Decisions and Solving Problems—Combining, evaluating, and analyzing information and data to make decisions and solve problems. Involves making decisions about the relative importance of information and choosing the best solution. Updating and Using Job-Relevant Knowledge—Keeping up-to-date technically and knowing the functions of one's own job and related jobs. Identifying Objects, Actions, and Events—Identifying information received by making estimates or categorizations, recognizing differences or similarities, or sensing changes in circumstances or events. Processing Information—Compiling, coding, categorizing, calculating, tabulating, auditing, verifying, or processing information or data.

Sports and Physical Training Instructors and Coaches

▲ Growth: 28%

▲ Annual Job Openings: 104,431

▲ Yearly Earnings: $22,230

▲ Education Required: Moderate-term O-J-T

▲ Self-Employed: 0%

▲ Part-Time: 42.5%

Fitness Trainers and Aerobics Instructors

Instruct or coach groups or individuals in exercise activities and the fundamentals of sports. Demonstrate techniques and methods of participation. Observe participants and inform them of corrective measures necessary to improve their skills. Selects, stores, orders, issues, and inventories equipment, materials, and supplies. Explains and enforces safety rules and regulations. Organizes and conducts competition and tournaments. Plans physical education program to promote development of participants' physical attributes and social skills. Organizes, leads, instructs, and referees indoor and outdoor games such as volleyball, baseball, and basketball. Teaches individual and team sports to participants, utilizing knowledge of sports techniques and of physical capabilities of participants. Advises participants in use of heat or ultraviolet treatments and hot baths. Teaches and demonstrates use of gymnastic and training apparatus such as trampolines and weights.

Personality Type: Social. Social occupations frequently involve working with, communicating with, and teaching people. These occupations often involve helping or providing service to others.

Abilities: Oral Expression—The ability to communicate information and ideas verbally so others will understand. Time Sharing—The ability to efficiently shift back and forth between two or more activities or sources of information such as speech, sounds, or touch. Speech Clarity—The ability to speak clearly so that what is said is understandable to a listener. Gross Body Coordination—The ability to coordinate the movement of the arms, legs, and torso together in activities where the whole body is in motion. Stamina—The ability to exert one's self physically over long periods of time without getting winded or out of breath. Multilimb Coordination—The ability to coordinate movements of two or more limbs together (for example, two arms, two legs, or one leg and one arm) while sitting, standing, or lying down. Does not involve performing the activities while the body is in motion.

Skills: Speaking—Talking to others to effectively convey information. Instructing—Teaching others how to do something. Coordination—Adjusting actions in relation to others' actions. Learning Strategies—Using multiple approaches when learning or teaching new things. Monitoring—Assessing how well one is doing when learning or doing something. Social Perceptiveness—Being aware of other people's reactions and understanding why people react the way they do.

Generalized Work Activities: Establishing and Maintaining Relationships—Developing constructive and cooperative working relationships with others. Coaching and Developing Others—Identifying developmental needs of others and coaching or otherwise helping others to improve their knowledge or skills. Teaching Others—Identifying educational needs, developing formal training programs or classes, and teaching or instructing others. Developing and Building Teams—Encouraging and building mutual trust, respect, and cooperation among team members. Performing General Physical Activities—Performing physical activities that require moving one's whole body, such as in climbing, lifting, balancing, walking, and stooping. Performing activities that often also require considerable use of the arms and legs, such as in the physical handling of materials.

Sprayers and Applicators

▲ Growth: 24%

▲ Annual Job Openings: 5,167

▲ Yearly Earnings: $21,650

▲ Education Required: Moderate-term O-J-T

▲ Self-Employed: 0%

▲ Part-Time: 28.5%

Pesticide Handlers, Sprayers, and Applicators, Vegetation

Mix or apply pesticides, herbicides, fungicides, or insecticides through sprays, dusts, vapors, soil incorporation, or chemical application on trees, shrubs, lawns, or botanical crops. Usually requires specific training and state or federal certification. Plants grass with seed spreader and operates straw blower to cover seeded area with asphalt and straw mixture. Cleans and services machinery to ensure operating efficiency, using water, gasoline, lubricants, and hand tools. Connects hoses and nozzles that have been selected according to terrain, distribution pattern requirements, type of infestation, and velocity. Gives driving instructions to truck driver, using hand and horn signals, to ensure complete coverage of designated area. Starts motor and engages machinery such as sprayer agitator and pump. Fills sprayer tank with water and chemicals, according to formula. Covers area to specified depth, applying knowledge of weather conditions, droplet size, elevation-to-distance ratio, and obstructions. Lifts, pushes, and swings nozzle, hose, and tube to direct spray over designated area. Sprays livestock with pesticides.

Personality Type: Realistic. Realistic occupations frequently involve work activities that include practical, hands-on problems and solutions. They often deal with plants, animals, and real-world materials like wood, tools, and machinery. Many of the occupations require working outside and do not involve a lot of paperwork or working closely with others.

Abilities: Arm-Hand Steadiness—The ability to keep the hand and arm steady while making an arm movement or while holding the arm and hand in one position. Trunk Strength—The ability to use one's abdominal and lower back muscles to support part of the body repeatedly or continuously over time without giving out or fatiguing. Dynamic Strength—The ability to exert muscle force repeatedly or continuously over time. This involves muscular endurance and resistance to muscle fatigue. Information Ordering—The ability to correctly follow a given rule or set of rules in order to arrange things or actions in a certain order. The things or actions can include numbers, letters, words, pictures, procedures, sentences, and mathematical or logical operations. Extent Flexibility—The ability to bend, stretch, twist, or reach out with the body, arms, and/or legs. Manual Dexterity—The ability to quickly make coordinated movements of one hand, a hand together with its arm, or two hands, to grasp, manipulate, or assemble objects.

Skills: Operation and Control—Controlling operations of equipment or systems. Equipment Selection—Determining the kind of tools and equipment needed to do a job. Mathematics—Using mathematics to solve problems. Equipment Maintenance—Performing routine maintenance and determining when and what kind of maintenance is needed. Reading Comprehension—Understanding written information in work-related documents.

Generalized Work Activities: Performing General Physical Activities—Performing physical activities that require moving one's whole body, such as in climbing, lifting, balancing, walking, and stooping. Performing activities that often also require considerable use of the arms and legs, such as in the physical handling of materials. Estimating Needed Characteristics—Estimating the characteristics of materials, products, events, or information; estimating sizes, distances, and quantities; determining time, costs, resources, or materials needed to perform a work activity. Controlling Machines and Processes—Using either control mechanisms or direct physical activity to operate machines or processes. Does not involve working with computers or vehicles. Handling and Moving Objects—Using one's hands and arms in handling, installing, forming, positioning, and moving materials, or in manipulating things. Includes the use of keyboards. Getting Information Needed to Do the Job—Observing, receiving, and otherwise obtaining information from all relevant sources.

Statisticians

- ▲ Growth: 2%
- ▲ Annual Job Openings: 1,635
- ▲ Yearly Earnings: $48,540
- ▲ Education Required: Bachelor's degree
- ▲ Self-Employed: 0%
- ▲ Part-Time: 5.2%

Financial Analysts

Conduct quantitative analyses of information affecting investment programs of public or private institutions. Draws charts and graphs to illustrate reports, using computer. Interprets data concerning price, yield, stability. Interprets data concerning future trends in investment risks and economic influences pertinent to investments. Calls brokers; purchases investments for company, according to company policy. Recommends investment timing and buy-and-sell orders to company or to staff of investment establishment. Analyzes financial information to forecast business, industry, and economic conditions, for use in making investment decisions. Gathers industry, regulatory, and economic information, company financial statements, financial periodicals, and newspapers.

Personality Type: Investigative. Investigative occupations frequently involve working with ideas and require an extensive amount of thinking. These occupations can involve searching for facts and figuring out problems mentally.

Abilities: Number Facility—The ability to add, subtract, multiply, or divide quickly and correctly. Written Comprehension—The ability to read and understand information and ideas presented in writing. Deductive

Reasoning—The ability to apply general rules to specific problems to come up with logical answers. Involves deciding if an answer makes sense. Mathematical Reasoning—The ability to understand and organize a problem and then select a mathematical method or formula to solve the problem. Written Expression—The ability to communicate information and ideas in writing so others will understand.

Skills: Reading Comprehension—Understanding written information in work-related documents. Information Gathering—Knowing how to find information and identifying essential information. Mathematics—Using mathematics to solve problems. Critical Thinking—Using logic and analysis to identify the strengths and weaknesses of different approaches. Information Organization—Finding ways to structure or classify multiple pieces of information.

Generalized Work Activities: Identifying Objects, Actions, and Events—Identifying information received by making estimates or categorizations, recognizing differences or similarities, or sensing changes in circumstances or events. Analyzing Data or Information—Identifying underlying principles, reasons, or facts by breaking down information or data into separate parts. Getting Information Needed to Do the Job—Observing, receiving, and otherwise obtaining information from all relevant sources. Providing Consultation and Advice to Others—Providing consultation and expert advice to management or other groups on technical, systems-related, or process-related topics. Interpreting Meaning of Information to Others—Translating or explaining what information means and how it can be understood or used to support responses or feedback to others. Communicating with Other Workers—Providing information to supervisors, fellow workers, and subordinates. This information can be exchanged face-to-face, in writing, or via telephone/ electronic transfer. Communicating with Persons Outside Organization—Communicating with persons outside the organization. Representing the organization to customers, the public, government, and other external sources. Exchanging information face-to-face, in writing, or via telephone/electronic transfer.

Statisticians

Engage in the development of mathematical theory. Apply statistical theory and methods to collect, organize, interpret, and summarize numerical data. Specialize in fields such as biostatistics, agricultural statistics, business statistics, economic statistics, or other fields. Presents numerical information by computer readouts, graphs, charts, tables, written reports or other methods. Investigates, evaluates, and reports on applicability, efficiency, and accuracy of statistical methods used to obtain and evaluate data. Evaluates reliability of source information, adjusts and weighs raw data, and organizes results into format that can be analyzed by computers or other methods. Develops statistical methodology. Examines theories such as those of probability and inference, to discover mathematical bases for new or improved methods of obtaining and evaluating numerical data. Describes sources of information. Describes limitations on reliability and usability. Analyzes and interprets statistics to identify significant differences in relationships among sources of information. Develops and tests experimental designs, sampling techniques, and analytical methods; prepares recommendations concerning their use. Conducts surveys utilizing sampling techniques or complete enumeration bases. Applies statistical methodology to provide information for scientific research and statistical analysis.

Plans methods to collect information and develops questionnaire techniques according to survey design.

Personality Type: Investigative. Investigative occupations frequently involve working with ideas and require an extensive amount of thinking. These occupations can involve searching for facts and figuring out problems mentally.

Abilities: Mathematical Reasoning—The ability to understand and organize a problem and then select a mathematical method or formula to solve the problem. Number Facility—The ability to add, subtract, multiply, or divide quickly and correctly. Deductive Reasoning—The ability to apply general rules to specific problems to come up with logical answers. Involves deciding if an answer makes sense. Written Expression—The ability to communicate information and ideas in writing so others will understand. Inductive Reasoning—The ability to combine separate pieces of information, or specific answers to problems, to form general rules or conclusions. Includes coming up with a logical explanation for why a series of seemingly unrelated events occur together. Near Vision—The ability to see details of objects at a close range.

Skills: Mathematics—Using mathematics to solve problems. Information Gathering—Knowing how to find information and identifying essential information. Critical Thinking—Using logic and analysis to identify the strengths and weaknesses of different approaches. Active Learning—Working with new material or information to grasp its implications. Solution Appraisal—Observing and evaluating the outcomes of a problem solution to identify lessons learned or to redirect efforts.

Generalized Work Activities: Analyzing Data or Information—Identifying underlying principles, reasons, or facts by breaking down information or data into separate parts. Getting Information Needed to Do the Job—Observing, receiving, and otherwise obtaining information from all relevant sources. Processing Information—Compiling, coding, categorizing, calculating, tabulating, auditing, verifying, or processing information or data. Identifying Objects, Actions, and Events—Identifying information received by making estimates or categorizations, recognizing differences or similarities, or sensing changes in circumstances or events. Evaluating Information against Standards— Evaluating information against a set of standards and verifying that it is correct.

Subway and Streetcar Operators

- ▲ Growth: 7%
- ▲ Annual Job Openings: 250
- ▲ Yearly Earnings: $43,330
- ▲ Education Required: Moderate-term O-J-T
- ▲ Self-Employed: 0%
- ▲ Part-Time: 2.3%

Subway and Streetcar Operators

Operate subway or elevated suburban train with no separate locomotive to transport passengers. Operate electric-powered streetcar to transport passengers. Handle fares. Drives rail-guided public transportation such as subways, elevated suburban train, or electric-powered streetcar to transport passengers. Records readings of coin receptor at beginning and end of shift, to verify amount of money received during shift. Collects fares from passengers and issues change and transfers. Opens and closes doors of train or streetcar to allow passengers to enter or leave vehicle. Answers questions from passengers concerning fares, schedules, and routes.

Personality Type: Realistic. Realistic occupations frequently involve work activities that include practical, hands-on problems and solutions. They often deal with plants, animals, and real-world materials like wood, tools, and machinery. Many of the occupations require working outside and do not involve a lot of paperwork or working closely with others.

Abilities: Reaction Time—The ability to quickly respond with the hand, finger, or foot to a signal such as a sound, a light, or a picture. Oral Expression—The ability to communicate information and ideas verbally so others will understand. Oral Comprehension—The ability to listen to and understand information and ideas presented verbally. Far Vision—The ability to see details at a distance. Control Precision—The ability to quickly and repeatedly make precise adjustments in moving the controls of a machine or vehicle to exact positions.

Skills: Operation and Control—Controlling operations of equipment or systems. Operation Monitoring— Watching gauges, dials, or other indicators to make sure a machine is working properly. Time Management— Managing one's own time and the time of others. Speaking—Talking to others to effectively convey information. Mathematics—Using mathematics to solve problems. Social Perceptiveness—Being aware of other people's reactions and understanding why people react the way they do. Active Listening—Listening to what other people are saying; asking questions as appropriate.

Generalized Work Activities: Operating Vehicles or Equipment—Running, maneuvering, navigating, or driving vehicles or mechanized equipment such as forklifts, passenger vehicles, aircraft, or water craft. Handling and Moving Objects—Using one's hands and arms in handling, installing, forming, positioning, and moving materials, or in manipulating things. Includes the use of keyboards. Getting Information Needed to Do the Job—Observing, receiving, and otherwise obtaining information from all relevant sources. Monitoring Processes, Materials, Surroundings— Monitoring and reviewing information from materials, events, or the environment, often to detect problems or to find out when things are finished. Performing for/ Working with Public—Performing for people or dealing directly with the public, including serving persons in restaurants and stores and receiving clients or guests.

Surgical Technologists

▲ Growth: 42%
▲ Annual Job Openings: 9,182
▲ Yearly Earnings: $25,780
▲ Education Required: Postsecondary vocational training
▲ Self-Employed: 0%
▲ Part-Time: 22.9%

Surgical Technologists

Assist in operations, under the supervision of surgeons, registered nurses, or other surgical personnel. Help set up operating room. Prepare and transport patients for surgery. Adjust lights and equipment. Pass instruments and other supplies to surgeons and surgeons' assistants. Hold retractors and cut sutures. Help count sponges, needles, supplies, and instruments. Puts dressings on patient following surgery. Cleans operating room. Hands instruments and supplies to surgeon; holds retractors; cuts sutures; performs other tasks as directed by surgeon during operation. Washes and sterilizes equipment, using germicides and sterilizers. Counts sponges, needles, and instruments before and after operation. Maintains supply of fluids such as plasma, saline, blood, and glucose, for use during operation. Scrubs arms and hands and dons gown and gloves. Assists team members in placing and positioning patient on table. Places equipment and supplies in operating room; arranges instruments according to instruction. Aids team in donning gowns and gloves.

Personality Type: Realistic. Realistic occupations frequently involve work activities that include practical, hands-on problems and solutions. They often deal with plants, animals, and real-world materials like wood, tools, and machinery. Many of the occupations require working outside and do not involve a lot of paperwork or working closely with others.

Abilities: Oral Comprehension—The ability to listen to and understand information and ideas presented verbally. Information Ordering—The ability to correctly follow a given rule or set of rules in order to arrange things or actions in a certain order. The things or actions can include numbers, letters, words, pictures, procedures, sentences, and mathematical or logical operations. Arm-Hand Steadiness—The ability to keep the hand and arm steady while making an arm movement or while holding the arm and hand in one position. Finger Dexterity—The ability to make precisely coordinated movements of the fingers of one or both hands to grasp, manipulate, or assemble very small objects. Number Facility—The ability to add, subtract, multiply, or divide quickly and correctly.

Skills: Information Organization—Finding ways to structure or classify multiple pieces of information. Active Listening—Listening to what other people are saying; asking questions as appropriate. Coordination—Adjusting actions in relation to others' actions. Reading Comprehension—Understanding written information in work-related documents. Mathematics—Using mathematics to solve problems.

Generalized Work Activities: Handling and Moving Objects—Using one's hands and arms in handling, installing, forming, positioning, and moving materials, or in manipulating things. Includes the use of keyboards. Assisting and Caring for Others—Providing assistance or personal care to others. Getting Information Needed to Do the Job—Observing, receiving, and otherwise obtaining information from all relevant sources. Implementing Ideas and Programs—Conducting or carrying out work procedures and activities in accord with one's own ideas or information provided through directions/instructions for purposes of installing, modifying, preparing, delivering, constructing, integrating, finishing, or completing programs, systems, structures, or products. Communicating with Other Workers—Providing information to supervisors, fellow workers,

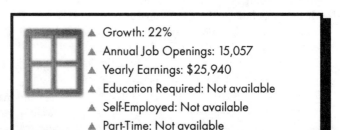

and subordinates. This information can be exchanged face-to-face, in writing, or via telephone/electronic transfer. Estimating Needed Characteristics—Estimating the characteristics of materials, products,

events, or information; estimating sizes, distances, and quantities; determining time, costs, resources, or materials needed to perform a work activity.

Surveying and Mapping Technicians

- ▲ Growth: 22%
- ▲ Annual Job Openings: 15,057
- ▲ Yearly Earnings: $25,940
- ▲ Education Required: Not available
- ▲ Self-Employed: Not available
- ▲ Part-Time: Not available

Mapping Technicians

Calculate map-making information from field notes. Draw and verify accuracy of topographical maps. Computes and measures scaled distances between reference points, to establish exact relative position of adjoining prints. Forms three-dimensional image of aerial photographs taken from different locations, using mathematical aides and plotting instruments. Verifies identification of topographical features and accuracy of contour lines by comparison with aerial photographs, old maps, and other reference materials. Supervises and coordinates activities of workers engaged in drafting maps or in production of blueprints, photostats, and photographs. Stores, retrieves, and compares map information, using computers and data banks. Analyzes aerial photographs to detect and interpret significant military, industrial, resource, or topographical data. Trims, aligns, and joins prints to form photographic mosaic, maintaining scaled distances between reference points. Marks errors and makes corrections, such as numbering grid lines or lettering names of rivers or towns. Lays out and matches aerial photographs in sequence taken, looking for missing areas. Traces contours and topographical details to produce map. Calculates latitude, longitude, angles, areas, and other information for mapmaking from survey field notes, using reference tables and computer.

Personality Type: Conventional. Conventional occupations frequently involve following set procedures and

routines. These occupations can include working with data and details more than with ideas. Usually there is a clear line of authority to follow.

Abilities: Near Vision—The ability to see details of objects at a close range. Written Comprehension—The ability to read and understand information and ideas presented in writing. Wrist-Finger Speed—The ability to make fast, simple, repeated movements of the fingers, hands, and wrists. Mathematical Reasoning—The ability to understand and organize a problem and then select a mathematical method or formula to solve the problem. Inductive Reasoning—The ability to combine separate pieces of information, or specific answers to problems, to form general rules or conclusions. Includes coming up with a logical explanation for why a series of seemingly unrelated events occur together.

Skills: Mathematics—Using mathematics to solve problems. Information Organization—Finding ways to structure or classify multiple pieces of information. Information Gathering—Knowing how to find information and identifying essential information. Active Learning—Working with new material or information to grasp its implications.

Generalized Work Activities: Processing Information— Compiling, coding, categorizing, calculating, tabulating, auditing, verifying, or processing information or data. Identifying Objects, Actions, and Events—Identifying information received by making estimates or categorizations, recognizing differences or similarities, or sensing changes in circumstances or events. Getting Information Needed to Do the Job—Observing, receiving, and otherwise obtaining information from all relevant sources. Interacting with Computers—Controlling computer functions by using programs, setting up functions, writing software, or otherwise communicating with computer systems. Drafting and Specifying Technical Devices—Providing documentation, detailed instructions, drawings, or specifications to inform others about how devices, parts, equipment, or structures are to be fabricated, constructed, assembled, modified, maintained, or used.

Surveying Technicians

Adjust and operate surveying instruments such as the theodolite and electronic distance-measuring equipment. Compile notes, make sketches, and enter data into computers. Compiles notes, sketches, and records of survey data obtained and work performed. Directs work of subordinate members of party, performing surveying duties not requiring licensure. Obtains land survey data such as angles, elevations, points, and contours, using electronic distance-measuring equipment and other surveying instruments.

Personality Type: Realistic. Realistic occupations frequently involve work activities that include practical, hands-on problems and solutions. They often deal with plants, animals, and real-world materials like wood, tools, and machinery. Many of the occupations require working outside and do not involve a lot of paperwork or working closely with others.

Abilities: Written Expression—The ability to communicate information and ideas in writing so others will understand. Oral Expression—The ability to communicate information and ideas verbally so others will understand. Far Vision—The ability to see details at a distance. Spatial Orientation—The ability to know one's location in relation to the environment or to know where other objects are in relation to one's self.

Skills: Mathematics—Using mathematics to solve problems. Information Gathering—Knowing how to find information and identifying essential information. Reading Comprehension—Understanding written information in work-related documents. Writing—Communicating effectively with others in writing as indicated by the needs of the audience. Instructing—Teaching others how to do something. Information Organization—Finding ways to structure or classify multiple pieces of information.

Generalized Work Activities: Getting Information Needed to Do the Job—Observing, receiving, and otherwise obtaining information from all relevant sources. Documenting/Recording Information—Entering, transcribing, recording, storing, or maintaining information in either written form or by electronic/magnetic recording. Controlling Machines and Processes—Using either control mechanisms or direct physical activity to operate machines or processes. Does not involve working with computers or vehicles. Identifying Objects, Actions, and Events—Identifying information received by making estimates or categorizations, recognizing differences or similarities, or sensing changes in circumstances or events. Processing Information—Compiling, coding, categorizing, calculating, tabulating, auditing, verifying, or processing information or data.

Systems Analysts

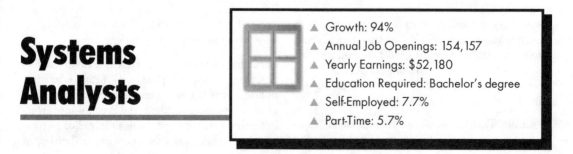

- ▲ Growth: 94%
- ▲ Annual Job Openings: 154,157
- ▲ Yearly Earnings: $52,180
- ▲ Education Required: Bachelor's degree
- ▲ Self-Employed: 7.7%
- ▲ Part-Time: 5.7%

Computer Systems Analysts

Analyze science, engineering, business, and all other data-processing problems for application to electronic data-processing systems. Analyze user requirements, procedures, and problems to automate or improve existing systems. Review computer system capabilities, workflow, and scheduling limitations. Analyze or recommend commercially available software. Supervise computer programmers. Modifies program to correct errors by correcting computer codes. Formulates and reviews plans, outlining steps required to develop programs to meet staff and user requirements. Consults with staff and users to identify operating procedure problems. Devises flow charts and diagrams to illustrate steps and to describe logical operational steps of program. Writes and revises program and system-design procedures, test procedures, and quality standards. Reviews and analyzes computer printouts and performance indications, to locate code problems. Trains staff and users to use computer system and its programs. Coordinates installation of computer programs and operating systems. Tests, maintains, and monitors computer system. Analyzes and tests computer programs or system to identify errors and ensure conformance to standard. Writes documentation to describe and develop installation and operating procedures of programs. Reads manuals, periodicals, and technical reports to learn how to develop programs to meet staff and user requirements. Assists staff and users to solve computer-related problems such as malfunctions and program problems.

Personality Type: Investigative. Investigative occupations frequently involve working with ideas and require an extensive amount of thinking. These occupations can involve searching for facts and figuring out problems mentally.

Abilities: Written Comprehension—The ability to read and understand information and ideas presented in writing. Mathematical Reasoning—The ability to understand and organize a problem and then select a mathematical method or formula to solve the problem. Written Expression—The ability to communicate information and ideas in writing so others will understand. Oral Comprehension—The ability to listen to and understand information and ideas presented verbally. Near Vision—The ability to see details of objects at a close range. Deductive Reasoning—The ability to apply general rules to specific problems to come up with logical answers. Involves deciding if an answer makes sense.

Skills: Programming—Writing computer programs for various purposes. Reading Comprehension—Understanding written information in work-related documents. Troubleshooting—Determining what is causing an operating error and deciding what to do about it. Testing—Conducting tests to determine whether equipment, software, or procedures are operating as expected.

Generalized Work Activities: Updating and Using Job-Relevant Knowledge—Keeping up-to-date technically and knowing the functions of one's own job and related jobs. Interacting with Computers—Controlling computer functions by using programs, setting up functions, writing software, or otherwise communicating with computer systems. Getting Information Needed to Do the Job—Observing, receiving, and otherwise obtaining information from all relevant sources. Thinking Creatively—Originating, inventing, designing, or creating new applications, ideas, relationships, systems, or products, including artistic contributions. Communicating with Other Workers—Providing information to supervisors, fellow workers, and subordinates. This information can be exchanged face-to-face, in writing, or via telephone/electronic transfer. Providing Consultation and Advice to Others—Providing consultation and expert advice to management or other groups on technical, systems-related, or process-related topics.

Tax Preparers

▲ Growth: 19%
▲ Annual Job Openings: 13,654
▲ Yearly Earnings: $27,960
▲ Education Required: Moderate-term O-J-T
▲ Self-Employed: Not available
▲ Part-Time: Not available

Tax Preparers

Prepare tax returns for individuals or small businesses. Do not have the background or responsibilities of an accredited or certified public accountant. Verifies totals on forms prepared by others, to detect errors in arithmetic or procedure, as needed. Computes taxes owed, using adding machine or personal computer; completes entries on forms, following tax-form instructions and tax tables. Calculates form preparation fee according to complexity of return and amount of time required to prepare forms. Consults tax-law handbook or bulletins to determine procedure for preparation of atypical returns. Reviews financial records such as income statements and documentation of expenditures, to determine forms needed to prepare return. Interviews client to obtain additional information on taxable income and deductible expenses and allowances.

Personality Type: Conventional. Conventional occupations frequently involve following set procedures and routines. These occupations can include working with data and details more than with ideas. Usually there is a clear line of authority to follow.

Abilities: Number Facility—The ability to add, subtract, multiply, or divide quickly and correctly. Mathematical Reasoning—The ability to understand and organize a problem and then select a mathematical method or formula to solve the problem. Oral Comprehension—The ability to listen to and understand information and ideas presented verbally. Oral Expression—The ability

to communicate information and ideas verbally so others will understand. Written Comprehension—The ability to read and understand information and ideas presented in writing. Deductive Reasoning—The ability to apply general rules to specific problems to come up with logical answers. Involves deciding if an answer makes sense.

Skills: Mathematics—Using mathematics to solve problems. Information Gathering—Knowing how to find information and identifying essential information. Reading Comprehension—Understanding written information in work-related documents. Problem Identification—Identifying the nature of problems. Active Listening—Listening to what other people are saying; asking questions as appropriate.

Generalized Work Activities: Getting Information Needed to Do the Job—Observing, receiving, and otherwise obtaining information from all relevant sources. Processing Information—Compiling, coding, categorizing, calculating, tabulating, auditing, verifying, or processing information or data. Performing Administrative Activities—Approving requests, handling paperwork, and performing day-to-day administrative tasks. Documenting/Recording Information—Entering, transcribing, recording, storing, or maintaining information in either written form or by electronic/magnetic recording. Communicating with Persons Outside Organization—Communicating with persons outside the organization. Representing the organization to customers, the public, government, and other external sources. Exchanging information face-to-face, in writing, or via telephone/electronic transfer.

Taxi Drivers and Chauffeurs

- ▲ Growth: 20%
- ▲ Annual Job Openings: 26,739
- ▲ Yearly Earnings: $15,540
- ▲ Education Required: Short-term O-J-T
- ▲ Self-Employed: 44.1%
- ▲ Part-Time: 21.5%

Taxi Drivers and Chauffeurs

Drive automobiles, vans, or limousines to transport passengers. Occasionally carry cargo. Maintains vehicle by performing such duties as regulating tire pressure and adding gasoline, oil, and water. Vacuums, sweeps, and cleans interior, and washes and polishes exterior of automobile. Performs errands for customers, such as carrying mail to and from post office. Delivers automobiles to customers from rental agency, car dealership, or repair shop. Makes minor repairs on vehicle, such as fixing punctures, cleaning spark plugs, or adjusting carburetor. Assists passengers in entering and exiting vehicle; assists with luggage; holds umbrellas in wet weather. Collects and documents fees, payments, and deposits determined by rental contracts or taximeter recordings. Communicates with taxicab dispatcher by radio or telephone, to receive requests for passenger service. Drives taxicab, limousine, company car, hearse, or privately owned vehicle to transport passengers. Tests performance of vehicle accessories such as lights, horn, and windshield wipers.

Personality Type: Realistic. Realistic occupations frequently involve work activities that include practical, hands-on problems and solutions. They often deal with plants, animals, and real-world materials like wood, tools, and machinery. Many of the occupations require working outside and do not involve a lot of paperwork or working closely with others.

Abilities: Oral Comprehension—The ability to listen to and understand information and ideas presented verbally. Number Facility—The ability to add, subtract, multiply, or divide quickly and correctly. Multilimb Coordination—The ability to coordinate movements of two or more limbs together (for example, two arms, two legs, or one leg and one arm) while sitting, standing, or lying down. Does not involve performing the activities while the body is in motion. Written Comprehension—The ability to read and understand information and ideas presented in writing. Reaction Time—The ability to quickly respond with the hand, finger, or foot to a signal such as a sound, a light, or a picture.

Skills: Operation and Control—Controlling operations of equipment or systems. Service Orientation—Actively looking for ways to help people. Active Listening—Listening to what other people are saying; asking questions as appropriate. Equipment Maintenance—Performing routine maintenance and determining when and what kind of maintenance is needed.

Generalized Work Activities: Operating Vehicles or Equipment—Running, maneuvering, navigating, or driving vehicles or mechanized equipment such as forklifts, passenger vehicles, aircraft, or water craft. Getting Information Needed to Do the Job—Observing, receiving, and otherwise obtaining information from all relevant sources. Communicating with Other Workers—Providing information to supervisors, fellow workers, and subordinates. This information can be exchanged face-to-face, in writing, or via telephone/electronic transfer. Repairing and Maintaining Mechanical Equipment—Fixing, servicing, aligning, setting up, adjusting, and testing machines, devices, moving parts, and equipment that operate primarily on the basis of mechanical, not electronic, principles. Performing for/Working with Public—Performing for people or dealing directly with the public, including serving persons in restaurants and stores and receiving clients or guests.

Teacher Assistants

▲ Growth: 32%
▲ Annual Job Openings: 343,831
▲ Yearly Earnings: $15,800
▲ Education Required: Short-term O-J-T
▲ Self-Employed: 0%
▲ Part-Time: 61.7%

Teacher Assistants

Perform duties that are instructional in nature or deliver direct services to students and/or parents. Serve in a position for which a teacher or another professional has ultimate responsibility for the design and implementation of educational programs and services. Presents subject matter to students, using lecture, discussion, or supervised role-playing methods. Discusses assigned teaching area with classroom teacher to coordinate instructional efforts. Confers with parents on progress of students. Prepares, administers, and grades examinations. Helps individual students or groups of students with their lesson assignments, to present or reinforce learning concepts. Prepares lesson outline and plan in assigned area; submits outline to teacher for review. Plans, prepares, and develops various teaching aids such as bibliographies, charts, and graphs.

Personality Type: Social. Social occupations frequently involve working with, communicating with, and teaching people. These occupations often involve helping or providing service to others.

Abilities: Oral Expression—The ability to communicate information and ideas verbally so others will understand. Written Expression—The ability to communicate information and ideas in writing so others will understand. Speech Clarity—The ability to speak clearly so that what is said is understandable to a listener. Oral Comprehension—The ability to listen to and understand information and ideas presented verbally. Written Comprehension—The ability to read and understand information and ideas presented in writing.

Skills: Instructing—Teaching others how to do something. Speaking—Talking to others to effectively convey information. Active Listening—Listening to what other people are saying; asking questions as appropriate. Learning Strategies—Using multiple approaches when learning or teaching new things. Reading Comprehension—Understanding written information in work-related documents.

Generalized Work Activities: Teaching Others—Identifying educational needs, developing formal training programs or classes, and teaching or instructing others. Communicating with Persons Outside Organization—Communicating with persons outside the organization. Representing the organization to customers, the public, government, and other external sources. Exchanging information face-to-face, in writing, or via telephone/electronic transfer. Establishing and Maintaining Relationships—Developing constructive and cooperative working relationships with others. Getting Information Needed to Do the Job—Observing, receiving, and otherwise obtaining information from all relevant sources. Communicating with Other Workers—Providing information to supervisors, fellow workers, and subordinates. This information can be exchanged face-to-face, in writing, or via telephone/electronic transfer.

Telephone and Cable TV Line Installers and Repairers

- ▲ Growth: 30%
- ▲ Annual Job Openings: 18,246
- ▲ Yearly Earnings: $32,750
- ▲ Education Required: Long-term O-J-T
- ▲ Self-Employed: 0%
- ▲ Part-Time: 0.9%

Telecommunications Line Installers and Repairers

String and repair telephone and television cable, including fiber optics and other equipment for transmitting messages or television programming. Digs holes, using power auger or shovel; hoists poles upright into holes, using truck-mounted winch. Collects installation fees. Computes impedance of wire from pole to house to determine additional resistance needed for reducing signal to desired level. Pulls lines through ducts by hand or with use of winch. Ascends poles or enters tunnels and sewers to string lines and install terminal boxes, auxiliary equipment, and appliances, according to diagrams. Repairs cable system, defective lines, and auxiliary equipment. Installs and removes plant equipment such as callboxes and clocks. Installs terminal boxes and strings lead-in wires, using electrician's tools. Explains cable service to subscriber. Connects television set to cable system, evaluates incoming signal, and adjusts system to ensure optimum reception. Measures signal strength at utility pole, using electronic test equipment. Cleans and maintains tools and test equipment. Fills and tamps holes, using cement, earth, and tamping device.

Personality Type: Realistic. Realistic occupations frequently involve work activities that include practical, hands-on problems and solutions. They often deal with plants, animals, and real-world materials like wood, tools, and machinery. Many of the occupations require

working outside and do not involve a lot of paperwork or working closely with others.

Abilities: Manual Dexterity—The ability to quickly make coordinated movements of one hand, a hand together with its arm, or two hands, to grasp, manipulate, or assemble objects. Control Precision—The ability to quickly and repeatedly make precise adjustments in moving the controls of a machine or vehicle to exact positions. Oral Comprehension—The ability to listen to and understand information and ideas presented verbally. Deductive Reasoning—The ability to apply general rules to specific problems to come up with logical answers. Involves deciding if an answer makes sense. Near Vision—The ability to see details of objects at a close range. Oral Expression—The ability to communicate information and ideas verbally so others will understand. Information Ordering—The ability to correctly follow a given rule or set of rules in order to arrange things or actions in a certain order. The things or actions can include numbers, letters, words, pictures, procedures, sentences, and mathematical or logical operations.

Skills: Installation—Installing equipment, machines, wiring, or programs to meet specifications. Repairing—Repairing machines or systems, using the needed tools. Troubleshooting—Determining what is causing an operating error and deciding what to do about it. Equipment Maintenance—Performing routine maintenance and determining when and what kind of maintenance is needed.

Generalized Work Activities: Repairing and Maintaining Electrical Equipment—Fixing, servicing, adjusting, regulating, calibrating, fine-tuning, or testing machines, devices, and equipment that operate primarily on the basis of electrical or electronic, not mechanical, principles. Performing General Physical Activities—Performing physical activities that require moving one's whole body, such as in climbing, lifting, balancing, walking, and stooping. Performing activities that often also require considerable use of the arms and legs, such as in the physical handling of materials. Getting Information Needed to Do the Job—Observing, receiving, and otherwise obtaining information from all relevant sources. Handling and Moving Objects—Using one's hands and arms in handling, installing, forming, positioning, and moving materials, or in manipulating things. Controlling Machines and Processes—Using either control mechanisms or direct physical activity to operate machines or processes. Does not involve working with computers or vehicles. Identifying Objects, Actions, and Events—Identifying information received by making estimates or categorizations, recognizing differences or similarities, or sensing changes in circumstances or events.

Tire Repairers and Changers

▲ Growth: 10%
▲ Annual Job Openings: 26,095
▲ Yearly Earnings: $16,810
▲ Education Required: Short-term O-J-T
▲ Self-Employed: 2.3%
▲ Part-Time: 30.2%

Tire Repairers and Changers

Repair and replace tires. Unbolts wheel, using lug wrench. Buffs defective area of inner tube, using scraper. Raises vehicle, using hydraulic jack. Hammers required counterweights onto rim of wheel. Rotates tires to different positions on vehicle, using hand tools. Places wheel on balancing machine to determine counterweights required to balance wheel. Removes inner tube from tire; inspects tire casing for defects such as holes and tears. Cleans sides of white-wall tires. Reassembles tire onto wheel. Inflates inner tube and immerses it in water to locate leak. Remounts wheel onto vehicle. Patches tube with adhesive rubber patch; seals rubber patch to tube, using hot vulcanizing plate. Separates tubed tire from wheel, using rubber mallet and metal bar or mechanical tire changer. Removes wheel from vehicle by hand or by use of power hoist. Seals puncture in tubeless tire by inserting adhesive material and expanding rubber plug into puncture, using hand tools. Locates puncture in tubeless tire by visual inspection or by immersing inflated tire in water bath and observing air bubbles. Glues boot (tire patch) over rupture in tire casing, using rubber cement.

Personality Type: Realistic. Realistic occupations frequently involve work activities that include practical, hands-on problems and solutions. They often deal with plants, animals, and real-world materials like wood, tools, and machinery. Many of the occupations require working outside and do not involve a lot of paperwork or working closely with others.

Abilities: Information Ordering—The ability to correctly follow a given rule or set of rules in order to arrange things or actions in a certain order. The things or actions can include numbers, letters, words, pictures, procedures, sentences, and mathematical or logical operations. Static Strength—The ability to exert maximum muscle force to lift, push, pull, or carry objects. Control Precision—The ability to quickly and repeatedly make precise adjustments in moving the controls of a machine or vehicle to exact positions. Near Vision—The ability to see details of objects at a close range. Manual Dexterity—The ability to quickly make coordinated movements of one hand, a hand together with its arm, or two hands, to grasp, manipulate, or assemble objects. Problem Sensitivity—The ability to tell when something is wrong or is likely to go wrong. Does not involve solving the problem, only recognizing there is a problem.

Skills: Repairing—Repairing machines or systems, using the needed tools. Equipment Selection—Determining the kind of tools and equipment needed to do a job. Operation and Control—Controlling operations of equipment or systems. Installation—Installing equipment, machines, wiring, or programs to meet specifications. Problem Identification—Identifying the nature of problems.

Generalized Work Activities: Handling and Moving Objects—Using one's hands and arms in handling, installing, forming, positioning, and moving materials,

or in manipulating things. Performing General Physical Activities—Performing physical activities that require moving one's whole body, such as in climbing, lifting, balancing, walking, and stooping. Performing activities that often also require considerable use of the arms and legs, such as in the physical handling of materials. Controlling Machines and Processes—Using either control mechanisms or direct physical activity to operate machines or processes. Does not involve working with computers or vehicles. Identifying Objects, Actions, and Events—Identifying information received by making estimates or categorizations, recognizing differences or similarities, or sensing changes in circumstances or events. Inspecting Equipment, Structures, Materials—Inspecting or diagnosing equipment, structures, or materials to identify the causes of errors or other problems or defects.

Travel Agents

- ▲ Growth: 18%
- ▲ Annual Job Openings: 17,019
- ▲ Yearly Earnings: $23,010
- ▲ Education Required: Postsecondary vocational training
- ▲ Self-Employed: 9%
- ▲ Part-Time: 31.7%

Travel Agents

Plan and sell transportation and accommodations for travel-agency customers. Determine destination, modes of transportation, travel dates, costs, and accommodations required. Books transportation and hotel reservations, using computer terminal or telephone. Prints or requests transportation carrier tickets, using computer printer system or system link to travel carrier. Collects payment for transportation and accommodations from customer. Converses with customer to determine destination, mode of transportation, travel dates, financial considerations, and accommodations required. Computes cost of travel and accommodations, using calculator, computer, carrier tariff books, and hotel rate books; quotes package-tour costs. Plans, describes, arranges, and sells itinerary tour packages and promotional travel incentives offered by

various travel carriers. Provides customer with brochures and publications containing travel information such as local customs, points of interest, or foreign country regulations.

Personality Type: Enterprising. Enterprising occupations frequently involve starting up and carrying out projects. These occupations can involve leading people and making many decisions. They sometimes require risk taking and often deal with business.

Abilities: Oral Expression—The ability to communicate information and ideas verbally so others will understand. Oral Comprehension—The ability to listen to and understand information and ideas presented verbally. Fluency of Ideas—The ability to come up with a number of ideas about a given topic. Emphasis is on the number of ideas produced and not the quality, correctness, or creativity of the ideas. Written

Comprehension—The ability to read and understand information and ideas presented in writing. Mathematical Reasoning—The ability to understand and organize a problem and then select a mathematical method or formula to solve the problem.

Skills: Coordination—Adjusting actions in relation to others' actions. Service Orientation—Actively looking for ways to help people. Speaking—Talking to others to effectively convey information. Implementation Planning—Developing approaches for implementing an idea. Information Gathering—Knowing how to find information and identifying essential information. Active Listening—Listening to what other people are saying; asking questions as appropriate.

Generalized Work Activities: Selling or Influencing Others—Convincing others to buy merchandise/goods, or otherwise changing their minds or actions. Performing for/Working with Public—Performing for people or dealing directly with the public, including serving persons in restaurants and stores and receiving clients or guests. Getting Information Needed to Do the Job—Observing, receiving, and otherwise obtaining information from all relevant sources. Communicating with Persons Outside Organization—Communicating with persons outside the organization. Representing the organization to customers, the public, government, and other external sources. Exchanging information face-to-face, in writing, or via telephone/electronic transfer. Assisting and Caring for Others—Providing assistance or personal care to others.

Truck Drivers

- ▲ Growth: 17%
- ▲ Annual Job Openings: 535,419
- ▲ Yearly Earnings: $24,300
- ▲ Education Required: Short-term O-J-T
- ▲ Self-Employed: 9.2%
- ▲ Part-Time: 9.9%

Tractor-Trailer Truck Drivers

Drive tractor-trailer truck to transport products, livestock, or materials to specified destinations. Drives tractor-trailer combination, applying knowledge of commercial driving regulations, to transport and deliver products, livestock, or materials, usually over a long distance. Loads or unloads truck, or assists in loading and unloading. Inventories and inspects goods to be moved. Wraps goods, using pads, packing paper, and containers; secures load to trailer wall using straps. Obtains customer's signature or collects payment for services. Services truck with oil, fuel, and radiator fluid to maintain tractor-trailer. Works as member of two-person team, driving tractor with sleeper bunk behind cab. Fastens chains or binders to secure load on trailer during transit. Reads bill of lading to determine assignment. Inspects truck before and after trips; submits report indicating truck condition. Maintains driver log according to I.C.C. regulations. Maneuvers truck into loading or unloading position, following signals from loading crew as needed. Gives directions to helper in packing and moving goods to trailer. Drives truck to weigh-station, before and after loading and along route, to document weight and conform to state regulations.

Personality Type: Realistic. Realistic occupations frequently involve work activities that include practical, hands-on problems and solutions. They often deal with plants, animals, and real-world materials like wood, tools, and machinery. Many of the occupations require working outside and do not involve a lot of paperwork or working closely with others.

Abilities: Far Vision—The ability to see details at a distance. Reaction Time—The ability to quickly respond with the hand, finger, or foot to a signal such as a sound, a light, or a picture. Response Orientation—The ability to choose quickly and correctly between two or more movements in response to two or more signals, such as lights, sounds, or pictures. Includes the speed with which the correct response is started with the hand, foot, or other body parts. Near Vision—The ability to see details of objects at a close range. Static Strength—The ability to exert maximum muscle force to lift, push, pull, or carry objects.

Skills: Operation and Control—Controlling operations of equipment or systems. Equipment Maintenance—Performing routine maintenance and determining when and what kind of maintenance is needed. Mathematics—Using mathematics to solve problems. Reading Comprehension—Understanding written information in work-related documents. Writing—Communicating effectively with others in writing as indicated by the needs of the audience.

Generalized Work Activities: Operating Vehicles or Equipment—Running, maneuvering, navigating, or driving vehicles or mechanized equipment such as forklifts, passenger vehicles, aircraft, or water craft. Documenting/Recording Information—Entering, transcribing, recording, storing, or maintaining information in either written form or by electronic/magnetic recording. Handling and Moving Objects—Using one's hands and arms in handling, installing, forming, positioning, and moving materials, or in manipulating things. Repairing and Maintaining Mechanical Equipment—Fixing, servicing, aligning, setting up, adjusting, and testing machines, devices, moving parts, and equipment that operate primarily on the basis of mechanical, not electronic, principles. Inspecting Equipment, Structures, Materials—Inspecting or diagnosing equipment, structures, or materials to identify the causes of errors or other problems or defects.

Truck Drivers, Heavy

Drive truck with capacity of more than three tons, to transport materials to specified destinations. Positions blocks and ties rope around items to secure cargo for transport. Assists in loading and unloading truck

manually. Obtains customer signature; collects payment for delivered goods and for delivery charges. Cleans, inspects, and services vehicle. Keeps record of materials and products transported. Maintains truck log according to state and federal regulations. Maintains radio or telephone contact with base or supervisor to receive instructions or be dispatched to new location. Drives truck with capacity of more than three tons, to transport and deliver cargo, materials, or damaged vehicles. Operates equipment on vehicle, to load, unload, or disperse cargo or materials.

Personality Type: Realistic. Realistic occupations frequently involve work activities that include practical, hands-on problems and solutions. They often deal with plants, animals, and real-world materials like wood, tools, and machinery. Many of the occupations require working outside and do not involve a lot of paperwork or working closely with others.

Abilities: Static Strength—The ability to exert maximum muscle force to lift, push, pull, or carry objects. Reaction Time—The ability to quickly respond with the hand, finger, or foot to a signal such as a sound, a light, or a picture. Spatial Orientation—The ability to know one's location in relation to the environment or to know where other objects are in relation to one's self. Far Vision—The ability to see details at a distance. Response Orientation—The ability to choose quickly and correctly between two or more movements in response to two or more signals, such as lights, sounds, or pictures. Includes the speed with which the correct response is started with the hand, foot, or other body parts.

Skills: Operation and Control—Controlling operations of equipment or systems. Equipment Maintenance—Performing routine maintenance and determining when and what kind of maintenance is needed. Writing—Communicating effectively with others in writing as indicated by the needs of the audience. Reading Comprehension—Understanding written information in work-related documents. Operation Monitoring—Watching gauges, dials, or other indicators to make sure a machine is working properly.

Generalized Work Activities: Operating Vehicles or Equipment—Running, maneuvering, navigating, or driving vehicles or mechanized equipment such as forklifts, passenger vehicles, aircraft, or water craft. Handling and Moving Objects—Using one's hands and arms in handling, installing, forming, positioning, and moving materials, or in manipulating things. Performing General Physical Activities—Performing physical activities that require moving one's whole body, such as in climbing, lifting, balancing, walking, and stooping. Performing activities that often also require considerable use of the arms and legs, such as in the physical handling of materials. Documenting/Recording Information—Entering, transcribing, recording, storing, or maintaining information in either written form or by electronic/magnetic recording. Repairing and Maintaining Mechanical Equipment—Fixing, servicing, aligning, setting up, adjusting, and testing machines, devices, moving parts, and equipment that operate primarily on the basis of mechanical, not electronic, principles.

Truck Drivers, Light or Delivery Services

Drive a truck or van with a capacity of under 26,000 GVW, primarily to deliver or pick up merchandise or to deliver packages within a specified area. Use automatic routing or location software. Load and unload truck. Inspects and maintains vehicle equipment and supplies. Presents billing invoice and collects receipt or payment. Performs emergency roadside repairs. Communicates with base or other vehicles, using telephone or radio. Drives truck, van, or automobile with capacity under three tons, to transport materials, products, or people. Maintains records such as vehicle log, record of cargo, or billing statements, in accordance with regulations. Loads and unloads truck, van, or automobile.

Personality Type: Realistic. Realistic occupations frequently involve work activities that include practical, hands-on problems and solutions. They often deal with plants, animals, and real-world materials like wood, tools, and machinery. Many of the occupations require working outside and do not involve a lot of paperwork or working closely with others.

Abilities: Reaction Time—The ability to quickly respond with the hand, finger, or foot to a signal such as a sound, a light, or a picture. Spatial Orientation—The ability to know one's location in relation to the environment or to know where other objects are in relation to one's self. Far Vision—The ability to see details at a distance. Static Strength—The ability to exert maximum muscle force to lift, push, pull, or carry objects. Extent Flexibility—The ability to bend, stretch, twist, or reach out with the body, arms, and/or legs.

Skills: Operation and Control—Controlling operations of equipment or systems. Operation Monitoring—Watching gauges, dials, or other indicators to make sure a machine is working properly. Equipment Maintenance—Performing routine maintenance and determining when and what kind of maintenance is needed. Reading Comprehension—Understanding written information in work-related documents. Writing—Communicating effectively with others in writing as indicated by the needs of the audience. Repairing—Repairing machines or systems, using the needed tools. Speaking—Talking to others to effectively convey information.

Generalized Work Activities: Operating Vehicles or Equipment—Running, maneuvering, navigating, or driving vehicles or mechanized equipment such as forklifts, passenger vehicles, aircraft, or water craft. Handling and Moving Objects—Using one's hands and arms in handling, installing, forming, positioning, and moving materials, or in manipulating things. Repairing and Maintaining Mechanical Equipment—Fixing, servicing, aligning, setting up, adjusting, and testing machines, devices, moving parts, and equipment that operate primarily on the basis of mechanical, not electronic, principles. Inspecting Equipment, Structures, Materials—Inspecting or diagnosing equipment, structures, or materials to identify the causes of errors or other problems or defects. Communicating with Persons Outside Organization—Communicating with persons outside the organization. Representing the organization to customers, the public, government, and other external sources. Exchanging information face-to-face, in writing, or via telephone/electronic transfer. Documenting/Recording Information—Entering, transcribing, recording, storing, or maintaining information in either written form or by electronic/magnetic recording.

Urban and Regional Planners

▲ Growth: 17%
▲ Annual Job Openings: 5,057
▲ Yearly Earnings: $42,860
▲ Education Required: Master's degree
▲ Self-Employed: 3.5%
▲ Part-Time: 18.1%

Urban and Regional Planners

Develop comprehensive plans and programs for use of land and physical facilities of local jurisdictions such as towns, cities, counties, and metropolitan areas. Compiles, organizes, and analyzes data on economic, social, and physical factors affecting land use, using statistical methods. Recommends governmental measures affecting land use, public utilities, community facilities, housing, and transportation. Prepares or requisitions graphic and narrative reports on land use data. Conducts field investigations, economic or public opinion surveys, demographic studies, or other research, to gather required information. Maintains collection of socioeconomic, environmental, and regulatory data related to land use, for governmental and private sectors. Advises planning officials on feasibility, cost effectiveness, regulatory conformance, and alternative recommendations for project. Determines regulatory limitations on project. Evaluates information to determine feasibility of proposals or to identify factors requiring amendment. Reviews and evaluates environmental impact reports applying to specific private and public planning projects and programs. Develops alternative plans, with recommendations for program or project. Discusses purpose of land use projects such as transportation, conservation, residential, commercial, industrial, and community use, with planning officials.

Personality Type: Investigative. Investigative occupations frequently involve working with ideas and require an extensive amount of thinking. These occupations can involve searching for facts and figuring out problems mentally.

Abilities: Inductive Reasoning—The ability to combine separate pieces of information, or specific answers to problems, to form general rules or conclusions. Includes coming up with a logical explanation for why a series of seemingly unrelated events occur together. Oral Expression—The ability to communicate information and ideas verbally so others will understand. Written Comprehension—The ability to read and understand information and ideas presented in writing. Speech Clarity—The ability to speak clearly so that what is said is understandable to a listener. Deductive Reasoning— he ability to apply general rules to specific problems to come up with logical answers. Involves deciding if an answer makes sense.

Skills: Judgment and Decision Making—Weighing the relative costs and benefits of a potential action. Implementation Planning—Developing approaches for implementing an idea. Information Gathering— Knowing how to find information and identifying essential information. Idea Evaluation—Evaluating the likely success of an idea in relation to the demands of the situation. Reading Comprehension—Understanding written information in work-related documents. Idea Generation—Generating a number of different approaches to problems. Systems Perception— Determining when important changes have occurred in a system or are likely to occur.

Generalized Work Activities: Getting Information Needed to Do the Job—Observing, receiving, and otherwise obtaining information from all relevant sources. Identifying Objects, Actions, and Events— Identifying information received by making estimates or categorizations, recognizing differences or similarities, or sensing changes in circumstances or events. Processing Information—Compiling, coding, categorizing, calculating, tabulating, auditing, verifying, or processing information or data. Analyzing Data or Information—Identifying underlying principles, reasons, or facts by breaking down information or data into separate parts.

Providing Consultation and Advice to Others—Providing consultation and expert advice to management or other groups on technical, systems-related, or process-related topics.

Ushers, Lobby Attendants, and Ticket Takers

- ▲ Growth: 18%
- ▲ Annual Job Openings: 22,505
- ▲ Yearly Earnings: $12,520
- ▲ Education Required: Short-term O-J-T
- ▲ Self-Employed: 0%
- ▲ Part-Time: 48.8%

Ushers, Lobby Attendants, and Ticket Takers

Collect admission tickets and passes from patrons at entertainment events. Assist patrons in finding seats, searching for lost articles, and locating such facilities as rest rooms and telephones. Monitors patrons' activities to prevent disorderly conduct and rowdiness and to detect infractions of rules. Verifies credentials of patrons desiring entrance into press box; permits only authorized persons to enter. Assists patrons in finding seats, searching for lost articles, and locating facilities such as rest rooms and telephones. Counts and records number of tickets collected. Serves patrons at refreshment stand during intermission. Assists other workers in changing advertising display. Distributes programs to patrons. Provides door checks for patrons temporarily leaving establishment. Greets patrons. Refuses admittance to patrons who do not have tickets or passes or who are undesirable for reasons such as intoxication or improper attire. Collects admission tickets and passes from patrons at entertainment events. Runs errands for patrons of press box, such as obtaining refreshments and carrying news releases. Examines tickets or passes to verify authenticity, using criteria such as color and date issued.

Personality Type: Social. Social occupations frequently involve working with, communicating with, and teaching people. These occupations often involve helping or providing service to others.

Abilities: Oral Expression—The ability to communicate information and ideas verbally so others will understand. Oral Comprehension—The ability to listen to and understand information and ideas presented verbally. Near Vision—The ability to see details of objects at a close range. Perceptual Speed—The ability to quickly and accurately compare letters, numbers, objects, pictures, or patterns. The things to be compared may be presented at the same time or one after the other. Includes comparing a presented object with a remembered object. Written Comprehension—The ability to read and understand information and ideas presented in writing.

Skills: Service Orientation—Actively looking for ways to help people. Speaking—Talking to others to effectively convey information. Active Listening—Listening to what other people are saying; asking questions as appropriate. Social Perceptiveness—Being aware of other people's reactions and understanding why people react the way they do. Reading Comprehension—Understanding written information in work-related documents.

Generalized Work Activities: Performing for/Working with Public—Performing for people or dealing directly with the public, including serving persons in restaurants and stores and receiving clients or guests. Communicating with Persons Outside Organization—

Communicating with persons outside the organization. Representing the organization to customers, the public, government, and other external sources. Exchanging information face-to-face, in writing, or via telephone/electronic transfer. Getting Information Needed to Do the Job—Observing, receiving, and otherwise obtaining information from all relevant sources. Assisting and Caring for Others—Providing assistance or personal care to others. Monitoring Processes, Materials, Surroundings—Monitoring and reviewing information from materials, events, or the environment, often to detect problems or to find out when things are finished. Handling and Moving Objects—Using one's hands and arms in handling, installing, forming, positioning, and moving materials, or in manipulating things. Identifying Objects, Actions, and Events—Identifying information received by making estimates or categorizations, recognizing differences or similarities, or sensing changes in circumstances or events.

Veterinarians

- ▲ Growth: 25%
- ▲ Annual Job Openings: 3,227
- ▲ Yearly Earnings: $50,950
- ▲ Education Required: First professional degree
- ▲ Self-Employed: 39.6%
- ▲ Part-Time: 10.5%

Veterinarians

Diagnose and treat diseases and dysfunctions of animals. Engage in a particular function such as research and development, consultation, administration, technical writing, sale or production of commercial products, or rendering of technical services to commercial firms or other organizations. Includes veterinarians who inspect livestock. Oversees activities concerned with feeding, care, and maintenance of animal quarters to ensure compliance with laboratory regulations. Conducts postmortem studies and analyzes results to determine cause of death. Inspects housing; advises animal owners regarding sanitary measures, feeding, and general care, to promote health of animals. Participates in planning and executing nutrition and reproduction programs for animals. Trains personnel in handling and care of animals. Examines animals to detect and determine nature of diseases or injuries; treats animals surgically or medically. Ensures compliance with regulations governing humane and ethical treatment of animals used in scientific research. Participates in research projects; plans procedures; selects animals for scientific research, based on knowledge of species and research principles. Establishes and conducts quarantine and testing procedures to prevent spread of disease and to ensure compliance with governmental regulations. Inspects and tests horses, sheep, poultry flocks, and other animals for diseases; inoculates animals against various diseases, including rabies. Exchanges information with zoos and aquariums concerning care, transfer, sale, or trade of animals, to maintain all-species nationwide inventory.

Personality Type: Investigative. Investigative occupations frequently involve working with ideas and require an extensive amount of thinking. These occupations can involve searching for facts and figuring out problems mentally.

Abilities: Deductive Reasoning—The ability to apply general rules to specific problems to come up with logical answers. Involves deciding if an answer makes sense. Problem Sensitivity—The ability to tell when something is wrong or is likely to go wrong. Does not involve solving the problem, only recognizing there is a problem. Inductive Reasoning—The ability to combine separate pieces of information, or specific answers to problems, to form general rules or conclusions. Includes coming up with a logical explanation for why a series of seemingly unrelated events occur together. Manual

Dexterity—The ability to quickly make coordinated movements of one hand, a hand together with its arm, or two hands, to grasp, manipulate, or assemble objects. Wrist-Finger Speed—The ability to make fast, simple, repeated movements of the fingers, hands, and wrists. Near Vision—The ability to see details of objects at a close range. Oral Expression—The ability to communicate information and ideas verbally so others will understand.

Skills: Science—Using scientific methods to solve problems. Critical Thinking—Using logic and analysis to identify the strengths and weaknesses of different approaches. Solution Appraisal—Observing and evaluating the outcomes of a problem solution to identify lessons learned or to redirect efforts. Problem Identification—Identifying the nature of problems. Judgment and Decision Making—Weighing the relative costs and benefits of a potential action. Reading Comprehension—Understanding written information in work-related documents. Active Listening—Listening to what other people are saying; asking questions as appropriate.

Generalized Work Activities: Identifying Objects, Actions, and Events—Identifying information received by making estimates or categorizations, recognizing differences or similarities, or sensing changes in circumstances or events. Making Decisions and Solving Problems—Combining, evaluating, and analyzing information and data to make decisions and solve problems. Involves making decisions about the relative importance of information and choosing the best solution. Getting Information Needed to Do the Job—Observing, receiving, and otherwise obtaining information from all relevant sources. Monitoring Processes, Materials, Surroundings—Monitoring and reviewing information from materials, events, or the environment, often to detect problems or to find out when things are finished. Assisting and Caring for Others—Providing assistance or personal care to others.

Veterinary Assistants

- ▲ Growth: 28%
- ▲ Annual Job Openings: 14,770
- ▲ Yearly Earnings: $16,200
- ▲ Education Required: Short-term O-J-T
- ▲ Self-Employed: 0%
- ▲ Part-Time: 38.1%

Veterinary Assistants and Laboratory Animal Caretakers

Feed, water, and examine pets and other nonfarm animals for signs of illness, disease, or injury, in laboratories, animal hospitals, and clinics. Clean and disinfect cages and work areas; sterilize laboratory and surgical equipment. Provide routine postoperative care; administer medication orally or topically; prepare samples for laboratory examination, under the supervision of veterinary or laboratory animal technologists or technicians, veterinarians, or scientists. Assists veterinarian during surgical procedures, passing instruments and materials in accordance with oral instructions. Prepares patient, medications, equipment, and instruments for surgical procedures, using specialized knowledge. Prepares examination or treatment room. Holds or restrains animal during procedures. Assists professional personnel with research projects in commercial, public health, or research laboratories. Inspects products or carcasses to ensure compliance with health standards, in food-processing plant. Assists veterinarian in variety of animal healthcare duties, including injections, venipunctures, and wound dressings. Completes routine laboratory tests; cares for and feeds laboratory animals.

Personality Type: Realistic. Realistic occupations frequently involve work activities that include practical, hands-on problems and solutions. They often deal with plants, animals, and real-world materials like wood, tools, and machinery. Many of the occupations require working outside and do not involve a lot of paperwork or working closely with others.

Abilities: Wrist-Finger Speed—The ability to make fast, simple, repeated movements of the fingers, hands, and wrists. Oral Comprehension—The ability to listen to and understand information and ideas presented verbally. Near Vision—The ability to see details of objects at a close range. Manual Dexterity—The ability to quickly make coordinated movements of one hand, a hand together with its arm, or two hands, to grasp, manipulate, or assemble objects. Finger Dexterity—The ability to make precisely coordinated movements of the fingers of one or both hands to grasp, manipulate, or assemble very small objects.

Skills: Science—Using scientific methods to solve problems. Equipment Selection—Determining the kind of tools and equipment needed to do a job. Active Listening—Listening to what other people are saying; asking questions as appropriate. Information

Organization—Finding ways to structure or classify multiple pieces of information. Reading Comprehension—Understanding written information in work-related documents. Information Gathering—Knowing how to find information and identifying essential information.

Generalized Work Activities: Assisting and Caring for Others—Providing assistance or personal care to others. Performing General Physical Activities—Performing physical activities that require moving one's whole body, such as in climbing, lifting, balancing, walking, and stooping. Performing activities that often also require considerable use of the arms and legs, such as in the physical handling of materials. Evaluating Information against Standards—Evaluating information against a set of standards and verifying that it is correct. Establishing and Maintaining Relationships—Developing constructive and cooperative working relationships with others. Communicating with Other Workers—Providing information to supervisors, fellow workers, and subordinates. This information can be exchanged face-to-face, in writing, or via telephone/electronic transfer. Handling and Moving Objects—Using one's hands and arms in handling, installing, forming, positioning, and moving materials, or in manipulating things. Includes the use of keyboards. Getting Information Needed to Do the Job—Observing, receiving, and otherwise obtaining information from all relevant sources.

Veterinary Technologists and Technicians

- ▲ Growth: 16%
- ▲ Annual Job Openings: 2,822
- ▲ Yearly Earnings: $19,870
- ▲ Education Required: Associate degree
- ▲ Self-Employed: 0%
- ▲ Part-Time: 11.7%

Veterinary Technologists and Technicians

Perform medical tests in a laboratory environment, for use in the treatment and diagnosis of diseases in animals. Prepare vaccines and serums for prevention of diseases. Prepare tissue samples, take blood samples, and execute laboratory tests such as urinalysis and blood counts. **Clean and sterilize instruments and materials and maintain equipment and machines.**

Note: The Department of Labor has not collected some data for this job, so it has fewer details than the other descriptions.

Vocational Education Teachers and Instructors

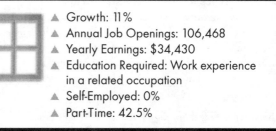

- ▲ Growth: 11%
- ▲ Annual Job Openings: 106,468
- ▲ Yearly Earnings: $34,430
- ▲ Education Required: Work experience in a related occupation
- ▲ Self-Employed: 0%
- ▲ Part-Time: 42.5%

Vocational Education Teachers, Middle School

Teach or instruct vocational or occupational subjects at the middle-school level. Prepares course outlines and objectives according to curriculum guidelines or state and local requirements. Assigns lessons and corrects homework. Develops and administers tests. Confers with students, parents, and school counselors to resolve behavioral and academic problems. Maintains discipline in classroom. Uses audiovisual aids and other materials to supplement presentations. Participates in faculty and professional meetings, educational conferences, and teacher training workshops. Selects, stores, orders, issues, and inventories classroom equipment, materials, and supplies. Keeps attendance records. Performs advisory duties such as sponsoring student organizations or clubs, helping students select courses, and counseling students with problems. Instructs students, using various teaching methods such as lecture and demonstration. Evaluates, records, and reports student progress.

Personality Type: Social. Social occupations frequently involve working with, communicating with, and teaching people. These occupations often involve helping or providing service to others.

Abilities: Oral Expression—The ability to communicate information and ideas verbally so others will understand.

Oral Comprehension—The ability to listen to and understand information and ideas presented verbally. Written Comprehension—The ability to read and understand information and ideas presented in writing. Written Expression—The ability to communicate information and ideas in writing so others will understand. Speech Clarity—The ability to speak clearly so that what is said is understandable to a listener.

Skills: Speaking—Talking to others to effectively convey information. Instructing—Teaching others how to do something. Learning Strategies—Using multiple approaches when learning or teaching new things. Reading Comprehension—Understanding written information in work-related documents. Active Listening—Listening to what other people are saying; asking questions as appropriate. Social Perceptiveness—Being aware of other people's reactions and understanding why people react the way they do.

Generalized Work Activities: Teaching Others—Identifying educational needs, developing formal training programs or classes, and teaching or instructing others. Communicating with Persons Outside Organization—Communicating with persons outside the organization. Representing the organization to customers, the public, government, and other external sources. Exchanging information face-to-face, in writing, or via telephone/electronic transfer. Getting Information Needed to Do the Job—Observing, receiving, and otherwise obtaining information from all relevant sources. Updating and Using Job-Relevant Knowledge—Keeping up-to-date technically and knowing the functions of one's own job and related jobs. Processing Information—Compiling, coding, categorizing, calculating, tabulating, auditing, verifying, or processing information or data. Interpreting Meaning of Information to Others—Translating or explaining what information means and how it can be understood or used to support responses or feedback to others. Documenting/Recording Information—Entering, transcribing, recording, storing, or maintaining information in either written form or by electronic/magnetic recording.

Vocational Education Teachers, Postsecondary

Teach or instruct vocational or occupational subjects at the postsecondary, prebaccalaureate level, to students who have graduated or left high school. Includes correspondence-school instructors; industrial, commercial, and government training instructors; adult-education teachers; and instructors who prepare persons to operate industrial machinery and equipment and transportation and communications equipment. Teach in public or private schools whose primary business is education or in a school associated with an organization whose primary business is other than education. Recommends advancement, transfer, or termination of student or trainee based on mastery of subject. Presents lectures and conducts discussions to increase students' knowledge and competence, using visual aids such as graphs, charts, videotapes, and slides. Plans course content and method of instruction. Determines training needs of students or workers. Corrects, grades, and comments on lesson assignments. Develops teaching aids such as instructional software, multimedia visual aids, computer tutorials, or study materials, for instruction in vocational or occupational subjects. Prepares reports and maintains records such as student grades, attendance, training activities, production records, and supply or equipment inventories. Arranges for lectures by subject-matter experts in designated fields. Participates in meetings,

seminars, and training sessions; integrates relevant information into training program. Solves operational problems; provides technical assistance with equipment and process techniques. Selects and assembles books, materials, supplies, and equipment, for training, courses, or projects. Administers oral, written, or performance tests to measure progress and to evaluate effectiveness of training. Prepares outline of instructional program and training schedule; establishes course goals. Observes and evaluates students' work to determine progress, to provide feedback, and to make suggestions for improvement. Conducts training sessions or classes, to teach and demonstrate principles, techniques, procedures, or methods of designated subjects. Reviews enrollment applications; corresponds with applicants.

Personality Type: Social. Social occupations frequently involve working with, communicating with, and teaching people. These occupations often involve helping or providing service to others.

Abilities: Oral Expression—The ability to communicate information and ideas verbally so others will understand. Oral Comprehension—The ability to listen to and understand information and ideas presented verbally. Speech Clarity—The ability to speak clearly so that what is said is understandable to a listener. Written Comprehension—The ability to read and understand information and ideas presented in writing. Written Expression—The ability to communicate information and ideas in writing so others will understand.

Skills: Speaking—Talking to others to effectively convey information. Instructing—Teaching others how to do something. Learning Strategies—Using multiple approaches when learning or teaching new things. Active Listening—Listening to what other people are saying; asking questions as appropriate.

Generalized Work Activities: Teaching Others—Identifying educational needs, developing formal training programs or classes, and teaching or instructing others. Updating and Using Job-Relevant Knowledge—Keeping up-to-date technically and knowing the functions of one's own job and related jobs. Getting Information Needed to Do the Job—Observing, receiving, and otherwise obtaining information from all relevant sources. Interpreting Meaning of Information to Others—Translating or explaining what information means and how it can be understood or used to support responses or feedback to others. Scheduling Work and Activities—Scheduling events, programs, activities, and the work of others.

Vocational Education Teachers, Secondary School

Teach or instruct vocational or occupational subjects at the secondary-school level. Keeps attendance records. Develops and administers tests. Prepares course outlines and objectives according to curriculum guidelines or state and local requirements. Assigns lessons and corrects homework. Uses audiovisual aids and other materials to supplement presentations. Participates in faculty and professional meetings, educational conferences, and teacher-training workshops. Performs advisory duties such as sponsoring student organizations or clubs, helping students select courses, and counseling students with problems. Selects, stores, orders, issues, and inventories classroom equipment, materials, and supplies. Maintains discipline in classroom. Evaluates, records, and reports student progress. Instructs students, using various teaching methods such as lecture and demonstration. Confers with students, parents, and school counselors to resolve behavioral and academic problems.

Personality Type: Social. Social occupations frequently involve working with, communicating with, and teaching people. These occupations often involve helping or providing service to others.

Abilities: Oral Expression—The ability to communicate information and ideas verbally so others will understand. Written Comprehension—The ability to read and understand information and ideas presented in writing. Written Expression—The ability to communicate information and ideas in writing so others will understand. Oral Comprehension—The ability to listen to and understand information and ideas presented verbally. Speech Clarity—The ability to speak clearly so that what is said is understandable to a listener.

Skills: Instructing—Teaching others how to do something. Speaking—Talking to others to effectively convey information. Learning Strategies—Using multiple approaches when learning or teaching new things. Reading Comprehension—Understanding written information in work-related documents. Social Perceptiveness—Being aware of other people's reactions and understanding why people react the way they do. Active Listening—Listening to what other people are saying; asking questions as appropriate.

Generalized Work Activities: Teaching Others—Identifying educational needs, developing formal training programs or classes, and teaching or instructing others. Communicating with Persons Outside Organization—Communicating with persons outside the organization. Representing the organization to customers, the public, government, and other external sources. Exchanging information face-to-face, in writing, or via telephone/electronic transfer. Getting Information Needed to Do the Job—Observing, receiving, and otherwise obtaining information from all relevant sources. Updating and Using Job-Relevant Knowledge—Keeping up-to-date technically and knowing the functions of one's own job and related jobs. Documenting/Recording Information—Entering, transcribing, recording, storing, or maintaining information in either written form or by electronic/magnetic recording. Interpreting Meaning of Information to Others—Translating or explaining what information means and how it can be understood or used to support responses or feedback to others. Processing Information—Compiling, coding, categorizing, calculating, tabulating, auditing, verifying, or processing information or data.

Water and Liquid Waste Treatment Plant and System Operators

- ▲ Growth: 14%
- ▲ Annual Job Openings: 12,735
- ▲ Yearly Earnings: $29,660
- ▲ Education Required: Long-term O-J-T
- ▲ Self-Employed: 0%
- ▲ Part-Time: 1.8%

Water and Liquid Waste Treatment Plant and System Operators

Operate or control an entire process or system of machines, often through the use of control boards, to transfer or treat water or liquid waste. Directs and coordinates plant workers engaged in routine operations and maintenance activities. Adds chemicals such as ammonia, chlorine, and lime, to disinfect and deodorize water and other liquids. Collects and tests water and sewage samples, using test equipment and color analysis standards. Cleans and maintains tanks and filter beds, using hand tools and power tools. Maintains, repairs, and lubricates equipment, using hand tools and power tools. Records operational data, personnel attendance, and meter and gauge readings on specified forms. Operates and adjusts controls on equipment to purify and clarify water, process or dispose of sewage, and generate power. Inspects equipment and monitors operating conditions, meters, and gauges, to determine load requirements and detect malfunctions.

Personality Type: Realistic. Realistic occupations frequently involve work activities that include practical, hands-on problems and solutions. They often deal with plants, animals, and real-world materials like wood, tools, and machinery. Many of the occupations require working outside and do not involve a lot of paperwork or working closely with others.

Abilities: Information Ordering—The ability to correctly follow a given rule or set of rules in order to arrange things or actions in a certain order. The things or actions can include numbers, letters, words, pictures, procedures, sentences, and mathematical or logical operations. Problem Sensitivity—The ability to tell when something is wrong or is likely to go wrong. Does not involve solving the problem, only recognizing there is a problem. Near Vision—The ability to see details of objects at a close range. Control Precision—The ability to quickly and repeatedly make precise adjustments in moving the controls of a machine or vehicle to exact positions. Deductive Reasoning—The ability to apply general rules to specific problems to come up with logical answers. Involves deciding if an answer makes sense. Time Sharing—The ability to efficiently shift back and forth between two or more activities or sources of information such as speech, sounds, or touch.

Skills: Operation and Control—Controlling operations of equipment or systems. Operation Monitoring—Watching gauges, dials, or other indicators to make sure a machine is working properly. Information Organization—Finding ways to structure or classify multiple pieces of information. Problem Identification—Identifying the nature of problems. Testing—Conducting tests to determine whether equipment, software, or procedures are operating as expected. Mathematics—Using mathematics to solve problems. Information Gathering—Knowing how to find information and identifying essential information.

Generalized Work Activities: Monitoring Processes, Materials, Surroundings—Monitoring and reviewing information from materials, events, or the environment, often to detect problems or to find out when things are finished. Controlling Machines and Processes—Using either control mechanisms or direct physical activity to operate machines or processes. Does not involve working with computers or vehicles. Handling and Moving Objects—Using one's hands and arms in handling, installing, forming, positioning, and moving materials, or in manipulating things. Includes the use of keyboards. Inspecting Equipment, Structures, Materials—Inspecting or diagnosing equipment, structures, or materials to identify the causes of errors or other problems or defects. Identifying Objects, Actions, and

Events—Identifying information received by making estimates or categorizations, recognizing differences or similarities, or sensing changes in circumstances or events. Documenting/Recording Information—Entering, transcribing, recording, storing, or maintaining information in either written form or by electronic/magnetic recording.

Water Vessel Captains and Pilots

- ▲ Growth: 3%
- ▲ Annual Job Openings: 3,581
- ▲ Yearly Earnings: $41,200
- ▲ Education Required: Work experience in a related occupation
- ▲ Self-Employed: 7.9%
- ▲ Part-Time: 3%

Pilots, Ship

Command ships. Steer ships into and out of harbors, estuaries, straits, and sounds. Steer ships on rivers, lakes, and bays. Must be licensed by U.S. Coast Guard, with limitations indicating class and tonnage of vessels for which license is valid and indicating route and waters that may be piloted. Directs course and speed of ship, based on specialized knowledge of local winds, weather, tides, and current. Orders worker at helm to steer ship. Navigates ship to avoid reefs, outlying shoals, and other hazards, utilizing navigational aids such as lighthouses and buoys. Signals tugboat captain to berth and unberth ship.

Personality Type: Realistic. Realistic occupations frequently involve work activities that include practical, hands-on problems and solutions. They often deal with plants, animals, and real-world materials like wood, tools, and machinery. Many of the occupations require working outside and do not involve a lot of paperwork or working closely with others.

Abilities: Far Vision—The ability to see details at a distance. Spatial Orientation—The ability to know one's location in relation to the environment or to know where other objects are in relation to one's self. Oral Expression—The ability to communicate information

and ideas verbally so others will understand. Control Precision—The ability to quickly and repeatedly make precise adjustments in moving the controls of a machine or vehicle to exact positions. Speech Clarity—The ability to speak clearly so that what is said is understandable to a listener.

Skills: Operation and Control—Controlling operations of equipment or systems. Monitoring—Assessing how well one is doing when learning or doing something. Operation Monitoring—Watching gauges, dials, or other indicators to make sure a machine is working properly. Judgment and Decision Making—Weighing the relative costs and benefits of a potential action. Systems Perception—Determining when important changes have occurred in a system or are likely to occur. Identification of Key Causes—Identifying the things that must be changed to achieve a goal.

Generalized Work Activities: Operating Vehicles or Equipment—Running, maneuvering, navigating, or driving vehicles or mechanized equipment such as forklifts, passenger vehicles, aircraft, or water craft. Monitoring Processes, Materials, Surroundings—Monitoring and reviewing information from materials, events, or the environment, often to detect problems or to find out when things are finished. Getting Information Needed to Do the Job—Observing, receiving, and otherwise obtaining information from all relevant sources. Identifying Objects, Actions, and Events—Identifying information received by making estimates or categorizations, recognizing differences or similarities, or sensing changes in circumstances or events. Making Decisions and Solving Problems—Combining, evaluating, and analyzing information and data to make decisions and solve problems. Involves making decisions about the relative importance of information and choosing the best solution.

Ship and Boat Captains

Command vessels in oceans, bays, lakes, rivers, and coastal waters. Inspects vessel to ensure safety of crew and passengers, efficient and safe operation of vessel and equipment, and conformance to regulations. Collects fares from customers or signals ferryboat helper to collect fares. Purchases supplies and equipment; contacts buyers to sell fish; resolves questions or problems with customs officials. Signals passing vessels, using whistle, flashing lights, flags, and radio. Tows and maneuvers barge, or signals tugboat to tow barge to destination. Interviews, hires, and instructs crew; assigns watches and living quarters. Maintains records of daily activities, movements, and ports-of-call; prepares progress and personnel reports. Calculates sighting of land, using electronic sounding devices and following contour lines on chart. Signals crew or deckhands to rig tow lines, open or close gates and ramps, and pull guard chains across entry. Computes position, sets course, and determines speed, using charts, area plotting sheets, compass, sextant, and knowledge of local conditions. Steers and operates vessel, or orders helmsperson to steer vessel, using radio, depth finder, radar, lights, buoys, and lighthouses. Directs and coordinates activities of crew or workers, such as loading and unloading, operating signal devices, fishing, and repairing defective equipment. Commands passenger and freight vessels, fishing vessels, yachts, tugboats, barges, deep-submergence vehicles, ferryboats, and other water vessels. Monitors sonar and navigational aids; reads gauges to verify sufficient levels of hydraulic fluid, air pressure, and oxygen.

Personality Type: Enterprising. Enterprising occupations frequently involve starting up and carrying out projects. These occupations can involve leading people and making many decisions. They sometimes require risk taking and often deal with business.

Abilities: Spatial Orientation—The ability to know one's location in relation to the environment or to know where other objects are in relation to one's self. Control Precision—The ability to quickly and repeatedly make precise adjustments in moving the controls of a machine or vehicle to exact positions. Far Vision—The ability to see details at a distance. Problem Sensitivity—The ability to tell when something is wrong or is likely to go wrong. Does not involve solving the problem, only recognizing there is a problem. Night Vision—The ability to see under low light conditions. Response Orientation—The ability to choose quickly and correctly between two or more movements in response to two or more signals, such as lights, sounds, or pictures. Includes the speed with which the correct response is started with the hand, foot, or other body parts. Near Vision—The ability to see details of objects at a close range. Number Facility—The ability to add, subtract, multiply, or divide quickly and correctly.

Skills: Operation and Control—Controlling operations of equipment or systems. Operation Monitoring—Watching gauges, dials, or other indicators to make sure a machine is working properly. Coordination—Adjusting actions in relation to others' actions. Speaking—Talking to others to effectively convey information. Management of Personnel Resources—Motivating, developing, and directing people as they work, identifying the best people for the job.

Generalized Work Activities: Operating Vehicles or Equipment—Running, maneuvering, navigating, or driving vehicles or mechanized equipment such as forklifts, passenger vehicles, aircraft, or water craft. Getting Information Needed to Do the Job—Observing, receiving, and otherwise obtaining information from all relevant sources. Identifying Objects, Actions, and Events—Identifying information received by making estimates or categorizations, recognizing differences or similarities, or sensing changes in circumstances or events. Communicating with Other

Workers—Providing information to supervisors, fellow workers, and subordinates. This information can be exchanged face-to-face, in writing, or via telephone/electronic transfer. Monitoring Processes, Materials, Surroundings—Monitoring and reviewing information from materials, events, or the environment, often to detect problems or to find out when things are finished. Making Decisions and Solving Problems—Combining, evaluating, and analyzing information and data to make decisions and solve problems. Involves making decisions about the relative importance of information and choosing the best solution.

Writers and Editors

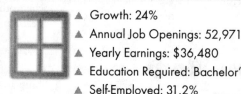

- ▲ Growth: 24%
- ▲ Annual Job Openings: 52,971
- ▲ Yearly Earnings: $36,480
- ▲ Education Required: Bachelor's degree
- ▲ Self-Employed: 31.2%
- ▲ Part-Time: 18.5%

Caption Writers

Write caption phrases of dialogue for hearing-impaired and foreign-language-speaking viewers of movie or television productions. Operates computerized captioning system for movies or television productions for hearing-impaired and foreign-language–speaking viewers. Writes captions to describe music and background noises. Translates foreign-language dialogue into English captions; translates English dialogue into foreign-language captions. Edits translations for correctness of grammar, punctuation, and clarity of expression. Watches production and reviews captions simultaneously, to determine which caption phrases require editing. Enters commands to synchronize captions with dialogue and place on the screen. Discusses captions with directors or producers of movie and television productions. Oversees encoding of captions to master tape of television production.

Personality Type: Artistic. Artistic occupations frequently involve working with forms, designs, and patterns. They often require self-expression, and the work can be done without following a clear set of rules.

Abilities: Written Expression—The ability to communicate information and ideas in writing so others will understand. Oral Comprehension—The ability to listen to and understand information and ideas presented verbally. Written Comprehension—The ability to read and understand information and ideas presented in writing. Near Vision—The ability to see details of objects at a close range. Oral Expression—The ability to communicate information and ideas verbally so others will understand.

Skills: Writing—Communicating effectively with others in writing as indicated by the needs of the audience. Reading Comprehension—Understanding written information in work-related documents. Active Listening—Listening to what other people are saying; asking questions as appropriate. Monitoring—Assessing how well one is doing when learning or doing something. Speaking—Talking to others to effectively convey information. Product Inspection—Inspecting and evaluating the quality of products.

Generalized Work Activities: Interpreting Meaning of Information to Others—Translating or explaining what information means and how it can be understood or used to support responses or feedback to others. Evaluating Information against Standards—Evaluating information against a set of standards and verifying that it is correct. Interacting with Computers—Controlling computer functions by using programs, setting up functions, writing software, or otherwise communicating with computer systems. Monitoring Processes, Materials, Surroundings—Monitoring and reviewing information from materials, events, or the environment, often to detect problems or to find out when things are finished. Communicating with Other Workers—Providing information to supervisors, fellow workers, and subordinates. This information can be exchanged face-to-face, in writing, or via telephone/electronic transfer. Identifying Objects, Actions, and Events—Identifying information received by making estimates or categorizations, recognizing differences or similarities, or sensing changes in circumstances or events.

Copy Writers

Write advertising copy for use by publication or broadcast media to promote sale of goods and services. Consults with sales media and marketing representatives to obtain information on product or service and to discuss style and length of advertising copy. Writes advertising copy for use by publication or broadcast media; revises copy according to supervisor's instructions. Reviews advertising trends, consumer surveys, and other marketing data, to formulate approach. Writes articles, bulletins, sales letters, speeches, and other related informative and promotional material. Prepares advertising copy, using computer. Obtains additional background and current development information through research and interview.

Personality Type: Artistic. Artistic occupations frequently involve working with forms, designs, and patterns. They often require self-expression, and the work can be done without following a clear set of rules.

Abilities: Written Expression—The ability to communicate information and ideas in writing so others will understand. Written Comprehension—The ability to read and understand information and ideas presented in writing. Oral Comprehension—The ability to listen to and understand information and ideas presented verbally. Originality—The ability to come up with unusual or clever ideas about a given topic or situation, or to develop creative ways to solve a problem. Oral Expression—The ability to communicate information and ideas verbally so others will understand. Fluency of Ideas—The ability to come up with a number of ideas about a given topic. Emphasis is on the number of ideas produced and not the quality, correctness, or creativity of the ideas. Near Vision—The ability to see details of objects at a close range.

Skills: Writing—Communicating effectively with others in writing as indicated by the needs of the audience. Reading Comprehension—Understanding written information in work-related documents. Idea Generation—Generating a number of different approaches to problems. Monitoring—Assessing how well one is doing when learning or doing something. Information Gathering—Knowing how to find information and identifying essential information.

Generalized Work Activities: Getting Information Needed to Do the Job—Observing, receiving, and otherwise obtaining information from all relevant sources. Judging Qualities—Making judgments about or assessing the value, importance, or quality of things, services, or other people's work. Evaluating Information against Standards—Evaluating information against a set of standards and verifying that it is correct. Communicating with Other Workers—Providing information to supervisors, fellow workers, and subordinates. This information can be exchanged face-to-face, in writing, or via telephone/electronic transfer. Analyzing Data or Information—Identifying underlying principles, reasons, or facts by breaking down information or data into separate parts. Identifying Objects, Actions, and Events—Identifying information received by making estimates or categorizations, recognizing differences or similarities, or sensing changes in circumstances or events.

Creative Writers

Create original written works such as plays or prose, for publication or performance. Selects subject or theme for writing project, based on personal interest and writing specialty or based on assignment from publisher, client, producer, or director. Writes humorous material such as comedy routines, gags, comedy shows, or scripts, for publication or performance by entertainers. Writes play or script for movies or television, based on original ideas or adapted from fictional, historical, or narrative sources. Writes fiction or nonfiction prose such as short stories, novels, biographies, articles, descriptive or critical analyses, or essays. Organizes material for project; plans arrangement or outline; writes synopsis. Conducts research to obtain factual information and authentic detail, utilizing sources such as newspaper accounts, diaries, and interviews. Collaborates with other writers on specific projects. Confers with client, publisher, or producer to discuss development changes or revisions. Develops factors such as theme, plot, characterization, psychological analysis, historical environment, action, and dialogue, to create material. Reviews, submits for approval, and revises written material to meet personal standards and to satisfy needs of client, publisher, director, or producer.

Personality Type: Artistic. Artistic occupations frequently involve working with forms, designs, and patterns. They often require self-expression, and the work can be done without following a clear set of rules.

Abilities: Written Expression—The ability to communicate information and ideas in writing so others will understand. Originality—The ability to come up with unusual or clever ideas about a given topic or situation, or to develop creative ways to solve a problem. Written Comprehension—The ability to read and understand information and ideas presented in writing. Fluency of Ideas—The ability to come up with a number of ideas about a given topic. Emphasis is on the number of ideas produced and not the quality, correctness, or creativity of the ideas. Near Vision—The ability to see details of objects at a close range.

Skills: Writing—Communicating effectively with others in writing as indicated by the needs of the audience. Reading Comprehension—Understanding written information in work-related documents. Idea Generation—Generating a number of different approaches to problems. Information Gathering—Knowing how to find information and identifying essential information. Monitoring—Assessing how well one is doing when learning or doing something.

Generalized Work Activities: Thinking Creatively—Originating, inventing, designing, or creating new applications, ideas, relationships, systems, or products, including artistic contributions. Judging Qualities—Making judgments about or assessing the value, importance, or quality of things, services, or other people's work. Communicating with Other Workers—Providing information to supervisors, fellow workers, and subordinates. This information can be exchanged face-to-face, in writing, or via telephone/electronic transfer. Getting Information Needed to Do the Job—Observing, receiving, and otherwise obtaining information from all relevant sources. Communicating with Persons Outside Organization—Communicating with persons outside the organization. Representing the organization to customers, the public, government, and other external sources. Exchanging information face-to-face, in writing, or via telephone/electronic transfer. Evaluating Information against Standards—Evaluating information against a set of standards and verifying that it is correct.

Editors

Lay out, index, and revise content of written materials, in preparation for final publication. Compiles index, cross references, and related information such as glossaries, bibliographies, and footnotes. Reads material to determine items to be included in index of book or other publication. Determines placement of stories based on relative significance, available space, and knowledge of layout principles. Reads copy or proof to detect and correct errors in spelling, punctuation, and syntax; indicates corrections, using standard proofreading and typesetting symbols. Selects and crops photographs and illustrative materials to conform to space and subject-matter requirements. Selects local, state, national, and international news items received by wire from press associations. Arranges topical or alphabetical list of index items, according to page or chapter, indicating location of item in text. Reviews and approves proofs submitted by composing room. Confers with management and editorial staff members regarding placement of developing news stories. Writes and rewrites headlines, captions, columns, articles, and stories to conform to publication's style, editorial policy, and publishing requirements. Reads and evaluates manuscripts or other materials submitted for publication; confers with authors regarding changes or publication. Plans and prepares page layouts to position and space articles, photographs, or illustrations. Verifies facts, dates, and statistics, using standard reference sources.

Personality Type: Artistic. Artistic occupations frequently involve working with forms, designs, and patterns. They often require self-expression, and the work can be done without following a clear set of rules.

Abilities: Written Comprehension—The ability to read and understand information and ideas presented in writing. Written Expression—The ability to communicate information and ideas in writing so others will understand. Near Vision—The ability to see details of objects at a close range. Oral Expression—The ability to communicate information and ideas verbally so others will understand. Oral Comprehension—The ability to listen to and understand information and ideas presented verbally. Problem Sensitivity—The ability to tell when something is wrong or is likely to go wrong. Does not involve solving the problem, only recognizing there is a problem. Deductive Reasoning—The ability to apply general rules to specific problems to come up with logical answers. Involves deciding if an answer makes sense. Information Ordering—The ability to correctly follow a given rule or set of rules in order to arrange things or actions in a certain order. The things or actions can include numbers, letters, words, pictures, procedures, sentences, and mathematical or logical operations.

Skills: Writing—Communicating effectively with others in writing as indicated by the needs of the audience. Reading Comprehension—Understanding written information in work-related documents. Product Inspection—Inspecting and evaluating the quality of products. Monitoring—Assessing how well one is doing when learning or doing something. Coordination—Adjusting actions in relation to others' actions. Information Organization—Finding ways to structure or classify multiple pieces of information.

Generalized Work Activities: Getting Information Needed to Do the Job—Observing, receiving, and otherwise obtaining information from all relevant sources. Judging Qualities—Making judgments about or assessing the value, importance, or quality of things, services, or other people's work. Communicating with Other Workers—Providing information to supervisors, fellow workers, and subordinates. This information can be exchanged face-to-face, in writing, or via telephone/electronic transfer. Making Decisions and Solving Problems—Combining, evaluating, and analyzing information and data to make decisions and solve

problems. Involves making decisions about the relative importance of information and choosing the best solution. Identifying Objects, Actions, and Events—Identifying information received by making estimates or categorizations, recognizing differences or similarities, or sensing changes in circumstances or events. Evaluating Information against Standards—Evaluating information against a set of standards and verifying that it is correct.

Poets and Lyricists

Write poetry or song lyrics for publication or performance. Writes words to fit musical compositions, including lyrics for operas, musical plays, and choral works. Adapts text to accommodate musical requirements of composer and singer. Writes narrative, dramatic, lyric, or other types of poetry for publication. Chooses subject matter and suitable form, to express personal feelings, experience, or ideas, or to narrate story or event.

Personality Type: Artistic. Artistic occupations frequently involve working with forms, designs, and patterns. They often require self-expression, and the work can be done without following a clear set of rules.

Abilities: Originality—The ability to come up with unusual or clever ideas about a given topic or situation, or to develop creative ways to solve a problem. Written Expression—The ability to communicate information and ideas in writing so others will understand. Fluency of Ideas—The ability to come up with a number of ideas about a given topic. Emphasis is on the number of ideas produced and not the quality, correctness, or creativity of the ideas. Near Vision—The ability to see details of objects at a close range. Oral Expression—The ability to communicate information and ideas verbally so others will understand.

Skills: Writing—Communicating effectively with others in writing as indicated by the needs of the audience. Reading Comprehension—Understanding written information in work-related documents. Idea Generation—Generating a number of different approaches to problems. Monitoring—Assessing how well one is doing when learning or doing something. Idea Evaluation—Evaluating the likely success of an idea in relation to the demands of the situation. Product Inspection—Inspecting and evaluating the quality of products.

Generalized Work Activities: Thinking Creatively—Originating, inventing, designing, or creating new applications, ideas, relationships, systems, or products, including artistic contributions. Implementing Ideas and Programs—Conducting or carrying out work procedures and activities in accord with one's own ideas or information provided through directions/instructions for purposes of installing, modifying, preparing, delivering, constructing, integrating, finishing, or completing programs, systems, structures, or products. Judging Qualities—Making judgments about or assessing the value, importance, or quality of things, services, or other people's work. Making Decisions and Solving Problems—Combining, evaluating, and analyzing information and data to make decisions and solve problems. Involves making decisions about the relative importance of information and choosing the best solution. Communicating with Persons Outside Organization—Communicating with persons outside the organization. Representing the organization to customers, the public, government, and other external sources. Exchanging information face-to-face, in writing, or via telephone/electronic transfer. Identifying Objects, Actions, and Events—Identifying information received by making estimates or categorizations, recognizing differences or similarities, or sensing changes in circumstances or events.

Technical Writers

Write technical materials such as equipment manuals, appendices, or operating and maintenance instructions. Assist in layout work. Confers with customer representatives, vendors, plant executives, or publisher to establish technical specifications and to determine subject material to be developed for publication. Analyzes developments in specific field to determine need for revisions in previously published materials and need for development of new material. Studies drawings, specifications, mock ups, and product samples, to integrate and delineate technology, operating procedure, and production sequence and detail. Interviews production and engineering personnel and reads journals and other material, to become familiar with product technologies and production methods. Assists in laying out material for publication. Reviews published materials; recommends revisions or changes in scope, format, content, and methods of reproduction and binding. Reviews manufacturers' and trade catalogs, drawings, and other data relative to operation, maintenance, and service of equipment. Arranges for typing, duplication, and distribution of material. Organizes material and completes writing assignment according to set standards regarding order, clarity, conciseness, style, and terminology. Selects photographs, drawings, sketches, diagrams, and charts to illustrate material. Maintains records and files of work and revisions. Observes production, developmental, and experimental activities to determine operating procedure and detail. Edits, standardizes, or makes changes to material prepared by other writers or establishment personnel. Draws sketches to illustrate specified materials or assembly sequence.

Personality Type: Artistic. Artistic occupations frequently involve working with forms, designs, and patterns. They often require self-expression, and the work can be done without following a clear set of rules.

Abilities: Written Expression—The ability to communicate information and ideas in writing so others will understand. Written Comprehension—The ability to read and understand information and ideas presented in writing. Near Vision—The ability to see details of objects at a close range. Information Ordering—The ability to correctly follow a given rule or set of rules in order to arrange things or actions in a certain order. The things or actions can include numbers, letters, words, pictures, procedures, sentences, and mathematical or logical operations. Originality—The ability to come up with unusual or clever ideas about a given topic or situation, or to develop creative ways to solve a problem.

Skills: Information Gathering—Knowing how to find information and identifying essential information. Reading Comprehension—Understanding written information in work-related documents. Writing—Communicating effectively with others in writing as indicated by the needs of the audience. Information Organization—Finding ways to structure or classify multiple pieces of information. Synthesis/ Reorganization—Reorganizing information to get a better approach to problems or tasks.

Generalized Work Activities: Getting Information Needed to Do the Job—Observing, receiving, and otherwise obtaining information from all relevant sources. Interpreting Meaning of Information to Others—Translating or explaining what information means and how it can be understood or used to support responses or feedback to others. Documenting/ Recording Information—Entering, transcribing, recording, storing, or maintaining information in either written form or by electronic/magnetic recording. Drafting and Specifying Technical Devices—Providing documentation, detailed instructions, drawings, or specifications to inform others about how devices, parts, equipment, or structures are to be fabricated, constructed, assembled, modified, maintained, or used. Communicating with Other Workers—Providing information to supervisors, fellow workers, and subordinates. This information can be exchanged face-to-face, in writing, or via telephone/electronic transfer.

Index
of Job Descriptions

N

O

P

R

S

T

U–Z